Teacher's Edition

PACEMAKER®

World History

Shoreview, MN

Reading Consultant

Timothy Shanahan, Ph.D., Professor of Urban Education, Director of the Center for Literacy, University of Illinois at Chicago, Author, *AMP*^{TM} *Reading System*

Reviewers

The publisher wishes to thank the following educators for their helpful comments during the review process for Pacemaker® *World History.* Their assistance has been invaluable. **Debora Hartzell,** Special Education and Vocational Teacher, Lakeside High School, Atlanta, GA; **Lenore Hoyt,** Social Studies Teacher, Centennial High School, Circle Pines, MN; **Stephen C. Larsen** (formerly of The University of Texas at Austin); **J. B. Whitten,** ESE Teacher, Lennard High, Ruskin, IL

Acknowledgments appear on page 798, which constitutes an extension of this copyright page.

1-800-992-0244
www.agsglobe.com

Contents

Contents

Pacemaker® World History

Pacemaker® *World History*

A fundamental understanding of world history should be important to everyone. Today, the people of the world are linked more closely than at any other time in history. As the global community becomes more interdependent culturally, economically, and politically, it is essential that students gain a better understanding of the past and connect the past to the present.

Pacemaker® *World History* helps students of all abilities understand world history. Through concise lessons and clear language, students are presented with a chronological approach to the major themes of world history from prehistory to modern times. Written at a fourth-grade reading level, the text uses the latest research on how students learn. The book is organized into an easy-to-understand format of units, chapters, and lessons with many special features to aid students.

Each chapter has well-defined learning goals and each lesson has specific learning objectives. Vocabulary

terms are highlighted and defined in sidebar boxes throughout the chapter to reinforce vocabulary instruction. All headings are written in the form of questions to increase comprehension and establish a purpose for reading. The review sections after each lesson and at the end of each chapter help students and teachers assess learning. Critical-thinking questions and a variety of other question types are included.

Special features in the text enhance student learning. Reading Strategies created by reading specialists help the students make sense of what they read. *Words from the Past* highlights written or spoken words related to the chapter that continue to affect the world today. *Great Names in History* features people who have made a difference in the past. *Learn More About It, Technology Connection, Geography Note, Remember,* and *History Fact* provide background material to support the content. Students gain point-of-use critical-thinking exposure from *You Decide* prompts. *Timeline Studies,* maps, and other high-interest visuals stimulate the reading experience.

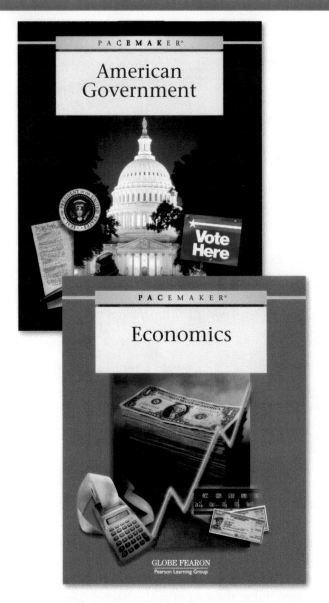

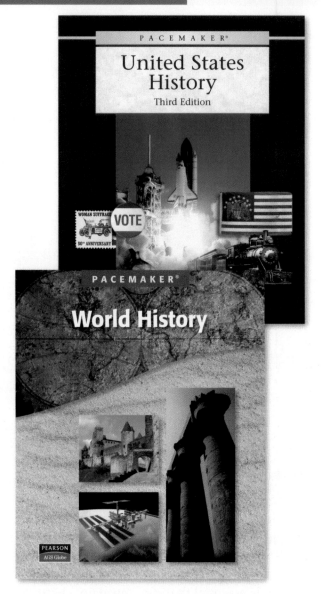

Enhance your social studies program with Pacemaker® textbooks. AGS Globe has four social studies Pacemaker® titles— *American Government, Economics, United States History,* and *World History*— that offer an easy, effective way to teach students the practical skills they need. Each Pacemaker® textbook builds and reinforces basic language skills. Written at a low reading level, these programs are ideal for students and adults who need help with language concepts, or those who are learning English as a second language. The full-color books use student-friendly text and real-world examples to show students the relevance of language in their daily lives. Each provides comprehensive coverage of skills and concepts. The short, concise lessons will motivate even reluctant students. With readabilities of all the texts below a fourth-grade reading level, students can concentrate on learning the content. AGS Globe is committed to making learning accessible to all students.

For more information on AGS Globe's textbooks and worktexts:
**call 1-800-992-0244, visit our Web site at www.agsglobe.com,
or e-mail AGS Globe at mail@agsglobe.com**

Skill Track

Skill Track monitors student progress and helps schools meet the demands of adequate yearly progress (AYP). Students using AGS Globe curriculum access multiple-choice assessments to see how well they understand the content of each textbook lesson and chapter. Skill Track is a tool available anytime. With timely and ongoing feedback from individual student and class reports, teachers can make informed instructional decisions. Administrators can use the reports to support teacher effectiveness and parents can keep up to date on what their students are learning.

Simple to use, Skill Track is secure and confidential. Students enter through three paths—lesson by lesson, at the end of a chapter, or by unit. Mastery is assessed by a variety of multiple-choice items; parallel forms are available for chapter assessments. Hundreds of items cover the content and skills in each textbook. Students may retake any assessment as often as necessary and scores are reported for each attempt. Accordingly, teachers can identify areas in need of reinforcement and practice for individual learners as well as the class.

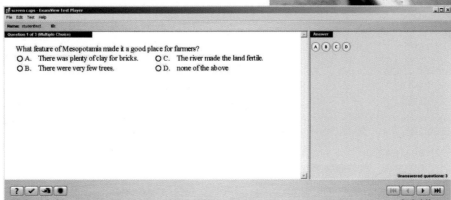

For more information about Skill Track:
call 1-800-992-0244 or visit our Web site at www.agsglobe.com

Student Edition Highlights

- Each lesson is clearly labeled to help students focus on the skill or concept to be learned.

- Maps, timelines, photos, and illustrations provide visual representations of the content.

- Goals for Learning at the beginning of each chapter and Objectives at the beginning of each lesson identify learner outcomes.

- Vocabulary terms are bold-faced and then defined in the margin on the page and in the glossary.

- In each chapter, students can focus on one of seven reading strategies. Reading strategy notes appear throughout the chapters to give students practice with applying the strategy.

- Learn More About It provides additional information related to the chapter.

- Great Names in History highlights people who have made contributions to the world.

- Technology Connection highlights inventions at the time that made life better or easier.

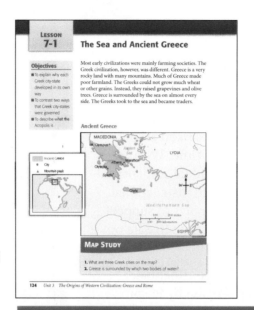

LESSON 7-1

The Sea and Ancient Greece

Objectives
- To explain why each Greek city-state developed in its own way
- To contrast two ways that Greek city-states were governed
- To describe what the Acropolis is

Most early civilizations were mainly farming societies. The Greek civilization, however, was different. Greece is a very rocky land with many mountains. Much of Greece made poor farmland. The Greeks could not grow much wheat or other grains. Instead, they raised grapevines and olive trees. Greece is surrounded by the sea on almost every side. The Greeks took to the sea and became traders.

Ancient Greece

MAP STUDY

1. What are three Greek cities on the map?
2. Greece is surrounded by which two bodies of water?

124   Unit 3   The Origins of Western Civilization: Greece and Rome

Ice Age
A period of time when much of Earth and Earth's water was frozen

Glacier
A large, slow-moving mass of ice and snow

Reading Strategy: Questioning

What do you think you will learn about in this lesson?

MAP STUDY

1. Which names of places are on both maps?
2. Look at both maps. In which present-day country was Sumer located?

GOALS FOR LEARNING

- To explain why the civilization of Sumer grew
- To discuss the growth of Sumerian city-states
- To name the most important Sumerian inventions
- To describe life in Sumer

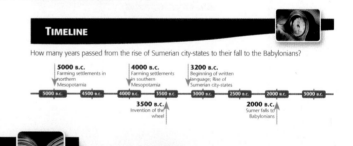

TIMELINE

How many years passed from the rise of Sumerian city-states to their fall to the Babylonians?

5000 B.C.	4000 B.C.	3200 B.C.
Farming settlements in northern Mesopotamia	Farming settlements in southern Mesopotamia	Beginning of written language; Rise of Sumerian city-states

5000 B.C. — 4500 B.C. — 4000 B.C. — 3500 B.C. — 3000 B.C. — 2500 B.C. — 2000 B.C. — 3000 B.C.

3500 B.C. Invention of the wheel

2000 B.C. Sumer falls to Babylonians

LEARN MORE ABOUT IT

The Slave Trade
In Africa, too, some Europeans were tr
animals. The Europeans discovered tha
made in the slave trade. The Spanish a
ships full of Africans to the Americas, v
into slavery.

For a time the Spanish and Portuguese
markets. Soon England and France join

An English naval commander, Sir John
English slave trader. In the 1560s, Haw
each one, he stopped in Africa to find
Then Hawkins carried these Africans to
Americas. There he sold them into slav
in setting up trade between England a

GREAT NAMES IN HISTORY

Hammurabi
Hammurabi was one of the greatest l
from about 1792 B.C. to 1750 B.C. Ha
laws called the **Code** of Hammurabi.
every aspect of life. There were nearly
marriage and divorce, property and b
military service, and so forth. For anyc
Code listed harsh punishments in the
when seeking justice. The Code was
of the individual citizen.

In time, the Babylonians were conque
However, some of their ideas about l
through the ages. Some are included
Code of Hammurabi can be seen in t

TECHNOLOGY CONNECTION

The Work of Archimedes
The Greeks lost a great thinker during the Punic Wars. Archimedes was a scientist, mathematician, philosopher, and inventor.

Archimedes worked for the state during the Punic Wars. During that time, he invented many weapons to defend his town of Syracuse, Italy. He developed a catapult that was used to throw stones at an enemy. Another tool he created could lift or tip an enemy's ship. Also, some claim that he invented a "burning mirror" to reflect the sun's ray toward an enemy.

However, Archimedes is most famous for another discovery. He learned that an item placed in water lost weight based on the amount of water it replaced. This idea was revolutionary for the time.

Archimedes eventually died at the hands of a Roman soldier.

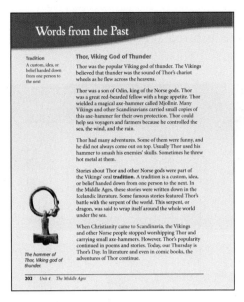

Words from the Past

Tradition
A custom, idea, or belief handed down from one person to the next

Thor, Viking God of Thunder

Thor was the popular Viking god of thunder. The Vikings believed that thunder was the sound of Thor's chariot wheels as he flew across the heavens.

Thor was a son of Odin, king of the Norse gods. Thor was a great red-bearded fellow with a huge appetite. Thor wielded a magical axe-hammer called Mjollnir. Many Vikings and other Scandinavians carried small copies of this axe-hammer for their own protection. Thor could help sea voyagers and farmers because he controlled the sea, the wind, and the rain.

Thor had many adventures. Some of them were funny, and he did not always come out on top. Usually Thor used his hammer to smash his enemies' skulls. Sometimes he threw hot metal at them.

Stories about Thor and other Norse gods were part of the Vikings' oral **tradition**. A tradition is a custom, idea, or belief handed down from one person to the next. In the Middle Ages, these stories were written down in the Icelandic literature. Some famous stories featured Thor's battle with the serpent of the world. This serpent, or dragon, was said to wrap itself around the whole world under the sea.

When Christianity came to Scandinavia, the Vikings and other Norse people stopped worshipping Thor and carrying small axe-hammers. However, Thor's popularity continued in poems and stories. Today, our Thursday is Thor's Day. In literature and even in comic books, the adventures of Thor continue.

The hammer of Thor, Viking god of thunder.

202 Unit 4 The Middle Ages

Test Tip

Be sure you understand what a test question is asking. Read it twice if necessary.

- Words from the Past presents written or spoken words related to the chapter that continue to affect the world today.

- Lesson Review questions allow students to check their understanding of key concepts presented in the text.

- Summaries at the end of each chapter and unit highlight main ideas for students.

- Chapter Reviews allow students and teachers to check for skill mastery. These cover the objectives in the Goals for Learning at the beginning of each chapter, and the Objectives at the beginning of each lesson.

- Group Activities appear at the end of each Chapter Review. They provide students with engaging activities to apply their knowledge.

- Test-Taking Tips at the end of each Chapter Review help reduce test anxiety and improve test scores.

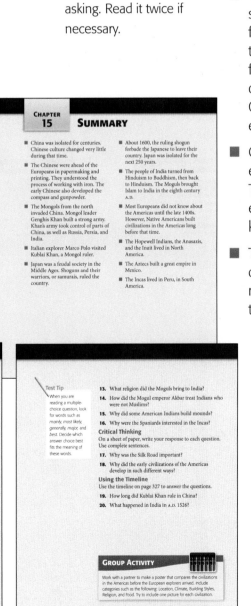

LESSON 15-1 REVIEW

On a sheet of paper, write the answer to each question. Use complete sentences.

1. What are three things the Chinese invented?
2. What was the route known as the Silk Road?
3. What lands did Genghis Khan conquer?
4. What role did Marco Polo have in teaching the Europeans about Chinese discoveries?

On a sheet of paper, write the letter of the answer that correctly completes each sentence.

5. The Mongols were _____ who roamed the vast plains of central Asia.
   A traders   B armies   C nomads   D farmers
6. The Mongols were among the fiercest _____ in history.
   A conquerors   B horsemen   C travelers   D rulers
7. _____ was a clever, ruthless ruler who built up a huge Mongol army.
   A Marco Polo   B Kublai Khan   C Babar   D Genghis Khan
8. _____ was one of the greatest rulers. He allowed religious freedom, ensured roads were good for travelers, and developed a postal service.
   A Marco Polo   B Kublai Khan   C Babar   D Genghis Khan
9. Marco Polo was an Italian _____ who traveled throughout China for 17 years.
   A trader   B farmer   C ruler   D inventor
10. The _____ dynasty followed the Mongol rule in China.
   A Khan   B Genoa   C Chinese   D Ming

CHAPTER 15 SUMMARY

- China was isolated for centuries. Chinese culture changed very little during that time.
- The Chinese were ahead of the Europeans in papermaking and printing. They understood the process of working with iron. The early Chinese also developed the compass and gunpowder.
- The Mongols from the north invaded China. Mongol leader Genghis Khan built a strong army. Khan's army took control of parts of China, as well as Russia, Persia, and India.
- Italian explorer Marco Polo visited Kublai Khan, a Mongol ruler.
- Japan was a feudal society in the Middle Ages. Shoguns and their warriors, or samurais, ruled the country.
- About 1600, the ruling shogun forbade the Japanese to leave their country. Japan was isolated for the next 250 years.
- The people of India turned from Hinduism to Buddhism, then back to Hinduism. The Moguls brought Islam to India in the eighth century A.D.
- Most Europeans did not know about the Americas until the late 1400s. However, Native Americans built civilizations in the Americas long before that time.
- The Hopewell Indians, the Anasazis, and the Inuit lived in North America.
- The Aztecs built a great empire in Mexico.
- The Incas lived in Peru, in South America.

CHAPTER 15 REVIEW

Word Bank
acupuncture
barter
forge
missionaries
mosaic
privileges
samurai
shogun
terraced

Vocabulary Review
On a sheet of paper, use the words from the Word Bank to complete each sentence correctly.

1. _____ were upper-class, feudal warriors who fought for the nobles.
2. A(n) _____ was a great general governing Japan.
3. The Japanese were suspicious of Christian _____, so the ruling shogun closed Japan's doors.
4. The Aztecs _____ their land to stop the soil from eroding.
5. The Aztecs would _____ for goods, exchanging them without the use of money.
6. Small pieces of stone or glass can be used to create a(n) _____.
7. The Chinese invented _____, which uses needles to treat pain and illness.
8. The Chinese knew how to _____ iron and mine salt.
9. Samurai were given many _____, including wealth and land.

Chapter Review Questions
On a sheet of paper, write the answer to each question. Use complete sentences.

10. Where did the Ming emperors of China live?
11. How did Marco Polo feel about what he had seen in China?
12. What were the classes in Japan during the Middle Ages?

Test Tip
When you are reading a multiple-choice question, look for words such as *mainly, most likely, generally, major,* and *best.* Decide which answer choice best fits the meaning of these words.

13. What religion did the Moguls bring to India?
14. How did the Mogul emperor Akbar treat Indians who were not Muslims?
15. Why did some American Indians build mounds?
16. Why were the Spaniards interested in the Incas?

Critical Thinking
On a sheet of paper, write your response to each question. Use complete sentences.

17. Why was the Silk Road important?
18. Why did the early civilizations of the Americas develop in such different ways?

Using the Timeline
Use the timeline on page 327 to answer the questions.

19. How long did Kublai Khan rule in China?
20. What happened in India in A.D. 1526?

GROUP ACTIVITY

Work with a partner to make a poster that compares the civilizations in the Americas before the European explorers arrived. Include categories such as the following: Location, Climate, Building Styles, Religion, and Food. Try to include one picture for each civilization.

330 Unit 6 The Age of Exploration and Conquest

1100–1700   To the East; To the West   Chapter 15   331

The comprehensive, wraparound Teacher's Edition provides instructional strategies at point of use. Everything from preparation guidelines to teaching tips and strategies are included in an easy-to-use format. Activities are featured at point of use for teacher convenience.

UNIT 1

PLANNING GUIDE

Looking at the World's History

	Student Pages	Vocabulary	Map Study	Reading Strategy	Lesson Review	Chapter Summary/Review
Chapter 1 What Is History?	2–17	✓		✓		15–17
Lesson 1–1 History Is All About Change	4–7	✓		✓	7	
Lesson 1–2 Historians and Archaeologists	8–10	✓		✓	10	
Lesson 1–3 Maps and Timelines	11–14	✓	✓	✓	14	
Chapter 2 Early Humans: The Story Begins	18–35	✓		✓		33–35
Lesson 2–1 The Hunters	20–23	✓		✓	23	
Lesson 2–2 The Agricultural Revolution	24–27	✓		✓	27	
Lesson 2–3 The Fertile Crescent	28–32	✓	✓	✓	32	

Student Text Features / Teaching Strategies / Learning Styles / Teacher's Resource Library

	Words from the Past	Learn More About It	Great Names in History	Technology Connection	Geography Note	You Decide/Remember/History Fact	Timeline Study	ELL/ESL Strategy	Background Information	Common Error	Life Skills Connection	Key Vocabulary Words	Study Skills	Applications (Home, Career, Community)	Online Connection	Teacher Alert	World Cultures	Auditory/Verbal	Body/Kinesthetic	Interpersonal/Group Learning	Logical/Mathematical	Visual/Spatial	Activities/Modified Activities	Workbook Activities	Self-Study Guide	Chapter Outline
Chapter 1													3	3											✓	✓
Lesson 1–1						5, 6		5	4	5					6	5	5	5						1	1	
Lesson 1–2	8	9						9	9				9	10						9			2	2		
Lesson 1–3						13		13	12	13								12		11	13	3	3			
Chapter 2							19	19														✓	✓			
Lesson 2–1	22	21						22	21	23								21			21, 22	4	4			
Lesson 2–2			25			24, 26		25	25	25, 26			25, 26	24		26						5	5			
Lesson 2–3			30	28	30	30		29	31			28			31			30	30			6	6			

Chapter Activities

Teacher's Resource Library
Life Skills Connection 1–2
Key Vocabulary Words 1–2

Assessment Options

Student Text
Chapter Reviews 1–2
Teacher's Resource Library
Chapter 1 Mastery Tests A and B
Chapter 2 Mastery Tests A and B
Unit 1 Mastery Test
Teacher's Edition
Chapter Projects 1–2

Modified Activities

The Teacher's Resource Library (TRL) contains a set of lower-level worksheets called Modified Activities. These worksheets cover the same content as the standard Activities but are written at a lower reading level.

Skill Track

Use Skill Track for *World History* to monitor student progress and meet the demands of adequate yearly progress (AYP). Make informed instructional decisions with individual student and class reports of lesson and chapter assessments. With immediate and ongoing feedback, students will also see what they have learned and where they need more reinforcement and practice.

xxxiiA   Unit 1   Looking at the World's History   Looking at the World's History   Unit 1   xxxiiB

Chapter Planning Guides

- The Planning Guide saves valuable preparation time by organizing all materials for each chapter.

- A complete listing of lessons allows you to preview each chapter quickly.

- Assessment options are highlighted for easy reference. Options include:

  Chapter Reviews

  Chapter Mastery Tests, Forms A and B

  Midterm and Final Mastery Tests

- Page numbers of Student Text and Teacher's Edition features help you customize lesson plans to your students.

- Many teaching strategies and learning styles are listed to support students with diverse needs.

- Activities in the Teacher's Resource Library are listed.

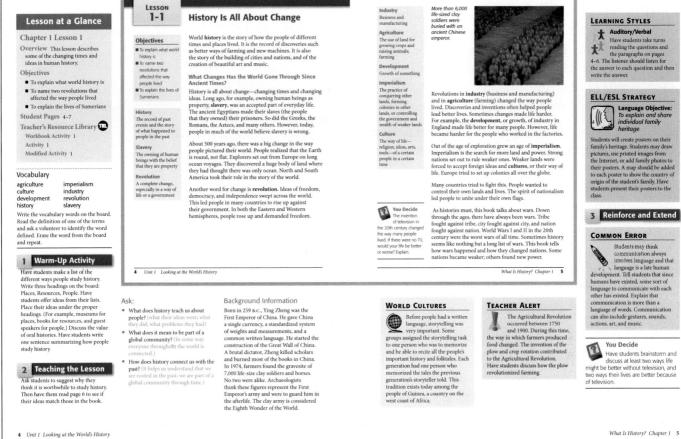

Lessons

- Quick overviews of chapters and lessons save planning time.

- Lesson objectives are listed for easy reference.

- Page references are provided for convenience.

- Easy-to-follow lesson plans in three steps save time: Warm-Up Activity, Teaching the Lesson, and Reinforce and Extend.

- Teacher Alerts and Common Error highlight content that may need further explanation.

- Students use social studies concepts in real-life applications through Life Skills Connection activities.

- Applications: Three areas of application—At Home, Career Connection, and In the Community—help students relate language to the world outside the classroom. Applications motivate students and make learning relevant.

- Online Connections list relevant Web sites.

- Learning Styles activities provide teaching strategies to help meet the needs of students with diverse ways of learning. Modalities include Auditory/Verbal, Visual/Spatial, Body/Kinesthetic, Logical/Mathematical, and Interpersonal/Group Learning. Targeted teaching activities are provided for ELL students.

- Answers are provided in the Teacher's Edition for all reviews in the Student Text. Answers to the Teacher's Resource Library and Student Workbook are provided at the back of this Teacher's Edition and on the TRL CD-ROM.

- Several worksheets, including Activities, Workbook Activities, and Chapter Mastery Tests from the Teacher's Resource Library, are shown at point of use in reduced form.

Support for Students Learning English

Increasing numbers of students learning English are among the students in most schools and classrooms. The purpose of the ELL/ESL Strategy feature in this Teacher's Edition is to incorporate the language and content needs of English Language Learners in a regular and explicit manner.

ELL/ESL Strategy activities promote English language acquisition in the context of content area learning. Students should not be separated or isolated for these activities and interaction with English-speaking peers is always encouraged.

The ELL/ESL Strategy helps the teacher scaffold the content and presentation in relation to students' language and skill proficiency. Each activity suggests to the teacher some ideas about how to adjust the presentation of content to meet the varying needs of diverse learners, including students learning English. *Scaffolding* refers to structuring the introduction of vocabulary, concepts, and skills by providing additional supports or modifications based on students' needs. Ideally, these supports become less necessary as students' language proficiency increases and their knowledge and skill level becomes more developed.

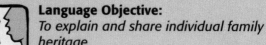

ELL/ESL STRATEGY

Language Objective:
To explain and share individual family heritage

Students will create posters on their family's heritage. Students may draw pictures, use printed images from the Internet, or add family photos to their posters. A map should be added to each poster to show the country of origin of the student's family. Have students present their posters to the class.

Each activity includes a language objective and strategy related to *listening, speaking, reading,* or *writing.* The language objective and activity relate to one or more content objectives listed in the Teacher's Edition under Lesson at a Glance. Some examples of language objectives include: reading for meaning, understanding different styles or purposes of writing, identifying and practicing common grammar structures, learning vocabulary specific to the content area, preparing and giving a group presentation, speaking in front of a group, or discussing an assigned topic as a small group.

Strategies That Support English Learners

- Identify and build on prior knowledge or experience; start with what's familiar and elaborate to include new content and new connections, personal associations, cultural context
- Use visuals and graphic organizers—illustrations, photos, charts, posters, graphs, maps, tables, webs, flow charts, timelines, diagrams
- Use hands-on artifacts (realia) or manipulatives
- Provide *comprehensible input*—paraphrase content, give additional examples, elaborate on student background knowledge and responses; be aware of rate of speech, syntax, and language structure and adjust accordingly
- Begin with lower-level, fact recall questions and move to questions that require higher-order critical-thinking skills (application, hypothesis, prediction, analysis, synthesis, evaluation)
- Teach vocabulary—pronunciations, key words or phrases, multiple meanings, idioms/expressions, academic or content language

- Have students create word banks or word walls for content (academic) vocabulary
- Teach and model specific reading and writing strategies—advance organizers, main idea, meaning from context, preview, predict, make inferences, summarize, guided reading
- Support communication with gestures and body language
- Teach and practice functional language skills—negotiate meaning, ask for clarification, confirm information, argue persuasively
- Teach and practice study skills—structured note-taking, outlining, use of reference materials
- Use cooperative learning, peer tutoring, or other small group learning strategies
- Plan opportunities for student interaction—create a skit and act it out, drama, role play, storytelling
- Practice self-monitoring and self-evaluation—students reflect on their own comprehension or activity with self-checks

How Do AGS Globe Textbooks Support Students Learning English?

AGS Globe is committed to helping all students succeed. For this reason, AGS Globe textbooks and teaching materials incorporate research-based design elements and instructional methodologies configured to allow diverse students greater access to subject area content. Content access is facilitated by controlled reading level, coherent text, and vocabulary development. Effective instructional design is accomplished by applying research to lesson construction, learning activities, and assessments.

AGS Globe materials feature key elements that support the needs of students learning English in sheltered and immersion settings.

Key Elements	*AGS Globe Features*
Lesson Preparation	■ Content- and language-specific objectives
Building Background	■ Warm-Up Activity ■ Explicit vocabulary instruction and practice with multiple exposures to new words ■ Background information; building on prior knowledge and experience
Comprehensible Input	■ Controlled reading level in student text (Grades 3–4) ■ Highlighted vocabulary terms with definitions ■ Student glossary with pronunciations ■ Clean graphic and visual support ■ Content links to examples ■ Sidebar notes to highlight and clarify content ■ Audio text recordings (selected titles) ■ Modified Activity pages (Grade 2 reading level)
Lesson Delivery	■ Teaching the Lesson/3-Step Teaching Plan ■ Short, skill- or content-specific lessons ■ Orderly presentation of content with structural cues
Strategies	■ ELL/ESL Strategy activities ■ Learning Styles activities ■ Writing prompts in student text ■ Teaching Strategies Transparencies provide additional graphic organizers ■ Study skills: Self-Study Guides, Chapter Outlines
Interaction	■ Vocabulary-building activities ■ Language-based ELL/ESL Strategy activities ■ Learning Styles activities ■ Reinforce and Extend activities
Practice/Application	■ Skill practice or concept application in student text ■ Reinforce and Extend activities ■ Career, home, and community applications ■ Student Workbook ■ Multiple TRL activity pages
Review and Assessment	■ Lesson reviews, chapter reviews, unit reviews ■ Skill Track monitors student progress ■ Chapter, Unit, Midterm, and Final Mastery Tests

For more information on these key elements, see Echevarria, J., Vogt, M., & Short, D. (2004). *Making content comprehensible for English language learners: The SIOP model* (2nd ed.). Boston, MA: Allyn & Bacon.

Learning Styles

Differentiated instruction allows teachers to address the needs of diverse learners and the variety of ways students process and learn information. The Learning Styles activities in this Teacher's Edition provide additional teaching strategies to help students understand lesson content by teaching or expanding upon the content in a different way. The activities are designed to help teachers capitalize on students' individual strengths and learning styles.

The Learning Styles activities highlight individual learning styles and are classified based on Howard Gardner's theory of multiple intelligences: Auditory/Verbal, Body/Kinesthetic, Interpersonal/Group Learning, Logical/Mathematical, and Visual/Spatial.

Following are examples of activities featured in the Pacemaker® *World History* Teacher's Edition:

Logical/Mathematical
Students learn by using logical/mathematical thinking and problem solving in relation to the lesson content.

LEARNING STYLES

Logical/Mathematical

Ask students to use the distance key to determine how many miles or kilometers (km) early people might have traveled on foot to migrate from South Africa to North America. (1.5 centimeters (cm) = 3,000 miles, and 1 cm = 3,000 km. The distance on the map is approximately 7 cm = 21,000 km or about 13,500 miles.

Visual/Spatial
Students learn by viewing or creating illustrations, graphics, patterns, or additional visual demonstrations beyond what is in the text.

LEARNING STYLES

Visual/Spatial

The timeline on page 13 covers a great deal of time. Divide the timeline into shorter periods and assign them to groups. Have students create posters with their period's date and labels. Have them skim later chapters in the book for things to draw or paint in their time period. When the groups have finished, have the class connect all the posters in order to make one complete timeline.

Auditory/Verbal
Students learn by listening to text read aloud or from an audiorecording, and from other listening or speaking activities. Musical activities related to the content may help auditory learners.

LEARNING STYLES

Auditory/Verbal

Have students take turns reading the questions and the paragraphs on pages 4–6. The listener should listen for the answer to each question and then write the answer.

Interpersonal/Group Learning
Students learn from working with at least one other person or in a cooperative learning group on activities that involve a process and an end product.

LEARNING STYLES

Interpersonal/Group Learning

To reinforce students' understanding of primary and secondary sources, divide the class into small groups. Have each group make a poster with the headings "Primary Source" and "Secondary Source." Have them select a lesson from the U.S. Declaration of Independence, the *Gettysburg Address*, or another historic document and place it under the heading "Primary Source." Then have them paraphrase the primary source by writing it in their own words under the "Secondary Source" heading. Students can then read their source material.

Body/Kinesthetic
Students learn from activities that include physical movement, manipulatives, or other tactile experiences.

LEARNING STYLES

Body/Kinesthetic

Have students find maps of the world as the world was at various times in the past. For example, have them find on the Internet a map that shows Pangaea, the route Columbus took to discover the Americas, or the route that Darwin sailed on the Beagle. Then have them create a poster of their map by cutting out the continents and marking landmarks. Remind them to include a key. Display the posters in the classroom.

Teacher's Resource Library Highlights

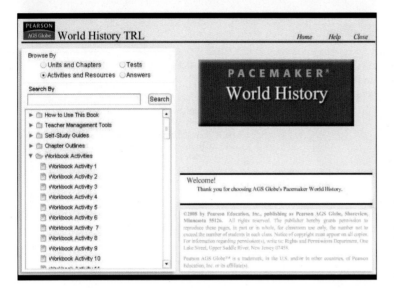

All of the activities you'll need to reinforce and extend the text are conveniently located on the Teacher's Resource Library (TRL) CD-ROM. All of the reproducible activities pictured in the Teacher's Edition are ready to select, view, and print. You can also preview other materials by linking directly to the AGS Globe Web site.

Workbook Activities
Workbook Activities are available to reinforce and extend skills from each lesson of the textbook. A bound workbook format is also available.

Activities
Activities for each lesson of the textbook give students additional skills practice.

Modified Activities
These activities cover the same content as the Activities but are written at a lower reading level.

Life Skills Connections
Relevant activities help students extend their knowledge to the real world and reinforce concepts covered in class.

Self-Study Guides
An assignment guide provides teachers with the flexibility for individualized instruction or independent study.

Mastery Tests
Chapter, Unit, Midterm, and Final Mastery Tests are convenient assessment options. Critical-thinking items are included.

Teacher Management Tools
These resource tools can assist teachers with lesson planning and classroom management.

Answer Key
All answers to reproducible activities are included in the TRL and in the Teacher's Edition.

Workbook Activities

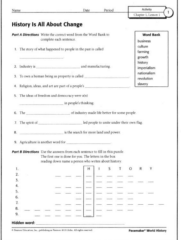

Activities

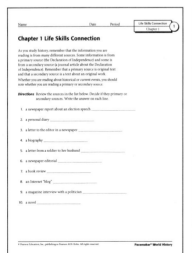

Life Skills Connections

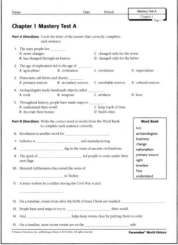

Mastery Tests

Synopsis of the Scientific Research Base

Research-Based Principles	AGS Globe Textbooks	References
Standards Alignment		
Subject area instruction needs to be based on skills, concepts, and processes represented by common standards for that subject area.	■ Textbook content and skills aligned with national standards and state grade-level or course-specific content standards, where available	Matlock, L., Fielder, K., & Walsh, D. (2001). Building the foundation for standards-based instruction for all students. *Teaching Exceptional Children, 33*(5), 68–72. Miller, S. P., & Mercer, C. D. (1997). Educational aspects of mathematics disabilities. *Journal of Learning Disabilities, 30*(1), 47–56. Reys, R., Reys, B., Lapan, R., Holliday, G. & Wasman, D. (2003). Assessing the impact of standards-based middle grades mathematics curriculum materials on student achievement. *Journal of Research in Mathematics Education, 34*(1), 74–95.
Readability		
Many students struggle to learn from core content-area textbooks that are written too high above their reading level. Students need access to textbooks written at a level they can read and understand, where the reading level is within the students' range of comprehension.	■ Grade 4.0 or lower readability using the Spache formula ■ Controlled vocabulary matched to student reading ability and use of synonyms to replace non-essential difficult words above grade 4 ■ Simple sentence structures ■ Limited sentence length	Allington, R. L. (2002). You can't learn much from books you can't read. *Educational Leadership, 60*(3), 16–19. Chall, J. S., & Conard, S. S. (1991). *Should textbooks challenge students? The case for easier or harder textbooks.* New York: Teachers College Press. *Readability calculations.* (2000). Dallas: Micro Power & Light Company.
Language Complexity and Sequence		
Students struggling with vocabulary and text comprehension need textbooks with accessible language.	■ Simple, direct language using an active voice ■ Clear organization to facilitate understanding ■ Explicit language signals to show sequence of and links between concepts and ideas	Anderson, T. H., & Armbruster, B. B. (1984). Readable texts, or selecting a textbook is not like buying a pair of shoes. In R. C. Anderson, J. Osborne, & R. J. Tierney (Eds.), *Learning to read in American schools* (pp. 151–162). Hillsdale, NJ: Lawrence Erlbaum Associates, Inc. Curtis, M. E. (2002, May 20). *Adolescent reading: A synthesis of research.* Paper presented at the Practice Models for Adolescent Literacy Success Conference, U.S. Department of Education. Washington, DC: National Institute of Child Health and Human Development. Retrieved September 15, 2003, from http://216.26.160.105/conf/nichd/synthesis.asp McAlpine, L., & Weston, C. (1994). The attributes of instructional materials. *Performance Improvement Quarterly, 7*(1), 19–30. Seidenberg, P. L. (1989). Relating text-processing research to reading and writing instruction for learning disabled students. *Learning Disabilities Focus, 5*(1), 4–12.
Vocabulary Use and Development		
Students need content-related vocabulary instruction in the context of readable and meaningful text.	■ New vocabulary boldfaced on first occurrence, used in context, and defined in a sidebar ■ Glossary with pronunciation, definition, and relevant graphic illustrations for all vocabulary words ■ Direct vocabulary instruction introduced in the Teacher's Edition and reinforced in context throughout ■ Multiple exposures to new vocabulary in text and practice exercises	Ciborowski, J. (1992). *Textbooks and the students who can't read them: A guide to teaching content.* Cambridge, MA: Brookline. Kameenui, E. J., & Simmons, D. C. (1990). *Designing instructional strategies.* Columbus, OH: Merrill Publishing Company. Marzano, R. J. (1998). *A theory-based meta-analysis of research on instruction.* Aurora, CO: Mid-Continent Research for Education and Learning. Retrieved October 1, 2003, from http://www.mcrel.org/topics/productDetail/asp?productID=83 McAlpine, L., & Weston, C. (1994). The attributes of instructional materials. *Performance Improvement Quarterly, 7*(1), 19–30. National Reading Panel. (2000). *Teaching children to read: An evidence-based assessment of the scientific research literature on reading and its implications for reading instruction.* Reports of the subgroups. Washington, DC: National Institute of Child Health and Human Development. Taylor, S. E., Frackenpohl, H., White, C. E., Nieroroda, B. W., Browning, C. L., & Birsner, E. P. (1989). *EDL core vocabularies in reading, mathematics, science, and social studies.* Austin, TX: Steck-Vaughn.

Research-Based Principles	AGS Globe Textbooks	References

Text Organization: Presentation and Structure

Students need an uncluttered page layout, with easy-to-read print, that clearly directs the reader to main ideas, important information, examples, and comprehensive practice and review.

Reading comprehension is improved by structural features in the text that make it easier for learners to access the content.

Print characteristics and page layout:
- Serif font for body copy; sans serif font for boxed features, examples
- Maximum line length of 5" for ease of reading
- Unjustified (ragged) right margins
- Major/minor column page design presents primary instructional information in the major column and support content in the sidebar or in a box

Presentation characteristics:
- Lesson introductions, summaries
- Explicit lesson titles, headings, and subheadings label and organize main ideas
- Signals alert readers to important information, content connections, illustrations, graphics
- Cues (e.g., boldface type) highlight important information

Text structure:
- Lesson heads in question or statement format guide comprehension
- Text written to explicitly link facts and concepts within and across lessons; text cohesiveness
- Each skill or concept linked to direct practice and review

Armbruster, B. B., & Anderson, T. H. (1988). On selecting "considerate" content area textbooks. *Remedial and Special Education, 9*(1), 47–52.

Beck, I. L., McKeown, M. G., & Grommoll, E. W. (1989). Learning from social studies texts. *Cognition and Instruction, 6*(2), 99–158.

Chambliss, M. J. (1994). Evaluating the quality of textbooks for diverse learners. *Remedial and Special Education, 15*(5), 348–362.

Ciborowski, J. (1992). *Textbooks and the students who can't read them: A guide to teaching content.* Cambridge, MA: Brookline.

Dickson, S. V., Simmons, D. C., & Kameenui, E. J. (1995). *Text organization and its relation to reading comprehension: A synthesis of the research* (Technical Report No. 17) and *Text organization: Curricular and instructional implications for diverse learners* (Technical Report No. 18). National Center to Improve the Tools of Educators. Eugene, OR: University of Oregon. Retrieved January 26, 2000, from http://idea.uoregon.edu/~ncite/documents/techrep/tech17.html and http://idea.uoregon.edu/~ncite/documents/techrep/tech18.html

Dickson, S. V., Simmons, D. C., & Kameenui, E. J. (1998). Text organization: Research bases *and* Text organization: Instructional and curricular basics and implications. In D. C. Simmons & E. J. Kameenui (Eds.), *What reading research tells us about children with diverse learning needs: Bases and basics* (pp. 239–278; 279–294). Mahwah, NJ: Lawrence Erlbaum Associates, Inc.

Mansfield, J. S., Legge, G. E., & Bane, M. C. (1996). Psychophysics of reading. XV: Font effects in normal and low vision. *Investigative Ophthalmology and Vision Science, 37*, 1492–1501.

McAlpine, L., & Weston, C. (1994). The attributes of instructional materials. *Performance Improvement Quarterly, 7*(1), 19–30.

McNamara, D. S., Kintsche, E., Songer, N. B., & Kintsche, W. (1996). Are good texts always better? Interactions of text coherence, background knowledge, and levels of understanding in learning from text. *Cognition and Instruction, 14*(1), 1–43.

Tyree, R. B., Fiore, T. A., & Cook, R. A. (1994). Instructional materials for diverse learners: Features and considerations for textbook design. *Remedial and Special Education, 15*(6), 363–377.

Differentiated Instruction and Learning Styles

Student learning is more successful when tasks are aligned with academic skill levels and developmental stage, and adjustments are made to allow students multiple means to engage and express their learning strengths and styles at appropriate levels of challenge and support.

Differentiated instruction allows teachers to organize instruction to adjust for diverse learning needs within a classroom.

Learning activities that capitalize on students' learning styles can structure planning for individual differences based on multiple intelligences theory.

- Multiple features, including Learning Styles activities, help teachers match assignments to students' abilities and interests
- Variety of media to select from—print, audio, visual, software
- Step-by-step, part-by-part basic content and skill-level lessons in the Student and Teacher's Editions
- Modified Activities written at a Grade 2 (Spache) readability in the Teacher's Resource Library
- Variety of review materials, activities, sidebars, and alternative readings
- Multiple assessments—lesson or chapter reviews, end-of-chapter tests, cumulative midterm/final mastery tests, alternative assessment items

Learning Styles activities include:
- Auditory/Verbal
- Body/Kinesthetic
- Interpersonal/Group Learning
- Logical/Mathematical
- Visual/Spatial

ELL/ESL Strategies provide support for students who are learning English and lesson content concurrently.

Allington, R. L. (2002). You can't learn much from books you can't read. *Educational Leadership, 60*(3), 16–19.

Carnine, D. (1994). Introduction to the mini-series: Diverse learners and prevailing, emerging, and research-based educational approaches and their tools. *School Psychology Review, 23*(3), 341–350.

Forsten, C., Grant, J., & Hollas, B. (2003). *Differentiating textbooks: Strategies to improve student comprehension and motivation.* Peterborough, NH: Crystal Springs Books.

Gardner, H. (1983). *Frames of mind: The theory of multiple intelligences.* New York: Harper and Row.

Gersten, R., & Baker, S. (2000). The professional knowledge base on instructional practices that support cognitive growth for English-language learners. In R. Gersten, E. P. Schiller, & S. Vaughn (Eds.), *Contemporary special education research: Syntheses of the knowledge base on critical instructional issues* (pp. 31–80). Mahwah, NJ: Lawrence Erlbaum Associates, Inc.

Hall, T. (2002, June). *Effective classroom practices report: Differentiated instruction.* Wakefield, NJ: National Center on Accessing the General Curriculum. Retrieved September 29, 2003, from http://www.cast.org/cac/index.cfm?i=2876

Lazear, D. (1999). *Eight ways of knowing: Teaching for multiple intelligences* (3rd ed.). Arlington Heights, IL: Skylight Training and Publishing.

Orlich, D. C., Harder, R. J., Callahan, R. C., & Gibson, H. W. (2001). *Teaching strategies: A guide to better instruction* (6th ed.). Boston: Houghton Mifflin Company.

Roderick, M. & Camburn, E. (1999). Risk and recovery from course failure in the early years of high school. *American Educational Research Journal, 36*(2), 303–343.

Tomlinson, C. A. (1999). *The differentiated classroom: Responding to the needs of all learners.* Alexandria, VA: Association for Supervision and Curriculum Development.

Synopsis of the Scientific Research Base

Research-Based Principles	AGS Globe Textbooks	References

Instructional Design: Lesson Structure and Learner Support Strategies

Instruction that includes the components of effective instruction, utilizes effective strategies and interventions to facilitate student learning, and aligns with standards improves learning for all students, especially diverse learners and students who are struggling.

Elements of effective instruction:

Step 1: Introduce the lesson and prepare students to learn
Step 2: Provide instruction and guided practice
Step 3: Provide opportunities for applied practice and generalization

Organizational tools:
Advance organizers
Graphic organizers

Instructional process techniques:
Cooperative learning
Student self-monitoring and questioning
Real-life examples
Mnemonics

Step 1: Introduce the lesson and prepare students to learn
In the Student Edition:
- "How to Use This Book" feature explicitly teaches text organization
- Chapter and lesson previews with graphic and visual organizers
- Goals for Learning
- Sidebar notes review skills and important facts and information

In the Teacher's Edition:
- Lesson objectives
- Explicit *3-Step Teaching Plan* begins with "Warm-Up Activity" to inform students of objectives, connect to previous learning and background knowledge, review skills, and motivate students to engage in learning

Step 2: Provide instruction and guided practice
In the Student Edition:
- Short, manageable lessons break content and skills into smaller, step-by-step, part-by-part pieces
- Systematic presentation of lesson concepts and skills
- Chapter and lesson headings presented as questions or statements
- Graphic organizers arrange content visually—charts, graphs, tables, diagrams, bulleted lists, arrows, graphics, mnemonics, illustrations, and captions
- Models or examples link directly to the explanation of the concept
- Multiple opportunities for direct practice throughout

In the Teacher's Edition:
- *3-Step Teaching Plan* for each lesson includes "Teaching the Lesson" with direct instruction, and helps teachers present and clarify lesson skills and concepts through guided practice and modeling of important ideas
- Supplemental strategies and activities, including hands-on modeling, transparencies, graphic organizers, visual aids, learning styles

Step 3: Provide opportunities for applied practice and generalization
In the Student Edition:
- Each skill or concept lesson is followed by direct practice or review questions
- Multiple exercises throughout
- Generalization and application activities in sidebars and lessons link content to real-life applications
- Chapter reviews and summaries highlight major points

Allsopp, D. H. (1990). Using modeling, manipulatives, and mnemonics with eighth-grade math students. *Teaching Exceptional Children, 31*(2), 74–81.

Chambliss, M. J. (1994). Evaluating the quality of textbooks for diverse learners. *Remedial and Special Education, 15*(5), 348–362.

Ciborowski, J. (1992). *Textbooks and the students who can't read them: A guide to teaching content.* Cambridge, MA: Brookline.

Cole, R. W. (Ed.). (1995). *Educating everybody's children: Diverse teaching strategies for diverse learners.* Alexandria, VA: Association for Supervision and Curriculum Development.

Curtis, M. E. (2002, May 20). *Adolescent reading: A synthesis of research.* Paper presented at the Practice Models for Adolescent Literacy Success Conference, U.S. Department of Education. Washington, DC: National Institute of Child Health and Human Development. Retrieved September 15, 2003, from http://216.26.160.105/conf/nichd/synthesis.asp

Dickson, S. V., Simmons, D. C., & Kameenui, E. J. (1995). *Text organization: Curricular and instructional implications for diverse learners* (Technical Report No. 18). National Center to Improve the Tools of Educators. Eugene, OR: University of Oregon. Retrieved January 26, 2000, from http://idea.uoregon.edu/~ncite/documents/techrep/tech18.html

Dixon, R. C., Carnine, D. W., Lee, D., Wallin, J., & Chard, D. (1998). *Review of high quality experimental mathematics research: Report to the California State Board of Education.* Sacramento, CA: California State Board of Education.

Jarrett, D. (1999). *The inclusive classroom: Mathematics and science instruction for students with learning disabilities—It's just good teaching.* Portland, OR: Northwest Regional Educational Laboratory.

Johnson, D. W., Johnson, R. T., & Stanne, M. B. (2000, May). *Cooperative learning methods: A meta-analysis.* Minneapolis: The Cooperative Learning Center, University of Minnesota. Retrieved October 29, 2003, from http://www.cooplearn.org/pages/cl-methods.html

Kameenui, E. J., & Simmons, D. C. (1990). *Designing instructional strategies.* Columbus, OH: Merrill Publishing Company.

Lovitt, T. C., & Horton, S. V. (1994). Strategies for adapting science textbooks for youth with learning disabilities. *Remedial and Special Education, 15*(2), 105–116.

Marzano, R. J. (1998). *A theory-based meta-analysis of research on instruction.* Aurora, CO: Mid-Continent Research for Education and Learning. Retrieved October 1, 2003, from http://www.mcrel.org/topics/productDetail/asp?productID=83

Marzano, R. J., Pickering, D. J., & Pollock, J. E. (2001). *Classroom instruction that works: Research-based strategies for increasing student achievement.* Alexandria, VA: Association for Supervision and Curriculum Development.

Miller, S. P., & Mercer, C. D. (1993). Mnemonics: Enhancing the math performance of students with learning difficulties. *Intervention in School and Clinic, 29*(2), 78–82.

Montague, M. (1997). Cognitive strategy instruction in mathematics for students with learning disabilities. *Journal of Learning Disabilities, 30*(2), 164–177.

Reiser, R. A., & Dick, W. (1996). *Instructional planning: A guide for teachers* (2nd ed.). Boston: Allyn and Bacon.

Roderick, M., & Camburn, E. (1999). Risk and recovery from course failure in the early years of high school. *American Educational Research Journal, 36*(2), 303–343.

Steele, M. (2002). Strategies for helping students who have learning disabilities in mathematics. *Mathematics Teaching in the Middle School, 8*(3), 140–143.

Swanson, H. L. (2000). What instruction works for students with learning disabilities? Summarizing the results from a meta-analysis of intervention studies. In R. Gersten, E. P. Schiller, & S. Vaughn (Eds.), *Contemporary special education research: Syntheses of the knowledge base on critical instructional issues* (pp. 1–30). Mahwah, NJ: Lawrence Erlbaum Associates, Inc.

Tyree, R. B., Fiore, T. A., & Cook, R. A. (1994). Instructional materials for diverse learners: Features and considerations for textbook design. *Remedial and Special Education, 15*(6), 363–377.

Vaughn, S., Gersten, R., & Chard, D. J. (2000). The underlying message in LD intervention research: Findings from research syntheses. *Exceptional Children, 67*(1), 99–114.

Instructional Design: Lesson Structure and Learner Support Strategies, *continued from previous page*

In the Teacher's Edition:

- 3-Step Teaching Lesson Plan concludes with "Reinforce and Extend" to reinforce, reteach, and extend lesson skills and concepts
- Unit or chapter projects link and apply unit or chapter concepts
- Multiple supplemental/alternative activities for individual and group learning and problem solving
- Career, home, and community application exercises

In the Teacher's Resource Library:

- Multiple exercises in Student Workbook and reproducibles offer applications, content extensions, additional practice, and modified activities at a lower (Grade 2 Spache) readability

Skill Track:

- Monitors student learning and guides teacher feedback to student

Ongoing Assessment and Tracking Student Progress

Textbooks can incorporate features to facilitate and support assessment of learning, allowing teachers to monitor student progress and provide information on mastery level and the need for instructional changes.

Assessment should measure student progress on learning goals over the course of a lesson, chapter, or content-area textbook.

Students and teachers need timely and ongoing feedback so instruction can focus on specific skill development.

- Test-taking tips and strategies for students who benefit from explicit strategy instruction
- Lesson and chapter reviews check student understanding of content
- Workbook and reproducible lesson activities (Teacher's Resource Library) offer additional monitoring of student progress
- Discussion questions allow teachers to monitor student progress toward lesson objectives
- Self-Study Guides (Teacher's Resource Library) allow teacher and student to track individual assignments and progress
- Chapter assessment activities and curriculum-based assessment items correlate to chapter Goals for Learning:
  - Chapter reviews
  - End-of-chapter tests
  - Cumulative midterm and final mastery tests
  - Alternative chapter assessments
  - Skill Track assesses and tracks individual student performance by lesson and chapter

Deshler, D. D., Ellis, E. S., & Lenz, B. K. (1996). *Teaching adolescents with learning disabilities: Strategies and methods* (2nd ed.). Denver, CO: Love Publishing Company.

Jarrett, D. (1999). *The inclusive classroom: Mathematics and science instruction for students with learning disabilities—It's just good teaching.* Portland, OR: Northwest Regional Educational Laboratory.

Reiser, R. A., & Dick, W. (1996). *Instructional planning: A guide for teachers* (2nd ed.). Boston: Allyn and Bacon.

Tyree, R. B., Fiore, T. A., & Cook, R. A. (1994). Instructional materials for diverse learners: Features and considerations for textbook design. *Remedial and Special Education, 15*(6), 363–377.

For more information on the scientific research base for AGS Globe Textbooks, please go to www.agsglobe.com or call Customer Service at 1-800-992-0244 to request a research report.

Pacemaker® World History Skills Chart

World History Skills	HTUTB	SH	Unit 1	Unit 2	Unit 3	Unit 4	Unit 5	Unit 6	Unit 7	Unit 8	Unit 9	Unit 10
Prehistory			1–2									
Beginnings of Human Society			1–2									
Agricultural Revolution			1–2			12						
Middle Eastern Civilizations			1–2	3–6								
Greek Civilizations			1		7–9							
Roman Civilizations			1		9	10						
The Middle Ages						10–12						
African Civilizations				4						24		
American Civilizations				6				15				
Asian Civilizations				6				15–16				
The Renaissance & the Reformation							13					
Monarchies							14					
Exploration			1	5–6	8	10, 12	13–14	15–16		20–24		34
The Age of Reason									17–18			
The Industrial Revolution										19		34
Nationalism							14				25	
Imperialism			1						19–24			
World War I										26–27		
Aftermath of World War I										26		
World War II										28		
Aftermath of World War II										27–28	29	
Contemporary Issues												30–34

The numbers on this chart refer to the chapter number.

Social Studies Skills	HTUTB	SH	Unit 1	Unit 2	Unit 3	Unit 4	Unit 5	Unit 6	Unit 7	Unit 8	Unit 9	Unit 10
Charts		●		3							26	
Communication			2	3–5	9	10, 12	13		17	24	25, 27–28	34
Critical Thinking			1–2	3–6	7–9	10–12	13–14	15–16	17–18	19–24	25–28	29–34
Economics			2	5		10–12	13–14	15–16		19–24	25–28	29–34
Geography Notes			2	4	9	10	14	15	18	21	28	32
Government/Civics			1	3–6	7–9	10–12	13–14		17–18	20–24	25–28	29–34
Group Activities			1–2	3–6	7–9	10–12	13–14	15–16	17–18	19–24	25–28	29–34
Maps		●	1–2	3–6	7–9	12		15–16	18	19–24	25–28	29–33
Reference Materials	●											
Technology			2	6	9	12	13	15	17	24	25	34
Timelines			1–2	3–6	7–9	10–12	13–14	15–16	17–18	19–24	25–28	29–34
Study Skills	HTUTB	SH	Unit 1	Unit 2	Unit 3	Unit 4	Unit 5	Unit 6	Unit 7	Unit 8	Unit 9	Unit 10
Note-Taking	●											
Outlines	●											
Test-Taking Tips	●		1–2	3–6	7–9	10–12	13–14	15–16	17–18	19–24	25–28	29–34
Vocabulary Development			1–2	3–6	7–9	10–12	13–14	15–16	17–18	19–24	25–28	29–34
Reading Skills	HTUTB	SH	Unit 1	Unit 2	Unit 3	Unit 4	Unit 5	Unit 6	Unit 7	Unit 8	Unit 9	Unit 10
Summarizing		●	1		8			15		22		29
Questioning		●	2		9			16		23		30
Predicting		●		3	10				17	24		31
Text Structure		●		4	11				18		25	32
Visualizing		●		5	12					19	26	33
Inferencing		●		6		13				20	27	34
Metacognition		●		7		14				21	28	

The numbers on this chart refer to the chapter number.

HTUTB=How to Use This Book   **SH**=Skills Handbook

World History

Shoreview, MN

Reading Consultant

Timothy Shanahan, Ph.D., Professor of Urban Education, Director of the Center for Literacy, University of Illinois at Chicago, Author, *AMP™ Reading System*

Reviewers

The publisher wishes to thank the following educators for their helpful comments during the review process for Pacemaker® *World History.* Their assistance has been invaluable. **Debora Hartzell,** Special Education and Vocational Teacher, Lakeside High School, Atlanta, GA; **Lenore Hoyt,** Social Studies Teacher, Centennial High School, Circle Pines, MN; **Stephen C. Larsen** (formerly of The University of Texas at Austin); **J. B. Whitten,** ESE Teacher, Lennard High, Ruskin, IL

Acknowledgments appear on page 798, which constitutes an extension of this copyright page.

1-800-992-0244
www.agsglobe.com

Table of Contents

Reading Strategies

Maps

Maps, cont.

Timelines

Words from the Past

Learn More About It

Great Names in History

Technology Connection

How to Use This Book: A Study Guide

Overview This portion of the book may be used to introduce the study of world history, to preview the book's features, and to review effective study skills.

Objectives

- To introduce the study of world history
- To preview the student textbook
- To review study skills

Student Pages xviii–xxv

Teacher's Resource Library TRL
How to Use This Book 1–7

Introduction to the Book

Have volunteers read aloud the three paragraphs of the introduction. Discuss with students why studying world history is important and what kinds of things people can learn from it.

How to Study

Read aloud each bulleted statement, pausing to discuss with students why the suggestion is part of good study habits. Distribute copies of How to Use This Book 1, "Study Habits Survey." Read the directions together and then have students complete the survey. After they have scored their surveys, ask students to make a list of the study habits they plan to work on improving. After three or four weeks, have students complete the survey again to see if they have improved their study habits. Suggest that they keep the survey and review it every month or so to see whether they are maintaining and improving their study habits.

How to Use This Book: A Study Guide

Welcome to the study of world history. You may be asking yourself, "Why do I need to know about people, places, and events that happened a long time before I was even born?" When we study the past, we can have a better understanding of why some things happened the way they did. We can learn from the mistakes and the successes of the past.

This book is a story about the world. As you read the units, chapters, and lessons of this book, you will learn about the important people and events that shaped world history.

Before you start to read this book, it is important that you understand how to use it. It is also important that you know how to be successful in this course. Information in this first section can help you achieve these things.

How to Study

These tips can help you study more effectively:

- Plan a regular time to study.

- Choose a desk or table in a quiet place where you will not be distracted. Find a spot that has good lighting.

- Gather all the books, pencils, paper, and other equipment you will need to complete your assignments.

- Decide on a goal. For example: "I will finish reading and taking notes on Chapter 1, Lesson 1, by 8:00."

- Take a five- to ten-minute break every hour to keep alert.

- If you start to feel sleepy, take a break and get some fresh air.

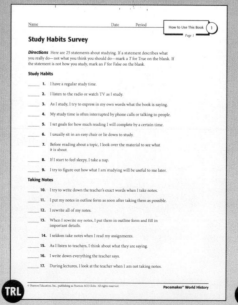

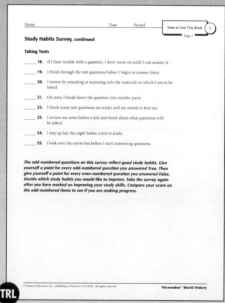

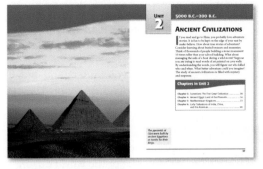

Before Beginning Each Unit

◆ Read the unit title and opening paragraph(s).

◆ Study the photograph. Do you recognize anything in the photo? Also read the caption and try to connect the ideas to the picture.

◆ Read the titles of the chapters in the unit.

◆ Read the Chapter Summaries to help you identify key ideas.

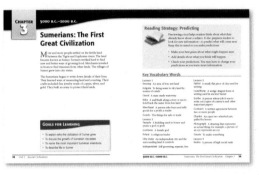

Before Beginning Each Chapter

◆ Read the chapter title and dates, as well as the opening paragraphs.

◆ Review the Goals for Learning. The Chapter Review and tests will ask questions related to these goals.

◆ Study the timeline(s). Timelines help you see the order in which key events in the chapter occurred.

◆ Read the information in the Reading Strategies box; it will help you become a better reader. Reading Strategy notes in each lesson will help you apply the strategy as you read.

◆ Read the words and definitions in the Key Vocabulary Words box. They are important vocabulary terms for the chapter.

◆ Read the Chapter Summary to help you identify key themes.

◆ Look at the Chapter Review. The questions cover the most important information in the chapter.

How to Use This Book: A Study Guide **xix**

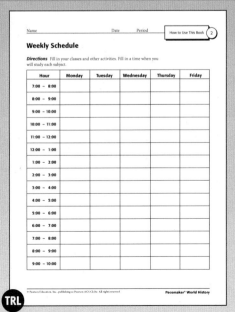

Before Beginning Each Unit

When students begin their study of Unit 1, you may wish to have them read aloud and follow each bulleted suggestion on page xix. Actually trying the suggestions will help students understand what they are supposed to do and recognize how useful the suggestions are when previewing a unit. At the beginning of other units, refer students to page xix and encourage them to follow the suggestions. You may wish to continue to do this as a class each time or allow the students to work independently.

Before Beginning Each Chapter

When students begin their study of Chapter 1, you may wish to have them read aloud and follow each bulleted suggestion on page xix. Read aloud the first bulleted statement under "Before Beginning Each Chapter." Have students turn to page 2, and have a volunteer read aloud the title of Chapter 1, as well as the opening paragraphs. Then read aloud the second bulleted statement and have volunteers take turns reading the Goals for Learning for Chapter 1. Discuss with students why knowing these goals can help them when they are studying the chapter. After reading aloud the remainder of the bulleted points, explain that all these tools—timelines, Reading Strategies, Key Vocabulary Words, Chapter Summaries, and Chapter Reviews—are there to help the students gain as much as they can from the chapter.

Unit and Chapter Introductions organize information into easy-to-read formats. To help students organize their time and work in an easy-to-read form, have them fill out How to Use This Book 2, "Weekly Schedule." Encourage them to keep the schedule in a notebook or folder where they can refer to it easily. Suggest that they review the schedule periodically and update it as necessary.

How to Use This Book: A Study Guide **xix**

Note These Features

Have students skim their textbooks and find one of each of the listed features. You may wish to remind students of a book feature that can help them with this activity—the Table of Contents. Ask volunteers to tell the page numbers of the features they have found. Have the other students check to see that the features do appear on those pages.

Students may use How to Use This Book 3 as they complete assigned writing activities throughout the book.

Note These Features

You can find complete listings of these features in this textbook's table of contents.

Reading Strategy:
Summarizing

Reading Strategy
Tips to help you understand and make sense of what you read

Map Study
Helps locate important features in a certain area of the world during a certain time period

Timeline Study
Aids in understanding the order of events in the chapter or lesson

Words from the Past
Presents written or spoken words related to the chapter that continue to affect the world today

Learn More About It
Provides additional information related to the chapter

Great Names in History
Highlights people who have made contributions to the world

Technology Connection
Highlights inventions at the time that made life better or easier

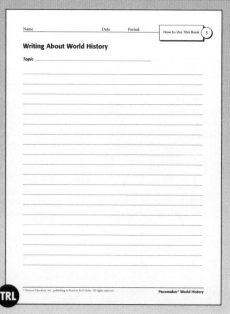

Before Beginning Each Lesson

Read the lesson title and restate it in the form of a question. For example, write: *What changes have happened throughout history?*

Look over the entire lesson, noting the following:

◆ bold words

◆ text organization

◆ photos and maps

◆ Lesson Review questions

As You Read the Lesson

◆ Read the major headings.

◆ Read the subheads and paragraphs that follow.

◆ Study the maps.

◆ Before moving on to the next lesson, see if you understand the concepts you read. If you do not, reread the lesson. If you are still unsure, ask for help.

◆ Practice what you have learned by completing the Lesson Reviews.

Artifact
A handmade object, such as a tool or weapon

Using the Bold Words

Knowing the meaning of all the boxed words in the left column will help you understand what you read.

These **vocabulary words** appear in **bold type** the first time they are mentioned in the text and are often defined in the paragraph.

> They find handmade objects, called **artifacts,** that have long been underground.

All of the words in the left column are also defined in the **Glossary**.

> **Artifact** (är´ tə fakt) A handmade object, such as a tool or weapon (p. 9)

Before Beginning Each Lesson

Read through the information on page xxi with students. Then assign each of the three lessons in Chapter 1 (pages 2–17) to a small group of students. Have them read each of the headings in their lesson. Then have students report on the specifics of what they expect to learn about in their lesson to the rest of the class.

As You Read the Lesson

Have students turn to page 4 in their textbooks. Read aloud the first bulleted point on page xxi and have a volunteer read aloud the first subhead in Lesson 1 of Chapter 1—"What Changes Has the World Gone Through Since Ancient Times?" Then read the second bulleted comment and have volunteers read the paragraph under the subhead in the textbook. After reading the next two bulleted statements, ask students to answer the question in the subhead in their own words. You may wish to repeat this procedure using the other subheads in Lesson 1 of Chapter 1. Then read aloud the last bulleted statement and have students turn to the Lesson 1–1 Review on page 7. Discuss how the questions in the subheads are related to the questions in the Lesson Review.

Using the Bold Words

Read aloud the information on page xxi. Make sure students understand what the terms *bold type, vocabulary,* and *glossary* mean. Then ask them to look at the boxed words on page 4. Have a volunteer read the first boxed word (history) and then find and read the sentence in the text in which that word appears in bold type. Have another volunteer read the second boxed word and then find and read the definition given in the text. Have another volunteer find and read the definition of this word in the glossary at the back of the book.

Point out that boxed vocabulary words may appear on other pages in a lesson besides the first page. Have students turn to page 5 and look at the boxed words on that page. Explain that these words appear in a box here because they are used in the text on this page. Have volunteers find and read the sentences in the text in which the five vocabulary words on page 5 are used.

Word Study Tips

Have a volunteer read aloud the Word Study Tips on page xxii. You may wish to demonstrate how to make a vocabulary card by filling out an index card for the word *culture* and its definition (page 5). Point out that students can use words they list on How to Use This Book 4 to make their vocabulary cards.

Taking Notes

Ask students why note taking is an important study skill. Encourage them to tell what method they use to take notes during class discussions or when reading. Then have volunteers read the information on page xxii. Suggest that students who do not have a method for taking notes try one of the methods mentioned and see how it works for them.

Suggest to students that they can use How to Use This Book 5 and 6 to help them organize information as they read.

Word Study Tips

◆ Start a vocabulary file with index cards to use for review.

◆ Write one term on the front of each card. Write the definition, chapter number, and lesson number on the back.

◆ You can use these cards as flash cards by yourself or with a study partner to test your knowledge.

> ### History
>
> #### Chapter 1, Lesson 1
>
> The record of past events and the story of what happened to people in the past.

Taking Notes

It is helpful to take notes during class and as you read this book.

◆ Outline each lesson using the subheads as the main points.

◆ Always write the main ideas and supporting details.

◆ Keep your notes brief.

◆ Write down important information only.

◆ Use your own words.

◆ Do not be concerned about writing in complete sentences. Use phrases.

◆ Do not try to write everything the teacher says.

◆ Use the same method all the time. Then when you study for a test, you will know where to go to find the information you need to review.

◆ Review your notes to fill in possible gaps as soon as you can after class.

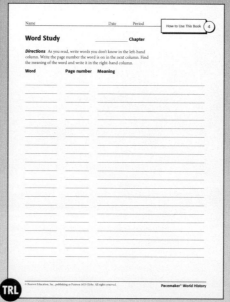

How to Use This Book 4

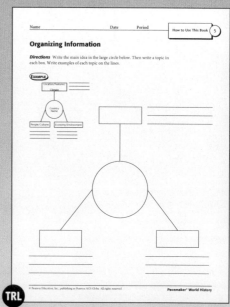

How to Use This Book 5

Using a Three-Column Chart

One good way to take notes is to use a three-column chart. Make your own three-column chart by dividing a sheet of notebook paper into three parts. In Column 1, write the topic you are reading about or studying. In Column 2, write what you learned about this topic as you read or listened to your teacher. In Column 3, write questions, observations, or opinions about the topic, or write a detail that will help you remember the topic. Here are some examples of different ways to take notes using the three-column chart.

The topic I am studying	What I learned from reading the text or class discussion	Questions, observations, or ideas I have about the topic
Sumer	• civilization grew between the Tigris and Euphrates rivers • Sumerians invented many things that we use today	• It makes sense that Sumer grew between two rivers because water is important to all life. • I wonder what people did before the wheel was invented.

Vocabulary word	Definition	Sentence with vocabulary word
Merchant	a person who buys and sells goods for a profit; a trader	Sumerian ~~merchants~~ traded crops for gold, silver, and pearls from other lands.

Topic	Facts	Page number
Sumerian city-states	each city-state was independent and had its own government	p. 43
	built walls around their city-states (for protection)	p. 43
	Ur was one of the greatest Sumerian city-states; it had a ziggurat (a gigantic temple)	p. 44

Using a Three-Column Chart

Have students read the information about making a three-column chart on page xxiii. Then demonstrate to students how to correctly divide the paper into thirds and to label each section. Ask students to create a three-column chart such as one of those on page xxiii and use it as they read and explore Chapter 1.

Explain to students that the three-column chart is one of many good organizational tools. Pass out the How to Use This Book 7 worksheet and discuss with students certain ways this three-column chart could be used to organize information.

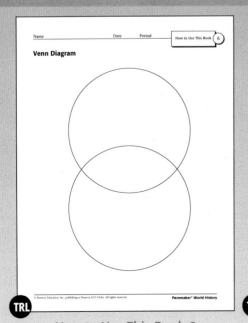

How to Use This Book 6

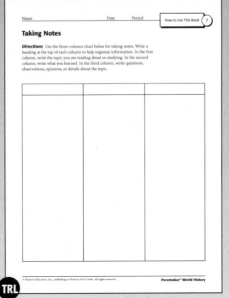

How to Use This Book 7

Using the Summaries

Have students turn to page 15. Point out that a Chapter Summary gives the main ideas covered in the chapter in the form of bulleted statements. Then read aloud the statements on page xxiv that suggest how to use the Chapter Summary when studying for a test.

Using the Reviews

Ask students to turn to page 16. Point out that a Chapter Review is intended to help them focus on and review the key facts and main ideas of a chapter before they are tested on the material. Suggest that they may want to complete the review after studying their notes, vocabulary lists, worksheets, and the Chapter Summary.

Preparing for Tests

Encourage students to offer their opinions about tests and their ideas on test-taking strategies. What do they do to study for a test? List their comments on the board. Then read the bulleted statements on page xxiv. Add these suggestions to the list on the board if they are not already there.

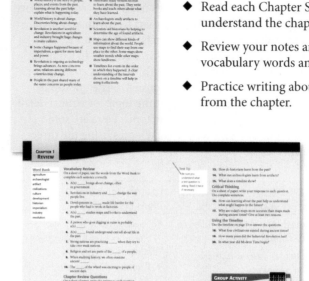

Using the Summaries

◆ Read each Chapter Summary to be sure you understand the chapter's main ideas.

◆ Review your notes and test yourself on vocabulary words and key ideas.

◆ Practice writing about some of the main events from the chapter.

Using the Reviews

◆ Answer the questions in the Lesson Reviews.

◆ In the Chapter Reviews, answer each fill-in-the-blank, short-answer, critical-thinking, and timeline question.

◆ Review the Test-Taking Tips.

Preparing for Tests

◆ Complete the Lesson Reviews and Chapter Reviews. Make up similar questions to practice what you have learned. You may want to do this with a classmate and share your questions.

◆ Review your answers to Lesson Reviews and Chapter Reviews.

◆ Reread the Chapter Summaries.

◆ Test yourself on vocabulary words and key ideas.

Reading Checklist

Good readers do not just read with their eyes. They read with their brains turned on. In other words, they are active readers. Good readers use strategies as they read to keep them on their toes. The following strategies will help you to check your understanding of what you read. A strategy appears at the beginning of each chapter of this book.

- **Summarizing** To summarize a text, stop often as you read. Notice these things: the topic, the main thing being said about the topic, important details that support the main idea. Try to sum up the author's message using your own words.

- **Questioning** Ask yourself questions about the text and read to answer them. Here are some useful questions to ask: Why did the author include this information? Is this like anything I have experienced? Am I learning what I hoped I would learn?

- **Predicting** As you read, think about what might come next. Add in what you already know about the topic. Predict what the text will say. Then, as you read, notice whether your prediction is right. If not, change your prediction.

- **Text Structure** Pay attention to how a text is organized. Find parts that stand out. They are probably the most important ideas or facts. Think about why the author organized ideas this way. Is the author showing a sequence of events? Is the author explaining a solution or the effect of something?

- **Visualizing** Picture what is happening in a text or what is being described. Make a movie out of it in your mind. If you can picture it clearly, then you know you understand it. Visualizing what you read will also help you remember it later.

- **Inferencing** The meaning of a text may not be stated. Instead, the author may give clues and hints. It is up to you to put them together with what you already know about the topic. Then you make an inference—you conclude what the author means.

- **Metacognition** Think about your thinking patterns as you read. Before reading a text, preview it. Think about what you can do to get the most out of it. Think about what you already know about the topic. Write down any questions you have. After you read, ask yourself: Did that make sense? If not, read it again.

Reading Checklist

Read the title and first paragraph on page xxv to students. Then ask a volunteer to read each of the reading strategies listed on the page. Go through each strategy one by one, making sure students understand the concepts behind each term. Then give examples of each strategy through the text. Have students participate. After reading a paragraph ask one volunteer for a summary. Ask another volunteer for a question that came from the reading. Ask another volunteer to make a prediction based on the text. Continue this way until all strategies are explained.

Using Globes and Maps

Present a globe for students to study. Explain that a globe accurately shows the geography of Earth. Then ask a volunteer to find the equator and the prime meridian. Ask another volunteer to find the international date line. Then ask students to find where you are on the globe. Ask them to find the closest lines of latitude and longitude.

Ask:

● What advantages does a globe have over a map? (Since both the globe and Earth are round, a globe accurately shows the shape of Earth and the size of physical features.)

Using Globes and Maps

A globe is a model of Earth. Looking at the globe, you can see that Earth is round. You can see Earth's features and surfaces. A globe is the best way to show Earth. However, how do you show the round features of a globe on a flat page? You use a map.

You also can see that geographers divide Earth into halves or **hemispheres**. The **equator** divides Earth into the Northern Hemisphere and the Southern Hemisphere. The equator is an imaginary line that circles the middle of Earth.

The **prime meridian** and the **international date line** divide Earth into the Eastern Hemisphere and the Western Hemisphere. The prime meridian is an imaginary line that circles Earth from the North Pole to the South Pole. The international date line is on the side of Earth you cannot see here. It is directly opposite the prime meridian.

Geographers measure distances from the equator and the prime meridian. These distances are imaginary lines called **latitude** and **longitude**.

The Hemispheres

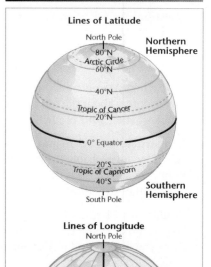

Lines of Latitude

North Pole
80°N
Arctic Circle
60°N
40°N
Tropic of Cancer
20°N
0° Equator
20°S
Tropic of Capricorn
40°S
South Pole

Northern Hemisphere

Southern Hemisphere

Lines of Longitude
North Pole
80°W
60°W
40°W
20°W
0° Prime Meridian
20°E
40°E
60°E
80°E
South Pole

Western Hemisphere

Eastern Hemisphere

Cartographers, or mapmakers, have created different map projections. Some of these map projections show the true size of a place, but distort, or change, the shape. Others show the true shape, but distort the size. All maps show some kind of distortion. Therefore, geographers must choose the best maps for their purposes.

A **Mercator projection** stretches the lines of latitude apart. It does not show the true size of landmasses. A Mercator projection does show true shape, however.

Landmasses in a **Robinson projection** are not as distorted as in a Mercator projection. However, there is some distortion in the size of the landmasses.

Mercator Projection

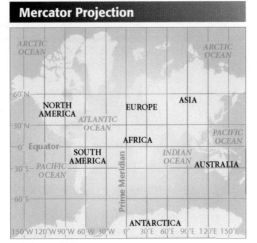

Robinson Projection

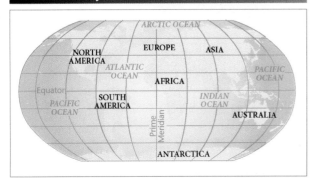

Critical Thinking

Why would a mapmaker choose to use a Robinson projection instead of a Mercator projection?

Explain that globes are not always available or detailed enough for a specific situation. In these cases, a map is a useful tool. Present a map of the world for students to study. Explain that it is impossible to correctly show both size and shape by using a map. Therefore, every map has some sort of distortion.

After reading page xxvii of the text, ask students to identify the type of map you have displayed. (Answers will vary. *Either Mercator projection or Robinson projection.*)

Ask students to find your location on the map and pinpoint the latitude and longitude as closely as possible.

Critical Thinking

Answers will vary. Sample answer: A mapmaker might choose a Robinson projection over a Mercator projection if they were more interested in accurately showing the shape of the landmasses.

Reading a Map

Have students read page xxviii of the text. Explain that knowing how to read maps is one of the most important skills in learning geography.

Ask:

- What are the main parts of a map? (a title, a key, a compass rose, and a scale)

Tell students to look at the political map of the Middle East on page xxviii.

Ask:

- How are the countries differentiated from one another? (borderlines and color)
- What country is directly west of Jordan? (Israel)
- What is the capital of Iran? (Tehran)

Reading a Map

To understand history, you need to know how to read maps. To read a map, you need to understand its parts. The main parts of a map are a title, a key, a compass rose, and a scale. Many of the maps you see are **general purpose maps**. These are political maps and physical maps. A **political map** shows features that people determine, such as country boundaries, cities, and capitals.

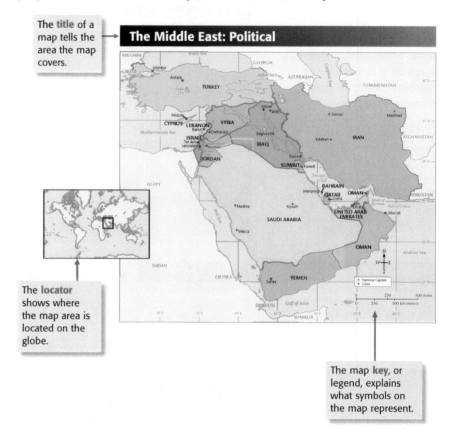

The **title** of a map tells the area the map covers.

The Middle East: Political

The **locator** shows where the map area is located on the globe.

The map **key**, or legend, explains what symbols on the map represent.

A **physical map** shows how high a landmass is. It also shows natural features such as rivers and oceans. Some of the maps you see show specific kinds of information. These maps are called **special purpose maps**. There are many types of special purpose maps. For example, a map that shows where early civilizations lived is a special purpose map. Look at the Early Civilizations of North America map on page 323.

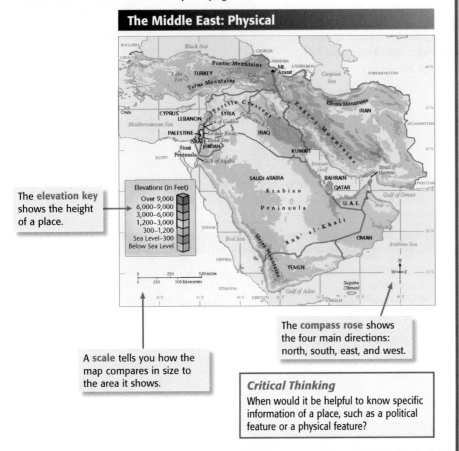

The Middle East: Physical

The **elevation key** shows the height of a place.

A **scale** tells you how the map compares in size to the area it shows.

The **compass rose** shows the four main directions: north, south, east, and west.

Critical Thinking
When would it be helpful to know specific information of a place, such as a political feature or a physical feature?

Have a volunteer read the paragraph on page xxix. Then explain to students that a physical map, unlike a political map, shows elevation, or how high a landmass is. It also shows natural features, such as mountains, lakes, rivers, and oceans.

A special purpose map is designed to show one specific piece of information.

Ask:

- What are some possible topics for a special purpose map? (climate, resources, population, language, ethnicity)

Ask students which type of map would be most useful under the following circumstances:

- Discovering the highest region in America (physical map)
- Finding out the population density of Egypt (special purpose map)
- Finding the capital of the Philippines (political map)
- Discovering the natural resources of China (special purpose map)

Critical Thinking

Answers will vary. Sample answer: It would be helpful to know specifics when studying a region of the world. Learning from a map about physical features (such as deserts, mountains, or rivers) would help explain why the population size is low or high in a certain area.

Reading Graphs and Charts

Explain to students that graphs and charts are excellent ways to show information. Different graphs and charts can be used in different circumstances. Ask a volunteer to read the paragraph about circle graphs on page xxx.

Ask:

- What country is the single largest energy user in the world? (the United States)

Ask a second volunteer to read the paragraph about bar graphs at the bottom of page xxx.

Ask:

- Which country is larger: Canada or Brazil? (Canada)

Reading Graphs and Charts

Graphs and charts organize and present information in a visual way. There are different types of graphs and charts.

A **circle graph** is sometimes called a pie graph. It is a good way to show the sizes of parts as compared to a single whole. This single whole is represented as a circle. Each piece of the circle represents a part of the whole.

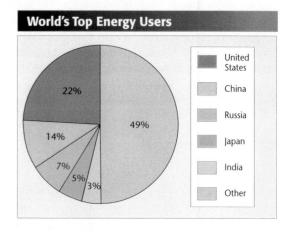

World's Top Energy Users

- United States
- China
- Russia
- Japan
- India
- Other

A **bar graph** is a good way to show information visually. Each bar represents a set of facts. You can compare sets of facts by looking at the different sizes of the bars.

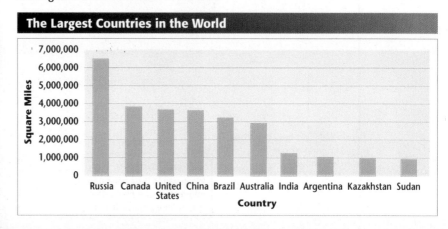

The Largest Countries in the World

World Facts

Fact	Place	Location	Size
Highest Mountain	Mount Everest	Nepal and China	29,035 feet high
Longest River	Nile	North and East Africa	4,160 miles long
Largest Island	Greenland	North Atlantic	840,000 square miles
Largest Body of Water	Pacific Ocean	From west of North and South America to east of Asia and Australia	63,800,000 square miles

A **chart** can also be called a table. Charts are organized into rows and columns. Charts can help you to compare information.

A **line graph** shows the relationship between two sets of information. A point is placed at the intersection of every fact. When all the points are on the graph, a line is drawn to connect them. You can get a quick idea as to the trend, or direction, of information by looking at the ups and downs of the line.

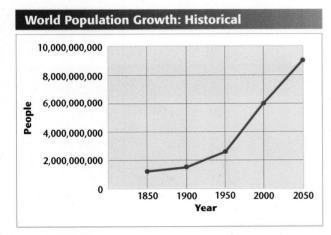

World Population Growth: Historical

Critical Thinking

If you were to organize information about your classmates into categories such as age and gender, would you use a chart or a graph? Explain.

Ask a volunteer to read the paragraph about charts on page xxxi.

Ask:

- Where is Greenland, the world's largest island, located? (in the North Atlantic)

Ask a volunteer to read the paragraph about line graphs at the bottom of page xxxi.

Ask:

- Is the world's population expected to increase or decrease in the future? (increase)

Have students look over the graphs on pages xxx and xxxi. Then ask the following questions:

- Which is the best type of graph to use if you want to show a trend? (a line graph)
- Which is the best type of graph to use if you want to compare parts of a whole? (a circle graph)

Critical Thinking

Answers will vary. Sample answer: It would be best to use a chart if I were organizing information about my classmates because a chart shows off multiple categories. I can create as many rows and columns as necessary to fit all the information I want to show. The other graphs are best for showing one piece of information.

UNIT 1

PLANNING GUIDE

Looking at the World's History

	Student Text Lesson					
	Student Pages	Vocabulary	Map Study	Reading Strategy	Lesson Review	Chapter Summary/Review
Chapter 1 What Is History?	2–17	✔		✔		15–17
Lesson 1–1 History Is All About Change	4–7	✔		✔	7	
Lesson 1–2 Historians and Archaeologists	8–10	✔		✔	10	
Lesson 1–3 Maps and Timelines	11–14	✔	✔	✔	14	
Chapter 2 Early Humans: The Story Begins	18–35	✔		✔		33–35
Lesson 2–1 The Hunters	20–23	✔		✔	23	
Lesson 2–2 The Agricultural Revolution	24–27	✔		✔	27	
Lesson 2–3 The Fertile Crescent	28–32	✔	✔	✔	32	

Chapter Activities

Teacher's Resource Library
Life Skills Connection 1–2
Key Vocabulary Words 1–2

Assessment Options

Student Text
Chapter Reviews 1–2
Teacher's Resource Library
Chapter 1 Mastery Tests A and B
Chapter 2 Mastery Tests A and B
Unit 1 Mastery Test
Teacher's Edition
Chapter Projects 1–2

Student Text Features							Teaching Strategies										Learning Styles					Teacher's Resource Library			
Words from the Past	Learn More About It	Great Names in History	Technology Connection	Geography Note	You Decide/Remember/History Fact	Timeline Study	ELL/ESL Strategy	Background Information	Common Error	Life Skills Connection	Key Vocabulary Words	Study Skills	Applications Home, Career, Community	Online Connection	Teacher Alert	World Cultures	Auditory/Verbal	Body/Kinesthetic	Interpersonal/Group Learning	Logical/Mathematical	Visual/Spatial	Activities/Modified Activities	Workbook Activities	Self-Study Guide	Chapter Outline
										3	3													✔	✔
					5, 6		5	4	5					6	5	5	5					1	1		
	8	9					9	9				9	10						9			2	2		
						13	13	12	13									12		11	13	3	3		
										19	19													✔	✔
22	21						22	21	23									21			21, 22	4	4		
			25		24, 26		25	25	25, 26				25, 26	24		26						5	5		
			30		28	30	30	29	31			28			31				30	30		6	6		

Modified Activities

The Teacher's Resource Library (TRL) contains a set of lower-level worksheets called Modified Activities. These worksheets cover the same content as the standard Activities but are written at a lower reading level.

Skill Track

Use Skill Track for *World History* to monitor student progress and meet the demands of adequate yearly progress (AYP). Make informed instructional decisions with individual student and class reports of lesson and chapter assessments. With immediate and ongoing feedback, students will also see what they have learned and where they need more reinforcement and practice.

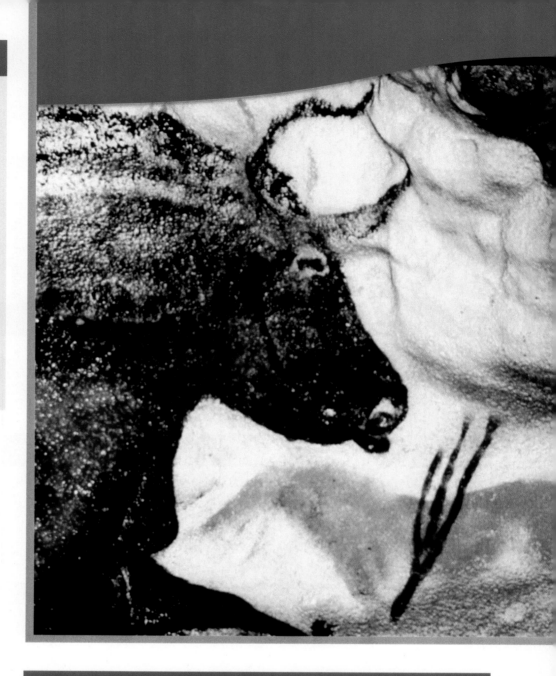

Other Resources

Books for Teachers

Aldred, Cyril. *Ancient People And Places: Egyptians.* New York: Thames and Hudson, 1999.

Homer. *The Iliad.* New York: Penguin Books USA Inc., 1990.

Whitley, James. *The Archaeology of Ancient Greece.* London: Cambridge University Press, 2001.

Books for Students

National Geographic Student Atlas of the World. Washington, DC: National Geographic Children's Books, 2005.

Adkins, Jan. *What If You Met a Knight?* New York: Roaring Brook Press, 2006

Clements, Gillian. *The Picture History of the Great Inventors.* London: Francis Lincoln Children's Books, 2000.

CD-ROM

My First Amazing History Explorer, DK Multimedia, 2001. (This game teaches basic world history.)

LOOKING AT THE WORLD'S HISTORY

When two people want to get to know one another, they may ask, "Where were you born? Where did you go to school? From what city did you move?" They want to know history. It could seem that studying world history is not important, but it is. Like many leaders from history, you may want power. That power could well be the power to understand. You can have the power to better relate to today's world news. You can travel to far-off places and have a clearer idea of how a another culture developed. You can plan your future with a broader vision of how you want to create your own history.

Chapters in Unit 1

This cave painting in Lascaux, France, is thousands of years old. People of Stone Age cultures often painted pictures of animals they hunted.

1

Introducing the Unit

Tell students that this first unit introduces them to the study of history. Discuss the photograph and caption on the opening page. Read the title and the first paragraph on page 2 to students. Then have them read the next paragraph to find out how we learn about history in the time before written records.

Ask:

- What clues did these people leave about the way they lived? (paintings on the walls of caves and artifacts)

- What type of scientists explores the lives of ancient people? (archaeologists)

- What do you think archaeologists might find at a site where prehistoric people once lived? (Answers will vary; students might say bones, fossil footprints, or cave paintings.)

- The art on this page was drawn on the wall of a cave by a prehistoric artist. What kind of animal do you think the artist drew? (Students may say a cow or a bull.)

- If you have ever been in a cave, you know it is pitch dark as soon as you can no longer see light from the opening. How do you think the prehistoric artist was able to see and draw in the cave? (Students will probably say the artist must have had fire.)

- With what do you think the artist might have drawn the picture? (Answers will vary; students may say the artist used charcoal, or paint made out of grinding rocks and minerals.)

Videos

Greece: Secrets of the Past. (45 minutes) MacGillivray Freeman, 2006. (A documentary video of ancient Greek civilization; downloadable at www.agsglobepmwh.com/page1a.)

The Discoverers. (39 minutes). Image Entertainment, 1993. (Based on Pulitzer Prize winning book of the same title by Dr. Daniel J. Boorstin.)

Web Sites

www.agsglobepmwh.com/page1b (This site provides links to readings about ancient civilizations.)

www.agsglobepmwh.com/page1c (This site provides information to help students and teachers evaluate Internet sources and the quality of online primary materials.)

www.agsglobepmwh.com/page1d (The Center for Teaching History with Technology aims to help K–12 history and social studies teachers incorporate technology effectively into their courses.)

Introducing the Chapter

History did not begin with the first written word. There was no written word for most of human history. There was a time when the latest advance was a new way to hit a flint to make a sharper spear point.

Ask:

- What may have caused excitement in ancient times? (A hunt or an attack may have been exciting.)

- Why did early people mark on cave walls? (They wanted to tell a story or talk about an idea or their life.)

- How can we show graphically a location or a sequence of events over time today? (Through discussion, lead students to suggest maps and timelines.)

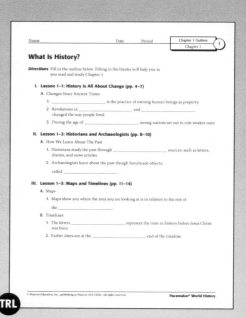

CHAPTER 1

What Is History?

You are reading a book about the history of the world. For centuries, now, your ancestors have been recording their history for future generations. Their forefathers did the same for them. Before those people, however, earlier inhabitants of the planet were not writing history books. They were too busy trying to live.

The information in this first chapter comes from clues left in or on the earth. Thanks to the efforts of curious explorers such as archaeologists, you can learn quite a bit about the earliest people. Who knows? Your own curiosity may someday cause you to go exploring, too.

GOALS FOR LEARNING

- To explain why life in ancient times was just as exciting as life today

- To describe how historians and archaeologists learn about the past

- To explain why people make maps and how to use a timeline

Reading Strategy: Summarizing

When readers summarize, they ask questions about what they are reading. As you read the text in this chapter, ask yourself the following questions:

- Who or what is this chapter about?
- What is the main thing being said about this topic?
- What details are important to the main idea?

Key Vocabulary Words

Lesson 1

History The record of past events and the story of what happened to people in the past

Slavery The owning of human beings with the belief that they are property

Revolution A complete change, especially in a way of life or a government

Industry Business and manufacturing

Agriculture The use of land for growing crops and raising animals; farming

Development Growth of something

Imperialism The practice of conquering other lands, forming colonies in other lands, or controlling the government and wealth of weaker lands

Culture The way of life—religion, ideas, arts, tools—of a certain people in a certain time

Lesson 2

Historian Someone who writes about the past; an expert in history

Border The dividing line between two countries

Primary source A first-hand account of a historical event

Civilization A group of people who have cities and government

Archaeologist A scientist who studies cultures of the past by digging up and examining the remains of ancient towns and cities

Artifact A handmade object, such as a tool or weapon

Lesson 3

B.C. (Before Christ) Dating from before the time Jesus Christ was born

A.D. (Anno Domini) Dating from the time Jesus Christ was born

---

Reading Strategy:
Summarizing

Explain to students that a summary captures the general ideas presented in the chapter. Have students page through the chapter. Have them read the chapter headings. Point out and discuss the visuals found in the chapter. Direct students to read the questions.

Ask:

- Who or what is this chapter about? (It is the story of how people of different times and places lived.)

....

Key Vocabulary Words

Point out that these chapter words are presented in the order they appear in each lesson. They are also found in the glossary.

LIFE SKILLS CONNECTION

Students learn the difference between primary and secondary sources. Students decide if the listed items are primary or secondary sources. Bring in examples of both to class for students to discuss.

KEY VOCABULARY

In Part A of the Key Vocabulary Words 1 worksheet, students write the correct word from the Word Bank to complete each sentence. In Part B, students match each definition to the correct word.

CHAPTER PROJECT

Have each student look up a well-known historian or archaeologist. Students should research their subject and learn about the individual's background, education, important discoveries, published works, and so on. Have students write biographies of their subjects. Students should summarize the significance of the subjects' contributions to historical study.

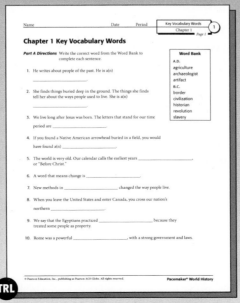

Life Skills Connection 1 **Key Vocabulary Words 1, pages 1–2**

Lesson at a Glance

Chapter 1 Lesson 1

Overview This lesson describes some of the changing times and ideas in human history.

Objectives

- To explain what world history is
- To name two revolutions that affected the way people lived
- To explain the lives of Sumerians

Student Pages 4–7

Teacher's Resource Library

Workbook Activity 1

Activity 1

Modified Activity 1

Vocabulary

agriculture	imperialism
culture	industry
development	revolution
history	slavery

Write the vocabulary words on the board. Read the definition of one of the terms and ask a volunteer to identify the word defined. Erase the word from the board and repeat.

1 Warm-Up Activity

Have students make a list of the different ways people study history. Write three headings on the board: Places, Resources, People. Have students offer ideas from their lists. Place their ideas under the proper headings. (For example, museums for places, books for resources, and guest speakers for people.) Discuss the value of oral histories. Have students write one sentence summarizing how people study history.

2 Teaching the Lesson

Ask students to suggest why they think it is worthwhile to study history. Then have them read page 6 to see if their ideas match those in the book.

History Is All About Change

Objectives

- To explain what world history is
- To name two revolutions that affected the way people lived
- To explain the lives of Sumerians

History
The record of past events and the story of what happened to people in the past

Slavery
The owning of human beings with the belief that they are property

Revolution
A complete change, especially in a way of life or a government

World **history** is the story of how the people of different times and places lived. It is the record of discoveries such as better ways of farming and new machines. It is also the story of the building of cities and nations, and of the creation of beautiful art and music.

What Changes Has the World Gone Through Since Ancient Times?

History is all about change—changing times and changing ideas. Long ago, for example, owning human beings as property, **slavery**, was an accepted part of everyday life. The ancient Egyptians made their slaves (the people that they owned) their prisoners. So did the Greeks, the Romans, the Aztecs, and many others. However, today, people in much of the world believe slavery is wrong.

About 500 years ago, there was a big change in the way people pictured their world. People realized that the Earth is round, not flat. Explorers set out from Europe on long ocean voyages. They discovered a huge body of land where they had thought there was only ocean. North and South America took their role in the story of the world.

Another word for change is **revolution.** Ideas of freedom, democracy, and independence swept across the world. This led people in many countries to rise up against their government. In both the Eastern and Western hemispheres, people rose up and demanded freedom.

Ask:

- What does history teach us about people? (what their ideas were; what they did; what problems they had)
- What does it mean to be part of a global community? (In some way everyone throughout the world is connected.)
- How does history connect us with the past? (It helps us understand that we are rooted in the past; we are part of a global community through time.)

Background Information

Born in 259 B.C., Ying Zheng was the First Emperor of China. He gave China a single currency, a standardized system of weights and measurements, and a common written language. He started the construction of the Great Wall of China. A brutal dictator, Zheng killed scholars and burned most of the books in China. In 1974, farmers found the gravesite of 7,000 life-size clay soldiers and horses. No two were alike. Archaeologists think these figures represent the First Emperor's army and were to guard him in the afterlife. The clay army is considered the Eighth Wonder of the World.

Industry
Business and manufacturing

Agriculture
The use of land for growing crops and raising animals; farming

Development
Growth of something

Imperialism
The practice of conquering other lands, forming colonies in other lands, or controlling the government and wealth of weaker lands

Culture
The way of life—religion, ideas, arts, tools—of a certain people in a certain time

More than 6,000 life-sized clay soldiers were buried with an ancient Chinese emperor.

Revolutions in **industry** (business and manufacturing) and in **agriculture** (farming) changed the way people lived. Discoveries and inventions often helped people lead better lives. Sometimes changes made life harder. For example, the **development**, or growth, of industry in England made life better for many people. However, life became harder for the people who worked in the factories.

Out of the age of exploration grew an age of **imperialism**. Imperialism is the search for more land and power. Strong nations set out to rule weaker ones. Weaker lands were forced to accept foreign ideas and **cultures**, or their way of life. Europe tried to set up colonies all over the globe.

Many countries tried to fight this. People wanted to control their own lands and lives. The spirit of nationalism led people to unite under their own flags.

As histories must, this book talks about wars. Down through the ages, there have always been wars. Tribe fought against tribe, city fought against city, and nation fought against nation. World Wars I and II in the 20th century were the worst wars of all time. Sometimes history seems like nothing but a long list of wars. This book tells how wars happened and how they changed nations. Some nations became weaker; others found new power.

You Decide
The invention of television in the 20th century changed the way many people lived. If there were no TV, would your life be better or worse? Explain.

What Is History? Chapter 1 **5**

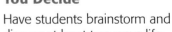

Reading Strategy:
Summarizing

Have students list two things that they have learned about revolution. (Possible answers: New ideas led people to rise up against their government. Changes in industry and in agriculture changed the way people lived. We are still in the process of revolution.)

Remember
Have students imagine and discuss what it might have been like to have a simple breakfast in ancient times. (Students will understand that having a granola bar was not an option in ancient times. Early people might, instead, have had a handful of gathered seeds and nuts.)

ONLINE CONNECTION

Students can gain additional information by accessing the following Web sites:

www.agsglobepmwh.com/page6a
(This British Web site discusses the people, culture, and changes that occurred during the Bronze Age.)

www.agsglobepmwh.com/page6b
(Several links on this Minnesota State University Web site take students to a variety of museum exhibits and maps on early civilizations in North and South America, Asia, and Europe.)

www.agsglobepmwh.com/page6c
(This Web site explains how and where to access primary sources.)

Reading Strategy:
Summarizing

What does this lesson tell you about revolution?

Remember
All human beings have the same basic needs for food, clothing, and shelter. In different times and places, people have met these needs in different ways.

We are still in the process of revolution. Each day, there are changes in science, in technology, and in relations between countries. There are still many difficult problems that need to be solved.

To us, ancient times may seem simple. That is not really so. About 5,000 years ago, the Sumerians in the city of Ur were very busy. They worried about feeding their people and making lands produce crops. They struggled to defend themselves against their enemies. They also faced the dangers of nature, like floods. They invented new ways to get from one place to another faster. They set up governments and made laws. They tried to explain their existence through religion. They also educated their children. They celebrated life through art and writing.

Are we really so different today? People go into space. They use the great power of the tiny atom. However, the events of ancient days were just as exciting to the people who lived then. What about the day a human being first put ideas down in writing? Was the first wheel any less exciting than the first rocket engine? People in ancient times must have found discovery and changes to be just as exciting as we do today.

Christopher Columbus claimed land in the West Indies for Spain in October 1492.

The cultures of the past are our best clues to history. By looking at yesterday's people, we can better understand the world as it is today—and as it might be tomorrow.

Match the definition in Column A with the term in Column B.
Write the correct letter on a sheet of paper.

Column A

1. the way of life of a certain people in a certain time

2. a complete change, especially in a way of life or government

3. the practice of conquering, forming colonies, or controlling the government and wealth of weaker lands

4. the use of land for growing crops and raising animals; farming

Column B

A agriculture
B culture
C imperialism
D revolution

On a sheet of paper, write the letter of the answer that correctly completes each sentence.

5. In ancient times, Egyptians, Greeks, _____, and Aztecs made people their slaves.

   A Romans   **B** Sumerians   **C** English   **D** French

6. In ancient times, revolutions in _____ and agriculture changed the way people lived.

   A exploration **B** industry   **C** science   **D** slavery

7. World War I and _____ were the worst wars in human history.

   A Civil War   **C** World War II
   B Seven Years' War   **D** Gulf War

On a sheet of paper, write the answer to each question. Use complete sentences.

8. What change has taken place over the years in the way people feel about slavery?

9. What did Europeans discover after they knew the world was round?

10. How was life in ancient times like life today?

What Is History? Chapter 1   **7**

Lesson 1–1 Review Answers

1. B **2.** D **3.** C **4.** A **5.** A **6.** B **7.** C
8. People in much of the world now believe slavery is wrong. **9.** They discovered North and South America. **10.** Ancient people faced the same dangers of nature as we do now. Like today, they made laws and set up governments. They came up with new ways to get from place to place faster. They also had religion, education, art, and writing.

Lesson at a Glance

Chapter 1 Lesson 2

Overview This lesson describes some of the ways historians and archaeologists learn how people lived before written records.

Objectives

■ To identify types of documents historians use to learn about the past

■ To identify types of objects archaeologists use to learn about cultures of the past

Student Pages 8–10

Teacher's Resource Library

Workbook Activity 2

Activity 2

Modified Activity 2

Vocabulary

archaeologist   civilization
artifact   historian
border   primary source

Randomly read the definition of each word. Have students guess the words that match the definitions.

1 Warm-Up Activity

Have students share a favorite event from the past. This may be as recent as a current event, or much farther back in time. Write their ideas on various places on the board. Draw lines making connections between events. For example, the causes of the American Revolution could be connected to a current effort to promote representative government.

2 Teaching the Lesson

Invite students to share stories about events and people that are a part of history. Then have students read pages 8–9 to find out the sources of those stories and how historians evaluate the sources.

Historians and Archaeologists

Objectives

■ To identify types of documents historians use to learn about the past

■ To identify types of objects archaeologists use to learn about cultures of the past

Historian
Someone who writes about the past; an expert in history

Border
The dividing line between two countries

Primary source
A first-hand account of a historical event

We find out about the people of the past by looking at the things they left behind.

How Do We Learn About the Past?

The easiest way we can look into the past is by reading papers and books of days gone by. **Historians** look at old maps that tell how the dividing line between countries, or **borders,** and the names of countries have changed. They study letters, diaries, speeches, news articles, and other documents. These types of writings are called **primary sources.** Then they write books about their findings.

LEARN MORE ABOUT IT

The Trojan War

Thousands of years ago, the Greek poet Homer wrote the *Iliad.* It was about a mighty city called Troy. He wrote that Paris, son of the king of Troy, was visiting Sparta in Greece. There, Paris fell in love with Helen, the wife of King Menelaus. Paris took Helen home with him to Troy. The Greeks swore revenge. A huge army set sail for Troy. For 10 years the Greeks fought the Trojans, but the Greeks were not able to capture the city. Then they built a gigantic wooden horse. The Greek soldiers hid inside it. The Trojans were curious about the horse and dragged it inside the city walls. The Greeks climbed out and killed most of the Trojans, including Paris. Then the Greeks looted and burned the city. Helen returned to Menelaus in Sparta.

Did all of this really happen? Was there ever a city called Troy? A German archaeologist named Heinrich Schliemann believed there was such a place. In 1870 he traveled to Turkey with a team of assistants. There they began digging in a mound that seemed to fit the location described in Homer's *Iliad.* Sure enough, they uncovered the ruins of several cities piled on top of each other. At least one of the cities had massive stone walls. Schliemann had discovered Troy!

8   *Unit 1 Looking at the World's History*

Ask:

● What are some ways you could learn about people who lived long ago? (Answers will vary; students may suggest books, museum artifacts, or the Internet.)

● What is an example of a primary source? (Answers will vary; students may say an eyewitness account is a primary source.)

LEARN MORE ABOUT IT

Around 1870 it was generally agreed that the Trojan War never had happened and Troy never existed. Then Heinrich Schliemann discovered the ruins of Troy. Today many scholars agree that the Trojan War is based on a Greek expedition against the city of Troy, but most agree that the Homeric poems did not represent the actual events of the war.

Have students use the Internet to read about Troy. Ask them to list the numerous poets and ancient historians who wrote about Troy.

Civilization
A group of people who have cities and government

Archaeologist
A scientist who studies cultures of the past by digging up and examining the remains of ancient towns and cities

Artifact
A handmade object, such as a tool or weapon

Reading Strategy:
Summarizing

What is the main idea of this lesson?

This hoe was used for farming by an ancient Plains people in North America. It was made from the shoulder blade of a buffalo.

What about the cities and governments of people, or **civilizations,** from long ago? There were times when no one wrote books or drew maps. How do we know so much about the ancient days? People called **archaeologists** dig in the ruins of ancient civilizations. They find handmade objects, called **artifacts,** that have long been underground. They study each artifact they find and piece bits of information together. In this way, they come up with a picture of the past.

Scientists have many ways of deciding how old things are. A piece of cloth, an iron tool, and a painting on a wall may all be pieces of the puzzle. As the pieces come together, bit by bit the story is told!

GREAT NAMES IN HISTORY

Louis Leakey and Mary Leakey
Louis and Mary Leakey made exciting discoveries about early humans. Louis Leakey believed that humankind had developed in Africa. The two British scientists worked in East Africa for about 40 years. They collected stone tools and pieces of bone, skulls, and teeth. These were clues to what early people were like.

Background Information

Louis and Mary Leaky pioneered excavation work at Olduvai Gorge in the 1950s. The Olduvai Gorge is known as "The Cradle of Mankind." It is a steep ravine in the Great Rift Valley in eastern Africa. The Olduvai Gorge is about 30 miles long and 295 feet deep. Objects found at the site range from 2,100,000 to 15,000 years old. The area is distinguished by lava flows, volcanic–ash deposits, and other sediments. Fossils of the area show it was rich in plant life and that some human life located along streambeds. Tools and animal bones and teeth are among the items that have been discovered.

GREAT NAMES IN HISTORY

To discover more about Mary Leakey's research and the contribution it has made to science, have students research Mary Leakey in the library or on the Internet.

STUDY SKILLS

Have students use the World Atlas on page 760 to find out the names of the nations in which archaeologists found skeletons. Ask them to group the finds by continent. Then have them list the nations of each continent along with their respective archaeological discoveries.

Reading Strategy:
Summarizing

(This lesson tells how we find out about people of the past.)

LEARNING STYLES

 Interpersonal/Group Learning
To reinforce students' understanding of primary and secondary sources, divide the class into small groups. Have each group make a poster with the headings "Primary Source" and "Secondary Source." Have them select a lesson from the U.S. Declaration of Independence, the *Gettysburg Address*, or another historic document and place it under the heading "Primary Source." Then have them paraphrase the primary source by writing it in their own words under the "Secondary Source" heading. Students can then read their source material.

ELL/ESL STRATEGY

 Language Objective: *To practice common grammar structures by comparing and contrasting foods from different countries*

Review that scientists can tell a great deal about the life of a person from their bones, including diseases they have had, injuries, the approximate age of a person, and much about the person's diet. Often, scientists can determine the region a person lived in as a child based on diet factors found in his or her bones. Have ELL students think about food that is particular to their family's country of origin. Ask students to describe one food item that is enjoyed by many people. Have students use complete sentences. Write the food items on the board. Have the ELL students compare favorite foods by using a sentence that shows comparison. Students may also bring in a favorite dish to share with the class. Students might enjoy explaining how the dish is prepared.

AT HOME

The development of pottery provided a way for humans to store surplus food and protect it from hungry animals. Ask students to investigate the containers used at home to store and protect food. Ask students to sketch five or six containers and list the unique features of each. Then have students compare their findings.

CAREER CONNECTION

Anthropologists study the way humans live now and the way they lived in the past. They look for the patterns of behavior, such as family life, that people share. Anthropologists usually need several college degrees to qualify for their work. Have students use library and Internet resources to research education requirements for anthropologists.

IN THE COMMUNITY

Investigate the resources of your local or state historical society. It may be possible to do so over the Internet. Find and list some of the primary and secondary sources available on a sample topic, such as early settlers in your state or area.

Lesson 1–2 Review Answers

1. B **2.** C **3.** D **4.** A **5.** primary sources
6. maps **7.** weapons **8.** Homer **9.** Troy
10. horse

LESSON 1-2 REVIEW

Match the definition in Column A with the term in Column B. Write the correct letter on a sheet of paper.

Column A

1. a handmade object
2. a group of people who have cities and government
3. someone who writes about the past
4. a scientist who studies past cultures by digging up and examining the remains of ancient towns and cities

Column B

A archaeologist
B artifact
C civilization
D historian

Word Bank

Homer
horse
maps
primary sources
Troy
weapons

On a sheet of paper, write the word from the Word Bank to complete each sentence correctly.

5. Writings from the time about things that happened are called _____.

6. Historians often use _____ to learn how borders and country names have changed.

7. Tools and _____ are examples of artifacts.

8. _____ was a Greek poet.

9. The *Iliad* is about a mighty city called _____.

10. In the *Iliad,* the Greeks hid inside a gigantic wooden _____. They built it to trick the Trojans.

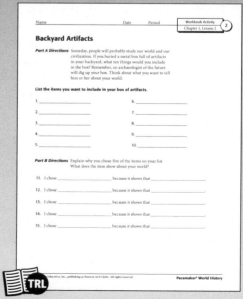

LESSON 1-3

Maps and Timelines

Objectives

- To explain why maps are important
- To describe the information that maps can show
- To explain how a timeline works
- To identify the different units and intervals that can be used on a timeline

You will notice many maps and timelines as you read. The maps will help you locate the part of the world you are learning about. Locators and other features on the maps will help guide you. They show you where the area you are looking at is in relation to the rest of the world. Timelines in each chapter help you understand the order of the events you read about.

What Do Maps Show?

The maps in this book show how countries have changed and how groups of people have moved. They show that cities were built along rivers and on seacoasts. They show how waterways made it possible for different people to come together.

The World

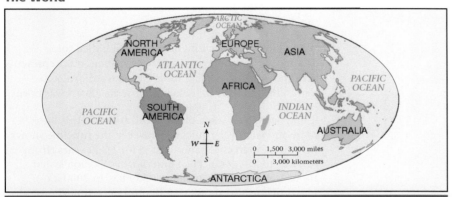

MAP STUDY

1. What are the names of the continents?
2. Which oceans border Africa?

What Is History? Chapter 1   **11**

Ask:

- Did early people walk this distance all at one time? (It took thousands of years for early people to move to the rest of the world.)

LEARNING STYLES

Logical/Mathematical

Ask students to use the distance key to determine how many miles or kilometers (km) early people might have traveled on foot to migrate from South Africa to North America. (1.5 centimeters (cm) = 3,000 miles, and 1 cm = 3,000 km. The distance on the map is approximately 7 cm = 21,000 km or about 13,500 miles.

MAP STUDY

Answers:

1. North America, South America, Europe, Asia, Africa, Australia, Antarctica

2. Atlantic Ocean, Indian Ocean

Ask:

- Which direction on the map is up? (north)
- Which continent on the map is the farthest east? (Australia)
- Which continent is the farthest west? (North America)

Lesson at a Glance

Chapter 1 Lesson 3

Overview This lesson explains how maps help locate the part of the world you are learning about, and timelines help you understand the order of the events you are reading about.

Objectives

- To explain why maps are important
- To describe the information that maps can show
- To explain how a timeline works
- To identify the different units and intervals that can be used on a timeline

Student Pages 11–14

Teacher's Resource Library TRL

Workbook Activity 3

Activity 3

Modified Activity 3

Vocabulary

A.D. (Anno Domini)
B.C. (Before Christ)
Discuss the meanings of these two abbreviations and how they are used to denote a period of time.

PRONUNCIATION GUIDE

Use this list to help students pronounce difficult words in this lesson.

Anno Domini (a nō dä mə nē)

1 Warm-Up Activity

Have students write five important dates, such as a birthday or an important holiday. Have students create a new calendar based on some natural occurrence, like the rising and setting of the sun, or the seasons. Discuss how time would be divided and dates would be determined. Talk about the importance of having some uniform system of measuring time.

What Is History? Chapter 1   **11**

Have students flip through their books to find different maps and timelines. Have students compare a map or timeline they found to one another student found. How are they different?

Ask:

- What are some things that a map can show? (oceans, continents, borders between countries, trade routes, migration patterns, etc.)
- What are some things that a timeline can show? (length of time periods, order of historical events)

Background Information

In some cultures, years or time periods are named after an event that characterized that year or time period. A count of years from an initial event helps to maintain a consistent chronology. An example is the adoption of the birth of Christ as the initial event in the development of the Christian calendar. Dionysius Exiguus, a sixth-century scholar, established the Christian era or A.D. However, he could not establish an accurate date for the birth of Christ. Most scholars believe that Christ was born some years before A.D. 1.

LEARNING STYLES

Body/Kinesthetic

Have students find maps of the world as the world was at various times in the past. For example, have them find on the Internet a map that shows Pangaea, the route Columbus took to discover the Americas, or the route that Darwin sailed on the Beagle. Then have them create a poster of their map by cutting out the continents and marking landmarks. Remind them to include a key. Display the posters in the classroom.

Reading Strategy:
Summarizing

(Different kinds of maps show different details: landforms, weather, continents, countries, and cities.)

B.C. (Before Christ)
Dating from before the time Jesus Christ was born

A.D. (Anno Domini)
Dating from the time Jesus Christ was born

Reading Strategy:
Summarizing

What are some important details about things different types of maps may show?

People have been making maps for a long time. They drew maps to try to understand their world. They also used maps to find their way from one place to another. Since ancient times, the art of mapmaking has come a long way. Maps of today are more accurate, or correct. Now there are maps to show landforms, maps to show weather, and maps that picture continents, countries, and cities.

Mapmakers, however, have more work ahead. Think about the maps of the future. Will maps be needed to help people find their way among the stars?

What Do Timelines Show?

The history of the people of the world is a long and exciting story. The timelines in each chapter will help you keep events clear and in order. Look at the timeline on page 13. It gives some idea of just how long the story is. The timeline shows some of the time periods and people you will read about as the story unfolds. If you look closely at it, you should be able to find where you fit on the timeline of history.

When looking at the timeline, you will notice some differences in the way the dates are written. B.C. represents the time in history *before* Jesus Christ was born. A.D. represents the time in history *after* Jesus Christ was born.

It may seem as if some of the civilizations in this book came and went very quickly. However, the timeline shows that the Roman civilization lasted for 1,250 years (from 750 B.C. to A.D. 500). The Sumerian civilization lasted about 1,500 years (from about 3500 B.C. to 2000 B.C.). The timeline also shows that the "modern times" period is only about 500 years old so far. How does the period in history that we call ancient times compare in length with medieval times and with modern times?

You can use the same method to read most timelines.

1. Look at the whole timeline to figure out how much time it covers. Look for the earliest date. It is the first date on the left. Look for the latest date. It is the last date on the right. To read most timelines correctly, you will read the dates from left to right.

Reading Strategy:
Summarizing

What are some important details that help you read timelines?

2. Remember that a timeline is like a ruler. It is divided into equal units. These equal units are called intervals. An interval may be one day, one month, one year, five years, or any other amount of time. To read any timeline correctly, you need to know how much time each unit or interval represents.

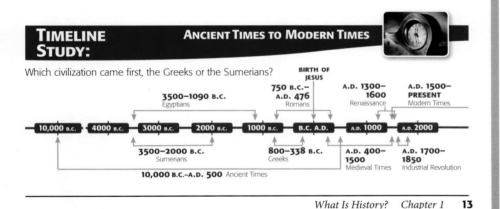

TIMELINE STUDY: ANCIENT TIMES TO MODERN TIMES

Which civilization came first, the Greeks or the Sumerians?

What Is History? Chapter 1 **13**

LEARNING STYLES

Visual/Spatial

The timeline on page 13 covers a great deal of time. Divide the timeline into shorter periods and assign them to groups. Have students create posters with their period's date and labels. Have them skim later chapters in the book for things to draw or paint in their time period. When the groups have finished, have the class connect all the posters in order to make one complete timeline.

ELL/ESL STRATEGY

Language Objective: *To learn vocabulary specific to the use of maps and timelines, such as* map, border, label, timeline, unit, *and* interval.

Have students create their own maps and timelines. Have students create a map of their classroom, school, or neighborhood. Encourage the use of borders, labels, and different colors. Then have students create a timeline of a typical day. When they are finished, have students explain their map or timeline aloud using the proper vocabulary.

3 Reinforce and Extend

COMMON ERROR

Students may think the continents have always been in the same position on the earth. Explain that a map of the earth as it was about 237 million years ago showed one single landmass we call *Pangaea*.

Reading Strategy:
Summarizing

(Look at the dates, events, and where an event is on a timeline.)

TIMELINE STUDY

Answer: Sumerians

An important feature of a timeline is the way it shows the order of historical events. Timelines can often show how significant events or times overlap.

Ask:

- Four great civilizations existed during ancient times. How did these civilizations overlap? (The Egyptian and the Sumerian civilizations overlapped. The Romans and the Greeks overlapped. The Egyptian and Sumerian civilizations did not overlap with the Roman and Greek civilizations.)

COMMON ERROR

Students may think that events in ancient history were faithfully recorded when they happened. Explain that many stories were told orally and were written centuries after the event. To help them understand how stories can change, have small groups sit in a circle. Have one student whisper a short story to the next student. Have that student repeat the story to the next student, and so on. Ask the last student in the circle to tell the story aloud.

REVIEW

On a sheet of paper, write the answer to each question. Use complete sentences.

1. What are two reasons why people first started making maps?

2. What information can a map show? (List at least three things.)

3. Why is a timeline useful?

On a sheet of paper, write the word from the Word Bank to complete each sentence correctly.

Word Bank

A.D.

B.C.

events

intervals

left

rivers

way

4. People make maps to find their _____ from one place to another.

5. Maps can show many things, including: country borders, cities, and _____.

6. _____ represents a time in history before Christ was born.

7. _____ represents a time in history after Christ was born.

8. On a timeline, the earliest date is on the _____.

9. The equal units on a timeline are called _____.

10. Timelines list _____ in the order in which they happened.

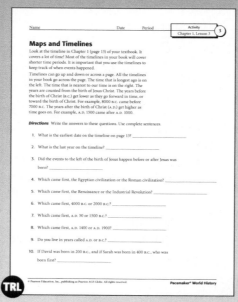

Activity 3

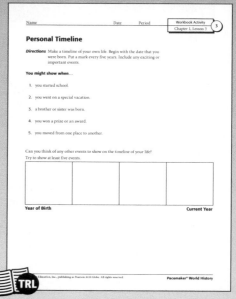

Workbook Activity 3

- World history is the story of people, places, and events from the past. Learning about the past helps explain what is happening today.

- World history is about change. Discoveries bring about change.

- Revolution is another word for change. Revolutions in agriculture and industry brought huge changes to many cultures.

- Some changes happened because of imperialism, a quest for more land and power.

- Revolution is ongoing as technology brings advances. As new concerns arise, relations among different countries may change.

- People in the past shared many of the same concerns as people today.

- Historians study written records to learn about the past. They write books and teach others about what they have learned.

- Archaeologists study artifacts to learn about the past.

- Scientists aid historians by helping to determine the age of found artifacts.

- Maps can show different kinds of information about the world. People use maps to find their way from one place to the other. Some maps show weather trends while other maps show landforms.

- Timelines list events in the order in which they happened. A clear understanding of the intervals shown on a timeline will help in using it effectively.

Chapter 1 Summary

Have students read the Chapter Summary on page 15 to review the main ideas presented in Chapter 1.

Ask:

- Why should people learn about the past? (The past helps explain what is happening today.)

- What effect do discoveries have on world history? (Discoveries bring about change, and world history is about change.)

- Revolutions in what two areas helped to bring major changes to many cultures? (The two areas are agriculture and industry.)

- What is imperialism? (It is the quest for more land and power.)

- How can the development of new technology be a revolution? (Technology brings advances. This may change relations among countries.)

- What do archaeologists do? (They study artifacts to learn about the past.)

- What kinds of information can maps show? (Maps can show how to find the way from place to place, weather, or landforms.)

- What does a timeline show? (It lists events in the order in which they happened.)

CHAPTER PROJECT FOLLOW-UP

 Have students read their biographies aloud to the class. Allow students to use transparencies to show photos, maps, or other visuals. Students should provide detailed biographies of the individual they chose. Pertinent details should include education, significant discoveries, published articles or books, and past or current projects. Students should be able to relate the subject's work to something touched upon in the chapter.

TEACHER'S RESOURCE

The AGS Globe Teaching Strategies in Social Studies Transparencies may be used with this chapter. The transparencies add an interactive dimension to expand and enhance the Pacemaker® *World History* program content.

Chapter 1 Review

Use the Chapter Review to prepare students for tests and to reteach content from the chapter.

Chapter 1 Mastery Test

The Teacher's Resource Library includes two forms of the Chapter Mastery Test. Each test addresses the chapter Goals for Learning. An optional third page of additional critical-thinking items is included for each test. The difficulty level of the two forms is equivalent.

Chapter 1 Review Answers

Vocabulary Review

1. revolution
2. agriculture
3. industry
4. historian
5. archaeologist
6. artifact
7. imperialism
8. culture
9. civilizations
10. development

Chapter Review Questions

11. World history is the story of how the people of different times and places lived.

12. The events of ancient days were exciting to the people who lived them.

Word Bank

agriculture
archaeologist
artifact
civilizations
culture
development
historian
imperialism
industry
revolution

Vocabulary Review

On a sheet of paper, use the words from the Word Bank to complete each sentence correctly.

1. A(n) _____ brings about change, often in government.

2. Revolutions in industry and _____ change the way people live.

3. Developments in _____ made life harder for the people who had to work in factories.

4. A(n) _____ studies maps and books to understand the past.

5. A person who goes digging in ruins is probably a(n) _____.

6. A(n) _____ found underground can tell about life in the past.

7. Strong nations are practicing _____ when they try to take over weak nations.

8. Religion and art are parts of the _____ of a people.

9. When studying history, we often examine ancient _____.

10. The _____ of the wheel was exciting to people of ancient days.

Chapter Review Questions

On a sheet of paper, write the answer to each question. Use complete sentences.

11. What is world history?

12. What made life exciting during ancient times?

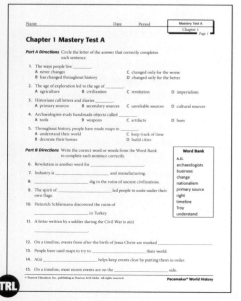

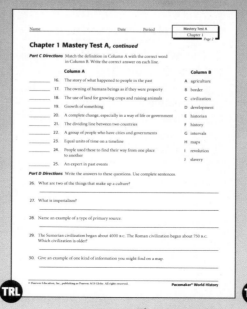

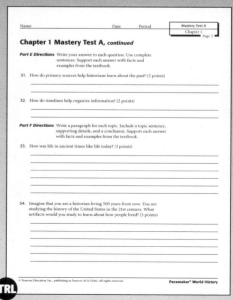

13. How do historians learn from the past?

14. What can archaeologists learn from artifacts?

15. What does a timeline show?

Critical Thinking

On a sheet of paper, write your response to each question. Use complete sentences.

16. How can learning about the past help us understand what might happen in the future?

17. Why are today's maps more accurate than maps made during ancient times? Give at least two reasons.

Using the Timeline

Use the timeline on page 13 to answer the questions.

18. What four civilizations existed during ancient times?

19. How many years did the Industrial Revolution last?

20. In what year did Modern Time begin?

GROUP ACTIVITY

Work in groups of two or three. Suppose you are archaeologists who have uncovered the remains of an ancient city. What artifacts do you hope to find? Make a list of the top 10 artifacts that you think will tell you the most about life in the ancient city.

What Is History? Chapter 1 **17**

---

13. Historians study papers and books of days gone by to learn about the past.

14. Archaeologists learn about cultures of the past from artifacts.

15. A timeline shows the intervals between events in the order that they happened.

Critical Thinking

16. Learning about civilizations, wars, and how cultures change can help us understand the world today. It can also help us understand the world as it might be tomorrow.

17. We have explored most of the world. We use accurate technology to make maps.

Using the Timeline

18. Sumerian, Egyptian, Roman, and Greek

19. 50 years

20. A.D. 1500

GROUP ACTIVITY

Answers will vary but should include 10 artifacts that tell how people lived, such as tools, paintings, weapons, and cooking utensils.

Chapter 1 Mastery Test B, pages 1–3

What Is History? Chapter 1 **17**

Introducing the Chapter

Have students preview the chapter by reading the titles and by looking at illustrations (on pages 20, 25, and 29), the timeline (on page 30), and the maps (on page 31). Write the chapter title on the board: Early Humans: The Story Begins. As a class, discuss what students have previously learned, read, or seen about Stone Age people.

Ask:

- How do you think early humans lived? (Answers will vary. Accept all reasonable answers.)

- When and where did the Agricultural Revolution begin? (around 9000 B.C. in the Fertile Crescent)

Early Humans: The Story Begins

Millions of years ago most of the world was frozen. This was the Ice Age.

Over time the ice began to melt. Small groups of people hunted for food in the warmer, southern parts of the world. This time is known as the Stone Age.

People started to plant food. They learned how to tame animals. They started to build homes in small villages. Much of the earliest farming took place in an area known as the Fertile Crescent. This was the area of the Middle East between the Tigris and Euphrates rivers.

GOALS FOR LEARNING

- To understand how humans began to hunt and what happened after the Ice Age
- To explain how the development of agriculture changed the world
- To describe the area known as the Fertile Crescent

18   *Unit 1   Looking at the World's History*

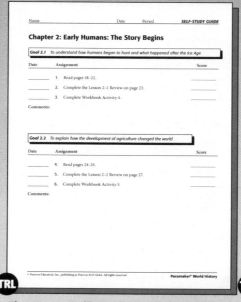

Chapter 2 Self-Study Guide, pages 1–2

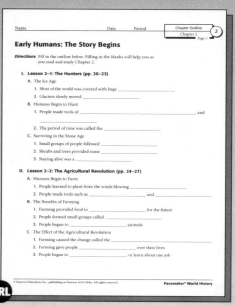

Chapter 2 Outline, pages 1–2

Reading Strategy: Questioning

Asking questions as you read will help you understand and remember more of the information. Questioning the text will also help you to be a more active reader. As you read, ask yourself:

- What is my reason for reading this text?
- What decisions can I make about the facts and details in this text?
- What connections can I make between this text and my own life?

Key Vocabulary Words

Lesson 1

Ice Age A period of time when much of Earth and Earth's water was frozen

Glacier A large, slow-moving mass of ice and snow

Stone Age The earliest known period of human culture where people used tools and weapons made from stone

Lesson 2

Settlement A small group of homes in a newly established place or region

Specialize To work in, and know a lot about, one job or field

Craft A trade or art that takes special skill with the hands

Lesson 3

Fertile Crescent The area of land in the Middle East shaped like a quarter moon

Fertile Able to produce large crops, as in rich soil

Remind students to look for answers in the text as they develop questions about their reading.

Key Vocabulary Words

Point out that these chapter words are presented in the order they appear in each lesson. They are also found in the glossary.

LIFE SKILLS CONNECTION

Students learn about what things to consider when moving and settling down in a new city. Direct students to the Web sites of their chosen cities. Even smaller cities and towns may have an official Web site with a great deal of information.

KEY VOCABULARY

Assist students as they work through the Key Vocabulary Words 2 Worksheet. In Part A, students match the words to the correct meaning. In Part B, students choose the answer that best completes the statement.

CHAPTER PROJECT

Divide the class into small groups of three or four. Have each group find an image of a Stone-Age artifact, such as a spear point, in reference materials or on the Internet. Each group should create a plan stating how they intend to study the history and purpose of the artifact.

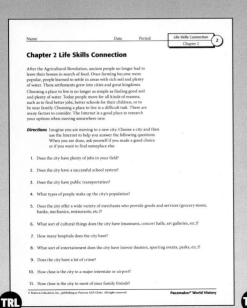

Life Skills Connection 2   Key Vocabulary Words 2

Lesson at a Glance

Chapter 2 Lesson 1

Overview This lesson describes the environment and culture of the Stone Age.

Objectives

- To define the Ice Age and glacier
- To describe the people of the Stone Age

Student Pages 20–23

Teacher's Resource Library **TRL**

Workbook Activity 4

Activity 4

Modified Activity 4

....

Vocabulary

glacier   Stone Age
Ice Age

Ask a volunteer to write one of the vocabulary words from this lesson on the board. Have a second volunteer read the definition aloud. Have a third student restate the definition in his or her own words. Ask a fourth student to use the word in a sentence. Continue until all vocabulary words are on the board. Place students in pairs, and have them use as many vocabulary words as they can in a brief conversation.

1 Warm-Up Activity

Have students work in small groups to develop a "call system" to communicate simple commands and identify common objects. Have each group demonstrate their system to the class. The class should attempt to interpret each group's call system.

Reading Strategy:
Questioning

Have students brainstorm about what they might learn in this lesson.

The Hunters

Objectives

- To define the Ice Age and glacier
- To describe the people of the Stone Age

Reading Strategy: Questioning

What do you think you will learn about in this lesson?

Ice Age
A period of time when much of Earth and Earth's water was frozen

Glacier
A large, slow-moving mass of ice and snow

Our story of the world's history begins more than one million years ago. It was a time called the **Ice Age.** Most of the world was frozen then. It was covered with thick sheets of ice called **glaciers.** These glaciers had formed in the north.

In the northern parts of Europe, Asia, and North America, ice piled up about 10,000 feet thick. The weight of all that ice caused the glaciers to spread out. As they moved, the glaciers pushed soil and rocks out of their way. Many valleys and lakes were formed. Slowly, the glaciers moved farther and farther south.

People of the Stone Age lived in caves and used simple weapons to hunt.

Stone Age
The earliest known period of human culture where people used tools and weapons made from stone

How Did Humans Begin to Hunt?

Over time, in the southern parts of the three continents, the ice melted some during the short summers. Little groups of people lived there, scattered about. They were hunters. They had learned to make spears and other simple weapons and tools. They used wooden sticks, bones, and stones. They had not yet learned how to use metal. So historians call these people and their way of life the **Stone Age** culture.

Such was life on Earth for tens of thousands of years. The hunters left their caves in the summer to move around. They could not settle down for good. They had to follow the herds of wild animals. They also gathered some food from shrubs and trees, such as nuts, berries, and fruits. However, they mainly counted on animals for food and clothing. Hunting was the most important thing in their lives. Without a good hunt, they would die. Just staying alive was a constant struggle for people during this time.

LEARN MORE ABOUT IT

Cave Artwork

Stone Age art has been discovered in caves in France, Spain, Italy, and other places. Most of the time, the caves were discovered by mistake. In 1940, for example, three teenage boys stumbled down a hole and discovered Lascaux Cave in France.

In 1994, three men discovered Chauvet Cave in France. Some of the paintings were created more than 30,000 years ago! The artwork included animals not usually pictured on cave walls. Horses and bison were there, but so were leopards, hyenas, rhinos, and bears. In addition, there were many pictures of cave lions. These pictures showed that the artists knew the habits of the cave lions well.

It is possible that even older cave art has been discovered. In 2000, painted slabs of rock were found at Fumane Cave in Italy. The art, which includes a half-human, half-beast figure, may be 32,000–36,500 years old.

Early Humans: The Story Begins Chapter 2 **21**

Background Information

Historians often describe the earliest humans in terms of the tools and weapons they used. The following chart describes the early eras of the human race.

Old Stone Age	Middle Stone Age	New Stone Age
• 150,000 to 10,000 years ago	• 10,000 to 8,000 years ago	• 8,000 to 6,000 years ago
• made weapons and tools of stone and wood	• life much the same as Old Stone Age	• learned to farm
• fished and hunted for food	• certain animals were domesticated (dogs and goats)	• raised animals
• sewed clothing of animal skins		• learned to weave baskets, to make clothing from plant fibers and wool, and to make clay pots
• lived in caves		• invented the wheel
• used fire for warmth and cooking		

Encourage students to think about the daily challenges faced by people of the Ice Age.

Ask:

- How did people of the Ice Age meet most of their needs? (by hunting)
- Where did people of the Ice Age live during the winter? (in caves)

LEARNING STYLES

Visual/Spatial
Have students create their own cave art. On large sheets of paper taped to a classroom wall, have students describe the people and places in their own community. Remind students not use words, only pictures.

LEARNING STYLES

Body/Kinesthetic
Have students research signs used for communication among different Native American tribes who lived on the Great Plains during the 19th century. Ask them to demonstrate the signs, explaining the message conveyed by each sign.

LEARN MORE ABOUT IT

Remind students that cave artwork tells stories with interesting information about the people who created them and the times they lived in.

Ask:

- What was significant about cave artwork? (Sample answer: People began to record and communicate their experiences.)
- Why do you think people painted on cave walls? (Sample answer: They painted to tell stories or to share what they knew.)

Before students read page 22, have them brainstorm ways that people can communicate without writing or speaking. (Sample answers include gestures such as waving, universal icons on road signs, or the sign language of the hearing impaired.) Then have students read "Humans Learn to Say 'Hello'" to find out how anthropologists think human speech may have developed.

LEARNING STYLES

Visual/Spatial

Have students make up their own call system, as described in the "Words from the Past" feature on page 22. Students should assign a meaning to each sound and practice communicating.

ELL/ESL STRATEGY

Language Objective: *To help students visualize important concepts in the text*

To help ELL students comprehend how long ago Stone-Age people lived, work with students to make a timeline that shows in proportion 15,000 B.C., 10,000 B.C., 5000 B.C., and A.D. 2000. Have students make a mark for every thousand years. Have students take turns naming and pointing out on the timeline a year that marks the turn of a millennium B.C. or A.D. (for example, 1200 B.C. or A.D. 900).

Words from the Past

Humans Learn to Say "Hello"

What did early humans sound like? What language did they speak? No one can be sure. Scientists think that humans developed language over millions of years. Very early humans probably used a "call system." They made sounds with a certain meaning, like those that some animals use. Calls showed feelings. "Look out! There's a lion!" "I'm scared." "This plant tastes good."

Then life changed for early humans. For one thing, they began to walk upright on two feet. This allowed their hands to be free to make tools. People also began to live in larger groups. They worked together to find wild plants. Groups of hunters tracked animals. Now people needed a better way to share ideas. Hunters had to plan for the next day's hunt. A skilled potter needed to teach younger workers their art. The bodies of humans also changed. Their brains and larynx, or voice box, developed. By about 100,000 years ago, some early humans were ready for a different kind of human speech.

On a sheet of paper, write the letter of the answer that correctly completes each sentence.

1. The Ice Age was more than one _____ years ago.

   A hundred   **B** thousand   **C** million   **D** billion

2. A glacier is a _____.

   A cave painting   **B** thick sheet of ice   **C** valley   **D** shrub

3. The _____ Age was a time when people hunted and made simple weapons and tools.

   A Ice   **B** Information   **C** Cave   **D** Stone

4. People of the Stone Age did not yet learn how to use _____.

   A metal   **B** sticks   **C** bones   **D** stones

5. People of the Stone Age hunted wild animals, and _____ food from shrubs and trees.

   A armed   **B** planted   **C** cooked   **D** gathered

On a sheet of paper, write the answer to each question. Use complete sentences.

6. Where did the glaciers form?

7. What caused the glaciers to spread out?

8. What helped form the valleys and lakes during the Ice Age?

9. Where did people live during the Stone Age?

10. Name three countries where Stone Age art has been found.

Early Humans: The Story Begins   Chapter 2   **23**

---

3 **Reinforce and Extend**

COMMON ERROR

Students may think that the Ice Age was an isolated occurrence. Explain that ice ages have occurred periodically throughout Earth's history.

COMMON ERROR

Students might not realize that animals, other than humans, use signs and sounds to communicate. Show students a video on animal communication. Afterwards, have students compare and contrast different types of communication systems among living things.

Lesson 2–1 Review Answers

1. C **2.** B **3.** D **4.** A **5.** D **6.** The glaciers formed in the north. **7.** The weight of all the ice in the northern parts of Europe, Asia, and North America caused the glaciers to spread out. **8.** Slow-moving glaciers pushed soil and rock out of their way, forming valleys and lakes. **9.** People lived in the southern parts of the three continents. **10.** Stone Age art has been found in France, Spain, and Italy.

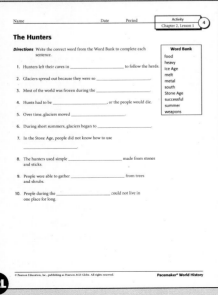

Activity 4

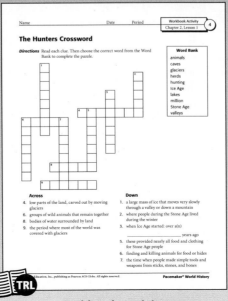

Workbook Activity 4

Lesson at a Glance

Chapter 2 Lesson 2

Overview This lesson discusses the impact of the Agricultural Revolution.

Objectives

- To explain two things people learned when the glaciers melted
- To describe how taming animals helped people in their everyday life
- To explain why the Agricultural Revolution helped develop trading
- To name the three basic human needs that were met because of the Agricultural Revolution

Student Pages 24–27

Teacher's Resource Library **TRL**

Workbook Activity 5

Activity 5

Modified Activity 5

Vocabulary

craft   specialize
settlement

Ask students to preview the lesson and identify five unfamiliar words or phrases, including the vocabulary words. Tell students to write the words in their notebooks. Then have students use dictionaries to define the terms.

Objectives

- To explain two things people learned when the glaciers melted
- To describe how taming animals helped people in their everyday life
- To explain why the Agricultural Revolution helped develop trading
- To name the three basic human needs that were met because of the Agricultural Revolution

Settlement
A small group of homes in a newly established place or region

 Remember
The earliest farmers had no system of writing. We learn about them from the artifacts that archaeologists find.

The Ice Age ended about 10,000 B.C. The glaciers began melting. The land was no longer frozen. People now learned how to grow food. They no longer had to chase wild animals across the lands. Once they learned to raise their own food, they could settle down. That change, from hunting to farming, made civilization possible.

How Did Humans Begin to Farm?

The people of long ago watched the winds blow seeds across the ground. They noticed that new plants grew where the seeds landed. This is how the people learned to farm. They tried planting seeds themselves. They broke up the ground to make it soft. They chose the best seeds, and they grew plants. Next, they made tools to use in farming. They used flint sickles to cut grain and wooden plows to help them dig up the ground.

Once the glaciers were gone, life became easier for people. Now they could count on a ready food supply. Often they grew more than they could eat in one winter. They could store food for the future. They would not have to move away from their homes to search for food. People began to form small groups of homes, called **settlements,** and live there.

They also learned to tame animals. Some say the dog was the first animal tamed. Next came cows, goats, sheep, and pigs. With their own herds, people had a steady supply of meat, milk, and wool. They now had animals that could live side by side with them. The animals could carry loads and help people work.

---

 1   **Warm-Up Activity**

Have students discuss what they would eat to survive if they had to depend on food that is available naturally in their area.

Remember
Archaeologists can make assumptions about ancient farming based on artifacts they discover. For example, they can tell from the size and shape of a tool what it may have been used for.

---

2   **Teaching the Lesson**

As students read this lesson, point out examples of how the Agricultural Revolution changed where and how people lived.

Ask:

- Why did people choose to farm near rivers? (They needed a steady supply of water to grow crops.)
- How did tamed animals help early people? (The animals provided meat, milk, and wool. They also carried loads and helped people work.)

ONLINE CONNECTION

 Students can gain additional information by accessing the following Web sites:

www.agsglobepmwh.com/page24a
(This Web site from Washington State University includes helpful questions and answers that complement the student text.)

www.agsglobepmwh.com/page24b
(This Web site provides a detailed history of farming, including the development of important tools and mechanisms.)

TECHNOLOGY CONNECTION

Ancient Farming

The earliest known farmers had some interesting methods. They used short-handled hoes, or sickles, to loosen soil and plant seeds. This was difficult work.

Farmers harvested grain using sickles made of flint. They gathered the grain onto areas of hard-packed earth. Then oxen, pulling sleds with flint points underneath, crushed the husks away from the grain. Grain was moved in bags carried by people, oxen, or donkeys.

Carts with solid wood wheels were used by about 3500 B.C. Wheels with spokes were invented by 2000 B.C. for two-wheeled carts. Farming wagons with either type of wheel were not likely used by the early farmers.

What Effect Did the Agricultural Revolution Have on People?

When people began to farm about 11,000 years ago, their lives changed. The change brought about by agriculture was great. For this reason, the change is often called the Agricultural Revolution. Now people could settle in large groups, in one place. They chose areas with plenty of water and good soil. They built houses out of whatever materials were nearby. Often the houses were built of mud.

Now the people could plan on how much food to plant each year. They could decide on how many animals to raise in the herds. Now they had more control of their own lives.

For thousands of years, people have tamed animals to carry loads and help them with work.

3 Reinforce and Extend

COMMON ERROR

Students may think that dogs, sheep, pigs, goats, cows, and other domesticated animals have always been tame. Divide the class into small groups. Assign each group a different domesticated animal to research. Have them trace the evolution of the animal, and share their results with the class.

CAREER CONNECTION

Show students how farming has changed since the Agricultural Revolution. Today, farmers use many kinds of technology to plant and harvest crops. There are a diverse number of careers in agriculture. Fields such as Biotechnology, Engineering, Pest Management, and Environmental Science are just a few areas of agriculture today.

Background Information

Some groups of people did not take part in the Agricultural Revolution described in this lesson. They did not settle down in permanent homes. Instead, they continued to live a nomadic lifestyle.

There are three basic nomadic ways of life today. Some nomads hunt and gather. Others live in one place much of the time but move with the seasons to find pasture for their herds. Still others move about selling or trading their goods and their work. Today, some Kalahari San in Africa are hunters and gatherers. Some Nenets and Khanty in Siberia are reindeer herders. Some Roma, or Gypsies, move from place to place selling goods they have made and also hiring out for work.

ELL/ESL STRATEGY

Language Objective: *To describe how inventions and discoveries made life easier for people*

Have each ELL student choose an ancient discovery or invention, such as discovering fire, taming a dog, or inventing the wheel. They should give a class presentation describing the invention or discovery. Students may draw pictures or show magazine pictures to present their ideas. They may also want to tell how the invention or discovery impacted their native country. Class presentations should include a description of how the invention or discovery made life easier for early people. For example, the plow enabled people to cultivate land more easily. Thus, people could grow more food and were better nourished.

TECHNOLOGY CONNECTION

Tools and transportation in agriculture have changed significantly since sickles and two-wheeled carts. Farmers now have advanced technology such as tractors, combines, and harvesters that eliminate the need to work the land by hand.

You Decide

Ask students to list craftworkers in their neighborhood. Have students brainstorm about the types of crafts they would like to create.

Reading Strategy:
Questioning

Have students relate jobs from Agricultural Revolution to jobs of today.

COMMON ERROR

Students might be surprised to know that some ancient crafts are still being practiced today. Arrange a field trip to a studio where artisans create pottery, beaded jewelry, or handwoven baskets. Encourage students to make a list of questions to ask the artisans.

AT HOME

To develop more familiarity with timelines, ask students to create a personal timeline by recording five to ten important events in their lives. Then, have students illustrate their timelines with drawings, photos, or magazine cutouts.

WORLD CULTURES

Before writing evolved, storytelling was very important. Some groups assigned the storytelling task to one person who was responsible for memorizing and reciting the culture's important history and folktales. Each generation, the responsibility was passed to a new person. This tradition exists today among the people of Guinea, a country on the west coast of Africa.

Specialize
To work in, and know a lot about, one job or field

Craft
A trade or art that takes special skill with the hands

You Decide
There are still craftworkers today. Are craftworkers needed as much today as they were long ago? Why or why not?

Reading Strategy:
Questioning
What sort of job might you have wanted to have those thousands of years ago? Why?

Having a large enough food supply and staying in one place gave people spare time. Not everyone in the group was needed to raise food or care for the animals. This allowed people to learn a lot about one job, and they began to **specialize.** Some people farmed. Others took care of the animals.

Now there were also chances to do things they had never done before. People had time to work on their **crafts.** Weavers wove grass into fine baskets. Others made pottery from mud and clay and baked it in ovens. With wool from the sheep, some people learned to spin thread and to weave cloth.

As different jobs developed, so did trading. Weavers might trade their cloth for food from farmers. A goat might be traded for an ax from the toolmaker. First, trading was carried on within the village. Later, people traded from one village to the next.

With the Agricultural Revolution, people's most important needs—food, shelter, and clothing—were easier to meet. However, now people owned things. Potters had their jars and bowls. Herders had their animals. Now there were things to protect! New laws were needed. Most likely a group of the oldest, wisest people in the village would meet. They would decide on rules for the rest of the people.

People started to worry when their villages grew rich. Someone might attack them and try to steal some of their riches. Therefore, people formed armies to protect their villages.

As time went on, villages grew into cities. Later, cities joined together to form small kingdoms. Agriculture is what made this development possible.

IN THE COMMUNITY

Have students visit a farm or local garden in your community. Students should explore the basic steps for growing crops or other food sources. Help students make the connection between the agricultural industry and the food they buy in a store.

REVIEW

Word Bank

farming

kingdoms

laws

specialize

tame

On a sheet of paper, write the word from the Word Bank to complete each sentence correctly.

1. The change from hunting to _____ made civilization possible.

2. The Agricultural Revolution allowed people to _____.

3. People learned to grow food and to _____ animals when the Ice Age ended.

4. When people started to own things, new _____ were needed.

5. As time went on, villages grew into cities, which grew into _____.

On a sheet of paper, write the answer to each question. Use complete sentences.

6. Why were people able to live in settlements?

7. How did taming animals help people in their everyday life?

8. How did the Agricultural Revolution help develop trading? (Provide examples.)

9. What three basic human needs were met because of the Agricultural Revolution?

10. Why did people start to form armies?

1. farming **2.** specialize **3.** tame **4.** laws **5.** kingdoms **6.** They no longer had to move away from their homes in search of food. **7.** Animals gave people a steady supply of meat, milk, and wool. Also, animals could carry loads and help people work. **8.** People had the time to work on crafts and to specialize. As different jobs developed, trading began. For example, weavers might trade their cloth for food from farmers. **9.** The Agricultural Revolution met people's needs for food, shelter, and clothing. **10.** People formed armies to protect their villages.

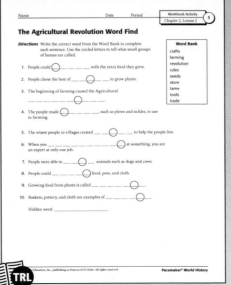

Activity 5

Workbook Activity 5

Chapter 2 Lesson 3

Overview This lesson discusses the location and the culture of the Fertile Crescent.

Objectives

■ To locate the Fertile Crescent on a map

■ To explain how the people of ancient Jericho tried to protect their town

Student Pages 28–32

Teacher's Resource Library 🔵 **TRL**

Workbook Activity 6

Activity 6

Modified Activity 6

Vocabulary

fertile   **Fertile Crescent**

Using graph paper, have students develop crossword puzzles incorporating the vocabulary words in this chapter, including the words for this lesson. Challenge students to create challenging clues that are not copied directly from the text. Have students share their puzzles with their classmates.

PRONUNCIATION GUIDE

Use this list to help students pronounce difficult words in this lesson.

Euphrates (yù frā´tēz)

Mesopotamia (mes´ ə pə tā´ mē ə)

Jericho (jer´ i kō)

History Fact

Compare the population of the students' town or city with that of Jericho. Ask them to describe what differences there may have been or what it would have been like to live there.

The Fertile Crescent

Objectives

■ To locate the Fertile Crescent on a map

■ To explain how the people of ancient Jericho tried to protect their town

Fertile Crescent
The area of land in the Middle East shaped like a quarter moon

Fertile
Able to produce large crops, as in rich soil

History Fact
By about 8000 B.C., Jericho had between 1,000 and 2,000 people. Archaeologists have found wheat and barley in the remains of the town.

The success of farming depends on rich soil and the presence of water. For this reason, early human settlements arose near rivers.

What Is the Fertile Crescent?

The earliest known farming took place along the great rivers of the Middle East. These lands include what are now the countries of Jordan, Syria, Iraq, Iran, Kuwait, Lebanon, Israel, and Turkey. This area is called the **Fertile Crescent** because it is shaped like a quarter moon. The Tigris and Euphrates rivers provided plenty of water for the land. The soil was rich, or **fertile**. The land between the Tigris and Euphrates was called Mesopotamia. That name means "land between two rivers."

Within the Fertile Crescent was the town of Jericho. It is one of the earliest known towns. By about 8000 B.C., Jericho was probably a farming village. Its people built rounded houses of mud and bricks. Archaeologists have found remains showing that the people of Jericho buried their dead right under their houses.

The land around Jericho was very fertile. The people grew many crops and became rich. The town grew. Jericho now had to protect itself. The people built a stone wall around their town.

---

1   Warm-Up Activity

Discuss how archaeologists learn about ancient civilizations. Have students identify some of the things archaeologists may have discovered in the Fertile Crescent. Describe a dig in which archaeologists uncover the ruins of buildings and entire villages. Show students photographs of excavated buildings at archaeological digs.

STUDY SKILLS

Outlining helps students organize a large amount of information. Review proper outlining techniques with the class. Then have students outline the lesson. Encourage them to use the subheads in the text as titles for each Roman numeral in their outlines. Remind students to focus on main points and supporting key details.

The wall was not enough protection. Around 7000 B.C., archaeologists say, Jericho was probably captured. The houses built after that time were no longer round but had square corners. This clue suggests that a new group of people must have taken over and settled there.

The wall built to protect Jericho was destroyed and the town was captured.

Review uses for maps. Make sure all students understand a map scale and can easily locate places on a map.

Ask:

- Look at the maps on page 31. What are the names of the bodies of water? (the Nile River, the Tigris River, the Euphrates River, the Persian Gulf, the Black Sea, the Caspian Sea, the Arabian Sea, the Red Sea, and the Mediterranean Sea)

- Look at the section entitled "What Is the Fertile Crescent?" Have students answer that question. (It is the land where the earliest known farming occurred along the great rivers of the Middle East.)

Background Information

Much of what we know about the ancient cultures of the Fertile Crescent comes from archaeological and anthropological studies. Archaeologists study the remains of past civilizations. They excavate sites to uncover buildings, temples, and homes of prehistoric and ancient people. Their discoveries often add to the historian's understanding of the way people lived.

Anthropological studies also contribute to our knowledge of history. Anthropologists study the way humans live now and the way they lived in the past. They look for the patterns of behavior, such as family life, that people share.

Geography Note

Relate the loss of suitable farming land in the Nile to current environmental concerns such as soil erosion and drought caused by global warming.

Reading Strategy:
Questioning

Have students copy the timeline on a separate piece of paper and write the main points from the lesson in the corresponding space to use as a reference when asking questions.

TIMELINE STUDY

Answer: 6000 years

Ask students to create their own timeline with events such as when they started school, joined the school band, or learned to drive.

Geography Note

Archaeologists believe that people were farming the Nile Valley as early as 10,000 B.C. By 6000 B.C., farmers there were harvesting grains such as sorghum, millet, and barley. Beginning in about 4000 B.C., the area became increasingly dry. The Sahara grew. Many of the former Nile Valley farmers moved to southwest Africa.

Reading Strategy:
Questioning

Study the maps and the timeline. Ask yourself how they relate to what you just read.

More is known about the early farming villages of the Fertile Crescent than anywhere else. However, farming was developing in other parts of the world, too. By 6000 B.C., farming had spread to Europe. By 5000 B.C., a culture of rice farmers had grown up in China. Between 5000 B.C. and 2000 B.C., agriculture spread across northern Africa.

People began to settle wherever there was good soil and plenty of water. Now they had food and clothing. They had time to learn. Certain cities began to grow into great civilizations.

Compare the maps on the next page. Notice how the Middle East changed over time.

TIMELINE STUDY:

THE AGRICULTURAL REVOLUTION

How many years passed between the beginning of agriculture and the first use of the wheel?

10,000 B.C. End of Ice Age	**6000 B.C.** Farming spreads to Europe	**5000 B.C.** Rice farming develops in China

10,000 B.C. — 9000 B.C. — 8000 B.C. — 7000 B.C. — 6000 B.C. — 5000 B.C. — 4000 B.C. — 3000 B.C. — 2000 B.C. — 1000 B.C. — B.C. A.D.

9000 B.C. Taming of animals and beginning of agriculture in Fertile Crescent

7000 B.C. Pottery-making begins; Jericho probably captured

5000 B.C. Agriculture spreads across northern Africa

3500 B.C. First use of wheel

BIRTH OF JESUS

The Middle East: Then

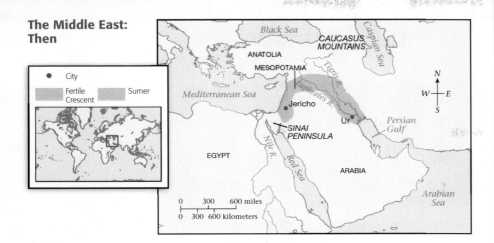

City

Fertile Crescent   Sumer

The Middle East: Now

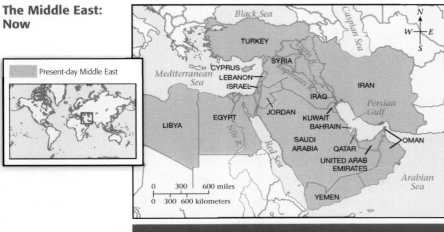

Present-day Middle East

MAP STUDY

1. Which names of places are on both maps?
2. Look at both maps. In which present-day country was Sumer located?

COMMON ERROR

The Fertile Crescent is shaped like a quarter moon. Students might be confused about the shape of this moon phase. Show them a photograph of a quarter moon.

COMMON ERROR

Students might not realize that the names of countries, cities, rivers, and other geographic features can change over time. Have them compare the ancient and modern names of several features on the maps on page 31.

TEACHER ALERT

In the Chapter Review, the Vocabulary Review activity includes a sample of the chapter's vocabulary terms. The activity will help determine students' understanding of key vocabulary terms and concepts presented in the chapter.

MAP STUDY

Answers:

1. Persian Gulf, Arabian Sea, Caspian Sea, Black Sea, Mediterranean Sea, Red Sea, Euphrates River, Tigris River, Nile River, Egypt

2. Iraq

Lesson 2–3 Review Answers

1. C **2.** B **3.** A **4.** C **5.** D **6.** A **7.** A
8. The area known as the Fertile Crescent includes Jordan, Syria, Iraq, Iran, Kuwait, Lebanon, Israel, and Turkey. **9.** They buried their dead under their homes. **10.** The houses built after 7000 B.C. were no longer round.

On a sheet of paper, write the letter of the answer that correctly completes each sentence.

1. The land with rich soil and that produced large crops was known as the _____.

   A Middle East   **B** Mesopotamia   **C** Fertile Crescent   **D** Jericho

2. The land between the Tigris and _____ was called Mesopotamia.

   A Jordan   **B** Euphrates   **C** Iraq   **D** Lebanon

3. _____ means *land between two rivers*.

   A Mesopotamia   **B** Tigris   **C** Euphrates   **D** Iraq

4. A town within the Fertile Crescent was _____.

   A Israel   **B** Iraq   **C** Jericho   **D** Tigris

5. People in Jericho built rounded houses made of _____ and bricks.

   A sticks   **B** straw   **C** bones   **D** mud

6. The people of Jericho tried to protect their town by building a stone _____.

   A wall   **B** weapon   **C** house   **D** road

7. By _____ B.C., farming had spread to Europe.

   A 6000   **B** 5000   **C** 4000   **D** 2000

On a sheet of paper, write the answer to each question. Use complete sentences.

8. What Middle Eastern countries does the area known as the Fertile Crescent include?

9. What do archaeologists believe the people of Jericho did with their dead?

10. What evidence is there to suggest that Jericho was captured?

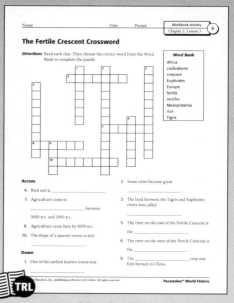

Activity 6   Workbook Activity 6

SUMMARY

- During the Ice Age, most of the world was frozen. In some places, the ice was 10,000 feet thick.

- In southern areas, groups of people hunted for food during the short summers.

- Hunters could not form long-term settlements. They had to follow the animals. They gathered some wild foods such as nuts and berries.

- People began to see that the wind scattered seeds and became new plants. They started to plant seeds on their own. They made tools for farming.

- People began to tame animals.

- Farming meant people could control their own food supply. They could build houses and settle in one place. Some people call this the Agricultural Revolution.

- In the new settlements, people had different jobs. New crafts developed.

- As people created more and different products, trading began and villages became richer.

- Villages formed armies to protect their valuables.

- Villages grew into cities, cities joined to form kingdoms.

- One of the earliest areas of farming was in the Middle East, along two great rivers. This area is called the Fertile Crescent.

Early Humans: The Story Begins   Chapter 2   **33**

Chapter 2 Summary

Have students read the Chapter Summary on page 33 to review the main ideas presented in Chapter 2.

Ask:

- How did people in southern areas get food during the short summers of the Ice Age? (They hunted and gathered nuts and berries.)
- What did people do when they noticed that the wind scattered seeds that grew into plants? (They began to plant seeds.)
- What happened during the Agricultural Revolution? (People grew their own food and began to tame animals. They settled in one place and built homes.)
- What happened when people created a wide variety of products? (They began to trade with one another.)
- Why did villages form armies? (to protect their valuables)
- Cities join together to form what? (kingdoms)
- What is the Fertile Crescent and where is it found? (It was one of the earliest areas of farming. It was located in the Middle East.)

CHAPTER PROJECT FOLLOW-UP

 Have groups of students give multimedia presentations on the Stone Age artifacts they researched earlier. Presentations might include videotapes, posters, drawings, audio recordings, or models. The presentations should explain the history and purpose of the artifacts.

TEACHER'S RESOURCE

The AGS Globe Teaching Strategies in Social Studies Transparencies may be used with this chapter. The transparencies add an interactive dimension to expand and enhance the Pacemaker® *World History* program content.

Chapter 2 Review

Use the Chapter Review to prepare students for tests and to reteach content from the chapter.

Chapter 2 Mastery Test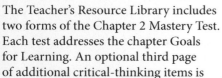

The Teacher's Resource Library includes two forms of the Chapter 2 Mastery Test. Each test addresses the chapter Goals for Learning. An optional third page of additional critical-thinking items is included for each test. The difficulty level of the two forms is equivalent.

Chapter 2 Review Answers

Vocabulary Review

1. Fertile Crescent

2. craft

3. fertile

4. specialize

5. glacier

6. settlement

Chapter Review Questions

7. The Stone Age was the earliest known period of human culture where people used tools and weapons made of stone.

8. People were able to live in settlements because they developed farming and no longer had to move around in search of food.

9. People learned how to grow their own food.

10. Sample answer: People had a steady supply of food. They did not have to move around. They had more control of their lives.

11. They built the wall to protect their town.

12. The shape of the houses changed.

13. The earliest known farming took place in the Fertile Crescent.

14. Mesopotamia is the land between the Tigris and Euphrates Rivers.

Word Bank

craft

fertile

Fertile Crescent

glacier

settlement

specialize

Vocabulary Review

On a sheet of paper, use the words from the Word Bank to correctly match each definition below.

1. The area of land in the Middle East where the earliest farming took place

2. Arts and skills such as weaving and making baskets

3. Rich soil that is suitable for farming

4. To work in a job that takes a certain kind of knowledge

5. A moving body of ice and snow

6. A small village in a newly established place or region

Chapter Review Questions

On a sheet of paper, write the answer to each question. Use complete sentences.

7. What was the Stone Age culture?

8. Why were people able to live in settlements?

9. What did people begin to do after the Ice Age ended?

10. How did farming make life easier for people after the Ice Age ended?

11. Why did the people of Jericho build a wall around their town?

12. How did archaeologists know Jericho was captured?

13. Where did the earliest known farming take place?

14. What is Mesopotamia?

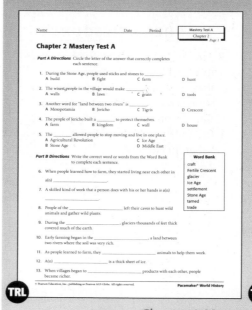

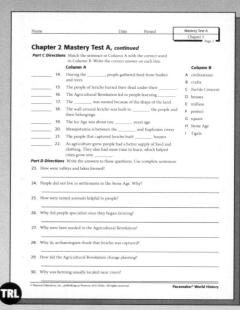

Critical Thinking

On a sheet of paper, write your response to each question. Use complete sentences.

15. Why do you think people made pictures in caves thousands of years ago?

16. Why did trading develop after people began to specialize?

17. Why is the change from hunting to farming called the Agricultural Revolution?

Using the Timeline

Use the timeline on page 30 to answer the questions.

18. Which came first, pottery-making or the first use of the wheel?

19. Where and when did rice farming develop?

20. How many years after the end of the Ice Age was Jesus born?

GROUP ACTIVITY

Form a group of three or four students. Discuss the ways life in early villages was like life in towns and cities today. Make a list of the ways they were alike. Share the list with the rest of the class.

Early Humans: The Story Begins   Chapter 2   **35**

Critical Thinking

15. Possible answer: pictures were to record experiences, or express creativity.

16. Possible answer: People had the time to work on crafts and to specialize. As different jobs developed, trading began. For example, weavers might trade their cloth for food from farmers.

17. Possible answer: The change brought about by agriculture was great, so it was called a revolution.

Using the Timeline

18. pottery-making

19. Rice farming developed in China in 5000 B.C.

20. about 10,000 years

GROUP ACTIVITY

Students' lists should include similarities such as the following: settled in large groups, built homes, had spare time, specialized in type of work, traded things, owned things, needed laws, needed protection.

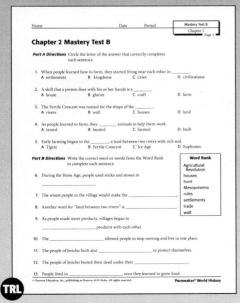

Chapter 2 Mastery Test B, pages 1–3

Early Humans Chapter 2   **35**

Ancient Civilizations: 5000 B.C.–200 B.C.

	Student Text Lesson					
	Student Pages	Vocabulary	Map Study	Reading Strategy	Lesson Review	Chapter Summary/Review
Chapter 3 Sumerians: The First Great Civilization	38–55	✔		✔		53–55
Lesson 3–1 The Sumerian Civilization	40–42	✔	✔	✔	42	
Lesson 3–2 Sumerian City-States	43–45	✔		✔	45	
Lesson 3–3 Sumerian Inventions	46–49	✔		✔	49	
Lesson 3–4 Life in Sumer	50–52	✔		✔	52	
Chapter 4 Ancient Egypt: Land of the Pharaohs	56–71	✔		✔		69–71
Lesson 4–1 Egypt and the Nile	58–61	✔	✔	✔	61	
Lesson 4–2 The Pyramids	62–64	✔		✔	64	
Lesson 4–3 Egyptian Culture	65–68	✔		✔	68	

(Unit Planning Guide is continued on next page.)

Chapter Activities

Teacher's Resource Library
Life Skills Connection 3–6
Key Vocabulary Words 3–6

Assessment Options

Student Text
Chapter Reviews 3–6
Teacher's Resource Library
Chapter 3 Mastery Tests A and B
Chapter 4 Mastery Tests A and B
Chapter 5 Mastery Tests A and B
Chapter 6 Mastery Tests A and B
Unit 2 Mastery Test
Teacher's Edition
Chapter Projects 3–6

Student Text Features							Teaching Strategies										Learning Styles					Teacher's Resource Library			
Words from the Past	Learn More About It	Great Names in History	Technology Connection	Geography Note	You Decide/Remember/History Fact	Timeline Study	ELL/ESL Strategy	Background Information	Common Error	Life Skills Connection	Key Vocabulary Words	Study Skills	Applications Home, Career, Community	Online Connection	Teacher Alert	World Cultures	Auditory/Verbal	Body/Kinesthetic	Interpersonal/Group Learning	Logical/Mathematical	Visual/Spatial	Activities/Modified Activities	Workbook Activities	Self-Study Guide	Chapter Outline
										39	39													✔	✔
			41				41	41					42				42					7	7		
							45	44	43							45		44				8	8		
48					47		47	47	47, 48			49		48	48				48		48	9	9		
						51	51	51					52									10	10		
										57	57													✔	✔
	60				60		60	59	60			61	60						59			11	11		
							63	63				64	63	63	64			63				12	12		
67			65		66	66	67	66	65				67			68	67					13	13		

Modified Activities

The Teacher's Resource Library (TRL) contains a set of lower-level worksheets called Modified Activities. These worksheets cover the same content as the standard Activities but are written at a lower reading level.

Skill Track

Use Skill Track for *World History* to monitor student progress and meet the demands of adequate yearly progress (AYP). Make informed instructional decisions with individual student and class reports of lesson and chapter assessments. With immediate and ongoing feedback, students will also see what they have learned and where they need more reinforcement and practice.

Ancient Civilizations: 5000 B.C.–200 B.C. *(continued)*

	Student Pages	Vocabulary	Map Study	Reading Strategy	Lesson Review	Chapter Summary/Review
Student Text Lesson						
Chapter 5 Mediterranean Kingdoms	72–95	✔		✔		93–95
Lesson 5–1 The Phoenicians	74–77	✔	✔	✔	77	
Lesson 5–2 The Israelites	78–82	✔		✔	82	
Lesson 5–3 The Babylonians	83–85	✔		✔	85	
Lesson 5–4 The Hittites	86–88	✔		✔	88	
Lesson 5–5 The Assyrians	89–92	✔		✔	92	
Chapter 6 Early Civilizations of India, China, and the Americas	96–119	✔		✔		117–119
Lesson 6–1 Ancient India	98–101	✔	✔	✔	101	
Lesson 6–2 Buddhism	102–105	✔		✔	105	
Lesson 6–3 Early China	106–110	✔	✔	✔	111	
Lesson 6–4 Early America	112–116	✔	✔	✔	116	

	Student Text Features							Teaching Strategies										Learning Styles					Teacher's Resource Library			
Words from the Past	Learn More About It	Great Names in History	Technology Connection	Geography Note	You Decide/Remember/History Fact	Timeline Study	ELL/ESL Strategy	Background Information	Common Error	Life Skills Connection	Key Vocabulary Words	Study Skills	Applications Home, Career, Community	Online Connection	Teacher Alert	World Cultures	Auditory/Verbal	Body/Kinesthetic	Interpersonal/Group Learning	Logical/Mathematical	Visual/Spatial	Activities/Modified Activities	Workbook Activities	Self-Study Guide	Chapter Outline
---	---	---	---	---	---	---	---	---	---	---	---	---	---	---	---	---	---	---	---	---	---	---	---	---	---
										73	73													✔	✔
						76	76	75	76			76	76						75			14	14		
79					81	81	79	79	80						80	80	80			81		15	15		
		84			83, 84	84	84	84	85				85	85							84	16	16		
					86		87	87	87				87									17	17		
						91	90	89									90					18	18		
										97	97													✔	✔
							99	99	100				101	100							99	19	19		
					104	104	104	103	104				104			105	103					20	20		
		110			109		108	107	109					110	109		110	108				21	21		
			114		112, 114	115	115	114	113											114		22	22		

Unit at a Glance

Audio Library

Skill Track for World History

Teacher's Resource Library

Unit 2 Mastery Test

(Answer Keys for the Teacher's Resource Library begin on page 809 of the Teacher's Edition.)

Other Resources

Books for Teachers

Doyle, Arthur Conan and Leslie S. Casson, Lionel. *The Ancient Mariners.* Princeton, NJ: Princeton University Press, 1991.

Nemat-Nejat, Karen Rhea. *Daily Life in Ancient Mesopotamia.* Westport, CT: Greenwood Press, 1998.

Books for Students

Bauer, Susan Wise. *The History of the Ancient World: From the Earliest Accounts to the Fall of Rome.* New York: W. W. Norton, 2007.

Morley, Jacqueline. *You Wouldn't Want to Be a Sumerian Slave! A Life of Hard Labor You'd Rather Avoid.* New York: Franklin Watts, 2007.

CD-ROM

Ancient Egypt and the Middle East. Fairfield, CT: Queue. (Multimedia presentation takes the viewer to the site of archaeological digs.

ANCIENT CIVILIZATIONS

I f you read and go to films, you probably love adventure stories. It is fun to be kept on the edge of your seat by make-believe. How about true stories of adventure? Consider learning about buried treasure and mummies. Think of thousands of people building a stone monument 10 times taller than your school building. What about managing the sails of a boat during a wild storm? Suppose you are trying to read words of art painted on cave walls. By understanding the words, you will figure out who killed who and when. What better adventure could you imagine? The study of ancient civilizations is filled with mystery and suspense.

Chapters in Unit 2

The pyramids at Giza were built by ancient Egyptians as tombs for their kings.

37

Introducing the Unit

Call attention to the photo on page 36. Ask students to suggest how they think the photo relates to the title "Ancient Civilizations." Tell students they will read about these buildings and many others constructed by great civilizations all over the world.

Videos

Great Cities of the Ancient World: The Pyramids and the Cities of the Pharaohs. (75 minutes). Questar, 1994. (The rise of Egyptian civilization from the sand to monumental heights.)

Mayas, Aztecs, and Incas. (27 minutes). (Three parts show the last phases of pre-Conquest urban culture in the New World.)

Web Sites

www.agsglobepmwh.com/page37a (British Museum site with well-presented information on Mesopotamia. Includes history, explorations, and interactive challenges on the subjects of writing, beliefs, geography, and time.)

www.agsglobepmwh.com/page37b (Pages for prehistory and prehistoric technology include India, Mesopotamia, Egypt, and early Americas.)

Introducing the Chapter

Some of the first civilizations developed
in the Middle East about 7,000 years ago.
Have students create a list of things that
are necessary for civilizations to develop.
(Answers may include fertile land for
farming, written language to record
information, and natural resources to
build shelter.) As they read this chapter,
have students add to their lists.

Ask:

• When and where did the Sumerians
first begin farming? (5000 B.C.,
Mesopotamia)

Sumerians: The First Great Civilization

More and more people settled on the fertile land
between the Tigris and Euphrates rivers. The land
became known as Sumer. Farmers worked hard to find
new and better ways of growing food. Merchants traveled
in boats to find treasures from other lands. The villages of
Sumer grew into city-states.

The Sumerians began to write down details of their lives.
They learned ways of measuring land and counting. Their
crafts included fine jewelry made of copper, silver, and
gold. They built an army to protect their lands.

GOALS FOR LEARNING

• To explain why the civilization of Sumer grew
• To discuss the growth of Sumerian city-states
• To name the most important Sumerian inventions
• To describe life in Sumer

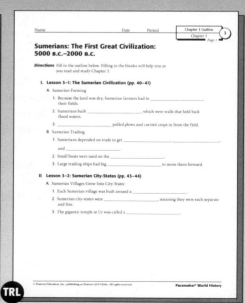

Chapter 3 Self-Study Guide, pages 1–2   Chapter 3 Outline, pages 1–2

Reading Strategy: Predicting

Previewing a text helps readers think about what they already know about a subject. It also prepares readers to look for new information—to predict what will come next. Keep this in mind as you make predictions:

- Make your best guess about what might happen next.
- Add details about what you think will happen.
- Check your predictions. You may have to change your predictions as you learn more information.

Key Vocabulary Words

Lesson 1

Swamp An area of low, wet land

Irrigate To bring water to dry land by means of canals

Canal A man-made waterway

Dike A wall built along a river or sea to hold back the water from low land

Merchant A person who buys and sells goods for a profit; a trader

Goods The things for sale or trade

Lesson 2

Temple A building used to honor and praise a god or gods

Goddess A female god

Priest A religious leader

City-state An independent city and the surrounding land it controls

Independent Self-governing, separate, free

Lesson 3

Tablet A small, flat piece of clay used for writing

Cuneiform A wedge-shaped form of writing used in ancient Sumer

Scribe A person whose job it was to write out copies of contracts and other important papers

Contract A written agreement between two or more people

Chariot An open two-wheeled cart, pulled by horses

Pictograph A drawing that represents an actual thing; for example, a picture of an eye represents an eye

Create To make something

Lesson 4

Noble A person of high social rank

- Identify three major accomplishments of the Sumerians. (They developed city-states, invented writing, and used wheels.)

Reading Strategy: Predicting

Encourage students to skim the lesson and section titles ahead to gather information in order to form predictions.

....

Key Vocabulary Words

Point out that these chapter words are presented in the order they appear in each lesson. They are also found in the glossary.

LIFE SKILLS CONNECTION

Students learn how to create a resume. Students also learn about the importance of using professional language in a resume. Provide students with some sample resumes to give them an idea of style and format.

KEY VOCABULARY

Work with students as they choose vocabulary words to complete each statement.

CHAPTER PROJECT

On a sheet of plain paper, have each student create a chart with two columns and five rows. The heading for the left-hand column should be "Sumer" and the heading for the right-hand column should be "Modern America." The headings for the rows should be "Cities," "Government," "Rights of Children," "Religion," and "Inventions." As they read the chapter, students should write one or two key facts for each row under the Sumer column. Then, drawing on their own observations, students should write one or two facts for each row under the Modern America column.

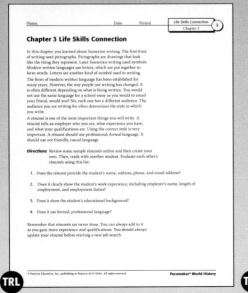

Life Skills Connection 3

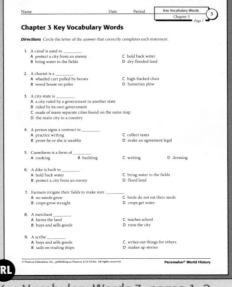

Key Vocabulary Words 3, pages 1–2

Chapter 3 Lesson 1

Overview This lesson describes where the Sumerians lived, and how they farmed and traded.

Objectives

- To locate the land of Sumer on a map
- To describe the Sumerian method of farming and irrigating
- To name three items Sumerians got through trading
- To identify how Sumerians carried goods to and from Sumer

Student Pages 40–42

Teacher's Resource Library

Workbook Activity 7

Activity 7

Modified Activity 7

Vocabulary

canal	irrigate
dike	merchant
goods	swamp

Have each student make flashcards for the vocabulary words. The front of the card should contain the word, and the back of the card should contain the corresponding definition. Give the students a few minutes to silently learn the definitions using their flashcards. Then pair them up and have them quiz each other aloud.

PRONUNCIATION GUIDE

Use this list to help students pronounce difficult words in this lesson.

Sumerian (sü mir´ ē ən)

Mesopotamia (mes´ ə pə tā´ mē ə)

Tigris (ti´ grəs)

Euphrates (yü fra´ tēz)

The Sumerian Civilization

Objectives

- To locate the land of Sumer on a map
- To describe the Sumerian method of farming and irrigating
- To name three items that Sumerians got through trading
- To identify how Sumerians carried goods to and from Sumer

The land that would one day be called Mesopotamia lay between two rivers. The rivers were the Tigris and the Euphrates. Sometimes the rivers flooded and washed rich bottom-soil up on the land. This made the land good for farming. People settled on this rich land. They grew their crops and raised animals. In the south, in a land called Sumer, a great civilization grew.

How Did the Sumerians Farm?

The people of Sumer were called Sumerians. Although the land they settled was fertile, it was not a perfect place to live. The weather was very hot in the summer. In spring there was always the danger of the rivers flooding.

The Sumerians

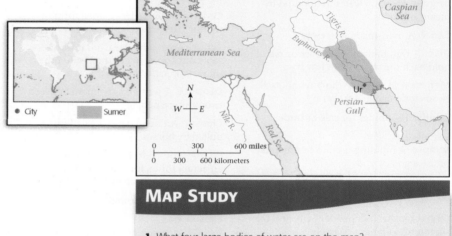

City   Sumer

MAP STUDY

1. What four large bodies of water are on the map?
2. What three rivers are on the map?

---

1   Warm-Up Activity

Have students study the map on page 40. Ask them to use the map to write a description of where the Sumerians lived. Then have them answer the Map Study questions.

MAP STUDY

Answers:

1. Mediterranean Sea, Red Sea, Caspian Sea, Persian Gulf

2. Nile, Euphrates, and Tigris rivers

2   Teaching the Lesson

Ask students to look for the new technologies that contributed to the Sumerians' success in farming and trade.

Ask:

- How did the Sumerians control water on their land? (They used canals to bring water to their fields. Dikes prevented flooding in low areas.)

- What did merchants trade for the Sumerian crops? (goods such as metals, stone, and timber)

Swamp

An area of low, wet land

Irrigate

To bring water to dry land by means of canals

Canal

A man-made waterway

Dike

A wall built along a river or sea to hold back the water from low land

Merchant

A person who buys and sells goods for a profit; a trader

Goods

The things for sale or trade

History Fact
Sumerians with the same jobs often lived and worked on the same street.

Reading Strategy: Predicting

Based on what you have just read, predict what you think you may learn from the next lesson.

Sometimes whole villages would be washed away. Many people would die.

Part of Sumer was **swamp** land, meaning it was quite wet. Other parts were very dry. Land that was flooded in the spring dried hard under the late summer sun. It was necessary to make the land ready for crops. The Sumerian farmers had to get water from the rivers to their fields.

The farmers found a way to **irrigate,** or bring water to, their fields. They made cuts in the river banks and dug waterways, called **canals.** The canals carried the river water out to the crops. The Sumerians also built a wall, called a **dike,** to hold back the flood waters.

A Sumerian farmer worked hard from early morning until late at night. Oxen were the farmer's treasure. They pulled the farmer's plow and carried the crops in from the field. Sumer was a wealthy, or rich, land. Its wealth lay in farming.

How Did the Sumerians Trade?

The people of Sumer had different jobs. While some were farmers, others were traders, or **merchants.** Sumer had little metal, stone, or timber of its own. Sumerians depended on trading to get these things. They sent their fine crops to other lands. In return, they brought back the **goods,** the things for sale or trade, they needed at home.

Boats carried the goods to and from Sumer. The Sumerian boats were among the first ever used. There were two kinds of boats. River boats were small. They moved along under the power of long oars or poles. Trading ships were much longer, and they were narrow. They had big sails. The trading boats brought home treasures of gold, silver, pearls, and copper from other lands.

Background Information

Durable Sumerian writing tablets have greatly helped archaeologists in learning about Sumerian culture. Henry Rawlinson first deciphered cuneiform (Assyrian) in 1835, starting with a long inscription that included a king's name, Darius. This name unlocked the cuneiform puzzle. The tombs of Ur, some 1,800 graves excavated by C. Leonard Woolley from 1922 to 1934, held many writings and other artifacts. At the Ur site, a ziggurat, other temple buildings, and ordinary houses were also unearthed, giving a broad perspective on Mesopotamian life.

History Fact
Discuss the benefits of living where you work, and of being on the same street as others in the same trade. Ask students to compare present-day job locations to the Sumerian clustering of trades.

Reading Strategy: Predicting

Ask students what questions they now have about the Sumerians. Encourage them to use their own questions in predicting what the next lesson might address.

ELL/ESL STRATEGY

To describe how Sumerian inventions made life easier for them

Have each ELL student choose a device that Sumerians invented and give a class presentation describing the invention. Students may draw pictures or show magazine pictures of their device. They may also want to tell how the device is used in their native country. Class presentations should include a description of how the device made life easier and better for the Sumerian people. For example, the invention of the plow enabled people to cultivate land more easily. Thus, people could grow more food and were better nourished.

LEARNING STYLES

Auditory/Verbal

Sumerian music has been reconstructed and performed by the Ensemble De Organographia. and several composers have set Sumerian texts to music. Get a recording of Sumerian music or poetry and play it for your class.

3 Reinforce and Extend

IN THE COMMUNITY

Not all archaeological digs involve very old material. In fact, some are quite recent, such as 18th-century cellar holes in New England and 19th-century abandoned mining towns in the West. Have students find out what archaeological digs or research (if any) is going on in your county. Suggest that they check the local historical association and the local history section in the library.

CAREER CONNECTION

Today, people who plan and supervise the construction of canals are called civil engineers. Civil engineers work on other major construction projects as well, including bridges, dams, tunnels, airports, highways, sewer systems, and railroads. Encourage interested students to research the training needed to become a civil engineer and the job opportunities that are available in their area.

Lesson 3–1 Review Answers

1. A 2. D 3. B 4. C 5. E 6. D 7. B 8. A 9. C 10. A

Match the definition in Column A with the term in Column B. Write the correct letter on a sheet of paper.

Column A

1. a man-made waterway
2. a person who buys and sells goods for profit; a trader
3. a wall built along a body of water to prevent flooding
4. to bring water to dry land by means of canals
5. an area of low, wet land

Column B

A canal
B dike
C irrigate
D merchant
E swamp

On a sheet of paper, write the letter of the answer that correctly completes each sentence.

6. The land of Sumer is located between the Tigris and _____ rivers.

   A Mediterranean   B Caspian   C Nile   D Euphrates

7. _____ were the farmer's treasure. They pulled the plow and carried crops in from the field.

   A Slaves   B Oxen   C Children   D Boats

8. The people of Sumer had to trade to get metal, _____, and timber.

   A stone   B weapons   C crops   D slaves

9. _____ were used to carry goods to and from Sumer.

   A oxen   B canals   C boats   D plows

10. Sumerians used two kinds of boats: river boats and _____.

    A trading ships   B canals   C plows   D merchants

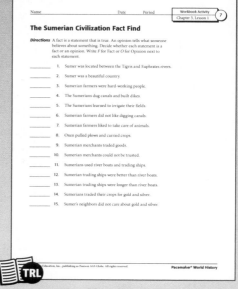

Sumerian City-States

Objectives

- To describe the earliest Sumerian houses
- To name and describe one of Sumer's greatest city-states

Temple
A building used to honor and praise a god or gods

Goddess
A female god

Priest
A religious leader

City-state
An independent city and the surrounding land it controls

Independent
Self-governing, separate, free

In the beginning, the Sumerians lived in the hills northeast of Mesopotamia. Gradually, however, they moved into the river valleys.

How Did the Villages Grow Into City-States?

The earliest Sumerians lived in houses made from reeds. The reeds, or tall grasses, grew in the swamps. Later, the people learned to make bricks from mud. They dried the bricks in the sun and built houses from them. The brick houses stayed cool inside during the hot summers.

Each Sumerian village was built around a **temple.** The temple was where people would honor and praise a god or **goddess,** a woman god. The people believed a god or goddess lived in the temple and protected the village. The farmers took part of their crops to the temple to offer to the god or goddess. The **priests,** or religious leaders, of the temple became very wealthy and powerful.

Over the years, the villages grew. They became **city-states,** each one with its own government. The city-states were **independent,** meaning they were each separate and free. A temple still stood at the center of each city-state. There was farmland all around the edge of the city. The city-states often fought among themselves. For protection, the Sumerians built walls around their cities.

Chapter 3 Lesson 2

Overview This lesson describes the evolution of villages into cities, and the structures of those cities.

Objectives

- To describe the earliest Sumerian houses
- To name and describe one of Sumer's greatest city-states

Student Pages 43–45

Teacher's Resource Library

  Workbook Activity 8

  Activity 8

  Modified Activity 8

Vocabulary

city-state   priest
goddess   temple
independent

Have students write a definition for each vocabulary word in this lesson. Suggest they use a dictionary if they need help.

PRONUNCIATION GUIDE

Use this list to help students pronounce difficult words in this lesson.

ziggurat (zig´ ū rat)

COMMON ERROR

 Students may only associate priests with the Roman Catholic religion. Explain that the term is also used in a more general way when referring to early religious leaders.

1 Warm-Up Activity

Review with students the work of archaeologists and how they learn about ancient civilizations. Have students identify some of the things archaeologists may have discovered in Mesopotamia that told them how the Sumerians lived. Describe a dig in which archaeologists uncover the ruins of buildings and entire villages. Show students photographs of Sumerian dwellings that have been discovered.

2 Teaching the Lesson

As students read the lesson, have them draw a diagram of a village and of a city. They should include ordinary houses as well as important structures.

Ask:

- How can a city also be a state? (It has its own government and surrounding land, makes its own laws, and has its own army.)
- Why was each Sumerian village built around a temple? (The people believed a god or goddess lived in the temple and protected the village.)

Background Information

The base of a ziggurat was composed largely of the ruins of previous temples built on the same spot. Before rebuilding the temple, the old mud-brick walls were knocked down. The remains formed a platform that was used as the foundation for the new building. The platform for the temple at Eridu comprises the foundations of buildings going back for hundreds of years. Later builders constructed new temples on top of a constructed base, rather than on ruins.

LEARNING STYLES

Body/Kinesthetic

As an extra challenge, invite students to construct a model of a ziggurat (a four-sided pyramid) using wood blocks or any material of their choice. Encourage students to strive for detail and historical accuracy. They may find it useful to do some research on the construction of ziggurats.

Reading Strategy:
Predicting

Have students review their predictions and revise them. Tell them they'll revisit them in Lesson 3–4.

Reading Strategy:
Predicting

Think about what you predicted earlier. Does your prediction still work, or do you need to revise your prediction?

One of the greatest city-states of Sumer was called Ur. A gigantic temple, called a *ziggurat,* was built in Ur. This tall temple-tower was built to honor the god who watched over the city. The people of Ur came in great numbers to bring gifts to the temple. They believed that if their god was happy, the city would be wealthy.

The ziggurat was built to honor the Sumerian god who watched over the city of Ur.

Word Bank

bricks
city-state
gifts
god
government
reeds
temple
Ur
walls
ziggurat

On a sheet of paper, write the word from the Word Bank to complete each sentence correctly.

1. Early Sumerians lived in houses made of _____.

2. Sumerians learned to make houses from _____ that they made from drying mud in the sun.

3. Sumerian villages were built around a(n) _____.

4. A(n) _____ is an independent city and the surrounding land it controls.

5. Each city-state had its own _____.

6. Sumerians built _____ around their cities for protection.

7. _____ was one of the greatest city-states of Sumer.

8. A gigantic temple is known as a(n) _____.

9. Large temples were built to honor the _____ that watched over the city.

10. Sumerians brought _____ to gods to make sure they were happy.

ELL/ESL STRATEGY

Language Objective:
To learn vocabulary relevant to the Sumerian city-states

Pair English proficient students with ELL students. Ask each pair to create a word game with the vocabulary words. Suggest matching games, crosswords, concentration, word scrambles, and word scans. To play the games successfully, students must know the meanings of the words.

3 Reinforce and Extend

WORLD CULTURES

 Iraq presently occupies the land of the Sumerians. Like their predecessors, the Iraqis must irrigate much of their farmland, fight salinization of the land, and try to control flooding of the Tigris River. In the 20th century, they built canals that drained most of the enormous swamps that existed in ancient Mesopotamia. Draining the swamps has destroyed habitat for many birds and other animals, turning the drained areas into dry salty flats. Since 2003, restoration of the swamps is slowly going forward.

Lesson 3–2 Review Answers

1. reeds **2.** bricks **3.** temple **4.** city-state **5.** government **6.** walls **7.** Ur **8.** ziggurat **9.** god **10.** gifts

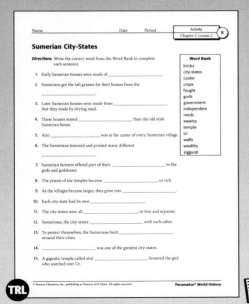

Activity 8

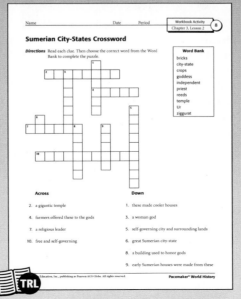

Workbook Activity 8

Sumerian Inventions

Lesson at a Glance

Chapter 3 Lesson 3

Overview This lesson describes important Sumerian inventions, such as ways to measure time and area, their own form of writing, and the wheel.

Objectives

- To describe cuneiform and why it was so important
- To understand the role of a scribe
- To name three gifts, besides writing, that Sumerians gave to the world

Student Pages 46–49

Teacher's Resource Library

Workbook Activity 9

Activity 9

Modified Activity 9

Vocabulary

chariot   pictograph
contract   scribe
create   tablet
cuneiform

Point out that some of the vocabulary words have a suffix or prefix. Ask students to use a dictionary to find out what *-let* (small one), *-form* (resembling), *picto-* (picture), and *-graph* (something written or drawn) mean.

Objectives

- To describe cuneiform and why it was so important
- To explain the role of a scribe
- To name three gifts, besides writing, that Sumerians gave to the world

Reading Strategy: Predicting

Think about what you have read in the previous lessons. What do you expect you will learn in the rest of this chapter?

Tablet
A small, flat piece of clay used for writing

Cuneiform
A wedge-shaped form of writing used in ancient Sumer

Scribe
A person whose job it was to write out copies of contracts and other important papers

---

The Sumerians' inventions were their gifts to the world. All the civilizations that followed used inventions of the Sumerians. There are still things in the world today that date back to Sumer.

What Was the Greatest Gift the Sumerians Gave to the World?

The greatest gift the Sumerians gave to the world was the invention of writing. The Sumerians were a wealthy people. They needed some way to keep track of what they owned. They began by drawing pictures. They used a reed as a pen. They drew on soft pieces of clay. The soft clay was then dried in the sun. The small, flat piece of clay, called a **tablet,** became a permanent (lasting) record. Later, the Sumerian drawings changed into wedge-shaped symbols. This kind of writing is called **cuneiform.** By putting symbols together, the Sumerians could write whole sentences.

Not all Sumerians knew how to write. Only wealthy parents could afford to send their children to school. Very few girls received an education, so students were often called school-sons. Their teachers were called school-fathers. Specially trained people called **scribes** learned how to write. The school-sons learned to write by copying texts over to tablets of clay.

A clay tablet

---

1   Warm-Up Activity

Lead a discussion on the longevity of media such as CDs, magnetic tapes, and paper. Ask students if they think people will read about them 1,000 years from now. Point out that they'll read about Sumerian writings that are more than 5,000 years old.

Reading Strategy: Predicting

Ask to explain how reviewing what you've already learned may help in predicting the lesson.

---

2   Teaching the Lesson

Discuss why clay tablets were such a useful invention. Ask students whether people in the United States and Canada play roles similar to scribes in Sumer. (Today's equivalents might be court reporters, accountants, and lawyers.)

Ask:

- Why were scribes so important in Sumer? (Writing was very useful in trade and government. As it was difficult to learn, the people who knew how to write were scarce and important.)

Contract

A written agreement between two or more people

Chariot

An open two-wheeled cart, pulled by horses

Remember

Before the Agricultural Revolution, most people did not have other jobs besides farming.

You Decide

What if the wheel had never been invented? What would the world be like today? How would people travel?

The scribes were paid well for their special skill. They were among the richest of the Sumerians. They drew up business agreements, called **contracts,** for the farmers and merchants. Some scribes learned to add, subtract, and multiply; they could become tax collectors.

We know a great deal about this earliest of civilizations. This is because Sumerian scribes wrote down their ideas and kept records.

What Other Gifts Did the Sumerians Give the World?

The Sumerian farmers had to pay a tax on their property. To figure the taxes, they invented a way of measuring land. Fields were divided into even squares. Then the squares were counted to decide how much tax a farmer owed. Since the Sumerians used silver as money, payments were made in silver. The value of the silver was measured by its weight.

The Sumerians also learned to measure time. The 60-second minute and the 60-minute hour probably come from the Sumerian way of counting time.

Historians believe that the wheel was first used in Sumer. Sumerian armies rode in wheeled **chariots.** A chariot is an open two-wheeled cart, usually pulled by horses. However, there were no horses in all of Sumer. Therefore, wild donkeys were taught to pull the chariots.

Irrigation canals came to us from the Sumerian farmer. Sailboats came from the traders.

There was little metal in Sumer itself, so the Sumerians traded for metal. They became skilled metalworkers. They learned to make fine jewelry of copper, silver, and gold.

Sumerian ideas and Sumerian inventions brought about changes that would affect life for ages to come.

Remember

Only wealthy boys had a classroom education. Most families, including the children, worked in the fields.

You Decide

Encourage students to use their imaginations about these alternative modes of transportation. They should keep in mind that gears, pulleys, etc. would also not exist.

COMMON ERROR

Students may have trouble recognizing that agricultural and other technologies used by the Sumerians developed over long periods of time. Point out that boats and drawings existed in rudimentary form before the Sumerians made improvements to them.

Background Information

While the Sumerians are credited with inventing cuneiform, subsequent civilizations, including the Akkadians, Babylonians, and Persians, continued using it, making important changes along the way. At first, cuneiform was written in columns, read from right to left. This later changed to lines, read from left to right. In addition, the symbols were rotated 90 degrees, so that they appeared horizontally rather than vertically. These changes made it faster and easier to write cuneiform. Archaeologist Sir Henry Creswicke Rawlinson began the long process of deciphering cuneiform texts in the 19th century, and the work continues to this day.

ELL/ESL STRATEGY

Language Objective: *To compare the effects of Sumerian inventions*

Ask students to read "What Other Gifts Did the Sumerians Give the World?" on page 47. Ask students to decide which Sumerian invention—the wheel or writing—is more important for us today. Have students give three reasons to support their choices.

Pictograph
A drawing that represents an actual thing

Create
To make something

How Writing Changed

If you were trying to communicate with someone and you did not have a written language, how would you do it? You might use pictures to tell a story. That is how writing began in Sumer.

At first, **pictographs,** or drawings that represent actual things, were used. For example, a picture of a fish represented a fish. These early pictographs were drawn in vertical columns with a pen made from a sharpened reed.

In time, these pictographs began to look less like the real objects they represented. Instead, they became simple symbols that were easier to draw. These marks eventually became wedge-shaped strokes, or cuneiform. The Latin word for "wedge" is *cuneus.* People then began to write in horizontal rows. A new type of pen was used. It was pushed into the clay, forming the wedge-shaped symbols.

Writing eventually developed into something closer to an alphabet by other groups of people. However, it was the Sumerians who **created,** or made, the first efficient form of writing. There were symbols, or cuneiform writing, for thousands of words!

Word	Early Pictograph	Late Pictograph	Cuneiform
Bird			
Fish			
Ox			
Sun			

This chart shows how writing changed from simple pictures to symbols, called cuneiform.

Match the definition in Column A with the term in Column B.
Write the correct letter on a sheet of paper.

Column A

1. a legal written agreement between two or more people

2. an open two-wheeled cart, pulled by horses or donkeys

3. a person whose job was to write out copies of contracts and other important papers

4. a small, flat piece of clay used for writing

5. a wedge-shaped form of writing used in ancient Sumer

Column B

A chariot
B contract
C cuneiform
D scribe
E tablet

On a sheet of paper, write the answer to each question. Use complete sentences.

6. Why was cuneiform so important?

7. How could a Sumerian become a scribe?

8. Why did Sumerians have to invent a way to measure land?

9. What animal pulled the chariots in Sumer?

10. What are three gifts, besides writing, that the Sumerians gave to the world?

STUDY SKILLS

Outlining is a useful way to organize a large amount of information. After reviewing proper outlining techniques with students, have them outline Lessons 1–3 of this chapter. You might encourage them to use the subhead questions as the titles for each Roman numeral in their outline. Remind students that outlines should not contain every piece of information. Instead, they should contain main points and some key details.

Lesson 3–3 Review Answers

1. B **2.** A **3.** D **4.** E **5.** C **6.** Cuneiform helps us understand early civilizations. We know so much about the Sumerian civilization because scribes wrote down their ideas and kept records. **7.** Wealthy families would send their sons to school to learn to write. They learned to write by copying texts over to tablets of clay. **8.** Sumerians had to measure land in order to pay taxes on their property. **9.** Wild donkeys were taught to pull the chariots. **10.** Sumerians invented a way to measure land, how to measure time, the wheel, and irrigation canals.

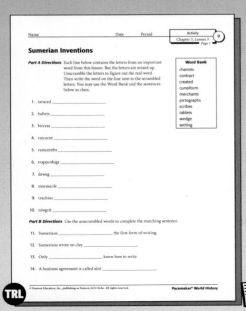

Activity 9, pages 1–2   Workbook Activity 9

Overview This lesson describes life in Sumer and the decline of the Sumerian city-states.

Objectives

- To identify the people who ruled or helped rule the city of Ur
- To explain what the people of Ur believed would happen when they died
- To explain why Sumer grew weak
- To identify the group of people that attacked the Sumerian city-states

Student Pages 50–52

Teacher's Resource Library **TRL**

Workbook Activity 10

Activity 10

Modified Activity 10

Vocabulary

noble
Read aloud the sentences below, letting students fill in the missing vocabulary words.

Since the land was very dry in the summer, Sumerian farmers brought water to the fields in _____. (canals)

Sumerians built a _____ at the center of their cities. (ziggurat)

Ur was a Sumerian _____. (city-state)

A king ruled Ur, with the help of _____, _____, and _____. (priests, scribes, and nobles)

PRONUNCIATION GUIDE

Use this list to help students pronounce difficult words in this lesson.

Babylonian (ba´ bə lō nē ən)

Life in Sumer

Objectives

- To identify the people who ruled or helped rule the city of Ur
- To explain what the people of Ur believed would happen when they died
- To explain why Sumer grew weak
- To identify the group of people that attacked the Sumerian city-states

Although it may be hard to imagine, life in Sumer was quite exciting.

What Was Life Like in Sumer?

A Sumerian boy might awaken to a hot, dry summer day in the city of Ur. If his father were a farmer, the boy would go with him to work in the fields. The two of them would leave their small house with the earliest rays of the sun. Perhaps that day the father and son would clean the irrigation canals. Even if the day were very hot, the boy would work hard. Those canals were important to the farm. Without them, nothing would grow. The boy might work alongside other farmers. They would have help from the slaves from one of the larger farms.

Boys from wealthy families could go to school. If a boy learned well, he might become a scribe. A scribe could work in the king's palace or perhaps in the great temple itself.

Sumerian boys from wealthy families went to school, where they learned to write.

---

1   Warm-Up Activity

Ask students whether they would prefer to work in the fields or study in a classroom, if they had a choice. Discuss their answers and tell them they will learn in this lesson what boys' lives were like in Sumer.

Noble
A person of high social rank

The king ran the city of Ur. He ruled in the name of the city's god. Priests, scribes, and **nobles** helped him rule. These people were very rich. They lived a fine life. They were members of the highest classes in Sumer.

The people of Ur believed that when they died, they went to another world. Archaeologists have discovered graves filled with fine gold jewelry. Some graves of the nobles hold many skeletons. It may be that other people killed themselves, or were killed, when the nobles died. This way they could follow the dead nobles to that other world.

What Brought an End to the Sumerian Civilization?

The Sumerian city-states fought with each other. That is why, after a while, Sumer grew weak. Around 2000 B.C., Sumerian cities came under attack. The Sumerian armies, even with their wheeled chariots, were not strong enough to save Sumer. Ur was destroyed. The city's wealth was stolen. Men and women were killed. Children were taken as slaves.

Reading Strategy:
Predicting

Think about your prediction. What details can you now add to make your prediction more specific?

Soon other Sumerian cities fell, too. The invaders (attackers), called the Babylonians, built new cities. Later, some of those cities died away. Dust and dirt covered them over. Today archaeologists dig into great mounds that still stand in the Middle East. Under the mounds of dirt lay all that is left of these ancient civilizations.

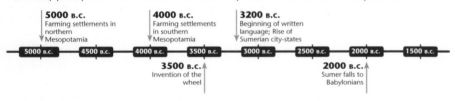

TIME LINE STUDY: SUMER: 5000 B.C.–2000 B.C.

How many years passed from the rise of Sumerian city-states to their fall to the Babylonians?

5000 B.C.
Farming settlements in northern Mesopotamia

4000 B.C.
Farming settlements in southern Mesopotamia

3200 B.C.
Beginning of written language; Rise of Sumerian city-states

| 5000 B.C. | 4500 B.C. | 4000 B.C. | 3500 B.C. | 3000 B.C. | 2500 B.C. | 2000 B.C. | 1500 B.C. |

3500 B.C.
Invention of the wheel

2000 B.C.
Sumer falls to Babylonians

---

2 Teaching the Lesson

As students study the lesson, have them note which people's lives aren't described. (girls, women, slaves) Point out that the lives of Sumerians were apparently quite similar from generation to generation for hundreds of years.

Ask:

- Who worked in the fields of Sumer? (slaves and other men and boys)
- Why do you think that only wealthy Sumerian families could send their sons to school? (Families relied on their children to work from an early age.)
- What led to the decline of Sumer? (Fighting among city-states weakened them, so that outsiders could take over.)

Background Information

Sumerians lived as families, most in their own small houses. Children were the property of their parents, and could be sold into slavery. Parents decided whom a young person should marry. A young man's father gave a gift to a young woman's father. After that, the young people were engaged to be married. Wives had some rights, such as property ownership. A husband could easily get a divorce from his wife, however, or take a second wife. When family members died, they were buried with items such as food, clothing, tools, weapons, musical instruments, and games, to help them in the next world.

Reading Strategy:
Predicting

Discuss how reading content earlier in the chapter makes it possible to make more specific predictions later in the chapter.

TIMELINE STUDY

(Answer: 1,200 years)

Help students comprehend the amount of time between the rise of Sumerian city-states and the fall to the Babylonians by comparing the age of the present-day country. The Sumerian city-states lasted over 1,000 years, while the United States of America is less than 250 years old.

ELL/ESL STRATEGY

Language Objective:
To use visuals for reading comprehension

Ask students to study the timeline entitled Sumer, 5000 B.C.–2000 B.C. on this page. Ask students to use the key dates and information from the timeline to write a paragraph about the Sumerians.

AT HOME

In Sumer, as in many cultures today, young people had little or no choice about education and occupation. Ask students what choices they have, and whether the number and type of choices have changed since their grandparents' time. Encourage students to interview their parents and grandparents about this question. Invite students to share the results of the interview in class discussion.

Lesson 3–4 Review Answers

1. C **2.** D **3.** B **4.** A **5.** B **6.** D **7.** C
8. A Sumerian farm boy would wake up very early and go to work in the fields with his father. Part of their work might include cleaning the irrigation canals. **9.** They believed that when they died they went to another world. **10.** Sumer grew weak because Sumerian city-states fought with each other.

On a sheet of paper, write the letter of the answer that correctly completes each sentence.

1. On a typical day, boys from wealthy families might _____.

  A work on the farm   **C** go to school
  B praise their god in the temple   **D** go sailing

2. A _____ could work in the king's palace or even in a temple.

  A boy   **B** farmer   **C** king   **D** scribe

3. The _____ ran the city of Ur.

  A gods   **B** king   **C** nobles   **D** farmers

4. Priests, scribes, and _____ also helped rule Ur.

  A nobles   **B** slaves   **C** farmers   **D** young boys

5. Archaeologists have found graves filled with _____.

  A weapons   **B** gold jewelry   **C** chariots   **D** mummies

6. Sumerian cities came under attack around _____ B.C.

  A 5000   **B** 4000   **C** 3000   **D** 2000

7. The _____ invaded Sumerian cities and built new cities.

  A slaves   **B** scribes   **C** Babylonians   **D** archaeologists

On a sheet of paper, write the answer to each question. Use complete sentences.

8. What was a typical day like for a Sumerian farm boy?

9. What did the people of Ur believe happened to them when they died?

10. Why did Sumer grow weak?

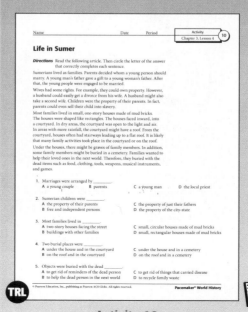

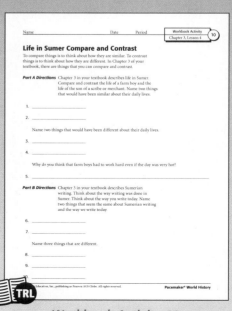

Activity 10   Workbook Activity 10

- The first great civilization grew up between the Tigris and Euphrates rivers in the land of Sumer.

- The Sumerian civilization was based on farming. The Sumerians had to irrigate their land. They dug canals and built dikes to control the water supply.

- The Sumerian merchants traded with other lands for the goods they needed. They traveled in some of the world's first boats.

- Sumerians lived in brick houses built around temples. They honored gods and goddesses with their own crops as gifts.

- The Sumerians lived in city-states. Each city-state had its own government.

- One of the greatest Sumerian city-states was called Ur. The people there built a huge ziggurat, or temple, there.

- The Sumerians invented writing. They used wedge-shaped symbols in a kind of writing called cuneiform. Their trained writers, or scribes, became wealthy by writing down records and helping with business agreements.

- The Sumerians also invented the wheel, the sailboat, irrigation, canals, and a way of measuring.

- The Sumerian city-states were attacked and fell, but their ideas lived on.

- The invaders, the Babylonians, built new cities.

Chapter 3 Summary

Use the Chapter Summary on page 53 to review the main ideas presented in Chapter 3.

Ask:

- Why did people settle the lands between the Tigris and Euphrates rivers? (Floods made the land good for farming.)
- How did Sumerian farmers control water? (with dikes and irrigation canals)
- What did Sumerian merchants do with the Sumer crops? (traded them for goods from other lands)
- What did Sumerians use to build homes and temples? (mud bricks)
- When did the city-states appear? (about 3200 B.C.)
- What was the most important building in Ur? (the ziggurat, or temple)
- Why were scribes important in Sumer? (They kept track of taxes, created contracts, and kept trade records.)
- What two inventions helped Sumerians travel? (the wheel and the sailboat)
- When did the city-states fall? (about 2000 B.C.)
- Who brought 1,200 years of Sumerian city-states to an end? (the Babylonians)

CHAPTER PROJECT FOLLOW-UP

 Have students complete their chart comparing life in Sumer and in America. Lead a discussion on the similarities and differences between life in Sumer and life in America today.

TEACHER'S RESOURCE

The AGS Globe Teaching Strategies in Social Studies Transparencies may be used with this chapter. The transparencies add an interactive dimension to expand and enhance the Pacemaker® *World History* program content.

Chapter 3 Review

Use the Chapter Review to prepare
students for tests and to reteach content
from the chapter.

Chapter 3 Mastery Test **TRL**

The Teacher's Resource Library includes
two forms of the Chapter 3 Mastery Test.
Each test addresses the chapter Goals
for Learning. An optional third page
of additional critical-thinking items is
included for each test. The difficulty level
of the two forms is equivalent.

Chapter 3 Review Answers

Vocabulary Review

1. temple

2. merchants

3. city-state

4. goods

5. cuneiform

6. scribe

7. contracts

8. swamp

9. irrigate

10. chariot

Chapter Review Questions

11. They irrigated the land by a
system of canals. They used dikes to
hold back floods. They used oxen to
pull the plow and carry crops from
the land.

12. Sumerians depended on trading
to get things they needed, such as
metal, stone, and timber.

13. They used silver as money.

Word Bank

chariot

city-state

contracts

cuneiform

goods

irrigate

merchants

scribe

swamp

temple

Vocabulary Review

On a sheet of paper, use the words from the Word Bank to
complete each sentence correctly.

1. Sumerians believed a god or goddess lived in the
_____ and protected the village.

2. Sumerians depended on _____ to get metal, stone,
and timber.

3. Each _____ had its own government.

4. Sumerians used boats to carry _____ to and from
Sumer.

5. The Sumerian system of writing based on wedge-
shaped symbols was called _____.

6. A(n) _____ was a person who was trained to write.

7. Scribes would draw up business _____ for farmers
and merchants.

8. Sumer had fertile land; some parts were _____ land
and other parts were very dry.

9. Sumerian farmers found a way to _____ their fields.

10. Sumerians used wild donkeys to pull their _____.

Chapter Review Questions

On a sheet of paper, write the answer to each question.
Use complete sentences.

11. How did Sumerians farm the land?

12. Why did the Sumerians trade with other lands?

13. What did the Sumerians use for money?

14. How did the Sumerians invent writing?

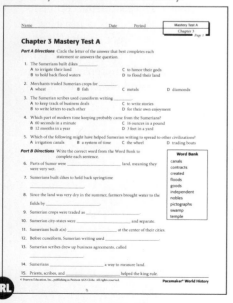

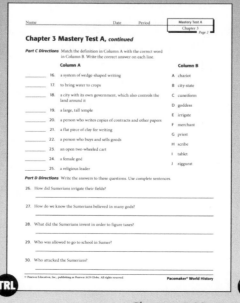

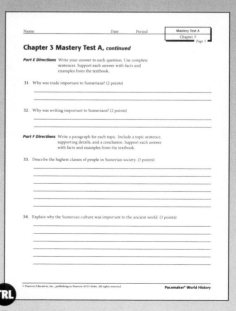

Test Tip

Do not wait until the night before a test to study. Plan your study time so that you can get a good night's sleep before a test.

15. What were five inventions of the Sumerians?

16. Why were scribes members of the richest and highest class of Sumerian culture?

Critical Thinking

On a sheet of paper, write your response to each question. Use complete sentences.

17. How do you think the Sumerians might have been able to prevent the fall of their cities?

18. How were Sumerian schools different from schools today?

Using the Timeline

Use the timeline on page 51 to answer the questions.

19. What two things were invented between 3500 B.C. and 3000 B.C.?

20. How many years passed between settlements in northern and southern Mesopotamia?

GROUP ACTIVITY

Choose five items found in your classroom and draw a symbol for each. Work in small groups to see if you can guess what one another's symbols represent. Once you have determined what each symbol means, create a sentence by putting certain symbols next to each other in a row. Present your group's sentence to the class to see if your classmates can guess what it says.

14. The Sumerians invented writing by drawing objects less and less like the real things they represented. The drawings became symbols that were wedge-shaped from the reed they were drawing with.

15. Inventions of the Sumerians include writing, counting time, the wheel, irrigation, canals, and sailboats.

16. Scribes had the special skill of writing, which was needed by farmers and merchants.

Critical Thinking

17. Possible answers: The Sumerians might have tried to bargain with their enemies. They could have hidden their riches outside the cities. They could have expanded their military and stationed their armies outside the cities.

18. Possible answer: In Sumer, the best students became scribes. In present-day schools, the best students go into many types of work.

Using the Timeline

19. Written language and the wheel

20. 1,000 years

GROUP ACTIVITY

Students should create symbols that show some relationship to an object, but not be a drawing of it. The sentences should be easy to understand once classmates know what each symbol means.

Chapter 3 Mastery Test B, pages 1–3

Chapter at a Glance

Introducing the Chapter

Like the Sumerians, ancient Egyptians built great civilizations that lasted several thousand years. After settling in the fertile Nile River Valley, ancient Egyptians cultivated the land, built great cities and pyramids, and established a complex civilization ruled by wealthy and powerful pharaohs.

Ask:

- Why did people settle along the Nile River? (fertile farmland, reliable source of water)

- Why were the Egyptian pharaohs mummified and buried in pyramids? (They believed that after death they would go on to another life; they would need their bodies and their worldly possessions.)

Ancient Egypt: Land of the Pharaohs

The story of the ancient Egyptians is quite interesting. The first farmers there lived in the Nile River Valley. Their villages joined to form larger settlements. By 3100 B.C., all of Egypt was ruled by King Menes. He became the first of the great Egyptian pharaohs.

Egyptian pharaohs led lives of great wealth and power. When they died, their bodies were preserved as mummies. They were buried in tombs surrounded by giant pyramids. The pharaoh's favorite things were buried with him or her. The Egyptians believed that after death people went on to another life.

GOALS FOR LEARNING

- To explain why people settled along the Nile River
- To explain why the pharaohs had their people build the pyramids
- To describe Egyptian culture

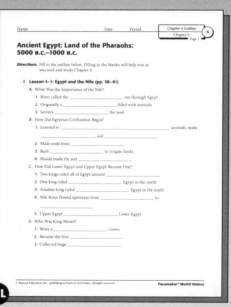

Reading Strategy: Text Structure

Understanding how text is organized helps readers decide which information is most important. Before you begin reading this chapter, look at how it is organized.

- Look at the title, headings, boldfaced words, and photographs.
- Ask yourself: Is the text a problem and solution, description, or sequence? Is it compare and contrast or cause and effect?
- Summarize the text by thinking about its structure.

Key Vocabulary Words

Lesson 1

Desert Dry, sandy land with little or no plant life

Upstream In the direction against the flow of the river; at the upper part of a river

Unite To bring together as one

Pharaoh A ruler of ancient Egypt

Tax Money paid to support a government

Lesson 2

Tomb A grave, usually one that is enclosed in stone or cement

Pyramid A huge stone structure with a square base and four triangular sides that meet in a point at the top; Egyptian rulers were buried in the pyramids

Transport To move from one place to another

Mummy A dead body kept from rotting by being treated with chemicals and wrapped in cloth

Lesson 3

Hieroglyphics A system of writing using pictures or symbols to represent objects, ideas, or sounds

Papyrus A writing paper the Egyptians made from water plants of the same name

Translate To change the words of one language to another

Reading Strategy:
Text Structure

Introduce the reading skill *organizing.* Explain that when you study how a text is organized, you are attempting to organize your thoughts and understanding of that text so that you may better decide which information is most important.

Key Vocabulary Words

Point out that these chapter words are presented in the order they appear in each lesson. They are also found in the glossary.

LIFE SKILLS CONNECTION

Students learn about museum curators. Students research the skills and qualifications required of the career they wish to pursue. Help students by directing them to appropriate Web sites for career research.

KEY VOCABULARY

After students have created their puzzle, have them write a brief clue for each word. Encourage students to swap puzzles and work individually to complete them. Consider giving a small prize to the student who correctly completes the puzzle first.

CHAPTER PROJECT

The daily lives of the pharaohs and their subjects were very different. While the pharaohs had lives of great power, their subjects lived simple lives defined by hard work. As students read the chapter, have them write down at least 5–10 details from the text that illustrate how the pharaohs lived. Then, have them write down at least 5–10 details that illustrate the lives of the peasants.

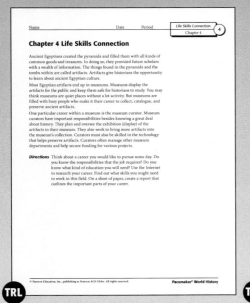

Life Skills Connection 4

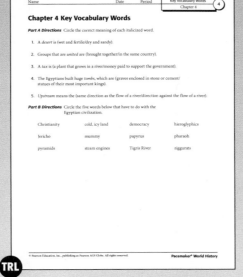

Key Vocabulary Words 4

Chapter 4 Lesson 1

Overview Students will learn how the fertile Nile River, with its consistent pattern of flooding, made development of civilization along its banks possible.

Objectives

■ To describe what happened to the Nile River Valley every July

■ To locate upper and lower Egypt on a map

■ To describe what a pharaoh did

Student Pages 58–61

Teacher's Resource Library (TRL)

Workbook Activity 11

Activity 11

Modified Activity 11

Vocabulary

desert	unite
pharaoh	upstream
tax	

Have each student make flashcards for these vocabulary words. On the front of each card, they should write a vocabulary word. The back of each card should contain the correct definition. Give students a few minutes to review silently the definitions on their flashcards. Then have pairs of students quiz each other aloud.

PRONUNCIATION GUIDE

Use this list to help students pronounce difficult words in this lesson.

Egyptian (ē′ jip shun)

Menes (mē′ nēz)

Egypt and the Nile

Objectives

■ To describe what happened to the Nile River Valley every July

■ To locate upper and lower Egypt on a map

■ To describe what a pharaoh did

Reading Strategy:
Text Structure

Preview this lesson, including the headings, features, and boldfaced words.

Desert

Dry, sandy land with little or no plant life

At one time the area now called the Sahara was a green plain. People lived there. There was water and wildlife. Over time the weather changed. The plain dried up and became a **desert**—a dry, sandy land with little or no plant life. The people living there went looking for water. Some of them went to a land called Egypt.

What Was the Importance of the Nile?

A great river called the Nile ran through Egypt. The Nile River Valley was a swampland. It was a dark jungle filled with dangerous animals. The people needed water badly, so they cleared the land anyway. They built their villages along the river where the jungle used to be.

Like the Sumerians, the people of Egypt built a civilization along a river. They were able to do this because the land along the Nile had what they needed. The Egyptians learned to farm, to tame animals, to make pottery, and to weave. They learned to make tools from metal.

The weather in Egypt was hot. Each year, in July, the Nile River spilled over its banks in a great flood. Land that stood dry all year was suddenly under water for several weeks. The floods left the land very fertile.

Farmers learned to use the floods to help them. They saved some of the flood waters to water their crops the rest of the year. Like the Sumerians, they learned to dig canals to irrigate their fields.

Each July the farmers moved to higher ground, taking their animals with them. They knew that the floods would be over in a few weeks. They waited until the Nile once again flowed peacefully within its banks. Then they planted their seeds in the rich, soft ground.

58 *Unit 2 Ancient Civilizations*

---

1 Warm-Up Activity

Remind students that the Nile River, which begins in central Africa and flows for 4,000 miles north to the Mediterranean Sea, is the longest river in the world. Tell students that historians often call Egypt "The Gift of the Nile." Ask them why they think this is so.

Reading Strategy:
Text Structure

Have students use the headings, features, and boldfaced words to build an outline on a separate piece of paper.

Upstream
In the direction against the flow of the river; at the upper part of a river

Reading Strategy:
Text Structure

Study the map in this lesson. How does it help you to understand what the lesson is about?

How Did Lower Egypt and Upper Egypt Become One?

The civilization along the Nile did well. Villages joined together to form larger settlements. There came a time, around 3200 B.C., when two kings ruled all of Egypt. One king ruled Lower Egypt, in the north. Another king ruled Upper Egypt, in the south. A look at the map below shows each of these areas. The Nile River flows northward. A person in Lower Egypt who followed the Nile south, or **upstream,** would come to Upper Egypt.

Upper and Lower Egypt

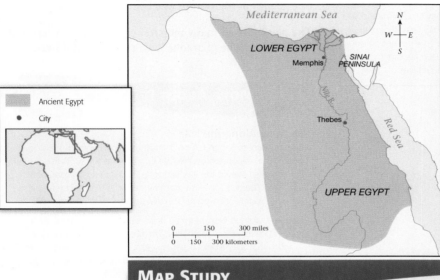

MAP STUDY

1. What are two ancient Egyptian cities on the map?
2. Which part of Egypt, Upper or Lower, bordered on the Mediterranean Sea?

LEARNING STYLES

Interpersonal/Group Learning

In the text we learn that the survival and success of the Egyptians depended on animals such as oxen, sheep, goats, and cattle. Have students gather in small groups to discuss how these animals contributed to daily life in cultures along the Nile River. What role do animals play in students' lives today? Ask students to make a list that compares the tasks and importance of animals then with the tasks and importance of animals today.

MAP STUDY

Answers:

1. Thebes and Memphis
2. Lower Egypt

2 Teaching the Lesson

As students read the information on pages 58–60, ask them to compare and contrast the daily lives of the peasants and the pharaohs. Encourage students to pay careful attention to the boxed information on page 60 ("Farming Along the Nile") for a more in-depth description of what life was like for Egyptian peasants.

Ask:

- What factors contributed to the success of Egyptian civilization? (Answers may vary: success at farming, reliable source of water, movement away from nomadic lives, strong leadership, small villages joining together to form large settlements.)
- How did King Menes become the first great ruler of Egypt? (He conquered Lower Egypt around 3100 B.C.)
- How did pharaohs secure their access to "rich, splendid lives." (They collected huge taxes from their subjects and had many men to carry out their orders.)

Reading Strategy:
Text Structure

Have students copy all the labels from the map into their notebook with a description of each one.

Background Information

Modern Egyptians put an end to the unpredictable flooding of the Nile by building the Aswan Dam. Completed in 1970, the dam brought great benefits to the Egyptians in the form of improved navigation on the river and hydroelectric power. The reservoir behind the dam now supports a fishing industry. Before the Aswan Dam was built, a massive engineering project supported by international funds disassembled the monumental temples at Abu Simbel and moved them piece by piece to a new site on high ground where they continue to be appreciated by tourists and scholars.

ELL/ESL STRATEGY

Language Objective:
To empower students to seek out definitions for unfamiliar words

Explain to students that the vocabulary words in each chapter, while useful, should not be viewed as the final word on vocabulary acquisition. Ask students to preview the chapter for five unfamiliar words or phrases and to record them in their notebooks. Once students have identified the words and phrases, ask them to use their dictionaries to define them.

Encourage students to combine vocabulary words with the five words in their notebooks to compose original sentences that further illuminate the chapter materials. (For example, pharaohs—vocabulary word—and towering—unfamiliar word—might be put together to create this sentence: The pyramids were towering monuments to the pharaohs.)

---

3 Reinforce and Extend

AT HOME

Food for the ancient Egyptians came from the harvests of farmers along the Nile River. Ask students to think of one meal that they have at home and then list the places from which that food comes. Have them compare their findings with those of their classmates.

You Decide

Remind students that pharaohs depended in large part on the taxes they collected to ensure their continued wealth and power. Encourage them to discuss the question posed in this section: *What do you think would happen if a government official used tax money to live a rich life?* (Answers may vary.)

Unite
To bring together as one

Pharaoh
A ruler of ancient Egypt

Tax
Money paid to support a government

 You Decide
People today still have to pay taxes. What do you think would happen if a government official used tax money to live a rich life?

The king of Lower Egypt wore a red crown. The king of Upper Egypt wore a white crown. The two kings ended up fighting to control all of Egypt. Around 3100 B.C., King Menes of Upper Egypt conquered Lower Egypt. Now Menes wore a "double" crown. He ruled and **united,** or brought together, all of Egypt.

King Menes became the first great ruler, or **pharaoh,** of Egypt. The Egyptians called their ruler *pharaoh,* meaning "The Great House."

The pharaohs were powerful rulers. Each year they collected **taxes**—huge taxes—from all the people to support the government. Farmers had to give the pharaoh a large part of their crops as a tax.

The pharaoh had many men to help carry out orders and collect taxes. The pharaohs lived rich, splendid lives.

LEARN MORE ABOUT IT

Farming Along the Nile
Egypt's success depended on thousands of peasants. But raising good crops depended on the Nile flooding every year. These floodwaters covered the land along its banks, making a strip of rich farmland. The rich soil came from farther up the river. The Nile also provided water for irrigation. The rest of Egypt was desert.

Men and women worked in the fields during the day. They grew grains such as wheat and barley. The flour from these grains was mixed with honey to make sweet bread. Farmers grew grapevines and picked dates too. Other peasants tended herds of sheep, goats, or cattle. They also hunted deer and water birds.

Besides food crops, Egyptian farmers grew cotton and flax, a plant that was used for its fibers. They spun the fibers to make cotton and linen cloth. Most farmwork was done by hand. Tomb paintings show farmers using metal tools to cut grain. Oxen were used for heavy work, such as turning water wheels.

LEARN MORE ABOUT IT

Call students' attention to the title. Remind them that farming was key to the Egyptians' survivals. Ask students to review the Reading Strategy on page 57. Read the selection aloud, then ask students whether the passage is primarily an example of text as a problem and solution, description, or sequence? (The text is primarily descriptive.) Then ask students if it is primarily compare and contrast or cause and effect? (The text is primarily cause and effect.)

COMMON ERROR

Students often confuse *desert* with *dessert.* Remind students that the word *desert* (dry, sandy land with little or no plant life) contains only one *s*, while *dessert* (a sweet course or dish usually served at the end of a meal) contains two *s's*. One easy trick for remembering this detail is to remind students that they might very well wish for two desserts (two *s's*), but rarely would they wish for two deserts (one *s*).

On a sheet of paper, write the answer to each question. Use complete sentences.

1. Why did people settle along the Nile River?

2. How did farmers use the floods to help them?

3. What was the life of a pharaoh like?

On a sheet of paper, write the letter of the answer that correctly completes each sentence.

4. The Nile River Valley flooded every July, leaving the land very _____.

    A dry   **B** sandy   **C** barren   **D** fertile

5. Upper Egypt was in the south, and Lower Egypt was in the _____.

    A north   **B** east   **C** west   **D** bottom

6. King _____ was the first great pharaoh of Egypt.

    A Tut   **B** Menes   **C** Cleopatra   **D** Nile

Match the definition in Column A with the term in Column B. Write the correct letter on a sheet of paper.

Column A

7. in the direction against the flow of the river

8. money paid to support a government

9. dry, sandy land with little or no plant life

10. a king of ancient Egypt

Column B

A desert

B pharaoh

C tax

D upstream

STUDY SKILLS

 Outlining is a useful way for students to organize a large amount of information. Review proper outlining techniques with students and then have them outline Lesson 4–1 of this chapter. You might encourage them to use the subhead questions as the titles for each Roman numeral in their outline. Remind students that outlines should not contain every piece of information. Rather, they should contain main points and some key details.

Lesson 4–1 Review Answers

1. The land had what they needed: water. **2.** The farmers learned to save up some of the flood waters to use during the rest of the year. They dug canals to irrigate their fields. Every July they would move to higher ground with their animals. A few weeks later, when the flood was over, they moved back and planted their seeds in the rich, soft ground. **3.** Pharaohs lived rich, splendid lives. They had many men to help them carry out order and collect taxes. **4.** D **5.** A **6.** B **7.** D **8.** C **9.** A **10.** B

Activity 11   Workbook Activity 11   *Ancient Egypt Chapter 4* **61**

Chapter 4 Lesson 2

Overview From about 2650 B.C. until 1637 B.C., the pharaohs of Egypt were buried deep within great tombs called pyramids. Many of these buildings still stand today. In this section students will learn how and why the pyramids were built and what archaeologists have found in these enormous, ancient constructions.

Objectives

- To explain how archaeologists think the Egyptians built the pyramids
- To tell what archaeologists found inside Egyptian tombs
- To detail how Egyptians prepared a dead body to be placed in a tomb

Student Pages 62–64

Teacher's Resource Library

Workbook Activity 12

Activity 12

Modified Activity 12

Vocabulary

mummy   tomb
pyramid   transport

Challenge all students to write original sentences that correctly use each word. Ask volunteers to share their sentences with the class.

PRONUNCIATION GUIDE

Use this list to help students pronounce difficult words in this lesson.

Cairo (kī´rō)

Herodotus (hĭ rŏd´ə təs)

1 Warm-Up Activity

Explain to students that pharaohs were often called "god-kings" and citizens believed their leaders would also rule in the next life. Ask students to speculate about what effect it might

---

LESSON 4-2   The Pyramids

Objectives

- To explain how archaeologists think the Egyptians built the pyramids
- To tell what archaeologists found inside Egyptian tombs
- To detail how Egyptians prepared a dead body to be placed in a tomb

Tomb
A grave, usually one that is enclosed in stone or cement

Pyramid
A huge stone structure with a square base and four triangular sides that meet in a point at the top

Transport
To move from one place to another

The Egyptian pharaohs wanted people to remember just how rich and how powerful they were. Some had huge statues of themselves made. They also had their people build great **tombs,** or graves, for them. When the pharaohs died, their bodies were placed in the tombs. Jewelry, food, clothing—all the pharaoh's favorite things—went into the tomb, too. The Egyptians believed that a person would need those things in the next world.

These great, towering Egyptian tombs are called **pyramids.** The pharaohs of Egypt, from about 2650 B.C. until 1637 B.C., were buried within those huge pyramids. There are many pyramids still standing in Egypt today. They are considered one of the Seven Wonders of the Ancient World.

How Were the Pyramids Built?

The most famous pyramid is the Great Pyramid near Cairo. It covers an area larger than 10 football fields. It contains more than 2 million stone blocks, each weighing about 2.5 tons. Somehow, the stones had to be cut into shape and then moved, or **transported,** to the building site. Then the stones were raised into place. They were laid so that they fit together exactly. From a distance, the pyramid looks as if it were cut out of a single stone. The Egyptians of 4,500 years ago had no machinery or iron tools. So how did they do it? We do not know for certain. In fact, we do not know if we would be able to build pyramids today, even with our modern building methods.

The ancient Egyptians did use copper chisels. They also probably hauled the stones on some sort of wooden sled.

---

have on a citizenry to think of its leaders as "god-kings."

2 Teaching the Lesson

Call students' attention to the lesson's subtitles. Ask one student to read each subtitle aloud (How Were the Pyramids Built? What Else Has Been Found in Tombs?) Then have students read both sections. After students have read the sections, ask for volunteers to briefly summarize the contents of each.

Ask:

- How does the illustration on page 63 illuminate what you have read? (Answers will vary, but students

may say that the illustration shows the wealth of the pharaoh's tomb and the dedication of the pharaoh's subjects.)

- What artifacts have been discovered in the pyramids? (bowls, pictures, food, jewelry, clothing—and the bodies of the pharaohs or nobles)
- What is a mummy? (a body treated with special chemicals and wrapped in cloth bandages)
- Why did Egyptians go to so much trouble to prepare pharaohs and wealthy Egyptians for burial? (Egyptians believed that they would need their bodies in the next life; because only the wealthy could afford such treatment.)

Mummy
A dead body kept from rotting by being treated with chemicals and wrapped in cloth

Most likely, they built a system of ramps and wooden planks to haul the stones into place. Mostly they had to rely on human muscle power. The ancient Greek historian Herodotus wrote about the pyramids. He said that 100,000 men worked each year for 20 years to build the Great Pyramid. Archaeologists doubt these numbers, but we will never know for sure.

Tombs within the pyramids have served as a wonderful record of the Egyptian civilization. However, robbers have broken into some tombs and stolen the artifacts. Fortunately, archaeologists have discovered some tombs still filled with goods from daily Egyptian life. The walls of the tombs are covered with picture-writing. The pictures tell the story of the ancient Egyptian world.

What Else Has Been Found in Tombs?

Archaeologists found more than bowls, pictures, jewelry, and pottery within the tombs. They found the pharaohs themselves! The Egyptians used certain chemicals to keep the dead body from rotting away. Of course, only the rich Egyptians could afford this special treatment.

Reading Strategy:
Text Structure

Notice that the section headings are written as questions. After you read each section, try to answer the question asked in the heading.

This Egyptian tomb contains the mummy of Tutankhamen, an Egyptian pharaoh.

Burying people this way was not a simple matter in ancient Egypt. First, the brain and organs had to be removed from the body. Then the body was treated with a special chemical. It was then wrapped around and around in cloth bandages. A body wrapped like this is called a **mummy.** Many mummies were found deep within the Egyptian tombs. Scientists have removed Egyptian mummies and artifacts from these tombs. They are on display today in museums around the world.

Background Information
How to Build a Pyramid

- Work 20,000 men for 20 years; feed them.
- Have 10,000 workers make about 26 million mud bricks for the inside of the pyramid.
- Have the other 10,000 workers cut huge stone block.
- Transport these blocks—about 12,600 of them—up the river to the building site.
- Dig a canal to connect the site to the river.
- Find a rock base, clear it of sand, and make it level.
- Make the sides of the stone block smooth; polish them.
- Build ramps upon which to haul the stone blocks higher and higher.
- Remove the building ramps as you work back downward.
- Build a funeral temple, the surrounding walls, a valley temple, and smaller pyramids for family members.

LEARNING STYLES

Body/Kinesthetic
Have students who learn well through tactile experience make a model of an Egyptian burial chamber. They can include miniature replicas of artifacts typically found in Egyptian tombs. Encourage students to write short explanations of various artifacts they include.

ELL/ESL STRATEGY

Language Objective: *To encourage students to learn and use the words provided in the Word Bank*

Call students' attention to the words provided in the Word Bank on page 64. Ask them to record each word in their notebook along with the word's definition and a short, original sentence.

Reading Strategy:
Text Structure

Have students write the answers to the heading questions on a separate piece of paper.

3 Reinforce and Extend

ONLINE CONNECTION

Students can gain additional information by accessing the following Web site:
www.agsglobepmwh.com/page63
(National Geographic Web site to learn more about the pyramids.)

CAREER CONNECTION

The modern career counterpart to the rudimentary embalming techniques of the ancient Egyptian is the mortician or undertaker. Students interested in careers that involve preparing the dead for burial and arranging for funerals can find out more information about this career online or in their local library.

Lesson 4–2 Review Answers

1. The pyramids were built to bury the dead Egyptian pharaohs—the pharaohs wanted people to remember how rich and powerful they were. **2.** They believed that a person would needs things like jewelry, food, and clothing in the next world. **3.** Egyptians had copper chisels. They probably used wooden sleds to haul the stones of the pyramids. They also likely built a system of ramps and wooden planks to put the stones into place. But mostly they used human muscle power. **4.** First, Egyptians would remove the brains and organs. Then they treated the body with a special chemical and wrapped it in cloth bandages. **5.** They found bowls, pictures, jewelry, and pottery. They also found mummies. **6.** Herodotus **7.** rich **8.** iron tools **9.** picture-writing **10.** wonders

On a sheet of paper, write the answer to each question. Use complete sentences.

1. Why did the Egyptians build the pyramids?
2. Why did the pharaohs want all of their favorite things to be buried with them?
3. How do archaeologists think the Egyptians built the pyramids?
4. How did Egyptians prepare a dead body for burial?
5. What did archaeologists find inside Egyptian tombs?

Word Bank

Herodotus
iron tools
picture-writing
rich
wonders

On a sheet of paper, write the word from the Word Bank to complete each sentence correctly.

6. Greek historian _____ wrote about the pyramids.
7. Only _____ Egyptians could afford to bury a mummy.
8. Egyptians did not have machinery or _____ to build the pyramids.
9. Tomb walls are covered with _____ that tell the story of the ancient Egyptian world.
10. The pyramids are considered to be one of the _____ of the world.

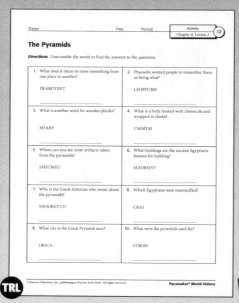

Activity 12

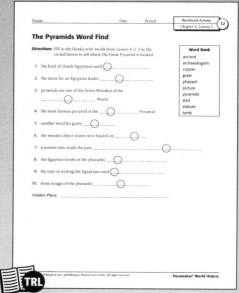

Workbook Activity 12

Egyptian Culture

Objectives

- To explain how we know the Egyptians were concerned about the way they looked
- To describe what the Egyptians believed about death
- To describe how Egyptians wrote
- To name three Egyptian inventions, besides writing

Geography Note

Many ancient Egyptian writings tell of voyages through the Red Sea to the Land of Punt. This land had beehive-shaped houses on stilts. Travelers returned with new and different plants and items. They brought back the skins of animals such as giraffes or cheetahs. Many believe the Land of Punt was in eastern Africa, probably in present-day Ethiopia.

The Egyptian pharaohs and their nobles lived rich lives. However, all the rest of the people led very simple lives.

What Was Egyptian Life and Religion Like?

The farmers worked hard in their fields. There was usually plenty of food. This meant that Egypt's craftworkers had more time to improve their skills.

The Egyptians were concerned about the way they looked. Drawings and statues show Egyptian women with long, dark hair worn in many braids and ringlets.

Both men and women wore makeup. They painted their lips red. They drew around their eyes with a dark green or gray paste called *kohl*. The Egyptians also liked perfume. Both men and women rubbed sweet-smelling oils into their skin.

Most ancient Egyptians believed in many gods. Just as in the land of Sumer, each city had its own special god. Osiris was the powerful god of death.

The river played an important part in Egyptians' lives and their belief about death. They believed that the dead were ferried, or transported, across a great river. There they would meet Osiris in the next world.

Egyptians cared about their looks. Both men and women lined their eyes with kohl.

Lesson at a Glance

Chapter 4 Lesson 3

Overview The rich, fertile soil around the Nile River, combined with the hard work of farmers, provided Egyptians with an abundance of food. This allowed them to devote their time and talents to cultivating a complex culture.

Objectives

- To explain how we know the Egyptians were concerned about the way they looked
- To describe what the Egyptians believed about death
- To describe how Egyptians wrote
- To name three Egyptian inventions, besides writing

Student Pages 65–68

Teacher's Resource Library

Workbook Activity 13

Activity 13

Modified Activity 13

Vocabulary

hieroglyphics   translate
papyrus

Have students fill in the blank with the correct vocabulary word. Then, ask students to write a new sentence using each vocabulary word.

The Egyptians invented a system of picture-writing called _____. (hieroglyphics)

The word *paper* comes from the word _____. (papyrus)

To _____ is to change the words of one language to another. (translate)

PRONUNCIATION GUIDE

Use this list to help students pronounce difficult words in this lesson.

kohl (kōl)

Osiris (ō sī´ rĭs)

Champollion (chä pol yo)

COMMON ERROR

Words such as *papyrus*, *hieroglyphics*, and *pharaoh* may present a spelling challenge to many students. Explain to students that many words cannot be neatly explained by the rules of Standard English. Instead, students must simply work hard to memorize these difficult words. One strategy for memorizing a difficult word is to write it over and over again until the student has committed it to memory.

Geography Note

Historians have known for years that Egyptians traveled to the mysterious Land of Punt—Egyptians also called it "Ta Netjer" or God's Land—to bring back incense and other treasures they found there. But there has been much debate over whether Egyptians traveled by land or by sea. Recently, the discovery of wooden planks, cargo boxes, and ropes in a series of caverns near the Red Sea were determined to be the remnants of Egyptian seafaring ships that most likely traveled to and from the Land of Punt.

Point out to students that in this lesson, (and every lesson) subheadings are worded as questions rather than statements. Ask students to read the information below each subheading, then briefly answer the question in their own words.

2 **Teaching the Lesson**

Ask students to write several details they remember from the previous chapter on the Sumerians. Guide a discussion where students compare and contrast Sumerian culture with Egyptian culture. What do these two cultures have in common? How are they different?

Ask:

• What evidence do we have that Egyptians were concerned about the way they looked? (Drawings and statues show women with elaborate hairstyles; both men and women wore makeup and perfumes.)

• What role did the river play in the Egyptian concept of death? (They believed that the dead were ferried across a great river to the underworld where they would meet Osiris.)

Background Information

Although the Egyptians charted the stars and decide that there were 365 days in a year, their calendar differed from modern calendars in important ways. The Egyptians followed a calendar system that corresponded with the cycles of the Nile. Their "year" consisted of 360 days, with three seasons, each comprised of four months, with 30 days in each month. These three seasons were known as Inundation (from June 21st to October 21st), Emergence (from October 21st to February 21st), and Summer (from February 21st to June 21st). The beginning of each year was marked with five additional days, which were times of feast and celebration for the Egyptians.

Hieroglyphics
A system of writing using pictures or symbols to represent objects, ideas, or sounds

Papyrus
A writing paper the Egyptians made from water plants of the same name

History Fact
The Egyptian calendar was based on the sun. There were three seasons of 120 days each. There was a five-day celebration at the end of the year.

Reading Strategy:
Text Structure

How does the timeline help you understand this chapter?

What Did Egyptians Invent?

The Egyptians invented a system of picture-writing called **hieroglyphics.** They learned to make paper from river reed called **papyrus.** Our word *paper* comes from the word *papyrus.*

The Egyptians learned to chart the stars. They also decided that there were 365 days in a year.

The Egyptians made jewelry of gold and precious stones. They used metals for tools and weapons. The Egyptians made music, too. Archaeologists have found ancient Egyptian instruments and the words to songs. The Egyptians built ships. They traded with other people.

Most of all, the ancient Egyptians are remembered as the builders of the pyramids. The Egyptian builders have left us what may be the most amazing works of any civilization. Most likely, many of their secrets still lie buried within the pyramids.

TIMELINE STUDY: **EVENTS IN ANCIENT EGYPT**

How many years did it take for a unified Egypt to become the world's greatest power?

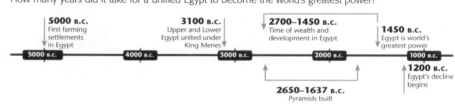

5000 B.C.
First farming settlements in Egypt

3100 B.C.
Upper and Lower Egypt united under King Menes

2700–1450 B.C.
Time of wealth and development in Egypt

1450 B.C.
Egypt is world's greatest power

5000 B.C.   4000 B.C.   3000 B.C.   2000 B.C.   1000 B.C.

1200 B.C.
Egypt's decline begins

2650–1637 B.C.
Pyramids built

Reading Strategy:
Text Structure

Show students how the timeline is another way to structure text.

TIMELINE STUDY

Answer: 1,650 years

History Fact
Ask students why the Egyptian calendar only had three seasons. As a hint, they should consider the climate in Egypt.

Words from the Past

Translate
To change the words of one language to another

The Rosetta Stone

Hieroglyphics can still be seen in many places in Egypt. Yet for many hundreds of years, nobody could read them. The meaning of these ancient Egyptian symbols had been lost sometime in the distant past. Then in 1799, a French engineer in Egypt discovered a large stone. It was half buried near the mouth of the Nile River.

The Rosetta Stone, as it came to be called, was completely covered with writing. Carved into the stone were three languages: hieroglyphics, a second Egyptian language, and Greek. A French historian named Champollion **translated** (changed the words from one language to another) the Greek portion first. Then he carefully compared this to the other languages. He realized that the same message was written in the three languages. He was finally able to learn the meaning of the hieroglyphics. In 1822 he published the results of his work.

Champollion had developed a system of sounds and meanings that could be applied to other hieroglyphics. For the first time, scholars could go into an Egyptian tomb or temple and read the name of a king and something about him. With hard work, a skilled translator could read a papyrus roll that had not been read for thousands of years.

Today, the Rosetta Stone is in the British Museum in London, England. Many visitors come to see the black stone that provided the key to understanding ancient Egyptian hieroglyphics.

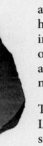

The Rosetta Stone has the same message written in three languages.

5000 B.C.–1000 B.C.   *Ancient Egypt: Land of the Pharaohs*   Chapter 4   **67**

WORDS FROM THE PAST

As an activity, have students create their own form of writing. As a class, create symbols for each letter in the alphabet. Have students spell their names, or even write sentences, with their new language.

LEARNING STYLES

Auditory/Verbal

Have a student—or several students—read aloud the information about the Rosetta Stone on page 67. Then ask a volunteer to describe how Champollion was able to decipher the writing on the Rosetta Stone. Ask a second volunteer to describe the importance of this accomplishment for scholars and future generations.

ELL/ESL STRATEGY

Language Objective: *To learn the definitions of unfamiliar words in the "Words from the Past" selection*

Students may encounter several unfamiliar words in the "Words from the Past" selection on page 67. Have small groups of students work together to compile a list of all unfamiliar words. Using a dictionary, students should write a definition for each word. Encourage students to reread "The Rosetta Stone" when their lists are complete, using the lists as a guide.

3   Reinforce and Extend

IN THE COMMUNITY

One of the many gifts from Egyptians to the modern world was their use of papyrus, a reed from the Nile River, used to make paper. Encourage your students to think about the importance of this contribution by having them make a list of the many ways paper helps make their lives easier.

WORLD CULTURES

The mythical sphinx is a symbol often associated with ancient Egypt. Some modern nations adopt real animals as national symbols. For the United States, the national symbol is the bald eagle. Have students use the World Atlas to find modern nations located near the eastern end of the Mediterranean Sea. Then have them research animals that are the national symbols of these countries. Have students display the symbols on an area map showing the nations they researched.

Lesson 4–3 Review Answers

1. They believed there was life after death. They thought the dead were ferried across a great river to meet Osiris in the next world. **2.** Egyptians invented a form of picture-writing called hieroglyphics. They also learned to chart the stars, decided there was 365 days in a year, and used metals for tools and weapons. **3.** By translating the Rosetta Stone, a French historian learned the meaning of hieroglyphics. Now, scholars could go into an Egyptian tomb or temple and read the name of a king and something about him—something that had not been done for thousands of years! **4.** looked **5.** kohl **6.** perfume **7.** Osiris **8.** hieroglyphics **9.** papyrus **10.** music

LESSON 4-3 REVIEW

On a sheet of paper, write the answer to each question. Use complete sentences.

1. What was the Egyptian belief about death?

2. What were some important Egyptian inventions?

3. How did translating the Rosetta Stone help scholars?

On a sheet of paper, write the word from the Word Bank to complete each sentence correctly.

4. Egyptians were quite concerned about the way they _____.

5. The green or gray paste Egyptians used to draw around their eyes was called _____.

6. Egyptians used _____ to smell good.

7. _____ was the powerful god of death.

8. The Egyptian system of picture-writing is known as _____.

9. _____ was the writing paper made from river reed that Egyptians used.

10. Archaeologists have found instruments and words to songs, suggesting that Egyptians made _____.

Word Bank

hieroglyphics
kohl
looked
music
Osiris
papyrus
perfume

68   *Unit 2   Ancient Civilizations*

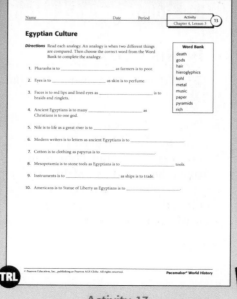

Activity 13

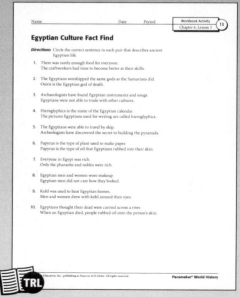

Workbook Activity 13

SUMMARY

- When the Sahara became a desert, people went to live along the Nile River. They cleared jungle land there and built villages.

- The river flooded each year. This caused the land around it to become more fertile. Farmers used the rich land and dug canals to bring water to their crops.

- Lower Egypt and Upper Egypt were united under King Menes. Menes was the first great ruler, or pharaoh, of Egypt.

- Egyptians paid taxes to their powerful pharaohs who, in turn, became wealthy.

- The pharaohs' tombs were inside giant pyramids. The most famous is the Great Pyramid near Cairo.

- Ancient Egyptians believed in life after death. Many of the things they owned were buried with wealthy Egyptians.

- A special treatment was used to bury the bodies of some wealthy Egyptians. A wrapped body treated with chemicals is called a mummy.

- We know a lot about Egyptians from the mummies and artifacts found in their tombs. We know they made jewelry, tools, weapons, and musical instruments.

- Both men and women of Egypt wore makeup and perfumes.

- The Egyptians invented a system of picture-writing called hieroglyphics.

- The Egyptians made paper from a reed called papyrus.

5000 B.C.–1000 B.C.   *Ancient Egypt: Land of the Pharaohs*   Chapter 4   **69**

TEACHER'S RESOURCE

The AGS Globe Teaching Strategies in Social Studies Transparencies may be used with this chapter. The transparencies add an interactive dimension to expand and enhance the Pacemaker® *World History* program content.

CHAPTER PROJECT FOLLOW-UP

As students complete the chapter, ask them to write two short letters to a friend. In the first letter, have students describe their daily lives as if they were pharaohs living in ancient Egypt. In the second letter, have students describe their daily lives as if they were farmers or workers. Remind students to provide plenty of specific examples from their notes and readings. Encourage students to share their letters with the class.

Chapter 4 Summary

Have students read the Chapter Summary on page 69 to review the main ideas presented in Chapter 4.

Ask:

- Why did people originally settle along the Nile River? (They were seeking water and the Nile River provided rich farmland.)

- What was the importance of the yearly flooding along the banks of the Nile River? (The floods caused the land around the river to become more fertile and provided a reliable source of water.)

- What does it mean to pay taxes? (Taxes are monies given to a government.)

- What was the impetus for building pyramids? (to honor pharaohs and nobles; to provide them with the things they would need in the next life; to preserve and protect their bodies)

- Why did Egyptians include such things as jewelry, food, money, and pottery in the tombs? (They believed the dead would need those things in the next life.)

- How did the Egyptians prepare their dead pharaohs and nobles for burial? (First, they removed their brains and organs. Next, they treated the body with a special chemical for preservation. Then, they wrapped the body in cloth bandages.)

- Why did both men and women wear makeup and perfumes? (Appearance was important to them.)

- What condition most likely made it possible for the Egyptians to dedicate time and energy to music, religion, art, and architecture? (the abundance of food)

- What are hieroglyphics? (a system of picture-writing)

- Name two important contributions Egyptians made to the modern world. (paper, a 365-day calendar)

Chapter 4 Review

Use the Chapter Review to prepare students for tests and to reteach content from the chapter.

Chapter 4 Mastery Test

The Teacher's Resource Library includes two forms of the Chapter 4 Mastery Test. Each test addresses the chapter Goals for Learning. An optional third page of additional critical-thinking items is included for each test. The difficulty level of the two forms is equivalent.

Chapter 4 Review Answers
Vocabulary Review

1. desert

2. tomb

3. pyramid

4. mummy

5. papyrus

6. hieroglyphics

7. upstream

8. pharaoh

9. tax

10. united

Chapter Review Questions

11. It was a swampland—a dark jungle filled with dangerous animals. But it was also a hot climate that provided water that people needed so badly.

12. The Nile River flooded and left the land very fertile.

13. King Menes was from Upper Egypt. He conquered Lower Egypt, giving him a "double" crown as he ruled all of Egypt. He was the first pharaoh of Egypt.

Word Bank

desert
hieroglyphics
mummy
papyrus
pharaoh
pyramid
tax
tomb
united
upstream

Vocabulary Review

On a sheet of paper, use the words from the Word Bank to complete each sentence correctly.

1. The area called the Sahara changed from a green plain to a(n) _____.

2. When pharaohs died, their body was placed in a(n) _____.

3. An Egyptian ruler was buried in a(n) _____, which is a great towering structure.

4. The dead body of a rich Egyptian might be preserved as a(n) _____.

5. The Egyptians made writing paper from a plant called _____.

6. A system of writing used by the Egyptians is called _____.

7. Follow the Nile River _____, and you will reach Upper Egypt.

8. Long ago, an Egyptian ruler was called a(n) _____.

9. Farmers gave a large part of their crops to the pharaoh as a(n) _____.

10. Egypt was _____ under King Menes.

Chapter Review Questions

On a sheet of paper, write the answer to each question. Use complete sentences.

11. What was the Nile River Valley like?

12. What happened to the Nile River every year in July?

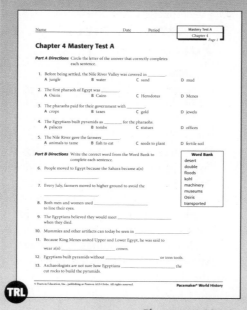

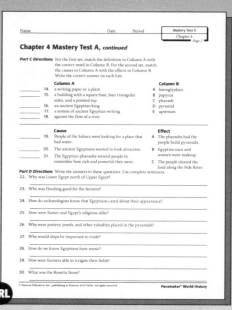

Test Tip

When studying for a test, use a marker to highlight key words and important concepts in your notes. For a final review, read what you highlighted.

13. How did King Menes come to wear a "double" crown?

14. What clues show that Egyptians were concerned about their looks?

15. How did the Egyptian pharaohs pay for their rich way of life?

Critical Thinking

On a sheet of paper, write your response to each question. Use complete sentences.

16. Why do you think so many people are fascinated by the Egyptian pyramids today?

17. Why is it important to understand the written records of ancient civilizations?

Using the Timeline

Use the timeline on page 66 to answer the questions.

18. How many years passed between the first farming settlements in Egypt and the unification of Upper and Lower Egypt?

19. When the pyramids were built, was Egypt rich or poor?

20. What year was Egypt the world's greatest power?

GROUP ACTIVITY

With a small group, create a trivia game about the pyramids of Egypt. Use information from this chapter, encyclopedias and other books, and the Internet. New information about the pyramids is available from ongoing archaelogical digs.

5000 B.C.–1000 B.C.   *Ancient Egypt: Land of the Pharaohs*   *Chapter 4*   **71**

---

14. There are drawings and statues of Egyptian women who wore their long, dark hair in many braids and ringlets. Also, both men and women wore makeup and used perfume.

15. They made people pay taxes.

Critical Thinking

16. Possible answer: Many people are fascinated by the pyramids because they do not know exactly how they were built. Also, they are interesting because of the reason they were built, the shape is pleasing, and they are very old.

17. Without understanding the written records, we are left to guess at the meaning of many of the artifacts that archaeologists find. Also, through ancient writings we gain understanding of the ideas as well as the lifestyle of people of the past.

Using the Timeline

18. 1,900 years

19. rich

20. 1450 B.C.

GROUP ACTIVITY

The trivia game should include questions and answers about topics such as how the pyramids may have been built, how large they are, where they are located, and number of visitors each year.

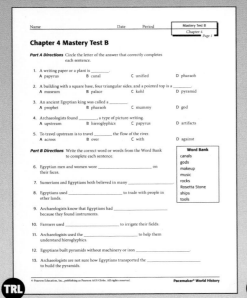

Chapter 4 Mastery Test B, pages 1–3

Introducing the Chapter

From around 2000 B.C. to 500 B.C. several groups of people lived near the shores of Mediterranean Sea. This chapter discusses five kingdoms. The Phoenicians, the Israelites, the Hittites, the Babylonians, and the Assyrians.

Mediterranean Kingdoms

Many groups of people settled near the shores of the Mediterranean Sea. The Phoenicians sailed seas from their colonies on the eastern shore, trading with people in many lands. The ancient Israelites also lived on the eastern shores; they believed in one god called *Yahweh.* The Hittites, from the area of present-day Turkey, were warriors who made weapons with iron.

The Babylonians built a huge civilization near the Euphrates River inland, to the east of the Mediterranean. The Assyrians built their kingdom nearby, on the banks of the Tigris River. Like the Hittites, they were fierce warriors.

GOALS FOR LEARNING

- To explain the importance of the sea in the Phoenician civilization
- To explain the importance of religion to the ancient Israelites
- To understand why Babylon was one of the greatest cities of the ancient world
- To understand why the Hittites were so powerful in the eastern Mediterranean
- To describe the military society of the Assyrians

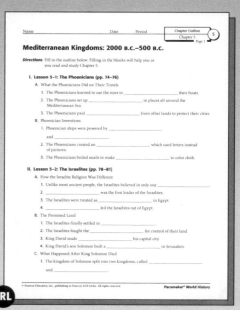

Reading Strategy: Visualizing

Visualizing is another strategy that helps readers understand what they are reading. It is like creating a movie in your mind. Use the following ways to visualize a text:

- Look at the photographs, illustrations, and words.
- Consider how your experiences may add to the images.
- Notice the order in which things are happening and what you think might happen next.

Key Vocabulary Words

Lesson 1

Navigate To plan the course of a ship; to sail or steer

Colony A group of people who settle in a far-off land but are still under the rule of the land they came from

Lesson 2

Worship To honor and praise a god

Bible The ancient Israelite and Christian book that is thought to be holy

Nomad A person who moves from place to place

Commandment A law or order, most often a religious law

Judaism The religion developed by the ancient Israelites that Jews practice today

Christianity The religion based on the teachings of Jesus Christ and the Bible

Conquer To get control by using force, as in a war

Capital A city or town where the government of a nation or state is located

Religious Having to do with a belief in a higher being

Lesson 3

Empire A group of lands all ruled by the same government or ruler

Code A group of laws

Lesson 4

Treaty An agreement, usually having to do with peace or trade

Lesson 5

Military Having to do with soldiers or the armed forces

Siege The surrounding of a city by soldiers who are trying to capture it so that food, water, and other supplies cannot get in or out

Tribute A payment or gift demanded by rulers of ancient kingdoms

Ask:

- What factors that are necessary for civilizations to develop. (Answers may include fertile land for farming, written language to record information, and natural resources to build shelter.)
- What did each of these five kingdoms have in common? (All settlements occurred near a major body of water.)

Reading Strategy: Visualizing

Encourage students to study the photographs, illustrations, timelines, and maps in Chapter 5. As students look at each, ask them to close their eyes and pretend they are filmmakers. Ask them to create a short scene in their minds, and then write a short description of each scene.

Ask:

- How did the information in the text help you to visualize the scene?
- How did your personal experiences contribute to your visualizations?

Key Vocabulary Words

Point out that these chapter words are presented in the order they appear in each lesson. They are also found in the glossary.

LIFE SKILLS CONNECTION

Students learn about the importance of laws in civilization. Students discuss various traffic laws. Provide students with a *Rules of the Road* booklet to review the many traffic laws in your state.

KEY VOCABULARY

In Part A, students choose the correct vocabulary term from the Word Bank to complete each sentence. In Part B, students match the vocabulary term to its definition.

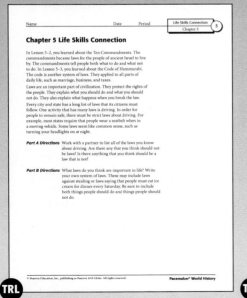

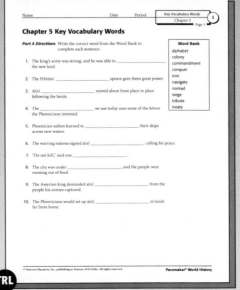

Life Skills Connection 5

Key Vocabulary Words 5, pages 1–2

Chapter 5 Lesson 1

Overview This lesson describes the Phoenicians, a civilization that settled along the eastern shores of the Mediterranean and excelled in sailing and trading.

Objectives

- To locate Phoenicia on a map
- To describe what Phoenicians would do on their travels
- To name two important Phoenician inventions

Student Pages 74–77

Teacher's Resource Library

Workbook Activity 14

Activity 14

Modified Activity 14

Vocabulary

colony   navigate

Have students fill in the blank with the correct vocabulary word.

The Phoenicians used the stars to _____. (navigate)

A _____ is a group of people that settle in a far-off land. (colony)

PRONUNCIATION GUIDE

Use this list to help students pronounce difficult words in this lesson.

Phoenician (fe nish´ ən)

Mediterranean (me de te rā´ nē ən)

Gibraltar (jə bról´ ter)

Tyre (tīr´)

Sidon (sīd´ n)

1 Warm-Up Activity

Review with students the work of archaeologists and how they learn about ancient civilizations. Have students identify some of the things archaeologists may have discovered in the Mediterranean that told them how the Phoenicians lived.

LESSON 5-1

The Phoenicians

Objectives

- To locate Phoenicia on a map
- To describe what Phoenicians would do on their travels
- To name two important Phoenician inventions

Navigate

To plan the course of a ship; to sail or steer

Colony

A group of people who settle in a far-off land but are still under the rule of the land they came from

The Phoenician civilization grew up along the eastern shores of the Mediterranean. It was unlike most of the other Mediterranean civilizations. The Phoenicians were not farmers. They built their cities on rocky shores; they were people of the sea. They were sailors and traders.

Few farm crops grew in Phoenicia. However, there were plenty of trees. The people cut down the trees to use as wood to build sailing ships.

What Did the Phoenicians Do on Their Travels?

The Phoenicians were the best sailors in the ancient world. They learned to use the stars to **navigate** (to sail or steer). This made it possible for them to sail beyond the sight of land. The Phoenicians sailed where no other people dared to go. Their ships went to every corner of the Mediterranean. They reached the coast of Spain. They even sailed out into the Atlantic Ocean, beyond Gibraltar. They sailed along the west coast of Africa. Then they probably went all the way around the continent of Africa.

Wherever they traveled, the Phoenicians set up **colonies.** A colony is a group of people who settle in a far-off land but are still under the rule of the land they came from. Their people settled in places all around the Mediterranean Sea. The Phoenician colonies became trading centers. One of the largest Phoenician colonies was Carthage. It was on the north coast of Africa. The people of Carthage traded their gold, ivory, and ebony for Phoenician pottery, glass, and beads.

---

2 Teaching the Lesson

As students read the information on pages 74–77, remind them that, unlike most Mediterranean civilizations, the Phoenicians were not farmers. Because the land in Phoenicia was rocky and little could grow there, the Phoenicians had to rely on other means for surviving and thriving along the shores of the Mediterranean.

Ask:

- Where did the people get the wood to build their sailing ships? (They cut down trees.)

CHAPTER PROJECT

Divide the class into five groups, one for each of the kingdoms explored in Chapter 5. Tell students that they are going to become experts on their assigned kingdom. By the end of the chapter, each group should be prepared to present a brief, oral presentation on their subject that includes information from the chapter and their own independent research.

Reading Strategy:
Visualizing

What words in this lesson help you visualize Phoenician life?

The colonies paid taxes to the Phoenician homeland. Great Phoenician cities—like Tyre, Sidon, and Byblos— grew rich and strong.

The Phoenicians were traders and sailors, not warriors. They paid soldiers from other lands to protect their cities. They built high stone walls to protect themselves from attack.

What Are Some Phoenician Inventions?

The Phoenician ships were powered by oars and sails. They sailed all about the ancient world. As the Phoenicians traded goods, they also traded ideas.

Phoenician Trading Routes

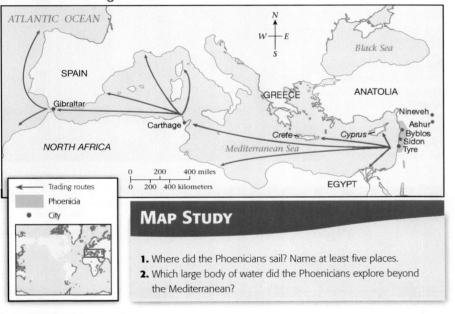

MAP STUDY

1. Where did the Phoenicians sail? Name at least five places.
2. Which large body of water did the Phoenicians explore beyond the Mediterranean?

- What was one of the largest Phoenician colonies? Where was it located? (Carthage, north coast of Africa)
- Name three Great Phoenician cities. (Tyre, Sidon, Byblos)
- What is the importance of the Phoenician invention of the alphabet to modern peoples? (Our alphabet comes from the letters they invented.)
- The color purple is often called a royal color. Why is this so? (Answers may vary. The dye used to make purple was costly and required great numbers of small snails to make a tiny amount. Royalty used purple to decorate their palaces. Purple came to stand for wealth and power.)

Background Information

We remember the Phoenicians for two important reasons: First, they developed a simple alphabet of 22 letters. These few letters took the place of the 550 letters of the cuneiform alphabet. The Greeks and Romans used this alphabet to build their own. The English and Spanish languages also use it. Second, the Phoenicians spread the culture and products of the Mediterranean to many places. They did this through their trade and their colonies. Because of this, important ideas spread around the world.

Reading Strategy:
Visualizing

Have students list the words that help them visualize Phoenician life.

MAP STUDY

Answers:

1. Gibraltar, Carthage, Crete, Cyprus, and Egypt (Students name at least five places.)
2. The Atlantic Ocean

Ask:

- What three large bodies of water are represented on this map? (Atlantic Ocean, Black Sea, Mediterranean Sea)
- What five countries are named? (Spain, North Africa, Greece, Anatolia, Egypt)
- How do we know that a place is a city? (It is marked with a small red dot.)

LEARNING STYLES

Interpersonal/Group Learning

In small groups of three or four, have students examine the map on page 75 and discuss the many trade routes the Phoenicians traveled. Using the mileage chart on the map, have them calculate the distance between Carthage and Gibraltar as well as several other major cities and landmarks. Encourage students to discuss how navigation made it possible for the Phoenicians to sail beyond the sight of land. Why is this important? Encourage students to speculate about how the first sailors might have felt about this.

These are the Phoenician letters for A, B, C, D, and E.

One of the most important ideas the Phoenicians spread was the alphabet. They turned pictures into letters. In fact, our own alphabet comes from the letters the Phoenicians invented.

The Phoenicians became famous for another invention, too. It was a secret dye used to color cloth. The dye was made from snails that lived along the coast. The Phoenicians boiled thousands of snails to make just a tiny bit of dye. The dye was very costly. Named after the city of Tyre, it was called Tyrian purple.

The Phoenicians traded the purple cloth. Only rich people could buy it. Royalty decorated their palaces with it. They wore robes of Tyrian purple. The color purple came to stand for power and wealth. It became a royal color.

Phoenician explorers were the first people who could sail beyond the sight of land. They spread their ideas and inventions throughout the ancient world.

TIMELINE STUDY: THE PHOENICIANS

How many years passed from the time the Phoenicians developed the alphabet until they rose to power?

1500 B.C. Phoenicians develop the alphabet	1100 B.C. Phoenicians rise to power	600 B.C. Phoenicians may have sailed around Africa

2000 B.C. ———————— 1500 B.C. ———————— 1000 B.C. ———————— 500 B.C.

76   *Unit 2   Ancient Civilizations*

Lesson 5–1 Review Answers
1. C **2.** B **3.** D **4.** B **5.** A **6.** D **7.** C **8.** D
9. A **10.** B

On a sheet of paper, write the letter of the answer that correctly completes each sentence.

1. Phoenician civilization developed along the _____ shores of the Mediterranean.

   A northern   **B** southern   **C** eastern   **D** western

2. Phoenicians were sailors and _____.

   A farmers   **B** traders   **C** warriors   **D** trappers

3. Phoenician sailors used the _____ to navigate.

   A compass   **B** map   **C** oars   **D** stars

4. Phoenicians would set up _____ wherever they traveled.

   A ships   **B** colonies   **C** temples   **D** crops

5. One of the largest Phoenician colonies was _____.

   A Carthage   **B** Tyre   **C** Sidon   **D** Byblos

6. Phoenicians paid _____ to protect their cities.

   A slaves   **B** farmers   **C** craftsmen   **D** soldiers

7. Phoenicians built _____ to protect themselves from attack.

   A weapons   **B** pottery   **C** stone walls   **D** ships

8. Phoenician ships were powered by oars and _____.

   A oil   **B** wood   **C** snails   **D** sails

9. One of the most important ideas Phoenicians spread was the _____.

   A alphabet   **B** ivory   **C** pottery   **D** ships

10. Another important Phoenician invention was a(n) _____ made from snails.

    A alphabet   **B** purple dye   **C** glass   **D** beads

---

2000 B.C.–500 B.C.   *Mediterranean Kingdoms*   Chapter 5   **77**

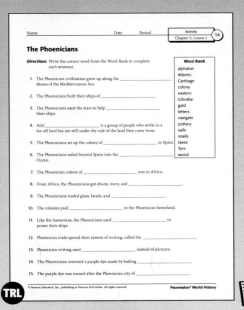

Activity 14   Workbook Activity 14

Overview The ancient Israelites differ from the other four kingdoms of the Mediterranean in several important ways. First, the Israelites worshipped a single God rather than the many gods of their counterparts. Second, their civilization sprang up in response to their attempt to escape slavery. Finally, the Israelites sought to establish permanent residence in the land of Canaan, which they believed to be their "Promised Land."

Objectives

- To explain how the Israelites' religion was different from that of other Mediterranean people
- To describe the ancient Israelites' "Promised Land"
- To name the two kingdoms that formed after King Solomon died
- To explain why there is fighting over Jerusalem's land

Student Pages 78–82

Teacher's Resource Library

Workbook Activity 15

Activity 15

Modified Activity 15

Vocabulary

Bible	Judaism
capital	nomad
Christianity	religious
commandment	worship
conquer	

Have volunteers take turns reading the words and their definitions. Then challenge all students to write original sentences that correctly use each word. Ask volunteers to share their sentences with the class.

LESSON 5-2

The Israelites

Objectives

- To explain how the Israelites' religion was different from that of other Mediterranean people
- To describe the ancient Israelites' "Promised Land"
- To name the two kingdoms that formed after King Solomon died
- To explain why there is fighting over Jerusalem's land

Worship
To honor and praise a god

Bible
The ancient Israelite and Christian book that is thought to be holy

Nomad
A person who moves from place to place

Commandment
A law or order, most often a religious law

The ancient Israelites lived along the east coast of the Mediterranean Sea. Their civilization grew up just south of Phoenicia.

What Was Different About the Israelite Religion?

The ancient Israelites wanted their own land where they could honor and praise, or **worship,** their god. In the Mediterranean world, most people believed in many gods. There were gods of death, sun, and rain. The ancient Israelites believed in one god, Yahweh.

Their holy book, the **Bible,** says that a man named Abraham was the father of the Israelites. One day he left with his family to become a **nomad.** Abraham and his people moved from place to place, following their herds. They came to a land called *Canaan.*

Abraham's people were eventually treated as slaves in Egypt. The Egyptian pharaoh was cruel. A man named Moses became the ancient Israelites' leader. He led them out of Egypt, into the desert, away from the cruel pharaoh. On Mt. Sinai, Moses received the Ten **Commandments.**

PRONUNCIATION GUIDE

Use this list to help students pronounce difficult words in this lesson.

Israelite (ĭz´ rē ə līt)

Yahweh (yä wā wě)

Canaan (kā´ nən)

---

1 | Warm-Up Activity

Ask students to recall what they learned about the ancient Egyptians and their religious beliefs from Chapter 4. Remind students that in the Mediterranean world, most people believed in many gods that represented important aspects of daily living—sun, rain, death, and the river. Have students keep this in mind as they read the information on pages 78–81.

Words from the Past

Judaism
The religion developed by the ancient Israelites that Jews practice today

Christianity
The religion based on the teachings of Jesus Christ and the Bible

The Ten Commandments

The ancient Israelites did not find their land of freedom right away. They wandered, searching, for many years. The Bible says that during that time, Moses was given the Ten Commandments. It says that the commandments came directly from God.

The commandments are laws to live by. They became laws for the people of ancient Israel. The first commandment says that people must believe that their god is more important than any other gods. "The Lord is One," the Bible reads.

The Ten Commandments also tell people how they must act toward each other. For example, children must honor their parents. The commandments forbid unfaithfulness, killing, stealing, or wanting what belongs to someone else.

Over time, the Ten Commandments became an important part of **Judaism** and **Christianity.** Today, some people want to display the commandments in public schools to remind students of the things they should not do. Other people feel that displaying them in school would make it look like the government is supporting a particular religion.

Moses holds the stone tablets which contain the Ten Commandments.

2000 B.C.–500 B.C.

Mediterranean Kingdoms Chapter 5 **79**

---

2 | Teaching the Lesson

Both the Phoenicians and the Israelites moved around a lot. Invite students to list the different places this group moved to and the reasons for their movements. Encourage students to make a list of the leaders of the Israelites as they moved from place to place.

Ask:

- Who was the father of the Israelites? (Abraham)
- What is a nomad? (one who moves from place to place, usually to follow a herd or in search of food)
- Who led the Israelites out of Egypt and why? (Moses; to take them away from slavery under the Egyptian pharaoh)

Background Information

One of the most compelling and controversial stories from the Hebrew Bible is that of Abraham and his son Isaac. In Genesis 22, God asks Abraham to sacrifice his beloved son Isaac on Mount Moriah. The "Binding of Isaac," as the story is sometimes called, has been the subject of countless theological debates and speculation as well as the inspiration for a number of paintings, essays, stories, and songs.

WORDS FROM THE PAST

Ask four volunteers to read each paragraph of this section aloud in turn. After the section has been read in its entirety, encourage students to discuss the final paragraph of the section. Do students think displaying the Ten Commandments in public schools is a good idea? Why or why not? What is problematic about the appearance of a government supporting a particular religion?

ELL/ESL STRATEGY

Language Objective: *To encourage students to contemplate and understand the meanings of abstract words*

Have students identify several words in the "Words from the Past" selection that describe abstract concepts. Examples of these may be: believe, honor, unfaithfulness. Next, have students look these words up in their dictionaries and write them in their notebooks. Encourage students to compose original sentences to accompany each word.

Body/Kinesthetic

Divide students into small groups of 3–4 students and have them write, direct, and produce a one-act play that dramatizes some aspect of the lesson. For example, students may wish to dramatize Moses leading the people out of Egypt and into the desert; or, they may wish to dramatize the story of David and Goliath described on page 80.

Reading Strategy:
Visualizing

Have students write their own paragraph about the ancient Israelites using descriptive words.

3 Reinforce and Extend

TEACHER ALERT

Discussing the history and ongoing conflicts in and around the city of Jerusalem can pose a challenge to many teachers. In 2001, PBS produced a short series called PROMISES, which provides lesson plans, resources, films, and background on the conflicts in Jerusalem as well as the areas known as the West Bank and the Gaza Strip. Their Web site provides lesson plans and further information.

WORLD CULTURES

Thousands of Jews from around the world moved to Israel when it was created in 1948. Israel's official language is Hebrew, which was brought back after not being spoken for nearly 1,800 years. Although Jews make up more than four-fifths of the population, Israel is home to other religious groups as well, including Muslims and Christians.

Conquer
To get control by using force, as in a war

Capital
A city or town where the government of a nation or state is located

Religious
Having to do with a belief in a higher being

Reading Strategy:
Visualizing

What words in this section help you to visualize what happened with the ancient Israelites?

What Is the Promised Land?

The ancient Israelites finally reached Canaan again. They called it the "Promised Land." They believed it was the land that God had promised them. They settled there and built towns. They followed their religion.

Holding onto the Promised Land was not always easy. The Philistines lived nearby. The Philistines fought the ancient Israelites for their land.

There were 12 tribes of ancient Israelites. At first, the Philistines were able to gain control, or **conquer,** some of the tribes. Divided, the ancient Israelites were weak. In time, the tribes joined together under one king to fight the Philistines.

There is a famous story of a shepherd boy named David. He fought a Philistine giant called Goliath. David killed Goliath with a rock from a slingshot. The ancient Israelites then won the war against the more powerful Philistines.

David later became king of the ancient Israelites. The town of Jerusalem became his **capital** city and was a **religious** center.

When David died, his son, Solomon, became king. Solomon built a beautiful temple in Jerusalem. He built a group of fine sailing ships. King Solomon was known to be good and wise. Under his rule, Jerusalem became a mighty city.

COMMON ERROR

Students may be tempted to assume that "religious" must always refer to a belief in a single higher power. Remind students that although most of the peoples in the Mediterranean worshipped many gods, there also were significant forms of religious expression with their own highly stylized rituals and beliefs.

COMMON ERROR

Students often confuse the words *capital* and *capitol.* Write these two words on the board and underline the second "a" in the first word as well as the "o" in the second. Tell students that capital is a city or town where the government of a nation or state is located. For example, "Austin is the capital of Texas."

Capitol describes a building in which a state legislative body meets or where legislative functions are carried out. For example, "Austin is the capital of Texas, and the Texas State Capitol Building is located in Austin."

History Fact

The citizens of Israel are sometimes referred to as Israelites. The citizens of Judah were called Jews.

What Happened When King Solomon Died?

When King Solomon died, his kingdom split. The tribes in the north made their own kingdom. They called it Israel. The tribes in the south formed the kingdom of Judah. Jerusalem was in Judah. The name of the Jewish religion came from the word *Judah*.

The two kingdoms were in danger! For the next 200 years they fought each other. They fought the powerful kingdoms that were all around them. These were the Egyptians, the Hittites, the Assyrians, the Babylonians, and the Persians. They all wanted control of the lands around Jerusalem.

At last the fierce neighbors were too strong. In 722 B.C., the Assyrians took over Israel. The Israelites were moved out or taken as slaves. In 587 B.C., Judah fell to a Babylonian people known as Chaldeans. The Babylonian king destroyed Solomon's fine temple in Jerusalem.

So it went. One power after another fought for the city that everyone wanted to control. Jerusalem was right in the middle of things. It came under many different rulers. Today it is more than 2,500 years since the Babylonians destroyed the temple. Very little has changed. Different groups of people continue to argue over who should control Jerusalem.

TIMELINE STUDY: THE ANCIENT ISRAELITES: STORY OF A PEOPLE

How many years passed before the ancient Israelites returned to Canaan?

1240 B.C. Ancient Israelites follow Moses out of Egypt

1200 B.C. Ancient Israelites return to Canaan

722 B.C. Assyrians conquer Israel

2000 B.C. — 1500 B.C. — 1000 B.C. — 500 B.C.

920 B.C. Israel and Judah become separate kingdoms

587 B.C. Babylonians take Jerusalem

LEARNING STYLES

Logical/Mathematical

Have students study the timeline on page 81 and figure out how many years after the Assyrians conquered Israel did the Babylonians take over Jerusalem. (135 years)

History Fact

Today, people who follow the Jewish religion—no matter where they live—are called Jews.

TIMELINE STUDY

Answer: 40 years

2000 B.C.–500 B.C.   *Mediterranean Kingdoms*   Chapter 5   **81**

Lesson 5–2 Review Answers

1. A **2.** G **3.** F **4.** D **5.** E **6.** C **7.** B
8. While most people in the Mediterranean people believed in many gods, the ancient Israelites believed in one god, Yaweh. **9.** Israel formed from the tribes in the north, and Judah formed from the tribes in the south. **10.** Fighting continues over Jerusalem's land because everyone wants to control the city.

LESSON 5-2 REVIEW

Match the description in Column A with the term in Column B. Write the correct letter on a sheet of paper.

Column A

1. the father of the Israelites, according to the Bible
2. the name of the one god the ancient Israelites believed in
3. the set of rules ancient Israelites lived by; came directly from God
4. the ancient Israelites' leader; led them out of Egypt, into the desert, to escape slavery
5. the son of David
6. the capital city and religious center; grew to be a mighty city
7. "The Promised Land"

Column B

- **A** Abraham
- **B** Canaan
- **C** Jerusalem
- **D** Moses
- **E** Solomon
- **F** The Ten Commandments
- **G** Yahweh

On a sheet of paper, write the answer to each question. Use complete sentences.

8. How was the religion of ancient Israelites different from that of other Mediterranean people?
9. What two kingdoms formed after King Solomon died?
10. Why is there fighting over Jerusalem's land?

82   *Unit 2   Ancient Civilizations*

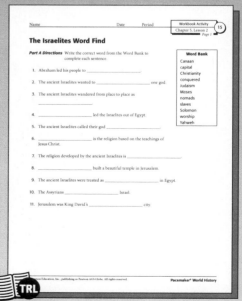

82   *Unit 2 Ancient Civilizations*

Activity 15, pages 1–2   Workbook Activity 15, pages 1–2

The Babylonians

Objectives

■ To describe what was happening around the time when Babylon became an important city
■ To explain the Code of Hammurabi

The Babylonians built a great civilization in Mesopotamia, along the Euphrates River. Their empire eventually grew to include the land that had once belonged to the Sumerians.

What Do We Know About the Babylonians?

Babylon was the capital city of the Babylonians. It stood on the banks of the Euphrates River. Little remains of it today. There are a few ruins in the middle of some dirt mounds. Archaeologists have been digging through the ruins. They have learned that Babylon was one of the greatest cities of the ancient world. It contained some of the most beautiful temples and palaces to be found anywhere. They were decorated with blue glazed bricks and pictures of made-up beasts. People entered and left the city through huge bronze gates. Bronze is a hard metal made by blending copper and tin.

Near the center of the city stood the great Tower of Babel. This tower is mentioned in the Bible. Not far from the tower were the Hanging Gardens of Babylon. The gardens were one of the Seven Wonders of the Ancient World. They were built by a Babylonian king for his wife. She had been homesick for the beauty of her homeland in the mountains.

> **Remember**
> The Nile, another one of the Seven Wonders of the Ancient World, is in Egypt.

Beautiful gates such as this existed in ancient Babylon, which is now in Iraq.

2000 B.C.–500 B.C.   *Mediterranean Kingdoms* Chapter 5   **83**

---

2 Teaching the Lesson

Remind students that archaeologists piece together a civilization's story by digging through ruins. Today, little remains of Babylon, but archaeologists are studying the ruins of the city for information about the ancient Babylonian culture.

Ask:

● How do we know that Babylon was one of the greatest cities of the ancient world? (Answers may vary. Findings of glazed bricks and pictures as well as remnants of bronze gates all serve as evidence of Babylon's beauty.)

● What were the Hanging Gardens of Babylon? (gardens built by a Babylonian king for his wife and one of the Seven Wonders of the Ancient World)

● What civilization did the Babylonians destroy? (the Sumerians)

Mediterranean Kingdoms Chapter 5   **83**

Background Information

Hammurabi's Code shows what life in Babylonia was like. Property was important. Ordinary people were valued less than nobles. Harming a common person brought a small fine. Harming a noble meant harsh punishments. This code was important because the laws were written out. Written laws were fairer because people knew what the law was. A ruler could not change laws without telling people. Laws were the same from case to case. People could defend themselves.

Today nearly every modern country has a written code of laws. Ideas about the laws have changed over time, though. In general, penalties for small crimes are not harsh like those in Hammurabi's Code.

LEARNING STYLES

Visual/Spatial

Call your students' attention to the timeline on page 84 and then divide them into groups of three or four. On a large, blank sheet of paper, have them create a pictorial timeline that corresponds to the dates provided. For example, the first entry on the timeline—2000 B.C.—might contain drawings of the Tower of Babel or the Hanging Gardens of Babylon while the second entry—1792–1750 B.C.—might depict images from the rule of King Hammurabi. Encourage students to conduct outside research into the rise and fall of the Babylonian empire.

ELL/ESL STRATEGY

Language Objective:
To empower students to seek out and learn unfamiliar words

Have students identify five words in the lesson that are unfamiliar to them and add those words to their notebooks. Encourage students to look up each word in their dictionaries, and then compose five original sentences using the words.

Empire
A group of lands all ruled by the same government or ruler

Code
A group of laws

Reading Strategy:
Visualizing

Draw a picture to help you visualize some part of Babylon, such as the Hanging Gardens. How does this image help you remember what you are reading?

 You Decide
How do laws today protect the rights of individual citizens?

Babylon became an important city about 2000 B.C. This was nearly the same time that the Babylonians were destroying the Sumerian civilization. The Babylonians went on to build a large **empire** in what had been the land of the Sumerians. An empire is a group of lands all ruled by the same ruler.

GREAT NAMES IN HISTORY

Hammurabi

Hammurabi was one of the greatest kings of Babylonia. He ruled from about 1792 B.C. to 1750 B.C. Hammurabi created a system of laws called the **Code** of Hammurabi. These laws dealt with almost every aspect of life. There were nearly 300 laws. They applied to marriage and divorce, property and business, taxes, wages, loans, military service, and so forth. For anyone who broke a law, the Code listed harsh punishments in the form of an "eye for an eye" when seeking justice. The Code was created to protect the rights of the individual citizen.

In time, the Babylonians were conquered by other civilizations. However, some of their ideas about laws and justice have lasted through the ages. Some are included in our own laws today. The Code of Hammurabi can be seen in the Louvre in Paris, France.

TIMELINE STUDY: THE BABYLONIAN EMPIRE

How long did the Babylonian empire last?

2000 B.C. Beginning of Babylonian empire

1595 B.C. Babylonians conquered by Hittites

550 B.C. Babylonians conquered by Persians

1792–1750 B.C. Hammurabi rules

612 B.C. Babylonians (Chaldeans) conquer Assyrians

2000 B.C.   1500 B.C.   1000 B.C.   500 B.C.

84   *Unit 2   Ancient Civilizations*

GREAT NAMES IN HISTORY

After students read this section, ask them to summarize the Code of Hammurabi in their own words. Why was the Code created? What were the penalties for those who broke the law?

Reading Strategy:
Visualizing

What important person is introduced in this section?

3   Reinforce and Extend

 You Decide

Ask students to think about ancient laws, such as Hammurabi's Code and the Ten Commandments. Have them write a code of ten laws for their school. Encourage individuals to read their code aloud to the class and have students discuss their codes as a group.

TIMELINE STUDY

Answer: 1,450 years

LESSON 5-3 REVIEW

Word Bank

Babylon
blue
bronze
citizen
Euphrates
greatest
Hammurabi
Hanging Gardens
Sumerian
Tower of Babel

On a sheet of paper, write the word from the Word Bank to complete each sentence correctly.

1. _____ was the capital city of the Babylonians.

2. Babylon was on the banks of the _____ River.

3. Babylon was one of the _____ cities of the ancient world.

4. Babylonian temples and palaces were decorated with _____ glazed bricks and pictures of made-up beasts.

5. People entered Babylon through huge _____ gates.

6. At the center of the city was the _____.

7. The _____ are one of the Seven Wonders of the Ancient World.

8. Babylon was an important city around 2000 B.C. This was at the same time the Babylonians were destroying the _____ civilization.

9. The Code of _____ was a system of laws. It addressed many aspects of life and was named for a great king of Babylon.

10. The Code was created to protect the rights of the individual _____.

IN THE COMMUNITY

In the time of Hammurabi, members of the military and those who answered directly to the king enforced the laws. Today, police officers enforce most laws in individual communities. Students may wish to interview a local law enforcement officer to find out how he or she maintains a commitment to the fair enforcement of laws.

ONLINE CONNECTION

Students can gain additional information by accessing the following Web site:
www.agsglobepmwh.com/page85
(This Web site encourages readers to learn more about the Code of Hammurabi.)

COMMON ERROR

Remind students that quickly and successfully accessing a web address depends upon their commitment to accurately copying down the Web site information.

COMMON ERROR

It is easy to forget how much time elapsed between the rise of the Babylonian empire and its final decline. Ask students to figure out the number of years that elapsed between the beginning of the empire and the Persians' conquering of the Babylonians (about 1,450 years).

Lesson 5–3 Review Answers

1. Babylon 2. Euphrates 3. greatest
4. blue 5. bronze 6. Tower of Babel
7. Hanging Gardens 8. Sumerian
9. Hammurabi 10. citizen

Name _____ Date _____ Period _____ Activity 16 Chapter 5, Lesson 3

The Babylonians

Directions Write the correct word from the Word Bank to complete each sentence.

1. Babylon was the _____ city of the Babylonians.

2. Babylon stood on the banks of the _____ River.

3. Babylon contained beautiful _____ and palaces.

4. Palaces in Babylon were decorated with blue glazed _____

5. The gates of the city were made of _____.

6. Babylon's great _____ of Babel is mentioned in the Bible.

7. The _____ of Babylon were built by a Babylonian king for his wife.

8. The Babylonians built a great _____ in what had been the land of the Sumerians.

9. _____ was a great Babylonian king.

10. Hammurabi created the _____ of Hammurabi to protect the rights of the citizens.

Word Bank
bricks
bronze
capital
code
empire
Euphrates
Hammurabi
Hanging Gardens
temples
Tower

Activity 16

Name _____ Date _____ Period _____ Workbook Activity 16 Chapter 5, Lesson 3

Comparing Civilizations

The Sumerians and Babylonians both built civilizations in Mesopotamia. The chart below compares some of the facts of the two civilizations.

Sumer	Babylon
5000 B.C. to 2000 B.C.	2000 B.C. to 1595 B.C.
capital city of Ur on Euphrates River	capital city of Babylon on Euphrates River
built temples many stories tall	built temples decorated with blue glazed bricks and pictures of made-up beasts
learned to irrigate fields by digging canals	learned to make bronze by blending copper and tin
built dikes to hold back floods	built the Hanging Gardens of Babylon, one of the Seven Wonders of the Ancient World
developed writing	wrote a code of laws
conquered by the Babylonians	conquered by the Hittites

Directions Answer the questions below by writing the name of the civilization that correctly completes the statement. Some statements may be true of both civilizations. If so, write "both."

1. the older civilization _____

2. built a capital on the Euphrates River _____

3. built one of the wonders of the ancient world _____

4. invented irrigation _____

5. built temples _____

6. decorated temples with blue glazed bricks _____

7. used bronze _____

8. learned to control flooding _____

9. developed writing _____

10. was/were conquered by another civilization _____

Workbook Activity 16

TRL   TRL

Lesson at a Glance

Chapter 5 Lesson 4

Overview This lesson describes the Hittites, a mysterious people of uncertain origin who settled in the eastern Mediterranean around 2000 B.C. and created an empire that lasted until around 1200 B.C.

Objectives

- To describe the secret knowledge of the Hittites
- To explain the peace treaty the Hittites and Egyptians signed
- To explain what brought about the end of the Hittite empire

Student Pages 86–88

Teacher's Resource Library TRL

Workbook Activity 17

Activity 17

Modified Activity 17

Vocabulary

treaty

Explain to students that a thesaurus is an excellent source for finding synonyms for a word. Have them look up "treaty" in a thesaurus and report back with the words they find. Some words they find may include pact, agreement, and truce.

PRONUNCIATION GUIDE

Use this list to help students pronounce difficult words in this lesson.

Anatolia (a nə tō´ lē ə)

Reading Strategy:
Visualizing

Have students work together to rewrite the lesson.

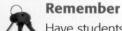
Remember
Have students discuss what it would be like to build a house with no machines or iron tools, like the pyramids.

The Hittites

Objectives
- To describe the secret knowledge of the Hittites
- To explain the peace treaty the Hittites and Egyptians signed
- To explain what brought about the end of the Hittite empire

Reading Strategy:
Visualizing

How could this lesson be written differently to create a stronger picture in your mind?

Remember
When the Egyptians built the pyramids, they had no machines or iron tools.

The Hittites were warriors who came to the eastern Mediterranean around 2000 B.C. No one knows for sure where they came from, but they quickly swept through the lands called Anatolia. They found city-states already there. They conquered one after another. By 1650 B.C., the Hittites ruled all of these lands. Today this area is the country Turkey.

The Hittites were mighty fighters. They used their might to create an empire. After they conquered Anatolia, they began attacking neighboring lands.

What Was the Secret Knowledge of the Hittites?

The Hittites had a secret that gave them great power. For hundreds of years, they were the only people who knew how to make iron. Iron was a strong, heavy metal that was easy to shape. It made better weapons. No other people could beat the Hittite warriors and their iron spears.

The Egyptians looked upon the Hittites with great respect. They thought of the Hittites as the only other great power in the Mediterranean. In about 1269 B.C., after years of fighting with each other, the Hittites and the Egyptians made peace. To help keep the peace, a Hittite princess married an Egyptian pharaoh.

---

1 Warm-Up Activity

Point out to students that in this lesson, as in the previous lesson, the subhead is worded as a question. Ask students to read the information below the subhead, then answer the question briefly using their own words.

2 Teaching the Lesson

Ask students to write several details they remember from the previous chapter on the Egyptians. Guide a discussion where students speculate about why the Egyptians had such great respect for the Hittites.

Ask:

- Why was iron so important to the Hittite warriors? (It was a strong, heavy metal that was easy to shape and made formidable spears.)
- By 1650 B.C., the Hittites ruled all of the lands around Anatolia. What is this area called today? (Turkey)
- Who finally conquered the Hittites around 1200 B.C.? (the *Sea Peoples*)

Treaty
An agreement, usually having to do with peace or trade

The Hittites and the Egyptians signed an agreement to keep the peace. It became the first recorded peace **treaty**, or agreement.

In time other people learned the secret of making iron. The Hittites were no longer the strongest. Around 1200 B.C., new people came and attacked the Hittites. They were called the *Sea Peoples*. They came from islands in the Mediterranean. They brought about the end of the Hittite empire.

The Hittites were mighty warriors. The ability to make iron was the secret to their power.

Background Information

Clever, curious people have always made inventions and discoveries. Very early in history, people learned to control floods. They built impressive buildings. Before 1500 B.C., technology was moving ahead in the ancient Middle East.

One giant step was learning to work with iron. Much earlier, people had mixed copper and tin to make bronze. Iron, however, was stronger than bronze. It made better knives and tools. Iron swords had a sharper edge. But it was harder to work with, too. It took a very hot fire to melt, or smelt, iron out of the rock. Then a worker called a *smith* hammered it into shape while it was red-hot.

ELL/ESL STRATEGY

Language Objective:
To practice writing from different viewpoints

Encourage students to write a short paragraph in which they recreate the peace treaty between the Egyptians and the Hittites. Remind students that although the Egyptians and Hittites fought for years, the Egyptians had great respect for the warrior Hittites. Suggest that students look carefully at the text on pages 86–87 to assist them with composing their peace treaty. When students have completed the assignment, ask for volunteers to share their treaties with the class.

---

3   Reinforce and Extend

COMMON ERROR

Students sometimes become so enamored with a thesaurus that they misunderstand the connotations and denotations of a particular word. Have students look at a list of synonyms for "treaty" that you have written on the board and discuss the connotations of each. For example, is there a difference in common usage between "pact" and "truce"? Encourage students to discuss the nuances of synonyms they have chosen and to create original sentences for each.

CAREER CONNECTION

Students have learned that the Hittites had the "secret" of iron. They developed a way to create weapons out of the strong, heavy metal. Working with iron is still an important profession today. Traditionally, people who work with iron are called *welders*, but they also work with materials such as steel, aluminum, or brass. Welders use extreme heat and pressure to join and shape metal. It can be a dangerous job, so safety equipment is essential! Welders are found in a variety of industries, such as engineering or auto mechanics.

Lesson 5–4 Review Answers

1. B 2. C 3. A 4. B 5. D 6. C 7. B 8. C
9. D 10. A

On a sheet of paper, write the letter of the answer that correctly completes each sentence.

1. The Hittites were _____.

    A farmers   B warriors   C traders   D trappers

2. The Hittites came to the _____ Mediterranean around 2000 B.C.

    A northern   B southern   C eastern   D western

3. The Hittites quickly _____ city-state after city-state in Anatolia.

    A conquered   B built   C traded with   D farmed

4. By _____ B.C., the Hittites ruled all of the lands in present-day Turkey.

    A 2000   B 1650   C 1258   D 1200

5. _____ was the secret that the Hittites had that gave them their great power.

    A The Code   B The Bible   C Sailing ships   D Iron

6. Even though they fought, the _____ looked upon the Hittites with great respect.

    A Sea Peoples   B Babylonians   C Egyptians   D Assyrians

7. To help keep the peace, a Hittite princess married an Egyptian _____.

    A king   B pharaoh   C god   D mummy

8. The peace agreement that the Egyptians and Hittites signed was the first recorded peace _____.

    A law   B tax   C treaty   D stone

9. In _____ B.C., new people came and attacked the Hittites.

    A 2000   B 1650   C 1258   D 1200

10. The _____ brought an end to the Hittite empire.

    A Sea Peoples   B Babylonians   C Egyptians   D Assyrians

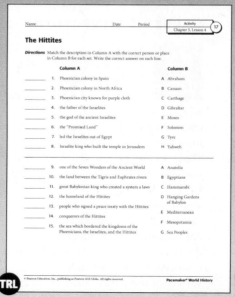

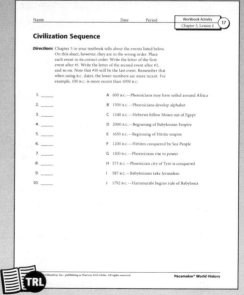

The Assyrians

Objectives

■ To describe how the Assyrian Empire grew
■ To tell what the Assyrians did when they captured a city
■ To name three Assyrian inventions

Military
Having to do with soldiers or the armed forces

Siege
The surrounding of a city by soldiers who are trying to capture it so that food, water, and other supplies cannot get in or out

The Assyrians were another warrior civilization. At first Assyria was a small kingdom. When the Hittite civilization ended, the Assyrians began to want an empire of their own.

The Assyrians built their capital city on the banks of the Tigris River. The city was named Ashur, after one of the Assyrians' many fierce gods.

Assyrian kings were hard rulers. They made their people pay heavy taxes. Assyrians lived under strict laws. Anyone who broke a law could be cruelly punished. Many law breakers were beaten. Some even had their ears cut off!

How Did the Assyrians Build Up Their Empire?

The Assyrians built up a great army. It was the best trained army of the ancient world. The Assyrians sent their army to attack the neighboring kingdoms. As more and more cities were captured, the Assyrian Empire grew.

The Assyrian civilization was a **military** one. Assyrian boys knew what their future held. Men had to go into the army. The Assyrians needed soldiers in order to keep their power. The Assyrians were builders as well as fighters. They built military equipment to help them conquer cities. They beat down city walls and gates with their huge machines called siege engines. They would surround a city with soldiers and try to capture it so that food, water, and other supplies could not get in or out. A city under **siege** from fierce Assyrians stood little chance.

Chapter 5 Lesson 5

Overview The Assyrians were warriors who sought an empire through conquering neighboring kingdoms. Known for their merciless conquests and harsh laws, the Assyrians used a great army to defeat enemies, but were also known for erecting fine buildings and statues.

Objectives

■ To describe how the Assyrian Empire grew

■ To tell what the Assyrians did when they captured the city

■ To name three Assyrian inventions

Student Pages 89–92

Teacher's Resource Library

Workbook Activity 18

Activity 18

Modified Activity 18

Vocabulary

military   tribute
siege

Remind students that these terms are as much a part of the modern vocabulary as they are a way to describe events in ancient history. Have students brainstorm modern uses for each term.

PRONUNCIATION GUIDE

Use this list to help students pronounce difficult words in this lesson.

Ashur (ä´shər)

Nineveh (ni´ nə və)

Chaldean (kăl dē´ ən)

1   Warm-Up Activity

Ask students to think about the civilizations they have encountered in Chapter 5. Encourage students to compare and contrast each of these civilizations.

2   Teaching the Lesson

Ask students to consider the factors that led to the Assyrians' success and to their downfall.

Ask:

● What factors contributed to the success of the Assyrian Empire? (Students may mention their powerful army, iron weapons, division of territory into provinces, the collection of tributes and taxes, and their merciless treatment of the conquered.)

● What is a siege engine? (an enormous machine used to beat down city walls and gates)

● What contribution did the Assyrians make to the world of letters? (They were among the first people to have a library.)

Background Information

The library that was established in Nineveh contained not only dictionaries of other languages, but also copies of religious texts from temple libraries and texts on the behavior of men and animals, plants, mathematics, chemistry, astronomy, literature, fables, and proverbs.

Reading Strategy:
Visualizing

Have students point out features of the photo on page 90 that help them visualize the Palace of Nineveh.

Tribute
A payment or gift demanded by rulers of ancient kingdoms

Reading Strategy:
Visualizing

Study the photo of the sculpture from the Palace of Nineveh. How does this image help you visualize what you have read?

The Assyrians were not kind to the cities that they took. Sometimes they burned the city and killed the people who lived there. Often they took the people as slaves.

Sometimes, after they captured a city, the Assyrians acted as its new rulers. The people from the city had to pay **tribute** (give gifts or payments) to the Assyrian king. If they did not pay the high price, they were punished.

A relief, or sculpture, from the Palace of Nineveh shows an Assyrian king.

What Are Some Assyrian Developments?

The Assyrian civilization did leave some things behind besides a successful military record. They built fine buildings and statues. They invented machines that beat down walls and gates. They also built machines to help lift water from the river into canals.

The Assyrians were among the first people to have a library. The library stored clay tablets with writings from the ancient world.

Even the fierce Assyrians were defeated at last. By 670 B.C., the empire was so big that it was hard to control. It began to break up. In 612 B.C., the Assyrian city of Nineveh was under siege itself. The Assyrian Empire came to an end. The Assyrians had been conquered by a new Babylonian people—the Chaldeans.

Reading Strategy:
Visualizing

Study the timeline below. How does it help you visualize the change from Hittite to Assyrian power?

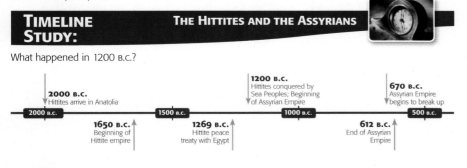

TIMELINE STUDY: THE HITTITES AND THE ASSYRIANS

What happened in 1200 B.C.?

2000 B.C.
Hittites arrive in Anatolia

1650 B.C.
Beginning of
Hittite empire

1269 B.C.
Hittite peace
treaty with Egypt

1200 B.C.
Hittites conquered by
Sea Peoples; Beginning
of Assyrian Empire

612 B.C.
End of Assyrian
Empire

670 B.C.
Assyrian Empire
begins to break up

2000 B.C. 1500 B.C. 1000 B.C. 500 B.C.

Reading Strategy:
Visualizing

Ask students if they think the timeline is complete. What else could they add?

TIMELINE STUDY

Answer: The Sea Peoples, or Assyrians, conquered the Hittites and established the Assyrian Empire.

3 Reinforce and Extend

Lesson 5–5 Review Answers

1. Tigris **2.** Ashur **3.** taxes **4.** laws
5. military **6.** builders **7.** Chaldeans
8. The Assyrians built military
equipment to help them conquer
cities. Siege engines would help
them beat down city walls and gates.
A city under siege from the Assyrians
stood little chance. **9.** Sometimes
the Assyrians burned the city they
captured. Other times, they took the
people as slaves. In other cases, they
would act as the city's new rulers,
and force the people of the city to
pay tribute to the Assyrian king.
10. The Assyrians built fine buildings
and statues, siege machines, and
machines to help lift water from the
river into canals.

LESSON
5-5 REVIEW

Word Bank

Ashur
builders
Chaldeans
laws
military
taxes
Tigris

On a sheet of paper, write the word from the Word Bank to complete each sentence correctly.

1. The Assyrians built their capital city on the banks of the _____ River.

2. The capital city of Assyria was named _____, after one of their many fierce gods.

3. Assyrian kings were hard rulers and made their people pay heavy _____.

4. Assyrians lived under strict _____.

5. The Assyrians had a(n) _____ civilization.

6. The Assyrians were _____ as well as fighters.

7. In 612 B.C., the _____ brought an end to the Assyrian Empire.

On a sheet of paper, write the answers to each question. Use complete sentences.

8. What did the Assyrians build to help them conquer a city?

9. What did the Assyrians do when they captured a city?

10. What are three things the Assyrians invented?

92   Unit 2   Ancient Civilizations

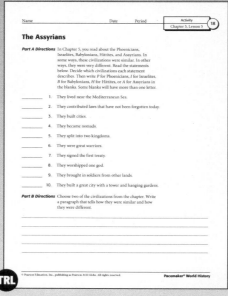

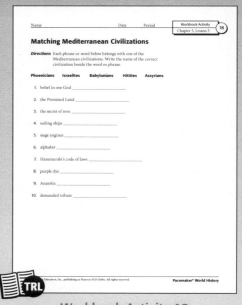

Activity 18   Workbook Activity 18

92   Unit 2 Ancient Civilizations

- There were many kingdoms around the eastern Mediterranean Sea.

- The Phoenicians were expert sailors. They used the stars to help them navigate the seas.

- The Phoenicians were also active traders. They were not farmers or warriors.

- The Phoenicians set up many colonies. The colonies paid taxes to the Phoenician homeland. One of the largest colonies was Carthage.

- The Phoenicians developed an alphabet much like ours.

- The ancient Israelites gave us the Jewish religion. They were among the first to believe in one god.

- The ancient Israelites left slavery in Egypt to follow Moses to the Promised Land. They lived by rules called the Ten Commandments.

- David became king of the ancient Israelites. Jerusalem was his capital and religious center.

- David's son Solomon became a powerful king of the Israelites. When Solomon died, his kingdom split into Israel and Judah.

- A Babylonian King, Hammurabi, created one of the earliest systems of laws.

- The Hittites and the Assyrians were two groups who controlled the eastern Mediterranean Sea.

- The Hittites and the Assyrians both had warlike civilizations.

2000 B.C.–500 B.C.

Mediterranean Kingdoms   Chapter 5   **93**

Chapter 5 Summary

Have students read the Chapter Summary on page 93 to review the main ideas presented in Chapter 5.

Ask:

- What were the Phoenicians well known for? (They were sailors and explorers who navigated the seas using the stars to guide them.)

- What distinguished the Phoenicians from several of the other civilizations in the chapter? (They were neither farmers nor warriors; rather, they were active traders who established colonies in the lands they visited.)

- What was the most significant contribution of the ancient Israelites? (They gave us Judaism and the Ten Commandments. They are among the first people to worship a single god.)

- Why did the Israelites leave Egypt? (to escape slavery and find "The Promised Land")

- Who was Solomon? (a powerful king of the Israelites)

- What is the legacy of King Hammurabi? (his Code of conduct, which became one of the earliest legal systems)

- What two civilizations were most known as warriors and conquerors? (the Hittites and the Assyrians)

- What region did both the Hittites and Assyrians control at different times? (the eastern Mediterranean Sea)

CHAPTER PROJECT FOLLOW-UP

Have students present short oral reports on their assigned civilization from Chapter 5. Encourage them to use information both from the text as well as any independent research they may have conducted. Students may wish to present their findings in the form of a short skit, a brief debate, or a television newscast.

Chapter 5 Review

Use the Chapter Review to prepare students for tests and to reteach content from the chapter.

Chapter 5 Mastery Test

The Teacher's Resource Library includes two forms of the Chapter 5 Mastery Test. Each test addresses the chapter Goals for Learning. An optional third page of additional critical-thinking items is included for each test. The difficulty level of the two forms is equivalent.

Chapter 5 Review Answers

Vocabulary Review

1. conquer
2. siege
3. treaty
4. tribute
5. empire
6. colony
7. capital
8. nomad
9. navigate
10. worship

Chapter Review Questions

11. The Phoenicians were not farmers, they were sailors and traders.

12. Only the very rich and royalty could afford it.

Word Bank

capital
colony
conquer
empire
navigate
nomad
siege
treaty
tribute
worship

Vocabulary Review

On a sheet of paper, use the words from the Word Bank to correctly match each definition below.

1. To defeat an enemy in war

2. In war, surrounding a city to prevent necessary items from getting in or out

3. An agreement, like the one the Hittites and Egyptians made to keep the peace

4. Something a ruler demands from the people

5. A large area of land controlled by a single ruler or government

6. A group of people who settle in a far-off land but are still under the rule of the land they came from

7. The city where the government of a nation or state is located

8. A person who moves from place to place

9. To plan the route of a ship

10. To honor and praise a god

Chapter Review Questions

On a sheet of paper, write the answer to each question. Use complete sentences.

11. How was the Phoenician civilization different from other civilizations on the shores of the Mediterranean?

12. How did purple become a royal color?

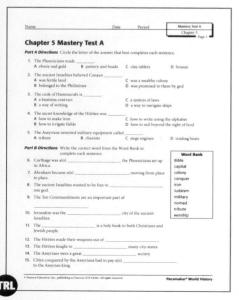

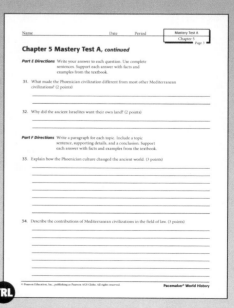

Before you begin
a test, look it over
quickly. Try to set
aside enough time
to complete each
section.

13. How were ancient Israelite beliefs different from those of most other people in the Mediterranean world?

14. What was the "Promised Land"?

15. How did the Egyptians and Hittites finally make peace with each other?

16. What other things, besides a successful military record, did the Assyrians leave behind?

Critical Thinking

On a sheet of paper, write your response to each question. Use complete sentences.

17. Why did the Hittites keep their ability to make iron a secret?

18. Do you think people liked living under the harsh rule of the Assyrians? Why or why not?

Using the Timelines

Use the timelines on pages 76, 81, 84, and 91 to answer the questions.

19. What period of time is covered on the four timelines?

20. How many years after the Phoenicians rose to power did Moses lead the ancient Israelites out of Egypt?

GROUP ACTIVITY

In a group of three or four, make a poster promoting one of the Mediterranean kingdoms. Be sure to talk about the religion, laws, or any special developments of that empire. Discuss what you think life would have been like in that kingdom. Share with the class the information from your poster about your chosen empire.

---

13. The ancient Israelites believed in one God.

14. The ancient Israelites believed that Canaan was the land God promised them.

15. They signed a peace treaty (the first ever recorded) and a Hittite princess married an Egyptian pharaoh.

16. The Assyrians built fine buildings and statues, siege machines, and machines to help lift water from the river into canals.

Critical Thinking

17. Possible answer: The Hittites kept the secret of making iron so that nobody could defeat them in war.

18. Possible answers: Yes, soldiers probably had a high place in society. No, the rulers were too strict and punishments were not fair.

Using the Timelines

19. 140 years

20. 2000 B.C. to 500 B.C.

GROUP ACTIVITY

Project should include accurate, interesting material about the empire.

Introducing the Chapter

As early as 6000 B.C., great civilizations grew in India and China, and later America. Have students brainstorm a list of everything that comes to mind when they think of China, India, and the early Americas. Have each student keep a copy of this list in a folder. As students read, have them check off those items that the chapter discusses.

Ask:

- What geographical feature was needed to begin farming in China and India? (rivers)

Early Civilizations of India, China, and the Americas

Another strong civilization grew up in the Indus River Valley of Asia. This culture thrived peacefully for more than 1,000 years. The Aryans gained power, bringing with them a system of separate social classes.

At about the same time, a civilization developed in the Huang He Valley of present-day China. These people wrote about history. Many dynasties, or ruling families, controlled China for hundreds of years.

Across the Pacific Ocean, the Olmecs were building a society in what is now Mexico. This civilization lasted for more than 1,000 years. The Maya people followed the Olmecs.

GOALS FOR LEARNING

- To describe civilization along the Indus River Valley
- To understand Buddhism and how it came about
- To describe the early Chinese civilization that lived in the Huang He Valley
- To understand life in the early Americas

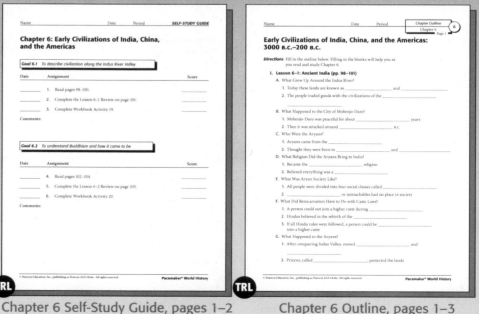

Chapter 6 Self-Study Guide, pages 1–2   Chapter 6 Outline, pages 1–3

Reading Strategy: Inferencing

Sometimes the meaning of a text is not directly stated. You have to make an inference to figure out what the text means.

What You Know + What You Read = Inference

To make inferences, you have to think "beyond the text." Predicting what will happen next and explaining cause and effect are helpful strategies for making inferences.

Key Vocabulary Words

Lesson 1
Conqueror A person who gains control by winning a war

Hinduism The main religion of India; Hindus worship many gods

Class A group of people according to social rank

Caste A social class in India

Soul A person's spirit

Reincarnation A belief that living souls are reborn in a new body

Lesson 2
Buddhism A religion based on the teachings of Buddha

Buddha A name meaning the "Enlightened One;" the name given to Siddhartha Gautama, the founder of Buddhism

Enlightened Knowing the truth

Emperor A person who rules a group of different countries, lands, or peoples

Foreign From another country; having to do with another country

Lesson 3
Ancestor A person from whom one is descended

Dynasty A family that rules a country for a long period of time

Barrier Something that blocks the way; a wall

Raid To attack suddenly; a surprise attack

Isolate To set apart from others; alone

Collapse To fall apart

Lesson 4
Shrine A place of worship believed to be sacred or holy

- What does "Buddha" mean? (Enlightened One)
- How long did the Shang dynasty last? (about 500 years)
- How do scientists think people reached America from Asia? (They traveled across a land bridge.)

Reading Strategy:
Inferencing

Explain to students that to infer means to draw conclusions that are not stated explicitly in text. They should use what they have learned in previous chapters along with the current lessons to infer the intended conclusion.

Key Vocabulary Words

Point out that these chapter words are presented in the order they appear in each lesson. They are also found in the glossary.

LIFE SKILLS CONNECTION

Students discuss exploration and travel. Students study maps and learn the basic features of maps. Providing maps of your school's town may help students since they are already familiar with the geography of the area.

KEY VOCABULARY

In Part A, students will match the vocabulary term to the correct definition. In Part B, students will choose the correct term to finish each sentence.

CHAPTER PROJECT

Brainstorm a list of research topics with students. They might include Mohenjo-Daro, caste system, Great Wall of China, Confucius, Olmecs, and Maya. Ask each student to choose one of the topics to research on the Internet. Review search words and good encyclopedia, history, archaeology, and travel Web sites.

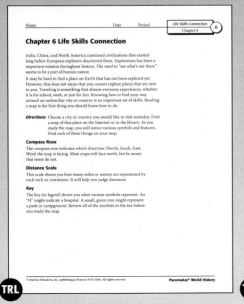

Life Skills Connection 6

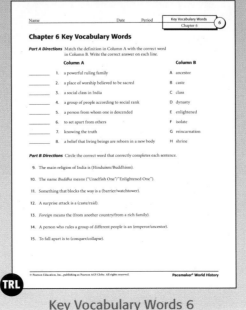

Key Vocabulary Words 6

Overview This lesson describes the geography, culture, and religion of ancient India.

Objectives
- To describe life in the city of Mohenjo-Daro
- To describe the Aryan people
- To explain the Hindu religion
- To name the social classes of the Indian caste system

Student Pages 98–101

Teacher's Resource Library

Workbook Activity 19

Activity 19

Modified Activity 19

Vocabulary

caste   Hinduism
class   reincarnation
conqueror   soul

As a class, scan the lesson to locate each vocabulary word. Discuss the pronunciation and meaning of each word. Then have students create a four-column chart using the following headings: Vocabulary Word, Meaning Clues from the Text, Definition, and My Sentence. As students read the lesson, have them fill in the chart.

PRONUNCIATION GUIDE

Use this list to help students pronounce difficult words in this lesson.

Mohenjo-Daro (mō hen´jō - där´ō)

Indus (in´dəs)

Shiva (shē´və)

Brahma (brä´mə)

Vishnu (vish´nü)

Objectives
- To describe life in the city of Mohenjo-Daro
- To describe the Aryan people
- To explain the Hindu religion
- To name the social classes of the Indian caste system

Reading Strategy:
Inferencing

What do you already know about present-day India or India of long ago?

One of the world's earliest civilizations grew up around the Indus River. These lands are now known as India and Pakistan. The people, like so many others, settled near the river. They learned to irrigate their fields and to grow crops. They made pottery, jewelry, and statues. They traded goods and ideas with the civilizations of the Fertile Crescent.

What Happened to the City of Mohenjo-Daro?

One of the main cities in the Indus River Valley was Mohenjo-Daro. Mohenjo-Daro was a neat, well-planned city. It had long, straight main streets. Covered drainage systems ran under the streets. The people built brick houses. They even built apartment houses.

Life was good in Mohenjo-Daro. There were public swimming pools and bath houses. People could cool off on hot Indus Valley days. Brick courtyards circled shaded wells so that people and animals could drink in comfort. Many houses in Mohenjo-Daro had their own indoor wells and tile-lined baths. Wheat and date palms grew on farms outside the city.

Mohenjo-Daro stood peacefully for close to 1,000 years. Then, around 1500 B.C., the city was attacked. People from the north, the Aryans, swooped down on Mohenjo-Daro. The Aryans showed no mercy. They ran through the streets of Mohenjo-Daro killing most of the people.

The Aryans believed that they were born to conquer and control. The word *Aryan* meant "nobleman" or "owner of land." The Aryans soon controlled all of the Indus River Valley.

---

1   Warm-Up Activity

Ask students to describe their neighborhood or town. Ask them if it has a swimming pool, brick courtyards, or apartment buildings. Tell them that the city of Mohenjo-Daro had these and other "modern" conveniences. Read aloud the description of Mohenjo-Daro on page 98. Have students compare and contrast the city with their own area.

Reading Strategy:
Inferencing

Have students make a three-column chart using the following headings: What I Know, What I Want to Know, and What I Learned. Before they read the lesson about India, have students fill in the first two columns.

2   Teaching the Lesson

As students read this section, have them list characteristics of life in Mohenjo-Daro before and after the Aryan invasion.

Conqueror
A person who gains control by winning a war

Hinduism
The main religion of India; Hindus worship many gods

The Aryans were fierce **conquerors** who gained control of lands by winning a war. However, they also brought new ideas. They became known for making beautiful cloth decorated with gold and silver. They also became known for their skilled doctors and mathematicians.

What Religion Did the Aryans Bring to India?

The Aryans' religion was based on the idea that some people are born "better" than others. Their religion developed into the Hindu religion. Hindus, the people who practice **Hinduism,** worship many gods.

Ask:
- How was Mohenjo-Daro similar to cities today? (It had straight main streets, covered drainage systems under the streets, brick houses, apartments, swimming pools, and bath houses.)
- What did the Aryans do to all people? (They put them in a caste system.)

Background Information

Hindu religious festivals are ancient traditions. Many are still practiced today. They might include religious ceremonies, worship, prayer, music, dances, eating and drinking, and feeding the poor. To celebrate the Hindu New Year, objects representing the impurities of the previous year are thrown into a bonfire. Hindu festivals are community events. They involve young and old, and can last for several days.

The Indus River Valley

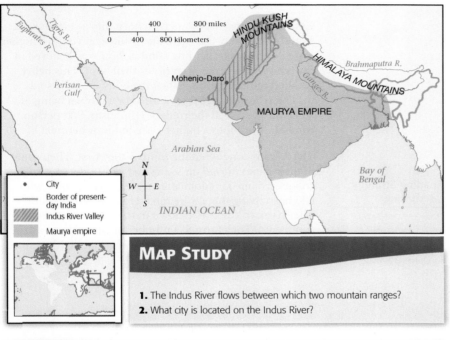

MAP STUDY

1. The Indus River flows between which two mountain ranges?
2. What city is located on the Indus River?

LEARNING STYLES

Visual/Spatial

Have students work in pairs to create a "pocket travel guide." Explain that the purpose of the guide is to persuade tourists to visit Mohenjo-Daro on their next vacation. Students can illustrate the booklets with drawings and captions. Encourage them to have fun with the project—the goal of the travel guide is to highlight the beauty and attractions of this ancient Indian city.

MAP STUDY

Answers:

1. The Hindu Kush and Himalaya mountains

2. Mohenjo-Daro

ELL/ESL STRATEGY

Language Objective:
To classify vocabulary relative to different aspects of daily life

Have the ELL students choose from the following categories: farming, life at home, architecture, religion, or city life. Have them create word banks related to their category. Each word bank should have words and a drawing or photo related to each word. Students should include a caption with each word and accompanying image.

COMMON ERROR

Students may not know that many ancient and modern cities were built next to rivers. Explain that rivers provide a steady source of water for drinking, growing crops, and cleanliness. They also are used to move people and goods from place to place. Have students look at a world map, then make a list of large cities found near rivers.

Reading Strategy:
Inferencing

Have students return to their three-column chart and tell them to fill in the third column.

ONLINE CONNECTION

Students can gain additional information by accessing the following Web sites:

www.agsglobepmwh.com/page100a
(This site on ancient India, similar to the ancient China site, is part of the British Museum online presentation of ancient civilizations.)

www.agsglobepmwh.com/page100b
(This site provides information on the history, beliefs, and holy days of Hinduism and allows students to easily access similar information on other religions.)

www.agsglobepmwh.com/page100c
(This interactive site allows students to access information on the geography, art, lifestyle, and writing of ancient China with simply a click.)

Class
A group of people according to social rank

Caste
A social class in India

Soul
A person's spirit

Reincarnation
A belief that living souls are reborn in a new body

Reading Strategy:
Inferencing

How does what you already know about India add to what you have just read?

Hindus believe that everything is God, or Brahman. They believe that Brahma, Vishnu, and Shiva are different faces of God. Brahma creates, or makes, life. Vishnu preserves life, and Shiva destroys it. Hindus believe these three faces show us the main powers of God.

The Aryans divided all people into four groups according to social rank, or social **classes.** They called these social classes **castes.** The highest caste consisted of priests and scholars. Rulers and warriors were the next in rank, followed by craftworkers, merchants, and farmers. Unskilled workers made up the lowest caste.

The Aryans called the people they conquered *outcastes* or *untouchables.* The outcastes had no place in society. Any Aryan who married one of the conquered people would also become an outcaste.

Caste laws were strict. A person born into a certain caste would always stay there. No one could ever rise to a higher caste during his or her life. Hindus, however, believed in the rebirth of a person's spirit, or their **soul.** This belief is called **reincarnation.** When the body dies, the soul may be reborn in either an animal or a human being. If a person obeyed all the rules of Hinduism, that person would be born into a higher caste in his or her next life.

The Aryans conquered the Indus Valley first. Then some of their tribes moved on to the east and to the south. They conquered one kingdom after another. The people who had been living there were forced to flee farther south. The Aryan tribes settled down in the lands that they conquered. They formed a number of city-states. Each one was ruled by a *raja,* or prince, who had highly trained armies to protect the lands.

Match the description in Column A with the term in Column B.
Write the correct letter on a sheet of paper.

Column A

1. a social class in India

2. prince

3. the God of the Hindu religion

4. a belief that living souls are reborn in a new body

5. a word that means "nobleman" or "owner of the land"

Column B

A Aryan

B Brahman

C caste

D raja

E reincarnation

On a sheet of paper, write the answer to each question. Use complete sentences.

6. What was life like in the city of Mohenjo-Daro?

7. What were the Aryan people like?

8. What are three different faces of God in the Hindu religion?

9. What are the four social classes of the Indian caste system?

10. How could a person change to a different social class?

AT HOME

The pottery, statues, and jewelry that archaeologists have discovered around the Indus River are called artifacts. Artifacts are objects that tell us how people lived. Ask students to collect a set of artifacts from their homes that future historians could study to learn about American life in the early 21st century. Students can put the artifacts in a shoebox and label it with the date and their address. Have students show their artifacts to the class, explaining why they chose each object.

Lesson 6–1 Review Answers

1. C **2.** D **3.** B **4.** E **5.** A **6.** People had a good life. The city had drainage systems, straight streets, and apartments. There were public swimming pools, bath houses, and brick courtyards. **7.** They were fierce conquerors. They gained control of lands by winning a war. They were also known for their skilled doctors and mathematicians. **8.** Brahma creates life. Vishnu preserves life. Shiva destroys life. **9.** The highest social class is made up of priests and scholars. Next are rulers and warriors. Craftworkers, merchants, and farmers follow. The lowest social class is made up of unskilled workers. **10.** A person could change by obeying all the rules of Hinduism. Then that person could be born into a higher caste in the next life.

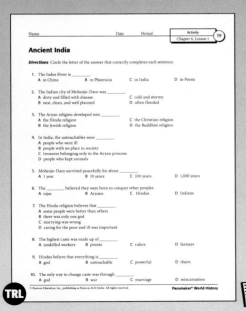

Activity 19

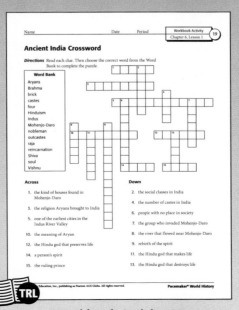

Workbook Activity 19

Early Civilizations Chapter 6 **101**

Buddhism

Lesson at a Glance

Chapter 6 Lesson 2

Overview This lesson describes Siddhartha Gautama, and the beliefs and practices of Buddhism. It also compares and contrasts Buddhism and Hinduism.

Objectives

- To describe the life of Siddhartha Gautama
- To explain why Buddhism is called a gentle religion
- To name two countries Buddhism spread to

Student Pages 102–105

Teacher's Resource Library

Workbook Activity 20

Activity 20

Modified Activity 20

Vocabulary

Buddha   enlightened
Buddhism

Have students write each vocabulary word and its definition on one side of an index card. On the other side of the card, students should write sentences incorporating each word. Ask volunteers to read their sentences aloud to the class.

1 Warm-Up Activity

Challenge students to draw a picture of nirvana. Then have students add the concept of a soul to their drawings. Stress that these abstract terms mean different things to different people. Have students share their drawings with their classmates. Lead a class discussion about how Buddhism affected the caste system in India.

Objectives

- To describe the life of Siddhartha Gautama
- To explain why Buddhism is called a gentle religion
- To name two countries Buddhism spread to

Buddhism
A religion based on the teachings of Buddha

Buddha
A name meaning the "Enlightened One"

Enlightened
Knowing the truth

Buddhism is a religion based on the teachings of a man named **Buddha**. It began in India before Christianity or Islam, and quickly spread throughout Asia.

Who Was Buddha?

The man who would one day be called Buddha was born about 563 B.C., long before Jesus or Muhammad. He was the son of a wealthy Hindu in India. His father was a raja. Therefore, the boy, Siddhartha Gautama, was considered a prince. His life should have been one of riches and plenty. Instead, Gautama chose a different path.

He saw many of his people living in poverty and sorrow. He saw beggars in the streets. Gautama felt sorry for the unhappy people. Human life was full of suffering. The rich had so much; the poor had so little.

When he was a young man, Gautama gave up his own wealth. He left his father's palace and went to live in the forest. For about six years he lived simply, wandering around India. He spent his time thinking about how life could be better for people.

It is said that the truth came to Gautama one day as he sat under a fig tree. "The sorrows of the world are caused by selfishness," Gautama decided. If people could put aside their desire for riches, Gautama thought, the world would be a better place. So he developed a new religion, Buddhism, which is based on brotherly love. Gautama was called Buddha, which means the "**Enlightened** One." When someone is said to be enlightened, it means they know the truth.

What Did the Buddhist Religion Teach?

The Buddhist religion is known as a "gentle" religion. It teaches that the sacred (holy) life is found in unselfishness. People who get rid of all greed and selfishness will reach a state of mind known as *nirvana*. Like Hindus, Buddhists also believe in reincarnation. They believe that living beings, including animals, are reborn in another form after death. They see life as a continuing cycle of death and rebirth. A person can only break the cycle of death and suffering by reaching nirvana. Buddhists hope to reach nirvana someday. It is their idea of heaven.

Buddha, the "Enlightened One," had many followers.

3000 B.C.–200 B.C.   *Early Civilizations of India, China, and the Americas*   *Chapter 6*   **103**

2 Teaching the Lesson

Have students read the lesson, and then compare and contrast Buddhism and Hinduism. Each student should draw a Venn diagram. They should write similarities between the religions in the overlapping section of the circles. In the two sections that do not overlap, students should list the main features of Buddhism and Hinduism.

Ask:

- **Who was Gautama?** (He was a young man who gave up his wealth to live according to the four noble truths. He became known as Buddha, or Enlightened One.)
- **Who was Asoka?** (the third emperor of the Maurya who followed Buddha's teachings about brotherly love)
- **Why is a caste system not part of Buddhism?** (Buddha taught that all people are alike.)

Background Information

Karma, or a belief that all actions have consequences, is central to Buddhism. As such, Buddhists believe that the lives of people are influenced by their past actions. People are responsible for their actions and the effects of those actions. Thus, every individual is responsible for his or her life, and the joy or pain they impose on others. Karma is linked to all past lives and affects future lives through reincarnation.

LEARNING STYLES

Auditory/Verbal

Ask a volunteer to orally summarize the information about Buddhism. Ask another volunteer to do the same for the Maurya empire. This exercise will make it easier for auditory/verbal learners to understand and retain the information presented in this lesson.

3 Reinforce and Extend

Emperor
A person who rules a group of different countries, lands, or peoples

Foreign
From another country; having to do with another country

You Decide
Do you think that Asoka was a wise ruler? Why or why not?

Reading Strategy:
Inferencing

What can you infer about the way the Indians reacted to the rise of Buddhism?

In 321 B.C., a new empire was created in northern India. It was called the Maurya empire. The third Maurya **emperor** was named Asoka. Asoka's rule began in about 268 B.C. He followed Buddha's teachings about brotherly love. Asoka made Buddhism the state religion. He taught that all people and animals were to be loved.

Buddha's teachings were very different for the Indians. They were used to Hindu ways. However, the Hindu caste system weakened during Asoka's rule. New laws treated all people more equally.

India's Maurya empire came to an end about 185 B.C. Then one **foreign** land after another invaded India. Most Indians went back to the Hindu religion. Buddhism, however, had spread. Followers of Buddha carried their ideas to China, Japan, and other parts of Asia. Beautiful Buddhist temples and pagodas are still standing today. They show that the gentle religion is still an important part of Asia's culture.

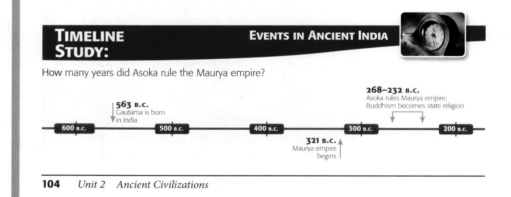

TIMELINE STUDY: **EVENTS IN ANCIENT INDIA**

How many years did Asoka rule the Maurya empire?

268–232 B.C.
Asoka rules Maurya empire; Buddhism becomes state religion

563 B.C.
Gautama is born in India

600 B.C.   500 B.C.   400 B.C.   300 B.C.   200 B.C.

321 B.C.
Maurya empire begins

Reading Strategy:
Inferencing

Remind students that inferences are conclusions based on observations, facts, or experiences. In this case, most Indians went back to the Hindu religions, so one can infer that they were against the rise of Buddhism.

TIMELINE STUDY

Answer: 36 years

Make copies of the timeline and distribute them to students. Encourage students to add additional details to the timeline as they read the lesson.

REVIEW

On a sheet of paper, write the letter of the answer that correctly completes each sentence.

1. Siddhartha Gautama was born about _____ B.C., which was long before Jesus or Muhammad.

   A 563   **B** 321   **C** 268   **D** 185

2. Although Gautama was born a _____, he chose a different path.

   A slave   **B** farmer   **C** warrior   **D** prince

3. Gautama believed the sorrows of the world are caused by _____.

   A war   **B** selfishness   **C** unskilled workers   **D** kings

4. Gautama was called Buddha, which means _____.

   A "Enlightened One"   **C** "untouchable"
   B "nobleman"   **D** "gentle one"

5. The Buddhists believed that people should work to get rid of all greed and selfishness. In doing so, a person will reach a state of mind known as _____.

   A religion   **B** reincarnation   **C** nirvana   **D** Vishnu

6. The Mauryan emperor _____ made Buddhism the state religion.

   A Aryan   **B** Asoka   **C** Gautama   **D** Siddhartha

7. Buddhism has spread to China, _____, and other parts of Asia.

   A Egypt   **B** Babylon   **C** Japan   **D** Turkey

On a sheet of paper, write the answer to each question. Use complete sentences.

8. Why did Gautama give up his wealth and go to live in the forests?

9. What is Buddhism based on?

10. What does Buddhism teach?

WORLD CULTURES

All art of Buddha has similar attributes of symmetry and a sense of peace. Images of Buddha range from man to god. In sculptures of Buddha during the third century B.C., he is dressed in flowing robes, showing the influence of Greek culture. Some sculptures and paintings show Buddha in the yoga position. The lower part of the body is hidden, but the upper body is strong and depicted in perfect proportion.

Lesson 6–2 Review Answers

1. A **2.** D **3.** B **4.** A **5.** C **6.** B **7.** C
8. He saw many poor people and much human suffering. He gave up his wealth and lived simply. During this time, he thought about how life could be better for people.
9. Buddhism is based on brotherly love. **10.** It teaches that the sacred life is found in unselfishness. This means that people must get rid of all greed and selfishness.

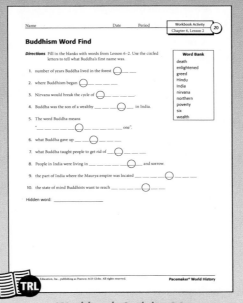

Activity 20   Workbook Activity 20

Lesson at a Glance

Chapter 6 Lesson 3

Overview This lesson describes the achievements of the early Chinese dynasties and the isolation of the Chinese culture.

Objectives

- To explain why the Chinese empire remained separated from the rest of the world
- To tell why Chinese culture did not change for thousands of years
- To explain why the Great Wall of China was built
- To name three dynasties that ruled China during ancient times

Student Pages 106–111

Teacher's Resource Library

Workbook Activity 21

Activity 21

Modified Activity 21

Vocabulary

ancestor	dynasty
barrier	isolate
collapse	raid

Have each student create a graphic organizer for Early China using the vocabulary words for this lesson. Suggest that they place the phrase "Early China" in the center of the organizer. Different aspects of Early China can branch off from the center. Remind students that a graphic organizer can take different shapes as long as it presents information in a clear, concise manner.

PRONUNCIATION GUIDE

Use this list to help students pronounce difficult words in this lesson.

Huang He (hwäng´ hě´)

Yangtze (yang´ sē)

Shi Huangdi (shoe´ hwäng dē)

Early China

Objectives

- To explain why the Chinese empire remained separated from the rest of the world
- To tell why Chinese culture did not change for thousands of years
- To explain why the Great Wall of China was built
- To name three dynasties that ruled China during ancient times

Reading Strategy:
Inferencing

What sorts of things can you infer the early Chinese wrote about?

Ancestor
A person from whom one is descended

They called themselves the *Black-haired People.* They lived in the valley of the Huang He, or Yellow River, in China. Their civilization grew up apart from the rest of the world. Steep mountains, wide deserts, and deep seas circled their lands. Northern China and the people of the Huang He Valley were cut off from other civilizations.

What Was Life Like in the Huang He Valley?

Most of the people in the Huang He Valley were farmers. They fought floods that were so terrible that the Huang He became known as "China's Sorrow."

They dug pitlike houses in the ground and wove roofs of grass. Their kings lived in palaces made of wood and mud.

In 1700 B.C., these early Chinese learned to write. They cut letters, or characters, into animal bones. They kept a record of their own history. It is one of the world's oldest written histories.

The people of the Huang He Valley made fine cloth. They raised silkworms. They carefully unwound the long, thin threads that the silkworms spun. They wove the threads into silk cloth.

The Chinese had a special feeling for their **ancestors,** the people from whom they were descended. They also showed honor toward their homes, their families, and their land. There were many rules of courtesy in the Chinese culture. Those rules made it possible for large families to live together happily.

---

1 Warm-Up Activity

Have students locate the Chang Jiang (Yangtze) and Huang He (Yellow) rivers on the map on page 107. On a small piece of a paper, have each student write one reason why people settle along rivers. Have students fold their paper and place it in a cup. Mix up the papers. Each student should pull out a piece of paper and read the reason. Place those with the same reason in small groups. Each group should discuss their reason, and then report on how the reason applies to the Chang Jiang or Huang He River.

Reading Strategy:
Inferencing

Point out that people often write about the things that most affect them. Many early Chinese were strongly affected by the Huang He River, with its terrible floods. The Chinese also place great emphasis on family and ancestors.

Dynasty
A family that rules a country for a long period of time

The Chinese culture did not change for many thousands of years. This is because people honored the ways of their ancestors. Also, the land was cut off from the rest of the world.

What Dynasties Ruled China During Ancient Times?

A period of rule in China is called a **dynasty.** For about 500 years, Shang kings ruled the Huang He Valley. This period is called the Shang dynasty.

**The Shang Dynasty,
Huang He (Yellow River) Valley, China**

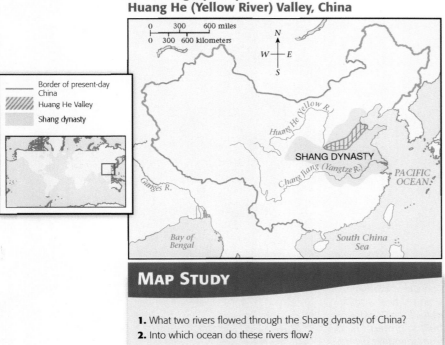

Border of present-day China
Huang He Valley
Shang dynasty

MAP STUDY

1. What two rivers flowed through the Shang dynasty of China?
2. Into which ocean do these rivers flow?

Have students read the section about Chinese dynasties. Students should then make a timeline, showing the dynasties in chronological order. Have students write two or three details about each dynasty next to the name of the dynasty on their timelines.

Ask:

- **What were the four great dynasties of China?** (Shang, Zhou, Qin, and Han)
- **Why didn't Chinese culture change for many thousands of years?** (People honored the ways of their ancestors, and the land was cut off from the rest of the world.)

Background Information

In addition to the Great Wall of China, early Chinese built the Grand Canal. The 1,100-mile waterway joined the Huang He and Chang Jiang rivers. Work on the canal began about 2,400 years ago. During the course of construction, some two million workers died, became ill, or ran away. The Grand Canal is the oldest human-made waterway and is still in use. In the mid-20th century, workers straightened and widened the canal, allowing it to carry bigger ships. Ask students to brainstorm a list of other famous canals. (Possibilities include the Erie, the Suez, and the Panama canals.)

MAP STUDY

Answers:

1. Huang He (Yellow River) and Chang Jiang (Yangtze River)

2. The Pacific Ocean

Around 1028 B.C., a warlike people, the Zhou, came to power. The Zhou leaders developed systems of irrigation and flood control. They also extended their rule southward. Chinese civilization now reached from the Huang He to the Chang Jiang, or Yangtze River. The powerful Zhou dynasty lasted for more than 750 years.

The name *China* may have come from Qin. The Qin family ruled China from 221 B.C. until 206 B.C. This period was called the Qin dynasty. Shi Huangdi was the first Qin emperor. His empire was the first Chinese empire with a strong central government.

The Great Wall of China is over 4,000 miles long. It was built to protect China from invading armies.

Barrier
Something that blocks the way; a wall

Raid
To attack suddenly; a surprise attack

Isolate
To set apart from others; alone

Collapse
To fall apart

Reading Strategy:
Inferencing

What did you already know about the Great Wall of China? Did this help you with your understanding?

History Fact
The Great Wall of China was built to prevent people from entering China. Another famous wall—the Berlin Wall—was built by East Germany in 1961 to prevent people from leaving the country. You will read about this in Chapter 29. The Berlin Wall was torn down in 1989.

Shi Huangdi planned the Great Wall of China. China had many natural **barriers** to keep people from other countries, or foreigners, out. Mountains and deserts lay all around. The only border that could be easily crossed was to the north. Enemies crossed this northern border to **raid,** or attack, Chinese farms. The Chinese of an earlier period had also tried to protect the border. Short walls had been built by the Zhou dynasty. Shi Huangdi decided to connect these walls. He wanted to build one great stone wall. Work on the wall continued on and off until around A.D. 1600.

The Great Wall of China is over 4,000 miles long. It is the longest structure ever built! The Great Wall is 30 feet high and about 20 feet wide at the top. The wall once had 2,500 watchtowers. It helped to protect the northern borders from invaders, especially those on horseback. It also further set China apart, or **isolated** them, from the rest of the world.

Shi Huangdi had planned a wall that would last for thousands of years. Unfortunately, the Qin dynasty only lasted a few years. It was expensive to build the wall. So Shi Huangdi forced people to pay high taxes. Many people began to hate the Qin dynasty. Soon after the emperor died in 210 B.C., a civil war broke out. The Qin dynasty quickly fell apart, or **collapsed.** By 206 B.C., the Han dynasty had gained control of China.

The Han dynasty is known as the first Golden Age of China. For more than 400 years, the Han dynasty (206 B.C.–A.D 220) changed China in important ways. The Han military expanded China's empire by conquering large areas of land. Today, the influence of the Han can be seen in the culture and people of China. More than 90 percent of people identify themselves as the "People of the Han."

3000 B.C.–200 B.C. *Early Civilizations of India, China, and the Americas* Chapter 6 **109**

Reading Strategy:
Inferencing

Have students make a three-column chart with the following headings: What I Know, What I Want to Know, and What I Learned. Before they read the lesson about China, have students fill in the first two columns. After reading, have them fill in the third column.

History Fact
Show students photos of the Berlin Wall before and after it was torn down. Discuss the advantages and disadvantages of using walls and other barriers to isolate people.

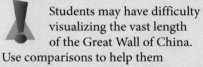

3 **Reinforce and Extend**

COMMON ERROR

Students have been raised in a world of rapid transportation. They may not realize the barriers posed by geographic features in ancient times. Remind them that early people only had a few means of available transportation, such as boats, horses, and animal-drawn carts. They often walked from place to place. Discuss the difficulties presented by traveling long distances over mountains and deserts on foot.

TEACHER ALERT

Students may have difficulty visualizing the vast length of the Great Wall of China. Use comparisons to help them understand. For example, the Great Wall is more than 4,000 miles long. From sea to sea, the United States is about 2,400 miles across.

COMMON ERROR

Students may read about the reaction of Chinese people to Shi Huangdi's taxes and infer that all taxes are bad. Explain that taxes help finance many worthwhile programs, including those that provide aid for the poor and the elderly. Taxes help support the military and education. They pay for crucial infrastructure, such as highways and bridges. They also help provide disaster relief. Lead a class discussion on programs financed by taxes that benefit students directly or indirectly.

Early Civilizations Chapter 6 **109**

LEARNING STYLES

Auditory/Verbal

After students read about Confucius on page 110, have them work in groups to research five of the teachings of this philosopher. Ask each group to create a visual presentation of their work. Arrange with another teacher to have the groups present their projects to a younger class. Students should be prepared to answer questions from the younger students.

CAREER CONNECTION

The Chinese honor and revere their ancestors. Keeping an accurate record of a family's ancestry was difficult in early civilizations. Today we have genealogists to study ancestry. Genealogists do extensive research to discover the ancestry of a family. They may examine public records to learn where people lived, what jobs they performed, how many children they had, or what property they owned. Genealogists also seek out and interview living family members. The information they gather can lead to a better understanding of a family's past history or lifestyle. It may also bring together families who have been separated by immigration, war, or adoption. On a larger scale, genealogists contribute to historical studies by showing how families change and move within a community or even a nation.

GREAT NAMES IN HISTORY

Confucius

Confucius was born in 551 B.C. For more than 2,000 years, his ideas were the single strongest influence on Chinese life. Confucius gave people rules to live by. He was most interested in how people treated each other.

"Never do to others what you would not like them to do to you," Confucius taught. He taught that family life was most important. In China, large family groups lived together. Grandparents, parents, and children usually shared the same house. Therefore, if family members loved and honored each other, the family would enjoy good fortune. Old people were honored. Ancestors were respected. Respect for the ways of the ancestors kept Chinese culture from changing.

Confucius prized scholarship, or knowledge, and taught that a ruler should govern by good example. He thought that if a ruler used force to govern, the ruler had failed. In China, only well-educated people could be government officials. The greatest honor came to a family if a son became a scholar. Then he could study to take the government exams. The examination was based on the teachings of Confucius. A young man who passed the exams could become an official.

For centuries in China, people had to take tests to hold government jobs. China had the world's first civil service system.

The teachings of Confucius were so important that they were made the state religion of China.

GREAT NAMES IN HISTORY

Confucius was the most important philosopher in Chinese history. He emphasized character and morals, and greatly influenced the culture of Asia, including China, Japan, Korea, and Vietnam. Some of his more famous sayings are listed below:

- [A good man] does not worry about not being known by others but rather worries about not knowing them.
- If one's acts are motivated by profit, he will have many enemies.
- The superior man is ashamed that his words exceed his deeds.

On a sheet of paper, write the letter of the answer that correctly completes each sentence.

1. The Huang He Valley was surrounded by steep mountains, wide deserts, and deep seas. Because of this, the people _____ the rest of the world.

   A were connected to   **C** traded with
   B were isolated from   **D** fought with

2. People of the Huang He Valley fought terrible _____.

   A armies   **B** rodents   **C** floods   **D** storms

3. People in the Huang He Valley made fine _____ cloth.

   A silk   **B** reeds   **C** grass   **D** cotton

Word Bank

Han
Qin
Shang
Zhou

On a sheet of paper, write the word from the Word Bank to complete each sentence correctly.

4. The _____ dynasty ruled the Huang He Valley for about 500 years.

5. The _____ dynasty, a warlike people, spread their rule south toward the Chang Jiang.

6. Shi Huangdi, from the _____ dynasty, planned the Great Wall of China.

7. When the Qin dynasty collapsed, the _____ dynasty gained control of China.

On a sheet of paper, write the answer to each question. Use complete sentences.

8. Why did the Chinese culture remain the same for thousands of years?

9. Why was the Great Wall of China built?

10. What were three things that Confucius taught?

Lesson 6–3 Review Answers
1. B **2.** C **3.** A **4.** Shang **5.** Zhou
6. Qin **7.** Han **8.** The Chinese culture remained the same for thousands of years because people honored the ways of their ancestors and because the land was physically cut off from the rest of the world. **9.** The Great Wall of China was built to prevent people from entering China from the north. **10.** Confucius taught people to treat others as you would like to be treated, that family life was most important, and that old people were to be honored and respected.

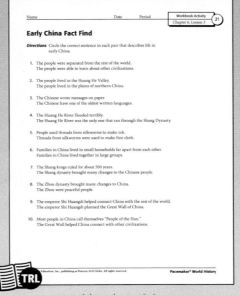

Lesson at a Glance

Chapter 6 Lesson 4

Overview This lesson describes the first Americans and where they likely came from. Students will learn about the early cultures of the Americas.

Objectives

■ To describe how scientists believe people came to the Americas
■ To name two early civilizations in the Americas
■ To name three new crops grown in the Americas

Student Pages 112–116

Teacher's Resource Library

Workbook Activity 22

Activity 22

Modified Activity 22

Vocabulary

shrine

Have students work in pairs to write a paragraph using the vocabulary word. The word should be underlined for emphasis each time it is used. Ask students to read their paragraphs aloud.

1 Warm-Up Activity

Have students examine the map on page 113. Point out the Bering Strait. Note how close Asia and North America are to one another. Ask students to infer how ancient people might have migrated from Siberia into North America. (The strait was covered with ice during the migration.)

You Decide

Explain that some historical and scientific questions may never be answered with complete certainty. Regardless of the position students take, they should base their answers on logic and facts.

Early America

Objectives

■ To describe how scientists believe people came to the Americas
■ To name two early civilizations in the Americas
■ To name three new crops grown in the Americas

 You Decide

Nobody knows for sure that American Indians migrated to North America over a land bridge. What do you think? Why?

There were faraway lands that the people of the Middle East and Asia knew nothing about. For the most part, these lands were wild, with thick woods and deep rain forests. They were lands that would one day be known as North and South America.

What Was the Land Bridge?

American Indians lived in the Americas. Many American Indians believe that their people have always lived there. Many scientists believe that the Indians first came from Asia. They say that the Indians traveled across a bridge of land and ice at the Bering Strait. Such a land bridge would have stretched 56 miles between Asia and Alaska. No trace of a land bridge exists now.

Why would these people have crossed the land bridge? Perhaps they were following animal herds. Then, over thousands of years, they kept on traveling south. Some stayed in North America. Others continued on to Central and South America.

For a long time, the people hunted and fished for their food. Then farming settlements began to spring up. This took place about 5,000 years after the people of the Middle East and Asia began farming. The new lands produced new crops. Farmers grew *maize,* or Indian corn. They grew squash, tomatoes, and beans.

South American farmers grew cotton as early as 3000 B.C. They raised herds of tall, woolly animals called llamas. They wove the llama wool into beautiful cloth.

Possible Route to the Americas

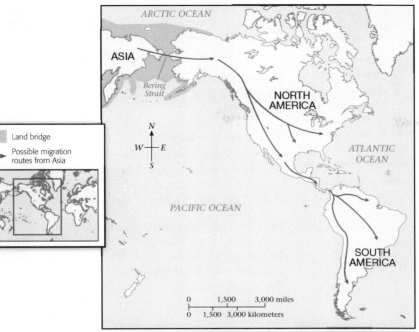

Land bridge

→ Possible migration routes from Asia

MAP STUDY

1. Which body of water did the land bridge cross?
2. Which America did the people from Asia reach first?

Who Were the Olmecs?

A people called the Olmecs built what might have been the first real city in the Americas. Their city was in Mexico, just west of the Gulf of Mexico. Archaeologists have discovered Olmec jade and pottery dating back to 1200 B.C.

Have students examine a globe or world map to find out where the Olmecs and Maya were located. Then have students read the lesson to learn about the cultures of these early American civilizations.

Ask:

- **Where were the Olmec and Maya civilizations?** (Mexico and Central America)
- **What was impressive about the way the Olmecs did their carvings?** (They made their carvings without metal tools and without the wheel.)
- **When was the Mayan civilization strongest?** (from about 250 B.C. to A.D. 800)

COMMON ERROR

Students may think that people have always been in the Americas. Have them trace the possible path of migration on the map on page 113. Have interested students research the evidence that leads scientists to believe that humans migrated to the Americas. Ask them to share their research with the class.

MAP STUDY

Answers:

1. Bering Strait

2. North America

Background Information

The Olmecs created the first great civilization in Mesoamerica. Mesoamerica is a term for Mexico and Central America together. The Olmecs may have been the mother culture of later Native American civilizations in the area, meaning that later civilizations were influenced by the Olmec culture.

The Olmecs are especially known for their art. They carved huge heads from single blocks of stone. They also made tiny figures out of jade and other gemstones. Some figures are less than three inches tall.

The Olmecs' mammoth stone heads have flat faces, full downturned lips, and almond-shaped eyes. The heads all wear a kind of helmet that is tied at the back with a knot. Many scientists think the heads are of Olmec kings. The most famous head is called el Rey, or "the King," by people in the area of San Lorenzo, Mexico, where it was discovered.

The Olmecs liked to carve figurines, masks, and ornaments out of dark blue jade. A group of 16 figurines made from jade and other materials was found at La Venta, Mexico, in 1955. The largest figurine was 7 inches tall. All the figurines have faces like the huge stone faces. The heads are shaved and misshapen by binding in infancy. The figurines are arranged as if they are at a meeting.

Shrine
A place of worship believed to be sacred or holy

Remember
Historians believe the Sumerians first used the wheel in 3000 B.C. on their chariots.

Reading Strategy:
Inferencing

What inferences can you make in comparing the Olmecs and the Mayas?

The Olmecs carved giant heads out of stone. Some of their carvings are more than nine feet tall. The Olmecs also built places to worship, called **shrines,** atop high mounds of earth. The Olmecs did an amazing job. They worked without metal tools and without the wheel.

The Olmecs had a system of counting. They also invented a simple calendar. The Olmec civilization lasted for more than 1,000 years.

Who Were the Maya?

Just as the Olmec civilization ended, the Maya arose. The Maya civilization began in southern Mexico and Central America. The Maya cleared rain forests and built towns. They built temples to the gods of rain and of earth.

The Maya used what the Olmecs had learned. They studied the Olmec calendar. Then they watched the sun, the moon, and the stars. They made their own calendar. It showed many feast days set aside to honor their gods. The Maya civilization was strongest from about 250 B.C. until A.D. 800.

TECHNOLOGY CONNECTION

State-of-the-Art Communication

The Maya had one of the most detailed communication systems of their time. Their language had more than 800 different symbols. Their writings were carved on buildings, pillars, stairways, and wooden objects. They were written on paper as well as on walls and pottery.

The Maya wrote about cycles of time in detailed calendars. They wrote about traditions and customs. They described flowers and animals.

The Maya kept records of history, particularly their own rulers and ancestors. They told of victories over other cultures that usually included bloody human sacrifices to the gods.

Researchers have been studying Maya writings for over 100 years. About 85 percent of the writing found has been translated. Computers help compare findings in order to make more new discoveries.

114   *Unit 2   Ancient Civilizations*

LEARNING STYLES

Interpersonal/Group Learning
Place students in small groups. Have each group work cooperatively to write a page of a Mayan or Olmec newspaper. The pages might include a sports section, a weather report, a local news item, and an advertisement. Encourage groups to use the information in this lesson to compile their newspapers. Students should do additional research on their selected culture.

Remember
Direct students back to Chapter 3 and the discussion on Sumerians. Have them list other achievements by the Sumerians, such as the invention of writing.

Reading Strategy:
Inferencing

Students should infer that both civilizations were religious, innovative, and interested in the natural world.

3   Reinforce and Extend

TECHNOLOGY CONNECTION

Have students work in small groups to develop symbols that represent the spoken word. For example, students might use a picture of a hawk to represent *bird* or a smiling face to represent *happy*. Challenge students to form a sentence using only symbols. Have students exchange sentences and try to interpret each other's work.

The Maya temple is in Chichén Itzá, Mexico.

When the Olmecs built shrines in Mexico, what crop had been farmed there for 1,900 years?

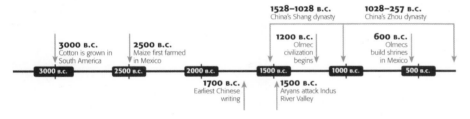

1528–1028 B.C.
China's Shang dynasty

1028–257 B.C.
China's Zhou dynasty

3000 B.C.
Cotton is grown in
South America

2500 B.C.
Maize first farmed
in Mexico

1200 B.C.
Olmec
civilization
begins

600 B.C.
Olmecs
build shrines
in Mexico

3000 B.C.   2500 B.C.   2000 B.C.   1500 B.C.   1000 B.C.   500 B.C.

1700 B.C.
Earliest Chinese
writing

1500 B.C.
Aryans attack Indus
River Valley

3000 B.C.–200 B.C.   *Early Civilizations of India, China, and the Americas*   *Chapter 6*   **115**

ELL/ESL STRATEGY

 Language Objective:
*To learn more about
the first Americans*

Have ELL students
write the three questions that form
the headings in this lesson in their
notebooks. Then ask students to
scan through each section to find
the answer to the question. Have
them write the answer in their own
words below the question. When
students have finished, they will have
an outline of the lesson, which they
can use as a study tool. Students can
repeat this activity for other lessons
in upcoming chapters.

TIMELINE STUDY

Answer: maize

Make copies of the timeline and
distribute them to students. Challenge
them to place events in ancient India on
the timeline of ancient China and the
Americas.

Lesson 6–4 Review Answers
1. A **2.** D **3.** C **4.** B **5.** A **6.** B
7. Scientists believe that people came to America by walking across a bridge of land and ice at the Bering Straight. The first Americans might have been following animal herds. **8.** Farmers grew maize, squash, tomatoes, beans, and cotton. **9.** The Olmecs worked without metal tools and without the wheel. **10.** The Maya studied the Olmec calendar to make their own calendar.

REVIEW

On a sheet of paper, write the letter of the answer that correctly completes each sentence.

1. Olmec jade and pottery have been discovered dating back to _____.

   A 1200 B.C.   **B** 600 B.C.   **C** 250 B.C.   **D** A.D. 800

2. The Olmecs built places of worship, known as _____, atop high mounds of earth.

   A rocks   **B** anthills   **C** temples   **D** shrines

3. The Olmec civilization lasted over _____ years.

   A 50   **B** 100   **C** 1,000   **D** 5,000

4. The Maya civilization began as the Olmec civilization _____.

   A began   **C** was at its height
   B ended   **D** started growing maize

5. The Maya built towns after clearing away _____.

   A rainforests **B** swampland **C** crops   **D** rocks

6. The Maya built _____ to the gods of rain and earth.

   A shrines   **B** temples   **C** churches **D** stone walls

On a sheet of paper, write the answer to each question. Use complete sentences.

7. How and why do scientists believe people came to the Americas?

8. What crops were grown in early America?

9. Why are the shrines the Olmecs built considered to be so amazing?

10. What did the Maya borrow from the Olmecs?

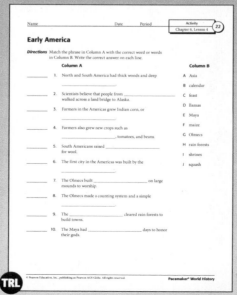

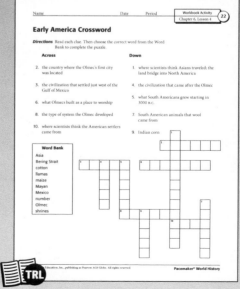

Activity 22   Workbook Activity 22

- An early civilization developed along the Indus River Valley in what is now India and Pakistan. One major city was Mohenjo-Daro. It grew peacefully for about 1,000 years.

- The Aryans from the north destroyed Mohenjo-Daro around 1500 B.C. They brought a caste system to India. The Aryans' religion developed from the Hindu religion. They believed in rebirth, or reincarnation.

- A prince named Siddhartha Gautama gave up his wealth to help the poor. He developed a new religion called Buddhism.

- The Maurya empire began in northern India in 321 B.C. Its emperor, Asoka, made Buddhism the official religion of the empire. The empire ended in 185 B.C. Followers of Buddha spread the religion to other parts of Asia.

- An early Chinese civilization grew up along the Huang He, or Yellow River. These people learned to write in about 1700 B.C. They left one of the world's oldest written histories.

- The Shang dynasty ruled China for about 500 years.

- The warlike Zhou dynasty came to power around 1028 B.C. The Chinese civilization grew under the Zhou leaders for about 750 years.

- The Qin dynasty ruled China from 221 B.C. to 206 B.C. Its first emperor, Shi Huangdi, began work on the Great Wall of China. Work on the wall continued on and off until around A.D. 1600.

- The Great Wall of China, at 4,000 miles long, is the longest structure ever built.

- American Indians may have descended from people who crossed a land bridge from Asia to the North American continent.

- The Olmecs of Mexico were one of the earliest civilizations in America. Their civilization lasted for more than 1,000 years.

- The Maya built cities in southern Mexico and Central America.

3000 B.C.–200 B.C. *Early Civilizations of India, China, and the Americas* Chapter 6 **117**

Chapter 6 Summary

Have students read the Chapter Summary on page 117 to review the main ideas presented in Chapter 6.

Ask:

- Who destroyed the city of Mohenjo-Daro? (the Aryans)

- What did Siddhartha Guatama develop? (a new religion called Buddhism)

- Which emperor made Buddhism the official religion of northern India? (Asoka)

- Name one achievement of the early Chinese civilization that grew up along the Huang He, or Yellow River. (They created one of the world's oldest written histories.)

- Which Chinese dynasty came after the warlike Zhou? (the Qin dynasty)

- Describe the historic accomplishment of the first Qin emperor, Shi Huangdi. (He began work on the Great Wall of China. The wall is 4,000 miles long. It is the longest structure ever built.)

- How did American Indians likely reach North America? (They crossed a land bridge from Asia to North America.)

- Name two early America civilizations. (the Olmecs of Mexico and the Maya of southern Mexico and Central America)

TEACHER'S RESOURCE

The AGS Globe Teaching Strategies in Social Studies Transparencies may be used with this chapter. The transparencies add an interactive dimension to expand and enhance the Pacemaker® *World History* program content.

CHAPTER PROJECT FOLLOW-UP

Have a study fair in which students display the results of their research on tables set up around the room. Have students present information about their topic in the form of models, posters, drawings, or photo collages. For example, a calendar can represent the Mayan civilization. A model of the Great Wall can represent early Chinese dynasties. Have each student give a brief oral presentation about their topic.

Chapter 6 Review

Use the Chapter Review to prepare students for tests and to reteach content from the chapter.

Chapter 6 Mastery Test

The Teacher's Resource Library includes two forms of the Chapter 6 Mastery Test. Each test addresses the chapter Goals for Learning. An optional third page of additional critical-thinking items is included for each test. The difficulty level of the two forms is equivalent.

Chapter 6 Review Answers

Vocabulary Review

1. class

2. ancestors

3. enlightened

4. caste

5. shrine

6. reincarnation

7. dynasty

8. isolated

9. foreign

Chapter Review Questions

10. The Aryans believed they were better than the people they conquered.

11. Buddhism teaches unselfishness and love for all people and animals.

12. Farmers had to fight terrible floods.

13. The Chinese honored their ancestors and showed courtesy toward their homes, families, and lands. Rules helped family members live together happily.

Word Bank

ancestors

caste

class

dynasty

enlightened

foreign

isolated

reincarnation

shrine

Vocabulary Review

On a sheet of paper, use the words from the Word Bank to complete each sentence correctly.

1. Unskilled workers are the lowest _____, or caste, according to the Indians.

2. All people are descended from their _____.

3. A(n) _____ person knows the truth.

4. A social class in India is called a(n) _____.

5. A(n) _____ is a place of worship.

6. According to the belief of _____, a person who dies is reborn.

7. The Shang kings were a(n) _____.

8. The mountains and deserts surrounding China kept the Chinese _____.

9. India was invaded by many _____ lands.

Chapter Review Questions

On a sheet of paper, write the answer to each question. Use complete sentences.

10. What did the Aryans believe about the people they conquered?

11. Why is Buddhism known as a gentle religion?

12. Why was the Huang He, or Yellow River, known as "China's sorrow"?

13. What helped family members live together happily in China?

14. What is the longest structure ever built?

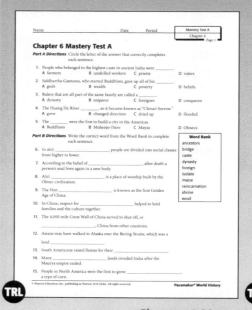

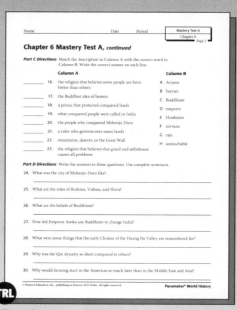

Chapter 6 Mastery Test A, pages 1–3

15. How might Asians have first traveled to North America?

16. What were four American Indian crops?

Critical Thinking

On a sheet of paper, write your response to each question. Use complete sentences.

17. Was it good or bad for China to be isolated for a long time?

18. How were the Olmecs and Maya like ancient civilizations in India and China?

Using the Timelines

Use the timelines on pages 104 and 115 to answer the questions.

19. Which was grown first in the Americas, cotton or maize?

20. How many years passed between the time the Olmecs built their shrines in the Americas and Gautama was born in India?

GROUP ACTIVITY

Form groups of three or four. Create a guidebook to the most interesting structures around the world. You might begin with the Great Wall of China or the Great Pyramid of Egypt. Ask classmates to name places they have been to or know about. Do some further research. Arrange your guidebook in some kind of order, such as alphabetical or geographical.

3000 B.C.–200 B.C.   *Early Civilizations of India, China, and the Americas*   **Chapter 6**   **119**

---

14. The Great Wall of China is the longest structure ever built.

15. Asians may have traveled to North America over a bridge of land and ice at the Bering Strait.

16. American Indians grew maize, squash, tomatoes, and beans.

Critical Thinking

17. Possible answers: It was good, because people honored the ways of their ancestors and lived happily with their families. Also, a culture of learning developed. It was bad, because someday foreigners would come and the Chinese might not have the experience to deal with them.

18. Possible answers: The civilizations in the Americas moved from hunting to farming. The people were religious; they built temples to their gods.

Using the Timelines

19. cotton

20. 37 years

GROUP ACTIVITY

Students' guidebooks may feature any important or beautiful buildings or other structures around the world. The book should be attractive and in some kind of order, such as geographical.

Chapter 6 Mastery Test B, pages 1–3

Early Civilizations Chapter 6   **119**

UNIT 3

PLANNING GUIDE

The Origins of Western Civilization: Greece and Rome: 1500 B.C.–A.D. 400

	Student Pages	Vocabulary	Map Study	Reading Strategy	Lesson Review	Chapter Summary/Review
Chapter 7 Greek City-States and the Golden Age	122–141	✔		✔		139–141
Lesson 7–1 The Sea and Ancient Greece	124–127	✔	✔	✔	127	
Lesson 7–2 Athens and Sparta	128–131	✔		✔	131	
Lesson 7–3 Fighting in Greece	132–135	✔		✔	135	
Lesson 7–4 The End of an Empire	136–138	✔		✔	138	
Chapter 8 Alexander the Great	142–157	✔		✔		155–157
Lesson 8–1 King Philip and Alexander	144–146	✔		✔	146	
Lesson 8–2 Alexander's Conquests	147–151	✔	✔	✔	151	
Lesson 8–3 The End of an Empire	152–154	✔		✔	154	

(Unit Planning Guide is continued on next page.)

Chapter Activities

Teacher's Resource Library
Life Skills Connection 7–9
Key Vocabulary Words 7–9

Assessment Options

Student Text
Chapter Reviews 7–9
Teacher's Resource Library
Chapter 7 Mastery Tests A and B
Chapter 8 Mastery Tests A and B
Chapter 9 Mastery Tests A and B
Unit 3 Mastery Test
Teacher's Edition
Chapter Projects 7–9

	Student Text Features							Teaching Strategies										Learning Styles					Teacher's Resource Library			
	Words from the Past	Learn More About It	Great Names in History	Technology Connection	Geography Note	You Decide/Remember/History Fact	Timeline Study	ELL/ESL Strategy	Background Information	Common Error	Life Skills Connection	Key Vocabulary Words	Study Skills	Applications Home, Career, Community	Online Connection	Teacher Alert	World Cultures	Auditory/Verbal	Body/Kinesthetic	Interpersonal/Group Learning	Logical/Mathematical	Visual/Spatial	Activities/Modified Activities	Workbook Activities	Self-Study Guide	Chapter Outline
											123	123													✔	✔
								125	125	126			126							125	125		23	23		
		130				128–129		129	129	128, 130					130	130		129				129	24	24		
						133		133	133	134				134									25	25		
							137	137	137	138				137, 138		137				137			26	26		
											143	143													✔	✔
						144		145	145	146				146	146		146	145				145	27	27		
		148						149	148	150			150	150		149					149		28	28		
						152	153	153	152					153						153	153		29	29		

Modified Activities

The Teacher's Resource Library (TRL) contains a set of lower-level worksheets called Modified Activities. These worksheets cover the same content as the standard Activities but are written at a lower reading level.

Skill Track

Use Skill Track for *World History* to monitor student progress and meet the demands of adequate yearly progress (AYP). Make informed instructional decisions with individual student and class reports of lesson and chapter assessments. With immediate and ongoing feedback, students will also see what they have learned and where they need more reinforcement and practice.

The Origins of Western Civilization: Greece and Rome: 1500 B.C.–A.D. 400 *(continued)*

	Student Pages	Vocabulary	Map Study	Reading Strategy	Lesson Review	Chapter Summary/Review
			Student Text Lesson			
Chapter 9 The Rise of Rome	158–187	✔		✔		✔
Lesson 9–1 How Rome Grew Powerful	160–164	✔		✔	164	
Lesson 9–2 Julius Caesar	165–168	✔		✔	168	
Lesson 9–3 The Roman Empire	169–171	✔	✔	✔	171	
Lesson 9–4 Roman Society	172–176	✔		✔	176	
Lesson 9–5 Christianity in Rome	177–182	✔	✔	✔	182	
Lesson 9–6 The End of the Empire	183–184			✔	184	

Student Text Features							Teaching Strategies										Learning Styles					Teacher's Resource Library			
Words from the Past	Learn More About It	Great Names in History	Technology Connection	Geography Note	You Decide/Remember/History Fact	Timeline Study	ELL/ESL Strategy	Background Information	Common Error	Life Skills Connection	Key Vocabulary Words	Study Skills	Applications Home, Career, Community	Online Connection	Teacher Alert	World Cultures	Auditory/Verbal	Body/Kinesthetic	Interpersonal/Group Learning	Logical/Mathematical	Visual/Spatial	Activities/Modified Activities	Workbook Activities	Self-Study Guide	Chapter Outline
										159	159													✔	✔
		163	162		161, 162		162	161	162				163								161	30	30		
		166					167	166	168							167	167					31	31		
		169					170	170	171													32	32		
175				173			174	173	175			175	174, 176	175	174							33	33		
					178, 179	181	179	178	180								179	179				34	34		
						183	184	184													184	35	35		

Audio Library 🎧

Skill Track for World History

Teacher's Resource Library **TRL**

Unit 3 Mastery Test

(Answer Keys for the Teacher's Resource Library begin on page 809 of the Teacher's Edition.)

Other Resources

Books for Teachers

Connolly, Peter, and Hazel Dodge. *The Ancient City: Life in Classical Athens and Rome.* New York: Oxford University Press, 1998.

Fantham, Elaine, et al. *Women in the Classical World: Image and Text.* New York: Oxford University Press, 1995.

Books for Students

Freeman, Charles. *The Ancient Greeks.* New York: Oxford University Press, 1996.

Nardo, Don. *The Roman Republic.* San Diego: Lucent Books, 1994.

Videos

Great Cities of the Ancient World: Rome and Pompeii. Questar, 1993. 70 minutes. Recreates the Roman Empire through computer graphics, archival film, and classic art.

Video Visits: Discovering Greece, Questar, 1994. 120 minutes. Focuses on buildings past and present; includes history of the sites.

THE ORIGINS OF WESTERN CIVILIZATION: GREECE AND ROME

Many everyday elements of our world came from the ancient Greeks and Romans. As a theater audience member, you may smile at the plays from the ancient Greeks. You may stop at a post office building which is similar to the style of the Romans' buildings. Perhaps you are learning a foreign language that came from Latin of ancient Rome. By learning about the cultures of these ancient lands, you may better understand some things they gave us.

Chapters in Unit 3

The Colosseum, a brilliant example of ancient Roman architecture, still stands in Rome, Italy.

121

Introducing the Unit

Have students examine the picture of the ruins. Greek and Roman architecture, such as the Coliseum and the Parthenon, still influences the design of buildings today. Explain that in this unit students will learn about the history of ancient Greece and Rome. Ask students what other ways these ancient cultures are reflected in America. (Possible answers: in our democratic government, our legal system, art, vocabulary based in Latin and Greek, the Latin alphabet)

Ask:

- What years will this unit cover? (1500 B.C. to A.D. 400)
- Which ancient civilization provided us with a model for government? (Greece)
- Which ancient civilization is remembered for its legal system? (Rome)

CD-ROM/Software

The Greek and Roman World. Omaha, NE: Educational Software Institute, 1999. Traces the customs and accomplishments of the ancient Greeks and Romans.

Web Sites

www.agsglobepmwh.com/page121a
(This site features interactive activities in ten topics pertaining to life in ancient Greece.)

www.agsglobepmwh.com/page121b
(This site includes links to museums, archeological sites, and monuments of ancient Greece and Rome.)

Greek City-States and the Golden Age

The people of ancient Greece were bold and determined. This was especially true in Greece's two most powerful city-states, Athens and Sparta. Athens was a city-state where its people asked questions. They thought about life and the power of gods, among many other things. They wanted to learn and create beautiful objects of art. The Athenians set up a democracy in which all of its citizens could vote.

Sparta was a very different city-state. Its leaders were members of the military. They focused on building a strong army to defend their lands. Citizens could not vote and many people kept slaves. Eventually the two city-states went to war against each other.

GOALS FOR LEARNING

- To explain the importance of the sea and trading in Greek life
- To compare life in Sparta and Athens
- To describe the series of wars the Greeks fought
- To identify the gifts that Greeks gave us that are part of life today

---

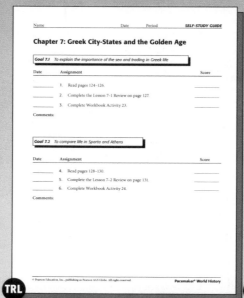

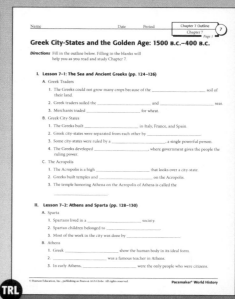

Reading Strategy: Metacognition

Metacognition means "thinking about your thinking." Use metacognition to become a better reader:

- Preview the text.
- Make predictions and ask yourself what you already know about the topic.
- Write the main idea, details, and any questions you have.
- Visualize what is happening in the text. If something does not make sense, go back and read it again.

Key Vocabulary Words

Lesson 1

Govern To rule

Tyrant A ruler who has complete power

Democracy A government that gives the people the ruling power

Citizen A person who has certain rights and duties because he or she lives in a particular city or town

Vote To choose leaders and pass laws

Expand To grow; to stretch

Hostility Feelings of hate or acts of war

Acropolis The hill on which the people in a Greek city built their main temple

Lesson 2

Myth A story, often about gods or goddesses, that is handed down through the years and sometimes used to explain natural events

Laborer A person who does hard work with his or her hands

Revolt To rise up against a government; to refuse to obey the people in charge

Constitution The basic laws and rules of a government

Jury A group of people who listen to the facts and decide if a person on trial is guilty or not guilty

Lesson 3

Democratic Having to do with a government in which all people have equal rights

Plague A deadly disease that spreads quickly

Lesson 4

Architecture The art of building

Athlete A person trained to take part in competitive sports

Introducing the Chapter

Use the word *democracy* to explain to students the profound influence that ancient Greek civilization has had on our language. Ask students to describe how we use the word *democracy* today. Tell students that this form of government had its beginnings in the city-states of ancient Greece. Have students study the goals for the chapter.

Ask:

- Where else have you seen city-states? (Sumer)
- Who governed these earlier city-states? (kings)
- Who rules in a democracy? (the people)

Reading Strategy:
Metacognition

Give students a short newspaper article to read. Have them practice metacognition with the article before reading the chapter. Remind students of the main points of metacognition.

Key Vocabulary Words

Point out that these chapter words are presented in the order they appear in each lesson. They are also found in the glossary.

LIFE SKILLS CONNECTION

Students learn about voting and how to register to vote. Hold mock elections in your class to familiarize students with voting.

KEY VOCABULARY

Students complete the sentences with words from the Word Bank.

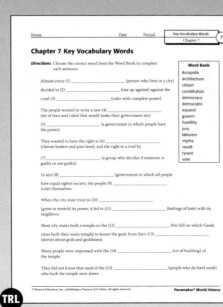

Life Skills Connection 7   Key Vocabulary Words 7

The Sea and Ancient Greece

Lesson at a Glance

Chapter 7 Lesson 1

Overview This lesson describes the development of Greek city-states and their different forms of government.

Objectives

■ To explain why each Greek city-state developed in its own way

■ To contrast two ways that Greek city-states were governed

■ To describe what the Acropolis is

Student Pages 124–127

Teacher's Resource Library

Workbook Activity 23

Activity 23

Modified Activity 23

Vocabulary

Acropolis	govern
citizen	hostility
democracy	tyrant
expand	vote

Have students create a crossword puzzle on graph paper using these vocabulary words. Suggest using the definitions or fill-in-the-blank sentences as clues. Allow students to exchange and solve the puzzles.

PRONUNCIATION GUIDE

Use this list to help students pronounce difficult words in this lesson.

Athena (ə thē´ nə)

Parthenon (pär´ thə non)

1 Warm-Up Activity

Have students study the map on page 124 and answer the questions. (1. Athens, Olympia, Sparta, Marathon. 2. Aegean Sea, Mediterranean Sea) Ask them to look at a modern map of the area to determine which place names are the same and which have disappeared. (Marathon and Olympia

Objectives

■ To explain why each Greek city-state developed in its own way

■ To contrast two ways that Greek city-states were governed

■ To describe what the Acropolis is

Most early civilizations were mainly farming societies. The Greek civilization, however, was different. Greece is a very rocky land with many mountains. Much of Greece made poor farmland. The Greeks could not grow much wheat or other grains. Instead, they raised grapevines and olive trees. Greece is surrounded by the sea on almost every side. The Greeks took to the sea and became traders.

Ancient Greece

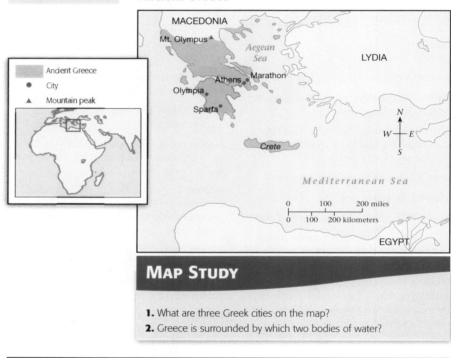

MAP STUDY

1. What are three Greek cities on the map?
2. Greece is surrounded by which two bodies of water?

are gone; Lydia is now Turkey; Sparta and Athens are still cities; Macedonia is smaller.)

2 Teaching the Lesson

Point out that sea travel was easier than overland travel. Show students a relief map of the area, if possible. As students read the chapter, have them keep notes about how the geography of Greece influenced its cities and towns, trade, and farming.

Ask:

● Why did so many Greeks become traders? (Farming was poor, so people's needs had to be met in large part through trade with other places. This meant lots of work for traders. Because Greece was surrounded by the sea, trade could be conducted with other parts of the Mediterranean world.)

● Why did city-states develop many different governments? (They were isolated by mountains and didn't have much contact with each other.)

● What buildings were often built at the Acropolis? (temples and theaters)

Govern
To rule

Tyrant
A ruler who has
complete power

Reading Strategy:
Metacognition

Notice the structure
of this lesson. Look at
the title, headings, and
boldfaced words.

What Did Greek Traders Do?

The Aegean and the Mediterranean seas made perfect
travel lanes. The Greeks traded with most of the
Mediterranean world. Greek traders set up colonies in the
lands they visited. Greek culture spread across the seas.

Greek harbors were always busy. The air was filled with
sounds. There was the clink of Greek coins and foreign
coins. There was the chatter of many different languages
as people of the world met. Merchants traded olive oil for
wheat. Ships from Egypt unloaded papyrus. Ebony and
ivory came in from Africa.

What Were Greek City-States Like?

The earliest people who settled in Greece began to build
villages about 1500 B.C. As time passed, the small villages
grew into city-states. Through trading, the city-states
became wealthy. By about 750 B.C., the Greeks had begun
to build colonies in other areas of the Mediterranean.
Some Greeks settled on the Greek islands. Many others,
however, traveled as far as southern Italy, France, Spain,
and Portugal. They built cities there. Naples, Syracuse, and
Marseilles began as Greek cities. Cities were also built in
western Turkey and on the shores of the Black Sea.

On the Greek mainland, the city-states were becoming
more powerful. The city-states were separated from each
other by rugged mountain ranges. For this reason there
was limited contact between the city-states. Each one
developed in its own way.

Each city-state had its own government. Each had its
own ideas about the way people should live. Some of the
city-states were **governed,** or ruled, by a **tyrant,** a single
powerful person. Some of the tyrants were cruel and
unjust, while others ruled fairly.

1500 B.C.–400 B.C.   *Greek City-States and the Golden Age*   Chapter 7   **125**

Background Information

In ancient Greece, most roads were for
pedestrians, pack animals, and horses.
They were impassable by wheeled
vehicles. Hence, the sea was usually a
less expensive and quicker way to ship
goods. Merchant ships used sails, rather
than oars, and so were at the mercy of the
winds. When ships were sailing into the
wind, travel times between ports could
increase dramatically. At ports, ships were
usually towed in and out of the harbor.

LEARNING STYLES

Logical/Mathematical
Ask students to use the
map on page 124 to answer
questions that you ask.
For example, what direction from
Greece is Lydia? (east) What is
the approximate distance between
the southern tip of Greece and the
western tip of Crete? (about 80 miles
or 120 kilometers)

LEARNING STYLES

**Interpersonal/Group
Learning**
Have students imagine that
they are going on a vacation
to Greece. Tell them to visit a travel
agency and collect brochures and
pamphlets about Greece. They
should decide which cities and towns
they will visit and which sights they
would like to see. Have them prepare
a travel plan for a one-week stay in
Greece.

Reading Strategy:
Metacognition

Explain that when you read something,
you often make a picture of the
information in your mind. You might
also think of questions about the text as
you read. Your mind tries to organize the
information as you read. When you think
about all of these things that you are
thinking about as you read, you are using
metacognition.

ELL/ESL STRATEGY

Language Objective:
To read for meaning

Go over the basics
of outlining, or give
students a skeleton outline to
complete. As students read the
chapter, ask them to use the headings
and subheadings to outline the
chapter.

3 Reinforce and Extend

CHAPTER PROJECT

Students may work individually or in small groups on a topic of their choosing from this list.

- Daily life in ancient Greece (Describe the occupations, housing, food, and economic and social classes of the different groups of Greeks. What did the children do? What was the status of women?)

- Geography of ancient Greece (Use salt-dough or modeling clay that dries to construct a relief map of the Aegean area that shows elevations of various landforms based on a scale of measurement. Paint the map in colors associated with an elevation key. Label the seas surrounding Greece, and the cities of Athens, Sparta, and Marathon. In a presentation, show trade routes and routes taken by ships in war.)

- Weapons of ancient Greece (Describe and illustrate the construction of weapons and how they were used.)

- Ships of ancient Greece (Construct models or drawings of ships used by different groups of ancient Greeks. How and where were they built? How were they powered?)

- Student-proposed topic approved by the teacher (The student should submit a one-paragraph proposal describing the topic and plan of action to the teacher for approval.)

- Suggest different types of products for the projects, such as written and illustrated reports, skits, videos, poems, songs, graphics on mural or chart paper, newspaper articles or newscasts of ancient Greece, and speeches.

Democracy
A government that gives the people the ruling power

Citizen
A person who has certain rights and duties because he or she lives in a particular city or town

Vote
To choose leaders and pass laws

Expand
To grow; to stretch

Hostility
Feelings of hate or acts of war

Acropolis
The hill on which the people in a Greek city built their main temple

Reading Strategy: Metacognition

Remember to look at the photographs and other graphics while you are reading. Also note the descriptive words. This will help you visualize what you are reading.

The first **democracy,** where the government gives people the ruling power, developed in the city-state. There, **citizens** could **vote** and have a say in government.

Because the city-states were so different from each other, they often fought among themselves. Tyrants with big ideas would decide that the time had come to grow, or **expand,** their rule. They would make plans to attack a nearby city-state. They might convince other city-states to join them. There was a constantly shifting pattern of friendship and **hostility** between the different city-states. This was a very unstable political situation. It would later lead to a major war between two of the largest city-states, Athens and Sparta.

What Is the Acropolis?

Each city-state was made up of a city circled by villages and farms. The farms provided food for the citizens. The city offered protection from invaders.

The Greeks usually built their city-states near a high hill. The hill was called the **Acropolis.** On that hill, they built special buildings, such as temples and theaters.

The people who lived in Athens built a beautiful temple atop their Acropolis. It was built to honor the goddess Athena. The temple was called the Parthenon.

The ancient Greeks built the Parthenon on a hill high above the city of Athens.

Reading Strategy: Metacognition

Ask students to point out examples of descriptive words in the section, "What Were Greek City-States Like?" (*small, rugged, powerful, cruel, unjust, fair, unstable*) Discuss how these words help them visualize the city-states.

STUDY SKILLS

On a separate sheet of paper, have students write a single sentence about the main idea of each paragraph in Lesson 1. Tell students that their sentences should answer the subhead questions.

COMMON ERROR

Students may think that sea travel was always faster than land travel. But the Mediterranean has changeable winds, with prevailing winds changing with the seasons or even, locally, with the time of day. When winds were blowing in the wrong direction, sail-powered travel was time-consuming.

REVIEW

Match the description in Column A with the term in Column B.
Write the correct letter on sheet of paper.

Column A

1. a ruler who has complete power

2. a government that gives the people the ruling power

3. the temple built in Athens to honor the goddess Athena

4. the sea Greece was surrounded by (other than the Mediterranean Sea)

5. the high hill the Greeks built their city-states near; they often built special buildings, such as temples and theaters, atop this hill

Column B

A Acropolis
B Aegean
C democracy
D Parthenon
E tyrant

On a sheet of paper, write the answer to each question. Use complete sentences.

6. Why was farming difficult for the Greeks, and what did they do instead?

7. How did Greek traders help to spread Greek culture across the seas?

8. What were some items the Greeks traded?

9. Why did each Greek city-state develop in its own way?

10. Why did Greek city-states often fight with each other?

Lesson 7–1 Review Answers

1. E **2.** C **3.** D **4.** B **5.** A **6.** Greece was a very rocky, mountainous land that made farming difficult. The crops they could raise successfully were grapevines and olive trees. Instead, since Greece is surrounded by the sea on almost every side, the Greeks took to the sea and became traders. **7.** The Greeks traded with most of the Mediterranean world, and set up colonies in the lands they visited. **8.** Merchants would trade olive oil for wheat. They would also trade to get ebony, ivory, and papyrus. **9.** The city-states were separated from each other by rugged mountain ranges, which limited the contact between the city-states. Thus each developed in their own way. **10.** They fought because they were so different from each other. Sometimes, tyrants would want to expand their rule and would plan to attack a nearby city-state. They would try to convince other city-states to join them. This created an unstable political situation.

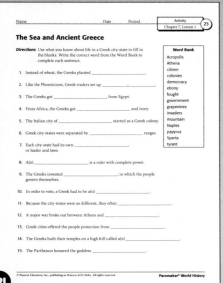

Activity 23

Workbook Activity 23

Lesson at a Glance

Chapter 7 Lesson 2

Overview This lesson describes life in two Greek city-states, Athens and Sparta.

Objectives

- To explain life in Sparta
- To describe the Athenian way of thinking
- To talk about democracy in Athens
- To name two Greek gods or goddesses

Student Pages 128–131

Teacher's Resource Library TRL

Workbook Activity 24

Activity 24

Modified Activity 24

Vocabulary

constitution   myth
jury   revolt
laborer

Ask volunteers to read the definitions of the vocabulary words. Then have each student write a paragraph that correctly uses all the words.

....

1   Warm-Up Activity

Begin the class by announcing that today, all girls with brown eyes (or all girls wearing a certain color, or all girls with another characteristic) will have certain privileges that no one else in the class will have. Describe the privileges (choose things that are looked upon positively as privileges by students in your school). Do not give a reason for this action. If students ask for an explanation, tell them that they will soon be able to figure it out.

2   Teaching the Lesson

Have students create a table with two columns, one for Athens and one for Sparta. As students read this lesson, have them list characteristics of each city. Then have them use their entries to compare the cities.

LESSON 7-2   Athens and Sparta

Objectives

- To explain life in Sparta
- To describe the Athenian way of thinking
- To talk about democracy in Athens
- To name two Greek gods or goddesses

Myth
A story, often about gods or goddesses, that is handed down through the years and sometimes used to explain natural events

History Fact
Today we use the word *spartan* to mean "harsh" or "strict." The word comes from the Spartans of ancient Greece.

Athens and Sparta were the most powerful Greek city-states. Their citizens spoke the same language. They believed in the same gods. They told **myths** or stories about their gods and goddesses. However, life in Athens was quite different from life in Sparta.

What Was Sparta Like?

The Spartans lived in a military society. Sparta's government was led by a small group of men. They were most interested in keeping Sparta a great military power. Spartan children belonged to the state. A healthy boy was turned over to the government at the age of seven. He was raised to be a soldier. He was taught to fight and to stand up under pain. He had to obey orders without question. Soldiers defeated in battle were not allowed to return home.

If a baby boy were born with something wrong, he might be left on a hillside to die. The Spartans only wanted boys who could grow up to be soldiers. Spartans had little use for girls. Girls and women were seldom seen in public. They kept to their houses. The Spartans were great warriors. However, they left the world little in the way of ideas, art, or music.

The Spartans, like most of the Mediterranean peoples, kept slaves. Most of the work in the city was done by slave labor. The Spartan army was often kept busy fighting other city-states. At other times it had the job of keeping rebel slaves in line.

Although life was harsh in Sparta, things were very different in Athens. The Athenians gave less thought to warfare. They were more interested in enjoying life.

Ask:

- What was the main focus of Sparta's government? (maintaining military strength)
- Who could be a citizen in Athens? (men who were not slaves)
- Which city allowed slavery? (both)
- What animal were the Greek gods and goddesses most like? (humans)

History Fact

Have students think of a place or person that they would describe as *spartan*. Ask them to describe their choice.

COMMON ERROR

Students may think that all the Greek gods lived on Mount Olympus. Greeks thought that gods were everywhere, however. Every place, including rivers and springs, had an associated god or a nymph. (A nymph was a female spirit who personified a natural feature.)

The Greeks carved outdoor theaters into hillsides.

What Was Athens Like?

Athens was a wealthy city. The Athenians decided that their wealth gave them more time to enjoy the beauties of life. They wanted their city to be glorious. They built the Parthenon. Their marble statues show the human body in its ideal form. The Athenians put on plays in huge outdoor theaters. For the first time, plays were written about how people thought and acted. Some of these plays are still performed today.

The Athenians took time to ask questions about their world. Great teachers, like Socrates, led the Greeks to ask, "What makes people good? What makes people evil?" "Always ask questions," Socrates taught. So the Greeks questioned, and they learned.

Some Greeks even questioned slavery. That slavery might be wrong was a brand new idea. Most of the ancient world used slaves to do hard work as **laborers.** In Athens, too, work was done by slaves. A few Athenian thinkers, however, were possibly the first to ask, "Is it right for people to own other people? Is it right to force a person to labor for another?"

You Decide
It is wrong for one person to own another. Why do you think slavery has existed, even though it is wrong?

Background Information

There were about a dozen Olympian gods, including Zeus, Hera, Poseidon, Athena, Apollo, Artemis, Dionysius, and Aphrodite. Other deities lived all over Greece, and were regularly consulted about every aspect of life. The gods and goddesses provided for human needs, protected people from danger, and cured illness. Different gods had special areas of authority and power.

You Decide
Although slavery has always been wrong, it wasn't recognized as such until the Greeks started questioning it. Point out that sometimes people need a change in perspective to recognize ethical or moral problems.

LEARNING STYLES

Auditory/Verbal
Encourage students to tell myths, legends, or stories that explain something in nature. Point out that these stories are like Greek myths, which also explained things in nature. Then ask small groups to write myths that explain things in nature such as why it thunders and where rainbows come from.

LEARNING STYLES

Visual/Spatial
If students are unfamiliar with Venn diagrams, show a simple example on the board. Ask students to create a Venn diagram and label the sections Sparta, Athens, and Both. Have students compare and contrast Sparta and Athens by listing details in the appropriate sections of the diagram. Ask students to use their completed Venn diagrams to write a summary.

ELL/ESL STRATEGY

Language Objective:
To classify words by meaning

Explain that organizing words into categories is a good way to understand and remember the meaning of words. Write the following categories on the board: People, Gods, Actions, and Society. Have the class read through the Word Bank on page 131 and put each word in a category. Have students copy the words into their notebooks.

Reading Strategy:
Metacognition

Have students write their prediction. Tell them they will review it later in this chapter.

COMMON ERROR

Students may think that Spartan women were unimportant in that culture. Although women did not participate in public events, their rights were greater in Sparta than in Athens. They were able to own and inherit property, for example. And they were encouraged to exercise to make their bodies strong.

ONLINE CONNECTION

Students can gain additional information by accessing the following Web site:

www.agsglobepmwh.com/page130

(This site is a good resource for additional information on ancient Athens.)

TEACHER ALERT

Students may ask where the slaves in Greece came from. They were mostly foreigners who were captured in war or by pirates. The war slaves came from defeated armies and the general population of defeated states. Piracy also contributed large numbers of captives. The children of slaves were themselves slaves. If students are interested in learning about the life of a slave, suggest they read *You Wouldn't Want to Be a Slave in Ancient Greece!* by Fiona MacDonald and David Antram.

Revolt

To rise up against a government; to refuse to obey the people in charge

Constitution

The basic laws and rules of a government

Jury

A group of people who listen to the facts and decide if a person on trial is guilty or not guilty

Reading Strategy:
Metacognition

Make a prediction as to what you think will happen next. Check your prediction as you continue reading and revise as needed.

In the early years of Athens, government was in the hands of landowners. If a man owned land, he was a citizen. He had a voice in running the city-state. As the city grew, many merchants and businesspeople, shippers and traders became wealthy. They did not own land, but they wanted a say in city government. They wanted to be citizens. Athenians rose up against their government. This **revolt** led to a new government. In 508 B.C., this government drew up an Athenian **constitution.** Under the new laws, all free men were citizens. Women and slaves, however, did not have the rights of citizenship.

A citizen had the right to vote. He was also expected to hold office if called upon, sit on a **jury,** and serve in the army. The Athenian democracy was a government "by the people." The problem was that so many of "the people" (women and slaves) were not allowed to be citizens.

LEARN MORE ABOUT IT

Greek Religion
The Greeks believed that people were important. They celebrated the human mind and the human body. Therefore, their gods were much like humans. The Greeks worshipped many gods and goddesses. They gave each one a name and a humanlike form and personality. The gods and goddesses, according to the Greek storytellers, lived on top of Mount Olympus. This is the highest mountain in Greece. There, they enjoyed life. They laughed and they argued just as humans do. They played tricks on each other and on the humans they ruled.

Zeus was the king of the Greek gods. His wife was Hera, queen of the gods. The Parthenon on the Athenian Acropolis was built to honor Athena. She was the goddess of wisdom and learning.

The Greeks told myths, which explained things in nature. They told of the doings of the gods and goddesses. Myths were told about jealous and angry gods and goddesses. Some fell in love with humans and others helped humans. Greek myths made exciting stories.

LEARN MORE ABOUT IT

Greek gods and goddesses were identified by distinct characteristics. Have students research them in the library or online. Have each student choose one god or goddess with whom they identify.

Word Bank

Athena

citizens

democracy

enjoying life

military

slaves

soldier

vote

women

Zeus

On a sheet of paper, write the word from the Word Bank to complete each sentence correctly.

1. Sparta was a(n) _____ society.

2. Athens was governed by a(n) _____.

3. Spartan children belonged to the state and boys were raised to be a(n) _____.

4. Athenians were less interested in warfare, and more interested in _____.

5. Spartans had little use for _____.

6. The Athenian constitution gave all free men citizenship and allowed them to _____.

7. In Athens, women and slaves were not allowed to be _____.

8. People in both Athens and Sparta had _____.

9. _____ was the king of the Greek gods, and Hera was the queen.

10. _____ was the goddess of wisdom and learning.

Lesson 7–2 Review Answers
1. military 2. democracy 3. soldier
4. enjoying life 5. women 6. vote
7. citizens 8. slaves 9. Zeus
10. Athena

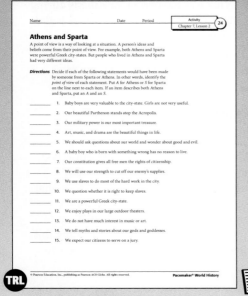

Lesson at a Glance

Chapter 7 Lesson 3

Overview This lesson describes two major conflicts, the Persian Wars and the Peloponnesian War, as well as the Golden Age that separated them.

Objectives

■ To describe how the Greeks eventually defeated the Persians

■ To explain the reason for the name "Golden Age"

■ To tell who won the Peloponnesian War and why

Student Pages 132–135

Teacher's Resource Library

Workbook Activity 25

Activity 25

Modified Activity 25

Vocabulary

democratic   plague

Write *democratic* and *democracy* on the board. Ask students how the words are related. (The first is the adjectival form of the second, which is a noun.) Ask for other examples of words that have a noun and adjectival form (e.g., atom/atomic, strategy/strategic, geometry/geometric)

PRONUNCIATION GUIDE

Use this list to help students pronounce difficult words in this lesson.

Darius (də ri´əs)

Peloponnesian (pel´ə pə ne´zhən)

Pericles (per´i klez´)

Salamis (sal´ə mis)

Xerxes (zûrk´ sez)

---

1 | Warm-Up Activity

Ask students about the reasons a country decides to go to war. Choose a recent war and have students read news reports and opinion pieces that give the official and unofficial motives for entering a conflict.

LESSON 7-3 — Fighting in Greece

Objectives

■ To describe how the Greeks eventually defeated the Persians

■ To explain the reason for the name "Golden Age"

■ To tell who won the Peloponnesian War and why

Reading Strategy: Metacognition

Remember to ask yourself questions as you read. This will help make sure that you understand what you are reading.

Between 500 and 400 B.C., the Greek empire was tested in a series of wars. The first battles united the city-states as they fought the great Persian Empire. The next war set the Athenians against the Spartans. The war lasted 27 years and is known as the Peloponnesian War.

What Were the Persian Wars?

As Greek city-states grew strong and wealthy, another land began to look toward Greece. The Persian Empire under Cyrus the Great had become the strongest military power in the world. In 546 B.C., Persia attacked and conquered the Greek colonies in Lydia. This was along the coast of what is now called Turkey. About 50 years later, the Greeks in Lydia revolted. King Darius I of Persia crushed their uprising. Then he sent his huge army to invade Greece.

In 490 B.C., the Persian armies headed for Athens. On the plain of Marathon, the Athenians beat the mighty Persians! An excited Greek citizen ran 25 miles (about 40 kilometers) to Athens to spread the good news. An Olympic event of today is named after that run from Marathon to Athens.

But the Persians were not ready to give up. Darius's son, Xerxes, continued the war. About 10 years later, Xerxes led an even stronger force into Greece. The Greek city-states put aside their quarrels to fight the common enemy. Xerxes's navy attacked. The Greeks fought the Persian invaders long and hard. Yet the Persians were too strong. Xerxes's men attacked the city of Athens next. In 480 B.C., they destroyed the Parthenon and burned much of the beautiful city.

---

2 | Teaching the Lesson

Discuss the reasons the Greeks and Persians went to war and why Sparta and Athens fought the Peloponnesian War. If students do the At Home activity, invite them to compare the Greeks' reasons with their rationale for modern wars. Have them write a short essay on what they find.

Ask:

● Who invaded Greece in 490 B.C.? (Darius I)

● How did the Athenians defeat the Persians at Salamis? (Their navy destroyed Persia's ships.)

● What was happening in Athens during the Golden Age? (growing wealth and power, cultural progress, continued development of democracy)

● Who won the Peloponnesian War? (Sparta)

Reading Strategy: Metacognition

Ask students to think of different ways they use to remember names (e.g., mnemonics, visualization). Discuss what they usually try to do, and what they could try as an alternative. Ask them to study the names in this section using this alternative and use the lesson review to evaluate how well it works.

You Decide

If the Persians had conquered Greece, our lives today might be very different. Why do you think this is so?

History Fact

Athenians created their greatest art and architecture during the Golden Age.

Xerxes left Athens thinking that he had won the war. He was in for a surprise, however. His men met the Athenian navy off the harbor of Salamis. There was a great sea battle. The Persians were defeated. The Greeks sent the Persians back across the Aegean Sea. Greece was then left to enjoy a time of peace.

What Was the Time Known as the Golden Age?

The peace following the Persian Wars lasted for about 50 years. During that time, Athens grew in power and strength. It became the greatest city-state in Greece.

Athens collected money from the other city-states. The Athenians insisted that their navy must be kept strong in order to protect all of Greece.

A great Athenian leader named Pericles rose to power in 461 B.C. Pericles helped the Athenians continue their government in which all people have equal rights—their **democratic** government. He used some of the money collected from other city-states to rebuild the Parthenon.

Athens flowered with Pericles as its leader. It was a time known as the Age of Pericles, or the Golden Age of Athens. The Athenians, at peace now, had time to study science and geography. They wrote their greatest plays and created their finest statues.

Athens of the Golden Age was one of the most beautiful cities in the world. Many other Greek city-states followed the Athenians' way of life and their ideas of democracy.

Sparta, however, continued as a military state. The Spartans did not like the way Athens was building and growing. They were also angry that Athens had been collecting money from the rest of Greece.

Pericles helped Athenians fight for democracy.

Background Information

Athens and a group of other city-states formed the Delian League to fight the Persians. The league also put down revolts among its own members. This league did not disband at the end of the Persian wars, but became the base of the Athenian Empire. Athens used its power to establish colonies around the Mediterranean and to collect tribute from its allies. Eventually, this expansion led to wars with Sparta.

ELL/ESL STRATEGY

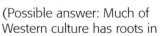

Language Objective: *To write for a variety of purposes: to express feelings, ideas, and opinions*

Discuss what being a "great leader," like Pericles, means. Ask students if they can think of contexts other than government where a person can be a great leader. Have students meet in small groups and describe to each other someone in their lives who they think is an inspiring leader. What are the characteristics of this person? What is one thing that this person has done that you consider great? Each student should write a short essay describing the person and his or her leadership qualities. Have volunteers share their essays with the class.

You Decide

(Possible answer: Much of Western culture has roots in Greek ideas and art. If it were based on Persian ones instead, our culture would likely be very different.)

History Fact

Have students list the basic essentials of life. Discuss how these essential needs were met in Athens. Point out that wealth and peace make it possible to spend money on cultural pursuits.

COMMON ERROR

Students may think that the marathon race dates back to ancient Greek games. However, the marathon race was first run in 1896, when the Olympic games were revived in Athens.

AT HOME

Have each student interview three adults—friends, family members, or community members—asking the question, "During your lifetime, for what reasons has your country gone to war?" and record the answers. During class, instruct students in small groups about how to combine and classify the responses that they collected. Categories might include fighting to protect life, property, or beliefs or values. Combine the results of all groups into a whole-class chart, and calculate the percentage of responses in each category. Refer to this information when discussing the reason for the Persian and Peloponnesian wars.

Plague
A deadly disease that spreads quickly

What Was the Result of the Peloponnesian War?

Peace ended in 431 B.C., when Sparta led some of the other city-states against Athens. Sparta was a land power with a strong army. Athens was a sea power. Most of its strength was in its navy. Both cities fought for control of Greece. The war between Athens and Sparta was called the Peloponnesian War. It was named after the Peloponnesus, the part of Greece in which Sparta was located. This war went on for 27 years!

The Spartans tried to cut off supplies to Athens to starve the people. The Athenians held on even though the Spartans were among the world's best fighters.

Then a terrible disease, a **plague,** broke out in the city of Athens. One-fourth of the Athenian people died during the plague. Their leader, Pericles, was among those who died.

Athens could no longer hold out against Sparta. In 404 B.C., Athens surrendered to Sparta.

On a sheet of paper, write the letter of the answer that correctly completes each sentence.

1. The Persian Empire under Cyrus the Great was the strongest _____ power in the world.

   A military   **B** land   **C** sea   **D** weapons

2. After the Athenians beat the Persians, an excited Greek citizen ran 25 miles to Athens. The _____, an Olympic event, is named for that run.

   A triathlon   **C** marathon
   B discus throwing   **D** chariot racing

3. _____ led the Persian army in destroying the Greek Parthenon in 480 B.C.

   A Cyrus   **B** Darius   **C** Xerxes   **D** Pericles

4. The Persian Wars lasted about _____ years.

   A 10   **B** 27   **C** 31   **D** 50

5. The Peloponnesian War lasted _____ years.

   A 10   **B** 27   **C** 31   **D** 50

6. _____ was the great Athenian leader who helped Athens thrive under its democratic government.

   A Cyrus   **B** Darius   **C** Xerxes   **D** Pericles

7. Athens and Sparta fought the Peloponnesian War for _____.

   A control of Greece   **C** a democratic government
   B power over the sea   **D** the right to own slaves

On a sheet of paper, write the answer to each question. Use complete sentences.

8. How did the Greeks eventually defeat the Persians?

9. What is the reason for the name "Golden Age"?

10. Who won the Peloponnesian War and how did they do so?

Lesson 7–3 Review Answers

1. A **2.** C **3.** C **4.** D **5.** B **6.** D **7.** A
8. The Persians attacked the city of Athens, destroying the Parthenon and burning much of the city. The Persians left Athens thinking they had won, but were surprised by an attack from the Athenian navy off the harbor of Salamis. After a great sea battle, the Persians were defeated.
9. The time in Athens after the Persian Wars and under the rule of Pericles was known as the "Golden Age." This is because the Athenians were at peace and had time to study science and geography. It is the time when they wrote their greatest plays and created their finest statues.
10. Sparta won the Peloponnesian War after a terrible plague broke out in Athens and one-fourth of the people died, including their leader Pericles. Athens could no longer hold out against Sparta, and surrendered.

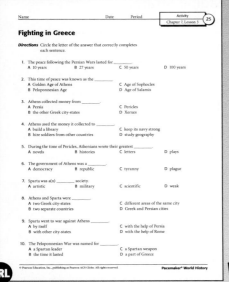

Activity 25

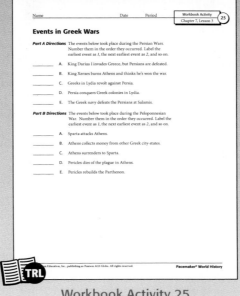

Workbook Activity 25

Gifts from the Greeks

Lesson at a Glance

Chapter 7 Lesson 4

Overview This lesson describes ancient Greek contributions to architecture, sculpture, sports, and philosophy.

Objectives

- To name three Greek thinkers
- To explain how democracy helped develop Athens

Student Pages 136–138

Teacher's Resource Library TRL

Workbook Activity 26

Activity 26

Modified Activity 26

Vocabulary

architecture   athlete

Write the vocabulary words on the board and ask volunteers to provide their own definition for each. Write their definitions. Then have students read each definition from the text and compare it to those on the board.

PRONUNCIATION GUIDE

Use this list to help students pronounce difficult words in this lesson.

Aristarchus (ar' ə stär' kəs)

Eratosthenes (er' ə tos' thə nez')

Pythagoras (pi thag' ər əs)

1 Warm-Up Activity

Have students review the prediction they made in Lesson 2 (page 130). Ask if it helped them think about the events they have been reading about.

Objectives

- To name three Greek thinkers
- To explain how democracy helped develop Athens

Architecture
The art of building

Reading Strategy:
Metacognition

Note the main ideas and important details in this lesson. Summarize what you have read to make sure you understand it.

The Doric, Ionic, and Corinthian columns are examples of classical Greek architecture.

The art and **architecture** of the Golden Age demonstrates the Greeks' love of beauty. In addition, it was a time when Greek thinkers questioned the world around them. The progress they made in art and their search for truth are their greatest gifts to civilization.

What Are Some Gifts the Greeks Gave Us That Are Part of Life Today?

Greek thought and Greek works are very much a part of life today. Greek ideas in building can be seen in modern buildings. Greek statues still influence today's artists. The style of art and architecture the Greeks developed is called the "classical" style.

Today's students still read the works of Greek thinkers like Socrates, Plato, and Aristotle. "Know yourself," the great teachers said. "Ask questions. Search for the truth."

The Greeks were the first people to ask, "What is the world made of? Why is it the way it is?" They developed ideas about the sun, the earth, and the stars.

"The earth is round," Eratosthenes said. "The earth moves around the sun," Aristarchus said. Euclid and Pythagoras helped invent geometry.

We can also thank the Greeks for a model of a democracy. "Our government is called a democracy because power is in the hands of the whole people," said the Athenian leader Pericles.

Greek words and ideas show up in our own language. *Astronomy, biology, geography,* and *geology* are all taken from the Greek language. So are the words *music, theater, drama, comedy,* and *tragedy.*

136   *Unit 3   The Origins of Western Civilization: Greece and Rome*

2 Teaching the Lesson

As students read this section, have them keep a running list of the great contributions the ancient Greeks made to world civilization. Then have them speculate what great contributions, if any, Canada and the United States have made to world civilization.

Ask:

- In what areas of study do we often refer to Greek works? (architecture, math, geometry, philosophy)
- Why did the Greeks convene games? (to honor the gods)

Reading Strategy:
Metacognition

Have students verbally summarize the lesson to another student, or write down their summary. The other student should critique the summary; it should be brief and include all the main points. Then have students swap partners and assume the other role.

Athlete
A person trained to take part in competitive sports

The word **athlete** comes from the Greeks, too. It means "one who tries to win a prize in a contest." Our Olympic Games are athletic contests. They are modeled after those played by Greek athletes so long ago.

The first known Olympic games took place in 776 B.C. Early Olympic games were held to honor the gods and goddesses. They were held every four years at the temple of Zeus in Olympia. All wars in Greece had to stop when it was time for the games. The athletes came from Athens and Sparta and all the other city-states.

The earliest Olympic games were just foot races. Later the Greeks added events such as boxing, wrestling, jumping, discus throwing, and chariot racing.

Today, just as in early Greece, it is a great honor to win an Olympic event. Winners get medals of gold, silver, and bronze. In ancient Greece the winners were crowned with a circle of laurel leaves. The athletes brought glory to their city-state and themselves.

The Greek leader Pericles saw the greatness of Greece in the Golden Age. "Mighty indeed are the marks and monuments of our empire . . . ," Pericles said. "Future ages will wonder at us."

TIMELINE STUDY: ANCIENT GREECE

What wars were going on when the Athenian Constitution was written?

776 B.C. First Greek Olympic Games

800 B.C. — **700 B.C.** — **600 B.C.** — **500 B.C.** — **400 B.C.**

546–449 B.C. Persian Wars

431–404 B.C. Peloponnesian War

508 B.C. Athenian Constitution

461–429 B.C. The Age of Pericles

1500 B.C.–400 B.C.   *Greek City-States and the Golden Age*   Chapter 7   **137**

Ancient Greek Olympic competitions were quite different from today's Olympic Games. For example, Greek wrestlers could do almost anything to their opponents, including kicking and hitting. The only rules were no biting and no sticking a thumb in the opponent's eye. Students may be interested to know that most Greek athletes participated wearing no clothing!

LEARNING STYLES

Body/Kinesthetic
Have students work in a small group to prepare and present a skit of a Greek comedy or a Greek tragedy performed with a chorus.

ELL/ESL STRATEGY

Language Objective:
To work together to use the new vocabulary

Have students use each vocabulary word in a sentence. Then have them erase the vocabulary word in each sentence and exchange sentences with a partner. After partners fill in the appropriate words, they discuss and correct the sentences.

TIMELINE STUDY

Answer: Persian Wars

3 Reinforce and Extend

WORLD CULTURES

The ancient Greek emphasis on education can be seen in modern Greece, where nine out of ten adults can read and write. All children must attend school between the ages of six and fifteen. Free public schools are available at all levels, including college, where enrollment has increased significantly in recent decades.

CAREER CONNECTION

Architects design buildings and supervise their construction. To become an architect, students undergo rigorous training. Earning a bachelor's degree in architecture generally takes about five years. After graduation, students must pass a design test, work as an intern in the office of a licensed architect, and pass a state licensing examination. Licensed architects can work independently, join a firm, or work for the government. Encourage interested students to take courses in history, mathematics, mechanical drawing, and computer science.

Lesson 7–4 Review Answers

1. C 2. D 3. B 4. A 5. D 6. B 7. Plato
8. Eratosthenes 9. Aristarchus 10. Pythagoras

On a sheet of paper, write the letter of the answer that correctly completes each sentence.

1. Greeks developed the _____ style of art and architecture.

   A "Athenian"   **B** "Spartan"   **C** "classical"   **D** "artistic"

2. The word *comedy* is an example of a word taken from the Greek _____.

   A Olympics   **B** theater   **C** government   **D** language

3. The Greeks provided us a model of democracy. In this model, the power of the government is in the hands of the _____.

   A nobles   **B** people   **C** king/queen   **D** military

4. Early Olympic games were held to _____.

   A honor the gods and goddesses   **C** win money for the athlete's city-state
   B keep the peace between city-states   **D** test the limits of the human body

5. In ancient Greece, all _____ had to stop when it was time for the Olympics.

   A thinking   **B** building   **C** governments **D** wars

6. Winners of an Olympic event in ancient Greece received _____.

   A medals of gold, silver, and bronze   **C** a bouquet of flowers
   B a crown of laurel leaves   **D** a trophy of Zeus (the Greek god)

Word Bank

Aristarchus

Eratosthenes

Plato

Pythagoras

On a sheet of paper, write the word from the Word Bank to complete each sentence correctly.

7. Great Greek thinkers, like Socrates, _____, and Aristotle, questioned their world.

8. _____ claimed the earth is round.

9. _____ said that the earth moves around the sun.

10. Euclid and _____ helped invent geometry.

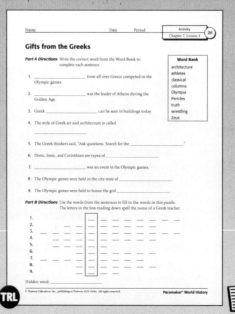

CHAPTER 7 SUMMARY

- Most of Greece's wealth came from trading rather than from farming. Traders set up colonies in places they visited.

- Greece was divided into city-states, each one with its own government. The city-states were very different from one another.

- Athens and Sparta were two powerful city-states. Athens was a democracy. Athens worked to make itself enlightened and beautiful.

- Sparta was a military government. Slaves were kept and most of life there focused on preparing for war.

- The Greeks worshipped many gods and goddesses with human qualities.

- The Persians attacked Greece many times beginning in 546 B.C. In 480 B.C., they destroyed much of Athens, but the Greek army drove the Persian army away.

- Pericles became leader of Athens in 461 B.C. This period became known as the Age of Pericles. People studied science and geography and created works of art. They made the city beautiful.

- Quarrels between Athens and Sparta turned into the Peloponnesian War. Sparta won.

- The Greeks were great thinkers. Because they questioned their world, they learned. The works of great thinkers such as Socrates, Plato, and Aristotle, are still read today.

- The first known Olympic games took place in Greece in 776 B.C.

Chapter 7 Summary

Have students read the Chapter Summary on page 139 to review the main ideas presented in Chapter 7.

Ask:

- Where did most of Greece's wealth come from? (trading)
- Why were city-states in Greece so different from each other? (They were isolated by mountains, and therefore had little contact with one another.)
- Where was the first democracy? (Athens)
- How were Spartans different from Athenians? (They did not care about trade or the arts.)
- What were the Greek gods like? (human characteristics, only more powerful)
- Did the Greek city-states or the Persians win the Persian wars? (the Greeks)
- What happened in Athens during the Golden Age? (The Athenians grew wealthy and devoted much money to arts, architecture, and science.)
- Who fought in the Peloponnesian War and who won? (Athens and Sparta; Sparta)
- Name three aspects of Greek culture that are still important today. (Greek philosophy, democracy, architectural styles, art, language)
- Who took part in the early Olympic games? (athletes from all over Greece)

TEACHER'S RESOURCE

The AGS Globe Teaching Strategies in Social Studies Transparencies may be used with this chapter. The transparencies add an interactive dimension to expand and enhance the Pacemaker® *World History* program content.

CHAPTER PROJECT FOLLOW-UP

 Have students present their chapter projects while they study this lesson. Encourage students to include some class participation in their presentations, and schedule presentation topics as near to the times of related chapter study as possible. Display project products in the classroom throughout the teaching of the chapter.

Chapter 7 Review

Use the Chapter Review to prepare students for tests and to reteach content from the chapter.

Chapter 7 Mastery Test

The Teacher's Resource Library includes two forms of the Chapter 7 Mastery Test. Each test addresses the chapter Goals for Learning. An optional third page of additional critical-thinking items is included for each test. The difficulty level of the two forms is equivalent.

Chapter 7 Review Answers

Vocabulary Review

1. tyrant
2. myths
3. democracy
4. citizen
5. plague
6. constitution
7. revolt
8. jury
9. athlete
10. architecture

Chapter Review Questions

11. The Acropolis was the high hill where Greeks built their city-states near. Oftentimes, special buildings, such as temples and theaters, were built atop this hill.

12. Greek culture spread because the Greeks were sailors and traders who set up colonies where they visited.

Word Bank

architecture
athlete
citizen
constitution
democracy
jury
myths
plague
revolt
tyrant

Vocabulary Review

On a sheet of paper, use the words from the Word Bank to complete each sentence correctly.

1. Some Greek city-states were ruled by a powerful ruler called a(n) _____.

2. The Greeks told _____ about their gods and goddesses.

3. Athens developed a form of _____, or rule of the people.

4. In Athens, a woman was not a(n) _____.

5. A deadly disease that spreads quickly is known as a(n) _____.

6. A basic set of rules and laws is a(n) _____.

7. When citizens _____, they are refusing to obey the people that are in charge.

8. A(n) _____ is a group of people who decide whether a person has disobeyed the law.

9. In ancient Greece, the word _____ means "one who tries to win a prize in a contest."

10. The Greeks developed a style of _____ called the "classical" style.

Chapter Review Questions

On a sheet of paper, write the answer to each question. Use complete sentences.

11. What was the Acropolis in Greek city-states?

12. Why did Greek culture spread?

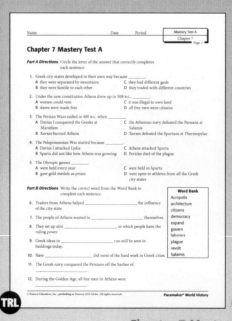

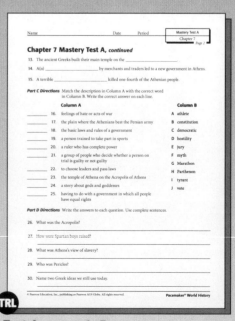

Chapter 7 Mastery Test A, pages 1–3

13. How did democracy develop in Athens?

14. What was the result of the Peloponnesian War and the plague in Athens?

15. Who participated in the Olympic Games in ancient Greece?

Critical Thinking

On a sheet of paper, write your response to each question. Use complete sentences.

16. Would you rather have lived in Sparta or in Athens? Give at least two reasons why.

17. Why is the period after the Persian Wars called the Golden Age of Athens?

Using the Timeline

Use the timeline on page 137 to answer the questions.

18. When were the first Olympic Games?

19. When did the Athenians get a constitution?

20. What came after the Age of Pericles?

GROUP ACTIVITY

Form a group of three or four. Make a poster about the most recent Olympics. Feature your group's favorite Olympic stars.

1500 B.C.–400 B.C.   *Greek City-States and the Golden Age*   **Chapter 7**   **141**

---

13. Democracy developed in Athens after businesspeople without land decided they wanted a say in government. They revolted, and a constitution was drawn up.

14. Athenians held out against the strong Spartan army at the end of the Peloponnesian War. But then a terrible plague broke out, killing one-fourth of the Athenian people. Because of this, Athens surrendered to Sparta.

15. Athletes from the various city-states in Greece participated in the ancient Olympic games.

Critical Thinking

16. Possible answer: Most students will probably choose Athens. They may mention that Sparta was a harsh military society, while people in Athens enjoyed plays, created beautiful buildings and statues, asked basic questions, and enjoyed life.

17. Possible answer: After the Persian Wars, Athens became the greatest city-state in Greece. Athenians studied, wrote plays, and built their best statues.

Using the Timeline

18. 776 B.C.

19. 508 B.C.

20. The Peloponnesian War

GROUP ACTIVITY

Projects should include accurate, interesting material about the Olympics.

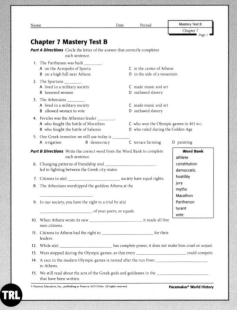

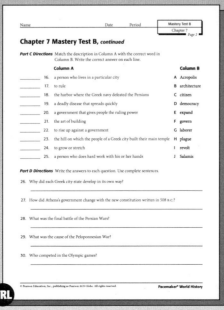

Chapter 7 Mastery Test B, pages 1–3

Introducing the Chapter

During his short life, Alexander the Great sought—through determination and military might—to conquer the world. Have students read the chapter to discover whether Alexander was successful at conquering the world and what influence his conquests had on civilization.

Ask:

- What was Macedonia like before King Philip built up its army? (poor, struggling)
- How did Alexander become ruler of Greece? (He inherited the position when his father Philip died.)

CHAPTER 8

360 B.C.–320 B.C.

Alexander the Great

King Philip II of Macedonia built up the army of his poor, struggling kingdom. He conquered the Greek city-states, in hope of going on to win the Persian Empire. Upon his death, his son Alexander went on to carry out his father's wishes.

Alexander showed great power and even greater determination. The Macedonians under Alexander conquered many lands from Egypt to the Middle East. Alexander the Great defeated the Persian Empire before conquering the Aryans in the Indus River Valley.

GOALS FOR LEARNING

- To explain how Alexander became ruler of Greece
- To tell why Alexander was called the Great Conqueror
- To explain the reason for the end of Alexander's empire

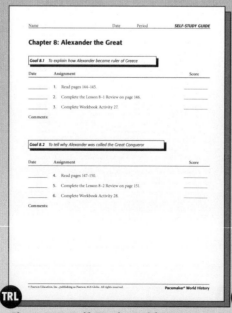

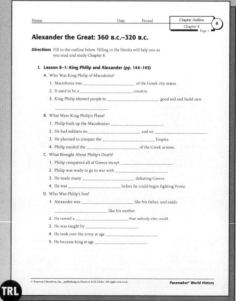

Reading Strategy: Summarizing

As you read the text in this chapter, you will want to ask yourself questions to help you understand what you read.

- What is the chapter about?
- What new ideas am I being introduced to?
- Why is it important that I remember these ideas?

Key Vocabulary Words

Lesson 1

Assassinate To murder a leader or other important person

Campaign A series of battles all aimed at one military end

Ambition The drive to become powerful, successful, or famous

Lesson 2

Founded To have begun a country or city; to have built a city

General A high-ranking military officer

Tell students that the purpose of a summary is to concisely and accurately explain the main points, facts, and information from a paragraph or section of a text. Remind students that *to summarize* something means that they must explain it using their own words.

Ask:

- What are some ways to ensure that you accurately summarize information? (Students may say that they have to read carefully or compare their completed summary with the actual text.)

LIFE SKILLS CONNECTION

Students learn about the importance of planning a journey. Discuss the differences there might be in packing for a trip Alaska and packing for a trip to Mexico.

KEY VOCABULARY

In Part A, students match the definition to the correct word. In Part B, they circle the words that relate to Alexander the Great.

CHAPTER PROJECT

Divide students into three groups and tell them that each group is going to create a class presentation about the life of Alexander the Great. The first group will focus on Alexander's birth, family, and early childhood including his relationship with his teacher. The second group will focus on Alexander's life as an adult—the death of his father, his military conquests, and his plan to conquer the world. The third group will focus on the lasting impact of Alexander's attempts to spread Greek culture and customs. Tell students that they may present their work in the form of a short play, a short film, or a series of lectures and debates. They should attempt to entertain as well as to inform their audience.

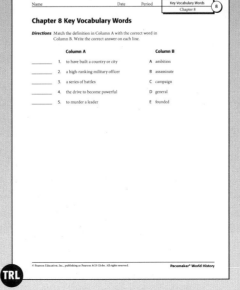

Life Skills Connection 8   Key Vocabulary Words 8

Lesson at a Glance

Chapter 8 Lesson 1

Overview This lesson introduces two figures: King Philip II, who turned the impoverished land of Macedonia into a military powerhouse and made plans to conquer the Persian Empire; and his son Alexander, an ambitious boy who took over as king of Macedonia at age 20 following his father's assassination.

Objectives

- To explain how King Philip II of Macedonia became ruler of Greece
- To explain events that allowed Alexander to take over as king of Macedonia
- To identify Alexander's teacher

Student Pages 144–146

Teacher's Resource Library **TRL**

Workbook Activity 27

Activity 27

Modified Activity 27

Vocabulary

ambition   campaign
assassinate

Read each word and its definition aloud. Now write the following sentences on the board and ask students to fill in the blanks.

The _____ against Persia was delayed by King Philip's death.

_____ without wisdom can be a dangerous character trait.

Was the plot to _____ King Philip II successful?

PRONUNCIATION GUIDE

Use this list to help students pronounce difficult words in this lesson.

Peloponnesian (pel´ ə pə ne´ zhən)

Aristotle (ar´ ə stot´ l)

King Philip and Alexander

Objectives

- To explain how King Philip II of Macedonia became ruler of Greece
- To explain events that allowed Alexander to take over as king of Macedonia
- To identify Alexander's teacher

Reading Strategy:
Summarizing

Who is being introduced in this section?

You Decide
Philip never conquered Sparta. What do you think stopped him?

The Peloponnesian War was over. The Greek city-states were now under Sparta's rule. They still argued with each other, however.

Who Was King Philip of Macedonia?

To the north was a land called Macedonia. It was ruled by a king named Philip II. Macedonia had always been poor. Things changed, however, when Philip became king. Philip saw to it that Macedonians farmed their good soil. He sent out Macedonian traders. He built new roads. King Philip II had ideas.

Philip built up the Macedonian army. He built war machinery. He taught his men new ways of fighting. Philip soon had a strong army of foot soldiers and soldiers on horseback.

King Philip's plan was to conquer the great Persian Empire. To do that, Philip needed military strength.

He needed more strength than he had with only Macedonia behind him. Philip wanted the power of all the Greek armies.

King Philip told some of the nearby city-states about his plan. They agreed to join him. Philip, however, needed more power. He needed the largest city-states, Athens and Thebes, behind him. For that reason he used all his military know-how along with his well-trained men and their fine machinery. With this support, Philip conquered Athens and Thebes.

Soon all of Greece fell under Macedonian control—all except Sparta, that is. Philip never conquered Sparta.

You Decide

Answers will vary. Students may say that the Spartans were too fierce to be subdued by Philip's army or that Philip decided it was more important to conquer the Persian Empire.

Reading Strategy:
Summarizing

Have students compose a short summary (2–3 sentences) that answers this question. Next, encourage volunteers to share their summaries with the class.

1 **Warm-Up Activity**

Encourage students to think about what qualities a great leader must possess. They may want to write some of these qualities down. Now ask students if they believe—based on their reading from the lesson—that King Philip II was a great leader.

2 **Teaching the Lesson**

As students read the information on pages 144–145, ask them to keep in mind this sentence: "King Philip II had ideas." Have students consider what steps he took to turn his ideas into realities. Remind them that, at the beginning of Philip's rule, Macedonia had been a poor, struggling civilization.

Assassinate
To kill a leader or other important person

Campaign
A series of battles all aimed at one military end

Ambition
The drive to become powerful, successful, or famous

Reading Strategy:
Summarizing

What are some important details about King Philip that help you understand this lesson?

Aristotle was a great thinker and teacher.

Now Philip was ready for war with the Persians. Yet King Philip II would never lead his men into Persia. By now he had made enemies. There was a plot to kill, or **assassinate**, him. Before he could begin his **campaign** against (or begin fighting with) Persia, he was killed.

Who Was Philip's Son?

Philip had a son, Alexander. Alexander was not an ordinary boy. From his father, Alexander inherited, or got, **ambition** and a love of power. Philip taught his son all about warfare and leadership. Alexander's mother, Olympias, was smart and hot-tempered. Alexander, too, was bright and easily angered.

As a boy, Alexander seemed almost fearless. Stories tell of the young Prince Alexander taming a certain horse. No other person in the kingdom could ride it. Alexander named that horse Bucephalus. Bucephalus would carry Alexander across an empire!

King Philip always thought highly of the Greek way of life and of Greek ideas. His son, Alexander, was to have the best of teachers—the Greek thinker, Aristotle. At age 13, Alexander began his lessons.

Aristotle taught Alexander to love Greek stories of heroes and adventure. He taught the boy about far-off lands and about other cultures. Aristotle saw to it that Alexander took part in sports, too.

By the time Alexander was 18, he was able to take a command in his father's army. Alexander was 20 when his father was killed. Now he was ready to take over as king of Macedonia and to become a conqueror.

360 B.C.–320 B.C.

Alexander the Great Chapter 8 **145**

- What were some of Philip's first steps toward improving the lives of Macedonians? (He encouraged farming, increased trade, built roads, and built up the army.)
- What was Philip's plan when he was killed? (to conquer Persia)
- What do we know about Alexander as a child? (Answers may vary. He was extraordinary, brave, ambitious, and intelligent. Aristotle was his teacher. He took over as king of Macedonia at age 20.)

Background Information

The taming of the horse Bucephalus by the boy Alexander is a story with great emotional resonance that can yield insight into both the character of Alexander and the relationship between father and son. For more information, look up Plutarch online and print information about Alexander. Have students read each section aloud.

Reading Strategy:
Summarizing

Call students' attention to the question on page 145. How does information about King Philip tell us more about Alexander? What does it tell us about him?

ELL/ESL STRATEGY

Language Objective: *To encourage students to think about the difference between fact and opinion*

Explain to students that a fact is a piece of information that can be measured or proven with evidence, and an opinion is an idea that other people can agree or disagree with. Then, have students copy five factual statements about Philip II and write an opinion for each of those facts. You might wish to provide the following example as a model: *Fact:* Macedonia was ruled by a king named Philip II. *Opinion:* He was a brilliant king.

LEARNING STYLES

Auditory/Verbal

Plutarch's writing may also be used to further reinforce information from the lesson for students who learn well by hearing information read aloud. Encourage students to listen carefully as you read the excerpt aloud. Then, ask them to talk about what this excerpt tells us about both Alexander's character and his relationship with his father.

LEARNING STYLES

Visual/Spatial

Have students study the portrait and caption of Aristotle on page 145. Ask students to draw a picture that dramatizes a scene from the chapter. For example, students may wish to draw Alexander taming Bucephalus; Aristotle teaching the child Alexander; or King Philip enjoining nearby city-states to form a coalition.

3 Reinforce and Extend

Lesson 8–1 Review Answers

1. D 2. B 3. A 4. B 5. C 6. C 7. A 8. D
9. B 10. C

COMMON ERROR

Students may confuse the words *ambition* and *ambitious*. Write each word on the board. Explain to students that ambition is a noun (*names* the drive to be powerful, successful, or famous) while ambitious is an adjective (*describes* the desire to be powerful, successful, or famous.)

CAREER CONNECTION

History is full of stories about beloved teachers and the influence they had on their pupils. In this lesson we read about Aristotle's influence on Alexander. Students interested in a career that involves teaching should contact their school counselor to find out about courses they can take to prepare themselves for a career in education.

WORLD CULTURES

For the ancient Greeks, food had many religious and philosophical meanings. For instance, the Greeks never ate meat unless it had been sacrificed to a god. In Greek culture, a meal is made up of more than just the food. The conversation, the setting, and the company are all important parts of sharing a meal. The main ingredients in Greek food usually include olive oil, honey, yogurt, fresh fruits and vegetables, lamb, and fish.

ONLINE CONNECTION

Students can gain additional information by accessing the following Web site: www. agsglobepmwh.com/page146 (Students will learn more about the life and times of Alexander the Great.)

146 *Unit 3 Greece and Rome*

LESSON 8-1 REVIEW

On a sheet of paper, write the letter of the answer that correctly completes each sentence.

1. Philip II ruled a land called _____.

   A Athens   **B** Sparta   **C** Thebes   **D** Macedonia

2. Philip constructed _____ and taught his men new ways of fighting.

   A new roads   **B** war machinery   **C** an empire   **D** boats

3. To conquer the _____, Philip needed the military strength of all the Greek armies.

   A Persian Empire   **B** Bucephalus   **C** Spartans   **D** Tyre

4. Philip II conquered all of Greece except for _____.

   A Athens   **B** Sparta   **C** Thebes   **D** Macedonia

5. Before Philip could lead his men into Persia, he was _____.

   A defeated   **B** made king   **C** assassinated   **D** campaigned

6. Philip's son, _____, inherited his father's ambition and love of power.

   A Aristotle   **B** Olympias   **C** Alexander   **D** Bucephalus

7. _____ was the great Greek thinker who taught young Alexander.

   A Aristotle   **B** Olympias   **C** Philip   **D** Bucephalus

8. Alexander was a fearless boy. _____ was the horse he tamed that no other person in the kingdom could ride.

   A Aristotle   **B** Olympias   **C** Philip   **D** Bucephalus

9. Alexander took command of his father's army at age _____.

   A 13   **B** 18   **C** 20   **D** 33

10. Alexander was only _____ years old when his father died.

   A 13   **B** 18   **C** 20   **D** 33

146   *Unit 3   The Origins of Western Civilization: Greece and Rome*

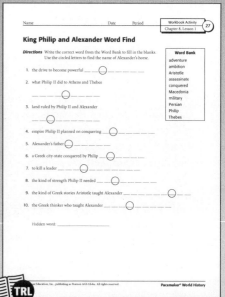

Activity 27   Workbook Activity 27

Alexander's Conquests

Objectives

- To tell what battle is considered to be one of Alexander's greatest military victories
- To locate Alexander's empire on a map
- To explain why Alexander had to give up his campaign

Philip II had planned to conquer an empire. Greece would be the center of that empire. Now that job fell to his son, Alexander.

What Is Considered One of Alexander's Greatest Military Victories?

Since birth, Alexander had been raised to be a ruler and a warrior. He was ready for the job. Alexander and the Macedonian army headed for Persia.

The next two years saw Alexander and his men crossing the Middle East. They conquered one land after another. Then in 334 B.C., Alexander began his campaign against Persia. In 333 B.C., Alexander did battle with the king of the Persian Empire, Darius III. Alexander won the battle, but King Darius escaped.

Alexander was the king of Macedonia at age 20. By the time he died at age 33, he expanded his empire and the whole world had heard of him.

360 B.C.–320 B.C.

Alexander the Great   Chapter 8   **147**

Lesson at a Glance

Chapter 8 Lesson 2

Overview This section describes the empire of Alexander the Great and the spreading of Greek culture that resulted from his conquests.

Objectives

- To tell what battle is considered to be one of Alexander's greatest military victories
- To locate Alexander's empire on a map
- To explain why Alexander had to give up his campaign

Student Pages 147–151

Teacher's Resource Library

Workbook Activity 28

Activity 28

Modified Activity 28

Vocabulary

founded   general

Have students write original sentences using each word. Ask volunteers to write their sentences on the board.

PRONUNCIATION GUIDE

Use this list to help students pronounce difficult words in this lesson.

Ptolemy (tol′ ə me)

1   Warm-Up Activity

Have students study the illustration on page 147 and the map on page 150. Lead a discussion in which students talk about how these two pieces of information affect their perspective on Alexander. What kind of leader do they think he was?

2 Teaching the Lesson

Have students read this section to find out whether Alexander was successful at conquering the world and what influence his conquests had on civilization.

Ask:

- What was Alexander's goal? (to conquer the world)
- What happened as Greek culture spread? (It blended with other cultures; this blend is called *Hellenism*.)
- What was the greatest city in the Hellenistic Age? (Alexandria in Egypt)
- Does Alexander deserve the name "Alexander the Great"? (Answers will vary; students may say yes, because he took over so much of the world.)

Background Information

Students may be interested to learn the name "Alexander" is derived from the Greek words "alexo" (refuge, dense, protection) and "aner" (man)—hence, "refuge of man," "protector of man," or, if you like, "dense man." But he was also known throughout the Persian Empire as "the accursed Alexander."

Reading Strategy:
Summarizing

Call students' attention to the question on page 148, "What are some important details about Alexander's accomplishments?" Encourage them to discuss these as a class.

LEARN MORE ABOUT IT

Ask students to read Learn More About It: Alexandria on page 148 of the Student Edition. Tell students to look at the second paragraph, which mentions the lighthouse, one of the wonders of the world. Ask students to work with a partner to research other wonders of the world. Ask students, *What are the other wonders of the world? What do you think makes them wonders of the world?* You may wish to ask students to illustrate the wonders of the world on a poster.

Founded
To have begun a country or city; to have built a city

Reading Strategy:
Summarizing

What are some important details about Alexander's accomplishments?

On through the Persian Empire, to Syria, swept the conquering Macedonians. They attacked the great Phoenician city of Tyre. Alexander ordered his men to build a raised road over the sea to reach the city. The battle at Tyre was one of his greatest military victories.

What Was Egypt Like After Alexander Conquered It?

After taking over Phoenicia, Alexander moved south, toward Egypt. Alexander's army easily took Egypt.

The Egyptians had been under harsh Persian rule. They were glad to have Alexander as their new ruler. Some Egyptians even hailed Alexander as the son of an Egyptian god.

Alexander built a city on the Mediterranean coast of Egypt. He named it after himself, like many other cities he had built. Egypt's *Alexandria* became the most famous of the Alexandrias.

LEARN MORE ABOUT IT

Alexandria

Alexander drew up plans for building the city of Alexandria in Egypt in 332 B.C. After his death, the ruling family carried out his plan. The city grew rapidly. It became one of the largest and most important cities of the ancient world. Within 200 years after it was **founded** (built), more than a million people were living in Alexandria.

It was a beautiful city. Many of its buildings were Greek in style. A giant lighthouse rose over 370 feet high. It was built of white marble and was known as one of the Seven Wonders of the Ancient World. The huge fire at the top of the lighthouse could be seen by sailors 30 miles away.

Alexandria was also famous for its fine schools and its library. The library contained more than 700,000 scrolls. A scroll is a roll of paper or parchment with writing on it. Scrolls were used instead of books. The library of Alexandria was the largest in the world. It became a famous center of learning and culture. The glory of Greece had come to Egypt.

General
A high-ranking military officer

One of Alexander's **generals** (a high-ranking military officer) was named Ptolemy. Alexander chose him to rule Egypt. Ptolemy's family would rule Egypt for 300 years.

What Brought About the End of the Persian Empire?

Alexander was more interested in conquering than in ruling. Just as with Ptolemy in Egypt, he would set up many more rulers in other lands. When Alexander felt his work in Egypt was done, he moved on. He still wanted the whole world.

In 331 B.C., Alexander met King Darius III of Persia again. Alexander defeated Darius. Once again, however, Darius escaped. Yet Alexander had no more trouble with his old enemy. King Darius was to die that same year, killed by his own men. With Darius gone, Alexander was the ruler of all of the Persian Empire.

The city of Persepolis, in southwestern Persia, was the greatest city of the Persian Empire. Much of the wealth of the empire was stored in the palaces of Persepolis. Alexander and his army easily captured the city. They killed most of the people who lived there. They took the rest as slaves. The Macedonians took all the treasures and then burned the Persian palaces. In 480 B.C., the Persians had burned Athens. Now Alexander had gotten even.

Then Alexander looked east. What was left for him in the world? India would be next.

What Happened in the Valley of the Indus?

In 326 B.C., Alexander the Great arrived in India. The Aryan rajas (princes) along the Indus River battled the Macedonian soldiers. The Aryans rode great, lumbering war elephants. Yet Alexander's men, riding horseback, were faster. Alexander conquered the Indus River Valley. He wanted to go deeper into India, but his men were tired.

---

360 B.C.–320 B.C.

Alexander the Great   Chapter 8   **149**

LEARNING STYLES

Logical/Mathematical
Distribute copies of a modern map of the region formerly occupied by Alexander's empire. Have students work in small groups to make a list of the countries that now occupy the area that was Alexander's empire. Alexander's army began its march in Macedonia and traveled eastward into India. Have students calculate the number of miles that the army marched before they turned back to return to Babylon (over 11,000 miles).

ELL/ESL STRATEGY

Language Objective: *To speak for a variety of purposes including to express feelings, ideas, and opinions; to explain, report, and inform; to describe; to influence and persuade*

Have a group of students role-play a scene in which the men of Alexander's army beg him to turn back after they had marched as far as India. More proficient students can write the skit themselves, giving reasons for their pleas. Less proficient students can act in a skit written by the teacher or other students.

3   Reinforce and Extend

TEACHER ALERT

Remind students that they will be presenting a short film, play, or presentation for their chapter project at the end of Chapter 8. Encourage them to work together to conduct research outside the class that will assist them in creating a well informed and entertaining chapter project.

Have students study the map on page 150. Alexander's empire covered parts of three continents. Have students use maps in the World Atlas to determine the three continents. (Africa, Asia, and Europe)

COMMON ERROR

Remind students that their knowing what part of speech a word is—noun, adjective, verb, or adverb—can help them to understand the same word in different contexts. For example, the word *general* is a noun; however, the word *general* may also be used as an adjective, and then has an entirely different meaning. Encourage students to look up *general* in their dictionaries—both as a noun and as an adjective.

STUDY SKILLS

Encourage students to make a list of the central characters in Lesson 2. Write Alexander, King Darius III, and Ptolemy on the board; have students write two or three details about each.

AT HOME

Students who come from immigrant families may have personal experiences in the blending of two cultures. Have them create a list of things from home that represent a blend of their own culture and American culture. Possibilities may include clothing, art objects, and food. Use this activity to help students understand Hellenism, which was a blending of Eastern and Western cultures following Alexander's conquests.

Heavy rains had come, and marching was hard. They wanted to go home.

"Back to Greece," the soldiers cried.

"On through India," Alexander demanded.

Alexander's armies insisted on turning back. They would go no farther. For that reason, Alexander had to give up his campaign.

Alexander's Empire

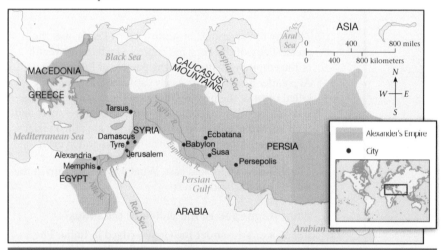

MAP STUDY

1. What are two cities in Egypt?
2. Which three rivers did Alexander have to cross to get to India (east of Persia)?

COMMON ERROR

The stories of Alexander the Great and his conquests are exciting and interesting. Much film, art, and myth has sprung up around the figure of Alexander the Great. That he successfully conquered the known world is undeniable. Yet, students often forget that Alexander's conquests came at great cost to those who were conquered. Ask students, "What happened to the citizens of Persepolis when Alexander and his army captured the city?" (Most of the people there were killed, and the rest were taken as slaves.)

REVIEW

Word Bank

Darius III

Egypt

Egyptian god

India

Indus River Valley

Ptolemy

Tyre

On a sheet of paper, write the word from the Word Bank to complete each sentence correctly.

1. The battle at _____ is considered to be one of Alexander's greatest military victories.

2. Alexander conquered Persia and then went on to Egypt and _____.

3. The Egyptians were glad to have Alexander as their new ruler. Some even hailed Alexander as the son of a(n) _____.

4. Alexandria is the city Alexander built on the Mediterranean coast of _____.

5. Alexander chose his general _____ to rule Egypt.

6. King _____ of the Persian Empire escaped death when Alexander conquered Persia. Unfortunately, he was killed by his own men a few years later.

7. Alexander conquered the _____ easily. This is because his men, riding horses, were faster than the Aryans who rode elephants.

On a sheet of paper, write the answer to each question. Use complete sentences.

8. How did Alexander defeat the city of Tyre?

9. How did the Persian Empire come to an end?

10. Why did Alexander have to give up his campaign?

Lesson 8–2 Review Answers

1. Tyre 2. India 3. Egyptian god 4. Egypt 5. Ptolemy 6. Darius III 7. Indus River Valley 8. Alexander ordered his men to build a raised road over the sea to reach the city. 9. Alexander took over as the ruler of the Persian Empire when King Darius III was killed by his own men. Then Alexander and his army captured the city of Persepolis (the greatest city in the Persian Empire) and killed most of the people that lived there. They took the rest of the people as slaves. Then they took all the treasures and burned the palaces, ending the Empire. 10. His men were tired and refused to go further. Thus he was forced to give up his campaign.

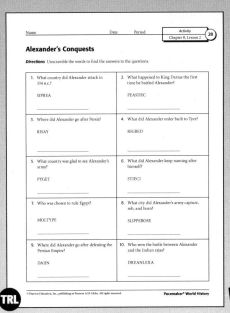

Chapter 8 Lesson 3

Overview After conquering the Aryan kingdoms in India, Alexander continued to spread Greek culture and ideas across the known world; however, after his sudden death at age 33, Alexander's empire quickly fell into disarray.

Objectives
■ To tell why Alexander made Babylon the capital of his empire
■ To describe what happened to Alexander's empire after his death

Student Pages 152–154

Teacher's Resource Library

Workbook Activity 29

Activity 29

Modified Activity 29

Remember
Ask students what Hammurabi and Alexander the Great may have in common.

1 Warm-Up Activity

Ask students to study carefully the illustration at the bottom of page 152. Have them describe what they see there and ask them how the caption affects their view of the information they've read in Lesson 8.

2 Teaching the Lesson

Have students read this section to discover how Alexander's empire came to an end.

Ask:
● How did Alexander attempt to create one culture from the two (Europe and Asia) that he had conquered? (Answers may vary. He rewarded intermarrying; he introduced Greek ideas, architecture, and politics; he introduced new plants.)
● What happened to Alexander's empire after his death? (His lands were divided among generals and the empire disappeared.)

The End of an Empire

Objectives
■ To tell why Alexander made Babylon the capital of his empire
■ To describe what happened to Alexander's empire after his death

Remember
At a much earlier date Hammurabi, a great ruler of Babylon, drew up a code of laws.

Alexander was 30 years old when he conquered the Aryan kingdoms in India. He had been fighting and building his empire for 12 years. In all that time he had never lost a single battle!

Alexander made his father's dreams real. He spread Greek culture and ideas over a large part of the world. Alexander's empire was the largest the ancient world had ever known.

Alexander imagined Europe and Asia as one big country, united under his rule. He wanted to blend the two into one. He chose Babylon as his capital city because it was in the center of his empire. He had plants brought in from one continent and planted on the other. Alexander married an Asian woman. He also rewarded his soldiers if they did the same.

Detail found on the tomb of Alexander the Great shows Persians and Greeks hunting together. It represents his desire for unity between people even after the fighting during his lifetime.

152 *Unit 3   The Origins of Western Civilization: Greece and Rome*

Background Information

After Alexander's death, his three generals divided the kingdom into three empires—Macedon, Egypt, and Syria. These three kingdoms often fought each other. But one thing held them together—their Greek culture. Throughout the Middle East, people adopted Greek customs. They spoke Greek, they built their buildings as the Greeks did, and they gave themselves Greek names. As Greek culture spread eastward, it blended with other cultures. We call this blend of eastern and western cultures "Hellenism." The word comes from the Greek word "Hellas," which means "their own land."

What Happened After Alexander's Death?

Alexander ruled a giant empire from his palace in Babylon. He had big plans for his empire. Then, in 323 B.C., he fell sick. He had a high fever. No medicines of the day could help him. Within a few days, 33-year-old Alexander the Great was dead. His soldiers placed his body in a gold coffin. It was taken to Alexandria in Egypt to be buried.

After his death, Alexander's lands were divided among some of his generals. The great empire was gone forever, split into separate smaller empires.

Yet the man who set out to conquer the world had left his mark. The lands Alexander touched would always show something of Greek style and Greek customs.

Reading Strategy: Summarizing

What important event in history is this lesson about?

TIMELINE STUDY:

ALEXANDER THE GREAT

What does the timeline show about Alexander's short life?

| 356 B.C. Alexander is born | 338 B.C. Philip of Macedonia wins control of Greece | 336 B.C. King Philip is assassinated | 326 B.C. Alexander invades India |

360 B.C.   350 B.C.   340 B.C.   330 B.C.   320 B.C.

334 B.C. Alexander begins Persian campaigns   332 B.C. Alexander conquers Egypt   323 B.C. Alexander dies

360 B.C.–320 B.C.

Alexander the Great   Chapter 8   **153**

LESSON 8-3 REVIEW

On a sheet of paper, write the letter of the answer that correctly completes each sentence.

1. Alexander was _____ years old when he conquered the Aryans in India.

   A 12   **B** 23   **C** 30   **D** 33

2. In his _____ years of fighting, Alexander had not lost a single battle.

   A 12   **B** 23   **C** 30   **D** 33

3. Alexander's _____ was the largest the ancient world had ever known.

   A army   **B** family   **C** empire   **D** slave population

4. Alexander wanted to rule Europe and _____ as one big country.

   A Asia   **B** Egypt   **C** Macedonia   **D** Persia

5. Alexander married a(n) _____ woman and rewarded his soldiers if they did the same.

   A Asian   **B** Egyptian   **C** Macedonian   **D** Persian

6. Alexander made _____ the capital city because it was the center of his empire.

   A Alexandria   **B** Babylon   **C** Persepolis   **D** Tyre

7. Alexander died at the age of _____.

   A 12   **B** 23   **C** 30   **D** 33

8. Alexander was buried in a gold coffin in the city of _____.

   A Alexandria   **B** Babylon   **C** Persepolis   **D** Tyre

9. After his death, the lands Alexander conquered were _____.

   A free to govern themselves   **C** divided among some of his generals
   B left to fight wars with each other   **D** given to his son

10. Alexander's empire _____ after his death.

    A turned to democracy   **C** grew
    B fought each other   **D** was over

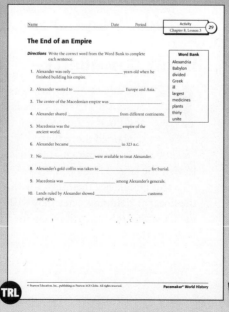

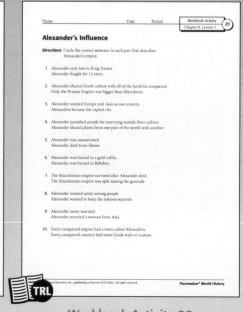

Activity 29   Workbook Activity 29

- King Philip of Macedonia built up his army. He taught his men new ways of fighting. He planned to conquer the Persian Empire.

- Because Philip needed all of Greece behind him, he first conquered the Greek city-states of Thebes and Athens. He did not conquer Sparta.

- King Philip was assassinated, then his son Alexander led the Macedonian armies into Persia.

- Alexander set out to conquer the world.

- Alexander had a great victory at Tyre in Phoenicia.

- Alexander conquered Egypt. He built Alexandria on its Mediterranean coast.

- Alexander chose Ptolemy, one of his generals, to rule Egypt.

- Alexander became ruler of the Persian Empire after destroying the city of Persepolis.

- Alexander conquered the Indus River Valley area in India.

- Alexander brought Greek ideas and culture to the lands he conquered.

- Alexander died at the age of 33.

- After Alexander's death, his lands were split up among his generals.

360 B.C.–320 B.C.   *Alexander the Great*   *Chapter 8*   **155**

Chapter 8 Summary

Have students read the Chapter Summary on page 155 to review the main ideas presented in Chapter 8.

Ask:

- Why did King Philip build up his army? (Answers may vary. Students may say that it was because Macedonia was poor or so he could conquer the Persian Empire.)

- Why did King Philip conquer the Greek city-states? (He needed an enormous army to conquer the Persian Empire.)

- What civilization was King Philip unable to conquer? (Sparta)

- What prevented King Philip from conquering Persia? (He was assassinated.)

- What did Alexander wish to do? (conquer the world)

- What was one of Alexander's greatest military victories (the victory at Tyre)

- Where was Alexandria built? (on the Mediterranean coast)

- Who was chosen to rule Egypt? (Ptolemy)

- What city was destroyed in the Persian Empire? (Persepolis)

- What did Alexander bring to the lands he conquered? (Greek ideas and culture)

- What befell his empire after Alexander died at age 33? (It was split up among his generals.)

TEACHER'S RESOURCE

The AGS Globe Teaching Strategies in Social Studies Transparencies may be used with this chapter. The transparencies add an interactive dimension to expand and enhance the Pacemaker® *World History* program content.

CHAPTER PROJECT FOLLOW-UP

Set aside class time for each group to present its chapter project. Encourage those students who are listening to a project to take notes. At the end of each project, ask for volunteers to summarize the information they have received.

Chapter 8 Review

Use the Chapter Review to prepare students for tests and to reteach content from the chapter.

Chapter 8 Mastery Test

The Teacher's Resource Library includes two forms of the Chapter 8 Mastery Test. Each test addresses the chapter Goals for Learning. An optional third page of additional critical-thinking items is included for each test. The difficulty level of the two forms is equivalent.

Chapter 8 Review Answers

Vocabulary Review

1. ambition
2. founded
3. general
4. campaign
5. assassinate

Chapter Review Questions

6. King Philip needed the military strength of all the Greek armies in order to conquer the Persian Empire.

7. Philip used his military know-how and his well-trained men to conquer Athens and Thebes. Then all of Greece, except Sparta, fell under his control.

8. King Philip thought highly of Greek ideas and the Greek way of life. The Greeks were known as scholars.

9. Alexander was called the Great Conqueror because he and his soldiers conquered one land after another.

10. The battle at Tyre was one of Alexander's greatest military victories because Alexander and his army built a raised road over the sea to reach (and conquer) the city.

11. The Egyptians were suffering under harsh Persian rule.

12. Alexander chose Babylon because it was at the center of his empire.

Word Bank

ambition
assassinate
campaign
founded
general

Vocabulary Review

On a sheet of paper, use the words from the Word Bank to complete each sentence correctly.

1. Alexander the Great had the _____ to take over the world.

2. Alexandria was _____ in 332 B.C.

3. A(n) _____ has a top position in the military.

4. To win a war, a military leader must plan a(n) _____ of a number of battles.

5. The people who _____ a leader are murderers.

Chapter Review Questions

On a sheet of paper, write the answer to each question. Use complete sentences.

6. What did King Philip II of Macedonia need in order to conquer the Persian Empire?

7. How did Philip become ruler of Greece?

8. Why did Philip choose a Greek teacher for young Alexander?

9. Why was Alexander called the Great Conqueror?

10. What battle is considered to be one of Alexander's greatest military victories, and why?

11. Why did the Egyptians welcome Alexander the Great?

12. Why did Alexander choose Babylon as the capital of his empire?

---

156   Unit 3   *The Origins of Western Civilization: Greece and Rome*

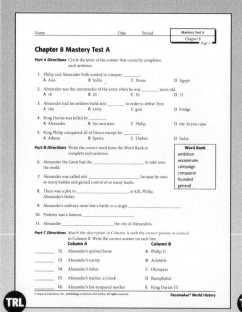

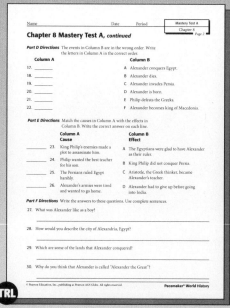

Always read test directions more than once. Underline words that tell how many examples or items you must provide.

13. What was Alexander's vision for his empire?

14. What happened to Alexander's empire after he died?

15. How did Alexander the Great leave his mark on the world he conquered?

Critical Thinking

On a sheet of paper, write your response to each question. Use complete sentences.

16. Why was Aristotle a good teacher for Alexander?

17. What was Alexander's greatest accomplishment? Explain why.

Using the Timeline

Use the timeline on page 153 to answer the questions.

18. What year was King Philip assassinated?

19. How old was Alexander when he began the Persian campaigns?

20. What is the order of the following: the conquest of Egypt, the invasion of India, the Persian campaigns?

GROUP ACTIVITY

In a group of three or four, write a mini-biography of Alexander the Great. Include basic information, such as his birth, accomplishments, and death. Include information from this chapter and from other books. In the last paragraph of your biography, express your opinion of Alexander. Tell why you think he was able to do so much during his short life.

360 B.C.–320 B.C.

Alexander the Great Chapter 8 **157**

---

13. Alexander wanted to rule Europe and Asia as one big country, united under his rule.

14. After Alexander died, the empire was divided among his generals.

15. The lands Alexander conquered had some Greek style and customs.

Critical Thinking

16. Possible answers: Aristotle taught Alexander about Greek heroes and adventure, and also about far-off lands. He had Alexander take part in sports. All these things prepared Alexander for leadership.

17. Possible answers: Students may mention Alexander's conquests, the important city of Alexandria with its excellent library, or the spread of Greek style and customs.

Using the Timeline

18. 336 B.C.

19. 22 years old

20. The Persian campaigns, the conquest of Egypt, the invasion of India

GROUP ACTIVITY

The biography of Alexander the Great should present information about his life in an organized way, plus an informed opinion about his accomplishments.

Chapter 8 Mastery Test B

Name _____ Date _____ Period _____

Mastery Test B
Chapter 8
Page 1

Part A Directions Circle the letter of the answer that correctly completes each sentence.

1. As a boy, Alexander was _____.
   A slow   B carefree   C fearless   D timid

2. The city of _____ was filled with libraries and schools.
   A Alexandria   B Persepolis   C Tyre   D Sparta

3. Alexander did not conquer _____.
   A Persia   B Syria   C Egypt   D India

4. Alexander's nickname was "Alexander the _____."
   A Fearless   B Great   C Son   D Conqueror

5. Alexander was able to tame _____ when nobody else could.
   A Aristotle   B Bucephalus   C Ptolemy   D Darius

Part B Directions Write the correct word from the Word Bank to complete each sentence.

6. Philip hired Aristotle to _____ Alexander.

7. Philip was assassinated before he could _____ Persia.

8. Alexander was welcomed by the people of _____.

9. Alexander was not able to conquer _____ as he had planned.

10. Philip defeated all the Greek city-states except _____.

11. Both Alexander and Philip were kings of _____.

Word Bank
conquer
Egypt
India
Macedonia
Sparta
teach

Part C Directions Match the description in Column A with the correct word in Column B. Write the correct answer on each line.

	Column A	Column B
___ 12.	the drive to become powerful	A assassinate
___ 13.	to completely destroy	B campaign
___ 14.	to kill a person of power	C general
___ 15.	a series of battles in a war	D ambition
___ 16.	a high-ranking military officer	E conquer

© Pearson Education, Inc., publishing as Pearson AGS Globe. All rights reserved.

Pacemaker® World History

Chapter 8 Mastery Test B, *continued*

Name _____ Date _____ Period _____

Mastery Test B
Chapter 8
Page 2

Part D Directions The events in Column B are in the wrong order. Write the letters in Column A in the correct order.

Column A	Column B
17. _____	A Alexander works with Aristotle.
18. _____	B Darius is killed by his own men.
19. _____	C Alexander destroys Persepolis.
20. _____	D Alexander battles in the Indus River Valley.
21. _____	E Philip reigns in Macedonia.
22. _____	F Alexander leads the Macedonian army.

Part E Directions Match the causes in Column A with the effects in Column B. Write the correct answer on each line.

	Column A Cause	Column B Effect
___ 23.	Alexander wanted to be remembered.	A Alexander set out to conquer Persia.
___ 24.	Alexander's mother, Olympias, had a quick temper.	B He founded the city of Alexandria.
___ 25.	Philip was assassinated before conquering Persia.	C Alexander was quick to become angry.
___ 26.	King Darius escaped the first time he fought Alexander.	D Alexander and Darius fought a second time.

Part F Directions Write the answers to these questions. Use complete sentences.

27. What was both Philip's and Alexander's dream?

28. What did Alexander do to make the defeat of Tyre so great?

29. What happened to King Darius?

30. Why did Alexander not conquer India?

© Pearson Education, Inc., publishing as Pearson AGS Globe. All rights reserved.

Pacemaker® World History

Chapter 8 Mastery Test B, pages 1–3

Alexander the Great Chapter 8 **157**

Introducing the Chapter

From the founding of Rome through the fall of the Roman Empire, this chapter chronicles Rome's vast contributions to civilization. Despite several bad emperors, the Roman Empire lasted 500 years and reigned over nearly 100 million people before its fall in A.D. 476. During this period, one of the world's great religions was born.

The Rise of Rome

Over a period of 500 years, Rome grew to be a republic. It started as a group of villages and grew to be a mighty city. Its empire included lands on all sides of the Mediterranean.

The Romans had a strong civilization. They developed language, architecture, laws, and religion of wide range and strength. Their civilization was larger and more powerful than any that had come before it. The Roman Empire would have deep effects on many cultures that followed it.

GOALS FOR LEARNING

- To describe how Rome grew powerful
- To explain the role of Julius Caesar in early Rome
- To describe the beginnings of the Roman Empire
- To describe Roman society
- To explain the rise of Christianity in Rome
- To explain why the Roman Empire began to fall

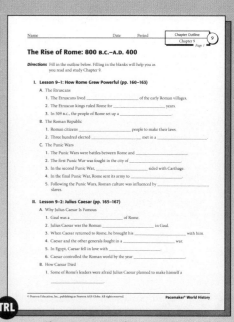

Reading Strategy: Questioning

As you read, ask yourself questions. This will help you understand more of the information and become a more active reader. Ask yourself:

• What do I hope to learn from this text?

• What do the facts and details in this text tell me?

• Are there any people or situations in this text that connect to my life?

Key Vocabulary Words

Lesson 1

Peninsula A long piece of land almost completely surrounded by water

Republic A government in which the citizens have the right to choose their representatives to make laws

Elect To choose someone for an office by voting

Representative A person who is chosen to act or speak for others

Senate A governing or lawmaking body

Lesson 2

Province A part of a country, with its own local government

Governor A person chosen to run a province or territory

Civil war Fighting between people who live in the same country

Forum A public square in an ancient Roman city; lawmakers met there

Lesson 3

Pax Romana The Roman peace that began during the reign of Augustus Caesar

Lesson 4

Aqueduct A channel that carries flowing water over a long distance

Lesson 5

Gospel One of four books of the New Testament part of the Bible

Enslaved When a person is forced to become a slave

Persecute To treat in a cruel way

Convert Change from one religion to another

Bishop A high-ranking church official in charge of other priests and a number of churches

Pope The head of the Roman Catholic Church

Ask:

• When was Rome founded? (753 B.C.)

• Who was Julius Caesar? (He was a Roman general who later ruled the Roman world.)

• Who was Rome's first emperor? (Octavian)

• What was the language of the Romans? (Latin)

• What did Constantine do for Christians? (He made Christianity legal.)

Reading Strategy: Questioning

Introduce the reading skill *questioning*. Explain that when you ask questions about something you are reading, you make connections between what you have just read and what you are about to read. Asking questions can also help you make inferences and predictions.

Point out that when we ask questions about what we are reading, we can anticipate finding the answers to our questions in the paragraphs to come. This feeling of anticipation heightens our interest and makes reading fun.

Ask:

• What questions can you ask about the information in the paragraph? (Sample answer: How did Rome change from a village into a great city?)

Key Vocabulary Words

Point out that these chapter words are presented in the order they appear in each lesson. They are also found in the glossary.

LIFE SKILLS CONNECTION

Students learn about the cost of owning property. They also discuss the responsibility of home ownership. Direct students to Web sites that provide mortgage calculators.

KEY VOCABULARY

Students will write the correct word from the Word Bank to complete each sentence.

Chapter 9 Life Skills Connection

The members of the Roman Senate were usually wealthy landowners. Many battles were fought over land in Roman times. Throughout history, the owning of land has started all sorts of conflicts.

Today, the value of owning land or property is just as high. While most people do not fight over land anymore, they do work hard to purchase it. Owning a home is a goal that most people work towards for many years. It is not a simple task. Most people take out loans, or mortgages, to buy a home. A mortgage is a big responsibility. If you cannot pay your mortgage, you could lose your home. The responsibility of owning a home is more than just the initial purchase. That is only the first step.

Once you own a home, you must pay annual property taxes. This is usually a percentage of the home's value. Property taxes help pay for resources in your community like schools, law enforcement, and transportation. Another cost of owning a home is insurance. Insurance protects you from losing money if your home is damaged by fire or a natural disaster. It is also a lot of work to maintain a home. Things like electrical wiring, plumbing, and heating and cooling can break and must be fixed right away. You must be responsible for keeping your home clean, safe, and running properly.

Directions Find the real estate ads in the newspaper or online. Choose a home you might like to live in one day. Use the Internet to find a calculator that will show you the real cost of owning that home. These calculators can show you what your mortgage payment would be along with taxes and insurance. Compare the cost of the home you chose to that of other students.

Chapter 9 Key Vocabulary Words

Directions Write the correct word from the Word Bank to complete each sentence.

Word Bank
aqueducts
bishop
civil war
elected
emperor
Gospels
governors
peninsula
pope
provinces
representative
republic
senators

1. The Italian _____ is almost completely surrounded by water.

2. Roman citizens _____ leaders to make their laws.

3. A(n) _____ is a person who is chosen to speak for others.

4. The Roman _____ was governed like a democracy.

5. The Romans built _____ to bring fresh water into the city.

6. Rome chose _____ to run its provinces.

7. Julius Caesar fought the other Roman generals in a(n) _____

8. Julius Caesar was killed by a group of Roman _____

9. The Roman _____ ruled many countries.

10. The lands controlled by Rome were divided into _____

11. The four _____ tell the story of the life of Jesus.

12. The head of the Roman Catholic Church has the title of _____

13. A(n) _____ is a high-ranking church official.

Lesson at a Glance

Chapter 9 Lesson 1

Overview This lesson traces the rise of Rome as a world power.

Objectives

- To tell about the effect the Etruscans had on early Rome
- To describe how the Roman Republic was governed
- To explain what the Punic Wars were and what they did for Rome

Student Pages 160–164

Teacher's Resource Library

Workbook Activity 30

Activity 30

Modified Activity 30

Vocabulary

elect	republic
peninsula	senate
representative	

Ask students to find the vocabulary words and their definitions in the lesson. Have them write each vocabulary word on an index card. Read aloud the definitions in random order and have students hold up the card with the corresponding vocabulary word. Continue the activity until students are thoroughly familiar with all vocabulary words.

1 Warm-Up Activity

Have students scan the section titled "How Was the Roman Republic Governed?" As a class, discuss similarities between the Roman Republic and the United States government (we both have elected representatives and a senate). Tell students that our system of government was based on the government of the Roman Republic.

How Rome Grew Powerful

Objectives

- To tell about the effect the Etruscans had on early Rome
- To describe how the Roman Republic was governed
- To explain what the Punic Wars were and what they did for Rome

Reading Strategy: Questioning

What do you already know about Rome?

Peninsula
A long piece of land almost completely surrounded by water

Republic
A government in which the citizens have the right to choose their representatives to make laws

Seven hills rose up along the Tiber River in the center of Italy. Small villages dotted the seven hills. One of those villages was called Rome. It had been built by the Latins in 753 B.C. The Latins, or Romans, were one of several groups of people that had moved down from central Europe. They settled in the Italian **peninsula** around 1000 B.C. A peninsula is a long piece of land almost completely surrounded by water. Rome was not very important then. However, it would one day grow into a great city. That city would become the center of an empire.

Who Were the Etruscans?

From 750 B.C. to 600 B.C., the little Italian villages were ruled by a series of Roman kings. During those years, the Romans lived in peace. They were mainly farmers and herders. Things changed in about 600 B.C. North of the Tiber River lived a people called the Etruscans. They decided to conquer Rome and the other villages. The Romans did not stand a chance against them.

For about the next 100 years, Rome was ruled by Etruscan kings. The Etruscans had many skills. They built a wall around the city. They drained nearby swamps and laid the first sewer to carry away dirty water and human waste. The Romans even adopted the Etruscan alphabet. Slowly, Rome changed from a little farming village into a city-state.

Then, in 509 B.C., the people of Rome rose up against a severe Etruscan king. They took the government of Rome into their own hands and set up a **republic.**

---

160 Unit 3 *The Origins of Western Civilization: Greece and Rome*

Reading Strategy: Questioning

Have students write the following question in their notebooks: *What do I already know about Rome?* Then have them make a list of facts and stories they know about Rome.

Elect
To choose someone for an office by voting

Representative
A person who is chosen to act or speak for others

Senate
A governing or lawmaking body

History Fact
Not all Roman citizens had equal rights. Poor people did not win political equality until 287 B.C.

Reading Strategy: Questioning

As you read, notice the details in the text. What questions can you ask yourself about those details?

How Was the Roman Republic Governed?

In a republic, the government is controlled by the people and there is no king. Roman citizens **elected,** or chose, men to make their laws and run their government. Three hundred elected **representatives** met in a **senate.** The senate was the part of the government that made laws. The Republic was democratic because citizens voted for the people who would represent them. The Roman Republic was a model for our own democratic system of representative government.

The members of the Roman Senate were usually wealthy landowners. Once elected, they held office for life. Some of the Senate members were quite old. The people thought them very wise. The word *senate* comes from the Latin word that means "old."

The early years of the Republic were not peaceful. At first Rome was attacked by armies from other lands. However, Rome grew more and more powerful. After a time, Rome wanted to gain more land.

What Did the Punic Wars Do for Rome?

The Romans became skilled soldiers. Almost every Roman male spent some time in the army. Rome's military power grew. The Romans began battling for more land. By about 270 B.C., Rome had taken over the whole Italian peninsula.

One of Rome's greatest enemies was Carthage. Carthage was on the north coast of Africa. It was a city settled by the Phoenicians. Carthage and Rome quarreled over Mediterranean trade routes.

Rome fought three wars with Carthage. These were called the Punic Wars. The first clash between the two states came in Sicily. They battled for the city of Messina. Rome finally won this war in 241 B.C., after 23 years of fighting!

Have students describe in their own words how Rome was transformed from a farming village into a powerful city-state.

Ask:

- For how many years was Rome ruled by Etruscan kings? (about 100 years)
- What is the main difference between the government of early Rome and the government of the Roman Republic? (Early Rome was ruled by Etruscan kings, and the Roman Republic was controlled by the people and the leaders they elected.)
- What did Rome hope to gain by entering into wars? (more land)

Background Information

The Etruscans were eventually overthrown by the Romans, but the former conquerors left behind a unique legacy. They created the Doric column, an architectural feature still used in modern times. They also developed the toga, the loose-fitting draped garment that the ancient Romans wore. In early Rome, the color of a toga denoted a person's status. Senators, for example, wore white.

LEARNING STYLES

Visual/Spatial
After students read the first paragraph of Lesson 1, have them make a map of Italy showing the Tiber River and Rome.

Reading Strategy: Questioning

Have students work with a partner to find the answers to their questions in the text. If the answers are not found in the text, encourage students to do additional research.

History Fact
Tell students that poor people often face political inequality. Have them discuss reasons why this happens.

ELL/ESL STRATEGY

Language Objective: *To improve students' recognition of common words*

Have students make a "Roman Dictionary" of vocabulary words and any other difficult words in this lesson. For each entry in the dictionary, students should write a definition and a sentence that includes the entry word. Encourage students to repeat the activity for each lesson in the chapter.

3 Reinforce and Extend

COMMON ERROR

Students may assume that elected representatives serve for a limited number of years. Point out that members of the senate in the Roman Republic served for life. Members of the U.S. Supreme Court serve for life. However, they are appointed. They are not elected.

Remember

Have students review their notes from Chapter 8 to refresh their memories about Philip II and Alexander.

TECHNOLOGY CONNECTION

Challenge interested students to make a working model of one of the inventions of Archimedes. Archimedes, a Greek scientist, used the concept of simple machines to create useful tools and weapons.

Remember
Philip II and Alexander the Great were Macedonians.

During the second war between Carthage and Rome, Macedonia had sided with the Carthaginians. Macedonia was still the most powerful state in Greece. After taking Carthage, Rome sent armies into Greece. Roman armies conquered the Greek city-states. They brought Greek treasures back to Rome, introducing Roman citizens to Greek art and style.

The Romans made slaves of the conquered Greeks. Many of the slaves were used as laborers. Some of the Greek captives, however, were well educated. They became teachers and doctors in Rome. Many Greek slaves found themselves with kind Roman masters, masters who respected them. Some Greeks were able to earn their freedom. Therefore, in many ways, Roman culture was influenced by the Greeks.

Over the next 50 years, Carthage grew strong again. Once more, Rome felt threatened. So Rome declared war and sent its army back to Africa. This time, in the final Punic War, the city of Carthage was totally destroyed.

TECHNOLOGY CONNECTION

The Work of Archimedes
The Greeks lost a great thinker during the Punic Wars. Archimedes was a scientist, mathematician, philosopher, and inventor.

Archimedes worked for the state during the Punic Wars. During that time, he invented many weapons to defend his town of Syracuse, Italy. He developed a catapult that was used to throw stones at an enemy. Another tool he created could lift or tip an enemy's ship. Also, some claim that he invented a "burning mirror" to reflect the sun's ray toward an enemy.

However, Archimedes is most famous for another discovery. He learned that an item placed in water lost weight based on the amount of water it replaced. This idea was revolutionary for the time.

Archimedes eventually died at the hands of a Roman soldier.

By 140 B.C., Rome controlled all of the Mediterranean lands. Citizens of the Republic thought of the Mediterranean Sea as a Roman sea.

GREAT NAMES IN HISTORY

Hannibal

In 218 B.C., a fierce Carthaginian general named Hannibal arrived in Spain. He brought a huge army with him. He led his soldiers over the Pyrenees and the Alps. Many of Hannibal's soldiers rode elephants. The mountains were hard on the huge animals. Many elephants lost their footing on the narrow mountain paths and fell to their deaths. Most of them, however, made it to the Po Valley of Italy. Hannibal was a clever general. He caught the Romans by surprise and beat the Roman army. Thus began the second of the Punic Wars.

For the next 13 years, Hannibal led his army up and down Italy. He won more battles against Roman forces. Nevertheless, little by little the Romans grew stronger. Finally Hannibal was driven out of Italy. Then the Romans invaded Africa and defeated Hannibal's army in 202 B.C.

Hannibal crossed the Alps to invade Rome because he knew the Romans would be surprised.

GREAT NAMES IN HISTORY

Draw a graphic organizer on the board. Ask students to copy the organizer in their notebooks. They should write Hannibal as the central topic, and words and phrases that describe Hannibal and his actions in the surrounding circles. Ask students if they think that Hannibal was a good leader. Have them explain their answer.

CAREER CONNECTION

Early Romans put great emphasis on rule by law. Today, a variety of careers are related to the law, including paralegals. Paralegals work in law firms and government agencies and for public-interest groups, such as environmental and civil rights organizations. To become a paralegal, a person must obtain a college degree and demonstrate proficiency in word processing. In addition, one must complete a postgraduate course of study.

CHAPTER PROJECT

Divide the class into six small groups. Assign one lesson in this chapter to each group. Have the groups create short skits based on the content in their lessons. Be sure students develop a script and assign roles to each member of the group. Encourage students to do additional research concerning the dress and lifestyles of the people they will represent.

Lesson 9–1 Review Answers

1. B **2.** A **3.** E **4.** C **5.** D **6.** They built a wall around the city, drained nearby swamps, and laid the first sewer. The Romans also adopted the Etruscan alphabet. The Etruscans slowly changed Rome from a farming village to a city-state. **7.** In a republic, the government is controlled by the people. Citizens elected people to make their laws and run their government. They elected representatives to meet in a senate. Usually the Roman Senate was made up of wealthy landowners and, once elected, they held office for life. **8.** The Punic Wars were the three wars Rome fought with Carthage. The Romans, in their quest to expand, quarreled with Carthage over Mediterranean trade routes. **9.** In the second Punic War, the Romans captured Greek city-states. They brought back Greek treasures, introducing Romans to Greek art and style. Romans made slaves of the Greeks and forced many of them to work as laborers. Others who were educated became teachers and doctors in Rome. Thus, Roman culture was influenced by the Greeks in many ways. **10.** The Romans thought of the Mediterranean Sea as a Roman sea because by 140 B.C., Rome controlled all of the Mediterranean lands.

Match the description in Column A with the term in Column B. Write the correct letter on a sheet of paper.

Column A

1. the Carthaginian general who helped start the second Punic War

2. the people that ruled Rome for 100 years

3. the river Rome rose up along

4. the people who built Rome in 753 B.C.

5. the government the Romans set up after rebelling against a harsh king

Column B

A Etruscans
B Hannibal
C Latins
D republic
E Tiber

On a sheet of paper, write the answer to each question. Use complete sentences.

6. What effect did the Etruscans have on early Rome?

7. How was the Roman Republic governed?

8. What were the Punic Wars and why were they fought?

9. What did the Punic Wars do for Roman culture?

10. Why did the Romans think of the Mediterranean Sea as a Roman sea?

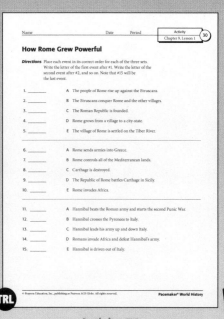

Julius Caesar

Objectives

■ To explain the role of armies in Roman provinces
■ To name some things Julius Caesar did for Rome
■ To tell how Julius Caesar died

Province
A part of a country, with its own local government

Governor
A person chosen to run a province or territory

Senator
A person who is a member of the senate

Rome conquered many lands. Some of them were far from the city itself. To make the lands easier to govern, they were divided into sections called **provinces.** Each province had its own local government and was ruled by its own **governor.** Some people in the provinces accepted the Roman rule. Others were not happy with their new rulers. Furthermore, they did not like Roman customs.

To keep the people in order, Rome sent large armies to each province. A general was at the head of each of these armies. The soldiers in the provinces were a long way from Rome. They often felt more loyalty to their generals than they did to Rome. The generals became powerful men.

Sometimes the generals and their armies fought among themselves. The most powerful of the generals was a man named Julius Caesar.

Who Was Julius Caesar and Why Is He So Famous?

Julius Caesar was the Roman general in the province of Gaul. Gaul was a land to the northwest of Rome. It would one day be called France. People liked Julius Caesar. His soldiers were loyal to him. The people of Rome admired his success. He won many battles in Gaul and expanded Roman control. After a while, members of the senate in Rome, or **senators,** began to worry about Caesar's popularity. Was Julius Caesar becoming too powerful?

Chapter 9 Lesson 2

Overview This lesson tells the rise and fall of Julius Caesar.

Objectives

■ To explain the role of armies in Roman provinces
■ To name some things Julius Caesar did for Rome
■ To tell how Julius Caesar died

Student Pages 165–168

Teacher's Resource Library

Workbook Activity 31

Activity 31

Modified Activity 31

Vocabulary

civil war   province
forum   senator
governor

Have students write definitions for the vocabulary words on index cards. Suggest that they use the definitions in the chapter and the Glossary as references. Students can use the cards as study tools as they read this lesson.

1 Warm-Up Activity

Show students a map that illustrates the lands conquered by Rome. Remind them that many of these lands were very different from Rome, both culturally and geographically. Discuss what it might have been like to be governed by a power that had different rules and customs.

As students read about the life of Julius Caesar, have them consider his strengths and weaknesses.

Ask:

- Who was Julius Caesar? (the Roman general in the province of Gaul)

- Why did Rome send large armies to each province? (to keep people in order)

- Why was Caesar killed? (Some powerful people were afraid of Caesar. They thought he planned to make himself a king.)

Background Information

Spartacus was born in Thrace, a Roman province that had been captured from the Greeks. As a boy, Spartacus lived the peaceful life of a shepherd. When he was older, he had to join the Roman army. He was brave and strong. But he did not want to fight as a Roman soldier. He left the army, and was arrested soon after.

The Romans took Spartacus as a slave. He was trained to fight as a gladiator. He used his training against the Romans, escaping with other slaves in 73 B.C. The band of runaways settled in at a hideout on Mt. Vesuvius. There they planned a rebellion and their army grew. They fought for three years against the Roman army and won many battles. Overconfident, the rebels attempted an attack on Rome. Spartacus and his band were overpowered by the Roman army. He was wounded and died bravely. His body was never found. The Roman army, at last, had crushed the rebels.

You Decide

Write "Julius Caesar" on the board. Stand in front of the class and hold up a calendar. As you say each month, have students vote as to which month was named after Caesar. (July)

Civil war
Fighting between people who live in the same country

The senate called Caesar back to Rome. "Leave your army in Gaul," the senators ordered. Caesar returned to Rome, but he brought his army with him. It was 49 B.C. The common people welcomed Caesar as a hero. Soon Caesar and his army took control of the Roman government.

Some of the other generals were not happy about this. They challenged Caesar's power. This led to **civil wars,** with one Roman army fighting another.

Julius Caesar was always the winner. He won battles in Greece, in Spain, and in North Africa. While fighting in Egypt, Caesar met the beautiful Egyptian princess, Cleopatra. He found time to fall in love with her. He helped her win the throne of Egypt.

By 45 B.C., Caesar controlled the Roman world. The people hailed him as their ruler. For the most part he used his power wisely. He made citizens of many of the people in the provinces. He even allowed some to sit in the Senate. He made sure the governors ruled the provinces fairly. Caesar made more jobs for the people of Rome. He set up colonies where poor Romans could start their own farms.

You Decide

Julius Caesar named a month after himself. What do you think it was?

Caesar even improved the Roman calendar. Borrowing from the Egyptians, he changed it to a system of 365 days in a year. He added an extra day every fourth year, creating "leap year." The new calendar was much better than the old one.

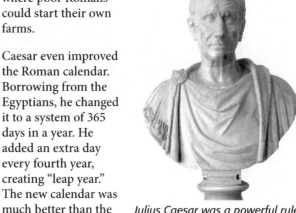

Julius Caesar was a powerful ruler in ancient Rome.

Forum
A public square in an ancient Roman city; lawmakers met there

The people of Rome cheered Caesar. They stamped his picture on Roman coins and built a temple in his name. At the Roman **Forum** (the public square where lawmakers met), Mark Antony offered Caesar the crown of king. Mark Antony was a senator and Caesar's friend. Caesar refused the crown.

How Did Caesar Die?

Many of Rome's leading citizens were worried. It did not help that Caesar had not accepted the crown. They were still afraid he planned to make himself a king and put an end to the Republic.

Reading Strategy:
Questioning

What details are important to understanding what this lesson is about?

Some of the Roman senators, led by Brutus and Cassius, plotted to kill Caesar. Many of these men had been Caesar's friends. They did not want to lose the Republic, however. Their first loyalty was to Rome. On March 15, 44 B.C., Julius Caesar was stabbed to death as he entered the Roman Senate.

LEARNING STYLES

Auditory/Verbal
Use a tape recorder to record the description of Julius Caesar on pages 165–166. Allow students who learn best by listening to use the tapes as they study this lesson.

ELL/ESL STRATEGY

Language Objective:
To help students identify lesson content using manipulatives

Distribute index cards to students. As students read this chapter, have them write the name of a famous Roman leader on the front of an index card and one or two interesting facts about that leader on the back of the index card. Then have students work in pairs to practice identifying the leaders referred to by the facts on each card.

Reading Strategy:
Questioning

Point out that the headings for the lesson are in question format. Important details include those that answer the questions in each section.

3 Reinforce and Extend

WORLD CULTURES

The toga served as a sort of Roman uniform. Romans could infer a man's social class and, more rarely, his occupation by the color and style of his toga. In modern times, a person's uniform is a clue to his or her occupation or recreational activities. Have students brainstorm a list of modern uniforms. Ask them to classify the uniforms into groups. Examples might include uniforms for sports teams, religious orders, medical professionals, and the military.

COMMON ERROR

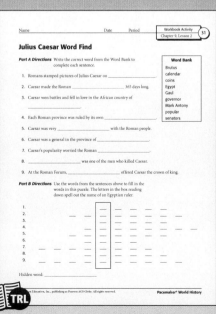

Students may not understand why our calendar includes leap years. Explain that it takes the earth slightly longer than 365 days each year to revolve around the sun. This extra time equals about ¼ of a day each year, adding up to a full day every four years. If the calendar did not account for this difference, the calendar date would not align with the seasons. For example, in 200 years, Christmas would occur in the fall. By adding one day to the calendar every four years, the calendar date stays consistent with the seasons.

Lesson 9–2 Review Answers

1. B 2. D 3. C 4. C 5. C 6. A 7. B
8. Armies were sent to Roman provinces to keep people in order.
9. Caesar made more jobs for Romans and set up colonies where Romans could start their own farms. He made citizens of many of the people in the provinces, and even let some sit in the Senate. He also improved the Roman calendar, changing it to 365 days in a year and creating a "leap year" every four years. 10. Although he refused the crown, some Roman senators worried that Caesar would make himself king and end the Republic. So they stabbed him to death as he entered the Roman Senate.

On a sheet of paper, write the letter of the answer that correctly completes each sentence.

1. Julius Caesar was the Roman general in the province of _____.

  A Carthage   **B** Gaul   **C** Greece   **D** Rome

2. Caesar was well-liked and popular, and soon he and his army took control of _____.

  A the province of Gaul   **C** the Mediterranean Sea
  B the Forum   **D** the Roman government

3. _____ were not happy about Caesar's control, which led to civil wars.

  A Other generals   **C** Roman senators
  B Citizens   **D** Farmers

4. Caesar controlled the Roman world by _____ B.C., and people hailed him as their ruler.

  A 202   **B** 140   **C** 45   **D** 44

Match the description in Column A with the person in Column B. Write the correct letter on a sheet of paper.

Column A	Column B
5. a senator who offered Caesar the crown of king	**A** Brutus
6. a Roman senator who, along with Cassius, plotted to kill Caesar	**B** Cleopatra
7. the Egyptian princess with whom Caesar fell in love	**C** Mark Antony

On a sheet of paper, write the answer to each question. Use complete sentences.

8. What was the role of armies in Roman provinces?

9. What are three things Julius Caesar did for Rome?

10. Why and how did Julius Caesar die?

168   *Unit 3   The Origins of Western Civilization: Greece and Rome*

Julius Caesar (Activity 31, Chapter 9, Lesson 2)

Name _____ Date _____ Period _____   Activity 31   Chapter 9, Lesson 2

Julius Caesar

Directions Circle the letter of the answer that correctly completes each sentence.

1. Lands far from Rome were divided into _____.
   A provinces   B city-states   C countries   D democracies

2. Julius Caesar was a Roman _____ in Gaul.
   A governor   B emperor   C senator   D general

3. Caesar's soldiers were _____.
   A afraid of him   C disrespectful of him
   B loyal to him   D angry with him

4. Members of the Senate told Caesar to _____.
   A conquer France   C send his army home
   B attack Egypt   D return to Rome

5. Caesar's army fought against _____ in civil wars.
   A the Greeks   C other Roman armies
   B the Egyptians   D the Assyrians

6. Caesar helped Cleopatra win the throne of _____.
   A Greece   B Egypt   C Spain   D Macedonia

7. Caesar improved the Roman _____.
   A aqueducts   B roads   C Senate   D calendar

8. The people of Rome built a _____ in Caesar's name.
   A temple   B forum   C palace   D statue

9. Roman senators, led by _____, plotted to kill Caesar.
   A Brutus and Antony   C Brutus and Cassius
   B Antony and Cassius   D Antony and Octavian

10. Caesar was _____ to death.
   A shot   B stabbed   C drowned   D beaten

© Pearson Education, Inc., publishing as Pearson AGS Globe. All rights reserved.   Pacemaker® World History

Julius Caesar Word Find (Workbook Activity 31, Chapter 9, Lesson 2)

Name _____ Date _____ Period _____   Workbook Activity 31   Chapter 9, Lesson 2

Julius Caesar Word Find

Part A Directions Write the correct word from the Word Bank to complete each sentence.

Word Bank
Brutus
calendar
coins
Egypt
Gaul
governor
Mark Antony
popular
senators

1. Romans stamped pictures of Julius Caesar on _____.

2. Caesar made the Roman _____ 365 days long.

3. Caesar won battles and fell in love in the African country of _____.

4. Each Roman province was ruled by its own _____.

5. Caesar was very _____ with the Roman people.

6. Caesar was a general in the province of _____.

7. Caesar's popularity worried the Roman _____.

8. _____ was one of the men who killed Caesar.

9. At the Roman Forum, _____ offered Caesar the crown of king.

Part B Directions Use the words from the sentences above to fill in the words in this puzzle. The letters in the box reading down spell out the name of an Egyptian ruler.

1. __ __ __ __ __
2. __ __ __ __ __
3. __ __ __ __ __
4. __ __ __ __ __
5. __ __ __ __ __
6. __ __ __ __ __
7. __ __ __ __ __
8. __ __ __ __ __
9. __ __ __ __ __

Hidden word: _____

© Pearson Education, Inc., publishing as Pearson AGS Globe. All rights reserved.   Pacemaker® World History

The Roman Empire

Reading Strategy: Questioning

As you read, notice details about the development of the Roman Empire. What questions do you ask yourself about these details?

Pax Romana

The Roman peace that began during the reign of Augustus Caesar

You Decide

Do you think it is a good idea to allow one person to have complete power? What would happen if that person were not a wise ruler?

Now that Julius Caesar was dead, the days of the Roman Republic were numbered. Most of the people had been happy under Caesar. They wanted a ruler who would continue with Caesar's policies and plans.

Who Was Augustus?

Once again there was a struggle for power, and civil wars shook Rome. First Brutus and Cassius fought against Mark Antony and Octavian. Mark Antony and Octavian had remained loyal to Caesar. When Octavian and Mark Antony won, they turned against each other.

Mark Antony fell in love with none other than Egypt's Cleopatra. They were determined to rule Rome together. Yet they were defeated by Octavian. The defeat led Antony and Cleopatra to kill themselves.

Now Octavian ruled all of the Roman world. It was the beginning of a new age for Rome. It was the start of the Roman Empire. Octavian became Rome's first emperor.

An emperor had even more power than a king. To his people, he was only one step below a god. In 27 B.C., the Roman Senate gave Octavian the title of "Augustus." The title meant that he was above all others. He was to be worshipped.

The Roman Senate continued to meet, but the Republic was as dead as Caesar. Augustus chose new senators to make his laws. Augustus, indeed, held complete power.

Under Emperor Augustus the Roman Empire thrived as never before. Augustus ended the civil wars. The time of peace that he brought about was called the *Pax Romana* (Roman Peace).

800 B.C.–A.D. 400   *The Rise of Rome*   *Chapter 9*   **169**

You Decide

Encourage students to use examples of historical figures to support their views. Suggest that they look for examples in their textbooks. Or, they can research the Internet and reference books.

Vocabulary

Pax Romana

Ask students to study the vocabulary word and definition for this section. Then write the vocabulary word on the board and ask a volunteer to define it. If the class agrees that the definition is correct, have the volunteer select an unfamiliar word from the lesson and write it on the board. Repeat the activity until all unfamiliar words have been defined.

1   Warm-Up Activity

Before students read this lesson, ask them to imagine that they rule a population of millions spread over a large area. Discuss the best ways to manage the empire. Then have students read the lesson to discover how Augustus Caesar brought peace and order to the Roman Empire.

Reading Strategy: Questioning

Have students write their questions on a separate sheet of paper. Have them share their questions with a partner. Then have the pairs make a master list using both sets of questions.

2 Teaching the Lesson

Encourage students to provide written responses in complete sentences to the following questions.

Ask:

- What date marks the beginning of the Roman Empire? (27 B.C.)
- Why was the period after the civil wars called the *Pax Romana*? (It was a time of Roman peace during which the Roman Empire flourished as never before.)

Background Information

Cleopatra was an ambitious ruler. When Julius Caesar came to Egypt with his army, she entered into a romantic relationship with him, one that ultimately furthered her own interests. After Caesar's death, Cleopatra began a relationship with Mark Antony; the two married. Unfortunately, Mark Antony was already married to the sister of his rival, Octavian. Mark Antony's marriage to Cleopatra, which was invalid according to Roman law, infuriated Octavian and unified Romans against Mark Antony. Romans supported Octavian's conquest of Egypt, which ended in the joint suicide of Antony and Cleopatra.

Augustus chose good, honest men as government leaders. He built roads connecting all the provinces with Rome. He improved harbors and made trade easier. Life became better for most people.

The Roman Empire Under Augustus

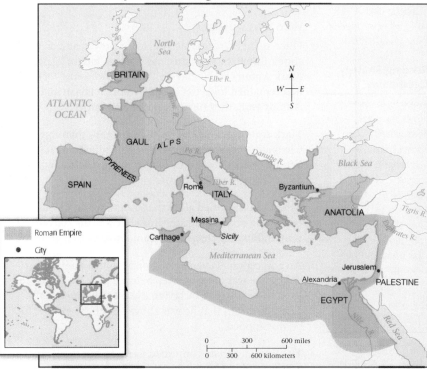

MAP STUDY

1. What five lands bordering the Mediterranean Sea were ruled by Rome?

2. Which two rivers formed the northern border of the Roman Empire?

170   *Unit 3   The Origins of Western Civilization: Greece and Rome*

MAP STUDY

Answers:

1. Gaul, Spain, Egypt, Palestine, and Anatolia

2. Rhine and Danube

Word Bank

Augustus
Cleopatra
emperor
king
Mark Antony
Octavian
power

On a sheet of paper, write the word from the Word Bank to complete each sentence correctly.

1. After Caesar's death, there was a struggle for _____.

2. Brutus and Cassius fought against Mark Antony and _____.

3. When Octavian and _____ won, they turned against each other.

4. Mark Antony fell in love with _____ and they were determined to rule Rome together.

5. Octavian became Rome's first _____.

6. In Rome, an emperor had more power than a(n) _____. He was one step below a god.

7. Octavian was given the title of "_____" by the Roman Senate. It meant he was above all others and should be worshipped.

On a sheet of paper, write the answer to each question. Use complete sentences.

8. Why did Mark Antony and Cleopatra kill themselves?

9. What changes did Augustus make to the Roman government?

10. Why did the Roman Empire thrive under Augustus?

COMMON ERROR

Students may see the name "Augustus Caesar," and assume he was the biological son of Julius Caesar. In fact, Augustus Caesar was the grand-nephew of Julius Caesar. Caesar had adopted Octavian in his will, to pass on the name of Caesar after the death of Julius Caesar. Octavian, now known as Augustus Caesar, adopted his successor and stepson and successor, Tiberius, passing on the name of Caesar once more. Eventually the family name of Caesar became a title bestowed on Roman emperors.

Lesson 9–3 Review Answers

1. power **2.** Octavian **3.** Mark Antony **4.** Cleopatra **5.** emperor **6.** king **7.** Augustus **8.** They were defeated by Octavian. **9.** Augustus had complete power, and he chose new senators who were good, honest men to make his laws. He built roads connecting all the provinces. He improved harbors and made trade easier. **10.** The empire thrived because Augustus ended the civil wars, which brought about a time of peace known as *Pax Romana*.

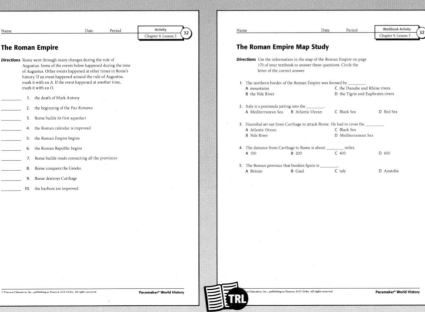

Chapter 9 Lesson 4

Overview This lesson describes Rome's contributions to art, architecture, language, and law.

Objectives

- To describe Roman life
- To tell some things the Romans built
- To name the languages of the Romans

Student Pages 172–176

Teacher's Resource Library TRL

Workbook Activity 33

Activity 33

Modified Activity 33

Vocabulary

aqueduct
Have students work in pairs to create crossword puzzles using the vocabulary words in this lesson and in preceding lessons. Clues can be definitions or fill-in-the-blank sentences. Have the pairs exchange and solve each other's puzzles.

Reading Strategy:
Questioning

Encourage students to consider all aspects of their lives, including school, family, social activities, government, sports, and religion. Stress that there are no wrong answers. At the same time, encourage students to be thoughtful and articulate.

1 Warm-Up Activity

Ask students what they might see if they visited Rome in 27 B.C. What places would they go to? What events would they see? After students read this lesson, discuss how their views of Rome have changed.

LESSON 9-4

Roman Society

Objectives

- To describe Roman life
- To tell some things the Romans built
- To name the language of the Romans

Aqueduct
A channel that carries flowing water over a long distance

Reading Strategy: Questioning

What experiences from your own life give you a better understanding of Roman society?

As the largest city in the Roman Empire, Rome was a busy place. A million people lived in or near the city.

What Was Life Like in Rome?

Indeed, Rome had come a long way from that tiny village on a hill. It was a fine and beautiful place. The wide main streets were paved with stone. Fresh water came to the city through overhead **aqueducts.** The water was piped into houses and public fountains.

The Romans built beautiful temples to their many gods and goddesses. There were 300 temples in Rome alone. One of the most famous of these was the Pantheon.

The Roman Forum was a gathering place. It was there that the Senate met in the Senate House. Columned temples lined the edges of the Forum. Merchants built shops there.

The Romans also built huge public baths. They were more than a place to bathe in hot and cold pools. The baths were also a center of social life. The baths held libraries, gymnasiums, and even small theaters. The public baths were free of charge.

Wealthy Romans lived in big houses. These houses had swimming pools and large dining halls for parties. Many rich people also had country homes. They hired workers to live there and look after the land.

The average Roman family lived in a small house or apartment. The poorer people lived in tiny rooms in big apartment buildings. They often had to struggle for enough to eat.

Appius Claudius Caecus became censor of Rome in 312 B.C. The censor was in charge of public works. He directed construction of the first major road from Rome. The Appian Way ran 132 miles (212 km) from Rome to ancient Capua. It was made of cemented lava stone and domed in the center for runoff of rainwater. In 244 B.C. the road was extended to Brindisi in the far southeast near the Adriatic coast. The road became a common route for Roman armies and merchants.

Reading Strategy: Questioning

What details about ancient Roman society tell you about its future?

Rich and poor people alike enjoyed the free entertainment provided by the emperors. The Romans celebrated many holidays—to honor their gods and goddesses or to honor military heroes. On these days they often held chariot races. These exciting races took place at a sports stadium called the Circus Maximus. The Romans loved to watch these events. They also enjoyed more violent forms of entertainment.

What Shaped Roman Art and Architecture?

The Romans admired the Greeks. They put up statues taken from Greek city-states. They copied Greek style in statues of their own. Many of the great buildings in Rome were also based on Greek style and form.

Roman builders liked to use arches, curved openings that supported something. Arches spanned streets, supported bridges, and held up great aqueducts. Visitors often passed under a great arch to enter a Roman city.

The Romans wanted their art and architecture to be useful. The 14 aqueducts that carried water into Rome were certainly beautiful. They were also useful—and they were built to last. Some aqueducts built more than 2,000 years ago still stand today.

Some roads of ancient Rome are in use today, too. "All roads lead to Rome," a famous saying goes. That means that Roman highways, paved layer upon layer, linked all the provinces to Rome. The Romans were fine builders. They built a sewer system to serve ancient Rome. Parts of it are still being used in the modern city.

Tell students that Romans were a practical people. They built things to last, some of which are still in use today.

Ask:

- How many people lived in or near Rome? (about 1 million)
- In addition to beauty, what did Romans want from their art and architecture? (to be useful)
- What is Vulgar Latin? (the spoken Latin of ordinary Romans)

Background Information

The Roman aqueducts were built over a period of 500 years. They brought fresh water to Rome from 57 miles away. Only 30 miles of the total 260-mile system were above the ground; the remainder was underground. The Romans also built aqueducts in Greece, Italy, France, Spain, North Africa, and Asia Minor. Many of these aqueducts fell into disrepair following the collapse of the empire.

Today, aqueducts are much longer and can carry more water than their ancient counterparts. For example, New York City uses a system that carries nearly 2 billion gallons of water a day from 120 miles away.

Geography Note

Tell students that Romans used concrete to build roads and other structures. The concrete was a mixture of sand, water, and other materials. It hardened to a rocklike consistency, and made the roads strong and long lasting.

Reading Strategy: Questioning

Have students make a list of details about ancient Roman life. Then have them use this list to answer the question on page 173. A sample answer may be that ancient Romans had libraries in their public baths. This indicates that they might emphasize education in their future.

This aqueduct was built more than 2,000 years ago to bring water to dry lands.

What Were the Languages and Laws of the Romans?

Italian, French, Spanish, Portuguese, and Romanian are all called Romance languages. They all come from Latin, the language of the Romans.

There are many words that we have taken from the Romans. We have *colosseums* today. Our government has a *senate*. The Russians changed the word Caesar to *Czar,* the Germans to *Kaiser.*

"Justice for all!" was an idea that came from the Roman Senate. Many of our ideas about laws and courts of law came from the Romans. Roman laws and lawmaking served as a model for many other nations.

Words from the Past

Borrowed Words

English-speakers use many words and phrases borrowed from Latin, the Romance languages, and other languages. In fact, about half of the words in present-day English come from languages other than English.

The Romance languages developed from Vulgar Latin. This was the spoken Latin of ordinary Romans. Soldiers and settlers brought Latin to areas throughout the Roman Empire. In each area, the language became a dialect of Latin. Over time, the dialect became a separate language. Italian, French, Spanish, Portuguese, and Romanian are national languages that developed from Latin.

England was a part of the Roman Empire, too. However, the English language developed from the language of Germanic tribes that invaded England in the fifth century A.D. Ever since that time, English has borrowed words from other languages.

Many words about the church came from Latin, such as *priest* and *bishop.* Many English words for technology also come from Latin. Even the word *computer* has Latin beginnings.

Many words about law and society come from French. A few words are *judge, jury, parliament, duke,* and *baron.* During one period of English history, the French-speaking Normans ruled England. English people cooked for the Normans. English names for animals, such as *cow, sheep,* and *swine,* are real English words. However, the names of meats from those animals—*beef, mutton, pork,* and *bacon*—are from French.

WORDS FROM THE PAST

The English language has two main sources: German and Latin. Many people in early England spoke the language of the Angles, Saxons, and Jutes—Germanic languages. When the Normans conquered England in 1066, they added many Latin-derived French words to the English language. Additional Latin words came from scholars and scientists, who still use Latin today for plant and animal names. Following the Norman conquest, most common people continued to use Saxon words, while the wealthy and educated used Latin-derived words. Eventually, the two forms blended together into the modern English language.

COMMON ERROR

Students might think that languages are static and do not change over time. Point out that the English language continues to evolve today. For example, the invention of the computer has added new words to our vocabulary, such as Web site. Have students brainstorm a list of new words that stem from the invention of computers.

STUDY SKILLS

Have students set up a four-column chart titled "Roman Life." Students should title the columns as follows: "Art," "Architecture," "Language," and "Law." As students read this section, have them add information about each category to their chart.

ONLINE CONNECTION

Students can gain additional information by accessing the following Web site: www.agsglobepmwh.com/page175 (This Web site offers information about books, museums, magazines, videos, CD-ROMs, and other Web sites that discuss early Rome.)

Lesson 9–4 Review Answers

1. C **2.** B **3.** C **4.** D **5.** A **6.** B **7.** D **8.** A **9.** B **10.** C

LESSON 9-4 REVIEW

On a sheet of paper, write the letter of the answer that correctly completes each sentence.

1. The Romans built _____ to bring water to houses and public fountains.

   A arches   **B** public baths   **C** aqueducts   **D** sewer systems

2. The Romans built beautiful _____ to honor their gods and goddesses.

   A houses   **B** temples   **C** arches   **D** aqueducts

3. The Romans built huge _____ that were the center of social life.

   A forums   **B** arches   **C** public baths   **D** temples

4. On the holidays Romans would celebrate, _____ would often be held.

   A Olympic Games   **B** school   **C** big feasts   **D** chariot races

5. Roman builders admired the Greeks, and liked to use _____ when building.

   A arches   **B** aqueducts   **C** marble   **D** sewer systems

6. The Romans wanted their art and architecture to be beautiful as well as _____.

   A marble   **B** useful   **C** romantic   **D** big

7. The Romans built _____ in ancient Rome. Some parts are still being used today.

   A public baths   **B** houses   **C** apartment buildings   **D** a sewer system

8. Italian, French, Spanish, Portuguese, and Romanian are _____ languages.

   A Romance   **B** European   **C** Roman   **D** Greek

9. The Romans spoke _____, which is what the Romance languages come from.

   A Romanian   **B** Latin   **C** Italian   **D** English

10. Many of our ideas about _____ come from the Romans.

   A romance   **B** language   **C** laws   **D** sewer systems

---

176   Unit 3   *The Origins of Western Civilization: Greece and Rome*

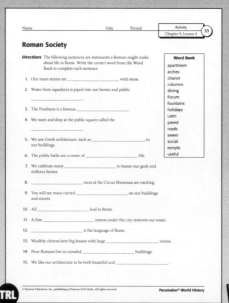

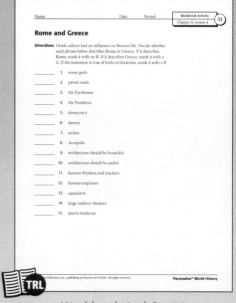

Christianity in Rome

Objectives

- To explain why Jesus's teachings appealed to the poor
- To tell how the Romans persecuted the Christians
- To describe how the Emperor Constantine helped the Christian religion grow in Rome

Gospel
One of four books of the New Testament part of the Bible

Enslaved
When a person is forced to become a slave

Reading Strategy: Questioning

What are the most important details that you will want to remember about the earliest days of Christianity?

Look at any of the timelines in this book. Each one shows how important a man named Jesus was to history and to the calendar we use today. All the dates before the birth of Jesus Christ are labeled B.C., or "Before Christ." All the dates after the birth of Christ are labeled A.D. The letters A.D. stand for the Latin words *Anno Domini,* or "in the year of our Lord."

Who Was Jesus Christ?

The Christian religion began with Jesus. Jesus was a Jew. He lived during the time of the Roman Emperor Augustus. He was born in Bethlehem, a little town south of Jerusalem. This was in a far-off province of the Roman Empire. Much of what we know about Jesus comes from the Bible. The first four books of the New Testament are about his life. These books are called the **Gospels.** The Gospels contain stories passed down over the years.

The Gospels say that Jesus taught people to love one another, to do good deeds, and to love God. If people were good, Jesus taught, they would be rewarded in an afterlife.

The teachings of Jesus were most popular with poor and **enslaved** people. His teachings offered some hope for happiness, if not in this life, then in the next. While other religions spoke of an afterlife, they said that princes would remain princes. Commoners would keep their lowly station—even after death. In contrast, Jesus spoke of a happy afterlife for all who were good on Earth.

Jesus's followers called him "Christ," or messiah. Jesus was 33 years old when he was sentenced to die on a cross. His crucifixion did not end his teachings. In the next years, the Christian religion spread to many lands.

Overview This lesson discusses the rise of Christianity, and the changing attitude of the Roman Empire toward the rapidly expanding religion.

Objectives

- To explain why Jesus's teachings appealed to the poor
- To tell how the Romans persecuted the Christians
- To describe how the Emperor Constantine helped the Christian religion grow in Rome

Student Pages 177–182

Teacher's Resource Library

  Workbook Activity 34

  Activity 34

  Modified Activity 34

Vocabulary

bishop	legal
convert	persecute
enslaved	pope
gospel	

Ask students to draw two columns on a sheet of paper. Have them write the vocabulary words in the left column. The definitions of the words go in the right column in random order. Tell students to exchange papers with a classmate, and to draw lines matching the words and their definitions.

PRONUNCIATION GUIDE

Use this list to help students pronounce difficult words in this lesson.

Diocletian (di´ ə kle´ shən)

Byzantium (by zan´ tē əm)

Constantinople (kon´ stan tn o´ pəl)

1   Warm-Up Activity

Some students may already know details about the birth of the Christian religion. Ask interested students to share what they know. Then have the class read pages 177–179 to learn about the beginnings of Christianity and how the Roman Empire responded to the growing religion.

Reading Strategy: Questioning

Details may include the names of important figures who played a role in early Christianity, the teachings of the growing religion, the dates and places of where it began and where it spread, and the reactions of other cultures to Christianity.

2 | Teaching the Lesson

Tell students that *Gospel* means "good news." Discuss the good news Jesus offered to common people.

Ask:

● Why did Jesus's message appeal to the poor? (Other religions said that the poor would remain poor in the afterlife. Jesus spoke of a happy afterlife for all who were good on Earth.)

● How did the Roman Empire first react to the new religion? (The emperors let the Christians worship as they pleased. Later, the emperors decided that the Christians were a threat. They began to treat the Christians cruelly.)

● What happened to the church under the rule of Constantine? (Sample answer: The church was strengthened, the government and church were no longer separate, and the office of the pope was created.)

Background Information

In the years immediately following Jesus's death, his disciples preached only to Jews. Saul, or Paul as he was later called, was among the first to preach to gentiles (non-Jews). Saul had originally condemned the new religion. He had a religious experience, however, in which he saw a vision of the risen Christ. Saul promptly took the name Paul and converted to Christianity. In addition to his extensive travels, he wrote letters to numerous Christian groups throughout the ancient world. These letters were later incorporated into the New Testament. His tireless efforts paid off—Paul was instrumental in moving Christianity from a cult to a world religion.

Persecute
To treat in a cruel way; to hurt or injure

The Bible explains how Jesus taught others and performed good deeds as he traveled.

One man who carried word of the Christian religion was named Paul. Paul spent almost 30 years of his life traveling the Mediterranean world. He told people about Jesus's teachings. Paul could speak Greek. Therefore, he could take Christian beliefs to Athens and to other Greek cities. Paul started churches wherever he traveled. Even in Rome, Paul found people willing to listen. People were ready to accept a new religion that spoke of equal rights and hope.

How Were Christians Treated in the Roman Empire?

The Roman Empire had many religions. At first, one more religion did not seem too important. Therefore, the emperors allowed the Christians to worship as they pleased.

 You Decide
Can you do anything to help when the wrong people are being blamed for something? Explain.

However, the Christians would not bow down to the Roman emperor. They would not call the emperor a god. Therefore, the Roman government decided that the Christians were a threat. The Roman emperors began to treat the followers of Christ cruelly, or to **persecute** them. They blamed the Christians for everything that went wrong.

178 *Unit 3 The Origins of Western Civilization: Greece and Rome*

You Decide
Answers will vary. The penalty for people who followed a new religion, such as the early Christians, might have been death. Explain that in most modern Western countries, it is possible to defend those unjustly accused without fear of physical harm. Students might suggest several remedies, including institutional change, media exposure, and legal recourse.

A terrible fire burned in Rome in A.D. 64. This was the time when Nero was emperor. "The Christians started the fire!" Nero shouted. As a result, many Christians were killed. Paul, one of the men who had spread Jesus's teachings, was one of those killed.

The Romans persecuted the Christians for 300 years. Christian men and women were forced into Roman arenas to fight wild animals. Some of the emperors worried more about Christianity than others. Sometimes Christians were safe; other times they were in danger.

 You Decide
Why do you think people risk their lives sometimes to follow their religion?

Christians often held secret church meetings. They met in tunnels, called catacombs, deep under the city of Rome. It was dangerous to follow the Christian religion. Yet even though it could mean death, people continued to join the Christian religion. At first only the poor Romans and slaves turned to Christianity. After a time, however, some of the Roman leaders became interested, too.

What Did the Emperor Constantine Do for the Christians?

Constantine became emperor of Rome in A.D. 306. In A.D. 312, a Roman general named Maxentius threatened to seize the throne. One night, Constantine dreamed that he saw a cross in the sky. He thought it was the Cross of Christ. He dreamed that if he carried that cross into battle, he would win a great victory. In response, Constantine rode into battle against Maxentius. He carried a flag that pictured the cross. He won that battle and Maxentius was defeated.

Roman Emperor Constantine was the first Christian emperor of Rome.

At the time Constantine became emperor, he had to share power with others. The Roman Empire had been divided into an eastern and a western part. In A.D. 286, the Emperor Diocletian decided the empire had grown too big to be ruled by just one man. Thus he set up a system of shared rule.

 You Decide
Answers will vary. Students may realize that some people feel very strongly about their religious beliefs. These people might think that death is preferable to renouncing their beliefs.

LEARNING STYLES

 Body/Kinesthetic
Have students work in small groups to create posters titled "The Rise of Christianity." The posters should trace the growth of Christianity, from Jesus's birth to Constantine's conversion in A.D. 337. Posters should describe key figures, dates, and events. Encourage students to be creative. Tell them to include captions for all illustrations.

LEARNING STYLES

Auditory/Verbal
Some students may benefit from summarizing the rise of Christianity in their own words. Have them record their summaries on tape and use it later to review this lesson.

ELL/ESL STRATEGY

Language Objective:
To learn strategies to clarify text

Choose a section of text from Lesson 9–5 that ELL/ESL students are struggling to comprehend. Think aloud about strategies they could use to clarify that text. For example, refer students to page 180. Say: *I don't understand what the word "legal" means in the sentence, "Constantine had made Christianity legal." I can do a few different things to figure out the meaning. I can look at the sentences around it to see if I can figure out what "legal" means. If that doesn't work, I can look up "legal" in the dictionary or Glossary. I can also ask a classmate or my teacher to explain the meaning to me.* Encourage students to try out these strategies as they read the lesson.

COMMON ERROR

Students may not understand the meaning of the phrase "bow down" as used in the following sentence: Christians would not bow down to the Roman emperor. Explain that the phrase means that early Christians resisted the authority of the emperor. They would not accept that the emperor had power over them. Ask students to picture the act of bowing down. The gesture is used to show respect. A refusal to bow down is an act of defiance.

MAP STUDY

Answers:

1. Anatolia, Palestine, Egypt

2. Britain, Spain, Gaul, and Italy

Legal
Lawful; based on the law of the government

Convert
Change from one religion to another

Constantine was not happy with shared rule. In A.D. 324, he clashed with Licinius, the ruler of the eastern part of the empire. That same year, Constantine became the sole ruler of the Roman Empire. In A.D. 330, he set up a new capital at Byzantium in the east. He renamed the city Constantinople. Today this city is known as Istanbul.

In A.D. 313, Constantine had made Christianity **legal.** Christians were no longer persecuted. More and more Romans now turned to the religion. Constantine himself **converted,** or changed, to Christianity. In A.D. 337, he was baptized and became the first Christian emperor of Rome. He built the first great Christian cathedral in Rome. He then built churches in Constantinople and in other cities.

The Eastern Roman Empire and the Western Roman Empire

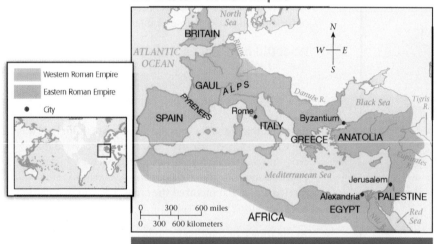

MAP STUDY

1. What are three countries in the Eastern Roman Empire?

2. What are four countries in the Western Roman Empire?

Bishop

A high-ranking church official in charge of other priests and a number of churches

Pope

The head of the Roman Catholic Church

The Roman government and the Christian church became very much a part of one another. Officials of the church were powerful men. The largest churches chose **bishops** as their leaders. The bishop of the Church of Rome became the head of the Roman Catholic Church, and was known as the **pope.** While the government of the Roman Empire was weakening, the Christian church was gaining power.

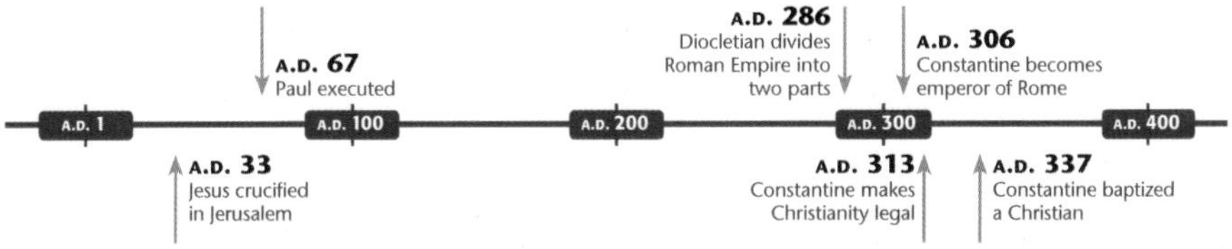

TIMELINE STUDY

Answer: A.D. 313

After students have studied the timeline on page 181, have them close their books while you write the following events on the board: Constantine makes Christianity legal; Paul is executed; Jesus is crucified; Constantine converts to Christianity; Jesus is born. Have students place the events in proper chronological order. (Jesus is born; Jesus is crucified; Paul is executed; Constantine makes Christianity legal; Constantine converts to Christianity.)

TIMELINE STUDY: CHRISTIANITY AND ROME

When did Christianity become legal in Rome?

A.D. 67
Paul executed

A.D. 286
Diocletian divides Roman Empire into two parts

A.D. 306
Constantine becomes emperor of Rome

A.D. 1   A.D. 100   A.D. 200   A.D. 300   A.D. 400

A.D. 33
Jesus crucified in Jerusalem

A.D. 313
Constantine makes Christianity legal

A.D. 337
Constantine baptized a Christian

800 B.C.–A.D. 400

The Rise of Rome   Chapter 9   **181**

Lesson 9–5 Review Answers

1. Jesus 2. Gospels 3. Paul
4. Maxentius 5. Constantine 6. His
teachings were popular with
the poor and enslaved people
because they offered some hope
for happiness. He spoke of a happy
afterlife for all who were good on
Earth, no matter their station in life.
7. The Christians would not call the
emperor a god, and thus the Roman
government decided that they were
a threat. They began to persecute
the Christians and blame them for
everything that went wrong. 8. Some
Christians were executed. For other
men and women, the Romans
forced them to fight wild animals
in arenas. As a result, Christians
were forced to hold secret church
meetings to practice their religion.
9. The Roman Empire was split
because it had grown too big to be
ruled by one man. 10. Constantine
made Christianity legal, ending the
persecution of the Christians. He
converted to Christianity and became
the first Christian emperor of Rome.
The Roman government and the
Christian church became a part of
one another.

Word Bank

Constantine

Gospels

Jesus

Maxentius

Paul

On a sheet of paper, write the word from the Word Bank to complete each sentence correctly.

1. _____ was an important man in history. He is so important, that the dates on our calendar are named after him.

2. The books known as the _____ contain stories about Jesus's life.

3. A man named _____ carried the word of the Christian religion after Jesus's death.

4. A Roman general named _____ threatened to seize Constantine's throne, but was defeated in battle.

5. In A.D. 324, _____ became sole ruler of the Roman Empire.

On a sheet of paper, write the answer to each question. Use complete sentences.

6. Why did Jesus's teachings appeal to the poor?

7. Why did the Romans persecute the Christians?

8. How did the Romans persecute the Christians?

9. Why did the Emperor Diocletian divide the Roman Empire into an Eastern and Western Empire?

10. How did Emperor Constantine help the Christian religion grow in Rome?

182 Unit 3 *The Origins of Western Civilization: Greece and Rome*

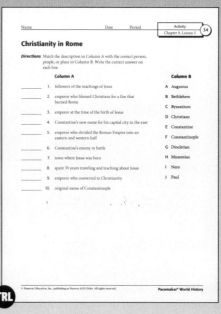

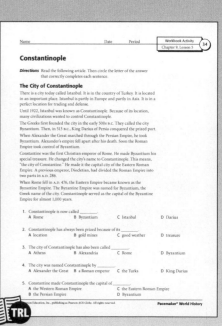

Activity 34   Workbook Activity 34

The End of the Empire

Reading Strategy: Questioning

In what ways does the timeline help you understand the order of events that led up to the end of the Roman Empire?

Not all of the emperors that followed Augustus were wise and good. Indeed, some were mad with power. Some were greedy. Royal families often fought among themselves over who would get the throne. Yet there were always skilled men to do the actual work of running the empire. The *Pax Romana* lasted for two centuries. During that time there were no serious threats to Rome's power.

How Did the Roman Empire Weaken?

Around A.D. 180, however, things began to go wrong. The Roman world faced invaders from northern and eastern Europe. Rome had to double the size of its army to protect the empire. A bigger army meant higher taxes—taxes that people could not pay! Prices of goods rose. Trading fell off. People were out of work. Life in the city was no longer good. More and more wealthy people left Rome to live in the country.

The Roman Empire did not fall in a day, or in a month, or even in a year. Yet the empire grew weaker with each passing year. Its fall was coming.

TIMELINE STUDY: RISE AND FALL OF THE ROMAN EMPIRE

How many years passed between the founding of Rome and its fall? (Remember to account for the change from B.C. to A.D.)

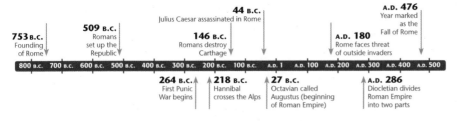

753 B.C.
Founding of Rome

509 B.C.
Romans set up the Republic

264 B.C.
First Punic War begins

218 B.C.
Hannibal crosses the Alps

146 B.C.
Romans destroy Carthage

44 B.C.
Julius Caesar assassinated in Rome

27 B.C.
Octavian called Augustus (beginning of Roman Empire)

A.D. 180
Rome faces threat of outside invaders

A.D. 286
Diocletian divides Roman Empire into two parts

A.D. 476
Year marked as the Fall of Rome

800 B.C. 700 B.C. 600 B.C. 500 B.C. 400 B.C. 300 B.C. 200 B.C. 100 B.C. A.D. 1 A.D. 100 A.D. 200 A.D. 300 A.D. 400 A.D. 500

800 B.C.–A.D. 400

Reading Strategy: Questioning

Remind students that timelines can help them visualize events in their correct order. Ask them to think of other events to add to the timeline that may have led to the fall of Rome.

TIMELINE STUDY

Answer: 1,229

Rome was founded in 753 B.C. The fall of Rome was in A.D. 476. About 1,229 years passed between the founding of Rome and its fall.

Background Information

Rome had its share of good rulers, such as Augustus, Claudius, Trajan, and Hadrian. But it also had extremely bad rulers, including the insane Caligula and the cruel Nero. The people were not patient with incompetence. Between A.D. 180 and 284, a staggering 25 out of 29 emperors were murdered.

LEARNING STYLES

Interpersonal/Group Learning

Have students work in groups to create a large format timeline combining the events shown on the timelines on pages 181 and 183.

ELL/ESL STRATEGY

Language Objective: *To understand different purposes for writing*

Place students in pairs. Have each pair read the first paragraph on page 183. Have them discuss its purpose. (to summarize the *Pax Romana*) Then ask each pair to examine the timeline on page 183. Have them discuss its purpose. (to show the events that led to Rome's fall in proper order) Finally, ask the pairs to scan the review questions on page 184. Have them discuss the purpose for that writing. (to assess students' knowledge of lesson content)

3 Reinforce and Extend

Lesson 9–6 Review Answers

1. D 2. B 3. D 4. C 5. A 6. B 7. B 8. C 9. D 10. A

LESSON 9-6 REVIEW

On a sheet of paper, write the letter of the answer that correctly completes each sentence.

1. The emperors that followed Augustus were sometimes power hungry and _____.

   A wise   B good   C fair   D greedy

2. Emperors struggled with each other over power. Still, _____ were always available to do the actual work of running the empire.

   A slaves   B skilled men   C nobles   D kings

3. The *Pax Romana* lasted for _____.

   A two weeks   B two months   C 20 years   D two centuries

4. There were no threats to Rome's _____ during the *Pax Romana*.

   A Republic   B trading   C power   D architecture

5. Rome faced _____ around A.D. 180.

   A invaders   B floods   C civil wars   D persecution

6. To protect its empire, Rome had to double the size of its _____.

   A empire   B army   C land   D aqueducts

7. As a result, _____ were raised.

   A weapons   B taxes   C animals   D churches

8. The price of goods increased while trading _____.

   A did not change   B increased   C decreased   D doubled

9. Thus, more people left Rome to live in _____.

   A Gaul   B Greece   C the city   D the country

10. The _____ of Rome was coming.

    A fall   B rise   C reign   D peak

---

184   *Unit 3   The Origins of Western Civilization: Greece and Rome*

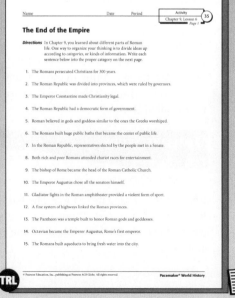

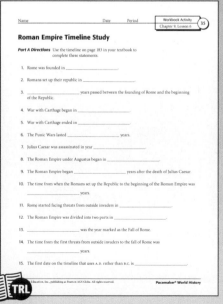

Activity 35, pages 1–2   Workbook Activity 35

CHAPTER 9

SUMMARY

- Rome grew out of settlements on seven hills along the Tiber River. For about 100 years it was ruled by Etruscans.

- In the Roman Republic, laws were made by elected representatives who met in a senate. There was no king. Members of the Roman Senate were usually wealthy landowners.

- Roman armies conquered many peoples. During the Punic Wars they took over the Carthaginians. They went on to conquer the Greeks.

- Conquered lands became Roman provinces. Each province was ruled by its own governor.

- Julius Caesar was a powerful general in the province of Gaul. He became the leader of the Roman Republic.

- Caesar won battles all around the Mediterranean. He met a princess named Cleopatra and he helped her gain the throne of Egypt.

- Roman armies battled one another, often over disagreements about Caesar's power. Some senators killed Caesar because they feared that he had too much power.

- Civil wars ended with Octavian as the head of the Roman Empire. The people called Octavian the Emperor Augustus.

- The reign of Augustus began a period of peace and growth known as the *Pax Romana*.

- The ancient Romans were great builders, lawmakers, and students of language.

- The Christian religion is based on the teachings of Jesus. Some Roman emperors persecuted the Christians.

- Constantine became the first Christian emperor of Rome.

800 B.C.–A.D. 400   *The Rise of Rome*   Chapter 9   **185**

Chapter 9 Summary

Have students read the Chapter Summary on page 185 to review the main ideas presented in Chapter 9.

Ask:

- Who first ruled the city of Rome? (the Etruscans)

- Describe a typical member of the Roman Senate. (The typical member was a wealthy landowner.)

- What happened to lands conquered by Rome? (The lands became Roman provinces.)

- Why was Julius Caesar killed? (Some senators feared that he had too much power.)

- When did the civil wars end? (They ended when Octavian became head of the Roman Empire.)

- What accomplishments were ancient Romans known for? (They were great builders, lawmakers, and students of language.)

- The Christian religion is based on whose teachings? (The Christian religion is based on the teachings of Jesus.)

- Who was the first Christian emperor of Rome? (Constantine)

CHAPTER PROJECT FOLLOW-UP

 Have student groups present their skits about the lesson they studied in this chapter. Assess the accuracy of their information, how well they present the key facts, and their ability to hold the interest of their audience.

TEACHER'S RESOURCE

The AGS Globe Teaching Strategies in Social Studies Transparencies may be used with this chapter. The transparencies add an interactive dimension to expand and enhance the Pacemaker® *World History* program content.

The Rise of Rome   *Chapter 9*   **185**

Chapter 9 Review

Use the Chapter Review to prepare students for tests and to reteach content from the chapter.

Chapter 9 Mastery Test

The Teacher's Resource Library includes two forms of the Chapter 9 Mastery Test. Each test addresses the chapter Goals for Learning. An optional third page of additional critical-thinking items is included for each test. The difficulty level of the two forms is equivalent.

Chapter 9 Review Answers

Vocabulary Review

1. peninsula

2. aqueducts

3. province

4. senate

5. forum

6. convert

7. pope

8. bishop

9. persecute

10. republic

Chapter Review Questions

11. In the Roman Republic, the government was controlled by the people.

12. Julius Caesar made citizens of many people in the provinces and let some of them sit in the Senate, assured fair government in the provinces, created more jobs in Rome, set up colonies for poor people, and improved the calendar.

13. Sample answer: Augustus held complete power, but he made life better for most people.

Word Bank

aqueducts
bishop
convert
forum
peninsula
persecute
pope
province
republic
senate

Vocabulary Review

On a sheet of paper, use the words from the Word Bank to complete each sentence correctly.

1. The Romans settled on a piece of land called a(n) _____ around 1000 B.C.

2. The Romans built huge _____ to transport water.

3. The Romans conquered Greece, making it a Roman _____.

4. The Roman _____ made laws.

5. In ancient Rome, lawmakers met in a(n) _____.

6. Constantine chose to _____, or change his religion, to Christianity.

7. The _____ is the head of the Roman Catholic Church.

8. A(n) _____ is a high-ranking official of a church.

9. Roman emperors would _____ Christians.

10. In a(n) _____, citizens have the right to elect their own representatives.

Chapter Review Questions

On a sheet of paper, write the answer to each question. Use complete sentences.

11. Who controlled the government in the Roman Republic?

12. What were some of Julius Caesar's accomplishments as ruler of the Roman world?

13. What kind of leader was Augustus?

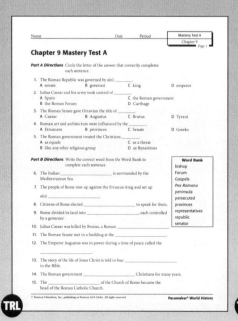

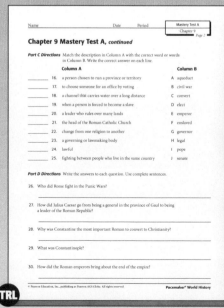

Chapter 9 Mastery Test A, pages 1–3

14. What happened to the language of Rome as the Roman Empire grew?

15. Who did Jesus's teachings appeal to and why?

16. What were two reasons for the fall of the Roman Empire?

Critical Thinking

On a sheet of paper, write your response to each question. Use complete sentences.

17. What was Nero trying to do after the fire in Rome?

18. Why was Constantine's conversion to Christianity important to the future of the Roman Empire?

Using the Timelines

Use the timelines on pages 181 and 183 to answer the questions.

19. What happened about 280 years after Jesus was crucified?

20. How many years passed between the founding of Rome and the setting up of the Republic?

GROUP ACTIVITY

Form a group of five or six. You are some of Rome's leading citizens in the Roman Republic. Caesar has been doing some good things in Rome, and he has just refused the crown. Still, you are worried that the end of the Republic is in sight. What will you say to your friends about your concerns? Write and perform a skit for the rest of the class.

800 B.C.–A.D. 400   *The Rise of Rome*   *Chapter 9*   **187**

---

14. Latin, the language of Rome, was taken to many parts of the empire. Romance languages, such as Italian, French, Spanish, Portuguese, and Romanian, developed from Latin.

15. Jesus's teachings appealed to the poor and enslaved people. This is because he said that everyone would be happy in the afterlife, not just those who were rich or had high status on Earth.

16. Any two of the following are acceptable: Invaders came from the north and the east. Higher taxes were needed to pay for protection ruined the economy. Life in Rome itself worsened, and many people left the city.

Critical Thinking

17. By blaming the fire on the Christians, Nero had an excuse to get rid of many of them.

18. Possible answer: After Constantine's conversion, the government of the Roman Empire and the Christian Church were part of one another. As time went on, the government weakened and the church grew stronger.

Using the Timelines

19. Christianity was made legal.

20. 244 years

GROUP ACTIVITY

The skit should show understanding of the situation Caesar's friends were in, and the conflict that can exist between friendship and some larger goal.

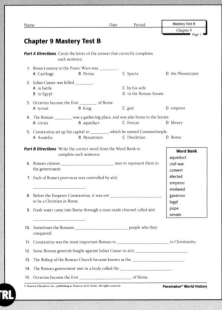

Chapter 9 Mastery Test B, pages 1–3

UNIT 4

PLANNING GUIDE

The Middle Ages:
A.D. 400–1400

	Student Pages	Vocabulary	Map Study	Reading Strategy	Lesson Review	Chapter Summary/Review
Chapter 10 The Barbarians and the Vikings	190–207					205–207
Lesson 10–1 The Fall of the Western Roman Empire	192–196	✔		✔	196	
Lesson 10–2 The Byzantine Empire	197–199			✔	199	
Lesson 10–3 The Vikings	200–204	✔		✔	204	
Chapter 11 The Lords and the Serfs	208–221					219, 221
Lesson 11–1 Feudalism	210–212	✔		✔	212	
Lesson 11–2 Religion During the Middle Ages	213–215	✔		✔	215	
Lesson 11–3 Life in the Middle Ages	216–218	✔		✔	218	

(Unit Planning Guide is continued on next page.)

Chapter Activities

Teacher's Resource Library
Life Skills Connection 10–12
Key Vocabulary Words 10–12

Assessment Options

Student Text
Chapter Reviews 10–12

Teacher's Resource Library
Chapter 10 Mastery Tests A and B
Chapter 11 Mastery Tests A and B
Chapter 12 Mastery Tests A and B
Unit 4 Mastery Test

Teacher's Edition
Chapter Projects 10–12

Words from the Past	Learn More About It	Great Names in History	Technology Connection	Geography Note	You Decide/Remember/History Fact	Timeline Study	ELL/ESL Strategy	Background Information	Common Error	Life Skills Connection	Key Vocabulary Words	Study Skills	Applications Home, Career, Community	Online Connection	Teacher Alert	World Cultures	Auditory/Verbal	Body/Kinesthetic	Interpersonal/Group Learning	Logical/Mathematical	Visual/Spatial	Activities/Modified Activities	Workbook Activities	Self-Study Guide	Chapter Outline
										191	191													✔	✔
					193, 195		193	193	194		194		195						193			36	36		
					197, 198		198	198	198							198		198				37	37		
202			201			203	202	201	202, 203				202	203	203		201			201	201	38	38		
										209	209													✔	✔
					211		211	211	211, 212						211					211		39	39		
	214						214	213	215			213	214, 215			215	214	214			214	40	40		
						217	217	216	217, 218				217						217			41	41		

Modified Activities

The Teacher's Resource Library (TRL) contains a set of lower-level worksheets called Modified Activities. These worksheets cover the same content as the standard Activities but are written at a lower reading level.

Skill Track

Use Skill Track for *World History* to monitor student progress and meet the demands of adequate yearly progress (AYP). Make informed instructional decisions with individual student and class reports of lesson and chapter assessments. With immediate and ongoing feedback, students will also see what they have learned and where they need more reinforcement and practice.

	Student Pages	Student Text Lesson				
		Vocabulary	Map Study	Reading Strategy	Lesson Review	Chapter Summary/Review
Chapter 12 Islam and the Crusades	222–253	✔		✔		251–253
Lesson 12–1 Muhammad and Islam	224–230	✔	✔	✔	230	
Lesson 12–2 The Crusades	231–236	✔	✔	✔	236	
Lesson 12–3 The Costs of the Crusades	237–239	✔		✔	239	
Lesson 12–4 Changes in Agriculture	240–242	✔		✔	242	
Lesson 12–5 Changes in City Life	242–247	✔		✔	247	
Lesson 12–6 The Magna Carta	248–250	✔		✔	250	

	Student Text Features							Teaching Strategies										Learning Styles					Teacher's Resource Library			
	Words from the Past	Learn More About It	Great Names in History	Technology Connection	Geography Note	You Decide/Remember/History Fact	Timeline Study	ELL/ESL Strategy	Background Information	Common Error	Life Skills Connection	Key Vocabulary Words	Study Skills	Applications Home, Career, Community	Online Connection	Teacher Alert	World Cultures	Auditory/Verbal	Body/Kinesthetic	Interpersonal/Group Learning	Logical/Mathematical	Visual/Spatial	Activities/Modified Activities	Workbook Activities	Self-Study Guide	Chapter Outline
											223	223													✔	✔
	229						228	226	226	227				227	229	227		226					42	42		
		235	234			232, 234		233	233				233	234						233			43	43		
		237						238		238							239					238	44	44		
								241	240	241											241		45	45		
					245	244		243	244	243				245					245				46	46		
	249						248	249	249	249						249							47	47		

Audio Library

Skill Track for World History

Teacher's Resource Library

Unit 4 Mastery Test

(Answer Keys for the Teacher's Resource Library begin on page 809 of the Teacher's Edition.)

Other Resources

Books for Teachers

Sykes, Bryan. *Saxons, Vikings, and Celts: The Genetic Roots of Britain and Ireland.* New York, NY: W.W. Norton, 2006.

Huff, Toby E. *The Rise of Early Modern Science: Islam, China and the West.* Cambridge, UK: Cambridge University Press, 2003.

Books for Students

DK Eyewitness Books. *Viking.* New York, NY: DK Publishing, 2005.

Elliott, Lynne. *Children and Games in the Middle Ages.* New York, NY: Crabtree Publishing Company, 2004.

Videos

Medieval Siege. (60 minutes) Nova, 2000.

The History Channel Presents the Crusades—Crescent & the Cross. (180 minutes) A&E Home Video, 2005.

CD-ROM/Software

History of the City of Rome in the Middle Ages; Ferdinand Gregorovius; Italica Press. 2004. A CD-ROM that expands in greater detail the city of Rome.

THE MIDDLE AGES

The picture of a knight in armor atop a horse may get you interested. You may become more interested if a second knight is charging toward him with a lance. The Middle Ages was a period unlike any other before or after it. People were divided into classes to serve nobles and to protect the king. Traveling through many European countries you can still see the leftovers of many medieval estates. Throughout those same countries, you may still see shiny sets of armor or long threatening lances. However, the knights who once owned them are long gone with the Middle Ages.

Chapters in Unit 4

A country estate such as this included a feudal manor house. It was a place where a noble family could feel safe from enemies. Many estates included small villages and fields for growing crops.

189

Introducing the Unit

By A.D. 500, the once-mighty Roman Empire had fallen. The next 1,000 years of history are known as the Middle Ages. At its height, the Middle Ages was a time when people's thinking centered on their religion. For some, it was also a time of little travel. Have students study the picture on page 188. Tell them that in a feudal estate, like the one depicted, poor farm workers were tied to the land and could not leave if they wanted. Explain to students that they will learn about what happened in Europe and Asia during the Middle Ages. Have a student read aloud the unit introduction on page 189.

Ask:

- What is happening in the picture? (People are working in the fields tending crops.)
- What years are covered in this unit? (A.D. 400–1400)
- What event marks the beginning of the Middle Ages? (the fall of the Roman Empire)

TEACHER ALERT

Students will learn about feudal estates, as shown on page 188, in Chapter 11. A feudal estate is a large piece of land with a large home on it. The home, along with the farmland and village, is part of a manor. A manor is all the lands belonging to the lord (king or noble).

Web Sites

www.agsglobepmwh.com/page189a
(This site includes information on Viking culture, religion, money, women, weapons, colonists, and food.)

www.agsglobepmwh.com/page189b
(This site includes a directory of educational sites about the Crusades.)

Introducing the Chapter

The Middle Ages in Europe span nearly a millennium. This chapter discusses the fall of the Roman Empire, prompted by waves of barbarian invasions.

Ask:

- What did Germanic tribes wear? (rough cloth and animal skins)

- What did the barbarian invaders want? (adventure, power, and riches)

- What ended with the collapse of the Roman Empire? (fine cities; schools; the study of art, science, and literature)

The Barbarians and the Vikings

As the Roman Empire grew weaker, enemies beyond its borders were growing stronger. German tribes from the north, called *barbarians* by the Romans, threatened their borders. At last a tribe called the Huns invaded the Roman Empire. Meanwhile, other groups of warriors swept through Italy, Gaul, and Britain. The Western Roman Empire fell. The east became the Byzantine Empire. Strong new leaders such as Charlemagne came forward. Changes would begin with a new period called the Middle Ages.

GOALS FOR LEARNING

- To explain the role of barbarian tribes in the fall of the Western Roman Empire
- To tell why the Eastern Roman Empire did so well
- To explain how the Vikings influenced many parts of the world

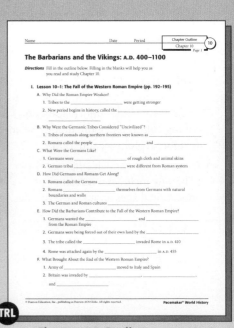

Chapter 10 Self-Study Guide, pages 1–2   Chapter 10 Outline, pages 1–3

Reading Strategy: Predicting

As you read a text, you can make predictions about what will happen next. It helps to preview the text and think about what you already know about the topic. As you make predictions, keep these things in mind:

- Make your best guess about what will happen next.
- Use what you know to predict what will take place next.
- Check your predictions. As you learn more information, you may find you need to change your predictions.

Key Vocabulary Words

Lesson 1

Middle Ages The period of European history extending from the Fall of Rome in A.D. 476 to about A.D. 1450

Frontier Land just beyond the border of a country

Uncivilized Without training in arts, science, or government

Primitive Of long ago; very simple

Barbarians Uncivilized, primitive people; people living outside Greece or Rome in the days of the Roman Empire

Lesson 3

Exiled Forced to live away from home in a foreign land

Saga A long story of brave deeds

Tradition A custom, idea, or belief handed down from one person to the next

---

Review the reading skill *predicting*. Remind students that making a prediction involves recognizing patterns and adding new details to what they already know about a subject. In the process, they make educated guesses about what will happen next. Predicting helps readers to analyze and comprehend subject matter.

Ask:

- Predict when you will have a test on this chapter. Explain your prediction. (Students might pick Friday, explaining that they always have a chapter test on that day.)

Key Vocabulary Words

Point out that these chapter words are presented in the order they appear in each lesson. They are also found in the glossary.

LIFE SKILLS CONNECTION

Students learn about modern day plundering—identity theft. Students learn and research common tips about how to avoid identity theft.

KEY VOCABULARY

In Part A, students match the definition to the correct word. In Part B, they circle the correct answers to complete the statements.

CHAPTER PROJECT

Have students research the Vikings using the Internet and reference materials. Several Scandinavian museums are online. Also, the Smithsonian and the Canadian government provide information about the Vikings online. Ask students to find a myth about a Viking god or goddess. Students will use their research to write a myth of their own, incorporating what they have learned from this chapter.

Barbarians and Vikings Chapter 10   **191**

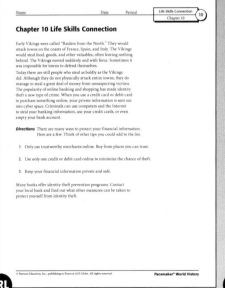

Life Skills Connection 10

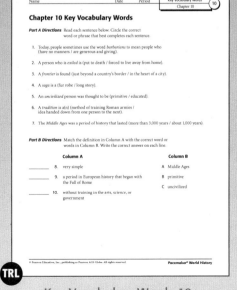

Key Vocabulary Words 10

Lesson at a Glance

Chapter 10 Lesson 1

Overview This lesson describes various reasons for the fall of the Western Roman Empire.

Objectives

- To describe the lifestyle of Germanic tribes
- To explain why the barbarians invaded the Roman Empire
- To describe what happened to Rome

Student Pages 192–196

Teacher's Resource Library TRL

Workbook Activity 36

Activity 36

Modified Activity 36

Vocabulary

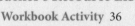

barbarians · primitive
frontier · uncivilized
Middle Ages

Place students in pairs. Have each pair create a crossword puzzle, using the vocabulary words in this lesson. Students can use definitions from the textbook or write their own. Tell pairs to exchange puzzles with other pairs. Challenge students to solve the puzzles.

Reading Strategy:
Predicting

Have students repeat this activity using the headings throughout this lesson. Students should write each prediction. After they read the lesson, have them review their predictions to see if they were correct. Tell students to revise their predictions if necessary.

LESSON 10-1

The Fall of the Western Roman Empire

Objectives

- To describe the lifestyle of Germanic tribes
- To explain why the barbarians invaded the Roman Empire
- To describe what happened to Rome

Reading Strategy:
Predicting

Preview the lesson title. Predict what you will learn in this lesson.

Middle Ages
The period of European history extending from the Fall of Rome in A.D. 476 to about A.D. 1450

Frontier
Land just beyond the border of a country

Uncivilized
Without training in arts, science, or government

Primitive
Of long ago; very simple

The Roman Empire was growing weaker. The tribes that lived beyond the northern borders were growing stronger. The day was coming when these tribes would sweep across the borders. The empire would be destroyed. New people would come into power. These people had cultures very different from the Roman culture. A new period in history was being born—the **Middle Ages.** This period would last about 1,000 years.

Why Were the Germanic Tribes Considered "Uncivilized"?

Tribes of nomads lived just beyond the border of the Roman Empire—along the northern **frontiers.** These people were known as Germans. The Romans called the Germanic tribes **uncivilized** and **primitive.** The Germans wore clothing of rough cloth and animal skins. They carried spears, swords, and battle-axes.

The Germans' tribal laws were different from the well-ordered Roman system of law. An assembly of men ruled each German village. When villagers broke the law, the assembly would ask, "Guilty or not guilty?" If the villager said he or she was not guilty, a test was used to prove innocence or guilt. For example, the villager's hand might be thrust into boiling water. If the burn healed easily, innocence was proven. If not, he or she was guilty. The gods had spoken! This was not at all like the Roman courts of justice.

---

1 Warm-Up Activity

Ask students what characteristics come to mind when they hear the word *barbarian.* (sample answers: rough and violent) Write their responses on the board. Then have students brainstorm a list of characteristics of early Romans. (sample answers: educated and refined) Compare and contrast the lists.

2 Teaching the Lesson

Have students predict why the Western Roman Empire collapsed. Then have them read pages 193–195 to see if their predictions were correct.

Ask:

- How were the Romans and Germans different? (Sample answer: They differed in dress, lifestyle, education, values, law, and government.)
- Why did the Romans believe that the Germanic tribes were uncivilized? (The Germanic tribes dressed in animal skins, carried battle-axes, and had harsh tribal laws.)
- What organization managed to keep its power after the empire fell? (the Christian church)

Barbarians
Uncivilized, primitive people; people living outside Greece or Rome in the days of the Roman Empire

You Decide
Under which system of laws would there be more justice—the German or the Roman? Why?

Germanic tribes often fought each other. The men took pride in their bravery in battle. They had fierce loyalty to the tribal chief. "I am a man now!" a German boy would shout when he received his first spear and shield. To lose his shield in battle would be his greatest disgrace.

The Romans called these German outsiders **barbarians.** Today this word is used to describe any uncivilized person. The Roman frontiers were protected from the barbarians by natural boundaries such as rivers and mountains. Where there were no natural boundaries, the Romans built forts and stone walls. The Roman Emperor Hadrian, who ruled between A.D. 117 and A.D. 138, built a huge wall. Hadrian's wall stretched across northern England.

The Germanic tribes lived just on the edge of the frontier. They were bound to cross over the borders. Therefore, the cultures mixed. The Germans learned to use Greek and Roman letters to write their own language. The Romans began to wear furs, as the Germans did. Many Roman women wore blond wigs made from German hair.

The Romans recognized the Germans' war skills. Some Germans joined the Roman armies. German soldiers sometimes married Roman women. It was all very neighborly at first. However, the Germans would not be friendly neighbors for long.

How Did Barbarians Contribute to the Fall of the Western Roman Empire?

The tribes from the north grew impatient. They wanted adventure. They wanted power of their own. They saw that they could take power, and riches, too, from the weakening Roman Empire. Barbarian armies began pouring across the frontier.

A.D. 400–1100   *The Barbarians and the Vikings* Chapter 10   **193**

You Decide
Students will likely note that the Romans had a more just system of laws than the Germans. The Roman system was based on facts and logic, while the Germanic system was based on superstition.

Background Information

The Huns were a non-Germanic tribe that invaded Eastern Europe around A.D. 375. Led by the fierce Attila, they were ruthless warriors. The Huns rode across Europe, defeating all Germanic tribes in their path. One tribe, the Goths, turned to Rome for help. Rome agreed to let the Goths move into the empire and to give them land. The Goths, in turn, promised to be peaceful and to leave their weapons behind. Neither side kept its promise, and the Goths later invaded Rome.

LEARNING STYLES

Interpersonal/Group Learning

Place students in small groups. Have each group select one of the following events related to the fall of Rome: raids by Attila the Hun, the Goths' invasion of Rome, the Vandals' invasion of Rome, and the overthrow of the last Roman emperor by Odoacer. Tell students to create a skit about their chosen event. Students should assign roles to each group member, and then perform their skit to the class.

ELL/ESL STRATEGY

Language Objective: *To learn specific content vocabulary*

Place students in pairs. Have one partner write each vocabulary word from this lesson on an index card. The other partner should then write the definition for each word on a separate index card. Tell students to place the word cards and the definition cards facedown on a desk in random order. They can play a memory game by turning over two cards and trying to match a word to its definition. When students find a match, they should read the word and definition aloud to their partner. They should keep matching pairs of cards, and turn down cards that do not match. Have students continue the activity until all cards are matched.

COMMON ERROR

Students might wonder how rivers formed natural boundaries that protected the Roman Empire. Remind them that there were no large metal bridges spanning the rivers. Rivers had to be crossed on horse or on boat—the boats themselves had no engines. The invaders were carrying heavy shields and battle-axes, making the crossing even more difficult. A fast-flowing river, in particular, formed an effective barrier against invading armies.

COMMON ERROR

Make sure students understand the meaning of the word *loot*. To loot means to take valuable items by force. Looting often occurs during wars, when the victors go through defeated cities and towns, taking whatever they please. Looting has also occurred in large cities during riots, natural disasters, and blackouts. Usually, buildings and other structures are damaged during looting. Have students discuss whether victorious armies should be allowed to loot. Some students may believe that "to the victor go the spoils." Lead them to understand that looting is stealing, and that most governments have laws in place to discourage looting by soldiers and citizens alike.

STUDY SKILLS

Have students create a four-column chart titled "Barbarian Invasions." As students read this lesson, they should fill in the chart with the name of each barbarian tribe, who they invaded, from whom they were fleeing (if applicable), and where they settled.

Besides being driven by greed, the Germans were fleeing an enemy of their own. A tribe of wild horsemen, called Huns, had swept out of Asia. Later, they were led by their fierce leader, Attila. They took more and more German lands. They forced the German tribes into the Roman Empire.

Barbarian invaders from the north attacked Rome in hopes of defeating the powerful empire.

A barbarian tribe called the Goths marched into Italy. Germans who had become Roman soldiers left their armies to join the Goths. In A.D. 410, the Goths, led by Alaric, entered Rome. The city was weak. The Goths took Rome with little trouble. They destroyed much of the city and stole what they could. Then they went on, leaving the ruins of Rome behind them.

Now other tribes of Germans swept through the Roman Empire. In A.D. 455, the city of Rome was attacked—this time by the Vandals. Like the Goths, they looted and destroyed everything in their path. Then they moved on into Spain and northern Africa.

Another army of Goths settled in Italy and Spain. Then the Angles, Saxons, and Jutes invaded the island of Britain. The Angles gave England its name. Their language would be called English. A tribe known as the Franks were on the move, too. The Franks settled in Flanders, just north of the province of Gaul.

The Roman Empire fell. Many Romans buried their treasures—including art and religious objects. They tried to save things from the barbarians. Long after that, people were still finding remains of the great empire. The treasures of Rome were buried in the fields and pastures of Europe.

The days of the Western Roman Empire were over. In A.D. 476, the German chief Odoacer overthrew the last of the Roman emperors. The fine cities were gone. There were no new schools. Few people studied art or literature or science. Barbarians set up new states. Their kings ruled, blending Roman law with tribal law. The Latin language changed. It became different in each of the different states. Only the Christian church kept its power and its organization.

History Fact

Tell students that most historians mark the fall of the Western Roman Empire as the beginning of the Middle Ages. Have students research why this period of history is called the Middle Ages. (The one thousand year period falls between the collapse of the Western Roman Empire and the beginning of the Renaissance in Europe.)

Reading Strategy: Predicting

Details might include the warlike culture of the various Germanic tribes, the mixing of the Germanic and Roman cultures, and the weakening of Rome by repeated invasions. Accept all reasonable answers.

AT HOME

Have students find out which languages their ancestors spoke. How many generations ago were these languages used? Are they still being used now? If so, by whom? Ask bilingual students to discuss the advantages of knowing a second language. Have them share how their native language influences their English.

CAREER CONNECTION

Most modern countries depend on the military to defend their interests, just as the Romans and the Germanic tribes did. In the United States, there are four branches of the military: the Army, the Air Force, the Marines, and the Navy. A military career encompasses a vast array of options. Have interested students conduct research in the library or on the Internet about military careers.

History Fact

By A.D. 476, the Roman Empire was over. Barbarians had conquered all the Roman cities and states and set up their own states.

Reading Strategy: Predicting

Think about your prediction. What details can you now add to make your prediction more specific?

Lesson 10–1 Review Answers

1. nomads **2.** assembly **3.** mix
4. Attila **5.** buried **6.** Odoacer
7. Christian church **8.** He built the
wall to protect the Romans from
barbarian invaders—everywhere
else there were natural boundaries
such as rivers and mountains. **9.** The
German tribes started to move into
the Roman Empire because they
wanted the power and riches of the
weakening empire, and because
they were fleeing a tribe of wild
horsemen. **10.** The Goths and the
Vandals attacked Rome.

LESSON 10-1 REVIEW

Word Bank

assembly
Attila
buried
Christian church
mix
nomads
Odoacer

On a sheet of paper, write the word from the Word Bank to complete each sentence correctly.

1. The Germanic tribes were _____ who lived along the northern frontiers of the Roman Empire. They were considered by the Romans to be uncivilized.

2. According to German tribal laws, a(n) _____ tested villagers to prove their innocence or guilt.

3. Because the Romans and Germans lived so close, their cultures began to _____.

4. _____ was the fierce leader of the Huns.

5. Romans _____ their treasures to save them from barbarians when the Roman Empire was falling.

6. In A.D. 476, the German chief _____ overthrew the last of the Roman emperors. It brought about the end of the Western Roman Empire.

7. The barbarians took over the Western Roman Empire. After, the _____ was the only piece to keep its power and organization.

On a sheet of paper, write the answer to each question. Use complete sentences.

8. Why did the Emperor Hadrian build a wall across northern England?

9. What are the two reasons the German tribes moved into the Roman Empire?

10. What were two barbarian tribes that attacked Rome?

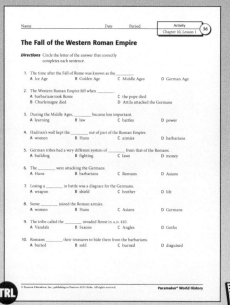

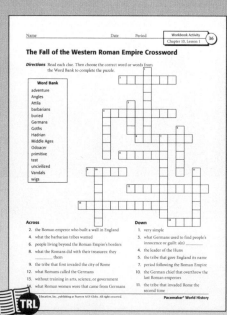

The Byzantine Empire

Overview This lesson compares the Byzantine and Roman empires, and discusses the life and times of Charlemagne.

Objectives

■ To describe the Byzantine Empire

■ To tell why Charlemagne proved to be a fine ruler

Reading Strategy: Predicting

As you begin reading about the Byzantine Empire, make a prediction about what will happen with it.

Remember The language of the Roman Catholic Church was Latin.

The Western Roman Empire fell to the barbarians. The Eastern Empire, with Constantinople as its capital, resisted attack. The Eastern Empire was known as the Byzantine Empire. It would last for almost 1,000 years after German tribes took the Western Roman Empire. Life in the Western Empire was grim. The Byzantine Empire, however, put up fine buildings trimmed in gold. A new university was built there. The people grew wealthy from trading.

The language of the Byzantine Empire was Greek. This became the official language of the Eastern church. In A.D. 1054, the Christian church split into two sections. The church in the west was called Roman Catholic. The church in the east was called Eastern Orthodox.

Who Was Charlemagne?

"A giant of a man! About seven feet tall! He had blond hair and a merry face." That is the way a writer of the time described Charles the Great, or Charlemagne. Charlemagne was king of the Franks, the German tribe that took Flanders. The Franks had continued their conquests. They ended up ruling all the lands that would one day be France.

Charlemagne's father was called Pepin the Short. He had died in A.D. 768. Charlemagne proved to be a fine ruler when he became king of the Franks. He conquered more land—much of Germany and part of Italy. He showed an interest in education and in the Christian religion, and won favor with the pope.

Objectives

■ To describe the Byzantine Empire

■ To tell why Charlemagne proved to be a fine ruler

Student Pages 197–199

Teacher's Resource Library

Workbook Activity 37

Activity 37

Modified Activity 37

Vocabulary

Have students preview the lesson for five unfamiliar words or phrases. Tell them to record the terms in their notebooks. As students read, have them use dictionaries to define the words. Students can also rely on textual clues, such as surrounding sentences, to infer the meanings of the words.

1 Warm-Up Activity

Tell students that the Byzantine Empire was relatively peaceful, while lawlessness reigned in the former Western Roman Empire. Ask them what school might be like without laws or rules. As a class, discuss how just, equitable laws help society to function effectively.

Reading Strategy: Predicting

Tell students that headings, captions, and illustrations are clues to what the lesson is about. Have them scan the lesson before they make their predictions.

Remember Use a dictionary to show students that many modern words have either Latin or Greek roots. This fact serves as a reminder of the vast influence of ancient Rome and Greece on our culture.

2 Teaching the Lesson

Place students in pairs. Give each partner the option of answering the questions verbally or in writing.

Ask:

● Who was Charlemagne? (He was the leader of the Franks who later became Emperor of the Holy Roman Empire.)

● Why was Charlemagne's empire a good one? (He built schools, encouraged artists, learned Latin, and worked with the church.)

Background Information

Justinian was one of the greatest Byzantine emperors. He ruled from A.D. 527 to 565. Justinian was born in the Balkan Mountains region of the empire. As a young man, he went to Constantinople where his uncle, the future emperor Justin I, held an important military position. Justin adopted Justinian. After his uncle's death, Justinian became emperor.

As emperor, Justinian's most important achievement was reforming the laws of ancient Rome. Justinian appointed scholars who worked for 10 years collecting, revising, and organizing Roman laws. Finally, the laws were arranged into codes. These codes are known as the Justinian Code. The Justinian Code became the legal foundation for nearly every modern European nation.

LEARNING STYLES

Body/Kinesthetic
One of the world's most beautiful churches, the Hagia Sophia, was built in Constantinople during the Byzantine Empire. Have students research the architecture of the Hagia Sophia. Tell them to create drawings or clay models to illustrate the church's unique features. Display students' work around the class.

ELL/ESL STRATEGY

Language Objective:
To read text for meaning and to practice public speaking

Place students in small groups. Have each group read Lesson 2 together. Then ask each student in the group to form a question based on the text. Students should write their question on an index card. Have students share their questions with one another. Each student should take a turn answering a question in his or her own words. Students should discuss the answers to assess if they are correct.

You Decide
Do you think Charlemagne was a fine ruler? Why or why not?

On Christmas Day, A.D. 800, the pope crowned Charlemagne "Emperor of the Holy Roman Empire." Although the empire was called "Roman," Charlemagne was still a barbarian. He dressed in the Frankish style and spoke the language of the Franks. His was a Germanic land rather than a Roman one.

Charlemagne's empire was a good one. Charlemagne built schools and encouraged artists. He learned to read Latin and worked closely with the church.

When Charlemagne died, his empire went to his son, Louis I. The empire began to crumble. It was finally divided among Charlemagne's three grandsons—Charles the Bald, Lothair, and Louis the German. The divided lands would one day become France, Germany, and part of Italy.

Charlemagne was crowned emperor of the Holy Roman Empire by the pope.

You Decide
Have students offer facts from the text to support their views. For example, students might say that Charlemagne was a good ruler because he built schools, encouraged artists, and conquered much of Germany and Italy.

3 Reinforce and Extend

COMMON ERROR

Students may assume that Charlemagne could write Latin, as well as read it. The great ruler did try to learn to write late in life, but he never quite mastered the task. He could speak both Latin and old Teutonic, the language of the Franks. He also understood Greek.

LESSON 10-2 REVIEW

On a sheet of paper, write the letter of the answer that correctly completes each sentence.

1. The Eastern Empire resisted the barbarians' attack and would not fall for another _____ years.

    A 100   **B** 1,000   **C** 1,050   **D** 2,000

2. The Eastern Empire is known as the _____ Empire.

    A Greek   **B** German   **C** Frank   **D** Byzantine

3. _____ was the official language of the Eastern Empire.

    A Greek   **B** Roman   **C** Latin   **D** German

4. The Christian church split into two sections in A.D. _____.

    A 768   **B** 800   **C** 1054   **D** 2100

5. The church was called Roman Catholic in the west and _____ in the east.

    A Eastern Catholic   **C** Greek Orthodox
    B Roman Orthodox   **D** Eastern Orthodox

6. _____ was the king of the Franks.

    A Charlemagne   **B** Charles the Bald   **C** Lothair   **D** Louis the German

7. The Franks ruled all the lands that one day would be known as _____.

    A Italy   **B** France   **C** Sweden   **D** Denmark

8. The pope crowned Charlemagne "Emperor of the Holy Roman Empire." However, he was still a _____.

    A Roman   **B** Vandal   **C** barbarian   **D** Viking

9. After his death, Charlemagne's empire began to crumble under _____.

    A Louis I   **B** Charles the Bald   **C** Lothair   **D** Pepin the Short

10. Charlemagne's empire was divided, becoming France, _____, and part of Italy.

    A Norway   **B** Sweden   **C** Denmark   **D** Germany

A.D. 400–1100   *The Barbarians and the Vikings*   Chapter 10   **199**

WORLD CULTURES

Iconography, or the painting of icons, was very popular in Russia for about 300 years. The icons reflected Byzantine culture. In the 15th century, however, Russians began to change the images on their icons. They painted backgrounds that more closely matched their own surroundings. The backgrounds might include local vegetation and churches similar to the ones in which they worshipped. By the 17th century, outside cultural influences influenced Russian artists and again changed the character of the icons.

Lesson 10–2 Review Answers
1. B 2. D 3. A 4. C 5. D 6. A 7. B 8. C 9. A 10. D

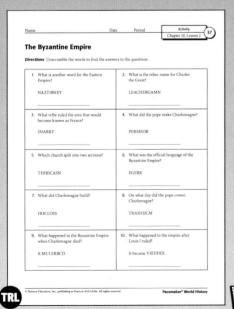
Activity 37

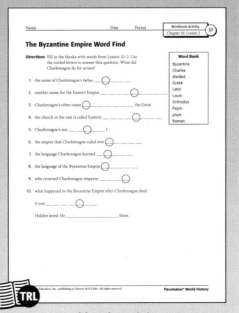
Workbook Activity 37

Barbarians and Vikings Chapter 10   **199**

Lesson at a Glance

Chapter 10 Lesson 3

Overview This lesson discusses the characteristics and achievements of the Vikings, including the branch that settled in France. This branch later became known as the Normans.

Objectives

- To name the places the Vikings explored, settled, or conquered
- To tell who William the Conqueror was and what he did
- To tell why the Vikings left their mark on many cultures

Student Pages 200–204

Teacher's Resource Library 🔵**TRL**

Workbook Activity 38

Activity 38

Modified Activity 38

Vocabulary

exiled   tradition
saga

As a class, review the definitions of the vocabulary words. Ask students to write sentences that use each word correctly.

PRONUNCIATION GUIDE

Use this list to help students pronounce difficult words in this lesson.

Valhalla (val hal´ ə)

Mjolnir (myòl´ nir)

1 Warm-Up Activity

Have students think of one example of how the Vikings influenced modern culture. If students are at a loss, write the word *Thursday* on the board. This day of the week is named after the Viking god of thunder, Thor.

Objectives

- To name the places the Vikings explored, settled, or conquered
- To tell who William the Conqueror was and what he did
- To tell why the Vikings left their mark on many cultures

Reading Strategy:
Predicting

As you begin your reading of this section, what predictions can you make about the Vikings?

Exiled

Forced to live away from home in a foreign land

People called the attackers Northmen because they sailed down from the north. They came from lands that are today Norway, Sweden, and Denmark. The Northmen were adventurers. They loved sailing and fighting. Their ships, powered by oars and sails, were swift. The sailors set their course by the stars and by the sun. They called themselves Vikings.

Who Were the "Raiders from the North"?

The Viking raids began in A.D. 793. The Vikings attacked an island off the east coast of England. This was followed by a wave of raids against England, Scotland, and Ireland. During the mid-800s the Vikings burned and looted towns on the coasts of France, Spain, and Italy.

For many years the Vikings kept on the move. They stole and took by force, or plundered, many towns, then sailed back home. Later, they settled in the lands that their ships reached.

Swedish Vikings settled in Russia. Other Vikings found homes in England and along the coast of France. The Vikings in France became known as the Normans. Their new land was called Normandy.

Some Vikings sailed the Atlantic Ocean and set up colonies in Iceland. In about A.D. 982, a red-haired Viking, Erik the Red, was **exiled.** In other words, he was forced to live away from his home in Iceland. In response, Erik decided to sail to Greenland to set up a colony.

200   *Unit 4   The Middle Ages*

Reading Strategy:
Predicting

Tell students to make a list of predictions about the Vikings. Then read aloud the introductory paragraph of this lesson. Afterwards, ask students to revise or expand their predictions based on new details in the paragraph.

2 Teaching the Lesson

Have students examine the timeline on page 203. Point out that the timeline summarizes important events they have learned about throughout this chapter. Ask them to brainstorm additional events to add to the timeline.

Ask:

- What were the Northmen like? (They were adventurers who loved sailing and fighting.)
- With what did the Vikings decorate buildings and ships? (carved animals)
- Why was the Battle of Hastings in 1066 important? (William, Duke of Normandy, conquered England and became its king.)

Geography Note

Normandy is a region in northwestern France. It became a Roman province in about 50 B.C. The Franks took power in about A.D. 500. Vikings kept raiding the area until France gave it to them in A.D. 911. It was an independent kingdom for over 200 years. Due to several wars, control passed back and forth between England and France. It has remained part of France since A.D. 1450.

Erik had a son named Leif Eriksson. In A.D. 1000, Eriksson sailed as far as the east coast of North America. The Vikings stayed there for several years. Eriksson called the land Vinland (or Wineland), possibly for the grapes he found.

We do not know why the Vikings left Vinland. For centuries afterward, they made trips to North America, but they did not stay. They had to give up their colony in Greenland during the 1400s. By that time, the climate had become much colder.

Songs and stories of Leif Eriksson, Erik the Red, and other Viking heroes are called **sagas.** Much of what we know about the Vikings comes from these sagas. Some sagas tell of Norse gods like Odin and Thor. They tell of Valhalla, the hall of the gods, where dead Viking warriors live forever.

Many Vikings sailed from their homeland in the north in search of food and treasure.

Background Information

From archaeological evidence, historians know that about A.D. 1000, Leif Eriksson and a small group of Vikings spent a winter at L' Anse aux Meadows, in present day Newfoundland, Canada. According to legend, Leif was on his way home from Normandy when a raging storm blew his ship off course. They were lost for 40 days before a sailor spotted land.

The Vikings landed in Newfoundland, becoming the first Europeans to explore the Americas. However, they did not build permanent settlements there. Historians do not know for certain why the colony in Newfoundland was abandoned after about three years. It would be almost 500 years before an Italian named Christopher Columbus would reach the new land again.

LEARNING STYLES

Auditory/Verbal

Ask the class to close their textbooks. Have a volunteer read aloud two events from the timeline on page 203. The volunteer should not give the dates of the events. Then have the class verbally vote on which event came first. Continue the activity until all events on the timeline have been covered.

LEARNING STYLES

Logical/Mathematical

Ask students to draw three timelines on a piece of paper. Tell them to label the first timeline "Rome," the second timeline "Europe," and the third timeline "North America." Then refer students to the timeline on page 203 of the Student Edition. Ask them to separate the events into three groups—Rome, Europe, and North America—and place the information from the text's timeline onto their own appropriate timelines.

Geography Note

Tell students that Normandy finally passed into France's hands during the Hundred Years' War, which they will learn about later. This war began in 1337 when the English King Edward III landed in Normandy to stake a claim to the throne of France. The war spanned the reigns of five English kings and five French kings.

LEARNING STYLES

Visual/Spatial

Have each student place a piece of tracing paper over a map of Europe. Tell them to trace the outline of the countries, including Norway, Sweden, Denmark, France, Germany, Spain, England, Scotland, Ireland, and Italy. Students should label major rivers, oceans, mountains, and cities. Then have students use symbols to indicate the movements and conquests of the Vikings. Students should create a map key that explains their symbols.

Barbarians and Vikings *Chapter 10*   **201**

Tradition
A custom, idea, or belief handed down from one person to the next

Thor, Viking God of Thunder

Thor was the popular Viking god of thunder. The Vikings believed that thunder was the sound of Thor's chariot wheels as he flew across the heavens.

Thor was a son of Odin, king of the Norse gods. Thor was a great red-bearded fellow with a huge appetite. Thor wielded a magical axe-hammer called Mjollnir. Many Vikings and other Scandinavians carried small copies of this axe-hammer for their own protection. Thor could help sea voyagers and farmers because he controlled the sea, the wind, and the rain.

Thor had many adventures. Some of them were funny, and he did not always come out on top. Usually Thor used his hammer to smash his enemies' skulls. Sometimes he threw hot metal at them.

The hammer of Thor, Viking god of thunder.

Stories about Thor and other Norse gods were part of the Vikings' oral **tradition**. A tradition is a custom, idea, or belief handed down from one person to the next. In the Middle Ages, these stories were written down in the Icelandic literature. Some famous stories featured Thor's battle with the serpent of the world. This serpent, or dragon, was said to wrap itself around the whole world under the sea.

When Christianity came to Scandinavia, the Vikings and other Norse people stopped worshipping Thor and carrying small axe-hammers. However, Thor's popularity continued in poems and stories. Today, our Thursday is Thor's Day. In literature and even in comic books, the adventures of Thor continue.

Who Were the Normans?

The Normans were adventurous, like their Viking ancestors. In 1066 William, the Duke of Normandy, decided to make himself King of England. He waited for fair breezes to blow his ships across the English Channel. At last the moment came.

There was a savage fight known as the Battle of Hastings. William killed the English king, Harold. William became king of England and was named "William the Conqueror."

Why Did the Vikings Leave Their Mark on So Many Lands?

With new settlements and new languages, the Vikings turned to a new religion. They became Christians, leaving behind the Norse gods of the sagas. The Viking days of raiding ended.

The Vikings kept sea trade alive and booming. They used their fine ships and sailing skills to travel oceans and rivers. Their art is found throughout Europe. They decorated buildings, as well as ships, with carved animals and beasts. The adventurous Vikings settled in many lands; they left their mark on many cultures.

TIMELINE STUDY: THE NORTHERN INVADERS

How many years after Erik the Red settled in Greenland did Leif Eriksson reach North America?

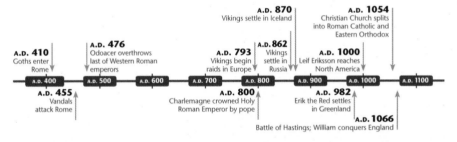

A.D. 410 Goths enter Rome

A.D. 455 Vandals attack Rome

A.D. 476 Odoacer overthrows last of Western Roman emperors

A.D. 793 Vikings begin raids in Europe

A.D. 800 Charlemagne crowned Holy Roman Emperor by pope

A.D. 870 Vikings settle in Iceland

A.D. 862 Vikings settle in Russia

A.D. 982 Erik the Red settles in Greenland

A.D. 1054 Christian Church splits into Roman Catholic and Eastern Orthodox

A.D. 1000 Leif Eriksson reaches North America

A.D. 1066 Battle of Hastings; William conquers England

A.D. 400 — A.D. 500 — A.D. 600 — A.D. 700 — A.D. 800 — A.D. 900 — A.D. 1000 — A.D. 1100

A.D. 400–1100   *The Barbarians and the Vikings*   Chapter 10   **203**

If students have difficulty answering the question, model how to find the answer using the timeline. Say, "According to the timeline, Erik the Red settled Greenland in A.D. 982. Leif Eriksson reached North America in A.D. 1000. That's a difference of about 18 years."

TEACHER ALERT

Some students may have difficulty reading the fine print in the timeline. Make enlarged copies of the timeline and pass them out to students. You can also make a transparency, and display the timeline on an overhead projector. Repeat this activity for other timelines throughout the book.

ONLINE CONNECTION

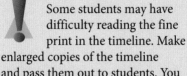

Students can gain additional information by accessing the following Web site: www.agsglobepmwh.com/page203 (This site has additional information on Viking life, including sagas and decorated boats.)

COMMON ERROR

Students might not understand why people are exiled from their homelands. Explain that exile can be a punishment for breaking the law or some cultural taboo. Leaders may use exile to banish potential threats to their power. Community bonds were strong in tribal cultures. To be banished from family and friends served as a powerful deterrent against wrongdoing.

Word Bank

Christians
Denmark
Iceland
Normans
raiding
sagas
sailing
settled
Thor
William

On a sheet of paper, write the word from the Word Bank to complete each sentence correctly.

1. The Northmen, also known as Vikings, were attackers that came from Norway, Sweden, and _____.

2. The Vikings were adventurers who loved _____ and fighting.

3. The Vikings kept on the move, _____ towns and then sailing back home.

4. Vikings in France became known as the _____.

5. The Vikings explored and settled in many lands, including: Russia, France, England, _____, and Greenland.

6. The songs and stories about the brave deeds of Viking heroes are called _____.

7. _____ was the Viking god of thunder.

8. The Battle of Hastings made _____, the Duke of Normandy, the king of England.

9. The new settlements and new languages turned the Vikings into _____.

10. The Vikings left their mark on many cultures because they _____ in so many lands.

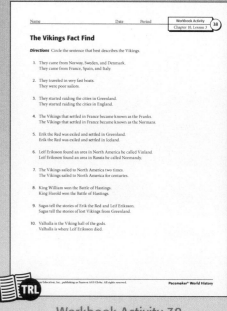

Activity 38   Workbook Activity 38

- Tribes of Germans lived along the northern border of the Roman Empire. The Romans called those people barbarians. German armies often fought one another. This made Romans fear invasion.

- Roman Emperor Hadrian built a huge wall that stretched across northern England. In other places, natural barriers provided some protection from the barbarians.

- A barbarian tribe called the Goths attacked and destroyed much of Rome. They were followed by the Vandals who destroyed much more. Angles, Saxons, Jutes, and Franks invaded and plundered Britain and other areas of the Western Roman Empire.

- The Western Roman Empire fell in A.D. 476.

- The Eastern Roman Empire was known as the Byzantine Empire. It lasted for another 1,000 years after the fall of the Western Roman Empire.

- Charlemagne, king of the Franks, ended up ruling the area that would become France.

- The pope crowned Charlemagne "Emperor of the Holy Roman Empire."

- Vikings sailed to other parts of Europe from Norway, Denmark, and Sweden. The Vikings settled in many of the places they raided. The Viking Leif Eriksson started a colony in North America.

- William the Conqueror, Duke of Normandy, conquered England.

- The Vikings influenced cultures in many parts of the world.

A.D. 400–1100   *The Barbarians and the Vikings*   Chapter 10   **205**

Chapter 10 Summary

Have students read the Chapter Summary on page 205 to review the main ideas presented in Chapter 10.

Ask:

- Which border of the Roman Empire did the German tribes threaten? (the northern border)

- What did the Roman Empire rely on to protect itself from invaders? (natural boundaries and human-built structures such as walls)

- Name two tribes that attacked Rome. (the Goths and the Vandals)

- How long did the Eastern Roman Empire last after the fall of the Western Roman Empire? (about 1,000 years)

- What title did the pope give Charlemagne? (Emperor of the Holy Roman Emperor)

- What is Leif Eriksson known for? (He started a colony in North America.)

- Who was William the Conqueror? (the Duke of Normandy who conquered England)

CHAPTER PROJECT FOLLOW-UP

Ask each student to orally present their myth to the class. Encourage students to use props. For example, they might want to make hats out of construction paper or weapons out of cardboard. Assess students' myths based on originality and creativity.

TEACHER'S RESOURCE

The AGS Globe Teaching Strategies in Social Studies Transparencies may be used with this chapter. The transparencies add an interactive dimension to expand and enhance the Pacemaker® *World History* program content.

Chapter 10 Review

Use the Chapter Review to prepare students for tests and to reteach content from the chapter.

Chapter 10 Mastery Test

The Teacher's Resource Library includes two forms of the Chapter 10 Mastery Test. Each test addresses the chapter Goals for Learning. An optional third page of additional critical-thinking items is included for each test. The difficulty level of the two forms is equivalent.

Chapter 10 Review Answers

Vocabulary Review

1. barbarian
2. sagas
3. exiled
4. uncivilized
5. tradition
6. frontier
7. Middle Ages

Chapter Review Questions

8. They were the Germanic tribes that invaded the island of Britain.

9. They wore clothing of rough cloth and animal skins. They carried spears, swords, and battle-axes. Villages had laws that did not seem fair. They often fought each other.

10. The Germanic tribes wanted the riches of the Roman Empire. They were also running away from the Huns.

Word Bank

barbarian
exiled
frontier
Middle Ages
sagas
tradition
uncivilized

Vocabulary Review

On a sheet of paper, use the words from the Word Bank to complete each sentence correctly.

1. A person living outside Greece or Rome was called a(n) _____.

2. The Vikings told _____ about their heroes, gods, and goddesses.

3. Erik the Red went to Greenland because he was _____, or forced from his homeland.

4. The Romans thought the Germans were _____ because they were more primitive.

5. The Vikings had an oral _____ of telling stories of Norse gods.

6. Explorers go beyond their country's borders to the next _____.

7. The period of history known as the _____ lasted about 1,000 years.

Chapter Review Questions

On a sheet of paper, write the answer to each question. Use complete sentences.

8. Who were the Angles, Saxons, and Jutes?

9. How did the Germanic tribes live before they invaded Rome?

10. What are two reasons that Germanic tribes attacked the Western Roman Empire?

11. Why was Charlemagne a fine ruler?

12. What was the Byzantine Empire like after the fall of Rome?

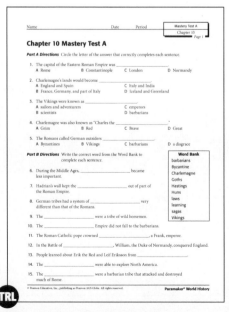

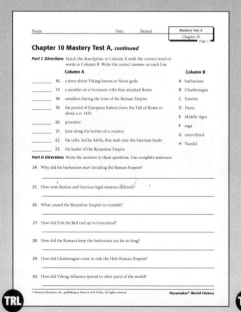

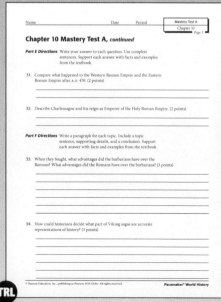

13. Where did the Vikings come from?

14. What are three places the Vikings explored or settled?

15. Why did the Vikings influence so many cultures?

Critical Thinking

On a sheet of paper, write your response to each question. Use complete sentences.

16. Could a barbarian become an excellent ruler in the Roman Empire? Explain your answer, using examples.

17. Are the sagas reliable sources of information about the Vikings? Explain why or why not.

Using the Timeline

Use the timeline on page 203 to answer the questions.

18. How many years after the Goths attacked Rome did the Vandals do the same?

19. When was Charlemagne crowned Holy Roman Emperor?

20. The Vikings began their raids in Europe before they reached North America. How many years passed between those two events?

GROUP ACTIVITY

In a group of two or three, research Viking life. Write a short account—a skit, story, or other piece of creative writing—about your topic. Then present your findings to the class. Sample subjects are:
- a news story of a Viking trade voyage or raid;
- a journal of a Viking discovering and settling in a new land;
- a Viking saga; and
- a skit about life in a Viking village.

11. He built schools and encouraged artists. He learned to read Latin and worked closely with the church.

12. After the fall of Rome, the Byzantine Empire continued to grow. The people built great buildings, including a university. Trade grew.

13. The Vikings came from lands that are today Norway, Sweden, and Denmark.

14. Answers should include three of the following: Russia, England, France, Iceland, Greenland, east coast of North America.

15. They settled in many lands, so they influenced many cultures.

Critical Thinking

16. Possible answer: Yes, Charlemagne was a barbarian and an excellent ruler.

17. Possible answer: Sagas are like myths. They may contain basic truths and some history, but they may not be entirely accurate.

Using the Timeline

18. 45 years

19. A.D. 800

20. 207 years

GROUP ACTIVITY

The final product should show an understanding of Vikings and specific information about Viking life.

Chapter 10 Mastery Test B, pages 1–3

Barbarians and Vikings Chapter 10   **207**

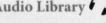
Introducing the Chapter

The fall of the Roman Empire in the West changed people's lives in many ways. The Roman Catholic Church filled much of the cultural and religious void. Feudalism introduced a new form of government based on land ownership. As students read the chapter, they should note how roles changed from the social structures of the Romans and Greeks. (Serfs replaced slaves. Cities shrank, as people moved into the countryside. There was less trade.)

Ask:

- What were the roles of knights, monks, and nuns in the religious life of the Middle Ages? (They supported the church by providing protection, prayer, and service.)

The Lords and the Serfs

The strength and power of the Roman Empire had faded. So had the colorful way of life that the Romans spread throughout much of Europe, Asia, and northern Africa. Like the Athenians before them, the Romans had explored new ideas. They had created works of art and grand new buildings. They had set ambitious goals.

The next 1,000 years brought much change in the way people lived. Many lived a country life within the new feudal class system. In many cases, people were not "on the move" as much and life became more predictable. This would be a colorful time, but in a much different way.

GOALS FOR LEARNING

- To understand the feudal system people lived under during the Middle Ages
- To explain the role of religion in feudal life
- To describe the hard life of the Middle Ages

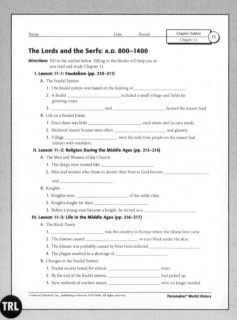

Reading Strategy: Text Structure

Before you begin reading this chapter, look at how it is organized. Look at the title, headings, boldfaced words, and photographs. Ask yourself:

- Is the text a description or sequence?
- Is it compare and contrast or cause and effect?

Key Vocabulary Words

Lesson 1

Organize To set up; to get a series or number of things in order

Feudalism A political and military system based on the holding of land

Vassal A noble who received land from a king in return for loyalty and service

Homage A pledge of loyalty; a promise to serve that was made to kings and lords during the Middle Ages

Lord A king or noble who gave land to someone else

Manor The lands belonging to a medieval lord, including farmland, a village, and the home of the owner

Estate A large piece of land with a large home on it

Freemen People who are free, not slaves, and who have the rights of citizens

Serf A poor farm worker who was bound to the land and whose life was controlled by the lord of the manor

Medieval Belonging to the Middle Ages

Fortress A building with strong walls for defense against an enemy

Lesson 2

Clergy The people who lead a religion

Monk A man who has taken religious vows and usually lives in a monastery

Nun A woman who has taken religious vows and enters a convent

Knight A high-ranking soldier of the Middle Ages who received his title from a noble

Lesson 3

Artisan A person who works with his or her hands to create something

Peasant A poor farmer or farm worker

- What classes existed in the feudal system? (serfs, nobles, clergy)
- How did the Black Death and gunpowder weaken the feudal system? (Plague depopulated the countryside and created a labor shortage. Gunpowder made it harder to defend land.)

Reading Strategy:
Text Structure

Have students skim the lessons in the chapter. Then have them fill out the Teacher's Resource Library outline. An outline will give students an overall picture of the text structure.

Key Vocabulary Words

Point out that these chapter words are presented in the order they appear in each lesson. They are also found in the glossary.

LIFE SKILLS CONNECTION

Students learn about independent farmers and how to find locally grown produce in their own communities. They also discuss the benefits of choosing locally grown foods.

KEY VOCABULARY

Students choose the correct word from the Word Bank to complete the sentences.

CHAPTER PROJECT

Have students divide into the following groups based on personal interest: books based on the Middle Ages, serf, peasant, page, squire, knight, vassal, or lord. Have each group research their topic to learn as many details as possible about their category. Tell students that their research will culminate in a class literary work of fiction.

TRL Life Skills Connection 11

TRL Key Vocabulary Words 11, pages 1–2

Lesson at a Glance

Chapter 11 Lesson 1

Overview This lesson describes feudalism, a new system of government in the Middle Ages, and the everyday life of serfs and nobles.

Objectives

- To describe the life of the lord of the manor
- To describe the life of a serf
- To name the three classes in feudal society

Student Pages 210–212

Teacher's Resource Library TRL

Workbook Activity 39

Activity 39

Modified Activity 39

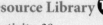

Vocabulary

estate   manor
feudalism   medieval
fortress   organize
freeman   serf
homage   vassal
lord

Have students create flashcards for the vocabulary words, placing the words on one side of the cards and the definitions on the other. Allow a few minutes for students to study their cards. Then have them quiz each other.

Objectives

- To describe the life of the lord of a manor
- To describe the life of a serf
- To name the three classes in feudal society

Reading Strategy:
Text Structure

Preview the lesson. Notice the headings, features, and boldfaced words.

Organize
To set up

Feudalism
A political and military system based on the holding of land

Vassal
A noble who received land from a king in return for loyalty and service

Homage
A pledge of loyalty

When the Roman Empire fell, the period of European history known as the Middle Ages began. Many people in Europe moved from the cities to the country. The splendor of the great cities faded. After a time, some towns no longer existed. Trade all but disappeared. People no longer used money. Education and learning became less and less important. Only in the church was there an effort to continue the reading and writing of Latin. The church also saved many writings from ancient times.

What Was the Feudal System?

Life was now set up, or **organized,** under a new system called **feudalism.** In a feudal society, a king ruled a whole country. He divided the land among important men, or of nobles. These nobles were called **vassals** of the king. In exchange for land, the nobles paid **homage,** or pledged loyalty, to the king. This meant that they promised to serve the king. They swore to fight for and protect him.

A noble, or **lord,** lived in a **manor** house on a large piece of land. This land was called an **estate.** The estate included a small village and fields for growing crops. **Freemen** and **serfs** lived on the feudal estate. They depended on the ruling noble and his land for their living.

The manor fields were divided into strips of land. Freemen were allowed to buy and farm their own strips. In return they had to pay the lord of the manor a part of their crops. Also, they had to promise to fight for the lord. A noble always had to worry about attacks by neighboring estates.

The serfs did not own their own land. They worked for the lord of the manor, farming his land. Serfs were tied to the land on which they were born. They could not leave the estate, even if they wanted to.

210 *Unit 4 The Middle Ages*

---

1 Warm-Up Activity

Some students may already know about life on a manor from books, television, or movies. Before they read this section, have students brainstorm anything that comes to mind. (Students may mention castles, moats, drawbridges, kings, and queens.) Write their ideas on the board. After students read the section, lead a discussion on whether books, television, and movies give an accurate picture of life on a manor.

2 Teaching the Lesson

Have students draw a pyramid showing the power structure in the feudal system. Tell them to write the most powerful people at the top of the pyramid, the next most powerful group in the middle, and the least powerful group at the base. (At the top should be the king, then the vassals, and the peasants at the base.)

Ask:

- Under the feudal system, who owned all the land? (the king)
- Who were serfs? (peasant farmers who had to work on the manor on which they were born)

Reading Strategy:
Text Structure

Tell students that using the structure of a text can help them figure out which pieces of information are the most important. Stress the importance of reading the headings in text, and studying the photographs, charts, and illustrations that accompany the text. Explain that the headings in a text will often provide a hint about the most important information. Sometimes the headings are written as questions. After reading the text, students should be able to answer the question.

Lord
A king or noble who gave land to someone else

Manor
The lands belonging to a medieval lord

Estate
A large piece of land with a large home on it

Freemen
People who are free and who have the rights of citizens

Serf
A poor farm worker who was bound to the land and whose life was controlled by the lord of the manor

Medieval
Belonging to the Middle Ages

Fortress
A building with strong walls for defense against an enemy

You Decide
Even rich people lived under harsh conditions during the Middle Ages. Would you have liked living in a castle? Why or why not?

The serfs provided every service for the lord of the manor and his family. The serfs grew crops and gathered wood. They took care of the lord's lands and his house. In the feudal system, each class owed loyalty and service to the class just above it.

What Was Life Like on a Feudal Estate?

Very little trade went on under the feudal system. Each feudal estate had its own village and met its own needs. Each village had a blacksmith who made tools and weapons, and a miller who ground grain into flour. The serfs had to use the services of the manor. They also had to pay whatever price was asked for these services.

Many nobles and their families lived in great houses made of stone. Some **medieval** manor houses were real castles. They were cold, however, and often gloomy. They had no glass in the windows or running water. They were dimly lit by burning torches made of twigs. The damp, shadowy castles were cold **fortresses** in which noble families could feel safe from enemies.

Many of the lords had several manors. They lived part of the year at one and part of the year at another. The lords chose managers to oversee the land when they were away.

While the noble family lived in the manor house, the villagers lived in small, smoky huts. They ate from wooden bowls and sat on backless, three-legged stools. They could not read or write. Their only contacts from outside the manor came when the village held a fair. Then merchants from around the countryside might bring their wares, or goods.

A manor lord could treat his serfs much as he pleased. "Between you and your serf there is no judge but God" was a medieval saying. Serfs had little protection from the lord's treatment.

Background Information

Before 1100, castles were made of wood and mud. Castle builders switched to stone in the 1100s to better protect against enemy invaders, fire, and weather. In some cases, the stone walls could be as wide as 33 feet. While stone provided better protection, it also had its disadvantages. Stone walls became cold and wet, and they failed to protect inhabitants from the cold drafts of harsh European winters.

LEARNING STYLES

Logical/Mathematical
To give students the idea of land division, hand one student a square piece of paper the size of a small note. Tell the student that he or she is a lord and the paper represents a land holding. Have the student divide his or her "land" among vassals by tearing the paper and giving it away to a vassal. The "lord" can have many vassals each with a small piece of land, or fief, or perhaps only two vassals, each with a larger fief. The vassals repeat the activity, choosing other vassals and dividing land (the paper) between them. Make it clear that vassals are loyal to higher vassals, and ultimately to the lord. Taxes are paid and goods provided by one vassal to another and then to the lord. Have students speculate on whether it is better for a lord to have a few or many vassals.

You Decide
Ask for volunteers to give their reasons for wanting to live in a castle.

TEACHER ALERT

The Middle Ages are subject to both romantic idealization and depictions of unalleviated squalor. Look for opportunities to debunk myths such as King Arthur's Camelot. Encourage students to imagine themselves in the life situations they are studying.

COMMON ERROR

A common misconception about medieval farmers is that they were mere laborers, without particular skills. In fact, the serfs and other villagers had to know how to produce the best crops possible, breed and manage domesticated animals, brew beer, mill grain, work iron, and produce cloth.

ELL/ESL STRATEGY

Language Objective:
To learn vocabulary using a concept map

Explain that organizing words in a concept map is a good way to understand and remember their meaning. Have the class read through the vocabulary words and place each word in a concept map. If students are new to this strategy, create a concept map on the board with the class, or give students a partial map that they can complete.

COMMON ERROR

Students may have the misconception that everyone in the Middle Ages wore highly decorated clothing, furs, and leather. Point out that the few garments that have been preserved from the Middle Ages and that appear in paintings are the exceptionally fine articles worn by nobles, not what ordinary people wore. Most clothing was simply cut and made of relatively inexpensive, wool cloth.

Lesson 11–1 Review Answers

1. B **2.** A **3.** C **4.** B **5.** D **6.** C **7.** A
8. Lords lived in a manor house on a country estate that included a small village and fields for growing crops. In exchange for land, they had to promise to serve the king and swear to fight for him and protect him.
9. The serfs grew crops and gathered wood. They took care of the lord's lands and his house. **10.** The castles were made of stone and were very cold and sometimes gloomy. There was no glass in the windows or running water. They were dimly lit by burning torches.

On a sheet of paper, write the letter of the answer that correctly completes each sentence.

1. The Middle Ages began when _____.

   A the Vikings invaded England   **C** the church grew
   B the Roman Empire fell   **D** Charlemagne died

2. There were many changes during the Middle Ages. _____ practically disappeared, money was no longer used, and education and learning became less important.

   A Trade   **B** The church   **C** The Vikings   **D** The sun

3. _____ was/were the main place where education and learning took place during the Middle Ages.

   A Huts   **B** Manor houses   **C** The church   **D** Fortresses

4. Life during the Middle Ages was organized under a system called _____.

   A homage   **B** feudalism   **C** manor houses   **D** country estates

5. In return for land, nobles had to _____ to the king.

   A give crops   **B** pay money   **C** give a serf   **D** pay homage

6. While freemen were allowed to buy and farm their own land, _____ could not.

   A nobles   **B** lords   **C** serfs   **D** clergy

7. The noble family lived in manor houses, the villagers lived in small _____.

   A huts   **B** estates   **C** castles   **D** fortresses

On a sheet of paper, write the answer to each question. Use complete sentences.

8. What was the life of the lord of a manor like?

9. What jobs did the serfs have to do for the lord of the manor?

10. What were the castles like that some nobles and their families lived in?

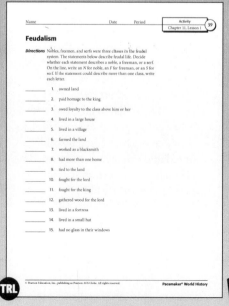

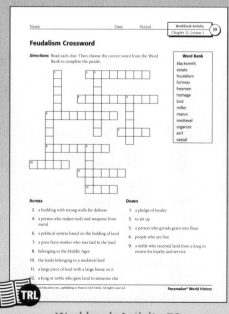

LESSON 11-2

Religion During the Middle Ages

Objectives

■ To provide two examples of clergy in the Middle Ages

■ To describe the life of a knight

Clergy
The people who lead a religion

Monk
A man who has taken religious vows and usually lives in a monastery

Nun
A woman who has taken religious vows and enters a convent

Knight
A high-ranking soldier of the Middle Ages who received his title from a noble

When the Roman Empire crumbled in A.D. 476, Europe broke into hundreds of small governments. Despite the unrest, the Church remained strong.

Who Were the Men and Women of the Church?

Medieval society was a Christian society. Higher officials in the church were nobles. Large pieces of land were often given to the leaders of the church, the **clergy**. The highest-ranking clergy were as wealthy and powerful as the most important lords.

Some men and women wished to devote their entire lives to serving God. These men became **monks** and lived in monasteries. These women became **nuns** and lived in convents. In monasteries and convents, they spent their days studying, praying, working, and taking part in religious services.

What Was the Purpose of a Knight?

Except for the church leaders, every important man in feudal society was a fighter. Even the kings were warriors. The estates fought each other. There were bands of robbers to be controlled. Tribes of people from other parts of the country often came looking for new lands.

Warriors of the noble class were known as **knights.** Knights fought to defend their own manors. They fought for their king as they had promised. They also fought to protect Christianity from being threatened.

A.D. 800–1400   *The Lords and the Serfs*   *Chapter 11*   **213**

Ask:

● What were the duties of nuns and monks? (They studied, prayed, and worked for the church.)

● Who could become a knight? (the son of a noble)

● What promises did a knight make? (to defend the church, the king, and his land)

Background Information

Besides having strong religious faith, monks and nuns were from well-to-do families, usually with several siblings. Women had to have a dowry to enter a convent, and some were widows with nowhere to go. Different orders attracted different types of people; some monastic orders welcomed boys, while others were

filled with mature men who wanted to retire from busy lives to serve God. Convents and monasteries could be a good choice for particularly intelligent children who wanted an education or to learn an art.

STUDY SKILLS

Call attention to the first subhead question on this page. Explain that you can rephrase this question as a statement that begins, "Men and women of the church were . . . ." Tell students they can find information to complete the sentence by reading the paragraph.

Lesson at a Glance

Chapter 11 Lesson 2

Overview This lesson describes the importance of the Christian religion in the Middle Ages and the roles played by monks, nuns, and knights.

Objectives

■ To provide two examples of the clergy in the Middle Ages

■ To describe the life of a knight

Student Pages 213–215

Teacher's Resource Library
   Workbook Activity 40
   Activity 40
   Modified Activity 40

....

Vocabulary

clergy   monk
knight   nun

Review the definitions of these words. Ask volunteers to come up with original sentences that correctly use each word. As an extra challenge, ask students to use all four words in a single sentence.

1   Warm-Up Activity

Tell students that they will learn about nuns, monks, and knights in this lesson. Ask what they know about present-day nuns and monks. (Nuns and monks exist in nearly every modern religion. Students may perceive them as always living in isolation, devoting all their time to religious observances.)

2   Teaching the Lesson

As students read, have them consider why someone would want to become a monk, nun, or knight in the Middle Ages. Point out that religion, though important, may not have been the only reason. Ask them to come up with other motives that might have been in play. (desire for power, education, security)

The Lords and the Serfs   *Chapter 11*   **213**

Reading Strategy:
Text Structure

Supply students with sample organizers to get them started, such as a sequence-of-events chart or a word web.

LEARN MORE ABOUT IT

The Queen of England still selects honorable people to be knights. The occasion is purely ceremonial, but the title is a great honor in England. Have students look up people who have been knighted by the Queen in recent years.

LEARNING STYLES

Visual/Spatial
Have students make a model or draw a large picture of a feudal manor or a castle.

LEARNING STYLES

Body/Kinesthetic
Invite several students to perform a simulation of a knighting ceremony. One student should play the role of a lord and the others should play the roles of squires. Have the lord explain his or her expectations to the future knights and have the squires recite their promises. Then have the lord officially pronounce them knights.

LEARNING STYLES

Auditory/Verbal
Hildegard of Bingen was a German abbess in the 12th century. She wrote poetry and set some of it to music. We have 77 of her songs, written in medieval musical notation. This music is still performed today.

Knights were noble warriors. They tested their skills in tournaments called jousts.

Reading Strategy:
Text Structure

As you read about becoming a knight, use a graphic organizer such as a word web to help organize the details.

LEARN MORE ABOUT IT

Knights in Armor

Being a knight was a costly business. Armor (the metal covering that protected a knight's body in battle) and weapons were elaborate and expensive. Serfs had to work hard to pay for their lord's fancy armor, many horses, and fine weapons. If a boy wanted to grow up to be a knight, he began training at age 7. He started out as a page. He learned to fight and to have the proper knightly manners.

The next step in becoming a knight was acting as a squire. A squire served a knight. He helped the knight with his armor and weapons. The squire also rode with his knight into battle. When he was 21, a worthy squire was "knighted"—or made a knight—by a noble.

The young squire became a knight when a sword was tapped on his shoulder.

Knighthood was both a military and a religious honor. A young man spent the night before he was knighted in a church. There he kept watch over his armor, as he knelt and prayed. He thought about the honor he was about to receive.

Knights kept their fighting skills ready by entering jousts, or tournaments. Two knights on horseback would fight each other with long lances. The goal of each knight was to knock the other one off his horse. The winner's honor was not only for himself. It was also for his favorite "lady," whose ribbon he wore into battle.

ELL/ESL STRATEGY

Language Objective:
To be able to use transition words to define a sequence of events

Transition words include *then, after, next, before, first, second,* and similar words that define time or sequence. Divide the class into small groups. Have ELL students work with native speakers to explain how a boy became a knight. To begin, have each group make a list of transition words. Have native speakers use the transition words in sample sentences. Then have the ELL student describe knighthood.

3 Reinforce and Extend

CAREER CONNECTION

The monks and nuns who decorated books with bright colors and pictures may have been the first graphic artists. Today, graphic artists rely on sophisticated equipment to create advertisements in newspapers and magazines. Graphic artists also work in art reproduction, computer game design, bookmaking, and fashion design. Encourage artistic students to research the education and training needed to become a graphic artist.

REVIEW

Word Bank

Christian
church leaders
clergy
king
monks
nuns
religious
7
squire
21

On a sheet of paper, write the word from the Word Bank to complete each sentence correctly.

1. Medieval society was a _____ society.

2. People trained or ordained for religious work are called _____.

3. Men who devoted their entire lives to serving God became _____ and lived in monasteries.

4. Women who devoted their entire lives to serving God became _____ and lived in convents.

5. Every important man in feudal society was a fighter except for _____.

6. The knights fought to defend their manors, their _____, and Christianity.

7. A boy wanting to be a knight started training at age _____ as a page.

8. The step after a page is a _____.

9. At age _____, the worthy knight-in-training would become a knight. It happened when a sword was tapped on his shoulder.

10. Knighthood was both a military and _____ honor.

COMMON ERROR

Students may imagine that medieval armies comprised mostly knights on horseback. Most people fought on foot, however, and most soldiers were not knights, but low-born infantry (freemen and serfs).

IN THE COMMUNITY

Take the class on a field trip to a museum that displays medieval suits of armor. Show students the weaponry of a medieval knight. Have the students draw pictures of armor and weapons used by knights.

WORLD CULTURES

The tradition of knights lives on in modern Great Britain. The British government recommends a person of high achievement or service to the queen, then the queen officially selects the person to be knighted. Male knights adopt the title "Sir" and their wives are called "Lady." Women who receive the honor adopt the title "Dame." These titles carry no responsibility; they are purely honorary.

Lesson 11–2 Review Answers

1. Christian 2. clergy 3. monks
4. nuns 5. church leaders 6. king
7. 7 8. squire 9. 21 10. religious

Name _____ Date _____ Period _____   **Activity** 40
Chapter 11, Lesson 2

Religion During the Middle Ages

Directions Write the correct word from the Word Bank to complete each sentence.

Word Bank
Christian
church
clergy
convents
land
monks
nobility
powerful
studying
warriors

1. When the Roman Empire crumbled, the _____ remained strong.

2. Medieval society was a _____ society.

3. Higher officials of the church were members of the _____.

4. The leaders of the church were often given _____.

5. The people who lead a religion are called _____.

6. Church officials were often wealthy and _____.

7. Church leaders were the only important men in feudal society who were not _____.

8. _____ devoted their lives to God and lived in monasteries.

9. Nuns were religious women who lived in _____.

10. Monks and nuns spent their days _____ and praying.

   Pacemaker® World History

Name _____ Date _____ Period _____   **Workbook Activity** 40
Chapter 11, Lesson 2

Knights During the Middle Ages

Directions Circle the letter of the answer that correctly completes each statement.

1. Knights were _____.
   A nobles   B clergy   C freemen   D serfs

2. Knights fought _____.
   A bands of robbers   C tribes from other parts of the country
   B warriors from other estates   D all of the above

3. Knights wore _____ into battle.
   A lances   B armor   C tunics   D squires

4. Knights began their training _____.
   A at age 7   B at age 14   C at age 21   D with a page

5. A squire _____.
   A fought against knights   B made armor   C served with a knight   D served in the church

6. A man was knighted _____.
   A by his lady   B by the clergy   C only by the king   D by a noble

7. A young man spent the night before he was knighted _____.
   A fighting   B praying   C jousting   D sleeping

8. Knights kept their fighting skills ready _____.
   A by entering tournaments   C by raiding other estates
   B by training with serfs   D by entering a monastery

9. In jousts, knights fought each other with _____.
   A spears   B swords   C lances   D gunpowder

10. Knighthood was both a military honor and _____.
    A a religious chore   B a religious honor   C a feudal system   D a medieval duty

   Pacemaker® World History

Activity 40   Workbook Activity 40   *The Lords and the Serfs Chapter 11*   **215**

Overview This lesson describes the changes in feudal life that came over time because of plague, new methods of warfare, and repopulation of cities and towns.

Objectives

- To explain the Black Death and its result
- To describe new methods of warfare

Student Pages 216–218

Teacher's Resource Library **TRL**

Workbook Activity 41

Activity 41

Modified Activity 41

Vocabulary

artisan   peasant

Have students use a dictionary to find where the words *peasant* and *serf* came from (from Old French *paisant*, whose root means "country"; from the Latin *servus*, which means "slave"). Discuss how knowing the origins of these words helps to distinguish their meanings: serfs were farm workers bound to stay on the land, while peasants were farmers who were legally free to move.

1 Warm-Up Activity

Tell students that a terrible plague killed millions of Europeans in the 14th century. Have them speculate about what the results of such a plague might have been for the average farmer and for Europe as a whole. Then have students read the lesson to find out about the Black Death and its effects

2 Teaching the Lesson

As students read the lesson, encourage them to envision the consequences of these changes. For example, what would the villages have been like when a third of the population had died? Would there have been enough people

---

Life in the Middle Ages

Objectives

- To explain the Black Death and its result
- To describe new methods of warfare

The feudal way of life was most widespread during the 1100s and 1200s. Life on a feudal manor was hard. There were floods and years of bad crops. There were always battles to fight. There were plagues, too.

What Was the Black Death?

In A.D. 1348, a ship from the east docked at an Italian port. Some sick sailors came ashore. They brought with them a terrible plague. This disease became known as the Black Death. It got its name because it caused spots of blood to turn black under the skin.

Little was known about medicine during the Middle Ages. There were few doctors, and those doctors that were around did not understand the causes of diseases or how diseases were spread. The villages were not very clean. A large population of rats lived off the garbage. Doctors today think that bites from infected rat fleas caused the plague. Doctors in the 1300s, however, did not know much about the prevention or treatment of disease. They had little help to offer.

The Black Death quickly spread across Europe killing thousands of nobles and serfs alike.

---

to support the manor and the church? (Many deaths would leave the village short of labor and without critical skills.)

Ask:

- How did people get the disease known as the Black Death? (from fleas)
- How did the decrease in population affect artisans and peasants? (They earned higher wages.)
- Why weren't knights needed any more in 1400 A.D.? (Warfare had changed, with gunpowder and foot soldiers becoming more important.)

Background Information

The Black Death was caused by *Yersenia pestis,* a bacterium that is still endemic in Asia and America. Its hosts in North America are prairie dogs, who live in communities where fleas can spread the disease. During 1347–1351, about one third of Europe's population died of plague. The Black Death was considered to be a punishment for people's sins, and dealing with its consequences led to a massive recruitment of new clergy, monks, and nuns.

As a result of the plague, nobles and serfs alike fell sick and died. The Black Death also resulted in a shortage of labor. Because there were fewer workers, wages increased for **artisans** and **peasants.**

What Changes Were Happening in the Feudal System?

Feudal society lasted for almost 700 years. By A.D. 1400, however, the great manors had almost disappeared. Trade had picked up. Money had come back into use. Nobles no longer received land for services. People moved back to the towns.

New methods of warfare were being developed. Gunpowder and new weapons, such as cannons, were now available. In addition, foot soldiers were being used more effectively. Because of these changes, knights were no longer needed.

For hundreds of years, the picture of life in Europe had been the feudal manor. It was a world where most people fit into one of three classes: nobles, clergy, or serfs. "Some fight," a medieval bishop wrote. "Others pray. And others work."

TIMELINE STUDY: THE MIDDLE AGES

How long did the Middle Ages last?

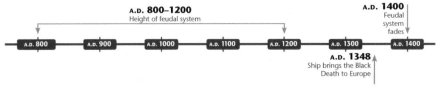

A.D. **800–1200**
Height of feudal system

A.D. **1400**
Feudal system fades

A.D. 800   A.D. 900   A.D. 1000   A.D. 1100   A.D. 1200   A.D. 1300   A.D. 1400

A.D. **1348**
Ship brings the Black Death to Europe

A.D. **800–1400**   *The Lords and the Serfs*   *Chapter 11*   **217**

Lesson 11–3 Review Answers

1. D **2.** C **3.** A **4.** D **5.** B **6.** A **7.** A **8.** D
9. C **10.** B

LESSON 11-3 REVIEW

On a sheet of paper, write the letter of the answer that correctly completes each sentence.

1. Nobles, _____, and serfs were the three classes in feudal society.

  A knights   **B** kings   **C** lords   **D** clergy

2. Life on a feudal manor was hard with floods, bad crops, battles, and _____.

  A fires   **B** cannons   **C** plagues   **D** persecution

3. In A.D. 1348, a ship from the east brought _____.

  A the Black Death   **B** medicine   **C** cannons   **D** gunpowder

4. _____ were dirty and there were large populations of rats that lived off of garbage.

  A Manor houses   **B** Castles   **C** Estates   **D** Villages

5. There was little known about _____ during the Middle Ages.

  A farming   **B** medicine   **C** Christianity   **D** warfare

6. Doctors today think the plague was caused by _____.

  A bites from infected rat fleas   **C** the serfs
  B garbage   **D** bad crops

7. Feudal society lasted almost _____ years.

  A 700   **B** 1,100   **C** 1,300   **D** 1,400

8. Trade picked up, money was used again, and people moved back into towns by A.D. _____.

  A 700   **B** 1100   **C** 1300   **D** 1400

9. New methods of warfare were developed, such as _____ and cannons.

  A spears   **B** knives   **C** gunpowder   **D** bombs

10. Knights were not needed when _____ were being used more effectively.

  A serfs   **B** foot soldiers   **C** monks   **D** nobles

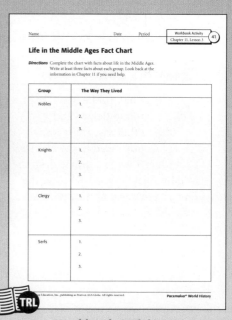

- During the Middle Ages many people lived under the feudal system. Each class owed loyalty to the class above it.

- Most medieval society was divided into three classes: the nobles, the clergy, and the serfs.

- In return for land, nobles were called vassals of the king. They paid homage to their king by agreeing to protect him.

- Medieval estates, or manors, included a manor house, a village, and fields. The noble was lord of the manor and the absolute ruler of the feudal estate.

- The manor house was like a fortress, designed to protect the noble from enemies.

- Serfs worked the land for the lord of the manor. They owned no land of their own.

- Members of the clergy were often given large pieces of land.

- Knights were warriors of the noble class. They were trained to protect the king and the king's interests.

- A plague called the Black Death killed many Europeans in the Middle Ages.

- By about A.D. 1400 the feudal system was weakening. Trade had increased and more people were living in towns. Better weapons meant that knights were no longer needed because armies were becoming more effective.

TEACHER'S RESOURCE

The AGS Globe Teaching Strategies in Social Studies Transparencies may be used with this chapter. The transparencies add an interactive dimension to expand and enhance the Pacemaker® *World History* program content.

CHAPTER PROJECT FOLLOW-UP

 Have each group share details they learned about the different levels of society during the Middle Ages. Have the class create a story line for a class literary work on the Middle Ages. Have each group add interesting details to the story based on what they learned in their group research. Students who enjoy artwork can create illustrations for the story. Have interested students publish the story using a computer publishing program that inputs text and images.

Chapter 11 Summary

Have students read the Chapter Summary on page 219 to review the main ideas presented in Chapter 11.

Ask:

- What was feudalism? (a new political and military system based on the holding of land)

- List the three levels in feudal society, from fewest to most people. (king, vassals or nobles, serfs)

- What were vassals responsible for? (serving and protecting the king)

- What did a feudal estate include? (a noble's manor house, village, and fields)

- Why did nobles build castles? (to protect themselves from their enemies)

- Who worked on a manor and what did they do? (Serfs worked as farmers and laborers.)

- What were the leaders of the church called? (clergy)

- Describe the steps the son of a noble needed to take to become a knight. (First he learned religion, manners, obedience, and loyalty and became a page; next he learned to ride a horse and use weapons and became a squire; at age 21 he became a knight.)

- What was the Black Death? (a plague that killed millions of Europeans in the mid-1300s)

- Give two reasons for the weakening of the feudal system. (Answers may include two of the following: changes in warfare, increasing trade, movement of population into towns, land no longer given as a reward for services.)

Chapter 11 Review

Use the Chapter Review to prepare students for tests and to reteach content from the chapter.

Chapter 11 Mastery Test

The Teacher's Resource Library includes two forms of the Chapter 11 Mastery Test. Each test addresses the chapter Goals for Learning. An optional third page of additional critical-thinking items is included for each test. The difficulty level of the two forms is equivalent.

Chapter 11 Review Answers

Vocabulary Review

1. serf
2. vassal
3. homage
4. knight
5. estate
6. feudalism
7. medieval
8. clergy
9. manor
10. fortress

Chapter Review Questions

11. The Middle Ages began. Cities, towns, trade, and money almost disappeared. Learning was concentrated in the church.

12. The main social classes were nobles, clergy, and serfs.

Word Bank

clergy
estate
feudalism
fortress
homage
knight
manor
medieval
serf
vassal

Vocabulary Review

On a sheet of paper, use the words from the Word Bank to correctly match each definition below.

1. A peasant who was almost a slave during the Middle Ages

2. A noble who received land from the king in return for loyalty and service

3. A pledge of loyalty that a noble gave to the king

4. A warrior trained to defend the manor, the king, and Christianity

5. A large piece of land that nobles, freemen, and serfs lived on

6. A way of life during the Middle Ages

7. Something that belongs to the Middle Ages

8. People who do religious work as their job

9. The house where a noble, or lord, lived

10. A building constructed so noble families would feel safe from enemies

Chapter Review Questions

On a sheet of paper, write the answer to each question. Use complete sentences.

11. What happened in Western Europe after the Roman Empire fell?

12. What were the main social classes in the feudal system?

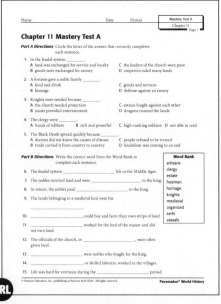

Chapter 11 Mastery Test A, pages 1–3

13. Why was the feudal life hard for the serfs?

14. Where was the main place that education and learning were carried on during the Middle Ages?

15. What did men and women do if they wanted to give their lives to serving God?

16. Why did the Black Death strike all classes of feudal society?

Critical Thinking

On a sheet of paper, write your response to each question. Use complete sentences.

17. Why were knights so important in feudal society?

18. Do you think the serfs were more slave than free? Tell why or why not.

Using the Timeline

Use the timeline on page 217 to answer the questions.

19. When was the feudal system at its height?

20. When the feudal system faded, how long had it been since the Black Death arrived in Europe?

GROUP ACTIVITY

During the Middle Ages, each noble family had a coat of arms. The coat of arms used shapes, colors, and symbols to represent the family. Form a group with two or three other students. Brainstorm ideas and then design your own coat of arms. Use a favorite background color, or field. Draw a band of another color across the field. Draw a symbol for each family member.

A.D. 800–1400

The Lords and the Serfs   Chapter 11   **221**

13. They were tied to the land. They had to provide for the lord. There were few protections from the lord's treatment.

14. Education and learning mainly went on within the church.

15. Some men became monks, and some women became nuns.

16. Medical knowledge was poor. Doctors did not now how to prevent the disease or how to cure it. They did not understand the relationship between cleanliness and health.

Critical Thinking

17. Possible answer: Knights were important because manors had to be defended from robbers and invading tribes. Also, knights fought to protect Christians.

18. Possible answer: Most students will probably say that serfs were more slave than free because they were tied to the land and had to work for the lord.

Using the Timeline

19. A.D. 800–1200

20. 52 years

GROUP ACTIVITY

Students should be able to explain the meaning of their coat of arms.

Introducing the Chapter

Ask students to preview the chapter by reading the headings and subheadings and by looking at the art and photos, the maps, and the timelines. Ask students to focus on the timeline entitled "The Crusades" on page 248 of the Student Edition.

Ask:

- How much time passed from the beginning to the end of the Crusades? (196 years)

Islam and the Crusades

The Middle Ages is sometimes thought of as a time of darkness, of little forward progress. In some ways, in some places, this was the case. However, there were major strides taken in many areas of Europe. The Crusades, or Holy Wars, caused a lot of people to move from one land to another. With the Crusades came new ideas and interests, as well as some new struggles. People began to question and challenge the people in power, such as kings. They also began to question the class structure they lived in. Christianity, Judaism, and the rise of Islam had large effects, too, particularly in the Mediterranean areas.

GOALS FOR LEARNING

- To discuss the importance of Muhammad
- To explain the struggle for power of the Holy Land
- To realize the costs of the Crusades
- To explain the changes in agriculture
- To describe the changes in city life
- To tell why the Magna Carta was important

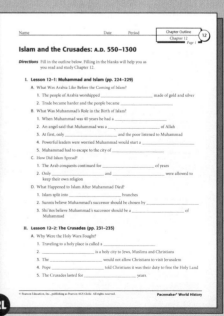

Reading Strategy: Visualizing

Visualizing is like creating a movie in your mind. It will help you understand what you are reading. Use the following ways to visualize a text:

- Think about the order in which things are happening. That may be a clue to what will happen next.
- Look at the photographs, illustrations, and descriptions.
- Think about experiences in your own life that may add to the images.

Key Vocabulary Words

Lesson 1

Idol An image of a god that is used as an object of worship

Muslim A follower of the religion that Muhammad founded in Arabia in the seventh century

Prophet A religious leader who claims to speak for God; one who tells what will happen in the future

Holy Land Palestine

Koran The holy book of the Muslims that contains the teachings of Islam

Faith To believe in God; a religion

Lesson 2

Pilgrimage A visit to a holy place

Crusade Any of the military journeys taken by Christians to win the Holy Land from the Muslims

Truce A time when enemies agree to stop fighting

Lesson 3

Exploration The act of looking around some unknown place

Lesson 4

Surplus More than what is needed

Lesson 5

Migrate To move away from one country or region to settle in another

Guild An organization formed to protect the interests of workers in one craft or trade

Apprentice A person who learns a trade under a master

Lesson 6

Human rights The right to life, liberty, and pursuit of happiness

Charter A constitution

- What two groups fought against one another in the Crusades? (Muslims and Christians)
- What effect might the Crusades have had on the world at that time? (Answers may vary. Students may say that many people died, that the Crusades were costly, or that new products and ideas were exchanged.)

Reading Strategy: Visualizing

Ask students what tools in the chapter might be useful for thinking about chronology. (the timelines) Have them choose one photograph, illustration, or description from the chapter and discuss why it is compelling to them. Then ask students why experiences from their own lives might help them learn new information.

Key Vocabulary Words

Point out that these chapter words are presented in the order they appear in each lesson. They are also found in the glossary.

LIFE SKILLS CONNECTION

Students learn how to more effectively use search engines on the Internet. Give students some other topics to research and let them compare their results.

KEY VOCABULARY

Assist students as they choose the correct words from the Word Bank to complete the sentences in the paragraph.

CHAPTER PROJECT

Have student groups research the contributions Arabs have made in science, mathematics, and literature. Have each group choose one contribution and write a report describing it. Student reports should explain why the contribution has been important to world civilizations.

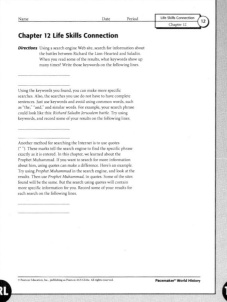

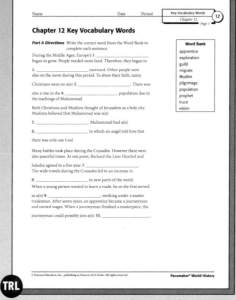

Life Skills Connection 12   Key Vocabulary Words 12, pages 1–2

Chapter 12 Lesson 1

Overview This lesson discusses the beginning of and the spread of Islam.

Objectives

- To explain how Muhammad gained followers
- To describe the spread of Islam
- To tell why the Arab armies allowed Jews and Christians to keep their religion
- To explain the beliefs of the two branches of Islam

Student Pages 224–230

Teacher's Resource Library

Workbook Activity 42

Activity 42

Modified Activity 42

Vocabulary

faith	Muslim
Holy Land	prophet
idol	vision
Koran	

Have students create a flash card for each vocabulary word. Have them write the word on one side of a card. Then have students write the definition and an original sentence using the word on the other side. Encourage them to compare their flash cards with each other.

PRONUNCIATION GUIDE

Use this list to help students pronounce difficult words in this lesson.

Sunni (soon´ ē)

Shi'ite (shē´ īt)

1 Warm-Up Activity

Have students locate Mecca on a world map. Tell them that this is where Muhammad, the founder of Islam, was born. Then have them read pages 224–229 to find out about Muhammad's life and the beliefs of Islam.

Muhammad and Islam

Objectives

- To explain how Muhammad gained followers
- To describe the spread of Islam
- To tell why the Arab armies allowed Jews and Christians to keep their religion
- To explain the beliefs of the two branches of Islam

Idol
An image of a god that is used as an object of worship

**Reading Strategy:
Visualizing**

Draw a picture to help you visualize what this section is about.

In A.D. 570, Arabia was a vast desert southeast of the Mediterranean Sea. The people who lived there, the Arabs, believed in many gods. They worshipped **idols**—images of a god—made of gold and silver. Tribes of nomads lived on the edges of the desert in tent camps. They drove caravans of camels across the sands. Wealthy people lived in fine homes in the cities. They dressed in rich silks and wore bright jewels.

It was not a peaceful land. Bands of thieves rode into the cities, waving swords. They looted and killed, taking riches off into the desert. The nomadic tribes also fought among themselves. More and more trouble spread throughout Arabia. Trade became harder and the people became poorer. Fewer people lived in fine palaces; more people struggled for even enough to eat.

Arabian people still ride camels great distances across empty deserts.

Muslim
A follower of the religion that Muhammad founded in Arabia in the seventh century

Vision
Something seen in the mind or in a dream

Prophet
A religious leader who claims to speak for God; one who tells what will happen in the future

Reading Strategy:
Visualizing
Create a graphic organizer of the stages in Muhammad's life and the growth of Islam.

The **Muslim** religion was born in the desert land of Arabia. Today this land is called Saudi Arabia.

What Was Muhammad's Role in the Birth of Islam?

Around the year A.D. 570, in the Arabian city of Mecca, a man named Muhammad was born. Not much is known about Muhammad's early life. Yet Muhammad was to become a religious figure who would change the shape of the world.

When Muhammad was 40 years old, it is said, he had a **vision**. Muhammad believed he saw an angel on a hillside outside of Mecca. The angel spoke to him, saying that Muhammad was a **prophet** of God. "Teach your people," the angel said, "that there is one God, and that God is Allah."

Like Jesus, Muhammad became a teacher. He tried to teach people that Allah was the one true god. Most Arabs would not listen. They still worshipped their many gods.

Muhammad did have some followers. They heard his words about Allah. Muhammad promised that Allah would reward people for good deeds with a wonderful life after death. Poor people listened. Slaves listened. People whose lives were hard or sad listened to Muhammad.

The powerful leaders of Mecca began to worry. They had laughed at him at first, this man called Muhammad. Now he was growing popular. What if he stirred the commoners into a rebellion (revolution)? The leaders began to persecute Muhammad and his followers. The Muslims were forced to flee the city of Mecca.

Reading Strategy:
Visualizing

Have students complete the suggested activities on pages 224–225. Then, compare and discuss their drawings and graphics.

2 Teaching the Lesson

After students read Lesson 1, draw their attention to the subheads on pages 225, 227, and 228. Point out that each of these subheads is a question. Encourage the class to answer each question in a few short sentences.

Ask:

- What was life like in Arabia at the time of Muhammad's birth? (Bands of thieves rode into cities, looting and killing people. The nomadic tribes fought each other. There were many poor people.)

- What did the angel say to Muhammad? (The angel said Muhammad was a prophet of God. The angel said Muhammad should teach "that there is one God, and that God is Allah.")

- Who were some of the people who listened to Muhammad's message? (People who listened had hard or sad lives—they were poor or slaves.)

- What are followers of Muhammad's teachings called? (Muslims)

- What was Arabia like by the time Muhammed died? (Most of Arabia had one religion. The religion of the Muslims was called Islam. Huge armies of Muslims were ready to promote Islam throughout the world.)

- What two branches of Islam arose after Muhammad's death? (Sunnis and Shi'ites)

- Why were Jews and Christians allowed to keep their religions? (Jews and Christians also worshipped one God.)

Background Information

The Angel Gabriel gave the Koran to the prophet Muhammad in the Arabic language. Because of this, Muslims always study their holy book in Arabic. Translations could be wrong or the reader might not understand them. As Islam spread across the world, so did the Arabic language. Muslims still use Arabic for their religious services, even in non-Arab countries.

The Koran lists five duties, or pillars, for each Muslim—announcement of faith, prayer, giving of alms, fasting, and the Hajj (pilgrimage to Mecca).

In A.D. 622, Muhammad took his people to the Arabian city of Medina. Still, the number of Muslims grew. New converts became soldiers for Islam. With an army of followers, Muhammad returned to Mecca. They took the city in A.D. 630.

In A.D. 632, Muhammad died. By the time of his death, the prophet Muhammad had done his job. Most of Arabia was united under one religion. The religion of the Muslims was called Islam. The Islamic religion promised that any followers who died battling for Allah would go to paradise, or heaven. This idea alone created huge armies of enthusiastic soldiers. The Muslim soldiers were ready to carry the word of Allah throughout the world.

The Muslim Empire, About A.D. 750

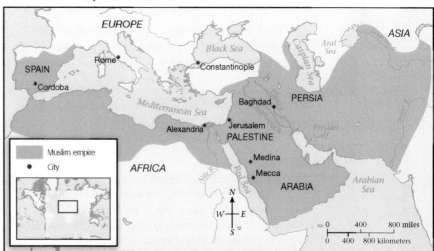

MAP STUDY

1. The Muslim empire extended across parts of which three continents?
2. Medina and Mecca were near which body of water?

Holy Land

Palestine; the area where Jesus of Nazareth lived

Koran

The holy book of the Muslims that contains the teachings of Islam

How Did Islam Spread?

Then came one of the greatest series of conquests, or take-overs, the world had ever seen. Between A.D. 640 and A.D. 660, Arab armies swept through Syria, Persia, and Egypt. They conquered Palestine, or the **Holy Land.** It included the holy city of Jerusalem. The Arab conquests continued for hundreds of years. Arab lands would stretch from North Africa and Spain to the Indus River and Central Asia.

Some of the conquered people welcomed the new religion with its hope of paradise. The Arabs, however, gave them little choice—the people must become Muslims or die. Only Jews and Christians were allowed to keep their own religion. The Muslims respected those who also worshipped one God and followed the words of a holy book.

Indeed, Muhammad was influenced early in his life by the Jews and Christians he knew. His God, Allah, was the one God of the Jews and Christians. According to Muhammad, God revealed himself to humanity through his chosen prophets. The major prophets were Adam, Noah, Abraham, Moses, Jesus, and, finally, Muhammad. God gave the Ten Commandments to Moses, the Gospels to Jesus, and the **Koran** to Muhammad. (Koran is also spelled *Qur'an.*) Even so, the Christians and Jews were forced to pay tribute to the new Arab rulers.

These are early Arabic numerals representing the numbers 1 through 5.

The conquering Arabs brought their culture as well as their religion. They built fine cities, new schools, and beautiful places of worship called mosques. Their language and writing became part of world culture. The Arabs made their mark on the world in many ways. The numerals that are used in the United States and Canada, for example, are Arabic numerals.

A.D. 550–1300

Islam and the Crusades *Chapter 12* **227**

COMMON ERROR

Remind students to go beyond their textbook to do research on their topic. Encourage them to go to their school or local library and ask a librarian for help.

COMMON ERROR

Words such as *faith* and *vision* are abstract words. Students may have difficulty grasping these abstract concepts. Encourage them to keep a list of these and other abstract words that appear in the chapter and add them to their Word Banks.

TEACHER ALERT

You can find more information on the Five Pillars of Islam and photos on the Internet: www.agsglobepmwh. com/page227

IN THE COMMUNITY

Have students find out if there is a mosque in or near their community. If there is, students can ask permission to visit. They should ask to have someone give them a tour and point out the features of the mosque. Students should observe the art in the mosque. They should observe that there are no drawings of animals and humans.

Answer: They went on to conquer other lands and spread Islam.

Ask:

- How old was Muhammad when he had his vision of the angel? (40 years)
- How old was Muhammad when he died? (62 years)
- What four regions were conquered by Muslims in the years between A.D. 640–660? (Syria, Jerusalem, Egypt, and Persia)

Faith
A religion

What Happened to Islam After Muhammad Died?

Muhammad died in A.D. 632. His death raised the question of who should succeed him. Different answers to that question led to the formation of two branches of Islam, the Sunnis and the Shi'ites. The Sunnis believe that Muhammad did not appoint (choose) a successor. Therefore, a new religious leader could be chosen by vote. The new leader did not have to be a relative of Muhammad. Shi'ites believe that Muhammad appointed Ali as his successor. Ali was married to Muhammad's daughter. Shi'ites believe that a new religious leader should be related to Muhammad. Eventually, these two branches developed different laws and religious practices.

Today Islam is one of the world's great religions. Most Muslims live in the Middle East, Pakistan, India, North Africa, and parts of Asia. They live in lands that the Arabs conquered during the seventh and eighth centuries. It is estimated that 1 percent of the U.S. population (5.75 million people) follows the Islamic **faith**. In Canada, that number is about 1.9 percent. It is believed that about 90 percent of Muslims are Sunnis.

TIMELINE STUDY: MUHAMMAD AND THE GROWTH OF ISLAM

After Muhammad died, what did the Muslims do?

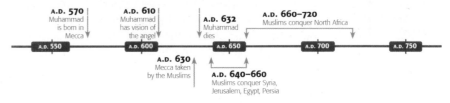

A.D. 570 Muhammad is born in Mecca

A.D. 610 Muhammad has vision of the angel

A.D. 632 Muhammad dies

A.D. 660–720 Muslims conquer North Africa

A.D. 550   A.D. 600   A.D. 650   A.D. 700   A.D. 750

A.D. 630 Mecca taken by the Muslims

A.D. 640–660 Muslims conquer Syria, Jerusalem, Egypt, Persia

Words from the Past

The Koran

The Koran (also spelled *Qur'an*) is the sacred, or holy, book of Islam. The book is a collection of verses. The verses are said to be revealed (made known) to Muhammad by the angel Gabriel. His followers memorized his words or wrote them down. Later they were collected to form the Koran. Muslims believe the Koran is the word of God and cannot be changed in any way, although translations are permitted.

The Koran is made up of verses revealed to Muhammad.

The Koran says that Allah is the one and only God. Muslims must obey Allah and his word. Allah will judge each person by his or her deeds and obedience to him.

There are several things a good Muslim must do, according to the Koran. A Muslim must pray five times a day, facing toward Mecca. A Muslim must give to the poor. A Muslim must not eat or drink during daylight hours of one special month called *Ramadan*. A Muslim should, if at all possible, make at least one visit to Mecca. Today Muslim pilgrims from many lands still journey to the holy city of Mecca.

"There is no God but Allah," a Muslim declares, "and Muhammad is His prophet!"

Students may benefit from hearing this information read aloud. Have different volunteers read the paragraphs aloud. Then ask students to study the illustration on page 229. Have them discuss how this information affects what they knew—or thought they knew—about Islam.

ONLINE CONNECTION

Students can gain additional information by accessing the following Web site: www.agsglobepmwh.com/page229 (This Web site offers additional information about the Koran and misconceptions of Islam.)

Lesson 12–1 Review Answers

1. Mecca **2.** poor **3.** conquests **4.** culture **5.** Koran **6.** The Arabs believed in many gods, and worshipped idols made of gold and silver. **7.** Muhammad believed he saw an angel on a hill outside of Mecca. The angle told him he was a prophet of God and that he should teach his people that there is one God—Allah. **8.** The Islamic religion promised that any followers who died battling for Allah would go to paradise; in essence, they would have a wonderful life after death. **9.** Jews and Christians were allowed to keep their own religion because Muslims respected those who also worshipped one God and followed the words of a holy book. **10.** The Sunnis believe that Muhammad did not appoint a successor and that they should choose a new religious leader by a vote. The new leader did not have to be a relative of Muhammad. On the other hand, the Shi'ites believe that Muhammad appointed Ali (who was married to Muhammad's daughter) as his successor. They believe that the new religious leader should be related to Muhammad.

LESSON 12-1 REVIEW

Word Bank

conquests
culture
Koran
Mecca
poor

On a sheet of paper, write the word from the Word Bank to complete each sentence correctly.

1. Muhammad was born in the Arabian city of _____.

2. Muhammad's teachings appealed to the _____ and enslaved.

3. Islam spread by a series of _____ that lasted for over 100 years.

4. Conquering Arabs brought their _____ as well as their religion.

5. The _____ is the sacred book of Islam.

On a sheet of paper, write the answer to each question. Use complete sentences.

6. What did the Arabs worship in A.D. 570?

7. What did Muhammad see in his vision?

8. How does Allah reward good deeds?

9. Arab armies allowed Jews and Christians to keep their religion after they were conquered. Why?

10. What are the differences between the Islamic beliefs of the Sunnis and the Shi'ites?

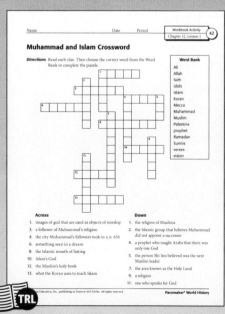

Activity 42

Workbook Activity 42

The Crusades

Objectives

- To give four reasons people went on Crusades
- To describe the terms of the truce between Saladin and Richard
- To tell how the Holy Land came to be under Muslim rule

Pilgrimage

A visit to a holy place

Reading Strategy:
Visualizing

What clues help you to get a feeling about the way the Crusades progressed?

During the Middle Ages, the Christian religion was the strongest force in Europe. People made visits to a holy place, or **pilgrimages,** to show their faith. From Germany, France, England, and Italy they traveled to holy shrines. Thousands of pilgrims went on foot and on horseback.

Pilgrims traveled east to the holy city of Jerusalem. Jerusalem had been a holy city for the Jews since the days of Solomon's splendid temple. The Muslims had also called Jerusalem a holy city. Now it was a holy city for the Christians as well. Christian pilgrims flocked to Jerusalem. They went to see the place where Jesus had lived and taught.

Why Were the Holy Wars Fought?

When the Christian pilgrims of the Middle Ages journeyed to Jerusalem, that city was under Muslim control. The Arab Muslims respected the Christian religion. They allowed Christian pilgrims to visit Jerusalem.

In 1071, the Seljuk Turks, who dominated Syria, took power in Jerusalem. The Turks were Muslims, too. The Turks were not as friendly to the Christians. The Turks would not allow Christians to visit their city. They would not let them worship at the holy shrines.

An angry pope named Urban II stirred Europeans to action in 1095. He spoke before a gathering of important people. He reminded them that the Turks held Jerusalem. He told them that Christians there were in danger. It was their Christian duty, he said, to free the Holy Land.

Overview This lesson describes the Crusades fight between Christians and Muslims between A.D. 1096 and A.D. 1291.

Objectives

- To give four reasons people went on Crusades
- To describe the terms of the truce between Saladin and Richard
- To tell how the Holy Land came to be under Muslim rule

Student Pages 231–236

Teacher's Resource Library

   Workbook Activity 43

   Activity 43

   Modified Activity 43

Vocabulary

Crusade   truce
pilgrimage

Remind students that definitions for their vocabulary words are in the glossary at the end of the textbook. Read each vocabulary word aloud and write it on the board. Have students write a definition and an original sentence for each word.

PRONUNCIATION GUIDE

Use this list to help students pronounce difficult words in this lesson.

Seljuk (sel jook´)

Saladin (sal´ ə din)

Reading Strategy:
Visualizing

Draw attention to the Reading Strategy on page 231. Ask students to keep this question in mind as they read about the Crusades and how they progressed.

Review with students the basic beliefs of Judaism and Christianity. Have students make a chart with three columns labeled Judaism, Christianity, and Islam. Ask students to write some of the basic beliefs of Judaism and Christianity in the first two columns. As they read the lesson, they should fill in the third column about Islam.

2 Teaching the Lesson

As students read, remind them that it is useful to organize their thoughts using the Five Ws—who, what, when, where, and why. Encourage students to make a written list and take notes to answer questions about the lesson. Then have them create several of their own questions beginning with who, what, when, where, or why.

Ask:

- Who first stirred Europeans to begin the Crusades? (Pope Urban II)

- Why did Pope Urban II stir Europeans to begin the Crusades? (The Turks held Jerusalem. Christians in Jerusalem were now in danger. The Pope told Europeans that it was their Christian duty to free the Holy Land.)

- When was the earliest Crusade and who led it? (1096, Peter the Hermit)

- What kinds of people joined the Crusades? (Some people had strong religious feelings. Some people were looking for adventure. Others wanted wealth in new lands. Soldiers wanted military glory. Merchants wanted new markets for their goods. Criminals wanted a safe place to hide. Serfs wanted to escape feudal manors.)

- What was life like for the crusaders? (Crusaders had to steal food to keep from starving. Many died from hunger and disease. They had to fight many battles along the way.)

- How many years elapsed between the speech of Pope Urban II and the last Crusade? (196 years)

Crusade
Any of the military journeys taken by Christians to win the Holy Land from the Muslims

 You Decide
If you were a Christian during those days, would you have wanted to go on the Crusades? Why or why not?

People listened. Feudal lords, knights, and commoners were all moved to action. Word spread across Europe. Soon armies of Christians were ready to travel to the Holy Land. They wore crosses on their clothing as a symbol of their mission. Then the Christian armies set forth on the **Crusades.** The Crusades were the military journeys the Christians took to win the Holy Land from the Muslims. The Holy Wars they started were to last for 200 years.

Many crusaders marched because of strong religious feelings. Some went on the Crusades for other reasons. Some were looking for adventure. Others were looking for wealth in new lands. Soldiers wanted military glory. Merchants wanted new markets for their goods. Criminals wanted a safe place to hide.

Crusaders came from every social class—kings and nobles, knights and lords. The serfs saw a chance to escape feudal manors. They joined the march, too. They all set out to take Jerusalem from the Muslims.

The earliest Crusade, in 1096, was led by a man called Peter the Hermit. This Crusade was made up of French and German peasants. They started out for the Holy Land before the huge armies of knights did. The peasants were not well organized. They had to steal food along the way to keep from starving. The Turks had little trouble defeating them. Most of the peasants were killed before they reached Jerusalem.

In the autumn of 1096, several armies of knights set out from Europe. Nobles from France led the march. It was a hard trip. Over the next two years, many died from hunger and disease. The knights had to fight many battles along the way. Those who made it to Jerusalem were ready for another fight. They started a bloody battle. It lasted six weeks. When it was over, the crusaders had taken Jerusalem and much of the Holy Land from the Muslims.

232 Unit 4 The Middle Ages

 You Decide
Lead a class discussion in which students describe how they might have acted if they had been Christians during the Crusades. Ask if they would have joined the Crusades and why. Ask if they feel people today would join in Holy Wars.

The Crusades

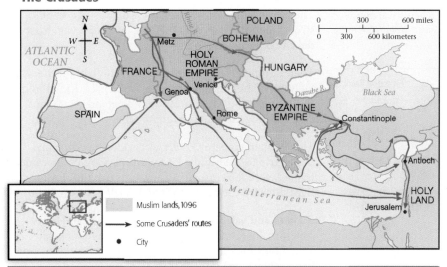

MAP STUDY

1. Which bodies of water did the crusaders cross on their way to the Holy Land?

2. According to the map, who did the Holy Land belong to in 1096?

The crusaders had killed many of the people who lived there—Jews and Muslims. The year was 1099.

The nobles from Europe set up several small states in the Holy Land. Christians back home were pleased. The Holy Land was under Christian control. Most of the crusaders returned to Europe.

Then European leaders in the Holy Land began to quarrel among themselves. The Turks launched new attacks. In response, more crusaders went off to help protect the Holy Land.

A.D. 550–1300

Islam and the Crusades Chapter 12 **233**

Background Information

Although Saladin is remembered most for resisting Christian crusaders, his other accomplishments should not be overlooked. Saladin made Egypt the most powerful empire in the Muslim world. Under his firm leadership, education grew, population increased, Egypt became financially stable, and culture flourished. He was also known for his generosity. At his death, Saladin did not even leave enough money to pay for his own grave.

LEARNING STYLES

Interpersonal/Group Learning

Have small groups of students summarize the results of the Crusades in their own words. They may want to prepare a short skit, a debate, a mock newscast, or a brief lecture to present their ideas.

ELL/ESL STRATEGY

Language Objective: *To encourage students to use writing to think about their own practices and traditions*

Remind students that two pillars of Islam are fasting and pilgrimage. Encourage students to learn more about these concepts from their textbooks, dictionaries, and Web sites. Ask students if their cultural or religious backgrounds encourage these traditions. If yes, have them write a short paragraph about the significance of the fast or the pilgrimage. If no, have them write a short paragraph about what it might be like to practice one or both of these traditions.

MAP STUDY

Answers:

1. Mediterranean Sea, Rhine River, Danube River, Atlantic Ocean

2. Muslim peoples

STUDY SKILLS

Have small groups of students write three cause-and-effect statements based on this section. For example, because Pope Urban II wanted to free Palestine from Muslim control, he started a Crusade against the Muslims. On a different sheet of paper, have groups write only the causes. Have students exchange papers with other groups, who will fill in the effects.

History Fact
Encourage students to do research in the library or on the Internet to learn more about these European rulers.

GREAT NAMES IN HISTORY

Share the Background Information about Saladin with students. Then lead a discussion in which students discuss the complexity of the lives of many of the central figures of world history. Have them compare Saladin with some of the other leaders they have studied. Ask them to describe characteristics many of these leaders share.

3 Reinforce and Extend

AT HOME

Have students interview older relatives or friends who are war veterans. Students should find out why the veteran joined the armed forces and fought in a war. Are any of these reasons the same reasons the crusaders fought? Are any reasons different? Students may discover that in many cases, unlike the crusaders, veterans did not choose to fight but were drafted. Have students record their findings and report them to the class.

Truce
A time when enemies agree to stop fighting

History Fact
The German emperor Frederick I was called Barbarossa, King Philip II of France was called Philip Augustus, and King Richard of England was called Richard the Lion-Hearted.

Saladin, a Muslim leader, seized Jerusalem from the Christian crusaders in 1187.

What Was the Truce Between Saladin and Richard?

The Muslims' leader was Saladin, who was said to be strong and wise. Saladin's soldiers, or troops, won back the city of Jerusalem in 1187.

Then European rulers joined together to fight for the Holy City. The German emperor Frederick I, King Philip II of France, and King Richard I of England set off on a Crusade. Together they fought to take back Jerusalem.

The German emperor Frederick accidentally drowned on the trip to the Middle East. France's King Philip came home before the Crusade was over; he was too sick to fight. Richard the Lion-Hearted was left to face Saladin.

Richard and Saladin were both great leaders and brave warriors. They had much respect for each other's skills. When they met in battle, Saladin's forces gained the upper hand. Then word came that Richard was needed back in England. Saladin agreed to a five-year **truce** to stop fighting. Under the terms of the truce, Christians would be allowed to visit Jerusalem. They could also keep control of a few cities on the coast.

GREAT NAMES IN HISTORY

Saladin
Saladin was a Muslim leader. He became the ruler of Egypt and Syria. Saladin built schools and mosques (places of worship) there. He was so brave and honest that even crusaders admired him.

For years, the crusaders held Palestine. Saladin wanted those Muslim lands back. He united Muslims against the crusaders. His forces captured Jerusalem in 1187. Then they took back most of Palestine.

As a result, the Third Crusade began. It ended Saladin's two-year siege of the crusaders at Acre. But they never won back Jerusalem. Finally, Saladin and crusade leader Richard the Lion-Hearted met. Their truce let Christian pilgrims visit Jerusalem.

How Did the Ottomans Gain Control of the Holy Land?

When Saladin died, the truce weakened. By 1291 the Muslims again held all of the Holy Land. In 1453, the Ottoman Turks took power in Constantinople and much of Anatolia. Like the Seljuk Turks, the Ottomans were Muslims. The Holy Land fell under their rule. The Ottomans also put an end to the Byzantine Empire. They changed the name of their capital city, Constantinople, to Istanbul. By 1500 the Ottomans would rule over a huge empire. The Middle East, North Africa, and much of eastern Europe fell to the Ottomans. The Ottoman Empire would last for hundreds of years.

LEARN MORE ABOUT IT

Remind students that in 1453 the Ottoman Turks conquered Constantinople and changed its name to Istanbul. Have students look at a contemporary map of Turkey and compare it with the description of the Ottoman Empire from their textbook.

LEARN MORE ABOUT IT

The Ottoman Empire

The Ottoman Turks first appeared in Asia Minor in the late 1200s. They were named Osmanli or Ottoman after their leader, Osman. It was under Osman that the Ottomans began to conquer the Byzantine Empire. The ruler of the Ottoman Empire was called a *sultan.* The sultan was a powerful man who ruled through a group of high officers.

The Ottoman Empire continued to grow after Osman's death. By the early 1400s, Constantinople was a Christian city surrounded by Muslim lands. Then the Ottomans, under the rule of their sultan, Mehmed II, captured Constantinople. Mehmed's troops also captured Bulgaria and parts of Hungary, and Mehmed II became known as "the Conqueror." In the 1400s and 1500s, the Ottoman Empire

extended into Asia and Africa. The Ottoman sultans took the title of *caliph,* or spiritual leader of Islam. Under the caliph known as "Suleiman the Magnificent," the Ottoman Empire grew. It now included Palestine, Egypt, and parts of Arabia, North Africa, Europe, and Persia.

The Ottomans continued to rule their vast empire for hundreds of years. During the 1800s, however, they began to lose territory. The government grew harsher. Minority groups in all parts of the empire suffered persecution. Many people wanted freedom, or **independence,** from Ottoman rule.

The Ottoman Turks joined Germany and Austria in World War I (1914–1918). With defeat came the loss of all non-Turkish lands. A free republic of Turkey was declared in 1923.

LESSON 12-2 REVIEW

On a sheet of paper, write the letter of the answer that correctly completes each sentence.

1. Pope _____ stirred Europeans to action. He did so by telling them that Christians in the Holy Land were in danger.

   A Peter the Hermit   **B** Philip II   **C** Urban II   **D** Richard I

2. Christian crusaders fought to win Jerusalem from the _____.

   A Turks   **B** Ottomans   **C** Germans   **D** Muslims

3. Armies of Christians wore _____ on their clothing as a symbol of their mission.

   A Jesus   **B** crosses   **C** crowns   **D** hearts

4. In _____, the crusaders took Jerusalem and much of the Holy Land from the Muslims.

   A 1071   **B** 1096   **C** 1099   **D** 1187

5. Muslim leader _____ won back the city of Jerusalem in 1187.

   A Saladin   **B** Philip II   **C** Frederick I   **D** Allah

6. The truce weakened when Saladin died. By _____, the Muslims held all of the Holy Land.

   A 1187   **B** 1291   **C** 1453   **D** 1500

7. In 1453, the Holy Land fell under _____ rule (who were also Muslim).

   A Ottoman   **B** Byzantine   **C** Turk   **D** German

On a sheet of paper, write the answer to each question. Use complete sentences.

8. Why did Christians go on pilgrimages?

9. What are four reasons people went on the Crusades?

10. What were the terms of the truce between Saladin and Richard?

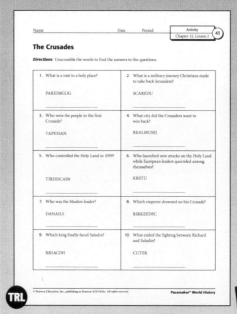

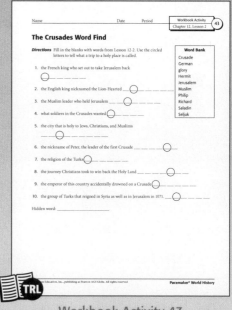

The Costs of the Crusades

Objectives

■ To name two ways the Crusades negatively affected people and their lives

■ To explain how the Crusades affected European trade

Reading Strategy:
Visualizing

Create a graphic organizer to list your own description of changes (new foods, for instance) that occurred with the Crusades.

Europeans found the Crusades costly in many ways. It took a lot of money to equip the warriors and send them such great distances. The Crusades were also costly in terms of lives. Many people—Christians, Muslims, and Jews—died bloody deaths fighting for the Holy Land. In the name of God, people looted, burned, and killed.

In the beginning, people thought the Crusades would lead them to glory. The Holy Wars, however, caused much suffering and misery. And this was all in the name of religions based on brotherhood and love.

LEARN MORE ABOUT IT

The Children's Crusade

One of the saddest of the Crusades became known as the Children's Crusade. In 1212, an army of 30,000 French boys and girls set out to fight. Most of them were 12 years old or younger. They were gathered together and led by a shepherd boy named Stephen.

At first it must have seemed like an adventure for the children. Sadly, however, few of them ever returned home. Nearly all of the 30,000 children died. Most fell sick along the way, or they starved to death.

Another army of German youths headed for Jerusalem. Led by a boy named Nicholas, these 20,000 children never saw the Holy Land either. When seven ships offered to take them to Jerusalem, they accepted. How lucky, they thought, to get a ride!

Unfortunately, the free ride was bad luck indeed. Two of the ships were wrecked in storms. All of the children aboard drowned. The rest of the ships were not headed for Jerusalem at all. The children had been tricked. The ships took them to Egypt, where they were sold as slaves.

A.D. 550–1300

Islam and the Crusades Chapter 12 **237**

LEARN MORE ABOUT IT

Have students silently read *The Children's Crusade*. Then have them write several adjectives to describe what happened to the children who participated in the Crusades. Lead a discussion in which students talk about how this reading affected their perceptions of the Crusades.

Chapter 12 Lesson 3

Overview This lesson describes how the Crusades affected people, trade, and culture.

Objectives

■ To name two ways the Crusades negatively affected people and their lives

■ To explain how the Crusades affected European trade

Student Pages 237–239

Teacher's Resource Library

Workbook Activity 44

Activity 44

Modified Activity 44

....

Vocabulary
exploration

Have students use both the vocabulary word and the list of words from the Word Bank on page 239 to write original sentences. Encourage volunteers to share their sentences with the class.

Reading Strategy:
Visualizing

As students read the lesson, have them add to their graphic organizers. Encourage them to use descriptive and specific language. After the lesson, you may have students share their graphic organizers with the class.

1 Warm-Up Activity

The Crusades brought new ideas and technology back to Europe. Have students think about what sorts of things have been brought to their country from somewhere else. Have students brainstorm a list and note the country where each item came from.

Reading Strategy:
Visualizing

Ask students to write several descriptive words in the lesson that show their understanding of the Crusades.

2 Teaching the Lesson

Have students read the information on pages 237–238. Then have them study the illustration about the Crusades on page 238.

Ask:

- Who were the people killed in the Crusades? (Christians, Muslims, and Jews)

- Did Christians keep any of the lands they once held in the Middle East? (no)

- Name some of the products that were introduced to Europeans because of the Crusades. (lemons, rice, apricots, melons, ginger, pepper, cloves, cinnamon, and colorful dyed silks)

- What were some of the ideas the crusaders absorbed from their journeys? (Europeans had a new interest in travel and exploring new places. People learned to make better maps. Crusaders returned with new weapons and better battle skills. People shared cultures and increased trade.)

Exploration
The act of looking around some unknown place

Reading Strategy:
Visualizing

What words in this section help you visualize what you are reading?

What Changes Did the Crusades Bring to Europe?

By 1291 the Christians had lost all of the lands they once held in the Middle East. The crusaders brought back Middle Eastern ideas. Crusading merchants also brought home new products. The Crusades created a new Europe.

The merchants introduced Europeans to foods like lemons, rice, apricots, and melons. New spices, such as ginger and pepper, cloves and cinnamon, now seasoned European food. The merchants brought fine cloth. Europeans began wearing brightly dyed silks. With the new trading, Europe's whole economy became stronger.

When the crusaders left Europe, their journeys gave them fresh ideas. There was a new interest in travel and exploring new places, or **exploration.** People learned to make better maps. All the fighting that went on encouraged even more interest in warfare. Crusaders returned with new weapons and better battle skills.

The feudal society had kept medieval people tied down to the manors. The Crusades sent them out into the world. The Crusades were sad and costly. However, they also increased trade and brought a sharing of cultures.

Christians joined the Crusades to recapture the Holy Land from the Muslims.

3 Reinforce and Extend

REVIEW

Word Bank

children
economy
fine cloth
ideas
lives
maps
misery
spices
weapons
world

On a sheet of paper, write the word from the Word Bank to complete each sentence correctly.

1. The Crusades cost the Europeans a lot of money and _____.

2. The Crusades were meant to bring glory. Instead, the Holy Wars caused much suffering and _____.

3. _____ from France and Germany also went to fight.

4. The Crusaders brought back Middle Eastern _____ and new products.

5. The merchants introduced new food and _____ to the Europeans.

6. The merchants brought _____ and the Europeans began to wear brightly dyed silks.

7. With new trading, Europe's whole _____ became stronger.

8. The Crusades sparked people's interest in travel and exploration. As a result, people learned to make better _____.

9. The fighting also increased interest in warfare. The Crusaders brought back _____ and better battle skills.

10. In feudal society people were tied to their manors. The Crusades sent them out into the _____.

The Arab people of the Middle Ages have given us many wonderful gifts. In science, they gave us books on medicine, studies on light and lenses, chemistry, and the globe. In mathematics, they gave us Arabic numbers and zero and the decimal system we use today. In literature, they gave us beautiful poems about nature and love and wonderful adventure stories from the Arabian Nights. In art, they gave us beautiful designs that we see in their mosques, rugs, leather goods, and swords.

Lesson 12–3 Review Answers

1. lives 2. misery 3. children 4. ideas
5. spices 6. fine cloth 7. economy
8. maps 9. weapons 10. world

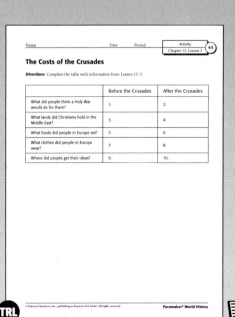

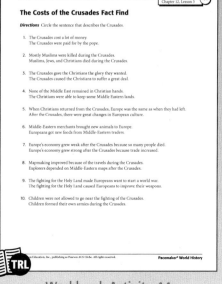

Lesson at a Glance

Chapter 12 Lesson 4

Overview Sweeping changes in agriculture during the Middle Ages created a farming revolution that changed society.

Objectives

- To name three new developments in farming in the Middle Ages
- To describe new tools that farmers started using

Student Pages 240–242

Teacher's Resource Library

Workbook Activity 45

Activity 45

Modified Activity 45

Vocabulary

surplus

Read the vocabulary word aloud and its definition. Have students write a sentence using the word.

1 Warm-Up Activity

Have students recall previous chapters that discuss the importance of farming and agriculture to ancient peoples. Lead a discussion in which students consider the importance of farming to medieval citizens.

2 Teaching the Lesson

Tell students that about 90 percent of the people who lived during the Middle Ages were peasants. A few peasants were free, but most were serfs. Serfs were not free, but they were not slaves either. Serfs had to stay on the manor on which they had been born, where they worked the manor farms from early in the morning until late at night. They did the farming, cut wood, and built fences. About 60 percent of what each serf raised went to the lord of the manor and to the church.

LESSON 12-4

Changes in Agriculture

Objectives

- To name three new developments in farming in the Middle Ages
- To describe new tools that farmers started using

Surplus
More than what is needed

The world's first agricultural revolution had taken place long ago. It occurred along the Mediterranean Sea when people began planting seeds and raising animals. During the Middle Ages another farming revolution was going on. Now people were learning about new and better methods of growing food. These changes in agriculture also changed society as a whole.

How Did Farming Change During the Middle Ages?

During the Middle Ages, Emperor Charlemagne opened new iron mines. With more iron available, farm tools improved. Now there were new metal axes and hoes.

The new tool that most changed farming in the Middle Ages was the plowshare. A plowshare is the broad blade of the plow that cuts through the soil. Early plows had been little more than large sticks. These sticks were dragged across the ground by one or two oxen. They only scratched the earth. It took hours and hours of work to break up even a small field.

The new plowshare was made of sharp, curved iron. The plow itself was fastened to a heavy, wheeled frame. Eight oxen were needed to pull the plowshare. With the new, heavier equipment, farmers could till even the heaviest soil. Working in long, narrow strips, they could plow the land more quickly.

The plowshare meant that more land could be farmed and more food could be grown. People did not have to eat all that they grew. They had more food than they needed, or a **surplus** of food. They could use this surplus to trade for other goods.

Ask:

- How did iron improve farm tools? (gave farmers sharper plowshares, better axes and hoes)
- Why were horses better workers than oxen? (They could work longer without rest and moved faster.)
- What was the importance of the three-crop rotation? (allowed the land to rest; provided for a second crop to be grown)
- How might the presence of a surplus affect the daily lives of citizens? (Answers may vary—more food means more opportunities to trade for other goods; citizens are less likely to succumb to the deprivations of hunger.)

Background Information

Even with new metal axes and hoes, farming in the Middle Ages was still very difficult. The threat of drought or pest infestation was always imminent. Also, farms were usually the property of a lord, who charged a tax to the farmers in order to use the land.

Medieval farmers discovered that horses were better workers than oxen. Horses could work longer without rest. They moved faster. With more iron around, it was easy to make enough horseshoes.

The farmers invented a new kind of harness to fasten their horses to a plow. It fit over the horse's shoulders instead of across its chest. Now the horse could breathe easier and could pull heavier weights. It took fewer horses than oxen to pull the new plowshare.

Farmers learned to get more out of their fields. They maintained three fields now. They planted one field in the autumn and one in the spring. A third field was not used and lay fallow, or bare, each season. Each field was given a season to be fallow. This let the soil rest and grow rich again.

The three-field method of crop rotation worked well. If one crop failed, there was always a second crop to rely on. More food was produced.

Reading Strategy:
Visualizing

Study the art in this lesson. What does it say about agriculture in the Middle Ages?

During the Middle Ages, new tools changed the way people farmed.

Reading Strategy:
Visualizing

Have students study the art on page 241, then write a short paragraph that describes the lives of the people in the illustration. Encourage volunteers to share their paragraphs with the class.

LEARNING STYLES

Logical/Mathematical

After students read about the three-field system, have them solve this problem:

Suppose three fields can produce 900 pounds of food each year. Under the three-field system, how many years would it take to produce 3,000 pounds of food? (because only two-thirds of the fields are planted at a time, 600 pounds of food would be produced each year; it would therefore take five years to produce 3,000 pounds of food)

ELL/ESL STRATEGY

Language Objective: *To encourage students to learn synonyms and antonyms for words they encounter in their reading*

Have students read the lesson. Then ask them to write several unfamiliar words on a separate sheet of paper. Ask them to look up the words in their dictionaries and write them in their notebooks. Have them write a minimum of one synonym and one antonym in context for each word. For example, a synonym for the vocabulary word *surplus* is *excess* and an antonym is *shortfall*.

3   Reinforce and Extend

COMMON ERROR

Once students discover the value of using a thesaurus, encourage them to use synonyms for more colorful writing.

LESSON 12-4 REVIEW

On a sheet of paper, write the answer to each question. Use complete sentences.

1. What was the new tool that changed farming the most during the Middle Ages?

2. What was the new method farmers learned for growing crops?

3. Why did they let one field rest each season?

On a sheet of paper, write the letter of the answer that correctly completes each sentence.

4. The _____ revolution of the Middle Ages taught people new, better methods for growing food. It also changed society.

   A industrial   **B** farming   **C** feudalism   **D** warfare

5. Because _____ opened new iron mines, there was more iron available and farm tools improved.

   A Charlemagne   **B** Richard I   **C** Philip II   **D** Frederick I

6. The new plowshare, made of _____, allowed farmers to till heavy soil.

   A sticks   **B** stone   **C** leather   **D** iron

7. The plowshare created _____ food, which farmers could use to trade.

   A different types of   **B** a loss of   **C** a surplus of   **D** more demand for

8. Farmers discovered that horses were better workers than _____.

   A dogs   **B** oxen   **C** children   **D** slaves

9. Horses could work longer without rest _____.

   A and they moved faster   **C** but they were unproductive
   B and they complained less   **D** but they were ineffective

10. The farmers invented a new _____. It allowed the horse to breathe easier and pull heavier weights.

   A plowshare   **B** iron   **C** harness   **D** horseshoe

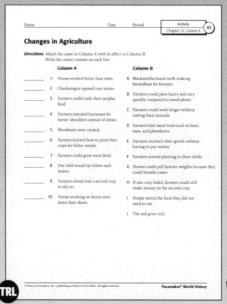

Activity 45   Workbook Activity 45

Changes in City Life

Objectives

- To describe what life was like in a medieval town
- To explain how the feudal system weakened
- To tell how a person could become a member of a guild
- To describe how cities like Constantinople and Antwerp grew during the Middle Ages

Population

People living in a place, or the total number of those people

Migrate

To move away from one country or region to settle in another

Reading Strategy: Visualizing

Draw a picture of a medieval town to help you visualize the ideas in this lesson.

During the 1000s, the number of people living in Europe, or Europe's **population**, began to grow. More people meant a need for even more farmland. Farmers cleared forests and drained swamplands in England and France. People began to **migrate**, or move, eastward. Germans colonized new lands in eastern Europe. Changes in agriculture caused people to live in new places.

What Was the Result of the Growth in Population?

As farm production increased, workers had more food to trade for goods. Beginning in the 1000s, craftworkers and traders began to settle in medieval villages to sell their goods. In addition to the blacksmith and the miller, there were now new shops in the villages. The villages grew into towns.

Medieval towns were usually surrounded by stone walls. Their narrow streets were often just mud. Sometimes the streets were paved with cobblestones. The towns were often dirty and dark.

With walls closing them in, the towns were small and crowded. People threw their garbage into the streets. There were no fire departments, no police departments, and no health services. Most of the houses were just huts made of wood. With these conditions, there was always a danger of fire and disease. The town of Rouen in France burned to the ground six times between 1200 and 1225! It is easy to see how the plague spread so quickly in such crowded, dirty towns.

Chapter 12 Lesson 5

Overview Changes in agriculture resulted in widespread changes, not only in the way people lived but where they lived. This lesson examines life in medieval towns and explains the feudal system. It also examines the incursion of rural peoples into cities.

Objectives

- To describe what life was like in a medieval town
- To explain how the feudal system weakened
- To tell how a person could become a member of the guild
- To describe how cities like Constantinople and Antwerp grew during the Middle Ages

Student Pages 243–246

Teacher's Resource Library

Workbook Activity 46

Activity 46

Modified Activity 46

Vocabulary

apprentice	migrate
guild	population

Write each vocabulary word on the board. Then give students the following sentences and have them fill in the blanks.

It is difficult to _____ from one's hometown. However, people in the Middle Ages moved around more and more.

The _____ of Europe began to grow during the 1000s.

The early _____ were similar to labor unions.

A(n)_____ often lived in the master's house and worked in the master's shop.

ELL/ESL STRATEGY

Language Objective: *To teach students how words function as different parts of speech and how this affects their meanings and placement in sentences*

Point out the word *apprentice* in the vocabulary list. Ask whether *apprentice* in the following example is a noun or as a verb: Jose is the new *apprentice* at the pottery shop. (It is a noun.) Explain that apprentice can also be a verb. It can mean *to serve as an apprentice*. Ask whether *apprentice* is a noun or verb in this example: Philip apprentices as a woodworker. (It is a verb.)

COMMON ERROR

Students may confuse *guild* with *gild*. Have them look up both words in the dictionary and compare their meanings. Remind them that they often must memorize the meanings of similar words.

Reading Strategy:

Visualizing

Have students draw pictures of medieval towns based on the information in Lesson 5.

Encourage students to compare and contrast their drawings of medieval towns. Have them discuss what their drawings have in common and how they differ. Ask them to defend how they drew their medieval towns based on what they read in Lesson 5.

Point out the subheadings in this lesson. Read the four lesson subheadings aloud: What Was the Result of the Growth in Population?, Why Did the Feudal System Begin to Weaken?, What Was the Purpose of a Guild?, What Were Some Big Cities During the Middle Ages? Remind students that answering these questions is a good way to test themselves on the content of a lesson.

Ask:

- What were conditions like in most medieval towns? (Most medieval towns were small and crowded. They were often dirty and dark. Garbage was on the streets. Most of the houses were huts made of wood. There was always the danger of fire and disease.)

- Why did towns grow? (Serfs saw the town as a place to win freedom from manor lords. Business and trade increased and towns became stronger. People were freer than they had been on the feudal estates. They wanted to live in the towns. Towns offered opportunity. Peasants could work their way up in the world. They could learn a trade or a craft.)

- Why were guilds useful? (Guilds helped set prices. They set standards for workmanship. They offered a chance to learn. Boys and girls could become an apprentice and go to work for a guild member.)

- What city was the center of the Islamic world? (Baghdad)

- During the Middle Ages, some cities were known as centers for art, science, and education. How do you think modern tools such as the Internet have changed our

Guild
An organization formed to protect the interests of workers in one craft or trade

Apprentice
A person who learns a trade under a master

History Fact
In the Middle Ages, a town that had a cathedral was known as a cathedral city. Many cathedrals grew to be large and beautiful.

In spite of their problems, the medieval towns grew. As they did, the workers, merchants, and craftworkers became more specialized.

People used money more often now. On the manors, services had been exchanged for goods. Now people paid money for new leather shoes, a pottery bowl, or a cake.

Serfs saw the town as a place to win freedom from manor lords. Sometimes serfs ran away and hid within the walls of a town. "Live free for a year and a day," the rule went, "and go free." A serf who could manage to escape his lord for that long became a free person.

Why Did the Feudal System Begin to Weaken?
During the late Middle Ages, business and trade increased. As the towns became stronger, and the merchants became richer, the feudal system weakened. The towns wanted to govern themselves—to be free of the manor.

Some feudal lords sold deeds of freedom to the towns. No longer were so many people "tied" to the land. Most towns were dirty and crowded. People, however, were freer than they had been on the feudal estates. It was not so surprising that they wanted to live in the towns.

What Was the Purpose of a Guild?
The towns offered opportunity. Peasants could work their way up in the world. They could learn a trade or a craft.

Each trade and craft had its own group, or **guild**. The guild helped set prices. It also set standards for workmanship. The guilds decided how long shops should stay open each day.

The guilds also offered a chance to learn. Boys and girls could become an **apprentice** and go to work for a guild member. The apprentice lived in the master's house and worked in the master's shop.

perceptions of where opportunities may be found? (Answer will vary.)

Background Information

Life in a medieval town offered many advantages to people who came from farms owned by lords. The new class of merchants and the formation of guilds meant that young people could learn a trade and support themselves. There was also some protection by law enforcement. Constables helped to keep law and order. There were curfews that kept people off the streets after the "curfew bell" was rung. Another bell was rung to announce civic meetings, courts, and alarms in case of fire or attack. These and other advantages drew many people to towns and soon their populations increased dramatically.

History Fact
Have students read the information about cathedrals on page 244. Show the class several examples of large and beautiful cathedrals that were built during the Middle Ages. Tell students that some of these cathedrals still stand today.

An apprentice served for seven years and received no pay. After that time, the apprentice could become a journeyman and earn wages. When the apprentice became skilled enough, the journeyman made one special piece of work for the master. It was called a "masterpiece." If the masterpiece was good enough, the journeyman might become a master and join the guild.

Streets in medieval towns often were named after different guilds. *Tailors Row* and *Boot Street*, for example, were typical street names.

What Were Some Big Cities During the Middle Ages?

Most Europeans lived in small, walled towns during the late Middle Ages. However, there were a few fine, wealthy cities. Trade flourished, or did well, in those cities. There were theaters and hospitals, schools and libraries.

There were cities like Constantinople, capital of the Byzantine Empire. One million people lived there. As many as one thousand ships might dock at Constantinople's harbor at the same time.

TECHNOLOGY CONNECTION

Silver and Medieval Business

In the 1160s more silver mines opened across Europe. Many of these were in Germany. As the number of mines increased, so did people's knowledge. Mining became more efficient and effective. More silver was brought into trade.

French and English merchants traded for German silver. Italians and other merchants from the Mediterranean traded goods brought from the East. More business was being conducted using silver money. Bankers from the south moved to growing northern trade centers.

Mines were expanded, or made larger. Small operations learned new technologies to mine greater amounts of silver. Jobs in industry became available to people. Those who did not want to be farmers now had other choices.

A.D. 550–1300   *Islam and the Crusades* *Chapter 12* **245**

LEARNING STYLES

 Body/Kinesthetic

Divide students into two groups—serfs who stayed with their manor lords in rural areas and serfs who ran away to towns or cities. Have students create a skit to demonstrate the advantages and disadvantages of both choices.

3 Reinforce and Extend

CAREER CONNECTION

 The builders of cities such as Baghdad, Constantinople, Antwerp, and Venice all shared a love for beautiful and complicated architecture. Some of their architecture still stands today. Architects design buildings and supervise their construction. To become an architect, students undergo rigorous training. Earning a bachelor's degree in architecture generally takes about five years. After graduation, students must pass a design test, work as an intern in the office of a licensed architect, and pass a state licensing examination. Licensed architects can work independently, join a firm, or work for the government. Encourage interested students to take courses in history, mathematics, mechanical drawing, and computer science.

TECHNOLOGY CONNECTION

Have students read the Technology Connection. Then ask them to discuss the impact of more efficient mining techniques on medieval peoples.

There were cities like Baghdad, center of the Islamic world. There, scientists studied mathematics and astronomy. Doctors made new discoveries in medicine. Geographers mapped the world.

There were cities like Córdoba, Spain. It was called the *Lighthouse of Learning*. Spanish Muslims and Spanish Jews studied there.

There were cities like Venice and Antwerp. Trade and manufacturing made these places wealthy.

All these cities grew during the Middle Ages. Trade kept them powerful and rich. They were centers for art, science, and education.

Constantinople was the capital of the Byzantine Empire. During the Holy Wars, it was raided by Crusaders.

On a sheet of paper, write the letter of the answer that correctly completes each sentence.

1. As towns grew, workers, merchants, and craftworkers became more _____.

   A wealthy   B in demand   C gifted   D specialized

2. As the medieval town population grew, people used money to exchange goods, rather than _____.

   A gold   B weapons   C services   D slaves

3. Towns offered _____, as peasants could work their way up in the world.

   A risk   B opportunity   C trade   D food

4. Streets in medieval towns were often named after different _____.

   A lords   B knights   C guilds   D clergy

5. Constantinople, Baghdad, and Antwerp are some examples of wealthy _____ in the late Middle Ages.

   A cities   B towns   C estates   D farms

6. _____ flourished in cities and helped to keep them powerful and rich.

   A Farming   B Trade   C The population   D Services

7. The cities were centers for art, science, and _____.

   A education   B weapons   C religion   D farm tool factories

On a sheet of paper, write the answer to each question. Use complete sentences.

8. What was life like in a medieval town?

9. How did the feudal system weaken?

10. What steps would a boy or girl need to take to become a guild member?

Lesson 12–5 Review Answers
1. D 2. C 3. B 4. C 5. A 6. B 7. A
8. Medieval towns were small and crowded. They were usually surrounded by stone walls, and streets were either mud or cobblestone. The streets were littered with garbage, and the houses were huts made of wood. There were no fire departments, police departments, or health services. The conditions made a constant risk of fire and disease. 9. The feudal system weakened when business and trade increased, making the towns stronger and the merchants richer. The towns wanted to govern themselves and to be free of the manor. 10. First, a boy or girl would become an apprentice and work for a guild member for no pay. Once the apprentice had served for seven years, he/she could become a journeyman and earn wages. When the journeyman became skilled enough, he/she would make a special piece of work for the master. If the masterpiece was good enough, the journey could become a master and join the guild.

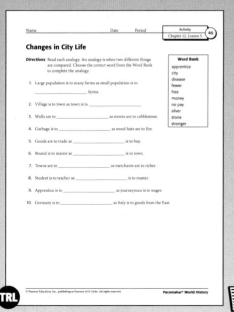

Activity 46   Workbook Activity 46

Lesson at a Glance

Chapter 12 Lesson 6

Overview This lesson describes the progress made concerning human rights during the Middle Ages.

Objectives

■ To discuss how the Magna Carta gave people justice

Student Pages 248–250

Teacher's Resource Library

Workbook Activity 47

Activity 47

Modified Activity 47

....

Vocabulary

charter   human rights
document

Write the vocabulary words on the board. Have students use their dictionaries to look up the words then ask them to compose original sentences that contain the words.

PRONUNCIATION GUIDE

Use this list to help students pronounce difficult words in this lesson.

Runnymede (run´ i med´)

Thames (temz)

---

1 Warm-Up Activity

Ask students what the term *human rights* means to them. Lead a discussion about how acknowledging human rights, even for a small minority of the population, paved the way for future talks.

2 Teaching the Lesson

Point out the illustration on page 249. Have students describe what they see. Remind them that when nobles drew up the Magna Carta, the Crusades were fighting in the Middle East.

LESSON 12-6

The Magna Carta

There was little concern with **human rights** during the early Middle Ages. Indeed, the right to life, liberty, and the pursuit of (the attempt to get) happiness was not granted to everyone. A lord had much power over the lives of serfs.

What Progress Was Made During the Middle Ages in Human Rights?

When King John ruled England, he showed no interest at all in anyone's rights. He did not even treat the nobles very well! Suppose that King John did not like a certain noble. Perhaps he thought that noble was becoming too powerful. He might very well have the noble put to death.

Nobles were angry. In 1213 some powerful men met in England. They drew up a list of rights that they wanted the king to grant them. The final **document** would make sure that justice, or fairness, would not be denied to freemen.

King John did not want to give up any power. He refused to sign the list. In 1215 the nobles sent an army after him. King John saw that he could not defeat the army, so he finally gave in. At Runnymede, near the Thames River, King John signed the list of rights, or the **charter**. It became known as the *Great Charter*, or the *Magna Carta*.

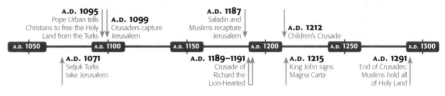

TIMELINE STUDY: THE CRUSADES

How many years passed from the time of Pope Urban's sermon to the end of the Crusades?

A.D. 1095	A.D. 1099	A.D. 1187	A.D. 1212
Pope Urban tells Christians to free the Holy Land from the Turks	Crusaders capture Jerusalem	Saladin and Muslims recapture Jerusalem	Children's Crusade

A.D. 1050 A.D. 1100 A.D. 1150 A.D. 1200 A.D. 1250 A.D. 1300

A.D. 1071	A.D. 1189–1191	A.D. 1215	A.D. 1291
Seljuk Turks take Jerusalem	Crusade of Richard the Lion-Hearted	King John signs Magna Carta	End of Crusades: Muslims hold all of Holy Land

---

Ask:

● What does Magna Carta mean? (Great Charter)

● What finally forced King John to sign the Magna Carta? (The nobles sent an army after him.)

● What rights did the authors of the Magna Carta insist on? (The Magna Carta said that a freeman must be tried by a jury of his equals before being sent to jail. It said taxes would be collected by legal means, not by force. It said punishment should fit the crime.)

● Who was guaranteed to receive these rights? (nobles and freemen)

Reading Strategy: Visualizing

After students have created their graphic organizers, invite several volunteers to share them with the class.

TIMELINE STUDY

Answer: 196 years

Ask:

● How much time elapsed between the Children's Crusade and the signing of the Magna Carta (3 years). Ask if these two events are related.

Words from the Past

The Magna Carta

When King John signed the Magna Carta in 1215, he gave some rights and liberties to the nobles, or barons. He also reformed the legal system and gave a few rights to freemen. Most people in England, however, were not free—they were serfs. None of the liberties in the charter applied to them.

How could a charter giving most rights to barons become such an important document? One reason was that when King John signed the charter, he was admitting that even the king had to obey the law. For another reason, over time many people came to believe that the rights in the charter belonged to all English people. In England, future laws granting liberties to all English people were based on the Magna Carta.

King John signed the Magna Carta.

The Magna Carta said that:

- A freeman must be tried by a jury of his equals before being sent to prison.
- Taxes would be collected by legal means, not by force.
- Punishment should fit the crime.

The Magna Carta was important to the development of a new nation, the United States of America. The Magna Carta inspired colonists to fight for their rights against King George and Great Britain. The Declaration of Independence, the U.S. Constitution, and many U.S. state constitutions were based partly on the ideas of the Magna Carta.

Background Information

Have students access the Magna Carta online to compare details found in the primary source document with the concepts presented in the "Words From The Past" section of page 249.

WORDS FROM THE PAST

The Magna Carta was the earliest influence of modern constitutional law. As seen in the United States Constitution and Bill of Rights, it laid the foundation for future democracies. Ask students to research the laws in their country to find if the three points listed in their book are represented. What are those laws called? What document are they found in?

ELL/ESL STRATEGY

Language Objective:
To encourage students to work together to discover new words

Have students silently read the selection from "Words From the Past" and write any words that are unfamiliar to them. Ask each student to share his or her list of words. Compile a master list of unfamiliar words on the board. Ask volunteers to define words they do know and write the correct definitions on the board next to the words. Then define any remaining unfamiliar words.

COMMON ERROR

Remind students of the importance of copying the addresses of Web sites exactly as they appear in a textbook, on the board, or on the Internet.

3   Reinforce and Extend

TEACHER ALERT

Remind students that, although the Magna Carta provided basic human rights for a small number of citizens in England, it had long lasting impacts on the modern world. Remind students that the Magna Carta inspired colonists to fight for their rights against King George and Great Britain several hundred years later.

Lesson 12–6 Review Answers
1. 1213 **2.** Great Charter **3.** freeman
4. 1215 **5.** serfs **6.** king **7.** equals
8. taxes **9.** punishment **10.** United
States of America

REVIEW

Word Bank

equals

freeman

Great Charter

king

punishment

serfs

taxes

1213

1215

United States of
America

On a sheet of paper, write the word from the Word Bank to
complete each sentence correctly.

1. In _____, a group of powerful men met and drew
up a list of rights. They wanted to ensure that justice
would not be denied to freemen.

2. The Magna Carta is also known as the _____.

3. King John signed the Magna Carta in _____.

4. The Magna Carta changed the legal system and
gave a few rights to _____.

5. None of the liberties in the charter applied to _____.

6. By signing the charter, King John admitted that
the _____ had to obey the law.

7. The Magna Carta said that a freeman must be tried
by a jury of his _____.

8. It also said that _____ should be collected by
legal means.

9. According to the charter, the _____ should fit
the crime.

10. The Magna Carta was important to the development
of the _____.

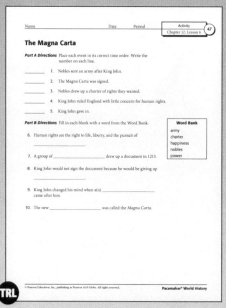

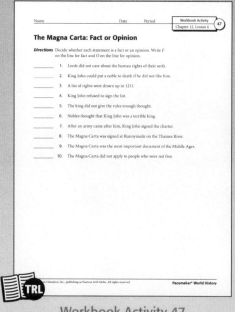

- During the Middle Ages, many Christians made pilgrimages to holy places such as the city of Jerusalem. Jesus Christ had lived and taught in Jerusalem.

- Muslims were followers of Muhammad. He was born in Mecca in A.D. 570. Muhammad taught the word of Allah. By the time Muhammad died in A.D. 632, he had many followers. Their religion was called Islam.

- Muslims conquered many lands, spreading Islam and the Arabic culture. They conquered Palestine (the Holy Land), which included the city of Jerusalem. Jews and Christians were also living in Jerusalem at that time.

- Christian crusaders fought to win Jerusalem from the Muslims. They fought a war that lasted for six weeks. They took control of the Holy Land.

- In A.D. 1167, the Muslims regained control of the Holy Land. They made a truce with the Christians, who would be allowed to visit Jerusalem.

- The Ottoman Turks took control of the Byzantine Empire, the Middle East, northern Africa, and much of eastern Europe by 1500. This included the Holy Land.

- The Crusaders brought back new ideas, new products, and new plans for trade throughout Europe.

- A medieval revolution in agriculture meant new tools and better methods of farming. Many people migrated to the east.

- Medieval towns saw an increase in craftworkers and merchants. The craftworkers formed guilds.

- In A.D. 1215, King John signed the Magna Carta, giving new rights to the English.

A.D. 550–1300   *Islam and the Crusades*   *Chapter 12*   **251**

TEACHER'S RESOURCE

The AGS Globe Teaching Strategies in Social Studies Transparencies may be used with this chapter. The transparencies add an interactive dimension to expand and enhance the Pacemaker® *World History* program content.

CHAPTER PROJECT FOLLOW-UP

 You may want to have students begin to present their chapter projects at the end of this lesson. Encourage them to share where they found further research on the contributions of Arabs to the rest of the world.

Chapter 12 Summary

Have students read the Chapter Summary on page 251 to review the main ideas presented in Chapter 12.

Ask:

- What is a pilgrimage? (a journey to a holy site)

- Who was Muhammad? (the founder of Islam, born in Mecca in A.D. 570)

- What happened after Muhammad's death? (Muslims began to spread Islam through the Middle East. They conquered Palestine and the city of Jerusalem.)

- Why did Pope Urban II urge Christians to engage in a holy war? (to regain control of Jerusalem)

- Who controlled the Byzantine Empire as well as the Middle East, northern Africa, and much of eastern Europe by 1500? (the Ottoman Turks)

- What were some of the benefits of the Crusades? (new ideas, new products, increased interest in travel and exploration, exchange of cultural information)

- Name several improvements made in farming techniques in the agricultural revolution during the Middle Ages. (use of iron to make better tools, improved plowshares, rotating crops, ability to grow a surplus of food)

- Why were guilds useful to medieval workers? (They provided standards for workmanship, programs for training and apprenticing, and standards for working hours.)

- Why was the signing of the Magna Carta a momentous event? (Answers may vary—because it was the first time authority acknowledged human rights; because it provided protections for certain citizens; because it regulated how taxes could be collected.)

Chapter 12 Review

Use the Chapter Review to prepare students for tests and to reteach content from the chapter.

Chapter 12 Mastery Test

The Teacher's Resource Library includes two forms of the Chapter 12 Mastery Test. Each test addresses the chapter Goals for Learning. An optional third page of additional critical-thinking items is included for each test. The difficulty level of the two forms is equivalent.

Chapter 12 Review Answers

Vocabulary Review

1. prophet

2. pilgrimage

3. faith

4. surplus

5. apprentice

6. guild

7. migrated

8. population

9. truce

10. independence

Chapter Review Questions

11. People of all classes went on the Crusades. Even children went on some Crusades.

12. The Ottomans took over the Holy Land. The Ottomans were Muslims.

13. Business and trade grew during the Middle Ages. Towns grew, and the towns wanted to be free of the manor. If serfs ran away to the towns and managed to escape for a year, they became free.

Word Bank

apprentice
faith
guild
independence
migrated
pilgrimage
population
prophet
surplus
truce

Vocabulary Review

On a sheet of paper, use the words from the Word Bank to complete each sentence correctly.

1. Muhammad was a(n) _____.

2. A religious person might make a(n) _____ to visit the Holy Land.

3. Millions of people of the Islamic _____ live in the United States and Canada.

4. The new plowshare resulted in a(n) _____ of food.

5. A boy or girl could work for a master as a(n) _____.

6. Master craftworkers could belong to a(n) _____.

7. Germans _____ to new lands in eastern Europe.

8. Europe's _____ began to grow during the 1000s.

9. Saladin signed a five-year _____ that allowed Christians to visit Jerusalem.

10. Minority groups suffering persecution wanted _____ from Ottoman rule.

Chapter Review Questions

On a sheet of paper, write the answer to each question. Use complete sentences.

11. Who went on the Crusades to the Holy Land?

12. After the Crusades, who controlled the Holy Land?

13. Why did the feudal system weaken?

14. How did farming change during the Middle Ages?

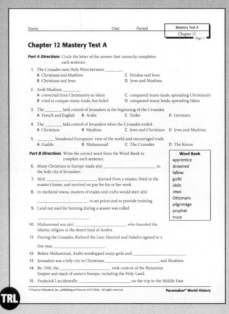

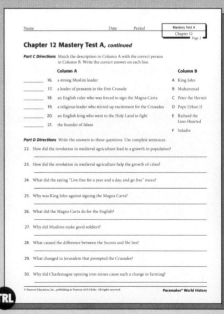

Chapter 12 Mastery Test A, pages 1–3

Read test questions carefully. Identify questions that require more than one answer.

15. Why did towns begin to grow in the 1000s?

16. What did the Magna Carta say about the relationship of the king to the laws of the land?

Critical Thinking

On a sheet of paper, write your response to each question. Use complete sentences.

17. How did Muhammad affect the world beyond his own followers?

18. What do you think was the most important right in the Magna Carta? Explain why.

Using the Timelines

Use the timelines on pages 228 and 248 to answer the questions.

19. How old was Muhammad when he died?

20. When was the Children's Crusade?

GROUP ACTIVITY

Form a group of five or six. Assign each person a role such as a merchant, soldier, king, noble, knight, serf, or child. Have each person write a speech about the reasons he or she wants to go on a Crusade. When the speeches are ready, perform them for the class.

A.D. 550–1300   *Islam and the Crusades   Chapter 12*   **253**

14. Farm tools, especially the plowshare, improved farming. Horses, with new harnesses, replaced oxen. Farmers learned to rotate their crops and were able to produce a surplus of food, which they could trade.

15. In the 1000s, towns grew because craft workers and traders began to move to the towns to sell their goods. Also, serfs moved there to win freedom from the lords.

16. It said that the king had to obey the laws; the king was not above them.

Critical Thinking

17. Possible answers: Islam became one of the world's great religions. It spread to many parts of the world. The Crusades would not have happened if the Muslims had not controlled the Holy Land.

18. Possible answers: Most students will probably say that a jury trial gives ordinary people a better chance of justice or that when punishment fits the crime, a person is not thrown in jail for a minor offense.

Using the Timelines

19. 62

20. A.D. 1212

GROUP ACTIVITY

Students' speeches should show understanding of the underlying motivations that people had for going on the Crusades.

Chapter 12 Mastery Test B, pages 1–3

UNIT 5

PLANNING GUIDE

The Renaissance: 1400–1650

	Student Pages	Vocabulary	Map Study	Reading Strategy	Lesson Review	Chapter Summary/Review
Chapter 13 New Ideas: The Renaissance	256–283					281–283
Lesson 13–1 A Time of New Ideas	258–260	✔		✔	260	
Lesson 13–2 Renaissance Art	261–264	✔		✔	264	
Lesson 13–3 Advances in Knowledge, Technology, and Science	265–270	✔		✔	270	
Lesson 13–4 The Renaissance Man	271–273			✔	273	
Lesson 13–5 The Reformation	274–277	✔		✔	277	
Lesson 13–6 The Counter-Reformation	278–280	✔		✔	280	
Chapter 14 Kings and Queens	284–303					301–303
Lesson 14–1 Rule by Monarchs	286–287	✔		✔	287	
Lesson 14–2 Spanish Monarchs	288–291	✔		✔	291	
Lesson 14–3 French Monarchs	292–294	✔		✔	294	
Lesson 14–4 English Monarchs	295–300	✔		✔	300	

Chapter Activities

Teacher's Resource Library
Life Skills Connection 13–14
Key Vocabulary Words 13–14

Assessment Options

Student Text
Chapter Reviews 13–14

Teacher's Resource Library
Chapter 13 Mastery Tests A and B
Chapter 14 Mastery Tests A and B
Unit 5 Mastery Test

Teacher's Edition
Chapter Projects 13–14

Words from the Past	Learn More About It	Great Names in History	Technology Connection	Geography Note	You Decide/Remember/History Fact	Timeline Study	ELL/ESL Strategy	Background Information	Common Error	Life Skills Connection	Key Vocabulary Words	Study Skills	Applications Home, Career, Community	Online Connection	Teacher Alert	World Cultures	Auditory/Verbal	Body/Kinesthetic	Interpersonal/Group Learning	Logical/Mathematical	Visual/Spatial	Activities/Modified Activities	Workbook Activities	Self-Study Guide	Chapter Outline
										257	257													✔	✔
					258		259	259	260											259		48	48		
					261		262	262	263			263	262			264			262			49	49		
267					265, 266, 268		267	266	268				269	269	268						266	50	50		
			272		276		272	272	273											272		51	51		
							276	275	276						276		276					52	52		
						279	279	278	279													53	53		
										285	285													✔	✔
							287	286					287						287			54	54		
	290		289	289			290	289	290, 291				291			290			290		289	55	55		
							293	292	294											293		56	56		
		299				297–299	296	296	297			297	298	298	298		296					57	57		

Modified Activities

The Teacher's Resource Library (TRL) contains a set of lower-level worksheets called Modified Activities. These worksheets cover the same content as the standard Activities but are written at a lower reading level.

Skill Track

Use Skill Track for *World History* to monitor student progress and meet the demands of adequate yearly progress (AYP). Make informed instructional decisions with individual student and class reports of lesson and chapter assessments. With immediate and ongoing feedback, students will also see what they have learned and where they need more reinforcement and practice.

Audio Library

Skill Track for World History

Teacher's Resource Library **TRL**

Unit 5 Mastery Test

(Answer Keys for the Teacher's Resource Library begin on page 809 of the Teacher's Edition.)

Other Resources

Books for Teachers

Ajmar, Marta. *At Home in Renaissance Italy*. London: Victoria and Albert Museum, 2006.

Hartt, Fred and Wilkins, David G. *History of Italian Renaissance Art*. New York: Prentice Hall, 1994.

Nicholl, Charles. *Leonardo da Vinci: Flights of the Mind: A Biography*. New York: Viking, 2004.

Books for Students

Rees, Fran. *Johannas Gutenberg: Inventor of the Printing Press*. Compass Point Books, 2005.

Saari, Peggy and Maurice, Aaron. *Renaissance and Reformation: Biographies Edition I*. UXL, 2002.

Videos

Florence: Cradle of the Renaissance, View Video, 1996, 30 minutes. (A look at Florence as the cradle of rebirth in art, architecture, and philosophy. Includes information on Michelangelo, Botticelli, Ghiberti, Cellini, Lorenzo de' Medici, and Leonardo da Vinci.)

Empires—the Medici, Godfathers of the Renaissance, PBS, 2004, 240 minutes. (A documentary that depicts the rise of the

THE RENAISSANCE

You will learn that the word *renaissance* has more than one definition. Beyond those, you might think of it as meaning "a bold, new start." The period in history called the Renaissance meant lots of new learning and new creations. It also meant many new opportunities for those wanting adventure. People faced challenges they had never known before. New kinds of kingdoms developed, under bold new leaders. Now groups competed for control of lands and the way people lived. Thus our recorded history was becoming more detailed and challenging.

Chapters in Unit 5

This detail from the Sistine Chapel illustrates the great thinking that happened during the Renaissance.

255

Introducing the Unit

Tell students that this unit introduces them to a time of many exciting changes. Ask students to study the picture on page 254 and describe what it shows. Then read the caption and introductory paragraph on page 255 to students. Have them consider what kinds of changes people experienced during the Renaissance.

Ask:

- What is one meaning of renaissance? (a bold, new start)

- What new experiences did people encounter during this period in history? (People encountered new learning and new creations. It meant new opportunities for adventure. People faced new challenges.)

- How did leadership change during the Renaissance? (New kinds of kingdoms developed under bold new leaders. Groups competed for control of lands.)

Medici family and their influence on the European Renaissance.)

CD-ROM/Software

Leonardo the Inventor 2.0 Broderbund, 2004. An animated environment filled with information about the inventor, his life, his inventions, and the world around him.

The Art of Renaissance Science: Galileo and Perspective CustomFlix, 2007. A presentation on the life of Galileo, the origin of perspective drawing and the interaction of art and science in the Renaissance.

Web Sites

www.agsglobepmwh.com/page255a (A catalog of 631 biographies of scientists from the 16th and 17th centuries.)

www.agsglobepmwh.com/page255b (A site on Leonardo da Vinci from the National Museum of Science and Technology.)

www.agsglobepmwh.com/page255c (Facts about Michelangelo for students.)

Introducing the Chapter

In the middle of the 14th century, the Middle Ages in Europe came to an end. A new interest in learning and creativity emerged. Scientists, artists, and the clergy gained more power. This period is called "the Renaissance."

New Ideas: The Renaissance

You have read that history is all about change. This could be moving to a different place or shifting focus to a new goal or way of thinking. It could also be the shift from a simple to a more difficult world.

The Middle Ages brought a growth in the Roman Catholic Church as well as in Islam. These religions attracted more and more people. They controlled larger areas and became more powerful. The Renaissance brought a return to learning and creativity. Scientists and artists had more power as did members of the clergy. They began to question their own relationships to religion and the power that came with it.

GOALS FOR LEARNING

- To understand the ideas behind the Renaissance
- To recognize the humanism in Renaissance art
- To describe the advances in knowledge during the Renaissance
- To describe what it means to be a Renaissance Man
- To understand how the Reformation came about
- To understand the ideas behind the Counter-Reformation

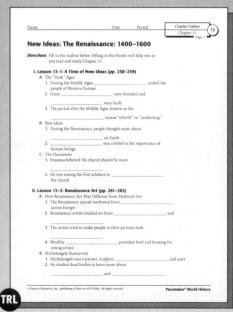

Chapter 13 Self-Study Guide, pages 1–3   Chapter 13 Outline, pages 1–3

Reading Strategy: Inferencing

Sometimes you have to make an inference to figure out what the text means. You have to make an inference because the meaning of a text is not directly stated.

What You Know + What You Read = Inference

You can make inferences by thinking "beyond the text." Add what you already know to what you read in the text. This is a helpful strategy for making inferences.

Key Vocabulary Words

Lesson 1
Renaissance The revival of art, literature, and learning in Europe in the 14th through 16th centuries

Humanism A concern with the needs and interests of human beings rather than religious ideas

Criticize To say that someone has done wrong; to find wrong in something

Lesson 2
Patron A wealthy person who supports artists

Sculptor A person who makes statues out of wood, stone, marble, or other material

Architect A person who draws plans for buildings

Masterpiece A piece of art that seems almost perfect

Lesson 3
Astronomer A person who keeps track of the sun, the planets, and the stars

Theory An explanation of how and why something happens, usually based on scientific study

Lesson 5
Reformation A movement that challenged and changed the Catholic religion in Europe

Authority Power

Lutheranism The religious movement founded by Martin Luther

Protestant A reformer who protested against the Catholic Church

Inquisition A special court set up by the Roman Catholic Church to question the beliefs of people to see if they were heretics

Heretic A person who is against the teachings of a church

Lesson 6
Counter-Reformation The Catholic Church's reforms that attempted to fight Protestant beliefs

Ask:

- How did religion change in the time leading up to the Renaissance? (The Roman Catholic Church and Islam attracted more and more people. They controlled larger areas and became more powerful.)
- What questions did scientists and artists begin to consider during the Renaissance? (They questioned their relationship to religion and the power that came with it.)

Reading Strategy:
Inferencing

Tell students that when they make an inference, they consider the material they have read and think about what else they can figure out based on that information. Tell them that sometimes making an inference is called "reading between the lines," because a reader interprets a meaning that is not spelled out in words.

Ask:

- How does making an inference help you when you are reading? (It can help you figure out what the text means.)

Key Vocabulary Words

Point out that these chapter words are presented in the order they appear in each lesson. They are also found in the glossary.

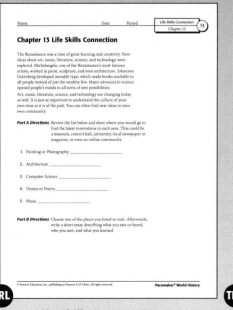

LIFE SKILLS CONNECTION

Students discuss the importance of learning and creativity in the Renaissance. They learn to explore the new ideas in their own communities. Help direct students to appropriate local cultural events they may not be aware of.

KEY VOCABULARY

In Part A, students circle the letter that correctly defines each word. In Part B, students match the definition to the correct word.

Lesson at a Glance

Chapter 13 Lesson 1

Overview This lesson describes the early days of the Renaissance and the beliefs of humanism.

Objectives

- To explain what the word *Renaissance* means
- To explain what the term *humanism* means

Student Pages 258–260

Teacher's Resource Library **TRL**

Workbook Activity 48

Activity 48

Modified Activity 48

....

Vocabulary

criticize   renaissance
humanism

On the board, write each vocabulary word with the letters scrambled. Have a volunteer read a definition aloud and ask another volunteer to unscramble the letters of the matching word. Continue until all words have been unscrambled.

PRONUNCIATION GUIDE

Use this list to help students pronounce difficult words in this lesson.

Renaissance (ren´ə säns)

1   Warm-Up Activity

Explain to students that the Renaissance was a time when Europeans realized that humans had a lot to offer to the world, so they should learn as much as possible. Have students make a list of different opportunities for learning that they have available today. Explain that the learning opportunities include more than just school. They can include athletics, art, music, etc. Then have students choose one learning opportunity from the list that they have never tried before. Have students explain why they are interested in that learning opportunity.

258   *Unit 5   The Renaissance*

LESSON 13-1

A Time of New Ideas

Objectives

- To explain what the word *Renaissance* means
- To explain what the term *humanism* means

Renaissance
The revival of art, literature, and learning in Europe in the 14th through 16th centuries

Humanism
A concern with the needs and interests of human beings rather than religious ideas

 History Fact
The Renaissance was a period of great thinking. The Renaissance lasted about 200 years.

During the Middle Ages, the culture and learning of the Greeks and Romans were all but forgotten. For most people it was as if Greece and Rome had never existed. For this reason, the Middle Ages, especially the early part, is sometimes called the Dark Ages.

Were the Middle Ages Really "Dark"?

During the Middle Ages, Christianity united the people of Western Europe. This was not, however, a Dark Age. Great universities were founded. Immense cathedrals were built. Toward the end of the Middle Ages, around A.D. 1300, trade and travel increased. New ideas exploded throughout Europe. The period after the Middle Ages became known as the **Renaissance.** *Renaissance* means "rebirth" or "awakening."

What New Ideas Sprang from the Renaissance?

The Renaissance was a time of new ideas. During the Middle Ages the Catholic Church was all-powerful. Thinking centered on God. Most well-educated people, or scholars, were also people of the church. During the Renaissance, people began to think about themselves as well as about God. People used to worry about whether or not they would go to heaven after they died. Now they thought more about making a good life on Earth. This new belief in the importance of human beings became known as **humanism.** The spirit of humanism sparked new ideas in art, science, literature, and philosophy.

---

2   Teaching the Lesson

Have students read pages 258–259 to learn about the early days of the Renaissance and humanism. Then ask students to think about humanists like Erasmus who questioned the church. Point out that such criticism was just one of the new ideas that emerged during the Renaissance.

Ask:

- What happened throughout Europe toward the end of the Middle Ages? (New ideas exploded throughout Europe.)

- What did Erasmus decide about the church? (The church was more concerned with wealth and power than helping people.)
- How did Erasmus spread his beliefs? (He wrote books.)

 History Fact
Renaissance thinkers wanted to emulate the values of classical times as expressed in classical literature, history, and philosophy. They tried to distance themselves from works written during the Middle Ages. They looked on this period negatively.

Criticize
To say that someone has done wrong; to find wrong in something

Who Were the Humanists?

Humanists began to question the church and its leaders. A Dutch scholar, Erasmus, eyed the church critically.

"It seems," Erasmus decided, "that the church is more concerned with wealth and power than with helping men find God."

Erasmus wrote books that questioned the church's practices. He believed that simple ways were best. There was too much ritual and ceremony in the church, he said. Erasmus was a humanist. He believed that if people were just shown what was right, they would live that way. Erasmus was among the first Renaissance scholars to **criticize**, or speak out against, the church. However, he certainly was not the last.

Reading Strategy:
Inferencing

After reading this lesson, what inferences can you make about the Renaissance?

1400–1600   *New Ideas: The Renaissance*   Chapter 13   **259**

Reading Strategy:
Inferencing

Have students reread the last sentence on page 259. Ask students what they can infer about future criticism against the church based on this sentence. They may say that people would criticize the church.

Background Information

Erasmus was sent to the school of a celebrated humanist when he was nine years old. His interest in humanism awakened. When Erasmus was 13 years old, his mother died. His father died a short time later. Erasmus was sent to a monastery school by his guardians. A few years later, Erasmus entered the monastery. He never felt a true religious vocation, he simply had nowhere else to go. Erasmus later described this turn of events as the "greatest misfortune" of his life. However, the benefit of the monastery was that Erasmus was free to pursue his studies. He devoted himself to the ancient classics.

LEARNING STYLES

Logical/Mathematical
Review with students the cultural achievements of the Middle Ages discussed on page 258. Then have students evaluate the claim that the Middle Ages were not a Dark Age. Does the evidence on page 258 support or refute that claim? Is it accurate to describe this period immediately following the Middle Ages as a renaissance, or rebirth? (Answers will vary; students may say that the term *renaissance*, or rebirth, is inaccurate because learning never stopped during the Middle Ages.)

ELL/ESL STRATEGY

Language Objective:
To identify and use the suffix –ism

Explain to students that a suffix is an ending that is added to the end of a word to give the word a new meaning. On page 258, the word *humanism* is introduced. Write *humanism* on the board. Then write *human + ism* on the board. Then write a definition for human on the board, such as "A human is a person." Write a definition for *–ism* on the board, such as, "An *–ism* is an attitude or a belief." Explain that when you put *human* and *–ism* together, you get a new word that means, "A belief that human actions, ideas, and works are important." Have students think of other suffixes that are added to the ends of words and discuss how those suffixes change the meanings of the root words.

New Ideas Chapter 13   **259**

COMMON ERROR

Students may be familiar with the word *practice* used as a verb, meaning "to train or drill." Point out that in the phrase *church's practices*, the word *practice* is used as a noun, meaning "a custom of the church."

CHAPTER PROJECT

Have pairs of students choose one artist, writer, leader, or historian from the Renaissance to research. Students can use reliable Internet and library sources to do their research. Have students prepare a presentation on their historical figure. The presentations should include visual aids, and should add to the knowledge presented in the textbook about each individual.

Lesson 13–1 Review Answers

1. C **2.** D **3.** B **4.** B **5.** A **6.** C **7.** A
8. Great universities were founded. Christianity united the people of Western Europe. Large cathedrals were built. **9.** Renaissance means "rebirth" or "awakening." The Renaissance period is the revival of art, literature, and learning in Europe in the 14th through 16th centuries. **10.** Humanism is a concern with the needs and interests of human beings rather than religious ideas.

LESSON 13-1 REVIEW

On a sheet of paper, write the letter of the answer that correctly completes each sentence.

1. The culture and learning of the Greeks and _____ seemed forgotten during the Middle Ages.

  A Macedonians   **B** Babylonians   **C** Romans   **D** Persians

2. During the Middle Ages, _____ united the people of Western Europe.

  A art   **B** literature   **C** philosophy   **D** Christianity

3. The period after the Middle Ages is known as _____.

  A humanism   **C** the Dark Ages
  B the Renaissance   **D** the Scientific Revolution

4. The Renaissance lasted about _____ years.

  A 100   **B** 200   **C** 1,300   **D** 1,500

5. During the Middle Ages, most scholars were _____.

  A people of the church   **C** knights
  B nobles   **D** kings

6. The Dutch scholar _____ questioned the church's practices.

  A Michelangelo   **B** Gutenberg   **C** Erasmus   **D** Galileo

7. The spirit of _____ sparked new ideas in art, science, literature, and philosophy.

  A humanism   **C** the Middle Ages
  B the Renaissance   **D** the Dark Ages

On a sheet of paper, write the answer to each question. Use complete sentences.

8. Why were the Dark Ages not a "Dark Age"?

9. What does the word *Renaissance* mean? What is the "Renaissance period"?

10. What does the term *humanism* mean?

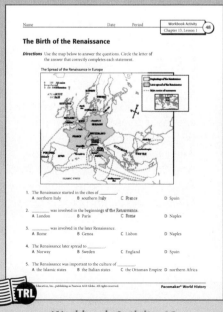

Renaissance Art

Objectives

■ To compare and contrast art of the Middle Ages with that of the Renaissance

■ To name three famous works of art crafted by Michelangelo

Reading Strategy: Inferencing

What do you already know about the cultures of ancient Greece and Rome?

Patron

A wealthy person who supports artists

History Fact
The spirit of humanism led Renaissance artists to make the people in their pictures lifelike.

The Renaissance began in Italy. Then it spread northwest across Europe. More and more people began to appreciate beautiful things. The work of Italian craftworkers became fine. People thought of it as art. Europeans showed a new interest in the civilizations of ancient Greece and Rome.

"Perhaps," people said, "that is when civilization was at its best!"

"Look at the art that came out of Greece," they said. "Look at the beautiful statues and the paintings. Look at the fine architecture of the Romans." At first Italian artists tried to copy the work of the ancient Greeks and Romans. Then they began to improve on it.

How Was Art During the Renaissance Different from Art During the Middle Ages?

During the Middle Ages, most paintings were of religious scenes. The people in these pictures were not very lifelike. Renaissance artists studied the human form. They tried to make the people in their pictures look more like real people. For the first time, artists used live models.

Craftworkers could make a good living from their work. It was harder for artists to earn a steady wage. Wealthy Italians served as **patrons** for promising young artists. A patron provided food, housing, and enough money for the artist to live on. Because of their patrons, artists were able to work and study to improve. Some of the world's finest artists lived during the Renaissance.

Lesson at a Glance

Chapter 13 Lesson 2

Overview This lesson describes the style of art that emerged during the Renaissance and the works of Michelangelo.

Objectives

■ To compare and contrast art of the Middle Ages with that of the Renaissance

■ To name three famous works of art crafted by Michelangelo

Student Pages 261–263

Teacher's Resource Library **TRL**

Workbook Activity 49

Activity 49

Modified Activity 49

Vocabulary

architect   patron
masterpiece   sculptor

Have students draw two columns on a sheet of paper. In the left-hand column, they should write the vocabulary words. In the right-hand column, they should write the definitions in random order. Have students exchange papers and match each word to its definition.

PRONUNCIATION GUIDE

Use this list to help students pronounce difficult words in this lesson.

Pietà (pyā tä′)

1 | Warm-Up Activity

Have students discuss their favorite types of art. Write the types of art on the board. Ask students to name artists they know who specialize in painting, sculpting, cartooning, or digital animation. Tell them they will be reading about an artist of the Renaissance who was a painter, sculptor, and architect. He is still so well known that people call him by his first name—Michelangelo.

2 | Teaching the Lesson

Review the meaning of *masterpiece*. Then have students read pages 261–263 to find out how art changed during the Renaissance. Tell students to take note of descriptions of the masterpieces created by Michelangelo that are described in this lesson.

Ask:

● Who was Michelangelo's patron? (Lorenzo de' Medici)

● How did patrons support the arts? (Patrons provided artists with food, housing, and enough money to live on. The artists could then work and study.)

● What do you think is Michelangelo's greatest work of art? (Answers will vary. Students should be able to provide an explanation of their choice.)

Reading Strategy: Inferencing

Have students share any background knowledge they might have about the ancient cultures of Greece and Rome.

History Fact

Renaissance painters studied mathematic ideas and observed the principles of natural light to portray realistic perspective in their paintings.

Background Information

Over the course of 500 years, a layer of soot and grime accumulated on the ceiling of the Sistine Chapel. Michelangelo's colorful frescoes were reduced to drab grays, obscuring many details of the paintings. In the early 1980s, the Vatican began what would become a 10-year restoration project. Sitting atop of scaffolding that reached all the way to the ceiling, conservators carefully applied a special cleaning paste. After the paste dried and the powder was brushed off, the fine details and bright colors that Michelangelo had painted were revealed.

LEARNING STYLES

Body/Kinesthetic

Have students tape a large piece of paper to the bottom of their desk. Provide watercolors or tempera paints and brushes. Have students lie underneath their desks and create a painting. Allow about 20 minutes for this activity. When students have finished, remind them that Michelangelo spent four years painting the Sistine Chapel lying on his back. Have students discuss their experience painting "upside down." Ask them to compare what they did to what Michelangelo accomplished. Have them draw conclusions about how four years of painting the ceiling might have affected Michelangelo's arms, back, and eyesight.

IN THE COMMUNITY

Working individually or with a partner, have students go on an "art treasure hunt," searching for examples of art in their community. Possibilities include sculptures, murals, and carvings. If possible, invite students to photograph what they find and organize the photos into an album or in a computer presentation. Otherwise, students might wish to write a description of the art and note its location in the community.

Sculptor
A person who makes statues out of wood, stone, marble, or other material

Architect
A person who draws plans for buildings

Sculpture
A carving from stone or other hard material

Masterpiece
A piece of art that seems almost perfect

Who Was Michelangelo Buonarroti?

One of the most famous artists of the Italian Renaissance was Michelangelo Buonarroti. During the Renaissance, people were encouraged to be good at many things. Michelangelo, in true Renaissance spirit, was more than just a fine painter. He was also a **sculptor,** a poet, and an **architect.**

Michelangelo earned his greatest fame for his **sculptures,** the carvings he made from stone. He studied the human body. He studied the human form at work and at rest. Michelangelo even studied dead bodies. This helped him understand the lines of bone and muscle. His sculptures seem alive and real. Each muscle is perfect. Each position is totally lifelike.

Michelangelo was born in 1475 in a mountain town in Italy. He began showing artistic talent as a young boy. A wealthy Italian, Lorenzo de' Medici, noticed Michelangelo's brilliance. He became Michelangelo's patron.

At age 24 Michelangelo created his first **masterpiece,** a huge statue called the *Pietà.* Michelangelo sculpted it for St. Peter's Church in Rome. In the *Pietà,* the body of Christ is shown held in his mother's arms. The word *Pietà* came from the Italian word for "pity."

Michelangelo's statue *David* is another of his most famous works. Completed in 1504, it is a perfect example of the Renaissance interest in the human form. "David" is strong and looks alive. The statue is 18 feet high and made of solid marble. Michelangelo's *David* is quite heavy. It took 40 men to move it from the workshop to a central square in Florence, Italy.

ELL/ESL STRATEGY

Language Objective:
To summarize information in texts

Explain to students that one of the best ways to make sure you remember information in text is to summarize it. Many students learning English may not be familiar with the idea of summarizing. Explain that summarizing means to tell the most important ideas about something you know. You can demonstrate how to summarize text by using the text on Michelangelo's sculptures and painting of the Sistine Chapel on pages 262–263. Read this text aloud. After each paragraph, pause and think aloud about the most important information in the paragraph. You may want to write that information on the board. After reading all of the paragraphs, write a short summary on the board. Take suggestions from students that are appropriate. Point out to students that your summary includes only the most important information from the paragraphs.

Pope Julius II hired Michelangelo to paint the ceiling of the Sistine Chapel in Rome. Michelangelo painted a series of pictures showing events in the Bible. Over 300 figures from the Bible appear on the 60-foot-high chapel ceiling. Michelangelo had to paint the scenes lying on his back. He laid on a platform held by ropes. He worked on that ceiling for four years.

Reading Strategy:
Inferencing

How did what you know about Greece and Rome add to what you have just read?

Later in his life, Michelangelo turned to architecture. He worked on the rebuilding of St. Peter's Church. He took no pay. He believed it was a task that would please God.

Michelangelo died when he was 90. He had lived a long life, sculpting, painting, and building. His art brought light and beauty to all of Europe.

One of Michelangelo's most famous works is the sculpture, Pietà.

Reading Strategy:
Inferencing

Have students share examples of how their prior knowledge of ancient Greece and Rome helped them better understand the text.

3 Reinforce and Extend

STUDY SKILLS

 Have students use reference sources such as books, encyclopedias, and the Internet to find information about one of these people from the Renaissance:

Shakespeare	Donatello
Cervantes	Michelangelo
Leonardo	Raphael

Ask students to write three facts about the work of the person they chose. Then compile a master list of all the facts about each person. Discuss similarities and differences between each artist.

COMMON ERROR

 Students sometimes confuse the words *sculptor* and *sculpture*. Write the words *sculptor* and *sculpture* on the board. Say the words and have students repeat them. Explain that a *sculptor* is one who sculpts, and the *sculpture* is what is created. Ask students to share ideas they have about how to remember the difference between the two words.

WORLD CULTURES

Today, Florence thrives on its Renaissance past and remains one of the world's leading cultural centers. Students come to the city to study at the University of Florence, the Academy of Fine Arts, or the Conservatory of Music. Native Florentines and tourists alike enjoy operas in the city's famous opera houses. Florence is also home to the Biblioteca Laurenziana, a library that dates back over 400 years and contains many important ancient texts. Many Florentines do the same work people did during the Renaissance—making and selling handicrafts such as pottery, straw products, and jewelry.

Lesson 13–2 Review Answers

1. D **2.** B **3.** A **4.** B **5.** C **6.** The Renaissance began in Italy. It spread northwest across Europe. **7.** The spirit of humanism made Renaissance artists want to make people look lifelike. **8.** Most art during the Middle Ages was paintings of religious scenes. The people in the pictures were not very lifelike. Renaissance artists studied the human form. They tried to make the people in their pictures look more like real people. **9.** A patron provided food, housing, and enough money to live on. **10.** Michelangelo crafted the *Pietà*, *David*, and the ceiling of the Sistine Chapel.

On a sheet of paper, write the letter of the answer that correctly completes each sentence.

1. Michelangelo was a fine painter, _____, poet, and architect.

  A engineer   **B** scientist   **C** explorer   **D** sculptor

2. Michelangelo studied _____, which helped to make his art so lifelike.

  A Middle Age art   **C** math books
  B the human body   **D** buildings

3. Lorenzo de' Medici, a wealthy Italian, noted young Michelangelo's artistic brilliance and became his _____.

  A patron   **B** scholar   **C** apprentice   **D** master

4. Michelangelo worked on _____ for four years.

  A *David*   **C** St. Peter's Church
  B the Sistine Chapel   **D** *Pietà*

5. Later in life, Michelangelo accepted no money when he worked to rebuild _____.

  A *David*   **C** St. Peter's Church
  B the Sistine Chapel   **D** *Pietà*

On a sheet of paper, write the answer to each question. Use complete sentences.

6. Where did the Renaissance begin and where did it spread to?

7. What led Renaissance artists to make the people in their art so lifelike?

8. Compare and contrast art in the Middle Ages with that of the Renaissance.

9. What is the role of a patron?

10. What are three famous works of art crafted by Michelangelo?

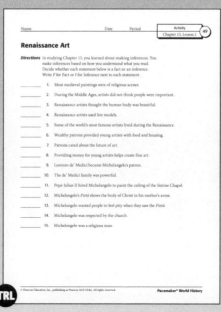

Activity 49

Workbook Activity 49

LESSON 13-3

Advances in Knowledge, Technology, and Science

Objectives

- To tell how the invention of movable type helped the spread of knowledge
- To tell about four other inventions that were discovered during the Renaissance
- To name four important people of the Renaissance
- To explain why Galileo was in trouble with the church

Reading Strategy: Inferencing

What can you infer about people's decision to learn how to read at this time?

Remember
Latin, the language of ancient Rome, became the language of the church. Rome was the first place that made Christianity its official religion.

All writing was done by hand during the Middle Ages. Books were copied on parchment made of animal skin. Therefore, books were beautiful, but they were also expensive and few in number. Only wealthy people could buy books of their own. Most books were written in Latin, the language of the church. The only scholars were clergy. The church was the main place where studying went on. The church controlled all learning.

Then things started to change.

How Did the Printing Press Help the Spread of Knowledge?

About 1450, secrets of making paper were brought to Europe from China. They were introduced by the Moors, or Spanish Muslims. Then a new invention eventually made books available to everyone! A German printer named Johannes Gutenberg discovered how to use movable type for printing.

With movable type, letters were molded onto small metal blocks. The letters could be moved around to spell different words. When inked and pressed onto paper, the movable type printed a whole page at one time.

Now books could be made quickly at low cost. Now many people could read the stories of the Greeks and Romans and tales of travel. The ideas of the past and the present were widely available. Books were translated into the languages of the common people, not just that of Latin scholars.

1400–1600   *New Ideas: The Renaissance*   Chapter 13   **265**

---

2 Teaching the Lesson

Set up a modern-day reenactment of Galileo's trial in front of church officials. Possible roles include Galileo, his lawyer, representatives from the church, lawyers for the church, a judge, a jury, and television reporters.

Ask:

- What new tool did Galileo use to make discoveries? (telescope)
- Did Galileo agree or disagree with Copernicus's theory? (He agreed.)
- Why did church authorities put Galileo on trial? (They saw his theories as an attack on church teachings.)

Reading Strategy: Inferencing

Have students infer that because books were more readily available after the invention of movable type, more people were able to learn how to read.

Remember
Point out that Latin is not a spoken language today. However, people still study Latin and translate ancient texts that were written in Latin. Many English root words, suffixes, and prefixes come from Latin.

Lesson at a Glance

Chapter 13 Lesson 3

Overview This lesson explains how the printing press, the telescope, and other inventions influenced progress in knowledge, technology, and science during the Renaissance.

Objectives

- To tell how the invention of movable type helped the spread of knowledge
- To tell about four other inventions that were discovered during the Renaissance
- To name four important people of the Renaissance
- To explain why Galileo was in trouble with the church

Student Pages 265–270

Teacher's Resource Library

Workbook Activity 50

Activity 50

Modified Activity 50

....

Vocabulary

astronomer
theory

Have students work in pairs. One student should read the definition of a vocabulary word and the other student should identify the word that matches the definition. After the words are identified, have students reverse roles and repeat this process.

1 Warm-Up Activity

Have a student stand in the center of the room. Have other students make a circle around the center student. Explain that the other students represent planets and the sun, while the student in the center represents Earth. Explain that long ago scientists believed all other planets and suns revolved around Earth. Have the student representing Earth remain stationary while the students in the circle revolve around him or her. Allow time for comments and discussion.

New Ideas Chapter 13   **265**

History Fact

Gutenberg printed 165 copies of the *Bible*, which was also called the *42-line Bible* for the number of lines on each page. Today, only 48 copies of *Gutenberg's Bible* exist.

Background Information

Galileo was born in 1564, in Pisa, Italy. Galileo went to school to become a doctor, but he switched to study math. Galileo's scientific methods were different from those of other scientists. He was often willing to change his views according to observations he made. The church condemned Galileo for proposing scientific theories that conflicted with church teachings. Galileo was forced to spend the end of his life on house arrest in Florence, where he went blind and died of natural causes in 1642. Almost 100 years after his death, Pope Benedict XIV allowed the publication of all Galileo's scientific works.

LEARNING STYLES

Visual/Spatial

Have students visit the science lab in school and have them view prepared slides under the microscope. Ask them to draw pictures of what they see. Tell them that they are scientists viewing these slides under one of the first microscopes. Have students discuss their drawings and what it would be like to be a Renaissance scientist discovering the world of "tiny creatures." What questions would the scientists have had about their observations? How would they feel about their discoveries? Have students discuss their ideas with a partner.

History Fact

The famous *Gutenberg Bible* was not discovered until 1760. It was found in Paris.

With the *Gutenberg Bible* Europeans could read the Bible for themselves. People did not have to rely on the church to tell them what the Bible said. The Bible was translated into English, Italian, French, and German.

It became important to be able to read. More schools opened. Schools that taught Greek and Latin grammar were called "grammar" schools. There were new universities. Studies went beyond religious thought. People studied the world. They also studied about their own place in the world.

What Were Some Other Inventions?

The Renaissance was a time for progress. There were some important changes during the Middle Ages. However, change had come slowly. Now new books—and new ideas—were available for anyone who could read. Universities were growing. With the spirit of the Renaissance, change came rapidly.

People explored new ideas. Gutenberg's printing press was just one of the new inventions. Inventors discovered how to make springs. Then they made watches that were small enough to be carried in a pocket. Before, the only clocks had been huge ones on public buildings. Now people could keep time at home.

New instruments helped sailors find their way on the open seas. New maps improved travel. People experimented with metals. Soon they came up with cast iron to replace expensive bronze.

In medicine, the English doctor William Harvey discovered that the heart pumps blood throughout the body. Around 1600, the microscope was invented. It led to a new look at the world. Suddenly people learned that there were tiny creatures—smaller than the eye could see!

Words from the Past

Newspapers Are Born

When Gutenberg invented movable metal type in the 15th century, printing became easier and cheaper. As a result, newspapers were born. Their purpose was to report news and information to people.

Early newspapers were small. They looked like newsletters. Papers usually consisted of one page. They were published weekly, not daily.

The first known newspaper started in Germany in 1609. It told about events in other countries. The first London paper began in 1622. Then in 1665, The *London News Gazette* started. It was published on a regular basis in newspaper format. The *Boston News-Letter* was the first continuously published American newspaper. It began in 1704. Like papers today, it had news about money and other countries. It also recorded births, deaths, and social events.

Give students time to silently read "Newspapers Are Born." Then ask a volunteer to read it aloud.

Ask:

- What invention made printing easier and cheaper? (movable metal type)
- What were early newspapers like? (one page in length; published weekly)
- Where and when did the first known newspaper start? (Germany; 1609)
- What kind of information did the *Boston News-Letter* contain? (news about money and other countries, births, deaths, and social events)

ELL/ESL STRATEGY

Language Objective: *To write the definitions of words from the lesson*

Have students find the terms *universe* and *heavens* in the lesson. Then have them write sentences that correctly use the words. Have students trade papers and discuss their definitions. After papers are returned to their owners, invite students to read their sentences aloud. Talk about the different definitions offered by students.

Reading Strategy:
Inferencing

Have students share any background knowledge they might have about astronomy. Point out that scientists continue to research and make new discoveries about the universe.

You Decide

Ask students to discuss why people were not willing to believe Copernicus. Answers may include the idea that people believed that their planet must be the center of the universe because they trusted the teachings of the church.

3   Reinforce and Extend

COMMON ERROR

Direct students' attention to the second sentence in the first paragraph on the page that defines *astronomy* as the study of the stars, planets, and other heavenly bodies. Explain that *astrology* is the study of interpreting the influence of stars and planets on human affairs. Tell students that astronomy is a recognized science, but astrology is not a recognized science.

TEACHER ALERT

You may want to save old newspapers or have students bring newspapers to school and incorporate them into the discussion of the newspaper activities. Not all students may be familiar with the local newspaper and its sections.

Astronomer
A person who keeps track of the sun, the planets, and the stars

Theory
An explanation of how and why something happens, usually based on scientific study

Reading Strategy:
Inferencing

What do you already know about the beginnings of the study of astronomy?

You Decide

Why do you think people were not willing to believe Copernicus?

What Did Scientists Suggest Was at the Center of the Universe?

Some of the greatest scientific discoveries of the Renaissance came in the field of astronomy. Astronomy is the study of the stars, planets, and other heavenly bodies. These new ideas changed people's thinking in many ways. Not only were there new ideas about the way the earth and stars moved. Now there was also a new way of seeing humanity's place in the whole system. These ideas shook up the scientific world as well as the church.

For hundreds of years people had believed that the earth was the center of the universe. They believed that the sun, moon, and stars all moved around the earth. Then, in 1543, the Polish **astronomer** Nicolaus Copernicus wrote a book. He said that the planets, including the earth, revolve around the sun.

Most people would not believe him!

Who Was Galileo Galilei?

The invention of the telescope challenged more old ideas. Now scientists could get a better look at the sky. An Italian scientist, Galileo Galilei, took up where Copernicus had left off. Galileo was born in Pisa in 1564. He made his first important scientific discovery at the age of 20. Galileo watched a great lamp swing from the ceiling of the cathedral in Pisa. Then he came up with the idea of the pendulum. A pendulum is a weight hung so that it swings freely back and forth.

Later, he discovered the "law of falling bodies." Galileo found that gravity pulls all bodies to the earth at the same speed, no matter what their weight. Galileo climbed to the top of the Leaning Tower of Pisa to prove his **theory.** Then he dropped a ten-pound weight and a one-pound weight. He showed that they both hit the ground at the same time.

Some people were angry. They were shocked that Galileo would dare to challenge the ideas of the wise Greek, Aristotle. Galileo's discoveries would bring him a lot of angry words.

The invention of the telescope brought another breakthrough. Galileo was not its inventor, but he was the first to use the telescope to study the heavens. With his telescope, Galileo discovered that the moon did not have its own light. It reflected light. He discovered moons around Jupiter and the mass of stars in the Milky Way. All of Galileo's discoveries led him to support Copernicus's theory. The earth was not the center of the universe. The earth was just another planet revolving around the sun!

No matter how well Galileo proved his theory, the church would not hear of it. Church members were ordered not to read Galileo's books. The church sent Galileo warnings. He was not to teach his theories. In 1632, Galileo was called to a church hearing. There was a long trial. Galileo had to promise that he would give up his belief in Copernicus's theory. The church forced him to say that the earth was the center of the universe. Church officials watched Galileo closely for the rest of his life. He became a prisoner in his own home.

Galileo first used the telescope to search the night sky. His discoveries changed the way people thought about the universe.

CAREER CONNECTION

Students interested in astronomy should take plenty of math and physical science courses in high school. To become a professional astronomer, students should major in astronomy or physics in college and then complete a PhD program. Some astronomers teach at colleges or universities while others conduct research at private or public institutions. Students might want to contact the American Astronomical Society to find out more about careers in astronomy.

AT HOME

Have students compare the contents of early newspapers to those of modern newspapers. At home, have them examine a newspaper and list its different content features. (Possibilities include local, national, and international news, sports, comics, weather, classified ads, horoscopes, and so on.) Which features also appeared in early newspapers? (news) Ask students why they think today's newspapers contain so many different features. (Answers will vary. Students may say that newspaper publishers want to appeal to as many people as possible so they can sell more newspapers.)

ONLINE CONNECTION

Students can gain additional information by accessing the following Web site: www.agsglobepmwh.com/page269 (This Web site gives information about the discoveries of William Harvey and his studies of the circulatory system.)

Match the description in Column A with the inventor/scientist in Column B. Write the correct letter on a sheet of paper.

Column A

1. invented the microscope

2. wrote a book that said the planets revolve around the Sun

3. the inventor of the printing press

4. a scientist who came up with ideas about gravity and the pendulum

Column B

A Nicolaus Copernicus
B Galileo Galilei
C Johannes Gutenberg
D William Harvey

On a sheet of paper, write the letter of the answer that correctly completes each sentence.

5. The Renaissance was a time for _____.

   A self-reflection   **C** religious worship
   B progress   **D** advancements in farming

6. Many of the greatest scientific studies during the Renaissance came in the field of _____. This is the study of stars, planets, and other heavenly bodies.

   A astronomy   **B** the human body   **C** engineering   **D** humanism

7. People were angry that Galileo would challenge the ideas of _____.

   A Copernicus   **B** Michelangelo   **C** William Harvey   **D** Aristotle

On a sheet of paper, write the answer to each question. Use complete sentences.

8. How did movable type help the spread of knowledge?

9. What are four other inventions, besides the printing press, that were discovered during the Renaissance?

10. Why was Galileo in trouble with the church?

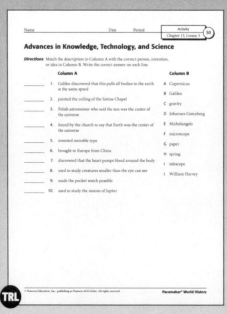

The Renaissance Man

Objectives

■ To explain the ways in which Leonardo da Vinci is a Renaissance Man

■ To name three things Leonardo da Vinci is famous for

The great artists, writers, and scientists of the Renaissance had many kinds of knowledge, talents, and skills. Michelangelo could paint, sculpt, write poetry, and build. Galileo studied medicine, physics, and astronomy.

Today we think of a Renaissance man as one who was expected to enjoy art, to write poetry, and to play a musical instrument. Renaissance education taught people to read and write Latin and to speak several other languages. People were expected to understand the politics of the day. They were supposed to ride well on horseback and to be good at sports.

A Renaissance man should be able to put up a good fight if necessary. A Renaissance man also had to learn proper manners of courtesy and grace. Great importance was placed on being well educated and well rounded. A perfect example of a Renaissance man was Leonardo da Vinci.

Who Was Leonardo da Vinci?

A list of what Leonardo da Vinci could not do would likely be shorter than a list of what he could do! Italian-born Leonardo was a Renaissance genius in not one field, but many. He was one of the world's greatest artists and scientists. Leonardo was a painter, a sculptor, an architect, and a musician. He was an inventor, an astronomer, and a geologist (he studied the history of the earth). He was one of the first to show an interest in "flying machines."

Leonardo's sketchbooks show drawings of many different machines. His ideas for flying machines were based on the flight of birds. These sketches also show great understanding of the human body and of engineering.

Leonardo da Vinci's sketchbook contains his ideas for machines. Da Vinci was one of the greatest inventors of all time.

1400–1600

New Ideas: The Renaissance Chapter 13 **271**

Chapter 13 Lesson 4

Overview This lesson describes the qualities of a Renaissance man and the talents and accomplishments of Leonardo da Vinci.

Objectives

■ To explain the ways in which Leonardo da Vinci is a Renaissance Man

■ To name three things Leonardo da Vinci is famous for

Student Pages 271–273

Teacher's Resource Library

Workbook Activity 51

Activity 51

Modified Activity 51

PRONUNCIATION GUIDE

Use this list to help students pronounce difficult words in this lesson.

da Vinci (də vin´chē)

---

1 Warm-Up Activity

Display the *Mona Lisa* and other paintings and sketches by Leonardo da Vinci. Ask students to discuss what the paintings and drawings have in common. Then tell students they were all created by the same artist. Write *Leonardo da Vinci* on the board. Tell students that they will read more about Leonardo in this lesson.

2 Teaching the Lesson

Ask students who invented the airplane and when it was invented. (the Wright brothers; early 1900s) Students may be surprised to learn that the idea for the airplane actually dates back to the Renaissance. Have students read pages 271–272 to find out about the achievements and ideas of a true Renaissance man, Leonardo da Vinci.

Ask:

● What were some of the characteristics of a Renaissance man? (A Renaissance man was one who enjoyed art, wrote poetry, and played a musical instrument. He could read and write Latin and speak several other languages. He could understand politics, ride on horseback, and be good at sports. He could fight well and learn good manners.)

● What other things did Leonardo da Vinci do besides paint? (He was a sculptor, an architect, a musician, an inventor, an astronomer, and a geologist. He could draw and he was an engineer.)

● How did Leonardo da Vinci use one talent to benefit another? (His scientific studies helped him understand people and world. This made his paintings seem more real.)

Background Information

Mystery surrounds the Mona Lisa. Who is she? Why is she smiling? Today, she is the most recognized woman on every continent. She is nearly 500 years old and still considered beautiful. Mona Lisa did not actually get her name until the 19th century. Italians have always called her by her original name *La Gioconda*, meaning "the playful one." There are many stories about her identity. Some people say she is the wife of a Florence businessman or a young widow. Other people say that da Vinci painted himself as a woman. The reason she smiles is also a mystery. These unsolved riddles only add to the popularity of this famous portrait.

Reading Strategy:
Inferencing

Students may infer that Leonardo da Vinci's talents were in great demand, since he worked for the Duke of Milan, the government of Florence, and then later for King Francis I. Students may also infer that Leonardo da Vinci's talents were valued by royalty and people in power.

TECHNOLOGY CONNECTION

Have students work in groups to look up pictures on the Internet of the first parachutes. Suggest that students search under "Louis Sebastien Lenormand" and "parachute" to find information on the parachute, its inventors, and the first jumps ever attempted.

The Mona Lisa *by Leonardo da Vinci.*

Reading Strategy:
Inferencing

After reading this section, what inferences can you make about Leonardo's contributions? What words helped you make your inference?

Leonardo had a sure sense of the way things worked. He understood the way parts joined together to form a whole. This great knowledge helped make him such a good artist.

Leonardo's *Mona Lisa* is a painting of a woman with a mysterious smile. It is one of the world's most famous masterpieces. Today it hangs in the Louvre Museum in Paris, France.

For 17 years Leonardo served the Duke of Milan. He worked as a painter, a sculptor, and an engineer. He was then hired as a painter by the government of Florence. For the last two years of his life, he lived in France at the invitation of King Francis I.

Leonardo, the Renaissance man, used one talent to benefit another. His scientific studies helped him understand people and the world. This understanding made his paintings seem all the more real. He had a desire to know more about everything. It was curiosity like Leonardo's that made the Renaissance a time of new ideas and new inventions.

TECHNOLOGY CONNECTION

Parachutes

Leonardo da Vinci imagined and sketched the parachute in 1514. His design called for a stiff frame shaped like a pyramid. The frame was then covered with a cloth. The cloth was coated to prevent a lot of air from passing through it. In his notes he had said that with his design, a person could safely jump from any height. Da Vinci also had thoughts about flight. Da Vinci's ideas are considered to have come about 400 years "ahead of their time."

A Croatian named Faust Vrancic built a device based on da Vinci's drawing. He jumped from a Venice tower using the parachute in 1617. A French physicist named Louis Sebastien Lenormand is usually credited for inventing the parachute. He made a successful jump from a Paris tower in 1783. Perhaps he gets noticed most often because he coined the word "parachute."

On a sheet of paper, write the answer to each question. Use complete sentences.

1. What is a Renaissance man?

2. Name a perfect example of a Renaissance man.

3. What fields did Leonardo da Vinci experiment in?

Word Bank

artist
Duke of Milan
France
Mona Lisa
painter
sketchbooks
talent

On a sheet of paper, write the word from the Word Bank to complete each sentence correctly.

4. Leonardo was such a great _____ because he understood the way things worked.

5. Leonardo's _____ had drawings for flying machines.

6. The _____ is the painting Leonardo is most famous for.

7. Leonardo served the _____ for 17 years as a painter, sculptor, and engineer.

8. He was also hired as a(n) _____ by the government of Florence.

9. Leonardo lived in _____ the last two years of his life.

10. As a Renaissance man, Leonardo used one _____ to benefit another.

---

3 Reinforce and Extend

COMMON ERROR

Students may confuse Leonardo da Vinci with Vincent van Gogh. Vincent van Gogh was a famous, post-impressionist artist who was born in the Netherlands. He painted about 300 years after da Vinci.

Lesson 13–4 Review Answers

1. A Renaissance man is well educated and well rounded. He enjoys art, writes poetry, and plays music. **2.** Leonardo da Vinci is a perfect example of a Renaissance man. **3.** Leonardo da Vinci was a painter, sculptor, musician, inventor, astronomer, and geologist. **4.** artist **5.** sketchbooks **6.** *Mona Lisa* **7.** Duke of Milan **8.** painter **9.** France **10.** talent

---

The Reformation

During the Middle Ages, most of the people in Western Europe were Roman Catholics. The Catholic Church held great power. It owned lands and collected taxes. Popes, bishops, and priests were wealthy men.

During the Renaissance, more people went to school and learned to read. They began to question many things, including the ways of the church.

Was it right for the clergy to be so interested in wealth? Was it right that church officials should have so much power? Some people also questioned the ceremonies and rituals that filled church services. They wondered what had become of the simple ways taught by Jesus.

The movement that questioned the practices of the Catholic Church was called the **Reformation**. Some Europeans set out to reform, or change, the church.

Who Was Martin Luther?

A German monk named Martin Luther became a leader among the reformers. Luther was born a German peasant. He grew up as a Roman Catholic. He studied at a university and became a monk. The more Luther studied religion, however, the more he worried. His concern was that the Catholic Church was headed in the wrong direction.

A person did not need fancy rituals or pilgrimages to find God, Luther said. He began to criticize the Catholic Church in public sermons. In 1517, Martin Luther wrote a list of 95 complaints about the church. He nailed it to the door of the Castle Church in Wittenberg, Germany.

Martin Luther led the Reformation that set out to change the Catholic Church.

Objectives
- To explain what the Reformation was
- To name two leaders of the Reformation
- To describe the Inquisition

Reformation
A movement that challenged and changed the Catholic religion in Europe

Chapter 13 Lesson 5

Overview This lesson describes Martin Luther's break from the Catholic Church and the resulting fractions known as the Reformation.

Objectives
- To explain what the Reformation was
- To name two leaders of the Reformation
- To describe the Inquisition

Student Pages 274–277

Teacher's Resource Library (TRL)

Workbook Activity 52

Activity 52

Modified Activity 52

Vocabulary
authority Lutheranism
heretic Protestant
Inquisition Reformation

Have students write a fill-in-the-blank sentence for each vocabulary word. Have volunteers write their sentences on the board. Have other students come to the board to fill in the blanks with the correct words.

1 Warm-Up Activity

Have students think about what they would do if leaders of their church or synagogue began doing things that they did not approve of or agree with. Ask how much they might be willing to accept before they objected. Ask what form their objections would take.

2 Teaching the Lesson

In this lesson, Martin Luther challenges the authority of the Catholic Church and starts a movement called the Reformation. Have students read pages 274–276 to find out how the church responded to the challenge.

Authority
Power; the right to tell someone what to do

Lutheranism
The religious movement founded by Martin Luther

Protestant
A reformer who protested against the Catholic Church

Reading Strategy:
Inferencing

What can you infer about the way different types of people reacted to Luther?

Luther continued to question church practices. In 1521, he spoke out against the power and **authority** granted the pope. This did not please the pope. Luther was told to recant, or take back, what he had said. Luther refused. He said that unless the Bible itself proved him wrong, he would not recant.

Luther was thrown out of the Catholic Church. Emperor Charles V declared Luther an outlaw. He said that anyone could kill Luther without punishment.

Several German princes supported Luther and his feelings about the church. One prince hid him in a castle. The church could not take him prisoner. Soon Luther had so many supporters that before long he was able to set up a whole new church.

The new church, based on Luther's ideas, simplified religion. Religious practices would be based on what was found in the Bible. In 1529, the Catholic Church declared that no one should practice **Lutheranism.** Lutheran princes decided to speak out, or protest. Because of this, they were called **Protestants.**

Other leaders across Europe also protested against Catholic practice. Other Protestant churches were started. The Reformation was under way.

What Was the Inquisition?

A man named John Calvin developed his own version of Protestantism in Switzerland, called Calvinism. He set up strict rules for Christians to live by. Calvin's teachings were followed in many parts of Europe.

Ask:

- Who was Martin Luther? (He was a German monk and a member of the Roman Catholic Church.)

- Why did Luther criticize the Catholic Church? (He believed that a person did not need fancy rituals or pilgrimages to find God.)

- How did Luther inform people about his beliefs? (He gave public sermons that criticized the Catholic Church. He wrote a list of 95 complaints that he nailed to the door of the Castle Church in Wittenberg, Germany.)

Background Information

Soon after 1517 and the beginning of the Protestant Reformation in Germany, the ideas of religious reform spread to France. French Protestants, called Huguenots, immediately were persecuted by the Catholic majority. In 1523, Jean Valliere was burned at the stake in Paris. He became the Huguenot's first martyr. Some Huguenots fled the persecution, many going to Strasbourg in Germany, which had been named a free city under the Holy Roman Empire. Among the Huguenot refugees in Strasbourg was John Calvin. Huguenot-Catholic conflicts continued until the French Revolution of 1789, when the National Assembly declared the principle of religious liberty.

Reading Strategy:
Inferencing

Students may infer that because Emperor Charles V declared Luther an outlaw, he was threatened by Luther's stand against the church. Students may also infer that German princes who supported Luther agreed with his beliefs.

History Fact
Queen Isabella and King Ferdinand of Spain authorized the expedition of Christopher Columbus. They are also the Catholic monarchs who established the Spanish Inquisition in 1478.

LEARNING STYLES

Auditory/Verbal
Have students act out the Inquisition. Ask volunteers to pose as members of the court. Have them ask questions to students who play the roles of heretics. After the role-play, have students discuss how people might have felt about being questioned on faith. Have them consider whether the experience would weaken or strengthen their faith.

ELL/ESL STRATEGY

Language Objective:
To understand how and why Luther wrote his 95 theses

Have ELL students choose a school or class rule that they don't think is fair. Possible examples could be not chewing gum in class, having to wear a school uniform, or not carrying a cell phone. Have students write a series of theses about the rule they have chosen. Each thesis should be a written statement that students can debate. Ask the student who wrote each thesis to lead a short class discussion in which both sides of the debate are heard.

Inquisition
A special court set up by the Roman Catholic Church to question the beliefs of people to see if they were heretics

Heretic
A person who is against the teachings of a church

History Fact
The Inquisition held secret trials, and people on trial were not told who their accusers were.

French Calvinists were called Huguenots. However, most French people were Catholic. They began to resent the Huguenots. On St. Bartholomew's Day, in August 1572, the Catholics carried out a plot. They murdered all the Protestants they could find in the city of Paris. The killing then spread throughout France. Thousands died during the next few days.

In Spain, the **Inquisition** was at work. The Inquisition was a special court set up by the Roman Catholic Church. Its purpose was to punish people who spoke out against the teachings of the church, or **heretics.** Besides Spain, the Inquisition was also going on in France, Germany, and Italy. The Inquisition hunted down anyone who was not a practicing Catholic. It forced people to confess their beliefs, often by torturing them. Some of those who would not accept the Catholic faith were burned to death.

---

3 Reinforce and Extend

COMMON ERROR

Draw a timeline on the board that extends from the 1500s through the 1900s. Write *Martin Luther* on the timeline at 1517. Write *Martin Luther King, Jr.* on the timeline at 1964, the year the Civil Rights Act passed. Explain that these two men both have similar names and fought for reform, but lived hundreds of years apart.

TEACHER ALERT

Some students may be sensitive to discussions about rejecting or questioning church teachings. Remind students that this chapter does not address today's beliefs. Instead, this chapter refers to the church of the past. Keep the discussion focused on history rather than any current religious controversy.

LESSON 13-5 REVIEW

On a sheet of paper, write the answer to each question. Use complete sentences.

1. What were Martin Luther's complaints about the church?

2. What happened in Paris on St. Bartholomew's Day in August 1572?

3. What is a heretic?

4. What was the Inquisition?

On a sheet of paper, write the letter of the answer that correctly completes each sentence.

5. As people became more educated during the Renaissance, they began to question many things. In particular, they questioned the ways of the _____.

A government   **B** church   **C** family   **D** universities

6. The movement that questioned the practices of the Catholic Church is known as _____.

A Protestants   **B** Lutheranism   **C** the Reformation   **D** Calvinism

7. Luther was thrown out of the Catholic Church and declared a(n) _____.

A pope   **B** monk   **C** scholar   **D** outlaw

8. After the Catholic Church banned the practice of Lutheranism, Lutherans began to complain. They became known as _____.

A Protestants   **B** Huguenots   **C** Calvinists   **D** Reformists

9. The people in France who followed John Calvin's teaching were called _____.

A Protestants   **B** Huguenots   **C** Catholics   **D** Lutherans

10. Some people who denied their beliefs to the Catholic faith were burned to death. This time was known as the _____.

A Inquisition   **B** Middle Ages   **C** Crusades   **D** early 1400s

---

1400–1600   *New Ideas: The Renaissance   Chapter 13*   **277**

Lesson 13–5 Review Answers

1. Martin Luther did not think people needed fancy rituals or pilgrimages to find God. He spoke out against the power and authority granted the pope. **2.** The Catholics murdered all the Protestants they could find in the city of Paris. The killings then spread throughout France. Thousands died over the next few days. **3.** A heretic is a person who is against the teachings of a church. **4.** The Inquisition was a special court set up by the Roman Catholic Church. Its purpose was to punish people who spoke out against the teachings of the church. **5.** B **6.** C **7.** D **8.** A **9.** B **10.** A

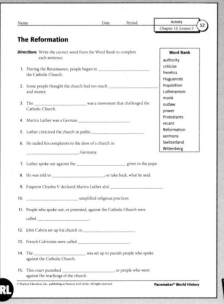

Activity 52   Workbook Activity 52

New Ideas Chapter 13   **277**

Lesson at a Glance

Chapter 13 Lesson 6

Overview This lesson explains the Counter-Reformation and the life of St. Ignatius Loyola, founder of the Jesuits.

Objectives

- To explain what the Counter-Reformation was
- To tell why St. Ignatius Loyola was a powerful leader in the Counter-Reformation

Student Pages 278–280

Teacher's Resource Library

Workbook Activity 53

Activity 53

Modified Activity 53

Vocabulary

Counter-Reformation

Have students use dictionaries to look up the etymology of the word *counter*. Discuss the origin of *counter* (Latin, *contra* meaning *against*) and point out that the Counter-Reformation was the movement against the Reformation. Then have students identify other words in which counter means against. (counterclockwise, counterculture)

1 Warm-Up Activity

Point out that many followers of the Catholic Church had broken off and started new religions. The church had been a powerful institution. Have students predict how the Catholic Church reacted to the Reformation. Tally the opinions of students on the board. Do more students think the church would accept the divide? How might an institution go about convincing its members to return? Ask students to discuss those questions and read the lesson to discover what happened.

The Counter-Reformation

Objectives

- To explain what the Counter-Reformation was
- To tell why St. Ignatius Loyola was a powerful leader in the Counter-Reformation

Counter-Reformation
The Catholic Church's reforms that attempted to fight Protestant beliefs

Many people who wanted change had turned away from the Catholic Church. Others hoped to make changes within the church itself. The movement for reform within the Catholic Church was called the **Counter-Reformation.** It is also known as the Catholic Reformation.

What Was the Council of Trent?

In 1545, the pope called a meeting of clergy at Trent in Italy. The Council of Trent looked for ways to keep the Catholic Church from losing followers. The Council clearly spelled out the beliefs of the church and insisted that people obey them. To reawaken faith among the people, church leaders approved of some new religious orders. One of these was the Society of Jesus.

The Council of Trent was formed to help reawaken faith among Catholics.

2 Teaching the Lesson

Have students read pages 278–279 to find out how the Catholic Church fought Reformation and how a former soldier spread Catholicism to far-off lands.

Ask:

- Who called the Council of Trent together? (the pope)
- What did the Council hope to do? (They wanted to keep the Catholic Church from losing followers.)
- Who started the Society of Jesus? (St. Ignatius Loyola)

Background Information

The turning point of Ignatius Loyola's life came in 1521. He was a soldier in battle when a cannonball tore open his left calf and broke his right shin. Ignatius read about the lives of Jesus Christ and the saints while he recovered. Sometimes Ignatius daydreamed about his life as a soldier. He began to believe that some of his ideas were God-sent, while others were ideas of the world. One night, Ignatius saw a vision of Mary holding the infant Jesus. He was filled with peace. Ignatius rejected his old ways, and from that day on would only speak of spiritual things.

Reading Strategy:
Inferencing

Consider what you know
about what happened
with the Counter-
Reformation. Then make
an inference about why it
happened.

Who Was St. Ignatius Loyola?

St. Ignatius Loyola was one of the most powerful leaders
of the Counter-Reformation. Once a Spanish soldier,
Loyola was crippled when a cannonball hit his leg. While
recovering, he read a book about the life of Jesus. He
decided to begin a spiritual life. He studied to become a
priest at the University of Paris.

In 1534, Loyola gathered six followers and formed the
Society of Jesus. Its members were called Jesuits. The
society quickly gained more members. Their mission was
to win Protestants back to the Catholic Church. The Jesuit
order, with ex-soldier Loyola at its head, was run much
like an army.

The Jesuits stopped the spread of Protestantism in
Europe. However, they carried Catholic ideas to far-off
lands. When Loyola died in 1556, the Jesuit order was
well established.

Throughout the Reformation, Catholics and Protestants
competed for religious control of Europe. The kings and
queens of Spain, England, and France became caught up
in the struggles of the Reformation. Religion played an
important part in shaping Europe's history.

TIMELINE STUDY:

THE RENAISSANCE

When was a council held to reform the Catholic Church?

1572
St. Bartholomew's
Day Massacre

1483
Martin Luther
is born

1452
Leonardo da Vinci
is born

1473
Copernicus
is born

1534
Loyola founds
Society of Jesus
(Jesuits)

1564
Galileo
is born

1400 — 1500 — 1600

1475
Michelangelo
is born

1517
Luther nails
95 complaints
to church door

1545–1563
Council of Trent

1578
Dr. William Harvey
is born

1400–1600

New Ideas: The Renaissance Chapter 13 **279**

Lesson 13–6 Review Answers

1. The Counter-Reformation was the Catholic Church's reforms that attempted to fight Protestant beliefs. **2.** The Council of Trent looked for ways to keep the Catholic Church from losing followers. **3.** The mission of the Jesuits was to win Protestants back to the Catholic Church. **4.** Italy **5.** Society of Jesus **6.** St. Ignatius Loyola **7.** Paris **8.** Europe **9.** Catholic ideas **10.** Religion

LESSON 13-6 REVIEW

On a sheet of paper, write the answer to each question. Use complete sentences.

1. What was the Counter-Reformation?

2. What was the purpose of the Council of Trent?

3. What was the purpose of the Jesuits?

On a sheet of paper, write the word from the Word Bank to complete each sentence correctly.

4. The 1545 meeting of clergy at Trent was in _____.

5. Church leaders at the Council of Trent approved a new religious order. The purpose of the _____ was to reawaken faith among the people.

6. One of the most powerful leaders of the Counter-Reformation was _____.

7. Loyola studied to become a priest at the University of _____.

8. The Jesuits stopped the spread of Protestantism in _____.

9. The Jesuits also carried _____ to other lands.

10. _____ played an important part in shaping Europe's history.

Word Bank

Catholic ideas

Europe

Italy

Paris

religion

Society of Jesus

St. Ignatius Loyola

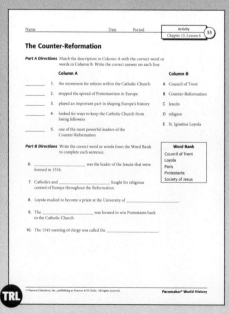

Activity 53

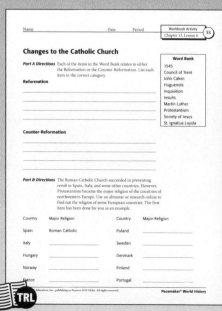

Workbook Activity 53

- Renaissance means "rebirth" or "awakening."

- Renaissance Europeans were interested in the art and ideas of the ancient Greeks and Romans.

- The spread of humanism sparked new ideas.

- During the Renaissance, great work was done in art and science. More books became available to more people.

- Human beings were considered important, and the human form in pictures and statues became realistic.

- Michelangelo was a brilliant painter and sculptor of the Renaissance.

- Scientist Galileo's theories caused trouble with the church. He was the first person to use the telescope to study the sky.

- Leonardo da Vinci was known for his many inventions and works of art.

- During the Renaissance, some people began to question the practices of the Catholic Church. Martin Luther led the Reformation.

- People who protested against the Catholic Church were called Protestants.

- Protestants and Roman Catholics competed for the control of Europe.

- The Catholic Church wanted to make changes within the Church itself. This was known as the Counter-Reformation.

Chapter 13 Summary

Have students read the Chapter Summary on page 281 to review the main ideas presented in Chapter 13.

Ask:

- What does the word *renaissance* mean? ("rebirth" or "awakening")

- What were people most interested in during the Renaissance? (Most people were interested in the art and ideas of the ancient Greeks and Romans.)

- How did humanism influence the Renaissance? (It sparked new ideas.)

- During the Renaissance, what became available to more people? (books)

- What became more realistic in pictures and statues? (the human form)

- Who was Michelangelo? (He was a painter and sculptor of the Renaissance.)

- Who was the scientist whose discoveries were banned by the church? (Galileo)

- What was Leonardo da Vinci known for? (his many inventions and works of art)

- Who led the Reformation? (Martin Luther)

- What were people who protested against the Catholic Church called? (Protestants)

- What was the Counter-Reformation? (the changes the Catholic Church wanted to make within the Church itself)

TEACHER'S RESOURCE

The AGS Globe Teaching Strategies in Social Studies Transparencies may be used with this chapter. The transparencies add an interactive dimension to expand and enhance the Pacemaker® *World History* program content.

CHAPTER PROJECT FOLLOW-UP

Have pairs of students give their presentations about the historical figure they chose. Assess students on the quality of their research by having students turn in a list of sources. Evaluate the quality of the presentation in terms of the quality of the delivery, visual aides, and enthusiasm of the students.

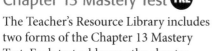

Chapter 13 Review

Use the Chapter Review to prepare students for tests and to reteach content from the chapter.

Chapter 13 Mastery Test **TRL**

The Teacher's Resource Library includes two forms of the Chapter 13 Mastery Test. Each test addresses the chapter Goals for Learning. An optional third page of additional critical-thinking items is included for each test. The difficulty level of the two forms is equivalent.

Chapter 13 Review Answers

Vocabulary Review

1. patron
2. masterpiece
3. sculptor
4. Renaissance
5. theory
6. astronomer
7. criticized
8. heretic
9. humanism
10. authority

Chapter Review Questions

11. The Renaissance began in Italy.

12. Renaissance means "rebirth" or "awakening."

13. The human form was more realistic in Renaissance art.

14. Books became available to more people.

Word Bank

astronomer
authority
criticized
heretic
humanism
masterpiece
patron
Renaissance
sculptor
theory

Vocabulary Review

On a sheet of paper, use the words from the Word Bank to complete each sentence correctly.

1. A wealthy person who helps an artist is a(n) _____.

2. *Pietà* was Michelangelo's first _____.

3. Among many other things, Michelangelo was a fine _____.

4. Leonardo da Vinci is a perfect example of a(n) _____ man. It seemed as if there was nothing he could not do.

5. A scientific explanation of why something happens is a(n) _____.

6. Copernicus was a(n) _____. He wrote a book that said the planets—including the earth—revolved around the sun.

7. Martin Luther _____ the Catholic Church.

8. A person who is against certain church teachings is often called a(n) _____.

9. The belief in the importance of human beings is called _____.

10. Luther did not like the power and _____ granted the pope.

Chapter Review Questions

On a sheet of paper, write the answer to each question. Use complete sentences.

11. Where did the Renaissance begin?

12. What is the meaning of the word *Renaissance*?

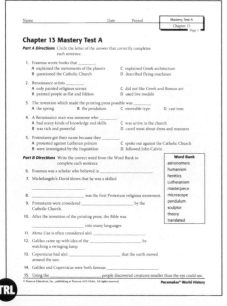

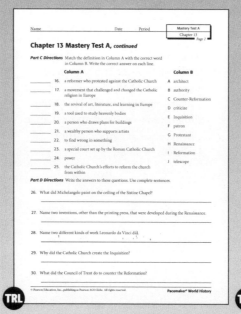

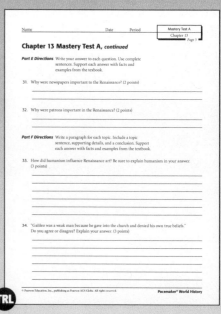

13. How was the art of the Renaissance different from the art of the Middle Ages?

14. What changes did the invention of movable type bring about?

15. How did the church react to Galileo's discovery?

16. Who were Martin Luther and John Calvin?

Critical Thinking

On a sheet of paper, write your response to each question. Use complete sentences.

17. How were the Reformation and the Counter-Reformation similar and yet different?

18. During the Renaissance, a well-rounded person was admired. Do you think the same thing is true today? Why or why not?

Using the Timeline

Use the timeline on page 279 to answer the questions.

19. Who was born first, Leonardo da Vinci or Michelangelo?

20. What event shows that some Protestants died for their faith?

GROUP ACTIVITY

Work in a small group to create a biographical dictionary of important people of the Renaissance. If possible, include copies of their works or pictures of their inventions. Be sure to tell why each person was important during the Renaissance and after.

---

15. The church did not want Galileo to say that the earth revolved around the sun. They put him on trail. They forced him to give up his belief in Copernicus's theory. Church officials watched Galileo closely for the rest of his life.

16. They were leaders in the Reformation. Luther started the Lutheran church in Germany. Calvin started a strict kind of Protestantism in Switzerland.

Critical Thinking

17. Both wanted reform in the Roman Catholic Church. Protestants left the Catholic Church due to the Reformation. The Catholic Church made some changes within the church because of the Counter-Reformation.

18. Possible answers: Yes, a well-rounded person can do many things and will have many interests. No, today a person needs to concentrate on a few areas because jobs are so specialized.

Using the Timeline

19. Leonardo da Vinci

20. St. Bartholomew's Day Massacre

GROUP ACTIVITY

Students' biographical dictionaries should provide a brief look at major Renaissance figures, including Erasmus, Michelangelo, Gutenberg, Galileo, Leonardo da Vinci, Martin Luther, St. Ignatius Loyola, and possibly others.

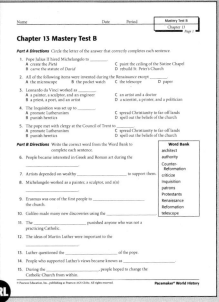

Chapter 13 Mastery Test B, pages 1–3

Introducing the Chapter

Europe in the 16th century made progress toward more modern political structures with the increase in a sense of nationalism. As nations formed, royal hopefuls and monarchs entered into a series of wars to increase their treasuries and territories. Throughout the 15th and 16th centuries, rulers and subjects struggled with the limits of power.

Ask:

- What is another word for the kings and queens who ruled kingdoms?
  (monarchs)

284 Unit 5 The Renaissance

CHAPTER

14

1450–1650

Kings and Queens

The borders of kingdoms were growing clearer. As this happened, the people living in them started feeling a sense of a homeland. People in different lands developed their own customs and languages. In Europe, most of those languages came from Latin.

Monarchs, the kings and queens of these early lands, wanted power. They often gained power by getting more land and goods, and controlling more people. Politics and religion were closely linked to one another. People, and the nations they loved, were certain to change by the power of religion.

GOALS FOR LEARNING

- To describe a country under monarch rule
- To explain the religious goal of the Spanish monarchs
- To describe what King Henry IV did to keep the peace in France
- To explain the struggle between the Catholics and Protestants in England

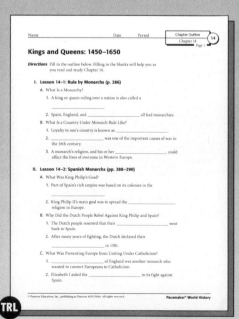

Reading Strategy: Metacognition

Metacognition means being aware of the way you learn. Use metacognition to become a better reader.

- Write the main idea, details, and any questions you have.
- Make predictions and ask yourself what you already know about the topic.
- Visualize what is happening in the text. If something does not make sense, go back and read it again.
- Summarize what you have read and make inferences about the meaning.

Key Vocabulary Words

Lesson 1
Monarch A ruler, like a king, queen, or emperor

Nationalism Love of one's nation; patriotism

Decline A period of increasing weakness

Lesson 2
Reign The rule of a monarch; to rule as a king, queen, or emperor

Fleet A group of warships under one command

Armada A large fleet of warships

Lesson 3
Massacre The act of killing many people who are often defenseless

Edict A public order by some authority

Lesson 4
Annul To cancel; to make something no longer binding under law

Parliament England's body of lawmakers

- What did kings and queens want and how did they get it? (The kings and queens wanted power. They got it by getting more land and goods and by controlling more people.)

Reading Strategy:
Metacognition

Explain that when you read something, you often make a picture of the information in your mind. You might also think of questions about the text as you read. Your mind also tries to organize the information as you read. When you think about how you learn as you read, you are using metacognition.

Ask:

- What do you predict this chapter is about? (the leaders of different kingdoms) Why? ("Kings and Queens" is the chapter title.)

Key Vocabulary Words

Point out that these chapter words are presented in the order they appear in each lesson. They are also found in the glossary.

LIFE SKILLS CONNECTION

Students discuss transportation. They list the benefits of public transportation versus the benefits of personal transportation.

KEY VOCABULARY

Students choose the correct words from the Word Bank to complete each sentence in the paragraph.

TRL   Life Skills Connection 14   TRL   Key Vocabulary Words 14

Lesson at a Glance

Chapter 14 Lesson 1

Overview This lesson describes how nations became unified under monarchs and how nationalism and religion shaped European history.

Objectives

■ To explain what a monarch is
■ To name and explain the two powerful forces that shaped 16th-century Europe

Student Pages 286–287

Teacher's Resource Library **TRL**

Workbook Activity 54

Activity 54

Modified Activity 54

Vocabulary

decline   nationalism
monarch

Have volunteers read a word and its definition. Have students write the word in a sentence. Have students work in groups of three to peer-edit their sentences.

---

1   Warm-Up Activity

"The Star-Spangled Banner," our national anthem, was written by Francis Scott Key after watching the bombardment of Fort McHenry during the War of 1812.

"La Marseillaise," the national anthem of France, was composed in one night during the French Revolution in 1792. Play the music for the class and distribute copies of the lyrics of both of these pieces (music and translation of the French is available on the Internet). Discuss the connection between national anthems and feelings of nationalism.

2   Teaching the Lesson

Ask students to share what they have heard, seen, or read about kings and queens.

Rule by Monarchs

Objectives

■ To explain what a monarch is
■ To name and explain the two powerful forces that shaped 16th-century Europe

Reading Strategy: Metacognition

Notice the structure of this chapter before you begin reading. Look at the titles, headings, and boldfaced words.

Monarch
A ruler, like a king, queen, or emperor

Nationalism
Love of one's nation; patriotism

Decline
A period of increasing weakness

Spain, France, and England had each become unified into nation-states. Now a separate government ruled each of these three lands. The rulers were **monarchs**—kings and queens who held power over a whole nation.

What Is a Country Under Monarch Rule Like?

The people of each nation were loyal to their rulers. They felt a bond with their country and with each other. Within a country everyone spoke similar languages and followed similar customs. This feeling of pride and loyalty toward one's nation is called **nationalism.** Nationalism and religious beliefs became important. Both were powerful forces that shaped 16th-century European history.

The monarchs of Spain, France, and England followed different religious teachings. Some were Roman Catholics. Some were Protestants. One ruler even started his own church. Because of their separate beliefs, the monarchs led their people into wars. They led them through times of peace, cultural growth, and **declines** (periods of increasing weakness).

Queen Mary I was one of the many monarchs that ruled England during the 16th century.

The history of each nation affected each of the others. The religions and the personalities of the monarchs changed the lives of the people of Western Europe.

Ask:

● What united people within a country? (They spoke similar languages and followed similar customs.)
● What forces shaped 16th-century Europe? (nationalism and religious beliefs)
● Why did monarchs sometimes lead their people into wars? (because of different religious beliefs)

Reading Strategy: Metacognition

Have students read the title and headings of Lesson 1. Then have students skim page 286 to find the words from the Word Bank.

Background Information

Monarchs serve as a symbol of national continuity and stability. The extent of a monarch's ruling power varies from monarchy to monarchy. For example, in England the Parliament holds most of the political power, while the Queen exercises mostly non-partisan powers. It is also noteworthy that while the European monarchies rule separate nations, they are often closely interconnected by marriage and family ancestry. This often affects political interactions among them.

REVIEW

Match the definition in Column A with the term in Column B. Write the correct letter on a sheet of paper.

Column A

1. love of one's nation; patriotism
2. a period of decreasing weakness
3. a ruler, like a king, queen, or emperor

Column B

A decline
B monarch
C nationalism

Word Bank

customs
decline
loyal
monarchs
nationalism
religious beliefs
Spain

On a sheet of paper, write the word from the Word Bank to complete each sentence correctly.

4. France, _____, and England are three nation-states that had monarchs in Europe during the 16th-century.
5. People were _____ to their ruler and nation.
6. Within a country, everyone spoke similar languages and followed similar _____.
7. _____ and religious beliefs were both powerful forces that shaped 16th-century European history.
8. The _____ of Western Europe followed different religious teachings.
9. Because of the different _____, the monarchs often led their people into war.
10. Monarchs ruled through times of peace, growth, and _____.

1450–1650   *Kings and Queens*   Chapter 14   **287**

LEARNING STYLES

Interpersonal/Group Learning

Have students work in small groups to research and plan a presentation about the dress and decoration of royalty. These items will vary between nations over hundreds of years. To organize the project, students could concentrate on a different country over a given period of time. Or, students could work together on only one country, and groups could present different aspects of its monarchy.

ELL/ESL STRATEGY

Language Objective: *To plan for writing and speaking in such ways as outlining, listing, or charting.*

Have students work in small groups to compare of one of our national holidays with a national holiday of another country. Have students research commemoration activities, traditional foods, music and dance, and any other categories suggested by the group.

3   Reinforce and Extend

AT HOME

Invite students to discuss with family members what countries their ancestors have lived in. Ask them to find out if these nations had a king, queen, or some other form of royalty when their ancestors lived there. Students with American Indian heritage might ask their parents which tribe their ancestors were a part of and what they know about the ruling structure of the tribe.

Lesson 14–1 Review Answers

1. C 2. A 3. B 4. Spain 5. loyal
6. customs 7. Nationalism
8. monarchs 9. religious beliefs
10. decline

Kings and Queens Chapter 14 **287**

Name _____ Date ____ Period ____   Activity 54
Chapter 14, Lesson 1

Rule by Monarchs

Directions Circle the letter of the answer that correctly completes each sentence.

1. Spain, France, and England each became _____.
   A conquered   B poor   C nation-states   D Catholic
2. Kings and queens are called _____.
   A monarchs   B nationals   C religions   D Europeans
3. People felt a(n) _____ to their country and rulers.
   A distance   B sadness   C anger   D bond
4. Each country had its own language and _____.
   A homes   B customs   C songs   D money
5. The feeling of national pride is called _____.
   A prejudice   B feudalism   C militant   D nationalism
6. The monarchs each had different _____.
   A religions   B titles   C names   D ideas
7. One ruler started his own _____.
   A customs   B church   C language   D country
8. The monarchs led their people into _____ over religious differences.
   A war   B arguments   C Jerusalem   D traps
9. When countries weakened, they were in _____.
   A disrepair   B decline   C conflict   D monarchy
10. The _____ of each country affected the other.
    A language   B religion   C cities   D history

© Pearson Education, Inc., publishing as Pearson AGS Globe. All rights reserved.   **Pacemaker® World History**

Activity 54

Name _____ Date ____ Period ____   Workbook Activity 54
Chapter 14, Lesson 1

Monarchs and Nationalism Match-Up

Directions Match the sentence in Column A with the correct word or phrase in Column B. Write the correct answer on each line.

Column A

____ 1. Spain, France, and England each formed _____.
____ 2. People felt a _____ with their ruler and their country.
____ 3. People in one country _____.
____ 4. They developed pride and _____ toward their nation.
____ 5. _____ was as important as religion.
____ 6. People in Spain, France, and England had different _____.
____ 7. Monarchs led people into _____ due to different religious beliefs.
____ 8. The _____ led their people in good and bad times.
____ 9. The religions and monarchs impacted people in _____.
____ 10. The _____ in Western Europe affected each other.

Column B

A bond
B loyalty
C nationalism
D nations
E nation-states
F religions
G rulers
H spoke a similar language
I war
J Western Euorpe

© Pearson Education, Inc., publishing as Pearson AGS Globe. All rights reserved.   **Pacemaker® World History**

Workbook Activity 54

Lesson at a Glance

Chapter 14 Lesson 2

Overview This lesson explains how Spain attempted to bring all of Europe under the Catholic Church.

Objectives

- To tell the goal of King Philip II of Spain
- To describe what happened when King Philip II wanted the Netherlands to accept Catholicism
- To describe the Spanish Armada and tell what happened to it

Student Pages 288–291

Teacher's Resource Library

Workbook Activity 55

Activity 55

Modified Activity 55

. . . .

Vocabulary

armada   reign
fleet

Have students write brief paragraphs that use the three vocabulary words correctly. Have volunteers read their paragraphs aloud to classmates.

. . . .

1   Warm-Up Activity

Display pictures of Spanish cathedrals, or have students search the Internet to find cathedrals built during the 15th and 16th centuries. Two examples are Segovia Cathedral (built on the spot where Isabella was proclaimed Queen) and Toledo Cathedral (stands on the site of an old Arab mosque). Point out that these cathedrals were built during the time King Philip II ruled Spain and promoted Catholicism.

2   Teaching the Lesson

Invite students to share what they know about King Ferdinand and Queen Isabella of Spain. Then have them read pages 288–290 to learn about the events that brought Spain to the brink of world power.

LESSON 14-2   Spanish Monarchs

Objectives

- To tell the goal of King Philip II of Spain
- To describe what happened when King Philip II wanted the Netherlands to accept Catholicism
- To describe the Spanish Armada and tell what happened to it

Reign

The rule of a monarch; to rule as a king, queen, or emperor

Reading Strategy: Metacognition

Remember to ask yourself questions about specific people as you read about them. This will help you make sure you understand what you are reading.

In the late 1400s, King Ferdinand and Queen Isabella ruled Spain. They were Roman Catholics. They wanted no one but Roman Catholics living in their nation.

There were not many Protestants in Spain, but there were Jews and Muslims. Spanish Muslims were called Moors. Ferdinand and Isabella called upon the Inquisition to hunt down anyone who was not Catholic. Many Jews and Moors were tortured and killed. Those who were lucky enough to escape the Inquisition had to flee the country. The Jews left for other European countries and the Middle East. Many of the Moors fled to North Africa.

What Was King Philip's Goal?

King Philip II ruled Spain from 1556 until 1598. He began his rule as the most powerful monarch in all of Europe. At that time, Spain was the strongest European nation. It held many other provinces. Spain controlled rich colonies in the Americas. However, Philip's **reign**, or rule as a monarch, marked the beginning of Spain's decline.

Like Ferdinand and Isabella, Philip II was a Catholic. He also supported the Inquisition and its methods. King Philip saw himself as a man with a job to do.

He wanted to see not only Spain, but all of Europe, under the Catholic Church. King Philip's goal was to crush Protestantism.

Ask:

- How did King Ferdinand and Queen Isabella treat non-Catholics? (They ordered the Inquisition to torture and kill Jews and Moors in Spain.)
- How did the Dutch people respond when King Philip tried to make the Netherlands Catholic? (The Dutch people rebelled. Later they declared independence from Spain.)
- What did the death of Queen Mary mean for a Catholic Europe? (Queen Elizabeth I was now leader of England. She was Protestant and saw King Philip as the enemy. She did not want Europe to be united under Catholicism.)

Reading Strategy: Metacognition

Have students pose a question about one of the people they read about on this page. Ask them if their question can be answered in the text, or if they would need to find the answer in another resource.

You Decide
Do you think that
Ferdinand and
Isabella were wise rulers?
Why or why not?

Reading Strategy:
Metacognition

Note the main idea and
important details about
Philip II. Summarize what
you read to make sure
you understand it.

**Geography
Note**

Andorra, located
between France and
Spain, is one of the
smallest countries in
Europe. It covers only
about 181 square miles
(468 square km) of
land. Beginning in 1278,
Andorra was governed
by both a French count
and a Spanish bishop.
In 1505, after the death
of Isabella, Spain's King
Ferdinand married the
daughter of the French
count. He brought
Andorra under the rule
of Spain.

Why Did the Dutch People Rebel Against King Philip and Spain?

Spain ruled the Netherlands. Many Protestants lived there. Philip II would not stand for Protestants living under his rule. He issued a royal command: "People of the Netherlands will accept the Catholic religion!"

Philip did not count on the spirit of the Dutch people. They wanted to worship as they chose. Even the Dutch who were Catholics did not like King Philip. He was a Spaniard, not Dutch. He expected them to send too much tax money to Spain.

The proud people of the Netherlands rebelled. A Dutch prince, William of Orange, led the rebellion in 1568. Things looked grim. However, the Dutch would not give in to Spain. In 1581, the Dutch declared independence. The Netherlands was on its way to freedom from Philip and from Spain.

What Was Preventing Europe from Uniting Under Catholicism?

King Philip was not alone in his dream of a Catholic Europe. Before he became king, Philip had married Queen Mary I of England. Mary was a loyal Catholic, too. She hoped to see all Protestants converted to Catholicism.

That was not to be. Queen Mary only reigned for five years. When she died, the English throne went to her Protestant half-sister, Elizabeth. Although Philip had been her brother-in-law, Elizabeth saw him as England's enemy. She sent aid to the Netherlands in its fight for freedom from Spain. She gave English ships permission to attack Spanish ships on the world's seas. Queen Elizabeth I was definitely getting in the way of Philip's plans to unite Europe under Catholicism.

Background Information

William of Orange was assassinated in 1584 after King Philip offered a reward of 25,000 crowns to whoever killed him. Despite the death of their leader, the Dutch forces continued to fight. They had strong naval resources and were victorious after plundering Spanish ships and blockading the southern provinces, which were controlled by Spain.

LEARNING STYLES

Visual/Spatial
Have students research the Alhambra, the building that was both palace and fortress for the Moors in Spain. Ask them to select one aspect of the building, such as the Court of the Lions, and make a model or drawing of it. Have students give their work a title and write notes on index cards that describe important features. Give students an opportunity to share their work with the class. They can use their index cards as prompts for their reports.

CHAPTER PROJECT

Divide the class into groups of 4–5 students. Have each group choose personalities from one of the European countries addressed in the chapter to role-play in an illustrated Living Timeline. Groups can use resource materials and the Internet to obtain background information about the personalities they are representing. Information gathered for role-playing should include political philosophies, physical characteristics, quotes, mannerisms, clothing, and attitudes of the people. Have students prepare illustrations of their subject to hang on the wall around the room as background for the presentations.

You Decide

Answers will vary. Some students may say that Ferdinand and Isabella were not wise rulers because they discriminated against Jews and Moors and used the Inquisition to torture and kill people. Other students may say that Ferdinand and Isabella were trying to unite those people who were alike, with a common religion and customs. Encourage students to listen to each opinion with respect.

Reading Strategy:
Metacognition

Have students identify the main idea and provide details from the text that support it. Ask volunteers to read their answers. (Answers will vary. Sample answer: King Philip II wanted to establish a Catholic Europe. He tried to crush Protestantism in the Netherlands.)

Geography Note

Have students use the Internet to search maps for Andorra. Students should identify the location of this country on a map and note its small size. Ask students to compare Andorra to the neighboring cities of Barcelona and Toulouse.

Students may benefit from making a poster-size drawing or a model of a Spanish galleon. Encourage students to research and identify the parts of the ship by adding labels to the drawing or model. Students could also list the ship's major statistics, such as average weight and length, possible cargo, and number of sailors required to sail it.

ELL/ESL STRATEGY

Language Objective:
To recognize that writing is a process of constructing meaning. To speak for the purposes of explaining, reporting, informing, and describing.

Students will work in a small group to create a mindmap on chart or mural paper with "Spanish Monarchs" indicated as the central topic. Using illustrations, labels, phrases, and directional symbols, students will chronicle the events and people involved in the processes of Spain's rise and fall between 1469 and 1588. Dates, locations, and illustrations of each significant event should be included. Hang the mindmap on the wall for a class presentation.

LEARN MORE ABOUT IT

Have the class discuss how King Philip might have felt when he first saw the small ships of the English navy. Have students discuss the outcome of the battle, noting that King Philip lost about half of his mighty fleet.

Fleet
A group of warships under one command

Armada
A large fleet of warships

By defeating the Spanish Armada, England's navy ruled the seas.

LEARN MORE ABOUT IT

The Spanish Armada

King Philip II decided to go to war with England. Philip built up a mighty **fleet,** or a group of warships under one command. It was called the **Armada.** The Armada was the largest fleet of ships that Europe had ever seen. In 1588, 130 Spanish ships set out against England. They were giant ships. There were crosses on their billowing sails. King Philip thought that his Armada could not be beaten.

The Armada reached the English Channel. English ships sailed out to meet it. The English ships were much smaller than the Spanish ships. At first it looked as if they would not stand a chance. However, the English crafts were fast. They could dart among the heavy Spanish galleons (large sailing ships with many decks), firing from all sides. The English had skilled captains like Sir Francis Drake. They kept

King Philip's Armada busy. The Spanish giants could not stop the quick, little English ships.

The fighting lasted for more than a week. Most of the Spanish ships were damaged. The crippled Armada fled to the North Sea. It escaped the English by sailing north around the British Isles. Heavy winds wrecked many ships off the coast of Ireland. What was left of Philip's once-glorious Armada headed back to Spain. Only 67 ships returned home.

Philip's dream of a Catholic Europe ended with the destruction (defeat) of his Armada. He had lost many soldiers. The Armada had cost Spain much money. Instead of conquering Europe, King Philip had sent Spain into a decline.

By defeating the Spanish Armada, England's navy ruled the seas.

COMMON ERROR

Students might not remember that the Netherlands is a separate area from Spain. Explain that although Spain ruled the Netherlands, it was not an area within Spain. The Netherlands is a separate country with its own leaders, religion, and customs. Point out the Netherlands on the map and its distance from Spain.

WORLD CULTURES

Spain left two lasting legacies with its former colonies in the Americas: its language and the Catholic faith. Because the Catholic Church allowed the indigenous peoples to maintain their beliefs, modern Latin Americans have been able to draw upon those beliefs. In Guatemala, the work of Nobel Prize-winning author, Miguel Angel Asturias, blends the modern yearning of his people for social justice with the mysticism of their ancestors, the Mayas.

LESSON 14-2 REVIEW

On a sheet of paper, write the answer to each question. Use complete sentences.

1. What did the Spanish Inquisition do to the Moors and Jews in Spain?

2. What was the goal of King Philip II of Spain?

3. What happened to the Spanish Armada when it reached the English Channel?

On a sheet of paper, write the letter of the answer that correctly completes each sentence.

4. King Philip would not stand for Protestants living under his rule in _____.

   A Portugal   **B** the Netherlands   **C** the West Indies   **D** England

5. William of Orange led the Dutch rebellion in 1568. In 1581, the Dutch declared _____.

   A independence   **B** a democracy   **C** war   **D** peace

6. King Philip of Spain married Queen Mary I of _____.

   A Portugal   **B** the Netherlands   **C** Italy   **D** England

7. Both King Philip and _____ wanted all Protestants to convert to Catholicism.

   A William of Orange   **B** Elizabeth   **C** Queen Mary   **D** Henry VIII

8. Elizabeth, who took the throne from her half-sister Mary, saw _____ as England's enemy.

   A the Netherlands   **C** the Catholic Church
   B King Philip   **D** William of Orange

9. King Philip's dream of a Catholic Europe ended with the destruction of the _____.

   A Protestant Church   **B** Catholic Church   **C** Armada   **D** Inquisition

10. Rather than conquering Europe, King Philip sent _____ into a decline.

    A England   **B** the Netherlands   **C** Spain   **D** France

---

COMMON ERROR

Point out that although countries were ruled by their own monarchs, these monarchs frequently wed to establish allies and keep peace between nations. For example, Mary I of England married King Philip II of Spain, giving him the title King of England and the King of Spain.

CAREER CONNECTION

Students interested in pursuing a career at sea might look into the education provided by the United States Merchant Marine Academy. Graduates receive a college degree and are eligible for licensing as officers for privately owned merchant ships. Academy graduates are commissioned as ensigns in the United States Naval Reserve, and many go on active duty in the Navy. Jobs are available on tugboats, on United States flag ships, and with land-based shipping companies. Encourage interested students to research other career opportunities available through the Merchant Marine Academy.

Lesson 14–2 Review Answers

1. The Inquisition tortured and killed many Jews and Moors. Those who could escape fled from Spain. **2.** King Philip II wanted to crush Protestantism. He wanted all of Spain and Europe under the Catholic Church. **3.** The English ships sailed out to meet the Armada at the English Channel. The English ships were much smaller than the Spanish ships. However, the English ships were fast and fired from all sides. The English and Spanish fought for a week. Most of the Spanish ships were damaged and fled to the North Sea. **4.** B **5.** A **6.** D **7.** C **8.** B **9.** C **10.** C

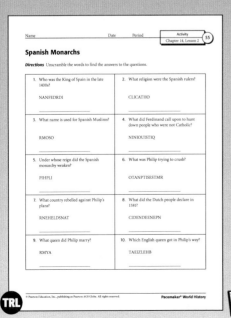

Activity 55

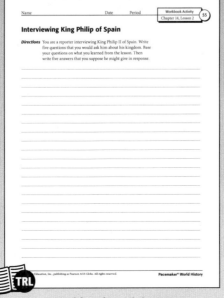

Workbook Activity 55

Lesson at a Glance

Chapter 14 Lesson 3

Overview This lesson describes the rise and reign of King Henry IV in France.

Objectives

- To tell why King Henry IV converted to Catholicism
- To name the good things that Henry IV did for France

Student Pages 292–294

Teacher's Resource Library

Workbook Activity 56

Activity 56

Modified Activity 56

Vocabulary

edict
massacre

Write the vocabulary words on the board and discuss their meanings. Ask a volunteer to choose a word and make up a sentence that is a clue to one of the words. Classmates should try to guess the word from the clue. Continue until the words have been guessed and all students who wish to volunteer have had an opportunity to do so.

1 Warm-Up Activity

Draw a timeline on the board with the years 1572, 1589, 1598, and 1610 on it. Have students recall what was happening in Spain during this time. Remind them that King Philip II wanted a Catholic Europe during this period. Tell students to note the above years as they read about the French monarchs and the role of religion in France during this time.

Reading Strategy:
Metacognition

Have students share strategies for understanding the text, such as visualizing what they read, asking questions about the topic, and summarizing the material after reading.

Objectives

- To tell why King Henry IV converted to Catholicism
- To name the good things that Henry IV did for France

Reading Strategy:
Metacognition

Before reading, think about what you can do to help you better understand the text.

Massacre

The act of killing many people who are often defenseless

Edict

A public order by some authority

France had problems of its own. There, too, wars broke out because of religion. Civil wars had torn the country apart for more than 30 years. The Protestant Reformation had started all the trouble. French Protestants, the Huguenots, fought the Catholics. King Philip of Spain and the pope supported the Catholics. England's Queen Elizabeth sent aid to the Huguenots.

In 1572, thousands of Protestants died in the **massacre** on St. Bartholomew's Day.

France's Catholic king was assassinated in 1589. Before he died, he named Henry of Navarre as the next king. Henry of Navarre became King Henry IV. Henry IV was a Huguenot!

What Did King Henry Do for France?

The French Catholics were in an uproar. A Huguenot was king! Henry IV had to fight to keep his throne. He won several battles, but he could not bring peace. The French, especially those in Paris, would not accept a Protestant as king.

To keep the peace, Henry IV declared himself a Catholic. Most French people welcomed this move. Henry IV was then officially crowned king of France. At last he was able to restore peace to the country.

Yet King Henry IV did not turn his back on the Huguenots. In 1598 he issued a public order, the **Edict** of Nantes. This gave religious freedom to the French Protestants. It was better, Henry said, than seeing France torn apart by civil war.

---

2 Teaching the Lesson

Ask students to think about what would happen if a Protestant became king of a Catholic country. Have students share their ideas with the class. Then have them read pages 292–293 to find out what happened when a Huguenot was made king of the French Catholics.

Ask:

- How did the French people respond when Henry of Navarre was named king? (They were in an uproar. Battles broke out.)
- What did Henry IV do to keep the peace? (He declared himself a Catholic.)

- How did Henry IV establish religious freedom for France? (He issued the Edict of Nantes. This gave religious freedom to the French Protestants.)

Background Information

Samuel de Champlain was a French explorer. In 1608 he founded Quebec City, Canada. Champlain built a fur trading outpost in Quebec. There he established both a business and military alliance with the Algonquin and Huron nations—the original inhabitants of the area. Years later, the king of France declared that only Roman Catholics could settle in the province of Quebec. Today, Quebec is primarily a Catholic province and French is the official language.

King Henry turned out to be a good king. Once there was religious peace, Henry worked hard to make France rich and strong. He passed laws to help the farmers. He built new roads. He also encouraged trade and manufacturing.

King Henry sent French explorers out on the seas. Under Henry's reign, the first French colony was founded in North America. It was called Quebec. Feelings of nationalism grew. The French called their king "Good King Henry."

Their "good king" was assassinated in 1610. However, the religious freedoms that he had brought to France lasted long after his death.

Thousands of Protestants died in the St. Bartholomew's Day massacre in 1572.

Kings and Queens   *Chapter 14*   **293**

3 | Reinforce and Extend

COMMON ERROR

Students may wonder why King Henry III, a Catholic, named a Protestant to succeed him. Explain that Henry IV was in line for the throne by birth, but he had to fight his way there. The transition between monarchs was not a smooth one.

Lesson 14–3 Review Answers

1. Protestant Reformation
2. massacre 3. Huguenot 4. Catholic
5. Edict of Nantes 6. rich 7. trade
8. Quebec 9. assassinated
10. religious freedoms

LESSON 14-3 | REVIEW

Word Bank

assassinated
Catholic
Edict of Nantes
Huguenot
massacre
Protestant Reformation
Quebec
religious freedoms
rich
trade

On a sheet of paper, write the word from the Word Bank to complete each sentence correctly.

1. The _____ started the civil wars in France.

2. Thousands of Protestants died in the _____ on St. Bartholomew's Day in 1572.

3. French Catholics were upset that King Henry IV was named king. This is because he was a(n) _____.

4. King Henry declared himself a(n) _____ to keep the peace.

5. King Henry issued the _____ that gave religious freedom to the French Protestants.

6. King Henry was a good king who made France _____ and strong.

7. King Henry passed laws to help farmers, built new roads, and encouraged _____ and manufacturing.

8. King Henry founded the first French colony in North America and named it _____.

9. King Henry was _____ in 1610.

10. The _____ that King Henry had brought to France lasted long after his death.

294 Unit 5 The Renaissance

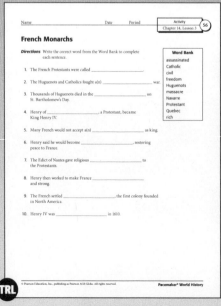

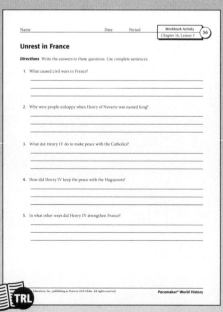

294 Unit 5 The Renaissance

Activity 56

Workbook Activity 56

English Monarchs

Objectives

- To explain why King Henry VIII set up a Church of England
- To compare life under "The Boy King" with that of "Bloody Mary"
- To explain why the English people called Queen Elizabeth "Good Queen Bess"
- To describe life in the Elizabethan Age

Reading Strategy:
Metacognition

Make a prediction to tell what you think will happen next. Check your prediction as you read this section and revise if needed.

In England in 1485, a man named Henry Tudor became King Henry VII. His reign ended years of civil war. He was the first of several monarchs from the Tudor family.

Henry VII was not a very colorful character, but he was well-liked. He kept England out of wars. He was good with business matters and built up the country's economy. King Henry VII saw to it that everyone, especially the nobles, paid their taxes.

When Henry VII died in 1509, his son became king of England. King Henry VIII was the second Tudor monarch. He had a more colorful personality than his father. He is well remembered for having six wives.

Why Did King Henry VIII Set Up a Church of England?

The story of Henry VIII and his wives involves religion. To begin with, Henry VIII was a Catholic. The people liked him. His father had been a good king. The new King Henry seemed good humored and kind.

Problems began when Henry no longer wanted to be married to his wife, Catherine of Aragon. Catherine had only been able to have one child. That child was a girl, the princess Mary, who later married King Philip of Spain. Henry wanted a son to follow him on the throne.

Henry showed an interest in Anne Boleyn. She had been one of his wife's maids of honor. Anne, he thought, was beautiful. She would make him a fine wife. She also might give him a son.

Chapter 14 Lesson 4

Overview This lesson describes the English monarchs from the Tudor family.

Objectives

- To explain why King Henry VIII set up a Church of England
- To compare life under "The Boy King" with that of "Bloody Mary"
- To explain why the English people called Queen Elizabeth "Good Queen Bess"
- To describe life in the Elizabethan Age

Student Pages 295–300

Teacher's Resource Library

Workbook Activity 57

Activity 57

Modified Activity 57

....

Vocabulary

annul
Parliament

Invite students to create a fill-in-the-blank game to play with other students. Have them study the definitions before writing a sentence that includes each vocabulary word. Students will substitute a blank line for the word. Then have them exchange papers with a partner and write the correct words in the blanks.

---

2   Teaching the Lesson

Remind students of the religious conflicts taking place in Europe that they have read about. Have them read pages 295–299 to learn how England broke from the Catholic Church and then switched from Protestant to Catholic under different leaders.

Ask:

- Why did Henry VIII break from the Catholic Church and start the Church of England? (He wanted the pope to annul his marriage. The pope refused.)

- What leader wanted to make England Roman Catholic again? (Queen Mary I)

- Who was the last monarch from the Tudor family? (Queen Elizabeth I)

Reading Strategy:
Metacognition

Students may predict that Henry VII ruled over a peaceful kingdom or that the next king to reign was Henry VIII.

1   Warm-Up Activity

Write the term "The Boy King" on the board. Tell students they will read about Edward VI who took the throne of England at the age of nine. Have students work in small groups to discuss what it would be like to be king of a powerful country at the age of 9. Have them make predictions about what England was like during the reign of King Edward VI.

Background Information

Parliament, the governing body that Henry VIII appealed to, is the law-making institution in the United Kingdom today. Parliament consists of the Crown, the House of Lords, and the House of Commons. The Prime Minister is the elected leader. The Crown, which is the King or Queen of England, can dissolve Parliament, make treaties, declare war, and award honors.

LEARNING STYLES

Auditory/Verbal

Explain that Shakespeare wrote 157 poems known as sonnets that deal with the topics of love, beauty, and politics. Have students search Shakespeare's sonnets on the Internet. There are several Web sites where they can be found. Have each student choose one sonnet to read aloud. Allow students time to practice. Invite volunteers to recite their sonnet for the class.

ELL/ESL STRATEGY

Language Objective: *To use art, music, or theater to express ideas.*

Have students work in a small group to find out why "Guy Fawkes Day" is celebrated in Britain with fireworks and bonfires, and the cellars of the Houses of Parliament are ceremonially searched before each State Opening of Parliament. Each group should use its information to create a poster of a political cartoon, a jingle that they will sing, or a skit to perform. (Guy Fawkes was an English conspirator in the Gunpowder plot to assassinate James I and blow up the Parliament in 1605. He was arrested in the cellar beneath Parliament and executed. The event has been celebrated in Britain each Nov. 5th ever since.)

Annul
To cancel; to make something no longer binding under law

Parliament
England's body of lawmakers

Reading Strategy: Metacognition

Remember to look at the timelines and illustrations. Also take note of the descriptive words. This will help you visualize what you are reading.

King Henry asked the pope to **annul**, or consent to end, his marriage to Catherine. The pope refused, so Henry VIII took matters into his own hands. In secret he married Anne Boleyn in 1533. His marriage to Catherine was annulled by the man who would become the Archbishop of Canterbury. Henry then broke with the Roman Catholic Church. In 1534, England's body of lawmakers, the **Parliament**, passed a law. The law made Henry the head of the Church of England.

The new Church of England was still Catholic in its practices and beliefs. However, it was not subject to any control by Rome. Henry's break with the church increased his own power and wealth. He seized all the lands, all the gold, and all the silver that had belonged to the Roman Catholic Church in England.

Things did not go so well for King Henry VIII and his new wife, Anne Boleyn. Like Catherine, Anne gave him a daughter, the princess Elizabeth. However, Henry still wanted a son. He wanted a new wife, too. He accused Anne of being unfaithful. He had her imprisoned in the Tower of London. She was sentenced to death and beheaded in 1536.

Henry married a third wife, Jane Seymour. At last Henry fathered a son, Prince Edward. Henry married again after Jane Seymour died. In fact, he married three more times. One wife, he divorced. Another, he ordered killed. The sixth and last wife outlived Henry.

Who Was "The Boy King"?

Prince Edward was Henry's only son. When Henry died, Edward took the throne of England. He became the monarch Edward VI at the age of nine.

Under Edward's rule, the number of Protestants increased in England. Protestantism became the state religion.

Reading Strategy: Metacognition

Have students identify the descriptive words that help them visualize what they are reading, such as *body of lawmakers* or *seized gold and silver.*

Because Edward was so young, the affairs of his country were handled by his uncle, Duke Edward Seymour.

Edward was called "The Boy King." He died after reigning for only six years. Now two women were next in line for the throne of England. They were Henry VIII's two daughters, Princess Mary and Princess Elizabeth.

Why Was Queen Mary Known as "Bloody Mary"?

Henry's older daughter, Mary, reigned after Edward's death. Queen Mary I was a strong Roman Catholic. She was determined to make England Roman Catholic again. First she struck down all the religious laws passed under Edward VI. She made new laws enforcing Catholicism. Mary married Philip II of Spain. Together they planned to reduce the strength of Protestantism in Europe.

History calls Queen Mary "Bloody Mary." She persecuted Protestants. She had more than 300 Protestants burned to death.

The English Parliament did not like it when Mary married Spain's King Philip. They were afraid of Spanish power. They refused Queen Mary's request to make Catholicism the state religion. Queen Mary I died after reigning for five years. Her spirit was broken because she never saw Protestantism crushed.

TIMELINE STUDY: REIGNS OF THE EUROPEAN MONARCHS: 1450–1650

During Elizabeth I's reign, England was united under what church?

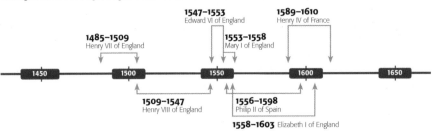

1485–1509
Henry VII of England

1547–1553
Edward VI of England

1589–1610
Henry IV of France

1553–1558
Mary I of England

1450   1500   1550   1600   1650

1509–1547
Henry VIII of England

1556–1598
Philip II of Spain

1558–1603 Elizabeth I of England

3 Reinforce and Extend

COMMON ERROR

Some students may assume that Henry VIII broke with the Catholic Church over his religious convictions. Henry VIII declared himself, with Parliament's approval, the head of the Church of England. However, he did not break with the Catholic Church over his religious conviction. Instead, he no longer wanted to follow the rules of the church.

COMMON ERROR

Some students may not realize that there are two queens of England named Elizabeth. Explain that the Queen of England who reigns today is called Queen Elizabeth, and she was named after Elizabeth I.

STUDY SKILLS

Have students write in their own words one key fact that is the main idea for each paragraph in Lesson 14–4. Then have students share their facts. Encourage them to write other students' facts when they hear one they think would be helpful when reviewing Lesson 14–4.

How Did England Finally Unite?

The next Tudor on the throne of England was Mary's half-sister, Elizabeth. Elizabeth declared that the Church of England was Protestant. The country became firmly united under the one church.

Elizabeth reigned for 45 years, until her death in 1603. Her reign became one of the most glorious periods in English history.

Nationalism grew during Elizabeth's reign. Trouble with Spain only served to strengthen that spirit. England's defeat of the Spanish Armada caused England to cheer.

Queen Elizabeth I did have her faults. She was said to be hot-tempered. She was also called vain. However, the English people loved Elizabeth. Most important, Queen Elizabeth, despite any other faults, loved her England!

Queen Elizabeth I was known as "Good Queen Bess."

Queen Elizabeth never married. Her reign ended the Tudor line. But the English remember her as "Good Queen Bess." She had brought a bright age to England.

What Was Life Like Under Elizabeth?

The reign of Queen Elizabeth became known as the Elizabethan Age. Great writers like William Shakespeare, Edmund Spenser, and Francis Bacon lived in England then. London's Globe Theater was built in 1599. Many of Shakespeare's plays were first performed there.

Elizabeth helped make her people wealthier and England's cities safer. Except for fighting the Spanish Armada, she kept the country out of expensive wars. This left more money to spend on other things. Elizabeth made new laws. The laws gave work to poor people and shelter for those who could not work.

During the Elizabethan Age, ship captains, like Sir Walter Raleigh, brought new products back to England. They brought tobacco and potatoes from America. Daring sailors, like Sir Francis Drake, captured treasures from Spanish ships. In Elizabeth's name, English sailors went out to explore the world.

GREAT NAMES IN HISTORY

William Shakespeare

William Shakespeare (1564–1616) wrote at least 37 plays. *Romeo and Juliet* is about two teenagers from warring families who fall in love. In *Macbeth,* the main character is too ambitious. *Hamlet* is the story of a prince who seeks revenge for his father's death. Although his plays are 400 years old, many are still performed today. Perhaps you have seen one done as a movie.

Many of Shakespeare's plays were first produced in London's Globe Theatre. It has been rebuilt and once again his plays are being performed there. Works by Shakespeare are often seen in major London and New York theaters, too. There are also many Shakespeare festivals. Stratford-upon-Avon, his birthplace, has hosted such an event since 1769.

GREAT NAMES IN HISTORY

Have several works of Shakespeare on hand, including *Romeo and Juliet, Hamlet, and Macbeth.* Ask students to read passages from the plays with a partner and then discuss the differences between the language of Shakespeare and the language of today.

TIMELINE STUDY

Answer: Philip II of Spain, Elizabeth I of England (Students may need to reference the timeline on page 297 for information on the monarchs.)

TIMELINE STUDY: ENGLAND: 1450–1650

When the Spanish Armada was defeated, who were the monarchs of Spain and England?

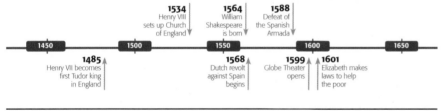

1534 Henry VIII sets up Church of England ▼
1564 William Shakespeare is born ▼
1588 Defeat of the Spanish Armada ▼

1450   1500   1550   1600   1650

1485 Henry VII becomes first Tudor king in England
1568 Dutch revolt against Spain begins
1599 Globe Theater opens
1601 Elizabeth makes laws to help the poor

LESSON 14-4 REVIEW

On a sheet of paper, write the letter of the answer that correctly completes each sentence.

1. King Henry VII was the first of several monarchs from the _____ family.

   A English   **B** Seymour   **C** Tudor   **D** Catholic

2. King Henry's son Edward became king at the age of _____.

   A 6   **B** 9   **C** 33   **D** 45

3. Under Edward's rule, _____ was the state religion.

   A Catholicism   **B** Hinduism   **C** Islam   **D** Protestantism

4. Queen Mary I made laws enforcing _____.

   A Catholicism   **B** the monarchy   **C** trade   **D** Protestantism

5. Queen Elizabeth I made the Church of England _____.

   A Catholic   **B** free   **C** Jewish   **D** Protestant

6. During Elizabeth's reign, _____ grew.

   A taxes   **B** civil wars   **C** nationalism   **D** the Armada

7. _____ brought a bright age to England, thus is known as "Good Queen Bess."

   A Catherine   **B** Elizabeth   **C** Anne   **D** Jane

On a sheet of paper, write the answer to each question. Use complete sentences.

8. Why did King Henry VIII set up a Church of England?

9. Why is Queen Mary known as "Bloody Mary"?

10. What was life in the Elizabethan Age like?

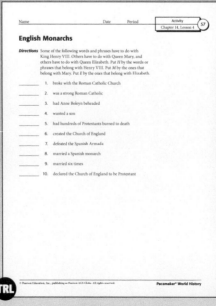

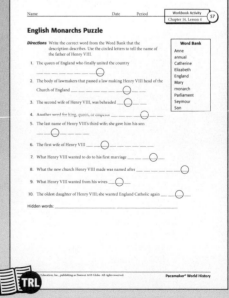

Activity 57   Workbook Activity 57

- During the 16th century, people throughout Europe developed a new sense of nationalism.

- King Philip II of Spain wanted to make all Europeans Catholic.

- Philip II sent his Armada out to conquer England. However, quicker, smaller English ships sent the Armada home in defeat.

- King Philip's reign sent Spain into a decline.

- The French King Henry IV converted to Catholicism to keep peace in France. Henry IV passed laws giving religious freedom to the Protestants in France.

- The Tudors ruled England from 1485 until 1603.

- King Henry VIII of England broke from the Roman Catholic Church and set up the Church of England.

- After Edward, "The Boy King" died, his sister Mary became queen. She tried to return England to Roman Catholicism by having Protestants put to death.

- The last Tudor monarch was Queen Elizabeth I. Elizabeth made the Church of England Protestant, and she encouraged English nationalism.

- The reign of Elizabeth, which became known as the Elizabethan Age, was one of exploration and relative peace.

- During the Elizabethan Age in England there were many writers who would become famous.

Chapter 14 Summary

Have students read the Chapter Summary on page 301 to review the main ideas presented in Chapter 14.

Ask:

- Where did nationalism grow during the 16th century? (Spain, France, and England)

- What was King Philip II's hope for Europe? (that all of Europe would follow the Catholic Church)

- What was the result of the battle between the English navy and the Spanish Armada? (the cost of the battle sent Spain into a decline and King Phillip's dream of a Catholic Europe failed)

- Who converted to Catholicism to keep the peace in France? (Henry IV)

- What family ruled England from 1485 to 1603? (the Tudors)

- Who established the Church of England? (Henry VIII)

- Who was called "Bloody Mary"? (Queen Mary)

- What monarch returned England to a Protestant nation? (Elizabeth I)

- Why was the reign of Elizabeth called the Elizabethan Age? (her reign lasted 45 years and England thrived culturally, economically, and politically)

TEACHER'S RESOURCE

The AGS Globe Teaching Strategies in Social Studies Transparencies may be used with this chapter. The transparencies add an interactive dimension to expand and enhance the Pacemaker® *World History* program content.

CHAPTER PROJECT FOLLOW-UP

Have students revisit the illustrated timeline on the walls. Ask students what information they can add to the descriptions of each person, based on what they read. Have students note the connections between different monarchs and countries through marriage or other alliances. Allow students to share any other relevant facts.

Chapter 14 Review

Use the Chapter Review to prepare students for tests and to reteach content from the chapter.

Chapter 14 Mastery Test

The Teacher's Resource Library includes two forms of the Chapter 14 Mastery Test. Each test addresses the chapter Goals for Learning. An optional third page of additional critical-thinking items is included for each test. The difficulty level of the two forms is equivalent.

Chapter 14 Review Answers

Vocabulary Review

1. nationalism

2. monarch

3. fleet

4. Parliament

5. decline

6. massacre

7. annul

8. reign

Chapter Review Questions

9. Two powerful forces that shaped European history are nationalism and religious beliefs.

10. Nationalism increased in England.

11. Henry IV restored peace. He gave religious freedom to the Protestants. He passed laws to help farmers. He built new roads and encouraged trade and manufacturing.

Word Bank

annul

decline

fleet

massacre

monarch

nationalism

Parliament

reign

Vocabulary Review

On a sheet of paper, use the words from the Word Bank to correctly match each definition below.

1. The feeling of pride and loyalty to one's nation

2. A king or queen who holds power over a nation or empire

3. A group of warships under one command

4. The English body of lawmakers

5. A period in which a nation loses strength

6. The act of killing many people who are often defenseless

7. To cancel something as if it had never been

8. The period of time that a monarch rules

Chapter Review Questions

On a sheet of paper, write the answer to each question. Use complete sentences.

9. What are two powerful forces that shaped 16th-century European history?

10. How did the defeat of the Spanish Armada affect England?

11. In what ways was Henry IV a good king of France?

12. Why did Henry VIII of England break with the Roman Catholic Church?

13. What did Henry VII, Henry VIII, Edward VI, Mary I, and Elizabeth I have in common?

14. What was Queen Mary's dream for England?

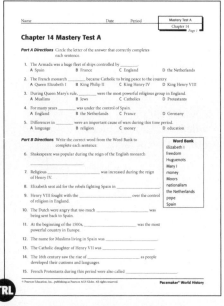

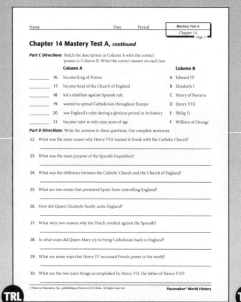

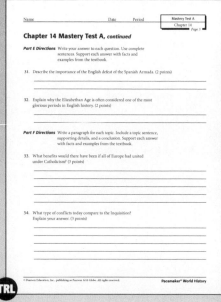

When studying for a test, learn the most important points. Practice writing this material or explaining it to someone.

15. Why was Queen Elizabeth I called "Good Queen Bess"?

16. In what age did Shakespeare live and write his plays?

Critical Thinking

On a sheet of paper, write your response to each question. Use complete sentences.

17. Which Tudor monarch is the most interesting? Give a reason for your answer.

18. Why did some monarchs want everyone in the nation to belong to one religion?

Using the Timelines

Use the timelines on pages 297 and 299 to answer the questions.

19. For how many years did Henry VIII rule England?

20. Did Elizabeth I make laws to help the poor early or late in her reign?

GROUP ACTIVITY

With your group, practice a scene from one of Shakespeare's plays. Perform it for the rest of the class.

1450–1650

Kings and Queens **Chapter 14** **303**

---

12. Henry VIII broke with the Roman Catholic Church because the pope refused to annul his marriage to Catherine.

13. They were all monarchs of England from the Tudor family.

14. Queen Mary wanted all the Protestants to convert to Catholicism.

15. Queen Elizabeth I brought a bright age to England. People were wealthier. Cities were safer. Nationalism grew.

16. Shakespeare lived and wrote during the Elizabethan Age.

Critical Thinking

17. Possible answers: Students may choose Henry VIII for his wives, Edward VI for his age, Mary I for her treatment of Protestants, or Elizabeth I for the achievements of the Elizabethan Age.

18. Possible answer: The monarchs thought that one religion would unify the nation. This would also bring loyalty to them.

Using the Timelines

19. 38 years

20. late

GROUP ACTIVITY

Students' performances should show the results of their practicing the scene and understanding it.

Name _____ Date _____ Period _____ | Mastery Test B Chapter 14 Page 1

Chapter 14 Mastery Test B

Part A Directions Circle the letter of the answer that correctly completes each sentence.

1. In the late 1500s, Spain tried to attack _____ with its huge fleet of ships.
   A France B Arabia C England D Italy
2. _____ is the feeling of loyalty or patriotism toward one's country.
   A Edict B Nationalism C Massacre D Reign
3. Thousands of people were killed in France on _____ in 1572.
   A New Year's Day C Easter Sunday
   B Christmas Day D St. Bartholomew's Day
4. Henry VIII left the Catholic Church because he did not get approval to _____.
   A build more ships C annul his marriage
   B increase taxes D go to war against Spain
5. King Philip II of Spain married _____.
   A Queen Mary I of England C Queen Elizabeth I of England
   B Anne Boleyn D Isabella

Part B Directions Write the correct word from the Word Bank to complete each sentence.

Word Bank
Armada
Catholic
Dutch
England
Huguenot
Inquisition
Mary
Orange
religion
Spanish

6. The Spanish _____ was not able to defeat the small, fast, English navy.
7. King Henry IV became _____ to bring peace to France.
8. Queen _____ had many English Protestants killed.
9. The _____ people wanted freedom from Spain as well as religious freedom.
10. Many wars during this time were based on _____.
11. King Henry of France was a(n) _____ before becoming king.
12. King Henry VIII created the Church of _____.
13. William of _____ led the Dutch revolt against Spain.
14. Sir Francis Drake brought money to England taken from _____ ships.
15. The Spanish _____ brought death to Jews and Moors.

© Pearson Education, Inc., publishing as Pearson AGS Globe. All rights reserved. **Pacemaker® World History**

Name _____ Date _____ Period _____ | Mastery Test B Chapter 14 Page 2

Chapter 14 Mastery Test B, *continued*

Part C Directions Match the description in Column A with the correct person in Column B. Write the correct answer on each line.

Column A | **Column B**
_____ 16. the queen that gave Henry VIII a son | A Catherine
_____ 17. a Spanish king who called upon the Inquisition | B Henry VII
_____ 18. a great writer of the Elizabethan Age | C Jane Seymour
_____ 19. the queen who tried to bring Catholicism back to England | D King Ferdinand
_____ 20. the English king who kept the country out of wars | E Queen Mary
_____ 21. the person whose marriage to Henry VIII was annulled | F William Shakespeare

Part D Directions Write the answers to these questions. Use complete sentences.

22. How did Henry IV bring religious freedom to France?

23. How did Elizabeth help the Dutch fight the Spanish?

24. Why did Henry VIII fight with the pope?

25. Why were the Dutch rebelling against Spain?

26. Why was Spain so powerful at the beginning of the 1500s?

27. Who were the Moors?

28. Who was the Catholic daughter of Henry VIII?

29. Why was Edward called "The Boy King"?

30. What was the difference between the Catholic Church and the Church of England?

© Pearson Education, Inc., publishing as Pearson AGS Globe. All rights reserved. **Pacemaker® World History**

Name _____ Date _____ Period _____ | Mastery Test B Chapter 14 Page 3

Chapter 14 Mastery Test B, *continued*

Part E Directions Write your answer to each question. Use complete sentences. Support each answer with facts and examples from the textbook.

31. Describe the differences between Mary and Elizabeth. (2 points)

32. Summarize the reign of the Tudors. (2 points)

Part F Directions Write a paragraph for each topic. Include a topic sentence, supporting details, and a conclusion. Support each answer with facts and examples from the textbook.

33. Which monarch had a greater impact on England's history, Henry VIII or Elizabeth I? Explain your answer. (3 points)

34. Imagine you are the pope. What arguments would you have to try to persuade Henry VIII to remain Catholic? (3 points)

© Pearson Education, Inc., publishing as Pearson AGS Globe. All rights reserved. **Pacemaker® World History**

Chapter 14 Mastery Test B, pages 1–3

Kings and Queens Chapter 14 **303**

	Student Pages	Vocabulary	Map Study	Reading Strategy	Lesson Review	Chapter Summary/Review
Student Text Lesson						
Chapter 15 To the East; To the West	306–331	✔		✔		329–331
Lesson 15–1 China	308–312	✔		✔	312	
Lesson 15–2 Japan	313–317	✔		✔	317	
Lesson 15–3 India	318–320			✔	320	
Lesson 15–4 The Americas	321–328	✔	✔	✔	328	
Chapter 16 Explorers, Traders, and Settlers	332–351	✔		✔		349–351
Lesson 16–1 Exploring New Lands	334–337		✔	✔	337	
Lesson 16–2 Conquering South America	338–340	✔		✔	340	
Lesson 16–3 Settling in North America	341–345	✔	✔	✔	345	
Lesson 16–4 Trading with the Colonies	346–348	✔		✔	348	

Chapter Activities

Teacher's Resource Library
Life Skills Connection 15–16
Key Vocabulary Words 15–16

Assessment Options

Student Text
Chapter Reviews 15–16

Teacher's Resource Library
Chapter 15 Mastery Tests A and B
Chapter 16 Mastery Tests A and B
Unit 6 Mastery Test

Teacher's Edition
Chapter Projects 15–16

Words from the Past	Learn More About It	Great Names in History	Technology Connection	Geography Note	You Decide/Remember/History Fact	Timeline Study	ELL/ESL Strategy	Background Information	Common Error	Life Skills Connection	Key Vocabulary Words	Study Skills	Applications Home, Career, Community	Online Connection	Teacher Alert	World Cultures	Auditory/Verbal	Body/Kinesthetic	Interpersonal/Group Learning	Logical/Mathematical	Visual/Spatial	Activities/Modified Activities	Workbook Activities	Self-Study Guide	Chapter Outline
										307	307													✔	✔
		310	309	309	309, 311		310	309	309, 311			311						310			310	58	58		
					314, 315		314	314	314, 315				315	316			314					59	59		
					319		319	318												319	319	60	60		
					322, 324	327	323	322	324				323, 324	326	325				322			61	61		
										333	333													✔	✔
		335					336	335	336			337			337					335	335	62	62		
	339	339					339	338	340				339			340	339					63	63		
		341					343	342	343, 344				344	343				342				64	64		
						347	347	347	347				347	347						347		65	65		

Modified Activities

The Teacher's Resource Library (TRL) contains a set of lower-level worksheets called Modified Activities. These worksheets cover the same content as the standard Activities but are written at a lower reading level.

Skill Track

Use Skill Track for *World History* to monitor student progress and meet the demands of adequate yearly progress (AYP). Make informed instructional decisions with individual student and class reports of lesson and chapter assessments. With immediate and ongoing feedback, students will also see what they have learned and where they need more reinforcement and practice.

Other Resources

Books for Teachers

Díaz del Castillo, Bernal. *The Discovery and Conquest of Mexico.* Trans. by A. P. Maudslay. Revised edition. New York: Da Capo Press, 2004.

Ebrey, Patricia Buckley, editor. *Chinese Civilization: A Sourcebook.* Second edition. New York: Free Press, 1993.

Whitfield, Roderick, Susan Whitfield, and Neville Agnew. *Cave Temples of Mogao: Art and History on the Silk Road.* Los Angeles: Getty Conservation Institute and J. Paul Getty Museum, 2000.

Books for Students

Fritz, Jean. *Around the World in a Hundred Years: From Henry the Navigator to Magellan.* New York: Putnam Publishing Group, 1998.

Hoobler, Dorothy, and Thomas Hoobler. *Captain John Smith: Jamestown and the Birth of the American Dream.* New York: Wiley, 2005.

Turnbull, Stephen. *Samurai: The Story of Japan's Great Warriors.* New York: PRC, 2004.

THE AGE OF EXPLORATION AND CONQUEST

People love to go exploring. How excited they may feel at discovering something new, often making it their own. Hundreds of years ago, explorers set out to broaden their horizons—and to become rich and powerful. Discovery often meant conquest, a new group of people found a place and made it their own. Too often this meant that one civilization fell victim to a stronger one. Some of those early civilizations disappeared, except for artifacts found today by archaeologists. Others fought back and continued to live on. Many had a deep effect on the world as it is today.

Chapters in Unit 6

The age of exploration brought together cultures and civilizations that had never crossed paths before.

305

Introducing the Unit

The exploration and discovery of other civilizations seemed to both expand and contract the world. Discuss why this might be. (Europeans discovered "new" lands, so the world expanded for them; some civilizations adopted new cultural ideas and the old ones disappeared, so the world became more uniform, or seemed to contract.) Discuss the meeting portrayed on page 304 in terms of expansion and contraction. How did the two parties react?

Ask:

- Did cross-cultural exchanges generate tolerance or isolation? (It varied for different civilizations and from time to time; e.g., Japan borrowed from Chinese culture for centuries, but isolated itself from Europe after the Middle Ages.)

- How does the spread of technology affect civilizations? (Possible answer: It can make them become more similar, but sometimes people adopt a technology and use it for a novel purpose.)

- What effect does trade have on the economy of a country? (usually makes it grow)

Videos

Ancient Americas: The Mayas and Aztecs. Culver City, CA: Social Studies School Services, 1998. (32 minutes; overview of Mayan and Aztec civilizations, complete with teacher's guide and handouts.)

Genghis Khan: Terror and Conquest. HistoryChannel.com. (50 minutes; extensive location footage, expert testimony, and period art and artifacts.)

CD-ROM/Software

Discovering America: The Adventure of Spanish Exploration. Culver City, CA: *Along the Silk Road: People, Interaction, and Cultural Exchange.* Palo Alto, CA: Stanford Program on International and Cross-Cultural Education. (Presents rich and colorful history of the Silk Road through the lives of historical figures.)

Social Studies School Service, 1993. (Fact-based game about history and the challenges faced by explorers.)

Web Sites

www.agsglobepmwh.com/page305a (Links for short biographies on India's early rulers, including Babar and Akbar.)

www.agsglobepmwh.com/page305b (Photographs, history, and detailed descriptions of an Indian village, depicting the daily lives of the people who once lived in Moundville.)

www.agsglobepmwh.com/page305c (Includes events and important figures in Mongol history, as well as the Mongols' way of life and governing ideas.)

Introducing the Chapter

The Middle Ages in India, China, and Japan saw the birth and adoption of new religions, a flowering of inventions, and momentous political changes. Discuss with students how that compares with the Middle Ages in Europe. Note that great American civilizations were flourishing at the same time. Although they have since disappeared, their monuments remain notable in the landscape.

Ask:

- What motivated people to explore new areas? (trade, conquest, looking for more or better land)

To the East; To the West

For many centuries the civilizations of the East had no contact with the kingdoms of Europe. As a result, China and Japan were not affected by Great Britain, France, or Spain. This all changed once the traders and missionaries started visiting. The world would start to feel smaller as civilizations became more aware of one another.

Across the ocean from both Europe and Asia lay the Americas. The early people there are thought to have been relatives of those who first settled parts of Asia. These people spread out across the wide open continents they discovered and formed various cultures.

GOALS FOR LEARNING

- To explain how China was advanced even though it was isolated for centuries
- To describe the isolated, feudal society in Japan
- To explain the changes in religion the people of India went through
- To name and describe the early American Indian civilizations

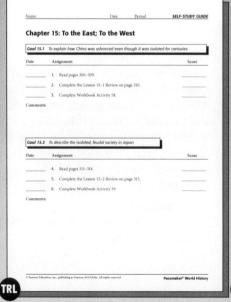

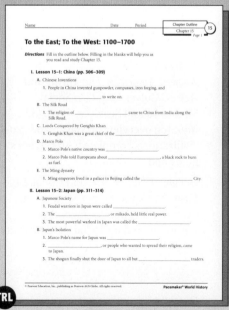

TRL Chapter 15 Self-Study Guide, pages 1–2

TRL Chapter 15 Outline, pages 1–2

Reading Strategy: Summarizing

When you summarize, you ask questions about what you are reading. That way you can review what you have just read. As you read the text in this chapter, ask yourself these questions:

- What details are most important to the people or this time in history?
- What is the main thing being said about the people?
- What events are pointed out about this time in history?

Key Vocabulary Words

Lesson 1

Forge To work into shape by heating and hammering

Acupuncture Treating pain or illness by putting needles into certain parts of the body

Compass A tool for finding direction by using a magnet

Lesson 2

Samurai A class of warriors in the Japanese feudal system

Privilege A special right given to a person or group

Shogun A great general governing Japan

Enforce To make sure that people follow the laws and rules

Missionary A person sent by a church to other countries to spread a religion

Lesson 4

Mesoamerica The area of North America (including Mexico and Central America) where civilizations developed before Europeans entered the continent

Dweller A person who lives in a place

Advanced Ahead of most others in knowledge, skill, or progress

Terraced Going upward like steps

Barter To trade goods or services without using money

Mosaic A design made by putting together small pieces of colored stone, glass, or other material

---

- What were the major religions in Europe and in east Asia at this time? (Christianity in Europe; many religions, including Islam, Buddhism, and Hinduism, in Asia)
- Who left the ruins of cities in Mesoamerica? (Incas, Aztecs, Mayans, mound builders, cliff dwellers)

Reading Strategy: Summarizing

Have students work in small groups and provide each group with a newspaper. Ask each group to choose an article that is at least five paragraphs long. As each volunteer describes an article, write the "who, what, when, where, why, and how" information on the board or on chart paper. Discuss the reasons for using this strategy for summarizing information. Have each group write a 20-word summary of its article, using the strategy.

Key Vocabulary Words

Point out that these chapter words are presented in the order they appear in each lesson. They are also found in the glossary.

LIFE SKILLS CONNECTION

Students learn about giving to charity and how to distinguish a charity from a business online. Have the class choose a charity and help them organize a fund raiser.

KEY VOCABULARY

In Part A, students match the definition to the correct word. In Part B, students choose the correct word from the Word Bank to complete each riddle.

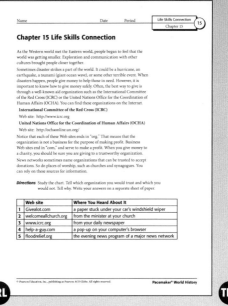

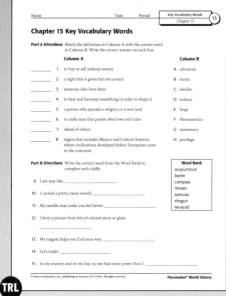

Life Skills Connection 15   Key Vocabulary Words 15

Lesson at a Glance

Chapter 15 Lesson 1

Overview This lesson describes the Chinese culture and how it slowly spread into the West, as well as the Mongol rule of China.

Objectives

- To name three Chinese inventions
- To explain the Silk Road
- To name the lands conquered by Genghis Khan
- To explain the role Marco Polo played in teaching the Europeans about Chinese discoveries
- To tell what dynasty followed the Mongol rule

Student Pages 308–312

Teacher's Resource Library

Workbook Activity 58

Activity 58

Modified Activity 58

Vocabulary

acupuncture   forge
compass

Ask students what parts of speech the word *forge* can be used as. (verb, noun) Have them use a dictionary if necessary. Ask for sentences that use the word as different parts of speech and with different meanings (e.g., to forge ahead, a forge for working steel, to forge a strong blade, forged steel). Have students select the meaning used in the text on this page.

PRONUNCIATION GUIDE

Use this list to help students pronounce difficult words in this lesson.

Kublai Khan (koo´ bli kän´)

Vasco da Gama (vas´ ko də gam´ ə)

Objectives

- To name three Chinese inventions
- To explain the Silk Road
- To name the lands conquered by Genghis Khan
- To explain the role Marco Polo played in teaching the Europeans about Chinese discoveries
- To tell what dynasty followed the Mongol rule

Forge

To work into shape by heating and hammering

Acupuncture

Treating pain or illness by putting needles into certain parts of the body

Compass

A tool for finding direction by using a magnet

European nations battled each other. Empires rose and fell. However, Chinese culture continued over the centuries with little change.

What Were Some Things the Chinese Invented?

The Chinese invented many things, but China was isolated. The rest of the world would not learn about Chinese discoveries for hundreds of years. The Chinese kept their secrets.

Papermaking first began during the Han dynasty. The Chinese made paper from wood ash and cloth pulp. The Chinese also knew how to melt iron and how to shape, or **forge,** it. They knew how to mine salt. They learned to use **acupuncture** to cure pain and disease. Later, the Chinese used woodblocks with carved characters to print books. Chinese sailors developed **compasses,** which they used to find their way when on the sea. Gunpowder also was invented in China. It was used first for fireworks. Not until A.D. 1161 were the first explosives used in actual battle.

The Chinese were among the first to use fireworks.

308 Unit 6   *The Age of Exploration and Conquest*

1 Warm-Up Activity

Show a compass to the class. Explain that the needle of the compass always points north. Tell students that the compass was invented by the Chinese. Have students speculate on how the compass affected Chinese sea travel, trade, and exchange of ideas between cultures. Explain that they will read about other Chinese inventions that had a great impact on the Chinese culture.

CHAPTER PROJECT

Divide the class into five groups of study: India, China, Japan, Aztecs, and Incas. Explain that each group will be researching inventions of these civilizations between A.D. 320 and A.D. 1630. Give students time to use the library and the Internet for their research. Ask them to create a display of the inventions. Allow group creativity to determine the scope of the display.

Geography Note

Macao is a province in southeastern China. It is made up of a city on a peninsula in the South China Sea and three nearby islands. The first European known to visit Macao was Vasco da Gama in 1497. The Portuguese established it as a trading port in 1557. The Portuguese paid the Chinese for the use of Macao until 1887 when it became a free port.

History Fact

People still like fine silk cloth. However, today it is made in many places in the world.

TECHNOLOGY CONNECTION

A Gift from the Chinese

A British agricultural advisor named Jethro Tull printed a book of farming methods in 1731. Among many other things, he insisted that planting crops in straight furrows (lines) was the best method. Tull is also thought to be the first European to develop the "seed drill."

However, the Chinese used a seed drill as early as the second century B.C. It was made up of plows that cut furrows in the ground. Seeds were then released from tubes connected to the plows. Then, in a third step, rollers on the plows covered the seeds with dirt. It is believed that visitors to China, probably traders, brought back ideas about farming over many hundreds of years. Eventually, the Europeans presented those ideas as their own.

What Was the Silk Road?

A route known as the *Silk Road* was China's main link to the Western world. A few traders traveled this road. They made their way across deserts and over mountains. They brought Chinese goods to the West. Many Europeans were fascinated with Chinese art and style. They especially liked the fine silk cloth. It was made from threads spun by silkworms.

The Silk Road was not a one-way road. Chinese products came out of China. New ideas filtered into China along this road. Buddhism came to China from India in the second century A.D. In the next centuries it spread across China.

What Lands Did Genghis Khan Conquer?

To the north of China are the vast plains of central Asia. In the second century, the people who lived there were called Mongols. They were nomads, loosely organized into groups. They wandered over their lands with their horses, sheep, camels, oxen, and goats. The Mongols were expert horsemen. They were also skilled at using the bow and arrow. In their camps they lived in felt tents called *yurts*.

1100–1700   *To the East; To the West*   *Chapter 15*   **309**

History Fact

The manufacture of silk was a carefully guarded secret in China. Over many years the secret leaked out and gradually moved across the Eurasian continent. Ask students why it was kept secret. (to protect China's lucrative trade) Ask students what they know about present-day trade secrets, their value, and their protection.

COMMON ERROR

The Western stereotype of Genghis Khan is that he was a barbaric plunderer who destroyed civilization. The Mongols, however, considered him a great national hero who initiated contacts between civilizations and encouraged the exchange of goods and ideas. Discuss with students why any national war hero is likely to be viewed differently from the other side's perspective.

2 Teaching the Lesson

Point out that by A.D. 1000, the Chinese people had a unique culture. Discuss how the lesson demonstrates that. Have students read to see whether outsiders affected the culture.

Ask:

- What important farming technique was invented in China? (planting in furrows with a seed drill)
- Who was Marco Polo? (an Italian trader who traveled extensively in China and later told Europeans about his experiences there)
- What was the main link between China and the West? (the Silk Road)
- Why did Genghis Khan invade China? (He wanted to establish and extend the Mongol Empire.)
- How long did the Mongols rule China? (for more than 100 years)

Background Information

The Silk Road may have been in use since about 1000 B.C. (the earliest date of silk found in Egyptian tombs). Silk was the main westward-traveling product; wool, gold, and silver traveled east. The Silk Road was not one road, but a network of caravan routes, connecting China to central Asia, India, Persia, and, indirectly, the Roman Empire. Individual travelers usually stayed in one region, rather than traveling the full length of the Silk Road. Traders abandoned the Silk Road during the Ming dynasty, when it was replaced by shipping.

TECHNOLOGY CONNECTION

Have students research current methods of farming and compare the Chinese seed drill to the automated technology used today.

Geography Note

Have students read about Macao. Have them find it on a map of China.

To the East; To the West Chapter 15   **309**

Reading Strategy:
Summarizing

(The main idea is that Mongol nomads lived on the plains north of China and conquered lands in China, Russia, Persia, and India. The next section introduces Marco Polo and describes his reactions to China's culture.)

LEARNING STYLES

Body/Kinesthetic

If students are recent immigrants or have visited a foreign country, invite them to share some of their experiences when they first arrived in America or other foreign place. Ask them to describe things that were new to them. Then have students role-play Marco Polo telling Europeans about the things he saw in China.

LEARNING STYLES

Visual/Spatial

Have a small group of students research the travels of Marco Polo. Encourage them to make a creative poster highlighting some of the information Marco Polo brought back to Europe about the court of Kublai Khan. Students might also include a map to show where Marco Polo traveled.

ELL/ESL STRATEGY

Language Objective:
To write a short summary, given a specific set of facts

Divide the class into small groups. Include ELL students in each group. Have students reread the box on Kublai Khan. Have each group list facts from the feature. Together, have students write a short summary based on the facts from the feature. Students should include ELL students in constructing the summary. Have each group read its summary of facts.

Reading Strategy:
Summarizing

What is the main idea of this section?

In A.D. 1206, a great chief took power over all the Mongols. His name was Genghis Khan. *Khan* was a title given to rulers. Genghis Khan believed that he was destined to rule a great empire. He built up a huge army of Mongol soldiers. They conquered many lands including parts of China, Russia, Persia, and India.

Genghis Khan had little education. Yet he was clever and ruthless. With his soldiers on horseback, he swept across the countryside. The thunder of hooves of Mongol horses was a terrifying sound. The Mongols were among the most fierce conquerors in history. If any city in their path tried to fight, the Mongols showed no mercy. Every single person in the city would be killed.

What Role Did Marco Polo Have in Teaching Europeans About the Chinese Culture?

Reading Strategy:
Summarizing

Who is being introduced in this section?

Marco Polo was a trader and a traveler. He lived in Venice, Italy. Marco Polo traveled to China with his father and his uncle. In about 1275 they went to see Kublai Khan. Khan's palace was in the city of Beijing, then called Cambaluc by Marco Polo.

GREAT NAMES IN HISTORY

Kublai Khan

Perhaps the greatest of the Khans was Kublai Khan. He was a grandson of Genghis Khan. Kublai Khan completed the conquest of China. Chinese farmers were no match for the Mongol armies. The Mongols ruled China from A.D. 1260 until A.D. 1368.

Kublai Khan ran his empire well. He was a Buddhist, but he allowed religious freedom. He saw to it that roads were good and travel was pleasant. There were stones to mark the way.

Trees were planted to give shade to travelers. Kublai Khan developed a postal service. He wanted to make it easy for people throughout his empire to communicate. Horsemen carried messages along China's Great Wall. A post house stood every 25 miles along the wall. At each post house messengers could change horses, and travelers could rest. The Grand Canal was built to transport goods from north to south. Chinese boats called junks carried goods along the miles of waterway.

GREAT NAMES IN HISTORY

After students have read the feature, discuss the things that Kublai Khan provided for his people. (A system of roads, a postal service, and mode to transport goods.) Have students research how those things were first provided in their own country.

History Fact
Kublai Khan's kingdom was huge. It extended as far as Russia.

Kublai Khan welcomed the traders. He allowed Marco Polo to travel about his empire. The young Italian stayed in China for 17 years. Marco Polo saw sights that no other European had ever seen.

Then Marco Polo returned to Italy. He got caught up in a war between Venice and another Italian city, Genoa. He was taken as a prisoner of war and thrown into jail in Genoa. There he told amazing tales to a fellow prisoner. The tales eventually became a part of his book, *Description of the World*. The book contained many stories of the great Chinese civilization and of the empire of Kublai Khan.

Many people did not believe Marco Polo's tales. Later, however, the stories proved to be true. Marco Polo had written a good description of his adventures in China.

Marco Polo was impressed with all he saw in China. The Chinese were using gunpowder and compasses, and coal for heat. Marco Polo wrote that coal was "a sort of black stone, which they dig out of the mountainside...." He was interested in their use of paper, especially for money. Europeans were still using heavy, metal coins. He had found China a rich land where travel was quite easy.

Marco Polo's stories gave Europeans their first glimpse of life inside China.

What Dynasty Followed the Mongol Rule?

In the 1300s, the Chinese revolted against Mongol rule. Mongol rule ended in China. The Mongols were driven away. The Ming dynasty reigned.

You Decide
Blue and white Ming porcelain is still much admired. Why do you think antiques, or old things, are often popular with people today?

Ming emperors lived in Beijing in a great palace known as the *Forbidden City*. The Mings ruled there for nearly 300 years. Chinese art and literature thrived during this time. Europeans found Ming art beautiful. They wanted to trade their European goods for the Ming art. China said no. The Chinese would only accept payments of gold and silver.

COMMON ERROR

A common misperception is that Marco Polo opened up China to the rest of the world. In fact, China and many other countries were connected by trade and religion by the time Polo arrived there.

STUDY SKILLS

Since students will read about many inventions made by Asians and Americans, have them organize this knowledge by creating a chart titled "Asian Inventions." They should set up three columns headed "Invention," "Date," and "Place of Discovery." Have students add information to the chart as they read the chapter.

History Fact
Many of Kublai Khan's innovations, which are listed on page 310, were important tools for ruling an enormous empire.

You Decide
The fine porcelain pottery of China inspired potters in other countries to make their own form of fine china. The English especially excelled at adapting the Chinese porcelain formula. In the 18th century, two firms, Spode and Wedgwood, began manufacturing china that still can be found in homes all over the world.

312

Lesson 15–1 Review Answers

1. Possible answers: The Chinese invented papermaking, compasses, and gunpowder. They also learned how to forge iron, mine salt, and cure pain and disease with acupuncture. Finally, they used woodblocks with carved characters to print books. **2.** The Silk Road was China's main link to the Western world. Traders traveled it, bringing goods to and from China. Also, new ideas, like Buddhism, were spread using this route. **3.** Genghis Khan and his army conquered parts of China, Russia, Persia, and India. **4.** Polo's tales of his adventures were told in his book, *Description of the World*. While no one believed him at first, the stories proved to be true. He gave the Europeans their first glimpse of life inside China. **5.** C **6.** A **7.** D **8.** B **9.** A **10.** D

On a sheet of paper, write the answer to each question. Use complete sentences.

1. What are three things the Chinese invented?

2. What was the route known as the Silk Road?

3. What lands did Genghis Khan conquer?

4. What role did Marco Polo have in teaching the Europeans about Chinese discoveries?

On a sheet of paper, write the letter of the answer that correctly completes each sentence.

5. The Mongols were _____ who roamed the vast plains of central Asia.

  A traders   **B** armies   **C** nomads   **D** farmers

6. The Mongols were among the fiercest _____ in history.

  A conquerors   **B** horsemen   **C** travelers   **D** rulers

7. _____ was a clever, ruthless ruler who built up a huge Mongol army.

  A Marco Polo   **B** Kublai Khan   **C** Babar   **D** Genghis Khan

8. _____ was one of the greatest rulers. He allowed religious freedom, ensured roads were good for travelers, and developed a postal service.

  A Marco Polo   **B** Kublai Khan   **C** Babar   **D** Genghis Khan

9. Marco Polo was an Italian _____ who traveled throughout China for 17 years.

  A trader   **B** farmer   **C** ruler   **D** inventor

10. The _____ dynasty followed the Mongol rule in China.

  A Khan   **B** Genoa   **C** Chinese   **D** Ming

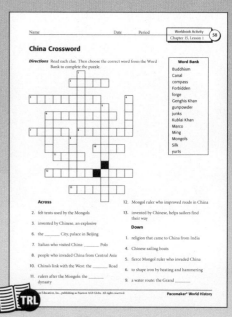

LESSON 15-2

Japan

Objectives

- To tell what the Japanese got from their Chinese neighbors
- To describe the role of samurai and shoguns in Japan
- To explain why the ruling shogun forbade the Japanese to leave their country

Samurai
A class of warriors in the Japanese feudal system

Privilege
A special right given to a person or group

Reading Strategy: Summarizing

What part of Japanese history is this section about?

Japan is a group of islands off the coast of China. Little is known about the early history of Japan. The reason is that the ancient Japanese had no system of writing. Writing first came to Japan from China during the fifth century A.D. Customs, crafts, arts, and ideas of government and taxes also came to Japan from China. The Japanese adapted the Chinese calendar system and the ideas of Confucius. About A.D. 552, Buddhism came to Japan from China and Korea.

The Japanese visited China. The Chinese came to Japan. The Japanese began to model their way of life after Chinese ways. In the seventh century, one Japanese emperor was especially drawn to Chinese ways. He ordered changes in Japanese life to make it more like Chinese life.

What Was Japanese Society Like?

Europeans of the Middle Ages lived under a system of feudalism. At the same time, so did the Japanese. Japanese feudal society was divided into classes.

Nobles were at the top. A class of warriors fought for the nobles. Japanese feudal warriors were called **samurai.** Samurai were given many special rights, or **privileges.** The nobles gave them wealth and land. The samurai were respected as an upper class. In return, samurai warriors pledged loyalty and protection to their nobles.

The samurai were highly trained soldiers. They were expected to die, if necessary, for their noble. Samurai fought with huge, two-handed swords. Before attacking, a samurai would first shout his own name. Then he would shout of the bravery of his ancestors. This was meant to scare his enemy.

1100–1700   *To the East; To the West*   Chapter 15   **313**

Lesson at a Glance

Chapter 15 Lesson 2

Overview This lesson describes the history and development of Japan from A.D. 500 to A.D. 1600.

Objectives

- To tell what the Japanese got from their Chinese neighbors
- To describe the role of samurai and shoguns in Japan
- To explain why the ruling shogun forbade the Japanese to leave their country

Student Pages 313–317

Teacher's Resource Library

Workbook Activity 59

Activity 59

Modified Activity 59

Vocabulary

enforce	samurai
missionary	shogun
privilege	

Have students generate synonyms and antonyms for the word *privilege*. Write the words on the board. Then have students create sentences interchanging the word *privilege* with its synonyms. Discuss how the meaning of the sentence changes slightly when different synonyms are used.

PRONUNCIATION GUIDE

Use this list to help students pronounce difficult words in this lesson.

Kamikaze (kä´mi kä´ze)

Tokugawa (tō ku gä´wä)

Reading Strategy: Summarizing

This section is about Japan's feudal period. Ask students to list the notable features of feudal Japan. (It had noble and peasant classes; samurai warriors, headed by the shogun; the head of state.)

---

1 Warm-Up Activity

Have students recall what they know about European feudalism. Create a graphic organizer on the board as students offer details about the structure of European feudalism. Explain that in this lesson students will learn about European and Japanese feudalism. Have students copy the graphic organizer into their notebooks for later comparison with the information in the lesson.

2 Teaching the Lesson

Have students outline the attitude of Japan toward outsiders. Discuss how it changed. (They borrowed a lot from the Chinese but tried to prevent any European influence.)

Ask:

- How has the geography of Japan shaped its history? (Possible answer: It is an island isolated and protected from the influence of other cultures.)
- What are two ways in which Japanese feudalism was like European feudalism? (Possible answer: They both had classes of nobles and peasants. The warrior class defended the nobles.)
- Who ruled Japan under feudalism? (the shogun)
- How did Japan resist European influence? (European entry was severely limited, and Japanese could not leave the country.)

To the East; To the West Chapter 15   **313**

Background Information

During the Tokugawa period, the Japanese experienced not only isolation from foreign influence, but also about 250 years of peace. Indigenous forms of literature developed. The Japanese had known about printing in the eighth century, but used it only for reproducing Buddhist writing. Readers of books preferred books that were handwritten in calligraphy, often with lavish illustrations. Eventually, demand for books brought change. The first non-Buddhist work was printed in Japan in A.D. 1591. Commercial publication began in 1609.

LEARNING STYLES

Auditory/Verbal

Have interested students listen to recordings of traditional Japanese music. They can compare the instrumentation, scales, and rhythms to Chinese music of the same period. Two good recordings are *The Music of Japan*, a CD from Passport International Music; and *Eleven Centuries of Traditional Music of China*, from Legacy.

ELL/ESL STRATEGY

Language Objective: *To prepare and give a group presentation*

The Japanese believed everyone could take part in the enjoyment and creation of art, literature, and music. Ordinary people often made up short poems to describe a lovely scene or a special occasion. They even held contests and games in which people made up short poems called *haiku*. A haiku is a poem containing 17 syllables—5 in the first line, 7 in the second, and 5 in the third. It captures a single moment. It may be sad, happy, or thoughtful. Have a group of ELL students find examples of haiku to read in translation and research the rules of composition. They should present the poems and enough information to the class, so that classmates can write their own haiku.

Remember

The European feudal warriors were called knights. Like the samurai, they defended their lords.

The nobles and samurai made up the upper classes of Japanese feudal society. However, most of the people in Japan were peasants. They raised the food for the nobles and warriors.

Japanese society also included craftworkers and a few traders. Traders were looked down upon. Buying and selling goods was not considered honorable.

Samurai warriors protected people. They fought with large, two-handed swords.

COMMON ERROR

Contrary to the barbaric image portrayed of samurai in movies, the samurai actually were connoisseurs of music, poetry, and other arts. The tea ceremony became an artform in the sixth century because of a samurai, Toyotomi Hideyoshi.

Remember

Have students study the picture on page 314. Ask how samurai weapons and armor compare to medieval weapons and armor in Europe. (They both include helmets and body protection; warriors carried swords. Samurai used bows and arrows.)

Shogun
A great general governing Japan

Enforce
To make sure that people follow the laws and rules

Missionary
A person sent by a church to other countries to spread a religion

History Fact
The shoguns were so powerful that they actually took over leadership from the emperors.

Over time, feudal clans, or families, united into larger groups. Eventually Japan became a nation-state under one emperor. The emperor was called the *mikado*. Japanese people honored their mikado. However, the mikado had no real power. The country was actually ruled by a warlord, a military leader.

One of those warlords was a man called Yoritomo. In A.D. 1192, he began to use the title of **shogun.** For almost 700 years, one powerful shogun after another ruled Japan. Highly trained samurai **enforced** the shogun's rule (they made sure that people followed the laws). Shogun rule lasted until 1867.

Kublai Khan, the Mongol emperor of China, tried twice to conquer Japan. He launched attacks in 1274 and in 1281. Both times, his fleet was defeated because of fierce storms. The Japanese called these raging storms *Kamikaze,* which means "Divine Wind."

Why Was Japan so Isolated from the Rest of the World?

A hermit is someone who lives alone, away from others. Japan under the shoguns could be called a hermit nation. Japan showed little interest in the rest of the world. For years it remained isolated, like China.

The Italian traveler Marco Polo first told Europeans about Japan. He called the country Cipango, land of gold and riches. Europeans liked the sound of "gold and riches"! Traders began to travel to Japan.

At first the Japanese allowed the trade. They even welcomed Christian **missionaries.** A missionary is a person sent by a church to another country to spread a religion. Soon, however, the shogun began to worry.

History Fact
There is still an emperor of Japan, Akihito, but the shoguns disappeared with feudalism, as Japan modernized in the 19th century.

3 Reinforce and Extend

COMMON ERROR

The primary samurai weapon was originally the longbow, not the sword. Samurai on horseback used longbows until the advent of guns.

IN THE COMMUNITY

Explain that, though Japan flourished for hundreds of years, for 250 years after the shogun expelled foreigners, Japan isolated itself from the outside world. Divide the class into small groups. Have each group discuss what life would be like if their community isolated itself from all other communities. Have them make a list of the consequences of isolation. Have the groups share their ideas with the class.

Reading Strategy:
Summarizing

(The Japanese showed little interest in other nations. The rulers refused to allow non-native people in or their own people out.)

TEACHER ALERT

Although there are many cultures in this chapter, there are common subjects for each civilization. Encourage students to see these themes, choose one that seems particularly interesting, and explore it further. They might focus on trade (money and goods), food (rice, corn, potatoes), roads, or written languages.

He thought that Christianity and European ways might upset the Japanese culture. Therefore, the ruling shogun of the Tokugawa family closed the doors to Japan. Only the Dutch were allowed to continue a little trade. Just one Dutch ship a year could come to the port of Nagasaki.

The Japanese were strict about their rules. Stories tell of foreign sailors shipwrecked on Japanese shores being put to death. Their crime was that they had dared to set foot on Japanese soil.

Reading Strategy:
Summarizing

What are some important details that relate to Japan as a "hermit nation"?

The shogun also did not allow the Japanese to travel outside of their country. Beginning in about 1600, Japan was totally separated from the rest of the world. For about the next 250 years, Japan remained alone.

On a sheet of paper, write the answer to each question. Use complete sentences.

1. How was the way of life in Japan influenced by its Chinese neighbors?

2. What was the role of the samurai in Japanese society?

3. Why did the ruling shogun family not allow the Japanese to trade with outsiders?

On a sheet of paper, write the letter of the answer that correctly completes each sentence.

4. Japan was a(n) _____ society.

   A feudal　　　　**B** friendly　　　　**C** democratic　　　　**D** artistic

5. Most Japanese were _____ who raised food for the nobles and warriors.

   A mikados　　　　**B** shoguns　　　　**C** samurai　　　　**D** peasants

6. The Japanese emperor, the _____, was honored by the people but had little power.

   A samurai　　　　**B** mikado　　　　**C** shogun　　　　**D** Kamikaze

7. The great general that governed Japan is known as a _____.

   A samurai　　　　**B** mikado　　　　**C** shogun　　　　**D** Kamikaze

8. Japan, like China, was quite _____ the rest of the world.

   A disliked by　　　　　　　　**C** friendly with
   B isolated from　　　　　　　 **D** open to

9. The ruling shogun of the Tokugawa family allowed only the _____ to trade with them.

   A Dutch　　　　**B** Italians　　　　**C** Chinese　　　　**D** Indians

10. The Japanese were not allowed to leave their country for _____ years.

   A 100　　　　**B** 250　　　　**C** 700　　　　**D** 1,600

Lesson 15–2 Review Answers

1. The Japanese adopted writing, customs, crafts, arts, and ideas of government and taxes from China. They also adapted the Chinese calendar system, as well as ideas from Confucius and Buddhism. **2.** The samurai were a class of warriors that fought for the nobles. The samurai were given many privileges and, in return, pledged loyalty and protection to their nobles. **3.** The ruling Japanese shogun thought that Christianity and European ways might upset the Japanese culture. **4.** A **5.** D **6.** B **7.** C **8.** B **9.** A **10.** B

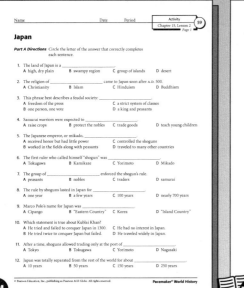

Activity 59, pages 1–2

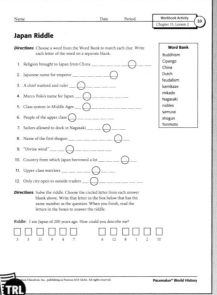

Workbook Activity 59

Chapter 15 Lesson 3

Overview This lesson describes the rise and fall of the Mogul Empire.

Objectives

- To explain why the people of India converted to Buddhism under the emperor Asoka
- To tell what the Moguls brought to India

Student Pages 318–320

Teacher's Resource Library

Workbook Activity 60

Activity 60

Modified Activity 60

PRONUNCIATION GUIDE

Use this list to help students pronounce difficult words in this lesson.

Shah Jahan (shä′ jə hän′)

Taj Mahal (täzh′ mə häl′)

---

1 Warm-Up Activity

Tell students that India's religions have played an important role in the country's history from early days right through the 20th century. Ask what they know about religion in India and how it has affected that country's history. (A notable 20th-century example was the division of India into Hindu India and Muslim Pakistan.)

2 Teaching the Lesson

Tell students to map the comings and goings of religions and Moguls as they read. Suggest that they use a flow chart or sequence-of-events chart to keep track of changes in the Mogul emperors and their religious ideas.

Ask:

- What did Asoka do? (He united India and established Buddhism as the state religion.)
- What empire did Babar set up in India? (the Mogul Empire)

LESSON 15-3 India

Objectives

- To explain why the people of India converted to Buddhism under the emperor Asoka
- To tell what the Moguls brought to India

Reading Strategy: Summarizing

What does this lesson have to say about Hinduism and Buddhism in India?

For a long time India was divided into different kingdoms. Wealthy princes ruled each one. The people followed the Hindu religion. But in about 268 B.C., Asoka became emperor. He converted to Buddhism. Most of India's people turned away from the Hindu religion with its strict caste laws. Many turned to the teachings of Buddha.

Later, however, the Hindu religion became popular in India again. Hindu believers flocked to the Ganges River to wash away their sins. The Hindus believed that all rivers came from the gods. They thought that the Ganges was especially holy.

What Was India Like Under Mogul Rule?

In the eighth century A.D., Muslim warriors began a series of invasions into India.

The first Muslims came from Arabia. Three hundred years later, the invaders came from Persia and Afghanistan. The city of Delhi was captured several times. In 1206, Muslims set up a government in Delhi. In 1398, the conqueror Tamerlane and his army from central Asia raided India and captured Delhi once again.

In 1526, a Muslim prince of Afghanistan named Babar invaded India. He was a direct descendant of Genghis Khan. Babar conquered most of northern India. He established the Mogul Empire and made himself emperor.

The greatest Mogul emperor was Babar's grandson, Akbar. He extended Mogul rule to most of India. He was a wise ruler. He was a Muslim, but he let others worship as they pleased. He tried to bring people of all religions together to live in harmony. Most of the empire remained Hindu.

- Who was the most famous Mogul ruler? (Akbar)
- Why did the Mogul Empire break up? (Aurangzeb persecuted the Hindus, who made up most of the population in India. They revolted and weakened the empire.)

Background Information

Although Buddhism arose in India and was an important religion there for hundreds of years, by the seventh century A.D. it had faded in importance. By then it had spread along trade routes to China, Korea, and Japan, as well as Southeast Asia, where it remains important. Later, it spread to Tibet. Each country developed a distinctive form or forms of Buddhism.

Reading Strategy: Summarizing

Have students read and answer the question. (India's population was largely Hindu; Buddhism was encouraged by some of the emperors, starting in the third century B.C., and by some Mogul emperors, who tolerated other religions.)

The Taj Mahal was built by Shah Jahan as a tomb for his wife.

History Fact
It took 20,000 workers 20 years, from 1630 to 1650, to complete the building of the Taj Mahal.

Reading Strategy: Summarizing

What leaders of India are mentioned in this lesson?

The Mogul Empire lasted for about 200 years. These were good years. The strong central government provided a time of peace. The arts thrived. A special blend of Middle Eastern and Indian culture developed. The Moguls left fine buildings. One of these is the famous Taj Mahal. It was built in Agra by Shah Jahan as a tomb for his wife, Mumtaz Mahal. Shah Jahan was the grandson of Akbar.

Shah Jahan had a son called Aurangzeb. In 1658, Aurangzeb took the throne. Aurangzeb was a harsh ruler. He threw his father in prison. He made Hindus pay a special tax. He destroyed many Hindu temples. Aurangzeb tried to force people to convert to Islam. In central India the Hindus revolted. The empire was weakened. Aurangzeb died in 1707. Shortly after, the Mogul Empire began to break up.

LEARNING STYLES

 Logical/Mathematical
Have students make a timeline that covers the events that led up to the Mogul occupation of India. Begin the timeline in the eighth century A.D. Have students use their timelines to quiz each other about the sequence of events in the occupation of India.

LEARNING STYLES

 Visual/Spatial
Encourage students to make a visual guide of the religions covered in this chapter. For each religion, suggest that students draw a trunk of a tree and label it with the name of the religion. Have students add branches to each tree with facts they already know. As students learn more about the religion, have them add additional branches with facts. Additional branches may grow from the trunk or from other branches.

ELL/ESL STRATEGY

 Language Objective: *To discuss and investigate a subject*

Ask students to study the photograph of the Taj Mahal on page 319. Ask students what kinds of details they can observe. Ask groups of students to list details that they can observe from the photo. Use the Who, What, Why, Where, When, and How method. Students may use these questions or create their own. Have students research the Taj Mahal in books or on the Internet and use the details they find to complete their charts. Ask them to use their charts to write a summary about what they learned about the Taj Mahal.

 History Fact
Students can learn more about the Taj Mahal and other buildings of the time at www.agsglobepmwh.com/page319.

Reading Strategy: Summarizing

(the Mogul princes: Babar, Akbar, Aurangzeb) You can also ask students to summarize the accomplishments of the Mogul emperors. (Their government presided over a time of peace and cultural progress.)

3 | Reinforce and Extend

Lesson 15–3 Review Answers

1. princes 2. Buddhism 3. rivers
4. Muslim 5. Arabia 6. Babar 7. Akbar
8. Aurangzeb 9. culture 10. Taj Mahal

LESSON 15-3

REVIEW

Word Bank

Akbar

Arabia

Aurangzeb

Babar

Buddhism

culture

Muslim

princes

rivers

Taj Mahal

On a sheet of paper, write the word from the Word Bank to complete each sentence correctly.

1. India was divided and ruled by wealthy _____ for a long time.

2. When Asoka became emperor he converted to _____, and many others did the same.

3. The Hindus believed that all _____ came from gods.

4. During the eight century A.D., _____ warriors began a series of invasions into India.

5. Invaders came from _____, Persia, and Afghanistan.

6. _____ conquered most of northern India, establishing the Mogul Empire and making himself emperor.

7. _____ extended Mogul rule to most of India.

8. _____ was a harsh ruler. He forced Hindus to pay a special tax and tried to convert people to Islam.

9. During the Mogul Empire, a strong central government provided peace and the arts thrived. Also, a special blend of Middle Eastern and Indian _____ developed.

10. One of the fine buildings the Moguls left is the famous _____.

320   Unit 6   The Age of Exploration and Conquest

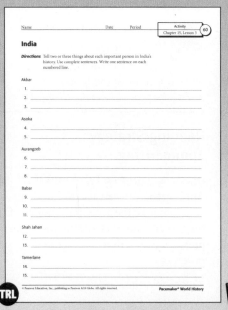

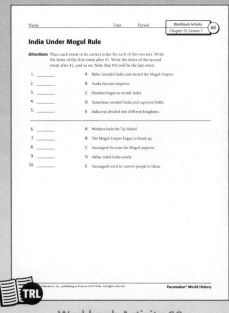

320   *Unit 6 Exploration and Conquest*   Activity 60   Workbook Activity 60

The Americas

Objectives

■ To provide examples of mound builders and cliff dwellers

■ To describe the climate the Inuits lived in and how it affected their daily lives

■ To explain why the Aztecs had one of the most advanced civilizations in the Americas

■ To describe the system of communication that the Incas developed

Mesoamerica
The area of North America (including Mexico and Central America) where civilizations developed before Europeans entered the continent

Dweller
A person who lives in a place

Until the end of the 15th century, most Europeans did not know about the Americas. Only the Vikings knew that land existed across the western sea. One day the Europeans would call these lands the New World. To the American Indians, however, the Americas were home. This area, at this time in history, is known as **Mesoamerica.** Mesoamerica refers to the area of North America (including Mexico and Central America) where civilizations developed before Europeans entered the continent.

Who Were the Mound Builders and the Cliff Dwellers?

Groups of American Indians lived in different parts of the Americas. From about 100 B.C. to A.D. 500, the Hopewell Indians lived in the Ohio River Valley. They built huge burial mounds. As many as 1,000 people were sometimes buried in a single mound. Other American Indians lived along the Mississippi River. They too built giant mounds of earth around A.D. 1000. They built their temples on top of the mounds. These Indians were called Mississippians. They lived mainly by farming.

To the west, in what is now New Mexico, Arizona, and Colorado, lived the cliff **dwellers.** As their name suggests, cliff dwellers were people who lived on a cliff. These Indians were called Anasazi. Some descendants of the Anasazi are called *Pueblo* Indians, from the Spanish word for "town." Around A.D. 1000, the Anasazi began building villages on the sides of cliffs. All building was done with sandstone blocks and mud. Some homes were on protected ledges. Others were in hollow spaces in the cliff walls. Most homes were two or three stories high. As many as 1,500 people lived in one of these villages.

Chapter 15 Lesson 4

Overview This lesson describes the civilizations that developed in Mesoamerica and the far north.

Objectives

■ To provide examples of mound builders and cliff dwellers

■ To describe the climate the Inuits lived in and how it affected their daily lives

■ To explain why the Aztecs had one of the most advanced civilizations in the Americas

■ To describe the system of communication that the Incas developed

Student Pages 321–328

Teacher's Resource Library

Workbook Activity 61

Activity 61

Modified Activity 61

....

Vocabulary

advanced	Mesoamerica
barter	mosaic
dweller	terraced

Ask volunteers to read the definitions of the vocabulary words. Then have each student write a paragraph that correctly uses all the words.

2 Teaching the Lesson

Have students study the map on page 323 to find out where the cliff dwellers, mound builders, Inuit, and Aztecs were located. Have students read this lesson to learn about the cultures of these civilizations and what their inhabitants' lives were like.

Ask:

● Where did the Anasazi live? (in the West, in mud and stone houses on cliffs)

● What is the biggest challenge the Inuit faced? (the cold)

● Why did the Aztecs practice human sacrifice? (They believed that the gods needed human sacrifice to be happy.)

● How did Incas get messages swiftly from place to place? (They used runners who passed messages by word of mouth.)

1 Warm-Up Activity

Ask students where corn, chocolate, tomatoes, and potatoes were first farmed. (Mesoamerica) Do they know who the farmers were? (Aztecs, Incas, Mayans) In this lesson, they'll read about American civilizations that have largely disappeared, though their legacy lingers on in some very important foods and cultural artifacts.

Reading Strategy:
Summarizing

(where they lived, how they fed themselves) If they find themselves unable to sift out the important details, discuss how to decide what they are.

Background Information

In spite of their reputation as fierce opponents, the Spaniards quickly conquered the Aztecs. A number of factors aided the Spanish in their conquest. By luck, their leader's appearance seemed to confirm the myth of a returning god for the Aztecs. The Spanish had guns and horses, and so were a superior force. They persuaded subjugated Indians to fight with the Spaniards against the ruling Aztecs. Also, they captured the head of state early on.

The Anasazi built dwellings in cliffs.

Reading Strategy:
Summarizing

What are the important details about the different groups of people who settled in North America?

No one knows why the Anasazi moved away by about A.D. 1300. They left behind their empty villages, which can still be seen today. Perhaps the climate had become too dry to allow farming.

These early American Indians did not have a system of writing. What we know about them comes from the findings of archaeologists.

Who Were the Inuit?

The Inuit, or Eskimos, lived in the far north of North America. The Inuit ate the meat of caribou, seals, whales, and birds. They also ate fish from icy northern waters. They had no greens to eat. They got their vitamins by eating every part of an animal. They often ate the meat raw. The word *eskimo* is an American Indian word. It means "eater of raw meat." The Eskimos call themselves *Inuit,* which means "people."

The Inuit lived in one of the coldest places in the world. They made tools and weapons to fit their cold land. They traveled in sleds made of driftwood and leather. The sleds were pulled by teams of dogs. In the summer the Inuit lived in tents made of animal skins. In winter they lived in houses made of blocks of snow. These houses were called *igloos.*

The Inuit loved feasts and celebrations. Their medicine men danced and sang to the spirits of the earth and the air.

The first Europeans to meet the Inuit were the Vikings. The Inuit arrived in Greenland about A.D. 1100. They found Vikings already living there.

Early Civilizations of North America

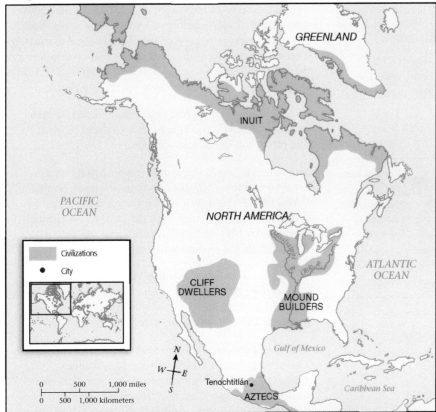

MAP STUDY

1. What were four early civilizations of North America?

2. The mound builders were located near which two rivers?

Language Objective:
To be able to use placement words

Placement words include *across, on top of, along, to the west, and on the sides*. Create a drawing of the school and surrounding streets and homes or businesses on the board. Make a list of placement words on the board. Have students use placement words to explain where buildings and streets are in relation to each other. Have students turn to the map of North America on page 323. Repeat the activity, noting the placement of civilizations and landforms in relation to each other.

3   Reinforce and Extend

MAP STUDY

Answers

1. Inuit, Aztecs, cliff dwellers, mound builders

2. Mississippi and Ohio rivers

AT HOME

The Aztecs had no coins, and instead bartered for goods. In our culture, with money constantly changing hands, bartering and bargaining, in general, is a lost art. Discuss where we allow bartering or bargaining. Have students talk to their families about if, when, and where they use bartering and bargaining.

Remember

Students studied these early Americans in Chapter 6. Have students refresh their memory of that chapter, then ask them how the Olmec and Maya were like the Aztecs. (Possible answer: They all built cities surrounded by farms. They all lived in Central America. They all used writing or hieroglyphics.)

COMMON ERROR

Students may think that all American Indians were illiterate. However, literacy was widespread among indigenous Mesoamerican peoples. They learned to write their own languages in Spanish after the Spaniards invaded.

CAREER CONNECTION

Radiocarbon dating is a technique used to determine the absolute age of a once-living thing. It measures the amount of radioactive carbon remaining in the specimen since death occurred. Since half the carbon in a specimen decays every 5,730 years, specimens older than about 50,000 years old cannot be dated because there is not enough remaining carbon to be measured.

The number of radiocarbon dating labs worldwide has grown; today there are more than 100 labs. Trained lab personnel perform radiocarbon assays for anthropologists, archaeologists, and other scientists. As the need for these assays increases, the demand for lab workers increases. Encourage interested students to research the career opportunities available for radiocarbon technicians and technologists.

Advanced

Ahead of most others in knowledge, skill, or progress

Terraced

Going upward like steps

Remember

The Olmecs and the Maya were some of the earliest civilizations in the Americas. They built their cities in Mexico and Central America.

Who Were the Aztecs?

The Aztecs were an important civilization. In the 1200s they settled in a large valley in Mexico. The Aztecs built one of the most **advanced** civilizations in the Americas. This means they were ahead of most other civilizations of the time in their knowledge, skill, and progress. Over time they conquered and ruled five to six million people.

"Find a place where a great eagle sits on a cactus," Aztec priests declared. "The eagle holds a snake in its beak. At that place, you shall build your temple."

The Aztecs followed the words of their priests. They believed that these words came from the gods. So that is how they decided on a site for the capital. Where they found the eagle, they built the city of Tenochtitlán. Modern-day Mexico City is on the same site as Tenochtitlán, the ancient Aztec capital.

The Aztecs were feared by other American Indians. During the 1400s, Aztec warriors conquered all the lands around Tenochtitlán. When Montezuma II came to the throne in 1502, he ruled the Aztec empire.

The Aztecs collected tributes from those they conquered. The tributes came in the form of gold and silver, craftwork, food, and human prisoners. Some prisoners were offered as sacrifices to Aztec gods. The Aztec religion called for sacrifices to keep the gods happy. The Aztecs developed advanced methods of farming. In mountainous areas, they **terraced**, or stepped, their land to stop the soil from eroding. In dry areas, they used irrigation canals. The Aztecs' greatest achievement, though, was the system of farming called *chinampa*. In this system, the Aztecs farmed in swamps and lakes. They dug drainage ditches and created islands of mud where they grew crops.

Barter

To trade goods or services without using money

Mosaic

A design made by putting together small pieces of colored stone, glass, or other material

Reading Strategy:
Summarizing

What is the main idea of this section on the Aztecs?

The Aztecs had a well-ordered society. They invented a form of picture-writing. They also developed a system of numbers to help them keep track of what they owned. They had a calendar stone that recorded time. They built temples and buildings in a pyramid style.

The Aztecs had no need for money since they **bartered**, or traded, for goods. Chocolate was a favorite drink. So cocoa beans were often traded. Our word *chocolate*, in fact, comes from the Aztec language.

The Aztecs made some beautiful craftwork. Archaeologists have found **mosaic** masks made of turquoise and jade. The Aztecs also used colorful feathers to make headdresses and cloaks.

The Aztecs liked games and contests of athletic strength and skill. One of their favorite games was called *tlachiti*. It was a combination of handball and basketball. The players had to put a bouncy rubber ball through rings at either end of a court.

The Aztec empire ended in 1521. Cortés and his army arrived in Tenochtitlán in 1519. They were amazed at what they found. Tenochtitlán was a beautiful city, with floating gardens, drawbridges, and markets. It was larger than any Spanish city of that time.

The Aztecs terraced their land for farming.

Reading Strategy:
Summarizing

Ask for two or three volunteers to answer the question and discuss any differences in their summaries.

WORLD CULTURES

Have students make a classroom display comparing the arts and crafts of civilizations discussed in this chapter. They should bring in items or pictures of items that represent the different cultures: Chinese, Japanese, Indian, American Indian, Mexican, Inuit, and South American. After the display is completed, have students compare the items. Do they see any similarities? Ask them to describe any clear differences in style, subject matter, use of color, or use of materials.

ONLINE CONNECTION

Have students suggest topics from the chapter—such as acupuncture, the Silk Road, Genghis Khan, Kublai Khan, Marco Polo, Japanese feudal system, samurai, Moguls, Taj Mahal, mound builders, cliff dwellers, Inuit, Aztecs, and Incas—for Internet research. Write these topics on the board. Assign half the class to research the East and half to research the Americas. Provide time for students to share their findings.

The Spaniards were welcomed in friendship. The Aztecs may have believed that Cortés was a long lost Aztec god. The god sailed away across the sea and was expected to return someday. Yet Cortés captured the emperor, Montezuma, and made him a prisoner. In 1520, Aztecs drove the Spaniards away. Montezuma died during the fighting. The next year Cortés returned and destroyed Tenochtitlán.

Who Were the Incas?

The earliest history of the Incas is only legend. What we know for sure is that the Incas lived in the mountains of what is now Peru in South America. Around A.D. 1200 they began to build their empire. In time, the Incas conquered much of western South America. They took over the rest of Peru and parts of what are now Colombia, Bolivia, Ecuador, and Chile.

One man ruled the entire Inca Empire. He was called the *Inca*. His people worshiped him as a direct descendant of the sun. The sun was the Inca people's most powerful god. The Inca's word was law. He had many officials to see that his laws were obeyed.

The Inca ruled over a giant empire from his capital at Cuzco. More than six million people lived under his rule. Communicating with all these subjects was a problem. Therefore, the Incas built a fine network of roads. These roads improved communication. They connected all corners of the empire.

The Incas also built bridges of twisted vines to stretch across steep rain forest valleys. They had no horses or wheeled vehicles. All traveling was done on foot. Llamas carried their goods.

Swift runners raced along the Inca roads to deliver messages. The Incas did not have a system of writing.

Messages were passed by word of mouth. Runners also carried *quipus*. These were different colored ropes with knots to stand for numbers. They used the quipus to keep track of things.

The Incas built rest stops along their roads. At each stop a tired runner could tell his message to a fresh runner. Then that messenger would hurry to the next stop. This relay system kept communication moving across the empire.

The Incas were fine builders. They used huge stone blocks. They fit the blocks together carefully. They needed no mortar or cement of any kind. Some of the stones fit together so tightly that the blade of a knife could not slide between them! Inca buildings still stand at Cuzco today, even after earthquakes have destroyed modern structures.

The Incas had plenty of gold and plenty of silver. Their temples were decorated with both of the valuable metals. Inca artists made beautiful objects of solid gold. These were often inlaid with precious jewels.

It is no wonder that the Spanish explorers were drawn to the Incas. In 1532, tales of great wealth brought Francisco Pizarro to South America. His visit was the beginning of the end of the Inca civilization.

Ask:

- What date did Kublai Khan's rule in China begin? (1260)
- How long did the Mongols rule in China? (108 years)
- In what year did the Moguls invade India? (1526)
- Spanish explorers invaded several Native American empires. Did Spanish explorers invade the Aztecs or the Incas first? (the Aztecs)
- In what year did Japan officially forbid trade with Europe? (1600)

TIMELINE STUDY:

ASIA AND THE AMERICAS: 1100–1600

When the Aztecs were first known to be in Tenochtitlán, what group ruled China?

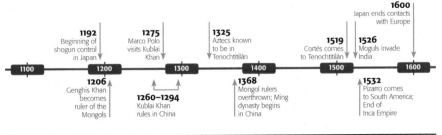

1192 Beginning of shogun control in Japan

1275 Marco Polo visits Kublai Khan

1325 Aztecs known to be in Tenochtitlán

1519 Cortés comes to Tenochtitlán

1526 Moguls invade India

1600 Japan ends contacts with Europe

1206 Genghis Khan becomes ruler of the Mongols

1260–1294 Kublai Khan rules in China

1368 Mongol rulers overthrown; Ming dynasty begins in China

1532 Pizarro comes to South America; End of Inca Empire

1100 | 1200 | 1300 | 1400 | 1500 | 1600

Lesson 15–4 Review Answers

1. B 2. B 3. A 4. D 5. A 6. C 7. A

8. The Inuits lived in one of the coldest places in the world. They made tools and weapons to fit their cold land, and traveled in sleds that were pulled by teams of dogs. In the summer they lived in tents made of animal skins, and in the winter they lived in igloos, which were houses made of blocks of snow. **9.** The Aztecs used terracing in mountainous areas, irrigation canals in dry areas, and *chinampa* in swamps and lakes. **10.** The Incas built a fine network of roads and bridges. Llamas would carry Inca goods and swift runners would race along the roads to deliver messages. There were rest stops along these roads, and a tired runner would pass his message to a fresh runner at these stops. In this way, the message spread across the empire.

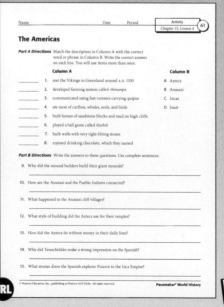

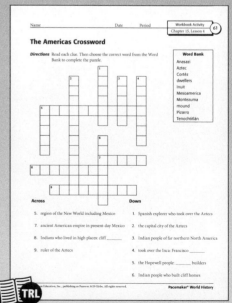

LESSON 15-4 REVIEW

On a sheet of paper, write the letter of the answer that correctly completes each sentence.

1. The _____ lived in the Ohio River Valley and built huge burial mounds.

- **A** Mississippians
- **B** Hopewell Indians
- **C** Pueblo Indians
- **D** Inuits

2. The _____ were cliff dwellers. They used sandstone blocks and mud to build their villages on the sides of cliffs.

- **A** Aztecs
- **B** Anasazi
- **C** Hopewell Indians
- **D** Mississippians

3. Early American Indians did not have a system of _____.

- **A** writing
- **B** farming
- **C** worship
- **D** building

4. The Inuits had no greens to eat, but got their vitamins from eating _____.

- **A** caribou
- **B** fish
- **C** birds
- **D** every part of an animal

5. The Aztecs conquered and ruled five to six million people. It was one of the most _____ civilizations in the Americas.

- **A** advanced
- **B** vicious
- **C** simple
- **D** dull

6. The _____ invented a form of picture-writing and a calendar stone that recorded time. They also had a number system to help them keep track of what they owned.

- **A** Inuits
- **B** Incas
- **C** Aztecs
- **D** Spaniards

7. _____ was the Inca people's most powerful god.

- **A** The sun
- **B** The Inca
- **C** Montezuma
- **D** The cocoa bean

On a sheet of paper, write the answer to each question. Use complete sentences.

8. How did the climate the Inuits lived in affect their daily lives?

9. What methods of farming did the Aztecs develop?

10. What was the system of communication that the Incas developed?

---

328 Unit 6 *The Age of Exploration and Conquest*

Activity 61

Workbook Activity 61

- China was isolated for centuries. Chinese culture changed very little during that time.

- The Chinese were ahead of the Europeans in papermaking and printing. They understood the process of working with iron. The early Chinese also developed the compass and gunpowder.

- The Mongols from the north invaded China. Mongol leader Genghis Khan built a strong army. Khan's army took control of parts of China, as well as Russia, Persia, and India.

- Italian explorer Marco Polo visited Kublai Khan, a Mongol ruler.

- Japan was a feudal society in the Middle Ages. Shoguns and their warriors, or samurais, ruled the country.

- About 1600, the ruling shogun forbade the Japanese to leave their country. Japan was isolated for the next 250 years.

- The people of India turned from Hinduism to Buddhism, then back to Hinduism. The Moguls brought Islam to India in the eighth century A.D.

- Most Europeans did not know about the Americas until the late 1400s. However, Native Americans built civilizations in the Americas long before that time.

- The Hopewell Indians, the Anasazis, and the Inuit lived in North America.

- The Aztecs built a great empire in Mexico.

- The Incas lived in Peru, in South America.

Chapter 15 Summary

Have students read the Chapter Summary on page 329 to review the main ideas presented in Chapter 15.

Ask:

- Why did Chinese culture remain the same for so long? (China was isolated for centuries.)

- What are three Chinese inventions? (Possible answer: papermaking, forging iron, and gunpowder)

- What Mongol leader invaded China? (Genghis Khan)

- Which Italian traveler visited Kublai Khan in Beijing? (Marco Polo)

- Describe the social organization in Japan in the Middle Ages. (It had a feudal society; warriors ruled the country.)

- Why was Japan isolated for 250 years? (The shogun forbade Japanese to leave the country.)

- What religions were important in India during the Middle Ages? (Hinduism, Buddhism, and Islam)

- When did Europeans discover American civilizations? (in the late 1400s)

- Where did the Hopewell Indians live? (North America)

- What great empire was in Mexico in the 15th and 16th centuries? (the Aztecs)

- Where did the Incas live? (Peru)

TEACHER'S RESOURCE

The AGS Globe Teaching Strategies in Social Studies Transparencies may be used with this chapter. The transparencies add an interactive dimension to expand and enhance the Pacemaker® *World History* program content.

CHAPTER PROJECT FOLLOW-UP

Put aside one day for groups to present their study and explain their displays on inventions from India, China, Japan, the Aztecs, or the Incas. Invite other members of the school staff to enjoy the displays. Have a student who has an interest in photography take photos for the school newspaper. Videotape displays for student portfolios, if students in your school are required to complete graduation portfolios.

Chapter 15 Review

Use the Chapter Review to prepare students for tests and to reteach content from the chapter.

Chapter 15 Mastery Test

The Teacher's Resource Library includes two forms of the Chapter 15 Mastery Test. Each test addresses the chapter Goals for Learning. An optional third page of additional critical-thinking items is included for each test. The difficulty level of the two forms is equivalent.

Chapter 15 Review Answers

Vocabulary Review

1. samurai
2. shogun
3. missionaries
4. terraced
5. barter
6. mosaic
7. acupuncture
8. forge
9. privileges

Chapter Review Questions

10. They lived in Beijing in a great palace called the Forbidden City.

11. Marco Polo was impressed with what he saw in China.

12. The classes were nobles, samurai, and peasants. There were also craftworkers and traders.

Word Bank

acupuncture
barter
forge
missionaries
mosaic
privileges
samurai
shogun
terraced

Vocabulary Review

On a sheet of paper, use the words from the Word Bank to complete each sentence correctly.

1. _____ were upper-class, feudal warriors who fought for the nobles.

2. A(n) _____ was a great general governing Japan.

3. The Japanese were suspicious of Christian _____, so the ruling shogun closed Japan's doors.

4. The Aztecs _____ their land to stop the soil from eroding.

5. The Aztecs would _____ for goods, exchanging them without the use of money.

6. Small pieces of stone or glass can be used to create a(n) _____.

7. The Chinese invented _____, which uses needles to treat pain and illness.

8. The Chinese knew how to _____ iron and mine salt.

9. Samurai were given many _____, including wealth and land.

Chapter Review Questions

On a sheet of paper, write the answer to each question. Use complete sentences.

10. Where did the Ming emperors of China live?

11. How did Marco Polo feel about what he had seen in China?

12. What were the classes in Japan during the Middle Ages?

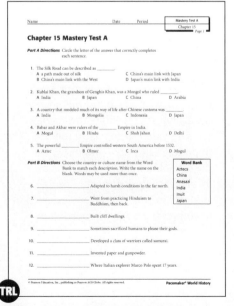

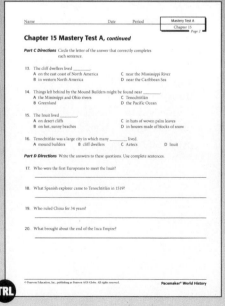

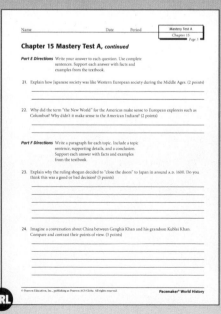

When you are reading a multiple-choice question, look for words such as *mainly, most likely, generally, major,* and *best.* Decide which answer choice best fits the meaning of these words.

13. What religion did the Moguls bring to India?

14. How did the Mogul emperor Akbar treat Indians who were not Muslims?

15. Why did some American Indians build mounds?

16. Why were the Spaniards interested in the Incas?

Critical Thinking

On a sheet of paper, write your response to each question. Use complete sentences.

17. Why was the Silk Road important?

18. Why did the early civilizations of the Americas develop in such different ways?

Using the Timeline

Use the timeline on page 327 to answer the questions.

19. How long did Kublai Khan rule in China?

20. What happened in India in A.D. 1526?

GROUP ACTIVITY

Work with a partner to make a poster that compares the civilizations in the Americas before the European explorers arrived. Include categories such as the following: Location, Climate, Building Styles, Religion, and Food. Try to include one picture for each civilization.

---

13. The Moguls brought Islam to India.

14. He let them worship as they pleased.

15. They built mounds for burial or as platforms for temples and other buildings.

16. They had heard that the Incas had lots of gold and silver.

Critical Thinking

17. Possible answer: During China's isolation from the rest of the world, the Silk Road was the country's main link to the outside.

18. Possible answer: Native American civilizations developed that were suited for the different climates, landforms, and resources of each area.

Using the Timeline

19. 34 years

20. Moguls invaded China.

GROUP ACTIVITY

Students' posters should present material comparing the Native American civilizations. The material should be organized, interesting, and attractive. Students should be able to explain the information on their posters if necessary.

Chapter 15 Mastery Test B, pages 1–3

Introducing the Chapter

From the mid-1400s to the mid-1600s, European explorers searching for trade routes sailed around the southern tips of Africa and South America and across the Pacific, Atlantic, and Indian oceans. By the first decade in the 17th century, European colonies had been established in the New World.

Ask:

- In which three centuries were these discoveries made? (15th, 16th, and 17th centuries)

Explorers, Traders, and Settlers

The explorers from Europe may have been curious about the world or may have wanted adventure. In most cases, they desired riches for themselves and their countries. On their explorations, they often came upon civilizations in the new lands. However, the explorers did not think about the rights of the people already living on the land. Instead, they forced their own culture on them, often making slaves of them.

Most settlers who journeyed to North America were not hoping to find great fortunes. They were seeking a better life and freedom to make their own choices about religion. As they moved onto lands for farming and trapping, they forced American Indians to surrender to them.

GOALS FOR LEARNING

- To explain the discoveries of explorers
- To tell about the Spanish conquistadors and the lands they claimed
- To explain what the English and French did upon coming to North America
- To explain the importance of trade with Europe and the Americas

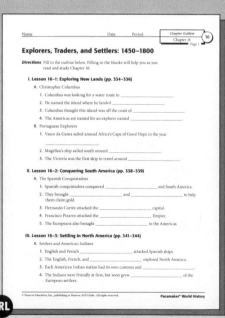

Chapter 16 Self-Study Guide, pages 1–2   Chapter 16 Outline, pages 1–2

Reading Strategy: Questioning

Ask yourself questions as you read. Questioning the text will help you to be a more active reader. You will remember more of what you read if you do this. As you read, ask yourself:

- Why am I reading this text?
- What connections can I make between this text and my own life?
- What decisions can I make about the facts and details in this text?

Key Vocabulary Words

Lesson 2
Conquistador A Spanish conqueror

Lesson 3
Piracy The robbing of ships on the ocean

Pilgrim A person who came to North America for religious freedom and settled in Plymouth, Massachusetts

Puritan A member of a 16th- or 17th-century English group of Protestants who wanted to make the Church of England simpler and stricter

Trapper A person who traps wild animals for their furs

Lesson 4
Stock Shares in a business or company

Shareholder A person who owns one or more parts (shares) of a business

Investment Money given to businesses in order to get even more money back

Interest Money paid for the use of other people's money

Insurance A guarantee that a person or company will be paid money to cover losses

---

- How did settlers who came to North America differ from some other explorers? (They were seeking freedom and a better life, rather than fortunes.)

Reading Strategy: Questioning

Have students brainstorm several questions that might help them to learn the material. For example: Who are the central historic figures in the chapter?

....

Key Vocabulary Words

Point out that these chapter words are presented in the order they appear in each lesson. They are also found in the glossary.

LIFE SKILLS CONNECTION

Students learn how to explore new places in their communities. They also learn how to find tourism information about places outside their own communities. Direct students to their state's tourism Web site. Also discuss traveling safely in new places.

KEY VOCABULARY

Students choose the correct word from the Word Bank to complete each sentence.

CHAPTER PROJECT

Write the following list of "minor characters" from the chapter on the board: Queen Isabella, Montezuma, the 18 survivors who sailed around the world, Amerigo Vespucci, the Incas, and the American Indians who helped the Pilgrims survive the first winter in Plymouth. Divide students into six groups and assign each the task of finding out more about their assigned characters. Have students find information that is not contained in the textbook.

Chapter 16 Life Skills Connection

When we read about explorers, we think of people discovering new lands. But you can be an explorer in your own city or town. You can explore other neighborhoods, and meet people who come from different backgrounds.

Directions Plan a trip to another part of town. Use the phone book or Internet to find places to visit. Many cities have a tourism office or a visitor's center. These can be good resources to find interesting places to visit. Here are some suggestions for places you might look for:

1. a restaurant that serves food you do not usually eat.
2. a museum or cultural center that serves people with a different background.
3. an arts organization you do not visit often, such as an opera hall.
4. a place of worship that serves a community of another faith.
5. an ethnic grocery store.

Some states have historic sites, where people live as they did in older times. For example, people in Virginia can see how settlers lived in Colonial Williamsburg. Your state tourism office will have information on similar places in your area. Visit one of these sites with your family. Report back to the class on what you learned.

Chapter 16 Key Vocabulary Words

Directions Write the correct word from the Word Bank to complete each sentence.

Word Bank
conquistadors
insurance
interest
investments
Pilgrims
piracy
Puritans
shareholders
stock
trappers

1. Massachusetts was settled by _____ looking for religious freedom.
2. Spanish _____ conquered civilizations in Mexico and South America.
3. The English and French used _____ to get a share of the Spanish gold.
4. The _____ wanted to make the Church of England simpler and stricter.
5. French _____ set up outposts all along the Mississippi River.
6. Traders bought _____ to protect their ships.
7. Trading companies sold _____ to raise money for their voyages.
8. The _____ of many people helped pay for the trips.
9. The people who paid this money were _____ in the company.
10. Banks charged _____ for the money they lent to the merchants.

Lesson at a Glance

Chapter 16 Lesson 1

Overview This lesson focuses on Spain and Portugal's efforts to find new trade routes to Asia. Christopher Columbus sailed westward from Spain in 1492, while the Portuguese explorers Vasco da Gama, Pedro Cabral, and Ferdinand Magellan explored several sea routes between 1497 and 1522.

Objectives

- To tell how Columbus came to land in America
- To name and tell about two Portuguese explorers and the things they discovered

Student Pages 334–337

Teacher's Resource Library

Workbook Activity 62

Activity 62

Modified Activity 62

PRONUNCIATION GUIDE

Use this list to help students pronounce difficult words in this lesson.

Amerigo Vespucci
(ə mer´i go´ ve spoo´che)

Magellan (mə jel´ən)

Reading Strategy:
Questioning

Draw students' attention to the Reading Strategy on page 334. Lead a discussion where students recall previous lessons and their own knowledge about the nature of exploration. Ask students what resources they believe a country must have to embark on explorations of new lands. (Answers may vary.)

1 Warm-Up Activity

Ask students to preview the chapter by reading the headings and subheadings and by looking at the art and photos (on pages 336, 338, and 342), the maps (on pages 335 and 343), and the timeline (on page 347). Then, ask

---

Objectives

- To tell how Columbus came to land in America
- To name and tell about two Portuguese explorers and the things they discovered

Reading Strategy:
Questioning

What do you already know about early explorations to new lands?

For centuries, the rest of the world did not know about the Americas or the people living there. Then the Vikings landed in North America. They met American Indians, but the Vikings did not stay long in North America. Much later, European explorers found the continent by accident. What they were really looking for was a quicker route to India and the Far East. The place they found instead seemed like a land of wealth and plenty. It seemed well worth exploring and conquering.

What Was Christopher Columbus Looking for and What Did He Find?

Christopher Columbus set sail from Spain in August 1492. He was not out to prove that the world was round, as stories often tell. He was also not out to conquer new lands. Columbus was looking for a water route to Asia. He believed that by sailing west he might find a shorter route to the treasures of Asia. He had convinced Queen Isabella of Spain to support his voyage. Queen Isabella and King Ferdinand gave Columbus three ships for the voyage. They were the *Niña*, the *Pinta*, and the *Santa Maria*.

Columbus sailed westward. Instead of reaching Asia, Columbus landed on an island in the Bahamas. There it was—a new world where no land should have been! Columbus claimed the land in the name of Spain. He named the land San Salvador.

Columbus thought he had reached an island off the coast of India. That is why he called the people living there "Indians." It was not too many years before people realized Columbus was wrong about the land's location. Those islands that Columbus explored are called the "West Indies."

---

students if they have ever explored something. Ask students, *What was it? What caused you to explore it?* Encourage students to share their stories and personal experiences. Then, ask students, *What is the purpose of exploring something?* Students should understand that exploration can happen, for example, out of need or out of curiosity. Ask students, *Why might explorers have been important during the course of history?*

2 Teaching the Lesson

Ask students why European countries sent explorers to discover new lands during this time period. Have students read pages 334–336 to find out about

the journeys of Columbus, da Gama, Cabral, and Magellan.

Ask:

- Who financed Columbus's voyage? (Queen Isabella)
- Why did Columbus call the American Indians he encountered on his journey "Indians"? (He thought he had reached an island off the coast of India.)
- Where does the word *America* come from? (Amerigo Vespucci)
- Who sponsored da Gama's journey to India? What route did he take? (Portugal; around Africa and then eastward)
- When did Cabral set out for India? What did he find? (1500; Brazil)

Early Voyages of Exploration

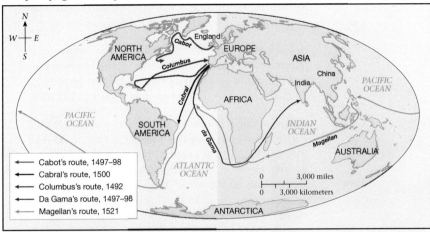

Cabot's route, 1497–98
Cabral's route, 1500
Columbus's route, 1492
Da Gama's route, 1497–98
Magellan's route, 1521

MAP STUDY

1. Which ocean did Columbus cross?
2. How would you describe da Gama's route to India?

Reading Strategy: Questioning

As you read about the early explorers, notice the details in the text. What questions can you ask yourself about these details?

 Remember
Marco Polo had introduced Europeans to the treasures of Asia.

Many places in the Americas have been named after Columbus. The word *America*, however, comes from the name of another explorer, Amerigo Vespucci. He was a European explorer who reached the mainland of South America in 1500. A mapmaker honored his accomplishment by naming the Americas after him.

What Did Portuguese Explorers Discover?

Other explorers searched for that water route to Asia. The Spaniards and the Portuguese led the way in voyages of discovery.

In 1497, Vasco da Gama sailed around Africa's Cape of Good Hope. Vasco da Gama was a Portuguese noble and sailor. He became the first explorer to reach India by a sea route.

1450–1800   *Explorers, Traders, and Settlers   Chapter 16*   **335**

 Remember
Remind students that information about Marco Polo appeared in Chapter 15. Ask them to recall some of the treasures of Asia that Marco Polo wrote about in his journals.

MAP STUDY

Answers:

1. The Atlantic Ocean

2. Da Gama went around the continent of Africa to reach India.

LEARNING STYLES

Visual/Spatial

Have students create a map on a large sheet of paper showing the routes in the map on page 335. Have them use different colors for each explorer. Be sure students label each part of the map correctly.

- What did Magellan's crew do that was a "first"? What country sponsored Magellan? (sailed around the world; Spain)
- What might these journeys have been like for the men who embarked on them? How do we know this from reading the text? (Answers may vary. Students may point out that Magellan was killed and only 18 "survivors" returned to Spain.)

Background Information

Although both Magellan and da Gama tried to reach India by sailing around Africa, the plan had two problems. First, the weather at the southern tip of Africa made the voyage dangerous. Second, reaching the southern tip of Africa took a long time. Sailing on to India would take even longer.

LEARNING STYLES

 Logical/Mathematical

Remind students that degrees of longitude begin with 0° at Greenwich, England, and become greater as one travels east or west. Further, starting with 0° at the equator, latitude degrees become greater as one travels north or south from the equator. Have students determine the approximate degrees of latitude and longitude for a ship entering the Pacific Ocean from the Atlantic Ocean through the Strait of Magellan (70°W longitude, 51°S latitude). Have students then calculate the same information for the modern shortcut from the Pacific to Atlantic oceans—through the Panama Canal (83°W longitude, 10°N latitude). Students should draw maps to illustrate their findings and share them with the class.

Reading Strategy: Questioning

Ask students to point out specific details from the text that illuminate the lives or travels of the early explorers. Lead a discussion in which students answer the question, *What questions can you ask yourself about these details?*

Language Objective:
To encourage students to speculate about the character of early explorers

Tell students that when Columbus died in 1506 he still believed that he had discovered a new route to Asia; he was certain that the area we call the "West Indies" was near China and Japan. What does this suggest about Columbus's character? What character traits do students believe are necessary for one to become an explorer? Have students write a brief paragraph that engages these questions, then encourage volunteers to share their work with the class.

COMMON ERROR

Legend and lore—especially in North America—might lead one to believe that Christopher Columbus was the premier explorer of the age. In fact, the explorations of both da Gama and Magellan were more extensive and "successful" than Columbus's. Encourage students to study the map and compare the distances traveled by each explorer.

COMMON ERROR

Students may not be fully aware of the difficulties and dangers inherent in the journeys taken by the early explorers. You may want to tell students that although Magellan began his journey with five ships and 241 men, only one ship and 18 men survived the trip and returned safely to Spain. Vasco da Gama left Portugal with four ships and 170 men; two ships and 54 men survived the journey and returned to Portugal.

Another Portuguese explorer, Pedro Cabral, set out for India in 1500. He sailed wide of Africa and found Brazil. Thanks to Cabral, Brazil was claimed in the name of Portugal.

In 1519, the Portuguese navigator Ferdinand Magellan began a voyage around the whole world. His own king had refused to give him money for his trip. However, the Spanish king agreed to supply five ships and 241 men.

Magellan sailed around South America and across the Pacific. However, Magellan himself did not make it all the way. In 1521, he was killed by people in the Philippine Islands. However, one of the ships, the *Victoria*, completed the trip around the world. With only 18 survivors, it returned to Spain in 1522. This was the first ship to have sailed completely around the world. The *Victoria's* voyage was the first proof that Earth is round.

The voyage of Magellan's ship, the Victoria, *was the first proof that Earth is round.*

LESSON 16-1 REVIEW

Match the description in Column A with the explorer in Column B.
Write the correct letter on a sheet of paper.

Column A

1. discovered Brazil and claimed it in the name of Portugal

2. first explorer to reach India by a sea route

3. discovered America when trying to find a water route to Asia

4. attempted to sail around the whole world

5. the word *America* is named for this explorer

Column B

A Amerigo Vespucci
B Christopher Columbus
C Ferdinand Magellan
D Pedro Cabral
E Vasco da Gama

On a sheet of paper, write the letter of the answer that correctly completes each sentence.

6. Columbus named the land he discovered _____.

   A Bahamas   **B** West Indies   **C** San Salvador   **D** Brazil

7. Columbus called the people living on the island he explored _____.

   A Indians   **C** American Indians
   B Americans   **D** Aztecs

8. The Spaniards and the _____ led the way in voyages of discovery.

   A Dutch   **B** Portuguese   **C** French   **D** English

9. A _____ king supplied five ships and 241 men on Magellan's voyage.

   A Spanish   **B** Portuguese   **C** French   **D** Dutch

10. While Magellan did not make the trip around the world, his ship _____ did.

   A *Niña*   **B** *Santa Maria*   **C** *Pinta*   **D** *Victoria*

1450–1800   *Explorers, Traders, and Settlers*   Chapter 16   **337**

---

3 Reinforce and Extend

STUDY SKILLS

Have students set up a separate sheet for notes about each group of people, set of city-states, and countries mentioned in this chapter. As they read the chapter, ask students to make notes about the role each played in this age of exploration.

TEACHER ALERT

As students work their way through Chapter 16, remind them to update their chapter notes and provide information about each group of people and the countries mentioned in the chapter.

Lesson 16–1 Review Answers

1. D **2.** E **3.** B **4.** C **5.** A **6.** C **7.** A **8.** B **9.** A **10.** D

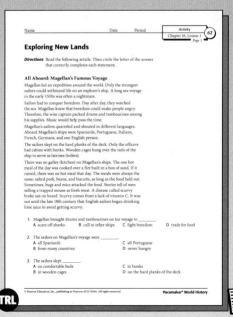

Activity 62, pages 1–2

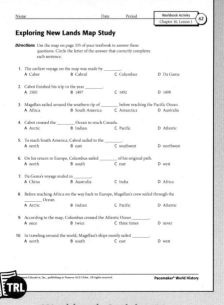

Workbook Activity 62

Explorers/Traders/Settlers Chapter 16   **337**

Chapter 16 Lesson 2

Overview By the time Spanish conquistadors arrived in Mexico and South America, vibrant and sophisticated cultures were already well established. Nevertheless, the Europeans failed to recognize these as legitimate civilizations. Both Cortés and Pizarro subjected the native peoples to great cruelty and hardship.

Objectives

- To describe the relationship between Spanish settlers and the American Indians
- To explain how the slave trade developed

Student Pages 338–340

Teacher's Resource Library 🆃🆁🅻

Workbook Activity 63

Activity 63

Modified Activity 63

Vocabulary

conquistador

Ask students to create a crossword puzzle using the vocabulary word above and the seven words from the Word Bank on page 340. Have students create clues by using information from the reading in Lesson 16–2. When students have completed their puzzles, have them trade with each other and complete one another's puzzles.

PRONUNCIATION GUIDE

Use this list to help students pronounce difficult words in this lesson.

Tenochtitlán (te nôch′ te tlän′)

Montezuma (mon ′tə zoo′mə)

1 | Warm-Up Activity

Ask students to recall what they know about slavery and the slave trade. Encourage a discussion in which students talk about the impact of slavery on African peoples.

Conquering South America

Objectives

- To describe the relationship between Spanish settlers and the American Indians
- To explain how the slave trade developed

Conquistador
A Spanish conqueror

Europeans quickly realized what a prize they had found in the new lands. They thought it did not matter that people already lived there. Europeans did not recognize that the natives had civilizations and cultures of their own. Europeans wanted the new lands for themselves.

What Things Did Spanish Conquistadors Bring to South America?

When the Spanish **conquistadors** (conquerors) arrived in Mexico and South America, they found great civilizations. The conquistadors brought guns and horses to help them claim gold. The American Indians had neither one.

Hernando Cortés met the Aztec ruler, Montezuma. Cortés went on to conquer the Aztec Empire.

---

2 | Teaching the Lesson

Have students say why people might feel threatened if outsiders were to take control of their country. Then have students read pages 338–339 to find out what happened when Spain took control of land in the Americas.

Ask:

- What name did Spain give its new land in the Americas? (New Spain)
- What two things helped the conquistadors conquer the American Indians? (guns and horses)
- What religion did the Spaniards try to force upon the Indians? (Christianity)

Background Information

When Cortés and his army arrived in Mexico, about 11 million American Indians lived there. By about 1650, fewer than two million were left. Cruel treatment and hard work had killed some. But diseases from Europe were the main killer. In Europe, disease, such as measles, were common. Over time, however, Europeans had built up a natural immunity to these illnesses. But because the peoples of South America had never been exposed to diseases such as smallpox, chickenpox, measles, and mumps, they had no immunity. Epidemics of these diseases swept through villages, killing people of all ages. Entire cultures disappeared.

Reading Strategy:
Questioning

What details are important to understanding what this lesson is about?

You Decide

Many people think the American Indians would have been better off if the Europeans had never set foot in the Americas. What do you think?

Hernando Cortés attacked the Aztec capital of Tenochtitlán in 1521. The Spaniards soon conquered all of Mexico. They called it New Spain.

In South America, Francisco Pizarro attacked the Inca Empire in 1532. Again, the Indians were no match for the new enemy they did not understand. The Spaniards tried to make the Indians accept the Christian religion. Many Indians who refused were burned to death.

The Spaniards treated the Indians cruelly in other ways, too. They used the Indians as slaves, working them harder than animals. Many Europeans thought these people were only savages.

The Europeans caused the Indians to suffer in yet another way. The Europeans brought their diseases with them to the Americas. Thousands of American Indians died from the new diseases.

LEARN MORE ABOUT IT

The Slave Trade

In Africa, too, some Europeans were treating people like work animals. The Europeans discovered that there was money to be made in the slave trade. The Spanish and Portuguese brought ships full of Africans to the Americas, where the Africans were sold into slavery.

For a time the Spanish and Portuguese controlled the slave markets. Soon England and France joined the slave trade, too.

An English naval commander, Sir John Hawkins, was the first English slave trader. In the 1560s, Hawkins made three voyages. On each one, he stopped in Africa to find the strongest, healthiest men. Then Hawkins carried these Africans to Spanish colonies in the Americas. There he sold them into slavery. Slave-trading led the way in setting up trade between England and the Americas.

Reading Strategy:
Questioning

Ask students: *What details are important to understanding this lesson?*

Encourage students to call out answers as you write them on the board.

You Decide

Lead a discussion in which students talk about the impact of European exploration on American Indians. Ask students to speculate about how the world might be different if the Europeans had stayed home.

LEARN MORE ABOUT IT

After students have read about the slave trade, tell them that for more than 300 years slave traders captured and sold into slavery more than 20 million Africans. Of these 20 million, one-fourth never reached the Americas. They died on the ships and the slave traders threw their bodies into the sea.

LEARNING STYLES

Auditory/Verbal

Have students listen as you read aloud the selection from "Learn More About It." Ask students to make notes as they listen. Ask students to summarize the main ideas from the reading.

ELL/ESL STRATEGY

Language Objective: *To familiarize students with another language*

If the first language of some students is Spanish, use the Spanish words in this section to give these students an opportunity to be in a leadership role. Ask Spanish-speaking students to provide a short pronunciation lesson for other students in the class. Encourage them to write the words on the board and pronounce them. Ask them to share other Spanish words that are similar in meaning to the words used in this section.

3   Reinforce and Extend

CAREER CONNECTION

Since Edward Jenner's development of a smallpox vaccination in 1790, many people have worked to prevent the spread of disease. Across the country, workers in public health facilities treat people with health problems and educate the public about ways to stay healthy. Have students research local colleges to find out about their public health curriculum and requirements for admission to classes. Students might also interview public health professionals to find out what they do in their jobs and how they trained for their work.

COMMON ERROR

It is a mistake to assume—as some students might—that the first explorers to the Americas encountered a wild, untamed land inhabited by uncivilized peoples (savages). Remind students that the indigenous peoples who lived in Mexico and South America had great civilizations evidenced by their own art, religion, language, and customs.

WORLD CULTURES

When the Europeans came to what is now known as Latin America, the population consisted of Indian groups such as the Aztecs, Incas, and Maya. Today, the people of Latin America have a varied ancestry. Throughout Latin America there are Indians, whites, and blacks, as well as people of mixed ancestry. People of mixed Indian and white descent are called *mestizos*.

Lesson 16–2 Review Answers

1. B **2.** C **3.** A **4.** Tenochtitlán
5. Christian **6.** slaves **7.** diseases
8. Portuguese **9.** Spanish **10.** England

LESSON 16-2 REVIEW

Match the description in Column A with the name in Column B. Write the correct letter on a sheet of paper.

Column A	Column B
1. conquered all of Mexico	**A** Francisco Pizarro
2. the first English slave trader	**B** Hernando Cortés
3. attacked the Inca Empire	**C** Sir John Hawkins

Word Bank

Christian
diseases
England
Portuguese
slaves
Spanish
Tenochtitlán

On a sheet of paper, write the word from the Word Bank to complete each sentence correctly.

4. Cortés attacked the Aztec capital of _____.

5. Spaniards tried to convert the Indians to the _____ religion.

6. The Spaniards used the Indians as _____.

7. The Europeans brought their _____ with them to the Americas. This caused thousands of American Indians to die.

8. The Spanish and _____ brought ships of Africans to the Americas.

9. Hawkins brought Africans to _____ colonies in the Americas.

10. Trading slaves set up trade between _____ and the Americas.

340   Unit 6   *The Age of Exploration and Conquest*

Activity 63

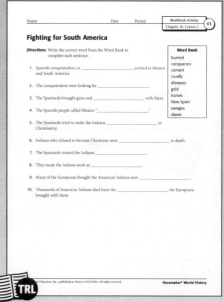

Workbook Activity 63

340   *Unit 6 Exploration and Conquest*

Settling in North America

Objectives

- To explain what a pirate is
- To name the groups of Europeans who settled the east coast of North America
- To tell how a person made money by trapping

Reading Strategy: Questioning

What do you already know about the settling of North America?

Piracy
The robbing of ships on the ocean

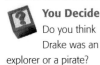

You Decide
Do you think Drake was an explorer or a pirate?

When the English and French set sail for the Americas, they were a little late. South American land had already been claimed. Therefore, they often turned to **piracy** to claim their share of South American treasures. In other words, they would get the treasures by robbing ships on the ocean.

Sir Francis Drake was English. He was the first English person to sail around the world. The English called him an explorer. The Spanish called him a pirate! Drake made daring attacks on Spanish ships and towns in the West Indies. He brought his treasures home to England. The English loved Drake, but the Spaniards feared his piracy. They called him "The Dragon."

By A.D. 1600, Spain had created an empire in present-day New Mexico, Florida, Central America, the Caribbean islands, and South America. The English, French, and Dutch explored and settled in North America.

How Did the Settlers and American Indians Divide Up the North American Land?

The first Europeans landed on the east coast of North America. There they found American Indians living in villages. Each nation had its own customs and culture. Most of the Indians farmed, hunted, and fished. They grew corn and other vegetables. Although the Indians were friendly at first, they did not fit in with the newcomers. The Europeans brought new ways, new religions, and new diseases. The Indians became wary, or overly cautious, of the settlers.

Overview Because the English and French began their explorations of the Americas late, they depended upon piracy to gain access to South American treasures. This lesson discusses the figure of Sir Francis Drake as well as the North American settlements established by the Spanish, French, English, and Dutch.

Objectives

- To explain what a pirate is
- To name the groups of Europeans who settled the east coast
- To tell how a person made money by trapping

Student Pages 341–345

Teacher's Resource Library

Workbook Activity 64

Activity 64

Modified Activity 64

Vocabulary

Pilgrim	Puritan
piracy	trapper

Have students look up the vocabulary words in the glossary at the back of the book. Then write the following sentences on the board and have students fill in the blanks.

A _____ makes his living by hunting animals and selling their furs.

The _____(s) wished that the Church of England were simpler and stricter.

In 1620, the _____(s) arrived on the *Mayflower*.

The English thought Sir Francis Drake was an explorer; however, the Spanish feared his _____.

Reading Strategy: Questioning

Lead a discussion in which students share their prior knowledge of the settlement of North America.

You Decide
Have students read about Sir Francis Drake and write three reasons he might be described as a pirate, and three reasons he might be described as an explorer.

1 Warm-Up Activity

Have students study the illustration on page 342. Ask if anything in the illustration surprises them. What figure, or figures, in the illustration are most compelling to them?

2 Teaching the Lesson

After students read the information on pages 341–344, ask them to share what they already know about the Pilgrims and Puritans and the other early colonies in the Americas.

Ask:

- Which groups of Europeans settled the east coast? (English, Dutch, French)

- If you had been one of the first Europeans to arrive in North America, which would you have preferred to be—Pilgrim, Puritan, trader, trapper, or farmer? Why? (Answers will vary.)

- What did the Spaniards call Sir Francis Drake? (The Dragon)

- What government controlled the 13 colonies? How did they thrive and grow? (English, through trade)

Background Information

In 1620, the Pilgrims, who wanted religious freedom, came to North America on the *Mayflower*. On board ship, they agreed to base their government on the rule of the majority of men settlers. Majority rule means that more than half of them had to agree on something to make it a law. Historians call their agreement the *Mayflower Compact*.

LEARNING STYLES

Body/Kinesthetic

Divide the class into two groups—the Spanish and the English. Then have each group compose a one-act play that either vilifies the Spanish or glorifies the English through the character of Sir Francis Drake. Have students stage and perform their play for the class. Students may need to conduct further research on Sir Francis Drake to successfully complete this project.

Pilgrim

A person who came to North America for religious freedom and settled in Plymouth, Massachusetts

Puritan

A member of a 16th- or 17th-century English group of Protestants who wanted to make the Church of England simpler and stricter

In 1607, a group of English colonists settled in Jamestown, Virginia. Another group of English, the **Pilgrims,** arrived on the sailing ship *Mayflower* in 1620. The Pilgrims landed at Plymouth, Massachusetts. They were seeking religious freedom. The **Puritans** were another religious group from England. The Puritans wanted to make the Church of England simpler and stricter. They built several settlements on Massachusetts Bay in the 1630s.

In 1626, the Dutch started a village at the mouth of the Hudson River, in present-day New York state. This village is New York City today. More Europeans came seeking religious freedom, a better life, and adventure. Most of the colonists became farmers. In the south, tobacco became a money-making crop. Slave traders brought Africans to help on the tobacco plantations.

Pilgrims celebrated their first year in Plymouth, Massachusetts, by holding a harvest festival with American Indians.

Reading Strategy:
Questioning

Ask yourself: "Did I understand what I just read?" If not, read the lesson again.

The settlers on North America's east coast formed 13 colonies. The colonies were under the control of the English government. Trade with Europe helped the colonies grow. Port towns like Boston sprang up.

The American Indians and the Europeans did not continue to live peacefully. Slowly, the Indians were driven westward. Over time, they lost their lands to the newcomers.

The 13 Original Colonies

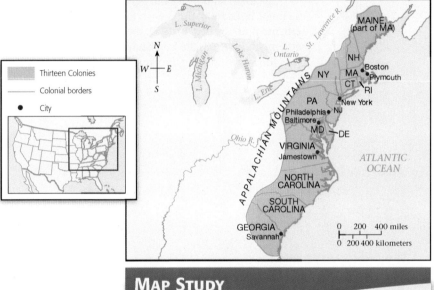

MAP STUDY

1. The colonies bordered on which mountain range?
2. What were the names of the 13 colonies?

MAP STUDY

Answers:

1. Appalachian Mountains

2. Georgia, South Carolina, North Carolina, Virginia, Maryland, Delaware, Pennsylvania, New Jersey, New York, Rhode Island, Connecticut, Massachusetts, New Hampshire

ELL/ESL STRATEGY

Language Objective:
To commit unfamiliar words and phrases to memory

Have students read the chapter and identify five unfamiliar words or phrases and then look them up in their dictionaries. Ask students to write down the words, their definitions, and a sentence that uses the word in their notebooks.

3 Reinforce and Extend

COMMON ERROR

Remind students that the words *Pilgrim* and *Puritan*, when used to describe the early settlers in North America, are capitalized. In fact, Puritan is almost always capitalized; pilgrim, however, is only capitalized when it refers to the specific group of settlers in North America.

TEACHER ALERT

Remind students of the Study Skills assignment mentioned in Lesson 16–1. They should be keeping a written record of the people, communities, and countries mentioned in Chapter 16.

Reading Strategy:
Questioning

Suggest to students that when they ask themselves the question, "Did I understand what I just read?" they might answer the question by providing specific examples of the reading material rather than just saying "Yes" or "No." Students may wish to re-frame the question like this: "What did I just read?"

Trapper
A person who traps wild animals for their furs

What Did Trappers Do?

Not all of the people who came to North America were interested in settling and farming. Some newcomers were **trappers.** These people made their living by hunting animals and selling the furs. Many French trapped along the Mississippi River. They explored the area, claiming lands in the name of France. Other French trappers went north to Canada. Hunting was good there, and fishing, too. The French created outposts from Canada to south of the mouth of the Mississippi River.

What Happened to Canadian Land?

The English also held land in Canada. This land had been claimed by John Cabot in 1497. Sometimes fights over Canadian land broke out between the French and the English. In 1608, the French founded the Canadian settlement of Quebec. In 1759, the English captured that settlement. By 1763, the English had taken all of Canada from the French during the French and Indian War.

Lesson 16–3 Review Answers
1. C **2.** D **3.** A **4.** A **5.** C **6.** B **7.** C **8.** D
9. B **10.** D

On a sheet of paper, write the letter of the answer that correctly completes each sentence.

1. Sir Francis Drake was known to the English as a(n) _____.

   A conquistador   **B** pirate   **C** explorer   **D** conqueror

2. A person who robs ships in the ocean is known as a(n) _____.

   A voyager   **B** conquistador   **C** explorer   **D** pirate

3. The English, French, and _____ explored and settled in North America.

   A Dutch   **B** Spanish   **C** Portuguese   **D** Indians

4. The Pilgrims landed in Plymouth, Massachusetts, on the sailing ship _____.

   A *Mayflower*   **B** *Pinta*   **C** *Victoria*   **D** *The Dragon*

5. The _____ were a religious group from England. They built several settlements on Massachusetts Bay during the 1630s.

   A Pilgrims   **B** Dutch   **C** Puritans   **D** colonists

6. _____ was a port town.

   A Quebec   **B** Boston   **C** Philadelphia   **D** Savannah

7. _____ made money by hunting animals and selling their furs.

   A Hunters   **B** Traders   **C** Trappers   **D** Farmers

8. _____ was an explorer who claimed land in Canada for the English.

   A Christopher Columbus   **C** Sir Francis Drake
   B Ferdinand Magellan   **D** John Cabot

9. The French founded the Canadian settlement of _____.

   A Jamestown   **B** Quebec   **C** Boston   **D** Baltimore

10. The English had taken all of Canada from the French by _____.

   A 1497   **B** 1608   **C** 1759   **D** 1763

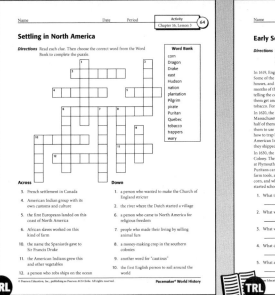

Activity 64

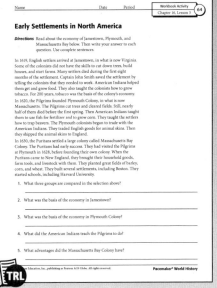

Workbook Activity 64

Chapter 16 Lesson 4

Overview In the early part of the 17th century, trade between Europe and the Americas became big business with the Netherlands, England, and France leading the pack. These ventures created growth opportunities in the Americas and resulted in the creation of a new middle class in Europe.

Objectives

- To name the three European countries that were leaders in trade
- To describe the effect successful trading with America had on the people in Europe

Student Pages 346–348

Teacher's Resource Library

Workbook Activity 65

Activity 65

Modified Activity 65

Vocabulary

insurance   shareholder
interest   stock
investment

Have students work in pairs to study the vocabulary words. Students should then write sentences using the vocabulary words. When they finish, have them check their partner's work. If students think word usage is not correct, have them offer corrections that will make it correct.

---

1   Warm-Up Activity

Bring to class copies of the business section from a newspaper that shows stock prices. Explain to students that many companies today offer shares of stock just like the trading companies did in the 1600s. Then, ask students to choose a stock that they could follow for the rest of the school year. You may wish to have students record their stocks' progress on a daily or a weekly basis and create a graph at the end of the year that shows the stocks' progress.

Trading with the Colonies

Objectives

- To name the three European countries that were leaders in trade
- To describe the effect successful trading with America had on the people in Europe

Stock
Shares in a business or company

Shareholder
A person who owns one or more parts (shares) of a business

Investment
Money given to businesses in order to get even more money back

Interest
Money paid for the use of other people's money

Insurance
A guarantee that a person or company will be paid money to cover losses

Trade between Europe and the Americas became big business. Merchants set up trading companies. The trading companies offered shares of their **stock** for sale. The people who owned the stocks were called **shareholders.** Sea voyages were expensive. Thus, the money the shareholders put in, their **investments,** helped pay for the trips. Profits from successful trips were divided among the shareholders. In 1611, the Amsterdam Stock Exchange was built. This was the first building meant just for the buying and selling of stocks.

What European Countries Were Leaders in Trade?

Three European countries became leaders in trade: the Netherlands, England, and France. These were the trading powers of the 1600s. Banks were set up to help pay for trading trips. They lent money to the merchants and charged a fee called **interest.** London and Amsterdam became important banking cities.

Shipping could be a risky business. There were storms and shipwrecks and lost cargoes. Although merchants could make a lot of money, they could also lose everything. The merchants paid companies a fee for **insurance** to protect their businesses. Then if their ships were lost at sea or attacked by pirates, the insurance companies covered the losses.

Three trading companies became powerful forces in the growing trade between Europe and the East Indies. These were the English East India Company, the Dutch East India Company, and the French East India Company. They brought home ships loaded with spices and rice, diamonds and ivory.

Reading Strategy:
Questioning

Think beyond the text.
Consider your own
thoughts and experiences
as you read.

Trading became a big business and powerful force during the 1600s.

What Did Successful Trade Create?

Successful trade ventures created a new, rising middle class in Europe. European merchants became wealthy. They often lived in the style of nobility. They built grand houses in the cities or settled on country estates. With their new-found wealth, some merchants became interested only in money, fashion, and fine living. Other merchants used their own good fortune to help others. They paid to set up hospitals, orphanages, and schools.

TIMELINE STUDY: EUROPEAN EXPLORERS IN THE AMERICAS

Were the Aztecs or the Incas conquered by Europeans first?

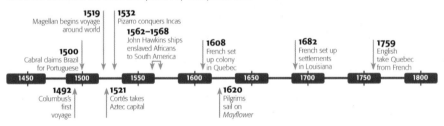

1519 Magellan begins voyage around world
1532 Pizarro conquers Incas
1562–1568 John Hawkins ships enslaved Africans to South America
1608 French set up colony in Quebec
1682 French set up settlements in Louisiana
1759 English take Quebec from French
1500 Cabral claims Brazil for Portuguese

| 1450 | 1500 | 1550 | 1600 | 1650 | 1700 | 1750 | 1800 |

1492 Columbus's first voyage
1521 Cortés takes Aztec capital
1620 Pilgrims sail on *Mayflower*

1450–1800   *Explorers, Traders, and Settlers*   Chapter 16   **347**

LEARNING STYLES

Interpersonal/Group Learning

Have students write one or two questions about something they learned in the chapter. Then, on small pieces of paper, write the names of each of the explorers, traders, and settlers. Place the pieces of paper into a box and ask students to choose one. Have students ask the questions they wrote and answer the questions from the viewpoint of the person they chose.

Reading Strategy: Questioning

Ask:

- What does it mean to "think beyond the text"? (Answers may vary.)
- What are some ways students can do this? (Answers may vary.)

2 Teaching the Lesson

As students read the lesson, have them write any words or phrases that are unfamiliar to them. Have students share their notes with the class and work together to discern the meanings of new words and phrases.

Ask:

- What was the first building set up for the sole purpose of buying and selling stocks? (Amsterdam Stock Exchange)
- What institutions were set up to help pay for trading trips? (banks)
- What were some of the risks of shipping? (Answers may vary—storms, shipwrecks, lost cargoes)
- What were some of the benefits of trade? (creation of a middle class in Europe, growth of the colonies)

Background Information

The Dutch East India Company operated from 1602 to 1798. Chartered by the States-General of the Netherlands to expand trade and assure close relations between the government and its colonial enterprises in Asia, the company was granted a monopoly on Dutch trade east of the Cape of Good Hope and west of the Strait of Magellan. From its headquarters at Batavia (founded 1619), the company subdued local rulers, drove the British and Portuguese from Indonesia, Malaya, and Ceylon (Sri Lanka), and arrogated to itself the fabulous trade of the Spice Islands. A colony, established (1652) in South Africa at the Cape of Good Hope, remained Dutch until conquered by Great Britain in 1814. The company was dissolved when it became scandalously corrupt and nearly insolvent in the late 18th century, and its possessions became part of the Dutch colonial empire in East Asia.

Lesson 16–4 Review Answers

1. The Netherlands, England, and France all became leaders in trade.
2. Merchants would pay insurance to protect their businesses, especially if their ships were lost at sea or attacked by pirates. The insurance would cover their losses.
3. Successful trading with America created a new, rising middle class in Europe. Merchants became wealthy.
4. stock **5.** interest **6.** Amsterdam
7. risky **8.** Dutch **9.** rice **10.** nobility

REVIEW

On a sheet of paper, write the answer to each question. Use complete sentences.

1. What were the three European countries that became leaders in trade?

2. Why might merchants want insurance on their business?

3. What effect did successful trade ventures in America have on the people in Europe?

On a sheet of paper, write the word from the Word Bank to complete each sentence correctly.

4. Trading companies sold shares of _____.

5. When banks give money to merchants, the fee they charge is called _____.

6. London and _____ were important banking cities.

7. Shipping could be a(n) _____ business.

8. Three trading companies helped trade grow between Europe and the East Indies. These include: the English East India Company, the _____ East India Company, and the French East India Company.

9. Common items to trade include: spices and _____, diamonds and ivory.

10. The new middle class in Europe often lived in the style of _____.

Word Bank

Amsterdam
Dutch
interest
nobility
rice
risky
stock

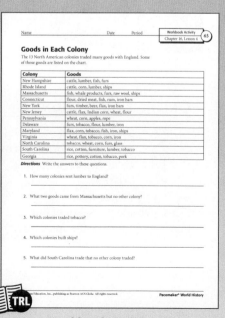

Activity 65   Workbook Activity 65

CHAPTER 16 SUMMARY

- Columbus was looking for a sea route to Asia when he landed in the Americas.

- The Spanish and Portuguese led the way in early explorations. Spanish conquistadors like Cortés and Pizarro claimed lands and gold for Spain.

- Europeans forced their own culture on American Indians and took their land.

- Africans were brought to the Americas to be sold into slavery.

- Sir Francis Drake was the first English person to sail around the world.

- The Spanish and Portuguese set up colonies in South America. The Spanish also settled in present-day New Mexico and Florida. The English, French, and Dutch also settled in North America.

- The Pilgrims and Puritans traveled to America from England. Many other groups from various European countries came seeking religious freedom.

- The settlers on North America's east coast formed 13 colonies.

- French trappers explored the Mississippi River and lands in Canada. England and France fought over the lands in Canada.

- The Netherlands, England, and France set up big trading companies. Successful trade created a new, wealthy middle class in Europe.

Chapter 16 Summary

Have students read the Chapter Summary on page 349 to review the main ideas presented in Chapter 16.

Ask:

- What was Columbus seeking when he landed in the Americas? (a faster route to Asia)

- What happened to American Indians as a consequence of their contact with Europeans? (They lost their land and their culture; many of them were killed.)

- Why were Africans brought to the Americas? (to be sold into slavery)

- What were conditions like for Africans on the slave ships? (harsh; many of them did not survive the journey)

- Who set up the first colonies in South America? (Spanish and Portuguese)

- What was a primary reason that the Pilgrims and Puritans traveled to North America? (religious freedom)

- What areas did French trappers explore? (Mississippi River and lands in Canada)

CHAPTER PROJECT FOLLOW-UP

 By the end of Lesson 16–3, students should be ready to present their "Minor Characters" project to the class. Set aside time for each group to share what they have learned about their person or group with the class.

TEACHER'S RESOURCE

The AGS Globe Teaching Strategies in Social Studies Transparencies may be used with this chapter. The transparencies add an interactive dimension to expand and enhance the Pacemaker® *World History* program content.

Chapter 16 Review

Use the Chapter Review to prepare students for tests and to reteach content from the chapter.

Chapter 16 Mastery Test

The Teacher's Resource Library includes two forms of the Chapter 16 Mastery Test. Each test addresses the chapter Goals for Learning. An optional third page of additional critical-thinking items is included for each test. The difficulty level of the two forms is equivalent.

Chapter 16 Review Answers

Vocabulary Review

1. conquistador
2. slavery
3. piracy
4. Puritans
5. stock
6. investment
7. shareholder
8. interest
9. trappers
10. insurance

Chapter Review Questions

11. Cortés attacked Tenochtitlán.

12. The word *America* comes from the name of an explorer, Amerigo Vespucci. He claimed to be the first European to reach the mainland of South America.

13. The Europeans started the slave trade to make money.

Word Bank

conquistador
insurance
interest
investment
piracy
Puritans
shareholder
slavery
stock
trappers

Vocabulary Review

On a sheet of paper, use the words from the Word Bank to complete each sentence correctly.

1. Hernando Cortés, a Spaniard who conquered the Aztecs, was a(n) _____.

2. The Spanish and Portuguese were the first to sell Africans into _____.

3. English and French explorers often turned to _____ to claim South American treasures.

4. The _____ wanted to make the Church of England simpler.

5. A person who buys shares of a company will own _____ in the company.

6. A person who makes a(n) _____ is giving money in the hopes of earning more.

7. A(n) _____ holds one or more parts of a business.

8. Merchants had to pay _____ when borrowing money from banks.

9. French _____ hunted animals for their fur.

10. When a business loses money, a(n) _____ company may pay for the losses.

Chapter Review Questions

On a sheet of paper, write the answer to each question. Use complete sentences.

11. What city in Mexico did Hernando Cortés attack?

12. Where does the name *America* come from?

13. Why did the Europeans begin the slave trade?

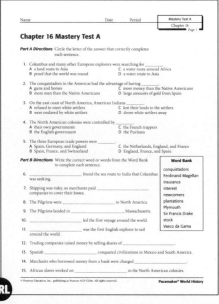

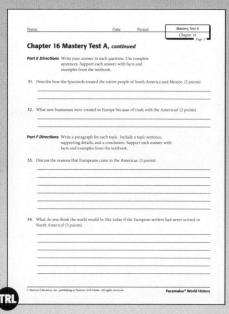

Test Tip

After you have completed a test, reread each question and answer. Ask yourself: Have I answered the question that was asked? Have I answered it completely?

14. Where did the first settlers in Virginia and Massachusetts come from?

15. Why did the first English colonists come to the eastern coast of North America?

16. What European countries were trading powers in the 1600s?

Critical Thinking

On a sheet of paper, write your response to each question. Use complete sentences.

17. This book uses the term "American Indian" to describe the first people in the Americas. Another term you might hear is "Native American." Why do you think different names are used to describe the same group of people?

18. Do you think trade with the Americas was important to Europe? Give at least one reason.

Using the Timeline

Use the timeline on page 347 to answer the questions.

19. Who conquered the Incas?

20. Did the French settle in Quebec or Louisiana first?

GROUP ACTIVITY

Discuss this question with a partner: What if the European explorers had traded with the American Indians but not conquered them? Write a description of what life might be like in the Americas today. Share your ideas with the rest of the class.

1450–1800   *Explorers, Traders, and Settlers*   Chapter 16   **351**

---

14. They were originally from England.

15. The first English colonists came for religious freedom.

16. The Netherlands, England, and France were the leading trading powers.

Critical Thinking

17. Possible answers: American Indian is more accurate because *Indian* is the name Columbus gave to the first people he met when arrived in what he believed was the "Indies." Native American is more accurate because, as the word *native* suggests, Native Americans were the first people in the Americas.

18. Possible answers: Yes, it gave them goods they needed or wanted, and it made some people rich. No, trade was risky, and the Europeans really wanted to trade with Asia.

Using the Timeline

19. Pizarro

20. Quebec

GROUP ACTIVITY

Answers will vary, but some students may describe a blending of European and American Indian cultures, or a multicultural society with American Indian as the majority culture.

Chapter 16 Mastery Test B, pages 1–3

Explorers/Traders/Settlers Chapter 16   **351**

UNIT 7

PLANNING GUIDE

The Birth of Democracy: 1200–1900

	Student Pages	Vocabulary	Map Study	Reading Strategy	Lesson Review	Chapter Summary/Review
Chapter 17 The Struggle for Democracy	354–371	✔		✔		369–371
Lesson 17–1 The Beginnings of Democracy	356–358	✔		✔	358	
Lesson 17–2 The King Tries to Limit Democracy	359–362	✔		✔	362	
Lesson 17–3 The Glorious Revolution	363–364	✔		✔	364	
Lesson 17–4 Revolution in America	365–368	✔		✔	368	
Chapter 18 Revolution in France	372–391	✔		✔		389–391
Lesson 18–1 The Age of Reason in France	374–375			✔	375	
Lesson 18–2 The King Tries to Limit Democracy	376–381	✔		✔	381	
Lesson 18–3 Napoleon Bonaparte	382–388	✔	✔	✔	388	

Chapter Activities

Teacher's Resource Library
Life Skills Connection 17–18
Key Vocabulary Words 17–18

Assessment Options

Student Text
Chapter Reviews 17–18

Teacher's Resource Library
Chapter 17 Mastery Tests A and B
Chapter 18 Mastery Tests A and B
Unit 7 Mastery Test
Chapters 1–17 Midterm Mastery Test

Teacher's Edition
Chapter Projects 17–18

Words from the Past	Learn More About It	Great Names in History	Technology Connection	Geography Note	You Decide/Remember/History Fact	Timeline Study	ELL/ESL Strategy	Background Information	Common Error	Life Skills Connection	Key Vocabulary Words	Study Skills	Applications Home, Career, Community	Online Connection	Teacher Alert	World Cultures	Auditory/Verbal	Body/Kinesthetic	Interpersonal/Group Learning	Logical/Mathematical	Visual/Spatial	Activities/Modified Activities	Workbook Activities	Self-Study Guide	Chapter Outline
										355	355													✔	✔
					357		357	357	357			358	358		357	357	357					66	66		
			359		359, 361		361	360	361				361					360		360	360	67	67		
							364	364														68	68		
367					366	366	366	366	367						367	367			366			69	69		
										373	373													✔	✔
					374		375	374					375									70	70		
					378, 380		378	377	378			379	379, 380	380			380			377	378	71	71		
	384			385	384	387	384	383	382, 385						383			386	384			72	72		

Modified Activities

The Teacher's Resource Library (TRL) contains a set of lower-level worksheets called Modified Activities. These worksheets cover the same content as the standard Activities but are written at a lower reading level.

Skill Track

Use Skill Track for *World History* to monitor student progress and meet the demands of adequate yearly progress (AYP). Make informed instructional decisions with individual student and class reports of lesson and chapter assessments. With immediate and ongoing feedback, students will also see what they have learned and where they need more reinforcement and practice.

Other Resources

Books for Teachers

Fraser, Rebecca. *The Story of Britain: From the Romans to the Present.* New York: W. W. Norton and Co., 2003.

Yalom, Marilyn. *Blood Sisters: The French Revolution in Women's Memory.* New York: HarperCollins, 1993.

Books for Students

Lacey, Robert. *Great Tales from English History, Book 2.* New York: Little, Brown and Co., 2005.

Murphy, Jim. *A Young Patriot: The American Revolution as Experienced by One Boy.* New York: Clarion Books, 1998.

Nardo, Don. *The French Revolution.* Turning Points in World History Series. San Diego, CA: Greenhaven Press, 1999.

Videos

Liberty! The American Revolution. Burbank, CA: PBS Home Video, 1997. (Ca. 6 hours; Explores the causes of the revolution and its effect on American life.)

A History of Britain. New York: A&E Television Networks, 2002. (Ca. 15 hours; thematic treatment with a focus on personalities; includes programs on the English civil war and Oliver Cromwell.)

THE BIRTH OF DEMOCRACY

As people became more aware of the world and their place in it, they began to ask questions. Government by a single powerful ruler could last for a time. Then, as a growing number of people began to ask questions, monarch rule started to weaken. It could not answer the questions. It could not give in to demands by the common people. The people listened to one another and heard familiar words. They found strength in their fellow citizens. Democracy would be government of a very different kind.

Fireworks explode over the crowning of William and Mary as king and queen of England. William and Mary signed a Bill of Rights that took away many of their royal rights and powers. The change came to be known as the Glorious Revolution.

353

Introducing the Unit

The Age of Reason in Europe was an exciting time. People found new ways of looking at the world and its place in the solar system. They also looked differently at government and its relationship to its people. European scholars and enlightened rulers contributed their views and implemented changes. These ideas eventually inspired people in England, America, and France to demand rights and fight for them. Ask students to study the picture on page 352. Point out that the celebration was in honor of the Bill of Rights. This bill was signed in the Bloodless Revolution in England. Ask them where two revolutions in the late 1700s were not bloodless. (America and Europe) Ask what the people were demanding. (to be free, to have the same rights for everyone, to have a voice in their government)

CD-ROM/Software

Censer, Jack R., and Lynn Avery Hunt. *Liberty, Equality, Fraternity: Exploring the French Revolution.* University Park: Pennsylvania State University Press, 2001. (CD-ROM of images, primary documents, and songs accompanies a text of the same name.)

Web Sites

www.agsglobepmwh.com/page353a (History of the British monarchy, including family trees, portraits, and palaces.)

www.agsglobepmwh.com/page353b (Includes essays, images, and original documents on the French Revolution and background on human rights and the Enlightenment.)

Introducing the Chapter

Democracy is not a static term. Have groups of students discuss what it means to them, then have each group write a definition. Ask the groups to read their definition to the class or to post it on a wall. Point out that they will read about early forms of democracy in this chapter.

Ask:

- How was democracy defined in the 1600s and 1700s in England? (having a voice in one's government)

The Struggle for Democracy

When you hear the word *democracy* you may think about people having a voice in their own government. This is not an idea that is new to the present time. Citizens of the 1600s and 1700s wanted their rights, too. It was a time called the *Enlightenment* or the *Age of Reason*.

Great thinkers at the time believed that every person was born with the ability to reason. They wrote that people should ask questions of their government. They spread ideas about democracy and equal rights for everyone. The ideas they raised sparked revolutions in Europe and in America.

GOALS FOR LEARNING

- To explain the beginnings of democracy
- To describe what happened in England when King Charles I tried to limit democracy
- To explain how the Glorious Revolution gained more power for the Parliament
- To explain why American colonists revolted against British rule

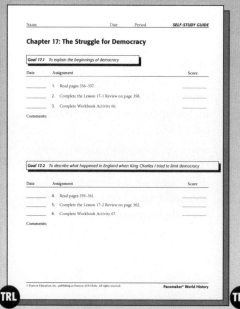

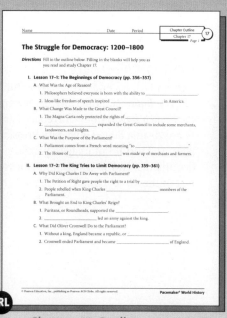

Reading Strategy: Predicting

Preview the text. Think about what you already know about a subject. Look for new information. These things will help you predict what will happen next.

Check your predictions as you read. As you learn more information, you may find you need to change your predictions.

Key Vocabulary Words

Lesson 1

Enlightenment A time in European history when thinkers and writers tried to solve the problems of society by using reason; also known as the Age of Reason

Equality The same rights for everyone

Lesson 2

Divine right The idea that a monarch's right to rule comes directly from God

Petition A written request, often with many signatures, to a person or group in authority

Petition of Right An English document that brought about more democracy

Consent To agree to something

Royalist A supporter of the king or queen during the English Civil War

Roundhead A Puritan who fought for Parliament in the English Civil War

Commonwealth A nation in which the people hold the ruling power

Lesson 3

Glorious Revolution The period in England that involved the overthrow of James II and the crowning of William and Mary

Lesson 4

Representation Sending one or more people to speak for the rights of others before a body of the government

American Revolution The American struggle against Great Britain for independence

Patriot A person who is loyal to his or her own country and shows a great love for that country

Liberty Freedom

Declaration of Independence A document the American colonists signed in which they declared their freedom from Great Britain

---

• Who made the laws for the English people from 1200 to 1600? (the monarchs)

Reading Strategy: Predicting

Explain that when you make a prediction, you add new details to what you already know about a subject. This process allows you to make an "educated guess" about what will happen next. Stopping to make predictions as you read will make you a more attentive reader and help you better analyze what you are reading.

Key Vocabulary Words

Point out that these chapter words are presented in the order they appear in each lesson. They are also found in the glossary.

LIFE SKILLS CONNECTION

Students learn how to find and take advantage of the benefits their government offers. Invite a local official to class to discuss what programs are available in your city.

KEY VOCABULARY

Students choose the correct word from Word Bank to complete each sentence.

CHAPTER PROJECT

Students will read about the English Bill of Rights in this chapter. Have students look up the U.S. Bill of Rights or the Canadian Charter of Rights and Freedoms in an almanac or an encyclopedia. Have them list five guaranteed freedoms. As they go through the chapter, have them note if and when these rights were acquired in England. Have them write a paragraph about a freedom or right and explain why it is important to them and to democracy in the United States or Canada.

Overview This lesson describes the Enlightenment ideas of equality and early steps toward democracy in England.

Objectives

- To list three main ideas from the Age of Reason
- To explain the revolutionary change King Edward I made to Parliament
- To name the two parts Parliament is divided into

Student Pages 356–358

Teacher's Resource Library

Workbook Activity 66

Activity 66

Modified Activity 66

Vocabulary

Enlightenment
equality

Write the parts of the word *enlightenment* on the board: en·light·en·ment. Have students share what they visualize when they think of the word *light*. Explain that *enlightenment* brings light to an idea through reason and knowledge. Have students create sentences using the word *enlightenment*. Write the sentences on the board.

PRONUNCIATION GUIDE

Use this list to help students pronounce difficult words in this lesson.

parliament (pär´ lə mənt)

Rousseau (rōō sō´)

Voltaire (vōl târ´)

1 Warm-Up Activity

Tell students that Voltaire was a French thinker who influenced many people, all over Europe. He defended a person's right to think and to say anything. He is reported to have said,

---

Objectives

- To list three main ideas from the Age of Reason
- To explain the revolutionary change King Edward I made to Parliament
- To name the two parts Parliament is divided into

Reading Strategy: Predicting

Preview the lesson title. Predict what you think you will learn in this lesson.

Enlightenment

A time in European history when thinkers and writers tried to solve the problems of society by using reason; also known as the Age of Reason

Equality

The same rights for everyone

The Beginnings of Democracy

"People have certain natural rights! They have the right to life, liberty, and property!"

"Man is born free! A monarch's right to rule is given to him not by God but by the people!"

"If a monarch rules badly, throw him out!"

Whoever heard of such wild ideas! These were shocking things to say in 17th-century Europe. Yet in the 1600s and 1700s, such ideas were being written and spoken in Europe. It was a time called the **Enlightenment** or the *Age of Reason*.

Philosophers at that time believed that every person is born with the ability to reason. Everyone had the power to decide what was true or false, or good or bad. They also said that people should use their abilities to question things. Why were things the way they were? How might they be better? Why should one person have so much power over others?

Questions like these were asked by the Englishman John Locke and the Frenchmen Voltaire and Jean Jacques Rousseau. These men were thinkers. They believed in freedom of thought, of action, and of speech. Their writings spread ideas of democracy and **equality** throughout the world. Their questions sparked flames of revolution in Europe and in America.

Why Was the Great Council Formed?

In 1215, King John of England was forced to sign the Magna Carta. This document limited certain powers of monarchs, and it granted certain rights. It served to ensure the rights of nobles. It did little for the common people.

"I disapprove of what you say, but I will defend to the death your right to say it." Ask students what that quotation means to them. Then ask how the viewpoint it expresses differs from that of a medieval person.

2 Teaching the Lesson

Explain that before people could struggle for rights, they had to have new ideas and develop new views about the world. This shift in views did not happen for everyone or all at once. King John was the first king to reverse himself after signing an agreement that guaranteed rights of nobles and commoners.

Ask:

- What did Enlightenment thinkers believe about a monarch's power? (The right of a monarch to rule is given by the people. A monarch who ruled badly could be taken out of power.)

- What did signing the Magna Carta do to English monarchy? (The Magna Carta limited the power of a monarch. It granted rights to nobles.)

Reading Strategy: Predicting

Ask students to write their predictions on a separate sheet of paper. Tell them they will review the accuracy of their predictions at the beginning of the next lesson.

Yet the ideas in the Magna Carta marked the beginning of democracy in England.

Now a king or queen could not simply go ahead and order new taxes. He or she first had to bring the matter before a council of nobles. That council was called the Great Council.

What Changes Did King Edward Make to Parliament?

Remember
Parliament is England's body of lawmakers.

The Great Council became known as Parliament. The word *parliament* comes from a French word, *parler*. It means "to speak." Members of Parliament could speak out, advise monarchs, and affect their decisions.

In 1272, King Edward I became king of England. In 1295, when Edward needed more money to fight a war, he called Parliament into session. Edward, however, made some changes. He invited not only nobles to Parliament, but also merchants, knights, and rich landowners. Now more people had a voice in the king's decisions.

After 1295, Parliament was divided into two parts. One group, called the House of Lords, was made up of nobles. Another group was called the House of Commons. Members of the middle class, such as merchants and rich farmers, served in the House of Commons. For those first few hundred years, the House of Lords held the most power. However, the day would come when the House of Commons became the real lawmaking body.

The changes King Edward I made to the Parliament gave more people a voice in his decisions.

1200–1800   *The Struggle for Democracy*   Chapter 17   **357**

Background Information

What made the Magna Carta more than just a piece of parchment? King John signed it under duress. He soon ignored the promises in it, until they were enforced by the nobles. Several times the Magna Carta was ignored by the monarchs of England, but it was held up as a guarantee of basic rights. Noblemen and commoners alike fought to maintain its articles. It remains a symbol of Britain and of struggle for rights and freedom.

LEARNING STYLES

Auditory/Verbal

To help students understand the events, have them listen to the audio of this lesson. As they do, have them write notes about important details. Students can fill in any missing information when they replay the audio. Encourage these students to study their notes as they prepare for the Chapter Review.

ELL/ESL STRATEGY

Language Objective:
To write questions that reinforce content

Write the words *who, what, when, where,* and *why* on the chalkboard. Model questions about the lesson that begin with these words. Ask students to write their own questions and answers beginning with these words.

3   Reinforce and Extend

COMMON ERROR

Students may think that the Magna Carta is a single document. The Magna Carta, originally written in 1215, was revised a number of times. It became a collection of documents, collectively referred to as the Magna Carta.

WORLD CULTURES

In Prussia, Frederick the Great tried to follow Enlightenment ideals. He said that he was king because he was the person best qualified to rule, not because he had a divine right to rule. He extended some new rights to his subjects. For example, he banned the use of torture to extract confessions, except in cases of murder or treason. He tried to set a standard for religious tolerance among his people. His way of rule is known as *enlightened despotism.* This means that he was still a despot (ruler), but he felt that he was governed by law and that he was personally responsible for the well-being of the country.

TEACHER ALERT

Students may need help keeping track of the monarchs of England. Genealogical trees are available at the official royal family Web site or in English history books, such as *Story of Britain* by Rebecca Fraser.

Remember
Point out that Parliament played an important role in the struggle for democracy both in England and in America, as students will learn in Lesson 17–4.

Lesson 17–1 Review Answers

1. It is known as the Age of Reason because of the wild ideas that were being written and spoken. **2.** They believed in freedom of thought, of action, and of speech—essentially democracy and equality. **3.** They were spread to America by writers like Locke, Voltaire, and Rousseau. **4.** Magna Carta limited certain powers and granted certain rights **5.** Magna Carta marked the beginning of democracy in England **6.** Before ordering new taxes, the king or queen had to bring the matter before a council of nobles, called the Great Council. **7.** King Edward I not only invited nobles to Parliament, but also merchants, knights, and rich landowners, giving more people a voice in the king's decisions. **8.** Members of the Parliament could speak out, advise monarchs, and affect their decisions. **9.** The two houses of Parliament are the House of Lords and the House of Commons. **10.** At first, the House of Lords had more power in Parliament.

LESSON 17-1 REVIEW

On a sheet of paper, write the answer to each question. Use complete sentences.

1. Why do we call this time in history the Age of Reason?

2. What did John Locke, Voltaire, and Jean Jacques Rousseau believe in?

3. How did ideas of democracy and equality spread to America?

4. What was the purpose of the Magna Carta?

5. What effect did the Magna Carta have in England?

6. What did a king or queen have to do before ordering new taxes?

7. What change did King Edward I make to Parliament in 1295?

8. What did members of the Parliament do?

9. What are the two houses of Parliament?

10. At first, which house of Parliament had the most power?

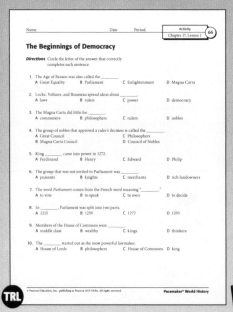

Activity 66

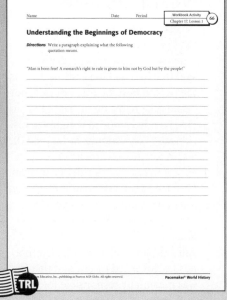

Workbook Activity 66

The King Tries to Limit Democracy

Objectives

■ To tell why a civil war began in England in 1642

■ To name and explain the two sides in the civil war

■ To describe who Cromwell was and how he ended the reign of King Charles I

■ To explain the republic Cromwell set up and what eventually became of the Parliament

Reading Strategy: Predicting

Predict what you think this lesson will be about.

Divine right

The idea that a monarch's right to rule comes directly from God

You Decide

Should any ruler ever be allowed to claim that he or she rules by "divine right"? Why or why not?

The power of Parliament grew. Some kings did not like that! King Charles I ruled England from 1625 until 1649. He did not want Parliament limiting his power.

In 1603, the line of Stuart kings had begun with the reign of James I. King Charles I was the son of James. He believed in the **divine right** of kings. In other words, he believed that God gave him the right to rule. He also thought he should rule with absolute power.

King Charles decided to ask people to pay higher taxes. When people did not pay the high taxes he demanded, he had them thrown in jail.

Parliament did not like that. "What about the Magna Carta?" Parliament asked. "Rulers must have our approval on new taxes!"

TECHNOLOGY CONNECTION

Halley's Astronomy

Edmond Halley was a British scientist and astronomer who made many of the first advances in the study of space. He drew the first map of the universe in 1686.

In 1705, Halley published a description of the orbits of 24 comets that were seen between 1337 and 1698. Three of these comets had followed the same orbit in 1531, 1607, and 1682. Halley predicted (guessed) that this comet would reappear in 1758. This comet is now known as Halley's Comet.

Halley studied eclipses of the sun by various planets. In 1716, an eclipse by the planet Venus helped him learn more about the solar system. After watching this eclipse, Halley was able to better determine the distance of Earth from the sun.

TECHNOLOGY CONNECTION

Halley's scientific discoveries were wide-ranging and influential. He had the Enlightenment view that his research should be aimed at "relief of man's estate." This means that he tried to find practical applications in science, such as improving navigation.

You Decide

You can use these questions to set up an informal debate. Assign groups of students to a side, and have them confer on their arguments. Have them present their arguments. Give each group a set amount of time for rebuttal.

Lesson at a Glance

Chapter 17 Lesson 2

Overview This lesson describes the struggle in England for power between King Charles I and Parliament.

Objectives

■ To tell why a civil war began in England in 1642

■ To name and explain the two sides in the civil war

■ To describe who Cromwell was and how he ended the reign of King Charles I

■ To explain the republic Cromwell set up and what eventually became of Parliament

Student Pages 359–362

Teacher's Resource Library

Workbook Activity 67

Activity 67

Modified Activity 67

Vocabulary

Commonwealth	Petition of Right
consent	Roundhead
divine right	Royalist
petition	

Have a few students make a word-find puzzle on the board, using all the vocabulary words. Have other students solve the puzzle.

1 Warm-Up Activity

Students might visit a city or county courtroom to learn more about how the jury system protects individual rights. They might also interview a person who has been on a jury. Have them write a brief report based on their visit or interview.

Reading Strategy: Predicting

Have students review their previous prediction. Then have them make a new prediction for this lesson. Students may want to use the headings in the lesson to help make their prediction.

Have students suggest rights that all people should have. Then have them read pages 359–361 to find out about a right that some English kings thought they had.

Ask:

- What right did Charles I say that he had as king? What did that mean? (divine right; God chose him to rule, and no one could question his decisions.)

- What document did Parliament make Charles I sign before it would give him any money? (the Petition of Right)

- In the English civil war, which side supported the king? Which side opposed the king? (Royalists; Roundheads)

- What action did Oliver Cromwell's Roundheads take against the king? (They tried him and beheaded him.)

Background Information

The civil war in England was largely a contest among wealthy landowners. Ordinary men served in the army for personal gain or on orders from their masters or landlords. During the civil war, the troops had freedom of worship and of speech. Radical groups in the army, such as the Levellers, asked for a republican constitution with a governing legislature. The legislature was to be chosen by male suffrage that included all men in the country except the poor and servants. The Diggers were even more radical. This group wanted to abolish private property and end government entirely. These radical groups, and freedom of speech, were suppressed at the end of the war.

Remember

Ask students to review how Parliament was created. (The Great Council was created by the Magna Carta. It became the Parliament.) After 1925, the Parliament was divided into two parts. One part was the House of Lords. The other part was the House of Commons.

Petition
A written request, often with many signatures, to a person or group in authority

Petition of Right
An English document that brought about more democracy

Consent
To agree to something

Royalist
A supporter of the king or queen during the English Civil War

Roundhead
A Puritan who fought for Parliament in the English Civil War

Remember

Parliament was created to limit a monarch's power.

Why Did King Charles I Do Away with Parliament?

In 1628, Parliament presented King Charles with a **petition,** or a written request. This petition is known as the **Petition of Right.** The petition said that a king could not demand new taxes without Parliament's **consent** or agreement. It also said the king could not throw people in jail without a jury trial.

King Charles agreed to the petition, but he did not keep his word. He kept raising taxes. When Parliament disagreed with King Charles about money, religion, and relations with other countries, Charles I decided to break up the whole group. King Charles ruled without a Parliament from 1629 until 1640.

Then trouble developed with Scotland. Charles I had been forcing the Scottish people to follow the English religion. Scotland rebelled. In response, Charles called Parliament back into session in 1640. He wanted money to go to war with Scotland.

Again Parliament tried to put reins on the king's power. Charles I reacted by arresting five of the leading members of Parliament. His troops marched right into a session of Parliament and made the arrest! That was too much. The people rebelled.

What Brought an End to King Charles' Reign?

In 1642, a civil war began in England. It lasted until 1649. The nobles who supported the king were called *Royalists.* The greatest supporters of Parliament were the Puritans. They were called *Roundheads* because they cut their hair short. They disagreed with King Charles about the church and other matters.

A man named Oliver Cromwell became a leading figure in the civil war. Cromwell was a member of Parliament. He led the Puritan army against the king.

LEARNING STYLES

Body/Kinesthetic

Distribute index cards to students. Have students write the name of an English monarch on the front of an index card and one or two interesting facts about that monarch on the back of the index card. Have students work in pairs to practice identifying the monarchs referred to by the facts on each card.

LEARNING STYLES

Visual/Spatial

Give students a graphic organizer for a concept, or draw one on the board as a model. Ask students to write the name of an important man or woman from their countries or cultures in the center shape. Have students write details that describe the person and his or her contributions to the culture in the surrounding shapes. Ask students to use their maps to develop a paragraph about the important man or woman from their countries or cultures that they chose and his or her contributions to that culture.

Cromwell's military victories meant the end of King Charles' reign. In 1649, Charles I was captured and tried by Parliament. He was found to be a "public enemy of the nation." Charles I was beheaded.

What Did Oliver Cromwell Do to the Parliament?

Parliament set up a republic. The republic, known as the **Commonwealth** of England, lasted from 1649 until 1660. Under the Commonwealth, England had no monarch. The country was governed by a committee of Parliament and its leader, Oliver Cromwell.

Cromwell, however, fought with Parliament. To solve the arguments, he put an end to Parliament in 1653. For the rest of the Commonwealth period, Cromwell ruled England alone.

Cromwell had believed in freedom. He had refused the title of king when Parliament once offered it to him. He had been against the total power of kings. Yet, now he had sole power in England. Cromwell's official title was Lord Protector of the Commonwealth. During his rule, he brought Ireland and Scotland under English control. His actions in Ireland were especially cruel.

Oliver Cromwell died in 1658. His son Richard tried to carry on his father's policies. Richard, however, was not as strong as his father. The people of England were also ready to return to the royal Stuart line.

Oliver Cromwell governed the Commonwealth of England. In 1653, he put an end to Parliament.

LEARNING STYLES

Logical/Mathematical

Halley's Comet still visits Earth about every 76 years. Have students calculate when the last visit was (1985–1986), and when the next is likely. (2061)

ELL/ESL STRATEGY

Language Objective:
To read for meaning and take notes

Ask students to read the section "Why Did King Charles I Do Away with Parliament?" Have students take notes on the steps that led up to the English civil war. Give students a graphic organizer for sequencing events, or draw a flow chart on the board. Ask students to make a chart showing the sequence of steps that led up to the English civil war. Have students use their charts to write a summary.

3 | Reinforce and Extend

IN THE COMMUNITY

Some English kings thought they ruled by divine right—they believed that God gave them the power to rule without any interference. In America, the power is vested in the people. Ask students to name people of authority in their community, province, or state. For example, students might mention the chief of police, mayor, state senator, or assemblyman. Have students list five state, provincial, or local government figures and, in a few sentences, explain how their power ultimately comes from the people.

COMMON ERROR

People often think that comets are balls of fire. Comets are not fiery. They are balls of ice and rock particles. Their tails are made of dust, and their glow is reflected light, not self-generated.

Lesson 17–2 Review Answers

1. divine **2.** absolute **3.** Royalists
4. Roundheads **5.** ended **6.** C **7.** B
8. A **9.** A **10.** C

Word Bank

absolute

divine

ended

Roundheads

Royalists

On a sheet of paper, write the word from the Word Bank to complete each sentence correctly.

1. King Charles believed in the _____ right of kings.

2. King Charles wanted to rule with _____ power.

3. The _____ supported the king during the civil war.

4. The _____ disagreed with the king during the civil war.

5. The reign of King Charles _____ in 1649.

On a sheet of paper, write the letter of the answer that correctly completes each sentence.

6. King Charles forced the people in _____ to follow the English religion.

  A England   **C** Scotland

  B Ireland   **D** Parliament

7. The civil war in England lasted until _____.

  A 1642   **C** 1653

  B 1649   **D** 1658

8. Under the Commonwealth, _____ led the Parliament.

  A Oliver Cromwell   **C** King Charles

  B Richard Cromwell   **D** the Roundheads

9. Oliver Cromwell's official title was _____.

  A Lord Protector of the Commonwealth

  B Roundhead

  C King Oliver

  D General Cromwell

10. Oliver Cromwell put an end to _____ in 1653.

  A military victories   **C** Parliament

  B higher taxes   **D** jury trials

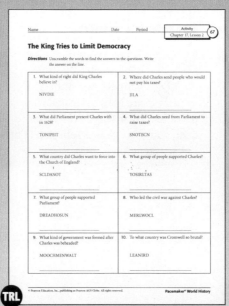

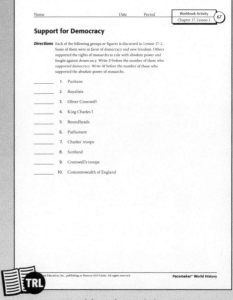

The Glorious Revolution

Objectives

■ To describe the Glorious Revolution

■ To explain the Bill of Rights that William and Mary signed

Glorious Revolution

The period in England that involved the overthrow of James II and the crowning of William and Mary

Reading Strategy: Predicting

Predict the impact the Bill of Rights will have.

William and Mary understood the importance of democracy and involved the Parliament in their decisions.

In 1660, Charles II became king. He restored Parliament, and things were quiet for a while. Unfortunately, new problems came up when James II came to the throne.

King James II became a Catholic. He asked for too much power. In response, Parliament sent word to James II's daughter Mary and her husband William of Orange. Parliament asked them to come from the Netherlands and take over James II's throne.

Did this anger King James? Yes. Did it cause another war? No. James II left the throne quietly. It was a bloodless takeover. Parliament persuaded William and Mary to sign over many of their royal rights and powers. The change came to be called the *Glorious Revolution.*

What Did the Bill of Rights Do for the English Government?

In 1689, William and Mary signed a Bill of Rights. This bill stated that the ruling monarch could act only after consulting Parliament. With that, England took another big step toward democracy. Now Parliament was truly a strong force in government.

One day the Americans would write their own Bill of Rights. The English Bill of Rights would serve as their model.

Over time, Parliament itself became more democratic. By the late 1600s, the House of Lords held less power. The House of Commons held more. Members of the House of Lords still inherited their positions. House of Commons members, however, were elected.

Ask:

● Who did the Parliament decide should become the Protestant rulers of England? (William and Mary)

● What were the two main points of the English Bill of Rights? (Only Parliament can make laws and the king must obey these laws.)

Reading Strategy: Predicting

Discuss how to check this prediction. (Read ahead in the chapter, or look at a history of the Bill of Rights.) Invite students to look on the Internet or in the library for more detailed history of the English Bill of Rights.

Lesson at a Glance

Chapter 17 Lesson 3

Overview This lesson describes the rule of William and Mary as monarchs of England and their signing of a Bill of Rights.

Objectives

■ To describe the Glorious Revolution

■ To explain the Bill of Rights that William and Mary signed

Student Pages 363–364

Teacher's Resource Library

Workbook Activity 68

Activity 68

Modified Activity 68

....

Vocabulary
Glorious Revolution

Have students look up the word *revolution* in the dictionary. Ask them to list other forms of the word *revolution*, such as *revolutionary* and *revolutionize*, and note what part of speech each is. Ask volunteers to write sentences on the board using all the *revolution* words.

---

1 Warm-Up Activity

Ask students what the word *revolution* means. Have students suggest possible meanings of the word and work with students to arrive at a clear explanation of the word. Ask students what changes might happen because of a revolution.

---

2 Teaching the Lesson

William and Mary signed a Bill of Rights. This bill determined who was to be Mary's successor, barred Roman Catholics from the throne (which eliminated the claim of divine right), took away the Crown's right to suspend laws, and declared that a standing army was illegal during peacetime. The monarchy upheld the Bill of Rights, as demonstrated by the lack of wars after 1689, as noted on the timeline on page 366.

Background Information

William of Orange was the nephew of James II, as well as his son-in-law. As the prince of Orange, he was a person of great importance in the Netherlands. When Mary and William were offered the Crown, they insisted that they both would reign. In turn, they were required to sign the Declaration of Rights, which Parliament soon reworked into the Bill of Rights.

ELL/ESL STRATEGY

Language Objective:
To discriminate between homonyms

The word *bill* has many meanings, including the following: a bird's mouthparts, a cap visor, an itemized list, an itemized costs of goods, a restaurant check, the draft of a law, a piece of paper money, to announce a play or event, to submit a charge, to caress, and to advertise. Have students write sentences using the word *bill* to mean these different things. Ask them to read their sentences aloud. Have other students identify the definition that is appropriate to the sentence. Discuss which definition is closest to the meaning in *bill of rights*. (an itemized list)

3 | Reinforce and Extend

Lesson 17–3 Review Answers

1. power **2.** daughter **3.** bloodless **4.** Glorious Revolution **5.** Bill of Rights **6.** Parliament **7.** democracy **8.** English **9.** House of Lords **10.** House of Commons

---

Word Bank

Bill of Rights
bloodless
daughter
democracy
English
Glorious Revolution
House of Commons
House of Lords
Parliament
power

On a sheet of paper, write the word from the Word Bank to complete each sentence correctly.

1. King James asked for a lot of _____.

2. William of Orange and Mary took over James II's throne; Mary was James II's _____.

3. King James was upset at having to give up his throne. Nonetheless, it was a(n) _____ takeover.

4. Parliament persuaded William and Mary to sign over many of their royal rights. It came to be known as the _____.

5. William and Mary signed the _____ in 1689.

6. The Bill of Rights stated that the ruling monarch could act only after consulting _____.

7. The Bill of Rights helped England move toward _____.

8. Americans would model their Bill of Rights after the _____.

9. By the late 1600s, the _____ held less power.

10. _____ members were elected to Parliament.

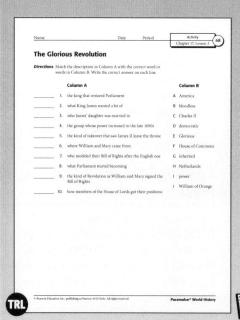

Activity 68

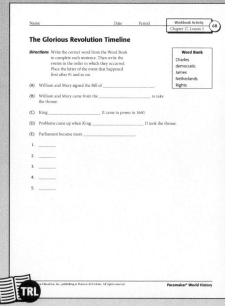

Workbook Activity 68

Revolution in America

Objectives

■ To list complaints that colonists in America had against King George III and Britain

■ To name five freedoms and rights that Americans won

Reading Strategy: Predicting

Think about King George's problems. Predict what you may read about next.

Representation

Sending one or more people to speak for the rights of others before a body of the government

American Revolution

The American struggle against Great Britain for independence

Patriot

A person who is loyal to his or her own country

Liberty

Freedom

George III became king of England in 1760. When he came to the throne, England had colonies in North America. George asked for the loyalty of his subjects in America. They seemed happy to give that loyalty.

Why Did the Colonists Revolt Against English Rule?

George III had wars to pay for. Great Britain had fought a major war, the Seven Years' War. In North America this war was sometimes called the French and Indian War. In 1763, the French and Indian War ended in America. The Americans and British had defeated the French and some American Indian nations. Now someone had to pay the bills for war costs. King George decided to demand high taxes from his subjects in the colonies.

"High taxes, but no rights!" the American colonists complained. They had seen that people had won new rights in England. They read the words of Locke, Rousseau, and Voltaire. The Americans wanted rights and freedom, too.

"No taxation without **representation!**" was their cry. If they paid taxes to King George, they wanted a say in the government.

Some colonists wanted more than representation. They wanted freedom!

Many colonists were willing to fight for that freedom. That fight for freedom from British rule was known as the **American Revolution. Patriots** like Thomas Jefferson spoke out for **liberty,** or freedom. Jefferson used his pen to fight for independence. He wrote that Parliament had no right to control the colonies. He also said that unfair acts by the king meant the colonists owed him no loyalty.

Overview This lesson describes the events leading up to the American Revolution.

Objectives

■ To list complaints that colonists in America had against King George III and Britain

■ To name five freedoms and rights that Americans won

Student Pages 365–368

Teacher's Resource Library

Workbook Activity 69

Activity 69

Modified Activity 69

Vocabulary

American Revolution
Declaration of Independence
liberty
patriot
representation

Ask students to write their own definitions after studying the definitions provided in the text. Have them trade papers with another student. Students will then read each other's definitions and approve or suggest corrections for their partner's definitions.

1 Warm-Up Activity

Have students recall the strategy that Parliament used to make the king sign the Petition of Right. (Parliament would not give him money to fight a war with Scotland.) Have students discuss instances of how control of revenues controls what someone can do. This could include international sanctions, conditions on lending, U.S. congressional control of funds for the executive branch, or withholding of an allowance. Ask students to predict how the issue of finances will affect the American colonies. Have them write their predictions on a separate sheet of paper.

2 Teaching the Lesson

Have students recall some of the rights, such as freedom of speech, that Enlightenment thinkers wrote about. Then have them read this section to find out what happened when the English colonists in the 13 English colonies in America felt England was taking their rights away.

Ask:

● What did colonists insist that they must do before they could be taxed? (agree to be taxed)

● What reason did colonists have for disobeying the king? (The King did not let the colonists have a say in the government. Unfair acts by King George meant the colonists owed him no loyalty.)

● Who was Jefferson aiming to represent when he wrote the Declaration of Independence? (all colonists)

Reading Strategy: Predicting

Have students fine-tune the predictions they wrote in the Warm-Up Activity.

Background Information

The unrest in the American colonies started over taxes that King George wanted the colonists to pay for the Seven Years' War. This war benefited the colonies and England. However, the colonists wanted their own assemblies to control internal policy and taxing. They wanted to be granted traditional British rights. The Declaration of Independence shifted the reason for the war from demanding these traditional rights to protecting *natural* rights against King George. The declaration adopted the Enlightenment program, described in Lesson 17–1.

Declaration of Independence
A document the American colonists signed in which they declared their freedom from Great Britain

History Fact
The American Revolution gave hope to people in other lands. It made them believe that one day they would also have freedom. They watched the United States become a nation that promised individual freedoms and a voice in government.

The colonies asked Jefferson to write a declaration of independence.

On July 4, 1776, the **Declaration of Independence** was approved. King George sent troops to the colonies. The colonists had to fight the British for their independence. General George Washington led the fight. Washington would later become the first president of the new United States of America.

Thomas Jefferson wrote the Declaration of Independence. Americans signed it on July 4th, 1776.

TIMELINE STUDY: FIGHTING FOR RIGHTS IN BRITAIN AND NORTH AMERICA

Who ruled England after the Commonwealth?

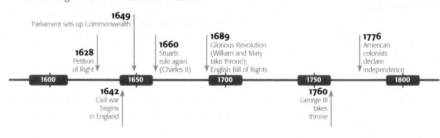

1649 Parliament sets up Commonwealth
1628 Petition of Right
1642 Civil war begins in England
1660 Stuarts rule again (Charles II)
1689 Glorious Revolution (William and Mary take throne); English Bill of Rights
1760 George III takes throne
1776 American colonists declare independence

1600 — 1650 — 1700 — 1750 — 1800

Words from the Past

The Declaration of Independence

In the Declaration that Thomas Jefferson wrote, he tried to speak for all colonists.

The Declaration was the colonists' announcement that the colonies were becoming a separate nation—the United States of America.

The following passages are from Thomas Jefferson's Declaration of Independence.

We hold these truths to be self-evident, that all men are created equal, that they are endowed by their Creator with certain unalienable Rights, that among these are Life, Liberty and the pursuit of Happiness.

That to secure these rights, Governments are instituted among Men, deriving their just powers from the consent of the governed.

That whenever any form of Government becomes destructive of these ends, it is the Right of the People to alter or to abolish it, and to institute new Government . . .

We, therefore, the Representatives of the United States of America . . . do . . . declare, That these United Colonies are, and of Right ought to be Free and Independent States . . . .

Students may benefit from hearing this excerpt read aloud. Have volunteers read the paragraphs aloud. Then ask students to study the illustration on page 366. Discuss any unfamiliar words or phrases until the entire passage is understood.

3   Reinforce and Extend

COMMON ERROR

A well-known story is that John Hancock said, "There, I guess King George will be able to read *that!*" as he boldly signed the Declaration of Independence. There is no evidence that he ever said this. There was only one other person with him when he signed, and neither he nor Hancock recorded what was said, if anything.

COMMON ERROR

Students may think that the Declaration of Independence sprang entirely from Jefferson's mind. Declarations of independence were written in several colonies before Jefferson wrote his famous declaration. Jefferson's ideas were not original. However, his declaration pulled together ideas from these earlier declarations and generalized them.

AT HOME

Ask students to check with merchants in their community to find out what taxes customers pay when they buy items such as newspapers and tea at a store. Have students report and compare their findings.

ONLINE CONNECTION

Students can gain additional information by accessing the following Web site:

www.agsglobepmwh.com/page367

(Use the search engine of this site to find information on the Declaration of Independence, as well as additional information on George Washington and Thomas Jefferson.)

REVIEW

On a sheet of paper, write the letter of the answer that correctly completes each sentence.

1. George III became king of England in _____.

   A 1689   **B** 1760   **C** 1763 **D** 1776

2. The Seven Years' War is also known as the _____.

   A Glorious Revolution   **C** Civil War
   B French and Indian War **D** Crusades

3. _____ wrote the Declaration of Independence.

   A George Washington   **C** Jean Jacques Rousseau
   B Oliver Cromwell   **D** Thomas Jefferson

4. The Declaration of Independence was approved on _____, 1776.

   A June 4   **B** August 6   **C** July 4 **D** December 25

Word Bank

freedom

patriot

representation

On a sheet of paper, write the word from the Word Bank to complete each sentence correctly.

5. Thomas Jefferson was a _____.

6. Colonists cried, "No taxation without _____.

7. Some colonists wanted more than representation, they wanted _____.

On a sheet of paper, write the answer to each question. Use complete sentences.

8. Why did King George demand high taxes from the colonies?

9. What complaints did American colonists have against King George III and Britain?

10. What were five rights that Americans won?

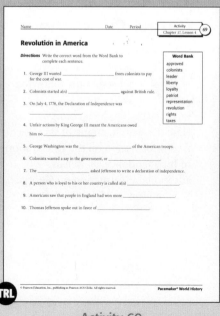

Activity 69

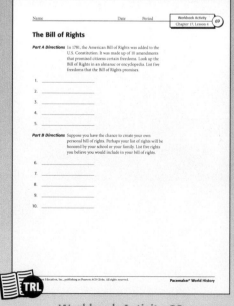

Workbook Activity 69

- Ideas of freedom, equality, and fairness came out of the Age of Reason.

- In 1295, the Parliament of England was made up of nobles, merchants, knights, and landowners.

- The English Parliament helped limit the powers of the monarch. Parliament has a House of Lords and a House of Commons. Some rulers did not like asking Parliament to allow them to raise taxes.

- During England's civil war, Oliver Cromwell led Parliament in overthrowing the king.

- After the war, Cromwell headed the Commonwealth from 1653 to 1658. He put an end to Parliament. He brought Ireland and Scotland under English control.

- The Stuart monarchy returned as Charles II took the throne in 1660. Charles restored Parliament. His reign was followed by James II.

- The Glorious Revolution was a bloodless takeover of the throne by William and Mary. The Glorious Revolution brought more power for Parliament and a Bill of Rights for the English people.

- King George III became king in 1760. He demanded high taxes of the American colonies to help pay off England's war debts.

- The English colonies in America resented paying taxes with no rights in return. They had thoughts of fighting for independence.

- In 1776, the American colonists declared their independence. They fought a war and won their freedom.

TEACHER'S RESOURCE

The AGS Globe Teaching Strategies in Social Studies Transparencies may be used with this chapter. The transparencies add an interactive dimension to expand and enhance the Pacemaker® *World History* program content.

Chapter 17 Summary

Have students read the Chapter Summary on page 369 to review the main ideas presented in Chapter 17.

Ask:

- What three ideas were important subjects of thought during the Age of Reason? (freedom, equality, and fairness)

- What people made up the Parliament of England? (The people who made up the Parliament were nobles, merchants, knights, and landowners.)

- What are the two parts of Parliament? (House of Commons and House of Lords)

- Who led the civil war against the king of England? (Oliver Cromwell and Parliament)

- What happened during the Commonwealth from 1653–1658? (Cromwell ended the Parliament. He brought Ireland and Scotland under English control.)

- What did Charles II do when he became king? (He restored Parliament.)

- Who reigned in England after the Glorious Revolution? (William and Mary)

- Why did George III demand high taxes from America? (He needed help to pay England's debts from the Seven Years' War.)

- Why did the English colonies not want to pay taxes? (They had no rights.)

- What happened in the English colonies in America in 1776? (The colonists declared their independence from England. They fought a war and won their freedom.)

CHAPTER PROJECT FOLLOW-UP

Have students prepare a short presentation on "their" right. They should include an example (recent or otherwise) of the freedom being upheld or violated. Have them present their examples to the class.

Chapter 17 Review

Use the Chapter Review to prepare students for tests and to reteach content from the chapter.

Chapter 17 Mastery Test

The Teacher's Resource Library includes two forms of the Chapter 17 Mastery Test. Each test addresses the chapter Goals for Learning. An optional third page of additional critical-thinking items is included for each test. The difficulty level of the two forms is equivalent.

Chapter 17 Review Answers

Vocabulary Review

1. Enlightenment

2. Declaration of Independence

3. divine right

4. consent

5. representation

6. liberty

7. Commonwealth

8. patriot

Chapter Review Questions

9. Their writing spread ideas of democracy and equality. They gave people the idea they could revolt.

10. The Roundheads were the Puritan supporters of Parliament.

11. Parliament wanted the king to have less power to demand taxes and throw people in jail. King Charles said he would abide by Parliament's Petition of Right, and then he did not. Instead, he got rid of Parliament.

Word Bank

Commonwealth

consent

Declaration of Independence

divine right

Enlightenment

liberty

patriot

representation

Vocabulary Review

On a sheet of paper, use the words from the Word Bank to correctly match each definition below.

1. A time when people questioned their way of life, and wanted freedom, equality, and fairness

2. A document American colonists signed; it declared their freedom from Great Britain

3. The idea that a monarch's right to govern comes from God

4. To agree to something

5. When one or more persons are chosen to speak for the rights of others

6. Freedom

7. A nation where people have the power to rule

8. A person, like Thomas Jefferson, who is loyal to his or her country

Chapter Review Questions

On a sheet of paper, write the answer to each question. Use complete sentences.

9. How did Voltaire, Rousseau, and Locke influence Britain and America?

10. Who were the Roundheads?

11. What was the problem between Parliament and King Charles I of England?

12. Who was Oliver Cromwell?

13. What was the Glorious Revolution in England?

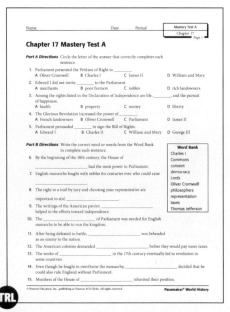

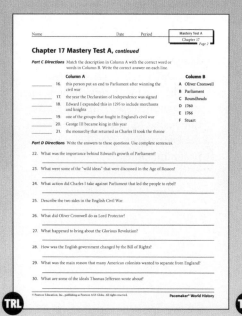

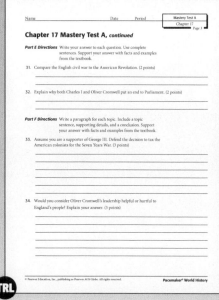

Test Tip

It is easier to learn new vocabulary words if you make them part of your speaking and writing in other discussions and subject areas.

14. Why did King George III try to get more money out of American colonists?

15. Why did the American colonists want to revolt against British rule?

16. Who wrote the Declaration of Independence?

Critical Thinking

On a sheet of paper, write your response to each question. Use complete sentences.

17. How were the new ideas of the Age of Reason different from the old idea of divine right?

18. Why were the American colonists affected by the British fight for freedom and rights?

Using the Timeline

Use the timeline on page 366 to answer the questions.

19. Which came first, the Petition of Right or the English Bill of Rights?

20. When the American colonists declared their independence, how long had George III been king of England?

GROUP ACTIVITY

Work with a partner. Read the passages from the Declaration of Independence on page 367. Discuss with your partner what each paragraph means. Look up words in a dictionary if you need to. Then rewrite the paragraphs in your own words.

---

12. He was a leader of the English civil war. He became the leader of the Commonwealth.

13. The Glorious Revolution was a bloodless takeover. James II left the throne, and William and Mary signed over many rights and powers to Parliament.

14. He wanted them to pay for the Seven Years' War.

15 Some wanted representation in the British government. Others wanted freedom.

16. Thomas Jefferson wrote the Declaration of Independence.

Critical Thinking

17. Possible answer: The ideas of the Age of Reason said that a monarch's right to rule came from the people, not from God.

18. Possible answer: The American colonists were British subjects. They wanted the same rights other British people had.

Using the Timeline

19. Petition of Right

20. 16 years

GROUP ACTIVITY

Students' paraphrases of the Declaration of Independence should show their understanding of the basic ideas.

Introducing the Chapter

Revolution brought dramatic change to France in the last quarter of the 18th century. Unlike the American Revolution, which was followed by a peaceful transition into democracy, the French Revolution was followed by the Reign of Terror. Napoleon rose to prominence as a military dictator, then as emperor of France. Nearly just as quickly, he fell from power and was exiled.

Ask:

- The French king believed they ruled by what right? (divine right)
- When did the French execute their king? (1793)
- When and where did Napoleon meet defeat? (1815; Waterloo)

Revolution in France

Most of the people of France had no voice in their government. They were at the bottom of a country ruled by the upper class. As a group, they could be strong, because their voices were loud and many.

The French Revolution was a colorful, heated time in world history. The common people spoke out against persecution. For many, this led to death for their cause.

The reign of Napoleon began a time in which France thrived. While the people did not gain the freedoms being enjoyed in America, change was being made.

GOALS FOR LEARNING

- To explain why the French began to want freedom and equality
- To explain how the storming of the Bastille led to bloody rebellion in France
- To describe Napoleon Bonaparte's role in French government and war

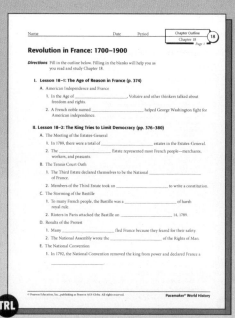

Reading Strategy: Text Structure

Understanding how text is organized helps you decide which information is most important. Before you begin reading this chapter, do these things:

- Look at how it is organized.
- Look at the title, headings, boldfaced words, and photographs.
- Ask yourself: Is the text a problem and solution, description, or sequence? Is it compare and contrast or cause and effect?
- Summarize the text by thinking about its structure.

Key Vocabulary Words

Lesson 2

Estates-General The French governmental body made up of representatives from the three estates

Oath A serious promise

Bastille A prison in Paris

Symbol An object that stands for an idea

Riot A violent disturbance created by a crowd of people

Arsenal A place where guns and ammunition are stored

French Revolution The war that the common people of France fought against the king, nobles, and one another to achieve freedom

Betray To give help to the enemy

Motto A word or phrase that expresses goals, ideas, or ideals

Fraternity Brotherhood

Execute To kill someone for a crime

Reign of Terror The one-year period in French history when radical leaders put many people to death

Guillotine An instrument used for cutting off a person's head

Lesson 3

Dictator A ruler who has total power

Napoleonic Code The constitution Napoleon set up that contained a single set of laws for all of France and its territories

Colonial Having settlements in far-off lands

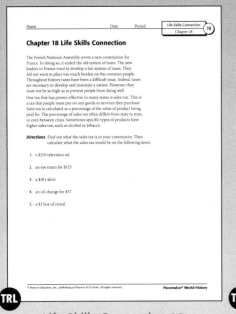

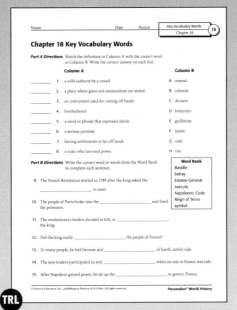

Reading Strategy:
Text Structure

Introduce the reading strategy *text structure*. Explain that text structure is an organizational technique that helps improve reading comprehension. Text structure helps the reader focus on key concepts and supporting details in the text. For example, the headings in the text are in the form of questions. These questions represent key concepts. The answers to the questions are found in the text, along with supporting details. Have students read the heading on page 374, then find the answer in the text.

Ask:

- How does the question structure help you to focus on important information? (Sample answer: The questions represent key concepts in the text. They help the reader figure out which details are important.)

Key Vocabulary Words

Point out that these chapter words are presented in the order they appear in each lesson. They are also found in the glossary.

LIFE SKILLS CONNECTION

Students learn about sales tax. Direct students to a municipal Web site that shows the local sales tax. Help students calculate the sales tax on various items. Tell students that some states, such as Oregon, do not have sales tax.

KEY VOCABULARY

In Part A, students match the definition to the correct word. In Part B, students choose the correct word from the Word Bank to complete each sentence.

Chapter 18 Lesson 1

Overview This lesson discusses the cultural climate that preceded the French Revolution.

Objectives

- To name two French writers in the 1700s who had new ideas
- To explain how the Age of Reason and American Revolution led to revolution in France

Student Pages 374–375

Teacher's Resource Library 🅣🅡🅛

Workbook Activity 70

Activity 70

Modified Activity 70

Reading Strategy:
Text Structure

Point out that the bulleted objectives are another example of text structure. They help focus the attention of readers on the main points of the lesson.

Remember

Have student volunteers summarize the beliefs of Rousseau and Voltaire. (Rousseau and Voltaire believed that people should be free. They believed people should have some rights.)

Objectives

- To name two French writers in the 1700s who had new ideas
- To explain how the Age of Reason and American Revolution led to revolution in France

Reading Strategy: Text Structure

Preview this chapter. Notice the question headings, features, and boldfaced words.

Remember

The British and the American colonists had also read Rousseau and Voltaire.

France, in the early 1700s, had a government that was still locked into the Middle Ages. French kings believed they ruled by divine right. No matter how unfair the rule, French people had to accept it. King Louis XIV is said to have declared, "I am the State."

Nobles led lives of luxury. They lived in fine palaces paid for by taxes collected from the lower and middle classes. While the nobles lived splendidly, the peasants often went without enough to eat.

How Did American Independence Affect the French?

By the 1780s, however, the French were listening to new ideas. They read the works of Rousseau and Voltaire. "Look at Britain," the writers said. "The people there are free. Look at the Americans, at their successful fight for freedom. We, too, deserve some rights!" Political conditions did not yet show it, but the Age of Reason had come to France.

The French had helped the Americans in their war for independence from British rule. French nobles were happy to see the British defeated by anyone. French peasants liked the idea of a fight against tyranny—the cruel and unjust use of power. The French noble, Lafayette, went to America and joined the colonists' battle. George Washington gave Lafayette command of a division, and the two fought side by side.

When the Americans won the war, the French began thinking about freedom for themselves.

---

1 Warm-Up Activity

Use an analogy to help students understand how the French may have felt before the revolution. Some students go to a strict school, and cannot speak freely. There are no extra activities. Other students go to an open school and decide the lunch menu and field trips. A student group helps plan student activities. Ask how students in the strict and open schools are similar to France before the revolution. (The French were like students in the strict school. Their voices were not heard. The British and Americans were like students in the open school. They could speak freely and helped run the school.)

2 Teaching the Lesson

Have student volunteers take turns reading this lesson aloud. Have volunteers read one paragraph each.

Ask:

- Why was life in France in the 1700s unfair? (Nobles lived splendidly; peasants often went hungry.)
- Why had the French helped the Americans in their war for independence? (The nobles wanted to see the British defeated; the peasants wanted to fight against tyranny.)

Background Information

King Louis XIV ruled France from 1643 until 1715. He reigned for 72 years, longer than any ruler in Europe. His reign began when he was only 4 years old. When he came of age, the king surrounded himself with splendor to ensure that people recognized him as a royal figure. He wore outrageously fancy clothes. He had a spectacular palace built at Versailles. Louis XIV and his court lived in the greatest of luxury, while the vast majority of his people languished in poverty.

On a sheet of paper, write the letter of the answer that correctly completes each sentence.

1. The French government in the early 1700s was still locked into _____.

   A war   **B** democracy   **C** the Revolution   **D** the Middle Ages

2. The French kings ruled by _____ and the French people had to accept it.

   A the constitution   **C** the Parliament
   B divine right   **D** the Third Estate

3. Nobles lived comfortable lives in palaces. The palaces were paid for by _____ collected from the lower and middle classes.

   A food   **B** crafts   **C** taxes   **D** goods

4. In contrast, the _____ often went without enough to eat.

   A Parliament   **B** craftworkers   **C** peasants   **D** merchants

5. The French looked at the freedom the _____ and Americans had, and wanted rights too.

   A Persians   **B** Germans   **C** Italians   **D** British

6. The _____ is when common sense began to take over people's thinking.

   A Age of Reason   **C** New Thinking
   B Revolution   **D** Tennis Court Oath

7. _____, a French noble, went to America and fought alongside the colonists.

   A King Louis XIV   **C** Rousseau
   B Lafayette   **D** George Washington

On a sheet of paper, write the answer to each question. Use complete sentences.

8. What did King Louis XIV mean when he declared, "I am the State"?

9. What are two French writers in the 1700s who had new ideas?

10. How did the Age of Reason and the American Revolution lead to revolution in France?

ELL/ESL STRATEGY

Language Objective:
To infer the meanings of words using prefixes and suffixes

Tell students that they can figure out the meaning of a word using prefixes or suffixes. For example, the word *unjust* has the prefix *un-*. *Un-* means "not or opposite of." So *unjust* means "not just." The word *successful* has the suffix *–ful*. This suffix means "full of or characterized by." So *successful* means "full of success." Have students look up the meaning of the suffix *–al*, found in the word *political*. (The suffix *–al* means "of or like." So *political* means "of politics.")

3   Reinforce and Extend

AT HOME

Have students work with a family member to cook a French meal. Students can find recipes in cookbooks or magazines. Have them describe the meal to their classmates.

Lesson 18–1 Review Answers

1. D **2.** B **3.** C **4.** C **5.** D **6.** A **7.** B
8. King Louis meant that the French people had to accept whatever rule he suggested—no matter how unfair—simply because he was king.
9. Rousseau and Voltaire wrote of new ideas. **10.** The French were inspired by the writers of the Age of Reason who opened their eyes to a new way of thinking—they realized they deserved rights. They were also inspired by the American colonists who won their freedom from Britain.

The Age of Reason in France

Part A Directions Tell why each person is important. Write one or more complete sentences about each person.

1. King Louis XIV

2. Rousseau

3. Lafayette

4. Voltaire

5. George Washington

Part B Directions Write the answers to these questions. Use complete sentences.

6. How did the nobles live under rule by the French kings?

7. How did the peasants live under the rule of the French kings?

8. What was the Age of Reason? Describe one important idea.

9. Why did French nobles support the American war for independence?

10. Why did French peasants support the American war for independence?

Pacemaker® World History

Activity 70

The Age of Reason in France Quiz

Part A Directions Match the quotation in Column A with the person or persons in Column B who could have said it. Write the correct answer on each line.

Column A	Column B
___ 1. "God made me king!"	A American citizens
___ 2. "I am happy to have Lafayette's help."	B French noble
___ 3. "Voltaire and I write about ideas of freedom."	C French peasants
___ 4. "I am proud to fight with George Washington."	D George Washington
___ 5. "We will thank Lafayette by naming towns after him."	E King Louis XIV
___ 6. "Rousseau and I support a new age of reason."	F Lafayette
___ 7. "We pay too many taxes to keep the nobles rich!"	G Rousseau
___ 8. "The peasants are dirty, and they smell bad."	H Voltaire

Part B Directions Circle the letter of the answer that correctly completes each statement.

9. King Louis XIV was on the throne _____.
  A in the 1500s   B in the early 1700s   C in the 1800s   D after 1900

10. The French kings believed that they ruled by _____.
  A a constitution   C permission of the middle and lower classes
  B cruelty   D divine right

11. The French nobles lived in _____.
  A drafty huts   C city apartment buildings
  B small houses   D palaces

12. Taxes paid by the lower and middle classes were used to _____.
  A pay for medical care   C keep the king and nobles rich
  B build public schools   D set up a system of social security

13. Thinkers such as Rousseau and Voltaire valued _____.
  A fancy carriages   C the divine right of kings
  B freedom   D the rights of nobles

14. France gave aid to the _____ in their fight for independence.
  A Americans   B British   C Germans   D Spanish

15. Two generals who fought side by side for freedom were Washington and _____.
  A Louis XIV   B Voltaire   C Rousseau   D Lafayette

Pacemaker® World History

Workbook Activity 70

The King Tries to Limit Democracy

Objectives

- To identify the Three Estates
- To explain what the Bastille was and what it stood for
- To describe how the rest of Europe reacted to the French Revolution
- To describe the time known as the Reign of Terror

Estates-General

The French governmental body made up of representatives from the three estates

Reading Strategy: Text Structure

Notice that the section headings are written as questions. After you read each section, try to answer the question asked in each heading.

By 1788, trouble was brewing in France. The peasants and the middle class were unhappy. The government was in trouble, too. It was out of money. Fancy living and too many wars had resulted in an empty treasury.

Why Was a Meeting of the Estates-General Called?

In 1789, King Louis XVI called a meeting of the **Estates-General.** This was a government body that was something like Britain's Parliament. The Estates-General had not met for 175 years. Now there was to be a meeting at Versailles. This was the name of the fine palace just outside of Paris where King Louis lived with his queen, Marie Antoinette. King Louis wanted the Estates-General to grant him more money in new taxes.

Three groups of people made up the Estates-General. Each group was called an *estate*. The First Estate included wealthy clergy. They arrived at King Louis's meeting dressed in fine clothing and riding in beautiful carriages.

Members of the Second Estate were the nobles. Many were wealthy and came from large country manors. Some of the nobles, however, had lost most of their wealth. They had only their titles left.

The First and Second Estates represented only a tiny part of the French population. The Third Estate represented most of the people of France. It represented a middle class of merchants and city workers and all the peasants.

Each of the three estates had one vote in meetings. This was hardly fair, since the Third Estate represented 98 percent of the population. The First and Second Estates could band together. They could then outvote the Third

Oath
A serious promise, often pledged in the name of God

Bastille
A prison in Paris

Symbol
An object that stands for an idea

Estate every time they wanted to. Members of the Third Estate were ready for change.

At the 1789 meeting in Versailles, the Third Estate asked for more votes. King Louis XVI refused.

What Was the Tennis Court Oath?

The Third Estate rebelled. The members called their own meeting. They declared themselves the National Assembly of France. The king refused to give them a government meeting hall. So the Third Estate held its own meeting at a nearby tennis court.

At the meeting, members of the Third Estate took the Tennis Court **Oath.** They swore that they would give France a constitution. The people of Paris celebrated. They supported the National Assembly. They wanted a constitution.

In the meantime, the king was organizing his troops. When he gathered an army near an assembly meeting, people began to worry. Was the king planning to stop the National Assembly by force? The people grew angry. Force, they said, would be met by force! France was now approaching the boiling point.

Why Did the French Storm the Bastille?

To the people of Paris, the **Bastille** was a terrible **symbol.** It stood for the tyranny of their king and for the injustices they faced. The Bastille was a gloomy fortress built in 1370. It was used as a prison. All that was needed to throw a French person into prison was the say-so of the king.

The Bastille was a dark, mysterious place. People were locked away there for disagreeing with the king or for failing to pay taxes. There were stories of men rotting away in the Bastille's dark dungeons and of terrible tortures. (A dungeon is a dark underground room used as a prison.)

1700–1900 Revolution in France Chapter 18 **377**

LEARNING STYLES

Logical/Mathematical

Have each student draw two pyramids. The first pyramid should illustrate the relative percentage of people in France's three estates, with the Third Estate at the bottom and the First Estate on top. The second pyramid should represent the percentage of votes each estate was given in the Estates-General. Discuss the discrepancies between the two pyramids—namely, the Third Estate made up 98 percent of the people in France, yet received only 33 percent of the votes in the Estates-General.

---

2 Teaching the Lesson

Review the causes of the American Revolution. Then have students read the lesson to find out how the French Revolution began.

Ask:

- What was the Estates-General? (a government body similar to Britain's Parliament)

- What event turned the revolutionaries against Louis XVI? (Austria and Prussia sent in armies to crush the revolution.)

- Why wasn't Robespierre a successful leader? (Answers will vary. Students might note that Robespierre led the dreaded Reign of Terror. Accept all reasonable answers.)

Background Information

The clergy who made up the First Estate owned about 10 percent of the land in France. The nobles who made up the Second Estate represented about 5 percent of the population and held all the important jobs in government. Neither the First or Second Estate paid taxes. Taxes were the sole responsibility of the three groups that made up the Third Estate. Farmers, for example, paid about half their income into taxes. They also were required to provide their labor once a year, without pay, to government projects.

The 1789 meeting of the Estates-General was sparked by King Louis XVI's attempt to tax nobles to raise funds for the government. The nobles themselves demanded the meeting. The Estates-General included 610 representatives of the Third Estate, and 591 representatives of the First and Second Estates combined. The existing system called for one vote per estate. The members of the Third Estate proposed that each person at the meeting receive one vote. This proposal was rejected by the king, opening the door for the creation of the National Assembly.

Revolution in France Chapter 18 **377**

LEARNING STYLES

Visual/Spatial

Show students pictures of several well-known symbols, such as the Lincoln Memorial, an eagle, and a smiley face. Have students discuss the meaning of each symbol. Then have each student choose an emotion or idea and sketch a symbol to represent the selection. Have students exchange their sketches with a classmate, and then determine the meaning of each other's symbols.

ELL/ESL STRATEGY

Language Objective: *To learn lesson vocabulary*

List the vocabulary words from Lesson 18–2 on the board. Say aloud each word or phrase as you point to it. Have students repeat each term after you. Then write the definition for each term on the board. Start a word wall for the lesson by writing the words and definitions on a sheet of butcher paper. Display the paper in the classroom. Add more words as needed as students read the chapter.

3 Reinforce and Extend

COMMON ERROR

Students may wonder why the French Revolution was a threat to Austria and Prussia. Remind them that freedom had spread to Britain and the United States. However, Austria and Prussia, along with several other European nations, were still ruled by kings, queens, or emperors.

Riot
A violent disturbance created by a crowd of people

Arsenal
A place where guns and ammunition are stored

History Fact
French people celebrate Bastille Day much as Americans celebrate the Fourth of July.

Actually, under earlier kings the prison had done away with dungeons and tortures. However, the horror stories remained. Most French people hated and feared the Bastille.

On July 14, 1789, a **riot** broke out in Paris. The people had become alarmed by the king's gathering of his troops. The people decided it was time to make a stand for freedom. They would attack the symbol of the king's unjust powers—the hated Bastille.

Early in the day, rioters broke into an **arsenal,** a place where guns and ammunition were stored. They took muskets and cannons. Then they attacked. "Down with the Bastille!" the excited rebels shouted. There was no stopping the large group of people, the mob. They murdered the governor of the prison. They carried his head on a stick through the streets.

The rebels then freed the prisoners. They opened the cells to find only seven prisoners inside! However, the Bastille had fallen, and the Revolution had begun.

On this same day, the king returned to his palace at Versailles after a day of hunting. Communication was slow in the 18th century. Therefore, he knew nothing of the riots and murders. It had been poor hunting that day. No deer had been killed. To describe his day, King Louis wrote only one word in his diary on July 14, 1789. He wrote *Rien*, a French word meaning "nothing."

The day that King Louis wrote *nothing* was a day that France would always remember!

An angry French mob stormed the Bastille, the royal prison, on July 14th, 1789. This marked the start of the French Revolution.

History Fact

Have students describe how Americans celebrate the Fourth of July. (People have fireworks, parades, and picnics.) Ask interested students to research how the French celebrate Bastille Day. Have students share the results of their research with the class.

French Revolution

The war that the common people of France fought against the king, nobles, and one another to achieve freedom

Betray

To give help to the enemy; to be unfaithful to

Motto

A word or phrase that expresses goals, ideas, or ideals

Fraternity

Brotherhood

Reading Strategy:
Text Structure

As you read the lesson, use a graphic organizer to organize the order of events in the French Revolution.

What Came Out of all the Protests?

Revolutionaries in France were excited by the storming of the Bastille. They began their own protests for freedom. Peasants rose up against feudal lords. Many nobles fled the country because they did not feel safe. In October, a group of women set out from Paris. They wanted the king to give the people more grain. To keep order, the king marched with them from Versailles to Paris.

During the next three years, 1789–1791, the National Assembly wrote the new constitution it had promised. New laws were made that did away with the feudal system. The nobles lost most of their rights and privileges. The king lost much of his power. The old system of taxes was also ended.

On August 26, 1789, the National Assembly adopted the Declaration of the Rights of Man. It was based on the English Bill of Rights and the American Declaration of Independence.

How Was the National Convention Formed?

Rulers throughout Europe saw what was happening in France. They were frightened. They worried that ideas of revolution could spread to their lands. The rulers of Austria and Prussia sent armies into France to try to crush the Revolution.

The leaders of the **French Revolution** were outraged. They thought that their own king had called for the outside armies. They accused Louis XVI of being unfaithful to, or **betraying,** France. They forced him off the throne. Then they held elections for a new lawmaking body called the *National Convention.*

In 1792, the National Convention declared France a republic. The **motto** of the new republic was "Liberty, Equality, and **Fraternity!**" In other words, they demanded freedom, the same rights for everyone, and brotherhood.

STUDY SKILLS

Tell students that many events led to the French Revolution. Suggest that they use index cards to track these events. On each card they should describe the event, and then write when it occurred and why it is important. Students should place the cards in chronological order. Encourage them to review the information on the cards as they study for the lesson and chapter tests.

CAREER CONNECTION

Point out that historians know what happened in Paris on July 14, 1789, in part because the event was reported by the press. On-site reporting by a free press is an important part of a healthy democracy. Explain that the press is often referred to as the Fourth Estate. Ask students to infer why this term is used. Tell students that most reporters have a bachelor's degree in journalism. Previous experience, even on school papers, is also helpful for a career as a reporter. Students should ask their guidance counselor which courses to take to prepare for a degree in journalism.

Reading Strategy:
Text Structure

Show students different examples of graphic organizers, such as concept maps, Venn diagrams, or outlines. Stress that they can design their own graphic organizer. Remind them that their graphic organizer must present information in a clear, concise way.

IN THE COMMUNITY

Have students research their local lawmaking body on the city or county level. What type of legislative entity enacts local rules? When was the entity formed? What kind of power does it have? Students can write to a member of the lawmaking body, asking for more information. They can also access the local library, historical society, or a community Web site. Tell each student to write a report about the lawmaking body. They should include references in their reports.

WORLD CULTURES

The Internet is a valuable tool for biologists to communicate with one another about their scientific findings. Have students find articles on the Internet about a global issue and present the information to the class.

ONLINE CONNECTION

Students can gain additional information by accessing the following Web site: www.agsglobepmwh.com/page380 (This Web site gives additional information about the French Revolution, including essays, maps, images, documents, songs, a timeline, and a glossary.)

Execute
To kill someone for a crime

Reign of Terror
The one-year period in French history when radical leaders put many people to death

Guillotine
An instrument used for cutting off a person's head

You Decide
Do you think Robespierre got what he deserved? Why or why not?

What Was Happening During the Reign of Terror?

Leaders of the new republic became fearful of their enemies. Their main goal was to seek out those enemies and to do away with them. The Revolution became bloodier.

Revolutionaries found King Louis XVI guilty of betraying his country. In 1793, Louis XVI and Marie Antoinette were **executed,** or killed for their crime. Throughout 1793 and 1794, the new leaders of France arrested and executed many people. Anyone suspected of being against the Republic was attacked. It was a time known as the **Reign of Terror.** "Off with their heads!" became the cry of that stage of the French Revolution.

A Frenchman had invented the **guillotine,** a machine for quickly cutting off heads! Hundreds of suspected enemies of the revolution were beheaded. Carts rolled through the streets of Paris, carrying victims to the guillotine.

A man named Robespierre was one of the most violent leaders of the Revolution. Robespierre believed the Republic would never be safe as long as one enemy lived. Later, the people turned on Robespierre himself. They blamed him for the bloodshed. After sentencing so many others to death, Robespierre lost his own head to the French guillotine.

The country was in turmoil—a state of great confusion. The leaders of the Revolution could not control the people or organize the government. The fighting and bloodshed went on and on.

Those considered to be enemies of the new French Republic were executed by guillotine.

On a sheet of paper, write the answer to each question. Use complete sentences.

1. What groups made up each of the Three Estates that met in Versailles in 1789?

2. Why was the National Assembly formed and what was their purpose? (Be sure to mention the oath they took.)

3. What is the Bastille and what does it stand for?

4. What happened on July 14, 1789?

5. What effect did the storming of the Bastille have on the rest of France?

6. What did the Declaration of the Rights of Man promise?

7. How did the rest of Europe react to the French Revolution?

8. Why was Louis XVI forced off the throne? What was formed to take over his position?

9. What did the National Convention declare in 1792? What affect did it have on the Revolution?

10. What was the time known as the Reign of Terror like?

Lesson 18–2 Review Answers

1. The First Estate included the clergy, the Second Estate included the nobles, and the Third Estate included the middle class of merchants and city workers, as well as the peasants. **2.** The National Assembly formed because the king denied the request of the Third Estate for more votes. They took the Tennis Court Oath and swore they would give the people of France a constitution. **3.** The Bastille was a gloomy fortress built in 1370. It was used as a prison. It was a symbol for the tyranny of their king and the injustices they faced. **4.** The people decided it was time to make a stand for freedom, so they stormed the Bastille. The rioters broke into an arsenal, murdering the governor of the prison and carrying his head on a stick through the streets. Then they freed the prisoners. **5.** Revolutionaries were excited by the storming of the Bastille and began their own protests for freedom. **6.** The new constitution did away with the feudal system. The nobles lost much of their rights and privileges, and the king lost much of his power. It also ended the old system of taxes. **7.** The rulers throughout Europe were frightened by what was happening in France. They worried that the ideas of revolution would spread to their lands. Austria and Prussia sent armies into France to try and stop the Revolution. **8.** The leaders of the French Revolution thought that he had called for outside armies, and accused him of betraying France. After forcing the king off the throne, they held elections for a new lawmaking body called the National Convention. **9.** The National Convention declared France a republic. It made the Revolution bloodier because their main goal was to seek out and destroy the enemies of the republic. **10.** During the Reign of Terror, anyone suspected of being against the Republic was attacked. It was an era of great confusion and bloodshed.

Napoleon Bonaparte

Lesson at a Glance

Chapter 18 Lesson 3

Overview This lesson covers Napoleon's impact on France and discusses the political climate following Napoleon's defeat at Waterloo.

Objectives

- To explain the Napoleonic Code and two good changes Napoleon made
- To explain the Battle of Waterloo
- To tell how many revolutions France went through in the years after Napoleon

Student Pages 382–388

Teacher's Resource Library

Workbook Activity 72

Activity 72

Modified Activity 72

Vocabulary

colonial
dictator
Napoleonic Code

Write the vocabulary words on the board and review their definitions with students. Ask a volunteer to make up a sentence that is a clue to one of the words. Have other students try to guess the word from the clue. Repeat the activity until all the words have been guessed.

---

1 Warm-Up Activity

Tell students that Napoleon created a code of laws for his country. Ask them what kind of laws they would include in a national code. Discuss which of these laws are currently in place and which are new. Also discuss the feasibility of implementing the students' suggestions.

2 Teaching the Lesson

As students read this lesson, have them think about how the French Revolution led the country into chaos and paved the way for Napoleon's rise to power.

Objectives

- To explain the Napoleonic Code and two good changes Napoleon made
- To explain the Battle of Waterloo
- To tell how many revolutions France went through in the years after Napoleon

Dictator
A ruler who has total power

Napoleonic Code
The constitution Napoleon set up that contained a single set of laws for all of France and its territories; it remains the basis of French law today

---

The Revolution had created a strong, new army. That army drove Austrian and Prussian forces out of France. One of the officers in the French army was a young man named Napoleon Bonaparte.

Meanwhile, the National Convention of France had been growing steadily weaker. In October 1795 it came under attack by an army of 30,000 national guardsmen. The guardsmen wanted to get rid of the National Convention and bring back the monarchy. The Convention called on General Napoleon Bonaparte to put down the uprising. Napoleon, a general at age 26, proved his military worth. On October 5, 1795, he brought in a battery of cannons. The uprising ended soon after.

The Directory soon replaced the National Convention in the leadership of France. The Directory eventually became corrupt, meaning it did not rule very honestly.

How Did Napoleon Come to Power?

As Napoleon won battles and gained power, the Directory began to worry. Was Napoleon trying to become the sole ruler of France?

That is exactly what Napoleon did. He pushed out the Directory. Then in 1799, he made himself **dictator** of France. As a dictator, he had total power. One of the first things Napoleon did as ruler was to set up the **Napoleonic Code.** This was a new constitution that contained a single set of laws for all of France and its territories. The Napoleonic Code remains the basis of French law to this day.

Ask:

- What event started Napoleon's rise to power? (He put down an uprising by 30,000 national guardsmen.)
- What did Napoleon do to take control of France? (He won battles, pushed out the Directory, and put himself directly in charge of the army. He also set up a police force responsible only to him.)
- Who defeated Napoleon at Waterloo? (the Duke of Wellington with troops from Britain, Belgium, Hanover, the Netherlands, and Prussia)

COMMON ERROR

Be sure that students understand the meaning of the word *battery* as used in the second paragraph on page 382. Explain that in this context, a battery is a set of cannons. Have students use their dictionaries to find other meanings of the word *battery*.

Reading Strategy:
Text Structure

Study the map. How does it help you to understand the changes in Napoleon's empire?

France soon discovered that Napoleon was a good politician as well as a good soldier. Napoleon put himself directly in charge of the army. He brought a quick end to the fighting within France. He set up a police force responsible only to him. He invited back the nobles who had fled France during the Revolution. "You will be safe," Napoleon told them, "if you are loyal to me."

Napoleon's Empire, 1812

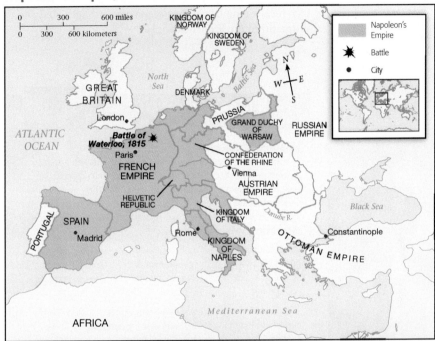

MAP STUDY

1. What are the names of three cities in lands ruled by Napoleon?

2. In which empire is Vienna?

Background Information

The British, Dutch, Belgians, and Germans were weary of years of Napoleonic wars. They were highly alarmed when they learned that Napoleon had escaped from exile and returned to France. The countries quickly joined their forces, assembling in Belgium under the command of the Duke of Wellington, an Englishman. When Napoleon was informed of this, he marched north to meet his foes. Historians disagree about why he was defeated at Waterloo. Some believe it was the timely arrival of the Prussian army. Others argue that his downfall came because he delayed his attack until noon on June 18, 1815. Regardless, the French army retreated. Napoleon's historic defeat has given rise to a well-known expression: a person who experiences a marked reversal of fate is said to be meeting her or his Waterloo.

Reading Strategy:
Text Structure

Answers will vary. Students may say that the map allows them to see how the borders of the empire changed over time. Accept all reasonable answers.

MAP STUDY

Answers:

1. Paris, Rome, Madrid

2. The Austrian Empire

TEACHER ALERT

Some students have a difficult time reading maps. Have students work cooperatively to interpret the map on page 383. Ask a volunteer to read the title, "Napoleon's Empire, 1812." Ask other volunteers to name the lands that were part of the empire. Have still other volunteers identify lands that were not part of the empire. Then have students read and answer the questions under the map.

Have small groups of students each design a mural showcasing Napoleon's accomplishments. Suggest that students first research the ruler's accomplishments individually. The group should then decide which accomplishments to include in the mural. Finally, they should designate a space on the mural for each accomplishment and assign painting tasks. Students should include short captions explaining each accomplishment.

ELL/ESL STRATEGY

Language Objective:
To learn vocabulary through constructive criticism

Have students read the definitions for each vocabulary word independently. Based on the definitions, they should then write a sentence that incorporates each word. Have students trade sentences with a partner. Tell them to read and critique one another's sentences. Encourage students to recommend changes in a supportive manner.

3 Reinforce and Extend

LEARN MORE ABOUT IT

Before students read "Learn More About It: Napoleon's Mistake" on page 384, ask them to create a Who, What, Why, Where, When, and How chart. As they read the feature, have them fill in the chart. For example, students should write "Napoleon Bonaparte" under *Who* in the chart, and "Napoleon's mistake" under *What* in the chart. Students should fill in the remaining columns, explaining why, where, when, and how Napoleon's mistake occurred. Suggest that students refer to the chart when they study for the lesson and chapter tests.

What Did Napoleon Do for France?

Napoleon put an end to the French Republic that the Revolution had won. In 1804, Napoleon had himself crowned emperor. He then crowned his wife, Josephine, empress. He let his ambition and desire for power spread war across Europe. Yet he also made some good changes in the French government.

Napoleon changed unfair tax laws. He required all people, rich and poor, to pay taxes under the same laws. The rich received no favors. Napoleon also strengthened and reorganized the French schools.

History Fact
For 15 years, the history of Europe was the history of Napoleon's conquests.

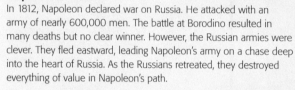

LEARN MORE ABOUT IT

Napoleon's Mistake

In 1812, Napoleon declared war on Russia. He attacked with an army of nearly 600,000 men. The battle at Borodino resulted in many deaths but no clear winner. However, the Russian armies were clever. They fled eastward, leading Napoleon's army on a chase deep into the heart of Russia. As the Russians retreated, they destroyed everything of value in Napoleon's path.

When Napoleon and his army reached Moscow, they found a deserted city. Most of the people had fled. Those who stayed behind set fire to the city. The French soon found themselves occupying a city of ruins.

Then winter came. It was an icy Russian winter. Napoleon's army had almost run out of food; they were starving and freezing. There was only one thing to do. Napoleon gave the orders to head for home. The Russians attacked again and again as Napoleon's weakened forces struggled toward France. The French suffered terrible losses during the retreat from Russia. Over 500,000 men were killed or died of illness or starvation. Others deserted or were captured. Many simply froze to death. The attack on Russia was Napoleon's big mistake.

Dictator and later emperor of France, Napoleon Bonaparte was very powerful.

History Fact
During the 15 years that Napoleon ruled France as a military dictator, he conquered most of Europe. Tell students that many historians call the period from 1800 to 1815 "the Age of Napoleon" because the ruler so thoroughly dominated European history.

Geography Note

Avignon is a city in southeastern France where the Rhone and Durance Rivers meet. It was a Phoenician trading port before it became a thriving city of the Roman Empire. In the 14th century it was home of the pope as the seat of the Roman Catholic Church. During much of this time, the Babylonian Empire controlled Rome. The city remained a territory of the pope for centuries. Its location encouraged a good deal of trading activity, as did its rare bridge over the Rhone River. Avignon was controlled by the Roman church until 1791. At that time, Revolutionary leaders took possession of the city for France.

Napoleon made most things, including education and the press, subject to strict government control. In fact, the French government *was* Napoleon!

Napoleon had a strong, wealthy France behind him now. He had the loyalty of the people. He now set out to conquer a European empire. He led France into war with Great Britain and most of the rest of Europe. Napoleon was a clever general. He won battle after battle. By 1812, Napoleon controlled most of Europe. However, he had been unable to invade and conquer Great Britain.

What Brought Napoleon's Rule to an End?

Other countries took heart when they heard of France's defeat in Russia. Napoleon could be beaten! These countries joined together. Prussia, Sweden, and Austria joined with Great Britain and Russia to march as allies against Napoleon.

The French saw that their emperor was beaten. The French Senate turned against Napoleon. It called for a new king to rule France. On April 11, 1814, Napoleon gave up his throne. Louis XVIII was crowned King of France. Napoleon was exiled and sent to live on the island of Elba off the coast of Italy.

Napoleon was not a man who gave up easily. In less than a year, he had escaped from Elba and returned to France. There he found supporters and actually ruled France again for 100 days. However, Napoleon's dream of ruling Europe was about to come to an end.

What Happened as a Result of the Battle of Waterloo?

The allies against Napoleon joined forces as soon as they heard of his return. With about 75,000 troops, Napoleon marched into Belgium to meet the allied forces. The Duke of Wellington had about 67,000 troops from Britain, Belgium, Hanover, and the Netherlands.

COMMON ERROR

Students may wonder why the French people, who fought so hard to be free, were willing to accept Napoleon as dictator. Remind them of the Reign of Terror. During this period, rebel leaders punished anyone suspected of opposing the revolution. Nearly 200,000 people were imprisoned, many without trial. Some 17,000 people were put to death. Discuss how the Reign of Terror might have made the French people willing to have a strong ruler again. (Answers will vary. Students might say that France wanted a strong ruler to end the bloody conflict.)

Geography Note

Have students locate Avignon on a map of France. Ask them why revolutionary forces might have wanted to capture this city for France. (Avignon had a rare bridge over the Rhone River. It was a thriving trading center.)

Play a recording of "The Marseillaise," the French national anthem. Have students listen closely to the lyrics. If possible, make copies of the lyrics and pass them out to students as you play the song. Tell them that the song became the national anthem of France in 1795. Napoleon later banned the song. But in 1875, it was renamed the national anthem of France. Have students discuss why the song is important to the French people, and why a French leader would ban it. (Sample answer: The song is important because it captures a feeling of hope and revolutionary change. Napoleon banned the song because it was connected to the French Revolution and he feared it would spark a revolt against him.)

The Battle of Waterloo brought the end to Napoleon's reign.

The fighting began on June 18, 1815, and is known as the Battle of Waterloo. The battle between the French and the allies was just about even for a few hours. Then Prussian troops arrived to back up the allies. That tipped the scale. After one last, fierce attack by France's famous *Old Guard*, the French had to retreat.

Again, Napoleon was sent away as a prisoner. The British sent him to far-off Saint Helena. This was a tiny island off the west coast of Africa. It was there on May 5, 1821, that Napoleon died.

What Was France Like After Napoleon?

A royal line of kings ruled France once more. Then, again, there was a revolution. For the next 55 years, France saw change after change—three revolutions in all. There was a Second Republic, a Second Empire, and then, in 1870, a Third Republic.

Under the Third Republic, France built a **colonial** empire. French colonies around the world strengthened French trade and industry. France's Third Republic lasted until World War II when Germany took over France.

After World War II, a Fourth Republic was set up—and then a Fifth. Social revolution continued. Women struggled to take their place in society, to hold property, and to take jobs. Minority groups looked for work, for fair pay, and for good housing. The French still worked toward "Liberty, Equality, and Fraternity."

Reading Strategy:
Text Structure

Study the timeline. How does it help you to understand the sequence of events in this chapter?

TIMELINE STUDY: **FRENCH REVOLUTIONS: 1750–1900**

Which came first, the Second Empire or the Second Republic?

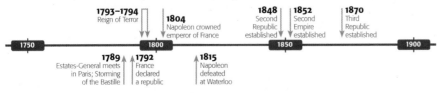

1793–1794 Reign of Terror

1804 Napoleon crowned emperor of France

1848 Second Republic established

1852 Second Empire established

1870 Third Republic established

1750   1800   1850   1900

1789 Estates-General meets in Paris; Storming of the Bastille

1792 France declared a republic

1815 Napoleon defeated at Waterloo

Reading Strategy:
Text Structure

Answers will vary. Students will likely say that the timeline shows events in chronological order. This helps them to understand the sequence in which the events occurred. Accept all reasonable answers.

TIMELINE STUDY

Answer: Second Republic

Lesson 18–3 Review Answers

1. The guardsmen thought that the National Convention wanted to bring back the monarchy, and started to attack. The National Convention had called on General Napoleon Bonaparte to put down the uprising. He did, but soon replaced the National Convention with the Directory. **2.** The Napoleonic Code was the new constitution Napoleon set up after he made himself dictator of France in 1799. It contained a single set of laws for all of France and its territories. **3.** Napoleon changed unfair tax laws and strengthened and reorganized the French schools. **4.** He attacked Russia. **5.** It was the battle that ended in Napoleon's defeat. **6.** C **7.** D **8.** B **9.** A **10.** B

LESSON 18-3

REVIEW

On a sheet of paper, write the answer to each question. Use complete sentences.

1. Why and how was the National Convention replaced?

2. What is the Napoleonic Code?

3. What are two good changes Napoleon made?

4. What was Napoleon's big mistake?

5. What was the Battle of Waterloo?

On a sheet of paper, write the letter of the answer that correctly completes each sentence.

6. In 1799, Napoleon made himself _____ of France.

   A head of the Directory   **C** dictator
   B a soldier   **D** emperor

7. In 1804, Napoleon made himself _____ of France.

   A head of the Directory   **C** dictator
   B a soldier   **D** emperor

8. By 1812, Napoleon controlled most of _____.

   A France   **B** Europe   **C** Russia   **D** Great Britain

9. _____ was crowned King of France after Napoleon gave up his throne.

   A Louis XVIII   **C** Louis XVI
   B Robespierre   **D** Duke of Wellington

10. France went through _____ revolutions in the 55 years after Napoleon.

   A two   **B** three   **C** four   **D** five

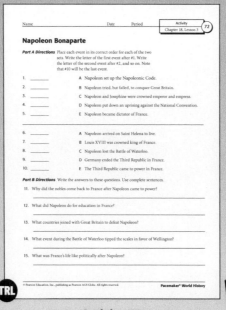

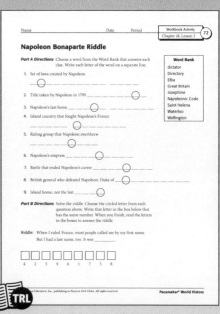

Activity 72   Workbook Activity 72

SUMMARY

- The government of France had changed little since the Middle Ages.

- The Age of Reason and the American Revolution gave the French people ideas about fighting for their own freedom.

- French kings, like Louis XVI, believed that they ruled by divine right.

- The First and Second Estates of the Estates-General represented a tiny piece of the French population. They were mostly wealthy clergy and nobles.

- The Third Estate of the French Estates-General represented all the common people.

- The French Revolution began on July 14, 1789, with the storming of the Bastille.

- King Louis XVI was found guilty of betraying his country. Louis XVI and Marie Antoinette were executed.

- The Reign of Terror from 1793 to 1794 led to increased fear and bloodshed.

- Napoleon Bonaparte stepped in to restore order in France. He conquered much of Europe and brought about many changes in the French government.

- France went through several revolutions in the late 1700s and the 1800s.

- The Third Republic built an empire of colonies. It helped strengthen France's trade and industry.

Chapter 18 Summary

Have students read the Chapter Summary on page 389 to review the main ideas presented in Chapter 18.

Ask:

- Where did the French get their ideas about fighting for freedom? (the Age of Reason and the American Revolution)

- Who was the king of France at the time of the revolution? (Louis XVI)

- Describe the First and Second Estates of the Estates-General. Compare them to the Third Estate. (The First and Second Estates were mostly wealthy clergy and nobles. The Third Estate represented all the common people.)

- What happened to King Louis XVI and Queen Marie Antoinette? (They were executed.)

- Who restored order to France following the Reign of Terror? (Napoleon Bonaparte)

- What is the Third Republic known for? (The Third Republic built an empire of colonies. It helped strengthen France's trade and industry.)

CHAPTER PROJECT FOLLOW-UP

Have members of each group take turns reading portions of their "Declaration of the Rights of Students" to the class. Each group should display their motto on a banner as they present their declaration. Assess students' work based on originality and clarity.

TEACHER'S RESOURCE

The AGS Globe Teaching Strategies in Social Studies Transparencies may be used with this chapter. The transparencies add an interactive dimension to expand and enhance the Pacemaker® *World History* program content.

Chapter 18 Review

Use the Chapter Review to prepare students for tests and to reteach content from the chapter.

Chapter 18 Mastery Test

The Teacher's Resource Library includes two forms of the Chapter 18 Mastery Test. Each test addresses the chapter Goals for Learning. An optional third page of additional critical-thinking items is included for each test. The difficulty level of the two forms is equivalent.

Midterm Mastery Test

The Teacher's Resource Library includes the Midterm Mastery Test. This test is pictured on page 805 of this Teacher's Edition. The Midterm Mastery Test assesses the major learning objectives for Chapters 1–17

Chapter 18 Review Answers
Vocabulary Review

1. symbol
2. dictator
3. oath
4. fraternity
5. riot
6. arsenal
7. betrayed
8. executed
9. motto
10. guillotine

Chapter Review Questions

11. Rousseau and Voltaire said French people should gain their freedom and rights like people in Britain and America.

12. They gave the French an idea that rule by the people was possible, that people deserved certain rights, and that freedom could be won.

CHAPTER 18 REVIEW

Word Bank

arsenal
betrayed
dictator
executed
fraternity
guillotine
motto
oath
riot
symbol

Vocabulary Review

On a sheet of paper, use the words from the Word Bank to complete each sentence correctly.

1. The Bastille was a(n) _____ of the injustices the people of France faced.

2. Napoleon took total power and became a(n) _____.

3. A(n) _____ is a serious promise, often given in the name of God.

4. The new French republic encouraged _____.

5. A(n) _____ broke out in July 1789, and the French attacked the Bastille.

6. Weapons are sometimes stored in a(n) _____.

7. When Revolution leaders thought Louis XVI _____ France, they forced him off the throne.

8. After King Louis XVI was found guilty of betraying his country, he was _____.

9. The _____ of the French Revolution was, "Liberty, Equality, and Fraternity!"

10. Robespierre, a violent leader of the Revolution, lost his head to the French _____.

Chapter Review Questions

On a sheet of paper, write the answer to each question. Use complete sentences.

11. What ideas did Rousseau and Voltaire give the French people?

12. What effect did the Age of Reason and the American Revolution have on the French people?

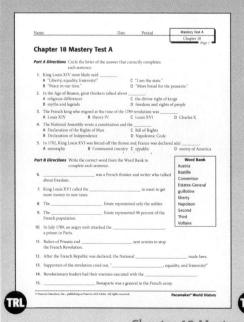

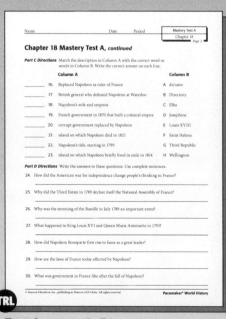

Chapter 18 Mastery Test A, pages 1–3

13. Why did members of the Third Estate think the Estates-General was unfair?

14. Why did so many people hate the Bastille?

15. What was one of the first things Napoleon did after he made himself dictator of France?

16. What did France do under the Third Republic, established in 1870?

Critical Thinking

On a sheet of paper, write your response to each question. Use complete sentences.

17. Why were European countries afraid the revolution would spread to them?

18. Overall, was Napoleon a success or a failure? Give reasons for your answer.

Using the Timeline

Use the timeline on page 387 to answer the questions.

19. What happened almost immediately after France became a republic?

20. When Napoleon was defeated at Waterloo, how long had he been emperor of France?

GROUP ACTIVITY

Form a group of three or four. Choose an event in the chapter. Write a skit about it. Practice performing the skit. Then present it to the rest of the class.

1700–1900 *Revolution in France* Chapter 18 **391**

---

13. The Third Estate represented 98 percent of the population, yet it had only one vote. The other estates often banded together and outvoted the Third Estate.

14. The Bastille was a prison, and in the past a person could be thrown in the Bastille on just the word of the king.

15. Napoleon set up the Napoleonic Code, a new constitution for France. It contained a single set of laws for all of France and its territories.

16. France built a colonial empire.

Critical Thinking

17. Possible answer: People in Europe were not free, and many felt oppressed. Revolution had already spread from Britain to America to France.

18. Possible answer: He was a success because the Napoleonic Code is still the basis of French law. He was not a success because he was defeated in war and was exiled.

Using the Timeline

19. The Reign of Terror began

20. 11 years

GROUP ACTIVITY

Skits should reveal some understanding of the events during the French Revolution.

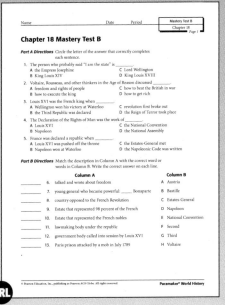

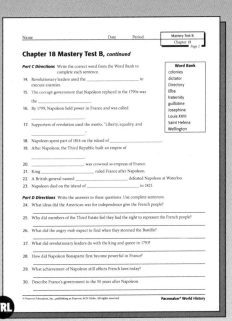

Chapter 18 Mastery Test B, pages 1–3

Revolution in France Chapter 18 **391**

The Age of Imperialism: 1500–1950

	Student Pages	Vocabulary	Map Study	Reading Strategy	Lesson Review	Chapter Summary/Review
Student Text Lesson						
Chapter 19 The Industrial Revolution	394–415	✔		✔		413–415
Lesson 19–1 Industries Develop	396–399	✔		✔	399	
Lesson 19–2 New Inventions	400–404	✔		✔	404	
Lesson 19–3 The Industrial Revolution Changes Life	405–409	✔		✔	409	
Lesson 19–4 The Industrial Revolution Spreads	410–412	✔		✔	412	
Chapter 20 Independence in Latin America	416–433	✔		✔		431–438
Lesson 20–1 Colonization	418–421	✔		✔	421	
Lesson 20–2 Colonies Fight for Independence	422–426	✔		✔	426	
Lesson 20–3 Latin American Culture	427–430	✔	✔	✔	430	

(Unit Planning Guide is continued on next page.)

Chapter Activities

Teacher's Resource Library
Life Skills Connection 19–24
Key Vocabulary Words 19–24

Assessment Options

Student Text
Chapter Reviews 19–24
Teacher's Resource Library
Chapter 19 Mastery Tests A and B
Chapter 20 Mastery Tests A and B
Chapter 21 Mastery Tests A and B
Chapter 22 Mastery Tests A and B
Chapter 23 Mastery Tests A and B
Chapter 24 Mastery Tests A and B
Unit 8 Mastery Test
Teacher's Edition
Chapter Projects 19–24

Words from the Past	Learn More About It	Great Names in History	Technology Connection	Geography Note	You Decide/Remember/History Fact	Timeline Study	ELL/ESL Strategy	Background Information	Common Error	Life Skills Connection	Key Vocabulary Words	Study Skills	Applications Home, Career, Community	Online Connection	Teacher Alert	World Cultures	Auditory/Verbal	Body/Kinesthetic	Interpersonal/Group Learning	Logical/Mathematical	Visual/Spatial	Activities/Modified Activities	Workbook Activities	Self-Study Guide	Chapter Outline
										395	395													✔	✔
					398		397	397	397			398					397					73	73		
					401, 402		401	401	403					403				401	402		402	74	74		
		407			405, 406, 407, 408		407	406	407				408		408	409				406		75	75		
						411	411	411														76	76		
										417	417													✔	✔
					420		418	420	418, 421					420			420	420				77	77		
		425			423		423	423					424				424			424		78	78		
						428	428	428	429			429	429, 430	430		430					428	79	79		

Modified Activities

The Teacher's Resource Library (TRL) contains a set of lower-level worksheets called Modified Activities. These worksheets cover the same content as the standard Activities but are written at a lower reading level.

Skill Track

Use Skill Track for *World History* to monitor student progress and meet the demands of adequate yearly progress (AYP). Make informed instructional decisions with individual student and class reports of lesson and chapter assessments. With immediate and ongoing feedback, students will also see what they have learned and where they need more reinforcement and practice.

UNIT 8

PLANNING GUIDE

The Age of Imperialism: 1500–1950 *(continued)*

	Student Text Lesson					
	Student Pages	Vocabulary	Map Study	Reading Strategy	Lesson Review	Chapter Summary/Review
Chapter 21 The United States Gains Power	434–453	✔		✔		451–453
Lesson 21–1 Imperialism and Growth	436–438	✔	✔	✔	438	
Lesson 21–2 Border Problems	439–442	✔		✔	442	
Lesson 21–3 The American Civil War	443–445			✔	445	
Lesson 21–4 U.S. Expansion	446–450	✔		✔	450	
Chapter 22 Imperialism and the Far East	454–473	✔		✔		471–473
Lesson 22–1 China Under Manchurian Rule	456–460	✔	✔	✔	460	
Lesson 22–3 Chinese Rebellion	461–465	✔		✔	465	
Lesson 22–4 Japan Opens Its Doors	466–470			✔	470	
Chapter 23 Imperialism and India	474–489	✔		✔		487–489
Lesson 23–1 The British East India Company	476–479	✔		✔	479	
Lesson 23–2 British Rule	480–482	✔		✔	482	
Lesson 23–3 Mahatma Gandhi	483–486	✔	✔	✔	486	
Chapter 24 Imperialism and Africa	490–511	✔		✔		509–511
Lesson 24–1 Early Kingdoms of Africa	492–497	✔	✔	✔	497	
Lesson 24–2 Africa After the First Century A.D.	498–500			✔	500	
Lesson 24–3 The African Slave Trade	501–504			✔	504	
Lesson 24–4 European Imperialism	505–508	✔			508	

Student Text Features							Teaching Strategies										Learning Styles					Teacher's Resource Library			
Words from the Past	Learn More About It	Great Names in History	Technology Connection	Geography Note	You Decide/Remember/History Fact	Timeline Study	ELL/ESL Strategy	Background Information	Common Error	Life Skills Connection	Key Vocabulary Words	Study Skills	Applications Home, Career, Community	Online Connection	Teacher Alert	World Cultures	Auditory/Verbal	Body/Kinesthetic	Interpersonal/Group Learning	Logical/Mathematical	Visual/Spatial	Activities/Modified Activities	Workbook Activities	Self-Study Guide	Chapter Outline
										435	435													✓	✓
							437	437							437					437		80	80		
				441	439		440	440	440, 441	441	442						440	440				81	81		
							444	444	445		445								444			82	82		
					447, 448	449	448	447	447, 449		449			449		449					447	83	83		
										455	455													✓	✓
					459		458	457	456, 457, 459		459							458		457		84	84		
	463				461, 464	464	464	462	462			465		463			463				463	85	85		
					467	469	468	467	468				469	469		469			469			86	86		
										475	475													✓	✓
	478						478	477	478				479		477							87	87		
							480	481	481, 482					482				481				88	88		
					483	485	485	484		484			486	485			485		484	484	485	89	89		
										491	491													✓	✓
					495	493	495	494	496				493	496					494	494		90	90		
					498		499	499	498, 499		500											91	91		
503							502	502						503	503	503	501					92	92		
					507	507	507	506		507	508			506				507			506	93	93		

Audio Library

Skill Track for World History

Teacher's Resource Library **TRL**

Unit 8 Mastery Test

(Answer Keys for the Teacher's Resource Library begin on page 809 of the Teacher's Edition.)

Other Resources

Books for Teachers

Beaudoin, Steven M. *The Industrial Revolution*. Problems in European Civilization series. Boston: Houghton Mifflin Co., 2003.

Elliott, John H. *Empires of the Atlantic World: Britain and Spain in America, 1492–1830.* New Haven: Yale University Press, 2006.

Rodriguez, Jaime E. *The Independence of Spanish America.* Cambridge: Cambridge University Press, 1998.

Books for Students

Fish, Bruce, and Becky Durost Fish. *South Africa: 1880 to the Present: Imperialism, Nationalism, and Apartheid.* New York: Chelsea House Publications, 2000.

Langley, Andrew. *The Industrial Revolution.* New York: Viking, 1994.

THE AGE OF IMPERIALISM

Changes in the world over hundreds of years were often connected to power over the earth's resources. In many cases, this meant conquering new lands and controlling new groups of people. As countries learned how to better manufacture different products, they needed more material. Similar knowledge helped them build better methods of transportation to travel to far-off places. Still other learning helped them take control of other lands, using new and stronger weapons. As people's abilities grew, so did their sense of imperialism. At the same time, changes in the makeup of the world seem to happen more rapidly all the time.

In 1900, the Chinese rebelled against all foreigners in China. This revolt is known as the Boxer Rebellion. It was one of the many uprisings brought on by imperialism during this time in history.

393

Introducing the Unit

Review the meaning of imperialism. Ask students which empires they have studied so far (e.g., Roman, Spanish, Byzantine). Have students study the picture on page 392. Ask them about people's reactions to imperialism in the countries they have studied. Explain that in this unit students will learn about imperialism, revolutions, industrialization, and nationalism, and how they are interconnected.

Ask:

- What appears to be happening in the illustration? (A battle is going on.)
- What kind of revolution was a factor in the spread of imperialism? (the Industrial Revolution)
- Where did European countries establish colonies in the 19th century? (Africa and Asia)

Videos

Imperial Ambition. Social Studies School Service (44 minutes; describes the history of Spanish rule in Latin America, the involvement of the British in India, and the motives behind the colonization of Africa.)

CD-ROM/Software

Imperialism. Culver City, CA: Social Studies School Service. (A study of imperialism and its effects in Latin America, India, and Africa.)

Web Sites

www.agsglobepmwh.com/page393a
(Archives of the magazine *Invention and Technology.*)

www.agsglobepmwh.com/page393b
(Devoted to the story of the Industrial Revolution.)

www.agsglobepmwh.com/page393c
(Imperialism by the United States, including the Boxer Rebellion and the Spanish-American War.)

Introducing the Chapter

In the middle of the 18th century, the
power of machines began to replace
the human hand in the production
of goods. Factories replaced home
workshops, and people left their farms
for jobs in the city. New inventions
allowed these changes to take place.
This period of rapid change from
farming to industry—from about 1750
to 1850—is known as the Industrial
Revolution.

The Industrial Revolution

The word *revolution* is an interesting one. In the last
chapter, it was a fiery battle to upset the unpopular
government of France. You have likely learned about
the *revolution* of the earth, or the way it moves around
the sun. Now, consider the definition you learned in
Chapter 1, that *revolution* is another word for "change."

The Industrial Revolution was a huge, rapid change
from making goods by hand to making them by machine.
It was about more products and a greater need for
materials to make those products. It was about more jobs
for more people. In some cases, it meant that more people
earned money to gain more freedom or, in some cases,
more power.

GOALS FOR LEARNING

- To tell why the Industrial Revolution began in
  Great Britain
- To explain inventions of the 1700s
- To explain how the Industrial Revolution changed life
- To explain how the Industrial Revolution made
  countries more dependent on each other

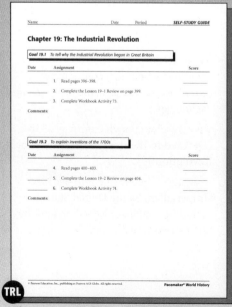

Chapter 19 Self-Study Guide, pages 1–2

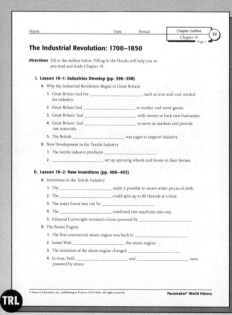

Chapter 19 Outline, pages 1–2

Reading Strategy: Visualizing

Visualizing is another way to help you understand what you are reading. When you visualize a text, you imagine how it looks. These things will help you visualize a text:

- Use the photographs, illustrations, and descriptive words to "set the stage" for the text.

- Think about experiences you may have faced that are similar to those described in the text.

- Notice the order in which things are happening; try to visualize what will happen next.

Key Vocabulary Words

Lesson 1

Profit The amount of money left over after paying for the cost of doing business

Industrial Revolution The important changes that took place in the way work was done during the 18th and 19th century

Natural resource Materials that are provided by nature

Energy Power that makes machines work

Locomotive A self-propelled vehicle that runs on rails

Investor A person who expects to make a profit by lending money to a business

Raw material Matter in its natural condition

Textile Cloth made by weaving

Import To bring into one country from another

Lesson 2

Internal combustion engine An engine that burns gasoline to produce power

Lesson 3

Labor union A group of workers who join together

Lesson 4

Developed country A nation that has many industries and that imports and exports products

Developing country A nation that is slowly growing its industry and economy

Export To send a product out of one country and into another to sell

Ask:

- Who invented the spinning jenny? (James Hargreaves)
- Which was invented first, the steam locomotive or the telegraph? (steam locomotive)
- Where did most British people live before the Industrial Revolution? After it? (on farms before, in cities after)

Reading Strategy: Visualizing

Draw students' attention to the definition. Tell students that visualizing helps you remember what you read by creating pictures in your mind about the topic. It is especially valuable in understanding how and where people lived.

Explain that visuals, such as drawings and photographs, will help them visualize what is described in the text. Encourage students to pay close attention to each illustration to further their understanding of the Industrial Revolution.

Key Vocabulary Words

Point out that these chapter words are presented in the order they appear in each lesson. They are also found in the glossary.

LIFE SKILLS CONNECTION

Students learn that labor unions are still active today. Students also research local unions. Try to have a local union representative visit your classroom to discuss modern unions.

KEY VOCABULARY

Have student review the vocabulary from each lesson before completing the exercise. Students choose a word from the Word Bank to complete each sentence.

Name _____ **Date** _____ **Period** _____   Life Skills Connection 19   Chapter 19

Chapter 19 Life Skills Connection

A vital product of the Industrial Revolution was labor unions. Workers banded together to demand fair wages and better working conditions. Labor unions are still active and important today. They are not just for factory workers, but for people in all kinds of jobs. Even people you might not think of, such as actors and teachers, have unions.

Part A Directions Using the Internet, find five different kinds of workers who are protected by unions.

1. _____
2. _____
3. _____
4. _____
5. _____

Part B Directions If you have a job, are there unions at your place of employment? If not, ask your family members if they belong to any unions. Try to find the answers to the questions below.

6. What do you have to do to join the union?
7. What protection does the union offer?
8. How much does it cost to be a member of the union?
9. How can you elect representatives to the union?
10. When and where does your local chapter of the union meet?

© Pearson Education, Inc., publishing as Pearson AGS Globe. All rights reserved.   **Pacemaker® World History**

Name _____ **Date** _____ **Period** _____   Key Vocabulary Words 19   Chapter 19

Chapter 19 Key Vocabulary Words

Directions Write the correct word from the Word Bank to complete each sentence.

Word Bank
cottage weavers
developed countries
developing countries
energy
export
import
Industrial Revolution
internal combustion engine
investors
labor unions
locomotives
natural resources
profits
raw materials
textile

1. The _____ changed the way people worked and lived starting in the 18th century.
2. Business owners often put their _____ back into their businesses.
3. Factories turn _____ into finished products.
4. Forests, minerals, and water are examples of _____.
5. Electricity is a new form of _____ developed during the Industrial Revolution.
6. Rich countries often set up colonies in _____.
7. Inventions such as the spinning jenny revolutionized the _____ industry.
8. Before the Industrial Revolution, _____ made cloth in their homes.
9. Great Britain and the United States are both _____.
10. _____ put money into businesses in order to make more money.
11. In Great Britain, _____ traveled over 6,600 miles of track.
12. Chile and Peru _____ copper to other countries.
13. Bad working conditions in factories made workers form _____.
14. The _____ made the invention of the automobile possible.
15. Other markets _____ the goods made by developed countries.

© Pearson Education, Inc., publishing as Pearson AGS Globe. All rights reserved.   **Pacemaker® World History**

Life Skills Connection 19   Key Vocabulary Words 19

Lesson at a Glance

Chapter 19 Lesson 1

Overview This lesson describes the beginning of the Industrial Revolution in Great Britain.

Objectives

- To tell reasons why the Industrial Revolution began in Great Britain
- To describe why British business leaders wanted to improve the production of textiles

Student Pages 396–399

Teacher's Resource Library

Workbook Activity 73

Activity 73

Modified Activity 73

Vocabulary

energy	market
factory	natural resource
import	profit
Industrial Revolution	raw material
investor	textile
locomotive	transportation

Write the headings "People," "Things," and "Events" in a three-column chart on the board. Read aloud each vocabulary word with students and discuss its definition. Have students classify each word under the correct heading. Once all words have been classified, invite students to use each word in a sentence. Write each sentence on the chart.

1 Warm-Up Activity

Divide the class into small groups. Read the definition of natural resources on page 396 to students. Have students make a list of all of the natural resources they can think of. Have students search the Internet for one of those resources and make a list of the products for which those natural resources are used. Have groups share the information they found with the class. If time permits, have students discuss which natural resources are renewable and which are nonrenewable.

Industries Develop

Objectives
- To tell reasons why the Industrial Revolution began in Great Britain
- To describe why British business leaders wanted to improve the production of textiles

Profit
The amount of money left over after paying for the cost of doing business

Industrial Revolution
The important changes that took place in the way work was done during the 18th and 19th century

Natural resource
Materials that are provided by nature, such as forests, minerals, and water

Energy
Power that makes machines work

The most dramatic changes in industry began in Great Britain in about 1750. It is true that people had been inventing things during earlier years. However, most of their work centered around scientific theories and ideas. Now science and invention took a more practical, or useful, turn. They developed machines especially designed to increase the production of goods and to help people make a **profit.**

Why Did the Industrial Revolution Begin in Great Britain?

The **Industrial Revolution** began in Great Britain for a number of reasons. For one thing, Britain had a large supply of workers. Women, as well as men, were ready to leave their homes and join the industrial workforce.

Great Britain also had the **natural resources** needed for industry. Natural resources are materials that are provided by nature, such as coal and iron. Indeed, Britain had a good supply of coal and iron. Coal could produce the **energy** to keep the new steam engines running. Coal was also needed to produce iron. Iron could be used to improve machines and tools. It could also be used to build railroad tracks, bridges, and ships.

Britain had the **transportation** that industry needed. Products had to be marketed and moved. Steam **locomotives** and steam-only ocean-going ships were developed in Britain in the 1700s and 1800s.

2 Teaching the Lesson

As students read the lesson, it may be challenging for them to understand what life was like prior to the Industrial Revolution. Explain that before the Industrial Revolution, most people made a living by farming, or by doing jobs related to farming. People who made things made them using hand tools. The Industrial Revolution was a time when a lot of machinery was invented that could help people with their jobs.

Ask:
- What four things did England have that helped it industrialize? (natural resources, workers, transportation, and investors)
- Why were colonies important to Britain? (They supplied raw materials and were a market for manufactured goods.)
- Why was cloth expensive? (It was in short supply because it was handmade.)

Transportation
The act of carrying from one place to another

Locomotive
A self-propelled vehicle that runs on rails

Investor
A person who expects to make a profit by lending money to a business

Market
A place to sell goods

Raw material
Matter in its natural condition, not changed by some human process

Factory
A building where goods are made by machinery

Textile
Cloth made by weaving

Import
To bring into one country from another

Britain had **investors.** These were people with money to back the new businesses.

Britain had colonies to serve as ready **markets** for the goods. British colonies also supplied **raw materials,** like cotton, to the **factories** in London and other cities. It was in the factories where the goods were made by machinery.

Finally, the British government was eager to support growing industry. For all these reasons, Great Britain saw a burst of industrial development. In the late 1700s and 1800s, Britain became known as the "Workshop of the World."

Why Was the Textile Industry in Need of New Development?

Britain's **textile** industry produced cloth. This industry is a good example of what the early Industrial Revolution was all about.

In the earliest days, British merchants **imported** cloth from other lands. Because of the cost of shipping finished goods, cloth was expensive.

Later, in the 1600s, Britain began importing raw cotton. The British spun their own threads and then wove their own cloth.

Farm families did the work. They set up spinning wheels and looms in their cottages. Both spinning wheels and looms were operated by hand. The families who worked this way were called *cottage weavers.*

1700–1850
The Industrial Revolution   *Chapter 19*   **397**

Background Information

Before the Industrial Revolution, cloth was expensive and clothing was all hand-made, usually to order. In most cases, families bought raw materials for fabric and spun thread and wove it themselves. Others bought cloth and hired tailors to make their clothes. Most people did not have many articles of clothing, and the ones they owned were carefully repaired and refurbished when necessary.

LEARNING STYLES

Auditory/Verbal
To help auditory learners process the information in this lesson, have students listen to the recording for Lesson 19–1. Encourage them to follow along in their book and to write key facts as they listen. Invite students to listen to sections of the lesson as many times as necessary to gain understanding of the concepts.

ELL/ESL STRATEGY

Language Objective: *To understand the main idea of a text*

Ask students to read "Why Did the Industrial Revolution Begin in Great Britain?" on page 396. Ask students to work with a partner and write the main idea in the center of an idea web. Then, have students find one important sentence and two details in each paragraph. They should write these in ovals connected to the web center. The fourth paragraph is short, so it will have no details.

3 Reinforce and Extend

COMMON ERROR

Students may think that the Industrial Revolution was the first or only great leap in technological inventions. Development of new technologies happened earlier in history, but they weren't accompanied by such widespread social changes.

CHAPTER PROJECT

Divide the class into pairs. Have each pair of students choose an invention from the era of the Industrial Revolution. The invention does not have to be one mentioned in this chapter. Have students use the Internet and the library to research their invention. Each pair of students should prepare a computer presentation on their invention that they will present to the class at the end of this chapter.

History Fact

Scotland united with England largely for strategic reasons: England needed support in its war with France. The Westminster Parliament absorbed Scotland's Parliament. Thereafter, Scotland gained free access to trade with England and its colonies.

Reading Strategy:
Visualizing

If students still need help using graphic organizers, discuss the type of organizer that lends itself to the subject of changes in the textile industry. Suggest that students keep their organizer and sketches for review at the end of the chapter.

History Fact
In 1707, Scotland joined England and Wales to become Great Britain, or Britain.

Reading Strategy:
Visualizing

Create a graphic organizer for making simple sketches to illustrate the changes in the textile industry.

Merchants would buy the finished cloth from the cottage weavers. The amounts of cloth produced were never very large. In order to meet their own needs, the weavers had to farm land, too. They could only make cloth in their spare time. There was never enough finished cloth for all the people who wanted to buy it. Therefore, British business leaders looked for ways to improve and increase the production of textiles.

During the 1600s, weavers set up spinning wheels and looms in their cottages. They sold the cloth they wove to merchants.

REVIEW

Word Bank

British

coal

cottage weavers

cotton

imported

small

steam

On a sheet of paper, write the word from the Word Bank to complete each sentence correctly.

1. Britain had a good supply of natural resources such as _____ and iron.

2. In the 1700s and 1800s, Britain developed locomotives and ships that were powered by _____.

3. British colonies supplied raw materials, like _____, to the factories in London and other cities.

4. At first, cloth was _____ from other lands to Britain, making it quite expensive.

5. In the 1600s, the _____ began to import raw cotton to weave their own cloth.

6. _____ operated the spinning wheels and looms by hand.

7. Weavers produced a(n) _____ amount of cloth, which they made in their spare time.

On a sheet of paper, write the answer to each question. Use complete sentences.

8. What dramatic changes in industry happened in Great Britain around 1750?

9. What are four reasons the Industrial Revolution began in Great Britain?

10. Why did British business leaders want to improve the production of textiles?

Lesson 19–1 Review Answers

1. coal **2.** steam **3.** cotton **4.** imported **5.** British **6.** cottage weavers **7.** small **8.** Rather than centering their work on scientific theories and ideas, inventors took a practical turn. They developed machines especially designed to increase the production of goods and to help people make a profit. **9.** There are actually six reasons the Industrial Revolution began in Great Britain: (any four of these answers are acceptable) Britain had a large supply of workers, it had the natural resources needed for industry, it had developed the transportation that industry needed, it had investors with money to back new businesses, it had colonies to supply raw materials to the factories, and the British government was eager to support a growing industry. **10.** There was never enough cloth for all the people who wanted to buy it.

Activity 73

Workbook Activity 73

Lesson at a Glance

Chapter 19 Lesson 2

Overview This lesson describes inventions that advanced the textile and transportation industries, and made energy in the form of petroleum and electricity more available.

Objectives

- To name five machines that improved the making of textiles
- To name two machines that were powered by steam
- To describe two uses for oil

Student Pages 400–404

Teacher's Resource Library

Workbook Activity 74

Activity 74

Modified Activity 74

Vocabulary

internal combustion engine

Have students look up each word in the vocabulary phrase. Ask them to write a sentence for each word (*internal*, *combustion*, and *engine*) as well as one for the whole phrase.

PRONUNCIATION GUIDE

Use this list to help students pronounce difficult words in this lesson.

Hargreaves (här´grēvz)

Newcomen (nōō kum´ən)

Trevithick (trev´ə thik)

1 Warm-Up Activity

There are many stories of inventions that were used for one purpose but developed a second purpose, or sequences of inventions that made subsequent inventions possible or desirable. Have students look at an example of an evolving invention, such as fiberglass or food preservation in cans.

Objectives

- To name five machines that improved the making of textiles
- To name two machines that were powered by steam
- To describe two uses for oil

Reading Strategy: Visualizing

Draw pictures to help visualize any of the new inventions. How do they help you remember?

In the 1700s some new machines were invented that changed the textile industry. Spinners and weavers left their cottages and went to work in new factories.

What Inventions Helped Move Textile-Making Out of Cottages?

The first important invention in the textile-making revolution was the *flying shuttle*. In 1733, a man named John Kay invented a shuttle, a device on a loom. The shuttle made it possible to weave wider pieces of cloth. Now one worker could do the work of two.

Soon more cotton yarn was needed than could be produced. Business leaders offered prizes to the inventor of a machine to spin yarn. In 1764, James Hargreaves came up with just such a machine. He named it after his wife. The *spinning jenny* used the same ideas as the spinning wheel. But it could spin as many as 80 threads at one time.

The biggest change came in 1769. In that year, Richard Arkwright invented a machine called the *water frame*. Now even more cotton thread could be spun at once. The water frame ran by water power. It was so big that it could not fit into a cottage. It was also an expensive piece of machinery. The water frame required a special building of its own.

New machines forced the textile business out of the English cottages. Mills and factories were built. Workers were no longer their own bosses. They became factory hands. They worked in large mills that often employed up to 600 people.

---

2 Teaching the Lesson

As students read, have them look for the connection where one technique or technological innovation made another one possible or essential. The Online Connection on page 403 may help them. Point out that the increased rate of spinning affected the pace of weaving, and visa versa. Ask students to build a concept map to help them visualize the connections among the inventions mentioned in this lesson.

Reading Strategy: Visualizing

Have students draw inventions and answer the question. Students may benefit from supplementing the text's illustrations with drawings of the water frame and other innovations. Have them search for these on the Internet or in an encyclopedia.

In 1779, Samuel Crompton put the spinning jenny and the water frame into one machine. He called it the *mule*. The mule could spin much finer threads very rapidly.

Now the weavers had to keep step with the spinners. With so much thread being produced, the textile industry needed a better loom. In about 1785, Edmund Cartwright invented a steam-powered loom.

History Fact
Workers who destroyed machines in the early 1800s were called *Luddites*. The name came from Ned Ludd, who reportedly led a mob which smashed some weaving machinery in the 1770s.

Workers sometimes feared the new machines. Would the machines completely replace the workers? Would they lose their jobs? At one point, antimachine riots broke out. Mobs smashed machines, shouting, "Men, not machines!" Sometimes progress was a frightening thing. The Industrial Revolution, however, could not be stopped.

Within 50 years, the textile industry had entirely changed. What had been a cottage industry had turned into a big business. As a result, a way of life had changed, too, for thousands of textile workers.

The spinning jenny made spinning yarn faster and easier.

Ask:

- Name four inventions that helped the textile industry. (flying shuttle, spinning jenny, water frame, mule)
- What fuel was used to drive steam engines? (coal)
- What was the connection between oil and the internal combustion machine? (Oil lubricated and provided fuel for the machine.)

Background Information

The construction of the transcontinental railroad in the United States had two starting points. The Union Pacific Railroad started laying tracks at Omaha, Nebraska, and headed westward. The Central Pacific Railroad started in Sacramento, California, and headed eastward. Conditions for the European and Chinese immigrants who laid the track were brutal: many lost their lives due to accidents, illness, and disputes with American Indians. Workers had to construct tunnels through mountains— sometimes making only a few feet of progress after a full day of work. Finally, after several years of grueling labor, the two railroad lines were joined at Promontory Point, Utah. This occasion was marked by a ceremony in which a golden spike was driven into the last link of track.

LEARNING STYLES

Body/Kinesthetic
Have students make a poster-size graphic organizer showing the different inventions and discoveries that fueled the Industrial Revolution. In addition to those discussed in this lesson, encourage students to include inventions or discoveries mentioned elsewhere in Chapter 19. Suggest that they include illustrations or diagrams that show how the inventions worked.

History Fact
Luddite is still a useful name for people who oppose technological change.

ELL/ESL STRATEGY

Language Objective:
To identify the versatility of a suffix

Ask students to read the History Fact on page 401. Explain to students that adding *-ites* to the end of a word identifies a person as part of a group. Therefore, a *Luddite* is someone who belongs to the group of workers who destroyed machines in the early 1800s. Tell students that other examples of this include *Moabite*, which means "a person from Moab"; *Labourite*, which means "a member of the Labour Party"; and *Israelite*, which means "a person from Israel." Ask students why it is useful to know the meaning of an ending that can be added to a word to change its meaning.

Reading Strategy:
Visualizing

(Possible answers: the illustration, previous knowledge of boats)

History Fact

Ask students what familiar household items are labeled with the number of watts they use. (Possible answer: lightbulb, hair dryer)

Reading Strategy:
Visualizing

What clues in this section help you to visualize the improvements to the steam engine?

History Fact

The power unit called the *watt* was named in honor of James Watt. He made steam power practical.

How Did the Steam Engine Change the Transportation Industry?

The new machines needed power. Water power was not strong enough to run heavy machines. During the 1600s, inventors had begun experimenting with "fire engines," or steam engines. In 1698, Thomas Savery built the first commercial steam engine. Around 1712, Thomas Newcomen improved on Savery's engine. It was, however, far from perfect. It used too much coal.

In 1769, a Scottish engineer named James Watt invented an improved steam engine. For several years only the textile industry made use of Watt's engine. By 1850, however, it was being used throughout Britain. Then it spread throughout the rest of Europe.

The invention of the steam engine completely changed transportation. In 1804, a British engineer, Richard Trevithick, built the first steam locomotive. Steam locomotives came into general use in Britain in the late 1830s. By 1850, Great Britain had 6,600 miles of railroad track. The United States, France, and Germany built their own rail systems during the next 10 years.

Early steam locomotives were simple but powerful.

Internal combustion engine

An engine that burns gasoline to produce power

An American, Robert Fulton, built the first successful steamboat in 1807. Within a few years, steamboats were being used on British rivers. By the mid-1800s, steam-powered ships were carrying raw materials and finished goods across the ocean.

What Were Some Advances in Electricity and Petroleum?

In 1831, an Englishman named Michael Faraday invented a machine called the *dynamo*. It generated an electric current by using magnets. Faraday's discovery led to the building of more powerful electric generators and electric motors. In time the use of electricity as a source of power would become widespread.

In the 1850s, Americans discovered that petroleum, or unrefined oil, could be used for many things. It could be used to make kerosene, and kerosene could be used for heat and light. Oil could make machinery run more smoothly. Fortunately, there was a good supply of crude oil available in the United States.

Oil was to become one of the most valuable resources in the world. This would come about with the invention of the **internal combustion engine** and the diesel engine. Petroleum could be turned into gasoline and diesel fuel to run those engines. Oil would give some nations new wealth and power.

COMMON ERROR

Coal, as well as other fuels, provided power to steam engines, although coal was most prevalent in Britain. In America, these engines were often fired with wood, especially in locomotives and boats.

COMMON ERROR

Students may think that inventors have to work in special fields. This is not always true. Have small groups develop an invention of their own. They are to think hard about what labor-saving, time-saving devices the world might need. Tell them to think about the kitchen, the office, the factory, and recreation. They should draw or diagram the new invention, or actually build it if they can! Have students present their inventions to the class.

ONLINE CONNECTION

Students can gain additional information by accessing the following Web site: www. agsglobepmwh.com/page403 (This Web site gives additional information about the early steam engines.)

LESSON 19-2 REVIEW

On a sheet of paper, write the letter of the answer that correctly completes each sentence.

1. The _____, invented in 1764, could spin as many as 80 threads at one time.

   A water frame
   B spinning jenny
   C steam-powered loom
   D mule

2. Edmund Cartwright's invention, the _____, helped the weavers keep up with the spinners.

   A steam-powered loom
   B spinning jenny
   C steam engine
   D dynamo

3. James Watt's new and improved _____ completely changed transportation.

   A steam locomotive
   B steam-powered loom
   C flying shuttle
   D steam engine

4. Because of the _____, many countries laid hundreds of miles of railroad track.

   A diesel engine
   B dynamo
   C spinning jenny
   D steam locomotive

5. The American Robert Fulton built the first successful _____.

   A water frame
   B steam-powered loom
   C river steamboat
   D diesel engine

6. Michael Faraday invented the _____, which generated an electric current by using magnets.

   A dynamo
   B flying shuttle
   C internal combustion engine
   D mule

On a sheet of paper, write the answer to each question. Use complete sentences.

7. What was the first important invention in the textile-making revolution and what did it do?

8. What machine did Richard Arkwright invent in 1769 and what did it do?

9. Why did workers sometimes fear new machines?

10. What are two things oil can be used for?

---

404 Unit 8 *The Age of Imperialism*

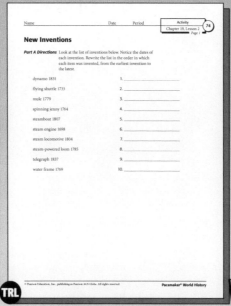

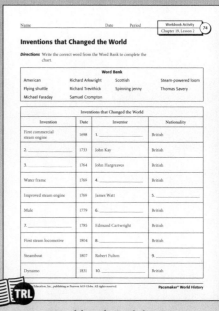

The Industrial Revolution Changes Life

Objectives

■ To explain how the Industrial Revolution encouraged imperialism
■ To describe how the Industrial Revolution affected people's lives
■ To describe the purpose of a labor union

Reading Strategy: Visualizing

What words in this lesson help you to visualize what you are reading about?

Remember
Imperialism is the practice of conquering other lands, forming colonies in other lands, or controlling the government and wealth of weaker lands.

As with any revolution, industrialization brought changes to Great Britain. While some of the changes were good, other times they were not.

How Did the Industrial Revolution Encourage Imperialism?

The Industrial Revolution meant new inventions and new products. It also meant new needs. As the ability to produce goods increased, so did the need for more raw materials. Britain needed even more coal to fire the steam engines. It needed more cotton to spin into thread. It also needed more iron to make railroad tracks and machinery.

Imperialism seemed to be a solution to the problems of getting raw materials. Britain took over land in Africa and Asia and formed colonies. The colonies were sources of raw materials. In addition, the colonies became markets for finished products from Britain.

Did the Industrial Revolution Improve Life?

Did the Industrial Revolution improve the lives of the British people? Or did it make life harder? A look at life in Great Britain in the late 1700s and early 1800s gives a mixed picture.

In many ways life was better. Average incomes tripled between 1700 and 1815. Between 1815 and 1836, incomes increased 30 times over! People had better food to eat. They had more meat, sugar, tea, and coffee. Coal not only fueled the industrial machines, it also heated homes and cooked food.

Lesson at a Glance

Chapter 19 Lesson 3

Overview This lesson describes both the positive and negative effects of industrialization.

Objectives

■ To explain how the Industrial Revolution encouraged imperialism
■ To describe how the Industrial Revolution affected people's lives
■ To describe the purpose of a labor union

Student Pages 405–409

Teacher's Resource Library

Workbook Activity 75

Activity 75

Modified Activity 75

· ·

Vocabulary

labor union

Have students look up synonyms for *labor union* in a thesaurus. (trade union, organized labor, craft union, industrial union) Assign different terms to small groups for them to determine how their term differs from *labor union*. They should write their results and report them to the class.

---

1   Warm-Up Activity

Once the Industrial Revolution began, many people gave up the farming lifestyle and moved to cities to work in factories. Divide the class into pairs. Have them role-play the parts of a farm worker and a factory worker at the time of the Industrial Revolution. Have each student describe their job to their partner. As students read, encourage them to determine if their thoughts on the job of the factory worker were accurate.

Reading Strategy: Visualizing

(Possible answer: list of foods, description of work conditions, living conditions)

Remember
Ask students for examples of colonizers and colonized countries that they've studied. (Greece, Rome, America)

As students read the lesson, have them think about the benefits and drawbacks of an industrialized society. You may want to have students include the information in a two-column chart that can be used to study for the chapter test.

Ask:

- Where did most people live before the Industrial Revolution? Where did they live after? (farms; cities)
- List the problems that arose as cities grew bigger. (Possible answer: Garbage piled up; bad water and poor sanitation caused disease.)
- Who worked in factories? (entire families, including young children)

Background Information

It should be noted that not all textile mills treated their workers unfairly. However, the standards of fair labor practices were different in the 1800s than they are now. At that time, children often worked 12 hours a day, and doctors disagreed over the length of time that would be okay. A law that limited the hours to 10 a day apparently was too lenient to pass in Parliament in 1832. Keeping track of hours worked may seem like a simple task today, but it cannot be done by people without watches. The few who owned a watch might even be forbidden to bring it to work.

LEARNING STYLES

Logical/Mathematical

Distribute copies of Morse code symbols to students. Explain that different combinations of long and short tones represent letters of the alphabet. Invite volunteers to write a short message using Morse code and have the class try to decipher it. If possible, have students send their messages using an electronic keyboard or other instrument. An alternate method for achieving the same effect is by flashing the classroom lights on and off.

For the merchants, bankers, shipowners, and factory owners, the Industrial Revolution meant wealth. The middle class now had a greater voice in the British government.

New inventions in communication let people learn what was going on in their world. In 1837, Samuel F. B. Morse invented the telegraph. He also invented a code to send telegrams—the Morse code. By 1866, a telegraph cable reached across the Atlantic.

Life, however, did not improve for everyone. As the Industrial Revolution went on, life got harder for many city workers. People spent long days in dirty, dangerous factories, working for poor wages.

At first factory work had paid well. But soon the owners found they could hire women and children for lower wages than men. Soon most of the factory workers were women and children. Many children were very young. Factory wages dropped.

History Fact
Most factory workers were poor and could not read or write.

Young children often worked at machines under dangerous conditions.

History Fact
Most families had to pay for schooling for their children. A good school wasn't cheap, and if the children were in school, they couldn't work and contribute to the family's income or food production.

LEARN MORE ABOUT IT

Child Labor

Many of the children working in factories came from orphanages or poor families. They were treated much like slaves. They often had to work from five in the morning until eight at night. Some factory owners treated the children quite well. Others beat the young workers for such crimes as falling asleep at their work or working too slowly.

In the 1800s there were new laws called Factory Acts. These laws took the very youngest children out of the factories. The laws also put limits on the number of hours children and women could work.

Despite the new laws, work could be dangerous. There were no safety measures or protection against industrial accidents. It is sad to imagine what happened to many little children working on dangerous machines with no safety devices.

Reading Strategy: Visualizing

Draw a simple sketch of city life showing how it has been shaped by industry. How do these drawings help you remember?

You Decide
If factory work and living conditions in the cities were so awful, why do you think so many people moved to the cities?

How Did the Living Conditions in the Cities Change?

Britain's cities were becoming dark with ash from the new coal-burning factories. As the skies blackened, the factories drew people to the cities. As a result, British cities went through a population explosion. In 1801, about 78 percent of people in Britain lived on farms. By 1901, about 75 percent lived in cities.

Where were all these people going to make their homes? Housing had to be built quickly and cheaply. The results were poorly built slum buildings. Inside were small apartments where whole families often shared one room. Sewage and garbage could not be disposed of properly. These conditions led to the outbreak and spread of disease.

1700–1850 *The Industrial Revolution* *Chapter 19* **407**

Reading Strategy:
Visualizing

Students should collect these sketches to use when they review the chapter.

You Decide
(Possible answer: There wasn't enough work in the countryside to support large families.) Ask for volunteers to give their answers and discuss them as a class. Point out that there were likely a number of reasons that someone might move to the city, just as there are today.

LEARN MORE ABOUT IT

Have students work in small groups to create a list of laws to protect children from unfair or dangerous working conditions. Ask them to consider the following questions: *What should be the minimum age for employment? When should young people be allowed to work? What type of work should young people be prohibited from doing?* Have groups share their laws with the class. Then have students read "Child Labor" to find out about the dangers of child labor and the laws that exist to protect children.

ELL/ESL STRATEGY

Language Objective:
To write to inform

In this lesson, students read about some of the challenges faced by factory workers during the Industrial Revolution, as well as some of the benefits the workers got from their work. Ask students to think about a profession they think would be interesting to pursue. Have students do research about that profession and find information on the education and training needed, the job description, the potential salary, and the challenges of the profession. Have students use their research to write a one-page report about the profession they chose. You may wish to post students' reports or have students read them to the class.

3 Reinforce and Extend

COMMON ERROR

People sometimes refer to the "traditional roles" played by men and women in the family—the men work outside the home, and the women inside. Before and during the Industrial Revolution, however, these distinct roles were not the status quo for the working class and farmers. As cottage weavers, men worked inside the house (as well as in farm fields), and women and children worked in the fields and in the factories.

COMMON ERROR

Child labor did not originate with the Industrial Revolution. Farm families had jobs that very young children could do, and older children usually worked alongside parents in the house and in the fields.

The Industrial Revolution Chapter 19 **407**

Although robots have taken over some of the factory jobs that people used to do, there are still many tasks modern technology cannot replace. As a result, the demand for product assemblers will continue. Product assemblers put together different kinds of products, usually working along a conveyor belt on an assembly line. Successful product assemblers have a minimum of a high school diploma, good math skills, and the ability to work with tools and machines. Encourage interested students to take shop, electronics, and computer classes in high school.

IN THE COMMUNITY

Have students research the influence of industrialization on the growth of their own town or city. Ask them to consider the following questions: *What industries developed in your town or city? What happened to the population when those industries grew? Has the population increased or decreased over time? What industries are located in your town or city today?* Students might call the local library or historical society to find this information. Have them summarize their findings in a brief report.

AT HOME

Some students may have family members who belong to labor unions. Have students interview them to find out why they choose to be a member. What benefits do they receive? Some students do not have family members in labor unions. Have those students interview a family member about the safety precautions that are taken so they can do their jobs safely. Have students summarize the interview in a brief report and share their findings with the class.

Labor union
A group of workers who join together to protect their wages, working conditions, and job benefits

Earning a living became difficult as more people moved into cities.

History Fact
An American visited a British textile mill in 1810. Within a few years he built the first textile factory in the United States. It was located in Waltham, Massachusetts.

It would not be long before people began to protest against this kind of life. They protested against factories that employed young children and paid terrible wages. They protested against having to work with dangerous machines that had no safety devices.

The Industrial Revolution taught workers that they had to band together. They formed **labor unions** to demand better, fairer conditions. Of course factory owners were not in favor of the workers' unions. Until 1825, unions were against the law in Great Britain.

TEACHER ALERT

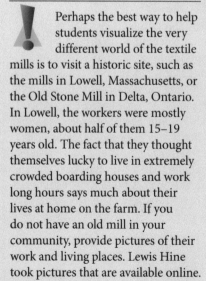

Perhaps the best way to help students visualize the very different world of the textile mills is to visit a historic site, such as the mills in Lowell, Massachusetts, or the Old Stone Mill in Delta, Ontario. In Lowell, the workers were mostly women, about half of them 15–19 years old. The fact that they thought themselves lucky to live in extremely crowded boarding houses and work long hours says much about their lives at home on the farm. If you do not have an old mill in your community, provide pictures of their work and living places. Lewis Hine took pictures that are available online.

History Fact
Frances Cabot Lowell was the manufacturer. His mill was the first to house all the processes that turned raw cotton into cloth. He passed away before the famed mills in Lowell, Massachusetts started operation.

Word Bank

children
coal
disease
incomes
middle
population explosion
telegraph

On a sheet of paper, write the word from the Word Bank to complete each sentence correctly.

1. Average _____ increased as a result of the Industrial Revolution.

2. _____ was used to heat homes and cook food.

3. The Industrial Revolution allowed the _____ class to have a greater voice in the British government.

4. The invention of the _____ allowed people to communicate across the ocean.

5. Factory wages dropped when factories began to employ women and _____.

6. The cities experienced a(n) _____ because of the Industrial Revolution.

7. Without a proper way to dispose of sewage and garbage, _____ spread more rapidly.

On a sheet of paper, write the answer to each question. Use complete sentences.

8. How did the Industrial Revolution encourage imperialism?

9. What were the Factory Acts?

10. What was the purpose of a labor union?

WORLD CULTURES

Manchester, England, is widely regarded as the first major urban center of the Industrial Revolution. While surrounding towns continue to depend on manufacturing today, the city itself has been turning away from its industrial past and turning toward a service economy. Banks and financial services have taken the place of factories. Almost half of the manufacturing jobs once available in the city are gone, resulting in high unemployment rates for unskilled workers.

Lesson 19–3 Review Answers

1. incomes 2. coal 3. middle 4. telegraph 5. children 6. population explosion 7. disease 8. An industrialized country needs more and more raw materials. One way to get them was to set up colonies as sources of raw materials. 9. The Factory Acts were new laws that took the very youngest children out of factories, and put limits on the number of hours children and women could work. 10. Labor unions were formed so workers could band together and demand better, fairer conditions.

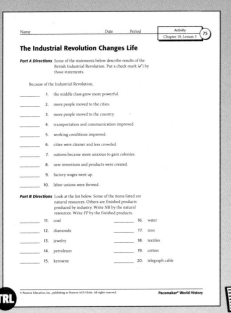

Activity 75   Workbook Activity 75

Lesson at a Glance

Chapter 19 Lesson 4

Overview This lesson describes the effects of the Industrial Revolution in various countries.

Objectives

- To explain the role of industrial countries
- To tell how the less-developed countries profited from the revolution

Student Pages 410–412

Teacher's Resource Library

Workbook Activity 76

Activity 76

Modified Activity 76

Vocabulary

developed country
developing country
export

Discuss with students the definitions of the vocabulary words. Then have them write two short paragraphs explaining how each word relates to industrialization. Encourage volunteers to read their paragraphs aloud.

1   Warm-Up Activity

Invite students to search the products in their home to find out where they were manufactured. Have them keep track of the countries and the number of products from each one. As a class, pool the information and graph the results.

2   Teaching the Lesson

Use the graph from the Warm-Up Activity to discuss the shift in factories from Britain to other developed countries, to colonies, to recently developed countries. Point out that this movement of factories affects what workers do and the relationships among nations.

The Industrial Revolution Spreads

Objectives
- To explain the role of industrial countries
- To tell how the less-developed countries profited from the revolution

Developed country

A nation that has many industries and that imports and exports products

Developing country

A nation that is slowly developing its industry and economy

Export

To send a product out of one country and into another to sell

Industrialization began in Great Britain. But during the 1800s, it spread to France, Germany, the United States, Russia, and finally Japan.

How Did the Relations Between Nations Change?

Over time industrialization forced nations of the world to depend on each other. Countries had to work out trade agreements. The more industrialized countries, known as **developed countries,** built the factories and produced the goods. They often depended on other nations for raw materials. Less developed countries, known as **developing countries,** needed finished products. Many of these countries profited from their natural resources.

The United States, Germany, Japan, and Great Britain are considered developed countries. They depend on Saudi Arabia, Mexico, Indonesia, Nigeria, and other developing countries for crude oil. They get uranium from nations in Africa. Chile and Peru **export** copper, meaning they ship copper to another country to sell.

The results of the Industrial Revolution can be seen in British coal mines, in Japanese electronics factories, in cities, and on farms. The Industrial Revolution has changed the way people live and where they live. It has changed the way they depend on each other.

Ask:

- What countries export most natural resources used in manufacturing? (developing countries)
- Why are companies building factories in developing countries? (because they have cheap labor)

Reading Strategy:
Visualizing

How could this lesson be written differently to create a stronger picture in your mind?

At one time, some people thought that the Industrial Revolution would come to an end. They thought that all the great changes and developments had already happened. In the late 1800s, it was actually suggested that the United States Patent Office be closed. Surely, some people thought, everything possible had already been invented. We know now that the revolution is far from over. New developments continue every day. In fact, in recent years, large international companies have made their finished products in developing countries. There, labor is cheap. Developed countries may produce many services and fewer finished products.

Background Information

Developing countries need four things to industrialize: natural resources, workers, transportation, and capital. They may lack one or more of these. "Catching up" to developed countries sometimes can seem impossible, as technology and energy costs are much higher now than they were during the Industrial Revolution.

Reading Strategy:
Visualizing

Have students follow up on their suggestions. For example, if they would have liked more illustrations, have them sketch something that would have been helpful.

ELL/ESL STRATEGY

Language Objective:
To practice common grammar structures

Give students practice with using proper punctuation. Photocopy the paragraph under the heading "How Did the Relations Between Nations Change?" and use white-out to delete all of the punctuation from the heading and the paragraph. Make a photocopy of this new page for each student. Have students read the selection independently and fill in the punctuation that they think best suits each sentence. When all students are finished, use choral reading to read the text again, with students saying the type of punctuation they used at the end of each sentence. Discuss with students what makes a complete sentence. Discuss why a period is appropriate for some sentences, while a question mark is appropriate for others.

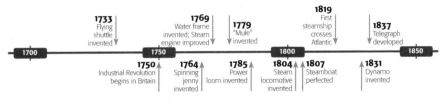

TIMELINE STUDY: THE INDUSTRIAL REVOLUTION

When was the machine invented that was a combination of the spinning jenny and the water frame?

1733 Flying shuttle invented
1769 Water frame invented; Steam engine improved
1779 "Mule" invented
1819 First steamship crosses Atlantic
1837 Telegraph developed

1700 — 1750 — 1800 — 1850

1750 Industrial Revolution begins in Britain
1764 Spinning jenny invented
1785 Power loom invented
1804 Steam locomotive invented
1807 Steamboat perfected
1831 Dynamo invented

1700–1850   *The Industrial Revolution*   Chapter 19   **411**

TIMELINE STUDY

Answer: 1779

Lesson 19–4 Review Answers
1. Industrialization **2.** trade agreements **3.** raw materials **4.** finished products **5.** crude oil **6.** live **7.** services **8.** France, Germany, the United States, Russia, and Japan joined in the industrialization that was started in Great Britain. **9.** Crude oil often comes from Saudi Arabia, Mexico, Indonesia, and Nigeria. Uranium comes from nations in Africa, and copper is exported from Chile and Peru. (Any three of these examples is acceptable.) **10.** People thought that all the great changes and developments were over.

LESSON 19-4 REVIEW

Word Bank

crude oil

finished products

industrialization

live

raw materials

services

trade agreements

On a sheet of paper, write the word from the Word Bank to complete each sentence correctly.

1. _____ forced nations to depend on each other.

2. Countries had to work out _____.

3. Industrialized countries depended on other nations for _____.

4. Less developed countries needed _____.

5. The United States and Great Britain relied on countries like Saudi Arabia and Nigeria for _____.

6. The Industrial Revolution changed the way and where people _____.

7. These days, developed countries may produce many _____ and fewer finished products.

On a sheet of paper, write the answer to each question. Use complete sentences.

8. What nations were affected by industrialization?

9. What are three countries that developed nations rely on for natural resources?

10. Why, in the 1800s, was it suggested that the U.S. Patent Office be closed?

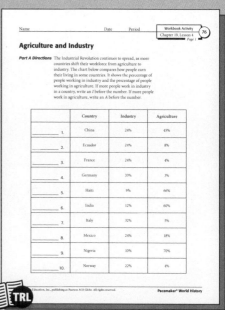

CHAPTER 19 SUMMARY

- During the Industrial Revolution, people went from making goods by hand to making goods by machine.

- Great Britain led the Industrial Revolution with rapid changes beginning around 1750.

- Great Britain had a good supply of resources such as coal and iron.

- Machines forced Britain's textile industry from country cottages to city factories.

- The invention of steam power changed manufacturing and transportation.

- To gain additional raw materials, Europe established new colonies.

- During the Industrial Revolution, people tried new things. Their discoveries led to important developments in electricity and the use of oil products in industry.

- Industrialization caused a rapid growth in city populations. Life for many people improved. A strong wealthy middle class grew. Life for many became harder.

- Working conditions in the factories were often unsafe and unhealthy. This eventually led people to form labor unions.

- By the late 1800s, France, Germany, the United States, Russia, and Japan became industrialized.

- Nations became dependent on each other for needed goods and services. Many wrote trade agreements for products such as oil, uranium, and copper.

CHAPTER PROJECT FOLLOW-UP

 Give student pairs some time to finish the preparation of their computer presentations on their chosen invention. Have students give their presentations to the class, and turn in a bibliography of reliable sources. Evaluate students on the accuracy of their research, the creativity of their presentation, and their ability to interest other students in their chosen invention.

TEACHER'S RESOURCE

The AGS Globe Teaching Strategies in Social Studies Transparencies may be used with this chapter. The transparencies add an interactive dimension to expand and enhance the Pacemaker® *World History* program content.

Chapter 19 Summary

Have students read the Chapter Summary on page 413 to review the main ideas presented in Chapter 19.

Ask:

- What term describes the change from making goods by hand to making them by machine? (Industrial Revolution)

- When and where did the Industrial Revolution start? (around 1750 in Great Britain)

- What made Great Britain a good place to develop industrialization? (good supplies of natural resources)

- What industry moved from the cottages to the factories in Britain? (textile making)

- Name two areas that profited from the invention of steam power. (Possible answer: transportation and manufacturing)

- When Europe needed more raw materials, how did they secure them? (They established colonies that could provide the materials.)

- How was oil used in industry in the Industrial Revolution? (to make machines run smoothly and to produce fuel)

- What positive effect did the Industrial Revolution have on people's lives? (Possible answer: People earned more money and ate better.)

- Why did people form labor unions? (They wanted better working conditions in the factories.)

- Which six countries were industrialized by the late 1800s? (Great Britain, France, Germany, the United States, Russia, and Japan)

- Where do most developed countries get natural resources to use in manufacturing? (from developing countries)

Chapter 19 Review

Use the Chapter Review to prepare students for tests and to reteach content from the chapter.

Chapter 19 Mastery Test

The Teacher's Resource Library includes two forms of the Chapter 19 Mastery Test. Each test addresses the chapter Goals for Learning. An optional third page of additional critical-thinking items is included for each test. The difficulty level of the two forms is equivalent.

Chapter 19 Review Answers

Vocabulary Review

1. factory

2. labor union

3. raw materials

4. energy

5. transportation

6. textile

7. import

8. natural resources

9. investors

10. Industrial Revolution

Chapter Review Questions

11. Britain had coal and iron.

12. Before the inventions, workers made cloth at home. After the inventions, people left their cottages and went to work in factories.

Word Bank

energy

factory

import

Industrial Revolution

investors

labor union

natural resources

raw materials

textile

transportation

Vocabulary Review

On a sheet of paper, use the words from the Word Bank to complete each sentence correctly.

1. A place where goods are made is a(n) _____.

2. A(n) _____ is an organization of workers.

3. Water, cotton, and wool are _____ that may be needed to make cloth.

4. Coal has the ability to supply the _____ needed to keep steam engines running.

5. The steam locomotive is an example of a development in _____ that helped advance industry.

6. Great Britain was a leader in the cloth, or _____ industry.

7. Many countries _____, or bring in, cloth from other countries.

8. Coal and iron are examples of _____.

9. _____ are people with money to back business.

10. During the _____, people stopped making goods by hand and instead made them with machines.

Chapter Review Questions

On a sheet of paper, write the answer to each question. Use complete sentences.

11. What natural resources did Britain have that were important for industry?

12. How did new inventions in the textile industry change the lives of workers?

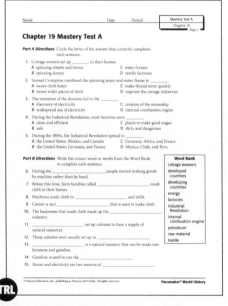

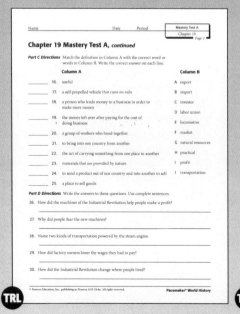

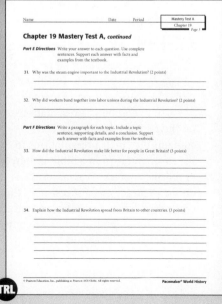

Test Tip

Learn from your mistakes. Review corrected homework and tests to understand your errors.

13. What are five inventions that changed industry in the late 1600s and in the 1700s?

14. How did industrialized nations get the raw materials that they so needed?

15. How did industrialization change relationships between nations?

Critical Thinking

On a sheet of paper, write your response to each question. Use complete sentences.

16. Why did factory owners like to hire women and children?

17. The Industrial Revolution made countries more dependent on each other. Do you think this was good or bad? Give at least one reason.

Using the Timeline

Use the timeline on page 411 to answer the questions.

18. When did the Industrial Revolution begin in Britain?

19. When was the steam locomotive invented?

20. How many years after the steamboat was perfected did the first steamship cross the Atlantic?

GROUP ACTIVITY

With a partner, debate this question: Should labor unions be allowed in Great Britain? One should take the part of a factory owner in 1810. The other should take the part of a factory worker. Before the debate, prepare some notes to help you remember the points you will make.

---

13. The flying shuttle, spinning jenny, water frame, steam engine, and mule were invented.

14. The industrialized nations set up colonies as sources of raw materials.

15. Because of industrialization, nations became dependent on each other for needed goods and services.

Critical Thinking

16. Possible answer: The factory owners could pay the women and children less money than the men.

17. Possible answers: Good: Nations had to cooperate with each other. Bad: One country could affect life and the economy in another country by refusing to sell it needed materials.

Using the Timeline

18. 1750

19. 1804

20. 12 years

GROUP ACTIVITY

Students' debates should show understanding of the points of view of a factory owner and worker. The factory owner may think that a labor union will force him or her to raise wages and cut profits. The worker may feel that a labor union gives workers more power to get improvements at work.

Chapter 19 Mastery Test B

Name _____ Date _____ Period _____   Mastery Test B / Chapter 19 / Page 1

Part A Directions Circle the letter of the answer that correctly completes each sentence.

1. The machines invented during the Industrial Revolution _____
   A made factories safer
   B allowed people to live in the country
   C increased the production of goods
   D made raw materials

2. People feared the new machines because _____
   A they thought the machines would break
   B people thought they would lose their jobs
   C the machines were so big
   D the factories were so dark

3. The steam engine provided power for _____
   A trains and ships
   B the dynamo
   C the water frame
   D the internal combustion engine

4. Factory owners lowered wages by hiring _____
   A women
   B children
   C people from other countries
   D women and children

5. During the Industrial Revolution, _____
   A farming increased
   B people moved from the country to the cities
   C people moved from the cities to the country
   D cities became cleaner

Part B Directions Write the correct word or words from the Word Bank to complete each sentence.

Word Bank: exported, imported, investors, labor unions, locomotives, markets, natural resources, practical, profit, transportation

6. During the Industrial Revolution, science and invention became more _____, or useful.

7. Machines increased production to help people make a(n) _____

8. _____ was important to keep goods moving.

9. _____ in Great Britain traveled over 6,600 miles of track.

10. British colonies were an important source of _____

11. Great Britain _____ raw materials from their colonies.

12. Colonies also served as _____ for the sale of goods.

13. British _____ provided the money to set up new businesses.

14. British _____ protested the working conditions in the factories.

15. Great Britain _____ finished goods to other countries to sell.

   Pacemaker® World History

Name _____ Date _____ Period _____   Mastery Test B / Chapter 19 / Page 2

Chapter 19 Mastery Test B, *continued*

Part C Directions Match the definition in Column A with the correct word or words in Column B. Write the correct answer on each line.

	Column A		Column B
16.	unrefined oil	A	cottage weavers
17.	power that makes machines work	B	developed country
18.	an engine that burns gasoline to produce power	C	developing country
19.	a building where goods are made by machinery	D	energy
20.	a nation that has slowly growing industry and economy	E	factory
21.	farm families who produced cloth by hand	F	Industrial Revolution
22.	material in its natural condition	G	internal combustion engine
23.	a nation that has many industries	H	petroleum
24.	cloth made by weaving	I	raw material
25.	the important changes that took place in the way work was done during the 18th and 19th century	J	textile

Part D Directions Write the answers to these questions. Use complete sentences.

26. Who were cottage weavers?

27. What did the "mule" do?

28. What effect did the dynamo have on industrialization?

29. What were factories like during the Industrial Revolution?

30. Name three countries to which the Industrial Revolution spread in the 1800s.

   Pacemaker® World History

Name _____ Date _____ Period _____   Mastery Test B / Chapter 19 / Page 3

Chapter 19 Mastery Test B, *continued*

Part E Directions Write your answer to each question. Use complete sentences. Support each answer with facts and examples from the textbook.

31. How did the Industrial Revolution increase imperialism? (2 points)

32. How did the Industrial Revolution make life harder for workers? (2 points)

Part F Directions Write a paragraph for each topic. Include a topic sentence, supporting details, and a conclusion. Support each answer with facts and examples from the textbook.

33. Discuss some of the reasons the Industrial Revolution began in Great Britain. (3 points)

34. Some people say the internal combustion engine was the most important invention to come out of the Industrial Revolution. Do you agree or disagree? Give reasons for your answer. (3 points)

   Pacemaker® World History

Chapter 19 Mastery Test B, pages 1–3

Introducing the Chapter

Have students preview the chapter by reading the headings and subheadings and by looking at the art and photos. Have them look at the timeline and the map. Then, ask students what *independent* and *dependent* mean. Encourage students to use their dictionaries, if necessary, to define the words and to work together as a class to arrive at a clear explanation of the words. Ask, *What does it mean to be independent? Why would a country want to win independence from another country?*

Ask:

• What countries ruled most of the colonies in Latin America?
(Spain and Portugal)

Independence in Latin America

Spain and Portugal ruled most of the colonies of Latin America. Their leaders were wealthy Europeans who took advantage of people who were native to the land. They became dictators who made slaves of the native people and Africans they had enslaved.

The desire for independence was felt not only by Europeans or the American colonies. People of the colonies of South America and Central America also wanted to gain their freedom. With the help of some rebel leaders, many of these countries found liberty during this time.

GOALS FOR LEARNING

• To explain the Latin American colonies' relationship with the countries that conquered them

• To describe the Latin American colonies' fight for independence

• To understand the influences on Latin America culture

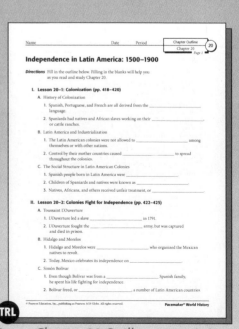

Reading Strategy: Inferencing

Sometimes the meaning of a text is not directly stated. You have to "read between the lines" to understand what is really being said.

What You Know + What You Read = Inference

As you read, look for clues that help you understand what is happening. Predicting what will happen next and explaining cause and effect are helpful strategies for making inferences.

Key Vocabulary Words

Lesson 1
Mother country A nation that controls a colony

Descendant A person who comes from a specific group of people; a family member

Discrimination Treating a person or people unfairly because of his or her race or religion

Lesson 2
Liberator One who frees a group of people

Viceroy The governor of a country or province who rules as the representative of the king

Political Having to do with governing

Lesson 3
Mural A large picture painted on a wall

Dominate To control; to be most important, most powerful, strongest

Influence The power to affect other people or things

- What is a dictator? (Answers may vary—a person who has absolute rule.)

Reading Strategy: Inferencing

Tell students that inferencing derives from the verb *infer*, which comes from the Latin *inferre* and means "to carry or bring into." When we infer something, we draw a conclusion—or speculate—based on the available facts or premises.

Key Vocabulary Words

Point out that these chapter words are presented in the order they appear in each lesson. They are also found in the glossary.

LIFE SKILLS CONNECTION

Students learn to read maps and then practice by creating a map of their school. Provide local maps for students to study.

KEY VOCABULARY

Students choose the correct word from the Word Bank to complete each sentence.

CHAPTER PROJECT

Although Latin American colonies fought hard to gain their independence from Spain and Portugal, often after independence dictators took over the government. They were unconcerned with the freedom of native peoples and mestizos. Divide students into small groups of two or three and, using the map on page 429, have them choose a Latin American country about which they would like to learn more.

Students should conduct research outside of class and prepare a 10-minute oral presentation about the history and culture of the peoples in their chosen country during the 20th and 21st centuries.

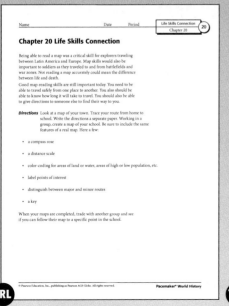

Overview This lesson describes the cultural and economic conditions of native peoples in the Americas under the rule of the Spanish, Portuguese, and French.

Objectives

- To explain how Central and South America came to be called "Latin America"
- To describe the control Spain and Portugal had over the Latin American colonies
- To tell why the Creoles and mestizos were ready to fight for independence

Student Pages 418–421

Teacher's Resource Library

Workbook Activity 77

Activity 77

Modified Activity 77

Vocabulary

descendant
discrimination
mother country

Write the vocabulary words on the board. Have students look them up in their dictionaries or in the textbook glossary. Next, have students create original sentences that use each word correctly. Ask volunteers write their sentences on the board.

PRONUNCIATION GUIDE

Use this list to help students pronounce difficult words in this lesson.

Hacienda (hä´sē en´də)

Creole (krē´ōl)

Mestizo (me stē´zō)

LESSON 20-1

Colonization

Objectives

- To explain how Central and South America came to be called "Latin America"
- To describe the control Spain and Portugal had over the Latin American colonies
- To tell why the Creoles and mestizos were ready to fight for independence

Reading Strategy: Inferencing

What do you already know about colonization?

Mother country
A nation that controls a colony

For 300 years, Spaniards built colonies in the Americas. From about 1500 until 1800, they controlled areas of Mexico, Central America, and South America. Some Portuguese settled in the eastern part of South America. The French also founded a few settlements. Most of the lands in this area are called *Latin America*. That is because the Spanish, Portuguese, and French languages came from Latin.

Wherever Spaniards settled, they took power. Many Spanish settlers came from wealthy families. They felt they should not do certain kinds of work. Therefore, they made the natives work for them. The Spaniards also brought Africans to the Americas to work as enslaved persons on farms and in mines.

Many wealthy Spaniards lived on *haciendas*. These were large cattle ranches with rich farmlands. Much of the work on the haciendas was done by native field hands or by enslaved Africans.

Why Was Latin America Late to Industrialize?

Spain and Portugal controlled all trade in their colonies. The colonies were not allowed to trade among themselves or with other nations. They were kept dependent on the **mother country.** In addition, any effort to develop industry in the colonies was crushed. Latin America had to sell all its raw materials to Spain and Portugal. It had to buy all its finished products from them, too.

COMMON ERROR

Word endings are easy to misspell and words ending with *–ent* and *–ant* can pose special spelling challenges for students. Tell students that words ending in *–ent,* such as *magnificent* and *respondent* have a slightly different sound than words such as *significant* or *descendant.* Say these words slowly so students can hear the different sounds made by each word. Remind students that sounding a word out can help to provide clues about its spelling, but oftentimes it is best or necessary to commit difficult spellings to memory.

ELL/ESL STRATEGY

Language Objective:
To encourage students to seek out and learn unfamiliar words and phrases

Have students work in small groups to comb the material on pages 418–420 for unfamiliar words or phrases. Ask them to write these words and phrases in their notebooks. Then work together to find the definitions. Ask each group to compose original sentences for each word or phrase. When students have completed this task, you may want to have volunteers share their lists and sentences.

This kind of control kept industry from developing in Latin America. Eventually the people of Latin America rose up against their foreign rulers. The 1800s saw waves of revolution sweep through Latin America.

What Was the Social Structure in the Latin American Colonies?

Most people who had been born in Spain felt superior to the other Latin Americans. This means that they felt they were better than, or above, the other Latin Americans. The Spaniards did not adopt any native customs. Instead, they tried to make the new land as much like Spain as possible.

The Creoles were people of Spanish blood who were born and raised in Latin America. Many Creoles resented the self-important attitude of Spanish-born people. The Creoles would play a large part in the soon-to-come struggles for independence.

Many wealthy Spaniards lived on large cattle ranches with rich farmlands, called haciendas.

Reading Strategy:
Inferencing

Lead a discussion in which students talk about instances of colonization from previous chapters. Encourage students to talk about both positive and negative consequences of colonization.

1 Warm-Up Activity

Have students read the information on pages 418–420. As they read, ask them to keep in mind the subheads: *Why Was Latin America Late To Industrialize? What Was the Social Structure in Latin American Colonies?* Ask students to answer these questions in their own words when they have completed reading the section.

2 Teaching the Lesson

Draw students' attention to the timeline on page 428. Ask them how long native peoples and displaced Africans lived under European rule before they began to revolt (about 279 years). Write on the board: "economic conditions" and "social conditions." Next, lead a discussion in which students talk about the conditions in Latin America under European rule.

Ask:

- What conditions prevented Latin America from becoming industrialized? (Colonies were not allowed to control their own trade; they were only allowed to purchase raw materials from their mother countries.)
- Why is Latin America called "Latin America"? (The Spanish, French, and Portuguese languages all derive from Latin.)
- Who were the Creoles? Why were they important to the struggle for independence? (people of Spanish blood who had been born and raised in Latin America; they resented the attitudes of Spanish-born people)
- Who are mestizos? (people of mixed race)

Latin America Chapter 20   **419**

Background Information

European interest in Latin America was likely piqued by the plentiful natural resources in the regions that are today known as Mexico, Central America, and South America. Vast forests provided hardwoods and raw building materials. Rich and fertile farmlands provided coca, cotton, coffee, sugarcane, and other agricultural bounty. Great mineral deposits yielded copper, gold, iron, and silver. Slave labor made it possible for Europeans to reap the benefits of these rich lands.

Descendant
A person who comes from a specific group of people; a family member

Discrimination
Treating a person or people unfairly because of his or her race or religion

 You Decide
Is there discrimination against any groups of people in the United States today? If so, what kind of discrimination do they face?

Reading Strategy:
Inferencing

How does what you already know about colonization add to what you have just read?

Most of the Spaniards and Portuguese who settled in Latin America did not bring their families. Many were soldiers and fortune-seekers. They did not plan to stay any longer than it took to get rich. Some Spaniards fathered the children of native women. These children and their **descendants** became part of a large class of people of mixed race, called *mestizos*.

Many of the mestizos were angered by their lack of social standing. They hated the unfair treatment, or **discrimination,** they felt from their Spanish rulers. The mestizos were ready for freedom from European rule.

The native people and the enslaved Africans were certainly ready for a change of government. Year after year, they worked hard yet remained poor. They had nothing for themselves under European rule—no land, no wealth, no power, little hope.

The poor people of Latin America were now ready to fight for freedom. They saw Britain's colonies in North America win their freedom. They saw the people of France rise up against tyranny. Now they needed leaders to call them together and organize revolts.

Match the description in Column A with the term in Column B.
Write the correct letter on a sheet of paper.

Column A

1. large ranch or country home that wealthy Spaniards lived in
2. people of Spanish blood who were born and raised in Latin America
3. a mixed race; typically refers to one that is born from a Spanish father and a native mother

Column B

A Creole
B hacienda
C mestizos

On a sheet of paper, write the answer to each question. Use complete sentences.

4. How did Central and South America come to be called "Latin America"?

5. What kept industry from developing in Latin America?

6. What does it mean to discriminate against someone?

7. Why were the Creoles and mestizos ready to fight for independence?

On a sheet of paper, write the letter of the answer that correctly completes each sentence.

8. The Spaniards that settled in Latin America believed they were above certain kinds of work. They made the native people work for them and brought _____ to work as slaves.

    A Asians   B Europeans   C Africans   D Americans

9. The people born in Spain felt _____ to the other Latin Americans.

    A enslaved   B superior   C inferior   D equal

10. The British colonies in _____ and the French inspired the poor people of Latin America.

    A Europe   B Britain   C Germany   D North America

COMMON ERROR

Some students may think that if discrimination occurs it is based *solely* on race or religion.
Encourage students to think of other conditions or situations that might cause an individual to fall victim to discrimination.

Lesson 20–1 Review Answers

1. B **2.** A **3.** C **4.** The lands in the area are called Latin America because the Spanish, Portuguese, and French settled there—and those languages come from Latin. **5.** The mother countries controlled all of the trade in the colonies, which kept the colony dependent on the mother country. Also, Latin America was forced to sell all of its raw materials to Spain and Portugal, and it had to buy all of its finished products from them too. **6.** When you discriminate against someone, you're treating them unfairly because of his or her race or religion. **7.** They were angered by their lack of social standing, and hated the discrimination they felt from their Spanish rulers. **8.** C **9.** B **10.** D

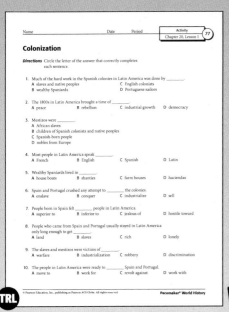

Activity 77

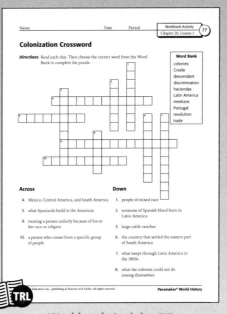

Workbook Activity 77

Chapter 20 Lesson 2

Overview This lesson describes the various revolutions that took place in Latin America from 1791 to about 1823.

Objectives

- To name six Latin American revolutionaries
- To describe the governments of the new, independent Latin American nations

Student Pages 422–426

Teacher's Resource Library 🆃🆁🅻

Workbook Activity 78

Activity 78

Modified Activity 78

Vocabulary

liberator
political
viceroy

Write the following sentences on the board. Have students choose the correct word to fill in the blank.

In Latin American colonies, the _____ held a position of great power and prestige. (viceroy)

To be a _____ of oppressed peoples, one must be dedicated to the fight for freedom. (liberator)

Most _____ systems encounter opposition from the governed at one time or another. (political)

1 Warm-Up Activity

Have students preview the subheads on pages 422–425 as well as the illustration on page 422. Remind them that one of their objectives for the lesson is to know the six Latin American revolutionaries who led the fights for independence. Encourage them to begin a chart with a column for each of the individuals named in Lesson 20–2—Toussaint L'Ouverture, Miguel Hidalgo, José Morelos, Simón Bolívar, Bernado O'Higgins, and Dom Pedro. Have them add information to each column as they read the lesson.

Colonies Fight for Independence

Objectives

- To name six Latin American revolutionaries
- To describe the governments of the new, independent Latin American nations

**Reading Strategy:
Inferencing**

What can you infer about the mood of people living in colonies?

Toussaint L'Ouverture led slaves in a rebellion.

The time for revolution in Latin America was ripe. The poor people were ready to back revolutionaries that would lead them to independence.

What Did Toussaint L'Ouverture Do?

Haiti covers the western third of the island of Hispaniola in the Caribbean Sea. Haiti was the first Latin American colony to fight for freedom. Haiti was a French colony. When news of revolution in France reached Haiti, the people of the colony got excited. They began to think about freedom, too.

In 1791, the enslaved people rebelled against their French masters. A black revolutionary named Toussaint L'Ouverture became a leader in Haiti's fight for freedom. L'Ouverture was an enslaved person himself until he was 50. He led the slave revolt until 1793, when France freed all enslaved people. In 1801, Napoleon sent a French army to Haiti. He planned to reestablish slavery in the country. War broke out again. The French threw L'Ouverture into prison, where he died in 1803. However, by 1804, the French army was defeated, and French rule in Haiti ended. Haiti declared its independence.

Wars of revolution continued. Other Latin American countries demanded freedom.

Reading Strategy:
Inferencing

Lead a discussion in which students answer the question, *What can you infer about the mood of people living in colonies?* Remind students that to infer means to make an educated guess based on information provided in the text.

2 Teaching the Lesson

A freed slave, a young man of privilege and wealth, a prince, a couple of Catholic priests—these were some of the men who led the fights for independence from Spanish and Portuguese rule. What did these men from such different backgrounds have in common? They shared a

desire to lead people to freedom and were disgusted with the conditions under European rule. As students read through the lesson, encourage them to think about the great risks and challenges posed to these revolutionaries.

Ask:

- What was the first Latin American colony to fight for freedom? Who led this revolt? (Haiti, Toussaint L'Ouverture)

- Who led Mexico's revolt against Spain? What was their fate? (Miguel Hidalgo and José Morelos; both died in the fighting)

- Who is known as the "George Washington of South America"? (Simón Bolívar)

Liberator
One who frees a
group of people

What Did Hidalgo and Morelos Do?

Miguel Hidalgo and José Morelos led Mexico's revolt against Spain. Both men were Catholic priests. They organized the native people in a revolution.

On September 16, 1810, in the town of Dolores, Miguel Hidalgo rang church bells. He shouted the *grito de Dolores*, or "cry of Dolores": "Long live independence! Down with bad government!"

Both Hidalgo and Morelos lost their lives fighting for Mexico's independence. By 1821, the fight was won. Now Mexico celebrates September 16th as its independence day. Furthermore, the town of Dolores is now called Dolores Hidalgo.

What Did Simón Bolívar Do?

Perhaps the best-known Latin American **liberator** was Simón Bolívar. Today he is called "The Liberator" and the "George Washington of South America."

Bolívar spent much of his life fighting for the independence of South American nations. He was a Creole, born in Venezuela. His parents were wealthy Spaniards. To keep his wealth and social position, Bolívar might have sided with Spain. Instead, he spent all his money backing revolutions because he believed in freedom from European rule. Starting in 1810, Simón Bolívar helped to organize an army. He then led the army in a series of victories against the Spanish. He liberated, or freed, one country after another. At one time he ruled the newly formed Republic of Gran Colombia. This was made up of Colombia, Venezuela, Ecuador, and Peru. Then, one by one, each country withdrew from the union. By 1828, Bolívar ruled only Colombia. His own people did not appreciate him. After a failed attempt on his life, he resigned as president in 1830.

History Fact
Bolívar died alone and poor. It was not until his death that he became honored as South America's liberator.

- What group revolted against O'Higgins' reforms in Chile in 1823? (wealthy landowners)
- Who was responsible for the only revolution that occurred without bloodshed in Latin America? (Dom Pedro)
- Did the struggles for independence yield free, democratic political systems? Why? (no; Answers may vary.)

Background Information

Students may be surprised to learn that some Catholic priests and missionaries played a large role in the fight for independence and advocating for better treatment of native peoples. The Catholic priest Bartolemé de las Casas, for example, was shocked at the cruelty of the Spaniards and by the working and living conditions of Native Americans who were forced to labor on plantations and in mines. He dedicated his life to working to defend Native Americans and to changing the policies of the Spanish government. An excerpt of his writings—*Brief Account of the Devastation of the Indies* (1542)—can be found online: www.agsglobepmwh.com/page423

ELL/ESL STRATEGY

Language Objective:
To understand the different roles words play in sentences

Write the words *political* and *liberator* on the board. Explain to students that each of these words may—with slight variations—function as different parts of speech. For example, the word *political* (adjective), which comes from the same Latin root as *police*, may also be a transitive verb (*politicize*) or an adverb (*politically*). Have students use their dictionaries to find other incarnations for the word *liberator*. (Answers may vary—*liberate* (verb), *liberation* (noun), and *liberating* (transitive verb) are possibilities.)

History Fact
What does this History Fact suggest about the nature of leadership and the place of great leaders in history? (Answers may vary, but this may lead to a discussion about how great leaders are often not recognized during their lifetimes.)

Ask students to listen carefully as you read aloud sections from Bartolemé de las Casas's *Brief Account of the Devastation of the Indies*. Lead a discussion in which students talk about the conditions that led to the revolts in Latin America.

LEARNING STYLES

 Logical/Mathematical

To help students understand how South America gained its freedom from Spain, have them create a graphic organizer that illustrates and outlines the events of the section. For example, students may want to write Simón Bolívar and José San Martín on opposite sides of a page and list the important events and dates of each. Students then may want to show how both men worked together by drawing arrows to the center of the page and listing the remaining events. Encourage students to be creative with their graphic organizers.

3 Reinforce and Extend

AT HOME

 Have students ask family members if they had ever attended a speech or rally in support of a political figure. Then have them ask if they had ever met or spoken with a political figure. Suggest that students consider how personal perceptions can change as distances are shortened.

Viceroy

The governor of a country or province who rules as the representative of the king

Political

Having to do with governing

What Did Bernardo O'Higgins Do?

Chile owes its liberation to the son of an Irishman. Bernardo O'Higgins's father had been a **viceroy**, or governor, of Peru. Bernardo O'Higgins led a revolution that began in 1810. After winning Chile's independence from Spain in 1818, O'Higgins acted as the country's dictator. He planned to bring about reform in Chile. He taxed wealthy landowners to pay for new schools and roads. He also tried to break up their big estates. A revolt by the landowners in 1823, however, sent O'Higgins into exile.

GREAT NAMES IN HISTORY

José de San Martín

Bernardo O'Higgins was helped in his struggle against Spain by another great leader, José de San Martín. San Martín was born in Argentina, but was educated in Spain. While in Spain, he fought with the Spanish army against Napoleon. When he returned to Argentina, the fight for independence had already begun in South America.

In 1812, San Martín took command of a rebel army. For the next several years he fought to free Argentina from Spain's rule. In 1816, Argentina declared its independence. Then San Martín decided to help the rest of South America become free. He planned a daring surprise attack against the Spanish army in Chile. In 1817, he joined forces with Bernardo O'Higgins. Together, they led their army across

the Andes Mountains. It was a difficult and dangerous march. Blizzards struck without warning. The men had to plow through deep snowdrifts. Slowly they made their way across the icy mountain passes. Many men died along the way. Finally, the brave leaders and their army came down from the mountains in Chile. There they attacked the Spanish army. The Spaniards were completely taken by surprise, and they were easily defeated.

San Martín then went on to help win independence for Peru in 1821. When he finally returned to Argentina, a fierce struggle for **political** power was going on. San Martín felt bad about this and would have nothing to do with it. He went back to Europe and lived in France for the rest of his life.

What Did Dom Pedro Do?

Dom Pedro led Brazil to independence without bloodshed. He was a Portuguese prince. He inherited the Brazilian kingdom when it was still under Portuguese rule. The Brazilian people wanted independence. They also wanted Dom Pedro to go home to Portugal.

"I remain!" he stated. Then on September 7, 1822, he declared Brazil an independent country. He took the throne of the newly independent nation as Pedro I.

What Were the Governments of the New Nations Like?

The Latin American countries' struggles for independence did not necessarily mean freedom for the people. Most of the countries did not become democracies. Life did not change much for many native peoples and mestizos in those lands.

Dictators ruled most of the new nations. These dictators were powerful men with strong armies behind them. Any changes in government usually came only by military takeovers.

GREAT NAMES IN HISTORY

Ask:

- What can be inferred from the information in the text about José de San Martín's upbringing and economic status? What suggests this? (His education in Spain suggests that he came from a privileged family and may have been Creole.)

- What country did San Martín first fight to free from Spanish rule? (Argentina)

- What was his relationship with Bernardo O'Higgins? (They joined forces in 1817 and, after an arduous journey across the Andes, defeated the Spanish army in Chile.)

- What can be inferred from the final paragraph of the reading? (Answers may vary: students may point out that San Martín appears to have become disillusioned by the fighting that occurred in Argentina after it had gained its independence from Spain.)

Lesson 20–2 Review Answers

1. F 2. E 3. D 4. B 5. A 6. C 7. B 8. D
9. C 10. B

Match the description in Column A with the revolutionary(ies) in Column B.
Write the correct letter on a sheet of paper.

Column A

1. a black revolutionary who led the slave revolt in Haiti

2. a Creole who helped organize an army in present-day
Colombia, Venezuela, Ecuador, and Peru; led them to
victories against the Spanish; known as "The Liberator"

3. the Catholic priests who led Mexico's revolt against Spain

4. the Portuguese prince who led Brazil to independence
without bloodshed

5. the son of a viceroy of Peru; led the revolution that won
Chile's independence from Spain

6. the leader who commanded a rebel army and helped
Argentina win freedom from Spain's rule

Column B

A Bernardo
O'Higgins

B Dom Pedro

C José de San
Martín

D Miguel
Hidalgo and
José Morelos

E Simón Bolívar

F Toussaint
L'Ouverture

On a sheet of paper, write the letter of the answer that correctly completes
each sentence.

7. A person who frees a group of people is known as a _____.

   A viceroy   B liberator   C descendant   D mestizos

8. A _____ is a governor of a country or province who rules as the
monarch's representative.

   A descendant   B dictator   C senator   D viceroy

9. Despite the Latin American countries' struggles for independence,
not all people were _____.

   A Creole   B liberators   C free   D in the army

10. _____ ruled most of the new nations.

   A Liberators   B Dictators   C Descendants   D Viceroys

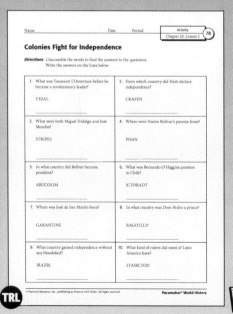

Activity 78   Workbook Activity 78

Latin American Culture

Objectives

■ To explain how the language, religion, and architecture of Latin America reflect European influence

■ To describe Latin American music and its influences

Mural
A large picture painted on a wall

Latin American culture is really more than one culture. It is a mixture of several different peoples: native people, Spanish, Portuguese, African, and French.

What Are the Influences of Latin American Culture?

Some native peoples who live in rural areas still live much like their ancestors. They wear woven shawls and take their goods to market along mountain roads on burros (small donkeys) and llamas. They play music on handmade wooden instruments and weave baskets of cane and reed. Native women still spin and weave colorful cloth. There is often a note of sadness to the native people's art. A **mural** in Mexico City shows natives suffering at the hands of Spanish conquistadors.

Although Spain colonized Latin America, native cultures are still strong. These natives of Peru are an example of people who have kept their own traditions.

1500–1900   *Independence in Latin America*   *Chapter 20*   **427**

Lesson at a Glance

Chapter 20 Lesson 3

Overview Latin American cultures are hybrids of may different cultures—Spanish, Portuguese, African, French, and native peoples. This lesson provides insight into the rich and diverse cultures of Latin America.

Objectives

■ To explain how the language, religion, and architecture of Latin America reflect European influence

■ To describe Latin American music and its influences

Teacher's Resource Library ⓣⓡⓛ

Workbook Activity 79

Activity 79

Modified Activity 79

Vocabulary

dominate
influence
mural

After students have found the definitions for the above words in their dictionaries or by looking in the glossary at the end of the textbook, have them create a crossword puzzle that uses all the vocabulary words listed in Chapter 20. Ask them to write clues for each word based on information they have read in the text. Then have students trade their puzzles and fill in the blanks.

Before students begin to read the lesson, ask them to preview the information by looking at the illustration and subhead on page 427, the timeline on page 428, and the map on page 429. Ask volunteers to speculate about what information they expect to learn based on these aspects of the lesson.

Reading Strategy:
Inferencing

Ask students to review the section and then volunteer specific words and phrases that helped them make their inferences and answer the questions.

TIMELINE STUDY

Answer: 1800–1900

Ask:

- During what era did Europeans colonize Latin America? (between 1521–1800)

2 Teaching the Lesson

As students read the information on pages 427–429, have them think about what they learned earlier in the chapter. Remind students that the revolts against the Europeans rarely yielded free and democratic political systems.

Ask:

- What factors contribute to the ability of some native peoples to continue living much as their ancestors did? (Answers may vary: rural isolation, determination, rebellion against the influence of European culture)
- What language do most people in Latin America speak? (Spanish)
- What religion do most people in Latin America follow? (Roman Catholicism)
- What country greatly influenced Latin American music? (Africa)

Background Information

Spain left two lasting legacies with its former colonies in the Americas: its language and the Catholic faith. Because the Catholic Church allowed the indigenous peoples to maintain their beliefs, modern Latin Americans have been able to draw upon those beliefs. In Guatemala, the work of Nobel prize-winning author, Miguel Angel Asturias, blends the modern yearning of his people for social justice with the mysticism of their ancestors, the Mayas.

Dominate
To control; to be most important, most powerful, strongest

Influence
The power to affect other people or things

Reading Strategy:
Inferencing

After reading this lesson, what can you infer about the lasting effects of the early Latin American culture? What words helped you make your inference?

The Spanish and Portuguese brought their languages and religion to Latin America. Most of the people of Latin America speak Spanish. Portuguese is the main language of Brazil. The different native groups speak their own native languages. Roman Catholicism is the main religion.

Spanish architecture is common in Latin America. Many homes, churches, and public buildings have a Spanish flavor. However, much Latin American music reflects the music of Africa. The Africans brought their songs and dances with them when they came to Latin America as enslaved people.

Different races and cultures **dominate** different areas of Latin America. In some countries, most of the people are natives. The art, music, dress, and customs in Guatemala, Bolivia, and Peru are strongly **influenced**, or affected, by the cultures of the native peoples. In some countries, like Haiti, the people are mostly descendants of Africans.

Latin America gets its name from the colonization and influence of Latin peoples—the Spanish, the Portuguese, and the French. However, the natives and Africans have played a large part in making Latin America what it is today.

TIMELINE STUDY: FROM COLONIES TO INDEPENDENCE IN LATIN AMERICA: 1500–1900

During what time period did many Latin American countries win their independence?

1521–1800
European colonization of Latin America

1800–1900
Many Latin American countries win independence

1500   1600   1700   1800   1900

1533 Pizarro conquers Incas in Peru

1521 Cortés conquers Aztecs in Mexico

428   Unit 8   The Age of Imperialism

LEARNING STYLES

Visual/Spatial

Have students conduct outside research using magazines, photocopies of art from books, and the Internet to create a collage of instruments, clothing, art, baskets, and tools that are still commonly found in some rural areas of Latin America. Encourage students to share their collages with the class and explain the origin of each item.

ELL/ESL STRATEGY

Language Objective:
To provide students with a concrete exercise for incorporating words from the Word Bank into their vocabularies

Have students work together in small groups to find definitions for the words in the Word Bank on page 430. After they have added the definitions to their notebooks, ask them to collaborate on a short story that uses all 10 words from the list. You may wish to have a volunteer from each group read the group's story aloud to the class.

Latin American Nations Become Independent

Year of Independence	
Antigua and Barbuda	1981
Argentina	1816
Bahamas	1973
Barbados	1966
Belize	1981
Bolivia	1825
Brazil	1822
Chile	1810
Colombia	1819
Costa Rica	1821
Cuba	1902
Dominica	1978
Dominican Republic	1844
Ecuador	1822
El Salvador	1841
Grenada	1974
Guatemala	1821
Guyana	1966
Haiti	1804
Honduras	1821
Jamaica	1962
Mexico	1821
Nicaragua	1838
Panama	1903
Paraguay	1811
Peru	1824
St. Kitts-Nevis	1983
St. Lucia	1979
St. Vincent	1979
Suriname	1975
Trinidad and Tobago	1962
Uruguay	1828
Venezuela	1821

MAP STUDY

1. In what year did Brazil become independent?

2. Which Latin American country shares a border with the United States?

MAP STUDY

Answers

1. 1822

2. Mexico

COMMON ERROR

Students may be tempted to confuse *guessing* with *inferring*. Remind them that, while inferring requires some speculation, it is speculation based on what they have read in the text. A student may *guess*, but it is an educated guess based on the information at hand.

STUDY SKILLS

Have students work in small groups of four. Assign each group a paragraph from Chapter 20. Give them the task of reading the selection and then drawing several inferences from the information provided.

You may want to have a spokesperson from each group read the selection aloud and then share with the class the inferences drawn from it.

COMMON ERROR

Many people believe— mistakenly—that the struggles for Latin American independence began and ended in the 19th century. Many countries did not achieve independence until the 20th century.

CAREER CONNECTION

Students who wish to travel, study, and work in Latin America may want to speak with a career counselor for information on teaching abroad or joining one of many service organizations that are working to improve the lives of native peoples in Mexico, Central America, and South America.

Lesson 20–3 Review Answers

1. African 2. ancestors 3. Burros
4. colorful 5. art 6. mural
7. Portuguese 8. Spanish 9. music
10. influence

Word Bank

African
ancestors
art
burros
colorful
influence
mural
music
Portuguese
Spanish

On a sheet of paper, write the word from the Word Bank to complete each sentence correctly.

1. Latin American culture mixes several different peoples: native people, Spanish, Portuguese, _____, and French.

2. Some people native to Latin America still live like their _____.

3. _____ are used to carry goods to market.

4. The cloth the native women weave is quite _____.

5. Native _____ often has a hint of sadness to it.

6. A(n) _____ is a large picture painted on a wall.

7. Most Latin Americans speak Spanish, but _____ is the main language of Brazil.

8. The architecture in Latin America has a(n) _____ flavor.

9. Latin American _____ reflects the customs that the Africans brought to Latin America.

10. When something has the power to affect other people or things, it has _____.

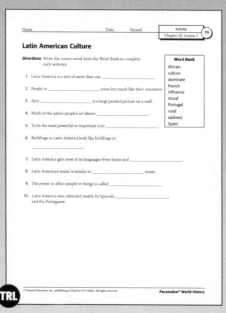

Activity 79

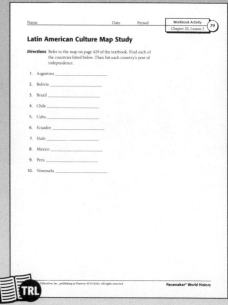

Workbook Activity 79

SUMMARY

- Most areas of Latin America were settled by the Spanish. The Portuguese settled some areas, particularly on the eastern side of South America.

- The European settlers made workers of the native people and enslaved Africans.

- Spain and Portugal, as colonial powers, did not allow industry to develop in Latin America. Their colonies could supply raw materials only to them.

- Between 1500 and 1900, Europeans, Creoles, mestizos, natives, and enslaved Africans lived in Latin America.

- As social classes developed in Latin America, many people became the victims of discrimination.

- During the 1800s, revolutions gained independence for many Latin American countries.

- Haiti was a French colony. With the help of Toussaint L'Ouverture, Haitians fought and gained their freedom in 1804.

- There were other Rebels, too, such as: Hidalgo, Morelos, Bolívar, O'Higgins, San Martín, and Dom Pedro. They helped lead countries of South America to independence.

- Newly formed countries in Latin America were often ruled by dictators.

- Latin American culture is a blend of Spanish, Portuguese, French, native, and African cultures.

Chapter 20 Summary

Have students read the Chapter Summary on page 431 to review the main ideas presented in Chapter 20.

Ask:

- What two European nations were responsible for the majority of colonies in Latin America? (Spain, Portugal)

- How did these nations treat the people who were already living in these regions? (Badly. They made workers of the native peoples and enslaved Africans.)

- How did Spain and Portugal prevent Latin American regions from gaining power? (Answers may vary: they did not allow colonies to trade on their own; they enslaved people; they forced colonies to buy raw materials only from their mother countries.)

- Even today, Latin America is a hybrid of many cultures. Name some of them. (Spanish, Portuguese, French, African, and native)

- What is discrimination? (Answers may vary: the text defines it as "treating a person unfairly because of his or her race or religion.")

- During what century did most revolutions for independence occur in Latin America? (19th)

- Where did the first revolt occur? Under whose leadership? (Haiti, Toussaint L'Ouverture)

- After the fights for independence, did most citizens in Latin American countries enjoy freedom, economic stability, and democracy? (no)

- Why do you think this is so? (Answers may vary.)

TEACHER'S RESOURCE

The AGS Globe Teaching Strategies in Social Studies Transparencies may be used with this chapter. The transparencies add an interactive dimension to expand and enhance the Pacemaker® *World History* program content.

CHAPTER PROJECT FOLLOW-UP

 Set aside time in class during this lesson for students to present their 10-minute oral projects on the Latin American country of their choice.

Chapter 20 Review

Use the Chapter Review to prepare students for tests and to reteach content from the chapter.

Chapter 20 Mastery Test

The Teacher's Resource Library includes two forms of the Chapter 20 Mastery Test. Each test addresses the chapter Goals for Learning. An optional third page of additional critical-thinking items is included for each test. The difficulty level of the two forms is equivalent.

Chapter 20 Review Answers

Vocabulary Review

1. mother country

2. political

3. discrimination

4. influence

5. descendant

6. liberator

7. mural

8. viceroy

9. dominate

Chapter Review Questions

10. Spain and Portugal controlled trade and industry. Spain and Portugal insisted the colonies sell them raw materials and buy finished materials from them.

11. They felt superior to the other Latin Americans, and refused to adopt any native customs.

Word Bank
descendant
discrimination
dominate
influence
liberator
mother country
mural
political
viceroy

Vocabulary Review

On a sheet of paper, use the words from the Word Bank to correctly match each definition below.

1. A nation that controls a country

2. Having to do with governing

3. Unfair treatment of a person, often based on race or religion

4. The power to affect the way that people or nations act

5. A person from a particular ancestor

6. A leader who frees a group of people

7. A large painting on a wall

8. A representative of the monarch that rules a country or province

9. To be most important, most powerful, or strongest

Chapter Review Questions

On a sheet of paper, write the answer to each question. Use complete sentences.

10. Why was Latin America late to industrialize?

11. How did the people born in Spain feel about Latin Americans and their culture?

12. Who were the Creoles and the mestizos?

13. What factors led the poor people of Latin America to fight for freedom?

14. Why does Mexico celebrate September 16th as independence day?

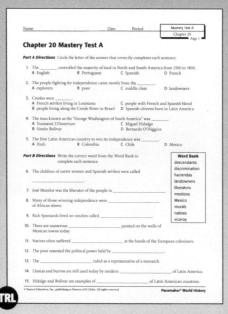

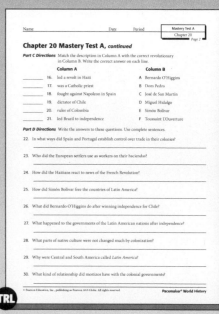

Chapter 20 Mastery Test A, pages 1–3

To study for a chapter test, use the headings within the chapter to write an outline. Review this outline to help you recall and organize the information.

15. What kind of leaders governed Latin American nations after independence?

16. Where does Latin American culture come from?

Critical Thinking

On a sheet of paper, write your response to each question. Use complete sentences.

17. How did the American and French revolutions affect Latin America?

18. Why do you think O'Higgins wanted to break up the big estates in Chile?

Using the Timeline

Use the timeline on page 428 to answer the questions.

19. How long did European colonization of Latin America last?

20. What happened in 1533?

GROUP ACTIVITY

Work with a group to make a large wall chart of Latin American revolutionaries. Include their personal background, nicknames, famous words, countries they liberated, and other information.

1500–1900   *Independence in Latin America*   Chapter 20   **433**

12. Creoles were people of Spanish blood born in Latin America. Mestizos were people of mixed race, Spanish and native South American.

13. The poor people were angered by their lack of social standing. They also did not like the discrimination they felt from their Spanish rulers.

14. Hidalgo started the revolution by ringing the church bells in Dolores and shouting, "Long live independence! Down with bad government!"

15. Mostly, military dictators governed the new Latin American nations.

Critical Thinking

16. Latin American culture is a mixture of cultures from native, Spanish, Portuguese, African, and French people.

17. Possible answer: The American and French revolutions encouraged them to fight for freedom.

18. Possible answer: He probably wanted to give land to more people instead of having land in the hands of a few.

Using the Timeline

19. 279 years

20. Pizarro conquered the Incas.

GROUP ACTIVITY

Charts should include Toussaint L'Ouverture, Miguel Hidalgo, José Morelos, Simón Bolívar, Bernardo O'Higgins, Dom Pedro, and José de San Martín.

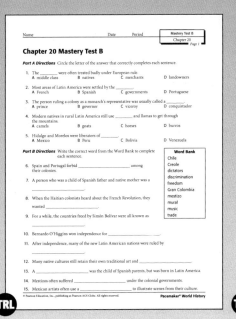

Chapter 20 Mastery Test B, pages 1–3

Introducing the Chapter

Many people came to the United States in search of new opportunities. The United States government wanted to expand the size of the country, while preventing European nations from claiming territory near United States boundaries. The Civil War divided the states for a time, but it did not prevent the country from expanding and moving forward as one nation.

The United States Gains Power

The new United States attracted more people who came in search of a new life. The Industrial Revolution brought growth in manufacturing, trade, and transportation. People were no longer on the move.

During the 1800s, the size of the United States grew. The growth was a result of a number of land purchases from other nations. The United States tried to protect the western hemisphere from further European involvement. In doing so, it also gained territories. However, the growth of America came with new problems.

GOALS FOR LEARNING

- To explain the growth of the United States in the early 1800s
- To list the problems the United States faced in establishing its northern and southern borders
- To identify the causes and main events of the American Civil War
- To explain the expansion of the United States

434   Unit 8   *The Age of Imperialism*

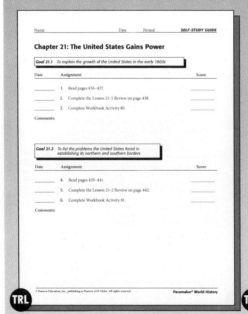

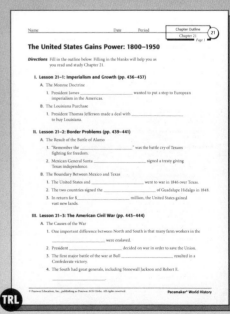

Reading Strategy: Metacognition

Metacognition means being aware of the way you learn. It will help you become a better reader.

- Preview the text, noting the main idea, details, and any questions you have.

- If you do not understand something, go back and read it again.

- Summarize what you have read. Make inferences about the meaning.

Key Vocabulary Words

Lesson 1
Monroe Doctrine The document stating that Europe should not try to get more territory in North or South America

Territory The land ruled by a nation or state

Lesson 2
Interfere To mix in another's affairs without being asked

Lesson 4
Expansion Growth; to increase in size

Sympathy Feeling sorry for another's suffering

Victor The winner of a battle, war, struggle, or contest

Rebellion A fight by people against a government; a struggle for change

Economic Having to do with money

International Having to do with many nations

Ask:

- What period of time brought growth in manufacturing, trade, and transportation to the United States? (the Industrial Revolution)
- How did the United States grow in the 1800s? (through a number of land purchases from other nations)

Reading Strategy:
Metacognition

Tell students that when you read something, you often note the main ideas and details in the text. You might also think of questions about the text as you read, and you can summarize the information after you read each lesson. When you think about how you learn as you read, you are using metacognition. Have students read the title of Chapter 21 on page 434.

Ask:

- What do you predict this chapter is about and why? (This chapter is how the United States grew more powerful. The terms *United States*, *gains*, and *power* are in the title.)

Key Vocabulary Words

Point out that these chapter words are presented in the order they appear in each lesson. They are also found in the glossary.

LIFE SKILLS CONNECTION

Students learn how to obtain a passport for traveling outside the country. Discuss both the benefits and the difficulties of traveling in a foreign country. Have students research a country they would like to travel to.

KEY VOCABULARY

Students choose the correct word from the Word Bank to complete each sentence.

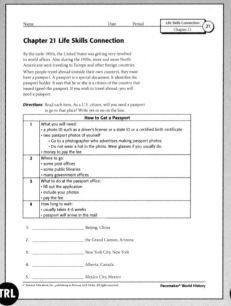

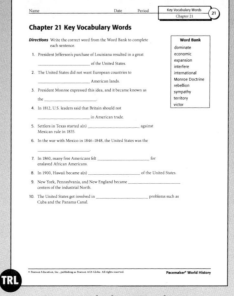

Life Skills Connection 21   Key Vocabulary Words 21

Lesson at a Glance

Chapter 21 Lesson 1

Overview This lesson describes the concept of imperialism and the terms of The Louisiana Purchase.

Objectives

- To explain European imperialism and the Monroe Doctrine
- To tell how the United States gained the Louisiana Territory

Student Pages 436–438

Teacher's Resource Library

Workbook Activity 80

Activity 80

Modified Activity 80

Vocabulary

Monroe Doctrine
territory

Have students write the vocabulary words on index cards. Read the definitions aloud and have students hold up the proper card for each definition. Repeat the process, reading a fill-in-the-blank sentence for each word. Then ask students to write one sentence of their own that uses both words.

1 Warm-Up Activity

Divide the class into two groups and award each group territory in an imaginary land. Tell one group that they aim to expand into the other group's territory. Have students in this group discuss the best way to acquire new land: by negotiating, waging war, or trying to purchase the land. Ask the second group to consider how willing they are to give up their territory. Ask them what a country would have to gain by giving up territory.

Reading Strategy:
Metacognition

Have students read the headings of each section and explain how each heading tells what the section will be about. (Each heading asks a question that the section will answer.)

LESSON 21-1

Imperialism and Growth

Objectives

- To explain European imperialism and the Monroe Doctrine
- To tell how the United States gained the Louisiana Territory

Reading Strategy: Metacognition

Notice the structure of this chapter. Look at the titles, headings, and boldfaced words.

Monroe Doctrine

The document stating that Europe should not try to get more territory in North or South America

Territory

The land ruled by a nation or state

Smaller nations are often threatened by larger and stronger nations. The new, independent countries in Latin America struggled to survive. The United States wanted these countries to remain independent.

What Is the Monroe Doctrine?

In 1823, James Monroe, president of the United States, spoke before Congress. He said that the United States would not allow Europe to set up new colonies in North or South America. The United States would also not allow any existing colonies to take over more land. The President's statement against European imperialism was later called the **Monroe Doctrine.**

How Did the United States Gain the Louisiana Territory?

The United States grew rapidly during the early 1800s. Settlers moved west, taking lands from the American Indians.

In 1803, Thomas Jefferson was president of the United States. He arranged for the United States to buy the Louisiana **Territory,** a large piece of land, from France. The United States paid about $15 million for 828,000 square miles of land. The Louisiana Purchase almost doubled the size of the United States.

American pioneers streamed into the new land. They settled first in what would become the states of Louisiana, Arkansas, and Missouri.

---

2 Teaching the Lesson

Explain that the early 1800s was a time of growth and expansion for the United States. President James Monroe wanted the country to become more powerful. However, he did not want other countries to settle land that he hoped would become part of the United States.

Ask:

- How did President Monroe prevent European countries from settling in North or South America? (He issued the Monroe Doctrine.)
- Thomas Jefferson purchased the Louisiana Territory from what country? (France)
- How did the Louisiana Purchase change the size of the United States? (It almost doubled the size of the United States.)

The Louisiana Purchase

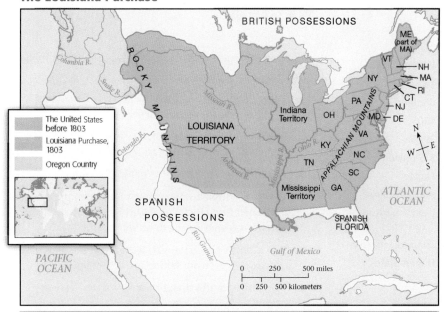

MAP STUDY

1. Which river formed the eastern border of the Louisiana Territory?

2. Which mountain range bordered the Louisiana Territory on the west?

MAP STUDY

Answers:

1. The Mississippi River

2. The Rocky Mountains

TEACHER ALERT

You may want to have a current map of the United States on hand, so students can compare and contrast with the map on page 437.

CHAPTER PROJECT

Have students choose one conflict described in this chapter: the Battle of the Alamo and the Mexican-American War, the Civil War, or the Spanish-American War. Tell students to imagine that they are journalists and reporters who lived during the time of their conflict. Have them work in small groups to research their topic, and then put together a newspaper with several stories and illustrations or copied photos that explain the "who, what, where, when, why, and how" of the conflict.

Background Information

Napoleon Bonaparte was the French emperor who sold the Louisiana Territory to Thomas Jefferson. Napoleon Bonaparte wanted to build a colonial empire in North America. Why did he change his mind? Napoleon Bonaparte was pressured to make this sale because of political consequences for Spain and England, as well as France and the United States. Napoleon Bonaparte needed money, and he did not think he could defend the Louisiana Territory if war broke out. So, he sold the territory, raised the money he needed, and gave up his plans for a New World empire.

LEARNING STYLES

Logical/Mathematical

The land that was sold in the Louisiana Purchase covered 828,000 square miles. The United States paid $15 million for the territory. Of this amount, $11.25 million went for the land, and the remainder was used to cover French debts. Give students this information, then ask them to figure out how much was used to pay off debts. ($3.75 million) Ask how much was paid per square mile for the land in the Louisiana Purchase. (about $18.12 per square mile)

ELL/ESL STRATEGY

Language Objective: *To use a map to describe the location of the states and territories of North America in the early 1800s*

Have students study the map on page 437. Ask them to describe the locations of New York, Georgia, Spanish Florida, the Indiana Territory, the Louisiana Territory, and the Mississippi Territory. Check students' understanding of geography as they describe these places on the map. Students may use words such as *northeast*, *southeast*, *Gulf of Mexico*, and *central* in their descriptions.

3 Reinforce and Extend

Lesson 21–1 Review Answers

1. Latin American countries **2.** James Monroe **3.** 1823 **4.** United States **5.** colonies **6.** France **7.** Thomas Jefferson **8.** 1803 **9.** $15 million **10.** doubled

LESSON 21-1

REVIEW

Word Bank

colonies

doubled

1803

1823

$15 million

France

James Monroe

Latin American countries

Thomas Jefferson

United States

On a sheet of paper, write the word from the Word Bank to complete each sentence correctly.

1. The United States wanted the newly independent _____ to remain independent.

2. The Monroe Doctrine was U.S. President _____'s statement against European imperialism.

3. The Monroe Doctrine was put into action in _____.

4. The _____ took a stand against European imperialism in the Monroe Doctrine. It said Europe could not set up new colonies in North or South America.

5. The Monroe Doctrine also forbid (did not allow) any existing _____ from taking over more land.

6. The United States bought the Louisiana Territory from _____.

7. President _____ arranged for the United States to buy the Louisiana Territory.

8. The Louisiana Territory was purchased in _____.

9. The United States paid _____ for the Louisiana Purchase.

10. The Louisiana Purchase practically _____ the size of the United States.

438 Unit 8 The Age of Imperialism

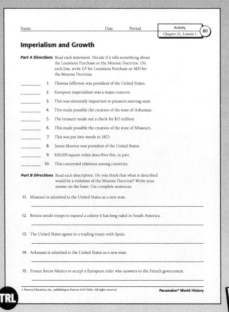

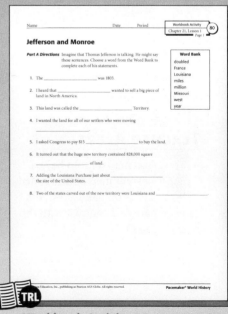

Activity 80

Workbook Activity 80, pages 1–2

LESSON
21-2

Border Problems

Objectives

■ To explain the reasons for the War of 1812
■ To describe the Battle of the Alamo
■ To explain the importance of the Treaty of Guadalupe Hidalgo

Reading Strategy:
Metacognition

Make a prediction to tell what you think will happen next. Check your prediction as you continue reading and revise if needed.

Interfere

To mix in another's affairs without being asked

History Fact
General Santa Anna made himself dictator of Mexico in 1834. Americans in Texas did not want to live under his rule.

The United States needed to set up clear northern and southern borders. Britain still controlled Canada to the north. War broke out between Britain and the United States in 1812. However, the United States-Canadian border was not the cause. Other problems had led to the war. Britain had been **interfering** with United States trade. In other words, Britain was mixing in U.S. trade without being asked. A peace treaty was signed in December 1814. The border remained the same.

In the southern United States, however, border disagreements *were* the cause of war. What is now the state of Texas once belonged to the Republic of Mexico. Many settlers from the United States moved into Texas.

The Mexicans worried about the large numbers of settlers from the North. They said that no more settlers could come in from the United States. In response, the settlers rebelled. In November 1835, they declared themselves free from Mexico. Then the battles began.

What Was the Result of the Battle of the Alamo?

The Battle of the Alamo was one of the most famous battles in the Texas war of independence. The Alamo was an old Spanish mission in San Antonio that the Texans were using as their fort.

1800–1950   *The United States Gains Power*   Chapter 21   **439**

---

2 Teaching the Lesson

Remind students that the 1800s was a period when the United States was aggressively expanding, which resulted in border conflicts. Have them read pages 439–441 to find out what happened when Mexico resisted settlers moving into their territory.

Ask:

● Who won the Battle of the Alamo? (Texan forces)

● When did Texas become a state? (1845)

● What was the result of the Treaty of Guadalupe? (The United States gained vast new territory that had belonged to Mexico.)

History Fact
Before returning to politics, Santa Anna declared himself retired "unless my country needs me." Santa Anna was elected president in 1833, at which point he threw his vice president out, suspended the constitution, and disbanded the Congress, thereby earning the title dictator.

Lesson at a Glance

Chapter 21 Lesson 2

Overview This lesson explains the War of 1812, the Battle of the Alamo, and the Treaty of Guadalupe Hidalgo.

Objectives

■ To explain the reasons for the War of 1812

■ To describe the Battle of the Alamo

■ To explain the importance of the Treaty of Guadalupe Hidalgo

Student Pages 439–442

Teacher's Resource Library

  Workbook Activity 81

  Activity 81

  Modified Activity 81

Vocabulary

interfere

Tell students that the word interfere comes from two French words. Write the following etymology on the board: *entre-* (between) + *ferir* (to strike). Ask students to explain the meaning of *interfere* in their own words, based on its origin. Then have students compare their definitions to the definition in the textbook.

1 Warm-Up Activity

Write the phrase "Remember the Alamo!" on the board. Have students share any background information they have about this phrase, the site of the battle, or the conflict between Texas and Mexico. Have students make predictions about the meaning of this battle cry.

Reading Strategy:
Metacognition

After reading the first section on this page, have students make a prediction about what will happen next. Students can write their prediction on an index card and reread it after completing the lesson.

Background Information

Life for a Mexican or American soldier was difficult. In both armies, food was scarce, living conditions were harsh, and diseases killed more soldiers than bullets. Most soldiers were illiterate. Only members of the officer corps kept diaries and wrote letters home. The wives, sisters, and girlfriends of soldiers moved with the army and served as cooks, maids, and nurses. There were only 8,600 officers and men in the United States army at the outbreak of the war with Mexico. Congress called for 50,000 volunteers to fight. Full-time soldiers looked down on the newcomers because of their lack of training.

The Alamo was a fort in San Antonio, Texas, where a famous battle was fought in 1836.

It was February of 1836. Around 5,000 Mexican soldiers stormed the fort. Inside the Alamo were fewer than 200 Texans, among them Davy Crockett and James Bowie. They managed to hold the fort for 13 days. In the end, nearly all the Texans defending the Alamo were killed. However, their brave fight gave spirit to the struggle and helped the Texan forces to win the war.

"Remember the Alamo!" became the battle cry of the Texan forces. By April 1836, the Mexican army was defeated. The Mexican general Santa Anna signed a peace treaty. Texas became an independent nation.

LEARNING STYLES

Body/Kinesthetic

Have students find several pictures of the Alamo fort in San Antonio, Texas. Using the pictures as a guide, have students work in groups to build models of the Alamo. Before they begin their models, have students discuss what materials would be best to create their models, and how they will construct their fort. Students can build the restored Alamo as it is today. Or, they may want to portray the fort at the time of the battle.

LEARNING STYLES

Auditory/Verbal

Have students do an Internet search for one of several songs written about the Alamo: "San Antonio Rose" by Patsy Cline; "Remember the Alamo," various recordings by Gianluca Zanna, Jane Bowers, The Kingston Trio, or Johnny Cash; or the traditional folk song "The Yellow Rose of Texas." Have students listen to one of these recordings and list words or phrases that represent the spirit of pride or rebellion associated with the Alamo. Then have volunteers share their lists with the class.

COMMON ERROR

Students may be more familiar with the commercial meaning of the word *Alamo* than the historical meaning. Explain that the word *álamo* is a Spanish word meaning "cottonwood trees."

Gold was discovered in California in 1848. More than 100,000 people moved west in search of their fortune. So many people settled in California that it was allowed to become a state the following year. Across the Pacific Ocean in 1851, gold was found in Australia. During the Australian Gold Rush of the 1850s, about 350,000 people traveled to that continent in search of gold. By the end of the 1850s, Australia was producing more than one-third of all gold in the world.

How Was the Boundary Between Mexico and Texas Decided?

In 1845, Texas became the 28th state to join the United States. Many in the Mexican government had not approved of the treaty Santa Anna had signed in 1836. As a result, the declaration of statehood led to war in 1846 between the United States and Mexico.

Mexico lost the war in 1848. The United States and Mexico signed the Treaty of Guadalupe Hidalgo. In the treaty, Mexico accepted the Rio Grande as the boundary between Mexico and Texas. Also, in return for $15 million, the United States gained vast new territory that had belonged to Mexico. This included what are now the states of Utah, California, Nevada, and most of Arizona, New Mexico, Wyoming, and Colorado.

Geography Note

Gold seekers from the eastern states followed three main routes to California. They sailed by way of the Isthmus of Panama, they sailed around Cape Horn, or they set out on the overland trail. In 1850, the average time from New York to San Francisco was three to five months. Travelers of this route risked catching malaria, yellow fever, and other deadly diseases.

ELL/ESL STRATEGY

Language Objective: *To compare and contrast similarities and differences*

Draw a three-column compare/contrast graphic organizer on the board. Have students copy it into their notebooks. Title the first column *Mexico*, the second column *Mexico and Texas*, and the third column *Texas*. Ask students to review the material on the Battle of the Alamo and list differences between the two sides in columns one and three, and similarities in column two. Get students started by writing *5,000 soldiers* under *Mexico* and 187 soldiers under *Texas*.

COMMON ERROR

Students may wonder who or what Guadalupe Hidalgo was. Guadalupe Hidalgo is the name of the city where the Mexican government fled when United States forces advanced. It was the site of the final negotiations between Mexico and the United States.

STUDY SKILLS

Have students pause at the end of the lesson to record details from the first two lessons in their own words. Then ask students to compare notes with a partner and add any information from their partner's list to their own notes. Direct students to repeat the process after reading the next two lessons.

3 Reinforce and Extend

AT HOME

Have students discuss their neighborhood or city with a parent or other family member. Have students find out the boundaries of their neighborhood or city. Tell them to discuss how boundaries might help or harm an area. Have them consider the questions: *How do people respect boundaries today? How do rivers, forests, or industrial areas function as built-in boundaries?*

Lesson 21–2 Review Answers

1. B 2. A 3. C 4. C 5. B 6. A 7. D 8. C 9. A 10. D

LESSON 21-2 REVIEW

On a sheet of paper, write the letter of the answer that correctly completes each sentence.

1. The War of 1812 began because Britain was interfering with U.S. _____.

A government   **B** trade   **C** borders   **D** wars

2. The state that is now Texas once belonged to _____.

A Mexico   **B** Britain   **C** France   **D** Santa Anna

3. The disagreements about _____ in the southern United States caused the war.

A government   **B** trade   **C** borders   **D** wars

4. The Alamo was a fort in San Antonio, _____.

A Louisiana   **B** Mexico   **C** Texas   **D** Oregon

5. The Battle of the Alamo gave Texans _____.

A another victory
B the determination to win
C independence from Mexico
D the land up to the Rio Grande

6. Mexican general _____ signed a peace treaty that made Texas independent.

A Santa Anna   **B** Davy Crockett   **C** James Bowie   **D** James Monroe

7. In 1846, _____ declared itself a state.

A Oregon   **B** Louisiana   **C** Mexico   **D** Texas

8. The Treaty of Guadalupe Hidalgo was signed in 1848 when Mexico _____.

A defeated the Texans
B won the Battle of the Alamo
C lost the war
D declared independence

9. The Treaty of Guadalupe Hidalgo said the _____ was the border between Mexico and Texas.

A Rio Grande   **B** Alamo   **C** Gulf of Mexico   **D** Mississippi River

10. The Treaty of Guadalupe Hidalgo also gave _____ new territory.

A Texas   **B** Mexico   **C** Louisiana   **D** the United States

---

442   Unit 8   *The Age of Imperialism*

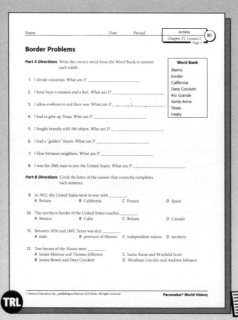

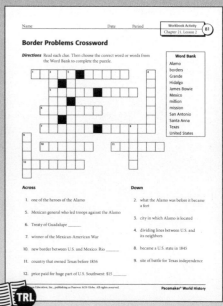

Activity 81, pages 1–2   Workbook Activity 81

---

442   Unit 8   *The Age of Imperialism*

The American Civil War

Objectives

■ To explain the reasons why the Civil War began

■ To describe the turning point of the war

Reading Strategy: Metacognition

Note the main idea and the important details of this section. Summarize what you have read to make sure you understand it.

History Fact
The word Union (with a capital U) means the Union of all the states. In the Civil War, Union also meant those on the side of the North, such as Union soldiers.

Like European history, American history is scarred with war. Between 1861 and 1865, Americans fought a bloody civil war between the northern and southern states.

What Caused the Civil War?

Slavery was an important issue between the North and South. However, it was not the immediate cause of the war. After Abraham Lincoln was elected president, the southern states broke away from the United States. They formed a separate nation called the Confederate States of America. Lincoln could not allow the South to break up the Union. He felt he had no choice but to go to war to save the Union.

The North had many more people than the South. The North also had more manufacturing and industry. It was able to produce more guns and cannons. The South was still mainly agricultural. Its main crops were cotton and tobacco. The southern plantations depended on enslaved workers.

Northerners expected the war to be over soon. They were also sure they would be the winners. However, they were in for a surprise. The first major land battle of the war, at Bull Run on July 21, 1861, was easily won by the South! Furthermore, the Confederate army went on to win one battle after another. The army was led by brilliant generals such as Robert E. Lee and Stonewall Jackson.

What Was the Turning Point of the War?

The turning point of the war came at Gettysburg, Pennsylvania. Lee and his forces retreated from the battlefield.

Chapter 21 Lesson 3

Overview This lesson describes the causes, turning point, and outcome of the Civil War.

Objectives

■ To explain the reasons why the Civil War began

■ To describe the turning point of the war

Student Pages 443–445

Teacher's Resource Library

  Workbook Activity 82

  Activity 82

  Modified Activity 82

1   Warm-Up Activity

Display a picture of Abraham Lincoln and ask students to share facts they know about the 16th President of the United States. Student ideas may include the *Emancipation Proclamation* and the fact that Lincoln was murdered by John Wilkes Booth. Explain that Lincoln was president during the Civil War, a time of great turmoil for the United States.

2   Teaching the Lesson

The strength of the United States came at a price: over 600,000 lives were lost in the four years of the Civil War. The war changed the face of the South and freed African Americans from slavery. Have students read pages 443–444 to learn more about the Civil War.

Ask:

● What was the cause of the Civil War? (The South wanted to break from the Union.)

● Who helped the South win early battles in the war? (brilliant generals such as Robert E. Lee and Stonewall Jackson)

● Who led the Northern army to victory? (Ulysses S. Grant)

Reading Strategy: Metacognition

Have students identify the main idea and find supporting details as they read the lesson. (Sample answer: The Civil War was a war between the northern and southern states.) Ask students to summarize the main points of the lesson after reading.

COMMON ERROR

Point out the first sentence in the second paragraph on page 443. Although it became an important issue during the war, slavery was not the cause of the Civil War. President Lincoln felt that war was the only way to convince the South that the United States must remain one country.

Background Information

With 12 more states and about 10 million more people, the North thought they could overpower the South and easily win the war. However, most military academies were located in the South. Brilliant leaders such as General Robert E. Lee and General Stonewall Jackson were trained in these schools. Additionally, Southerners were a rural, hunting people who were familiar with guns and living off the land. Most Northerners were from cities and not as familiar with the hardships war brought. For these reasons, the larger region was surprised by the strength of the smaller, and the South was initially victorious.

Reading Strategy:
Metacognition

Have students share questions that came to mind as they read. Have them suggest sources where they might find the answers to their questions.

The Union won the battle at Gettysburg, making it the turning point of the war.

Reading Strategy:
Metacognition

Remember to ask yourself questions as you read. This will help you make sure that you understand what you are reading.

In 1863, Lincoln's *Emancipation Proclamation* took effect, outlawing slavery in areas rebelling against the Union. By the end of the war, about 200,000 African Americans had fought for the North.

By 1864, Ulysses S. Grant had won many Union victories in the West. In that year, Lincoln appointed, or made, Grant commander of all Union forces. By 1865, much of the South lay in ruins. The southern armies had also become much weaker. The North had cut off all of the South's supply routes. Lee's army was trapped in Virginia by Grant's army. Lee decided it was hopeless to keep on fighting. He surrendered to Grant on April 9, 1865, at Appomattox Court House in Virginia.

The bloodiest war in American history was over. More than 600,000 people were killed. Many cities and farms were destroyed. However, the North had won the war and the Union was saved. All of the states were now united.

444   *Unit 8   The Age of Imperialism*

REVIEW

Word Bank

agricultural

Confederate States
of America

*Emancipation
Proclamation*

General Grant

General Lee

Gettysburg

industry

slavery

South

Union

On a sheet of paper, write the word from the Word Bank to complete each sentence correctly.

1. _____ was an important issue between the North and the South. It was not, however, the immediate cause of the Civil War.

2. When Abraham Lincoln was elected president, the southern states broke away from the United States. They formed the _____.

3. The main reason for the Civil War was to save the _____.

4. The North had more people and more manufacturing and _____.

5. The South was mainly _____ and depended on slave labor.

6. The _____ won the first battle of the war—Bull Run.

7. _____ was the turning point of the war.

8. Lincoln's _____ outlawed slavery in the south.

9. _____ was the commander of all Union forces.

10. After the North had cut off all of the South's supply routes, _____ surrendered.

CAREER CONNECTION

Have students do research on military academies in the South. Have them find out how military schools differ from regular high schools or colleges. Remind students that many successful generals in the Civil War attended military schools in the South. Have students research the various levels of service that people in the military must reach before becoming a general.

Lesson 21–3 Review Answers

1. slavery **2.** Confederate States of America **3.** Union **4.** industry **5.** agricultural **6.** South **7.** Gettysburg **8.** *Emancipation Proclamation* **9.** General Grant **10.** General Lee

Activity 82

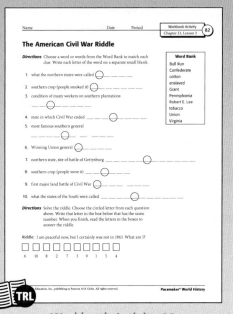

Workbook Activity 82

Lesson at a Glance

Chapter 21 Lesson 4

Overview This lesson explains how the United States grew after the Civil War was over.

Objectives

- To describe the impact of the transcontinental railroad in the United States
- To tell how the United States gained Alaska and Hawaii
- To explain the effects of the Spanish-American War
- To explain the importance of the Panama Canal

Student Pages 446–450

Teacher's Resource Library

Workbook Activity 83

Activity 83

Modified Activity 83

Vocabulary

economic   rebellion
expansion   sympathy
international   victor

Have students spend several minutes studying the vocabulary words and definitions with a partner. Then write the words on the board for reference. Have students number a sheet of paper 1–6. Read the definitions in random order and have students write the word for each definition next to the correct number. Then ask volunteers to define each word on their list. Have students check their answers as definitions are read.

Reading Strategy:
Metacognition

Have students share ideas about what they can do to better understand the text such as reading headings and boldface words first, asking questions as they read, and looking for main ideas and supporting details.

U.S. Expansion

Objectives

- To describe the impact of the transcontinental railroad in the United States
- To tell how the United States gained Alaska and Hawaii
- To explain the effects of the Spanish-American War
- To explain the importance of the Panama Canal

Reading Strategy:
Metacognition

Before you read this section, think about what you can do that will help you better understand the text.

Expansion
Growth; to increase in size

After the Civil War was over, the United States set its sights on **expansion,** or growth. With the battles of the country settled, the United States could finally grow its industry, territory, and control.

How Did Industry in the United States Change During the 1800s?

Many changes occurred in the United States during the early 1800s. The introduction of the steam locomotive led to great improvements in overland transportation. Samuel F. B. Morse's telegraph, first demonstrated in 1837, led to greatly improved communication. In 1834, Cyrus McCormick invented a mechanical reaper. This machine cut down and gathered crops, allowing farmers to harvest grain more quickly than before. Beginning in the early 1800s, some businesses began building factories. Inside the factories were machines that allowed workers to produce goods more rapidly.

After the Civil War, changes occurred more quickly. More and more factories were built. Machines began to replace hand labor as the main means of manufacturing. At this time, a new nationwide network of railroads was being built. In 1869, the transcontinental railroad was completed. This linked up the eastern and western parts of the country. It also helped speed up the settlement of the West.

The railroad system helped businesses distribute their goods more quickly. In addition, there were more goods available. Inventors developed new products. Businesses were able to make the products in large quantities. The United States now had its own industrial revolution.

446 Unit 8   *The Age of Imperialism*

1 Warm-Up Activity

Have students look at a map of the United States in a book or on a classroom wall map. Propose a trip from the east coast to the west coast. Ask students to discuss how they might make that trip. Answers include by car, train, or plane. Then ask students how travel differed during the 1800s. Explain that it was during this time that the transcontinental railroad was built, changing travel forever and speeding up settlement of the western states.

2 Teaching the Lesson

The time after the Civil War was one of industrial growth and increased expansion for the United States. Have students read pages 446–449 to learn about the transcontinental railroad, the acquisition of Hawaii and Alaska, and the construction of the Panama Canal.

Ask:

- What invention led to improvements in overland transportation? (the steam locomotive, or train)

Many big businesses developed during this period. Some involved the production of coal, petroleum, steel, and industrial machinery. New England, New York, and Pennsylvania became important industrial centers in the North. The United States was on its way to becoming an industrial giant.

Remember
The United States also made a huge land purchase in 1803, the Louisiana Purchase.

Reading Strategy:
Metacognition

Remember to look at the illustrations and to note the descriptive words. This will help you visualize what you are reading.

How Did the United States Gain Alaska and Hawaii?

"A foolish purchase!" "Who wants a hunk of frozen land?" Many Americans said that about the territory known as Alaska. In 1867, Secretary of State William Seward had persuaded the United States to buy Alaska from Russia. Its price was just over $7 million. In 1897, gold was discovered in Alaska. It was only then that Americans began to realize the value of the purchase.

The United States' interest in Hawaii began in 1820. That year a group of Protestant missionaries from New England arrived there. In 1835, the first sugar plantation began operating. It was owned by an American company. Commercial development of pineapple began in the mid-1800s. Also, around this time, hundreds of U.S. whaling ships began to visit Hawaii regularly. In 1887, the United States signed a treaty with Hawaii. It gave the United States the right to use Pearl Harbor as a naval base. The United States' interests were now well-established on the islands.

In 1893, the Hawaiians staged a revolution against Liliuokalani, queen of Hawaii. Americans, who by that time owned most of Hawaii's industry, encouraged and led the revolt. Queen Liliuokalani left her throne. In 1900, Hawaii became a territory of the United States.

The United States used the Monroe Doctrine to keep European interests out of the Americas. Meanwhile the United States gained more territory for itself.

After Queen Liliuokalani left her throne, Hawaii became a territory of the United States.

- What discovery in Alaska led Americans to think of the area as valuable territory? (the discovery of gold)
- Why did President Roosevelt want to build the Panama Canal? (as a transportation route for the U.S. Navy)

Background Information

When the United States purchased Alaska from Russia, it was the end of Russian efforts to expand trade and settlements in North America. Although they knew the area was rich in natural resources, Russia could not afford to fund further exploration or support major settlements. The purchase of Alaska was called "Seward's Folly" after the Secretary of State, until gold was discovered in Alaska. Alaska became a state in 1959.

COMMON ERROR

Explain that Alaska and Hawaii are not part of the continental United States. They are the only two states that are not connected by land. The continental United States is sometimes called "The Mainland" by Hawaiians and "The Lower 48" by people in Alaska.

LEARNING STYLES

Visual/Spatial
Remind students that the invention of the telegraph and Morse code revolutionized communication. Messages could be sent in minutes, rather than weeks. Find Morse code examples for the students. Then have students write messages in Morse code. Ask them to exchange messages and decode them on paper. You may want to allow students to also practice sending messages by Morse code in a series of taps as a telegraph would have done.

Remember

Have students revisit the map on page 437 to refresh their memory about how the Louisiana Purchase expanded the size of the United States. Ask students how the price of Alaska compared to the price of the Louisiana Territory.

Reading Strategy:
Metacognition

Have students close their eyes and imagine visiting a sugar plantation in Hawaii. Tell students to consider how a sugar cane plant looks, how it might taste, what sounds they would hear on the plantation, how the air smells, and what it might feel like to stand in the warm sun of Hawaii. Point out that readers can use their five senses to visualize what they are reading.

ELL/ESL STRATEGY

Language Objective:
To draw conclusions from a timeline of events

Have students draw a timeline representing January through December, 1898. Tell students to enter the events of the Spanish-American War from page 448 onto their timeline. Then ask students to draw a conclusion based on the timeline. Students will observe the short duration of this war. Have students suggest reasons why the war was a short one. (Students may conclude that the United States had greater military power than Spain.)

You Decide

Have students discuss their opinions about the war with a partner. Students may say that war was the only way to solve the conflict with Spain or that war was not the solution, and diplomatic discussions were another option.

Sympathy
Feeling sorry for another's suffering

Victor
The winner of a battle, war, struggle, or contest

 You Decide
Today some experts believe the explosion of the *Maine* was probably an accident. Were Americans right to declare war? Why or why not?

What Was the Outcome of the Spanish-American War?

A war broke out between the United States and Spain in 1898. As a result of this war, the United States gained still more territory.

The United States wanted Spain out of the Caribbean. Many Americans felt sorry, or **sympathy**, for the Cubans who lived under harsh Spanish rule. Some Americans also saw a chance for the United States to gain more power.

Relations between the United States and Spain were tense. Then, in February 1898, the U.S. battleship *Maine* exploded in the harbor at Havana, Cuba. Many Americans blamed Spain. By April the Spanish-American War had begun.

By August of that same year, the war was over. The United States was the winner, or **victor.** In December, Spain and the United States sent representatives to Paris to sign a treaty. The Treaty of Paris gave the United States possession of Puerto Rico, the Philippines, and the Pacific Island of Guam. Spain gave Cuba its freedom.

Why Was the Panama Canal so Important?

By the early 1900s, the United States was the strongest country on the American continents. It held control over lands gained in the Spanish-American War. During that war, the U.S. Navy sent a battleship from San Francisco to Cuba. It had to sail all the way around the tip of South America. This is a distance of 13,000 miles. If there had been a canal across Central America, the trip would have been about 5,000 miles.

U.S. President Theodore Roosevelt wanted to build such a canal across Panama. However, Colombia ruled Panama. Furthermore, Colombia would not grant the United States the land it needed for the canal. To get around this problem, the United States encouraged Panama to declare its independence from Colombia.

The Panama Canal was completed in 1914. Ships can now sail from the Atlantic to the Pacific Ocean without going around South America.

Rebellion
A fight by people against a government

Economic
Having to do with money

International
Having to do with many nations

Panama's **rebellion,** or fight against the government, in November 1903 was a success. The United States gained the right to build the canal. Panama sold the United States a canal zone that was 10 miles wide. The Panama Canal and the Canal Zone belonged to the United States. However, in 1977, the United States and Panama signed a treaty. In keeping with the treaty, Panama regained control of the Canal Zone in 1979. Then in 1999, Panama gained control of the canal itself.

With the canal built, the United States grew as an **economic,** military, and industrial power. It became important in **international** affairs. The United States was becoming a major force in the modern world.

TIMELINE STUDY:
THE U.S. GAINS POWER AND TERRITORY

From the information on the timeline, do you think the United States felt the Monroe Doctrine applied to itself? Why or why not?

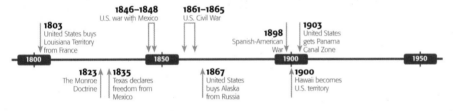

1803 United States buys Louisiana Territory from France

1823 The Monroe Doctrine

1835 Texas declares freedom from Mexico

1846–1848 U.S. war with Mexico

1861–1865 U.S. Civil War

1867 United States buys Alaska from Russia

1898 Spanish-American War

1900 Hawaii becomes U.S. territory

1903 United States gets Panama Canal Zone

1800　1850　1900　1950

Possible answer: No. The United States went to war with Mexico, fought the Spanish-American War, and obtained Hawaii and the Panama Canal.

3 Reinforce and Extend

WORLD CULTURES

In the Hawaiian language, words are thought to have *mana*—spiritual or divine power. The two most important words in the Hawaiian language are *aloha* and *mahalo.* These words are among the most sacred and powerful words, in part because they represent Hawaiian values. On a spiritual level, *aloha* invokes "the divine" and *mahalo* is "a divine blessing." Literally, *aloha* might be translated as "love, mercy, or grace" and *mahalo* as "thank you."

COMMON ERROR

Explain that although the Panama Canal was not in the United States, it was the property of the United States. In 1999, the United States made a deal with Panama, returning ownership of the canal to that country, almost 100 years after the canal was built.

ONLINE CONNECTION

Students can gain additional information by accessing the following Web sites:
www.agsglobepmwh.com/page449a
(This Web site provides a map of the Panama Canal.)
www.agsglobepmwh.com/page449b
(This Web site provides additional facts and pictures of the Panama Canal.)

IN THE COMMUNITY

Have students walk around their neighborhood, considering the trade and expansion they read about in this lesson. For example, what impact does a train have on their town? (People might take the train into the city for work; goods might be shipped into town by train.) Have students consider other modern advancements in transportation and how they impact life in their community.

Lesson 21–4 Review Answers

1. The transcontinental railroad linked the eastern and western parts of the country. It sped up the settlement of the West. It also helped businesses distribute their goods more quickly. **2.** Gold was discovered in Alaska. **3.** The United States used the Monroe Doctrine to keep European interests out and to gain more territory. **4.** The United States owned much of Hawaii's industry and had the right to use Pearl Harbor as a naval base. In 1893, Americans encouraged and led the revolt against Liliuokalani, queen of Hawaii. The queen left her throne. In 1900, Hawaii became a territory of the United States. **5.** Americans felt sorry for the Cubans who lived under harsh Spanish rule. Some Americans also saw a chance for the United States to gain more power. **6.** The Americans won the Spanish-American war. **7.** The United States and Spain signed the Treaty of Paris. It gave the United States possession of Puerto Rico, the Philippines, and the Pacific Island of Guam. Spain also gave Cuba its freedom. **8.** The United States encouraged Panama to declare its independence from Colombia. The rebellion in November 1903 was a success. **9.** Panama has had control of the Panama Canal since 1999. **10.** The canal allowed the United States to grow as an economic, military, and industrial power. It became important in international affairs. It helped the United States to become a major force in the modern world.

On a sheet of paper, write the answer to each question. Use complete sentences.

1. What impact did the transcontinental railroad have on the United States?

2. What made Americans change their minds about the "foolish" purchase of Alaska?

3. How did the United States keep European interests out of the Americas?

4. How did the United States gain Hawaii?

5. Why did the United States want Spain out of the Caribbean?

6. Who won the Spanish-American war?

7. Who signed the Treaty of Paris and what did it promise?

8. How did the United States gain the right to build the Panama Canal?

9. Who has control of the Panama Canal?

10. Why was the Panama Canal so important to the United States?

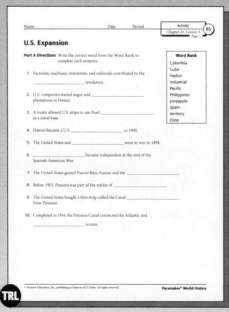

Activity 83, pages 1–2   Workbook Activity 83

- The Monroe Doctrine said that the United States would not allow Europeans to set up new colonies in the Americas.

- The United States expanded with the Louisiana Purchase.

- Great Britain and the United States went to war in 1812 over trade disagreements.

- In 1835, Texas went to war with Mexico. By 1845, Texas was a U.S. state.

- The United States fought with Mexico from 1846 to 1848. The United States purchased Mexican lands that later became the states of Utah, California, Nevada, and most of Arizona, New Mexico, Wyoming, and Colorado.

- The Treaty of Guadalupe Hidalgo established the southern border of the United States.

- The United States was torn apart by a bloody civil war from 1861 to 1865. The North won the war and the Union was preserved. More than 600,000 people died in that war.

- The completion of the transcontinental railroad aided business. It also helped speed up the settlement of the West.

- During the 1800s, farming methods improved, as did communication with the telegraph.

- Alaska (in 1867) and Hawaii (in 1900) became territories of the United States.

- In the Spanish-American War, the United States gained Puerto Rico, the Philippines, and Guam.

- The United States built the Panama Canal. It connected the Atlantic and Pacific Oceans.

Chapter 21 Summary

Have students read the Chapter Summary on page 451 to review the main ideas presented in Chapter 21.

Ask:

- What did the Monroe Doctrine say? (The United States would not allow Europeans to set up new colonies in the Americas.)

- How did the Louisiana Purchase change the size of the United States? (It doubled the size of the United States.)

- Who fought in the War of 1812 and why did the war start? (Great Britain and the United States went to war in 1812 over trade disagreements.)

- When did Texas go to war with Mexico? (1835)

- What states were established on land purchased from Mexico? (Utah, California, Nevada, and most of Arizona, New Mexico, Wyoming, and Colorado)

- What treaty established the southern border of the United States? (the Treaty of Guadalupe Hidalgo)

- Who won the Civil War? (the North)

- How did the transcontinental railroad change the United States? (It helped speed up the settlement of the West.)

- What lands did the United States gain in the Spanish-American War? (Puerto Rico, the Philippines, and Guam)

- Why did the United States want to build the Panama Canal? (to connect the Atlantic and Pacific Oceans)

TEACHER'S RESOURCE

The AGS Globe Teaching Strategies in Social Studies Transparencies may be used with this chapter. The transparencies add an interactive dimension to expand and enhance the Pacemaker® *World History* program content.

CHAPTER PROJECT FOLLOW-UP

Have each group of students exchange their newspapers and read the articles prepared by the other group. Allow students to read the newspapers of several groups. You may want to have students evaluate each other's newspapers with a peer review. Then ask students to provide examples of things they learned from writing and reading the papers that enhanced the material in the textbook.

Chapter 21 Review

Use the Chapter Review to prepare students for tests and to reteach content from the chapter.

Chapter 21 Mastery Test

The Teacher's Resource Library includes two forms of the Chapter 21 Mastery Test. Each test addresses the chapter Goals for Learning. An optional third page of additional critical-thinking items is included for each test. The difficulty level of the two forms is equivalent.

Chapter 21 Review Answers

Vocabulary Review

1. Monroe Doctrine

2. territory

3. sympathy

4. victor

5. rebellion

6. international

7. economic

Chapter Review Questions

8. The Monroe Doctrine did not allow Europe to get more territory in North or South America. It also did not allow any existing colonies from taking over more land.

9. The United States purchased the Louisiana Territory from France for $15 million.

10. The Treaty of Guadalupe said that the Rio Grande was the border between Mexico and Texas. It also gave the United States vast new territory that had belonged to Mexico.

11. The United States gained Utah, Nevada, and California for $15 million after winning the war with Mexico.

12. The South won the Battle of Bull Run.

Word Bank

economic

international

Monroe Doctrine

rebellion

sympathy

territory

victor

Vocabulary Review

On a sheet of paper, use the words from the Word Bank to complete each sentence correctly.

1. The _____ is the statement that the United States made against European imperialism.

2. Many thought that the purchase of the Alaska _____ was foolish.

3. The Cubans lived under harsh Spanish rule in 1898. Americans felt _____ for the Cubans.

4. The Union army was the _____ of the Civil War.

5. Americans encouraged _____ in Hawaii in hopes of gaining Hawaii as a territory.

6. The United States is an important power in _____ affairs.

7. The Panama Canal gave the United States _____, military, and industrial power.

Chapter Review Questions

On a sheet of paper, write the answer to each question. Use complete sentences.

8. What did the Monroe Doctrine forbid (not allow) Europe to do?

9. How did the United States gain the Louisiana Territory?

10. What did the Treaty of Guadalupe say?

11. How did the United States gain Utah, Nevada, and California?

12. Who won the Battle of Bull Run?

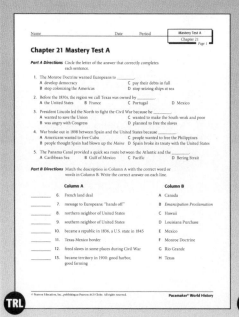

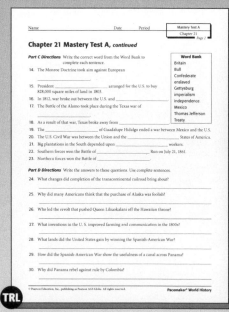

Chapter 21 Mastery Test A, pages 1–3

Test Tip

Take time to organize your thoughts before answering a question that requires a written answer.

13. How did the United States gain Alaska and Hawaii?

14. How did the United States gain Puerto Rico, the Philippines, and Guam?

15. In what ways was the transcontinental railroad good for the United States?

16. What events led to the building of the Panama Canal?

Critical Thinking

On a sheet of paper, write your response to each question. Use complete sentences.

17. What do you think would have happened to the United States if the South had won the Civil War?

18. Why might some countries have objected to the way the United States obtained the Panama Canal Zone?

Using the Timeline

Use the timeline on page 449 to answer the questions.

19. How many years passed between the time Texas declared freedom from Mexico and the U.S. war with Mexico?

20. How long did the Civil War last?

GROUP ACTIVITY

With a partner, debate the purchase of Alaska. One should be for the purchase, and the other should be against it. Before the debate, prepare a few notes to help you remember the points you hope to make. Make sure you review that information to support the argument on the opposing side. This will help prepare you to respond to the other person's arguments.

---

13. The United States bought Alaska from Russia. The United States supported a revolution against the queen of Hawaii. Later, Hawaii became a U.S. territory.

14. The United States gained Puerto Rico, the Philippines, and Guam in the Spanish-American War.

15. The transcontinental railroad linked the eastern and western parts of the country. This sped up the settlement of the West. It also helped businesses to distribute their goods more quickly.

16. The United States wanted to build the canal. However, Colombia ruled Panama. Columbia would not grant the United States the land for the canal. So, the United States encouraged Panama to declare its independence from Colombia. The rebellion in November 1903 was a success. The United States gained the right to build the canal.

Critical Thinking

17. Possible answers: The United States would have become two countries. The North and the South would have become the Union again. However, slavery would have stayed in the South.

18. Possible answer: The United States interfered between Columbia and Panama to get the Panama Canal Zone. It encouraged Panama to declare its independence from Columbia.

Using the Timeline

19. 11 years

20. 4 years

GROUP ACTIVITY

Students' debates should show understanding of the viewpoints for and against the purchase of Alaska. It should also include complete facts and be organized and persuasive.

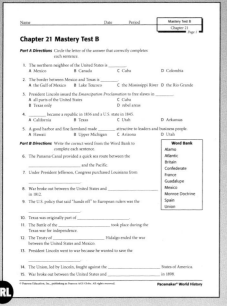

Chapter 21 Mastery Test B, pages 1–3

Introducing the Chapter

China and Japan remained isolated from the world for hundreds of years. However, the wave of imperialism that swept through Europe also affected Asia. Trade began to open between European and Asian countries. To keep trade thriving, the West aided Chinese leaders in their fight to crush a rebellion by peasants. During this time, Japan's economy and military grew strong.

Ask:

• Why did the Manchus limit trade in China? (They looked down on the rest of the world.)

• Why did China and Japan fight? (They both wanted Korea.)

Imperialism and the Far East

You have learned about how China and Japan spent many years isolated from other countries. Some contact developed as trade with Europe began. However, governments such as the Manchus in China put tight limits on trade. This kept most of the Far East in isolation.

The poverty of the Chinese peasants led to revolution. The Chinese were also at war with Japan over control of Korea. As a result, the Chinese government would struggle for many years. On the other hand, Japan was growing powerful. It was now open to trade with many countries. It gained a wealth of new materials from Korea to aid in its growing industries.

GOALS FOR LEARNING

• To describe China under Manchurian rule
• To explain the unrest in China under Manchurian rule
• To explain how Japan became less isolated

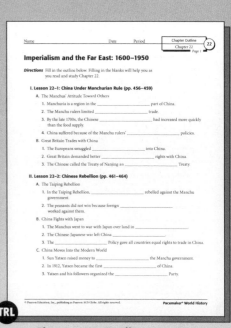

Chapter 22 Self-Study Guide, pages 1–2   Chapter 22 Outline, pages 1–2

Reading Strategy: Summarizing

When readers summarize, they look for key ideas and phrases. Then they rewrite them in their own words, using as few words as possible. A summary of key points will help you remember the important ideas you have read. As you read the text, ask yourself these questions:

- What are some important ideas or phrases in the text?
- How can I write these ideas or phrases in a few words?
- Will this remind me of the main idea in the section or the lesson?

Key Vocabulary Words

Lesson 1

Policy A rule; a method of action or conduct

Addicted Having a strong habit that is hard to give up

Smuggle To move something into or out of a country secretly because it is against the law

Lesson 2

Interference Mixing in another's affairs without being asked

Open-Door Policy The American approach to China around 1900 that allowed open trade relations between China and other nations

- What was Japanese imperialism? (Japan set up overseas colonies to supply itself with raw materials.)

Reading Strategy:
Summarizing

Tell students that a summary includes the main ideas presented in the chapter. Have them scan the chapter. Point out lesson titles, section headings, objectives, and illustrations. Explain that these elements are clues to the main ideas in each lesson.

Ask:

- What is this chapter about? (imperialism and the Far East)
- What are the main ideas in Lesson 22–1? (the Manchus' attitude toward other Chinese people and the world, the Opium War, and the Treaty of Nanjing)
- What was the name of a harbor city in China used by Danish, British, and American ships? (Canton)

Key Vocabulary Words

Point out that these chapter words are presented in the order they appear in each lesson. They are also found in the glossary.

LIFE SKILLS CONNECTION

Students discuss careers that involve the trade of goods or services. Students research one of the careers and request an informational interview with someone in the field. Help students create a list of questions to ask during their interviews.

KEY VOCABULARY

Students choose the word that correctly completes each sentence.

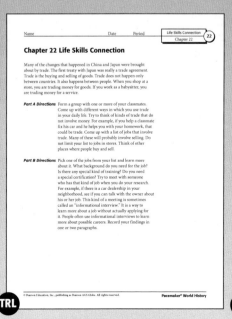

Life Skills Connection 22   Key Vocabulary Words 22

Overview This lesson describes the Manchu government and its interactions with the Chinese people and the West.

Objectives

- To describe the Manchus' attitude toward other Chinese people and the world
- To explain the Opium War and the Treaty of Nanjing

Student Pages 456–460

Teacher's Resource Library

Workbook Activity 84

Activity 84

Modified Activity 84

Vocabulary

addicted
policy
smuggle

Ask students to write a matching phrase for each of the vocabulary words. Then tell students to exchange papers and match the vocabulary words to the correct phrases. Students should assess one another's work.

PRONUNCIATION GUIDE

Use this list to help students pronounce difficult words in this lesson.

Manchuria (man choor´ē ə)

Qing (ching)

Guangzhou (gwäng´ jō´)

1 | Warm-Up Activity

Ask students if they have had an international visitor in their homes. What kind of welcome was the person given? What did they learn from the visitor? What did the visitor teach them? Tell them that in this lesson they will learn about the developing influence of the West on the Chinese and of the Chinese on the West.

China Under Manchurian Rule

Objectives

- To describe the Manchus' attitude toward other Chinese people and the world
- To explain the Opium War and the Treaty of Nanjing

Reading Strategy: Summarizing

What is the main idea of this first paragraph?

Empress Cixi, of the Qing dynasty, was a Manchu ruler who wanted to stop any change in China.

Manchuria is a region in the northeastern part of China. At one time, it did not belong to China. In 1644, the Manchus—the people of Manchuria—invaded northern China. They overthrew the Ming dynasty that was then in power. Then they conquered the rest of China. The Manchus set up their own dynasty called the Qing dynasty. The Manchus would remain in power for more than 250 years. However, the Qing dynasty would be the last of the Chinese dynasties.

What Was the Manchus' Attitude Toward Others?

The Manchus were a proud people—too proud, perhaps. They thought they were better than the other Chinese people. They passed a law saying that a Manchu could not marry a Chinese. They forced Chinese men to wear a Manchu hairstyle. This was a long braid down the back of the head. The British later called the long braid a *queue*. The word *queue* comes from a Latin word meaning "tail."

The Manchus not only looked down on other Chinese, they looked down on the rest of the world. Until the mid-1800s, foreign trade was allowed through only one Chinese city—Guangzhou, or Canton. When European nations and the United States asked for more trade with China, the Manchu rulers always refused.

Reading Strategy: Summarizing

(Sample answer: The Manchus overthrew the Ming dynasty and set up their own dynasty. It lasted 250 years.)

COMMON ERROR

Students might assume that the attitude of the Manchu toward foreigners was a new development in China. Remind them that the Ming emperors, who gained power in the 1300s, also worked to isolate China from the world. Like the Manchus, the Ming emperors considered foreigners barbarians.

CHAPTER PROJECT

Tell students that they will learn about various treaties between the West and Asia in this chapter. Have students form small groups. Ask each group to pair up with another group. Have the two groups choose an issue that affected either Japan or China and that country's relations with the West. Have one group represent Japan or China, and have the other group represent a Western power. Tell the groups to work together to create a treaty that is fair to both parties.

China Under the Qing Dynasty

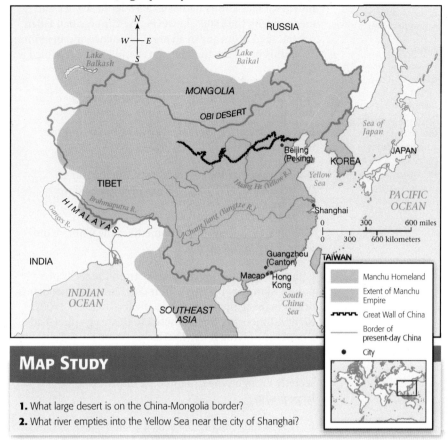

MAP STUDY

1. What large desert is on the China-Mongolia border?
2. What river empties into the Yellow Sea near the city of Shanghai?

During the first 150 years of Manchu rule, China enjoyed prosperity.

Agriculture increased, and the handicraft industry did, too. The population expanded rapidly. However, by the late 1700s, the times had changed. The population had increased more quickly than the food supply. Life became harder for most people.

Have students recall the characteristics of imperialism. Then have them read this lesson to discover the effects of the West's attempts to exert influence on China for economic reasons.

Ask:

- What were two laws the Manchus passed against the Chinese? (A Manchu could not marry a Chinese person, and Chinese men had to wear queues.)
- What were the terms of the Unequal Treaties? (China paid for the lost opium and the cost of the war. It opened ports to British trade. It gave the island of Hong Kong to Great Britain. British citizens could not be tried for any crime in a Chinese court.)

Background Information

Following the Treaty of Nanjing, Britain, France, Germany, and Russia took control of important Chinese harbors and lands. The four countries split China into different trading areas. Historians call such areas "spheres of influences." Each country controlled trade in its sphere of influence. On the surface, China remained an independent nation. In truth, however, its leaders were given no rights or powers in their trade relations with Europe.

COMMON ERROR

Students might wonder why two names are given in the text and on the map for some geographic features such as cities or rivers. Explain that the first name represents the modern Chinese name for the feature. The name in parentheses represents the traditional name or, in some cases, the Western name for the feature. Examples include the city of Guangzhou (Canton), and the Huang He (Yellow), and Chang Jiang (Yangtze) rivers.

MAP STUDY

Answers:

1. Gobi Desert

2. Chang Jiang (Yangtze) River

LEARNING STYLES

Logical/Mathematical
Have students look at the map key on page 457. Remind them that a map key includes symbols that represent different information. Ask students to make a list of the symbols found on the map on this page. The list should explain what each symbol represents. (Students might list the lines and colors to show borders, and the dots to show the locations of cities.)

Tell students to imagine that it is the year 1800. Some of them are merchants on a ship that has just docked at a Chinese port. Their job is to get supplies for their home voyage. Others in the class are Chinese traders. They have the supplies the merchants need. Have the merchants negotiate with the traders for supplies. The two sides must agree on items to be sold and the prices of the items.

ELL/ESL STRATEGY

Language Objective: *To understand cause-and-effect relationships*

Explain that the cause in a relationship is the factor that makes something happen. Then point out that the effect is the thing that happens because of the cause. Give students several events discussed in the lesson and have them identify the cause or effect of each event. For example, ask students why life became harder for most people in China by the late 1700s. (The population increased more quickly than the food supply.) Which was the cause and which was the effect of this event? (The cause was the increase in population. The effect was that life became harder for Chinese people.) Repeat the activity for other events, such as the war between China and Britain and the decline in Chinese science.

Policy
A rule; a method of action or conduct

Addicted
Having a strong habit that is hard to give up

Smuggle
To move something into or out of a country secretly because it is against the law

China also suffered because of the Manchus' isolationist **policies.** Once China had been a leader in science and medicine. By the 1800s, however, the Chinese had fallen behind the Europeans in all areas of science and invention. From this point on, the Manchus would rule a troubled China.

How Did Great Britain Finally Get to Trade with China?

Europeans wanted tea and silk from China. And they wanted a new source of raw materials.

"But there is nothing we want from you in return," the Manchus told the Europeans. "Why should we allow trade?"

Then the Europeans found something the Chinese did want. They found opium.

Opium is a dangerous drug made from the seeds of a poppy. Many poppies grew in India. European merchants began to bring opium to China during the early 1800s. Many Chinese became **addicted** to the drug—they had a hard time giving it up. Therefore, China passed a law making the opium trade illegal. However, the demand for opium was still there. Now the Europeans **smuggled,** or secretly brought, the drug into China, making large profits.

In 1839, a Manchu official seized 20,000 chests of opium from British merchants in Guangzhou. He had the opium burned. The British were angry. They said valuable property had been destroyed. Great Britain went to war with China, demanding better trading rights. China had little chance against Britain's armies. In 1842, the Chinese surrendered. They signed the Treaty of Nanjing.

You Decide
Do you think the major powers today would be more likely to go to war to protect the drug trade or to destroy it? Why?

This was the first of what the Chinese called the Unequal Treaties. China not only had to pay for the lost opium, but also for the cost of the war. China had to open five ports to British trade. China also had to give the island of Hong Kong to Great Britain. The new treaties totally protected British merchants from Chinese law. No British citizen could be tried for any crime in a Chinese court—even if the crime were committed in China. The Chinese felt helpless.

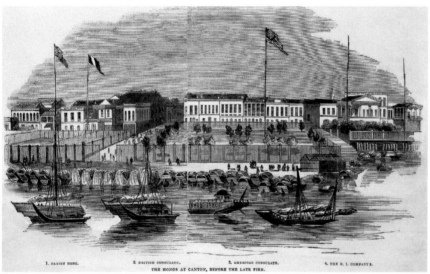

1. DANISH HONG.   2. BRITISH CONSULATE.   3. AMERICAN CONSULATE.   4. THE E. I. COMPANY'S.
THE HONGS AT CANTON, BEFORE THE LATE FIRE.

Danish, British, and American ships used harbors to trade with China, such as this one in Canton.

You Decide

Lead a class discussion in which students state their opinion about whether the major powers today would be more likely go to war to protect or destroy the drug trade. Be sure students give reasons for their opinions. For example, students might mention the "War on Drugs" in America.

3   Reinforce and Extend

AT HOME

Ask students to find a library book that is related to the content in this chapter. Have them look through the book with family members to find interesting facts that were not covered in the chapter. Students can share what they have learned with the class.

CAREER CONNECTION

There are many exciting careers in international relations. The government employs diplomats to establish and maintain relationships between nations. Companies hire businesspeople to work in trade and other financial issues. Environmental and social activists in non-profit organizations may help to set up programs and coordinate volunteers in host countries. Student interested in international relations go to college to learn the language, history, geography, economics, politics, and social structure of a region. Then they specialize in an area such as communications or marketing. Obtain undergraduate catalogs from nearby universities and allow interested students to examine them for ideas on international careers.

LESSON
22-1

REVIEW

Lesson 22–1 Review Answers

1. Qing **2.** Chinese **3.** trade
4. Agriculture **5.** food supply **6.** silk
7. opium **8.** China fell behind the
Europeans in all areas of science
and invention. Also, the population
increased more quickly than the food
supply, making life difficult. **9.** China
had to pay for the cost of war and
the cost of the opium. They had to
open ports to British trade and give
Hong Kong to Britain. The Chinese
could not try a British citizen for
crimes, even if they were committed
in China. **10.** Britain received Hong
Kong and did not have to pay for
the war. Five ports were opened to
British trade. British merchants were
protected from Chinese law.

Word Bank

agriculture
Chinese
food supply
opium
Qing
silk
trade

On a sheet of paper, write the word from the Word Bank to complete each sentence correctly.

1. The Manchu dynasty was known as the _____ dynasty.

2. The Manchus were proud people. They thought they were better than other _____ people and the rest of the world.

3. The Manchu rulers refused to _____ with the European nations and the United States.

4. _____, the handicraft industry, and the population increased in the first 150 years of Manchu rule.

5. Unfortunately, the population increased more quickly than the _____.

6. The Europeans wanted tea, _____, and a new source of raw materials from China.

7. The Europeans found that many Chinese wanted _____.

On a sheet of paper, write the answer to each question. Use complete sentences.

8. In what ways did China suffer from the Manchus' isolationist policies?

9. What did the Treaty of Nanjing force China to do?

10. In what ways did Great Britain benefit from the Unequal Treaties?

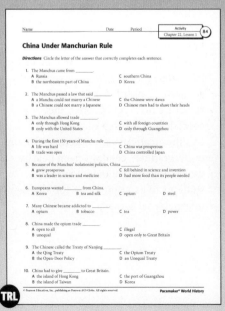

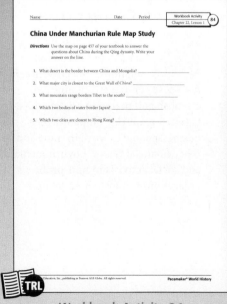

Activity 84

Workbook Activity 84

Chinese Rebellion

Reading Strategy: Summarizing

Write the main idea, details, and any questions you may have.

Remember
During the late 1700s, French peasants rose up against their lords.

The Manchus had trouble with foreigners as well as with people in China.

What Was the Result of the Taiping Rebellion?

Chinese farmers were not happy under Manchu rule. They said that the rulers were greedy and unfair. Most Chinese farmers were poor. Finally the peasants rebelled.

Peasants in China rose up against the Manchu rulers in 1850. By the end of the Taiping Rebellion in 1864, the Manchus were still in power.

1600–1950   *Imperialism and the Far East   Chapter 22*   **461**

Vocabulary

interference
Open-Door Policy

Read a definition of one of the vocabulary terms to students. Have a volunteer write the vocabulary word or phrase on the board. Do the same for the second vocabulary term. Have volunteers compare and contrast the terms. Ask them to explain how interference differs from the Open-Door Policy. Then ask how the terms are related. For example, would China have accepted the Open-Door Policy if the threat of interference did not exist? Have volunteers use the vocabulary terms in their explanations. Ask students whether the terms were used correctly, and if not, to recommend changes.

Reading Strategy: Summarizing

Suggest that students examine the lesson title for the main idea. The information under each section heading includes details that support the main idea.

Remember
After students have read this lesson, have them discuss similarities and differences between the French Revolution and the Chinese Rebellion. Students will find that both revolutions were followed by periods of unrest.

PRONUNCIATION GUIDE

Use this list to help students pronounce difficult words in this lesson.

Sun Yatsen (soon´ yät´sen´)

Yuan Shikai (yyän´ shē´ kī´)

Have students imagine that they are having a disagreement with a friend. Ask how they would feel if someone stepped in and took the friend's side. Relate the discussion to the interference of the West in the Taiping Rebellion.

Remind students that China was an isolated country. It refused to deal with foreigners. Have them read this lesson to find out how the United States began trading with this country.

Ask:

- Which countries interfered in the Taiping Rebellion? (Great Britain, the United States, and other Western nations)

- Why did the West interfere in the Taiping Rebellion? (They were afraid of losing their trade rights with China if the Manchus were overthrown.)

- Who was Sun Yatsen? (a Chinese doctor who led the revolution and overthrew the Manchu empire)

Background Information

China's Taiping Rebellion was an example of foreign interference changing the course of a nation's history. In 1851, Chinese peasants rebelled against the ruling Manchus. The Manchu rulers had been greedy and cruel. The peasants' cause was a just one, and their rebellion was strong. They might have won their fight, but foreign powers became involved.

The Manchus had granted favorable trade rights to many foreign countries. These foreign nations worried that if the Manchus were no longer in power, their trade rights might be endangered. The British government supported the Manchus. A British officer, Charles Gordon, earned the nickname "Chinese" Gordon leading the army that put down the peasants' revolt. When the rebellion ended in 1864, the Manchus were still in power.

Interference
Mixing in another's affairs without being asked

Open-Door Policy
The American approach to China around 1900 that allowed open trade relations between China and other nations

They called their rebellion *Taiping*, meaning "Great Peace." The Taiping Rebellion lasted from 1850 to 1864. Millions of lives were lost. When it was over, the Manchus still ruled China.

The peasants might have won their fight. They might have overthrown the Manchu government. Yet foreign **interference** worked against them. Western governments wanted to keep the Manchus in power. Western powers worried that they might lose their trade rights if the Manchus were overthrown. Great Britain, the United States, and other Western nations supported the Manchus. Western governments sent military help, and the peasants were defeated.

Why Did China Fight with Japan?

Next, the Manchus faced war with Japan. China had staked claims on Korea for hundreds of years. When a rebellion broke out in Korea in 1894, the Chinese sent troops in to crush it. Japan had interests in Korea, too. Japan also sent in its troops. The rebellion was put down. Then, neither Japan nor China would withdraw its troops. Instead, the two countries began fighting each other.

By April 1895, the Japanese had defeated the Chinese. China had to give up much of its claim on Korea. China also had to give the island of Taiwan to the Japanese. By 1910, Japan would take complete control of Korea.

The Chinese-Japanese war left China weak. From then on, Manchu rulers got little respect. The Manchus feared that European nations might step in and divide China into colonies. The United States suggested an **Open-Door Policy**. This meant that all countries would have equal rights to trade in China. The Manchus agreed to this policy. The Chinese had once kept everyone out. Now, they opened their ports to the world.

COMMON ERROR

Students might be confused by the title of the Chinese rebellion. The Taiping Rebellion, or the Great Peace, may seem a strange name to call a war. Explain that one of the main leaders of the Chinese revolt developed a unique brand of Christianity. He intended to set up a "Heavenly Kingdom of Peace" in China. The name of the rebellion can be traced to his beliefs.

The Boxer Rebellion

In 1898, the Manchu empress Cixi ruled the Qing dynasty. She was very old-fashioned. She wanted to stop any change in China. Perhaps she remembered China's glorious past. If she had her way, she would keep China the way it was.

Then something happened in 1900, during the empress's reign. A group of Chinese rebelled against all foreigners in China. The revolt was called the Boxer Rebellion. And the empress Cixi secretly supported the rebels.

The Boxers were members of a secret society. Westerners called them Boxers because they practiced Chinese exercises that resembled shadow-boxing. The Boxers attempted to kill all foreigners in China. They were put down by an international army that included soldiers from the United States.

China was forced to make payments to the foreign countries to make up for the rebellion. However, the United States used much of the money it received to educate Chinese students. Because of this, the United States won China's favor.

How Did China Move Into the Modern World?

The Qing dynasty would be the last dynasty to rule China. Rebellions had weakened the government. The war with Japan had cost China both land and power. Many foreign countries had interests in China now. In addition, the weak Manchus were unable to protect China against the foreigners. China needed a new government if it were to survive.

In 1911, a Chinese doctor named Sun Yatsen was in Denver, Colorado. He had been traveling throughout Japan, Europe, and the United States. He was trying to raise money to help overthrow the Manchu government. When he heard about sparks of revolution in China, he returned there. He led the revolution and overthrew the Manchu empire. On January 1, 1912, he became the first president of China's new republic. The last Manchu emperor, Puyi, gave up the throne on February 12, 1912. He was only six years old at the time.

Visual/Spatial

Before students read about China's move into the modern world, have them locate China on a globe. Ask questions that will help students understand China's place in the world. Questions might include the following: *What natural borders helped China remain isolated for so long? What countries border China? What countries are near China? How big is China compared to other countries of the world? How might imperialism affect a country as big as China?*

ONLINE CONNECTION

Students can gain additional information by accessing the following Web site: www. agsglobepmwh.com/page463 (This Web site offers a first-hand account of the rebellion written by Fei Ch'i-hao, a Chinese Christian who was friends with several foreigners.)

LEARNING STYLES

Auditory/Verbal

To give auditory learners a deeper understanding of the culture of the Far East, bring in a recording of Chinese or Japanese music. You can also ask a native speaker to visit the class and read a selection of his or her choosing in Chinese or Japanese. If you have students from China or Japan, give them the opportunity to address the class in their native tongue.

LEARN MORE ABOUT IT

Ask students to create a chart showing the sequence of events that led to the Boxer Rebellion. Students should write a title for the chart. Each event should be listed in chronological order. Students can use arrows showing how one event led to the next.

ELL/ESL STRATEGY

Language Objective:
To summarize text

After ELL students have read this lesson, draw a Venn diagram on the board. Have students copy the diagram in their notebooks. Model how to label the sections in the diagram using the following phases: *Qing Dynasty, Both,* and *Chinese Nationalists.* Then have students compare and contrast the Qing dynasty and the Chinese Nationalists by listing details in the appropriate sections of the diagram. Ask students to use their completed Venn diagrams to write a summary of the lesson. Students may wish to use the following topic sentence: *The Qing dynasty was different from the Chinese Nationalists because . . .*

3 Reinforce and Extend

History Fact

Have students explain why some people are referred to as the father or mother of a historical event. Have the class realize that these people played exceptionally crucial roles in the events in questions. In fact, the events might not have occurred if the people did not exist.

Reading Strategy:
Summarizing

Point out the strategy for summarizing on page 461 and have them complete the activity. Then lead a class discussion on the main idea, details, and student questions. Have them compare their questions. (Answers will vary. Students may say the outcome of the Taiping Rebellion, the terms of the Open-Door Policy, the outcome of the Boxer Rebellion, the overthrow of the Manchu dynasty, or the events that led to the rise of the Nationalist Party.)

TIMELINE STUDY

Answer: 267 years

History Fact
In China, Sun Yatsen is called "the father of the Revolution."

Reading Strategy:
Summarizing

What are the most important details that helped you understand this lesson?

Yatsen's term as president was short, less than two months. Then a strong military officer, Yuan Shikai, took over. Yatsen and his followers remained. They organized the Nationalist Party. For years the Chinese people suffered under harsh rulers who fought each other for power.

By 1922, the republic had failed and civil war was widespread. With the support of the Soviet Union and of Chinese Communists, Yatsen and his Nationalist Party trained an army. They set out to bring China together under a Nationalist government.

Sun Yatsen died in 1925, but his work was finished by Chiang Kai-shek. By 1928, Chiang was able to set up a Nationalist government in China.

More days of war and revolution were ahead. However, China had left its great dynasties behind and moved into the modern world.

TIMELINE STUDY: CHINA: 1600–1950

How long did the Qing dynasty last?

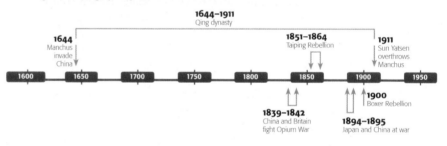

On a sheet of paper, write the answer to each question. Use complete sentences.

1. Why did the Chinese peasants rebel against the Manchus from 1850 to 1864?

2. What factors led to the Manchu victory over the peasants?

3. China was forced to make payments to make up for the Boxer Rebellion. What did the United States do with the money?

4. How did Sun Yatsen put an end to the Manchu rule in China?

On a sheet of paper, write the letter of the answer that correctly completes each sentence.

5. China and Japan fought for control of _____.

A Korea   **B** Taiwan   **C** Japan   **D** Hong Kong

6. The _____ gave all countries equal rights to trade with China.

A Taiping Rebellion   **C** Open-Door Policy
B Boxer Rebellion   **D** Treaty of Nanjing

7. The _____ was when a group of Chinese rebelled against all foreigners in China.

A interference   **C** Taiping Rebellion
B civil war   **D** Boxer Rebellion

8. _____ overthrew Sun Yatsen after less than two months as president.

A Puyi   **B** Cixi   **C** Chiang Kai-shek   **D** Yuan Shikai

9. Yatsen and his followers organized the _____.

A republic   **C** Boxer Rebellion
B Nationalist Party   **D** Taiping Rebellion

10. By _____, China had a Nationalist government.

A 1912   **B** 1922   **C** 1925   **D** 1928

1600–1950   *Imperialism and the Far East*   *Chapter 22*   **465**

Ask:

- How many years did the Taiping Rebellion last? (13 years)
- What year did the Boxer Rebellion begin? (1900)
- What came first: the war between China and Britain or the war between China and Japan? (The war between China and Britain started in 1839. The war between China and Japan started in 1894. So, the war between China and Britain came first.)

Lesson 22–2 Review Answers

1. The Chinese farmers were not happy under Manchu rule. Most farmers were very poor and the rulers were greedy and unfair. **2.** Western governments sent military help to the Manchus because they worried that they might lose their trade rights if the Manchus were overthrown. **3.** The United States used much of the money China paid to educate Chinese students. In this way, the United States won China's favor. **4.** Sun Yatsen traveled in an attempt to raise money to help overthrow the Manchu government. However, when he heard about the beginnings of rebellion in China, he returned. He led the revolution and overthrew the Manchu empire. He became the first president of China's new republic. **5.** A **6.** C **7.** D **8.** D **9.** B **10.** D

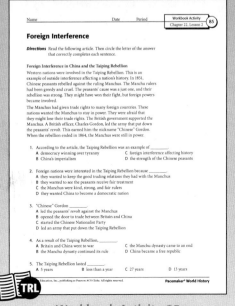

Activity 85   Workbook Activity 85

Lesson at a Glance

Chapter 22 Lesson 3

Overview This lesson traces Japan's transition from an isolated nation to an imperialistic power.

Objectives

- To tell how Commodore Matthew C. Perry opened the doors of trade to Japan
- To list the ways Japan modernized after a powerful emperor took over in 1867
- To explain how Japan's industrialization led to Japanese imperialism

Student Pages 466–470

Teacher's Resource Library

Workbook Activity 86

Activity 86

Modified Activity 86

1 Warm-Up Activity

Have students discuss the idea of change. What is good about holding onto traditional ways? What is good about embracing new ways of doing things? Relate the discussion to the rift that developed in Japan between people who clung to the past and people who demanded change.

Reading Strategy:
Summarizing

Both Commodore Matthew C. Perry and Townsend Harris are introduced in this lesson. Have students summarize how Perry convinced Japan to open its ports to U.S. ships. (Perry brought big ships and guns to Japan. This show of might impressed high-ranking officials. Perry himself also impressed Japanese rulers during negotiations.)

LESSON 22-3

Japan Opens Its Doors

Objectives

- To tell how Commodore Matthew C. Perry opened the doors of trade to Japan
- To list the ways Japan modernized after a powerful emperor took over in 1867
- To explain how Japan's industrialization led to Japanese imperialism

Reading Strategy:
Summarizing

What American is introduced in this lesson?

After 1600, Japan had become an isolated nation. The whole country was under the rule of the Tokugawa family. Foreign trade and travel were not allowed. Japan did not allow foreign products to enter its ports. Japan did not send any products to other lands either. Japan would not accept visitors from other countries. In fact, if a foreign seaman were shipwrecked on Japan's shores, he was in for trouble. He could be arrested or even killed.

How Did Commodore Perry Get Japan to Open Its Ports to Trade?

In 1853, an American naval officer, Commodore Matthew C. Perry, changed all that. Commodore Perry sailed four U.S. warships into Tokyo Bay. He brought a letter from the U.S. president. The letter asked the Japanese to change their policies. It asked for better treatment of any shipwrecked American sailors. It asked that American whaling ships be allowed to buy supplies at Japanese ports. It asked that Japan agree to trade with the United States.

The Japanese were impressed by Perry and his U.S. ships. They had never seen such large vessels or such mighty guns. Perry was a stern man. He met the Japanese with dignity. He refused to speak to anyone except the highest officials. Perry left his requests for the Japanese to consider.

The next year, Commodore Perry returned to Japan. This time, he brought even more ships. The ruling shogun spoke with Perry. Then the Japanese ruler signed a treaty with the United States. Japanese ports would be open to U.S. ships. It was the beginning of a new Japan.

466 *Unit 8 The Age of Imperialism*

2 Teaching the Lesson

Remind students that the Chinese also called their treaties with the West the "Unequal Treaties." As students read this lesson, have them look for other similarities to the West's interactions with Japan and China.

Ask:

- For how many years was Japan an isolated nation? (254 years)

- What were two different opinions about the West in Japan? (Some wanted to drive the foreigners out of Japan; others wanted to accept the West and learn from it.)

- Why was the Russo-Japanese War important for Japan? (For the first time, an Asian nation proved to be stronger than a European nation.)

Commodore Matthew C. Perry arrives in Tokyo in 1853 and is greeted by Japanese officials.

How Did Mutsuhito Modernize Japan?

In 1858, Townsend Harris, a U.S. diplomat, signed a more extensive treaty with Japan. That same year, Japan signed trade treaties with Great Britain, France, the Netherlands, and Russia. Japan was no longer an isolated nation.

Then came years of change. Japan was torn between its old ways and the new. Some Japanese wanted to drive the foreigners out of Japan again. They said the treaties Japan had signed were Unequal Treaties. Others wanted to accept the Western world and learn what they could. They realized that their feudal system of government was outdated. The rule of the shoguns with their samurai warriors had to end.

You Decide
Why do you think some Japanese considered the treaties to be "unequal"?

You Decide

Lead a class discussion in which students describe how they might have felt if they had lived in Japan during 1858, when Japan signed trade treaties with five countries. Ask if they would have wanted these trade treaties and why.

Background Information

Matthew Perry joined the navy at 16. He believed that the American navy could do more than simply fight wars. He believed the navy could help American trade.

In 1853, Commodore Matthew Perry arrived in Japan looking proud and sure of himself. He made it clear that his men were ready for military action. However, he also made it clear that he came as a friend. Perry refused to deal with anyone but the highest officials of the emperor. He left a letter from U.S. President Millard Fillmore and promised to return.

In February 1854, Perry was back in Japan. He came with gifts for the emperor. He brought American clocks, tools, books, plows, miniature train, stove, electric telegraphs, and telescopes. He even brought a kitchen sink.

The gifts impressed the emperor. On March 31, 1854, the emperor agreed to sign a treaty with the United States. Perry's expedition had opened the doors to Japan. It unlocked Japan's ports for trade with the United States. It also welcomed Japan into the modern world.

LEARNING STYLES

Interpersonal/Group Learning

The media includes people who report, write, and broadcast news for newspapers, radio, television, and the Internet. It has a great deal of influence on people's opinions. Ask students to work in small groups to find examples from newspapers and news magazines that imply that a country's actions are imperialistic. Suggest that groups look for opinion pieces, such as editorials, political cartoons, or columns. Photographs, headlines, and articles may also show examples of imperialism. Students should make copies of each feature. Have the groups work together to create a news magazine made of their features.

Refer ELL students to the timeline on page 469. Have them use index cards and different-colored pens to write the title and events on the timeline. Suggest that students use one color for the title, and a different color for the important events listed on the timeline. Each event should be listed on a separate card. Students should use a third color to represent details about the events. The details should also be listed on separate cards. Working in pairs, have students place the cards face down on a table. They should take turns selecting one card, and explaining how it relates to the timeline. For example, the card with the title tells the reader what the timeline is about.

3   Reinforce and Extend

COMMON ERROR

Students might think that the influence of the samurai disappeared in Japan following the end of shogun rule. Tell them that the samurai code of honor remained a part of Japanese life. The idea of dying for honor still existed during World War II, when young Japanese soldiers called *kamikazes* crashed their planes, loaded with bombs, into Allied ships.

In 1867, a young emperor named Mutsuhito came to power. He and his followers began to modernize Japan. Their motto was, "Knowledge shall be sought throughout the world." The emperor adopted *Meiji* as his title, which means "enlightened rule." He was to rule Japan until 1912. These years are known as the Meiji period. The Japanese traveled to other nations. They wanted to learn what they could about industry, education, transportation, and banking. They built thousands of schools and they invited foreigners to teach in Japan.

In 1889, Japan's first constitution was written. The Japanese still considered their emperor to be godlike. The emperor still held the power, but he accepted advice from elected representatives.

By the 1890s, Japan was keeping step with the modern world. Japan had done away with the samurai and now had a modern army and navy. Japan had steel mills, shipyards, and electrical power plants. In just over 25 years, Japan had made amazing progress. It had gone from an isolated, feudal nation to one of the world's industrial powers.

Reading Strategy:
Summarizing

What are some of the
ways in which Japan
changed during this time
in history?

What Brought About Japanese Imperialism?

As industry grew, Japan needed more raw materials. Like many strong nations, Japan decided to set up overseas colonies to supply those raw materials. However, gaining such colonies meant war.

From 1894 to 1895, Japan was at war with China. China and Japan had a strong difference of opinion over the control of Korea. Japan, with its new, modern military, easily defeated China, and took the island of Taiwan.

In 1904, Russia tried to stake claims in Korea. Japan declared war. The Russo-Japanese War was costly to both sides, but the war was over in 1905. Again the Japanese were the victors. Japan took over some lands in China that had been controlled by Russia. And in 1910, Japan took complete control of Korea. Japan's victory over Russia surprised the world. For the first time, an Asian nation had proved to be stronger than a European nation. And this was to be only the first chapter in the story of Japanese imperialism.

TIMELINE STUDY:

JAPAN: 1600–1950

From 1600 to 1854, Japan remained a relatively quiet country. Why are there few events on the timeline?

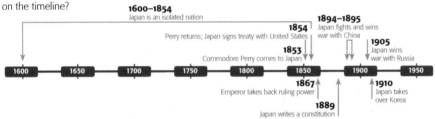

1600–1854
Japan is an isolated nation

1854
Perry returns; Japan signs treaty with United States

1853
Commodore Perry comes to Japan

1894–1895
Japan fights and wins war with China

1905
Japan wins war with Russia

1867
Emperor takes back ruling power

1910
Japan takes over Korea

1889
Japan writes a constitution

1600 | 1650 | 1700 | 1750 | 1800 | 1850 | 1900 | 1950

1600–1950

Imperialism and the Far East   Chapter 22   **469**

TIMELINE STUDY

Answer: Japan was isolated.

Ask:

- What happened in 1854? (Perry returned to Japan. Japan signed a treaty with the United States.)
- How many years was the war between Japan and China? (2 years)
- What year did Japan take over Korea? (1910)

IN THE COMMUNITY

 Have students go to local stores and make a list of 10 items made in Japan and China. Ask students to share their list with the class. As they read their lists, make a master list on the board. Afterwards, discuss how life would be different if we did not trade with these countries.

TEACHER ALERT

Direct students' attention to the illustration on page 467 and the timeline on page 469. Tell them that visuals such as illustrations, timelines, photographs, graphs, and tables help clarify content in the text. Ask them how the illustration of Perry's arrival in Tokyo helps them better understand this lesson. (Answers will vary. Students might say that the illustration shows the dignified and impressive manner in which Perry approached the Japanese rulers.)

WORLD CULTURES

 In Japan, tea ceremonies began in the 1400s. The ceremonies, which continue today, include rules that have evolved over time. The participants include a host and guests. They sit in a small room adorned with flowers and a hanging scroll. The host prepares the tea with great care, and then places the tea bowl before an honored guest. The guest sips the tea, complements the host on the tea's flavor, then passes the bowl to the next guest. The bowl is passed from guest to guest until it returns full circle to the host.

Reading Strategy:
Summarizing

As students read the lesson, have them make a list. Encourage them to use specific language. After the lesson, you may have students share their lists with the class.

Lesson 22–3 Review Answers

1. Commodore Perry sailed four U.S. warships into Tokyo Bay with a letter from the U.S. President. The letter asked Japan to change its policies. It wanted shipwrecked American sailors to be treated better, American whaling ships to be allowed to buy Japanese supplies in their ports, and Japan to agree to trade with the United States. A year later, Japan agreed and signed a treaty. **2.** As Japan's industry grew, so did its need for raw materials. To supply the need for raw materials, Japan set up overseas colonies. **3.** Japan declared war on Russia when they tried to stake claims in Korea. **4.** isolated **5.** treaties **6.** Mutsuhito **7.** Meiji **8.** constitution **9.** Taiwan **10.** Korea

REVIEW

On a sheet of paper, write the answer to each question. Use complete sentences.

1. How did Commodore Matthew C. Perry open the doors of trade to Japan?

2. Why did Japan need more raw materials and how did it solve that problem?

3. Why did Japan declare war on Russia?

On a sheet of paper, write the word from the Word Bank to complete each sentence correctly.

Word Bank

constitution
Korea
Meiji
Mutsuhito
isolated
Taiwan
treaties

4. Japan remained _____ after 1600, forbidding trade and foreign visitors.

5. Some Japanese thought the _____ they signed with other nations were good. Others thought they were unequal.

6. The emperor _____ worked to modernize Japan.

7. The emperor adopted _____ as his title, meaning "enlightened rule."

8. Japan's first _____ was written in 1889.

9. Japan won the island of _____ from China in 1895.

10. Japan took complete control of _____ by 1910.

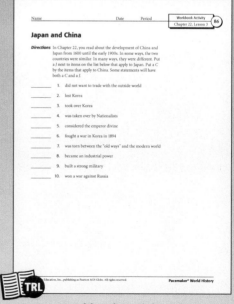

Activity 86   Workbook Activity 86

- The Manchus conquered China in 1644 and established the Qing dynasty.

- The Manchus tried to limit foreign trade in China.

- By the late 1700s, the population of China had grown too large for its food supply.

- Europeans started smuggling opium into China.

- Great Britain went to war against China for better trading rights.

- As a result of a treaty signed in 1842, China opened five ports to British trade. China had to give the island of Hong Kong to the British.

- Chinese peasants rebelled in the Taiping Rebellion of 1851. The rebellion was put down by the Manchus and the Westerners.

- Disagreements over claims to Korea led to a war between Japan and China. Eventually Japan gained control of all of Korea.

- The United States persuaded China to have an Open-Door Policy toward foreign trade.

- In 1900, the Boxers tried to drive foreigners out of China. They were crushed by foreign armies.

- In 1911, Chinese Nationalists overthrew the Manchus and ended dynasty rule in China.

- In 1853, Commodore Perry negotiated trade treaties with Japan.

- In 1867, a young emperor began to modernize Japan. It became a powerful industrial nation in just over 25 years.

- To gain raw materials, Japan began to practice imperialism. This led to costly wars with China and Russia.

Chapter 22 Summary

Have students read the Chapter Summary on page 471 to review the main ideas presented in Chapter 22.

Ask:

- What dynasty did the Manchus establish? (the Qing dynasty)

- What did the Manchus try to limit in China? (foreign trade)

- Why did China and Great Britain go to war? (Great Britain wanted better trading rights.)

- What were the terms of the treaty of 1842? (China opened five ports to British trade. China gave Britain the island of Hong Kong.)

- Why did Japan and China go to war? (over claims to Korea)

- How did dynasty rule end in China? (The Chinese Nationalists overthrew the Manchus in 1911.)

- Who negotiated trade treaties with Japan in 1853? (Commodore Perry)

- How long did it take Japan to become an industrial nation? (25 years)

CHAPTER PROJECT FOLLOW-UP

Have two of the student groups who worked cooperatively to forge a treaty come to the front of the class. Ask a representative from each group to present the terms of the treaty to the class. Then have the groups sit at a table and sign the treaty. Assess students' work on historical accuracy, ability to work cooperatively, and presentation.

TEACHER'S RESOURCE

The AGS Globe Teaching Strategies in Social Studies Transparencies may be used with this chapter. The transparencies add an interactive dimension to expand and enhance the Pacemaker® *World History* program content.

Chapter 22 Review

Use the Chapter Review to prepare students for tests and to reteach content from the chapter.

Chapter 22 Mastery Test

The Teacher's Resource Library includes two forms of the Chapter 22 Mastery Test. Each test addresses the chapter Goals for Learning. An optional third page of additional critical-thinking items is included for each test. The difficulty level of the two forms is equivalent.

Chapter 22 Review Answers

Vocabulary Review

1. interference

2. addicted

3. smuggle

4. Open-Door Policy

5. policy

Chapter Review Questions

6. The Manchu dynasty was known as the Qing dynasty.

7. The Manchus thought they were better than other Chinese.

8. The Chinese made the opium trade illegal because so many Chinese were becoming addicted to the drug. Not only was the drug dangerous, but the trading of the drug went against China's isolationist policies.

9. The Treaty of Nanjing was the first of what the Chinese called the Unequal Treaties.

10. The Manchus defeated the peasants because Western governments sent them military help.

11. The Chinese were afraid that if they did not agree to the Open-Door Policy, the European nations might divide China into colonies.

12. Sun Yatsen led the revolution that overthrew the Manchus. He then went on to become the first president of China's new republic.

Word Bank

addicted

interference

Open-Door Policy

policy

smuggle

Vocabulary Review

On a sheet of paper, use the words from the Word Bank to complete each sentence correctly.

1. Foreign _____ during the Taiping Rebellion in China may have changed the outcome of the uprising.

2. A person who is _____ to something must work hard to break the habit.

3. If you _____ goods into a country, they are not legal in that country.

4. The _____ gave all countries equal rights to trade with China.

5. A nation's foreign _____ determines the way the nation acts toward other nations.

Chapter Review Questions

On a sheet of paper, write the answer to each question. Use complete sentences.

6. What was the Manchu dynasty called?

7. How did the Manchus feel about other Chinese?

8. Why did the Chinese pass a law making opium trade illegal?

9. What was the Treaty of Nanjing known as?

10. Who won the Taiping Rebellion: the peasants or the Manchus? Why?

11. Why did the Manchus agree to the Open-Door Policy?

12. Who helped put an end to Manchu rule in China?

472 Unit 8 *The Age of Imperialism*

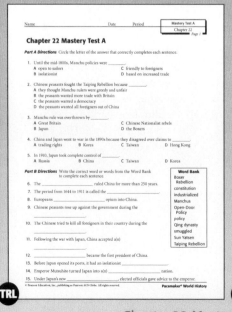

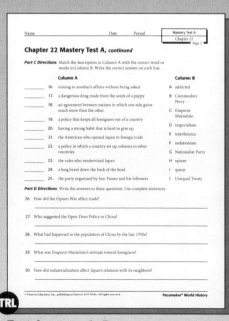

Chapter 22 Mastery Test A, pages 1–3

To answer a multiple-choice question, read every choice before you answer the question. Cross out the choices you know are wrong. Then choose the best answer from the remaining choices.

13. Who was the American naval officer who got Japan to sign a trade treaty?

14. How did Emperor Mutsuhito help to change Japan?

15. Why was Japan's victory over Russia so surprising to the world?

Critical Thinking

On a sheet of paper, write your response to each question. Use complete sentences.

16. Why did the dynasties come to an end in China?

17. Why did Japan become an imperialist nation?

Using the Timelines

Use the timelines on pages 464 and 469 to answer the questions.

18. What is the topic of each timeline?

19. How many years did the Taiping Rebellion last?

20. What happened in China one year after Japan took over Korea?

GROUP ACTIVITY

With a partner, create a large timeline that shows events in both China and Japan. Display the timeline on a wall of your classroom.

---

13. Commodore Matthew C. Perry got Japan to open its ports to U.S. ships.

14. Mutsuhito modernized Japan. He encouraged travel, industry, education, transportation, and banking. Under his rule, Japan's first constitution was written.

15. It was the first time that an Asian nation proved to be stronger than a European nation.

Critical Thinking

16. Possible answer: The Manchus were weakened by war and rebellions. Foreigners had interests in China, and the Manchus could not protect China against them.

17. Possible answer: Japan became imperialistic because it had few raw materials and it needed them for industry.

Using the Timelines

18. China: 1600–1950; Japan: 1600–1950

19. 13 years

20. Sun Yatsen overthrew the Manchus.

GROUP ACTIVITY

Students' timelines should combine events from the two timelines in the chapter. Encourage students to find additional events in encyclopedias and other books.

Chapter 22 Mastery Test B, pages 1–3

Introducing the Chapter

Remind students that they studied India in Chapter 15. Have them review their charts of changes in religion during the Mogul reign. Discuss how they think control of India would change from the Moguls to the present.

Ask:

- Why did the Mogul Empire break up? (Aurangzeb persecuted the Hindus, who made up most of the population in India. They revolted and weakened the empire.)

- Why were the British in India in the 1600s? (to pursue trade opportunities)

Imperialism and India

The situation in India during this time was far different from that of China and Japan. India had established strong trading ties with Europe for many years. Many Europeans had come to feel comfortable in India in various areas of trade. They had become quite powerful.

Like the native people of the Americas, the people of India wanted freedom from European control. They did not want to see their own culture taken over by another, especially the British. One man named Gandhi helped the people gain power using some very different methods.

GOALS FOR LEARNING

- To describe India after the fall of the Mogul Empire
- To explain the path of British rule in India
- To identify Mahatma Gandhi, and tell what was different about his way of revolution

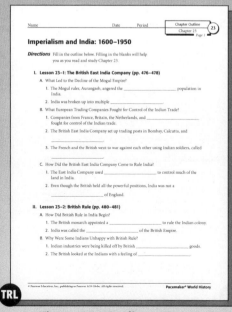

Reading Strategy: Questioning

You will understand and remember more information if you ask yourself questions as you read. As you read, ask yourself:

- What is my reason for reading this text?
- What connections can I make between this text and my own life, or something I have read before?

Key Vocabulary Words

Lesson 1

Agent A person who has the authority to act for some other person or company

Impose To force one's ideas or wishes on another

Indirectly In a roundabout way

Cartridge A small metal or cardboard tube that holds gunpowder and a bullet

Lesson 2

Superiority A feeling of being better than others

Lesson 3

Nonviolent resistance The act of opposing or working against without using force or causing injury

Civil disobedience The refusal to obey rules, orders, or laws

Fast To go without food

- How did Indian religions affect British rule? (They sparked the Sepoy Rebellion. British efforts to convert Indians to Christianity alienated many people.)

Reading Strategy: Questioning

Have students page through the chapter, noting the questions that divide the text in each lesson. Point out that the questions provide a reason for reading the text. The question in bold lettering should be answered after reading each section. Explain that a good study technique is to write the question in a notebook, read the section, and then write the answer. Explain that the same technique can be used with new vocabulary words.

Key Vocabulary Words

Point out that these chapter words are presented in the order they appear in each lesson. They are also found in the glossary.

LIFE SKILLS CONNECTION

Students learn about income tax and filing taxes. Help students find information about income tax on government Web sites.

KEY VOCABULARY

Students choose the correct word from the Word Bank to complete each sentence.

TRL Life Skills Connection 23   **TRL** Key Vocabulary Words 23

Imperialism and India Chapter 23   **475**

The British East India Company

Lesson at a Glance

Chapter 23 Lesson 1

Overview This lesson describes the events that led to British control of India.

Objectives

- To tell how the British East India Company came to rule India
- To explain how the Sepoy Rebellion began and how it led to direct British rule

Student Pages 476–479

Teacher's Resource Library

Workbook Activity 87

Activity 87

Modified Activity 87

Vocabulary

agent	impose
cartridge	indirectly

On the board, write each vocabulary word with the letters scrambled. Read aloud a definition and ask a volunteer to unscramble the letters of the matching word. Continue until all the words have been unscrambled.

PRONUNCIATION GUIDE

Use this list to help students pronounce difficult words in this lesson.

Aurangzeb (ôr´ əng zeb´)

Vasco da Gama (vas´ kō də gam´ə)

1 Warm-Up Activity

List these words on the board: *bandanna, bungalow, cot, khaki, loot, pajamas, sandal, veranda.* Ask students what they have in common. (All were adopted into English from Indian languages.) Ask students if they know of other adoptions of Indian words and add them to the list.

Objectives

- To tell how the British East India Company came to rule India
- To explain how the Sepoy Rebellion began and how it led to direct British rule

Reading Strategy: Questioning

What do you think you will learn about by reading this lesson?

Reading Strategy: Questioning

Have students answer the question. Ask them how they arrived at their answer.

Aurangzeb, the last powerful Mogul emperor, died in 1707. The Moguls had ruled India for almost 200 years. Aurangzeb, a Muslim, had been a harsh ruler. He had angered the Hindus by destroying many of their temples. He had tried to force non-Muslims to convert to Islam.

After the death of Aurangzeb, the Mogul Empire began to break up. Once again, India was divided into small kingdoms. The rajas of the different kingdoms quarreled with one another. The Mogul rulers no longer had any real power.

As the Moguls weakened, stronger countries saw their chance. Europeans would take advantage of the unsteady government in India.

What European Trading Companies Fought for Control of the Indian Trade?

Trading between Europe and India had been going on for a long time. In 1498, the Portuguese explorer Vasco da Gama reached India by sailing around Africa. From that time on, European merchants made regular voyages to India. Dutch, Portuguese, French, and British traders fought each other for control of Indian trade.

In 1600, a private business called the British East India Company was formed. Its purpose was to trade with India. It set up trading posts along India's coastline at Bombay, Calcutta, and Madras. At around this time, the Dutch East India Company was formed. It began operating out of Java, in Indonesia.

The Europeans gained little in India as long as the Mogul Empire was strong. But by the mid-1700s, there was no

CHAPTER PROJECT

Ask students to imagine that they are Indian students in Great Britain in the 1880s. How would they feel about British rule in India? What would it be like to return to India in the midst of the changes taking place at the time? Have groups of students write a skit in which Indian students express their feelings about British rule. Tell them that their skit may be chosen for a class performance to wrap up the chapter.

Agent
A person who has the authority to act for some other person or company

Impose
To force one's ideas or wishes on another

Indirectly
In a roundabout way

longer a strong central government in India. The British East India Company became involved in what went on in that country. It took sides in Indian civil wars. And it supported rulers who gave it favorable trade rights.

After the French began the French East India Company, the British went to war with the French. In 1757, Robert Clive led the British to victory against the French. Both Clive's army and the French army used Indian soldiers to fight their war. The Indian soldiers were called *sepoys*. The British drove the French out of India. After that, the British East India Company became a powerful force in India.

How Did the British East India Company Come to Rule India?

Soon, **agents** of the East India company became stronger than the local rajas. An agent is a person who has the authority to act for some other person or company. By 1850, the British agents controlled more than half of the land in India. The British put their own men into all the important positions. The British led sepoy armies. They became wealthy landholders.

The British **imposed,** or forced, their own ways on Indian society. They built Christian churches and spoke out

As ruler of Britain, Queen Victoria was eventually named empress of India.

against the Hindu caste system. Many of the Indians did not like the English ways. They did not like the East India Company either. For almost 100 years, Britain **indirectly** ruled India through the British East India Company. India was not officially a British colony, but the British held all the power.

Have students keep a two-column chart of changes to India and to Great Britain as they are described in the lesson. Have them draw connecting lines to show how one affected the other.

Ask:

- How did the East India Company get control of India? (It began by taking sides in Indian civil wars and supporting Indian rulers who gave it favorable trade rights.)
- Why did Great Britain and France go to war in 1757? (to determine who would control trade with India)
- What was the significance of the Sepoy Rebellion? (It convinced the government that the British East India Company couldn't be trusted with control of India.)

Background Information

As the Mogul Empire weakened, pockets of instability arose. In taking sides in local conflicts, European trading companies became involved in Indian politics and government. Eventually, the British East India Company took control, and started to rule parts of India. At first, Indian institutions were left in place, but the British were urging "improvements" in them by the end of the 18th century.

TEACHER ALERT

This chapter is a fine opportunity to discuss the unequal treatment of people. Some sources for the British feelings of superiority are described in the text. Point out that democracy ideally supports the equality of each person under the law. Imperialism often elicits or reinforces feelings of superiority, as the colonial people do not have rights equal to the ruling class.

ELL/ESL Strategy

Language Objective:
To compare cultures, using a Venn diagram

Ask students to read "Learn More About It: The Sepoy Rebellion" on page 478. Have students create their own Venn diagram, labeling the sections "The Sepoys," "Both," and "The British." If students are not familiar with Venn diagrams, model a simple example for them. Have students compare the Sepoys to the British, using the Venn diagram. Ask students to use their completed Venn diagrams to write a summary about the differences between the Sepoys and the British. They should start their topic sentence with "The Sepoys were different from the British because…"

Common Error

People sometimes think that all Indians are vegetarians. Although Hindus don't eat beef and Muslims don't eat pork, they may eat meat of other sorts.

Reading Strategy:
Questioning

(Possible answer: How does this connect with something I've read before?)

Learn More About It

Propose this headline to the class: Soldiers Refuse to Bite the Bullet. Ask students to write a short news article to fit the headline.

Cartridge
A small metal or cardboard tube that holds gunpowder and a bullet

Reading Strategy:
Questioning

As you read, notice the details in the text. What questions can you ask yourself about these details?

Learn More About It

The Sepoy Rebellion

To protect their own power, the East India agents from Britain built up armies of sepoys. Most of the British army officers did not try to understand Indian customs and culture. They insisted that the Indians accept British ways.

The sepoys grumbled about this. Then, in 1857, the British started using a new kind of bullet in India. To open the **cartridge,** a soldier had to bite off its end. A cartridge is the small metal or cardboard tube that holds gunpowder and a bullet. The new cartridges were greased with the fat from cows and pigs. The Muslim religion does not allow its followers to eat pork. Hindus are not allowed to eat the meat of a cow. Therefore, the sepoys refused to bite the bullets. When British officers ordered them to bite open the cartridges, the sepoys rebelled.

The British put down the Sepoy Rebellion in 1858. Many lives were lost in the battle. Britain saw that the East India Company could no longer be trusted with control of India.

Sepoys rebelled after they were ordered to bite bullets that were greased with animal fat.

On a sheet of paper, write the letter of the answer that correctly completes each sentence.

1. Europeans saw a chance to profit as the _____ power weakened.

   A sepoy   **B** Mogul   **C** trading   **D** Hindu

2. In 1600, the British East India Company was formed to _____.

   A get more soldiers for Britain   **C** trade with India
   B get more land from India   **D** convert Indians to Catholicism

3. By the mid-1700s, India no longer had a strong central _____.

   A religion   **B** government   **C** army   **D** trade route

4. At this time, the _____ became very involved with what went on in India.

   A sepoys   **C** French East India Company
   B Dutch East India Company   **D** British East India Company

5. Defeating _____ made the British East India Company powerful in India.

   A the French East India Company   **C** the Indians
   B the Dutch East India Company   **D** Clive's army

6. For almost _____ years, Britain indirectly ruled India.

   A 50   **B** 100   **C** 150   **D** 200

7. An Indian soldier is called a _____.

   A Bombay   **B** raja   **C** sepoy   **D** Java

8. The _____ imposed their ways and customs on Indian society.

   A British   **B** French   **C** Dutch   **D** sepoys

9. It went against the sepoys' _____ to bite the bullets greased with animal fat.

   A laws   **B** customs   **C** ways   **D** religion

10. Britain realized that the East India Company could not handle _____ India.

    A trade with   **B** control of   **C** treaties with   **D** war with

3   **Reinforce and Extend**

CAREER CONNECTION

In the 1700s the British East Indian Trading Company sold Indian silks throughout the world. That industry continues today as part of a larger textile industry. Workers in almost every country manufacture textiles. In developing nations such as India and Pakistan, many workers weave fabrics in their homes. In highly industrialized nations, textiles are produced in factories. Workers with specialized training supervise the process and run machinery. The textile industry provides many jobs for both skilled and unskilled workers. Have students research the requirements for beginning a career in the textile industry.

Lesson 23–1 Review Answers
1. B **2.** C **3.** B **4.** D **5.** A **6.** B **7.** C **8.** A **9.** D **10.** B

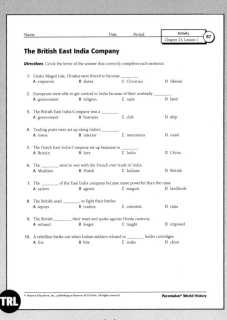

Activity 87

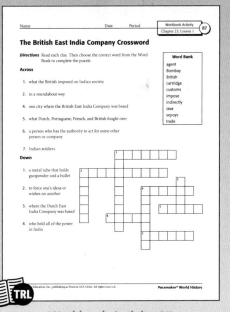

Workbook Activity 87

Imperialism and India Chapter 23   **479**

Chapter 23 Lesson 2

Overview This lesson describes India under British rule and why the Indians wanted independence.

Objectives

■ To list five good things Britain did for India

■ To explain why many Indians were unhappy with British rule

■ To tell of the turning point in British-Indian relations

Student Pages 480–482

Teacher's Resource Library

Workbook Activity 88

Activity 88

Modified Activity 88

Vocabulary

superiority

Have students look up the word *superiority* in the dictionary. Ask them to list phrases that use *superiority* and *superior* and to identify what the phrases mean. Call on volunteers to write sentences on the board, using the vocabulary word.

PRONUNCIATION GUIDE

Use this list to help students pronounce difficult words in this lesson.

Amritsar (əm rĭt´sər)

1   Warm-Up Activity

Ask students to compare British imperialism in India with Spanish imperialism in Latin America (Chapter 20). Discuss the ways the imperial powers gained control, as well as the attitudes of the imperial powers toward the native-born people. Have them compare the reactions of the native peoples to their rulers.

LESSON 23-2   British Rule

Objectives

■ To list five good things Britain did for India

■ To explain why many Indians were unhappy with British rule

■ To tell of the turning point in British-Indian relations

Reading Strategy: Questioning

What do the details of this section tell you about a likely outcome?

Superiority
A feeling of being better than others

Remember
In China the Manchus looked down on the rest of the people. In 1912, the Manchus were overthrown.

In 1858, the British Parliament took over the rule of India. India became a colony of Great Britain. It was now called "British India," or the "British Raj."

A viceroy ran the colony. He was appointed by the British monarch. In 1877, the British held a splendid ceremony in India. On this occasion, Queen Victoria was named empress of India.

The British profited from their Indian colony. They called India the "Jewel of the British Empire." In turn, the British government tried to treat Indians more fairly than the British East India Company had.

The British tried to solve the problems of poverty that had always troubled India. They helped farmers dig irrigation canals. They set up hospitals in cities and in some villages. They built railroads and factories, roads and schools. The British tried to do away with the harsh caste system that kept many people so poor.

Why Were Some Indians Unhappy with British Rule?

Many Indians were still unhappy. Some were poorer than ever. India's raw materials were all going to British industry. Manufactured goods were brought in from Britain, killing off India's own industries. Machine-made cloth poured in from Britain. This resulted in Indian spinners and weavers being put out of work. Furthermore, all of India's top jobs went to the British.

It was clear to the Indians that the British looked down on them. The British did not allow Indians in their restaurants or hotels. It seemed that British imperialism encouraged British feelings of **superiority**.

---

2   Teaching the Lesson

Ask students to consider each benefit or problem from both the Indian and the British point of view as they read the lesson.

Ask:

● How did the British government try to improve the life of Indians? (It tried to solve poverty; helped farmers; set up hospitals; built railroads, factories, roads, and schools; and tried to soften the caste system.)

● What was the Indian National Congress? (a group made up of educated Indians who wanted a revolution)

● What happened at the Amritsar Massacre? (British troops fired on an unarmed crowd and killed nearly 400 Indians.)

Reading Strategy: Questioning

Review the factors that lead to a revolution. Then have students answer the Reading Strategy question. (Possible answer: Indians were unhappy with British rule, and that would lead to a revolution.)

Remember
The Manchus controlled China from 1644 to 1912.

As Europeans moved into India, they brought Western ideas with them. They built railroad stations, such as this one in Agra, Utter Pradesh, India.

Where Did Indians Get Ideas of Independence?

The British chose some Indian students to send off to school in Great Britain. They planned to give the students "English" ideas and training. The plan backfired. Once the students from India learned about English democracy, they wanted independence for their own people.

In 1885, a group called the Indian National Congress was founded. It was made up of educated Indians. They said they were meeting to improve relations with Britain. In truth, they were discussing revolution. In the early 1900s, there were some violent uprisings. The British always crushed them. To improve the situation, the British allowed a few Indians to be included in the government. A few years later, the British increased the number of Indians in the government. But the protests continued.

Reading Strategy:
Questioning

Think beyond the text. Consider your own thoughts and experiences as you read.

On April 13, 1919, British troops fired on an unarmed crowd in Amritsar. Nearly 400 Indians were killed, and at least 1,200 were wounded. The Amritsar Massacre marked a turning point in British-Indian relations. From then on, Indians knew what they could expect from the British. They were determined to keep fighting for independence. No real progress toward independence came until leadership went to a man called Gandhi.

Background Information

British construction of transportation and communication networks always seemed to work against British control of India, as well as for it. The roads and railroads were first built to improve military transport, but they also made civilian movement cheaper and faster. A network of good transportation provided better access to raw materials and to markets. Other British improvements, such as speedy postal service, connected even small villages all over India. This service and a telegraph system allowed better control of India, but it also allowed Indians to connect with each other easily and to organize resistance to British rule.

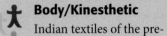

LEARNING STYLES

Body/Kinesthetic

Indian textiles of the pre-colonial days were spoken of in awe. Some of the more famous types of fabric were brocades, chintz, and very fine muslin. They were in great demand by the British people, whose government declared Indian fabrics contraband (illegal) in Great Britain in 1700. With students' help, collect samples of the type of fabrics India was famous for before their textile industry was gutted by British imports, as well as samples of fabrics produced now.

Reading Strategy:
Questioning

Point out that a question such as "how would I feel about Britain if I had been raised in its colony?" might be a good way to explore this lesson.

COMMON ERROR

Students may think that colonies never had industry, but produced only raw materials. Pre-colonial India had a thriving textile industry, which was destroyed when the British started manufacturing cloth from the raw cotton that India provided. Gandhi later encouraged spinning and making cloth so that India could once again supply its own clothing.

ELL/ESL STRATEGY

Language Objective:
To use context clues and a dictionary to learn vocabulary

Ask students to preview the lesson for three unfamiliar words or phrases and to write them on a sheet of paper. Once students have identified these words and phrases, ask them to use the context for clues to their meaning. If they still aren't sure what the words mean, have them use their dictionaries to define the words.

COMMON ERROR

There is no one "Indian" language. The many official languages include Kannada, Telugu, Tamil, and Malayalam. English is the official common language, a legacy from the British.

WORLD CULTURES

As of 2006, India made more movies than any other country in the world. Have students research Indian movies, find a movie that they want to rent, and watch it. After they watch the movie, have them make notes on how Bollywood (Indian) movies compare to Hollywood movies. Ask them to prepare a movie review.

Lesson 23–2 Review Answers

1. C **2.** C **3.** B **4.** A **5.** D **6.** B **7.** The British helped Indian farmers dig irrigation canals. The British set up hospitals. They built railroads, roads, factories, and schools. They tried to solve the problem of poverty. They tried to get rid of the caste system. **8.** Some Indians were poorer under British rule. All of India's raw materials were going to British industry, while India's own industries were dying. More people were out of work, especially when India's top jobs were given to the British. **9.** The Indian National Congress met to discuss revolution. **10.** The Amritsar Massacre was the turning point in British-Indian relations.

LESSON
23-2 REVIEW

On a sheet of paper, write the letter of the answer that correctly completes each sentence.

1. The British Parliament took control of India in 1858, making India a(n) _____ of Britain.

  A island   **B** republic   **C** colony   **D** supporter

2. The British monarch appointed a(n) _____ to run the colony.

  A raja   **B** empress   **C** viceroy   **D** queen

3. The British government tried to treat Indians more fairly than the _____ had.

  A French East India Company   **C** Dutch East India Company
  B British East India Company   **D** raja

4. The British _____ their hotels and restaurants.

  A did not allow Indians into   **C** forced Indians to build
  B allowed Indians into   **D** spent Indian money on

5. British _____ seemed to encourage British feeling of superiority.

  A religion   **B** democracy   **C** trade   **D** imperialism

6. When Indian students learned about _____, they wanted independence for their own people.

  A imperialism   **C** British railroads
  B English democracy   **D** British industry

On a sheet of paper, write the answer to each question. Use complete sentences.

7. What are five good things the British did in India?

8. Why were many Indians unhappy with British rule?

9. What was the Indian National Congress really meeting about?

10. What was the turning point in British-Indian relations?

---

482   Unit 8   *The Age of Imperialism*

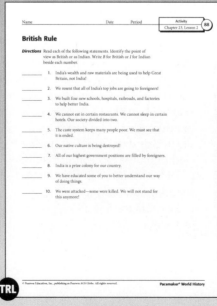

Mahatma Gandhi

Objectives

- To define and provide an example of nonviolent resistance
- To define and provide an example of civil disobedience
- To explain what happened after India won independence

Reading Strategy:
Questioning

What do you already know about Gandhi?

Nonviolent resistance

The act of opposing or working against without using force or causing injury

Civil disobedience

The refusal to obey rules, orders, or laws

You Decide

Do you think nonviolent resistance is a good way to make change today?

Mohandas K. Gandhi was born in 1869. He was a Hindu. His family belonged to the merchant caste. Gandhi studied law in London. He worked as a lawyer in South Africa for 21 years. At that time, South Africa was ruled by Great Britain. Gandhi worked for the rights of Indians who were being discriminated against. In 1914, Gandhi returned to India. There he began to work for independence from Britain. By 1920, he had become the leader of the Indian National Congress.

How Did Gandhi Suggest Indians Gain Their Independence?

Gandhi had new ideas. He said that the way to freedom was not through violence or bloodshed. Instead, Gandhi taught **nonviolent resistance** and **civil disobedience.**

Calmly and peacefully, Gandhi led Indians to refuse to obey the British government. "Conquer by love," he taught. His followers called him *Mahatma* Gandhi. *Mahatma* means "Great Soul."

"We cannot win against British guns," Gandhi said. "The British only know how to fight against guns. We will show them a new kind of resistance." Gandhi said that civil disobedience was a weapon stronger than guns. He told Indians to refuse to work in British mines, shops, and factories.

Gandhi led a revolution for independence. It was, for the most part, a revolution of the poor. Although he was a Hindu, he did not believe in the caste system. He lived among the poorest Indians, the untouchables, for many years. He lived simply, often wearing only a linen loincloth (a small cloth worn about the hips).

1600–1950   *Imperialism and India* *Chapter 23*   **483**

Lesson at a Glance

Chapter 23 Lesson 3

Overview This lesson describes how Gandhi led India toward independence.

Objectives

- To define and provide an example of nonviolent resistance
- To define and provide an example of civil disobedience
- To explain what happened after India won independence

Student Pages 483–486

Teacher's Resource Library **TRL**

Workbook Activity 89

Activity 89

Modified Activity 89

Vocabulary

civil disobedience
fast
nonviolent resistance

Have students write brief scenarios in which they could use passive resistance or civil disobedience to accomplish a political goal. Ask for volunteers to share these scenarios with their classmates. Discuss the difference between the two terms.

PRONUNCIATION GUIDE

Use this list to help students pronounce difficult words in this lesson.

Mahatma (mə hät´mə)

Mohandas Gandhi
(mō´ hən däs´   gän´ dē)

---

2 Teaching the Lesson

Ask students to share what they know about Mohandas Gandhi. Have them read the lesson to learn more about this dynamic individual and the role he played in unifying India.

Ask:

- Which two religious groups dominated India? (Hindus and Muslims)
- What major problems did Gandhi face in the unification of India? (religious differences)
- How did Gandhi protest the violence between Hindus and Muslims? (He fasted.)

Reading Strategy:
Questioning

(Possible answer: He led a nonviolent movement to free India from British rule.)

You Decide

Have students discuss the question in small groups. With the whole class, ask for the opinions formed in each group and the rationale behind them.

1 Warm-Up Activity

Have students write brief scenarios in which they could use passive resistance or civil disobedience to accomplish a political goal. Ask for volunteers to share these scenarios with their classmates. Discuss the difference between the two terms.

Imperialism and India Chapter 23   **483**

Background Information

More than 80 percent of the people of India are Hindus. Ninety-seven percent of the people of Pakistan are Muslims. Religious differences have caused conflict for many years.

In 1965, India and Pakistan fought a three-week war over Kashmir, a territory near the northern corner of India and Pakistan. Most of the people in Kashmir are Muslims, and Pakistan claimed the land as its own. India, too, claimed Kashmir. Both countries now control parts of that land.

In 1971, a civil war broke out between East and West Pakistan. As a result, Pakistan lost its eastern lands (East Pakistan). East Pakistan became a nation called Bangladesh. Today 83 percent of the people in Bangladesh are Muslims. In the 1990s, friction between India and Pakistan continued. In 2000, however, Pakistan sent supplies to help India after a major earthquake.

LEARNING STYLES

Logical/Mathematical

Have students use the map on page 484 to answer these questions.

- What are the present dimensions of India, east to west and north to south? (1,280 miles by 2,080 miles, or 2,050 kilometers by 3,330 kilometers)

- The main island of Great Britain is 480 kilometers (300 miles) east to west and 910 kilometers (570 miles) north to south. How many times would it fit into India? (about 15–16 times)

LEARNING STYLES

Interpersonal/Group Learning

Have students work in groups to research one of the boycotts or demonstrations that Gandhi led against the British. Have them work together to create a poster encouraging people to join the protest. Encourage volunteers to explain what makes their posters persuasive.

India and Pakistan, 1950

MAP STUDY

1. What are two cities in Pakistan?
2. What city in India is located near the Ganges River?

Reading Strategy:
Questioning

What problems in your own life can help you understand Gandhi and the struggles of the Indian people?

In one act of resistance, Gandhi led thousands of Indian women to the train tracks. There they lay down, stopping the British trains. When the British put an unfair tax on salt, Gandhi peacefully led a march 240 miles to the sea to get salt from the ocean.

Gandhi was often arrested for his activities. He spent a total of seven years in jail. But in time, the British began to listen to Gandhi and his followers.

MAP STUDY

Answers:

1. Karachi, Islamabad

2. New Delhi

Reading Strategy:
Questioning

Students may not want to answer the question publicly. Suggest that their answer might help them write their skits for the chapter project.

STUDY SKILLS

Ask students to study the map of India and Pakistan on page 484. Then, ask students to create a four-column chart with columns "Bodies of Water," "Cities," "Countries Bordering Pakistan," and "Countries Bordering India." Have students fill in the chart, using the information in the map.

What Did Gandhi Do to Keep the Peace in India?

Fast
To go without food

Mahatma Gandhi became an important leader in India's fight for independence.

The British knew that the Indian people no longer wanted them in their country. They knew it was just a matter of time before they would be forced to leave. So they offered independence to India. The Muslims however, demanded a separate nation. Their protests led to bloody rioting between Muslims and Hindus. As a result, India was divided into two nations. Pakistan would be a Muslim nation, and India would be Hindu.

Mahatma Gandhi saw his country gain independence in 1947. Unfortunately, more fighting between Hindus and Muslims came with independence. There was terrible loss of life. Entire villages were wiped out. Gandhi insisted that the fighting stop. He went on a **fast,** refusing to eat until the bloodshed ended. He almost starved to death. At last, Hindu and Muslim leaders promised to stop the fighting. They did not want their leader to die. Gandhi's fast had come to an end.

Shortly after Gandhi's fast ended, he was shot down by a Hindu gunman. Both Hindus and Muslims mourned their great leader.

TIMELINE STUDY: INDIA: 1600–1950

After Gandhi began nonviolent resistance against the British, how many years passed before Indian independence?

1877
Britain's Queen Victoria becomes empress of India

1948
Gandhi is assassinated

1858
Britain takes over India

1930
Gandhi leads march to the sea

1757
Clive's War

1857
Sepoy Rebellion

| 1600 | 1650 | 1700 | 1750 | 1800 | 1850 | 1900 | 1950 |

1600
British East India Company formed

1885
Indian National Congress formed

1920
Gandhi begins nonviolent resistance

1947
India gains its independence

1600–1950

Imperialism and India Chapter 23 **485**

TIMELINE STUDY

Answer: 27 years

LEARNING STYLES

Visual/Spatial
Ask students to study the picture of Gandhi on page 485, or bring in photographs or slides to show the class. Have them write a paragraph about how Gandhi's image compares to what they have learned about his actions. Provide an opportunity for students to share their observations with the class.

ONLINE CONNECTION

Have students brainstorm a list of questions about Mahatma Gandhi. Ask interested students to find the answers to these questions on the Internet. You may want to assign reports on topics such as his early life, religious beliefs, and family background.

LEARNING STYLES

Auditory/Verbal
The movie *Gandhi*, with Ben Kingsley as the protagonist, is excellent. It presents an interesting portrait of the Indian leader and of India during his life. Have students watch it at home (it is three hours long). Ask them to write their impressions for a class discussion.

ELL/ESL STRATEGY

Language Objective: *To explore the meaning of the vocabulary*

Some students may not know the meaning of the word *fast*. Explain that when people fast, they do not eat food for a certain period of time. In some cases, people may only eat some kinds of foods. Ask students whether their cultural or religious traditions require fasting.

Imperialism and India Chapter 23 **485**

AT HOME

Have students suppose that they are writing a letter to a Hindu teenager in India. What questions would they want to ask about the culture? How would they describe their own lives? They may include pictures (photographs or magazine pictures) that show life in America.

IN THE COMMUNITY

Ask students what the advantages of nonviolent protest is as a way to accomplish change. Have them search out people in their community who have participated in nonviolent protests, or leaders of groups that pursue their goals by nonviolent means. Ask students to write a paragraph about an environmental or social issue that they think could be changed by using nonviolent protest.

Lesson 23–3 Review Answers

1. B **2.** C **3.** A **4.** Gandhi **5.** conquer by love **6.** Great Soul **7.** Hindu **8.** Possible answer: Indians were practicing civil disobedience when they refused to work in British mines, shops, and factories. **9.** Possible answer: An example of nonviolent resistance was when Gandhi peacefully led a march 200 miles to the sea to get salt from the ocean. **10.** After India gained independence in 1947, the Hindus and Muslims began to fight. Many people died. Gandhi fasted until the bloodshed ended—almost starving to death. Eventually the fighting stopped.

Match the definition in Column A with the term in Column B. Write the correct letter on each line.

Column A

1. to go without food

2. the act of opposing without using force; working against without causing injury

3. to refuse to do as told, especially when the rule, order, or law is bad

Column B

A civil disobedience

B fast

C nonviolent resistance

Word Bank
conquer by love
Gandhi
Great Soul
Hindu

On a sheet of paper, write the word from the Word Bank to complete each sentence correctly.

4. _____ worked for the rights of Indians who were being discriminated against.

5. Gandhi taught Indians to _____.

6. *Mahatma* means "_____."

7. Gandhi was a _____, but did not believe in the caste system.

On a sheet of paper, write the answer to each question. Use complete sentences.

8. What is an example of civil disobedience?

9. What is an example of nonviolent resistance?

10. What happened after the British offered India independence?

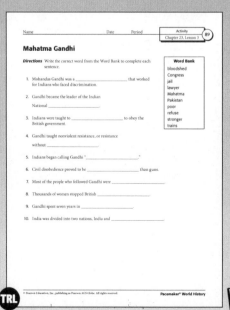

Activity 89   Workbook Activity 89

- Mogul rule in India weakened in the 1700s.

- The British East India Company gradually built a strong trading presence in India. It became involved in what took place in the country.

- When the French East India Company was formed, the British went to war against them. They were aided by Indians.

- The British East India Company began to rule India. They imposed British ways on Indian society.

- Indian soldiers, called sepoys, rebelled against the British East India Company in 1857.

- The British brought some improvements to India. However, the British felt superior to Indians and did not allow them to control their own country.

- A group of educated Indians formed the Indian National Congress to talk about gaining independence from Great Britain.

- In 1919, 400 Indians were killed and 1,200 wounded in the Amritsar Massacre. After that, the Indians were determined to end British rule.

- Mahatma Gandhi led India to independence by encouraging nonviolent civil disobedience.

- In 1947, India won independence and was divided into India and Pakistan.

- Unfortunately, independence brought more fighting between Hindus and Muslims.

Chapter 23 Summary

Have students read the Chapter Summary on page 487 to review the main ideas presented in Chapter 23.

Ask:

- When did the Moguls lose control over India? (in the 1700s)

- What company became deeply involved in India's trade? (British East India Company)

- Who fought against the French East India Company? (British and Indian troops)

- What happened to Indian society when the British East India Company ruled it? (It had to adopt British ways.)

- Describe the rebellion of 1857 in India. (The Sepoys rebelled against the British East India Company. They were suppressed in 1858.)

- What was one physical change that the British brought about in India? (Possible answer: They built railroads.)

- Why was the Indian National Congress formed? (to make India independent of Britain)

- What was the result of the Amritsar Massacre? (There were 1,600 Indian casualties. The massacre inspired Indians to end British rule.)

- What methods did Gandhi use to end British rule? (civil disobedience and nonviolent resistance)

- What countries emerged from India in 1947? (India and Pakistan)

- What are the relations like between the Hindus and Muslims in the Indian region? (They are often violent.)

TEACHER'S RESOURCE

The AGS Globe Teaching Strategies in Social Studies Transparencies may be used with this chapter. The transparencies add an interactive dimension to expand and enhance the Pacemaker® *World History* program content.

CHAPTER PROJECT FOLLOW-UP

Preview the skits. Choose one or two and have the authors perform them for the class.

Chapter 23 Review

Use the Chapter Review to prepare students for tests and to reteach content from the chapter.

Chapter 23 Mastery Test

The Teacher's Resource Library includes two forms of the Chapter 23 Mastery Test. Each test addresses the chapter Goals for Learning. An optional third page of additional critical-thinking items is included for each test. The difficulty level of the two forms is equivalent.

Chapter 23 Review Answers

Vocabulary Review

1. fast
2. civil disobedience
3. nonviolent resistance
4. impose
5. superiority
6. cartridge
7. indirectly
8. agent

Chapter Review Questions

9. The British East India Company's purpose was to trade with India.

10. The Mogul Empire was beginning to break up and the rajas were fighting.

11. It was clear that the British East India Company could no longer keep peace in India.

Word Bank

agent
cartridge
civil disobedience
fast
impose
indirectly
nonviolent resistance
superiority

Vocabulary Review

On a sheet of paper, use the words from the Word Bank to correctly match each definition below.

1. To go without eating for a considerable time
2. Refusal to obey bad rules, orders, or laws
3. Working against something without using force
4. To force one's will on another person or group
5. A feeling of being better than somebody else
6. A small tube that holds gunpowder and a bullet
7. To go about something in a roundabout way
8. A person who has the authority to act for someone or something else

Chapter Review Questions

On a sheet of paper, write the answer to each question. Use complete sentences.

9. What was the purpose of the British East India Company?
10. What gave the Europeans the chance to take advantage of India?
11. Why did the British Parliament take over rule of India?
12. Why was the Indian National Congress formed?
13. What two new ideas did Gandhi teach?
14. Why did Gandhi lead a march to the sea?
15. Why was India divided into two nations?

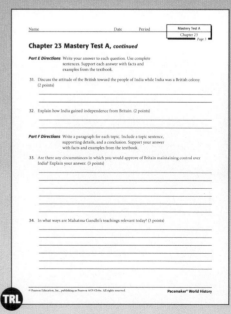

Test Tip

Studying together in small groups and asking questions of one another is one way to review for tests.

Critical Thinking

On a sheet of paper, write your response to each question. Use complete sentences.

16. Why do you think the British called India the "Jewel of the British Empire"?

17. Why do you think so many Indian people followed Gandhi?

Using the Timeline

Use the timeline on page 485 to answer the questions.

18. Did the Sepoy Rebellion take place before or after Britain took over India?

19. How many years after the British East India Company was formed did Britain officially take over India?

20. When was the Indian National Congress formed?

GROUP ACTIVITY

Form groups of four students. Discuss a problem in your community or nation. List some ways to solve the problem. Would nonviolent resistance help to solve it? Why or why not?

12. Although they said they were meeting to improve the relations with Britain, they were really formed to discuss revolution against the British.

13. Gandhi taught nonviolent resistance and civil disobedience.

14. In reaction to an unfair British tax on salt, Gandhi led a march to the sea to get salt.

15. India was divided into two nations—India and Pakistan—because the Muslims and Hindus could not get along.

Critical Thinking

16. Possible answer: India was as valuable as a jewel to the British.

17. Possible answers: Gandhi had a convincing argument. Gandhi's character and personality made him a great leader. The Indians knew they could not defeat the British in a fighting war.

Using the Timeline

18. before

19. 258 years

20. 1885

GROUP ACTIVITY

Students' lists should reflect contemporary concerns such as safety, health care, poverty, and education.

Chapter 23 Mastery Test B, pages 1–3

Introducing the Chapter

This chapter describes the early kingdoms of Africa, which began around 2000 B.C., as well as the impact of European imperialism on native Africans. One of these influences was the development of a slave trade, an industry that destroyed African life and cultures.

Ask:

- Who were the first Europeans to visit Africa? (traders)

- What is imperialism? (the control or influence a powerful nation has over a weaker country)

Imperialism and Africa

Many civilizations grew up south of the African Sahara beginning around 1000 B.C. Arabs were the first to trade with these civilizations. Later, traders from Europe began to visit these parts of Africa too. They made people aware of these civilizations. Trade increased and trading posts were established on the coast. Soon, the Africans, like the native people of the Americas, became affected by Europeans.

European explorers began to establish colonies. An increasing number of African people faced foreign control in their own land. Others became enslaved and many were taken away in ships, as if they were a raw material. It would be many years before much change would end outside control.

GOALS FOR LEARNING

- To name and describe the early kingdoms of Africa
- To describe Africa after the first century A.D.
- To describe the African slave trade
- To explain why Europeans wanted colonies in Africa

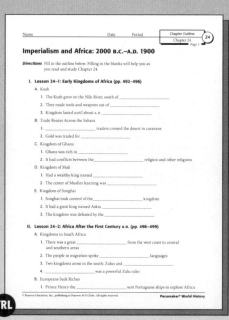

Chapter 24 Self-Study Guide, pages 1–2   Chapter 24 Outline, pages 1–2

Reading Strategy: Predicting

Previewing a text helps prepare readers to look for new information—to predict what will come next. A prediction is your best guess about what might happen next.

- As you read the text, notice details that could help you make predictions.
- While you read, check your predictions. You may have to change your predictions as you learn more information.

Key Vocabulary Words

Lesson 1

Caravan A group of people traveling together, often through a desert

Lesson 4

Dominance The act of ruling, controlling, or being most powerful

Prejudice Dislike of people just because they are of a different race or religion, or are from another country

Racism The idea that one race is better than another

Conference A meeting of people to discuss something

Inferior Not as good as someone or something else

- What made African civilizations susceptible to colonization by the Europeans? (Answers may vary.)

Reading Strategy:
Predicting

Tell students that when they make a prediction they are using their experience, observations, and attention to the details in the text to make an educated guess about what will happen next. Have students read carefully the goals for learning on page 490. Next, have them read the two introductory paragraphs on page 490. Finally, ask them to preview the chapter by looking at the subheads for each lesson. Ask, *What do you think you will learn about imperialism and Africa in this chapter?* Ask students to write a paragraph in which they make several specific predictions about the effects of imperialism on African cultures.

Key Vocabulary Words

Point out that these chapter words are presented in the order they appear in each lesson. They are also found in the glossary.

LIFE SKILLS CONNECTION

Students learn that there are laws in place to protect workers. Students research the labor laws in their own country and compare them to another country's laws. Direct students to government web sites for information about labor laws.

KEY VOCABULARY

Students choose the correct word from the Word Bank to complete each sentence.

Chapter 24 Life Skills Connection

Slavery was built on the idea of free labor. Slaves were purchased from a slave trader. Then they were forced to do work that free people would demand to be paid for. Slave owners did not have to provide rest periods or safe work environments. There were also no age limits for slaves; children worked alongside adults. While slavery in most countries has been abolished, the protection of workers is still an important issue. Laws that protect workers are known as labor laws.

Today most countries have a minimum wage, the lowest possible amount a person can be paid for work. This prevents employers from paying wages too low for people to live on. There are also federal organizations that monitor workplaces to make sure they are safe and healthy. In America, this organization is called the Occupational Safety and Health Administration (OSHA). Many countries have laws to prevent children from working before a certain age. There are also laws that require employers to give workers rest periods throughout the day.

Directions Use the Internet or library to research the labor laws in your country. Then research the labor laws in another country. How do they compare? Does one country offer more protection to workers than the other? Write your findings on a separate sheet of paper.

Chapter 24 Key Vocabulary Words

Directions Write the correct word from the Word Bank to complete each sentence.

1. We will schedule a(n) _____ so that everyone can share information and ideas.

2. The older, bigger kids tried to gain _____ over the younger, smaller ones.

3. Holding on to a(n) _____ may prevent you from making new friends.

4. We expressed _____ to Tim when his cat died.

5. If you try to _____ your wishes on your friends, they may stay away from you.

6. The _____ brought trade goods across the desert.

7. This broken old tennis racket is _____ to your strong new one.

8. Lena stopped practicing the trumpet so she would not _____ with our study time.

9. We can say no to _____ by accepting people of all colors as true equals.

10. Buying the lot next door created a(n) _____ of our yard.

Word Bank

caravan
conference
dominance
expansion
impose
inferior
interfere
prejudice
racism
sympathy

TRL   Life Skills Connection 24   **TRL**   Key Vocabulary Words 24

Overview This lesson describes four early kingdoms of Africa—the Kush civilization, which lasted from around 2000 B.C. until around A.D. 350; Ghana, which began during the A.D. 400s and lasted until the end of the 13th century; the wealthy kingdom of Mali; and the kingdom of Songhai.

Objectives

- To describe the Kush civilization
- To tell what the caravans brought and to explain their impact on Ghana
- To tell how Mali became a wealthy kingdom
- To describe the end of the kingdom of Songhai

Student Pages 492–497

Teacher's Resource Library

Workbook Activity 90

Activity 90

Modified Activity 90

Vocabulary

caravan

Ask students to preview the chapter to locate five unfamiliar words or phrases and to record them in their notebooks. Once students have identified these words and phrases, ask them to use their dictionaries to define them. Next, ask students to write a short paragraph that includes both the vocabulary word from the lesson and at least three of the words or phrases they discovered in the chapter. You may want to ask several volunteers to share their paragraphs with the class.

PRONUNCIATION GUIDE

Use this list to help students pronounce difficult words in this lesson.

Aksum (äk´soom)

Timbuktu (tim´buk tōō)

Songhai (song gī´)

Early Kingdoms of Africa

Objectives

- To describe the Kush civilization
- To tell what the caravans brought and to explain their impact on Ghana
- To tell how Mali became a wealthy kingdom
- To describe the end of the kingdom of Songhai

Reading Strategy: Predicting

Preview the lesson title. Predict what you think you will learn in this lesson and the lessons to follow.

One of the world's earliest civilizations was that of the ancient Egyptians in northern Africa. The Egyptian pharaohs built great pyramids and temples. In time, other nations founded colonies in northern Africa. The Phoenicians built the city of Carthage. Then the Romans came and built their own cities. Still later came the Arab conquerors. Their armies swept across northern Africa, bringing Islam with them.

All this happened in northern Africa. However, there were civilizations in the rest of the continent, south of the Sahara.

How Long Did the Kush Civilization Last?

Along the Nile River, just south of Egypt, is a country called Sudan. During the time of ancient Egypt, this land was called Nubia. A civilization arose there about 2000 B.C. The people of Nubia, or Kush, as it was also called, were black. In about 1500 B.C., Egypt conquered Kush. For the next 500 years, Kush was ruled by the Egyptians. The Kushites were greatly influenced by them. Kush became an important center of art, learning, and trade. But by about 1000 B.C., the Egyptians had lost much of their power. The Kushites were able to drive out the Egyptians.

At about this time, Kushites began mining iron. They used the iron to make tools and weapons. The Kushites kept growing stronger. In about 750 B.C., they conquered Egypt and ruled there until about 670 B.C.

Reading Strategy: Predicting

Students will probably predict that they will learn about the rise and fall of several African civilizations. Ask, *Were your predictions about what you would learn in Lesson 24–1 correct?*

After students have read the lesson, ask them to predict what they will learn in the lessons to follow.

CHAPTER PROJECT

Divide students into groups. Have each group research and write a report about the digging of the Suez Canal and how the canal influenced the spread of imperialism into Asia and Africa. Student reports should explain how Asia and Africa were changed by the canal. Suggest to students that each member of the group should focus on a different area, such as the digging of the canal, the fight to control the canal, the changes that occurred in Africa and in Asia as a result of the canal, and the changes that occurred in Europe.

Caravan
A group of people traveling together, often through a desert

The civilization of Kush lasted until about A.D. 350. Kush was then conquered by the neighboring kingdom of Aksum. By then, both Kush and Aksum had come under the influence of the Roman Empire and Christianity. Kush was to remain Christian until the 1300s when Arabs appeared in the region. The Kushites then converted to the Muslim religion.

How Were Goods Traded Across the Sahara?

In western Africa, on the southern side of the Sahara, is a vast area of grasslands. Great kingdoms of black Africans grew up there.

By about A.D. 1000, Arab traders from northern Africa began to cross the Sahara in **caravans**. The trade caravans brought goods that the people of western Africa needed. They brought tools and clothing. They also brought the thing that the people needed most—salt. The climate south of the Sahara is hot and dry. People needed salt to stay healthy. They needed salt to preserve their food. Salt was so important that the people were willing to trade gold for it. Luckily there was plenty of gold available in western Africa.

This ancient statue of a lion holding a shield dates back to the Kush civilization.

 TIMELINE STUDY: THE KUSHITES: 2000 B.C.–A.D. 500

How long did the Kush civilization last?

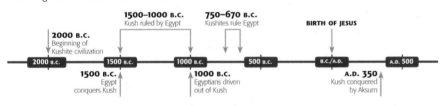

2000 B.C. Beginning of Kushite civilization
1500 B.C. Egypt conquers Kush
1500–1000 B.C. Kush ruled by Egypt
1000 B.C. Egyptians driven out of Kush
750–670 B.C. Kushites rule Egypt
BIRTH OF JESUS
A.D. 350 Kush conquered by Aksum

2000 B.C. | 1500 B.C. | 1000 B.C. | 500 B.C. | B.C./A.D. | A.D. 500

2000 B.C.–A.D. 1900   *Imperialism and Africa* Chapter 24   **493**

Have students preview the chapter by reading the headings and subheadings and by looking at the illustrations, the timelines, and the map. After students have studied the map ask, *What does this map tell you about the early civilizations in Africa?*

2 **Teaching the Lesson**

Lead a discussion in which students talk about what constitutes a civilization. Remind students that a civilization is defined by organization, government and, perhaps, a common language, art, and world view. As students read the lesson, have them try to keep in mind the chapter's title— Imperialism and Africa—to stimulate their thinking about the effects of Europeans on African civilizations.

Ask:
- What natural resource helped the Kushites conquer Egypt? How did this occur? (iron; stronger weapons)
- What religion did the Kushites convert to during the 1300s? (Islam)
- What did people in western Africa need most of all? (salt)
- What were they willing to trade for it? (gold)
- What destroyed the Kingdom of Ghana? (Muslim rulers tried to force Islam on its citizens, which weakened the kingdom.)
- How did Mansa Musa build wealth in the Mali kingdom? (He encouraged trade and then taxed the caravans.)
- Why did the Kingdom of Songhai fall into decline? (The weapons of the Songhai warriors were inferior to those of the Moroccans.)

TIMELINE STUDY

Answer: 2000 B.C. – A.D. 350 or 2,350 years

Ask:
- How long did Egypt rule Kush? (about 500 years)

ONLINE CONNECTION

 Students can gain additional information by accessing the following Web site: www.agsglobepmwh.com/page493 (The Web site provides excellent information which allows students and teachers to conduct in-depth research on a number of topics. Have students enter "Suez Canal" in the search field for information on their chapter projects.)

Divide students into five groups—one group for each of the subheads that appears in Lesson 24–1. Ask each group to read their section carefully, and then write a brief summary that answers the question posed in the subhead. Encourage students to share their summaries with the class. Then have each group lead a brief discussion about their portion of the lesson.

Background Information

Kush was the site of a highly advanced, ancient black African civilization that rivaled ancient Egypt in wealth, power, and cultural development. Here dwelt powerful and wealthy black kings who controlled the trade routes connecting central Africa with ancient Egypt. After the Kushites conquered Egypt in about 750 B.C., Kushite pharaohs promoted a renaissance in Egypt and incorporated Egyptian culture, art, and philosophy into their homeland. They built magnificent temples. The pyramid, abandoned as the proper tomb type by Egyptian kings a thousand years earlier, was revived by the Kushites and used by their monarchs for a thousand years, which is why today there are many more pyramids in the Sudan than in Egypt.

LEARNING STYLES

Logical/Mathematical

Remind students that maps usually have symbols to represent different information. Ask students to look at the map on this page and make a list of the symbols used, telling what information each symbol imparts. (Answers will vary; students may list the shading key to indicate kingdoms, scale to show distances, compass to show direction, and labels to name countries.) Have students suggest other symbols that might make the map more useful to them. (Answers will vary; students may suggest adding dates that each kingdom rose and fell.)

Ancient Kingdoms of Africa, 1500

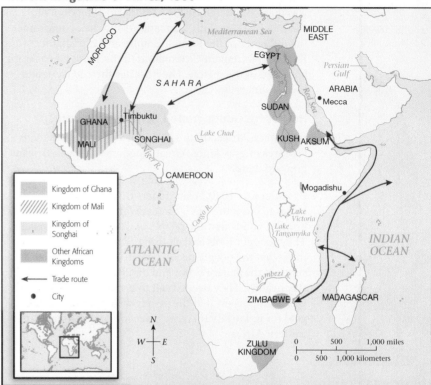

MAP STUDY

1. What large island is located off the coast of eastern Africa?

2. What are four rivers in Africa?

MAP STUDY

Answers:

1. Madagascar

2. The Niger, Congo, Nile, and Zambezi rivers

What Impact Did Arab Trading Caravans Have on the Kingdom of Ghana?

During the A.D. 400s, a kingdom called Ghana grew up in western Africa. The kingdom began to prosper about A.D. 1000. This is when the Arabs from northern Africa became interested in trade with Ghana. They had learned that Ghana was rich in gold. However, trade turned out to be a mixed blessing for Ghana. The Arab trading caravans brought not only goods but also religion to Ghana. In time, Ghana's rulers became Muslims. In contrast, most of the people living in Ghana did not convert. They still practiced their own ancient worship of many gods.

Muslim rulers tried to force the people to practice Islam. This weakened the kingdom. The Mandingo people of a kingdom called Mali took over Ghana near the end of the 13th century. By 1300, the kingdom of Ghana was gone.

How Did Mali Become a Wealthy Kingdom?

From 1312 to 1337, the Mali kingdom was ruled by a man named Mansa Musa. *Mansa* means "king." Mansa Musa was a good king. He built Mali's wealth by encouraging and then taxing caravan trade. Mansa Musa was a Muslim. He invited Arab scholars to come to Mali to teach. The city of Timbuktu became a center of Muslim learning.

Mansa Musa became famous when he made his pilgrimage to the holy city of Mecca, in Arabia. He decided to show the rest of the world just how wealthy his kingdom was. He took a splendid caravan with him on his pilgrimage to Mecca. Across the grasslands and deserts he went, along with thousands of his people. Mansa Musa also took thousands of enslaved people with him. Many of the slaves carried a solid gold staff, which was used for support when walking. He also took at least 80 camels, each loaded with bags of gold dust. Everywhere he went, the Mali ruler gave out gold and other gifts. Stories quickly spread about the fabulous wealth of the kingdom of Mali.

You Decide

 Would Mansa Musa's policies be good for a leader to follow today? Why or why not?

ELL/ESL STRATEGY

Language Objective: *To help students understand word endings and how these affect root words, especially of proper nouns*

A member of the Kush civilization was called a _____. (Kushite)

A Christian practices a religion called _____. (Christianity)

Citizens of ancient Egypt were called _____. (Egyptians)

A _____ cheetah is located in Sahara. (Saharan)

Citizens of Morocco are called _____. (Moroccans)

One who practices the religion of Islam is called a _____. (Muslim)

You Decide

Review with students the information on Mansa Musa. Then lead a discussion in which students speculate about the leadership qualities of Mansa Musa and how they might or might not be appropriate for a contemporary leader.

COMMON ERROR

Remind students that when they summarize material they need to use their own words to discuss information in the text.

TEACHER ALERT

The PBS series *Wonders of the African World* offers resources and information for teachers and students about early civilizations of Africa as well as handouts, photos, and support material for teachers seeking to enliven their lessons on Africa. Information on African cultures, the slave trade, and Africa today is abundant. This Web site can be accessed at: www.agsglobepmwh.com/page496

Reading Strategy:
Predicting

Ask volunteers to talk about ways they might make their predictions more specific.

Reading Strategy:
Predicting

Think about your prediction. What details can you now add to make your prediction more specific?

What Was the Kingdom of Songhai Like?

When Mansa Musa died, Mali weakened. A kingdom called Songhai took control of Mali during the 1400s. One of the Songhai rulers was a king named Askia Mohammed. Askia ruled from 1493 to 1528. This was a time of growth in Songhai power. The city of Timbuktu reached its height as an important center of trade and learning. Songhai remained strong until the late 1500s. At that time, the Moroccan king, Mohamed al-Mansur, The Victorious, attacked. The Moroccans had guns. The Songhai warriors fought with spears. Songhai was defeated.

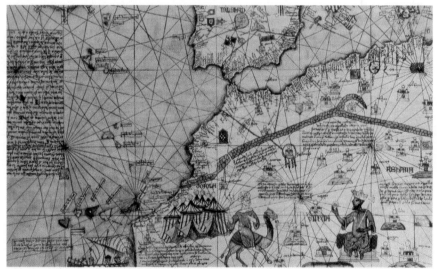

This Spanish map, created in 1375, includes a drawing of Mansa Musa. It gives clues about Musa's power, his wealth, and the extent of his rule.

Match the definition in Column A with the term in Column B.
Write the correct letter on a sheet of paper.

Column A

1. the civilization that arose around 2000 B.C. along the Nile River

2. a kingdom that began to prosper in A.D. 1000

3. the kingdom that took over Ghana near the end of the 13th century

4. the kingdom that took control of Mali during the 1400s

5. the ruler of the Mali kingdom from 1312 to 1337; was Muslim

6. the ruler of Songhai from 1493 to 1528

Column B

A Askia Mohammed
B Ghana
C Kush
D Mali
E Mansa Musa
F Songhai

On a sheet of paper, write the answer to each question. Use complete sentences.

7. What was the Kush civilization like during Egyptian rule (1500–1000 B.C.)?

8. What goods and ideas did the people of western Africa and the Arabs trade?

9. How did the ruler of Mali's kingdom from 1312 to 1337 build Mali's wealth?

10. What was the importance of the city of Timbuktu in the kingdom of Songhai?

Lesson 24–1 Review Answers
1. C **2.** B **3.** D **4.** F **5.** E **6.** A **7.** During that time, Kush became an important center of art, learning, and trade. **8.** The trading caravans brought tools, clothing, and, most important, salt. They also brought the Muslim religion. **9.** Mansa Musa built Mali's wealth by encouraging, and then taxing, a caravan trade. **10.** Timbuktu was an important center of trade and learning.

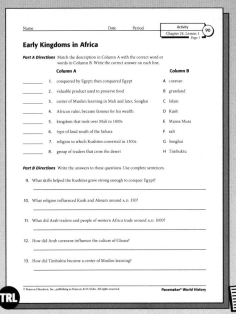

Activity 90, pages 1–2   Workbook Activity 90

Imperialism and Africa Chapter 24   **497**

Lesson at a Glance

Chapter 24 Lesson 2

Overview This lesson describes the migration of black peoples in Africa during the first century A.D., the rise in trading cities on the African coast, and the beginning of European influence in the region.

Objectives

■ To name two southern African kingdoms

■ To explain why Europe had little contact with southern Africa before the 1400s

Student Pages 498–500

Teacher's Resource Library

Workbook Activity 91

Activity 91

Modified Activity 91

PRONUNCIATION GUIDE

Use this list to help students pronounce difficult words in this lesson.

Mogadishu (mô´ gä dē´ shōo)

Swahili (swä hē´ lē)

Reading Strategy:
Predicting

Have students look again at the predictions they made at the beginning of the chapter. Encourage them to write a short revision of their initial predictions, if necessary.

1　Warm-Up Activity

Ask students to recall the chapter and information on the Renaissance. Then lead a discussion in which students speculate about what characteristics of the Renaissance caused people to be interested in travel and exploration. Remind students that one idea from the Renaissance was *humanism*. Ask students to talk about how the European notion of humanism was complicated by their actions in Africa. What attitude allowed Europeans to treat Africans differently than they treated other Europeans?

Africa After the First Century A.D.

Objectives

■ To name two southern African kingdoms

■ To explain why Europe had little contact with southern Africa before the 1400s

Reading Strategy:
Predicting

Think about what you predicted earlier. Does your prediction still work or do you need to revise your prediction?

History Fact
Swahili is a Bantu language that uses many Arabic words.

Early in the first century A.D., a great migration began in Africa. Black peoples of what is now Nigeria and Cameroon moved southward into the forests of central Africa. The population had been growing, and the people needed more land. Migration continued over the next 1,000 years. The people spoke Bantu languages. They settled in many parts of central, eastern, and southern Africa.

By about A.D. 1100, trading cities dotted the eastern African coast. A city called Mogadishu was one of the largest. The people living in coastal towns had frequent contact with Arab traders. They became Muslims, and they followed many Arabic customs. They spoke Swahili. The language is still used in much of central and southern Africa.

What Kingdoms Arose in South Africa?

A number of kingdoms arose in southern Africa. One of these was the kingdom of Zimbabwe. Another was the kingdom of the Zulus. The Zulus moved into southern Africa in the 1600s. They were powerful warriors. During the 1800s, they had a strong military under a fierce ruler named Shaka.

Shaka led his armies to conquer other kingdoms. Meanwhile, southern Africa was being settled by the Dutch and the British. The Zulus fought against European rule. In 1879, the British conquered the Zulu kingdom.

What Riches Did Europeans Find in Africa?

Africa was not an easy continent to explore. The Sahara kept many European traders from traveling south by land.

History Fact

Have students try to think of examples of foreign words being incorporated into their native language. For example, if a student's first language is English, he or she may suggest Spanish words such as *patio* or *salsa* that have become common English words. Ask, *What conditions must exist for a language to adopt foreign words into its lexicon?*

COMMON ERROR

Remind students that gathering more information should allow them to revise and refine their predictions so that they are more precise and expansive than initial predictions.

During the Renaissance, however, interest in travel grew. Seamen sailed better ships. In the 1400s, the Europeans began to arrive in Africa by sea routes.

The Portuguese were the first to sail the waters along Africa's coast. Prince Henry the Navigator sent ships along the west coast. He was searching for a trade route to India. Portuguese sailors soon learned of the gold in western Africa. They called a section of the African coastline the *Gold Coast*.

In 1497, the Portuguese sea captain Vasco da Gama discovered the sea route around Africa. Soon, Portugal set up trading posts along Africa's coasts. In 1571, Angola, in southwestern Africa, became a Portuguese colony.

Then the Portuguese found something in Africa that was a better money-maker than gold. They found that they could get rich by buying and selling human beings.

**Reading Strategy:
Predicting**

Think about the arrival of Europeans in Africa. What do you predict they will do?

This map from 1547 is of the Gold Coast in Africa. It is drawn upside-down as if viewed from Europe.

Background Information

What makes the Sahara such a formidable region? "The Great Desert," as the Arabs called it, is the world's largest non-polar desert in the world. It stretches for more than 3,000 miles across northern Africa, from the Atlantic Ocean in the west to the Red Sea in the east. The annual rainfall in the Sahara may be as little as three inches a year, with several years passing between rainfalls. With its high winds that blow from the northeast and temperatures as high as 136 degrees Fahrenheit (57.7 degrees Celsius), it has one of the harshest and hottest climates on Earth.

Reading Strategy:
Predicting

Lead a discussion in which students call upon their prior knowledge of colonization and imperialism to predict what will happen to African peoples. Answers will vary. Students will probably suggest that Africans will not do well under colonialism. They will not be respected, may lose their jobs, and will be poorly treated. However, health care and education may improve.

Before students begin reading the information on pages 498–499, write the following four topics on the board: migration, trade, war, and exploration. For each topic you have written on the board, ask students to write a sentence in their notebook that answers the questions *How, When, Where, Who,* and *Why.* You may want to have volunteers share their summaries with the class.

Ask:

- Why did the greater migration occur early in the first century? (population growth)

- People living in coastal towns had contact with what group? What were some of the impacts of this? (Arab traders; they became Muslims and adopted some Muslim customs)

- Name two of the kingdoms that arose in southern Africa. (Zimbabwe, Zulu)

- What made Africa a difficult continent to explore? How did Europeans solve this problem? (The Sahara prevented travel by land; Europeans began to arrive in Africa from the sea.)

ELL/ESL STRATEGY

Language Objective:
To encourage students to integrate words from the Word Bank into their vocabularies; to encourage collaboration and creativity

Divide students into several small groups. Then call their attention to the 10 words listed in the Word Bank on page 500. Have students look up the words using their dictionaries, the Internet, or the glossary at the end of the book. Next, ask each group to collaborate on a short story that uses at least seven of the words from the list. Have a volunteer from each group share the story with the class.

Because of its extreme dryness, the region called Antarctica is also considered to be a desert. In fact, it is the largest desert in the world. It is also the coldest, windiest, and driest place on the planet.

3 Reinforce and Extend

AT HOME

Ask students to find out—if they don't already know—how their families came to live in the town, state, nation where they currently reside. What factors influenced their family's choice to migrate? Encourage students to work with family members to chart the migration patterns of their ancestors. Have student write a brief biography of their family history that explains the patterns of migration as far back as they can trace them. Students may wish to share their findings with the class.

Lesson 24–2 Review Answers

1. south **2.** Mogadishu **3.** Zimbabwe
4. Zulus **5.** British **6.** Sahara
7. Portuguese **8.** Gold Coast **9.** Vasco da Gama **10.** human beings

---

LESSON 24-2 REVIEW

Word Bank

British
Gold Coast
human beings
Mogadishu
Portuguese
Sahara
south
Vasco da Gama
Zimbabwe
Zulus

On a sheet of paper, write the word from the Word Bank to complete each sentence correctly.

1. Africans began to migrate _____ in the first century A.D.

2. _____ was a large trading city on the eastern African coast around A.D. 1100.

3. The kingdom of _____ and the kingdom of the Zulus arose in southern Africa.

4. The _____ was a kingdom in Africa made up of powerful warriors.

5. The Zulus fought hard, but in 1879 the _____ conquered the Zulu kingdom.

6. Europe had little contact with Africa. This is because the _____ made it hard to travel south by land.

7. The _____ were the first to explore Africa's coast.

8. The western section of the African coast is known as the _____.

9. _____ discovered the sea route around Africa, which was then used for trading.

10. The Portuguese found that buying and selling _____ made better money than gold.

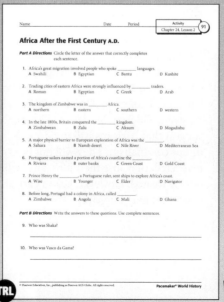

Activity 91

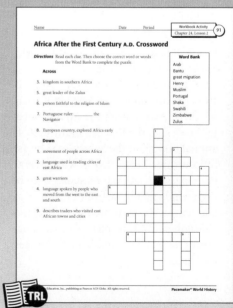

Workbook Activity 91

The African Slave Trade

Objectives

■ To explain the differences in the ways Africans and Europeans treated slaves

■ To list the European nations that took part in the slave trade

Reading Strategy: Predicting

Think about the slave trade by Europeans. What do you predict will happen to end this serious problem?

There had been enslaved people in Africa for a long time. When Africans conquered other Africans, they often made slaves of their captives. However, African slavery was quite different from the kind of slavery the Europeans practiced. The Africans treated enslaved people like human beings. Children of African slaves were free. But the Europeans treated their slaves like goods to be traded and sold, not like people.

How Did the African Slave Trade Come About?

The Portuguese were the first European slave traders. By the mid 1400s, the Portuguese were capturing Africans and packing them onto crowded ships. Many Africans died on the terrible voyages. Those who survived had to work as slaves in mines and on plantations in the West Indies. Soon the Spanish were also shipping slaves to the Americas.

PUBLIC SALE OF NEGROES.—Under the authority of a decree of the Circuit Court of Albemarle county, pronouced in the case of Michie's administrator and others, on the 8th day of October, 1855, I will offer for sale, at public auction, on MONDAY, the 5th day of May next, being Albemarle Court day, if a suitable day, if not, on the next suitable day thereafter, at the Court House of Albemarle county, *Five Negroes*, of whom the late David Tichis died possessed, consisting of a Negro Woman, twenty years of age and child two years old, a woman fifty-five years old, a negro man twenty-five years old, who has been working at the slating business, and a negro man twenty-two years old, a blacksmith.—The above lot of negroes is equal to any that has ever been offered in this market.
TERMS OF SALE—Five months credit, negotiable notes with approved endorsers, with the interest added.
ap24—ctds   GEO. DARR, Commissioner.

This 18th century slave trade ad demonstrates the horrors of slavery. Africans were sold like they were objects, rather than human beings.

Ask:

● Name at least two ways in which Africans treated slaves differently than Europeans. (Africans treated slaves as people; the children of slaves were free.)

● What were conditions like on Portuguese slave ships? (horrible; many slaves did not survive the trip)

● What countries participated in the slave trade? (Portugal, France, Britain, Denmark, United States)

● Why do you think the United States was the last to outlaw slavery? (Answers will vary.)

LEARNING STYLES

Auditory/Verbal

Have students preview the boxed feature on page 501 by skimming the text and reading the caption. Next, read aloud the advertisement for the *Public Sale of Negroes.* Lead a discussion in which students talk about how hearing the ad read aloud affected them. Ask, *What does this document reveal about the impact of the slave trade on families?*

Chapter 24 Lesson 3

Overview This lesson describes the beginning of the African slave trade and the impact of slavery on native communities and peoples in Africa.

Objectives

■ To explain the differences in the ways Africans and Europeans treated slaves

■ To list the European nations that took part in the slave trade

Student Pages 501–504

Teacher's Resource Library 🅣🅡🅛

  Workbook Activity 92

  Activity 92

  Modified Activity 92

Reading Strategy: Predicting

Students may say that European nations will eventually recognize that slavery is morally wrong; that slavery will be outlawed; or that the long-term consequences of slavery will continue to affect the African continent.

1   Warm-Up Activity

Have a student volunteer explain what a bully is and how he or she behaves. The students should give an example of how a bully would act in the classroom. Have a class discussion in which students compare imperialism with bullying. Ask if powerful nations act like bullies when they take over weaker countries.

2   Teaching the Lesson

Have students preview the lesson by reading the subheads, looking at the illustrations, and the "Words from the Past" information. As students read the lesson, ask them to think about the difference between slavery as it existed in Africa both before and after the arrival of Europeans.

Background Information

The enforced displacement of African peoples throughout the world created the Black *Diaspora*, the effects of which are still felt today. Diaspora is defined in the dictionary as "the movement, migration, or scattering of a people away from an established or ancestral homeland." Wherever they went, displaced Africans brought remnants of their own cultures—including music, food, dress, art, and stories—to the lands in which they found themselves displaced.

ELL/ESL STRATEGY

Language Objective: *To encourage creative writing skills and empathetic thinking*

After students have read the information on pages 501–503, have them write a letter to a slave trader from the point of view of an African citizen. The letter should describe the impact of the slave trade on the communities, families, and cultures of the African continent. Encourage volunteers to share their letters with the class.

By the mid-1600s, the French, English, and Dutch had joined in the profitable slave trade. Some Africans helped supply the Europeans with slaves. Sometimes, tribes fought each other to capture people to supply the slave traders. The fighting between tribes weakened Africa.

The slave markets wanted only the healthiest, strongest young Africans. Over time, at least 10 million men and women were taken out of Africa to be sold into slavery. The loss of some of its finest people also weakened Africa. Africa was in no position to defend itself against European imperialism.

Fortunately, people finally recognized that slavery was wrong. By the 1800s, many countries made slave trading illegal. In 1834, Britain outlawed, or did not allow, slavery in its colonies. Other European countries soon did the same. The United States abolished, or did away with, slavery in 1865. By 1888, slavery was illegal throughout the Americas.

Words from the Past

Songs of Slavery and Freedom

When enslaved Africans arrived in the Americas, they brought rich cultures with them. In the Americas, their cultures were forbidden. However, enslaved Africans created a rich culture of their own, based on their memories of Africa and their life on the plantations of America.

From the 1600s through the mid-1800s, enslaved Africans created songs called *spirituals*. Spirituals are religious songs that use African music and rhythms. The words of spirituals tell of enslavement and struggle.

This music served many purposes. As their ancestors had done in Africa, enslaved Africans sang while they worked.

During the mid-1800s, some spirituals helped enslaved people escape to freedom in the North on the Underground Railroad. For example, the song "Swing Low, Sweet Chariot," is about the Underground Railroad.

The spirituals were important to the development of today's gospel music, the blues, and jazz.

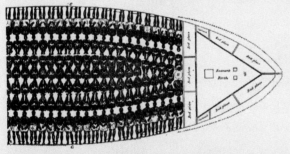

This is a diagram showing the inside of a slave ship.

IN THE COMMUNITY

Explain to students that, although most African nations are no longer colonies, their standard of living is much lower than that in Western countries. Many social and religious organizations send volunteers to these countries to help improve the native people's way of life. Have students find out if any churches or social organizations in their community have programs in Africa and what these programs try to accomplish. Give students an opportunity to share their findings.

TEACHER ALERT

Many scholars divide spirituals into roughly two types of song—*songs of sorrow* and *songs of joy*. You may wish to tell students this and encourage them to discuss examples of each in the spirituals they hear.

WORLD CULTURES

Negative effects of imperialism linger today. In South Africa, descendants of European colonists formed a white supremacist government and set up a system legally separating blacks from whites. They called this system apartheid. South Africa did not have an all-race parliamentary election until 1994. Efforts have been made in recent years to rectify abuses of human rights. On March 28, 1998, President Clinton became the first United States president to visit South Africa. Previous leaders had stayed away as an expression of their disapproval of apartheid.

WORDS FROM THE PAST

Bring in samples of spirituals. Then lead a discussion in which students talk about some of the themes they can distinguish in the songs. The University of Denver provides a good source of information and both text and audio samples of spirituals through its program called *Sweet Chariot: The Story of the Spirituals.*

LESSON 24-3 REVIEW

On a sheet of paper, write the letter of the answer that correctly completes each sentence.

1. The _____ were the first European slave traders.

   A Portuguese   **B** Spanish   **C** Dutch   **D** English

2. In the mid 1400s, slaves worked in mines and on plantations in _____.

   A the Americas   **B** France   **C** the West Indies   **D** Portugal

3. Sometimes, African tribes fought each other to capture people to _____, weakening Africa.

   A kill them   **C** get information from them
   B force them into the army   **D** supply the slave traders

4. Africans lost at least _____ men and women to slavery.

   A 10,000   **B** 1 million   **C** 10 million   **D** 100 million

5. Having lost many people, Africa was in no position to defend itself against European _____.

   A religion   **B** trade   **C** imperialism   **D** armies

6. Britain outlawed slavery in its colonies in 1834, and in 1865 _____ did the same.

   A Portugal   **B** the United States   **C** Spain   **D** France

7. Religious songs that use African music and rhythms, called _____, tell of enslavement and struggle.

   A spirituals   **B** musicals   **C** rap   **D** odes

On a sheet of paper, write the answer to each question. Use complete sentences.

8. What are the differences in the way Africans and Europeans treated slaves?

9. Which European countries were involved in slave trade in Africa?

10. What types of music of today are influenced by spirituals?

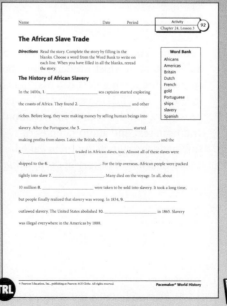

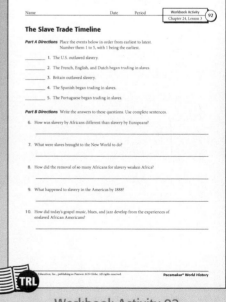

Activity 92   Workbook Activity 92

European Imperialism

Objectives

- To explain how and why racism led Europeans into Africa
- To detail how Europeans set up colonies in Africa
- To tell of ways that Europeans made Africans feel inferior

Dominance
The act of ruling, controlling, or being most powerful

Prejudice
Dislike of people just because they are of a different race or religion, or are from another country

Racism
The idea that one race is better than another

Conference
A meeting of people to discuss something

American and European slave trade in Africa finally came to an end. However, Africa had not seen the end of European **dominance** and **prejudice**. In the 1800s there had been an industrial revolution in Europe. Now Europeans needed raw materials and new markets for finished products. European nations wanted new colonies. These nations saw that the continent of Africa had lots of land.

The Industrial Revolution led to imperialism. However, there was another reason that led the Europeans into Africa. That was **racism**. Some Europeans simply thought they were better than the dark-skinned peoples of the world. Some thought it was their duty to bring their own culture to the black Africans. Therefore, the Europeans took over Africa.

How Were Colonies Set up in Africa?

In 1884, European nations held a **conference**, or a meeting, in Berlin, Germany. The United States and the Ottoman Empire sent representatives, too. No one invited African representatives. The conference set up rules for forming colonies in Africa. By 1914, Europeans had taken over almost all the land in Africa.

The Europeans formed some of their colonies easily. They made agreements with local tribal chiefs. They gave the chiefs presents and promised chances for trade. Some of the tribal leaders simply gave away their kingdoms.

Chapter 24 Lesson 4

Overview Although the European slave trade in Africa came to an end by the late 19th century, imperialism and colonialism continued to impact African peoples. The effects of imperialism on the nations, cultures, and peoples of Africa linger today.

Objectives

- To explain how and why racism led Europeans into Africa
- To detail how Europeans went about setting up colonies in Africa
- To tell of ways that Europeans made Africans feel inferior

Student Pages 505–508

Teacher's Resource Library

Workbook Activity 93

Activity 93

Modified Activity 93

Vocabulary

conference	prejudice
dominance	racism
inferior	

Write the vocabulary words on the board. Then ask students to create a crossword puzzle that contains hints for each word. Encourage students to use information from the chapter to develop their hints. Have students trade puzzles and work to fill in the blanks.

1   Warm-Up Activity

Discuss the definition of imperialism, and compare imperialism with nationalism. Have students suggest some differences between the two. Ask if nationalism has to come before imperialism. (Usually a country has to solidify the support of its people before it can conquer other countries.) Have students make a chart with two columns, labeled "Nationalism" and "Imperialism." Students should write some distinguishing features of each.

Have students read the information on pages 505–507. Ask them to pay careful attention to the subheads throughout the lesson. Remind students that many Europeans argued that imperialism had been good for Africa. Divide the class into two groups—those who will defend European imperialism in Africa and those who will condemn it. Have students work together in their groups to review Chapter 24 and develop at least three arguments that support their stance. Encourage a spokesperson from each group to present the group's findings to the class.

Ask:

- How did racism contribute to Europeans' desire to colonize Africa? (Answers will vary— Europeans thought they were superior; they thought it was their duty to bring European culture to black Africans; they wished to convert the native peoples to Christianity.)

- What was the purpose of the conference in Berlin in 1884? (to set up rules for forming colonies in Africa)

- How would you react if another country came to your homeland and established colonies there? (Answers will vary.)

Background Information

By the end of the 1800s Great Britain controlled what are now the nations of Sudan, Nigeria, Ghana, Kenya, and Uganda. South Africa became a British colony in 1909. France gained control of Algeria in 1847. This was the largest European empire in Africa. Spain and Portugal had the oldest colonies in Africa, while Belgium had a large empire in central Africa. Italy failed to take over Ethiopia, but took control of Tripoli in 1912. Liberia and Ethiopia were the only two independent countries left in Africa.

European missionaries helped set up colonies. They had come to convert the Africans to Christianity. Often they were unwelcome. Yet again, the Europeans felt it was their duty to show Africans the idea of a better way.

Soon there were only two independent countries left in all of Africa. Ethiopia, in the northeast, was the larger one. Liberia, on the west coast, was the other. Founded in 1822 by freed American slaves, Liberia had declared its independence in 1847.

TECHNOLOGY CONNECTION

The Suez Canal

The Suez Canal was built by a French company from 1859 to 1869. It was constructed under the direction of canal expert Ferdinand de Lesseps. This waterway linked the Gulf of Suez and the Red Sea with Port Said on the southeastern Mediterranean Sea. The total original cost of building the canal was about $100 million. It is 105 miles (169 km) long and 197 feet (300 meters) at its narrowest point. The Mediterranean and the Gulf of Suez are at about the same water level. Because of this, the canal was built without locks. (Locks are part of some canals. They are used to raise and lower boats as they move to different water levels.)

The Suez Canal revolutionized trade by providing a faster route from Europe to the Far East. The British government was responsible for protecting the Canal soon after it was completed. In 1956, Egypt took over that role. In recent years it has been widened so larger ships can pass through.

506 *Unit 8 The Age of Imperialism*

LEARNING STYLES

Visual/Spatial
Distribute outlines of a world map. Have students select a natural resource, such as coal, iron ore, tin, or copper, and research the parts of the world that are rich sources of the resource. Then, have students locate these parts of the world on the map and outline and shade them in with a colored pencil or marker. Students can mark more than one resource using different colors.

ONLINE CONNECTION

Draw students' attention to the information on the Suez Canal on page 506. After students have read the information ask them to compare what they learned with the independent research they conducted for the chapter project.

Remember

Religion came along with invaders at many points in history. Sometimes the new religion was welcomed. Often it was resisted.

How Did the Europeans Affect the Africans and Their Culture?

It is easy to see the wrongs and injustices of European imperialism in Africa. African culture was damaged. The Europeans did not understand tribal differences and tribal customs. Most did not even try to understand.

The Europeans forced the Africans to learn new ways. They tried to make the Africans feel **inferior**, or not as good as Europeans. They forced the Africans to accept European government, religion, and languages. They drew up colonial boundaries without giving any thought to splitting up tribes.

Some of the things the Europeans did in Africa helped the natives. However, most of those helped the Europeans. Railway systems, roads, and schools were built, and the continent of Africa was opened up to the rest of the world.

In the years ahead, new ideas would come to Africa. These would be ideas of freedom, of self-government—and, in some cases, of revolution.

TIMELINE STUDY:

CHANGES IN AFRICA: A.D. 400–1900

What happened 31 years after Britain outlawed slavery?

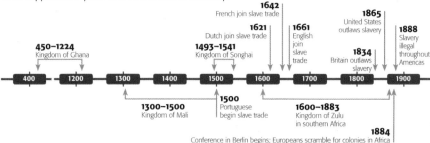

- **450–1224** Kingdom of Ghana
- **1300–1500** Kingdom of Mali
- **1493–1541** Kingdom of Songhai
- **1500** Portuguese begin slave trade
- **1642** French join slave trade
- **1621** Dutch join slave trade
- **1600–1883** Kingdom of Zulu in southern Africa
- **1661** English join slave trade
- **1834** Britain outlaws slavery
- **1865** United States outlaws slavery
- **1884** Conference in Berlin begins; Europeans scramble for colonies in Africa
- **1888** Slavery illegal throughout Americas

400 | 1200 | 1300 | 1400 | 1500 | 1600 | 1700 | 1800 | 1900

2000 B.C.–A.D. 1900

Imperialism and Africa Chapter 24 **507**

Body/Kinesthetic

Have students present a skit in which they are merchants on a ship that has just docked at a colonial port. Their job is to get supplies for the mother country. Have the merchants negotiate with the colonist traders for natural resources and other supplies. The two sides must agree on a price and terms of a sale.

ELL/ESL STRATEGY

Language Objective:
To research a subject

Pair ELL students with classmates who are proficient in English. Ask each pair to choose a country in Africa and find out more about how it was affected by imperialism. Students should research whether the country became a colony and which country took it over. They should also find out when and how it gained independence, and whether it is now independent. Have each pair of students work together to write a one-page summary of their research.

STUDY SKILLS

Tell students that the founding of Liberia, which means *Land of the Free*, can provide insight into the longing of slaves for both freedom and a return to their homeland. Have students go to the library and find a book or essay on the history of Liberia, and then write a brief summary of what they have learned. Ask students to bring both the original source and their summaries to class so they can share their summaries with their colleagues.

TIMELINE STUDY

Answer: The United States outlawed slavery.

Ask:

- Why do you think it took the United States an additional 31 years to follow Britain's lead? (Answers will vary: students may say that the relative isolation of the U.S. allowed slavery to continue; they may say that Europeans were able to more directly observe the devastating effects of slavery.)

Remember

Draw students' attention to the information on religion. Ask, *Why do you think some people resisted the influence of other religions?*

CAREER CONNECTION

The spread of imperialism resulted in increased trade between colonies and mother countries. Today, most countries have a global economy, which is based on trade with many countries. Some students may be interested in careers in international trade, sales, marketing, or banking. To be successful in any of these fields, a person should have a degree in business or public administration, international business, or a related field. Fluency in a foreign language and familiarity with multi-ethnic issues also are important. Invite students to find out which courses are needed to prepare for a career in international business.

Lesson 24–4 Review Answers

1. E **2.** C **3.** D **4.** B **5.** A **6.** As a result of the Industrial Revolution, Europeans needed raw materials and new markets for finished products. European nations wanted new colonies, and these nations saw that Africa had lots of land. **7.** Some Europeans thought they were better than the dark-skinned peoples of the world. Some thought it was their duty to bring their own culture to the black Africans. In this way, the Europeans took over Africa **8.** The European nations held a conference in Germany in 1884, but nobody invited African representatives. The conference set up rules for forming colonies in Africa. **9.** Ethiopia and Liberia are the two independent African countries. **10.** Europeans forced Africans to accept European government, religion, and languages. They also drew colonial boundaries without giving thought to splitting up tribes.

Match the definition in Column A with the term in Column B. Write the correct letter on a sheet of paper.

Column A

1. the idea that one race is better than another

2. not as good as someone or something else

3. disliking people because they are a different race or religion, or are from another country

4. the act of ruling, controlling, being most powerful

5. a meeting of people to discuss something

Column B

A conference
B dominance
C inferior
D prejudice
E racism

On a sheet of paper, write the answer to each question. Use complete sentences.

6. What factors (besides racism) led the Europeans into Africa?

7. How and why did racism lead Europeans into Africa?

8. How did Europeans go about setting up colonies in Africa?

9. What are the only two independent countries in Africa?

10. How did Europeans make Africans feel inferior?

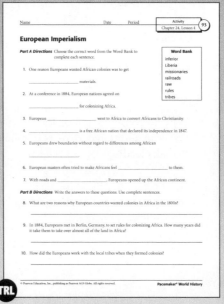

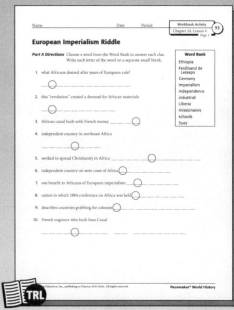

- The Kush civilization of ancient Egypt was one of the earliest in Africa.

- The Kushites were greatly influenced by 500 years of Egyptian rule, beginning in 1500 B.C.

- The Kush civilization lasted until about A.D. 350. At that time, it was taken over by the neighboring kingdom of Aksum.

- Ghana, Mali, and Songhai were rich kingdoms in western Africa.

- The population grew in what is now Nigeria and Cameroon. Thus more people moved into the forests of central Africa.

- European ships began arriving in Africa in the 1400s.

- The Portuguese found that they could make money by taking and selling Africans as slaves.

- The British, French, and Dutch soon joined the slave trade.

- The Industrial Revolution and racial prejudices played a part in European colonization of Africa.

- In 1884, a conference in Berlin laid down ground rules for colonizing Africa.

- By 1914, almost the entire continent of Africa had fallen under European imperialism.

2000 B.C.–A.D. 1900   *Imperialism and Africa*   *Chapter 24*   **509**

Chapter 24 Summary

Have students read the Chapter Summary on page 509 to review the main ideas presented in Chapter 24.

Ask:

- What is the importance of the Kush civilization in Africa? (It was one of the earliest in Africa.)

- Who ruled the Kushites for 500 years? What influence did this have on their civilization? (Egyptians; Students may point out that the Kushites adopted many cultural features of the Egyptians including building pyramids and having pharaohs as political leaders.)

- Name three African kingdoms in western Africa. (Ghana, Mali, and Songhai)

- What caused peoples to migrate early in the first century A.D.? (larger populations)

- Who were the first Europeans to sail along the African coast? (the Portuguese)

- Aside from gold, what "commodity" did the Portuguese discover in Africa? (human beings)

- Why was the Industrial Revolution a factor in the colonization of Africa? (Industrializing nations needed many of the raw materials that were abundant in Africa.)

- What was the fate of most of Africa? (By 1914, virtually the entire continent was under European rule.)

- What were the two exceptions to this? (Ethiopia and Liberia)

TEACHER'S RESOURCE

The AGS Globe Teaching Strategies in Social Studies Transparencies may be used with this chapter. The transparencies add an interactive dimension to expand and enhance the Pacemaker® *World History* program content.

CHAPTER PROJECT FOLLOW-UP

Encourage volunteers from each group to share the group's findings on the history and importance of the Suez Canal with the class.

Chapter 24 Review

Use the Chapter Review to prepare students for tests and to reteach content from the chapter.

Chapter 24 Mastery Test

The Teacher's Resource Library includes two forms of the Chapter 24 Mastery Test. Each test addresses the chapter Goals for Learning. An optional third page of additional critical-thinking items is included for each test. The difficulty level of the two forms is equivalent.

Chapter 24 Review Answers

Vocabulary Review

1. dominance

2. inferior

3. caravans

4. racism

5. conference

6. prejudiced

Chapter Review Questions

7. The Kush civilization was along the Nile River, just south of Egypt.

8. The Europeans did not want to cross the desert by land and they had not yet found a sea route.

9. The people of western Africa needed salt and the Arabs got gold in return. The Arabs also brought the Islam religion to Western Africa.

10. The Mali people took over Ghana.

11. The ruler, Mansa Musa, encouraged trade and taxed it.

Vocabulary Review

On a sheet of paper, use the words from the Word Bank to complete each sentence correctly.

Word Bank

caravans
conference
dominance
inferior
prejudiced
racism

1. When people show _____ toward others, they rule over them or use their power on them.

2. In colonial Africa, Europeans tried to make Africans feel _____, or not as good as Europeans.

3. About A.D. 1000, trade _____ crossed the desert to bring goods to Africa.

4. _____ is the mistaken idea that one race is better than another.

5. A(n) _____ is a meeting to discuss something.

6. Even though the slave trade had ended, Europeans were still _____ against Africans.

Chapter Review Questions

On a sheet of paper, write the answer to each question. Use complete sentences.

7. Where was the Kush civilization?

8. Why did Europeans have little contact with Africa south of the Sahara before 1400?

9. What goods and ideas did the people of western Africa and the Arabs trade?

10. Which people took over Ghana near the end of the 13th century?

11. How did the kingdom of Mali become rich?

12. During Songhai rule, what happened to Timbuktu?

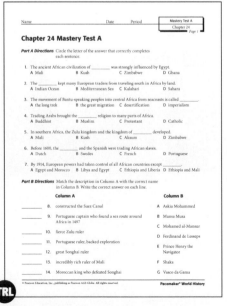

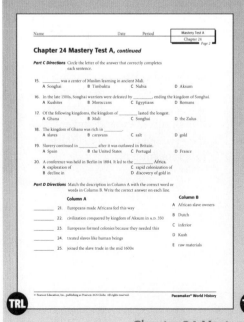

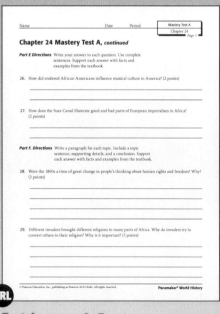

Test Tip

When answering a set of questions about a drawing or diagram, the answer to one question may be useful in answering the others.

13. What European nations took part in the slave trade in Africa during the 1600s?

14. What two factors led to European imperialism in Africa?

15. The Europeans colonized all but what two countries in Africa?

Critical Thinking

On a sheet of paper, write your response to each question. Use complete sentences.

16. How can salt be as valuable as gold?

17. How did the colonial powers show that they thought Africans were inferior?

Using the Timelines

Use the timelines on pages 493 and 507 to answer the questions.

18. How long did the Kushite civilization last?

19. Were the Kushites in power a longer time before or after the birth of Jesus?

20. How many years after the Dutch did the English join the slave trade?

GROUP ACTIVITY

Form groups of four students. Make a booklet of the early kingdoms of Africa. Describe the way of life and the accomplishments, or triumphs, of each kingdom.

---

12. Timbuktu became an even greater center of learning and trade.

13. The Portuguese, French, English, and Dutch took part in the slave trade.

14. Both the Industrial Revolution and racism led Europeans to colonize Africa.

15. Ethiopia and Liberia were the only two independent countries left in Africa after European colonization.

Critical Thinking

16. Possible answer: Salt can be as valuable as gold when people need salt to live. The people who lived south of the Sahara needed salt to preserve their food and to stay healthy.

17. Possible answers: Europeans enslaved some Africans. They split up Africa with no respect for the boundaries of kingdoms. They forced Africans to learn European ways.

Using the Timelines

18. 2,350 years

19. Before

20. 40 years

GROUP ACTIVITY

Students' brochures should include the Kushites, the Kingdom of Ghana, the Kingdom of Mali, and the Kingdom of Songhai. They may also include other African peoples.

Chapter 24 Mastery Test B

Part A Directions Circle the letter of the answer that correctly completes each sentence.

1. The _____ civilization was conquered by the kingdom of Aksum after A.D. 350.
   A Mali   B Kush   C Zimbabwe   D Ghana

2. African slave owners were different from European slave owners because they treated slaves like _____.
   A property   B kings   C criminals   D human beings

3. The French, the _____, and the Dutch joined the slave trade in the mid-1600s.
   A Germans   B Italians   C British   D Egyptians

4. The Europeans formed colonies in Africa because they needed _____.
   A raw materials for industry   B land for farming   C schools   D chiefs for their tribes

5. The Europeans thought Africans were _____ to them and forced them to learn European ways.
   A superior   B inferior   C smarter   D different

Part B Directions Match the description in Column A with the correct name in Column B. Write the correct answer on each line.

Column A		Column B
_____ 6.	great Songhai ruler	A Askia Mohammed
_____ 7.	ancient African civilization influenced by Egypt	B Bantu
_____ 8.	great, wealthy ruler of Mali	C Kush
_____ 9.	desert crossed by Arab caravans	D Mansa Musa
_____ 10.	powerful Zulu ruler	E Mohamed al-Mansur
_____ 11.	language of people in great migration	F Sahara
_____ 12.	Moroccan king, defeated Songhai warriors	G Shaka

Part C Directions Match the description in Column A with the correct word or words in Column B. Write the correct answer on each line.

Column A		Column B
_____ 13.	religion, spread by Arab traders	A Ferdinand de Lesseps
_____ 14.	kingdom of southern Africa	B Liberia
_____ 15.	Portuguese ruler, supported exploration	C Muslim
_____ 16.	discovered sea route around Africa in 1497	D Portuguese
_____ 17.	earliest European slave traders	E Prince Henry the Navigator
_____ 18.	French engineer, built Suez Canal	F Vasco da Gama
_____ 19.	independent African country in 1914	G Zimbabwe

Part D Directions Write the answers to these questions. Use complete sentences.

20. What was the kingdom of Ghana rich in?

21. What ancient African kingdom lasted the longest?

22. What African kingdom ended in a battle with Moroccans just before 1600?

23. What was the center of Muslim learning in ancient Mali?

24. What country outlawed slavery about 20 years later than Britain?

25. What event in 1884 led to the rapid colonization of Africa?

Chapter 24 Mastery Test B, continued

Part E Directions Write your answer to each question. Use complete sentences. Support each answer with facts and examples from the textbook.

26. In which century did attitudes toward African slavery change the most? Give at least two reasons for your choice. (2 points)

27. Compare and contrast the ways in which the Muslim religion and Christianity were spread in Africa. (2 points)

Part F Directions Write a paragraph for each topic. Include a topic sentence, supporting details, and a conclusion. Support each answer with facts and examples from the textbook.

28. Europeans kept control of the Suez Canal for nearly 100 years. How do you think the Europeans could have managed the canal more to Africans' benefit after they built it? (3 points)

29. Why do you think enslaved African Americans developed a new song form, the spiritual? Give at least three reasons. (3 points)

Chapter 24 Mastery Test B, pages 1–3

Nationalism and the Spread of War and Revolution: 1800–1950

	Student Text Lesson					
	Student Pages	Vocabulary	Map Study	Reading Strategy	Lesson Review	Chapter Summary/Review
Chapter 25 The Unifications of Italy and Germany	514–531	✔		✔		529–531
Lesson 25–1 Nationalism in Italy	516–522	✔	✔	✔	522	
Lesson 25–2 Nationalism in Germany	523–528	✔	✔	✔	528	
Chapter 26 World War I	532–549	✔		✔		547–549
Lesson 26–1 The War Begins in Europe	534–537	✔	✔	✔	537	
Lesson 26–2 The Fighting	538–541	✔		✔	541	
Lesson 26–3 The End of the War	542–546	✔	✔	✔	546	
Chapter 27 Revolution in Russia: The Birth of the Soviet Union	550–571	✔		✔		569–571
Lesson 27–1 The Early History of Russia	552–557	✔		✔	557	
Lesson 27–2 Unrest in the Early 1900s	558–561	✔		✔	561	
Lesson 27–3 Russia Becomes the USSR	562–568	✔	✔	✔	568	

(Unit Planning Guide is continued on next page.)

Chapter Activities

Teacher's Resource Library
Life Skills Connection 25–28
Key Vocabulary Words 25–28

Assessment Options

Student Text
Chapter Reviews 25–28
Teacher's Resource Library
Chapter 25 Mastery Tests A and B
Chapter 26 Mastery Tests A and B
Chapter 27 Mastery Tests A and B
Chapter 28 Mastery Tests A and B
Unit 9 Mastery Test
Teacher's Edition
Chapter Projects 25–28

	Student Text Features							Teaching Strategies										Learning Styles					Teacher's Resource Library			
Words from the Past	Learn More About It	Great Names in History	Technology Connection	Geography Note	You Decide/Remember/History Fact	Timeline Study	ELL/ESL Strategy	Background Information	Common Error	Life Skills Connection	Key Vocabulary Words	Study Skills	Applications Home, Career, Community	Online Connection	Teacher Alert	World Cultures	Auditory/Verbal	Body/Kinesthetic	Interpersonal/Group Learning	Logical/Mathematical	Visual/Spatial	Activities/Modified Activities	Workbook Activities	Self-Study Guide	Chapter Outline
---	---	---	---	---	---	---	---	---	---	---	---	---	---	---	---	---	---	---	---	---	---	---	---	---	---
										515	515													✔	✔
		521			517, 520		518	517	519			519	520	518	518		518				518	94	94		
525					523, 525, 526	527	527	524	524, 526							528		526	525	525		95	95		
										533	533													✔	✔
					535		536	535	535, 537			536	537				535			536		96	96		
	540				539, 540		540	539	541							541					540	97	97		
					542, 545	545	544	543	545				545	546	543				544	544		98	98		
										551	551													✔	✔
					556		555	554	553, 555					555			554	554				99	99		
560					558, 559		558	559	559, 560												560	100	100		
						567	565	564	565			565	566, 567		564	567				565	564	101	101		

Modified Activities

The Teacher's Resource Library (TRL) contains a set of lower-level worksheets called Modified Activities. These worksheets cover the same content as the standard Activities but are written at a lower reading level.

Skill Track

Use Skill Track for *World History* to monitor student progress and meet the demands of adequate yearly progress (AYP). Make informed instructional decisions with individual student and class reports of lesson and chapter assessments. With immediate and ongoing feedback, students will also see what they have learned and where they need more reinforcement and practice.

UNIT 9

PLANNING GUIDE

Nationalism and the Spread of War and Revolution: 1800–1950 *(continued)*

	Student Pages	Vocabulary	Map Study	Reading Strategy	Lesson Review	Chapter Summary/Review
Chapter 28 World War II	572–601	✔		✔		599–601
Lesson 28–1 The Rise of Dictators	574–578	✔		✔	578	
Lesson 28–2 World War II Begins in Europe	579–584	✔	✔	✔	584	
Lesson 28–3 The Holocaust and Allied Victories	585–590	✔		✔	590	
Lesson 28–4 The End of the War	591–594	✔		✔	594	
Lesson 28–5 The Results of the War	595–598	✔		✔	598	

Student Text Features							Teaching Strategies										Learning Styles					Teacher's Resource Library			
Words from the Past	Learn More About It	Great Names in History	Technology Connection	Geography Note	You Decide/Remember/History Fact	Timeline Study	ELL/ESL Strategy	Background Information	Common Error	Life Skills Connection	Key Vocabulary Words	Study Skills	Applications Home, Career, Community	Online Connection	Teacher Alert	World Cultures	Auditory/Verbal	Body/Kinesthetic	Interpersonal/Group Learning	Logical/Mathematical	Visual/Spatial	Activities/Modified Activities	Workbook Activities	Self-Study Guide	Chapter Outline
										573	573													✔	✔
					577		575	576	576, 577			577	577	574					576			102	102		
580					581, 583		581	581	582				582		581							103	103		
		587			586, 587, 588		588	587	589				589	589	590	588	587, 588					104	104		
				593			593	593	594									593				105	105		
					596	597	598	596												597	597	106	106		

Audio Library

Skill Track for
World History

Teacher's Resource Library **TRL**

Unit 9 Mastery Test

(Answer Keys for the Teacher's
Resource Library begin on page 809
of the Teacher's Edition.)

Other Resources

Books for Teachers

Collier, Martin. *Italian Unification 1820–71.* Heinemann Educational Publishers, 2003.

Merkl, Peter H. *German Unification.* Pennsylvania State University Press, 2004.

Riall, Lucy. *The Italian Risorgimento: State, Society and National Unification.* Routledge, 1994.

Books for Students

Abrams, Lynn. *Bismarck and the German Empire 1871–1918.* Routledge, 1995.

Landau, Elaine. *Napoleon Bonaparte.* Twenty-First Century Books, 2006.

Videos

Italy: Rome, Naples, and the Amalfi Coast. (52 minutes) Questar, 2002. (An overview of locations in Italy that are discussed in this chapter.)

NATIONALISM AND THE SPREAD OF WAR AND REVOLUTION

Nationalism is a feeling of strong loyalty to one's country. It may lead people to honor the flag or sing the anthem of that country. It may give them reason to risk their lives. The French had a sense of nationalism that made them fight for their rights within their country. The same was true of the American colonists.

Throughout history, a sense of nationalism gave even the poorest of people a real purpose. If they believed in their country, no government could abuse them in that country. They would revolt, if necessary, to make change. Sometimes the imperialism of one nation threatened the nationalism of another. This conflict often led to war.

Imperialism often leads to war. Japan thought the United States stood in the way of its control of the Pacific Ocean. So, Japan bombed the Pearl Harbor naval base in Hawaii, on December 7, 1941. The attack brought the United States into World War II.

Chapters in Unit 9

513

Introducing the Unit

Explain that the word *imperialism* is defined as "a powerful country seeking to expand into a smaller country" or "a powerful country seeking to dominate the policies of a smaller country." Imperialism may be met with nationalism, which is the pride and determination of the smaller country to maintain its independence. Have students read page 513 aloud to learn what can happen when these two forces intersect. Then have students study the photograph on page 512 and read the caption on page 513.

Ask:

- How was the reaction of the United States to the bombing of Pearl Harbor an example of nationalism? (It brought the United States into WWII to fight for its territory.)

- What is an example of nationalism practiced by people in a country? (honoring the flag, singing the anthem of that country)

- What has nationalism given people throughout history? (a sense of real purpose)

Web Sites

www.agsglobepmwh.com/page513a
(The history of Venice and Rome in A.D. 1866–1870.)

www.agsglobepmwh.com/page513b
(Facts on Bismarck and the unification of Germany.)

www.agsglobepmwh.com/page513c
(Additional information on the German empire.)

Chapter at a Glance

Chapter 25: The Unifications of Italy and Germany: 1800–1900
pages 514–531

Lessons

Audio Library

Skill Track for World History

Teacher's Resource Library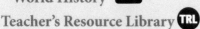

Workbook Activities 94–95

Activities 94–95

Modified Activities 94–95

Life Skills Connection 25

Key Vocabulary Words 25

Chapter 25 Self-Study Guide

Chapter 25 Outline

Chapter 25 Mastery Tests A and B

(Answer Keys for the Teacher's Resource Library begin on page 809 of the Teacher's Edition.)

Introducing the Chapter

Nationalism swept across Europe in the late 19th and early 20th centuries. Many changes occurred throughout the world as nationalism brought unification to Italy and Germany.

Ask:

• What unified the people of Italy and Germany? (They had a homeland. All around them were people with whom they shared a common language, customs, and culture.)

• Why did many Italians and Germans consider their country a homeland? (Their parents and grandparents were born in the same place they lived.)

• What is the word that made these people realize that they must defend their homeland, if necessary? (nationalism)

The Unifications of Italy and Germany

In the 19th century, the people of Italy and of Germany became much more unified. They had a homeland. Many were proud that their parents and grandparents were born in the same place they lived. All around them were people with whom they shared a common language, customs, and culture. Their sense of nationalism made them realize that they must defend their home, if necessary.

GOALS FOR LEARNING

• To tell how the spirit of nationalism led to the unification of Italy
• To tell how the spirit of nationalism led to the unification of Germany

514 *Unit 9 Nationalism and the Spread of War and Revolution*

Chapter 25 Self-Study Guide   Chapter 25 Outline, pages 1–2

Reading Strategy: Text Structure

Readers can look at the organization of the text to help them identify the most important information.

- Preview the chapter before you begin reading. Look at the chapter title and the names of the lessons and sections. Also review the boldfaced words and the maps and photographs.

- You will notice that the section titles are in the form of questions. The answer to each question is provided in the paragraph(s) in that section. In this way, the text is structured in a question and answer format.

Key Vocabulary Words

Lesson 1

Anthem The official song of a country

Unification Bringing together into one whole

Boundary The dividing line between one country and another

Unify To connect; to bring together as one

Society A group of people joined together for a common purpose

Prime minister The chief official of the government in some countries

Diplomat A person in government whose job is dealing with other countries

Lesson 2

Confederation A group of independent states joined together for a purpose

Legislature A group of people who make the laws of a nation or state

Reich The German word for "empire"

Kaiser The emperor of Germany

Chancellor The head of government, or prime minister, in some European countries

Militarism A national policy of maintaining a powerful army and constant readiness for war

Reading Strategy:
Text Structure

Explain that material in the text is organized to help the reader understand the content. Have students preview Lesson 25–1. Point out that the text is organized in sections according to topic. Each lesson has a title that tells what the lesson will be about, and each section has a subtitle. Explain that boldfaced words, maps, photographs, and captions are also part of the text structure.

Ask:

- Why do you think each section title is a question? (to grab students' interest, to direct students to the answer in the text)

Key Vocabulary Words

Point out that these chapter words are presented in the order they appear in each lesson. They are also found in the glossary.

LIFE SKILLS CONNECTION

Students learn about the military and discuss the different branches of the military.

KEY VOCABULARY

Students choose the correct word from the Word Bank to complete each sentence.

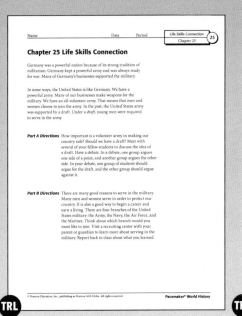

Life Skills Connection 25   Key Vocabulary Words 25

Lesson at a Glance

Chapter 25 Lesson 1

Overview This lesson describes nationalism, introduces the key people in the unification of Italy, and describes the contributions made by each person.

Objectives

- To define nationalism and explain why it develops
- To explain Napoleon's role in Italian nationalism
- To name three men who helped unify Italy
- To describe how Rome became a part of Italy

Student Pages 516–522

Teacher's Resource Library

Workbook Activity 94

Activity 94

Modified Activity 94

Vocabulary

anthem   society
boundary   unification
diplomat   unify
prime minister

Ask students to write each vocabulary word on a separate index card. As you read the definition for a vocabulary word, have students hold up the card on which the defined word is written. Repeat the definitions in a random order to be certain students understand the words.

1 Warm-Up Activity

Have students gather around a chess set. Using the pieces of the chess set, spread out the kings and queens on the board. Using the rest of the chess pieces, create groups around each king and queen. Place one knight in the center of the chess board. Explain that the knight's goal is to unite the four groups living under kings and queens who are very protective of their lands. Have students suggest why and how that goal could be accomplished. Explain that in this lesson, students will learn how three men united Italy.

Nationalism in Italy

Objectives

- To define nationalism and explain why it develops
- To explain Napoleon's role in Italian nationalism
- To name three men who helped unify Italy
- To describe how Rome became a part of Italy

Reading Strategy:
Text Structure

Preview this lesson. Notice the headings, features, and boldfaced words.

Anthem
The official song of a country

Unification
Bringing together into one whole

Nationalism is a feeling of strong loyalty to one's country and culture. Such a feeling often develops among people who speak the same language and follow similar customs. Nationalism leads people to honor their flag and to sing a national song, or **anthem**. It leads people to risk their lives to support their nation.

The spirit of nationalism helped the French fight off countries that were against their revolution. It gave the colonies in the Americas the strength to break away from the European imperialists.

In the 19th century, the spirit of nationalism led to the **unification** of Italy and of Germany. In each place, people were feeling the bonds of language, customs, and culture. They decided it was time to unite as a single nation.

What Role Did Napoleon Have in Italian Nationalism?

During the early Roman times, Italy had been a united country. It was the center of the Roman Empire. But late in the fifth century A.D., the Roman Empire fell. Italy was divided into many small kingdoms. For more than 1,000 years, different nations and monarchs fought for control of the Italian territories. French troops, Spanish troops, and German troops marched through Italy. Then in 1796, Napoleon Bonaparte invaded the Italian peninsula and took power.

Napoleon granted Venetia to Austria. Venetia was the kingdom that included the city of Venice. Napoleon put the rest of the small kingdoms under his own rule. In 1804, he crowned himself ruler of the new kingdom. The crown he wore had these words on it: "God gave it [the Italian peninsula] to me; woe to him who dares touch it."

Reading Strategy:
Text Structure

Allow students a few minutes to preview the lesson. Have them identify the differences in the maps on pages 518–519. Point out that the titles of the maps provide important information about their content.

CHAPTER PROJECT

Divide the class into two large groups. One group will study the unification of Italy. One group will study the unification of Germany. Explain that each group will need to create two puzzle boards that highlight the geography of unification and two games that highlight the events leading to unification. Allow students in each group to further divide according to their interests. Have students use library resources and the Internet to gather information for their puzzles or games.

Boundary
The dividing line between one country and another

Unify
To connect; to bring together as one

Society
A group of people joined together for a common purpose

 Remember
In India in the late 1800s, British leaders did not know their policy of sending Indians to school in Britain would encourage ideas of Indian independence.

Reading Strategy:
Text Structure

As you read this lesson, use three separate graphic organizers (such as webs) to gather details about Mazzini, Cavour, and Garibaldi.

Napoleon's actions gave rise to the spirit of nationalism. This spirit would one day carry Italy to independence. Napoleon did away with old **boundary** lines, the lines that divided one country from another. Then he joined the little kingdoms together. By doing this, he gave Italians a chance to look at themselves as members of one group. The idea that all of them were Italians began to grow.

Why Did Italians Form Secret Societies?

As feelings of nationalism grew, Italians began to think about unity. They dreamed about one independent Italy. However, by 1815, Italy was once again divided into many kingdoms and states. Most of these were ruled either by Austria or by the pope. The Italians who wanted to bring together, or **unify,** Italy had some barriers to overcome.

Austria tried to crush any ideas of unity. Austria wanted Italy to remain weak and divided. The pope also tried to crush any ideas of unity. He feared nationalism as a threat to his own power.

The people, however, wanted to be free. They wanted to join together as one nation. So secret revolutionary **societies**, groups of people joined together for a common purpose, sprang up. During the mid-1800s, three men became leaders of the movement toward a unified Italy. Italians called these men "The Soul," "The Brain," and "The Sword."

What Did "The Soul" Do?

"The Soul" of Italy was a man named Giuseppe Mazzini. In 1830, he joined a group that was working to unify Italy. That same year, he was exiled because of his political activities. He would remain in exile for 18 years. In 1831, Mazzini organized a secret society known as "Young Italy." The society's goal was to free the Italian peninsula from Austrian rule. Young Italy wanted to join the country together under one government.

Ask students to recall the definition of nationalism. Then have students read from pages 516–521 to learn about the "The Soul," "The Brain," and "The Sword" of Italy during the time of nationalism and unification.

Ask:

- Why did Giuseppe Mazzini's revolution fail? (Austrian and French armies helped put down the Italian revolt.)
- Which country helped Camillo di Cavour defeat Austria? (France)
- Who were the "Red Shirts?" (Garibaldi's army)

 Remember
India's rebellion against the British began in 1857. However, the British government continued to rule the country for the next 90 years. India became independent on August 15, 1947.

Reading Strategy:
Text Structure

Distribute a compare and contrast graphic organizer for students to use as they read the lesson. Have them keep notes about Giuseppe Mazzini, Camillo di Cavour, and Giuseppe Garibaldi on the graphic organizer.

Background Information

The Tiber River is the subject of many legends. The Roman king Tibernius Silvius was said to have drowned in the Abula River, so it was renamed Tiber in his memory. This king was sometimes depicted as a god of the river, with water streaming from his hair and beard. Another legend says that Romulus and Remus, twin boys, were thrown into the river. They were rescued by a she-wolf, who raised them. Later, Romulus founded the city of Rome in 753 B.C.

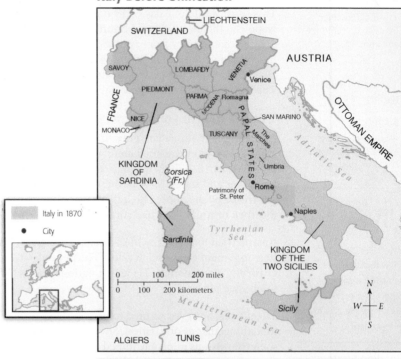

Italy Before Unification

MAP STUDY

Answers:

1. The Tyrrhenian Sea, Mediterranean Sea, Adriatic Sea

2. Sardinia and Sicily

MAP STUDY

1. Italy is bordered by which three seas?
2. Which main islands are part of Italy?

In 1848, revolutions broke out in many European countries. Mazzini returned to Italy to stir up a revolution there. The ruler of the kingdom of Sardinia favored the revolutionaries. He tried to help their cause by declaring war on Austria. However, Austrian and French armies helped put down the Italian revolt.

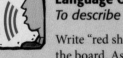

Italy Today

ITALY map showing: LIECHTENSTEIN, AUSTRIA, HUNGARY, SWITZERLAND, SLOVENIA, CROATIA, BOSNIA & HERZEGOVINA, FRANCE, Po R., Venice, ITALY, SAN MARINO, Tiber R., MONACO, Corsica (Fr.), Rome, Adriatic Sea, Naples, Sardinia, Tyrrhenian Sea, Sicily, Mediterranean Sea, ALGERIA, TUNISIA

Legend:
- Italy today
- ⊛ Capital city
- ● City

Scale: 0 100 200 miles / 0 100 200 kilometers

N W E S

MAP STUDY

1. What river runs through the capital of Italy?
2. What island off the coast of Italy is still under French control?

Not only did the revolution fail, but Sardinia was also defeated. Mazzini had to go into exile once again.

The Austrians forced the Sardinian king from his throne. His son, Victor Emmanuel II, became king of Sardinia in 1849.

Answers:
1. The Tiber River
2. Corsica

3 Reinforce and Extend

COMMON ERROR

Students may confuse Austria and Australia. Point out that Austria is a country and Australia is a continent. Display the two on a world map or have students investigate the locations of both on maps on the Internet.

STUDY SKILLS

To help students organize their material, ask them to create a chart with three columns and three rows. They can title the chart "Italian Nationalists." Have students write Soul, Brain, and Sword in the first column. In the second column, students should provide the names of the three Italian nationalists, placing them in the proper rows. (Mazzini; Cavour; Garibaldi) The third column should contain explanations as to why each term was associated with each nationalist. (stood for Italy's spirit of freedom; planned strategies; great military feats)

COMMON ERROR

Students may not make the connection between the nicknames of the Italian revolutionaries and their accomplishments. Explain that "The Soul" of Italy, Giuseppe Mazzini, represented the spirit of revolution, to become free and join together as one nation. "The Brain" was political mastermind Camillo di Cavour. "The Sword" was Giuseppe Garibaldi, a tough enforcer who finally brought Italy independence.

Prime minister
The chief official of the government in some countries

Diplomat
A person in government whose job is dealing with other countries

Giuseppe Garibaldi fought for Italian independence.

You Decide
The United States has a volunteer army today. Do you think this is a good idea? Why or why not?

What Did "The Brain" Do?

The new king of Sardinia was also in favor of Italian unity. He named Camillo Benso, Conte di Cavour, as his **prime minister,** the chief official of the government. This act moved Italy closer to freedom. Camillo di Cavour would soon be known as "The Brain," the leader of the unification movement.

Cavour was a **diplomat,** a master of foreign affairs. He recognized Austria as an enemy of unification. In 1858, he arranged a defense agreement between Sardinia and France. The next year Austria declared war on Sardinia. However, French and Italian soldiers pushed the Austrians almost as far east as Venice. Sardinia gained the nearby regions of Lombardy. Then in 1860, Romagna, Modena, Parma, and Tuscany showed their respect for Sardinia's accomplishments. They united with Sardinia and turned against Austria.

What Did "The Sword" Do?

Giuseppe Garibaldi was a revolutionary most of his life. When he was 26, he joined the secret society, Young Italy. Garibaldi was a soldier in the battle for freedom. His attempts to lead Italy to independence won him the nickname of "The Sword."

Failed rebellions forced Garibaldi to flee Italy or face death. He returned in 1848 to fight under Mazzini. When this revolution failed, he went into exile again.

In 1859, Garibaldi was back in Italy. He joined the fight for freedom led by King Victor Emmanuel of Sardinia. Garibaldi led an army of 1,000 volunteers to Sicily. His men were called "Red Shirts" because they wore red shirts as uniforms.

When Garibaldi and his army reached Sicily, many Sicilians joined them. Sicily was soon free.

Then Garibaldi, "The Sword," led his army north on the Italian mainland. He headed for Naples. Cavour, "The Brain," sent an army south. By the end of 1860, the two armies had freed most of Italy. In 1861, Victor Emmanuel II became ruler of an almost completely united Italy.

How Did Rome Become a Part of Italy?

Only Rome and the northern kingdom of Venetia were still not free. The pope ruled Rome, and Austria ruled Venetia. In 1866, the Italians helped Prussia defeat Austria in war. In return for its support, Italy was given Venetia.

Then came Rome. Garibaldi tried to take Rome twice, but failed. He was defeated by French troops who came to aid the pope. In 1870, Italy got another chance at Rome. France was fighting a war against Prussia. France took its troops out of Rome to help fight the Prussians. It was Italy's time to move! The pope's own small army could not fight off the Italian troops. Rome finally became part of the united nation of Italy. In 1870, Rome became the capital of Italy.

TECHNOLOGY CONNECTION

Marconi, the Telegraph, and the Radio

An Italian engineer named Guglielmo Marconi invented the wireless telegraph in 1895. In 1901, he transmitted, or sent, a signal on radio waves across the Atlantic Ocean. The signal went from England to Newfoundland. Marconi went on to build communication products for ships at sea. A few years later, Canadian Reginald Fessenden and American Ernst Alexanderson made related advances. They learned how to send speech and music on the same radio waves. Another American named Lee de Forest created a device to make these radio messages louder. By 1906, the beginnings of radio were established.

Large-scale worldwide radio broadcasting began about 1922. The number of radio stations in the United States grew from eight to nearly 600. Broadcasting services developed in Britain, Russia, and France about the same time.

Have a volunteer read the passage aloud. Point out that it has been fewer than 100 years since the early days of radio. Ask students to suggest ways radio changed and influenced society. (People could get news quickly. People could listen to programs on the radio for fun.) Then have students discuss other advances in audio technology that have taken place since the radio was invented, such as satellite radio, 3D sound, and other new sound technology. Ask volunteers to suggest ways they think radio technology might change in the next 100 years.

Lesson 25–1 Review Answers

1. Nationalism is a feeling of strong loyalty to one's country and culture. It often develops among people who speak the same language and follow similar customs. **2.** Napoleon did away with the old boundary lines. Then he joined the little Italian kingdoms together. By doing this, he gave Italians a chance to look at themselves as members of one group. **3.** France had taken its troops out of Rome to help fight the Prussians. The pope's own small army could not fight off the Italian troops. In this way, Rome became part of Italy. **4.** C **5.** A **6.** B **7.** B **8.** C **9.** A **10.** D

On a sheet of paper, write the answer to each question. Use complete sentences.

1. What is nationalism and why does it develop?

2. What role did Napoleon have in Italian nationalism?

3. How did Rome become a part of Italy?

Match the description in Column A with the revolutionary in Column B. Write the correct letter on a sheet of paper.

Column A

4. organized a secret society whose goal was to free the Italian peninsula from Austrian rule; known as "The Soul"

5. prime minister of Sardinia who is considered the leader of the unification movement; known as "The Brain"

6. led the "Red Shirts" and freed Sicily; known as "The Sword"

Column B

A Camillo di Cavour

B Giuseppe Garibaldi

C Giuseppe Mazzini

On a sheet of paper, write the letter of the answer that correctly completes each sentence.

7. "_____" was the secret society formed to free the Italian peninsula from Austrian rule.

    A Red Shirts   **B** Young Italy   **C** The Sword   **D** The Soul

8. In 1861, _____ was the ruler of an almost completely unified Italy.

    A the pope   **C** Victor Emmanuel II
    B Giuseppe Garibaldi   **D** Camillo di Cavour

9. Italy was given _____ in return for helping Prussia defeat Austria in war.

    A Venetia   **B** Rome   **C** Sicily   **D** Tuscany

10. Rome became the capital of Italy in _____.

    A 1848   **B** 1859   **C** 1866   **D** 1870

522   *Unit 9   Nationalism and the Spread of War and Revolution*

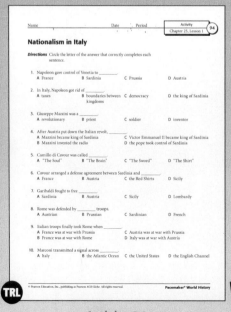

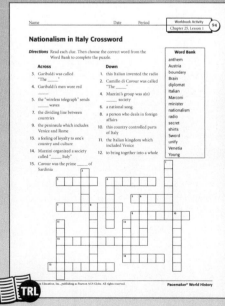

Nationalism in Germany

Objectives

■ To explain Napoleon's role in German nationalism
■ To tell how Bismarck united Germany under a Prussian kaiser
■ To describe two main features of the new German nation

Confederation
A group of independent states joined together for a purpose

Legislature
A group of people who make the laws of a nation or state

History Fact
The 39 states agreed to be members of the German Confederation, but each one remained an independent state.

Just as he did in Italy, Napoleon lit the first flames of nationalism in Germany. Napoleon took over large parts of Germany in 1806. These lands were made up of many small kingdoms. Napoleon decided to join them together to rule them more easily. He called the group of kingdoms the **Confederation** of the Rhine. A confederation is a group of independent states joined together for a purpose. People living within the Confederation began to have a sense of loyalty toward one another.

When Napoleon was defeated in 1815, a new German Confederation was formed. The Confederation joined 39 states together, including Austria and Prussia. Since Austria was large, it considered itself the leader. However, Prussia had a well-organized government and real strength—military strength.

Many Germans thought about unifying the states under a central government. Only Austria was against German unity. Austrians thought they could remain more powerful with the German states divided. It was not until 1862 that Germany moved toward becoming one nation.

Who Was Otto von Bismarck?

The king of Prussia, Wilhelm I, was having problems with his law-making group, the **legislature**. King Wilhelm wanted to add to his already mighty army. However, the legislature would not give him the money that he needed. King Wilhelm turned to a Prussian landowner and soldier to help him. His name was Otto von Bismarck. In 1862, Wilhelm appointed Bismarck prime minister.

History Fact
The purpose of the German Confederation was to guarantee the internal and external peace of Germany and the independence of its member states. The members pledged mutual aid to each other in the event that they were attacked.

Lesson at a Glance

Chapter 25 Lesson 2

Overview This lesson explains how the German states came together to form one nation.

Objectives

■ To explain Napoleon's role in German nationalism
■ To tell how Bismarck united Germany under a Prussian kaiser
■ To describe two main features of the new German nation

Student Pages 523–528

Teacher's Resource Library **TRL**

Workbook Activity 95

Activity 95

Modified Activity 95

Vocabulary

chancellor	legislature
confederation	militarism
kaiser	reich

Have students study the definitions of the vocabulary words. Then have them write the words in one column and the definitions in a second column. Tell students to write both words and definitions in random order. Have students exchange papers with a partner and match each word to its correct definition. Then have students correct each other's work.

1 Warm-Up Activity

Write three columns on the board: resources/nationalism/strategy. Have students brainstorm the factors that result in a country becoming a military might, such as availability of industry, natural resources, financial backing, soldiers, common heritage and history, leadership, and a strategy that will lead to victory over adversaries. Write their ideas under the proper columns. Have students copy the information and refer to it as they read through the lesson.

2 | Teaching the Lesson

Have students turn to the timeline on page 527. Ask them to find the year in which Germany became unified. (1871) Have students read pages 523–527 to learn about the steps that led to German unification.

Ask:

- Whose action lit the first flames of nationalism in Germany and what did he do? (Napoleon; he took over large parts of Germany in 1806)

- How did Otto von Bismarck become a leader in Germany? (He was appointed prime minister. He worked for German unification. Later, he became the chancellor, or head of government, of Germany.)

- What were the two main features of the new Germany? (The kaiser and chancellor had complete power of Germany. Germany had a strong tradition of militarism.)

Background Information

The Austro-Prussian War, also called the Seven Weeks' War, took place between June and August of 1866. Otto von Bismarck used this war to make Prussia the most powerful state in the German Confederation and to force Austria out of the Confederation. The Prussians' skillful use of new inventions such as the railroad and telegraph led them to victory.

Reading Strategy:
Text Structure

Have students share ideas about how the map is helpful to understanding the lesson. Answers may include that it is sometimes easier to comprehend the area and the land when looking at a map, instead of reading about it.

COMMON ERROR

 Direct students' attention to the title of the map on this page. Point out that this map shows Germany and its surrounding countries as they were in 1871. However, changes in boundaries and country names have occurred since then.

Otto von Bismarck had a strong sense of loyalty to Prussia. He was not interested in democracy or individual rights. He believed that duty to one's country was most important.

Reading Strategy:
Text Structure

Study the map of the unification of Germany. How does this map help you to understand what this lesson is about?

The Unification of Germany, 1871

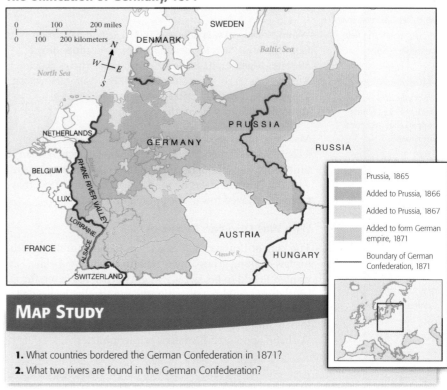

MAP STUDY

1. What countries bordered the German Confederation in 1871?
2. What two rivers are found in the German Confederation?

MAP STUDY

Answers:

1. the Netherlands, Belgium, Luxembourg, Alsace and Lorraine, Switzerland, Hungary, Russia

2. the Rhine River and the Danube River

You may want to use a present-day map to have students compare the countries and boundaries of 1871 with the countries of today.

Words from the Past

Otto von Bismarck expanded and unified Germany.

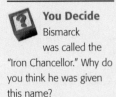

You Decide

Bismarck was called the "Iron Chancellor." Why do you think he was given this name?

Bismarck's Policy of "Blood and Iron"

Bismarck thought the goals of the individual and the state were the same. He promised the Prussian king a firm hand over the legislature and the people. The new prime minister thought that could be done with a strong army. "The importance of a state," Bismarck said, "is measured by the number of soldiers it can put into the field of battle . . . ."

Bismarck followed a policy of "blood and iron." In other words, it was a policy of war. "The great questions of our day," he said, "cannot be settled by speeches and majority votes, but by blood and iron."

Bismarck encouraged King Wilhelm to unite the German states under one rule—Prussian rule. "My highest ambition is to make the Germans a nation," Bismarck said.

How was this to be done? Bismarck's answer was war!

Logical/Mathematical

Ask students to create an outline of this section. Students may want to list prominent figures as main points and their accomplishments as subpoints. Alternatively, students could create a chronology of revolts and wars as main points and list the importance of each as subpoints.

 You Decide

Have students discuss their answers to the question with a partner. They may say that Bismarck was called the "Iron Chancellor" after the name of his policy, or because he was as cold and hard as iron.

LEARNING STYLES

Interpersonal/Group Learning

Divide the class into small groups. Explain that Alsace and Lorraine continued to be a region in dispute in future conflicts between Germany and France during the 20th century. Assign each group a characteristic of Alsace and Lorraine to research, such as natural resources, geography, agriculture, trade, language, and traditions. Have each group share what it learned. Discuss the importance of the region's attributes.

WORDS FROM THE PAST

Read aloud the passage about Bismarck's policy of "blood and iron." Have students explain in their own words what they think this policy means. Answers may include the ideas that blood is spilled when people are wounded or die in battle, and iron represents the weapons with which armies fight.

Reading Strategy:
Text Structure

Provide students with a sequence of events graphic organizer. Have them record the events that took Otto von Bismarck from prime minister to chancellor of Germany.

History Fact

The Latin word *Caesar* meant "an emperor." All Roman emperors were called *Caesar*, although the word is most commonly associated with Julius Caesar.

COMMON ERROR

Point out the word *rally* in the third paragraph on this page. Have students discuss their understanding of the word. Then explain that in the context of Bismarck's leadership, *rally* means "to call together for action."

Reich
The German word for "empire"

Kaiser
The emperor of Germany

Chancellor
The head of government, or prime minister, in some European countries

Reading Strategy:
Text Structure

Create an organizer (such as a simple chart) to record what Otto von Bismarck did during his reign. Be sure to put it in the correct order.

History Fact
The title *kaiser* came from the Latin word *Caesar*.

How Was the Second Reich Formed?

In 1864, Bismarck began a war with Denmark. After just seven months of fighting, Prussia seized two provinces from Denmark. In 1866, Prussia and Italy defeated Austria in the Seven Weeks' War. This brought the German Confederation to an end.

Then Prussia formed the North German Confederation in 1867, without Austria. Most of the German states joined. The Confederation's seat of power was Prussia, and at its head was Wilhelm I.

Bismarck would not be satisfied until all the German states were united under Wilhelm's rule. He decided on the best way to join the states. He would rally them together against one common enemy. For that purpose, in 1870, Bismarck started a war with France. Prussia's mighty armies won easily. They took the provinces of Alsace and Lorraine as their prize.

At the end of the war, all German states joined with Prussia. They formed a united German empire. On January 18, 1871, the new German empire was officially declared. It was also called the *Second Reich* (*reich* is the German word for "empire"). King Wilhelm I of Prussia was crowned its emperor, or *kaiser*.

What Were the Two Main Features of the New German Nation?

There were two main features of the new Germany. First, Germany was not a democratic nation. Germans accepted rule by a single person. Bismarck became the head of government, the **chancellor**, of Germany. He was responsible only to Kaiser Wilhelm I. Neither the kaiser nor the chancellor had to answer to any legislature or to any elected representatives. These two men alone had complete power in Germany.

Second, Germany had a strong tradition of **militarism**. Militarism was Germany's policy where they kept a powerful army and were always ready for war. Bismarck's "blood and iron" policy became the German way. German nationalism meant pride in a mighty military force.

Germans gave their soldiers respect and honor. It was a German's privilege to belong to a great army. It was an honor to fight for the glory of the empire.

Much of Germany was geared toward a strong military. Large businesses supported the army. Major industrialists, like Friedrich Krupp of the Krupp Iron and Steel Works, devoted factories to making war machines. Krupp built guns and cannons. The whole nation stood behind the military effort. Germany was ready for war!

TIMELINE STUDY:

UNIFICATION OF ITALY AND GERMANY

Which people had a revolution, the Italians or the Germans?

1849
Victor Emmanuel II becomes king of Sardinia

1860
Garibaldi and Red Shirts conquer Italy

1831
Young Italy founded

1848
Revolution in Italy

1870
Rome becomes capital of united Italy

1800   1850   1900

1861
Victor Emmanuel II becomes king of Italy

1871
German states unite; Wilhelm I becomes kaiser

1862
Bismarck becomes prime minister of Prussia

1800–1900   *The Unifications of Italy and Germany*   Chapter 25   **527**

3 Reinforce and Extend

WORLD CULTURES

 Throughout the second half of the 19th century, Germans represented the largest group of immigrants. Before the turn of the century, more than five million Germans arrived in the United States. Many settled in Ohio and in Wisconsin where farmland was plentiful, bringing their German heritage, foods, and traditions with them. The German word *burg*, meaning "castle" is found attached to a few small cities and villages in Wisconsin, such as *Reedsburg*, *Harrisburg*, and *Johnsburg*. Moreover, Amish living in Ohio, Wisconsin, and other states maintain their German heritage through their language and traditions.

Lesson 25–2 Review Answers

1. Napoleon joined the small kingdoms of Germany into the Confederation of the Rhine. People living within the Confederation began to have a sense of loyalty toward one another. **2.** Bismarck wanted all the German states united under Wilhelm's rule. He decided on the best way to join the states. He rallied them together against one common enemy. For that purpose, he started a war with France. **3.** The new German nation was ruled by a single person. It had a policy of militarism. **4.** Austria **5.** Otto von Bismarck **6.** war **7.** Second Reich **8.** King Wilhelm I **9.** chancellor **10.** military

---

LESSON 25-2 REVIEW

On a sheet of paper, write the answer to each question. Use complete sentences.

1. What role did Napoleon have in German nationalism?

2. Why did Bismarck start a war with France?

3. What are two features of the new German nation?

On a sheet of paper, write the word from the Word Bank to complete each sentence correctly.

Word Bank

Austria

chancellor

King Wilhelm I

military

Otto von Bismarck

Second Reich

war

4. _____ was the only state against German unity.

5. In 1862, Wilhelm I, king of Prussia, appointed _____ prime minister.

6. Otto von Bismarck believed in a policy of _____, and that duty to one's country was most important.

7. The new German empire formed in 1871 was known as the _____.

8. _____ was crowned kaiser of the new German empire.

9. In the new German nation, the kaiser and the _____ had complete power.

10. Germans placed great pride in their _____.

Activity 95

Workbook Activity 95

CHAPTER 25

SUMMARY

- The spirit of nationalism led the people of Italy to unite under a central government. During the 19th century, the Italians worked toward independence and unification.

- Giuseppe Mazzini was the leader of a secret society called "Young Italy," which worked to unify Italy.

- Camillo di Cavour was a diplomat and leader of the unification movement in Italy.

- Giuseppe Garibaldi led a revolutionary army that fought for a unified Italy.

- Almost all of Italy was united by 1860. Sardinia's king, Victor Emmanuel II, became its ruler.

- In 1870, Italy was totally united. Rome became its capital city.

- During the 19th century, many Germans wanted to see a unified Germany. Austria opposed the unification of Germany.

- The prime minister of Prussia, Otto von Bismarck, started a war to unify Germany.

- Bismarck won his wars, and in 1871 Germany was united. Prussia's Wilhelm I became the kaiser of the German empire.

- Germans accepted rule by a single person, known as the chancellor.

- Germany developed a tradition of militarism and loyalty to strong leaders.

Chapter 25 Summary

Have students read the Chapter Summary on page 529 to review the main ideas presented in Chapter 25.

Ask:

- What led Italy to unite under a central government? (the spirit of nationalism)

- Who was the leader of a secret society called "Young Italy?" (Giuseppe Mazzini)

- Who was a diplomat and leader of the unification movement in Italy? (Camillo di Cavour)

- Who led a revolutionary army in Italy? (Giuseppe Garibaldi)

- Who became the ruler of Italy after most of it was united in 1860? (Victor Emmanuel II)

- What city became the capital of Italy? (Rome)

- What country opposed the unification of Germany? (Austria)

- Who started the war that led to a united Germany? (Otto von Bismarck)

- Who became kaiser of the German empire? (Wilhelm I)

- What two traits defined the new Germany? (militarism and loyalty to strong leaders)

CHAPTER PROJECT FOLLOW-UP

 Provide time for students to share and explain their puzzle boards and games based on the unification of Italy or Germany. Provide time for the class to enjoy the puzzle boards and play the games.

TEACHER'S RESOURCE

The AGS Globe Teaching Strategies in Social Studies Transparencies may be used with this chapter. The transparencies add an interactive dimension to expand and enhance the Pacemaker® *World History* program content.

Chapter 25 Review

Use the Chapter Review to prepare students for tests and to reteach content from the chapter.

Chapter 25 Mastery Test

The Teacher's Resource Library includes two forms of the Chapter 25 Mastery Test. Each test addresses the chapter Goals for Learning. An optional third page of additional critical-thinking items is included for each test. The difficulty level of the two forms is equivalent.

Chapter 25 Review Answers

Vocabulary Review

1. prime minister
2. militarism
3. unification
4. anthem
5. diplomat
6. Reich
7. legislature
8. societies
9. confederation
10. kaiser

Chapter Review Questions

11. The purpose of Young Italy was to free the Italian peninsula from Austrian rule. Young Italy wanted to join the country together under one government.

12. Giuseppe Mazzini, Camillo di Cavour, and Giuseppe Garibaldi helped to unite Italy.

Vocabulary Review

On a sheet of paper, use the words from the Word Bank to complete each sentence correctly.

Word Bank

anthem
confederation
diplomat
kaiser
legislature
militarism
prime minister
reich
societies
unification

1. The _____ is the most important official in some countries, such as Britain.

2. Germany's strong tradition of _____ made them always ready for war.

3. Italians were interested in _____ to bring together people with a common language, customs, and culture.

4. A national _____ is a national song.

5. A(n) _____ is a person who deals with other countries for his or her own country.

6. _____ is the German word for "empire."

7. Prussia's _____ would not give King Wilhelm money to add to his army.

8. Many revolutionary _____ sprang up in Italy; they shared the same purpose: freedom.

9. Napoleon joined many small kingdoms of Germany together to rule them more easily. He called the group the _____ of the Rhine.

10. The emperor of Germany is the _____.

Chapter Review Questions

On a sheet of paper, write the answer to each question. Use complete sentences.

11. What was the purpose of Young Italy?

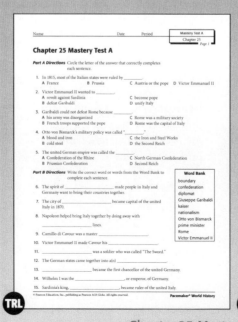

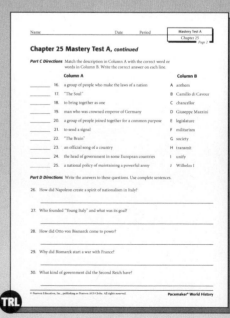

Chapter 25 Mastery Test A, pages 1–3

Test Tip

Pay special attention to key words in a set of directions—words such as *first*, *second*, *most important*, *least important*, *all*, *some*, *only*, *more than one*, *best*, and *none*.

12. What three men helped unify Italy?

13. How did the Italians take control of Rome?

14. How did Bismarck manage to form a united Germany?

15. What was the Second Reich?

16. How did German industry help the nation get ready for war?

Critical Thinking

On a sheet of paper, write your response to each question. Use complete sentences.

17. How did Napoleon help to develop a spirit of nationalism among Italians?

18. What are some positive ways to unite a country?

Using the Timeline

Use the timeline on page 527 to answer the questions.

19. When did Victor Emmanuel II become king of Italy?

20. When did Wilhelm I become kaiser of Germany?

GROUP ACTIVITY

Write a paragraph that compares and contrasts the way Italy and Germany became nations. Exchange your paragraph with a partner. Discuss the ideas in your paragraphs. Revise your paragraphs to make your ideas clearer.

---

13. The Italians tried twice to take Rome. They were defeated by French troops who came to aid the pope. Then in 1870, French troops were fighting the Prussians. The Italians defeated the pope's small army.

14. He united the people against a common enemy, France.

15. The Second Reich was the new German empire. It was a united German empire.

16. German industries made war machines for the military.

Critical Thinking

17. Possible answer: Napoleon did away with the boundaries of kingdoms. This encouraged the people of these kingdoms to see themselves as Italians.

18. Possible answer: A country can unite in positive ways. It could honor its history. It could honor its heroes or history.

Using the Timeline

19. 1861

20. 1871

GROUP ACTIVITY

Students' paragraphs should show understanding of similarities and differences in the road to unification. A similarity might be the small kingdoms of both places. A difference might be that the Italian people joined secret societies to work for independence from Austria and the pope. Otto von Bismarck, Germany's prime minister, decided on the best way to join the German states under King Wilhelm I's rule. He rallied them together against a common enemy. He started a war with France.

Chapter 25 Mastery Test B

Part A Directions Circle the letter of the answer that correctly completes each sentence.

1. Napoleon created nationalism in Italy by _____.
   A joining the Italian kingdoms together
   B conquering Austria
   C making Cavour his prime minister
   D forming "Young Italy"

2. The goal of "Young Italy" was to _____.
   A conquer France
   B free Sicily
   C free Italy from Austrian rule
   D free Italy from Sardinian rule

3. Wilhelm I made Otto von Bismarck the _____.
   A leader of the Confederation of the Rhine
   B prime minister of Austria
   C king of Sardinia
   D prime minister of Prussia

4. Bismarck brought the German states together by _____.
   A going to war with Denmark
   B starting a war with France
   C defending Prussia against Austria
   D becoming chancellor of the Reich

5. The Second Reich was a(n) _____.
   A democracy   B republic   C empire   D both A and B

Part B Directions Write the correct word or words from the Word Bank to complete each sentence.

6. _____ founded "Young Italy" to free the Italian peninsula.

7. "Young Italy" was a secret _____.

8. Marconi's "wireless telegraph" _____ radio waves.

9. People in Italy and Germany wanted to _____ their nations.

10. People show pride in their country by singing their national _____.

11. _____ was called "The Brain" of the unification movement.

12. The king of Prussia, _____, became emperor of Germany.

13. Since Germany was not democratic, it had no _____.

14. Wilhelm I and _____ ran the government of the united Germany.

15. Germany's strong army was supported by a tradition of _____.

Word Bank
anthem
Camillo di Cavour
Giuseppe Mazzini
legislature
militarism
Otto von Bismarck
society
transmitted
unify
Wilhelm I

Chapter 25 Mastery Test B, *continued*

Part C Directions Match the description in Column A with the correct word or words in Column B. Write the correct answer on each line.

	Column A	Column B
___ 16.	a group of independent states joined together for a purpose	A boundary
___ 17.	the chief official of the government in some countries	B confederation
___ 18.	"The Sword"	C diplomat
___ 19.	man who was chancellor of the Second Reich	D Giuseppe Garibaldi
___ 20.	the emperor of Germany	E kaiser
___ 21.	city that became capital of the united Italy in 1870	F nationalism
___ 22.	man who was king of the united Italy	G Otto von Bismarck
___ 23.	a feeling of strong loyalty to one's country and culture	H prime minister
___ 24.	the dividing line between one country and another	I Rome
___ 25.	a person in government whose job is dealing with other countries	J Victor Emmanuel II

Part D Directions Write the answers to these questions. Use complete sentences.

26. Who ruled most of the Italian kingdoms and states in 1815?

27. What did Victor Emmanuel II want to do?

28. Why did Garibaldi fail to take Rome?

29. What was the phrase that described Otto von Bismarck's military policy?

30. What was the Second Reich?

Chapter 25 Mastery Test B, pages 1–3

Introducing the Chapter

One incident—an assassination in
Sarajevo—set off a series of events
that climaxed with World War I. This
chapter discusses the tensions that
led to the war. It describes trench
warfare, and the devastation caused
by terrifying new weapons. In the end,
the winners came up with a treaty that
made the losers pay heavily.

Ask:

• Which incident began World
  War I? (the assassination of
  Archduke Ferdinand and his wife
  by a Serbian revolutionary)

• How did soldiers fight this war?
  (Many fought in a network of
  trenches on one of the three
  fronts.)

World War I

The major powers in Europe had been gathering
military strength for many years. For most countries,
a sense of national pride seemed to call for an army. Of
course, some built strong armies to help them conquer
weaker nations. Others needed armies simply to avoid
being conquered.

Finally, war began on July 28, 1914. It involved many
countries, most of them in Europe. The battles featured
modern weapons that caused great destruction. Years later
it would come to be called "World War I."

GOALS FOR LEARNING

• To describe the beginnings of World War I
• To describe the fighting during the war
• To describe the terms of peace at the end of the war

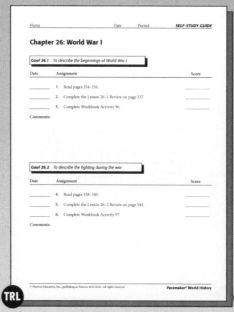

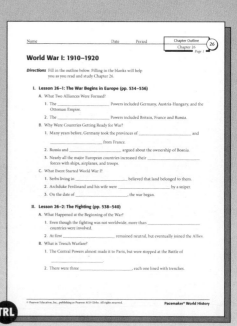

Chapter 26 Self-Study Guide, pages 1–2   Chapter 26 Outline, pages 1–2

Reading Strategy: Visualizing

When readers create pictures in their head about what they are reading, they are using visualization. This is another strategy that helps readers understand what they are reading. Use the following ways to visualize a text:

- Notice the order in which things are happening and what you think might happen next.
- Look at the photographs, illustrations, and words.
- Think about experiences in your own life that may add to the images.

Key Vocabulary Words

Lesson 1

Alliance A group of nations joined together for some purpose; an agreement to help one another

Central Powers The nations of Germany, Austria-Hungary, Turkey, and later Bulgaria

Allied Powers The nations of Great Britain, France, Russia, Italy, and eventually, the United States and Japan during World War I

Balance of power The condition that exists when all countries or all sections of government have equal strength

Sniper A person who shoots from a hidden spot

Lesson 2

Neutral Joining neither side in a war

Trench A long ditch dug in the ground to protect soldiers in battle

Front A place where the actual fighting is going on during a war

Torpedo To attack or destroy with a large, exploding, underwater missile

U-boat A German submarine

Lesson 3

Armistice An agreement to stop fighting; a truce before a formal peace treaty

Treaty of Versailles The treaty that ended World War I

Disarm To stop having armed forces or to reduce their size

Casualty A soldier who has been killed, wounded, captured, or is missing

Conflict Fighting

- What caused Russia to pull out of the war? (the Russian Revolution)

Reading Strategy: Visualizing

Tell students that visualizing helps them to connect prior knowledge to the content they are learning. It also helps to clarify text by linking images and words to key concepts. Have students look at the objectives for each lesson. Then have them scan the images and headings throughout the chapter. Have them note that each image and heading supports the main ideas of the lessons. Have them find words and phrases that help them to better visualize content.

Ask:

- What does a trench remind you of? (sample answer: a long ditch)
- What do you think it would be like to live for days in a trench? (Students will likely agree that it would be miserable to live in a trench for days.)

Key Vocabulary Words

Point out that these chapter words are presented in the order they appear in each lesson. They are also found in the glossary.

LIFE SKILLS CONNECTION

Students learn about conflict resolution services in their community. Students discuss lawyers and what questions to ask before hiring one. Explain to students that most lawyers do not work in courtrooms on a regular basis. Most lawyers work in an office for a law firm or a large company.

KEY VOCABULARY

Assist students as they work through the vocabulary words from the chapter. Students should match each definition with the correct word.

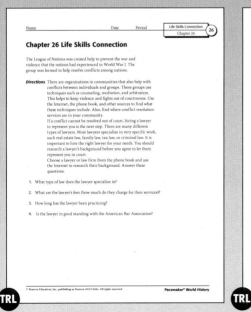

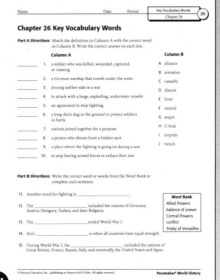

Chapter 26 Lesson 1

Overview This lesson discusses how the quarrels that existed between the two alliances in Europe led to World War I.

Objectives

- To explain what is meant by a "balance of power"
- To name the two alliances made by 1914
- To tell what event directly triggered World War I

Student Pages 534–537

Teacher's Resource Library

Workbook Activity 96

Activity 96

Modified Activity 96

Vocabulary

alliance	Central Powers
Allied Powers	sniper
balance of power	

Place students in pairs. Have one partner read a definition of a vocabulary word or phrase from the text. Have the other partner supply the correct term, and then use the term in a sentence. Have students take turns quizzing one another until they feel confident that they know the lesson vocabulary.

1 Warm-Up Activity

Ask students to brainstorm a list of things they already know about World War I. Write students' answers on the board. Afterwards, discuss why it is important to know why a war took place. Encourage students to speak freely. Some may argue that we need to know why wars take place in order to avoid future wars. Others may say that knowing the causes of wars has not stopped more wars from happening.

LESSON 26-1

The War Begins in Europe

Objectives

- To explain what is meant by a "balance of power"
- To name the two alliances made by 1914
- To tell what event directly triggered World War I

Alliance
A group of nations joined together for some purpose

Central Powers
The nations of Germany, Austria-Hungary, Turkey, and later Bulgaria

Allied Powers
The nations of Great Britain, France, Russia, Italy, and eventually, the United States and Japan during World War I

Balance of power
The condition that exists when all countries have equal strength

Relations between countries were strained in the early 1900s. By 1914, Europe had divided itself into two sides. Nations formed **alliances**. They promised to protect each other and to help each other in case of war.

What Two Alliances Were Formed?

One group of nations was called the **Central Powers**. The nations of the Central Powers included Germany, Austria-Hungary, the Ottoman Empire (Turkey), and, for a short time, Italy. (Bulgaria joined later.) The other group of nations was called the **Allied Powers**, or *Allies*. On that side were Britain, France, Russia, and many smaller nations.

Each alliance tried to keep the other from getting too strong. The two alliances wanted to keep a "**balance of power**" in Europe.

Why Were Countries Getting Ready for War?

As the year 1914 began, there was tension throughout Europe. France and Germany had been bitter enemies for years. France had lost a war against Bismarck's armies in 1871. Ever since then, France wanted to get back the provinces of Alsace and Lorraine.

Russia and Austria-Hungary had an ongoing quarrel. They disagreed about the territorial borders and control of areas, including Bosnia, in the Balkans. The Balkans is a southern peninsula of Europe.

CHAPTER PROJECT

 Tell students to imagine that they are war correspondents. Their job is to report on the events of World War I. Tell them that they are stationed in Europe, and they are writing for a newspaper based in the United States or Canada. Have them choose a crucial event or battle that took place during the war and research and write a news article about that event or battle.

Sniper
A person who shoots from a hidden spot

Remember
In 1871, Bismarck had attacked France to help unite Germany against a common enemy.

Reading Strategy: Visualizing

What words in these paragraphs help you visualize what you are reading?

Nations watched each other as each one built up its military forces. Airplanes, bigger warships, and machine guns made armies more capable of destruction or ruin. One country would build new arms. Then another would panic and race to keep up. No one wanted war, but everyone was getting ready for it.

What Event Started World War I?

It took a single incident in June 1914 to explode the already tense situation in Europe. The Austrian archduke Francis Ferdinand was assassinated. This is named as the incident that began the First World War.

Archduke Ferdinand was the next in line to the throne of Austria-Hungary. He and his wife, Sophie, were visiting Sarajevo, a city in the Austrian province of Bosnia. Many Serbs also lived in Bosnia. Some of them believed Bosnia should belong to Serbia.

The assassination of Archduke Francis Ferdinand led to the start of World War I.

Archduke Ferdinand and his wife were traveling by motor car on a road in Sarajevo. They were a fine-looking pair. The archduke wore a white uniform, and his wife wore a matching white gown. Riding in an open car, they were clear targets. As the royal procession drove through the streets, two shots rang out. Archduke Ferdinand and his wife were both killed by a **sniper**. A sniper is a person who shoots from a hidden spot.

The assassin, Gavrilo Princip, was a Serb. He was a member of a Serbian revolutionary group called the "Black Hand."

1910–1920   *World War I Chapter 26*   **535**

---

2 Teaching the Lesson

Ask students to recall which nations came together to defeat Napoleon. Then have them read this lesson to learn about the alliances formed by European countries prior to World War I.

Ask:

- Why did the nations of Europe form alliances? (to help and protect each other in case of war)
- Which countries belonged to the Allied Powers? Which countries belonged to the Central Powers? (Allied Powers: Great Britain, France, Russia, Italy, and eventually the United States and Japan; Central Powers: Germany, Austria-Hungary, Turkey, and later Bulgaria)

Background Information

Millions of people lost their lives in World War I. Millions more were wounded. The death toll would likely have been much higher were it not for the efforts of the Red Cross. The Red Cross was founded in 1863 by Jean Henri Dunant, a Swiss philanthropist. The organization offers medical care to the wounded and dying of all armies. According to the Geneva Conventions, no one can fire upon a Red Cross worker who is assisting a person in need—even if that person is an enemy soldier.

LEARNING STYLES

Auditory/Verbal

Place students in small groups. Ask each member of the group to take the point of view of one of the countries that participated in the war and role-play a leader of that country explaining the political reasons that led them to declare war.

Reading Strategy: Visualizing

Students might mention words and phrases such as *destruction, ruin, fine-looking pair, royal procession,* and *Black Hand.* If students have difficulty answering the question, point out some of the phrases listed here.

World War I Chapter 26   **535**

COMMON ERROR

Some students may confuse the words *alliance* and *Allies.* Explain that an *alliance* is a group of nations that join together for an agreed-upon purpose. The *Allies* was the name given to a specific alliance made up of Great Britain, France, Russia, Italy, the United States, and Japan. The Central Powers was also a specific alliance made up of Germany, Austria-Hungary, Turkey, and Bulgaria.

Remember

France was defeated by Bismarck's armies. As a result, France lost Alsace and Lorraine. Although this loss took place decades earlier, it primed France to enter World War I. Discuss how events can simmer and spark conflict many years later. Relate the discussion to the current conflict in the Middle East, which has its roots in policies and decisions that occurred in the previous century.

To help students better understand the cost of war, ask them to research the current price of barbed wire. Suggest that they call a local hardware store or search on the Internet. Students should then use the data to calculate how much it would cost to protect trenches along one mile of a front. Remind students that soldiers on both sides of the front need the wire for protection. Also point out that several parallel strands of wire are needed to protect each side. Have students share their findings with the class.

ELL/ESL STRATEGY

Language Objective:
To understand idioms

Explain that every language has idioms. An idiom can be a phrase with a meaning that differs from the literal meaning of its words. Give students an example, such as "straight from the horse's mouth" and explain what that this idiom means "from the highest authority." Then ask them to scan the lesson and make a list of phrases that they find confusing. Examples might be "clear target," "shots rang out," "race to keep up," and "came into play." Pair each ELL student with an English-language student. Ask the English-language speaker to help explain any confusing phrases to his or her partner.

MAP STUDY

Answers:

1. Spain, Sweden, Norway, the Netherlands, Switzerland, and Denmark

2. Allied Powers

Austria-Hungary blamed the Serbian government for the assassination. On July 28, 1914, it declared war on Serbia. Now the alliances came into play. Germany stood behind Austria-Hungary. Russia came to the aid of Serbia. France came to Russia's aid. Soon, Britain joined in to help its allies. World War I had begun.

Europe, 1914

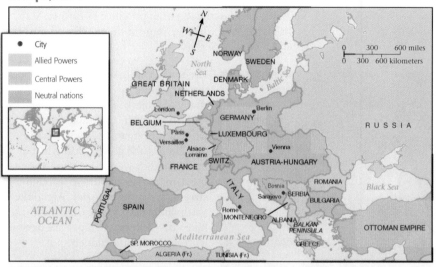

MAP STUDY

1. In 1914, which countries were neutral in Europe?
2. Did more nations belong to the Allied Powers or the Central Powers in 1914?

STUDY SKILLS

Have each student make a list of Allied nations and Central nations. Suggest that students make their lists on index cards, which they can later use as bookmarks. To strengthen self-evaluation skills, have students check their lists at least twice to be certain they are correct. Encourage students to refer to the cards as they read the chapter. The cards can also be used as study guides for lesson and chapter tests.

On a sheet of paper, write the answer to each question. Use complete sentences.

1. What nations were included in the Central Powers?

2. What nations were included in the Allies?

3. The European alliances wanted to keep a "balance of power." What does that mean?

4. What event directly triggered World War I?

On a sheet of paper, write the letter of the answer that correctly completes each sentence.

5. Tensions between countries were growing, and by 1914 _____ had divided itself into two sides.

    A Russia   **B** Germany   **C** Europe   **D** Austria-Hungary

6. France wanted to get back at _____ for losing the provinces of Alsace and Lorraine.

    A Russia   **B** Germany   **C** Europe   **D** Austria-Hungary

7. _____ and Austria-Hungary disagreed about the borders and control of areas, including the Balkans.

    A Russia   **B** Germany   **C** Europe   **D** Italy

8. Countries raced to keep up with the latest _____.

    A fashions   **B** computer technology   **C** weapons   **D** space technology

9. Archduke Ferdinand was the next ruler of _____.

    A Russia   **B** Germany   **C** Europe   **D** Austria-Hungary

10. Austria-Hungary blamed _____ for the killing, and declared war.

    A Serbia   **B** France   **C** Russia   **D** Italy

COMMON ERROR

Some students may think that an alliance serves only one purpose, which is that allied nations promise to protect one another in case of war. Point out that an alliance also acts as an effective deterrent against aggression. Other nations are less likely to attack a country that has allied partners.

CAREER CONNECTION

Students might be interested to know that spies played a pivotal role in World War I. They gathered sensitive information about other countries. Tell students that spying is still a widely accepted role of government in most parts of the world. In the United States, it is the career of choice for people who work for the U.S. Central Intelligence Agency (CIA) in Arlington, VA. One way to become a CIA employee is to enter the Clandestine Service. Applicants need college degrees and high academic marks. Proficiency in a second language is preferred. Interested students can meet with their counselor to map out which courses to take to prepare for college.

Lesson 26–1 Review Answers

1. The Central Powers included Germany, Austria-Hungary, Turkey, and later Bulgaria. **2.** The Allies included Britain, France, Russia, Italy, and eventually, the United States and Japan. **3.** Each alliance wanted to keep the other from getting too strong. **4.** The assassination of archduke Francis Ferdinand sparked the First World War. **5.** C **6.** B **7.** A **8.** C **9.** D **10.** A

Pacemaker® World History

Activity 96

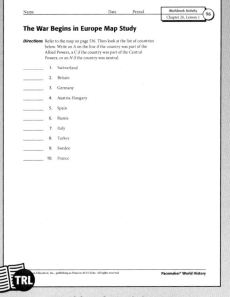

Pacemaker® World History

Workbook Activity 96

Lesson at a Glance

Chapter 26 Lesson 2

Overview This lesson describes life on the fronts, the United States participation in the war, and Russia's treaty with Germany.

Objectives

- To describe trench warfare
- To tell what event caused the United States to enter the war
- To tell how U.S. soldiers and supplies affected the outcome of the war

Student Pages 538–541

Teacher's Resource Library

Workbook Activity 97

Activity 97

Modified Activity 97

Vocabulary

front	trench
neutral	U-boat
torpedo	

Discuss the meaning of each term with students. Encourage them to make connections between the vocabulary word and their own background knowledge. Examples may include a war front, which is the boundary between two armies, and a weather front, which is the boundary between two air masses with different characteristics.

1 Warm-Up Activity

Remind students that airplanes were relatively new inventions in the early 1900s. Airplanes had not been used for war before World War I. Ask them to imagine how the planes flying overhead and dropping bombs may have affected the soldiers and civilians on the ground.

Reading Strategy: Visualizing

Lead a class discussion about the text on page 538 to help visualize the fight in France. Sample answers may include information on the length of the trenches, and the image of soldiers sleeping, eating, and dying in the trenches.

LESSON 26-2 The Fighting

Objectives
- To describe trench warfare
- To tell what event caused the United States to enter the war
- To tell how U.S. soldiers and supplies affected the outcome of the war

Neutral
Joining neither side in a war

Trench
A long ditch dug in the ground to protect soldiers in battle

Front
A place where the actual fighting is going on during a war

Reading Strategy: Visualizing

What clues on this page help you visualize the fight to take France?

World War I is sometimes called "The Great War." It was not really a "worldwide" war. Most of the fighting took place in Europe. Furthermore, not every country in the world was fighting. However, more than 30 countries, including all the major powers, were involved. The Great War's effects were certainly felt worldwide.

At first the Central Powers seemed to be winning. Germany and Austria-Hungary and their allies made gains. Italy had been allied with the Central Powers. However, Italy remained **neutral** in the early part of the war (they did not join either side). Then in 1915, Italy changed its alliance. It joined forces with the Allies.

What Is Trench Warfare?

The Central Powers wanted to take France. They came within 25 miles of Paris. However, the French and British held them off in a major battle, the Battle of the Marne. Then both sides dug in. The soldiers dug long **trenches**. Armies could hide in the trenches and shoot at each other. Some trenches were more than a mile long.

The **fronts** were lined with networks of trenches. A front is a place where the actual fighting is going on during a war. There were three fronts in Europe. The western front ran from Belgium to Switzerland. The eastern front ran from the Baltic Sea to the Black Sea. The Italian, or southern, front ran between Italy and Austria-Hungary.

The battle trenches along the fronts became home for the soldiers. They ate in the trenches and slept in the trenches. Many soldiers died in the trenches.

Torpedo
To attack or destroy with a large, exploding, underwater missile

History Fact
Switzerland was one of the few European nations to remain neutral throughout the war. It would also stay neutral during World War II.

Reading Strategy:
Visualizing

How could this section on the *Lusitania* be written differently to help you better visualize it?

Most of the battles of World War I were fought in Europe. However, there was also some fighting in Africa and in the Middle East. The powerful British navy kept control of most of the seas.

Why Did the United States Enter the War?

Despite Britain's great navy, German submarines were terrorizing the oceans. A submarine is a warship that travels under water. They attacked enemy merchant ships without warning. Then in 1915, Germany attacked a British luxury liner. The *Lusitania* was **torpedoed** (attacked with a large, exploding, underwater missile) and sunk. The death list of 1,198 people included 128 Americans. In 1917, German submarines began attacking ships of neutral nations. Several American merchant ships were sunk.

During World War I, soldiers dug trenches six to eight feet deep to hide and defend themselves.

Remind students that the native peoples in South America were amazed by the weapons of the Spanish conquistadors. Tell them that in this lesson, they will read about weapons and methods of fighting that no one had ever experienced before.

Ask:

- Who was the president of the United States during World War I? (Woodrow Wilson)
- Do you think that the United States would have entered the war if the *Lusitania* had not been torpedoed? (Answers will vary.)

History Fact
Have students research reasons why a country might remain neutral throughout a war. (Reasons vary from economic to social.) Then lead a class discussion on the pros and cons of remaining neutral.

Reading Strategy:
Visualizing

Answers will vary. Students may say that an illustration of the sinking of the *Lusitania* would help them to better visualize it. They may suggest more details about the actual attack.

Background Information

In a stunning move, Germany sank the British ocean liner *Lusitania* on May 7, 1915, off the coast of Ireland. Without warning, a German U-boat sent a torpedo into the side of the *Lusitania*. The ship was hopelessly damaged. It sank in 18 minutes. Some 1,200 people died, including 128 Americans. In the United States, posters soon circulated urging men to "Remember the *Lusitania*" and enlist in the army. U.S. reaction was so swift and hostile that Germany ceased U-boat attacks for a time. In 1917, the attacks resumed, prompting the United States to declare war against Germany.

U-boat
A German submarine

History Fact
The submarine was the most deadly military vessel of World War I.

In April 1917, U.S. President Woodrow Wilson made an announcement. He said that it was time to "make the world safe for democracy." The United States declared war on Germany and joined the Allies. The United States entered the battlefields just in time. The Allies needed help. The United States sent fresh soldiers and supplies of arms to Europe. The scale in the balance of power was now tipped in favor of the Allies.

Then in November 1917, a revolution took place in Russia. The new government signed a peace treaty with Germany and pulled out of the war.

LEARN MORE ABOUT IT

Wartime Inventions

The war brought many changes in the world. New inventions were perfected in a hurry to meet war needs. The Germans developed submarines to travel under the water, like sharks. The submarines were also called **"U-boats"** (underwater boats). Like a shark, they moved unseen, seeking their prey.

Allied countries could not find a defense against the submarines for the first three years of the war. Eventually depth charges were used to destroy the submarines. Fast British ships known as subchasers carried the depth charges. These ships also used zigzag courses to avoid German submarines.

The submarines were very successful. Only 203 German submarines were destroyed during the whole war. But the German submarines sank 6,604 Allied ships.

For the first time, airplanes were used for war. At first they were just used for scouting, watching the enemy, and taking pictures.

They were not used for fighting until later in the war.

Planes improved rapidly. In 1914, an airplane could go 60 to 70 miles an hour. By 1917, they were flying at 130 miles an hour or faster. They carried bombs and machine guns. Some pilots became famous as war aces for shooting down five or more enemy airplanes.

Germany used zeppelins in the air. Zeppelins were huge, cigar-shaped crafts, 600 feet long. They were filled with hydrogen gas and used in bombing raids over Britain and France.

British engineers invented the tank, an armored vehicle with caterpillar tracks. The big tanks rumbled their way across the battlefields of Europe. There were other new weapons, like poison gas and flame throwers. Each side tried to outdo the other with more powerful weapons.

On a sheet of paper, write the answer to each question. Use complete sentences.

1. Describe trench warfare.

2. Why did the United States enter the war?

3. What are three wartime inventions used during World War I?

Match the description in Column A with the term in Column B.
Write the correct letter on a sheet of paper.

Column A

4. the front that stretched from Belgium to Switzerland

5. the front that ran from the Baltic Sea to the Black Sea

6. the front that ran between Italy and Austria-Hungary

Column B

A eastern

B southern

C western

On a sheet of paper, write the letter of the answer that correctly completes each sentence.

7. More than 30 countries were involved in the Great War. Most of the fighting took place in _____.

A the ocean

B Germany

C Austria-Hungary

D Europe

8. The _____ kept control of most of the seas, even without submarines.

A Germans

B British

C French

D Russians

9. At first _____ remained neutral, but then in 1915 it joined forces with the Allies.

A France

B the United States

C Italy

D Serbia

10. U.S. soldiers and supplies helped tip the balance of power in favor of the _____.

A Allies

B Central Powers

C Germans

D Italians

1910–1920

World War I Chapter 26 **541**

COMMON ERROR

Students might think that the U.S. army in World War I was made up of professional volunteers, much like today's army. Explain that in the early 1900s, men usually became soldiers for the length of a war, and then returned to civilian life. Unlike today's army, a soldier did not join for a set number of years.

WORLD CULTURES

During the years of World War I, there was still a lot of prejudice toward African Americans in the United States. Racist attitudes carried over into the war. About 400,000 African Americans served in World War I. Tell students to research and write about the roles of black soldiers in the Great War. Students should share their reports with the class.

Lesson 26–2 Review Answers

1. During World War I, soldiers would dig long trenches where armies could hide and shoot at each other. Soldiers ate, slept, and died in the trenches. **2.** Germany attacked a British luxury liner, the Lusitania. Some 1,200 passengers died, including 128 Americans. German submarines began attacking ships of neutral nations, and several American merchant ships were sunk. So, to "make the world safe for democracy," the U.S. declared war on Germany. **3.** Submarines (U-boats), airplanes that carried bombs and machine guns, zeppelins, and tanks were all used for the first time during World War I. **4.** C **5.** A **6.** B **7.** D **8.** B **9.** C **10.** A

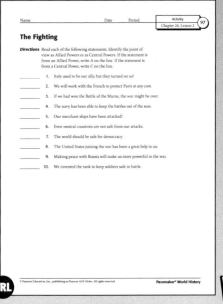

Activity 97

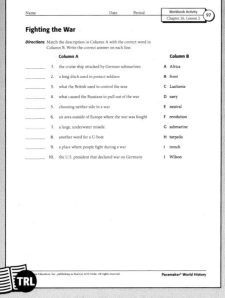

Workbook Activity 97

Lesson at a Glance

Chapter 26 Lesson 3

Overview This lesson explains the events that followed the end of the war, including the Treaty of Versailles and the League of Nations.

Objectives

- To describe how the war ended
- To explain the Treaty of Versailles
- To explain the League of Nations and why the Americans opposed it

Student Pages 542–546

Teacher's Resource Library

Workbook Activity 98

Activity 98

Modified Activity 98

Vocabulary

armistice   disarm
casualty   Treaty of Versailles
conflict

Write the vocabulary terms on the board. Ask students to work with a partner to find the definitions of the terms. Tell each student to write a question on an index card using one of the vocabulary words or phrases. Then have students exchange cards with their partners, and answer one another's question.

1   Warm-Up Activity

Remind students that they have read about treaties in previous chapters. Before they read this lesson, tell them that the Treaty of Versailles ended World War I. Based on what they have learned, ask students to predict what kind of terms Germany agreed to when it signed the treaty. (Students should realize that because Germany lost the war, it was forced to give up a great deal as part of the treaty.)

The End of the War

Objectives

- To describe how the war ended
- To explain the Treaty of Versailles
- To explain the League of Nations and why the Americans opposed it

Armistice

An agreement to stop fighting; a truce before a formal peace treaty

Treaty of Versailles

The treaty that ended World War I

Disarm

To stop having armed forces or to reduce their size

 History Fact When the German government finally agreed to the Allies' terms, Kaiser Wilhelm II gave up his throne.

With new American soldiers and supplies, the Allies began to push back the Germans. The other Central Powers had given up. Germany stood alone, and German armies were losing ground.

Germany asked for an end to the war. On November 11, 1918, an **armistice** was declared. All fighting was to stop at 11:00 A.M. that day.

What Demands Did the Treaty of Versailles Make?

After the war, leaders of the Allied nations and Germany met in Versailles, France. Their purpose was to write a peace treaty to end the war. The treaty, known as the **Treaty of Versailles**, was signed in 1919 and made many demands on Germany.

Germany lost all of its colonies and had to return Alsace and Lorraine to France. Germany took all blame for the war, so it had to pay for many of the war's costs. Germany also promised to **disarm**. The nation was not supposed to rebuild its navy or air force. It was allowed to maintain only a small army. This was quite a blow to a nation that had taken such pride in a powerful military.

Turkey was another big loser in the war. In 1919, most of the Middle East and North Africa was still ruled by the Ottoman Empire, or Turkey. However, the end of the war brought about the end of the Ottoman Empire. Most of the Arab lands that had been ruled by the Turks now fell under British control.

 History Fact

The people of Germany replaced Kaiser Wilhelm II with a democratic government. They drafted a constitution in the city of Weimar. Thus, the new government was called the Weimar Republic.

Europe After World War I

MAP STUDY

1. What were the new nations in Europe after World War I?
2. What countries now bordered Germany to the east?

MAP STUDY

Answers:

1. Poland, Yugoslavia, Czechoslovakia, Estonia, Latvia, Lithuania, East Prussia, Finland

2. Poland and Czechoslovakia

Ask students if they have ever heard of the United Nations. Tell them that the United Nations was formed to replace the League of Nations. Tell them that they will learn about the League of Nations in this lesson.

Ask:

- **What was the Treaty of Versailles?** (the peace treaty that ended World War I)

- **What were the terms of the Treaty of Versailles?** (Germany lost its colonies and Alsace and Lorraine. It took the blame for the war, paid many of the costs of the war, and promised to disarm. The Ottoman Empire ended, and Britain controlled Arab lands that had been ruled by the Turks.)

- **Why was it unlikely that the League of Nations could be a successful peacekeeper?** (Not all nations joined the League of Nations, and it had no army to enforce its decisions.)

TEACHER ALERT

To help students better visualize how Europe changed after World War I, refer them to the map on page 536. Have students compare and contrast the national boundaries shown on the maps on pages 536 and 543.

Background Information

Each nation wanted something slightly different from the Treaty of Versailles. The United States wanted an end to secret treaties, a policy of open waters in all seas and oceans, a global reduction in military might, and a global organization (the League of Nations) to help countries settle problems peacefully. France wanted revenge. It wanted Germany to pay for the cost of the war. It also wanted Alsace and Lorraine back. Britain wanted Germany's colonies in Africa. Like France, it wanted Germany to remain weak. However, Britain also wanted to limit French power. Italy wanted the land it was promised when it joined the war.

Casualty

A soldier who has been killed, wounded, captured, or is missing

Conflict

Fighting; not being able to agree on something

Some Casualties of World War I	
Allies	
Russia	9,150,000
British empire	3,190,235
France	6,160,800
Italy	2,197,000
United States	323,018
Central Powers	
Germany	7,142,558
Austria-Hungary	7,020,000
Turkey	975,000
Bulgaria	266,919

Reading Strategy: Metacognition

Create a graphic organizer of the events in the early years of the League of Nations. This will help you visualize the process.

Why Was the League of Nations Formed?

The Great War ended four years after it had begun. Those four years meant the loss of almost eight million soldiers. Millions of others died of disease and starvation, side effects of war. Russia suffered the most **casualties** in World War I. In other words, they had the most soldiers who had been killed, wounded, captured, or missing.

The total cost of the war to all countries involved was more than $337 billion. All of Europe was weakened.

When the war ended, leaders of the world's nations looked at the results. They decided there must be a better way to solve **conflicts**, or fights, between nations. President Wilson proposed setting up a League of Nations. European leaders welcomed the idea. They knew that their people would support such a league. Wilson was confident that the American people would support it as well.

In 1920, the League of Nations was set up. Its headquarters were in Geneva, Switzerland—a neutral, peaceful country. Representatives of member nations could meet there to discuss their problems. It was the first organization designed to keep the peace of the entire world.

The League of Nations was formed to keep the peace of the entire world.

Reading Strategy: Visualizing

Show students a minimum of four different types of graphic organizers. Include an outline, sequence-of-events chart, Venn diagram, and web chart. Allow students to choose the graphic organizer that best helps them to visualize events in the early years of the League of Nations.

Many nations joined the League. Some, including the United States, did not. Wilson was greatly disappointed. Many people in the United States did not like the idea of the League. In particular, Article Ten of the plan caused major problems. It mentioned threats to any member nation of the League. It said that if any threats were made, the other members would aid the threatened nation.

Americans felt they had seen too much of war. They did not want to have anything to do with Europe's problems. They thought Article Ten seemed to invite trouble.

 You Decide
Do you think the United States was right not to join the League of Nations? Why or why not?

President Wilson put up a strong fight. He made speeches all around the country. He did everything he could to try to convince Americans to join the League. However, the Senate voted against it in March 1920. Wilson died in 1924, a defeated man. He had warned that another world war was not far off. He had said that only the League of Nations could prevent it. Many Americans did not want to hear him.

The League of Nations had no army to enforce its decisions. The League was based on goodwill and the idea that nations wanted peace. The war years, 1914 to 1918, had left everyone fearful of war. Now the whole world was anxious to avoid war. People everywhere were hopeful that a war would never be fought again.

TIMELINE STUDY: WORLD WAR I AND AFTER

How long did World War I last?

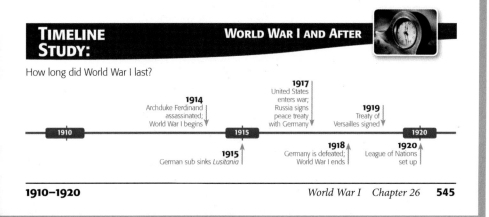

1914 Archduke Ferdinand assassinated; World War I begins

1917 United States enters war; Russia signs peace treaty with Germany

1919 Treaty of Versailles signed

1910

1915

1920

1915 German sub sinks *Lusitania*

1918 Germany is defeated; World War I ends

1920 League of Nations set up

1910–1920

World War I   Chapter 26   **545**

You Decide
Lead a class discussion on whether the United States was right not to join the League of Nations. Have students explain their answers. Some students may argue that the United States should have joined the League of Nations to help discourage future wars. Others may say that Article Ten of the plan made war a real possibility.

3 Reinforce and Extend

COMMON ERROR

 Students may think that the United States and its allies experienced roughly the same number of casualties during World War I. Have them study the table on page 544. Ask students to infer why the United States had so many fewer casualties than its allies did. (The United States entered the war late, and the war was not fought on American soil.)

IN THE COMMUNITY

 Have students check with county officials to find the locations of memorials to individuals who died in World War I. Have students visit the memorials, if possible. Suggest that they take pictures to share with the class. If there are no local memorials, students can contact local veterans' groups, and interview a member about events that honor World War I veterans.

AT HOME

 Suggest that students watch a video with their families about World War I. Students can select from a wide range of documentaries or feature-length films, such as *All Quiet on the Western Front*. Encourage students to discuss the video with their families afterwards. Was it an accurate picture of the war? What aspect of the war did it focus on? What parts did it leave out? Ask students to share their families' reactions with the class.

TIMELINE STUDY

Answer: 4 years

Lesson 26–3 Review Answers

1. All Central Powers except Germany gave up. Germany began to lose ground and asked for an end to the war. On November 11, 1918, an armistice was declared, and all fighting stopped. **2.** Germany lost all of its colonies, including Alsace and Lorraine, which it had to return to France. Germany had to pay for the war's costs, and promised to disarm. Germany was also not allowed to rebuild its navy or air force, and it could maintain only a small army. **3.** Americans thought that Article Ten invited trouble. This article stated that if threats were made to a member nation, the league members would aid the threatened nation. **4.** four **5.** Russia **6.** Turkey **7.** Wilson **8.** League of Nations **9.** Switzerland **10.** peace

---

On a sheet of paper, write the answer to each question. Use complete sentences.

1. How did World War I end?

2. What are three demands the Treaty of Versailles made on Germany?

3. Why was the United States against the League of Nations?

On a sheet of paper, write the word from the Word Bank to complete each sentence correctly.

Word Bank

four
League of Nations
peace
Russia
Switzerland
Turkey
Wilson

4. The Great War lasted _____ years.

5. _____ suffered the most casualties in World War I.

6. _____ lost control of most of its Arab lands as part of the peace treaty.

7. President _____ suggested setting up a League of Nations. Unfortunately, he died still fighting to convince Americans of its value.

8. The _____ was designed to keep the peace of the entire world.

9. The League of Nations was headquartered in _____ because it was a neutral, peaceful country.

10. The League of Nations had no army. It was based on goodwill and the idea that nations wanted _____.

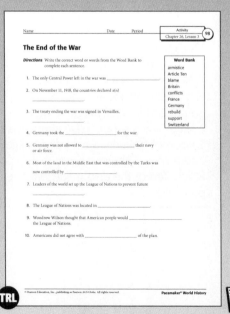

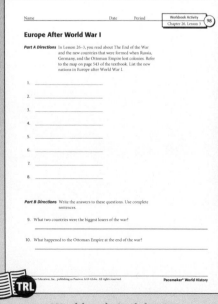

Activity 98   Workbook Activity 98

- World War I began in 1914. The assassination of the Austrian archduke Francis Ferdinand started World War I.

- The war was fought between the Central Powers and the Allies. The Central Powers included Germany, Austria-Hungary, and in the early part of the war, Italy. The Allies included Britain, France, and Russia.

- Italy joined the Allies in 1915.

- The United States entered the war on the side of the Allies in 1917.

- Most battles of World War I took place in Europe.

- For the most part, the strong British navy controlled the seas. German U-boats caused a good deal of damage to ships at sea.

- Wartime developments and inventions included submarines, special planes, zeppelins, tanks, and weapons such as poison gas.

- World War I ended in 1918. The Treaty of Versailles, signed in 1919, set up terms for peace.

- The League of Nations was founded after the war in hopes of maintaining world peace.

Chapter 26 Summary

Have students read the Chapter Summary on page 547 to review the main ideas presented in Chapter 26.

Ask:

- What event triggered the start of World War I? (the assassination of the Austrian archduke Francis Ferdinand)

- What two alliances formed during the war? (the Central Powers and the Allies)

- When did the United States enter the war? (1917)

- Where did most battles of World War I take place? (Europe)

- Describe how the war was fought on the seas. (The strong British navy controlled the seas most of the time. German U-boats caused a good deal of damage to ships at sea.)

- Name three wartime inventions. (any three of the following: submarines, special planes, zeppelins, tanks, and weapons such as poison gas)

- What was the main goal of the League of Nations? (to maintain world peace)

CHAPTER PROJECT FOLLOW-UP

Before students write their articles, have them look over several newspapers to become familiar with the structure of news articles. Point out that the first paragraph of a news article clearly states what the article is about, and when and where the event occurred. The headline and the first sentence should draw the reader in. Have volunteers read their news articles aloud to the class. Try to select articles that cover a variety of topics related to World War I. Assess students' work based on grammar, historical accuracy, and readability.

TEACHER'S RESOURCE

The AGS Globe Teaching Strategies in Social Studies Transparencies may be used with this chapter. The transparencies add an interactive dimension to expand and enhance the Pacemaker® *World History* program content.

Chapter 26 Review

Use the Chapter Review to prepare students for tests and to reteach content from the chapter.

Chapter 26 Mastery Test

The Teacher's Resource Library includes two forms of the Chapter 26 Mastery Test. Each test addresses the chapter Goals for Learning. An optional third page of additional critical-thinking items is included for each test. The difficulty level of the two forms is equivalent.

Chapter 26 Review Answers

Vocabulary Review

1. trench

2. fronts

3. alliance

4. U-boats

5. casualties

6. neutral

7. armistice

8. balance of power

9. conflict

10. disarm

Chapter Review Questions

11. The Central Powers and the Allies were the two alliances.

12. The Austrian Archduke Francis Ferdinand was assassinated by a Serb.

Vocabulary Review

On a sheet of paper, use the words from the Word Bank to complete each sentence correctly.

Word Bank
alliance
armistice
balance of power
casualties
conflict
disarm
fronts
neutral
trench
U-boats

1. A solider lived, fought, and often died in the long _____ he dug.

2. Three places where fighting went on, called _____, extended across much of Europe.

3. Nations could form a(n) _____ to protect and help each other in time of war.

4. German underwater ships, called _____, attacked enemy ships without warning.

5. Russia suffered the most _____ in World War I.

6. Some nations did not take sides in the war. They were _____.

7. An agreement to stop fighting is called a(n) _____.

8. A(n) _____ means that no one country becomes stronger than another.

9. Russia and Austria-Hungary had an ongoing quarrel, or _____, about territorial borders.

10. Germany promised to _____ after the war.

Chapter Review Questions

On a sheet of paper, write the answer to each question. Use complete sentences.

11. What two alliances were formed in Europe before World War I?

12. What event is usually named as starting World War I?

13. Why was World War I called the Great War?

Chapter 26 Mastery Test A

Part A Directions Circle the letter of the answer that correctly completes each sentence.

1. The event that started World War I was _____.
   A the Russian Revolution
   B the assassination of the Austrian Archduke Ferdinand
   C the German capture of Alsace and Lorraine
   D the sinking of the *Lusitania*

2. In the Battle of the Marne, _____.
   A the Germans took France
   B the Allied forces won the war
   C the machine gun was first used
   D the Germans were stopped from taking France

3. When the United States entered the war, the U.S. President was _____
   A Theodore Roosevelt   B Thomas Jefferson   C Herbert Hoover   D Woodrow Wilson

4. The country suffering the most casualties in World War I was _____
   A America   B Russia   C Great Britain   D Germany

5. The League of Nations met in _____
   A London, England   B Rome, Italy   C Geneva, Switzerland   D Paris, France

Part B Directions Write the correct word from the Word Bank to complete each sentence.

6. Before World War I, many European nations formed _____ with each other.

7. During World War I, _____ was a neutral nation.

8. The United States entered the war on the side of the _____ Powers.

9. According to the Treaty of Versailles, _____ took full blame for the war.

10. The nation of _____ was created after the war.

11. The Ottoman Empire was also known as _____.

12. Before the war began, Italy had an alliance with the _____ Powers.

13. The war was fought on three different _____

14. A(n) _____ is a formal agreement of peace between nations.

15. A(n) _____ nation is one that decides not to get involved in a war.

Word Bank: alliances, Allied, Central, fronts, Germany, neutral, Poland, Switzerland, treaty, Turkey

© Pearson Education, Inc., publishing as Pearson AGS Globe. All rights reserved.   **Pacemaker® World History**

Chapter 26 Mastery Test A, *continued*

Part C Directions Match the description in Column A with the correct date in Column B. Write the correct answer on each line.

Column A	Column B
_____ 16. the United States joins the war	A 1871
_____ 17. the League of Nations is established	B 1914
_____ 18. a revolution takes place in Russia	C 1915
_____ 19. the Austrian Archduke Ferdinand is assassinated	D April 1917
_____ 20. Germany defeats France	E November 1917
_____ 21. the Treaty of Versailles is signed	F 1918
_____ 22. Italy joins the Allied Powers	G 1919
_____ 23. an armistice is declared	H 1920

Part D Directions Write the answers to these questions. Use complete sentences.

24. Before World War I, what did many European nations do to ensure a balance of power?

25. How did Russia get out of the war?

26. What did the Germans do to get past the British navy in the seas?

27. What restrictions were put on Germany's military by the Treaty of Versailles?

28. Why was World War I called the Great War?

29. What was the main disagreement between Russia and Austria-Hungary before the war?

30. How were airplanes used during the war?

© Pearson Education, Inc., publishing as Pearson AGS Globe. All rights reserved.   **Pacemaker® World History**

Chapter 26 Mastery Test A, *continued*

Part E Directions Write your answer to each question. Use complete sentences. Support each answer with facts and examples from the textbook.

31. Explain why the shooting of Archduke Ferdinand is credited with starting World War I. (2 points)

32. Describe the way many Americans felt at the end of World War I. (2 points)

Part F Directions Write a paragraph for each topic. Include a topic sentence, supporting details, and a conclusion. Support each answer with facts and examples from the textbook.

33. Were Americans correct in staying out of the League of Nations? Explain your answer. (3 points)

34. What positive outcomes do you believe resulted from World War I? (3 points)

© Pearson Education, Inc., publishing as Pearson AGS Globe. All rights reserved.   **Pacemaker® World History**

14. How did the United States help the Allies beginning in 1917?

15. What was the peace treaty signed by the Allied nations and Germany in 1919?

16. What international organization was set up after World War I ended?

Critical Thinking

On a sheet of paper, write your response to each question. Use complete sentences.

17. Do you think the Treaty of Versailles made too many demands on Germany? Why or why not?

18. Do you think the League of Nations was a weak organization? Why or why not?

Using the Timeline

Use the timeline on page 545 to answer the questions.

19. After the Germans sank the *Lusitania*, how long did it take for the United States to enter the war?

20. What happened in 1919?

GROUP ACTIVITY

With a partner, prepare an illustrated talk about a ship, plane, or weapon of World War I. Prepare a drawing, with parts labeled. Have one person explain how the ship, plane, or weapon was used in war. Have the other person explain the drawing. Then switch roles if you wish.

1910–1920   *World War I   Chapter 26*   **549**

---

13. World War I was called the Great War because all the major powers were involved and the effects of the war were worldwide.

14. The United States joined the war, contributing fresh soldiers and supplies.

15. The Allied nations and Germany signed the Treaty of Versailles in 1919.

16. The League of Nations was founded after World War I ended.

Critical Thinking

17. Possible answers: No, because the Germans had been building up for the war, and they were the most to blame for it. Yes, because when a country is punished too much, the people might feel a lot of anger.

18. Most students will probably answer yes. They may point out that the United States did not join and that the League of Nations had no army and had to rely on goodwill.

Using the Timeline

19. 2 years

20. The Treaty of Versailles was signed.

GROUP ACTIVITY

Students' talks may feature submarines, planes, zeppelins, tanks, poison gas, or other World War I weapons.

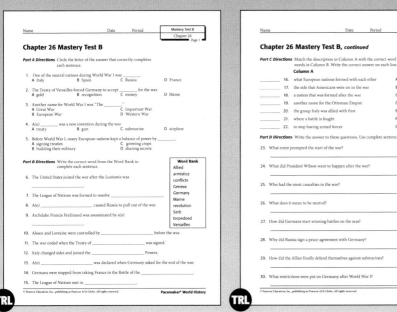

Introducing the Chapter

Russia's boundaries have been very fluid during much of its history. As students read the chapter, use maps to make them aware of the changing boundaries and character of the country—originally part of the Byzantine Empire, an expansionist country under the czars, later absorbed into the Mongol Empire, annexing "buffer" states, and then losing those buffer states after 1991.

Ask:

- What two empires was Russia once part of? (the Byzantine and Mongol empires)

Revolution in Russia: The Birth of the Soviet Union

In earlier chapters, you read about the Byzantine Empire that came out after the fall of Rome. You read how the empire fell to the Ottoman Turks in 1453. However, much of the Byzantine Empire continued on in a new nation in eastern Europe. That nation was Russia. The people of Russia are as varied as the geography of the country. Stories of their history are both exciting and colorful. This is especially true of the revolution that took place in Russia in the early 1900s.

GOALS FOR LEARNING

- To list the main events in Russia's early history
- To understand the reasons for unrest in Russia in the early 1900s
- To explain how Russia became the Union of Soviet Socialist Republics

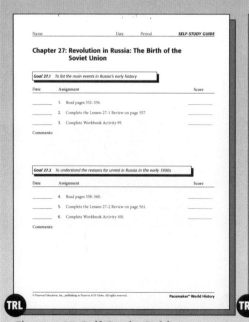

Chapter 27 Self-Study Guide, pages 1–2

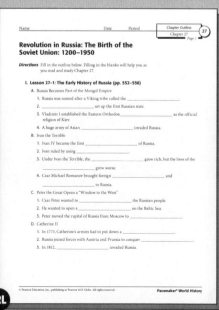

Chapter 27 Outline, pages 1–2

Reading Strategy: Inferencing

Sometimes the meaning of a text is not directly stated. You have to make an inference to figure out what the text means.

What You Know + What You Read = Inference

To make inferences, you have to think "beyond the text." Predicting what will happen next and explaining cause and effect are helpful strategies for making inferences.

Key Vocabulary Words

Lesson 1

Geography The natural surface features of the earth, or any part of it

Steppe A wide plain

Dialect A form of a language used only in a certain place or among a certain group

Czar The ruler of Russia; a Russian title that means "caesar"

Economy The system of making and trading things

Lesson 2

Socialism An economic and political system where the government owns and controls all industry

Communism A political system where there are no social classes and a common ownership of industries and farms, as well as a sharing of work and of goods produced

Shortage Too small an amount; not enough

Lesson 3

Bolshevik A revolutionary Communist group in Russia; means "member of the majority"

Soviet A Russian council

Collective Run by a group

Oppose To be against something

Censor To examine communications before they are released and to remove any parts that are objected to

Iron Curtain The invisible boundary between Western Europe and Eastern Europe after World War II

- How did Russia first get a port on the Baltic Sea? (Peter the Great got the port in 1721 in a treaty that ended a war with Sweden.)
- When did Russia reach all the way to the Pacific Ocean? (in the 1600s)
- When did Russia acquire part of Poland? (under Catherine the Great)

Reading Strategy: Inferencing

Ask for volunteers to read the strategy on page 551. Have students read the first two paragraphs on page 552. Remind them of the equation on page 551. Ask them what they already know about the material in the paragraphs. Ask what new information students read about. Now ask what inferences they can make. Have students write their inferences in a short paragraph.

Key Vocabulary Words

Point out that these chapter words are presented in the order they appear in each lesson. They are also found in the glossary.

LIFE SKILLS CONNECTION

Students learn about the different features of a newspaper, including news stories, editorials, letters to the editor, help wanted ads, and features. Students also compare local papers to national papers.

KEY VOCABULARY

Students complete each sentence with a word from the Word Bank.

Chapter 27 Life Skills Connection

One of the ways Joseph Stalin controlled the people of the USSR was by controlling the newspapers. Newspapers are a good way to learn about your world. They tell about things that are happening in your local area. They also carry stories about the rest of the country, and the rest of the world. When you are old enough to vote, newspapers are a good source of information about what people who are running for office think and believe.

Directions Get a copy of your local newspaper. Look for each of the following kinds of information.

1. *A news story.* This is a story about current events. It is about the facts, not about a person's opinion.

2. *An editorial.* This is a kind of article in which a writer gives his or her opinion about an event. Editorials are often located in a different part of the newspaper than news stories.

3. *A letter to the editor.* People who do not work for the newspaper write in letters expressing their ideas about current events.

4. *A "help wanted" ad.* A newspaper is a good source of information about jobs in your area.

5. *A feature story.* This is a story about something of interest that may not be a news story. For example, a story about students planning a school fundraiser would be a feature story.

Look at a national newspaper, such as the New York Times or the Wall Street Journal, at your local library. How is it the same as your local paper? How is it different?

Use the Internet to find five online news sites. For example, CNN.com is the online site for the CNN cable channel. How are these sites similar to print newspapers? How are they different?

Pacemaker® World History

Chapter 27 Key Vocabulary Words

Directions Write the correct word from the Word Bank to complete each sentence.

1. The _____ of Russia includes forests, deserts, and mountains.

2. The wide plains of Russia are called _____.

3. People who speak the same language may use different _____.

4. Ivan IV ruled using cruel punishment and other forms of _____.

5. The _____ of a nation depends on what it can make and sell.

6. Russia had food _____ during World War I.

7. Lenin was a leader of the _____ Revolution.

8. During the Russian Revolution, the _____ lost power.

9. Russia was governed by small councils called _____.

10. In _____, the government controls all industry.

11. Karl Marx wrote about a form of government called _____.

12. Joseph Stalin killed many people who _____ him.

13. Agriculture was organized into _____ farms.

14. Stalin would _____ any news he did not like.

15. The people of the Soviet Union lived behind a(n) _____.

Word Bank
Bolshevik
censor
collective
Communism
czar
dialects
economy
geography
Iron Curtain
opposed
shortages
socialism
soviets
steppes
terror

Pacemaker® World History

TRL Life Skills Connection 27   **TRL** Key Vocabulary Words 27, pages 1–2

Lesson at a Glance

Chapter 27 Lesson 1

Overview This lesson describes how Russia emerged as a country and who its rulers were from A.D. 882 to 1812.

Objectives

- To name the ancient civilization in eastern Europe that became Russia
- To explain why Ivan IV was so terrible
- To explain why Peter the Great wanted to open a "window to the West"
- To describe the reign of Catherine the Great

Student Pages 552–557

Teacher's Resource Library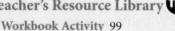

Workbook Activity 99

Activity 99

Modified Activity 99

Vocabulary

czar   geography
dialect   steppe
economy

Have students work with a partner and have them write definitions for each vocabulary word in their own words, without writing the actual vocabulary words. Have partners exchange papers with another pair of students and write the vocabulary word that matches each definition.

Reading Strategy:
Inferencing

(Possible answer: It was part of the USSR for most of the 20th century.)

The Early History of Russia

Objectives

- To name the ancient civilization in eastern Europe that became Russia
- To explain why Ivan IV was so terrible
- To explain why Peter the Great wanted to open a "window to the West"
- To describe the reign of Catherine the Great

Reading Strategy:
Inferencing

What do you already know about Russia?

Geography
The natural surface features of the earth, or any part of it

Steppe
A wide plain

Dialect
A form of a language used only in a certain place or among a certain group

The **geography** of Russia is varied. The country takes in frozen wastelands, thick forests, and wide plains known as **steppes**. There are also sandy deserts and huge snow-capped mountains. In addition, some of the longest rivers in the world are in Russia.

The people of Russia are just as varied as the geography. Some are tall and blond-haired, others are olive skinned and dark-haired. Some have European backgrounds, while others have Asian backgrounds. Altogether, Russian people speak dozens of different languages and **dialects**. A dialect is a form of language used only in a certain place or among a certain group.

Russia is the largest country on Earth. However, the country was not always so large or strong.

How Did Russia Become a Part of the Mongol Empire?

As far back as A.D. 400, a people known as Slavs lived in forests north of the Byzantine Empire. The Slavs became traders. Along their trade route, a town called Novgorod was established.

The Slavs of Novgorod were threatened by a wandering people of Turkish descent. The Vikings, a tribe of Northmen from Scandinavia, came to help the Slavs defend Novgorod. The Vikings were also called the Rus. In 862, Rurik the Viking became the ruler of Novgorod. The land of the Rus and the Slavs became known as Russia.

CHAPTER PROJECT

Divide the class into groups of three or four students. Have each group choose a leader discussed in the chapter. Have groups research that leader. Have students compile their research into a one-minute webcast on the leader's life, accomplishments, and role in history. Remind students that, when writing for their webcast, they will need to be concise and focus on the important information.

Czar
The ruler of Russia

Around 882, the Vikings captured the town of Kiev to the south of Novgorod. Kiev and Novgorod united under the rule of Viking Prince Oleg. Oleg set up the first Russian state and ruled from its capital at Kiev. The state was called Kievan Russia.

In 980, Vladimir I, great-grandson of Rurik, became the ruler of Kievan Russia. Vladimir wanted to unite Kievan Russia under one religion. He admired the Eastern Orthodox church and saw that it was established as the official religion of Kiev.

In 1019, the son of Vladimir I became the able ruler of Kievan Russia. He was known as Yaroslav the Wise because he made Kiev a center of learning.

Around 1237, a huge army of Asian warriors invaded Russia. Their leader was Batu Khan, a grandson of Genghis Khan. They destroyed one town after another, including Kiev. Russia became part of the Mongol Empire.

Why Was Ivan IV So Terrible?

The Mongols ruled for over 200 years. Then they grew weaker because of fighting among their leaders. Finally, in 1480, a group of Russian princes defeated the Mongols. Ivan III and his son, Basil III, led those princes. In 1547, Basil's son became the ruler, the first **czar** of all Russia. The first czar's name was Ivan IV. He became known as *Ivan the Terrible.*

Ivan IV changed Russian government. Earlier rulers, called Grand Dukes, had accepted advice and criticism from other nobles. Not Ivan IV—as czar, he moved the head of the government to Moscow and made himself all-powerful. It is said that one nobleman who dared to disagree with Ivan IV was tossed to the hounds (dogs). The hounds tore him to shreds!

Ivan the Terrible ruled by terror.

Ask students what the largest country in the world is. Use a globe or a world map to show Russia's size, relative to North America. (Russia is about the same size as all of North America.)

2   Teaching the Lesson

Ask students to preview the chapter by reading the headings and subheadings, and by looking at the art and photos, the map, and the timeline. Direct students to the title of the chapter, "Revolution in Russia: The Birth of the Soviet Union." Encourage students to recall the times when they have seen the word *revolution* in earlier chapters. Remind students that history is a collection of stories. Ask students what they think this story will be about, based on the chapter title? How can revolution lead to the birth of a new nation?

Ask:

- Who was Vladimir I? (ruler of Kievan Russia; grandson of Rurik, who established Russia)

- Name three ways that Peter the Great westernized Russia. (Possible answer: He brought experts from Europe to teach Russians; he opened an ice-free port for trade in the North Sea; he imposed cultural changes.)

- What happened to Russia during the reign of Catherine the Great? (Russian territory expanded to include part of Poland.)

COMMON ERROR

The historical account of the founding of the Russian royal family by the Viking Rurik around A.D. 880 is told in a chronicle that was compiled about 300 years later. Needless to say, some historians are skeptical of the validity of this chronicle. Some historians think that Rurik's son Igor, who founded Kiev as a principality, is the real founder of Russia's royal family.

Background Information

Kiev, which was one of the largest cities in the world in A.D. 1000, was a good defensive site and was surrounded by fertile farmlands. It was also a trading town from early in its history, and was on several trade routes. The north-south "water road" led from Byzantium to the Baltic, and other important trade routes led to the Caspian Sea and Central Asia. However, in 1240 the Mongols captured a weakened Russia and razed Kiev. Today Kiev is once again a large city, with more than 2.5 million people.

Economy
The system of making and trading things

Ivan ruled by terror. With threats of cruel punishment, he frightened the Russian people into doing what he wanted them to do. Hundreds of people were murdered by Ivan and his special police force. Ivan even killed his oldest son with his own two hands.

Ivan fought many wars. He increased Russia's territory. However, he made the daily lives of his people worse. Under Ivan the Terrible, the peasants were dreadfully poor. There was lots of land, but there were not enough people to keep the **economy** strong. The economy is the system of making and trading things.

Ivan did grant the right to trade in Russia. This brought in money for the upper classes. Yet it did little to improve the lives of the common people. After Ivan, most Russian rulers would seem kindly in comparison.

During the 1600s, Russia added to its territory. It took more of the Ukraine. It also extended its control of Siberia eastward to the Pacific Ocean. Slowly, Russia increased its contact with the rest of the world. Czar Michael Romanov took the throne in 1613. He encouraged trade with the Netherlands and England. He brought foreign engineers and doctors to Russia. Michael's son Alexis followed him. He, too, was open to European customs and cultures.

Why Did Peter the Great Want to Open a "Window to the West"?

Toward the end of the 17th century, a czar named Peter ruled in Russia. Peter had big plans. He wanted to make Russia more powerful. His goal was to make Russia equal to the nations of western Europe. Peter brought more Europeans into Russia. He brought engineers, artists, soldiers, and scientists to teach Russians the ways of western Europe.

Still, Peter did not learn all he wanted to know. To learn more, he went on a journey.

He traveled to the Netherlands to study shipbuilding. He continued his studies in England, where he visited factories, schools, and museums. He also visited France, Germany, and Austria.

When Czar Peter returned, he had many new ideas. He wanted to "westernize" his people. He ordered his subjects to wear European-style clothing instead of long, Asian-styled robes. He demanded that all Russian men cut off their beards to look more European. To set an example, Peter called his nobles together and cut off their beards himself. When people rebelled against Peter's no-beard orders, he demanded a tax from any man wearing a beard.

Peter changed the old Russian calendar to make it match the European calendar. He gave women more freedom. He put the Russian church under complete control of his government.

Peter the Great wanted to make Russia like the nations of western Europe. He wanted Russian men to cut off their beards to look more European.

1200–1950   *Revolution in Russia: The Birth of the Soviet Union   Chapter 27*   **555**

ELL/ESL STRATEGY

Language Objective: *To use maps as an aid for understanding text*

Have students practice reading maps and understand Peter the Great's point of view by illustrating the routes Russian ships took to reach European countries. Give each student a blank map, or have a group use a large classroom map. Instruct students to label or point to Russia, St. Petersburg, and the bodies of water that border Russia. Have students trace with their fingers or highlight with a pen the routes from the Baltic Sea to the Atlantic Ocean and from the Black Sea to the Mediterranean Sea. Ask students to explain what Peter the Great meant by calling St. Petersburg "a window for Russia to look at Europe."

3 | Reinforce and Extend

ONLINE CONNECTION

Brainstorm with students ways they might find out more about one of the monarchs mentioned in this chapter. Make sure students are aware of various Internet research strategies.

COMMON ERROR

Ask students to define *great*. Ask whether they think Peter and Catherine deserved this epithet. Discuss whose point of view lay behind the epithet: nobles or peasants?

(Possible answer: Russia arose and expanded several centuries before it became part of the USSR.)

History Fact

The brutal Russian winters have played a significant role in Russia's history at other times as well. For example, they were a stumbling block for the German army in World War II. They also helped to keep political dissidents isolated in Siberia.

Reading Strategy:
Inferencing

How does what you already know about Russia add to what you have just read?

History Fact

The great Russian author Tolstoy wrote about Napoleon's invasion of Russia in his famous novel, *War and Peace*.

Peter's desire to westernize Russia led him to seek a "window to the West." Peter wanted to open a Russian port on the ice-free Baltic Sea. Sweden stood in his way, so in 1700 he attacked Sweden. In 1721, a peace treaty gave Russia land along the eastern Baltic coast.

Meanwhile, in 1703, Peter began building the city of St. Petersburg. It would be Peter's European "window." It was built along the Neva River, where the river flows into the Gulf of Finland. In 1712, Peter moved the nation's capital from Moscow to St. Petersburg.

Peter brought new ideas, industrialization, and strength to Russia. That is why he was given the name *Peter the Great*. However, he did little for the common people. Russian peasants were still poor and completely at the mercy of their czar.

What Did Catherine II Do During Her Reign?

In 1762, Empress Catherine II became ruler of Russia. Catherine continued many of Peter's policies. She kept the "window to the West" open. She brought French culture to the nobles of Russia and improved their education. She was called *Catherine the Great*. However, she, too, did little for the peasants. In 1773, Catherine's armies had to put down a peasant revolt. Catherine ruled Russia for 34 years. She joined forces with the rulers of Austria and Prussia. Together they conquered Poland, and they divided up the land. Russia's territory was greatly increased during the reign of Catherine II.

In 1812, Russia's relations with the West took a turn for the worse. That year, France's Napoleon Bonaparte invaded Russia. In Chapter 18 you read how this turned out to be Napoleon's big mistake. After taking Moscow, Napoleon's army began to run out of supplies as the weather turned bitter cold. Napoleon had to order a retreat. Only about one out of six of the men in his army lived to reach France.

REVIEW

Word Bank

Byzantine

French

industrialization

Mongol

peasants

Sweden

territory

terror

trade

traveled

On a sheet of paper, write the word from the Word Bank to complete each sentence correctly.

1. During the 1400s, the _____ civilization in eastern Europe became Russia.

2. In 1237, Russia was invaded and became a part of the _____ Empire.

3. Ivan IV was the first czar after the Russians defeated the Mongols. He ruled by _____ and made the daily lives of people worse.

4. Although Ivan allowed _____ in Russia, it only brought in money for the upper classes.

5. Peter's goal was to make Russia equal to the nations of western Europe. Thus, he _____ to learn more about the western culture.

6. Peter fought _____ to win land along the eastern Baltic coast. The Russian port would serve as a "window to the West."

7. Peter brought new ideas, _____, and strength to Russia.

8. Catherine brought _____ culture and education to Russian nobles.

9. Catherine II greatly increased Russia's _____ during her reign.

10. Neither Peter nor Catherine did much for the _____ of Russia.

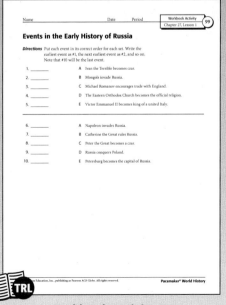

Lesson at a Glance

Chapter 27 Lesson 2

Overview This lesson describes the unrest in Russia from 1905 to 1917 and discusses Marx's Communist ideas.

Objectives

- To explain how Bloody Sunday started a revolution in 1905
- To describe how Russians felt about their country taking part in World War I
- To identify Karl Marx and define Communism

Student Pages 558–561

Teacher's Resource Library **TRL**

Workbook Activity 100

Activity 100

Modified Activity 100

Vocabulary

**Communism   socialism
shortage**

Have students read the vocabulary words and study their definitions. Ask volunteers to explain the differences between socialism and Communism. Classmates should concur with the definitions or offer corrections. Next, have students suggest things that they think contribute to shortages. Write students' suggestions on the board.

1 Warm-Up Activity

Ask students to recall the causes of the French and American revolutions. Have them read pages 558–559 to find out what life was like in Russia in the early 1900s.

Reading Strategy:
Inferencing

(They were angry about living in poverty and blamed the factory owners for it.)

Objectives

- To explain how Bloody Sunday started a revolution in 1905
- To describe how Russians felt about their country taking part in World War I
- To identify Karl Marx and define Communism

Reading Strategy:
Inferencing

What can you infer about the way the Russian peasants were feeling?

You Decide
Czar Nicholas II did not trust his people. In fact, he feared them. Do you think a ruler who fears the people can rule well? Why or why not?

Unrest in the Early 1900s

Russian peasants had lived under a feudal-type of system for hundreds of years. Wealthy nobles owned all the farmlands. In 1861, peasants were freed, but their lives were not much better.

How Did Bloody Sunday Prompt a Revolution in 1905?

As industrialization came to Russia, factories sprang up in the cities. Thousands of peasants left the farms. They moved to the cities to work in the factories. Often, the peasants found the factory owners as unfair and uncaring as the land-owning nobles had been. In 1905, many of the peasants protested to demand changes. On January 22, 1905, workers and their families marched in the streets of St. Petersburg. Workers wanted higher wages and a voice in government. In response, the czar's soldiers killed or wounded hundreds of men, women, and children that day. January 22, 1905, became known as Russia's "Bloody Sunday."

In 1905, protests by Russian workers led to violence in the streets.

You Decide
Ask volunteers for their opinions about these questions. Have them dig around in their text, in the library, or on the Internet for examples that support their opinions.

ELL/ESL STRATEGY

Language Objective:
To construct a chart to help students understand sequence of events

Ask students to read pages 558–559. Have them take notes on the steps that led up to the March 1917 revolt. Have them organize the steps in a sequence-of-events (flow) chart. Ask students to use their charts to write a summary about the steps that led to the revolt.

Reading Strategy: Inferencing

What inferences can you make about the Russian people's attitude? What words helped you make this inference?

 History Fact

In 1918, Czar Nicholas and his family were executed by a revolutionary Communist group called the Bolsheviks. The remains of the royal family were discovered in 1991.

Bloody Sunday was the end of any peaceful demand for change. Strikes, riots, and revolutionary battles broke out. In order to put a stop to the revolt, Nicholas II agreed to set up an elected Duma, or parliament. The Duma would have the power to rule on any proposals for new laws. Some people were satisfied with this change. Others felt that the Duma was not enough. The Duma lasted until 1917. The problems in Russia continued.

What Did the Revolutionaries Want?

Many Russians thought that **socialism** would solve Russia's problems. Socialism is an economic and political system where the government owns and controls all industry. Many of the revolutionaries in Russia had read the works of Karl Marx. Marx was a German thinker of the 1800s. Marx pictured a perfect world in which there would be no classes and in which government would be unnecessary. Marx's ideas were known as **Communism**. Communism is a form of socialism. Some of the revolutionaries in Russia wanted to see Marx's ideas become a reality in their country.

Why Were Russians Against Their Country's Involvement in World War I?

Russia entered World War I shortly after it began in 1914. The war brought severe food **shortages** to Russia (there was not enough food). The poor people became even poorer. The common people of Russia were not interested in fighting Germany. However, Czar Nicholas II had plunged Russia into the war.

In March 1917, the people of Russia demanded more food. The starving workers and peasants revolted. Czar Nicholas II was overthrown, and a new government took over. The czar and his family gave up the throne. The government promised democracy in Russia, but it did not end Russia's involvement in World War I. The people were against the war. It was draining supplies, killing men, and taking food.

Discuss what students learned about Russian peasants in Lesson 27–1. Ask them to infer what this lesson will recount of their demands and protests.

Ask:

- Why did the workers protest on Bloody Sunday? (They wanted higher wages and a voice in government.)
- Why did people want socialism in Russia? (They thought this new form of government would solve economic problems and give a political voice to more people.)
- What did the *Communist Manifesto* predict about workers? (They would revolt against factory owners.)

Background Information

From 1917 to 1998, no one knew for sure what had become of Czar Nicholas II and his family. Rumors that one or more of his children had survived persisted. Throughout the years, various individuals have claimed to be a surviving child of Nicholas II. In 1998 the remains of what was thought to be the czar and his family were identified. Two living relatives of the deceased royal family gave DNA samples that positively identified the skeletal remains discovered in a shallow grave near the city of Yekaterinburg in 1991 as those of the czar and his family. A formal reburial of the royal family took place on July 18, 1998, on what is thought to have been the 80th anniversary of their murder. The remains were interred in St. Petersburg's Saint Catherine Cathedral, where members of the Romanov dynasty have been interred since the time of Peter the Great.

Reading Strategy:
Inferencing

(People were poor, hungry, and angry with the government. They were "starved," "demanded" more food, and were "not interested in fighting.")

 ### History Fact

Much has been written and filmed about the last czar and his family. Interested students can find a plethora of information on the subject, but should be directed to look with a critical eye at the reliability of the sources.

 ### COMMON ERROR

Help students understand the difference between Communism, socialism, and capitalism. Point out that the United States and Canada are capitalist countries. Allow volunteers to share their families' experiences in a Communist or socialist nation.

3 Reinforce and Extend

WORDS FROM THE PAST

Remind students that an opinion is an idea that other people can agree or disagree with. Have students write three opinions that Karl Marx expressed, based on the information in the text. You might wish to provide the following opinion as a model: "A spirit is haunting Europe." Once students finish listing the opinions, ask them to write their opinion of Marx's beliefs (agree or disagree) and give one or two reasons that support their opinion.

COMMON ERROR

Students may have the idea that Marx was a Russian. Emphasize that he was, as the text says, a German and wrote his influential works in German.

COMMON ERROR

Most peasants and workers would not have read the *Communist Manifesto*. It affected them through the medium of more literate, well-educated leaders.

Karl Marx is often called the father of Communism.

Karl Marx and the *Communist Manifesto*

In 1848, Karl Marx and his friend Friedrich Engel wrote a pamphlet called the *Communist Manifesto*. "A spectre [spirit or ghost] is haunting Europe—the spectre of Communism," the *Manifesto* began. "Workingmen of all countries, unite," the *Manifesto* ended.

The *Manifesto* said that all history is the history of class struggles. It said that just as the serfs had gained their freedom from the nobles, workers in industry would revolt against the factory owners. The *Manifesto* described the first steps toward Communism. One step was that children would not be allowed to inherit their parents' money when their parents died.

Marx was born in Prussia (Germany) in 1818. His parents were middle class. Although they were Jewish, Marx's father converted to Christianity. Karl Marx was raised as a Christian. Later in life, he was famous for saying, "Religion is the opium [drug] of the people."

Das Kapital was Marx's most famous book. It was published in 1867. Part of the book described the poor conditions of the working class. Marx said that eventually capitalism would die and another better, classless, or Communist, society would take its place.

For most of Marx's adult life, he and his family lived in London, England. He researched his pamphlets and books at the British Museum. After Marx died in 1883, he was buried in Highgate Cemetery, in London. His ideas continue to have influence. They were important to the development of the USSR, a Communist state.

On a sheet of paper, write the answer to each question. Use complete sentences.

1. Why was January 22, 1905, called "Bloody Sunday"?

2. Who was Karl Marx and what was the main idea he promoted?

3. Why were the Russians against involvement in World War I?

On a sheet of paper, write the letter of the answer that correctly completes each sentence.

4. Russian peasants lived under a _____ type of system for hundreds of years.

   A feudal   **B** democratic   **C** republic   **D** monarch

5. More strikes, _____, and revolutionary battles followed Bloody Sunday.

   A trade   **B** riots   **C** peace   **D** farming

6. Nicholas II set up a parliament, called a _____, but it only lasted until 1917.

   A Manifesto   **C** Communist Party

   B soviet   **D** Duma

7. Many Russian revolutionaries read the works of _____.

   A Nicholas II   **B** Catherine II   **C** Karl Marx   **D** Lenin

8. Marx imagined a perfect world with a classless society and no _____.

   A trade   **B** government   **C** factories   **D** Communism

9. Russia entered World War I in 1914. As a result, poor people became even poorer and there were severe _____ shortages.

   A worker   **B** water   **C** soldier   **D** food

10. Even though _____ was overthrown in 1917, Russia stayed involved in World War I.

   A Czar Nicholas II   **C** the Duma

   B Karl Marx   **D** the working class

Lesson 27–2 Review Answers

1. That was the day workers and their families marched through the streets of St. Petersburg demanding higher wages and a voice in government. The czar's soldiers killed or wounded hundreds of men, women, and children. **2.** Marx was a German thinker of the 1800s. He said that capitalism would die and a Communist (classless) society would take its place. **3.** The war was draining supplies, killing men, and taking food—making life miserable for the Russians. **4.** A **5.** B **6.** D **7.** C **8.** B **9.** D **10.** A

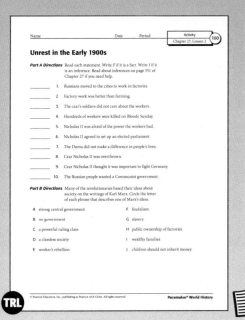

Activity 100

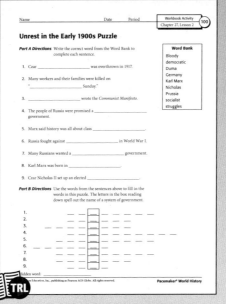

Workbook Activity 100

Revolution in Russia Chapter 27   **561**

Lesson at a Glance

Chapter 27 Lesson 3

Overview This lesson describes how Russia became the USSR and how Stalin led his country.

Objectives

- To identify the Bolsheviks, Lenin, and Stalin
- To explain the Bolshevik Revolution
- To identify the sides in the 1918 civil war and describe what each stood for
- To explain the Iron Curtain

Student Pages 562–568

Teacher's Resource Library

Workbook Activity 101

Activity 101

Modified Activity 101

Vocabulary

Bolshevik   Iron Curtain
censor   oppose
collective   soviet

Have students work with a partner, studying the definitions and making a three-column chart with words in the first column, definitions in the second column, and clues to the words in the third column. Have partners form a team and try to stump another two-person team. One team will put their paper face down and wait for the other team to give them a clue. If they can identify the word and define it, they get a point. Teams should alternate. The first pair to identify and define all the words correctly wins.

PRONUNCIATION GUIDE

Use this list to help students pronounce difficult words in this lesson.

Dzhugashvili (jōō´gəsh vē´lē)

Vladimir Ilyich Lenin (vlad´ə mēr´ il´yich len´in)

LESSON 27-3

Russia Becomes the USSR

Objectives

- To identify the Bolsheviks, Lenin, and Stalin
- To explain the Bolshevik Revolution
- To identify the sides in the 1918 civil war and describe what each stood for
- To explain the Iron Curtain

Reading Strategy: Inferencing

Use what you know about Russia to make inferences as you begin this lesson.

Bolshevik
A revolutionary Communist group in Russia

Soviet
A Russian council

In 1917, a man named Vladimir Ilyich Lenin returned to Russia from exile in Switzerland. Lenin had always hated the government of the czar. His brother had been hanged as a revolutionary. And Lenin himself had been exiled.

Lenin read Karl Marx. He became a Communist revolutionary who believed in rebellion and in a classless society. On his return to Russia, Lenin became the leader of a Communist group called the **Bolsheviks**. *Bolshevik* means "member of the majority." Lenin and the Bolsheviks promised to give the people what they wanted: "Peace, land, and bread."

What Was the Bolshevik Revolution?

In November 1917, the Bolsheviks overthrew the government. Karl Marx had pictured a society that would someday have no need for government. However, Lenin felt that a strict Communist Party should be in charge in Russia. The country would need a planned economy. Furthermore, the Communist Party would draw up the plans. The country would be governed by councils called *soviets*. The soviets would be headed by Bolsheviks.

What Was Life Like in the Union of Soviet Socialist Republics?

In 1918, Moscow became the nation's capital once again. That year, Russia was torn apart by a civil war. The Communists had taken power in the large cities of central Russia. However, resistance developed in many other parts of the country. The "Whites," or anti-Communists, had moved quickly to organize armies to fight the "Reds," or Communists. By 1921 most of the fighting was over. The Whites had been defeated.

---

562   *Unit 9   Nationalism and the Spread of War and Revolution*

Reading Strategy: Inferencing

Ask students to write down their inferences. Have them review the accuracy of their predictions at the end of the lesson.

Lenin led the Bolsheviks to power in Russia.

Reading Strategy:
Inferencing

Reread this section as necessary in order to make inferences about why Russia became the USSR.

In 1922, Russia became the Union of Soviet Socialist Republics (USSR). By then, Lenin had put the Communists firmly in charge. He had organized a strong police force. Every day, the police arrested, jailed, and even killed enemies of Communism. The police force often made their arrests secretly at night. Many members of the clergy were arrested. Communists believed that religion was in the way. Religion misguided people, the Communists said.

Have students share some things that they have learned or heard about the Communist form of government. Make a list of their ideas on the board. Make corrections to students' ideas as necessary. Explain that in this lesson, students will be reading about how Communism started in Russia.

2 **Teaching the Lesson**

As students read the lesson, have them make a list of all the reasons that the Russian people might have liked Lenin and supported him as a leader. This may help students understand why Lenin was able to gain so much control. Do the same for Stalin.

Ask:

- When did the Bolsheviks take over the Russian government? (fall of 1917)
- Who made up the "White" army and the "Red" army? (anti-Communists made up the White, Communists made up the Red)
- Who succeeded Lenin as head of the government? (Stalin)
- What was the Iron Curtain? (an invisible barrier between Western and Eastern Europe, enforced by walls, police, and lack of communication)

Reading Strategy:
Inferencing

Discuss the evidence students used to make inferences.

Background Information

Siberia is an enormous area, about twice the size of the United States. It has long, cold winters, but is teeming with wildlife. Bears, lynx, fox, sable, and ermine are trapped for their furs. It is a land rich in minerals like coal, iron, and gold. For a long time, Siberia was also a land of prisoners. Historically, it was home to political exiles sent from other parts of Russia and later the USSR. Peter the Great sent the first political prisoners to Siberia in 1710. Hundreds of thousands of Russians were sent to Siberia. They came from all walks of life and all social classes. Their crime was usually that they disagreed with the ruling government. So Siberia was colonized through an "exile system." The exiles worked for the government that imprisoned them. As they worked, they developed mining, manufacturing, and agriculture in Siberia.

The Soviet Union, 1922

MAP STUDY

1. What oceans border the Soviet Union?

2. Name two rivers in the Soviet Union.

Some members of the nobility and of the middle class were labeled enemies of the state. They were arrested, jailed, and executed. The government took their businesses. Lenin and his secret police ruled by fear.

The Bolshevik Revolution was supposed to help the peasants. Now Lenin ordered farmers to turn their crops over to the government. Some farmers rebelled. There was more fighting. Throughout the early 1920s, the Communists struggled to maintain power. For a brief period, the Communists let up on their hold over factories and farms in order to win support.

MAP STUDY

Answers:

1. Arctic Ocean, Pacific Ocean

2. The Volga River, the Ob River, the Yenisey River, the Lena River (Students name only two.)

Collective
Run by a group

Oppose
To be against
something

Then, in 1924, Lenin became ill and died. He is remembered as the "Father of the Revolution." After his death, Joseph Stalin, a well-known Communist Party member, took control.

What Did Joseph Stalin Do?

Joseph Stalin was born in 1879 in the country of Georgia. He was educated in a religious school. His mother wanted him to become a priest. Then Joseph Stalin read the works of Karl Marx. "There is no God!" he announced at age 13. When he grew up, he became a revolutionary and then a leader in the Communist Party.

Stalin's real name was Dzhugashvili. But in 1913, he adopted the name *Stalin*, which means "man of steel" in Russian. Stalin took power after Lenin's death. He ruled the Soviet Union from 1924 until his death in 1953.

Stalin built up Russia's economy and industry. He saw to the building of new factories and heavier machinery. The peasants were forced to work on farms run by a group, called **collective** farms. He insisted that farmers use the new government machines. However, he did not show the farmers how to operate them. Farm production went down. There were food shortages again.

Stalin made himself strong by destroying anyone who was against, or **opposed**, him. Suspected enemies were shot or exiled to Siberia. People learned to be loyal to the Communist Party and to Stalin.

Many people were unhappy living under such a tyrant. Stalin made life especially hard for Soviet Jews. Yet throughout the country, there were food shortages for everyone. In addition, certain goods, like clothing, were hard to come by.

1200–1950   *Revolution in Russia: The Birth of the Soviet Union*   *Chapter 27*   **565**

3 Reinforce and Extend

CAREER CONNECTION

Every government, whether a totalitarian state or a democracy, has a need for correctional institutions—places to incarcerate some people who violate the law. In the United States and Canada, corrections officers are needed for prisons at the federal, state, provincial, and local level. Students who might be interested in corrections work can search the Internet or the civil service department in their state or province to find out what a person needs to do to become a corrections officer.

IN THE COMMUNITY

Censorship is sometimes experienced at the community level. Have students interview or research comments by librarians, bookstore owners, local newspaper editors, and radio and TV managers about their experience with censorship. These might range from actual censorship of a book by a library board to responses to community pressure regarding the handling of news, display of magazines and books, or choices in programming. Give students an opportunity to report their findings.

Censor
To examine communications before they are released and to remove any parts that are objected to

Iron Curtain
The invisible boundary between Western Europe and Eastern Europe after World War II

Soviet newspapers and radio programs told nothing of the country's problems. Sources of news said only what Stalin wanted them to say. Also, Stalin would **censor** any news that came in from the rest of the world. This means that he would examine the news before it was released. Then, he would remove any parts he did not like. Stalin did not allow the Soviet people to travel outside the Soviet Union. This was one reason the Soviet Union was said to be surrounded by an **Iron Curtain**. The Iron Curtain refers to the invisible boundary between Western Europe and Eastern Europe after World War II.

Joseph Stalin controlled the Soviet Union through fear and terror.

British prime minister Winston Churchill made the term *Iron Curtain* popular. He used it in a speech in the United States in 1946.

Stalin had statues of himself put up all over Russia. He insisted that the statues be built to make him look taller and more handsome than he really was. Stalin actually rewrote Soviet history. He tried to make it sound as if the Russian people had actually chosen him to be their leader.

Russia has a long history of being ruled by tyrants. Ivan the Terrible, Peter the Great, and many other czars were cruel dictators. However, many people think that Stalin was the most destructive tyrant and dictator of all.

TIMELINE STUDY: HISTORY OF RUSSIA: FROM MONGOL RULE TO COMMUNISM

How long was Russia involved in World War I?

1237
Mongols invade Russia

1480
Russian princes defeat Mongols

1547
Ivan the Terrible becomes Russia's first czar

1703
Peter the Great founds St. Petersburg

1762
Catherine the Great becomes ruler of Russia

1812
Napoleon invades Russia

1848
Karl Marx publishes *Communist Manifesto*

1905
"Bloody Sunday," workers riot and strike

1914–1917
Russia involved in World War I

1917
Russian Revolution overthrows czar; Lenin becomes leader

1922
Russia becomes Union of Soviet Socialist Republics

1924–1953
Stalin rules as dictator

1200 | 1300 | 1400 | 1500 | 1600 | 1700 | 1800 | 1900 | 2000

Lesson 27–3 Review Answers

1. A **2.** C **3.** B **4.** B **5.** B **6.** C **7.** A

8. The Bolshevik Revolution did not help the peasants—in fact, Lenin ordered farmers to turn their crops over to the government. The farmers rebelled, and there was more fighting. **9.** Stalin censored news from Russia and the rest of the world. He also did not allow Soviets to travel outside of the Soviet Union. **10.** Stalin put up statues of himself all over the Soviet Union, and insisted that they make him look taller and more handsome that he really was. He also rewrote Soviet history and tried to make it sound as if the Soviet people had chosen him to be their leader.

LESSON 27-3 REVIEW

Match the description in Column A with the person in Column B. Write the correct letter on a sheet of paper.

Column A

1. known as the "Father of the Revolution"; he helped to overthrow the Russian government in 1917

2. British prime minister known for his speech about the Iron Curtain

3. a leader in the Communist Party who ruled the Soviet Union from 1924–1953; he helped build up Russia's economy and industry

Column B

A Lenin

B Stalin

C Winston Churchill

On a sheet of paper, write the letter of the answer that correctly completes each sentence.

4. The _____ were a Communist group whose name means "member of the majority."

   A Soviets   **B** Bolsheviks   **C** Reds   **D** Whites

5. The civil war that began in _____ put the "Whites" against the "Reds."

   A 1917   **B** 1918   **C** 1920   **D** 1921

6. The Whites, who were _____, were defeated in 1921.

   A Bolsheviks   **B** Soviets   **C** anti-Communist   **D** Communist

7. The Communists believed that _____ misguided people.

   A religion   **B** books   **C** governments   **D** factories

On a sheet of paper, write the answer to each question. Use complete sentences.

8. Did the Bolshevik Revolution help the peasants? Explain.

9. Why was it said that the Soviet Union was surrounded by an Iron Curtain?

10. What are two ways that Stalin made himself appear better than he really was?

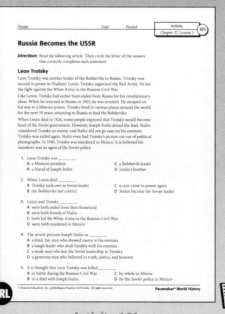

Activity 101

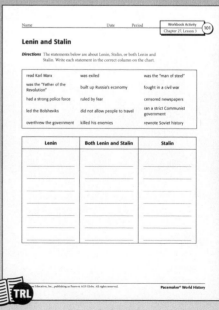

Workbook Activity 101

SUMMARY

- Much of the former Byzantine civilization lived on in Russia.

- Russia covers a good deal of land. It is home to many types of people. This includes descendants of the Vikings and Asian leader Genghis Khan.

- Russian czars came to power after 200 years of Mongol rule. Ivan the Terrible, who ruled by terror, was the first czar.

- Peter the Great westernized Russia. He brought teachers from Europe. He helped strengthen the industry of the country.

- Catherine the Great continued Peter's policies. She promoted education and culture.

- Bloody Sunday, in 1905, began a revolt of the Russian workers.

- Czar Nicholas II led Russia into World War I in 1914. The war was unpopular. In 1917, Nicholas II was overthrown.

- In 1917, the Bolsheviks took control of the government. The Bolsheviks, who followed Communist ideas, supported Lenin as head of Russia's government.

- In 1922, Russia became the Union of Soviet Socialist Republics.

- Joseph Stalin followed Lenin as leader of the Communist Party and the nation.

- Many Russians were hungry and unhappy living under the iron hand of Stalin.

TEACHER'S RESOURCE

The AGS Globe Teaching Strategies in Social Studies Transparencies may be used with this chapter. The transparencies add an interactive dimension to expand and enhance the Pacemaker® *World History* program content.

CHAPTER PROJECT FOLLOW-UP

 Have students perform their webcasts for the class. If the technology is available, tape the students during their webcasts and post them on a class Web site or burn them onto a CD that students can watch later. All students in a group should be responsible for reading a part of the one-minute webcast to the class. Evaluate students based on the quality of their research about their chosen leader as well as their performance delivery.

Chapter 27 Summary

Have students read the Chapter Summary on page 569 to review the main ideas presented in Chapter 27.

Ask:

- Russia grew out of what civilization? (the Byzantine Empire)

- Describe the land of Russia. (It is a huge country of frozen treeless lands, plains, and forests. It has people from many different ethnic groups.)

- Who was the first czar? (Ivan the Terrible)

- Which czar started to westernize Russia? (Peter the Great)

- How did Catherine the Great continue Peter's policies? (by encouraging cultural imports and European education)

- Why is Bloody Sunday important? (It launched the 1905 revolt of Russian workers.)

- How did World War I affect the leadership of Russia? (Because the czar refused to get out of the war, the Russians deposed him.)

- What organization advocated Communism in Russia? (the Bolsheviks)

- When did Russia become the USSR? (1922)

- Who was Joseph Stalin? (the leader of the Communist Party and of the USSR)

- Which policy of Stalin was hard on the Soviet people? (Possible answer: making the farms collective, which caused food shortages)

Chapter 27 Review

Use the Chapter Review to prepare students for tests and to reteach content from the chapter.

Chapter 27 Mastery Test

The Teacher's Resource Library includes two forms of the Chapter 27 Mastery Test. Each test addresses the chapter Goals for Learning. An optional third page of additional critical-thinking items is included for each test. The difficulty level of the two forms is equivalent.

Chapter 27 Review Answers

Vocabulary Review

1. Communism

2. geography

3. dialect

4. censor

5. Bolsheviks

6. economy

7. shortage

8. soviets

9. collective

10. opposed

Chapter Review Questions

11. Russia got its name from the Vikings, who were also known as the Rus.

12. Ivan IV was known as Ivan the Terrible because he ruled by terror. He had people murdered and punished in terrible ways.

Word Bank

Bolsheviks

censor

collective

Communism

dialect

economy

geography

opposed

shortage

soviets

Vocabulary Review

On a sheet of paper, use the words from the Word Bank to complete each sentence correctly.

1. _____ is a political system based on common ownership of industries and farms.

2. You can study _____ to learn about the natural features of the earth.

3. A(n) _____ is a form of language used in a certain place or by a certain group.

4. Stalin decided to _____ news so that Soviets would not know about events around the world.

5. The _____, a revolutionary Communist group, overthrew the Russian government in 1917.

6. Stalin built up Russia's _____, or system of making and trading things.

7. A(n) _____ is when there is not enough of something.

8. The Communist Party drew up a plan where Russia was governed by councils called _____.

9. Under Communism, peasants were forced to work on _____ farms (farms run by a group).

10. Stalin became powerful by destroying anyone who was against, or who _____, him.

Chapter Review Questions

On a sheet of paper, write the answer to each question. Use complete sentences.

11. Where did Russia get its name?

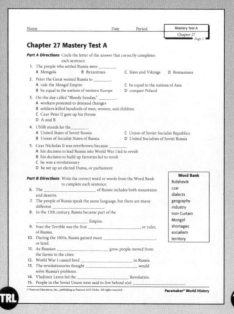

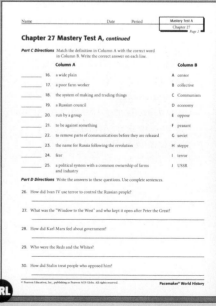

Chapter 27 Mastery Test A, pages 1–3

Test Tip

To choose the answer that correctly completes a sentence, read the sentence using each answer choice. Then choose the answer that makes the most sense when the entire sentence is read.

12. Why do you think Czar Ivan IV became known as *Ivan the Terrible?*

13. Why did Czar Peter want to open a "window to the West"?

14. What kind of government did Lenin think the Russians needed?

15. Why did Russian peasants revolt in 1917?

16. Lenin put Communists in charge in the Soviet Union. What was their attitude toward religion?

Critical Thinking

On a sheet of paper, write your response to each question. Use complete sentences.

17. Was life ever easy for Russian peasants? Why or why not?

18. What kind of person was Stalin? Give examples to support your answer.

Using the Timeline

Use the timeline on page 567 to answer the questions.

19. When did Peter the Great found St. Petersburg?

20. What happened in 1922?

GROUP ACTIVITY

Form a group of three or four. Write a skit about a person (or people) involved in the Russian Revolution. Base it on a historical event and make sure it follows some historical facts. You can also include fictional details (e.g., dialogue and actions). Perform your skit for the class.

---

13. Peter wanted a "window to the West" so new ideas could come into Russia. He wanted to modernize and westernize Russia.

14. Lenin thought the Communist Party should be in charge of government. He thought the economy should be planned.

15. Russian peasants revolted in 1917 because they were poor, starving, and not interested in fighting Germany.

16. The Communists believed religion misguided people. The Communists arrested many clergy.

Critical Thinking

17. Possible answer: Most students will probably answer no. They will point to poverty as serfs, miserable conditions as factory workers, and being forced to work on collective farms. There were food shortages throughout history.

18. Possible answer: Stalin ruled though fear. He tried to destroy everybody who opposed him. He did not allow freedom. He rewrote history to make it look as though he had been chosen to be leader.

Using the Timeline

19. 1703

20. Russia became the Union of Soviet Socialist Republics.

GROUP ACTIVITY

The skit should be historically accurate and show understanding of the person (people) and the event he/she (they) were involved in.

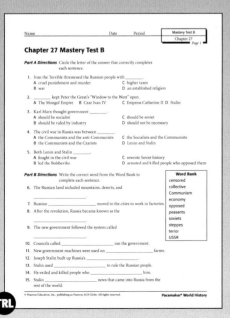

Chapter 27 Mastery Test B, pages 1–3

Introducing the Chapter

Officially, World War II began on September 3, 1939, when Great Britain and France declared war on Germany, and lasted until September 2, 1945, when Japan surrendered to Allied forces. The cost of the war—in human lives lost, in the destruction of cities, towns, histories, art, and literature, and in monies spent—was unparalleled in human history.

World War II

A fter World War I, many nations struggled with great economic depressions. People in various places were jobless and homeless. Nations such as China and Spain had civil wars. Other nations, such as Germany and Japan, had begun building empires.

World War I had been costly in lives and in money. No one was anxious for another war. Yet only 20 years after World War I ended, another war began.

GOALS FOR LEARNING

- To describe dictators who, in the years between the world wars, wanted an empire
- To understand how World War II began
- To describe the fighting during World War II
- To describe how the war ended
- To tell the results of the war

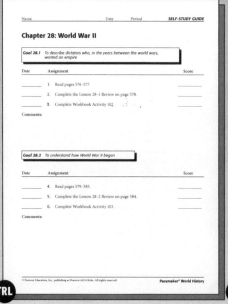

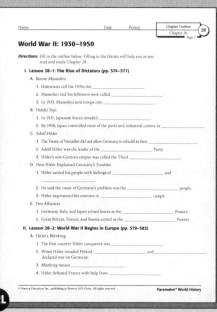

Reading Strategy: Metacognition

When you think about your thinking, you are using metacognition. Use metacognition to be a better reader.

- Preview the text. Ask yourself what you already know about the topic, and make predictions.

- Note the main idea, details, and any questions you have. Try to visualize what is happening in the text.

- Summarize and make inferences about what you read.

Key Vocabulary Words

Lesson 1

Depression A period of low business activity and high unemployment

Fascist People who follow the political system that honors the state over the individual

Anti-Semitism Prejudice against Jews

Scapegoat A person or group blamed for the mistakes and problems of others

Concentration camp A prison camp for people thought to be dangerous to a ruling group

Axis Powers The alliance of Germany, Italy, and Japan during World War II

Allied Powers The nations united against the Axis Powers in World War II; includes Britain, France, and later the United States and the Soviet Union

Lesson 2

Civilian A person who is not in the military

Lesson 3

Genocide An attempt to kill all the people of a certain race or religious group

Holocaust Hitler's killing of many of the Jews in Europe

Pact An agreement

D-Day The Allied invasion of France in 1944

Lesson 4

Kamikaze A Japanese pilot who crashed his plane into an enemy ship, destroying it and killing himself

Nuclear Having to do with atoms or energy from atoms

Atomic bomb A bomb that uses nuclear energy and has much destructive power

Lesson 5

Organization A group of people joined together for a common purpose

Ask:

- How much time elapsed from the end of World War I to the beginning of World War II? (about 20 years)

- What were some of the reasons for the start of World War II? (Students may say that many nations suffered from economic depressions; that civil wars contributed to political instability; or that there was a rise in nationalism and empire building.)

Reading Strategy: Metacognition

Tell students that Merriam Webster's Dictionary defines *metacognition* as "awareness or analysis of one's own learning or thinking processes." Using metacognitive skills can help them to become both better readers and more astute learners.

Key Vocabulary Words

Point out that these chapter words are presented in the order they appear in each lesson. They are also found in the glossary.

LIFE SKILLS CONNECTION

Students learn about income and spending by creating a budget. Students also learn the difference between fixed and variable expenses. Help students by providing realistic costs for expenses they may not be familiar with yet.

KEY VOCABULARY

Students choose the correct word from the Word Bank to complete each sentence.

Life Skills Connection 28

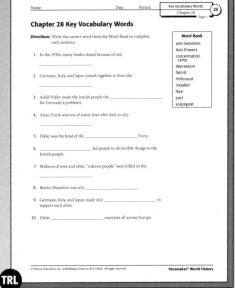

Key Vocabulary Words 28, pages 1–2

Lesson at a Glance

Chapter 28 Lesson 1

Overview In the years after World War I, dictators took control in many nations. These nations, fueled by nationalism and economic hard times, took steps that set the stage for another world war.

Objectives

- To name three dictators who came to power before World War II
- To identify the Axis and Allied Powers
- To describe the theory that Adolph Hitler used to explain Germany's troubles

Student Pages 574–578

Teacher's Resource Library

Workbook Activity 102

Activity 102

Modified Activity 102

Vocabulary

Allied Powers	depression
anti-Semitism	fascist
Axis Powers	invade
concentration camp	scapegoat

Write the vocabulary words on the board. Then ask students to find the definitions and write them in their notebooks. Next, have students create a crossword puzzle that uses information from the lesson to create a hint for each word. When students have finished their puzzles, have them swap with each other and fill in the blanks.

PRONUNCIATION GUIDE

Use this list to help students pronounce difficult words in this lesson.

Hideki Tojo (hē´ de kē tō jō)

Reich (rīk)

LESSON 28-1

The Rise of Dictators

Objectives

- To name three dictators who came to power before World War II
- To identify the Axis and Allied Powers
- To describe the theory that Adolf Hitler used to explain Germany's troubles

Depression
A period of low business activity and high unemployment

Fascist
People who follow the political system that honors the state over the individual

Benito Mussolini took control of Italy in 1922.

The 20 years between World War I and World War II were troubled years. In the early 1930s, nations struggled through **depressions**. Businesses went broke. Millions of workers were out of jobs. Farmers could not sell crops to unemployed people. Banks closed. Poverty spread throughout the world. Historians would call the 1930s the "Great Depression."

There were other troubles, too. In India, people were fighting for freedom from British rule. Civil wars were raging in China and Spain. In addition, Japan, Italy, and Germany began building empires.

The years between World War I and World War II brought new governments to several nations. They were governments ruled by dictators. The Great Depression created a perfect climate for the rise of dictators. Hungry, hopeless people wanted to see changes. They were ready to turn to a strong leader who promised a better future. Most of the dictators, however, were men with evil ideas and purposes. They wanted power and control.

Who Was Benito Mussolini?

A man named Benito Mussolini took control of Italy in 1922. He and his followers were called **fascists**. Fascists are people who honor the state over the individual. Mussolini won favor with his people by building roads and factories. He improved his country's economy and industry, but insisted on absolute rule. Anyone who refused to obey Mussolini was jailed or killed.

Mussolini wanted Italy to become a great empire. He wanted to win colonies, to make war, and to take new lands by force.

574 *Unit 9 Nationalism and the Spread of War and Revolution*

ONLINE CONNECTION

Students can gain additional information by accessing the following Web site: www.agsglobepmwh.com/page574 (This site provides additional information on the complex structure of the UN.)

CHAPTER PROJECT

Divide the class into small groups. Have the groups prepare reports on activities that the United Nations and its various councils and organizations are engaged in today. Students should search current newspapers, magazines, television newscasts, and the Internet for stories about the United Nations, write brief summaries of the articles or newscasts, and then compile the summaries into a report.

Invade
To attack or march into another country

General Hideki Tojo had all the power in Japan by 1941.

In 1935, Mussolini sent troops into Ethiopia, a free African country. The League of Nations protested. However, it could not stop Mussolini's drive into Africa.

Who Was General Hideki Tojo?

In Japan, General Hideki Tojo arose as a dictator. He wanted to build an empire in Asia. Under the leadership of Tojo and other generals, Japanese forces **invaded**, or attacked, the Chinese province of Manchuria in 1931. When the League of Nations protested, Japan left the League. By 1932, Japan had claimed Manchuria. Japan invaded China again in 1937, taking over miles of coastal lands. By 1938, Japan controlled all of China's major ports and industrial centers.

During the 1930s, Japanese military officers began taking over their own government. Anyone who got in their way or protested was either jailed or assassinated. By 1940, Tojo had become minister of war. Finally, in 1941, he became premier. Japan still had an emperor, but the emperor had no real power.

Who Was Adolf Hitler?

The country that was most willing to accept a dictator and to follow him without question was Germany. Germany had suffered greatly after World War I. German pride had been crushed. A country whose nationalistic spirit was based on military greatness had been beaten in war. German armies had been reduced to almost nothing. And the Treaty of Versailles had not allowed the Germans to rebuild their military.

The depression hit hard, and Germany still had war debts to pay. Germans were out of work and hungry. Many were angry and ready to get even.

Ask students to preview the chapter by reading the headings and subheadings and by looking at the photos. Have them study the map on page 582 and the timeline on page 597. Lead a discussion in which students talk about which photos in the chapter are most compelling to them, and why. Ask students, *Why is it important to understand the causes of a war?* Students may suggest that understanding the causes of a war might keep history from repeating itself.

2   Teaching the Lesson

As students read the information on pages 574–577, ask them to recall Napoleon's domination of Europe. Ask them to compare and contrast what they remember of Napoleon with the three dictators discussed in this lesson.

Ask:

● What did Benito Mussolini want for Italy? (that it would become a great empire)

● What free African country was invaded by Italy in 1935? (Ethiopia)

● Under the leadership of General Hideki Tojo, what Chinese province was invaded in 1931? (Manchuria)

● How did Adolf Hitler appeal to the German people? (Students may say that he appealed to their wounded pride, or to their nationalistic tendencies. They may say that he spoke of building a strong military and winning back lost territories. They may say that he appealed to their racism by suggesting that Germans were better than other races.)

● What group of people did Hitler blame for many of Germany's troubles? (the Jewish people)

● What were the Axis Powers? (an alliance formed among Italy, Germany, and Japan)

● What were the Allied Powers? (an alliance united against the Axis Powers comprised of Britain, France, and later the United States and the Soviet Union)

ELL/ESL STRATEGY

Language Objective:
To encourage students to seek out unfamiliar words and phrases

Begin by asking students to preview the chapter for five unfamiliar words or phrases other than those that appear in the vocabulary lists. Have students record the words and phrases in their notebooks, and then use their dictionaries to discover their meanings. Ask students to compose original sentences for each word or phrase.

● The text explains that blaming Jews for Germany's troubles provided a scapegoat for the German people. Why is the tendency to scapegoat others such a powerful one? Can you think of examples where a person or group of people has been turned into a scapegoat? If so, what was the outcome? (Answers will vary. Students might say that scapegoats provide a powerful distraction from conditions and situation over which people feel they have no control.)

Reading Strategy:
Metacognition

Ask several volunteers to share their predictions with the class. Encourage volunteers to talk about *how* they arrived at their predictions.

Background Information

The League of Nations was established in the aftermath of World War I with a singular mission—to ensure that war never broke out again. Based in Geneva, Switzerland, members of the League promised to defend all its member nations. Article 11 of the League's Covenant stated, "Any threat of war is a matter of concern to the whole League and the League shall take action that may safeguard peace . . ." The League of Nations' efficacy was tested in 1931, when Japan invaded Manchuria, and again in 1935 when Mussolini sent Italian troops into Ethiopia. In both cases, member nations of the League were unable to stop the aggressor states from taking over weaker nations and the League of Nations was unable to prevent the beginnings of World War II.

Anti-Semitism
Prejudice against Jews

Scapegoat
A person or group blamed for the mistakes and problems of others

Concentration camp
A prison camp for people thought to be dangerous to a ruling group

Reading Strategy:
Metacognition

Make a prediction as to what you think will happen next. Check your prediction as you read and revise if needed.

Adolf Hitler promised to win Germany's lost lands back.

This situation in Germany led people to accept Adolf Hitler as their leader in 1933. Hitler was the head of the National Socialist, or *Nazi*, party. The Nazis seemed to have an answer to Germany's problems. Hitler appealed to the Germans' wounded pride. He told them that they were a "super race" who should rule the world. He promised to return Germany to a position of power and glory.

Hitler spoke of winning back Germany's lost lands. He promised a new German empire, the Third Reich. In 1935, Hitler began rebuilding Germany's armed forces. This had been forbidden by the Treaty of Versailles. However, nothing was done to stop the Nazis from arming themselves.

As Hitler gave Germany new hope and national pride, he built his own strength. Few people dared speak out against Adolf Hitler!

How Did Hitler Explain Germany's Troubles?

Hitler tried to bind his people together with the feeling of hatred. He aimed that hate at all people who were not white and Germanic. Hitler believed that the German race was stronger, better, and smarter than any other. He gave fiery speeches that stirred German emotions. He told the people that Germans should be "masters of the world."

Hitler directed his fiercest hatred at the Jewish people. He encouraged **anti-Semitism**, a mindless hatred of Jews. He told the German people that the Jews were the cause of all their troubles. Hitler's lies gave the unhappy Germans a **scapegoat**. Now they had a simple way to explain away their troubles: they blamed them all on the Jews.

Hitler united Germany under a banner of hatred and fear. He made people afraid to disobey, or go against, him. Hitler's secret police backed his rule. They arrested anyone who spoke against him. **Concentration camps** were built to imprison Hitler's enemies. Many were killed in these camps.

Axis Powers

The alliance of Germany, Italy, and Japan during World War II

Allied Powers

The nations united against the Axis Powers in World War II; includes Britain, France, and later the United States and the Soviet Union

Remember

Long before Hitler, Alexander the Great wanted to conquer the world. Later, so did Napoleon.

Hitler won Germany's loyalty. Then he turned to the rest of Europe. "Today Europe," Hitler declared, "tomorrow the world!"

What Two Alliances Were Formed?

The three dictators—Hitler, Mussolini, and Tojo—each wanted an empire. In 1936, Hitler and Mussolini joined forces. They called their alliance the Rome-Berlin axis. They chose the name "axis" to suggest that all of Europe revolved around Germany and Italy. In 1940, Japan joined the **Axis Powers**. Germany, Italy, and Japan planned to conquer the world and divide it up!

On the other side, countries like Britain, France, and later the Soviet Union and the United States united against the Axis Powers. These nations were known as the **Allied Powers**.

With these two alliances formed, the sides were set for one of the worst wars in history.

Concentration camps imprisoned Hitler's enemies. Buchenwald concentration camp, pictured here, was one of the largest Nazi concentration camps.

1930–1950

World War II   *Chapter 28*   **577**

Remember

Ask students to recall what they learned about both Alexander the Great and Napoleon in earlier chapters. Ask, *What was the outcome of their campaigns to conquer the world?* (They failed and their leaders died (Alexander the Great) or died in exile (Napoleon).

---

3   **Reinforce and Extend**

COMMON ERROR

The word *fascist* may pose special spelling and usage problems for students. The following information may be useful to them.

Fascism comes from the Italian word *fascismo*, which means bundle or group.

Fascism is a noun. When it is used as a proper noun, it should be capitalized.

Fascist can be either a noun or an adjective. It is also often capitalized.

Fascistic is an adjective.

Fascistically is an adverb.

STUDY SKILLS

Reproduce a large version of the timeline from page 597 on the bulletin board. Leave plenty of space between the dates. As students study the chapter, ask volunteers to fill in the timeline with additional dates and events as they are discussed. Students may also wish to create icons to signify Allied and Axis powers.

AT HOME

To help students become aware of how events in history impact families, ask them to trace their family trees to two time frames: just before the entry of their nation into World War II and the early years of their nation's involvement in World War II. Students should ask family members where they lived, what kind of work they did, how World War II affected them, and other interesting facts. Ask students to write a report on their findings. Encourage students to illustrate their reports or include family photos and memorabilia.

World War II Chapter 28   **577**

Lesson 28–1 Review Answers

1. B **2.** C **3.** A **4.** B **5.** C **6.** A **7.** C
8. Hitler told the Germans that they were a "super race" that should rule the world. He believed the German race was stronger, better, and smarter than any other. He promised to return Germany to a position of power and glory. **9.** Britain and France were a part of the Allies. (The United States and the Soviet Union would join later.) **10.** Hitler believed that the Jews were the cause of all the German people's troubles. He bound people together with the feeling of hatred and fear.

Match the description in Column A with the dictator in Column B. Write the correct letter on a sheet of paper.

Column A

1. the fascist ruler who took control of Italy in 1922 and insisted on absolute rule

2. the man who, as premier of Japan in 1941, had more power than the emperor

3. head of the Nazis; believed Germans were a "super race" and should rule the world

Column B

A Adolf Hitler
B Benito Mussolini
C Hideki Tojo

On a sheet of paper, write the letter of the answer that correctly completes each sentence.

4. Germany's defeat in World War I had crushed German _____.

  A trade   **B** pride   **C** weapons   **D** inventions

5. _____ and Italy named their alliance "axis," suggesting that all of Europe revolved around them.

  A Britain   **B** France   **C** Germany   **D** Russia

6. In 1940, _____ joined the Axis Powers.

  A Japan   **B** Italy   **C** Russia   **D** the United States

7. By rebuilding Germany's armed forces, Hitler was going against the _____.

  A National Socialist party   **C** Treaty of Versailles
  B Axis Powers   **D** United Nations

On a sheet of paper, write the answer to each question. Use complete sentences.

8. How did Hitler appeal to the Germans' wounded pride?

9. What countries were included in the Allied nations?

10. What was Adolf Hitler's theory to explain Germany's troubles?

---

578   *Unit 9 Nationalism and the Spread of War and Revolution*

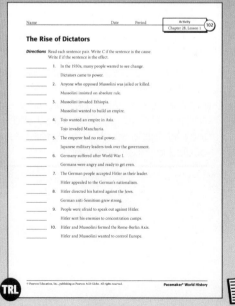

World War II Begins in Europe

Lesson at a Glance

Objectives

■ To explain how Germany helped to bring about World War II

■ To identify Hitler's style of warfare and explain what happened when Germany invaded France

■ To describe the Battle of Britain

■ To describe the problems Hitler had after his army invaded the Soviet Union

Reading Strategy:
Metacognition

Note the main idea and supporting details of *blitzkrieg*. Summarize what you have read to make sure you understand it.

In 1938, Hitler set forth on his conquest of Europe. His troops marched into Austria and took over the country. Austria was now a part of Germany.

"This is wrong," said Great Britain and France. "Hitler has broken the Treaty of Versailles." However, they did not act to stop him.

Next Hitler turned to Czechoslovakia. Hitler claimed that Germans living there were treated poorly. He asked for a border region in Czechoslovakia. He said that this would be his last request for territory. Great Britain and France had sworn to protect Czechoslovakia. To keep peace, however, they signed a treaty with Hitler. They gave him 11,000 square miles of Czech lands. This area was known as the Sudetenland. Six months later, Hitler took over the rest of Czechoslovakia. The British and French policy of trying to satisfy Hitler by giving in had not worked.

On September 1, 1939, German armies invaded Poland. This time Great Britain and France acted. On September 3, 1939, they declared war on Germany. World War II had begun.

What Was Hitler's *Blitzkrieg*?

The German army took Poland in less than a month. Then Hitler pushed west. Norway and Denmark fell to Germany, too.

Hitler's style of warfare was called a *blitzkrieg*, which means "lightning war." His armies moved fast, using quick attacks with planes, tanks, and troops. First, German planes bombed railroads, highways, and cities. Then, the armored cars moved in, followed by the Nazi foot soldiers.

Chapter 28 Lesson 2

Overview In 1938, Germany ignored the Treaty of Versailles and invaded neighboring countries. Britain and France attempted to stop Germany without fighting, but in 1939 both countries declared war on Germany. Before long, World War II spread throughout Europe.

Objectives

■ To explain how Germany helped to bring about World War II

■ To identify Hitler's style of warfare and explain what happened when Germany invaded France

■ To describe the Battle of Britain

■ To describe the problems Hitler had after his army invaded the Soviet Union

Student Pages 579–584

Teacher's Resource Library

Workbook Activity 103

Activity 103

Modified Activity 103

Reading Strategy:
Metacognition

Call students' attention to the reading strategy and ask them to write a short paragraph summarizing the information they learned about *blitzkrieg*. Next, ask students to write a sentence or two describing how they arrived at their summary.

Vocabulary

civilian

Write the vocabulary word on the board. Then have students compose an original sentence that uses the word in its proper context.

Draw students' attention to the Word Bank on page 584. Have students work in small groups to compose original paragraphs that include at least four of the Word Bank words as well as the vocabulary word. Encourage a volunteer from each group to read the paragraph aloud.

PRONUNCIATION GUIDE

Use this list to help students pronounce difficult words in this lesson.

Czechoslovakia (chek´ ə slə vä´ kē ə)

Blitzkrieg (blits´ krēg´)

1 Warm-Up Activity

Have students preview the lesson by reading the subheadings. Ask them to look at the photo on page 581 and map on page 582. Next, ask students to review the objectives on page 579. Remind students that their vocabulary for the lesson—civilian—first appears on page 581 and then again on page 583. Ask, *What role did civilians play in fighting the war?*

2 Teaching the Lesson

As students read the lesson, create a chart on the board with the following categories:

> Year
>
> Nation
>
> Reaction
>
> Outcome

Begin filling in the chart with information about Austria.

> **Year** (1938)
>
> **Nation** (Austria)
>
> **Reaction** (Great Britain and France condemn the invasion but do not act.)
>
> **Outcome** (Austria becomes part of Germany.)

As the class moves through the chapter, have students replicate this chart in their notebooks and fill in the categories as they learn more about the progress of World War II in Europe.

Ask:

- What is an example of appeasement in the lesson? (the treaty Great Britain and France signed with Hitler after Czechoslovakia was invaded)
- What is a *blitzkrieg*? (a quickly moving attack that begins with aerial bombing, then armored cars, and finally foot soldiers)
- What country helped Germany to defeat France? (Italy)
- What is the significance of the Battle of Britain? (It was the first major air war in history. It also marked Germany's first defeat in World War II.)

- What do you think life was like for the average British citizens during the eight months of the London Blitz? How do you think you might have coped if you had lived through this? (Students may say that average citizens tried to assist in the fighting; that they worked out plans to protect themselves.)
- What historical figure does the text compare Adolf Hitler within its discussion of the invasion of the Soviet Union? What was the outcome of this invasion? (Napoleon; students may say that Hitler underestimated both the ferocity of the Russian people's resistance and the harshness of the Russian weather.)

Words from the Past

Winston Churchill, June 4, 1940

Winston Churchill had become prime minister of Great Britain on May 10, 1940. That was the same day that Germany invaded Belgium, Luxembourg, and the Netherlands. Soon after that, Belgium surrendered to Germany. It looked as if it would only be a matter of days until France fell to the Nazis. People in Britain began to worry about what would happen to their own country.

On June 4, Churchill gave a speech to the British House of Commons. He wanted to raise the spirits of the British people. He said that even though all of Europe might fall, " . . . we shall not flag or fail. We shall go on to the end . . . we shall fight in the seas and oceans . . . we shall fight on the beaches, we shall fight on the landing-grounds, we shall fight in the fields and in the streets, we shall fight in the hills; we shall never surrender . . . ."

580   *Unit 9   Nationalism and the Spread of War and Revolution*

WORDS FROM THE PAST

After students have read the information on Winston Churchill on page 580, read aloud the excerpt from his speech to the British House of Commons. Ask, *What effect do you think this had on the British people?*

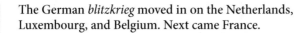

Civilian
A person who is not in the military

Remember
France had been Germany's bitter enemy since losing a war to Bismarck in 1871.

You Decide
Britain's spirit remained strong in spite of the constant bombing. Do you think your country would be as strong in this situation? Explain.

The German *blitzkrieg* moved in on the Netherlands, Luxembourg, and Belgium. Next came France.

When the Germans attacked France, they had some help from Italy. France's armies were unable to stop Hitler. With Germans at the gates of Paris and planes overhead, the French surrendered. In June 1940, the French admitted their defeat. It is said that Hitler received the news of France's surrender with great joy. A story went around that he danced a little "victory jig."

Who Won the Battle of Britain?

With the fall of France, only Britain remained in Hitler's way. Hitler decided not to attack the island of Great Britain by sea. Britain's navy was too powerful. Hitler would launch an air attack instead.

The Battle of Britain was the first major air war in history. Beginning in July 1940, thousands of German planes attacked Britain. They bombed cities and airfields. However, the British would not be defeated.

Readers choose books in a London library damaged by bombs.

British **civilians** (those not in the military) worked out air raid plans to protect their neighborhoods. Citizens even strung piano wire from balloons to catch Nazi planes. The skilled young pilots of the British Royal Air Force (RAF) fought hard. With speedy Spitfire planes and with newly developed radar, they fought off the German planes.

1930–1950   *World War II   Chapter 28*   **581**

Background Information

Hitler's willingness to wage total war was one reason many countries in Europe surrendered without battle. These countries knew what he would do and what their limitations were. Great Britain chose to go to war. Many people sent their children to stay with relatives in the countryside, because the cities, especially London, were being bombed day and night. Many who did not have relatives in the country sent their children to live with strangers. Some children spent the war years in the United States and other countries.

ELL/ESL STRATEGY

Language Objective:
To describe the meaning of the word appeasement

Tell students that another word for "keeping the peace" is *appeasement*. Have students look up this word in their dictionaries and lead a brief discussion about the different ways nations tried to use appeasement in the years leading up to World War II.

Ask an ELL student to come up before the class. Have a volunteer in the class give the ELL student a scenario from everyday life and ask the student to act out how he or she would use a policy of appeasement to prevent an argument. For example, if the student volunteer mentions that two children both want the last cookie, the ELL student might suggest that the cookie should be broken in half and half given to each child. Have the student narrate as he or she role-plays so the class knows what is happening.

You Decide

After students have discussed the question posed in this section, ask them to talk about how they arrived at the answer to the question. Ask, *What characteristics must a nation's citizens have—or fail to have—that would contribute to their reaction to warfare?*

TEACHER ALERT

Winston Churchill's speech to the British House of Commons on June 4, 1940, has been called one of the greatest speeches of the 20th century. You may want to have students hear or read the speech in its entirety by accessing it online. The *History Channel* provides both video and audio of Churchill's speech at the following Web site: www.agsglobepmwh.com/page581a

You may also wish to call students' attention to the BBC's archival Web site for further information and insight into Churchill's speeches during World War II. You can access the Web site at: www.agsglobepmwh.com/page581b

---

Remember

After students have read the information ask, *Do you think this affected France's decision to surrender to the Germans? Why or why not?*

Reading Strategy:
Metacognition

Ask students to recall their earlier predictions and, if necessary, have them read what they wrote for the previous lesson. Ask, *What changes are needed to refine and revise your prediction?*

3   Reinforce and Extend

COMMON ERROR

Although Hitler was the first to use aerial power to engage in "total war" against another nation, the practice of total war had been used for centuries. It is a military practice in which a nation, or nations, mobilizes all available resources to destroy an enemy's ability to wage war. Some early examples of total war include the Peloponnesian War, the French Revolution, and the American Civil War.

IN THE COMMUNITY

Arrange for students to go on a field trip to the local historical museum to view World War II artifacts and exhibits. If this is not an option, take a virtual field trip with students on the Internet or invite a veteran of World War II to speak to the class. Follow up with a class discussion on how World War II affected their communities.

MAP STUDY

Answers:

1. Sweden, Spain, Portugal, Turkey, Saudi Arabia, Ireland, and Switzerland

2. Leningrad, Moscow, and Stalingrad

Reading Strategy:
Metacognition

Review the prediction you made during the last lesson. Make changes to it as needed.

From September 1940 until May 1941, German planes bombed London almost every night. These attacks became known as the *London Blitz.* By May 1941, it was clear that the German bombing attacks had failed. Germany had lost more than 2,600 planes. It was Germany's first defeat in World War II.

World War II in Europe, 1942–1945

MAP STUDY

1. Which nations were neutral in World War II?
2. What three cities in the USSR were near the area of Axis control?

What Nations Did Hitler Conquer?

Unable to take Britain, Hitler's armies moved eastward. The Germans took Romania and its oil fields. Then Italy invaded Greece. Greece's armies fought bravely against the Italians. However, when Hitler joined the Italians, Greece had to surrender.

Next, the Axis nations invaded Yugoslavia. Most of Europe had now fallen under Hitler. His next goal would be the conquest of the Soviet Union. Germany had been allies with the Soviets, but Hitler decided to invade anyway.

What Happened When Hitler Invaded the Soviet Union?

Like Napoleon Bonaparte, Hitler chose June 22 as the day to attack Russia. Napoleon had attacked on June 22, 1812. Now Hitler attacked on June 22, 1941, with three million German soldiers. He expected Russia to fall in a matter of weeks.

The Russians surprised the world by fighting back with amazing strength and determination. Soldiers and civilians alike stood up against the Germans. However, the Germans advanced toward Moscow. Just as in the fight against Napoleon, Russians burned whatever they could not move. They destroyed food, supplies, machinery, and factories so the Germans could not use them. The Germans approached Moscow, but they were unable to take the city. People from all over Russia poured in to defend it.

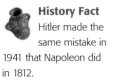

History Fact
Hitler made the same mistake in 1941 that Napoleon did in 1812.

Like Napoleon, Hitler did not count on the fierce Russian weather. Hitler's soldiers did not even have winter clothing. Furthermore, the winter of 1941–1942 turned out to be the worst in years. Nazi soldiers froze on the icy Russian plains. It was beginning to look as if Hitler might have made a mistake by invading Russia. Indeed, by 1944 the Soviets had pushed the Germans out of the Soviet Union.

History Fact
After students read the history fact, ask what mistakes both Hitler and Napoleon made. (They both underestimated the ferocity of the Russian people and the harshness of the Russian winter.)

Lesson 28–2 Review Answers

1. *Blitzkrieg* **2.** Czechoslovakia
3. France **4.** Britain **5.** Romania
6. Greece **7.** Moscow **8.** Germany
invaded Poland, causing Great Britain
and France to declare war. **9.** The
Battle of Britain, which eventually
became known as the London Blitz,
was the first major air war in history.
German planes bombed cities and
airfields, but the British would not
give up. Civilians would string piano
wire from balloons to catch Nazi
planes, and skilled pilots from the
British Royal Air Force fought hard
with speedy Spitfire planes and
radar. Eventually, Germany gave up.
10. When Hitler invaded the Soviet
Union he did not count on the fierce
Russian weather. His soldiers did not
even have winter clothing, and they
froze.

LESSON 28-2 REVIEW

Word Bank

blitzkrieg
Britain
Czechoslovakia
France
Greece
Moscow
Romania

On a sheet of paper, write the word from the Word Bank to complete each sentence correctly.

1. _____ was Hitler's style of warfare, which means "lightning war."

2. To keep peace, Britain and France signed a treaty that gave Hitler parts of _____. Ignoring the treaty, Hitler took over the rest of the nation six months later.

3. With help from Italy, Germany invaded _____ who surrendered, unable to stop Hitler.

4. Germany's loss to _____ was its first defeat in World War II.

5. Germany took _____ and its oil fields.

6. _____ surrendered to the Italians.

7. Germany was unable to take _____ because Russians from all over came to defend it.

On a sheet of paper, write the answer to each question. Use complete sentences.

8. What action by Germany started World War II?

9. What steps did the British take to defend their neighborhoods during the Battle of Britain?

10. What mistake did Hitler make when invading the Soviet Union in 1941?

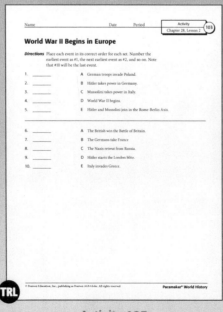

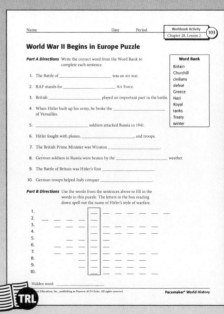

The Holocaust and Allied Victories

Objectives

- To explain Hitler's solution to the "Jewish problem"
- To explain how the United States became involved in the war
- To explain why the Battle of Stalingrad was a turning point in the war
- To describe the invasion of Normandy

Reading Strategy:
Metacognition

Before reading, think about what you can do to help you better understand the text.

Genocide
An attempt to kill all the people of a certain race or religious group

Holocaust
Hitler's killing of many of the Jews in Europe

Hitler forced his own ideas on the people he conquered. They were evil ideas of a "super race." People who did not fit Hitler's ideal of the super race were considered inferior. They were used as slave laborers or thrown into concentration camps.

What Was the Holocaust?

Some Europeans fought the Nazi ideas. They formed resistance groups and waged secret, undercover wars. They wrecked telephone and telegraph lines to stop German communication. They blew up bridges and derailed trains. They killed Nazi officers. They helped Allied prisoners escape.

The Nazis answered the resistance by murdering hundreds of innocent men, women, and children. Nazi terror was aimed most directly at Europe's Jews. First, Hitler forced Jews out of their jobs. He took their businesses and their property. Then Jews were made to live in special areas.

In 1941, Hitler's plans reached their evil peak. He announced his "final solution" to what he called the "Jewish problem." That solution was **genocide**—to kill all of Europe's Jews.

Hitler sent millions of people to concentration camps. Worse than any prison, these camps were slave-labor camps. In the camps, millions of men, women, and children were executed. Many people were spared execution only to be worked or starved to death.

Over six million Jews died in Nazi concentration camps. Hitler's efforts to destroy all Jews is called the **Holocaust**.

Lesson at a Glance

Chapter 28 Lesson 3

Overview This lesson describes the Holocaust, when more than six million Jews died in concentration camps, as well as the Japanese attack on Pearl Harbor and the continuing war in Europe.

Objectives

- To explain Hitler's solution to the "Jewish problem"
- To explain how the United States became involved in the war
- To explain why the Battle of Stalingrad was a turning point in the war
- To describe the invasion of Normandy

Student Pages 585–590

Teacher's Resource Library

   Workbook Activity 104

   Activity 104

   Modified Activity 104

....

Vocabulary

D-Day	Holocaust
genocide	pact

Have students record the vocabulary words and their definitions in their notebooks.

Reading Strategy:
Metacognition

Have students brainstorm aloud ways to better understand the text. Write their suggestions on the board.

The Nazis captured millions of Jewish men, women, and children and sent them to concentration camps.

History Fact
Healthy prisoners were sometimes hired out as slaves for private businesses. Often, they were worked and starved to death in factories and other businesses.

The Nazis also murdered millions of others—Russians, Poles, Gypsies, Slavs—all "inferior" enemies of Hitler.

The Nazi death camps are one of history's greatest horrors. "How could the world have let this happen?" question the ghosts of Hitler's victims. Survivors of the Holocaust tell of wishing for death in a world too evil to bear.

Why Did the United States Declare War on Japan?

The United States was a neutral nation from 1939 until 1941. It was not directly involved in the war.

Even so, the United States did send aid to Germany's enemies. The United States sent food, arms, and raw materials to Great Britain and Russia. However, it took a direct blow from Japan to bring the United States into World War II.

586 *Unit 9 Nationalism and the Spread of War and Revolution*

---

1 Warm-Up Activity

Have students read the objectives on page 585, then preview the lesson by looking at the photos as well as the History Facts and the Great Names in History. Then have students read the subheads.

Ask students to notice that there are three broad topics in the lesson—the Holocaust, the United States' entry into the War, and progress of the War in Europe. Lead a discussion in which students talk about ways to organize the lesson so they are sure to understand each topic in its entirety.

2 Teaching the Lesson

After students have read the lesson, lead a discussion in which students talk about the most compelling information they learned. Divide students into four groups—one for each topic in the lesson—and ask each group to prepare a short summary of the information contained in their assigned portion of the lesson. A spokesperson from each group should present the group's summary to the class.

Ask:

• What did resistance groups in Europe try to do? How did they do this? (They attempted to fight Nazism by waging secret wars. They interrupted German communication, blew up bridges, derailed trains, helped prisoners to escape, and killed Nazi officers.)

• What was Hitler's response to the resistance? (He punished the Jews.)

• Although Jewish people bore the brunt of Hitler's cruelty, millions of "other" enemies died as well. Who were they? (Russians, Poles, Gypsies, Slavs, the mentally or physically frail, homosexuals, and anyone else who was deemed "inferior.")

• What event precipitated the United States' entry into World War II? (the bombing of Pearl Harbor on December 7, 1941)

• Of the 350,000 German soldiers who attacked Stalingrad, how many were still alive five months later when the battle ended? (90,000)

• Who was the "Desert Fox"? (the German leader in Africa)

• What was the military goal for D-Day? (to free France from German rule)

History Fact
After students have read the information ask, *What does this information suggest about the submission of private citizens and businesses to Hitler's "Final Solution"?*

586 *Unit 9 Nationalism and Revolution*

You Decide

Why do you think the United States remained neutral until December 1941?

Japan was trying to create its empire in Asia. Japan felt that the United States stood in the way of its control of the Pacific Ocean. On December 7, 1941, Japanese planes bombed the Pearl Harbor naval base in Hawaii. The attack took the United States by surprise. Japan sank or damaged 13 ships and about 170 planes. Nearly 2,500 U.S. soldiers, sailors, and civilians died in the surprise attack.

In Japan, Emperor Hirohito declared war on the United States. In the United States, President Franklin D. Roosevelt asked Congress to declare war on Japan. After a vote in Congress, Roosevelt addressed the nation. "We are now in this war," he declared. "We are in it all the way."

Four days later, Germany and Italy honored their agreement, their **pact**, with Japan. They declared war on the United States.

By the end of 1941, the war really had become a world war. The Axis countries stood on one side. The Allied countries, which now included the United States, stood on the other.

GREAT NAMES IN HISTORY

Anne Frank

Anne Frank's diary has made her a symbol of Nazi cruelty. In July 1942, Nazi troops began rounding up Jews in Amsterdam. With her parents and sister, Anne went into hiding. She had just turned 13. The family and others lived in a secret attic above her father's former business. Anne also began a diary, writing about her hopes and dreams. For two years, non-Jewish friends brought them food. Then in August 1944, the secret police force, the Gestapo, found them. They sent them to concentration camps. Only her father lived past the horrors of the war. Anne died at Bergen-Belsen. After the war, her father found the diary and published it.

Background Information

The Nazis had created more than 100 concentration camps throughout Europe. By 1942, most of Europe's Jews had been shipped to one of them or murdered elsewhere. Other victims were members of the religious sect Jehovah's Witnesses, who were opponents of Hitler, and people with disabilities. In addition to murdering people, the Nazis performed medical experiments on their victims, especially women. Much of what became known of the Nazis' crimes was revealed immediately after the war. The Nazis apparently never considered that they might lose the war so, without fear or shame, they kept very detailed records of their own terrible actions.

LEARNING STYLES

Auditory/Verbal

Tell students that Hitler was an excellent public speaker—that some say he had an hypnotic effect on crowds. Explain that even listeners who do not know German can appreciate the roar of the crowds as they listen to Hitler. Encourage students to locate and listen to audio of Hitler's speeches and report back to the class about what they heard. One source is "Great Speeches of the Twentieth Century," a compact disc from Rhino World Beat, published in 1991.

Background Information

The *Diary of Anne Frank* has been made into a play and a movie. The diary has been translated into 55 languages and read by millions since it was discovered in the family's hiding place after the war. Suggest that interested students find out about a firsthand account of a teenager hiding from the Nazis in Holland during World War II.

GREAT NAMES IN HISTORY

Encourage a volunteer to read aloud the selection on Anne Frank. Then lead a discussion in which students talk about what life might have been like for the Frank family and for those who hid them during those two years.

You Decide

Lead a discussion in which students speculate about the reasons the United States was unwilling to enter World War II earlier. Students may say citizens in the U.S. were distracted by economic problems at home or that the horrors of World War I made them reluctant to enter another war. They may say that the relative geographic isolation of the U.S. made it easy to ignore problems in the world.

Play a recording of President Franklin D. Roosevelt's famous speech in which he declares that the United States is at war. Have students comment on the speech and ask them to describe how they might have felt at the time. Ask them to describe the emotions they hear in Roosevelt's voice, the emotions they feel Roosevelt is trying to create in his listeners, and the emotions he is trying to discourage.

History Fact

Encourage students to visit their local library or conduct independent research online to discover why the city of Leningrad changed its name back to St. Petersburg in 1991.

ELL/ESL STRATEGY

Language Objective:
To help students organize diverse material from a complex lesson

Write the four subheading questions from the lesson on the board—*What Was the Holocaust? Why Did the United States Declare War on Japan? Why Was the Battle of Stalingrad so Important?* and *What Was D-Day?* Next, write: *who, what, when, where, why.*

As students read the lesson, encourage them to create a learning chart for each question and to answer the questions *who, what, when, where,* and *why* as they appear in the text.

History Fact
The name *Leningrad* was changed back to St. Petersburg in 1991.

Why Was the Battle of Stalingrad so Important?

In 1942, Soviet and German armies were locked in battle. The battlefront stretched about 2,000 miles through the Soviet Union, from the Arctic to the Black Sea. In the north, Leningrad (formerly St. Petersburg) was under siege by the Nazis. The siege began in August 1941 and would last until January 1944. About a million Russians died during the siege, most of them from starvation.

In September 1942, the German Sixth Army attacked Stalingrad (now called Volgograd). For five months, Soviet soldiers fought the Germans. The battle raged back and forth from one block to the next. Finally, on January 31, 1943, the German Sixth Army surrendered. Only 90,000 of the original force of 350,000 German soldiers were still alive.

The Battle of Stalingrad marked a major turning point in the war. Now the Soviet army went on the offensive. The Soviets began to take back cities that had been captured by the Germans.

Meanwhile, fighting had been going on in northern Africa. Hitler had taken over most of Europe. Now he could be attacked only from Britain, the Soviet Union, or from North Africa. North Africa became important.

General Erwin Rommel, known as the clever "Desert Fox," led the Germans in Africa. Early in 1943, U.S. General Dwight D. Eisenhower set a trap for the Desert Fox and defeated the Germans. In May 1943, German and Italian forces in Africa surrendered.

The Allies invaded Italy next. It was, according to President Roosevelt, the "beginning of the end" for the Axis countries. The Allies accepted the Italian surrender in 1943. However, German forces continued to fight in Italy. Rome was finally freed on June 4, 1944.

WORLD CULTURES

On February 19, 1942, 10 weeks after Japan bombed Pearl Harbor, President Roosevelt authorized the military to identify citizens and aliens of Japanese heritage from specially designated areas for security reasons. The army proceeded to remove all Japanese-Americans living on the West Coast of the United States and place them in camps. About 110,000 Japanese-Americans were detained. Ironically while they were interned, 23,000 Japanese-American men fought in Italy. In 1998, Congress and the president signed a document stating that the Japanese-Americans were confined "without adequate security reason and without any acts of espionage or sabotage." Their heirs and the remaining survivors received $1.25 billion in reparations for the wrongs done to them.

What Was D-Day?

Hitler still felt sure of his strength in Europe. But the Allies were preparing an invasion. By 1944 they were ready to free France.

German forces protected the Normandy coast facing Great Britain. The Allies planned to invade Normandy. The day of the invasion was called "**D-Day**."

D-Day came at 2 A.M. on June 6, 1944. General Eisenhower was in charge of the attack. The first wave of troops crossed the English Channel. By 6:30 A.M. more than 150,000 Allied soldiers waded ashore on the beaches of Normandy. Within five days the Allies had fought many miles inland.

The Allies began their sweep through France. In August, they freed Paris. By October the Nazis were driven from all of France, as well as from Belgium and Luxembourg.

Allied soldiers landed in Normandy, France, for the longest land and sea attack in history.

1930–1950   *World War II*   *Chapter 28*   **589**

ONLINE CONNECTION

Students may gain additional information by accessing the following Web site: www.agsglobepmwh.com/page589 (The United States Holocaust Memorial Museum contains additional information on the Holocaust. Caution students that some information and images may be disturbing.)

Reading Strategy:
Metacognition

Encourage students to call out their predictions for what will happen in Lesson 28–4. Write their predictions on the board. After students have completed reading the next lesson, compare their predictions with the lesson's content.

3   Reinforce and Extend

COMMON ERROR

Oftentimes, students are surprised to learn that all kinds of people—for all kinds of reasons—perished in Hitler's concentration camps. Gypsies, the mentally ill, even artists and musicians were sent to the camps.

CAREER CONNECTION

Photojournalists played an important part in informing Americans about the grim events in Europe that preceded World War II. Photojournalism continues to be a dynamic career. It requires individuals to travel everywhere there is news to report. Candidates for this work need good eyesight and the ability to visualize scenes that will interest readers. Courses are available at trade schools, community colleges, and universities. Students interested in a career in photojournalism should check with their counselor to find out what high school courses they need to prepare for this career.

TEACHER ALERT

Many Jews today remember the Holocaust by observing Yom HaShoah (pronounced ha-SHOW-a), the Holocaust Martyrs' and Heroes' Remembrance Day. *Shoah*, Hebrew for "destruction," is another name for the Holocaust. This day commemorates the six million Jews who died during the Holocaust. It also marks the anniversary of the heroic Warsaw Ghetto uprising of 1943.

In Israel, a morning siren sounds, stopping all activity; people stand in honor of those who died. Jews around the world hold memorials and vigils, often lighting six candles in honor of the six million Holocaust victims. Many hold name-reading ceremonies to memorialize those who perished.

Lesson 28–3 Review Answers

1. A 2. B 3. D 4. C 5. D 6. C 7. A
8. Hitler's solution was genocide and he sent millions of people to concentration camps to be executed.
9. Japan bombed Pearl Harbor in an effort to gain control of the Pacific Ocean. The United States declared war on Japan and, to honor their pact with Japan, Germany and Italy declared war on the United States. 10. The Soviets outlasted the Germans in the Battle of Stalingrad, and the Germans surrendered. The Soviets went on the offensive and began to take back cities that the Germans had captured.

LESSON 28-3 REVIEW

On a sheet of paper, write the letter of the answer that correctly completes each sentence.

1. People who did not fit Hitler's ideal of the _____ were considered inferior. They were used as slave laborers or thrown into concentration camps.

   A super race   B Jewish   C Russian   D Gypsies

2. Some Europeans waged secret wars to fight the _____. It only seemed to fuel Hitler's purpose.

   A Russians   B Nazi ideas   C Italians   D Japanese

3. During the Holocaust, over _____ Jews died in Nazi concentration camps.

   A 600   B 6,000   C 60,000   D 6 million

4. German and Italian forces in _____ surrendered in May 1943.

   A Greece   B Romania   C Africa   D Britain

5. The Allies invaded _____ and accepted their surrender in 1943.

   A Japan   B France   C Belgium   D Italy

6. The day that the Allies planned to invade Normandy was called "_____."

   A Battle of Stalingrad   C D-Day
   B London Blitz   D Holocaust

7. By October 1944, the Nazis were driven from all of _____, Belgium, and Luxembourg.

   A France   B Russia   C Africa   D Germany

On a sheet of paper, write the answer to each question. Use complete sentences.

8. What was Hitler's solution to the "Jewish problem?"

9. How did the United States become involved in the war?

10. Why was the Battle of Stalingrad a major turning point in the war?

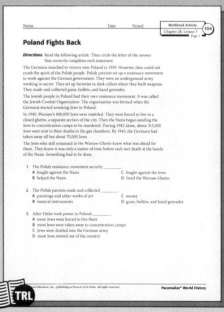

The End of the War

Objectives

- To explain the Battle of the Bulge and its outcome
- To explain what became of Mussolini and Hitler
- To tell the purpose of kamikaze pilots
- To describe how the war finally ended in Japan

Reading Strategy:
Metacognition

Note the main idea and important details about the ending of World War II. Summarize what you have read to make sure you understand it.

The Germans were soundly defeated in December 1944 in the Battle of the Bulge. According to Winston Churchill, it was the greatest U.S. victory of the war.

At last, early in 1945, the Allies invaded Germany. Germany's capital, Berlin, fell on May 2. On May 7, 1945, Germany surrendered. The war in Europe was over.

What Happened to Hitler and Mussolini?

The leaders of Germany and Italy had created terrible death and destruction. What became of the leaders of these fallen powers?

In Italy, fascist leader Benito Mussolini met an ugly end. Mussolini tried to escape from Italy, to run from the antifascists. When captured, he begged for his life.

Despite his pleas, Mussolini was executed—shot without a trial. His body was hung upside down outside a gas station in Milan, Italy. Italians shouted at the body, kicking it and throwing stones at it. A man who had lived by cruelty and terror met a cruel end.

Germany's Hitler died two days later. On April 30, 1945, reports came that the dictator had killed himself. He had been hiding in a bomb shelter beneath the flaming, shattered city of Berlin. Unable to face defeat, Hitler and his wife, Eva Braun, killed themselves.

Chapter 28 Lesson 4

Overview This lesson describes the end of World War II in both Europe and Japan.

Objectives

- To explain the Battle of the Bulge and its outcome
- To explain what became of Mussolini and Hitler
- To tell the purpose of kamikaze pilots
- To describe how the war finally ended in Japan

Student Pages 591–594

Teacher's Resource Library

  Workbook Activity 105

  Activity 105

  Modified Activity 105

Vocabulary

atomic bomb   nuclear
kamikaze

After students read the vocabulary words and their definitions, ask them to look back through the vocabulary words from the chapter and name the words that were created during World War II. (D-Day, atomic bomb, kamikaze, nuclear, *blitzkrieg*) Then have students write a paragraph about World War II using the vocabulary words.

Reading Strategy:
Metacognition

Ask students to write a brief summary about the ending of World War II. Then invite several volunteers to share their summaries with the class. You may also wish to ask students to write one or two sentences describing the thought processes they used to decide what information should be included in their summaries.

1   Warm-Up Activity

Have students review what they have learned so far about World War II by playing 20 Questions. One student should think of something related to the war—such as a battle, a country, or a place. The other students should ask questions that can be answered by yes or no. Students must identify the word in 20 or fewer questions.

2 Teaching the Lesson

Have a volunteer read the lesson title, as well as the subheads on pages 591 and 592. Ask students to consider the fates of Hitler, Mussolini, and General Tojo, as well as the fates of many Japanese people in the final days of the war. Explain to students that the decision to drop two atomic bombs on Japan in 1945 remains controversial in the minds of many people today. Ask, *Why do you think historians, scholars, and ethicists continue to debate the rightness of dropping the A-bombs on Japan even today?* (Students may say that it is because so many citizens were killed or that this ushered in the age of nuclear weapons.)

Ask:

- On what date did Germany surrender to Allied troops? (May 7, 1945)

- What fate befell Benito Mussolini? (He was shot and angry citizens degraded his corpse.)

- Why did the Japanese forces refuse to surrender to Allied troops? (Their highly cultivated sense of duty and honor demanded that they continue to fight.)

- What were Kamikazes? (Japanese pilots who flew suicide missions into U.S. warships)

- If you had been in President Harry S. Truman's shoes in the final days of World War II, how do you think you might have arrived at the decision to drop the A-bombs on Hiroshima and Nagasaki? Do you think you would have decided to do this? Why or why not? (Answers will vary.)

- What is the significance of September 2, 1945? (This was the day Japan surrendered to Allied forces; it was also the first Japanese military defeat in 2,000 years.)

Kamikaze
A Japanese pilot who crashed his plane into an enemy ship, destroying it and killing himself

Nuclear
Having to do with atoms or energy from atoms

Atomic bomb
A bomb that uses nuclear energy and has much destructive power

Why Did the Japanese Keep Fighting?

The war had ended in Europe, but not in the Pacific. After Pearl Harbor, the Japanese had taken the Philippines, most of Southeast Asia, and islands in the Pacific.

General Douglas MacArthur led the U.S. forces against the Japanese in the Pacific. Although his campaigns were successful, the Japanese would not give up. Most of Japan's navy and air force had been destroyed by August 1945. However, there was no surrender. The Japanese felt it was their duty and honor to fight to the very end.

The Japanese turned to desperate measures. **Kamikaze** pilots became human bombs. They did this by strapping themselves into planes filled with explosives. Then they flew their planes into U.S. warships.

It seemed time for the terrors of war to end. However, the greatest terror was still to come.

Why Did the United States Drop Two Atomic Bombs on Japan?

Scientists had discovered how to split the atom to create great energy, **nuclear** energy. This nuclear energy could be used as a weapon. By 1940, German scientists were working to develop an **atomic bomb**. An atomic bomb uses nuclear energy to create a powerful weapon.

In 1942, the Manhattan Project began to develop the bomb in the United States. Working on the project in the United States were scientists such as Enrico Fermi and J. Robert Oppenheimer. They, with the help of many others, finally built the powerful weapon.

U.S. President Harry S. Truman made the difficult decision. The atomic bomb would be the quickest way to end the war.

Geography Note

Hiroshima is on the southwest coast of Japan's Honshu Island. The River Ota splits into seven branches as it flows into the Seto Inland Sea. Hiroshima is made up of the six islands created by those branches. The islands are connected by 81 bridges. The Aioi Bridge was a T-shaped bridge connecting three of those islands. It was the target of the atomic bomb dropped in 1945. The bomb missed its target, but it damaged the bridge. After the war, the Japanese repaired the bridge. They replaced it many years later. Damaged pieces from the original bridge are preserved in Hiroshima's Peace Memorial Park.

Japan was warned, but the Japanese refused to surrender. Therefore, on August 6, 1945, an American plane dropped the atomic bomb on Hiroshima, Japan. In seconds, more than 60,000 people were killed, and Hiroshima was gone.

Still, Japan did not surrender, and three days later, a second A-bomb was dropped. This bomb fell on Nagasaki's 250,000 people.

At last, on September 2, 1945, the Japanese surrendered. It was their first military defeat in 2,000 years. General Tojo was arrested and convicted as a war criminal. He was hanged on December 23, 1948.

Background Information

One of the most controversial Allied actions of World War II was the bombing of Dresden, which took place between February 13 and February 15, 1945. The historian Frederick Taylor wrote, "The destruction of Dresden has an epically tragic quality to it. It was a wonderfully beautiful city and a symbol of baroque humanism and all that was best in Germany. It also contained all of the worst from Germany during the Nazi period. In that sense it is an absolutely exemplary tragedy for the horrors of 20th Century warfare . . ." During the two days of firebombing approximately 35,000 people were killed and much of the city was destroyed. In all, aerial bombings by allied forces are likely to have killed between 300,000 and 600,000 German civilians during the war.

LEARNING STYLES

Body/Kinesthetic

Invite students to work in two groups to create memorial models commemorating V-E Day (Victory over Europe Day) and V-J Day (Victory over Japan Day). Have students include facts from the text and other information found through research. Members of each group will decide who will plan the design, who will find the added research, and who will build the memorials.

ELL/ESL STRATEGY

Language Objective:
To compare and contrast D-Day, V-E Day, and V-J Day

Ask ELL students to make a three-part Venn diagram comparing and contrasting D-Day, V-E Day, and V-J Day. Within the ovals, students should write the name and date of each day and what each commemorates. Then, students should list some things that the three days have in common, such as Allied victories. Students should also list some things that are different. For example, V-J Day commemorates victory in Asia; the other two days commemorate victories in Europe.

Geography Note

After students have read the information, encourage them to learn more about Hiroshima's Peace Memorial Park by visiting the educational Web site of the Hiroshima Peace Memorial Museum. This site provides students and educators with a virtual museum tour of the Memorial Park as well as photos of the Aioi Bridge and the city of Hiroshima. The Web site may be accessed at:
www.agsglobepmwh.com/page593

COMMON ERROR

Remind students that not all of the citizens who perished in Hiroshima and Nagasaki died instantly. Many suffered for days, months, and even years from radiation poisoning and radiation sickness before they succumbed to death. They suffered horribly. In total, most scholars agree that approximately 140,000 people—most of them civilians—died in Hiroshima, either from the initial blast or the sickness that followed. In Nagasaki, approximately 74,000 people perished.

Even today, people continue to suffer from their injuries. They are called *Hibakusha*. In 2005, the Japanese government estimated that there were more than 266,000 Hibakusha living in Japan.

Lesson 28–4 Review Answers

1. Battle of the Bulge 2. Europe
3. executed 4. committed suicide
5. Pacific 6. surrender 7. Kamikaze
8. energy 9. atomic bombs
10. hanged

LESSON 28-4   REVIEW

Word Bank

atomic bombs
Battle of the Bulge
committed suicide
energy
Europe
executed
hanged
kamikaze
Pacific
surrender

On a sheet of paper, write the word from the Word Bank to complete each sentence correctly.

1. The Germans were soundly defeated in the _____.

2. When Berlin fell and Germany surrendered, the war in _____ was over.

3. Mussolini was _____.

4. Hitler and his wife Eva _____.

5. Although the war in Europe was over, the Japanese still had control of the _____.

6. Although most of Japan's navy and air force had been destroyed by August 1945, they did not _____.

7. _____ pilots became human bombs. They strapped themselves into planes filled with explosives and flew the planes into U.S. warships.

8. An atomic bomb uses the _____ from a split atom to create a powerful weapon.

9. After the United States dropped _____ on Hiroshima and Nagasaki, Japan finally surrendered.

10. General Tojo was convicted as a criminal and _____.

594   *Unit 9   Nationalism and the Spread of War and Revolution*

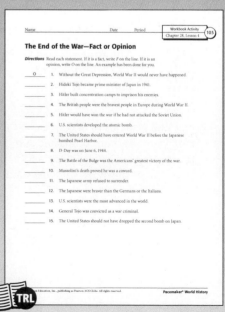

594   *Unit 9   Nationalism and Revolution*

Activity 105   Workbook Activity 105

The Results of the War

World War II was over at last. It was the most expensive war in history.

Objectives

■ To list three reasons why World War II was the most expensive war in history

■ To explain the pact known as the *Declaration by United Nations*

Reading Strategy: Metacognition

Remember to ask yourself questions as you read. This will help you better understand what you are reading.

What Were the Costs of the War?

The figures of World War II were shocking:

- Over a trillion dollars had been spent for arms and war machinery.

- About 55 million lives were lost. (This includes civilian and military losses.)

- Germany lost almost 3 million soldiers.

- Japan lost more than 2 million soldiers.

- Italy lost about 160,000 soldiers.

- Russia lost about 7,500,000 soldiers.

- Britain lost about 270,000 soldiers.

- The United States lost more than 400,000 soldiers.

- France lost about 200,000 soldiers.

Many millions of civilians had died. Millions of others were homeless. The world was left with questions to answer. How could people have so easily accepted the horrors of the Nazi concentration camps? What about the atomic bomb? What was to become of a world that possessed such a terrible and powerful weapon?

Why Was the United Nations Formed?

The League of Nations had tried to keep the peace after World War I. However, the League had failed. How could future wars be prevented?

Lesson at a Glance

Chapter 28 Lesson 5

Overview This lesson details the destruction caused by World War II and discusses the creation of the United Nations.

Objectives

■ To list three reasons why World War II was the most expensive war in history

■ To explain the pact known as the Declaration by United Nations

Student Pages 595–598

Teacher's Resource Library

Workbook Activity 106

Activity 106

Modified Activity 106

....

Vocabulary

organization

Ask students to use their dictionaries to identify the part of speech of the vocabulary word. (*Organization* is a noun.) Next, ask students to find the root of the word. It is the verb *organize*. Write the following words on the board: *organize, organization, organizational, organizationally, organizer, organizing*. Have students look each word up in their dictionaries to identify its part of speech, and then write a sentence for each word.

---

1 Warm-Up Activity

Have students discuss the reasons why they think world leaders felt it was so important to start an organization that would establish safety in the world. (Students may suggest that World War II devastated the world to such a great extent that world leaders felt it must never happen again.)

Reading Strategy: Metacognition

As students read the lesson, ask them to write at least two questions that occur to them as they read the material.

Have students read the information on pages 595–597 and study the timeline on page 597. Next, call students' attention to the figures of World War II on page 595. Ask students to add up the numbers of soldiers lost in Germany, Japan, Italy, Russia, Britain, France, and the United States (about 13,530,000 soldiers died in total). Have students subtract this number from the 55 million figure of lives lost (about 41,470,000 civilians were killed during World War II). You may want to call students' attention to the fact that no data is provided on the estimated loss of Chinese citizens during the Second World War (rough estimates are that between 3 and 4 million Chinese citizens and soldiers perished during World War II).

Ask:

- Approximately how much money was spent during World War II for arms and war machinery? (more than a trillion dollars)

- Why do you believe that people allowed the horrors of the Nazi concentration camps to continue without earlier intervention? (Students may say the world's citizens didn't know how bad things truly were; they may say there was a fair amount of bigotry world-wide regarding the Jewish people; or they may argue that people were distracted by fighting the war.)

- In January, 1942, 26 nations met in Washington, D.C.. There, they signed a pact calling for world peace and freedom for all people. What was this called? (the Declaration of the United Nations)

- Who were the five permanent members of the United Nations? (the United States, the Soviet Union, Great Britain, France, and China)

- What do the various branches of the United Nations work to do? (keep peace, work on problems of education, trade, labor, health, and economics)

Organization
A group of people joined together for a common purpose

History Fact
The name *United Nations* was created by U.S. President Franklin D. Roosevelt. Roosevelt died in 1945. Later, his wife, Eleanor Roosevelt, was a delegate to the United Nations.

U.S. President Franklin D. Roosevelt and other national leaders were thinking about how to keep peace. They had been since the beginning of World War II. Finally, in June 1941, representatives of nine countries met in London to talk about it. There, those officials signed a pledge to work for a free world. This pledge was called the *Inter-Allied Declaration*.

By early 1942, the idea of a "United Nations" gained wide support. In January, representatives from 26 nations met in Washington, D.C. There they signed a pact calling for world peace and freedom for all people. The agreement also called for eventual disarmament and economic cooperation. The pact they signed was called the *Declaration by United Nations*.

At that time, of course, there was still a world war going on. By 1944, however, it was clear that the Allies would win the war. Allied representatives began planning the new **organization**. In February 1945, a date was set for a United Nations meeting in San Francisco. As scheduled, the meeting was held on April 25.

At that first meeting of the United Nations, a constitution was established. Representatives from 50 nations signed the United Nations Charter. The delegates also set up a Security Council with permanent members from five countries. They were the United States, the Soviet Union, Great Britain, France, and China. Each member had veto power over any decision the Security Council made. Just one veto would keep a decision from going into effect.

On October 24, 1945, the United Nations became official. The new organization had a big job ahead of it. Its aim was to protect world peace and human rights throughout the world. In 1949, the cornerstone was laid for the UN headquarters in New York City.

- How well do you think the United Nations has fulfilled its mission? (Answers will vary, but students may say that violence, poverty, lack of education, and economic disparity continue to be major problems in the world today.)

Background Information

"Rosie the Riveter" was an American heroine of a World War II song. When Rosie's boyfriend was drafted, she went to work in a defense plant. Rosie became the symbol for female war workers. They made bombs and tanks. They welded battleships. Until then, most women had worked in traditional fields, such as teaching or nursing. The war opened up new kinds of work to women.

When the war ended, returning soldiers wanted their jobs back. Society and the media encouraged women to quit their jobs. The 1950s ideal for women centered on home and family.

American women never really left the workforce, however. In 2002, approximately 75% of women aged 25–54 had jobs. (U.S. Department of Labor)

History Fact
Encourage students to learn more about Eleanor Roosevelt's participation in United Nations by visiting their local library or by conducting independent online research.

The United Nations building is in New York City.

Whenever a world problem comes up, the United Nations meets to work for a peaceful settlement. Delegates from every member nation attend meetings of the United Nations' General Assembly. They try to solve problems without war. Other branches of the UN work on problems of education, trade, labor, health, and economics.

The weapons of the world have grown to unbelievable destructive power. The purpose of the United Nations has become more and more important. The United Nations has one victory as its major goal—the victory over war.

Reading Strategy:
Metacognition

Remember to look at illustrations such as this timeline. This will help you understand what you have read.

TIMELINE STUDY: WORLD WAR II

What event happened the same year that France fell to Germany?

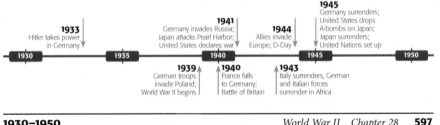

1933
Hitler takes power in Germany

1941
Germany invades Russia; Japan attacks Pearl Harbor; United States declares war

1944
Allies invade Europe; D-Day

1945
Germany surrenders; United States drops A-bombs on Japan; Japan surrenders; United Nations set up

1930   1935   1940   1945   1950

1939
German troops invade Poland; World War II begins

1940
France falls to Germany; Battle of Britain

1943
Italy surrenders, German and Italian forces surrender in Africa

1930–1950   *World War II   Chapter 28*   **597**

ELL/ESL STRATEGY

Language Objective:
To outline the structure of the United Nations

Ask ELL students to make a poster of a flow diagram that shows the structure of the United Nations. Have them present their diagrams to the class. Ask class members to describe fictitious problems and have the presenting student name the UN agencies that would handle the issues. For example, students may say that a certain area of a country is having trouble raising enough crops to feed the people. The presenting student should refer to the Food and Agricultural Organization (FAO).

Lesson 28–5 Review Answers

1. Over a trillion dollars were spent for arms and war machinery, about 55 million lives were lost, and the United States lost more than 400,000 soldiers. **2.** Representatives from nine countries met in June of 1941 to talk about preventing future wars. The officials signed a pledge to work for a free world. The pledge is known as the Inter-Allied Declaration. **3.** The United Nations signed a pact calling for world peace and freedom for all people. It also called for eventual disarmament and economic cooperation. **4.** C **5.** A **6.** D **7.** D **8.** B **9.** C **10.** A

On a sheet of paper, write the answer to each question. Use complete sentences.

1. What are three reasons why World War II was the most expensive war in history?

2. Describe the *Inter-Allied Declaration*.

3. What did the *Declaration by United Nations* call for?

On a sheet of paper, write the letter of the answer that correctly completes each sentence.

4. A _____ was established at the first meeting of the United Nations.

   A treaty   **B** war   **C** constitution   **D** trade agreement

5. The United Nations set up a Security Council from five countries. The countries were: the United States, the Soviet Union, Great Britain, France, and _____.

   A China   **B** Japan   **C** Germany   **D** Belgium

6. Each member of the Security Council had _____ power over any decision the council made.

   A little   **B** one-fifth   **C** unequal   **D** veto

7. The _____ became official on October 24, 1945.

   A *Inter-Allied Declaration*   **C** UN headquarters
   B Security Council   **D** United Nations

8. The UN headquarters are in _____.

   A Geneva   **B** New York City   **C** Moscow   **D** London

9. The UN has branches that address education, trade, labor, health, and_____.

   A religion   **B** air travel   **C** economics   **D** computer technology

10. The UN becomes important as _____ grow to even more destructive power.

   A weapons   **B** countries   **C** dictators   **D** computers

598   *Unit 9   Nationalism and the Spread of War and Revolution*

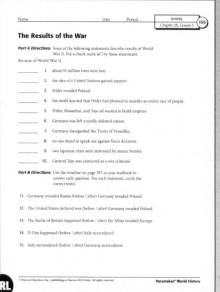

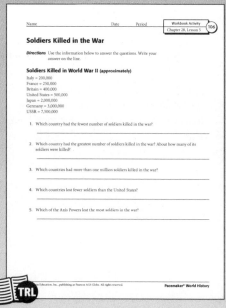

Activity 106   Workbook Activity 106

- Mussolini improved the economy and industry of Italy, then he became its dictator.

- Tojo rose up from the military to become dictator of Japan.

- Hitler, as head of the Nazi party, made bold promises to the people of Germany. The Germans were eager to regain their sense of national pride, so they made him their leader.

- Two alliances fought each other in World War II. The Axis Powers were Germany, Italy, Japan, and many smaller nations. The Allied Powers were Britain, France, Russia, the United States, and many smaller nations. The United States joined the war in 1941, after Japan attacked Pearl Harbor.

- Hitler had ideas of a "super race" that was meant to rule the world. He especially hated the Jews and he tried to destroy them. In the Holocaust, he imprisoned and murdered millions of Jews. He also murdered millions of other people who did not fit into his idea of the super race.

- World War II began in 1939, after Germany invaded Poland. The war was fought in Europe, Asia, and Africa.

- D-Day, in June 1944, began the Allied sweep to regain Europe. Within four months the Allies had freed France, Belgium, and Luxembourg.

- Terrible weapons, including two atomic bombs dropped by the United States on Japan, were used in the war.

- World War II ended after Germany surrendered in May 1945 and Japan surrendered in September 1945.

- About 55 million soldiers and civilians died in World War II.

- World War II cost more than any other war in history.

- The United Nations officially began in 1945. It was another attempt to promote world peace.

Chapter 28 Summary

Have students read the Chapter Summary on page 599 to review the main ideas presented in Chapter 28.

Ask:

- What is a dictator? (a person who rules a country with force and makes all the laws)

- What happened to citizens who disagreed with Mussolini's policies? (They were imprisoned or murdered.)

- Who was the dictator of Japan? (Tojo)

- Why were Germans susceptible to Hitler's propaganda? (Answers may vary, but students may say that the economic difficulties and post-World War I humiliations made them eager to regain their national pride.)

- What group in particular did Hitler blame for Germany's troubles? (the Jewish people)

- In what year did World War II begin? Where was it fought? (1939; Europe, Asia, and Africa)

- What was D-Day? (D-Day was a military offensive by allied forces that began in June, 1944, and sought to regain control of Europe.)

- How did the United States end the war in Japan? (Two atomic bombs were dropped on Hiroshima and Nagasaki.)

- Why does this decision continue to be controversial even today? (Answers may vary, but students may say the decision continues to be controversial because of the devastation caused and the loss of civilian life in Japan; or because the world entered a new age of terrifying and destructive new weapons.)

- In total, about how many people died in World War II? (about 55 million)

- What is the express purpose of the United Nations? (to promote world peace)

- How well do you believe the United Nations has lived up to its mission? (Answers will vary.)

TEACHER'S RESOURCE

The AGS Globe Teaching Strategies in Social Studies Transparencies may be used with this chapter. The transparencies add an interactive dimension to expand and enhance the Pacemaker® *World History* program content.

CHAPTER PROJECT FOLLOW-UP

 Student reports should contain accurate and current information about the activities of the United Nations and its councils. They should be factual, but students also may want to add their own opinions about whether the activities are accomplishing their goals or are successful. Have students display their reports or present them to the class.

Chapter 28 Review

Use the Chapter Review to prepare students for tests and to reteach content from the chapter.

Chapter 28 Mastery Test

The Teacher's Resource Library includes two forms of the Chapter 28 Mastery Test. Each test addresses the chapter Goals for Learning. An optional third page of additional critical-thinking items is included for each test. The difficulty level of the two forms is equivalent.

Chapter 28 Review Answers

Vocabulary Review

1. scapegoat
2. depression
3. pact
4. fascist
5. genocide
6. invaded
7. atomic bomb
8. anti-Semitism
9. organization
10. concentration camps

Chapter Review Questions

11. During the Great Depression, many people were hungry and hopeless. They wanted a strong leader who promised a better future.

12. Benito Mussolini ruled Italy, Hideko Tojo ruled Japan, and Adolf Hitler ruled Germany.

Word Bank

anti-Semitism
atomic bomb
concentration camps
depression
fascist
genocide
invaded
organization
pact
scapegoat

Vocabulary Review

On a sheet of paper, use the words from the Word Bank to complete each sentence correctly.

1. Hitler made the Jews into a(n) _____ by blaming them for all the troubles in Germany.

2. Business activity goes down and unemployment goes up during a(n) _____.

3. Germany, Italy, and Japan signed a(n) _____ to support each other in World War II.

4. A follower of the dictator Mussolini was a(n) _____.

5. The killing of people of a certain race or religion is _____.

6. Japan _____ China several times. By 1938 it controlled all of China's major ports and industrial centers.

7. Japan finally surrendered after a second _____ was dropped.

8. Hitler encouraged _____, or prejudice against Jews.

9. The United Nations is a(n) _____ formed to protect world peace and human rights.

10. Hitler sent millions of people to _____, which were built to imprison his enemies.

Chapter Review Questions

On a sheet of paper, write the answer to each question. Use complete sentences.

11. How did the Great Depression help the rise of dictators?

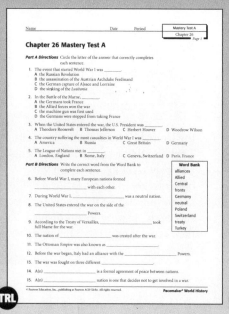

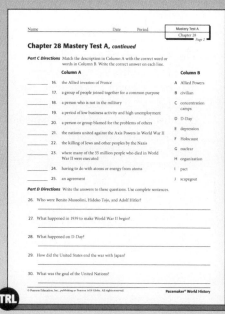

If you do not know
the meaning of a
word in a question,
read the question
to yourself, leaving
out the word. Try
to figure out the
meaning of the word
from its use in the
sentence.

12. What were the three Axis Powers and the dictators who ruled them?

13. How did Hitler use hate as a weapon?

14. How did Germany help cause World War II?

15. Which country lost the most soldiers in the war?

16. What are three world problems that the United Nations works to solve?

Critical Thinking

On a sheet of paper, write your response to each question. Use complete sentences.

17. Do you think the Holocaust could happen again? Why or why not?

18. How did the dropping of the atomic bombs on Japan change the world?

Using the Timeline

Use the timeline on page 597 to answer the questions.

19. When the United States entered the war, how long had it been going on?

20. When was D-Day?

GROUP ACTIVITY

Form a group of four. Make a large wall chart about World War II. Use the information in this chapter and in encyclopedias and other books. Suggested headings are: Battles, Weapons, Leaders, Nations and Their Flags, Famous Speeches, the Holocaust, the Atomic Bomb, Costs of War, the United Nations, and Winners and Losers.

1930–1950   *World War II   Chapter 28*   **601**

13. Hitler used hate to make people afraid to disobey him and to unite Germans against a scapegoat, the Jews.

14. Germany, under Hitler, set out to conquer the world. The more the French and British gave in to Hitler, the more he wanted. After he invaded Poland, both France and Britain declared war.

15. The Soviet Union lost the most soldiers in the war.

16. (Student pick three) Besides trying to solve problems without war, the United Nations also has branches that work on problems of education, trade, labor, health, and economics.

Critical Thinking

17. Possible answers: Some students may point out that in various parts of the world, there has been genocide. Other students may say that the Holocaust cannot happen again, because people have learned from history.

18. Possible answer: People understood that there were now weapons that might destroy the world.

Using the Timeline

19. 2 years

20. 1944

GROUP ACTIVITY

Students' charts should include several headings about World War II. Overall, the charts should provide a comprehensive picture of the war—including people, places, battles, weapons, participants, and outcomes.

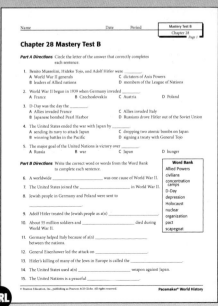

Chapter 28 Mastery Test B, pages 1–3

World War II Chapter 28 **601**

UNIT 10

PLANNING GUIDE

The World Since 1945: 1945–Present

	Student Pages	Vocabulary	Map Study	Reading Strategy	Lesson Review	Chapter Summary/Review
						Student Text Lesson
Chapter 29 The Cold War	604–621	✔		✔		619–621
Lesson 29–1 The World After World War II	606–609	✔	✔	✔	609	
Lesson 29–2 The Cold War Begins	610–615	✔		✔	615	
Lesson 29–3 Changing Relations Between the Soviets and Americans	616–618	✔		✔	618	
Chapter 30 Changes in Asia and Africa	622–657	✔		✔		655–657
Lesson 30–1 India	624–627	✔		✔	627	
Lesson 30–2 China	628–633	✔		✔	633	
Lesson 30–3 Korea	634–636			✔	636	
Lesson 30–4 Japan and Southeast Asia	637–639	✔		✔	639	
Lesson 30–5 Vietnam	640–645	✔		✔	645	
Lesson 30–6 Africa	646–654	✔	✔	✔	654	

(Unit Planning Guide is continued on next page.)

Chapter Activities

Teacher's Resource Library
Life Skills Connection 29–34
Key Vocabulary Words 29–34

Assessment Options

Student Text
Chapter Reviews 29–34
Teacher's Resource Library
Chapter 29 Mastery Tests A and B
Chapter 30 Mastery Tests A and B
Chapter 31 Mastery Tests A and B
Chapter 32 Mastery Tests A and B
Chapter 33 Mastery Tests A and B
Chapter 34 Mastery Tests A and B
Unit 10 Mastery Test
Chapters 1–34 Final Mastery Test
Teacher's Edition
Chapter Projects 29–34

Student Text Features							Teaching Strategies										Learning Styles					Teacher's Resource Library			
Words from the Past	Learn More About It	Great Names in History	Technology Connection	Geography Note	You Decide/Remember/History Fact	Timeline Study	ELL/ESL Strategy	Background Information	Common Error	Life Skills Connection	Key Vocabulary Words	Study Skills	Applications Home, Career, Community	Online Connection	Teacher Alert	World Cultures	Auditory/Verbal	Body/Kinesthetic	Interpersonal/Group Learning	Logical/Mathematical	Visual/Spatial	Activities/Modified Activities	Workbook Activities	Self-Study Guide	Chapter Outline
										605	605													✔	✔
							607	607	608				608	609					608		608	107	107		
					611, 612, 614		613	612	610, 614				614				613	612				108	108		
					617	617	617	617				617			616	618					617	109	109		
										623	623													✔	✔
					624, 626		626	626	625				627							626	626	110	110		
		632			628, 629		631	630	631			631					632	630				111	111		
							636	635	635										635			112	112		
					637		638	638	639				639									113	113		
					642		643	642	641						643	644						114	114		
					647, 648	653	650	648	650		653	651	652	651						649	650	115	115		

Modified Activities

The Teacher's Resource Library (TRL) contains a set of lower-level worksheets called Modified Activities. These worksheets cover the same content as the standard Activities but are written at a lower reading level.

Skill Track

Use Skill Track for *World History* to monitor student progress and meet the demands of adequate yearly progress (AYP). Make informed instructional decisions with individual student and class reports of lesson and chapter assessments. With immediate and ongoing feedback, students will also see what they have learned and where they need more reinforcement and practice.

The World Since 1945: 1945–PRESENT (continued)

	Student Text Lesson					
	Student Pages	Vocabulary	Map Study	Reading Strategy	Lesson Review	Chapter Summary/Review
Chapter 31 The Middle East	658–683	✔		✔		681–683
Lesson 31–1 The Fight for Palestine	660–666	✔	✔	✔	666	
Lesson 31–2 The Middle East Remains in Conflict	667–673	✔		✔	673	
Lesson 31–3 Oil	674–677			✔	677	
Lesson 31–4 Life in the Middle East	678–680			✔	680	
Chapter 32 The End of the Soviet Union	684–703	✔		✔		701–703
Lesson 32–1 Changes in the Soviet Union	686–689	✔		✔	689	
Lesson 32–2 The End of the Soviet Union and the Cold War	690–692	✔		✔	692	
Lesson 32–3 Changes in Eastern Europe	693–700	✔	✔	✔	700	
Chapter 33 Latin America After World War II	704–725	✔		✔		723–725
Lesson 33–1 The United States in Latin American Affairs	706–708	✔		✔	708	
Lesson 33–2 Unrest in Central America	709–714	✔		✔	714	
Lesson 33–3 Trouble in Mexico and Haiti	715–718	✔		✔	718	
Lesson 33–4 Latin America Today	719–722	✔	✔	✔	722	

(Unit Planning Guide is continued on next page.)

Words from the Past	Learn More About It	Great Names in History	Technology Connection	Geography Note	You Decide/Remember/History Fact	Timeline Study	ELL/ESL Strategy	Background Information	Common Error	Life Skills Connection	Key Vocabulary Words	Study Skills	Applications Home, Career, Community	Online Connection	Teacher Alert	World Cultures	Auditory/Verbal	Body/Kinesthetic	Interpersonal/Group Learning	Logical/Mathematical	Visual/Spatial	Activities/Modified Activities	Workbook Activities	Self-Study Guide	Chapter Outline
										659	659													✔	✔
	664	662			661, 664		663	662	661			663	664	662	664		662					116	116		
					670		670	668	670				671			672			669		670	117	117		
					674		676	675	676											676		118	118		
						679	679	679					680		680				679			119	119		
										685	685													✔	✔
					687		688	688	688			689	689	687						688		120	120		
							691	691	691, 692						692				691		691	121	121		
	695		698		694	699	697	695	695				698	699			696	696				122	122		
										705	705													✔	✔
							707	707	707, 708									707				123	123		
	710, 713				710, 712		711	711				711	712	712	712	713						124	124		
					716		715	716	716, 717											716	717	125	125		
	721					720	721	720					722				721		721			126	126		

UNIT 10

PLANNING GUIDE

The World Since 1945: 1945–PRESENT *(continued)*

	Student Pages	Student Text Lesson				
	Student Pages	Vocabulary	Map Study	Reading Strategy	Lesson Review	Chapter Summary/Review
Chapter 34 The World Today	726–759	✔		✔		757–759
Lesson 34–1 The Nuclear Age	728–731	✔		✔	731	
Lesson 34–2 The Space Age	732–735	✔		✔	735	
Lesson 34–3 The Computer Age	736–739			✔	739	
Lesson 34–4 Global Issues	740–744	✔		✔	744	
Lesson 34–5 Environment, Overpopulation, and Disease	745–749	✔		✔	749	
Lesson 34–6 The Threat of Global Terrorism	750–753	✔		✔	753	
Lesson 34–7 Looking to the Future	754–756			✔	756	

Student Text Features							Teaching Strategies										Learning Styles					Teacher's Resource Library			
Words from the Past	Learn More About It	Great Names in History	Technology Connection	Geography Note	You Decide/Remember/History Fact	Timeline Study	ELL/ESL Strategy	Background Information	Common Error	Life Skills Connection	Key Vocabulary Words	Study Skills	Applications Home, Career, Community	Online Connection	Teacher Alert	World Cultures	Auditory/Verbal	Body/Kinesthetic	Interpersonal/Group Learning	Logical/Mathematical	Visual/Spatial	Activities/Modified Activities	Workbook Activities	Self-Study Guide	Chapter Outline
										727	727													✔	✔
					728, 729		730	730	731			731									728	127	127		
		734			732		733	733	735					735					734			128	128		
738					736		738	737					738			739						129	129		
	743				741, 742		742	741	740				743							742		130	130		
	747						746	747					749		748			747				131	131		
							752	752									752					132	132		
						755	755	755	754													133	133		

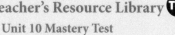

Other Resources

Books for Teachers

Gaddis, John Lewis. *The Cold War: A New History*. New York, NY: Penguin, 2006.

Montefiore, Simon Sebag. *Stalin: The Court of the Red Tsar*. London, UK: Vintage, 2005.

Powaski, Ronald E. *March to Armageddon: The United States and the Nuclear Arms Race, 1939 to the Present*. London, UK: Oxford University Press, 1989.

Books for Students

Cunningham, Kevin. *Joseph Stalin and the Soviet Union*. Greensboro, NC: Morgan Reynolds Publishing, 2006.

Fleisher, Paul. *Understanding the Vocabulary of the Nuclear Arms Race (Peacemakers)*. New York, NY: Dillon Press, 1988.

Lazo, Caroline Evensen. *Harry S. Truman*. Minneapolis, MN: Lerner Publishing Group, 2002.

THE WORLD SINCE 1945

Y

ou have read that history is all about change.
People move, people learn, and people develop
ideas. Disagreements among groups often lead to
wars. Countries change as their citizens change. That is the
history you read about in books. These last chapters cover
history that many people in the world recall as news. It is
history they remember. It is history they lived through.
It might even be history that affected their daily lives.
You may have some knowledge to bring to your reading.
Use your knowledge and experience when reading these
coming chapters.

Chapters in Unit 10

*The quality of life
on Earth is at risk
as overpopulation
threatens our
environment. It is
more important
than ever for
people to be
responsible citizens
of our planet.*

603

Introducing the Unit

Tell students to look at the picture on
page 602 and read the caption. Then have
a volunteer read page 603 aloud. Discuss
the relationship between news and history
as explained on this page. (History is
about change and people. News is history
that people remember. News is history
that people lived through. News is history
that affected the daily lives of people.) Ask
students how their own knowledge and
experience can help them when reading
about the history of the world.

Ask:

- What recent news stories may one
  day appear in history books and why?
  (Answers will vary. Have students
  provide reasons for their choices.)

- What causes events to be considered
  history? (events about change, people,
  and disagreements)

- How can history help people in the
  future? (Remembering past mistakes
  of others can help people not make the
  same mistakes again.)

Videos

*Cold War, Part 2, Iron Curtain, 1945–
1947.* (93 minutes). CNN Productions
and Warner Home Video, 1998.

Rivals: JFK vs. Khrushchev. (46 minutes).
Republic Pictures, 1998.

CD-ROM/Software

Sherlock Holmes—A Library. Pinehurst,
NC: CD-ROM NELLA_WARE, 2004.

Web Sites

www.agsglobepmwh.com/page603a
(This site includes information on the
Soviet Union.)

www.agsglobepmwh.com/page603b
(This site includes information on
President Harry S. Truman.)

www.agsglobepmwh.com/page603c
(This site includes information on the
Berlin Wall.)

Introducing the Chapter

After World War II, the world's two new superpowers, the United States and the Soviet Union, grew apart. Germany was divided. The Truman Doctrine was put into place in an effort to stop the spread of Communism and the Marshall Plan was established to help Europe rebuild. Reforms in the Soviet Union eventually led to the collapse of the Soviet Union and the establishment of independent countries.

Ask:

• How long did WWII last?
  (6 years)

The Cold War

After six years of fighting, World War II had come to an end. More than ever before, people all over the world hoped to see the end of war. Millions had lost loved ones. Millions of others were homeless or their cities had been destroyed. Many people and countries began to work for peace.

This time in history was not one without fear. New enemies were growing. New challenges were facing those who wanted to return to the happiness before the war. People wanted to live beyond war.

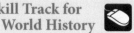

GOALS FOR LEARNING

• To describe the world after World War II
• To identify major crisis periods in relations between the Soviet Union and United States
• To describe the changing relations between the Soviets and Americans

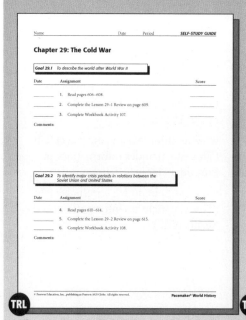

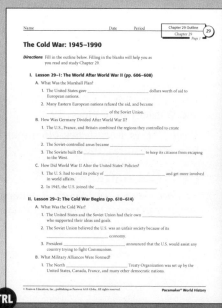

Chapter 29 Self-Study Guide, pages 1–2   Chapter 29 Outline, pages 1–2

Reading Strategy: Summarizing

When summarizing, a good reader asks questions about what he or she is reading. When reading this chapter, ask yourself these questions:

- Who or what am I reading about?
- Why am I reading about this topic?
- What is the most important idea related to this topic?

Key Vocabulary Words

Lesson 1

Marshall Plan The American plan to rebuild Europe after World War II

Satellite A country that depends on and is controlled by a more powerful country

Berlin Wall The wall that divided the people of East and West Berlin

Isolationism A policy of staying out of the affairs, or business, of other countries

Lesson 2

Superpower A nation that has more power and money than other countries

Cold war The tension and hostility between the United States and the Soviet Union after World War II; was a war of ideas

Capitalist Having business and industry privately owned and operated for profit

Truman Doctrine U.S. President Truman's plan to stop the spread of Communism

Currency The form of money a country uses

Nuclear weapon A powerful weapon, such as an atomic bomb or missile

Crisis A time of danger; a turning point in events

Lesson 3

Disaster Something that causes harm or problems

Détente An easing of tensions between countries

Ratify To formally approve

- What were some of the effects of the war? (Millions lost loved ones. Millions were homeless or their cities had been destroyed. Many people and countries began to work for peace.)

Reading Strategy: Summarizing

Ask volunteers to read the three bullet points on page 605. Explain that when readers summarize material, they find the answers to these questions and write them in their own words. A good summary includes the most important ideas related to the topic.

Ask:

- Who or what will we read about in this lesson? (the world after WWII)
- Why are we reading about this topic? (to learn more about how WWII changed the world)
- Looking at the section heads, what countries do you expect to read about in this lesson? (Germany and the United States)

Key Vocabulary Words

Point out that these chapter words are presented in the order they appear in each lesson. They are also found in the glossary.

LIFE SKILLS CONNECTION

Students learn about currency in other nations and how to determine exchange rates. Help students find exchange rate calculators online.

KEY VOCABULARY

Have students review the vocabulary from each lesson before beginning the exercise.

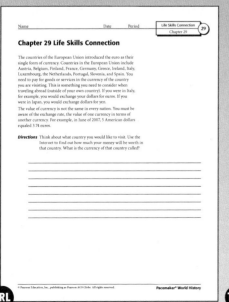

TRL Life Skills Connection 29

TRL Key Vocabulary Words 29, pages 1–2

Lesson at a Glance

Chapter 29 Lesson 1

Overview This lesson explains the Marshall Plan, the division of Germany after WWII, and the United States' policy of isolationism.

Objectives

- To explain the Marshall Plan
- To describe how Germany was divided after World War II
- To explain the change in the United States' connection to the world after the war

Student Pages 606–609

Teacher's Resource Library

Workbook Activity 107

Activity 107

Modified Activity 107

Vocabulary

Berlin Wall   Marshall Plan
isolationism   satellite

Write the vocabulary words on the board and discuss their meanings with students. Ask a volunteer to choose a word and make up a sentence that is a clue to one of the words. Classmates should try to guess the word from the clue. Continue until all the words have been guessed.

1 Warm-Up Activity

Have students imagine a wall dividing their city or town in half. Ask them to describe what it might be like to be forbidden to travel to the other side of the city. Then explain that Germany was divided into four sections after WWII. In addition, the city of Berlin was divided into East Berlin and West Berlin by a wall. Discuss problems societies may have when there is a dramatic change such as this.

Reading Strategy: Summarizing

Ask students to identify the main idea of the first section. (The Marshall Plan provided money for European recovery after WWII.)

The World After World War II

Objectives

- To explain the Marshall Plan
- To describe how Germany was divided after World War II
- To explain the change in the United States' connection to the world after the war

Marshall Plan

The American plan to rebuild Europe after World War II

Satellite

A country that depends on and is controlled by a more powerful country

Reading Strategy: Summarizing

What is the main idea of this first section?

Europe was weakened by World War II. European countries were no longer the powerful nations they had been. It was time for these nations to rebuild. Many nations, including Italy and France, set up democratic governments. Charles de Gaulle served as the first president of postwar France.

What Was the Marshall Plan?

U.S. President Harry S. Truman called for a plan to help put Europe back on its feet. The **Marshall Plan**, named for U.S. Secretary of State George C. Marshall, provided money for European recovery. From 1947 until 1951, the United States gave $13 billion of food, raw materials for industry, and machinery to European nations.

War-torn nations welcomed the aid. However, the Soviet Union and its Communist **satellites** refused to accept the Marshall Plan. This refusal was just one act that would divide the world into two camps.

The Eastern European countries did not turn to democracy. They became Communist satellites of the Soviet Union. They had been freed from the Germans by the Soviet Union at the end of the war. But they remained under Soviet control.

How Was Germany Divided After World War II?

Germany was a mess after World War II. Cities and farms had been bombed. The economy was ruined.

The winning nations divided Germany into four sections. Great Britain, France, the United States, and the Soviet Union each took control of a section. Each country put troops inside its zone to keep order.

---

2 Teaching the Lesson

WWII had weakened European countries. Many cities needed to be rebuilt. The United States came to the assistance of many nations. Have students read pages 606–608 to learn about the Marshall Plan and the division of Germany.

Ask:

- What type of aid did the Marshall Plan provide? (food, raw materials for industry, and machinery to help rebuild Europe)

- What nations refused to accept the Marshall Plan? (the Soviet Union and its Communist satellites)

- What countries controlled West Berlin and East Berlin? (The United States, France, and Britain controlled West Berlin. The Soviet Union controlled East Berlin.)

- What did the formation of the United Nations mean for the United States? (an end to its policy of isolationism)

After a few years the United States, France, and Britain tried to bring Germany together as one republic. However, the Soviet Union refused. As a result, the democratic nations combined their regions to form West Germany, or the Federal Republic of Germany. The Soviet-controlled zone became known as East Germany, or the German Democratic Republic.

The city of Berlin is located in the eastern part of Germany. It was divided into East Berlin, a Communist section, and West Berlin, under democratic West German control. In 1961, the Communists built the **Berlin Wall** to separate the city's two sections. They also wanted to keep East Berliners from leaving to live in the West.

The Division of Germany After World War II

MAP STUDY

1. What were the four sections of Germany after World War II?

2. What were the three parts of West Berlin?

Background Information

In 1945, Germany was divided into four sectors that were occupied by four separate armies. The entire city of Berlin was within the Soviet sector of Germany, which later became known as East Germany. A year later, Berlin held free elections, but the Soviets did not want that, so they cut off East Berlin from West Berlin, hoping to make Berliners accept Communism instead. The Allies came to the aid of West Berlin. In 1961, the Soviets began building the Berlin Wall to keep East Berliners who did not want to live under Communism from fleeing to West Berlin. Thus, West Berlin became an island of democracy within Communist East Germany.

ELL/ESL STRATEGY

Language Objective:
To be able to describe details shown on a map

Divide the entire class into small groups. Include ELL students in as many groups as possible. Each member of the group should describe a detail shown on the map on page 607 without naming it. Details might be a body of water, a country, or a map feature such as the scale of miles and kilometers. Other members of the group should try to identify what is being described. Each member of the group, including ELL students, should have at least one turn in describing a map detail.

MAP STUDY

Have students study the map on this page to see how Germany was divided after WWII. Point out the location of Berlin. Ask volunteers to provide the answers to the Map Study questions.

Answers:
1. Germany was divided into the French sector, Soviet sector, American sector, and British sector.
2. West Berlin was divided into the British sector, French sector, and American sector.

CHAPTER PROJECT

Divide the class into five groups. Assign each group a 10-year period from 1945 to 1995. Explain that many world events occurred related to the cold war. Have each group use library sources and the Internet to research its assigned time period. Explain that information learned from each group's research will be used to create a large timeline.

Isolationism
A policy of staying out of the affairs, or business, of other countries

Reading Strategy:
Summarizing

What are some important details to help you understand this section?

How Did World War II Alter the United States' Policies?

The United States, unlike Europe, was not shattered by World War II. No battles tore apart U.S. lands. Wide oceans kept the United States separate and safe. The United States also had the power of the atomic bomb. At the end of World War II, the United States was the strongest nation in the world.

Except for its involvement in World War I, the United States had mostly kept to its own business. It followed a policy of **isolationism**. World War II connected the United States with the rest of the world. In 1945, the United States became one of the first countries to join the United Nations. The world was changing. Countries were becoming more dependent on each other. The United States could no longer stand alone, minding its own business.

LESSON 29-1 REVIEW

On a sheet of paper, write the letter of the answer that correctly completes each sentence.

1. The Soviet Union and its Communist satellites refused to accept the _____.

   A peace treaty
   B policy of isolationism
   C Marshall Plan
   D détente

2. After World War II, the Eastern European countries were freed from the Germans. However, they remained under _____ control.

   A U.S.
   B Japanese
   C Soviet
   D German

3. _____ economy was ruined after its defeat in World War II.

   A The United States'
   B Japan's
   C The Soviet Union's
   D Germany's

4. The democratic nations combined their regions to form _____ Germany.

   A North
   B South
   C East
   D West

5. The Soviet-controlled zone became _____ Germany.

   A North
   B South
   C East
   D West

6. _____ was the strongest nation in the world at the end of World War II.

   A The United States
   B Japan
   C The Soviet Union
   D Germany

7. After World War II, the United States could no longer follow _____.

   A Communist rule
   B its policy of isolationism
   C the Marshall Plan
   D its democratic government

On a sheet of paper, write the answer to each question. Use complete sentences.

8. What was the Marshall Plan?

9. How was Germany divided after World War II?

10. Why was the Berlin wall built?

1945–1990   *The Cold War*   *Chapter 29*   **609**

ONLINE CONNECTION

Students can gain additional information by accessing the following Web sites:

www.agsglobepmwh.com/page609a (This is an interactive learning site about the cold war, including declassified documents.)

www.agsglobepmwh.com/page609b (This site provides audio and visual information about the Marshall Plan.)

www.agsglobepmwh.com/page609c (This site provides more information about East and West Berlin.)

Lesson 29–1 Review Answers

1. C **2.** C **3.** D **4.** D **5.** C **6.** A **7.** B
8. The Marshall Plan provided money for European recovery. The United States sent food, raw materials for industry, and machinery for European recovery. **9.** Germany was divided into four sections. Great Britain, France, the United States, and the Soviet Union each took control of a section. **10.** The Communists built the Berlin Wall to separate the city's two sections. East Berlin was a Communist section. West Berlin was under democratic control. The Communists also wanted to keep the East Berliners from leaving to live in the West.

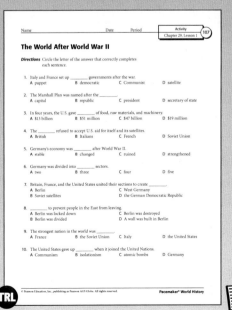

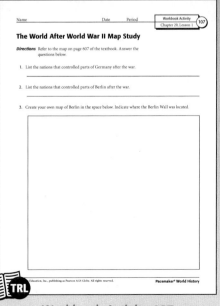

Activity 107   Workbook Activity 107

The Cold War Chapter 29   **609**

Chapter 29 Lesson 2

Overview This section explains the stages of the cold war, the development of nuclear weapons, and the growth of Communism and military alliances.

Objectives

- To explain why the cold war began
- To explain the alliances formed as a result of the cold war
- To name the bomb that was more powerful than the atomic bomb
- To describe life in the Soviet Union under Nikita Khrushchev
- To explain the Cuban missile crisis

Student Pages 610–615

Teacher's Resource Library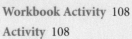

Workbook Activity 108

Activity 108

Modified Activity 108

Vocabulary

capitalist	nuclear weapon
cold war	superpower
crisis	Truman Doctrine
currency	

Have students work in pairs, taking turns giving the definitions and identifying the correct words. Then have them work individually to write definitions using their own words.

1 Warm-Up Activity

Write the word *IDEAS* on the board. Ask students to offer an idea of how government should run a country. Write that on the board. Then have students offer suggestions on how a government could use complete control to convince the people in the country that its idea of how to rule is correct. Discuss the pros and cons of allowing a government to control the flow of ideas in a country.

LESSON 29-2

The Cold War Begins

Objectives

- To explain why the cold war began
- To explain the alliances formed as a result of the cold war
- To name the bomb that was more powerful than the atomic bomb
- To describe life in the Soviet Union under Nikita Khrushchev
- To explain the Cuban missile crisis

Superpower

A nation that has more power and money than other countries

Cold war

The tension and hostility between the United States and the Soviet Union after World War II

Capitalist

Having business and industry privately owned and operated for profit

During World War II, the United States and the Soviet Union were allies. After World War II, the two countries became the most powerful nations on Earth. In fact, they were known as *superpowers*. This is because they had more money and power than other countries. Each had different ideas about what an ideal society should be like. Soviet peoples lived under Communism, while Americans lived in a free democracy. Disagreements and tensions between the two nations grew. The "**cold war**" had begun.

What Was the Cold War?

The cold war was not an outright conflict. It did not involve actual battles or bombings. The cold war was a war of ideas.

Both the Soviet Union and the United States had their own allies in the cold war. The United States and its allies thought Communism was bad. They pointed out that people in Communist countries usually had little freedom. The Communist nations criticized the United States for being a **capitalist** nation. A capitalist nation is one that has business and industry privately owned and operated for profit. They pointed out that some people in the United States were very rich and some were very poor. They said that because of this, the United States was an unfair society.

Americans worried about a Communist takeover of the whole world. President Truman announced that the United States would give aid to any country fighting Communism. He made a plan for military and economic support. This plan became known as the **Truman Doctrine**. Both Greece and Turkey were given aid under this plan.

COMMON ERROR

Be sure students understand that the term *cold war* has nothing to do with temperature. Explain that the cold war was a type of stand-off between countries because they were at war regarding their ideas and principals. No physical fighting occurred.

Reading Strategy: Summarizing

What are some important details about the Soviet idea of Americans? What are some important details about the American idea of Soviets?

You Decide
Do you think the Communist criticism of the United States was fair? Why or why not?

Remember
The world was also divided into alliances before and during the two world wars.

Communism often grew strong in poor countries. Financial aid under the Marshall Plan helped European nations resist Communist ideas.

What Military Alliances Were Formed?

In 1949, sides were clearly drawn in the cold war. The United States led the setting up of the North Atlantic Treaty Organization (NATO). Members of NATO included the United States, Britain, France, Italy, Canada, and several smaller nations. In 1954, West Germany became a member.

NATO began as a defense against Communism. Member nations promised to help each other. They said that an attack against any one of them would be taken as an attack against all.

In 1955, the Soviet Union created its own alliance to balance the NATO alliance. It was called the Warsaw Pact. It included the Soviet Union and its Communist allies in Eastern Europe.

What Economic Alliances Were Formed?

NATO and the Warsaw Pact were military alliances. The cold war also prompted European nations to form economic alliances. The Soviet Union developed ties with its European allies. These ties gave the Soviet Union a market for its manufactured products. The economic allies, in turn, supplied the Soviets with raw materials.

Many Western European countries joined together to promote trade and common interests. The organization that these countries formed was known as the European Union by the late 1990s. The European Union consisted of 15 full member nations: Austria, Belgium, Denmark, Finland, France, Germany, Greece, Ireland, Italy, Luxembourg, the Netherlands, Portugal, Spain, Sweden, and the United Kingdom.

Remember
Germany, Italy, and Austria-Hungary formed the Triple Alliance during WWI. The two major alliances during WWII were the Allied Powers made up of the United States, Great Britain, the Soviet Union, and China and the Axis Powers made up of Germany, Italy, and Japan. The Oslo group was an alliance of neutral countries.

Encourage students to discuss what they know about the cold war. When did it start? Who were the opponents? What nations were allies of each opponent? Then have students read pages 610–614 to learn more about the cold war and the development of nuclear weapons.

Ask:

- What type of war was the cold war? (a war of ideas)
- Why was NATO formed? (as a defense against Communism)
- How did the United States and the Soviet Union try to stay in step with each other? (by the buildup of weapons)
- What was Russian life like under Joseph Stalin? (Stalin set up labor camps, forcing workers to build a lot. There were shortages of food and clothing.)

Reading Strategy: Summarizing

Have students provide details about the Soviet idea of Americans, including the idea that Communist nations criticized the United States for being capitalist. Details on the American idea of Soviets might include that Americans worried about Communism taking over the world.

You Decide
Ask students to spend a few minutes discussing their opinion with a partner. Students should decide whether or not the Communist criticism was fair, and support their opinion with facts from the text.

Background Information

The rule of Joseph Stalin in the 1930s is sometimes called The Great Terror. Nikita Khrushchev was one of Stalin's top advisers during this time. When Stalin died, Khrushchev won a power struggle against Georgi Malenkov, Stalin's successor. Khrushchev became the dominant figure of the Communist party. He denounced Stalin for his crimes in a speech in 1956. However, Khrushchev never mentioned his own part in those crimes. Khrushchev promoted change and became an advocate for reform in Russia.

You Decide
Have students share any background knowledge they have about the nuclear arms race. Then have them discuss their answers to the question. Students may say that people felt safe because the United States was well defended. Or, they may say that people felt unsafe because there were enough weapons made to blow up the whole world.

Reading Strategy:
Summarizing

Students can summarize the event in history covered in this section in three words: nuclear arms race.

Currency
The form of money a country uses

The euro is the form of currency used in the European Union.

You Decide

Do you think the nuclear arms race made people feel safer? Why or why not?

Reading Strategy:
Summarizing

What event in history is this section about?

The atomic bomb killed everything in Nagasaki in a matter of seconds. With the discovery of the hydrogen bomb, the atomic bomb was no longer the most destructive weapon.

The European Union was best known as a supporter for a single form of **currency**, or money, called the euro. The euro has now been introduced in some member countries. The European Union also worked to lower trade barriers between the member countries.

Why Was There a Nuclear Arms Race?
The Soviet Union and the United States tried to stay in step with each other. Each superpower feared that the other would become more powerful.

One measure of power is the buildup of weapons. When the United States exploded the atomic bomb in 1945, it made America fearsome and powerful. Other nations wanted that power, too. In 1949, the Soviet Union exploded its first atomic bomb. By 1952, Great Britain also had the atomic secret. Then the United States pulled ahead again in the race for destructive power. In 1954, the United States tested a hydrogen bomb. It was thousands of times more powerful than the atomic bomb that had fallen on Hiroshima and Nagasaki. Soon Great Britain, France, and the Soviet Union had hydrogen bombs, too.

Nuclear weapon
A powerful weapon, such as an atomic bomb or missile

Now the People's Republic of China had the bomb. So did India, Israel, and Pakistan. The world had given itself something to fear. As nations struggled to keep pace in the cold war, the stakes became higher. There are now enough **nuclear weapons** in existence to destroy the world many times over.

What Was Life Like in the Soviet Union After World War II?

After World War II, Joseph Stalin worked to rebuild Soviet industry. He set up labor camps, forcing workers to build, build, and build some more. Between 1945 and 1965, Soviet industry boomed. Yet life was not easy for the Russian worker. Stalin had caused shortages of food and clothing with his stress on heavy industry.

After Stalin's death in 1953, there was a struggle for power. Then a new leader, Nikita Khrushchev, rose to the top of the Communist Party.

Khrushchev accused Stalin of the arrests and deaths of many citizens. Khrushchev promised that now the country would be led by the party rather than by a single dictator.

Under Khrushchev, life became better for the people of the Soviet Union. Khrushchev halted some of the activities of the secret police. The government allowed somewhat greater freedom of speech. The workweek was shortened to 40 hours. In addition, Khrushchev tried to raise the standard of living for ordinary people. His economic plan included a greater production of consumer goods. However, progress was slow.

LEARNING STYLES

Auditory/Verbal

Divide the class in half. Have half the class play the role of members of the North Atlantic Treaty Organization and the other half play the role of the Warsaw Pact members. Each group should prepare an explanation of the reasons why it joined the military alliance. Suggest that students refer to Chapter 28 if necessary. Have spokespersons present the case for each side. After students have heard both presentations, have them discuss why each side had legitimate fears for its security.

ELL/ESL STRATEGY

Language Objective: *To understand acronyms*

Write *NATO* on the board. Explain that NATO is an acronym, or word formed from the first letters of other words. Acronyms are easier to use as titles because they often stand for much longer titles. Divide the class into small groups. Have each group think of five acronyms and their meanings. Have each group share their acronyms and explain their meanings by writing the acronyms on the board. ELL students should add acronyms of interest to their notebooks.

COMMON ERROR

Explain to students that the Soviet Union, or USSR, no longer exists. The 15 republics that formed the Soviet Union all became independent by December, 1991.

CAREER CONNECTION

One of the effects of the cold war was the Space Race—the competition between the United States and the Soviet Union to be the first in space and to make the greatest advances in space technology. Today the National Aeronautics and Space Administration (NASA) continues to develop space technology. NASA employs many different specialists in science and engineering in its programs. Have students research NASA to find out what types of workers it employs. Then have them choose one specialty and find out more about that field and its educational requirements. They might use reference books, the Internet, or check a university catalogue. Have students write brief summaries of their findings and share them with the class.

IN THE COMMUNITY

Capitalism allows individuals to own and operate a private business for profit. Have students research how to obtain a business license in their community. Have students visit the local municipal office and speak to a city official about starting a business. Have students write about a business they would like to start in their community.

Crisis
A time of danger; a turning point in events

History Fact
Kennedy promised not to invade Cuba. He also said the United States would remove missiles from Turkey.

Where Did Communism Spread?

The Soviet Union helped spread Communism to other parts of the world. China, Mongolia, North Korea, and some nations in Southeast Asia and Africa, turned to Communism. Cuba, only 90 miles from the United States, became a Communist dictatorship under Fidel Castro.

In 1962, the Soviets tried to build missile bases in Cuba. To stop Soviet ships, U.S. President John F. Kennedy set up a blockade around Cuba. The cold war nearly turned hot at that point. The Cuban missile **crisis** brought the world to the edge of another big war. But Khrushchev agreed to take the missiles out of Cuba, and the situation cooled.

In 1963, Khrushchev's farm program fell apart. Russia had to buy a huge quantity of grain from the West. That year Soviet industrialization slowed down. Then Khrushchev came under heavy criticism for the way he had handled the Cuban situation. In 1964, he was forced to retire. Leonid Brezhnev and Alexei Kosygin replaced him as leaders of the Communist Party. Now life became worse for the people of the Soviet Union. Once again, people had to be careful about what they said.

History Fact
The Cuban missile crisis was a confrontation between the United States, the Soviet Union, and Cuba. It began on October 14, 1962, and ended 14 days later when Krushchev agreed to dismantle the nuclear missile installations in Cuba.

REVIEW

Word Bank

European Union

hydrogen bomb

NATO

superpowers

Warsaw Pact

On a sheet of paper, write the word from the Word Bank to complete each sentence correctly.

1. The United States and the Soviet Union were both _____.

2. _____ began as a defense against Communism.

3. To balance the NATO alliance, the Soviet Union and its Communist satellites formed the _____.

4. While NATO and the Warsaw Pact were military alliances, the _____ was an economic alliance. It is best known for its support of a single currency, the euro.

5. The United States tested the first _____, which was more powerful than the atomic bomb.

On a sheet of paper, write the answer to each question. Use complete sentences.

6. What was the cold war?

7. Why did the cold war begin?

8. What was the Truman Doctrine?

9. Life in the Soviet Union was better under the rule of Nikita Khrushchev. Name three reasons why.

10. What was the Cuban missile crisis?

1945–1990

The Cold War   Chapter 29   **615**

Lesson 29–2 Review Answers

1. superpowers **2.** NATO **3.** Warsaw Pact **4.** European Union **5.** hydrogen bomb **6.** After World War II, the United States and the Soviet Union were the most powerful nations on Earth. Each had different ideas about what an ideal society should be like. Soviet peoples lived under Communism. Americans lived in a free democracy. Disagreements and tensions between the two nations grew. This was the start of the cold war. **7.** The cold war was a war of ideas. It did not involve battles or bombings. **8.** The Truman Doctrine was U.S. President Truman's plan to stop the spread of Communism. President Truman said that the United States would give aid to any country fighting Communism. **9.** Students can list three of these reasons. Khrushchev stopped some of the activities of the secret police. The government allowed somewhat greater freedom of speech. The workweek was shortened to 40 hours. Khrushchev tried to raise the standard of living for ordinary people. His economic plan produced more consumer goods. **10.** The Soviets tried to build missile bases in Cuba. To stop Soviet ships, U.S. President John F. Kennedy set up a blockade around Cuba. A war could have started then. However, Khrushchev agreed to take the missile out of Cuba. The situation cooled.

The Cold War Begins

Directions Read each of the following statements. Identify the point of view as the United States or the Soviet Union. If the statement would likely come from the United States, write a U. If the statement would likely come from the Soviet Union, write an S.

____ 1. Communism is bad for people because they have so few freedoms.

____ 2. We will help any country fighting Communism.

____ 3. We will make a pact in answer to NATO.

____ 4. Our kind of government can help poor countries like Poland and Cuba.

____ 5. The Truman Doctrine is a great idea.

____ 6. Capitalism is bad because it is unfair to have so many poor people.

____ 7. We do not want to be a part of the European Union.

____ 8. We exploded our first atomic bomb in 1949.

____ 9. We will build a blockade around Cuba to keep our country safe.

____ 10. We are afraid that they will take over the world!

Activity 108

Alliances During the Cold War

Part A Directions The following countries are the member nations of NATO as of May 2007. When NATO was created by treaty in 1949, there were 12 original member nations. Use the Internet or an encyclopedia to find which 12 nations were charter, or original, members. Put an asterisk (*) beside the names of those 12 nations.

Belgium	Hungary	Portugal
Bulgaria	Iceland	Romania
Canada	Italy	Slovakia
Czech Republic	Latvia	Slovenia
Denmark	Lithuania	Spain
Estonia	Luxembourg	Turkey
France	the Netherlands	United Kingdom
Germany	Norway	United States
Greece	Poland	

Part B Directions Review Lesson 29–2 in your textbook. Also, check an encyclopedia, almanac, or the Internet to read more on the purpose of NATO and the Warsaw Pact. Explain why NATO and the Warsaw Pact exist.

_____

_____

_____

_____

_____

_____

_____

_____

Workbook Activity 108

Lesson at a Glance

Chapter 29 Lesson 3

Overview This lesson describes the relationship between the United States and the Soviet Union from the early 1970s to 1983.

Objectives

- To explain the SALT agreement
- To describe how the détente between the Soviet Union and the United States ended

Student Pages 616–618

Teacher's Resource Library **TRL**

Workbook Activity 109

Activity 109

Modified Activity 109

Vocabulary

disaster
détente
ratify

Have students write one fill-in-the-blank sentence for each vocabulary word. Then have students exchange papers with a partner and complete each other's sentences. Students can discuss the correct answers and review the definitions with their partner.

1 Warm-Up Activity

Ask volunteers to share examples of common quarrels or problems that classmates or siblings might have. How are these problems resolved? Who settles the argument when countries cannot get along? Tell students in this lesson they will read about how the struggles between the United States and the Soviet Union were resolved.

TEACHER ALERT

Explain that *détente* is a French word, meaning "a loosening or release." Point out that the tension between the United States and the Soviet Union was released during the time period known as détente.

Objectives

- To explain the SALT agreement
- To describe how the détente between the Soviet Union and the United States ended

Disaster
Something that causes harm or problems

Détente
An easing of tensions between countries

Reading Strategy: Summarizing

What important idea is being introduced in this section?

Changing Relations Between the Soviets and Americans

Both the United States and the Soviet Union realized that another world war would bring **disaster**. Between the quarrels and the peaks of tension, they met to try to solve their problems. The two countries even set up a "hot line" to prevent the cold war from turning into a "hot" war. The hot line was a telephone line between the leaders of the United States and the Soviet Union.

Soviet and American officials began to talk about more cooperation between their countries. The new relationship was called **détente**. The nations began to share ideas in science and space exploration. Trade relations improved.

U.S. President Richard M. Nixon and Leonid Brezhnev, general secretary of the Soviet Communist Party, signed the SALT agreement on May 26, 1972.

---

2 Teaching the Lesson

Ask students to remember what life was like for people in the Soviet Union under the rule of Stalin. Then have students read pages 616–617 to learn how relations between the Soviet Union and the United States changed.

Ask:

- What did both the United States and the Soviet Union want to avoid? (another world war)
- What did both countries agree to do during détente? (begin to talk about more cooperation between their countries)

- When did the period known as détente end? (when the Communists took over the government of Afghanistan)

Reading Strategy: Summarizing

Review the important ideas introduced in this lesson. Then have students summarize the most important idea—détente. Students may describe it in their own words as a period of time when the United States and Soviet Union worked cooperatively and got along better.

Ratify
To formally approve

History Fact
To protest the Soviet invasion of Afghanistan, the United States did not send its athletes to the Summer Olympics in Moscow in 1980. The USSR boycotted the Olympics in Los Angeles in 1984.

In 1972, the two powers held Strategic Arms Limitation Talks (SALT). They agreed to set some limits on nuclear arms. A second SALT agreement was later proposed. However, SALT II was never **ratified**, or approved, by the U.S. Senate.

What Ended the Détente?

In 1979, the Communists took over the government of Afghanistan. The Muslim people of Afghanistan rebelled. Soviet troops went in to put down the rebellion. The United States and many other nations were angered by the Soviet invasion of Afghanistan.

During the early 1980s, tensions between the United States and the Soviet Union continued to increase. The United States sent more missiles to Europe. Then, in 1983, a Korean Air Lines passenger jet was shot down over Soviet territory. More than 200 people were killed, many of them Americans. The Soviets said the jet was spying. The United States was angry. Détente was over, and Soviet–U.S. relations grew even colder.

TIMELINE STUDY: CHANGES IN EUROPE: 1940–1990

In what year was a wall built to separate East and West Berlin?

1947 Marshall plan sends aid to Europe

1961 Berlin Wall built

1962 Cuban missile crisis

1979 Soviet Union takes over Afghanistan

1940 — 1950 — 1960 — 1970 — 1980 — 1990

1949 Soviet Union explodes A-bomb

A.D. 1950 NATO is formed

1972 First SALT talks

1983 Korean Air Lines passenger jet shot down

1945–1990

The Cold War Chapter 29 **617**

History Fact
When President Carter announced the boycott of the Olympics, some athletes who had qualified found out while watching the news on television! About 60 teams boycotted the Moscow Olympics of 1980 in support of the policy of the United States. However, several allies such as Great Britain and France did send teams to compete.

TIMELINE STUDY

Answer: 1961

STUDY SKILLS

Have students study the timeline on this page. Have them write three observations about events occurring between 1949 and 1995. Then have students write three questions they could ask based on the information shown in the timeline. Tell students to list three sources other than the textbook they could use to find answers to their questions.

Background Information

Negotiations for the Strategic Arms Limitations Talk (SALT) started in Helsinki, Finland. They began in 1969 and lasted until the first treaty was signed in 1972. The treaty known as SALT I froze the number of nuclear weapons at the existing levels. The treaty known as SALT II was meant to limit the production of strategic nuclear weapons. It was signed in 1979, but the Soviet Union's invasion of Afghanistan prevented it from being ratified by the U.S. Senate. However, its terms were honored by both sides.

LEARNING STYLES

Logical/Mathematical
Have students create an outline of Lessons 29–1 and 29–2. Their outlines should show how the end of World War II led to the beginning of the cold war. They should cover the creation of NATO and the spread of Communism. After Lesson 29–3, have students add to their outlines. Encourage students to include dates for significant events.

ELL/ESL STRATEGY

Language Objective:
To compare and contrast currency systems

Divide students into small groups. Have each group research Russian currency and compare it with American currency. Each group should create a poster comparing and contrasting American and Russian currency. Provide the opportunity for ELL students to explain the currency of their native countries.

The Cold War Chapter 29 **617**

WORLD CULTURES

Cuba became embroiled in the cold war when the Soviets tried to build missile bases there. This led to the Cuban missile crisis and eventually to the U.S. embargo against Cuba. Despite their lack of commercial interaction with other nations, Cubans have a rich and diverse culture. Ethnically, they are a melting pot of cultures, mainly from Spain and Africa. Cuban music and dance is appreciated throughout the world. Musical styles such as salsa, rumba, and mambo have been influenced by Cuban culture. Cuban cuisine is also very popular. Typical Cuban meals include plantains, black beans, rice, tropical fruits, pork, and shredded beef called *ropa vieja*.

Lesson 29–3 Review Answers
1. A **2.** C **3.** D **4.** B **5.** B **6.** A **7.** C **8.** D
9. D **10.** B

On a sheet of paper, write the letter of the answer that correctly completes each sentence.

1. The _____ was an attempt to prevent the cold war from turning into a real war.

   A "hot line"   **B** Warsaw Pact **C** Marshall Plan **D** Truman Doctrine

2. The Soviet and _____ effort to improve relationships between their countries is known as *détente*.

   A German   **B** Muslim   **C** American   **D** Korean

3. Soviets and Americans tried to cooperate by sharing ideas in science and _____.

   A government   **B** capitalism   **C** nuclear arms **D** space exploration

4. In _____, the Soviet Union and United States held the Strategic Arms Limitation Talks (SALT).

   A 1970   **B** 1972   **C** 1979   **D** 1983

5. In the SALT agreement, the United States and Soviet Union set limits on _____.

   A space exploration **B** nuclear arms **C** Communism **D** trade

6. SALT II was never approved by _____.

   A the United States **B** Korea   **C** Afghanistan **D** the Soviet Union

7. The Communists took over the government of _____ in 1979.

   A the United States **B** Germany   **C** Afghanistan **D** Korea

8. The United States sent more _____ to Europe during the early 1980s.

   A hydrogen bombs **B** soldiers   **C** airplanes   **D** missiles

9. The Soviets shot down a Korean Air Lines passenger jet in _____.

   A 1970   **B** 1972   **C** 1979   **D** 1983

10. The shooting down of the Korean plane ended the _____.

   A SALT agreement **B** détente   **C** Warsaw Pact **D** Cuban missile crisis

618   *Unit 10 The World Since 1945*

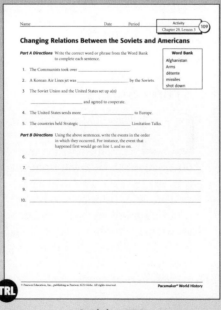

- Under the Marshall Plan, the United States gave aid to war-torn Europe.

- The Soviet Union and its Communist satellites refused Marshall Plan aid.

- The Soviet Union gained Communist satellites in Eastern Europe after World War II. The Soviet Union encouraged the spread of Communism throughout the world.

- After World War II, Germany was divided into two parts. West Germany was democratic and East Germany was controlled by Communists.

- The United States and the Soviet Union were allies during World War II. However, after the war a cold war began between the two nations.

- The two superpowers had different ideas about what a country should be. The Communist nations criticized the United States as a capitalist nation.

- The United States began the development of NATO, an alliance of defense against Communism.

- The Soviets formed the Warsaw Pact, an alliance of Communist nations.

- After World War II, a nuclear arms race began. Nations worked to develop powerful new types of weapons.

- The Soviet Union helped spread Communism to many different parts of the world.

- The two superpowers held peace talks to try to limit the buildup of nuclear arms.

Chapter 29 Summary

Have students read the Chapter Summary on page 619 to review the main ideas presented in Chapter 29.

Ask:

- What plan gave United States aid to war-torn European countries? (the Marshall Plan)

- Who refused Marshall Plan aid? (the Soviet Union and its satellites)

- How did the Soviet Union encourage the spread of Communism throughout the world? (by gaining satellite nations in Eastern Europe after WWII)

- What happened to Germany after WWII? (It was divided into two parts. West Germany was democratic. East Germany was controlled by Communists.)

- What countries were involved in a cold war and why? (A cold war began between the United States and the Soviet Union. The two countries had different ideas about what a country should be.)

- Why did Communist nations criticize the United States? (They said the United States was a capitalist nation.)

- What was NATO? (an alliance of defense against Communism)

- What was the Warsaw Pact? (an alliance of Communist nations)

- What was the nuclear arms race? (After World War II, nations worked to develop powerful new types of weapons.)

- What brought the two superpowers together? (peace talks to limit the buildup of nuclear arms)

TEACHER'S RESOURCE

The AGS Globe Teaching Strategies in Social Studies Transparencies may be used with this chapter. The transparencies add an interactive dimension to expand and enhance the Pacemaker® *World History* program content.

CHAPTER PROJECT FOLLOW-UP

Provide a banner paper to each group. Have students create a timeline of events occurring during their assigned time period. Have each group add visuals to its timeline. Connect the timelines to create a timeline mural. Discuss the events within each period and how the events of earlier years affected later events. Have students decide on a title for the timeline.

Chapter 29 Review

Use the Chapter Review to prepare students for tests and to reteach content from the chapter.

Chapter 29 Mastery Test

The Teacher's Resource Library includes two forms of the Chapter 29 Mastery Test. Each test addresses the chapter Goals for Learning. An optional third page of additional critical-thinking items is included for each test. The difficulty level of the two forms is equivalent.

Chapter 29 Review Answers

Vocabulary Review

1. ratify
2. capitalist
3. détente
4. isolationism
5. satellite
6. currency
7. cold war
8. disaster
9. crisis
10. nuclear weapon

Chapter Review Questions

11. The United States promised money for European recovery from World War II.

12. They built the Berlin Wall.

13. The Soviet Union and the United States were the superpowers.

Word Bank

capitalist
cold war
crisis
currency
détente
disaster
isolationism
nuclear weapon
ratify
satellite

Vocabulary Review

On a sheet of paper, use the words from the Word Bank to correctly match each definition below.

1. To officially approve

2. Running business and industry for profit

3. The relaxing of tensions between countries

4. The idea of staying out of international affairs

5. A country that is controlled by a more powerful country

6. The form of money a country uses

7. The war of ideas between the United States and the Soviet Union

8. Something that causes harm or problems

9. A dangerous time; a turning point in events

10. A powerful weapon, like a missile

Chapter Review Questions

On a sheet of paper, write the answer to each question. Use complete sentences.

11. What did the Marshall Plan promise?

12. How did the Communists decide to keep people from leaving East Berlin?

13. What nations were the superpowers after World War II?

14. What U.S. plan promised aid to any country fighting Communism?

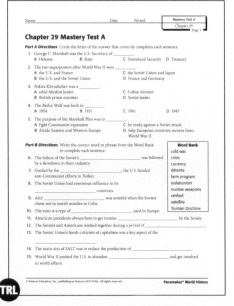

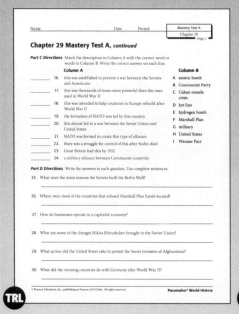

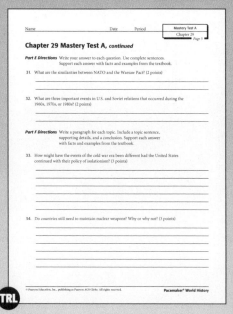

15. What is NATO?

16. What were the SALT treaties?

Critical Thinking

On a sheet of paper, write your response to each question. Use complete sentences.

17. Why do you think progress was slow when Khrushchev tried to improve the standard of living in the Soviet Union?

18. Suppose you lived in 1962. How do you think you would feel about the Cuban missile crisis?

Using the Timeline

Use the timeline on page 617 to answer the questions.

19. In what year was NATO formed?

20. In what year did the Soviets invade Afghanistan?

GROUP ACTIVITY

Form a group of three or four. Discuss whether you think the Olympics should be canceled or boycotted for political reasons. Write up your conclusion to share with the rest of the class.

1945–1990

The Cold War   Chapter 29   **621**

---

14. The Truman Doctrine promised military and economic support to any country fighting Communism.

15. NATO is the North Atlantic Treaty Organization. It was set up as a defense against Communism.

16. The SALT treaties were about setting some limits on nuclear arms.

Critical Thinking

17. Possible answer: The Communist system was very controlled. This makes change difficult.

18. Possible answer: Students may express fear about war. They may also have confidence in the leaders of the United States.

Using the Timeline

19. 1950

20. 1979

GROUP ACTIVITY

Students' conclusions will vary. Suggest that they give at least one reason for their conclusions. In their discussion, some students may emphasize individual competition. Other students may emphasize the fact that athletes represent their countries.

Chapter 29 Mastery Test B, pages 1–3

The Cold War Chapter 29   **621**

Introducing the Chapter

The period following World War II found many colonies struggling for independence from imperialistic rule. Gandhi led India to freedom, but assassinations and poverty hampered progress. China and Korea turned to Communism. Japan became a global economic force. War broke out in Vietnam, with repercussions back home. In South Africa, apartheid fell under the influence of Mandela.

Changes in Asia and Africa

The years after World War II brought huge changes to many countries of Africa and Asia. Some countries were forming new governments after winning their independence from large European powers. Some faced major upsets as different political groups struggled to gain control from within. Civil wars brought violence and ruin to many countries. Many people faced starvation and homelessness. Western nations such as the United States worked to fight the spread of Communism.

GOALS FOR LEARNING

- To describe India's problems of civil war, religious differences, and widespread poverty
- To describe China and Korea under Communist rule
- To explain why Korea is split into two parts
- To explain Japan and Southeast Asia after World War II
- To describe the conflict in Vietnam
- To understand Africa's progress after World War II

SELF-STUDY GUIDE

Name _____ Date _____ Period _____

Chapter 30: Changes in Asia and Africa

Goal 30.1 To describe India's problems of civil war, religious differences, and widespread poverty

Date	Assignment	Score
_____	1. Read pages 624–626.	_____
_____	2. Complete the Lesson 30–1 Review on page 627.	_____
_____	3. Complete Workbook Activity 110.	_____

Comments:

Goal 30.2 To describe China and Korea under Communist rule

Date	Assignment	Score
_____	4. Read pages 628–632.	_____
_____	5. Complete the Lesson 30–2 Review on page 633.	_____
_____	6. Complete Workbook Activity 111.	_____

Comments:

© Pearson Education, Inc., publishing as Pearson AGS Globe. All rights reserved.   *Pacemaker® World History*

Name _____ Date _____ Period _____   Chapter Outline / Chapter 30 / Page 1

Changes in Asia and Africa: 1945–present

Directions Fill in the outline below. Filling in the blanks will help you as you read and study Chapter 30.

I. **Lesson 30–1: India (pp. 624–626)**
   A. The Hindus and Sikhs Fight
      1. Hindus and Sikhs fought over the state of _____.
      2. Indira Gandhi and Rajiv Gandhi were both _____.
   B. Bangladesh
      1. India and Pakistan fought over the land called _____.
      2. Before 1971, Bangladesh was _____.
   C. India Works to End Poverty
      1. India faces food shortages because of its huge _____.
      2. The government brought in chemical plants to help increase _____.
      3. India is fighting poverty with programs for _____ growth.
      4. In 1950, the government outlawed the _____ category of the Hindu caste system.

II. **Lesson 30–2: China (pp. 628–632)**
   A. The Battle for Power in China
      1. The Communists felt Chiang Kai-shek showed favor to _____ and _____.
      2. Mao Zedong was supported by the _____.
      3. The Nationalists left mainland China to live in _____.
   B. Life Under Communist Rule
      1. Under the Communists, food was grown on _____.
      2. The government took over farming and _____.
   C. The Cultural Revolution
      1. Enemies of Communism were _____, or forced to accept the Communist way.
      2. Young students called the _____ helped Mao carry out his policies.
      3. Deng Xiaoping worked to make China more _____.
      4. In 1989, students gathered in _____ Square to demand more democracy.

© Pearson Education, Inc., publishing as Pearson AGS Globe. All rights reserved.   *Pacemaker® World History*

Reading Strategy: Questioning

Questioning what you are reading helps you understand and remember more information. It also makes you a more active reader. When reading this chapter, ask yourself:

- Why am I reading this text?
- What key points can be drawn from this text?
- How can I connect this text to my life experiences?

Key Vocabulary Words

Lesson 1
Security Safety

Violence Great physical force; actions that hurt others

Lesson 2
Corrupt Dishonest, evil, selfish

Commune A group of people working or living closely together, often sharing property and tasks

Lesson 4
Pollution Waste materials in the air or water

Invest To put money into something with the hope of making more money

Lesson 5
Guerilla One of a group of fighters who are not part of a regular army, and who usually make surprise raids behind enemy lines

Domino theory The belief that if one country became Communist, neighbors would fall to Communism too

Refugee A person who flees his or her country or home

Lesson 6
Starvation The condition of dying from not having enough food to eat

Famine A time when crops do not grow and there is no food

Minority Less than half

Sanction An action taken by one nation against another for breaking international law

Majority More than half

Apartheid The separation of races based mainly on skin color

Curfew A time after which certain people cannot be on the streets

Repeal To cancel; put an end to

Standard of living A way to judge how well a person or family is living

Ask:

- What religious groups controlled India and Pakistan? (Muslims in Pakistan and Hindus in India)
- Who was Mao Zedong? (the communist leader of the People's Republic of China)
- What happened after the Khmer Rouge lost its power in Cambodia? (National elections were held.)

Reading Strategy: Questioning

Tell students that when they ask questions while reading, they make connections between what they know and what they are about to learn. Asking questions can help good readers to make predictions and inferences.

Key Vocabulary Words

Point out that these chapter words are presented in the order they appear in each lesson. They are also found in the glossary.

LIFE SKILLS CONNECTION

Students learn about volunteering in developing nations, their own country, or their own community. Offer students extra credit for volunteer work they do in their spare time.

KEY VOCABULARY

Students complete each sentence with the correct word from the Word Bank.

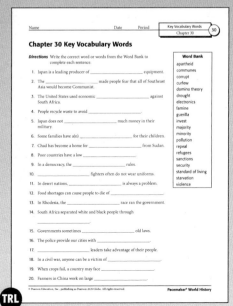

Life Skills Connection 30   Key Vocabulary Words 30

Lesson at a Glance

Chapter 30 Lesson 1

Overview This lesson traces India's transition from a colony to the world's largest democracy.

Objectives

- To describe the fighting between the Hindus and Sikhs over Punjab
- To explain the steps the Indian government has taken to end poverty

Student Pages 624–627

Teacher's Resource Library

Workbook Activity 110

Activity 110

Modified Activity 110

Vocabulary

security
violence

Have students locate the sentences in which the vocabulary words are found in the text. Have them read the surrounding sentences as well as gather additional meaning from context clues. Point out that the vocabulary terms have opposite meanings—one implies safety and one implies harm. Challenge students to use both vocabulary words in a single sentence that compares their meanings.

1 Warm-Up Activity

Ask students to brainstorm a list of strategies that they use to solve problems. Write the list on the board. The list will likely include both peaceful and hostile methods of problem solving, such as working cooperatively and fighting. Discuss how nations use similar strategies to solve their problems.

Objectives

- To describe the fighting between the Hindus and Sikhs over Punjab
- To explain the steps the Indian government has taken to end poverty

Reading Strategy: Questioning

What do you think you will learn about by reading this lesson?

Security
Safety

Violence
Great physical force; actions that hurt others

History Fact
With its population of about 1 billion, India is the world's largest democracy.

In Chapter 23, you read about India winning its independence from Britain in 1947. At that time, Indian leaders agreed to divide India into two separate nations, India and Pakistan. India fell under the control of the Hindus. The Muslims controlled Pakistan. Furthermore, Pakistan was divided into East and West Pakistan.

India held its first general election in 1951. Jawaharlal Nehru was elected as the first prime minister of the Republic of India. Nehru led India until he died in 1964. In 1966, his daughter, Indira Gandhi, was elected prime minister.

Why Did the Hindus and Sikhs Fight?

There were food shortages and labor strikes in India during Mrs. Gandhi's years as leader. For a time she lost her position. But she returned to power in 1980. In 1984, Indira Gandhi was assassinated by members of her own **security,** or safety, force. The assassins were members of the Sikh religion. Sikh rebels were seeking a separate state in Punjab, their region of India. After Gandhi's assassination, her son Rajiv became prime minister. Rajiv resigned (gave up his job) in 1989.

The late 1980s and early 1990s brought **violence,** or fighting, to several parts of India. A decision to bring the state of Punjab under control of the central government led to fighting between Hindus and Sikhs. Muslim and Hindu Indians clashed over possession of a holy temple. In 1991, Rajiv Gandhi made another bid for the office of prime minister. He was assassinated during that election campaign.

Reading Strategy: Questioning

Answers will vary. Students might say that they want to learn more about how India has changed since 1947. They might want to know the challenges that India faces today. Accept all reasonable answers.

History Fact

Before students read this lesson, discuss the difficulties the Indian government faces in providing services for a billion people. Then have students read the lesson to discover how India is dealing with these problems.

CHAPTER PROJECT

Place students in small groups. Tell them they are going to make a bulletin-board display or poster about the Korean War Memorial or the Vietnam Veterans Memorial. Let each group decide which memorial to research. Have students research basic facts about the memorials, such as where they are located, when they were built, what they look like, and number of visitors each year. Students should find several other interesting facts about the memorial. Tell them to include photographs or drawings in their displays.

Reading Strategy:
Questioning

As you read, notice the details in the text. What questions can you ask yourself about these details?

How Was Bangladesh Formed?

Over the years, India has had border disputes with its neighbors. This led to fighting between India and China in 1959 and in 1962. In 1965, India and Pakistan fought a three-week-long war. Both countries claimed the same land, called Kashmir, in northern India.

In 1971, civil war broke out in Pakistan. The people of East Pakistan complained because the center of government was based in West Pakistan. The war led to East Pakistan becoming a separate nation called Bangladesh. In 1998, India and Pakistan continued their fighting. Both nations tested nuclear weapons to prove they could launch a nuclear attack on each other.

How Is India Working to End Poverty?

India has always had to deal with poverty and food shortages. The country has a huge population. It must struggle to provide enough food for all its people. Even though India is a major producer of farm products, there is never enough food to go around. It is said that almost two-thirds of India's people go to bed hungry every night.

The government has tried to teach farmers new methods to increase production. They have allowed Western businesses to come in and build chemical factories. There was hope that the chemicals would increase crops. In general, India benefited from the chemicals. However, in 1984, an accident at one U.S. chemical plant caused the worst industrial disaster in history. There was an explosion at a factory in Bhopal, India. A cloud of highly toxic (deadly) gas spread into the heavily populated area around the plant. Several thousand people who breathed the poisonous fumes died horrible deaths.

2 Teaching the Lesson

Have students recall what they learned about Mohandas Gandhi. Tell them they will learn about how India fared following its successful bid for independence.

Ask:

- What happened to Indira Gandhi and her successor, Rajiv Gandhi? (They were both assassinated.)
- Why did India fight with its neighbors? (They had border disputes over areas such as Kashmir.)
- How is India attempting to end poverty? (by teaching farmers new methods to increase crop production, implementing programs to encourage economic growth, building dams, and educating people)

Reading Strategy:
Questioning

Answers will vary. Student questions may include the following: Why did both India and Pakistan claim Kashmir? Why did civil war break out in Pakistan? What caused the accident at the U.S. chemical plant?

COMMON ERROR

Students might know of other disasters that took more lives than the 1984 explosion in Bhopal, India. Be sure students understand that there are different types of disasters. Natural disasters, such as the 2004 tsunami that struck Indonesia and surrounding areas, often take a heavier toll than industrial disasters. The Bhopal explosion was an industrial disaster; it remains the largest disaster of its kind.

Background Information

Indira Gandhi became involved in politics at the young age of 12. She led the so-called Monkey Brigade in India, a children's group that worked to overthrow British rule. As a young mother, Gandhi was imprisoned by the British from 1942 to 1943 on charges of subversion. Several years later, India won its independence, and Gandhi's father was elected prime minister. Because her mother was no longer living, Gandhi traveled widely with her father and became well-versed in politics. In the 1960s and 1970s, she was elected on platforms dedicated to abolishing poverty, among other issues. However, she was a controversial figure in that she supported voluntary sterilization to help control India's growing population. She also limited civil liberties in an attempt to curb riots. Despite the controversy, Gandhi did much to improve life in India, particularly in the fields of economics, science, technology, and diplomacy.

Poverty and food shortages affect many people in India.

You Decide

Millions of poor people live on the streets of India's cities. How do you think rich countries can help homeless people?

India is trying to end its poverty with programs for economic growth. Indian leaders try to build industry. They want to make better use of their country's resources, such as coal and iron ore. And India spends billions of dollars building dams to provide power.

Age-old customs contribute to the food shortages. While India has tried to industrialize, some of its people still hold on to old ideas. In 1950, the government tried to improve life by outlawing the "untouchable" category in the Hindu caste system. Until then, people called *untouchables* had been forced to live in the dirtiest, poorest parts of villages. Their children were not allowed to go into schools. They had to sit on the steps outside and listen. When untouchables walked through village streets, they were supposed to brush away their footsteps with a broom. India has had to move beyond some old ideas to make life better for its people. In 1997, India's first lowest caste president, K. R. Narayan, took office.

LEARNING STYLES

Logical/Mathematical

Remind students that Indian has a population of one billion people. An estimated two-thirds of these people go to bed hungry every night. Have them calculate the actual number of people who go to bed hungry in India. (2/3 = 66.6 percent; 1,000,000,000 x 0.666 = 666,000,000 people)

You Decide

Students might suggest that rich countries can help poor people by sending money to feed, clothe, and shelter the poor. They might also suggest volunteering in developing nations or implementing programs that help to educate and train people. Accept all reasonable responses.

LEARNING STYLES

Visual/Spatial

Have students examine the photograph on this page. Ask them how the photo makes it easier to understand the content in the text. Have them select specific passages that were clarified by the photograph, such as the paragraph that discusses "the dirtiest, poorest parts of villages."

ELL/ESL STRATEGY

Language Objective:
To read and understand material from a variety of sources

Ask ELL students to find a newspaper or magazine article that reports on recent developments in India. Tell them to underline key sentences in the article. Ask each student to summarize his or her article for the class. The class as a whole should then discuss the various articles and relate them to what they have learned in this lesson.

Word Bank

Bangladesh
coal
disaster
Kashmir
population
Sikh
Western

On a sheet of paper, write the word from the Word Bank to complete each sentence correctly.

1. The people that assassinated Indira Gandhi were members of the _____ religion.

2. India and Pakistan both claimed the same land, called _____, in northern India.

3. A civil war led to East Pakistan becoming a separate nation called _____.

4. India has food shortages and poverty because of its large _____.

5. India's government has allowed _____ businesses to build factories to help increase production.

6. In 1984, an accident at a U.S. chemical plant caused the worst industrial _____ in history.

7. India is trying to make use of their natural resources, such as _____ and iron ore.

On a sheet of paper, write the answer to each question. Use complete sentences.

8. Why did a civil war break out in Pakistan in 1971?

9. What has India's government done to deal with poverty?

10. Before 1950, what was life like for the "untouchables"?

1945–PRESENT   *Changes in Asia and Africa   Chapter 30*   **627**

---

3 Reinforce and Extend

CAREER CONNECTION

During the 18th century, the British East Indian Trading Company sold Indian silks throughout the world. Trade in Indian silks has expanded in modern times to a global textile industry. Nearly every country manufactures textiles. Workers in developing nations such as India and Pakistan may weave fabrics in their homes. In the United States and other highly industrialized nations, textiles are produced in factories. Trained employees oversee the work and run the machinery. The textile industry provides many job opportunities for people of all abilities and educational backgrounds. Have students find out the requirements for a specific career in the textile industry.

Lesson 30–1 Review Answers

1. Sikh 2. Kashmir 3. Bangladesh 4. population 5. Western 6. disaster 7. coal 8. The people of East Pakistan were angry that the central government was located in West Pakistan. 9. The government has taught farmers new methods to increase crops, allowed Western businesses to build factories, and has added programs for economic growth. 10. The untouchables had to live in the poorest villages, were not allowed inside schools, and had to sweep away their footsteps with a broom.

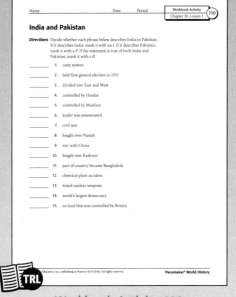

Activity 110   Workbook Activity 110

Lesson at a Glance

Chapter 30 Lesson 2

Overview This lesson describes changes in China following World War II, including the rise of Communism, the Cultural Revolution, and China's acquisition of Hong Kong.

Objectives

- To tell how Mao Zedong and the Communists took over China
- To explain the purpose of communes
- To describe the thinking behind the Cultural Revolution
- To describe how Hong Kong came under Chinese rule

Student Pages 628–633

Teacher's Resource Library TRL

Workbook Activity 111

Activity 111

Modified Activity 111

Vocabulary

commune
corrupt

Have students read the vocabulary words and find their definitions in the text. Ask each student to make a graphic organizer for the terms. The vocabulary term should be written in an oval in the center of the graphic organizer. Important details related to the term should be written in circles around the main oval. Lines should be drawn to link the circles to the main oval. Suggest that students repeat this activity for key concepts throughout the lesson.

PRONUNCIATION GUIDE

Use this list to help students pronounce difficult words in this lesson.

Deng Xiaoping (dung´ shou´ping´)

Myanmar (mī än´ mär)

Kowloon (kou´ lōōn)

Objectives

- To tell how Mao Zedong and the Communists took over China
- To explain the purpose of communes
- To describe the thinking behind the Cultural Revolution
- To describe how Hong Kong came under Chinese rule

Reading Strategy: Questioning

Think about the purpose of this text. Ask yourself what you hope to learn by reading it.

 History Fact
Chiang Kai-shek was the most powerful man in China for more than 20 years.

In the years after World War II, a power struggle was going on in China between two political parties. They were the Nationalists and the Communists.

Who Won the Battle for Power in China?

Back in 1928, Chiang Kai-shek and his Nationalist Party had come to power. Some members of the Nationalist Party believed in Communism. The Communists felt that Chiang showed favor to rich landowners and businesspeople. So the Communists broke away from the Nationalists. In 1927, they took over the city of Shanghai.

Chiang expelled (removed) the Communists from the Nationalist Party. A struggle began between Chinese Nationalists and Chinese Communists. Stalin and the Soviet Union supported the Communists. Stalin encouraged them to win the support of China's factory workers.

However, China's strength did not lie in the city workers. It lay in the farm peasants. A man named Mao Zedong, who had been born a peasant, turned to the peasants for support.

Mao Zedong set up a Communist government in mainland China.

Reading Strategy: Questioning

Answers will vary. Students will likely state that they want to learn more about the changes China experienced from World War II to the present.

 History Fact
Chiang Kai-shek, who is also known as Jiang Jieshi, continued to serve as leader of the Chinese Nationalists in Taiwan until his death in 1975.

Corrupt
Dishonest, evil, selfish

During World War II, the Communists helped defend the peasants of northern China against the Japanese. Mao and the Communists won the peasants' loyalty.

After the war, the Communists and Nationalists continued their struggle for China. There were four years of civil war. The Nationalists had better supplies and a larger army. However, they no longer had the support of the people. Many Nationalist leaders were dishonest, or **corrupt.** They wanted to become rich themselves while the Chinese people went hungry. The Communists divided land and food fairly among the people. In this way, they received the peasants' support.

By 1948, the war had turned in favor of the Communists. Chiang Kai-shek and the Nationalists decided it was time to get out. They left mainland China to live in Taiwan. In 1949, mainland China was taken over by Mao Zedong and the Communists. They called their nation the People's Republic of China.

The Soviet Union was quick to recognize the new government. So were many other nations. Yet the United States refused to recognize the Communist government.

You Decide
Why do you think it took so long for the United States to recognize the People's Republic of China?

The United States recognized the Nationalist government in Taiwan and supported it. Taiwan, calling itself the Republic of China, kept China's seat in the United Nations. In 1971, mainland China replaced Taiwan in the United Nations. In 1972, U.S. president Richard Nixon made an eight-day visit to the People's Republic. In 1979, the United States recognized the People's Republic of China, or mainland China, as the only legal government in China. However, the United States continued many unofficial contacts with Taiwan.

1 Warm-Up Activity

Remind students that India has a large population and struggles to provide enough food for its people. Tell them that China has an even larger population—1.25 billion people—and that in this lesson, they will learn about communes and other solutions used by the Chinese to feed its people.

2 Teaching the Lesson

Have students recall what they learned about Communism in Chapter 27. As they read this lesson, ask them to consider how Communism in Russia differed from Communism in China.

Ask:
- What was the purpose of the Cultural Revolution? (to build Communist loyalty)
- Why did so many peasants support the Communists in China? (The Chinese Nationalist leaders were corrupt, while the Communists divided land and food fairly among the people. Also, during World War II, the Communists helped defend the peasants against the Japanese.)

You Decide
Students might say that the United States was afraid that Communism would spread if it recognized the People's Republic of China. Accept all reasonable responses.

Background Information

Deng Xiaoping made broad changes in agriculture, industry, science, and the military. He encouraged private ownership of businesses and property. He courted foreign investors to help the economy grow. China's standard of living improved, but problems arose as well. The rich became richer and the poor became poorer. Food prices increased, as did rates of crime. Unemployment rose.

The discontent spilled over into universities. In May 1989, some 3,000 students staged a protest in Tiananmen Square. They went on a hunger strike to demand a democratic government. An estimated one million people took to the streets in support of the students. The protest was televised around the world.

In June 1989, the government responded. Soldiers attacked the protesters. Hundreds were killed. Many more were jailed, and then later tortured and killed.

Western countries were horrified, and called for increased human rights in China. The issue remains a point of contention between China and the West today.

Commune
A group of people working or living closely together, often sharing property and tasks

What Was Life Like Under Communist Rule?

More than one-fifth of the population of the world lives in China! Producing enough food to feed more than 1.25 billion people is no simple matter. The Communists knew they had to solve that problem. They took land away from rich farmers. They set up huge farm **communes.** A commune is a group of people working closely together, often sharing property and tasks. The peasants had to work on these communes. Sometimes as many as 10,000 people worked on a single commune. In addition, the government took over industries, built new factories, and trained workers.

The Communists insisted on the support and loyalty of all the people. Workers had to attend meetings where they read aloud from Mao Zedong's writings. They talked about how Mao's ideas could make them better citizens of a better China.

What Was the Cultural Revolution?

Mao and the Communists worried that people might prefer the Old China to the New China. They held meetings to teach people to think the Communist way. Enemies of Communism were punished. They were brainwashed, or forced to accept the Communist way of thought.

For a while, Mao's harsh policies worked. However, China's economy declined for a time. From 1965 to 1969, Mao called his policies a "Cultural Revolution." The Cultural Revolution was supposed to build loyalty for the Communists. Young students, called "Red Guards," became soldiers for Communism. They helped Mao carry out his policies.

Farm production fell. China closed its doors to visitors from the rest of the world. The Chinese leaders wanted to make sure that no anti-Communist ideas could filter in.

Red Guards helped Mao carry out his Communist policies.

After Mao's death in 1976, trade relations between China and the rest of the world improved. Under Deng Xiaoping and other leaders, China went through a period of modernization. In other words, they worked to make China more up-to-date and modern.

Deng was willing to give the Chinese more economic freedom. However, he was not willing to grant political freedom. In the spring of 1989, hundreds of thousands of students gathered in Tiananmen Square in Beijing to demand more democracy. The demonstration was crushed by the army, as tanks rolled through the square. Since then, China and the West have disagreed over China's treatment of protesters and others in the country. China had a fast-growing economy in the 1990s. China has allowed people to own businesses and trade with the West. In 2000, the U.S. Congress voted to give China permanent normal trade relations. Many people in the United States still worried about the lack of freedom and human rights in China.

WORLD CULTURES

The products that we use today, such as CD players and shoes, were likely made in Japan, China, or Korea. Following World War II, the economies of Asian countries have skyrocketed. Japan led the way with the fastest-growing economy of any nation after World War II. More recently, China, India, and Indonesia have seen upswings in their economies. In the beginning, the United States and Europe made up the market for Asian goods. Today, a thriving middle class has developed in many Asian countries. Asians themselves make up the fastest-growing market for Asian products.

Reading Strategy:
Questioning

Answers will vary. Students might mention any of the following: who was involved in the power struggle for China, who won the power struggle, how China changed under Communism, how China changed following Mao Zedong's death, how Hong Kong came under Chinese rule, and how the West views China. Accept all reasonable answers.

GREAT NAMES IN HISTORY

Early in life, Aung San Suu Kyi was inspired by the teachings of Mohandas Gandhi, India's great spiritual and political leader. She even lived in India as a teenager when her mother, who served in the government of independent Burma, was appointed ambassador to India. Suu Kyi went to college in England and then worked at the United Nations in New York. She did not return to Myanmar until 1988. The purpose of the trip was to visit her dying mother. However, Suu Kyi soon became involved in politics. She stayed true to Gandhi's teachings, relying on nonviolent protest to further the cause of peace and democracy in her country.

Reading Strategy:
Questioning
What details are important to understanding what this lesson is about?

GREAT NAMES IN HISTORY

Aung San Suu Kyi

Since 1988, Aung San Suu Kyi has led the fight for democracy in Myanmar (Burma). Leadership seems to run in her family. Her father, Aung San, is called the father of independent Burma.

In 1988, Myanmans protested against military rule. As a result, troops shot or arrested thousands. Aung San spoke out for human rights. She helped the National League for Democracy win 80 percent of the seats in Parliament. The rulers ignored the results and held her prisoner in her own home for six years. In 1991, she won the Nobel Peace Prize. However, the generals still limit her freedom to speak and travel.

How Did Hong Kong Come Under Chinese Rule?

China had to give Hong Kong to Britain in 1842. This was a part of the treaty that ended the Opium War. Britain got the mainland peninsula of Kowloon, a mainland region called the New Territories, and 230 small islands in the South China Sea. These areas became known as Hong Kong. Hong Kong lies off the southeastern coast of China.

After the Communist revolution in China, the population of Hong Kong grew rapidly. This is because people fled there from China. It became an important manufacturing and business center.

China and Britain signed an agreement in 1984. In it, Britain agreed to give up control of Hong Kong in 1997. The agreement stated that Hong Kong would become a protected region. It would also remain a free port. Britain returned Hong Kong to China on July 1, 1997.

Word Bank

commune

democracy

Hong Kong

Nationalists

peasants

population

United States

On a sheet of paper, write the word from the Word Bank to complete each sentence correctly.

1. The political parties that struggled for power after World War II were the _____ and the Communists.

2. The Communists gained strength with loyalty to the _____.

3. In 1949, the _____ did not recognize the Communist government in mainland China.

4. More than one-fifth of the world's _____ lives in China.

5. As many as 10,000 peasants worked at a single _____ to help feed its population.

6. In 1989, hundreds of thousands of students gathered in Tiananmen Square to demand more _____.

7. The area that lies off the southeastern coast of China is called _____.

On a sheet of paper, write the answer to each question. Use complete sentences.

8. What did the Communists do to gain the support and loyalty of their people?

9. Why did Mao Zedong create the "Red Guards"?

10. Why did China have to give Hong Kong to Britain in 1842?

Lesson 30–2 Review Answers
1. Nationalists 2. peasants 3. United States 4. population 5. commune 6. democracy 7. Hong Kong 8. Their workers had to attend meetings to teach people the benefits of Communism. Enemies of Communism were punished. 9. He wanted soldiers for Communism. The guards helped Mao carry out his policies. 10. China had to give Hong Kong to Britain because it was part of the treaty that ended the Opium War.

Name _____ Date ___ Period ___   Activity 111
Chapter 30, Lesson 2

China

Directions Each of the following statements is false. Rewrite the statement on the line so that it is now a true statement.

1. Chiang Kai-shek was the leader of the Communist Party.

2. Mao Zedong got his support from the city workers.

3. Mao Zedong left mainland China to live in Taiwan.

4. The United States still does not recognize the People's Republic of China.

5. Less than one-tenth of the population of the world lives in China.

6. Factory workers live and work in communes.

7. China's economy grew during the Cultural Revolution.

8. Deng Xiaoping gave the Chinese people political freedom.

9. China still does not trade with the West.

10. Great Britain will return Hong Kong to China in 2030.

Pacemaker® World History

Name _____ Date ___ Period ___   Workbook Activity 111
Chapter 30, Lesson 2

China Word Find

Part A Directions Write the correct word from the Word Bank to complete each sentence.

Word Bank
communes
Chiang
Cultural
Mao
Republic
students
Taiwan
Tiananmen
Xiaoping

1. In the 1960s, China went through the _____ Revolution.

2. Deng _____ wanted to make China more modern.

3. _____ Zedong was a Chinese leader.

4. Chinese farmers work on _____.

5. Mainland China is called the People's _____ of China.

6. _____ Kai-shek led the Nationalist Party.

7. In 1948, the Nationalists went to _____.

8. The Red Guard was made up of _____.

9. Students protested against the government in _____ Square.

Part B Directions Use the words from the sentences above to fill in the words in this puzzle. The letters in the box reading down spell out the kind of government in China.

1. _____
2. _____
3. _____
4. _____
5. _____
6. _____
7. _____
8. _____
9. _____

Hidden word: _____

Pacemaker® World History

Activity 111   Workbook Activity 111

Chapter 30 Lesson 3

Overview This lesson describes the three-year conflict commonly known as the Korean War, and discusses North Korea's nuclear plans.

Objectives

- To describe the separation between North and South Korea
- To explain the conflict surrounding North Korea's build up of nuclear weapons

Student Pages 634–636

Teacher's Resource Library

Workbook Activity 112

Activity 112

Modified Activity 112

---

1 | Warm-Up Activity

Show students a map of Korea and surrounding countries. Point out Korea, Japan, Russia, and China. Tell students that geography has influenced history. In Korea's case, its proximity to Japan and China helped shape its history. Note that the United States is not near Korea. Based on what they have learned so far, ask students to infer why the United States was drawn into a conflict over Korea. (Students should recall that the United States was against the spread of Communism, and so they sent troops to support South Korea.)

---

2 | Teaching the Lesson

Ask students how they think world leaders should deal with an unstable country that is acquiring nuclear power. Then have them read this lesson to see how North Korea fared in its negotiations with world leaders over the issue of nuclear arms.

Ask:

- How many years did the Korean War last? (three years)

LESSON 30-3 | Korea

Objectives

- To describe the separation between North and South Korea
- To explain the conflict surrounding North Korea's build up of nuclear weapons

Reading Strategy: Questioning

What do the details of Korea's past tell you about what happened there?

Korea, with its northern border on China, became a hot spot in the world in 1950. Korea had been controlled by the Japanese from 1910 to 1945. In 1945, the country was divided into two parts. North Korea had the support of Soviet Communists. South Korea had American support.

How Did Korea Become Divided Into Two Parts?

In 1950, North Korea suddenly attacked South Korea. The Communists threatened to take over the whole country.

South Korea turned to the United Nations for help. A UN army made up mostly of U.S. soldiers came to South Korea's aid. The UN troops and South Koreans pushed the Communists back, almost to the Chinese border. The Chinese sent 780,000 soldiers to help North Korea.

The U.S.-South Korean troops fought the Chinese-North Korean troops for three years. In 1953, a truce was finally declared. The division between North and South Korea remained. Today the United States supports efforts to reunify Korea. In 2000, North Korea and South Korea held a conference. Later, some family members who had been separated held reunions in the capitals of South Korea and North Korea.

Why Did North Korea Build Up Its Supply of Nuclear Weapons?

For many years, North Korean authorities insisted that the country needed its own nuclear weapons. Otherwise it would have no way to prevent or discourage other nations from attacking it.

- Why did the United States fight a war in Korea? (to stop the spread of Communism)
- What did Korea receive in return for shutting down its main nuclear facility? (approximately $400 million in economic aid, beginning with fuel oil)

Reading Strategy: Questioning

Answers will vary. Students might mention the struggle between China and Japan for Korea. Accept all reasonable answers.

It began building a supply of plutonium, a material used in making nuclear weapons. Then in 2002, North Korea forced UN inspectors looking for weapons out of the country. Leaders from five other nations began meeting with North Korea. They hoped to limit the country's production of nuclear weapons. In 2006, North Korea conducted its first nuclear missile test in eight years.

In February 2007, North Korea signed a deal with the United States and four other nations. It agreed to shut down its main nuclear facility, or factory, within 60 days. The other nations, in return, would send a total of $400 million in economic aid, beginning with fuel oil. This aid would help after severe floods in the late 1990s. The floods had left many North Koreans homeless and hungry. However, world nations became concerned almost immediately. North Korean authorities said the facility was being shut down "temporarily"—or for a short time.

North Korea's test of nuclear weapons drew much protest around the world. Here, protesters from South Korea rally against North Korea's 2006 nuclear missile test.

Background Information

General Douglas MacArthur led UN forces during the Korean War. He favored a drastic method to put an end to the war: drop an atomic bomb on China. This, he reasoned, would cut off supplies to the North Korean and Chinese troops who were fighting side by side. Then U.S. President Harry Truman disagreed, and eventually fired MacArthur over the issue. In the end, a truce was reached. The Korean War goes down in history as the first time the United Nations stopped an attack on a member nation. The war also proved that China was a force to reckon with.

LEARNING STYLES

Body/Kinesthetic
Place students in small groups. Have each group create a papier-mâché or clay model of North and South Korea. Direct students to the library to find physical and topographical maps of the region in atlases. Students should do additional research on the war, and include important features in their models, such as the Yalu River and the 38th parallel of latitude. Have each group present its model to the class. Groups should explain the importance of the features they included in their models. (The Yalu River marked the border between China and North Korea. The 38th parallel divided North Korea and South Korea.)

COMMON ERROR

Students may be confused by the phrase "hot spot," as used in the introductory paragraph of this lesson. Explain that in this context, a hot spot refers to an area that attracts world attention and has the potential to explode into violence—violence that may spill over into other nations.

ELL/ESL STRATEGY

Language Objective:
To improve listening skills

Place ELL students in small groups with students who are proficient in the English language. Make an audiotape of this lesson, or locate the lesson in the Audio Library, and distribute a copy to each group. Tell the groups to listen to the audio, following along in their text as they do. Have them come up with an answer to each subhead question. Encourage them to listen to the audio again to make sure that their answers are correct. If time permits, distribute audio for each lesson, and have students repeat the activity. They can make a list of questions and answers for each lesson to use as a study guide.

3 Reinforce and Extend

Lesson 30–3 Review Answers

1. B. **2** A **3.** C **4.** D. **5.** A **6.** B **7.** South Korea got help from the United Nations. The UN troops pushed the Communists back, almost to the Chinese border. **8.** North Korea had the support of the Soviet Communists. They also got help from the Chinese. The Chinese sent 780,000 soldiers to help North Korea. **9.** Plutonium is used to make nuclear weapons. North Korea was trying to make nuclear weapons to discourage other countries from attacking it. **10.** North Korean authorities said the facility was only going to be shut down for a short period of time. The five nations wanted it shut down permanently.

LESSON 30-3 REVIEW

On a sheet of paper, write the letter of the answer that correctly completes each sentence.

1. Korea was controlled by the _____ from 1910 to 1945.

  A French   **B** Japanese   **C** Chinese   **D** English

2. In 1950, North Korea suddenly attacked _____.

  A South Korea **B** Britain   **C** Japan   **D** China

3. The United Nations created an army made up of _____ soldiers.

  A Japanese   **B** British   **C** U.S.   **D** Vietnamese

4. The fighting in Korea lasted _____ years.

  A 30   **B** eight   **C** four   **D** three

5. North Korean authorities insisted that the country needed _____.

  A nuclear weapons   **C** stronger schools
  B economic growth   **D** more laws

6. Five nations sent aid to North Korea in the late 1990s. It was to help North Korea recover after severe _____.

  A drought   **B** floods   **C** crime   **D** poverty

On a sheet of paper, write the answer to each question. Use complete sentences.

7. How did South Korea defend itself against North Korea?

8. Who helped North Korea in trying to defeat South Korea?

9. Why was North Korea building up a supply of plutonium?

10. In 2007, North Korea signed a deal to shut down their main nuclear facility. Why were some nations concerned about the agreement?

636   *Unit 10 The World Since 1945*

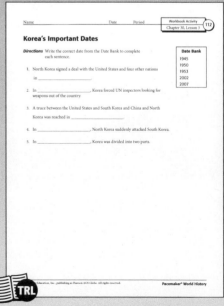

Activity 112   Workbook Activity 112

636   *Unit 10 The World Since 1945*

Japan and Southeast Asia

Objectives

- To name three Southeast Asian countries that gained independence from Japan after the war
- To describe Japan's role in the world economic community since World War II

Reading Strategy: Questioning

As you read, notice the details about Japan and Southeast Asia. What new questions can you ask yourself about this section?

You Decide

Japan is now one of the richest countries in the world. Why do you think Japan became a great industrialized country after its defeat in World War II?

The explosion of the atomic bomb left Japan in shock. Japan surrendered, and World War II was over. Then the Allied forces occupied Japan. U.S. general Douglas MacArthur was the supreme commander. His job was to build a democracy in Japan.

A new democratic constitution, written in 1946, gave power to an elected prime minister. It also gave women the right to vote. Japan would be allowed to keep its emperor, but he would have no power. In 1951, the government was put back into the hands of the Japanese. The Allied occupation had ended.

The new Japanese constitution stated that Japan would not maintain a strong military. As a result, the Japanese turned from a policy of war to one of industrial and economic growth.

What Southeast Asian Countries Gained Independence from Japan?

Japan took over much of Southeast Asia during World War II. Before the war all of the area, except Thailand, was colonized by European nations. After the war, anticolonial feelings were strong. The nations of Southeast Asia wanted to be free.

Some countries gained independence easily. Others had to struggle. When nations such as the Philippines, Burma (now Myanmar), Indonesia, Malaysia, and Singapore became independent, they all faced problems. In many of them, there were bitter civil wars.

Reading Strategy: Questioning

Students might mention the following questions: What role did the Japanese emperor have after World War II? What kind of problems did the newly independent Southeast nations face?

You Decide

Sample answer: The Japanese put the war behind them and instead focused on the future. The country also devised innovative ways to overcome the problems it faced, such as a lack of land and of resources.

Lesson at a Glance

Chapter 30 Lesson 4

Overview This lesson explains how Japan changed its focus from imperialism to economics, and describes the fate of several countries it once ruled.

Objectives

- To name three Southeast Asian countries that gained independence from Japan after the war
- To describe Japan's role in the world economic community since World War II

Student Pages 637–639

Teacher's Resource Library

Workbook Activity 113

Activity 113

Modified Activity 113

Vocabulary

electronics
invest
pollution

Ask students to use the glossary to look up the definition of the vocabulary words in this lesson. Then have them write the definitions in their own words. Tell students to write a paragraph that incorporates each vocabulary word. Ask volunteers to share their paragraphs with the class.

1 Warm-Up Activity

Ask students what they think of when they hear the word *pollution*. (Students will likely mention types of air pollution, such as smog, or water pollution.) Tell them that many industrialized nations have had to address pollution problems. Developing nations find themselves facing the same problems as they move toward a more industrialized economy.

Remind students that Germany was very bitter following World War I. This bitterness led, in part, to the rise of the Nazis and World War II. As they read this lesson, ask students to consider Japan's response to losing World War II. How did it differ from Germany's response following World War I?

Ask:

- What countries gained independence from Japan? (the Philippines, Burma, Indonesia, Malaysia, and Singapore)
- How is Japan affected by its geography? (It has little land to grow food and little natural resources, so it must depend on imports.)
- What was the goal of the trade agreement signed by Japan and the United States in 1990? (to make it easier for foreign countries to do business in Japan)

Background Information

Japan's economy is thriving; globally, it ranks second only to the United States' economy. Economists site several reasons for Japan's economic health in the years since World War II. The Japanese government works hand-in-hand with corporations to plan economic growth. The Japanese people save their money in banks, and the banks, in turn, invest heavily in businesses. In addition, Japan has a well-educated, skilled work force.

Electronic
Powered by electricity

Pollution
Waste materials in the air or water

Invest
To put money into something with the hope of making more money

What Is Japan's Role in the World Economic Community?

Today Japan has become a world leader in industry. Japan is one of the world's largest steel producers. It is the second largest manufacturer, or maker, of automobiles and **electronics** equipment. It is also a leading shipbuilder. This is quite an achievement since Japan has few natural resources of its own. The country's industrial success depends on trade, the import of raw materials, and the export of finished products.

Japan is a small, crowded country. There is little room to grow food. Again, Japan depends on imports, bringing in at least 30 percent of its food. Japan has also had to deal with problems caused by overcrowding, such as lack of housing. Another problem Japan faces is **pollution,** which is when waste materials get into the air and water. Despite these problems, Japan has made amazing progress.

Japan's economic success brought negative remarks from other nations. The Japanese were able to **invest** heavily in industry because of their very low defense budget.

Japan, a small, crowded country, faces pollution and lack of housing.

During the 1980s, some countries began to complain that the competition from Japanese exports was hurting their own industry. They also said that Japan was discouraging the import of foreign products. In 1981, Japan agreed to limit its exports of automobiles to Canada, the United States, and West Germany. It also began to remove some restrictions, or limits, on imports. In 1990, Japan and the United States signed a trade agreement. This made it easier for foreign companies to do business in Japan. By the late 1990s, Japan, like other world powers over the years, had trade and economic difficulties.

ELL/ESL STRATEGY

Language Objective:
To gather information from multiple sources

Place students in small groups. The groups will research how different countries deal with pollution. Each group should choose a different country to research. Encourage students to consider the countries of any international students in the class. Tell students to first research the sources of air, water, and land pollution in their country. They should then find out how the country addresses each type of pollution. What laws are in place? What programs encourage the reduction of pollution? Students should organize their information into an oral presentation with visual aids. After all groups have presented their reports, have students evaluate the different ways countries deal with pollution. As a class, decide which ways seem most effective.

REVIEW

Word Bank

atomic bomb
automobiles
democracy
free
imports
industry
invest

On a sheet of paper, write the word from the Word Bank to complete each sentence correctly.

1. The explosion of the _____ left Japan in shock.

2. Douglas MacArthur's job after the war was to build a(n) _____ in Japan.

3. Japan is now a world leader in _____.

4. Japan is the second largest maker of _____ and electronics equipment in the world.

5. Japan is a small, crowded country with few natural resources. Thus, it relies heavily on _____.

6. The Japanese have been able to _____ a lot in industry. This is because they spend very little on national defense.

7. After World War II, the other Southeast Asian countries wanted to be _____ from Japan.

On a sheet of paper, write the answer to each question. Use complete sentences.

8. What new laws did the Japanese constitution include?

9. What are some problems that Japan faces?

10. Why did Japan agree (in 1981) to limit its exports to Canada, the United States, and West Germany?

COMMON ERROR

Given Japan's role in World War II and the ban on a strong military in its constitution, students may not understand why some nations resent that Japan spends so little on defense. Students might think that Japan has no say in the matter. In reality, Japan can amend its constitution, and the issue of expanding its military force has arisen several times. It is a particularly relevant issue today in Japan, as North Korea continues to show signs of developing nuclear arms.

IN THE COMMUNITY

Suggest that students interview a community leader to learn how the community invests in local businesses. For example, a banker can discuss loans and lines of credit. The director of the small business development center can explain programs that aid small businesses. A county commissioner might talk about incentives given to businesses to encourage them to locate in the area. Students can choose whom they would like to interview, but the interview itself should focus on business investments.

Lesson 30–4 Review Answers

1. atomic bomb **2.** democracy **3.** industry **4.** automobiles **5.** imports **6.** invest **7.** free **8.** The constitution gave power to an elected prime minister. Women were allowed to vote. Japan would not maintain a strong military. **9.** There is very little room to grow food. They depend on imports. There is also pollution and a lack of housing. **10.** Other countries were complaining that the Japanese exports were hurting their own industries.

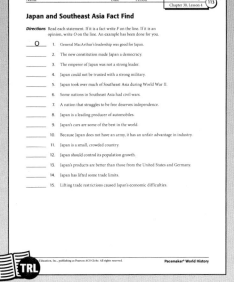

Activity 113   Workbook Activity 113

Lesson at a Glance

Chapter 30 Lesson 5

Overview This lesson describes the creation of North and South Vietnam, American involvement in the Vietnam War, and current relations between Vietnam and other countries.

Objectives

- To describe how Vietnam was divided
- To explain U.S. involvement in Vietnam and why so many Americans were against it
- To explain why there were so many refugees after the capital of South Vietnam fell

Student Pages 640–645

Teacher's Resource Library

Workbook Activity 114

Activity 114

Modified Activity 114

....

Vocabulary

domino theory
guerilla
refugee

Write the three vocabulary terms on the board. Have students locate the terms in the lesson. Have them brainstorm a list of related words for each vocabulary term. Examples for domino theory might include Communism, nations, U.S. policy, and South Vietnam. Write students' responses on the board. Keep the words on the board as you teach this lesson to help students understand how the vocabulary terms relate to the content of the lesson.

PRONUNCIATION GUIDE

Use this list to help students pronounce difficult words in this lesson.

Ho Chi Minh (hō´ chē´ min´)

Khmer Rouge (kmâr´ rōōzh´)

Objectives

- To describe how Vietnam was divided
- To explain U.S. involvement in Vietnam and why so many Americans were against it
- To explain why there were so many refugees after the capital of South Vietnam fell

Reading Strategy:
Questioning

What do you already know about Vietnam?

In the 1800s, France took over an area of Southeast Asia called Indochina. Indochina was made up of the countries of Vietnam, Laos, and Cambodia. During World War II, Japan took Southeast Asia from the French. Then France regained Southeast Asia after the war.

How Was Vietnam Divided?

Southeast Asia was not anxious to return to French rule. Nationalists and Communists had gained some support there. In 1946, the fighting began. The Vietnamese Communists wanted to force the French out of Vietnam. The French set up a government in the South. The Communists, under their leader, Ho Chi Minh, set up a government in the North. The Communists defeated the French in 1954.

Then a conference was held in Geneva, Switzerland, to decide what would happen next. Vietnamese Communists and representatives from France, Cambodia, Laos, China, Britain, the United States, and the Soviet Union all came to that conference. They made their decision. Vietnam was divided into two zones. Ho Chi Minh and the Communists would continue to rule the North. South Vietnam was supposed to hold an election to choose its own form of government.

But a free election never took place. Ngo Dinh Diem took leadership and refused to hold elections. Meanwhile, North Vietnam grew stronger with the support of Communist China and the Soviet Union. The political situation in South Vietnam remained unsettled.

Reading Strategy:
Questioning

Students might know that Vietnam is located in Southeast Asia. They probably know that a war was fought there, and that Americans were deeply divided over whether the United States should be involved in the war. Accept all reasonable answers.

Guerilla
One of a group of fighters who are not part of a regular army, and who usually make surprise raids behind enemy lines

Domino theory
The belief that if one country became Communist, neighbors would fall to Communism too

The Vietcong, Communist **guerilla** fighters, began an attempt to take over South Vietnam in 1957. Guerillas are a group of fighters who are not part of a regular army. In 1963, South Vietnam's leader, Diem, was assassinated. The country's problems increased. The government changed hands nine times in three years.

Why Did the United States Get Involved?

The Soviet Union and China continued to give aid to North Vietnam. In the 1960s, the U.S. government sent aid to South Vietnam because it believed in the **domino theory.** If dominoes are stood in a line together, the fall of one domino will knock down the others. The domino theory was the idea that if one country became Communist, neighbors would fall to the Communists, too.

At first, the United States sent money and supplies. Then in 1965, U.S. President Lyndon B. Johnson sent more than 3,500 U.S. marines to Da Nang, South Vietnam. They were the first United States combat troops to join the fight. Thousands more would follow. By 1969, there were more than 543,000 U.S. troops in Vietnam.

Why Were So Many Americans Against U.S. Involvement in Vietnam?

Many Americans did not want the United States to get into the war in Southeast Asia. When American soldiers began dying in Vietnamese jungles, the protests grew stronger. Hundreds of thousands of people marched against the war, in cities all across America. "Bring home our troops!" they shouted.

However, the war went on. More and more Americans were killed or wounded. The Vietcong remained strong. There did not seem to be any end in sight.

Show students a photograph of protestors marching against the war in Vietnam. Point out that many of the protestors were young people, not much older than the students in class. Ask students if there are any issues that they feel strongly about—so strongly that they would take to the streets in protest. During the discussion that follows, encourage students to respect each other's views.

2 | **Teaching the Lesson**

Students might know someone who fought in the Vietnam War, or who protested against American involvement in the war. Ask them to share what they have learned about the war. Then have students read this lesson to find out more about the war in Vietnam.

Ask:

- What was the domino theory? (The belief that if one country became Communist, others would too.)
- What risks did refugees face when escaping by boat? (Sample answer: The boat could fall apart or sink. The refugees could drown. The refugees could get lost or experience harsh weather, winds, or storms at sea.)

COMMON ERROR

Some students might not understand the analogy between dominoes and the spread of Communism. Bring a set of dominoes into class. Set up the dominoes, and demonstrate how knocking down one domino causes the others to fall. Afterwards, have students explain the domino theory in their own words to be certain they understand the concept.

Background Information

When many Americans think of Vietnam, they think of a war-torn, tropical nation. But most Vietnamese have put the war behind them. They are anxious to rebuild their nation and its economy. Since 1993, Vietnam has been the name of a country, not of a war.

In 1976, North and South Vietnam were unified under Communism. Though now under one government, divisions still remain between northern and southern Vietnam. The land itself differs from north to south. The South is lush and tropical with huge expanses of rice paddies. The North is cooler. Violent typhoons are common.

The seat of political power is in the North, but the South powers the economy. U.S.-built airports, highways, and ports encourage development in the South. The average yearly income in the South's Ho Chi Minh City is about $480, more than twice the national average. Signs of foreign investment and economic hope are everywhere in Ho Chi Minh City. For example, in recent years, trade has increased between the United States and Vietnam. In 2000, the two countries signed a new trade agreement.

Nearly half of the people in Vietnam have been born since the war ended and the country was unified. This new generation of people is looking ahead to their nation's future.

You Decide
Some students might believe that we did not have the right to get involved in another country's affairs. Other students might argue that we had to try to stop the spread of Communism. Accept all reasonable answers, but be sure students back up their opinions with historic facts.

History Fact
Show students pictures of the fall of Saigon, and the chaos that ensued as people attempted to leave the city. The photographs are particularly relevant given the United States' later involvement in the Middle East.

You Decide
Antiwar protesters felt that the war in Vietnam was a matter that should be fought and decided by the Vietnamese themselves. Do you think they were right to protest against the war? Why or why not?

History Fact
As the Communists closed in on Saigon, the remaining Americans were forced to flee the city.

By the end of the decade, the United States was a nation in turmoil, or unrest. The growing antiwar movement had helped to touch off a general youth protest movement. The middle-class youth of America were questioning and protesting against all the values of their parents.

Also during the 1960s, there had been a series of assassinations that had shocked the nation. President John F. Kennedy, in 1963, and his brother Robert F. Kennedy, in 1968, had been shot to death. So had African American leaders Malcolm X, in 1965, and Martin Luther King, Jr., in 1968. This was the last straw for many African Americans. They were becoming angry and frustrated at not being able to share in the success of white America. Now feeling that they had nothing to lose, they took their cause to the streets. Rioting occurred in many U.S. cities.

In 1973, the United States decided to take its troops out of Vietnam. About 58,000 Americans had been killed, and about 365,000 had been wounded. And the war had not been won.

How Did People Escape Communist Rule?

In 1975, Saigon, the capital of South Vietnam, fell to the Vietcong. The name of the city was changed to Ho Chi Minh City. Vietnam was united as a Communist country in 1976. Then the "dominoes" fell. Communists took power in Laos and Cambodia.

The Communist rulers of Cambodia, called the *Khmer Rouge,* murdered millions of Cambodians. The situation in Cambodia became very unstable. In 1978, Vietnam invaded Cambodia. For the next 10 years, Vietnam had control of the country. In 1989, Vietnam withdrew from Cambodia, giving in to pressure from the Soviet Union. The Khmer Rouge lost its power. National elections were held in 1998.

Refugee
A person who flees his or her country or home

Many people in Vietnam, Laos, and Cambodia did not want to live under Communist rule. They fled their homelands. These people, called **refugees**, escaped by boat. They became known as "boat people"—people who no longer had a home. A large number came to the United States. Some died making their escapes. All suffered hardships along their way. Today many boat people have made successful lives in the United States.

Reading Strategy: Questioning

Study the photographs as you read. Ask yourself how they relate to what you are reading.

Vietnamese refugees wanted freedom from Communism.

What Is Vietnam Like Today?

The Communist government of Vietnam continued through aid from the party's Central Committee. When the Soviet Union ended, much of that aid stopped. The government had to accept the development of private business to help the failing economy. The Vietnamese tried to encourage foreign investment in the country. The United States insisted on an updated account of American soldiers imprisoned or missing in Vietnam.

Reading Strategy: Questioning

Students will likely state that the photograph helps them better understand the plight of refugees. Discuss what questions students might have about the photo, and how they could go about finding the answers to their questions.

ELL/ESL STRATEGY

Language Objective: *To write a descriptive paragraph based on a visual*

Ask students to examine the photograph on page 643. Tell them to write a paragraph that describes the photograph. Before they write, give them the following guidance:

• Suggest that they divide the photo into sections and study each section. They should write a few words describing the people, objects, and activities in the photo.

• Next, they should describe their overall impression of the photo. What are the people doing? How are they accomplishing their goal?

• Based on their observations, tell students to infer how the people feel. Are they happy? Worried? Sad? Have them look for clues such as facial expressions or body language.

As a last step, students should use the information they have compiled to write a descriptive paragraph about the photograph. Ask volunteers to share their work with the class.

3   Reinforce and Extend

TEACHER ALERT

Students might not realize that veterans of the Vietnam War were treated differently than veterans of other wars. Explain that some Americans disapproved of their country's involvement in the war. Young people marched in antiwar demonstrations. Some young men left the country to avoid taking part in the war. Returning soldiers sometimes felt the brunt of this resentment against the Vietnam War. They were not greeted with parades and a hero's welcome when they came home. By and large, Vietnam veterans felt they were treated unfairly. Partly as an attempt to make amends, in 1982, the government dedicated the Vietnam Veterans Memorial in Washington, D.C.

WORLD CULTURES

 Many residents of Laos, called Hmong, helped U.S. troops during the Vietnam War. When Saigon fell, numerous Hmong soldiers and their families fled to America. The Hmong are skilled farmers—skills they learned from cultivating the mountainous regions of Southeast Asia. Thus, many Hmong opted to settle in rural areas, such as California's Central Valley. Others had to learn new trades. All Hmong faced the challenge of adapting to their new culture, while maintaining traditional ways. Their children are taught Hmong values and history to help them to remember their identity and to instill a sense of ethnic pride.

The Vietnamese gave in. In 1995, American firms began operating in Vietnam. Many Western nations opened factories and businesses in Vietnam, beginning in the late 1990s. The United States signed a long-term trade agreement with Vietnam. The Communist government wants to remain in control even though it allows private business in its country. In June 2005, Phan Van Khai was the first Vietnamese leader to visit the American White House.

On a sheet of paper, write the letter of the answer that correctly completes each sentence.

1. In 1946, the Vietnamese wanted to force the _____ out of Vietnam.

   A United States   **B** French   **C** Japanese   **D** Chinese

2. After the conference in Geneva, Vietnam was divided into _____ zones.

   A six   **B** four   **C** three   **D** two

3. North Vietnam grew stronger with support from Communist China and _____

   A Japan   **B** the United States   **C** the Soviet Union   **D** Africa

4. In the 1960s, the U.S. government sent aid to South Vietnam. This is because it believed in _____.

   A building leadership   **C** helping the poor
   B the domino theory   **D** expanding borders

5. By 1969, there were more than _____ U.S. troops in Vietnam.

   A 543,000   **B** 780,000   **C** 220,000   **D** 43,000

6. The United States decided to take its troops out of Vietnam in _____.

   A 1969   **B** 1972   **C** 1973   **D** 1978

7. To help the failing economy, Vietnam's Communist government had to accept the development of _____.

   A communes   **C** natural resources
   B a stronger military   **D** private business

On a sheet of paper, write the answer to each question. Use complete sentences.

8. Why did a free election never take place in South Vietnam?

9. How did Americans protest the war in Vietnam?

10. Why did the United States think South Vietnam would fall to Communism?

1945–PRESENT   *Changes in Asia and Africa*   Chapter 30   **645**

Lesson 30–5 Review Answers
1. B **2.** D **3.** C **4.** B **5.** A **6.** C **7.** D
8. Ngo Dinh Diem took leadership and refused to hold elections.
9. Hundreds of thousands of people marched against the war, in cities all across America. **10.** North Vietnam had a strong, united Communist Party who took over power in Laos and Cambodia. Because of this, they thought that South Vietnam would fall to Communism, too.

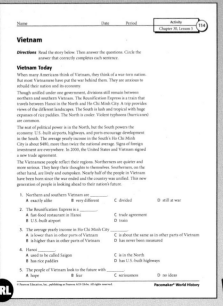

Activity 114

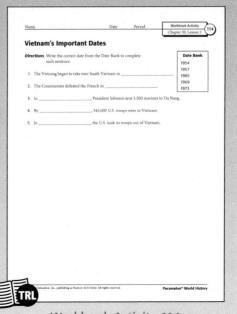

Workbook Activity 114

Chapter 30 Lesson 6

Overview This lesson describes the new African nations formed after World War II and the problems these nations face.

Objectives

- To describe the development of former colonies in Africa after World War II
- To explain the effects of apartheid inside South Africa
- To name three problems Africa faces today

Student Pages 646–654

Teacher's Resource Library

  Workbook Activity 115

  Activity 115

  Modified Activity 115

Vocabulary

apartheid	minority
curfew	repeal
drought	sanction
famine	standard of living
majority	starvation

Have each student look up the definitions of the vocabulary words in the text. Tell students to make a matching game using the words. Students should make a two-column chart. Suggest that they write the vocabulary words in the first column, and the definitions of the words in scrambled order in the second column. Have students exchange charts and complete one another's matching game.

PRONUNCIATION GUIDE

Use this list to help students pronounce difficult words in this lesson.

Idi Amin (ē′dē ämēn′)

Rwanda (rōō än′də)

Darfur (där foor′)

Africa

Objectives

- To describe the development of former colonies in Africa after World War II
- To explain the effects of apartheid inside South Africa
- To name three problems Africa faces today

Reading Strategy:
Questioning

Think about the purpose of this text. Ask yourself what you hope to learn by reading this lesson.

During the 19th century, Africa had been divided into European-ruled colonies. In 1945, at the end of World War II, most of Africa remained under European rule. Only the countries of South Africa, Ethiopia, Liberia, and Egypt were not. Many Africans had joined the armies of their European colonizers during the war. When they returned to Africa, they wanted independence.

How Did the African Colonies Gain Freedom?

The years after 1945 saw European colonies in Africa gain freedom, one by one. Some won their independence peacefully. For other nations, such as Algeria, freedom came only through struggle and revolt.

Several colonies ruled by the British gained independence during the 1950s. Sudan, the largest nation in Africa, won freedom from Britain in 1956. Some of the free nations changed their names. When the Gold Coast won its freedom in 1957, it became Ghana.

Kenya was an African nation that had to struggle for independence from Britain. A rebellion by a group known as the *Mau Mau* lasted from 1952 until 1956. Jomo Kenyatta was their leader. He was thrown in jail in 1953. Britain granted independence to Kenya in 1963. Kenyatta became the leader of the new, free nation. In the 1990s, Kenya suffered unemployment and conflict within the country. In 1998, the U.S. embassy in Nairobi was bombed.

Reading Strategy:
Questioning

Answers will vary. Students will likely want to learn more about the newly independent nations in Africa. Accept all reasonable answers.

Starvation
The condition of dying from not having enough food to eat

Famine
A time when crops do not grow and there is no food

Drought
A long period of time without much rain

Minority
A smaller number, less than half

Sanction
An action taken by one nation against another for breaking international law

 History Fact
In April 2000, Ethiopia's president Robert Mugabe introduced a new way to divide land. Violence against white farmers resulted. White people hold 70 percent of the land in Ethiopia, although they make up only 1 percent of the population.

What Problems Did Freedom Bring?

Freedom did not always mean an end to problems and unrest. The new nations had troubles of their own. In 1967, the eastern part of Nigeria separated and became a country called Biafra. This led to civil war. With the war came **starvation** (dying because of a shortage of food), disease, and death. Biafra was defeated by the Nigerian government in 1970. As a separate country, Biafra no longer existed.

Problems plagued Uganda when General Idi Amin took over the independent government in 1971. Amin arrested and executed anyone he thought was against him. Finally, the people revolted. In 1979, they forced Amin from power. Civil wars and military conflict have also taken place in Angola, Ethiopia, Rwanda, Sudan, and other countries. In Ethiopia, this conflict contributed to a **famine** that killed about one million people in the 1980s. Famine is a time when crops do not grow and there is no food. Again, in 2000, Ethiopia was threatened with famine after a three-year **drought**. A drought is a long period of time without rain.

How Was Zimbabwe Formed?

Independence did not bring an end to racial prejudice in some new African nations. Sometimes those nations had more problems with the new governments than with the European rulers. When Rhodesia gained independence from Britain in 1965, black Africans had no voice in government. Even though they were smaller in number, a white **minority** ruled for 15 years.

Britain wanted black Rhodesians to have rights. However, the new white rulers said no. Britain asked the United Nations to place **sanctions** on Rhodesia. A sanction is an action taken by one nation against another for breaking international law. Because of this request for a sanction, black revolutionaries began a guerilla war.

Ask students if they have a curfew. Discuss the purpose of curfews for students in elementary and secondary schools. (Curfews help parents to keep their children safe.) Explain that the South African government imposed a curfew on blacks in the decades during apartheid. Have students infer the purpose of this curfew. (to control blacks)

History Fact
Ask students if they think it is fair for 1 percent of a nation's population to own 70 percent of its land. (Most students will likely say no.) Have students discuss how they would address the inequity. What measures would they take if they were a part of the government? How could they ensure that these measures would be implemented peacefully?

2 Teaching the Lesson

Ask students to study the map on page 650. Point out that each African nation has a different physical landscape, as well as a unique culture. Tell students to read this lesson to learn more about modern Africa.

Ask:

- Look at the map on page 650. What country is farthest south? (South Africa)

- What were the apartheid laws in South Africa? (Races were separated by where they could live, what property they could own, and what businesses they could run. There were curfews and separate facilities for blacks.)

- What helped to bring about the end of apartheid in South Africa? (sanctions and other pressures from the United States and other countries of the world)

- What are some problems African nations face today? (poverty, disease, food shortages and starvation, lack of education and hospitals, and civil wars)

Background Information

Jomo Kenyatta was called Johnstone Kamau as a child. Born in Kenya in 1890, he went to a school run by Scottish missionaries. By adulthood, he was dedicated to working for black rule in Kenya. He joined a political group that wanted to end British colonial rule. Frustrated by the lack of progress, Kenyatta traveled to England in 1931 to further the cause of Kenyan independence. While in England he changed his name to Jomo, which translates as "burning spear." In 1946, Kenyatta returned home to continue fighting for Kenyan freedom. He was jailed, but not vanquished. In 1963, Kenya finally became independent, and Kenyatta became the first president of the country he had dedicated his life to helping.

Majority
A greater number, more than half

Apartheid
The separation of races based mainly on skin color

Curfew
A time after which certain people cannot be on the streets

 You Decide
What do you think were the worst aspects of apartheid?

In 1980, Rhodesia's first black **majority** government finally came to power through a general election. (It was a majority government because there was a greater number of blacks in Rhodesia.) The new government officially changed the nation's name. Rhodesia became Zimbabwe, an ancient African name for that part of the continent.

What Effects Did Apartheid Have on South Africa?

Of all the independent countries in Africa, South Africa was ruled by a white minority for the longest period of time. It was ruled by *Afrikaners* for many years. They were descendants of Dutch colonists who began settling in South Africa as early as 1652. The Afrikaners believe that the country belongs to them. They helped win South Africa's independence from Britain in 1910.

The Afrikaners wanted to keep white people in control. So in 1948, they set up a policy of **apartheid,** or separation of races. They passed laws to separate people according to race. By law, people of certain races can live, own property, or run businesses only in certain zones.

Curfews determined the time black people had to be off the streets of South Africa. Separate trains, beaches, schools, and other facilities were provided for blacks and whites. Laws did nothing to stop whites from getting the best facilities and blacks the worst.

Many people in South Africa and around the world were strongly against apartheid. However, many South Africans who protested were arrested, and apartheid continued.

During the 1980s, the United States and other countries placed sanctions on South Africa. The white South African government now came under growing pressure to do something about ending apartheid.

In 1990, South African president F.W. de Klerk decided to "unban" the African National Congress (ANC).

You Decide
Some students might feel that the curfews were the worst aspects of apartheid. Others might mention the laws that dictated where people could live. As students discuss the issue, stress that there is no right or wrong answer. However, explain that opinions should be based on facts.

Signs such as this were common in South Africa during apartheid.

Repeal
To cancel; put an end to

This meant that the ANC, a black anti-apartheid political party, would now be legal. De Klerk also released the jailed leader of the ANC, Nelson Mandela. Both leaders began working together on a difficult task. They had to find a way to end apartheid that would be acceptable to both blacks and whites.

In 1990 and 1991, the South African government **repealed,** or ended, its apartheid laws. No longer was separation of hotels, restaurants, and public places required by law. No longer could laws determine where a person could live. Nelson Mandela, as well as other anti-apartheid leaders, looked forward to the day when the black majority would be heard in government. A constitution giving nonwhites full voting rights was completed in 1994. After the repeal of the apartheid laws, countries around the world lifted most of their sanctions against South Africa.

LEARNING STYLES

Interpersonal/Group Learning

Place students in small groups. Have each group research Bishop Desmond Tutu and develop a skit about a different period in his life. One skit could focus on Tutu protesting against apartheid. A second skit could focus on his role as a leader while imprisoned. A third skit could show Tutu accepting the Nobel Peace Prize. A fourth skit could cover his time as president of South Africa. Students can play various roles in the skits, such as Tutu, other anti-apartheid leaders, and Nobel committee members. Set aside time for each group to perform its skit for the class.

650 *Unit 10 The World Since 1945*

LEARNING STYLES

Logical/Mathematical

Using the map on page 650 as a guide, have students work in small groups to create a bar graph that shows the populations of different African nations. Each group should research a different set of African nations. Tell students to plot the names of the countries on the horizontal axis and the population of the countries on the vertical axis. Display students' graphs around the classroom. Afterwards, discuss any trends or patterns in the graphs.

ELL/ESL STRATEGY

Language Objective:
To identify the main ideas and supporting details in the text

Partner each ELL student with a student who is proficient in English. Ask the pairs to read this lesson together. Tell them to write a brief answer to each subhead question. Suggest that students work cooperatively to identify the main idea in each section, and to look for supporting details in the text that follows. Let each pair take turns sharing their work with the class.

3 Reinforce and Extend

COMMON ERROR

Students might think all African nations are rural and undeveloped. Show them photographs of urban centers in different African nations. Explain that many Africans are moving to the cities in search of jobs. Rapid urbanization, which occurs when the growth of a city outstrips its ability to provide services to people, is one of Africa's most pressing problems.

African Nations Become Independent

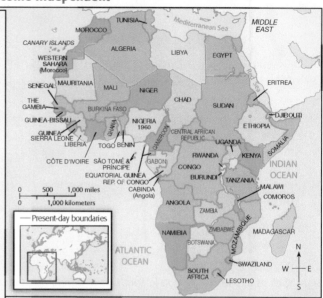

Year of Independence	
Algeria	1962
Angola	1975
Benin	1960
Botswana	1966
Burkina Faso	1960
Burundi	1962
Cameroon	1960
Central African Republic	1960
Chad	1960
Comoros	1975
Congo	1960
Côte D'Ivoire	1960
Djibouti	1977
Egypt	1922
Equatorial Guinea	1968
Eritrea	1993
Ethiopia	1941
Gabon	1960
Ghana	1957
Guinea	1958
Guinea-Bissau	1974
Kenya	1963
Lesotho	1966
Liberia	1847
Libya	1951
Madagascar	1960
Malawi	1964
Mali	1960
Mauritania	1960
Morocco	1956
Mozambique	1975
Namibia	1990
Niger	1960
Nigeria	1960
Rep. of Congo	1960
Rwanda	1962
São Tomé & Principe	1975
Senegal	1960
Sierra Leone	1961
Somalia	1960
South Africa	1910
Sudan	1956
Swaziland	1968
Tanzania	1961
The Gambia	1965
Togo	1960
Tunisia	1956
Uganda	1962
Zambia	1964
Zimbabwe	1980

MAP STUDY

1. What are two countries that became independent in 1960?
2. What are two countries that became independent in 1962?

Change does not often come easily. There were many South Africans who resisted the end of apartheid. However, change did come. A new constitution protected the rights of all South Africans. In 1994, Nelson Mandela became the president of South Africa. He served until 1999, when he chose not to run for reelection.

MAP STUDY

Answers:

1. Any two of the following: Benin, Burkina Faso, Cameroon, Central African Republic, Chad, Congo, Côte D'Ivoire, Gabon, Madagascar, Mali, Mauritania, Niger, Nigeria, Republic of Congo, Senegal, Somalia, Togo

2. Any two of the following: Algeria, Burundi, Rwanda, Uganda

South Africans celebrate the end of apartheid together.

Reading Strategy:
Questioning

Think again about the purpose of the text. Ask yourself, "Am I learning what I expected to learn when I began reading?"

There have been other political changes in South Africa, but they often came slowly. A conflict dating back to 1915 came to an end. In that year, South Africa took its neighbor, Namibia, away from Germany. For the next 75 years, South Africa ruled Namibia. The United Nations declared South Africa's rule of Namibia to be illegal. Black nationalists fought to rule their own country. In 1990, Namibia became independent.

Why Were So Many People Killed in Sudan?

Sudan is a large African country south of Egypt. Most of its people are native black Sudanese. For years the country has been controlled by the Arabic National Islamic Front. In 2003, native rebel groups began attacking government targets in Darfur, a western area of Sudan. They were protesting treatment by the government. The Janjaweed is a military group sponsored by the government. This group began attacking rebels as well as innocent civilians. More than 200,000 Sudanese were killed and more than two million were left homeless. Thousands of women and girls were sexually assaulted. Many have been taken as slaves by Janjaweed fighters.

AT HOME

Many large human rights groups have global memberships. Students can learn about local branches of these groups by conducting research on the Internet, or by searching through the phone book. Tell students to work with a family member to compile a list of groups in the area that work for human rights. Students can also include social service agencies in their lists. Examples might include homeless shelters or senior citizen centers. Students can write or email the organization of their choice, asking for more information. Students can also conduct phone interviews of local human rights leaders. Ask students to share their research with the class.

Reading Strategy:
Questioning

Have students refer back to their answers to the Reading Strategy question on page 646. Have them list the things they have learned about Africa thus far. Then have them compare this list to the things they hoped to learn at the beginning of the lesson. There may be discrepancies in the lists. Point out that some information might not be included in the text, but it can be found by conducting additional research.

TEACHER ALERT

The section titled "Why Were So Many People Killed in Sudan?" contains sensitive information concerning woman and girls who were sexually assaulted or taken as slaves by Janjaweed fighters. This information may not be age-appropriate for some students in the class. Use your discretion when teaching this section, and decide beforehand how you will address students' concerns.

ONLINE CONNECTION

 Students can gain additional information by accessing the following Web site:

www.agsglobepmwh.com/page652

(This site contains a variety of media pertaining to Africa, including slides, photographs, music, and documents.)

Many Sudanese fled to neighboring Chad, and that country was drawn into the fighting. Raids by Janjaweed into Chad have left many thousands of people from Chad homeless too.

Government representatives promised to give native Sudanese a greater representation in the government. United Nations and African Union groups have made unsuccessful attempts to bring peace to Sudan. Even into 2007, more than 14,000 aid workers from UN organizations fear for their lives as the fighting around them continues.

What Is Africa Like Today?

At one time, Africa was mistakenly called the "Dark Continent." To outsiders, it was an unexplored land of mystery. Later, it became a land to be owned, and it was divided up among strong European countries. Then World War II ended the days of European-ruled colonies in Africa. The new nations of Africa, however, continue to face serious problems such as poverty, disease, and food shortages. Many areas lack schools, hospitals, and medical equipment.

Severe droughts have added to Africa's food shortages. During the 1980s, many Africans starved to death in the worst drought in the continent's history. The death toll was especially high in Ethiopia.

In recent years, drought and civil war left over one million Africans starving in the tiny nation of Somalia. Since 1960, various Somali warlords had battled for control of parts of the country. Their armies blocked attempts to get food to starving people. In December 1992, the United States and the UN approved a plan to aid the Somalis. U.S. troops led an international force to Somalia. Soon after, UN forces left because of the fighting.

Standard of living

A way to judge how well a person or family is living

After continued violence and food shortages in Somalia, a peace agreement was signed in January 2004. In August of that same year, Somalia got its first legislature in 13 years. Despite the new parliament, the unrest continues.

Africa is the second largest continent on Earth. It has been slow to develop. Today, however, free African nations are growing stronger. More Africans are attending school. They are developing the skills needed to improve their **standard of living.** African nations are learning to work together. The Organization of African Unity (OAU) is an association of African nations that tries to find peaceful solutions to quarrels between African countries. They hope that unity will lead to economic and political progress. As the nations grow stronger, Africa takes a place of greater importance in the world.

TIMELINE STUDY

Answer: 1973

STUDY SKILLS

To help students better visualize how world events impacted Asia and Africa, suggest that they make two separate timelines, using the timeline on page 653 as a guide. One timeline can focus on events that occurred in Asia from 1945 to the present. The second timeline can show events that occurred in Africa during the same period.

TIMELINE STUDY:

ASIA AND AFRICA: 1945–2010

When did the United States first pull out of Vietnam?

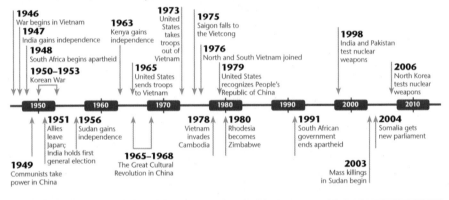

1946 War begins in Vietnam
1947 India gains independence
1948 South Africa begins apartheid
1950–1953 Korean War

1963 Kenya gains independence

1965 United States sends troops to Vietnam

1973 United States takes troops out of Vietnam

1975 Saigon falls to the Vietcong
1976 North and South Vietnam joined
1979 United States recognizes People's Republic of China

1998 India and Pakistan test nuclear weapons

2006 North Korea tests nuclear weapons

1950 | 1960 | 1970 | 1980 | 1990 | 2000 | 2010

1951 Allies leave Japan; India holds first general election
1956 Sudan gains independence

1965–1968 The Great Cultural Revolution in China

1978 Vietnam invades Cambodia
1980 Rhodesia becomes Zimbabwe

1991 South African government ends apartheid

2003 Mass killings in Sudan begin

2004 Somalia gets new parliament

1949 Communists take power in China

1945–PRESENT

Changes in Asia and Africa Chapter 30 **653**

Lesson 30–6 Review Answers

1. Europe **2.** Britain **3.** famine
4. apartheid **5.** Nelson Mandela
6. Darfur **7.** Africa **8.** Many Africans
had joined the armies of their
European colonizers during the war.
When they returned from the war,
they wanted their independence.
9. In some countries, civil wars
and conflicts broke out. The wars
brought starvation, disease, and
death. **10.** There was no longer
separation of hotels, restaurants,
and public places. Laws could no
longer determine where a person
could live. Nonwhites had the right
to vote. Countries lifted most of their
sanctions against South Africa.

REVIEW

Word Bank

Africa

apartheid

Britain

Darfur

Europe

famine

Nelson Mandela

On a sheet of paper, write the word from the Word Bank to complete each sentence correctly.

1. At the end of World War II, most of Africa remained controlled by _____.

2. In 1963, Kenya was granted independence by _____ after a long battle.

3. A time when crops do not grow and there is no food is called _____.

4. In 1948, the Afrikaners set up a policy of _____ to keep white people in control of South Africa.

5. In 1994, _____ became the president of South Africa.

6. Native rebel groups began attacking government targets in _____, a western area of Sudan.

7. _____ is the second largest continent on Earth.

On a sheet of paper, write the answer to each question. Use complete sentences.

8. Why did Africans want their independence after World War II?

9. What problems did nations have after gaining their independence?

10. How did the repeal of apartheid laws affect South Africa?

- India and its neighbors, Pakistan and Bangladesh, face many problems. These include: border disputes, religious conflicts, and food shortages.

- India is continually working to improve farming techniques. There is never enough food for the country's large population.

- Indian leaders are trying to build industry. They are doing this while learning to make better use of the country's natural resources.

- The Communists and the Nationalists fought a four-year civil war in China.

- In 1949, the Communists gained power in mainland China. They called their nation the People's Republic of China. The Nationalists left the mainland for Taiwan. They called their nation the Republic of China.

- Communist China has not granted its people political freedom, but it has allowed more private ownership and trade with the West.

- The United States fought wars in Korea and Vietnam on the anti-Communist side. Many Americans protested against U.S. involvement in the Vietnam War.

- Many European colonies in Africa gained independence after 1945.

- In South Africa, apartheid officially began in 1948 and ended in 1991. In 1990, Nelson Mandela, head of the African National Congress, was released from jail. He eventually became president of the country.

- African nations struggle to solve problems such as poverty, disease, and food shortages. Many are growing stronger, despite their history of colonial rule.

Chapter 30 Summary

Have students read the Chapter Summary on page 655 to review the main ideas presented in Chapter 30.

Ask:

- What problems do India, Pakistan, and Bangladesh face? (border disputes, religious conflicts, and food shortages)

- What are Indian leaders doing to help overcome the country's problems? (They are working to improve farming techniques. They are also trying to build industry and make better use of the country's resources.)

- How long did China's civil war last? (four years)

- What happened to the Chinese Nationalists? (They were defeated and moved to Taiwan where they set up the Republic of China.)

- What two wars did the United States fight against Communism? (the Korean War and the Vietnam War)

- What happened to many European colonies in Africa after World War II? (They became independent.)

- Which anti-apartheid leader eventually became president of South Africa? (Nelson Mandela)

- What problems do many African nations face? (poverty, disease, and food shortages)

TEACHER'S RESOURCE

The AGS Globe Teaching Strategies in Social Studies Transparencies may be used with this chapter. The transparencies add an interactive dimension to expand and enhance the Pacemaker® *World History* program content.

CHAPTER PROJECT FOLLOW-UP

 Have students present their displays of the Korean War Memorial or the Vietnam Veterans Memorial. Give each group an opportunity to share interesting facts about the memorial they researched. Keep students' displays around the class, and invite other classes to view them. Assess students' work on historical accuracy, and both visual and oral presentation.

Chapter 30 Review

Use the Chapter Review to prepare students for tests and to reteach content from the chapter.

Chapter 30 Mastery Test

The Teacher's Resource Library includes two forms of the Chapter 30 Mastery Test. Each test addresses the chapter Goals for Learning. An optional third page of additional critical-thinking items is included for each test. The difficulty level of the two forms is equivalent.

Chapter 30 Review Answers

Vocabulary Review

1. electronic
2. violence
3. sanction
4. majority
5. security
6. corrupt
7. curfew
8. minority
9. starvation
10. guerilla

Chapter Review Questions

11. The untouchable class in the Hindu caste system was outlawed.

12. The Communists helped defend northern peasants against the Japanese. Also, the Communists divided land and food among the people in a fair way.

Word Bank

corrupt
curfew
electronic
guerilla
majority
minority
sanction
security
starvation
violence

Vocabulary Review

On a sheet of paper, use the words from the Word Bank to correctly match each definition below.

1. Powered by electricity

2. Great physical force; actions that hurt others

3. An action taken by one nation against another for breaking international law

4. A greater number, more than half

5. Safety

6. Dishonest, evil, selfish

7. A time after which certain people cannot be on the streets

8. A smaller number, less than half

9. The act of dying from not having enough food to eat

10. One of a group of fighters who are not part of a regular army, and who usually make surprise raids behind enemy lines

Chapter Review Questions

On a sheet of paper, write the answers to each question. Use complete sentences.

11. What was outlawed in India in 1950?

12. How did Mao and the Communists win the support of the Chinese peasants?

13. How did the United Nations help South Korea?

14. Why did Japan and the United States sign a trade agreement in 1990?

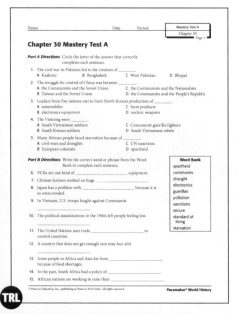

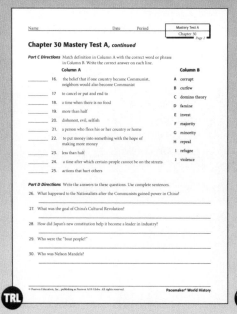

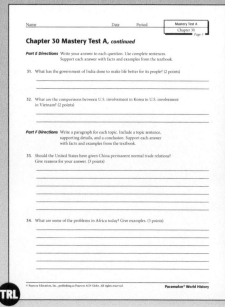

Test Tip

Restate test directions in your own words. Tell yourself what you are expected to do.

15. What major change happened in Africa after World War II?

Critical Thinking

On a sheet of paper, write your response to each question. Use complete sentences.

16. Do you think the limits on the Japanese military helped the Japanese economy after World War II? Give two examples to support your answer.

17. Do you think you would have liked being a young person in the 1960s? Be sure to include Vietnam and other important events in your answer.

Using the Timeline

Use the timeline on page 653 to answer the questions.

18. When did India gain its independence?

19. After World War II ended, how long did the Allies stay in Japan?

20. When did apartheid end in South Africa?

GROUP ACTIVITY

Work with a partner. Find a recent news story about one of the countries in this chapter. Write three questions that can be answered by the news story. Then read the story to your class, or tell about it in your own words. After you finish the story, ask your classmates the questions.

1945–PRESENT   *Changes in Asia and Africa*   **Chapter 30   657**

13. A UN army came to South Korea's aid.

14. They signed a trade agreement to make it easier for other countries to do business with Japan.

15. European colonies gained their freedom and became independent countries.

Critical Thinking

16. Possible answer: Yes. Japan did not need to spend much money on defense, so it could invest more money in industry. Japan could concentrate on consumer goods instead of materials for defense. The whole workforce could be employed in making goods for Japan and for export.

17. Possible answers: Yes, because it was an exciting time when young people were actively protesting and asking questions about the world around them. No, because many young people had to go to war. Also, it was a sad time when many people, including U.S. leaders, were killed.

Using the Timeline

18. 1947

19. 6 years

20. 1991

GROUP ACTIVITY

Students' stories should feature one of the countries in the chapter. Have students review relevant material in the stories if the class cannot answer a question.

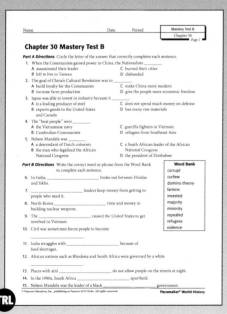

Chapter 30 Mastery Test B, pages 1–3

Changes in Asia and Africa Chapter 30 **657**

Chapter at a Glance

Audio Library 🎧

Skill Track for World History 🖱️

Teacher's Resource Library **TRL**

Workbook Activities 116–119

Activities 116–119

Modified Activities 116–119

Life Skills Connection 31

Key Vocabulary Words 31

Chapter 31 Self-Study Guide

Chapter 31 Outline

Chapter 31 Mastery Tests A and B

(Answer Keys for the Teacher's Resource Library begin on page 809 of the Teacher's Edition.)

Introducing the Chapter

In the last decades of the 20th century and into the 21st century, dramatic political change reshaped the world. The Middle East is an area that has experienced much conflict. These disagreements continue to the present day.

Ask:

- What subject has caused war in the Middle East for many centuries? (religion)

- What resource in the Middle East have countries fought over? (oil)

The Middle East

Religious differences have brought people to war against one another for many centuries. This is particularly true in the Middle East. Jews and Muslims have fought for the right to lands along the eastern Mediterranean. These disagreements continue. In countries such as Lebanon, Muslims and Christians fight for control. In other countries, Muslim groups with different beliefs fight one another. With the power of religion comes the power of money. The countries of the Middle East cover lands rich in valuable oil resources. Foreign nations are dependent on that oil, and thus become involved in the political struggles.

GOALS FOR LEARNING

- To explain why there is fighting over Palestine
- To list the conflicts that continue in the Middle East today
- To discuss the importance of oil to the Middle East and the world
- To describe life in the Middle East

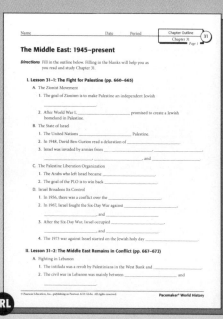

Chapter 31 Self-Study Guide, pages 1–2   Chapter 31 Outline, pages 1–3

Reading Strategy: Predicting

In order to predict what will come next, it is helpful to preview a text. Previewing helps readers think about what they already know about a subject. When making predictions, consider the following:

- Consider what you already know about the topic. Make your best guess as to what might happen next.

- Be sure to include details that support your prediction.

- As you read, you may learn new information that changes your prediction. Check your predictions from time to time.

Key Vocabulary Words

Lesson 1

Homeland The land that belongs to people

Zionism The movement to set up a Jewish nation in Palestine

Arms Weapons used to attack or defend

Cease-fire An end in military operations, especially to try and discuss peace

Hostile Unfriendly, showing hate or dislike

Traitor One who betrays a cause, a friend, or a nation

Lesson 2

Terrorist A fighter who hopes to achieve certain goals by using force or violence

Terrorism The use of force or random violence to frighten people or groups

Negotiate To talk together, make bargains, and agree on something

Stalemate To put in a position in which no action can be taken

Shah An Iranian ruler

Ayatollah A Muslim religious leader

Embassy The home and offices of a person sent to represent his or her government in another country

Hostages People held prisoner by an enemy until certain demands are met

Weapons of mass destruction A means of attack or defense that uses powerful weapons; an atomic bomb is an example

- Why do foreign nations sometimes get involved in the conflicts of the Middle East? (because they depend on oil from the region)

Reading Strategy:
Predicting

Explain that when readers make a prediction, they stop and think about what might happen next. Predictions are made before reading the text all the way through. Point out that readers include details to support their predictions. These details can come from what a reader already knows about the subject, or they may come from clues in the chapter title, section headings, or boldfaced words.

Key Vocabulary Words

Point out that these chapter words are presented in the order they appear in each lesson. They are also found in the glossary.

LIFE SKILLS CONNECTION

Students learn about emergency preparedness. Students work on creating home and car emergency kits. Direct students the Federal Emergency Management Agency's Web site.

KEY VOCABULARY

Students chose the correct word from the Word Bank to complete each sentence.

CHAPTER PROJECT

Explain that the Middle East is an area of the world that is regularly featured in the news. Remind students that the news stories of today become the history of tomorrow. Tell students to collect local or national newspapers as they read this chapter, and clip stories having to do with the Middle East. Direct students to keep a folder of stories that they will use at the end of the chapter.

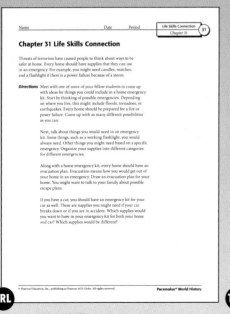

Life Skills Connection 31

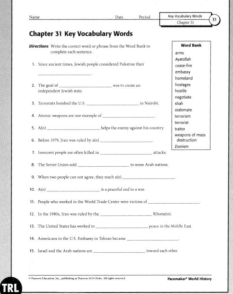

Key Vocabulary Words 31

The Fight for Palestine

Lesson at a Glance

Chapter 31 Lesson 1

Overview This lesson describes the
years of conflict between the Jews
and the Arabs in Palestine.

Objectives

■ To describe the conflict between
the Jews and Arabs over Palestine

■ To explain how Israel was
formed and how it became more
powerful

■ To explain why many Palestinians
ended up in refugee camps

Student Pages 660–666

Teacher's Resource Library

Workbook Activity 116

Activity 116

Modified Activity 116

Vocabulary

arms	hostile
cease-fire	traitor
homeland	Zionism

Have students read aloud definitions for
the vocabulary words. As each definition
is read, ask a volunteer to name the word,
define it in his or her own words, and
write it on the board. Have classmates
listen to the definitions students provide
and, if they are not accurate, explain how
to change them. Continue until all of the
words are listed.

1 Warm-Up Activity

Write the following questions on the
board or distribute to students:

Where is your homeland?

*Explain why you think of that
place as your homeland.*

Have students write their answers to
the questions and then discuss them.
On chart paper, list the students'
definitions of "homeland" and analyze
the results. Refer to this information
while reading the lesson.

Objectives

■ To describe the
conflict between the
Jews and Arabs over
Palestine

■ To explain how Israel
was formed and
how it became more
powerful

■ To explain why many
Palestinians ended
up in refugee camps

Reading Strategy:
Predicting

Preview the lesson title.
Predict what you think you
will learn in this lesson.

People in the Middle East were often ruled by other lands.
For hundreds of years, the Middle East was part of the
Ottoman Empire. After World War I, most of the Middle
East fell under British control. Egypt, however, gained its
independence from Britain in 1922. Meanwhile, France
took control of Syria and Lebanon.

World War II weakened the European countries. This left
the door open for Arab nationalists to gain independence
for their countries. However, with this independence came
conflict.

The Middle East Today

MAP STUDY

1. Which country borders the Red Sea and the Persian Gulf?
2. Turkey borders which two seas?

Reading Strategy:
Predicting

Have students read the title and ask
them to make a prediction about the
lesson. Call on volunteers to share their
predictions with the class. Most students
are likely to predict that the word *fight* in
the title indicates that the lesson will be
about conflicts over Palestine.

MAP STUDY

Answers:

1. Saudi Arabia

2. The Black Sea and the Red Sea

Homeland
The land that belongs
to people

Homeland
The land that belongs
to people

Zionism
The movement to set
up a Jewish nation in
Palestine

History Fact
This scattering
of the Jews is
called the *diaspora*.

What Was the Zionist Movement?

In ancient days, the Jews considered Palestine their
homeland. They called it a land promised to them by
God. They built a temple in Jerusalem, the holy city.

Almost 2,000 years ago, the Romans drove the Jews out of
Palestine. Some Jews settled in an area of Palestine called
Galilee. However, most of the Jews fled from Palestine.
They scattered around the world.

Many Jews never gave up their dream of the promised
homeland. In the late 1800s, Jews in eastern Europe
were persecuted. Some Jews started a movement
called **Zionism.** Their goal was to make Palestine an
independent Jewish nation. Jews from Europe began to
settle in Palestine, which at that time was ruled by the
Ottoman Turks.

By 1914, about 85,000 Jews were living there. After World
War I, Britain promised to create a Jewish homeland in
Palestine. Meanwhile, the Arab population of Palestine
had been increasing, too. There was a problem. The
Arabs living there did not like that Jews were moving into
Palestine.

After World War II, Zionism became more popular.
Jews who had felt Hitler's persecution were ready for a
homeland of their own. Many came to Palestine.

How Was the State of Israel Formed?

In 1947, the United Nations voted to end British rule over
Palestine. The UN knew there was a conflict between
Arabs and Jews in Palestine. Arabs said the land had been
theirs for 2,000 years. Jews said it had been theirs before the
Arabs. Therefore, the United Nations divided Palestine into
two parts. One part was for Jews and the other for Arabs.
The Jews agreed to the UN plan. However, the Arabs were
angry. They wanted all of Palestine to be an Arab state.

You Decide
Do you think the
United Nations
was wise to divide
Palestine into two parts?

Ask students to think about what
it would be like to have to give up
something of great importance to
them. Explain that they will be reading
about two groups of people that felt
strongly about the same territory.
Have students read pages 660–665 to
find out about these two groups.

Ask:

- In what year did the United
Nations divide Palestine into Jewish
and Arab states? (1947)
- Where were displaced Palestinian
Arabs forced to live? (in refugee
camps)
- What territories have many of the
wars been fought over? (The West
Bank, the Gaza Strip, and the Sinai
Peninsula)

History Fact
The word *diaspora* comes from
the Greek word *diaspeirein*,
meaning to scatter about or disperse.
Because the Jews were scattered
around the world, this word accurately
summarizes their plight.

You Decide
Have students discuss their
opinions of the United Nations'
decision to divide Palestine. Some
students may question the authority
of the United Nations in this situation,
while others may state that the idea
of a "homeland" is stronger than any
outside ruling. Some students may
decide that dividing Palestine was the
only fair and just solution.

COMMON ERROR

Students may be confused
by the names given to
those on both sides of the
conflict. Draw a chart on
the board and write Israelis/Jews on
one side of the chart and Palestinians/
Arabs on the other side. Point out
that both sides are referred to by both
titles throughout the lesson.

Background Information

The historic peace treaty signed in 1979 between Egypt and Israel is known as the Camp David Accords. Camp David is in Maryland, about 60 miles from Washington, D.C., in a scenic, wooded area. It is off-limits for everyone except the president of the United States, family members, and invited guests. The first president to use the camp was Franklin Roosevelt. President Eisenhower named the camp after his grandson.

LEARNING STYLES

Auditory/Verbal

Have students work in small groups to look up songs about peace on the Internet. Students can easily find songs by searching under songs about peace. Allow students 20–30 minutes to listen to these songs and then have each group choose their favorite song to share with the class. Have each group play their song for the class. If lyrics are available, you may want to have students discuss what it was about the lyrics that caught their attention.

ONLINE CONNECTION

Students can gain additional information about Golda Meir by accessing the following Web sites:

www.agsglobepmwh.com/page662a (This site provides a brief biography of Golda Meir's life.)

www.agsglobepmwh.com/page662b (This site provides a photo collection spanning her lifetime.)

www.agsglobepmwh.com/page662c (From the Jewish-American Hall of Fame, this site has a biography of Meir's life; it also includes a Golda Meir quiz.)

On May 14, 1948, David Ben-Gurion, the Zionist leader in Palestine, read a declaration of independence. He declared that the Jewish part of Palestine was the new state of Israel.

Israel was recognized immediately by the United States and then by the Soviet Union. The Arab nations declared war on Israel. On May 15, 1948, Israel was invaded by armies from the Arab nations of Syria, Egypt, Lebanon, Iraq, and Jordan.

GREAT NAMES IN HISTORY

Golda Meir

Golda Meir was born in Ukraine. Her family moved to Milwaukee in 1906. She later taught school there and worked with the Labor Zionist Party.

In 1921, Meir and her husband moved to Palestine. There she worked for the Zionist movement. After Israel became a nation, Meir was elected to the Knesset, the Israeli parliament. She was labor minister and then foreign minister. Later, she helped organize the Labor Party. As prime minister (1969–1974), Meir tried to bring peace to the Middle East.

Why Was the Palestine Liberation Organization Formed?

The Israelis were greatly outnumbered and had a shortage of weapons. However, Israel won the war against many odds. An agreement between Israel and Arab states was signed in 1949. The state of Israel was firmly established. The lands left to the Arabs became part of Jordan.

About 700,000 Arabs fled Israel, becoming refugees. The homeless Palestinian Arabs lived in crowded refugee camps outside of Israel. Many still live there. They believed that their homes were stolen. Some of them formed a group of fighters called the Palestine Liberation Organization (PLO). Their goal is to win back their land.

GREAT NAMES IN HISTORY

Have students read the passage independently or with a partner. Discuss the traits that might influence a person to move to another country to work for peace. You may want to have students do additional research on Golda Meir.

After the war in 1948, about 700,000 Jews living in Arab nations were forced to leave. Jews left Iraq, Yemen, Libya, and other countries. Most went to live in Israel.

Israel had won the 1948 war. However, the problems of the Middle East were far from settled.

How Did Israel Broaden Its Control?

Soon the superpowers became involved in the Israeli-Arab conflict. In 1955, the Soviets offered to sell weapons, or **arms,** to Egypt. This was followed by a conflict over the Suez Canal.

In 1956, Egypt took over the canal from Britain and France. Britain, France, and Israel then attacked Egypt. The United Nations arranged an end in military operations—a **cease-fire.** The Suez Canal was held by Egypt. The Arabs, however, became even more unfriendly and **hostile** toward Israel.

Families in the disputed area of Palestine live in sometimes hostile surroundings.

Reading Strategy:
Predicting

Have students revisit the predictions they made before reading. Allow them to revise their predictions based on what they have read. Have students make a prediction for the future of the region.

 You Decide

Ask students to share their opinions about Israel's fate if it had lost a war. Some students may think that Israelis would have been driven from their land, while others may think that a loss would have meant Palestinian leadership for Israel.

AT HOME

 Some students may have vague perceptions of the Middle East and Israel. You might suggest that these students invite their family members to rent a travel or documentary video that highlights Israel. Ask students to write a report that describes Israel's culture, history, and topography, and also its modern cities and high-tech features. For students who have traveled to Israel or the Middle East—or whose family members have visited—ask them to spend time with their families and select travel artifacts to bring to class. Students could feature their travel artifacts in their reports.

TEACHER ALERT

Keep in mind that the division of Palestine can be a controversial topic to this day. Refrain from passing judgment on either side of the issue. Be especially sensitive to students who are of Jewish or Arab descent, and help others to see that it is hard to fully understand a situation such as this one from afar.

Traitor
One who betrays a cause, a friend, or a nation

Reading Strategy:
Predicting

Think about what you predicted earlier. Does your prediction still work or do you need to revise your prediction?

 You Decide

What do you think would have happened to Israel if it had lost any of its wars?

LEARN MORE ABOUT IT

Have students follow along as you read the passage aloud. Discuss why Anwar Sadat's visit to Israel was a surprise. Explain that President Carter was considered part of the peace process for his role in the Camp David Accords in 1979. Have students discuss any questions they have after reading the passage. Ask them to consider what the assassination of Sadat might mean for future peacemakers.

In June 1967, another war began. Israel fought the Arab nations of Egypt, Jordan, and Syria. In the first few minutes of the war, Israeli planes attacked the Arab airfields. Almost all of the Arab airplanes were destroyed on the ground. Then the Israeli army pushed through the Sinai Peninsula all the way to the Suez Canal. The war was over in six days! Israel occupied all of the Sinai Peninsula, the Gaza Strip, and the West Bank. The West Bank was the section of Palestine that had become part of Jordan. Israel also took control of East Jerusalem.

Arab nations grew angrier. In 1973, Egypt, Syria, Jordan, and Iraq launched a surprise attack on Israel. It was called the *Yom Kippur War* because the Arabs attacked on the Jewish holy day called *Yom Kippur*. This time, the Arabs almost won. Israel managed to defend itself. However, it paid a high price in the number of lives lost.

LEARN MORE ABOUT IT

Anwar Sadat

In 1977, Egypt's President Anwar el-Sadat visited Israel. His visit surprised the world. It was the first move toward peace with Israel that any Arab leader had ever made. Then, U.S. President Jimmy Carter invited Sadat and Israel's prime minister, Menachem Begin, to the United States. There the three leaders held discussions on how to end the Israeli-Arab conflict. These meetings led to the signing of the Camp David Accords in 1979. Israel promised to return all of the Sinai Peninsula to Egypt in exchange for peace. Israel also promised to allow the Palestinians in Gaza and on the West Bank to govern themselves.

Much of the world praised Sadat. In 1978, Sadat and Begin shared the Nobel Peace Prize. However, many Arab nationalists were angry. They said that Sadat was a **traitor** to the Arab cause, meaning he betrayed it. In 1981, Sadat was assassinated by extremists.

Israel and Its Neighbors, After the Six-Day War

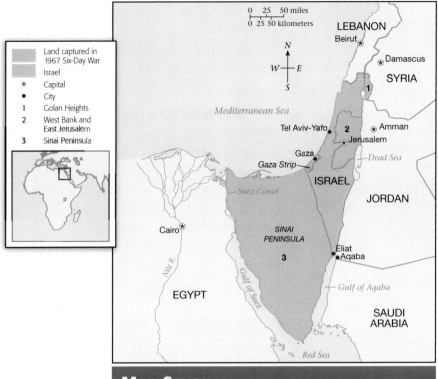

Legend:
- Land captured in 1967 Six-Day War
- Israel
- ⊛ Capital
- • City
- 1 Golan Heights
- 2 West Bank and East Jerusalem
- 3 Sinai Peninsula

Read the title of the map aloud and ask students to recall when the Six-Day War occurred. Then read the questions at the bottom of the map and ask volunteers to provide the answers.

Answers:

1. Golan Heights, West Bank, Sinai Peninsula

2. Suez Canal

MAP STUDY

1. What areas were captured by Israel in the 1967 Six-Day War?

2. What connects the Mediterranean Sea to the Red Sea?

LESSON 31-1 REVIEW

Word Bank

British
Egypt
homeland
Israel
refugees
Palestine

On a sheet of paper, write the word from the Word Bank to complete each sentence correctly.

1. Long ago, the Jews considered Palestine their _____.

2. The United Nations voted to end _____ rule over Palestine.

3. The United Nations divided _____ into two parts.

4. Palestinian _____ formed the Palestine Liberation Organization to win back their land.

5. After the United Nations arranged a cease-fire, _____ held control over the Suez Canal.

6. _____ gained the Sinai Peninsula, the Gaza Strip, and the West Bank after the Six-Day War.

On a sheet of paper, write the answer to each question. Use complete sentences.

7. What was the goal of the Zionist movement?

8. Why was Palestine divided by the United Nations?

9. Why did so many Palestinians end up in refugee camps after the war in 1948?

10. Why did Egypt, Syria, Jordan, and Iraq attack Israel on *Yom Kippur* in 1973? Who won?

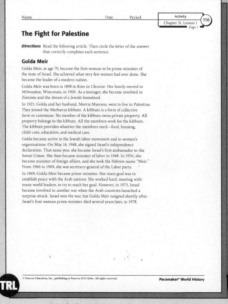

The Fight for Palestine

Directions Read the following article. Then circle the letter of the answer that correctly completes each sentence.

Golda Meir

Golda Meir, at age 70, became the first woman to be prime minister of the state of Israel. She achieved what very few women had ever done. She became the leader of a modern nation.

Golda Meir was born in 1898 in Kiev in Ukraine. Her family moved to Milwaukee, Wisconsin, in 1906. As a teenager, she became involved in Zionism and the dream of a Jewish homeland.

In 1921, Golda and her husband, Morris Myerson, went to live in Palestine. They joined the Merhavya kibbutz. A kibbutz is a form of collective farm or commune. No member of the kibbutz owns private property. All property belongs to the kibbutz. All the members work for the kibbutz. The kibbutz provides whatever the members need—food, housing, child-care, education, and medical care.

Golda became active in the Jewish labor movement and in women's organizations. On May 14, 1948, she signed Israel's independence declaration. That same year, she became Israel's first ambassador to the Soviet Union. She then became minister of labor in 1948. In 1956, she became minister of foreign affairs, and she took the Hebrew name "Meir." From 1966 to 1969, she was secretary-general of the Labor party.

In 1969, Golda Meir became prime minister. Her main goal was to establish peace with the Arab nations. She worked hard, meeting with many world leaders, to try to reach her goal. However, in 1973, Israel became involved in another war when the Arab countries launched a surprise attack. Israel won the war, but Golda Meir resigned shortly after. Israel's first woman prime minister died several years later, in 1978.

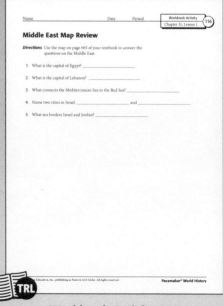

Middle East Map Review

Directions Use the map on page 665 of your textbook to answer the questions on the Middle East.

1. What is the capital of Egypt? _____

2. What is the capital of Lebanon? _____

3. What connects the Mediterranean Sea to the Red Sea? _____

4. Name two cities in Israel. _____ and _____

5. What sea borders Israel and Jordan? _____

Activity 116, pages 1–2   Workbook Activity 116

The Middle East Remains in Conflict

The fighting in the Middle East was not over. The Palestine Liberation Organization (PLO) still wanted a home for the Palestinians.

Why Was There Fighting in Lebanon?

In 1970, the PLO was forced out of Jordan. In 1975, it became involved in a civil war in Lebanon. From bases in Lebanon, the PLO carried out **terrorist** attacks into Israel. Terrorists use force or violence to achieve certain goals. Palestinian terrorists were also active in other parts of the world.

In 1982, Israel invaded Lebanon in order to destroy PLO bases. The PLO was forced to leave Lebanon. However, once the Israeli army withdrew from Lebanon, the PLO came back.

In December 1987, violent protests by Palestinians broke out in the West Bank and Gaza. The uprising, known as the *intifada,* continued until the 1990s. The Palestinians wanted an independent state. They were especially angry that Israel allowed Jewish settlers to take away some of their land. However, the Israelis have given control of some of the Gaza Strip and the West Bank back to the Palestinians.

Lebanon's civil war began in 1975 and lasted until 1990. Muslims battled Christians for power. Different Muslim groups also battled each other. In 1983, the United States became involved with the war. U.S. troops were taken out of Lebanon only after many U.S. Marines were killed by Muslim terrorists. Syria also sent troops into Lebanon, who used force to end the civil war in 1990.

Reading Strategy:
Predicting

Have students make a prediction about what the Palestinians might do next. Ask students to support their prediction with details from Lesson 31–1. You may want to have students write their predictions on an index card and use the card as a bookmark.

Lesson at a Glance

Chapter 31 Lesson 2

Overview This lesson explains the Middle East peace process, the revolution in Iran, the war between Iran and Iraq, the Persian Gulf War, and the influence of terrorists.

Objectives

■ To describe the conflict in Lebanon and Iran

■ To describe the events that led up to the Gulf War

■ To explain how terrorism spread to the larger world

Student Pages 667–673

Teacher's Resource Library

Workbook Activity 117

Activity 117

Modified Activity 117

Vocabulary

Ayatollah	stalemate
embassy	terrorism
hostages	terrorist
negotiate	weapons of
Shah	mass destruction

Have students write each vocabulary word on an index card. Read a sentence that describes each word or create a sentence that provides a clue about the word. Have students hold up the card with the correct answer. Continue until all the words have been used.

1 Warm-Up Activity

Display a world map and point out the region known as the Middle East. Discuss the geographic location of each country in the Middle East. Explain that oil has brought great wealth to some people of the Middle East while others live in extreme poverty. Have students speculate on the strategic importance of the Persian Gulf.

Ask students to name some nations that are in the Middle East. Then have them read pages 667–672 to find out about some conflicts that have led to violence in the Middle East.

Ask:

- Which United States president brought the Arab and Israeli leaders to Camp David for peace talks? (Jimmy Carter)
- What country captured American hostages in the 1970s? (Iran)
- Why did Iraq invade Kuwait in 1990? (Saddam Hussein wanted to take over the oil fields of Kuwait.)
- Where have terrorists struck outside the Middle East? (Kenya, the United States, Spain)

Background Information

Long ago, the term *Arab* referred to any of the Arabic-speaking people on the Arabian peninsula. However, after the rise of Islam in the seventh century, most Arabs converted and became Muslims. As Islam spread beyond its Arabian borders into central Asia and across the southern coast of the Mediterranean Sea into Spain, the Arabic language and culture traveled with it. As a result, many people who are Arabs belong to widely diverse cultures, some with Spanish, African, or Turkish traditions, among others. What links most Arabs together, however, are their religion and common language.

Terrorism
The use of force or random violence to frighten people or groups

Negotiate
To talk together, make bargains, and agree on something

Stalemate
To put in a position in which no action can be taken

The civil war all but destroyed Lebanon, leaving its cities in shambles. Beirut, the capital of Lebanon, had been known as the "Paris" of the Middle East. Much of it was left in ruins.

The PLO agreed to stop acts of **terrorism,** or the use of force or violence to frighten people. It also began talking and working toward agreement, or **negotiating,** with Israel. Israelis had a difficult choice to make as they negotiated with the Palestinians and Arabs. They could give up the occupied lands and hope that it would bring about a lasting peace.

In January 2001, hopes for peace seemed to be **stalemated** again (they were in a position in which no action could be taken). Despite U.S. President Bill Clinton's involvement, sticking points, such as Jerusalem's future, remained unresolved.

Israeli Prime Minister Yitzhak Rabin, left, and PLO chairman Yasser Arafat shake hands after signing a peace agreement. U.S. President Bill Clinton looks on.

Shah
An Iranian ruler

Ayatollah
A Muslim religious leader

Embassy
The home and offices of a person sent to represent his or her government in another country

Hostages
People held prisoner by an enemy until certain demands are met

Why Was Iran in Conflict?

The country of Iran has seen its share of conflict, too. Iranians were unhappy with their leader, the **Shah.** The Shah had a vicious secret police who made sure he kept power.

In 1979, a 76-year-old Muslim leader, the **Ayatollah** Khomeini, returned to Iran from exile in France. Khomeini led a successful revolution against the Shah. He then set up a Muslim republic following strict Islamic rules. Khomeini's followers wanted the Shah to stand trial for crimes they said he had committed. However, the Shah had fled to the United States. Then in November 1979, Iranians captured the U.S. **embassy** in Tehran, Iran's capital. An embassy is the home and offices of a person sent to represent their government in another country. They took American prisoners, called **hostages,** and they demanded the Shah's return.

Much of the world was angered by the Iranian action. However, Iran would not give up the hostages. The Shah died in Egypt in July 1980. Finally, in January 1981, the American hostages were freed.

Meanwhile, in 1980, Iran was attacked by its neighbor, Iraq. There had been bitter fights over territory. Iraq hoped to win a quick victory over Iran. Saddam Hussein, leader of Iraq, thought that Iran had been weakened by the Islamic revolution. However, neither nation could beat the other. The war dragged on for many years.

There were huge land battles. Then both sides began firing missiles at each other's cities. In addition, each country began to attack oil tankers in the Persian Gulf. In 1987, the United States sent its navy to the Gulf to protect the flow of oil.

Visual/Spatial

Have students use an atlas, classroom map, or the Internet to locate the countries involved in the Persian Gulf War. Have students identify Kuwait, Iraq, and Saudi Arabia. Discuss the size and proximity of the countries. Ask students to speculate on what type of defense system a small country like Kuwait might have, in comparison with Iraq and Saudi Arabia. Ask students why the United States became involved when Iraq threatened Saudi Arabia's borders. (The U.S. and Saudi Arabia have a cooperative relationship.) Remind students that the war ended when Kuwait was freed.

ELL/ESL STRATEGY

Language Objective:
To use a list of facts to write a summary

Divide the class into six groups. Assign a section of the lesson to each group. Each group should turn the question that leads its assigned section into a statement. One member of the group should read the assigned section aloud. Facts that support the statement should then be listed under the statement. Each group should write a short paragraph summarizing the facts. Then each group should use its list of facts and summary paragraph to generate three questions that could be answered by further research. Have groups share their paragraphs and questions.

Remember

Remind students that after reading Lesson 31–1, they shared their opinions about the United Nations' decision to divide Palestine. Ask them if they have changed their opinion after reading more about conflict in the Middle East. Have them discuss whether or not the division brought about the results that the United Nations envisioned.

Remember
The United Nations has been very involved in the Middle East relations. In 1947, the UN voted to end British rule over Palestine and divided Palestine into two parts.

Finally, in 1988, the United Nations was able to arrange a cease-fire between Iran and Iraq. Both countries had suffered such huge losses that they were willing to begin talking about ending the war.

Why Did Iraq Invade Kuwait?

In August 1990, Iraq invaded the small neighboring nation of Kuwait. Iraqi leader Saddam Hussein wanted to make Kuwait and its rich oil fields a part of his country. Kuwait fell only hours after the Iraqi attack.

The United Nations protested Iraq's capture of Kuwait. Then Iraq threatened the border of Saudi Arabia. The United States and other nations sent their own military forces to the Persian Gulf. They were ready to defend Saudi Arabia against a possible Iraqi invasion. They were also ready to liberate Kuwait.

On November 29, 1990, the United Nations sent Hussein a warning. It would use "all necessary means" if Iraq did not withdraw (pull out) from Kuwait. They gave Hussein until January 15, 1991 to do so. Hussein did not respond to the warning. So, on the evening of January 16, bombs and missiles began to fall on Iraq. A ground war began on February 23. By February 28, Kuwait was free, and a cease-fire had begun.

The Gulf War ended when Kuwait was freed. The war did not, however, destroy Saddam Hussein's control of Iraq or his threats of attack.

Saddam Hussein wanted to make oil-rich Kuwait a part of Iraq.

3 Reinforce and Extend

COMMON ERROR

Make sure that students understand that Iran and Iraq are two different countries. Have students find Iran and Iraq on a world map and identify their locations. Encourage students to spend time locating all the countries discussed in this lesson.

Hussein refused to cooperate with UN inspections to make sure he was not building **weapons of mass destruction.** An example of a weapon of mass destruction is an atomic bomb.

What Progress Did Peace Talks Bring to the Middle Eastern Nations?

In the 1990s, the United States and Russia sponsored peace conferences between Israel and the Arab nations of the Middle East. Israeli, Palestinian, and Arab leaders agreed to meet to try to cool heated conflicts. They wanted to make the Middle East more stable. Progress is slow. Israel has given the Palestinians control over some of the occupied lands. Israel and Jordan have also signed a peace treaty. In early 2000, the United States helped move Syria and Israel toward peace. However, by early 2001, the peace talks had broken down because Israel refused to give up the Golan Heights.

How Did Middle Eastern Terrorism Spread to the Larger World?

Many Middle Eastern countries have become home to terrorist groups. These people commit acts of violence against citizens of various countries. They often use bombs to kill people. Terrorists may disagree with the politics or religion of a particular nation or group. In some cases, they may not like the presence of foreign governments in their countries. Often this foreign presence is due to oil resources. Since 1998, there have been about 2,000 terrorist attacks worldwide.

As mentioned in Chapter 30, the U.S. Embassy in Nairobi, Kenya was bombed in 1998. Nearly 300 people were killed, and more than 5,000 were injured. Most victims were native Kenyans. The al Qaeda group, guided by Osama bin Laden, was blamed for these attacks.

On September 11, 2001, two planes crashed into the World Trade Center in New York City. Shortly afterward, another plane flew into the Pentagon. A fourth plane, redirected from another Washington target, crashed into a field in Pennsylvania. A total of 3,025 people were killed. Again, al Qaeda and Osama bin Laden were held responsible.

In March 2004, al Qaeda-related terrorists planted bombs in Madrid, Spain train stations. Three separate bombs there killed almost 200 people and wounded another 1,400.

Middle Eastern terrorism has spread to the larger world. On September 11, 2001, two planes crashed into the World Trade Center buildings in New York City.

Lesson 31–2 Review Answers
1. A **2.** D **3.** C **4.** B **5.** A **6.** B **7.** C **8.** D
9. C **10.** B

On a sheet of paper, write the letter of the answer that correctly completes
each sentence.

1. In 1975, the _____ became involved in a civil war in Lebanon.

   A PLO   **B** British   **C** United States   **D** Iranians

2. _____ use force or violence to achieve their goals.

   A Americans   **B** Iranians   **C** Israelites   **D** Terrorists

3. _____ sent troops into Lebanon to end the civil war in 1990.

   A The United States **B** Kuwait   **C** Syria   **D** Palestine

4. Iran had a leader called the _____. He had secret police to make sure he kept
his power.

   A president   **B** Shah   **C** prime minister   **D** dictator

5. In 1976, _____ returned to Iran from exile in France.

   A Ayatollah Khomeini   **C** Bill Clinton
   B David Ben-Guiron   **D** the Shah

6. In 1980, Iran was attacked by _____.

   A Lebanon   **B** Iraq   **C** Israel   **D** Russia

7. In 1987, the United States sent its military to the Gulf to protect the _____.

   A water   **B** people   **C** oil   **D** leader

8. The Gulf War ended when _____ was free.

   A Palestine   **B** Lebanon   **C** Chad   **D** Kuwait

9. In 2001, Israel broke down peace talks because it refused to give up _____.

   A Kuwait   **B** Iraq   **C** the Golan Heights **D** the oil fields

10. In 2001, two planes crashed into the World Trade Center in _____.

   A Washington, D.C. **B** New York City **C** Palestine   **D** Los Angeles

---

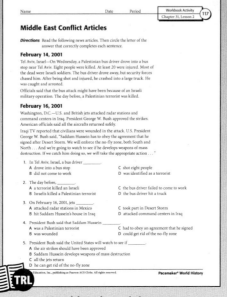

Lesson at a Glance

Chapter 31 Lesson 3

Overview This lesson explains where oil deposits are located, the role of OPEC, and how oil has played a role in the conflicts in the Middle East.

Objectives

- To explain how Middle Eastern nations manage their oil power
- To explain what happened when Libya tried to expand its borders
- To describe how Middle Eastern nations can impact oil prices

Student Pages 674–677

Teacher's Resource Library TRL

Workbook Activity 118

Activity 118

Modified Activity 118

---

1 | Warm-Up Activity

Ask students how they get to school every day. For many, getting to school requires a bus ride or a car trip. Have students think about all the people in the school building and the transportation that brings them together. Then, have students expand that to their neighborhood, city, state, and country. Point out that all the people who drive or ride the bus every day depend on one important natural resource to fuel their vehicles: oil. For this reason, oil is important to the whole country.

Reading Strategy:
Predicting

Have students share their ideas about what they think the lesson will be about. Encourage students to go beyond the chapter title, and state predictions that tell something about oil, such as where it's from, how we rely on it, or why the supply of oil is a source of conflict.

Objectives

- To explain how Middle Eastern nations manage their oil power
- To explain what happened when Libya tried to expand its borders
- To describe how Middle Eastern nations can impact oil prices

Reading Strategy:
Predicting

Preview the lesson title. Predict what you think you will learn in this lesson.

You Decide
Do you think it is good for the United States to be so dependent on Middle East oil?

As you may remember from Lesson 1, Arab nationalists gained independence for their countries after World War II. Most important, Arabs took control of their own oil fields. Oil deposits had been discovered in Iraq in 1927 and in Saudi Arabia in 1938. More huge oil fields were later found along the Persian Gulf. European and U.S. oil companies had moved in to control the oil fields. The Middle Eastern nations saw little of their own oil wealth. However, after World War II, many Arab nations gained tremendous riches and power because of their oil.

How Do Middle Eastern Nations Control Their Oil?

Much of the Middle East has oil. All nations need oil, and world supplies are limited. The Middle East's oil fields give Arab countries power.

An organization called OPEC (Organization of Petroleum Exporting Countries) manages that power. OPEC members include the oil-producing nations of the Middle East, Asia, and Africa, as well as the South American country of Venezuela.

OPEC sets the price of oil. OPEC can force up oil prices or deny oil from certain countries. This gives OPEC tremendous power. During the Israeli-Arab wars of 1967 and 1973, the Arabs used their oil as a weapon. They cut off the flow of oil to the West. In 1973, this resulted in a severe oil shortage in the United States. Drivers were forced to wait in long lines at the gas pumps. They also had to pay a much higher price for each gallon they bought. Through the 1990s and into the 21st century, OPEC used its power to control other countries.

You Decide
Ask students to share their opinions about whether or not it is good for the United States to be so dependent on Middle East oil. Have them share suggestions for reducing oil needs in the United States, by methods such as carpooling, using public transportation, or riding bicycles.

Oil pipelines run through Saudi Arabian oil fields. Saudi Arabia has the richest known oil reserves of any country in the world.

Some people in the Middle East are very, very wealthy because of oil. However, much of the oil wealth remains in the hands of a few. Most profits from oil sales go toward building a strong Arab military.

What Happened When Libya Tried to Expand Its Borders?

Most Middle East oil comes from Saudi Arabia. Another important oil producer is Libya. In 1969, Muammar al-Qaddafi came to power after he and his followers overthrew the king of Libya. Al-Qaddafi has shown great interest in expanding his country's borders. He tried to seize territory from Chad, the country that borders Libya on the south.

Explain that most of the world's oil supply comes from the Middle East. This gives oil-producing countries much power. The Organization of Petroleum Exporting Countries (OPEC) manages that power. Tell students they will read about OPEC and conflicts over oil in this lesson.

Ask:

- What is one responsibility of OPEC? (to set the price of oil)
- When was oil used as a weapon? (Arabs cut off the flow of oil to the West in the 1970s, resulting in a severe oil shortage.)
- What country did Muammar al-Qaddafi take over? (Libya)

Background Information

Muammar al-Qaddafi has been the leader of Libya since 1969. Since then, his leadership has gone from hostile to cooperative. For many years, Libya supported Palestinian independence. During the Reagan administration, there was an attempt to overthrow al-Qaddafi. Since then, al-Qaddafi has improved his relationships with Middle Eastern nations and the West. He was the first Arab leader to speak out against al Qaeda and terrorism after the September 11 attacks. He has cooperated with UN inspections of Libya. Because Libya does not have the oil wealth it once did, al-Qaddafi has changed his politics in order to work with other countries more effectively.

Reading Strategy:
Predicting

Have students look back at their predictions from Lesson 31–2. Ask them to discuss what they've learned in this lesson that either supports or refutes their predictions.

In April 1986, a disco in West Berlin that was popular with American service people was bombed. Two people were killed and 200 were injured. The United States learned that Libya was responsible for this act. In response, U.S. warplanes struck targets in Libya.

Al-Qaddafi spent much of Libya's oil profits on new weapons and a stronger army. He also supported terrorist actions against Americans and Israelis. However, in 2001, a top official in Libya said his country was prepared to restore its ties with the United States. By 2003, Libya announced that it would give up its nuclear weapons program. The United States returned to having full political relations with the country by 2006.

Why Do Oil Prices Continue to Change?

Oil prices rose sharply at the end of the Persian Gulf War. Hussein's Iraqi troops set fire to the oil fields of Kuwait as they left that country. This decreased the supply of oil exported from Kuwait. Other OPEC nations increased supplies and repairs to lines in Kuwait. This made prices come back down.

Reading Strategy:
Predicting

Think about the prediction you made in the last lesson. What details can you now add to make your prediction more specific?

During the 2000s, oil prices rose to an all-time high. The price per barrel of crude oil was $25 in September 2003. By August 2005, it had risen to $60 per barrel. It reached the highest price ever in July 2006, at $78.40 per barrel. Experts believe the prices may have risen due to fears about nuclear arms advances in North Korea and Iran. As those fears eased up a bit, the price of oil decreased slightly. However, oil prices continue to change and are still an issue today.

REVIEW

Word Bank

Kuwait

Libya

military

oil fields

OPEC

Saudi Arabia

weapon

On a sheet of paper, write the words from the Word Bank to complete each sentence correctly.

1. The Middle East's _____ give Arab countries power.

2. An organization called _____ manages the oil for several parts of the world.

3. During the Israeli-Arab wars, the Arabs used their oil as a(n) _____.

4. Most profits from oil go toward building a strong Arab _____.

5. Most of the oil in the Middle East comes from _____.

6. Muammar al-Qaddafi came to power after overthrowing the king of _____.

7. Hussein's Iraqi troops set fire to the oil fields of _____ before leaving the country.

On a sheet of paper, write the answer to each question. Use complete sentences.

8. Why did U.S. warplanes strike targets in Libya?

9. Why does OPEC have such tremendous power?

10. What do experts think caused oil to go up in price?

Lesson 31–3 Review Answers

1. oil fields **2.** OPEC **3.** weapon **4.** military **5.** Saudi Arabia **6.** Libya **7.** Kuwait **8.** The United States learned that Libya was responsible for an attack in West Berlin. **9.** OPEC sets the price for oil. OPEC can make oil prices go up or deny oil to certain countries. **10.** Experts believe prices have risen because of fears about nuclear arms advances in North Korea and Iran.

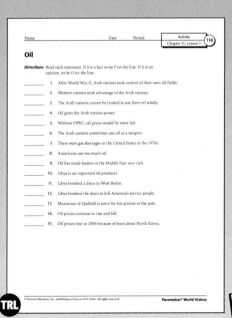

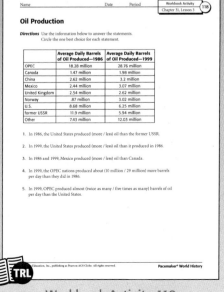

Life in the Middle East

Lesson at a Glance

Chapter 31 Lesson 4

Overview This lesson summarizes what life is like in Middle Eastern countries, particularly Israel.

Objectives

- To describe life in the Middle East today
- To explain how life in the Middle East is similar to life during ancient times

Student Pages 678–680

Teacher's Resource Library

Workbook Activity 119

Activity 119

Modified Activity 119

---

1 Warm-Up Activity

Write "Life in the Middle East" on chart paper and draw a three-column KWL graphic organizer. Have students give examples of things they *Know* about life in the Middle East, based on the previous lessons in the chapter. Ask students *What* they would like to know, and write their questions in the second column. Reserve the third column for things students have *Learned* after reading the chapter.

Reading Strategy:
Predicting

Ask students to make a prediction about what life in the Middle East is like. Encourage them to be specific, making a prediction about a topic such as work, school, industry, or recreation in the Middle East.

---

2 Teaching the Lesson

Point out that while much of the history of the Middle East revolves around conflict, it is a region where people continue to live and work in regular daily routines, despite the hardships of war. Tell students they will read more about life in the Middle East in this lesson.

Objectives

- To describe life in the Middle East today
- To explain how life in the Middle East is similar to life during ancient times

Reading Strategy:
Predicting

Based on what you have read in the previous lessons, predict what you think this lesson will be about.

The Middle East is, without a doubt, a land of war and conflict. It faces serious problems that will have to be dealt with. Still, the Middle East has fine, modern cities, well-educated people, farmlands, and productive industries.

What Is Life in the Middle East Like?

Israel is one of the most industrialized and advanced nations of the Middle East. About 85 percent of Israel's people live and work in modern cities. Israel's farms are a source of pride. Most of Israel's land is poor. Some of the land is too rocky or steep for farming. Other areas get little rainfall. Only through hard work and agricultural know-how could those lands be productive. Still, Israel produces most of its own food.

Huge irrigation systems pump in water through underground pipelines. Scientists experiment with turning saltwater from the Mediterranean and Red seas into fresh water to soak their fields.

The Israelis have not won the perfect land. However, they have worked hard to build their nation.

Long before the first century A.D., the first civilizations were forming along the Tigris and Euphrates rivers and along the Nile River. Those early peoples concerned themselves with producing food and irrigating dry lands. They battled invaders who would take their lands. They argued over how they would worship their gods. In some ways, those people had much in common with today's Middle Eastern people.

Land in Israel along the Sea of Galilee is fertile. This is because of irrigation systems and the hard work of the Israeli people.

Ask:

- What are the countries of the Middle East like? (They have fine, modern cities, well-educated people, farmlands, and productive industries.)
- Which country in the Middle East is one of the most industrialized? (Israel)
- How are the first civilizations of this region similar to the people of today? (Early people concerned themselves with producing food and farming; they battled invaders; they argued over how to worship gods.)

Background Information

The Sea of Galilee is Israel's largest freshwater source. The name Galilee refers to the region in which this body of water is located. Although it is called a sea by tradition, it is not really a sea, but a lake.

LEARNING STYLES

Body/Kinesthetic

Have students work with a partner or in a small group. Direct them to choose one thing they learned about the Middle East; ideas may be taken from the KWL chart generated in this lesson, or students may choose an event from the text. Have each group pantomime or role-play its event for the class. Then ask students to identify the event that was presented. You may want to have each group tell you what they are presenting beforehand, so that you can arrange the presentations in chronological order.

TIMELINE STUDY

Answer: 1979

TIMELINE STUDY:

THE MIDDLE EAST: 1945–2010

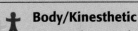

During which year did militant Iranians capture the U.S. embassy in Tehran?

1948
State of Israel declared; Israeli-Arab war

1960
OPEC is formed

1967
Six-Day War

1973
Yom Kippur War

1977
Anwar el-Sadat visits Israel

1980
Iran-Iraq war begins

1982
Israel invades Lebanon

1991
Persian Gulf War

2001
9/11—al Qaeda attacks United States

2004
al Qaeda bombs train stations in Madrid, Spain

1950 — 1960 — 1970 — 1980 — 1990 — 2000 — 2010

1956
Egypt takes control of Suez Canal

1979
Egypt-Israel peace treaty signed; Khomeini takes power in Iran; U.S. embassy in Tehran captured and hostages taken

1988
Cease-fire declared in Iran-Iraq war

1996
Arafat becomes president of Palestinian Authority

1945–PRESENT

The Middle East Chapter 31 **679**

ELL/ESL STRATEGY

Language Objective:
To compare and contrast life in North America with life in Israel

Distribute a compare and contrast graphic organizer with three columns. Title the first column *Life in North America*, the second column *Life in Israel*, and the third column *Life in North America and Israel*. Direct students to write facts about life in North America in the first column, and different facts about life in Israel in the second column. Students can refer to page 678 for facts about life in Israel. Then, have students use the text and draw conclusions to write similarities about life in both countries, such as *children go to school*. When students have finished their charts, have them share and discuss them with a partner.

TEACHER ALERT

Revisit the KWL chart students created with your guidance. Have students offer suggestions of things they have *Learned* about the Middle East, and write them in the third column. If there are questions students had that were not answered in the chapter, have volunteers suggest resources for additional research.

CAREER CONNECTION

The primary businesses in Israel include metal products, electronic, and biomedical equipment. Israel is known as one of the world's centers for diamond cutting and polishing. Israel is also a world leader in software development and the country continues to be a tourist destination. In 1998, the city of Tel Aviv was named on of the 10 most technologically advanced cities in the world.

Lesson 31–4 Review Answers

1. war **2.** Israel **3.** cities **4.** irrigation **5.** saltwater **6.** Nile **7.** land **8.** The Middle East has modern cities, educated people, fertile farmlands, and productive industries. **9.** The farms are productive because of hard work and agricultural know-how. **10.** There was fighting over land and religion.

LESSON 31-4 REVIEW

Word Bank
cities
irrigation
Israel
land
Nile
saltwater
war

On a sheet of paper, write the word from the Word Bank to complete each sentence correctly.

1. The Middle East is a land of _____ and conflict.

2. _____ is one of the most advanced nations in the Middle East.

3. About 85 percent of Israel's people work and live in modern _____.

4. Large _____ systems pump water through underground pipelines.

5. Scientists are experimenting with turning _____ into fresh water to soak their fields.

6. Early civilizations formed along the Tigris and Euphrates rivers and the _____ River.

7. Early civilizations battled invaders who would try and take their _____.

On a sheet of paper, write the answer to each question. Use complete sentences.

8. Despite the problems, what good things are happening in the Middle East?

9. How are Israel's farms productive even with poor land?

10. What do early civilizations have in common with today's Middle Eastern people?

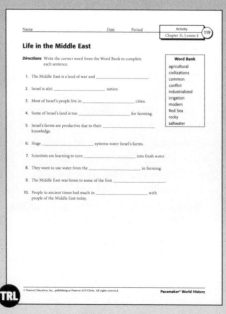

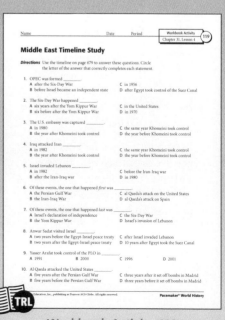

- Most Middle Eastern countries gained independence from Britain and France after World War II.

- Zionists wanted to set up a Jewish state in Palestine. The United Nations divided Palestine between Arabs and Jews.

- In 1948, the Jews set up the state of Israel. The remaining lands of Palestine became part of the Arab state of Jordan. Since 1948, Arabs and Israelis have fought wars for control of these lands. Conflict or the threat of conflict continues.

- Many Palestinians who had fled from Israel were forced to live in crowded refugee camps. They formed the PLO and demanded their lands back.

- Lebanon had a civil war between Muslims and Christians that lasted from 1975 to 1990.

- Iran captured the U.S. embassy in its capital in 1979. It happened after its former Shah came to the United States in exile. Americans from the embassy were taken hostage.

- Territory disputes caused a war between Iran and Iraq that lasted for nearly eight years.

- In 1990, Iraq invaded its neighbor, Kuwait. In the Persian Gulf War, the United States and other nations used military force to free Kuwait.

- Terrorism by Middle Eastern groups has spread to many other locations around the globe. Some of these places include: Spain, England, and the United States.

- Many nations of the Middle East have wealth and power because the world depends on their oil.

Chapter 31 Summary

Have students read the Chapter Summary on page 681 to review the main ideas presented in Chapter 31.

Ask:

- When did most Middle Eastern countries gain independence from Britain and France? (after WWII)
- Who wanted to set up a Jewish state in Palestine? (the Zionists)
- Who divided Palestine between Arabs and Jews? (the United Nations)
- Who controls the lands of Palestine? (Arabs and Jews continue to fight wars over who controls the land.)
- Where did Palestinians live when they fled from Israel? (in refugee camps)
- When was Lebanon's civil war? (from 1975 to 1990)
- What country captured U.S. hostages in 1979? (Iran)
- What caused a war between Iran and Iraq that lasted nearly eight years? (territory disputes)
- What countries fought in the Persian Gulf War? (the United States and Iraq)
- Name three countries that have been affected by terrorism. (the United States, England, and Spain)
- What gives many nations in the Middle East power? (the world's dependency on its oil)

TEACHER'S RESOURCE

The AGS Globe Teaching Strategies in Social Studies Transparencies may be used with this chapter. The transparencies add an interactive dimension to expand and enhance the Pacemaker® *World History* program content.

CHAPTER PROJECT FOLLOW-UP

 Have students sort through and read the stories about the Middle East they collected. Then have students organize the stories according to topics or countries. Have them choose one topic or country to write about. Students should write a summary describing what they learned from the current newspaper stories and how it might be related to the historical information in the text.

Chapter 31 Review

Use the Chapter Review to prepare students for tests and to reteach content from the chapter.

Chapter 31 Mastery Test

The Teacher's Resource Library includes two forms of the Chapter 31 Mastery Test. Each test addresses the chapter Goals for Learning. An optional third page of additional critical-thinking items is included for each test. The difficulty level of the two forms is equivalent.

Chapter 31 Review Answers

Vocabulary Review

1. negotiate

2. hostile

3. terrorism

4. homeland

5. Zionism

6. traitor

7. embassy

8. hostages

9. arms

10. stalemate

Chapter Review Questions

11. In ancient times the Jews considered Palestine their homeland, a land promised to them by God. They said they were in Palestine before the Arabs ever settled there.

12. Arabs said the land had been theirs for 2,000 years, so it should remain in their hands.

13. The Palestinians left Israel after Israel won the war with the Arab nations. The Palestinians were now homeless and they settled in refugee camps outside Israel.

Word Bank

arms

embassy

homeland

hostages

hostile

negotiate

stalemate

terrorism

traitor

Zionism

Vocabulary Review

On a sheet of paper, use the words from the Word Bank to complete each sentence correctly.

1. When countries _____, they begin to talk and work toward agreement.

2. The situation in Palestine has turned more _____, or unfriendly, over the years.

3. Middle Eastern _____ has spread to the larger world.

4. The Jews consider Palestine to be their _____.

5. _____ is the movement to set up a Jewish nation in Palestine.

6. Arab nationalists called Sadat a(n) _____ because they thought he had betrayed the Arab cause.

7. The U.S. _____ in Tehran, Iran was captured in 1979.

8. In 1979, Iranians took American _____ and demanded the Shah's return.

9. The Soviets offered to sell _____, or weapons, to Egypt in 1955.

10. Talks over the future of Palestine are at a(n) _____. They are in a position where no action can be taken.

Chapter Review Questions

On a sheet of paper, write the answers to each question. Use complete sentences.

11. Why did the Jews consider Palestine their homeland?

12. Why did the Arabs think Palestine belonged to them?

13. Why did many Palestinians end up in refugee camps in the late 1940s?

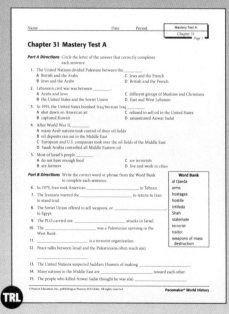

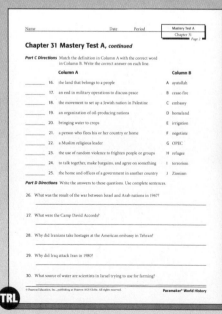

Chapter 31 Mastery Test A, pages 1–3

Test Tip

Be sure you understand what a test question is asking. Read it twice if necessary.

14. Why did the United States and other nations fight against Iraq in the Gulf War?

Critical Thinking

On a sheet of paper, write your response to each question. Use complete sentences.

15. Do you think the United States should try to help bring peace to the Middle East? Why or why not?

16. The United States and other countries are dependent on Middle Eastern oil. How do you think they could become less dependent?

17. Do you think it was right for the United Nations to divide Palestine into two parts?

Using the Timeline

Use the timeline on page 679 to answer the questions.

18. When did the oil-rich nations of the Middle East form their own organization?

19. Which came first, the Six-Day War or the Yom Kippur War?

20. When did Egypt take control of the Suez Canal?

GROUP ACTIVITY

Form a group of four or five. Assign group members to be either a news anchor or a field reporter. Choose an event that happened in the Middle East after 1945. Use that event as the basis for a 5-minute newscast. (Look at the timeline on page 679 for some major events in the Middle East.) The event should focus on at least two different religious groups in the city (e.g., Jews, Christians, Muslims). Report the news "live" to the class.

1945–PRESENT   *The Middle East*   *Chapter 31*   **683**

---

14. The United States and other nations fought the Gulf War to defend Saudi Arabia and free Kuwait from Saddam Hussein.

Critical Thinking

15. Possible answers: Yes, because the United States depends on oil, or because it is the right thing to try to assure peace for the people there. No, because the problems are too old and only the people there can solve them.

16. Possible answers: Students may say that drilling for oil in Alaska, developing other energy resources, or conserving energy will help reduce dependence.

17. Possible answers: Yes, dividing Palestine into two parts gives the Jews and the Arabs their own place to live so there is less fighting. No, dividing Palestine is wrong because people should not be divided by their ethnicity or religion.

Using the Timeline

18. 1960

19. Six-Day War

20. 1956

GROUP ACTIVITY

Students should work cooperatively to research and choose an event. The newscast should be accurate and balanced.

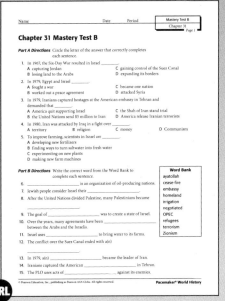

Chapter 31 Mastery Test B, pages 1–3

The Middle East Chapter 31   **683**

Chapter 32: The End of the Soviet Union: 1980–PRESENT
pages 684–703

Lessons

1. **Changes in the Soviet Union**
   pages 686–689

2. **The End of the Soviet Union and the Cold War**
   pages 690–692

3. **Changes in Eastern Europe**
   pages 693–700

Chapter Summary and Review, pages 701–703

Audio Library

Skill Track for World History

Teacher's Resource Library TRL

Workbook Activities 120–122

Activities 120–122

Modified Activities 120–122

Life Skills Connection 32

Key Vocabulary Words 32

Chapter 32 Self-Study Guide

Chapter 32 Outline

Chapter 32 Mastery Tests A and B

(Answer Keys for the Teacher's Resource Library begin on page 809 of the Teacher's Edition.)

Introducing the Chapter

From March 1985 until December 1991, Mikhail Gorbachev and the people of the Soviet Union gradually moved their nation toward greater freedom and increased interaction with the West. The cold war ended in February 1992 when Boris Yeltsin, the new leader of the republic of Russia, and U.S. President George H.W. Bush declared an end to hostilities between their nations.

Ask:

- How was life changing for the Soviet people during the late 1980s and early 1990s? (The Soviet people started having greater

---

The End of the Soviet Union

The Soviet Union began to change rapidly during the late 1980s and early 1990s. The Soviet people started having greater freedoms and focusing less on the strength of their army. The cold war, which had caused such fear among Americans, was coming to an end.

A man named Mikhail Gorbachev came to power in the Soviet Union in 1985. Like no Soviet leader before, he wanted to work together with other nations. He introduced bold new policies for the Soviet Union. Many nations would come to feel the effects of these historic changes.

GOALS FOR LEARNING

- To describe how Mikhail Gorbachev improved the Soviet Union's relations with Western nations
- To explain how the Soviet Union disbanded and became an alliance of independent republics
- To describe the freedom gained by Eastern European satellites and the unrest that often followed

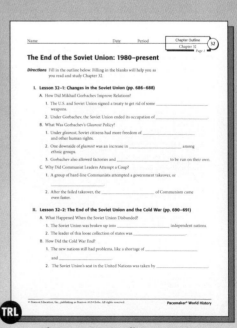

Reading Strategy: Text Structure

The way a text is organized can help readers determine which information is most important. Before you begin reading, page through this chapter to see how it is organized. When doing so, pay special attention to the title, headings, boldfaced words, maps, and photographs. When reading, ask yourself:

- How is this text organized?
- Is it a problem and solution, description, or sequence?
- Is it compare and contrast or cause and effect?

Think about the structure of the text and then summarize what you have just read.

Key Vocabulary Words

Lesson 1
Glasnost The Soviet policy of open discussion of political and social issues

Perestroika The Soviet policy of economic and government reform

Coup A bold, sudden move to bring about change in a government

Lesson 2
Disband To break up

Lesson 3
Reunification The act of joining together again

---

freedoms. They focused less on the strength of their army.)

- What was happening to the cold war between the Soviet Union and the United States during this time period? (The cold war was coming to an end.)
- As the new leader of the Soviet Union in 1985, what changes did Mikhail Gorbachev bring about? (He introduced bold new policies for the Soviet Union.)

Reading Strategy:
Text Structure

Teaching students to recognize common text structures found in expository texts can help students monitor their comprehension.

Key Vocabulary Words

Point out that these chapter words are presented in the order they appear in each lesson. They are also found in the glossary.

LIFE SKILLS CONNECTION

Students compare current maps of their communities to older ones and list the differences. Help student locate older maps in the library or town hall.

KEY VOCABULARY

Students choose the correct word from the Word Bank to complete each sentence.

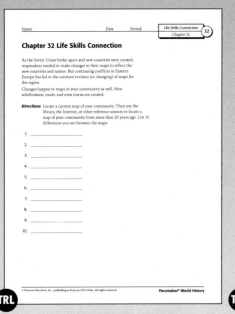

Chapter 32 Life Skills Connection

As the Soviet Union broke apart and new countries were created, mapmakers needed to make changes to their maps to reflect the new countries and names. But continuing conflicts in Eastern Europe has led to the constant revision (or changing) of maps for the region.

Changes happen to maps in your community as well. New subdivisions, roads, and even towns are created.

Directions Locate a current map of your community. Then use the library, the Internet, or other reference sources to locate a map of your community from more than 20 years ago. List 10 differences you see between the maps.

1. _____
2. _____
3. _____
4. _____
5. _____
6. _____
7. _____
8. _____
9. _____
10. _____

Chapter 32 Key Vocabulary Words

Directions Write the correct word from the Word Bank to complete each sentence.

Word Bank
coup
disbanded
glasnost
perestroika
reunification

1. Mikhail Gorbachev gave Soviet citizens more freedoms with his policy of _____

2. Gorbachev's government survived a _____ attempt by some unhappy Communist leaders.

3. Gorbachev called his economic reforms _____.

4. The two halves of Germany began the process of _____ after the fall of the Berlin Wall.

5. The Soviet Union was _____ into separate states during Gorbachev's administration.

Life Skills Connection 32   Key Vocabulary Words 32   *End of the Soviet Union Chapter 32*   **685**

Chapter 32 Lesson 1

Overview This lesson describes the enormous economic and social changes that swept through the Soviet Union and its satellite nations under Mikhail Gorbachev's leadership.

Objectives

- To list three changes in the Soviet Union for which Mikhail Gorbachev was responsible
- To describe the attempted coup and the effect it had on Communism in the Soviet Union

Student Pages 686–689

Teacher's Resource Library

Workbook Activity 120

Activity 120

Modified Activity 120

Vocabulary

coup
glasnost
perestroika

Challenge students to write a statement using each vocabulary word. For example, they might imagine themselves the newly elected leader of a country who is addressing the population for the first time. Invite volunteers to read their statements to the class.

PRONUNCIATION GUIDE

Use this list to help students pronounce difficult words in this lesson.

Mikhail Gorbachev
(mi kil´ gôr´ bə chôf´)

Azerbaijani (ä´ zər bī jä´ nē)

1 Warm-Up Activity

Have students create a list of factors that would cause the government of a country to dissolve. Write each idea on the board. Group the ideas into economic, political, and social factors. Query students as to where one factor

---

Changes in the Soviet Union

Objectives

- To list three changes in the Soviet Union for which Mikhail Gorbachev was responsible
- To describe the attempted coup and the effect it had on Communism in the Soviet Union

**Reading Strategy:
Text Structure**

Preview this lesson. Notice the headings, features, and boldfaced words.

Some of the biggest changes in recent history happened within the Soviet Union and its Eastern European satellites. Soviet policy turned from militarism and hostility to a freer and more open society. After years of cold war, the Soviet Union and the United States, the world's two superpowers, began to make peace.

Changes in the Soviet Union began in 1985 when a man named Mikhail Gorbachev came to power. Gorbachev introduced new policies within the Soviet Union and improved Soviet relations with other nations.

How Did Mikhail Gorbachev Improve Relations?

Friendly relations with Western countries were important to Gorbachev's plans for the Soviet Union. Good relations, he hoped, would lead to trade agreements and economic improvements. They might also lead to a more secure and peaceful world. In 1987, Gorbachev and U.S. President Ronald Reagan signed the INF Treaty (Intermediate-Range Nuclear Force Treaty). For the first time, both sides agreed to get rid of an entire class of nuclear weapons. In 1991, the Strategic Arms Reduction Treaty (START) was signed in Moscow. Gorbachev and U.S. President George Bush agreed to the treaty. It would reduce nuclear weapons on both sides by 30 percent.

Gorbachev took other steps to show that his country had changed its attitude toward the West. In 1989, he brought Soviet troops home from Afghanistan. He agreed to stop supplying military aid to the Communist Sandinista government in Nicaragua (see Chapter 33). He pressured Cuba's Communist leader, Fidel Castro, to bring home the Cuban troops from Angola in Africa. They had been involved in a civil war there. Gorbachev also persuaded Vietnam to withdraw its forces from Cambodia.

---

alone could cause a government to collapse, or if the interaction of all factors is required. Explain that in this lesson, students will learn about the collapse of the USSR.

Reading Strategy:
Text Structure

Draw students' attention to the Reading Strategy on page 686.

Ask:

- What is the structure of the headings on pages 686–688? (They are questions.)

- What is the significance of the boldfaced words? (They are vocabulary words.)

CHAPTER PROJECT

Give students a list of the Soviet Union's Eastern European satellite countries that split from the USSR in the late 1980s and early 1990s. This list may include: East Germany, Hungary, Czechoslovakia, Poland, Romania, and Bulgaria. Have students work in groups and choose one of the countries from the list. Encourage students to do independent research to learn about what conditions were like under Soviet rule and the details of that country's separation from the USSR. Have each group prepare a class presentation.

What Was Gorbachev's *Glasnost* Policy?

Although Mikhail Gorbachev was a Communist, he
encouraged his nation to be more open to information
and ideas from the democratic West. He put into action a
policy of *glasnost* or "openness." Suddenly, Soviet citizens
had more freedom of speech and basic human rights than
ever before.

A new branch of the government was set up. Its members
were directly elected by the people. Soviet citizens could
choose people they wanted to represent them in the
government. The newly elected people did not even have
to be members of the Communist Party. For the first time,
the Communist leaders had to listen to the opinions and
complaints of the Soviet people.

The policy of *glasnost* led many of the republics within the
Soviet Union to demand the right to manage their own
affairs. The Baltic states of Estonia, Latvia, and Lithuania
even went so far as to seek independence from Moscow.

One unfortunate result of *glasnost* was an increase in
hostilities between different national groups within
the Soviet Union. In many places, long-standing
disagreements boiled over into outbreaks of violence.
For example, violence broke out between Armenians and
Azerbaijanis as to who owned a particular territory in the
Caucasus Mountains. Many people were killed as a result.

Gorbachev knew that by the late 1980s, the Soviet
economy was in serious trouble. He also knew that
he would have to make major changes in order to see
any improvement. Therefore, he proposed a policy of
perestroika, or "restructuring." Factories and businesses
around the country would no longer be controlled by
Moscow. Each would be responsible for running its own
operations. In addition, individual Soviet citizens would
be allowed to engage in small-scale private business.

 You Decide

Lead a discussion in which
students speculate about how
they might have felt if they had been a
Soviet citizen voting for the first time.

Background Information

Mikhail Gorbachev was born in 1931, in a peasant village in the North Caucasus. As a young man, he worked in the wheat fields outside his hometown. In December 1990, Gorbachev was awarded the Nobel Peace Prize for his efforts in the Soviet Union. Here is an excerpt from his acceptance speech: "Mankind would one day be faced with a dilemma: either to be joined in a true union of nations or to perish in a war of annihilation ending in the extinction of the human race. Now, as we move from the second to the third millennium, the clock has struck the moment of truth." For Gorbachev's entire acceptance speech and other speeches, have students access the following Web site: www.agsglobepmwh.com/page688

LEARNING STYLES

Logical/Mathematical
Have students research the order in which republics broke away to become independent nations (they can reference the map on page 696). Students should research the dates for independence and number the new nations, beginning with 1 for the first republic to become independent, and so on. Have students use the dates to create a flow chart showing the sequence of events leading up to the last republic to become an independent country. Post students work for classmates to view.

Reading Strategy:
Text Structure

Have several volunteers give their answers to each question asked in the headings. You may want to lead a discussion in which students compare and contrast several answers to the same heading.

Coup
A bold, sudden move to bring about change in a government

Reading Strategy:
Text Structure

Notice that the section headings are written as questions. After you read each section, try to answer the question asked in the heading.

Mikhail Gorbachev introduced policies of openness and restructuring to the Soviet Union.

Gorbachev also welcomed U.S. corporations to set up joint operations in the Soviet Union. A number of U.S. companies signed agreements with the Soviets. In Moscow, the largest fast-food restaurant of a major U.S. chain of restaurants opened for business.

Many people in both the Soviet Union and the United States were declaring that the cold war was finally over. Yet in spite of all the changes taking place, Soviet citizens had questions. Would Gorbachev's plans be successful? What would happen if Gorbachev were to fall from power?

Why Did Communist Leaders Attempt a Coup?

Hard-line Soviet Communists criticized Gorbachev's new policies. During 1990, the Soviet Union was faced with a widespread economic crisis. Food shops in many cities were empty. Conflicts continued in some of the republics. Some Soviets believed that Gorbachev was changing things too quickly.

In August 1991, a group of hard-line Communist leaders made a move to take over power in the Soviet Union. They announced that Gorbachev had been "taken ill" and had left Moscow for a "rest." However, the **coup** failed. Since Gorbachev had begun reform in 1985, Soviet citizens had been introduced to new freedoms. Despite hard times, they were not ready to give up their rights.

Following the failure of the coup, change came even more rapidly. Citizens toppled statues of Communist heroes that had long stood in city squares. The city of Leningrad took back the name it held before the coming of Communism. It became St. Petersburg again. The country became known as the Union of Sovereign States. The attempted coup only sped up the death of Communism inside the Soviet Union.

ELL/ESL STRATEGY

Language Objective:
To encourage students to discover the meanings of unfamiliar words

Have students work in small groups to find a minimum of 10 words in the lesson that are unfamiliar to them. After students have identified 10 words and used their dictionaries to discover their meanings, ask each group to collaborate on a paragraph that uses at least five of the words. Have a volunteer from each group read the group's paragraph aloud and explain which words were unfamiliar.

COMMON ERROR

Students may assume that a coup happens through violence. On August 19, 1991, music played on state television and radio as the coup leaders announced that Gorbachev was sick, and they were taking control. In truth, Gorbachev had been detained by hardliners. Boris Yeltsin climbed aboard a tank outside the Russian parliament and defied the hard-liners' coup. Tens of thousands of people made barricades around the building where the Russian parliament met. Two days later, the tanks withdrew, the coup plotters fled, and Gorbachev returned to Moscow.

Word Bank

Afghanistan

cold war

coup

glasnost

Mikhail Gorbachev

Ronald Reagan

St. Petersburg

On a sheet of paper, write the word from the Word Bank to complete each sentence correctly.

1. The Soviet Union and the United States began to make peace in the 1980s. This peace was after years of _____.

2. Changes were made in 1985 when _____ came to power in the Soviet Union.

3. Gorbachev met with _____ in 1987 to begin limiting nuclear weapons.

4. In 1989, Soviet troops were taken out of _____ and brought home.

5. Gorbachev put into action a policy of _____ or "openness."

6. In 1991, a(n) _____ tried to take over the Soviet government and failed.

7. As Communism was dying, the city of Leningrad changed its name back to _____.

On a sheet of paper, write the answer to each question. Use complete sentences.

8. What was one bad result of *glasnost*?

9. What is the meaning of *perestroika*?

10. What changes occurred after the takeover of the Soviet government failed?

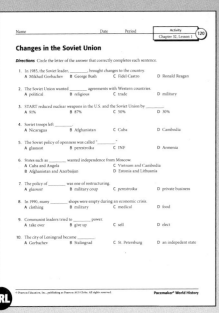

3   Reinforce and Extend

IN THE COMMUNITY

Invite a community leader to your class. Prior to the visit, have students brainstorm to create a list of questions to ask the community leader. Students should query the community leader about important community issues, how specific problems are being addressed, and what the leader sees for the future of the community.

AT HOME

Encourage students to talk to their family about their experiences in the cold war. Students can ask about family members' experiences in school with air raid drills and bomb shelters. Students should ask how children of the time felt about the cold war threat. Did they think the threat was serious? Were they afraid? Ask volunteers to share their findings with the class.

STUDY SKILLS

Have students find five facts about changes Gorbachev made in the Soviet Union. Ask students to write opinions about each of the facts they listed. Ask students, *Do you agree with what Gorbachev did?*

Lesson 32–1 Review Answers

1. cold war 2. Mikhail Gorbachev
3. Ronald Reagan 4. Afghanistan
5. glasnost 6. coup 7. St. Petersburg
8. There was an increase in hostilities between different national groups within the Soviet Union. There were many outbreaks of violence.
9. *Perestroika* means restructuring. It was the Soviet policy of economic and government reform. 10. Citizens took down statues of Communist heroes. The city of Leningrad changed its name back to St. Petersburg. The country became known as the Union of Sovereign States.

Lesson at a Glance

Chapter 32 Lesson 2

Overview This lesson describes the end of both the Soviet Union and the cold war.

Objectives

■ To discuss the importance of Boris Yeltsin as leader of an independent Russia

■ To explain the advances Vladimir Putin made with Western nations

Student Pages 690–692

Teacher's Resource Library

Workbook Activity 121

Activity 121

Modified Activity 121

Vocabulary

disband

Explain to students that a thesaurus can help them to find synonyms for words and phrases. Synonyms are words that have the same, or nearly the same, meanings. Ask student to look up the vocabulary word in a thesaurus and name several synonyms that they find. You may want to write a few of these synonyms on the board and talk about how each word has a slightly different connotation. Some synonyms for the word *disband* are: "disperse, scatter, break up, split apart, separate."

1 Warm-Up Activity

Have students preview the information on pages 690–692 by reading the subheads, studying the photo on page 690, and looking at the Word Bank words on page 692.

2 Teaching the Lesson

Ask students to remember what life was like for people in the Soviet Union under Stalin. Then have them read pages 690–692 to find out how the Soviet Union came to an end and what replaced it.

LESSON
32-2

Objectives

■ To discuss the importance of Boris Yeltsin as leader of an independent Russia

■ To explain the advances Vladimir Putin made with Western nations

Disband
To break up

Reading Strategy:
Text Structure

As you read this lesson, use a graphic organizer to help you understand the events leading up to the end of the Soviet Union.

The End of the Soviet Union and the Cold War

In December 1991, the Soviet Union **disbanded,** or broke up. It was replaced by 15 independent nations. Gorbachev had returned to power, but was unable to hold the union together. Three of the 15 republics that made up the Soviet Union—Latvia, Estonia, and Lithuania—had declared their independence earlier that year. On December 21, leaders of 11 of the 12 remaining republics signed agreements creating the Commonwealth of Independent States (CIS). This was a loose alliance of fully independent states. The Communist Party was no longer in charge. Mikhail Gorbachev stepped down. Boris Yeltsin, president of the republic of Russia, became a leader and spokesman for the new Commonwealth. Yeltsin had long been calling for an end to Communist rule.

Boris Yeltsin led Russia to democracy and freedom after the Soviet Union collapsed.

Ask:

• What party was no longer in charge as a result of the breakup of the Soviet Union? (Communist Party)

• When the Soviet Union disbanded, how many nations replaced it? (15)

• When Vladimir Putin was appointed prime minister in 1999, there had been five prime ministers in 18 months. Why do you think this was so? (Answers will vary. Students may suggest that this indicates how unstable politics in the Russian Federation were during that time.)

Reading Strategy:
Text Structure

Remind students that graphic organizers show patterns and relationships between words and ideas. Ask students to name a few of the graphic organizers they have used to help them learn and remember important information. These graphic organizers may include a Venn diagram, a timeline, an outline, a map, or a chart.

How Did the Cold War End?

On February 1, 1992, Boris Yeltsin met with U.S. President George H.W. Bush. The leaders declared an end to "cold war hostility." The United States and other nations of the free world pledged to send aid to help rebuild the economy of the new nations.

The Soviet Union died, and 15 new nations were born with many problems. The people still faced economic woes. Food and medicine continued to be in short supply. In some of the new nations, lives continued to be lost as different groups battled for control.

Russia, or the Russian Federation, is the largest and most powerful of the new nations. It took the seat at the UN that had been held by the Soviet Union.

What Did Vladimir Putin Do While In Office?

Yeltsin appointed Vladimir Putin prime minister in 1999. Putin was the fifth prime minister to be appointed in 18 months. The following year, Yeltsin resigned because of poor health. That same year, in 2000, Putin was elected president. He won more than half of all votes, as one of 11 candidates for president.

Vladimir Putin began his presidency by getting two weapons reduction agreements passed by the legislature. In talks with the United States and other Western nations, he said he wanted to reduce nuclear arms. He also wanted to take part in the fight against terrorism. Putin brought many important social reforms to Russia. He worked to build up Russia's vast energy supplies. He promoted changes to make the central Russian government stronger. Putin was reelected in 2004 for a four-year term.

Background Information

Reform in Russia has not been easy. Some new businesses and a new middle class have developed. But crime and dishonesty have also increased. Health care is poor. Also, factory workers are not producing as many goods. The government is unable to collect most taxes. It does not have money to take care of the old and poor. In 1998, the government could not even pay its bills.

LEARNING STYLES

Interpersonal/Group Learning

There is a wealth of history among the many ethnic groups within each state in the Commonwealth of Independent States. Have a small group research the history and ethnic composition of each of the CIS members. Have students divide responsibilities, with different students researching different states. Students can select one individual as moderator and present their information orally to the class in a panel-discussion format.

LEARNING STYLES

Visual/Spatial

Have students use the Internet to find photos of the Soviet Union during and after the cold war. Have students print the photos and create a collage showing the changes in the Soviet Union. Place photos taken during the cold war on the left and photos taken after the cold war on the right. Encourage students to look for pictures of students, families, workers, stores, schools, and factories among other things. Have each student present his or her collage in class and talk about a few of the photos that were found.

ELL/ESL STRATEGY

Language Objective:
To listen in order to gather information

Pair ELL students with English-speaking students. Have them listen to the audio for each section of this chapter, following along in their text as they do. Challenge them to agree on the answer to each subhead question. Students can listen to the audio again to make sure that their answers are correct. They should produce a list of questions and answers for each section and study the lists as they prepare for the Chapter Review.

COMMON ERROR

Students may assume that both the people and the leaders of the former Soviet Union have embraced their newfound freedoms unconditionally. In fact, the collapse of the Soviet Union has brought enough social and economic difficulties that some people have come to believe that the dissolution of the Soviet Union was a grave error.

3 | Reinforce and Extend

COMMON ERROR

Remind students that capitalism is a system that allows for private ownership of business.

WORLD CULTURES

Satellite nations of the Soviet Union often were made up of several ethnic groups. Soviet influence kept peace among these various groups. Following the breakup of the Soviet Union, some of these nations struggled violently for their own identity. The former Czechoslovakia separated peacefully into two nations—the Czech Republic and Slovakia. On the other hand, the former nation of Yugoslavia has had a stormy recent history. In the early 1990s, Croatia, Macedonia, Bosnia and Herzegovina, and Slovenia, all part of Yugoslavia, declared independence from the Yugoslavian government dominated by the Serbs. Since then, the former Yugoslavia has been plagued by ethnic and territorial wars, especially among Croatians, Muslims, and Serbs.

Lesson 32–2 Review Answers

1. independent 2. Boris Yeltsin 3. George Bush 4. Russia 5. Vladimir Putin 6. president 7. energy 8. There was economic trouble. Food and medicine were in short supply. People continued to die as different groups battled for control. 9. Yeltsin resigned because of poor health. 10. Possible answers: He has passed two weapons reduction agreements. He has taken part in the fight against terrorism. He worked to build Russia's energy supply. He promoted change to make the central Russian government stronger.

LESSON 32-2 REVIEW

Word Bank

Boris Yeltsin
energy
George H.W. Bush
independent
president
Russia
Vladimir Putin

On a sheet of paper, write the word from the Word Bank to complete each sentence correctly.

1. In 1991, the Soviet Union broke up into 15 _____ nations.

2. After Gorbachev stepped down from power, _____ became the leader of the new commonwealth.

3. Boris Yeltsin met with U.S. President _____ in 1991 to end the cold war.

4. The Soviet Union disbanded in 1991. The largest and most powerful of the new nations was _____.

5. Boris Yeltsin made _____ prime minister in 1999.

6. In 2000, Vladimir Putin was elected _____.

7. Putin has worked hard to build Russia's _____ supply.

On a sheet of paper, write the answer to each question. Use complete sentences.

8. When the Soviet Union ended, what problems did the 15 new nations have?

9. Why did Boris Yeltsin step down from office?

10. List two examples of what Vladimir Putin has done while in office.

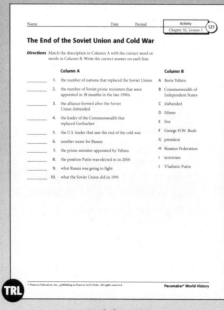

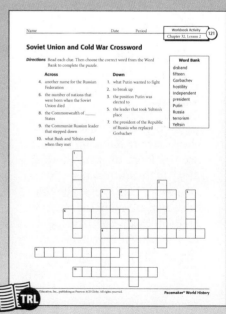

Activity 121   Workbook Activity 121

LESSON 32-3

Changes in Eastern Europe

Objectives

- To describe how Germany reunited
- To explain the unrest in Yugoslavia and Chechnya

Reading Strategy: Text Structure

As you read, look for words like *first, then, next, afterward,* and *finally.* These words will help you understand the sequence of events that changed Eastern Europe.

The Soviet Union was not the only country going through changes during the late 1980s and early 1990s. As a result of Gorbachev's *glasnost* policy, the Soviets loosened their control over their satellite countries in Eastern Europe.

How Did Soviet Satellites Gain Their Freedom?

Back in 1956, Hungary had tried to cut its ties with the Soviets. It wanted to set up its own government, free of Soviet influence. However, Soviet troops marched into Hungary, crushing the movement for independence.

Then in 1968, there was trouble in Czechoslovakia. The Soviet government felt that the Czechoslovakian Communist Party was losing control of the country. The Russians were afraid that too much freedom of speech would turn the people away from Communism. So in August 1968, Soviet tanks rumbled through Czechoslovakia. Soon, new people were running the Czech government—people chosen by Moscow.

During the 1970s, many workers rioted in Poland. They were demanding higher pay and better working conditions. They wanted a labor union, something unheard of under Communist rule. In 1980, the Polish government allowed the workers to form the union. The new workers' union was called Solidarity. Its leader was a man named Lech Walesa.

In 1982, the government began to fear that many of Solidarity's demands went against Communist ideals. That year, the Communists arrested Solidarity's leaders and declared the union illegal. Many people inside Poland and in the West insisted that the Soviet Union had forced the Polish government to outlaw Solidarity.

1980-PRESENT *The End of the Soviet Union* Chapter 32 **693**

Reading Strategy: Text Structure

Tell students that words such as *first, then, next, afterward,* and *finally* are words that signal chronology. They often tell us what will happen next, what happened first, and what will happen last. Ask students to find several examples of these words in the lesson, then explain how these words help them to better understand the text.

Lesson at a Glance

Lesson at a Glance

Chapter 32 Lesson 3

Overview This lesson describes the major changes that took place in the Soviet Union's satellite countries during the late 1980s and early 1990s, including the Solidarity movement in Poland, the reunification of Germany, and the unrest in Yugoslavia and Chechnya.

Objectives

- To describe how Germany reunited
- To explain the unrest in Yugoslavia and Chechnya

Student Pages 693–700

Teacher's Resource Library

Workbook Activity 122

Activity 122

Modified Activity 122

Vocabulary

Reunification

Write the vocabulary word on the board. Ask students to identify the root of the word. *(unify)* Tell students that the prefix *re-* comes from the Latin meaning *back* or *again* or *against.* When prefixes are added to words, they change the words' meanings in important ways. Some examples of this are as follows:

> call/recall
>
> tell/retell
>
> acquire/reacquire
>
> unification/reunification

Have students study these words, then lead a class discussion in which students discuss how the prefix *re-* changes the meaning of each word.

PRONUNCIATION GUIDE

Use this list to help students pronounce difficult words in this lesson.

Czechoslovakia (chek´ ə slə vä´ kē ə)

Nicolae Ceausescu
(nē´ kô lī´ chou shes´ kōō)

End of the Soviet Union Chapter 32 **693**

1 Warm-Up Activity

Ask students what they know about the fall of the Soviet Union and the radical changes that then happened in Eastern Europe. Have students preview the lesson by reading the subheads on pages 693–699, the information on the fall of the Berlin Wall (page 695), the History Fact (page 694), the map (page 696), and the timeline (page 699). Draw students' attention to the photos on page 694 and 697. Lead a discussion in which students speculate about what life might have been like for average citizens living in a satellite nation during the years just before independence from the Soviet Union.

History Fact

Encourage students to seek out more information on Slovakia and the Czech Republic by visiting their local library or conducting research on the Internet.

2 Teaching the Lesson

Ask students what they know about the Iron Curtain and the Berlin Wall. Have them read pages 693–699 to find out how these symbols of Communist repression were taken down.

Ask:

- What happened when Hungary tried to cuts its ties with the Soviet Union in 1956? (Soviet troops marched into Hungary. They crushed the movement for independence.)
- Name two other examples of satellite nations that tried to resist Soviet authority in the 1960s, 1970s, and 1980s. (Czechoslovakia in 1968; Poland in the 1970s and early 1980s)
- Who was Lech Walesa? (Lech Walesa was the leader of the workers' union called *Solidarity* in Poland. He became president of Poland. He lost the presidency in 1995.)

Reunification
The act of joining together again

History Fact
In 1993, the country of Czechoslovakia split into two separate nations: The Czech Republic and Slovakia.

In Germany, people celebrated the fall of the Berlin Wall.

Throughout the 1980s, economic conditions in Poland continued to worsen. By 1989, Polish leaders were ready to try a different approach. Encouraged by the radical changes taking place inside the Soviet Union, they made Solidarity legal again. Solidarity then formed a political party. When the first free elections in Poland were held, the union's leaders were voted into office to run the government. Lech Walesa became president. However, in 1995, after Poland experienced economic troubles, Walesa lost the presidency. A former Communist was elected president.

In 1990, free elections in East Germany led to a non-Communist government. East Germany and West Germany then began the process of **reunification.** Later that year, they were joined together again.

In Hungary and in Czechoslovakia, the Communist leaders decided to set up multi-party political systems through free elections. The Communist leaders of Bulgaria gave in to the wishes of their people and resigned. In Romania, a bloody revolt in 1989 ended in the arrest and execution of the Communist dictator, Nicolae Ceausescu, and his wife, Elena.

Eastern European countries wanted to establish closer ties with the West. It now seemed to people all over the world that the Iron Curtain had finally lifted.

- What does the word *solidarity* mean? (It is another word for unity.)
- What happened in Bosnia-Herzegovina from 1992 to 1995? (A civil war broke out between Serbs and Bosnians. Thousands of Bosnians were killed.)
- What was the fate of ethnic Albanians in Kosovo? (They were terrorized and killed by Serbs. This was under the leadership of Slobodan Milosevic.)
- Both the Russian army and Chechen fighters were criticized of what? (They have killed many innocent people.)

LEARN MORE ABOUT IT

The Fall of the Berlin Wall and the Reunification of Germany

For 28 years, a 26-mile-long wall had divided East Berlin from West Berlin. Ever since it had been built, East Berliners had been risking their lives to cross the wall to freedom. The Berlin Wall symbolized the split between a free, democratic West and an oppressed, nondemocratic East.

Then, in late 1989, democratic movements swept the Soviet Union and much of Eastern Europe. In September 1989, thousands of East Germans crossed the newly opened border from Hungary to Austria. From there they made their way to West Germany. The East German government recognized that it could no longer keep its citizens prisoners behind a wall.

After the East Germans agreed to open the gates to the Wall, people took matters into their own hands. They began to tear down the Wall.

In 1990, East Germany held its first free elections since World War II. The Communists were voted out of office. The new leaders of East Germany worked out a plan with West Germany to join into a single, reunified country. Helmut Kohl was elected the first chancellor of the reunified Germany. Once combined, the two Germanys had over 80 million people, more than any other nation in Europe. It would have a powerful economy and a strong military. A united Germany would be a mighty force in the European community.

Background Information

In 1945, Germany was divided into four sectors that were occupied by four separate armies. The entire city of Berlin was within the Soviet sector of Germany, which later became known as East Germany. A year later, Berlin held free elections, but the Soviets did not want that, so they cut off East Berlin from West Berlin, hoping to make Berliners accept Communism instead. The Allies came to the aid of West Berlin. In 1961, the Soviets began building the Berlin Wall to keep East Berliners who did not want to live under Communism from fleeing to West Berlin. Thus, West Berlin became an island of democracy within Communist East Germany.

LEARN MORE ABOUT IT

Have students read about the fall of the Berlin Wall. Discuss the symbolism of the wall.

Ask:

- When people risked their lives to cross the wall to freedom, what kinds of things did they want to be able to do? Write students' suggestions on the chalkboard. (Answers will vary.)
- When the Berlin Wall fell, what did that mean for people's personal freedom? (Possible answer: free elections)

COMMON ERROR

During the 28 years that the Berlin Wall separated East and West Germany, there were about 5,000 escape attempts and an estimated 239 people who died trying to cross the wall. Most of these people were shot by guards. The fall of the Berlin Wall during the weeks of November 1991 was a peaceful affair. People took pieces of the wall as mementoes and souvenirs.

Reading Strategy:
Text Structure

Draw students' attention to the question in the Reading Strategy.

Ask:

- How are visual tools such as maps and timelines useful ways to remember important information? (Answers may vary. Students may say that seeing information organized on a map helps them to better understand the sweep of the reforms in the Soviet Union.)

MAP STUDY

Answers:

1. Russia, Kazakhstan, Kyrgyzstan, Tajikistan, Uzbekistan, Turkmenistan, Azerbaijan, Armenia, Georgia, Ukraine, Estonia, Latvia, Belarus, Lithuania, Moldova (Students should list four.)

2. Ukraine and Kazakhstan

LEARNING STYLES

 Body/Kinesthetic

After students have studied the fall of the Berlin Wall, have them work in small groups to compose a one-act play that depicts the reunion between two people previously separated by the wall. Encourage students to consider what it might have been like for grandparents to see their grandchildren for the first time, or for cousins to meet one another. In preparation for this project, encourage students to view and listen to the stories of people whose lives were affected by the Berlin Wall. Set aside time in class for groups to present their performances to their peers.

Reading Strategy:
Text Structure

Study the map in this lesson. What is it showing you about this lesson?

Independent Republics

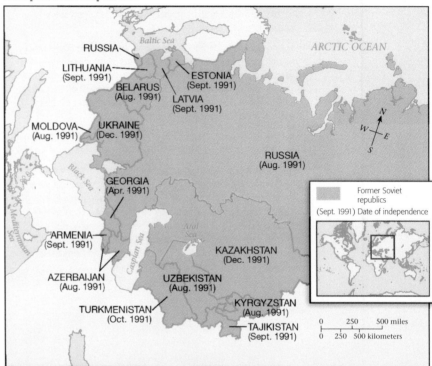

MAP STUDY

1. Name four former Soviet republics.
2. Which two former Soviet republics were the last to gain independence?

LEARNING STYLES

 Auditory/Verbal

Have students read, listen to, and view accounts of the fall of the Berlin Wall such as those found on this Web site: www.agsglobepmwh.com/page696

Students may want to visit their local library to view news footage from the days leading up to and during the dismantling of the Berlin Wall.

Why Did Yugoslavia Break Up?

New freedoms did not necessarily mean peace in Eastern Europe. As Communism released its hold on Yugoslavia, separate republics began declaring their independence. Yugoslavia was made up of six republics: Serbia, Croatia, Slovenia, Bosnia-Herzegovina, Macedonia, and Montenegro. Though it covered an area the size of Wyoming, it was home to 30 nationalities. The largest groups of people were Serbs and Croats. In Yugoslavia, 41 percent were Eastern Orthodox Christians, 32 percent were Roman Catholics, and 12 percent were Muslims.

Fierce fighting in Bosnia ended when the Dayton Accords was signed in 1995. Ten years later, a Bosnian man stands in front of a damaged building in Sarajevo.

In June 1991, the republics of Croatia and Slovenia formally declared themselves independent. Civil war began in Croatia as Croats and ethnic Serbs fought for control. By the end of 1991, at least 6,000 people had been killed and 15,000 wounded in the Serbian-Croatian conflict.

The republic of Bosnia-Herzegovina declared itself independent in February 1992. Independence was supported by the Bosnian Muslims. They made up about 44 percent of the republic's population. The Eastern Orthodox Serbs (about 34 percent of the population) opposed the declaration. Violence broke out between Serbs and Bosnians. Thousands of Bosnians were killed. Fierce fighting continued until 1995 when a peace plan called the Dayton Accords was signed. The plan was sponsored by the United States. NATO troops, including American troops, were sent to Bosnia to keep the peace.

ELL/ESL STRATEGY

Language Objective: *To help students organize information using charts*

Ask students to create a chart using the following headings: Satellite Country, Problems with Communism, Revolts and Fighting, Groups Involved, Reasons, and Outcome. Have them list the Soviet satellites and each republic of Yugoslavia discussed on pages 693–699 of the Student Edition under the first column of their chart. You may want to write the following example on the chalkboard for students to model:

Satellite Country: Hungary

Problems with Communism: 1956—tried to cut ties with Soviets

Revolts and Fighting: Soviet troops entered Hungary

Groups Involved: Soviets and Hungarians

Reasons: Wanted independence

Outcome: Movement was crushed

Geography Note

Ask students to find the Czech Republic on a map, then talk about any details that are striking to them. (Answers will vary. Students may be surprised by how small the Czech Republic is. They may note that it is landlocked. They may say that it is bordered by much larger countries.)

3 | Reinforce and Extend

CAREER CONNECTION

Since the cold war, the United Nations has worked to keep peace across the globe. The United Nations brings together leaders from many countries. These leaders do not always speak the same language. When leaders meet, they must use translators to communicate. To be a translator at the UN, you must be able to speak and write in at least three languages, including English and French. However there are many jobs that only require a bilingual translator. In a growing global economy, translators are more in demand every year. Translators are required to have a degree in a foreign language. To become fluent in a foreign language, it is also important to spend time living in a foreign country.

Geography Note

In the 9th century, Bohemia was an independent country in central Europe. Prague was its largest city. It later became part of the Holy Roman Empire. Under Emperor Charles IV (1347–1378), Prague grew into one of the most successful cities in Europe. After World War I, Bohemia, Moravia, and Slovakia became independent as Czechoslovakia. The country was taken over by Communists in 1948. Czechoslovakia broke up in 1993. Bohemia and Moravia joined to form the Czech Republic.

Trouble in the area that was once Yugoslavia has continued. Soon after Bosnia left Yugoslavia, another republic, Macedonia, declared its independence. Yugoslavia still appears on many maps, but now it only consists of two republics—Serbia and Montenegro. Ethnic Albanians living inside Serbia began to push for freedom.

In Serbia, the Serbs terrorized and killed many ethnic Albanians in Kosovo. Kosovo had been a self-ruling province in Serbia. Serbia's president, Slobodan Milosevic, started ruling Kosovo and forcing many ethnic Albanians to leave. In response, NATO bombed Serbia in 1999. More ethnic Albanians, or Kosovars, fled to nearby countries. After the bombing, NATO peacekeeping troops, including U.S. troops, went to Kosovo to protect the people. Many ethnic Albanians who had been forced from their homes returned to Kosovo.

A UN court charged Serbia's president, Slobodan Milosevic, with war crimes. In the year 2000, Serbs rejected him when he ran for president. When Milosevic would not accept election results, the Serbs protested. Milosevic finally accepted defeat in October 2000.

Why Was There War in Chechnya?

Chechnya is a region in southwestern Russia. After the fall of the Soviet Union, it remained part of Russia. However, in 1992 Chechnya declared its independence. Russian troops invaded the area to bring peace. Fighting continued until 1996, when troops left the area. Fighting began again in 1999. Heavy fighting took place on and off for years.

The Russian army was criticized for bombing civilian areas of Chechnya. Likewise, Chechen suicide bombers killed many innocent people throughout Russia. In 2002, Chechens held more than 800 hostages in a Moscow theater. Of the 800 hostages, 129 were killed. The number of civilian deaths in the two wars is not certain. Most sources estimate that anywhere from 100,000 to 200,000 people were killed in the two wars. In 2003, Russia approved a new constitution for Chechnya, giving it more power within the Federation.

TIMELINE STUDY: THE FALL OF COMMUNISM IN THE SOVIET UNION AND EASTERN EUROPE

Did the Soviet Union disband before or after reform swept Eastern Europe?

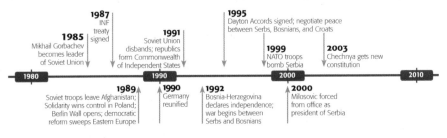

1985 Mikhail Gorbachev becomes leader of Soviet Union

1987 INF treaty signed

1991 Soviet Union disbands; republics form Commonwealth of Independent States

1995 Dayton Accords signed; negotiate peace between Serbs, Bosnians, and Croats

1999 NATO troops bomb Serbia

2003 Chechnya gets new constitution

1980 — 1990 — 2000 — 2010

1989 Soviet troops leave Afghanistan; Solidarity wins control in Poland; Berlin Wall opens; democratic reform sweeps Eastern Europe

1990 Germany reunified

1992 Bosnia-Herzegovina declares independence; war begins between Serbs and Bosnians

2000 Milosovic forced from office as president of Serbia

Lesson 32–3 Review Answers

1. C **2.** A **3.** D **4.** B **5.** B **6.** D **7.** A
8. Workers were demanding higher pay and better working conditions. They wanted a union.
9. Reunification is the act of joining together again. **10.** Croats and ethnic Serbs fought for control after Croatia declared independence.

LESSON 32-3 REVIEW

On a sheet of paper, write the letter of the answer that correctly completes each sentence.

1. In 1956, _____ tried to cut its ties with the Soviet Union.

   A Yugoslavia   **B** Moscow   **C** Hungary   **D** Romania

2. The Russians were afraid that Czechoslovakians had too much freedom of _____.

   A speech   **B** government   **C** Communism   **D** Moscow

3. In 1980, the Polish government allowed workers to form a(n) _____ to better working conditions.

   A government **B** coup   **C** army   **D** union

4. When the first free elections were held in Poland, _____ became president.

   A Nicolae Ceausescu   **C** Helmut Kohl
   B Lech Walesa   **D** Boris Yeltsin

5. In 1990, free elections in East Germany led to a non-_____ government.

   A radical   **B** Communist   **C** union   **D** political

6. Fierce fighting in _____ continued until a peace plan called the Dayton Accords was signed.

   A Serbia   **B** Albania   **C** Croatia   **D** Bosnia

7. NATO bombed _____ in 1999 because Slobodan Milosevic was forcing Albanians out of Kosovo.

   A Serbia   **B** Bosnia   **C** East Germany   **D** West Germany

On a sheet of paper, write the answer to each question. Use complete sentences.

8. Why did workers riot in Poland in the 1970s?

9. What is the meaning of the word *reunification?*

10. Why did civil war begin in Croatia?

---

700   *Unit 10 The World Since 1945*

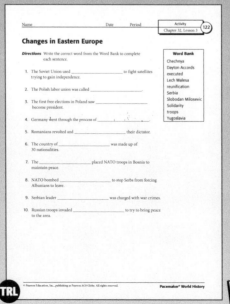

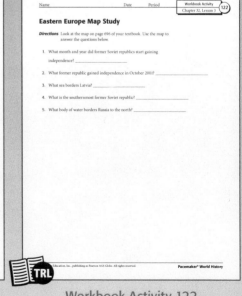

SUMMARY

- After he came to power in 1985, Mikhail Gorbachev introduced new policies. He gave Soviet citizens more freedoms and improved Soviet relations with Western nations.

- New treaties between the Soviet Union and the United States promised to reduce nuclear arms.

- Soviet citizens faced economic problems as well as shortages of food and medicine.

- During the late 1980s, democratic reform swept Eastern Europe, spurred by changes in the Soviet Union. The wave of freedom reached its height when the Berlin Wall fell in late 1989.

- In 1991, the Soviet Union disbanded. Eventually nations formed a loose alliance called the Commonwealth of Independent States. Boris Yeltsin became leader of independent Russia and the Commonwealth of Independent States.

- Upon the resignation of Yeltsin in 1999, Vladimir Putin became president of the Russian Federation. He was elected in 2000 and again in 2004.

- Putin made bold strides to begin social programs to help the people of his country. He worked to develop strong communication with Western nations.

- As the Soviet Union disbanded in 1991, Chechnya declared its independence from the Russian Federation. Two separate wars followed, during which at least 150,000 people have been killed to date.

- During the break up of the former Yugoslavia, the Serbian-Croatian conflict began. At least 6,000 people were killed and 15,000 were wounded.

- Parts of Eastern Europe have been unstable as nations and ethnic groups struggle to move forward.

Chapter 32 Summary

Have students read the Chapter Summary on page 701 to review the main ideas presented in Chapter 32.

Ask:

- What resulted from the new policies that Mikhail Gorbachev introduced when he came into power in 1995? (Soviet citizens got more freedom. The Soviet Union improved relations with Western nations.)

- What did the new treaties between the Soviet Union and the United States promise to do? (reduce nuclear arms)

- What were conditions like for Soviet citizens? (They faced economic problems and shortages of food and medicine.)

- What happened in 1991? (The Soviet Union disbanded.)

- Who became leader of independent Russia and the Commonwealth of Independent States? (Boris Yeltsin)

- What happened after Chechnya declared its independence from the Russian Federation in 1991? (Two separate wars followed, with at least 150,000 people killed to date.)

- When did the Serbian-Croatian conflict began? (during the breakup of the former Yugoslavia)

- Why have parts of Eastern Europe been unstable? (Nations and ethnic groups have struggled to move forward.)

TEACHER'S RESOURCE

The AGS Globe Teaching Strategies in Social Studies Transparencies may be used with this chapter. The transparencies add an interactive dimension to expand and enhance the Pacemaker® *World History* program content.

CHAPTER PROJECT FOLLOW-UP

Set aside class time during the lesson for groups to present their findings on the satellite countries that split from the Soviet Union.

Chapter 32 Review

Use the Chapter Review to prepare students for tests and to reteach content from the chapter.

Chapter 32 Mastery Test

The Teacher's Resource Library includes two forms of the Chapter 32 Mastery Test. Each test addresses the chapter Goals for Learning. An optional third page of additional critical-thinking items is included for each test. The difficulty level of the two forms is equivalent.

Chapter 32 Review Answers

Vocabulary Review

1. disband
2. reunification
3. *glasnost*
4. coup
5. *perestroika*

Chapter Review Questions

6. He made factories responsible for running themselves, allowed some private business, and welcomed U.S. corporations.

7. They formed the Commonwealth of Independent States.

8. East Germany voted the Communists out. East and West Germany were reunified into a single country.

9. The two countries introduced new treaties to reduce nuclear arms.

10. There was a widespread economic crisis. Some Soviets believed that Gorbachev was changing things too quickly.

11. Latvia, Estonia, and Lithuania declared independence from the Soviet Union in 1991.

12. The Russian Federation was the biggest and most powerful of the new nations.

Word Bank

coup
disband
glasnost
perestroika
reunification

Vocabulary Review

On a sheet of paper, use the words from the Word Bank to correctly match each definition below.

1. _____ is a word that means "to break up."

2. When the Berlin Wall fell, East and West Germany began the process of _____.

3. Gorbachev's policy of _____ led many republics in the Soviet Union to seek independence.

4. Hard-line Communist leaders attempted a _____ in 1991 to take over power in the Soviet Union.

5. Gorbachev's policy of _____ allowed other countries to open businesses in the Soviet Union.

Chapter Review Questions

On a sheet of paper, write the answers to each question. Use complete sentences.

6. How did Gorbachev change the Soviet economy?

7. What alliance did most of the former Soviet republics form?

8. What happened to Germany after the fall of the Berlin Wall?

9. How did the Soviet Union and the United States reduce nuclear arms?

10. Why did the hard-line Soviet Communists criticize Gorbachev's new policies?

11. In 1991, which three countries declared their independence from the Soviet Union?

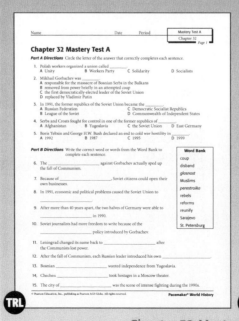

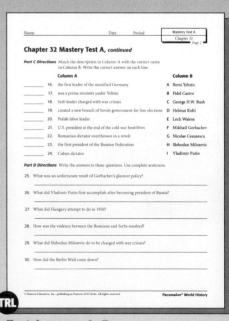

Chapter 32 Mastery Test A, pages 1–3

Test Tip

When a test item asks you to write a paragraph, make a plan first. Jot down the main idea of your paragraph. List supporting details to include. Then write your paragraph.

12. The Russian Federation took the seat in the UN that was held by the Soviet Union. Why?

13. What did the Soviet government do to limit Czechoslovakia's freedom of speech?

14. Why did Poland's government declare unions illegal?

Critical Thinking

On a sheet of paper, write your response to each question. Use complete sentences.

15. In your opinion, why has there been so much civil war in the area of former Yugoslavia?

16. In your opinion, why did the Soviet Union end?

17. Should the United States send troops to try to resolve conflicts in Eastern Europe? Explain.

Using the Timeline

Use the timeline on page 699 to answer the questions.

18. When did Solidarity win control in Poland?

19. What happened during the same year Bosnia-Herzogovina declared independence?

20. When did Mikhail Gorbachev become leader of the Soviet Union?

GROUP ACTIVITY

Form a group of four or five. Create a television newscast about the end of the Soviet Union and the fall of Communism in Eastern Europe. One classmate is the anchor. The three other classmates report from three different areas of Eastern Europe. Be sure to make notes to use during the newscast.

---

13. The Soviets brought tanks into Czechoslovakia. Soon, new people were running the government.

14. The government was beginning to fear that the union's demands were going against Communist ideals.

Critical Thinking

15. Possible answers: There were many different nationalities and many different types of religious beliefs. They were not used to their new freedoms.

16. Possible answers: The people of the Soviet Union had been held down for so long, a little freedom just made them want more. The country was too big and included too many republics to hold together in one country. Communism does not work.

17. Possible answers: Yes, the United States should try to resolve conflicts because otherwise there might be a world war again. No, the problems are too old and too hard to resolve.

Using the Timeline

18. 1989

19. War began between Serbs and Bosnians.

20. 1985

GROUP ACTIVITY

Students' newscasts should highlight important events in the Soviet Union, Hungary, Czechoslovakia, Poland, Germany, and Yugoslavia.

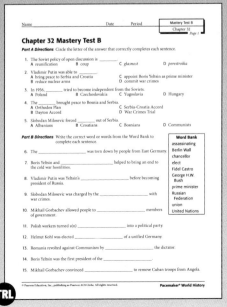

Chapter 32 Mastery Test B, pages 1–3

Latin America After World War II

Audio Library

Skill Track for World History

Teacher's Resource Library **TRL**

Workbook Activities 123–126

Activities 123–126

Modified Activities 123–126

Life Skills Connection 33

Key Vocabulary Words 33

Chapter 33 Self-Study Guide

Chapter 33 Outline

Chapter 33 Mastery Tests A and B

(Answer Keys for the Teacher's Resource Library begin on page 809 of the Teacher's Edition.)

Introducing the Chapter

Ask students what they remember about the Latin American countries featured in Chapter 20. Tell them that this chapter will cover Latin American history to the present. It will also describe the relationship between the U.S. and its Latin American neighbors.

Ask:

- What type of government did most Latin American countries have after they became independent?
  (dictatorship or military government)

After World War II, Communism began to grow throughout Asia and Europe. The United States grew more concerned about keeping the countries of Latin America free of Communist control. In 1948, the Organization of American States (OAS) was founded. The OAS members pledged to defend one another and to work out any problems among them peacefully. Since that time, the United States has sent billions of dollars to Latin American countries for education, industry, and health care programs.

GOALS FOR LEARNING

- To describe the United States' role in Latin American affairs
- To describe the unrest in Central America
- To explain the trouble in Mexico and Haiti
- To describe Latin America today

704 *Unit 10 The World Since 1945*

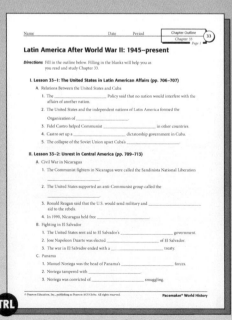

Chapter 33 Self-Study Guide, pages 1–2   Chapter 33 Outline, pages 1–2

Reading Strategy: Visualizing

It is often useful to create a movie in your mind as you read. This reading strategy is known as visualizing. It helps you better understand what you are reading. The following tips can help you visualize a text:

- Look at the maps, timelines, photographs, and illustrations.
- Think about your own experiences that may add to the images.
- Observe the order in which things are happening. Use your past knowledge and experiences to consider what you think might happen next.

Key Vocabulary Words

Lesson 1
Good Neighbor Policy The policy in which the United States said it would not interfere with Latin American affairs

Lesson 2
Stronghold A place dominated by a certain group which they have made safe and secure

Politics The work of government

Ban To get rid of; to make something not legal

Moderate To make or become less extreme or violent

Humane Kind; showing care for others

Lesson 3
Tariff A tax that countries put on goods they import or export

Immigration The act of coming into a country or region to live there

Refuge Shelter or protection from danger

Lesson 4
Global warming The heating up of Earth from the burning of wood, coal, oil, and gasoline

Environment The land, sea, and air of our world

- What organization formed in the early 20th century required American members to cooperate peacefully with each other? (the Organization of American States)
- How did the Latin American governments change toward the end of the 20th century? (Most countries turned toward democracy.)

Reading Strategy:
Visualizing

Tell students that visualizing helps you remember what you read by creating pictures in your mind about the topic. It is especially valuable in understanding how and where people live. Encourage students to use the pictures in this chapter to further their understanding of Latin America.

Key Vocabulary Words

Point out that these chapter words are presented in the order they appear in each lesson. They are also found in the glossary.

LIFE SKILLS CONNECTION

Students learn about endangered rain forests and how recycling helps prevent pollution across the globe. Students also learn about careers in waste management. Discuss your school's recycling program with students.

KEY VOCABULARY

Students choose the correct word from the Word Bank to complete each sentence.

CHAPTER PROJECT

Provide each group with poster board. Have students use images from the Internet, individual drawings, and images copied from magazines or newspapers to create a collage depicting current events in Latin America.

Life Skills Connection 33

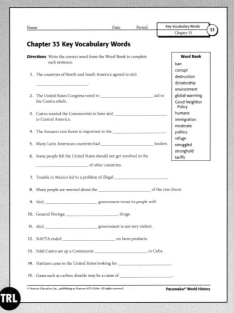

Key Vocabulary Words 33

Lesson at a Glance

Chapter 33 Lesson 1

Overview This lesson describes U.S. relations with Latin America, especially Cuba.

Objectives

- To explain why the Organization of American States was formed
- To describe the effect of Fidel Castro's takeover of Cuba on U.S.-Cuban relations

Student Pages 706–708

Teacher's Resource Library

Workbook Activity 123

Activity 123

Modified Activity 123

Vocabulary

Good Neighbor Policy

Ask students what they consider a good neighbor. Write on the board the qualities of a good neighbor that they suggest. Have students read the definition of *Good Neighbor Policy* in their text, and compare it to the class's list of qualities.

PRONUNCIATION GUIDE

Use this list to help students pronounce difficult words in this lesson.

Fulgencio Batista
(fōōl hen´syô bə tēst´)

Reading Strategy:
Visualizing

(Possible answer: The focus is on one person, which suggests his unique importance in the government.)

1 Warm-Up Activity

Ask students to create a two-column chart by writing in column 1 what they know about Latin America after World War II and in column 2 what they want to know about it. Ask students how Latin America was affected by World War II.

The United States in Latin American Affairs

Objectives

- To explain why the Organization of American States was formed
- To describe the effect of Fidel Castro's takeover of Cuba on U.S.-Cuban relations

Reading Strategy:
Visualizing

What clues on this page help you visualize the changes that took place in Cuba?

Good Neighbor Policy
The policy in which the United States said it would not interfere with Latin American affairs

Before World War II, representatives from the nations of the Americas met in a Pan-American conference. They pledged themselves to a **Good Neighbor Policy**. They promised that no nation would interfere with the affairs of another nation. Then came World War II. During the war all Latin American nations supported the Allies. Brazil and Mexico even provided troops.

When World War II ended, the United States took a renewed interest in Latin America. The U.S. government hoped to keep Communism out of the Western Hemisphere and to encourage good relations between the nations of the Americas. In 1948, the Organization of American States (OAS) was founded. Among its members were the United States and all the independent countries of Latin America. OAS countries pledged to join together in defending the Americas and in peacefully settling any quarrels.

Since the 1950s, the United States has sent billions of dollars to help Latin American countries solve their social and economic problems. Technical experts from the United States have helped improve Latin American agriculture, industry, education, and health care.

In more recent years, U.S. aid was sometimes unwelcome. Some Latin Americans said the United States was not really interested in helping them but was sending aid to protect its own interests. They said the United States should stay out of the affairs of other nations.

Why Are Relations Between the United States and Cuba Strained?

The first half of the 20th century was a time of change and instability in Latin America. Revolutions overthrew a number of dictators. However, the end of dictatorship did not always bring about stability. New governments did not always grant rights to its people.

A 1959 revolution led to major changes on the island nation of Cuba. A former lawyer named Fidel Castro and his army of guerrilla fighters overthrew the military dictatorship of Fulgencio Batista. Castro set up a Communist dictatorship. Under Communism, Cuba became closely allied with the Soviet Union. Castro pledged to help Communist rebels gain control in other Latin American countries. The United States refused to recognize the Castro government in Cuba. Friendly relations ended between the United States and the small country only 90 miles from its shores.

Thirty years later, the situation was not much better. The collapse of the Soviet Union and the end of Communism upset Cuba's economy. It left the country even more unstable. As a result, thousands of Cubans left Cuba for the United States. In recent years, this has strained Cuba's relationship with its U.S. neighbor.

Fidel Castro has been in power as the dictator of Cuba since 1959.

Tell students that they will be reading about the development of U.S.-Latin America relations since World War II. That war, though not fought in Latin America, influenced those countries and the United States' attitude toward them.

Ask:

- Describe what happened to the Good Neighbor Policy during World War II. (Latin American countries supported the Allies, ignoring their promise not to interfere in other nations' politics.)
- Which countries belonged to the Organization of American States? (independent Latin American countries and the United States)
- What kind of government did Cuba have before Castro came to power? (a military dictatorship)

Background Information

The trade embargo by the United States against Cuba went into effect under President Eisenhower in 1960. It excluded medicine, medical supplies, and food, and permitted Cuban exports to the United States. Under President Kennedy, the embargo became total: foreign merchant ships that went to Cuban ports were not allowed to dock in U.S. ports for a year, and U.S. citizens were forbidden to go to Cuba. Although there was some softening of restrictions (especially on travel) under President Clinton, the embargo remains in effect. At the United Nations in 2006, the estimated direct and indirect cost to Cuba was said to be $86 billion.

ELL/ESL Strategy

Language Objective: *To use an outline to organize thoughts about reading*

Have students write an outline of the chapter. If they need direction, suggest using the chapter headings as main topics. You may wish to ask students to use their completed outlines to write a summary about Latin America after World War II.

Common Error

Because Cuba has been under embargo for many years, it doesn't have up-to-date goods and technology. But that doesn't mean it is colorless or dull. Students might enjoy getting a glimpse of Cuban landscapes and the people's lives and music. Have them watch, "The Buena Vista Social Club" (1999; in Spanish with English subtitles). This documentary focuses on Cuban jazz musicians, with segments on their lives and music.

Learning Styles

Body/Kinesthetic

Students who play percussion or guitar may be interested in investigating Cuban music or that of other Latin American cultures. Arrange for them to perform some of the music for the class or the school.

Latin America Chapter 33 **707**

3 Reinforce and Extend

COMMON ERROR

A common misconception is that all Latin Americans speak Spanish. Brazil's principal language is Portuguese, and most countries have native populations who speak indigenous languages.

Lesson 33–1 Review Answers

1. Pan-American **2.** Good Neighbor Policy **3.** Communism **4.** Organization of American States **5.** dictatorship **6.** Cuba **7.** United States **8.** Possible answer: U.S. support has helped improve Latin American agriculture, industry, education, and health care. (Students name three.) **9.** Some Latin Americans thought that the United States was not interested in helping them, but was sending aid to protect U.S. interests. **10.** Cuba allied itself with the Soviet Union.

LESSON 33-1 REVIEW

Word Bank
- Communism
- Cuba
- dictatorship
- Good Neighbor Policy
- Organization of American States
- Pan-American
- United States

On a sheet of paper, write the word from the Word Bank to complete each sentence correctly.

1. The Good Neighbor Policy came out of the _____ conference held before World War II.

2. The _____ promised that no nation would interfere with the affairs of another nation.

3. The U.S. government took renewed interest in Latin America after World War II. They hoped to prevent _____ from entering the Western Hemisphere and to encourage good relations.

4. The _____ pledged to defend the Americas and peacefully settle any quarrels.

5. When Castro came to power after the 1959 revolution, he set up a Communist _____.

6. The United States refused to recognize the Castro government in _____.

7. After Castro came to power, friendly relations between the _____ and Cuba ended.

On a sheet of paper, write the answer to each question. Use complete sentences.

8. The United States has sent billions of dollars to help solve problems in Latin America. What are three social and economic problems U.S. support has helped improve?

9. Why was U.S. aid unwelcome in recent years?

10. Under Fidel Castro, Cuba allied itself with what superpower?

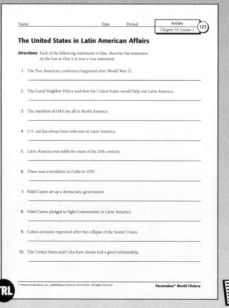

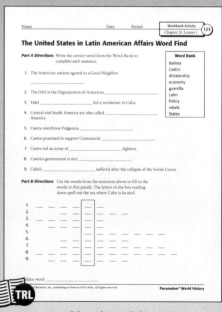

Activity 123

Workbook Activity 123

Unrest in Central America

Objectives

- To explain why the United States aided Nicaraguan rebels in their fight against the Sandinistas
- To describe why the United States helped the government of El Salvador stay in power
- To discuss the reasons the United States invaded Panama in 1989

Reading Strategy: Visualizing

Create a graphic organizer with boxes and arrows to help you understand the sequence of events in Nicaragua.

Stronghold

A place dominated by a certain group which they have made safe and secure

Politics

The work of government

The social and economic situation of Latin American countries is unstable at times. The United States has provided aid to some countries, but that aid is not always welcome. However, the United States is physically close to Central America. It is not surprising, then, that the United States continues to get tangled in Latin American affairs.

Why Did a Civil War Break Out in Nicaragua?

After the Castro revolution, Communist activity increased in Latin America. In 1979, Cuban Communists supported a revolution in Nicaragua. A Communist group called the Sandinista National Liberation Front overthrew Nicaragua's dictator, Anastasio Somoza. The Sandinistas took control of the government. Although Somoza had done little to improve life for his people, he had supported U.S. policies throughout Central America. The United States criticized Somoza's use of violence. The United States also feared that a new Sandinista government would provide a Communist **stronghold** in Central America. A stronghold is a place dominated by a certain group that has been made safe and secure. The United States accused the Nicaraguan Sandinistas of helping Communist rebels in neighboring El Salvador. They also accused the Sandinistas of relying on Soviet aid and support.

A group called the Contras (*contra* means "against" in Spanish) rebelled against the Sandinistas. U.S. President Ronald Reagan announced that the United States would provide military and economic aid to the Contras. Many Latin Americans criticized the United States for interfering in the **politics** of another nation. In other words, they did not think the United States should mix in the workings of another nation's government.

Lesson at a Glance

Chapter 33 Lesson 2

Overview This lesson describes recent wars in Nicaragua, El Salvador, and Panama and the role the United States played in them.

Objectives

- To explain why the United States aided Nicaraguan rebels in their fight against the Sandinistas
- To describe why the United States helped the government of El Salvador stay in power
- To discuss the reasons the United States invaded Panama in 1989

Student Pages 709–714

Teacher's Resource Library

Workbook Activity 124

Activity 124

Modified Activity 124

....

Vocabulary

ban	politics
humane	stronghold
moderate	

Have students work in pairs. One student should read the definition of a vocabulary word, and the other student should identify the word that matches the definition. After all words are identified, have students reverse roles and repeat this process.

PRONUNCIATION GUIDE

Use this list to help students pronounce difficult words in this lesson.

Sandinista (san´də nē´stə)

Reading Strategy: Visualizing

When students have made their charts, pair them up. Have them compare their charts and make improvements, if they can.

1 Warm-Up Activity

Have students look at the map on page 719. Have them find Central America on the map. Have them locate Nicaragua, Panama, and El Salvador. Ask them what they already know about these countries.

2 Teaching the Lesson

This lesson tells about dictators or the military being in control of Nicaragua, El Salvador, and Panama. As students go through the chapter, have them note the similarities and differences among the countries, and how the United States reacted to their civil wars or military takeovers. Encourage students to use an outline to keep track of details, or a table for comparing the three countries.

Ask:

- Why did the United States support the Contras? (They were fighting against Communists.)

- What two groups started the civil war in El Salvador? (the Communists and the military government)

- Why did the United States intervene in Panama? (to get rid of a corrupt leader who was exporting drugs to the United States)

 Remember

Ask students where else the theory has been applied. (Southeast Asia)

LEARN MORE ABOUT IT

Members of the National Security Council responsible for the Iran-Contra affair were fired and prosecuted.

Ban
To get rid of; to make something not legal

 Remember

Ronald Reagan feared that the domino theory, one nation after another falling to Communism, could apply to Latin America.

Some U.S. citizens also questioned their country's involvement. In 1984, the U.S. House of Representatives voted to **ban** aid to the Contras—they made giving aid to the Contras illegal. However, it was later discovered that in spite of the ban, illegal aid continued for several years.

A civil war went on in Nicaragua until 1989. Then President Daniel Ortega signed a treaty with Contra rebels. The Contras agreed to lay down their arms and refuse outside aid. Ortega promised that Nicaragua would hold democratic elections in 1990. That year, in a surprise victory, Violeta Barrios de Chamorro defeated Ortega and became the new president of Nicaragua.

LEARN MORE ABOUT IT

The Iran-Contra Affair

The United States Congress banned military aid to the Nicaraguan Contras in 1984. However, in 1986, the American people learned of a secret arms deal that gave money to Nicaragua. The affair had two parts.

Part One: It was discovered that U.S. officials secretly sold missiles and missile parts to the Middle Eastern nation of Iran. This was at a time when the United States was publicly speaking out against Iran, calling it a terrorist nation. As a result of the weapons sales, Iranians persuaded terrorists in Lebanon to release some U.S. hostages. U.S. policy, however, strictly forbade (did not allow) trading arms for political hostages.

Part Two: The U.S. Congress had specifically refused military aid to the Contras. However, profits from the Iranian arms sales were illegally used to aid the Contras in Nicaragua.

Reading Strategy:
Visualizing

What words about
El Salvador help you
visualize what you are
reading?

Why Was There Fighting in El Salvador?

Nicaragua was not the only Central American country engaged in a civil war during the 1980s. Unrest had rocked El Salvador for many years. In 1979, the military took control of the government. Anti-government rebels were backed by Cuba and by the Communists in Nicaragua. The United States sent aid to El Salvador's military government. President Reagan said the United States had to defend itself against Communism. Again, some U.S. citizens protested the aid. They said that the military government was not worthy of support because it promoted violence that had killed thousands of Salvadoran civilians.

Soldiers fought a civil war in El Salvador for over 12 years.

Reading Strategy:
Visualizing

(Possible answer: "rocked," "violence . . . killed thousands," "attacks continued")

Background Information

The United States had a military presence in Panama from 1903 on, when it signed a treaty and began building the Panama Canal. The Canal Zone was a 10-mile swath that cut Panama in two. It was occupied by thousands of U.S. troops, who not only guarded the important transportation link, but also intervened in drug-trafficking control. The Panamanians gained control of the canal in 1999, after 20 years of negotiations and planning.

ELL/ESL STRATEGY

Language Objective:
*To help students
monitor their learning*

Have students use their outline for this chapter as a study aid, then answer the review questions. Have small groups work together to check their answers for correctness and completeness. If their outlines did not cover the subject matter in the review or were incorrect, they should note what was missing.

STUDY SKILLS

Ask students to study the section "Why Was There Fighting in El Salvador?" Have students work in small groups and write three questions from the information in that section. Distribute index cards and have students write each question on the front of an index card and the answer to that question on the back of the index card. Students can use the cards to practice answering questions about Latin American leaders.

You Decide

Ask volunteers to state their opinions and the reasons they have for them.

3 Reinforce and Extend

IN THE COMMUNITY

Encourage students to take the lead in discussions of current events in their home countries. They may also want to invite relatives or other knowledgeable people in the community to speak with the class. If so, have ELL students and students who are proficient in English work together to prepare questions to help the speakers with their presentations.

AT HOME

Pass out outline maps of Latin America to students and ask them to play a game with their families. Each family member takes a turn placing a label with the name of a Latin American country on the correct spot on the map. Ask students to share their families' game experiences with classmates. You may want students to work in groups to complete the family game maps.

TEACHER ALERT

Although each Latin American country has unique qualities and history, students may have trouble keeping the countries' histories straight by the end of this chapter. Throughout the chapter, encourage students to use their skills in organizing information. Sequence charts for a country's changes in government, maps with annotations about its history or economy, content outlines, and charts that compare two countries could all be useful.

Moderate
To make or become less extreme or violent

Humane
Kind; showing care for others

In 1984, El Salvadoran voters elected Jose Napoleon Duarte to the presidency. He promised a more **moderate** and **humane** government. A moderate government is one that is less extreme or violent; a humane government is one that is more kind and shows care for people. However, rebel guerrilla attacks continued. The civil war finally ended in 1992.

A peace treaty between the government and rebel forces promised military and political reform. The war in El Salvador had lasted about 13 years and took the lives of nearly 75,000 people.

Why Did the United States Invade Panama?

As civil war raged in El Salvador, a storm was brewing in the Central American nation of Panama. In 1987, General Manuel Noriega was commander of the Panamanian defense forces. Although Panama's president was Eric Arturo Delvalle, all the real power lay in the hands of General Noriega.

You Decide

Do you think the United States had the right to send troops to Panama to drive Noriega from power? Why or why not?

Noriega was corrupt. He was an accused drug smuggler (he secretly brought illegal drugs into and out of the country). He was known to tamper with election votes so his candidates would win. In other words, he would interfere with votes so his candidates would be elected. When a national election was held in May 1989, the man who ran against him, Guillermo Endara, won the most votes. Noriega ignored the election results. He claimed victory.

The U.S. government wanted to see General Noriega removed from power. On December 23, 1989, U.S. President George H.W. Bush sent 24,000 U.S. troops to Panama to drive Noriega from power. At a U.S. military base, Guillermo Endara was sworn in as president.

ONLINE CONNECTION

Students can gain additional information by accessing the following Web site: www.agsglobepmwh.com/page 712 (This Web site has additional information on Latin American countries.)

General Noriega spent 10 days in hiding before he surrendered to American military forces. He was brought back to the United States to stand trial on drug charges. In 1992, a U.S. District Court in Miami, Florida, convicted Noriega of drug trafficking.

Throughout the 1980s, protest against military governments grew in several Latin American countries. In many cases, these protests brought free elections. By the early 1990s, civilian leaders elected by the people had replaced military governments in such places as Guatemala, Argentina, Brazil, Chile, and Paraguay.

LEARN MORE ABOUT IT

Have students locate the Falklands on a map. The island economy depends on sheep and, to a much lesser degree, tourism.

WORLD CULTURES

Encourage students to learn a few basic words in Spanish and Portuguese. They can go to the following Web site for help: www.agsglobepmwh.com/page713. Some ELL students may also be tutors for this activity. Ask students to create a chart of the same basic words in English, Spanish, and Portuguese.

LEARN MORE ABOUT IT

War in the Falklands

In April 1982, Argentina launched an attack on a British colony in South America. The Falklands, a group of islands off the Argentinian coast, had been a British colony since 1833. Most of the people living there are British. When Argentina tried to seize control of the Falklands, Margaret Thatcher, Britain's prime minister, sent forces to protect the colony. It was a short but bloody war. On June 14, Argentina surrendered. The Falklands remained under British control.

Today the Falkland Islands are a territory of the United Kingdom. The islands are also claimed by Argentina.

Lesson 33–2 Review Answers

1. B **2.** C **3.** C **4.** A **5.** B **6.** D **7.** Reagan believed it was the role of the United States to keep Communism out of the Western Hemisphere. He feared the domino theory could apply to Latin America. **8.** Some U.S. citizens were upset because El Salvador's military government promoted violence that killed thousands of Salvadoran citizens. **9.** U.S. President Bush sent troops to Panama to drive General Manuel Noriega from power. Noriega was a known drug smuggler, and although he did not win the May 1989 election, he still claimed victory. The U.S. government wanted to remove him from power. **10.** Possible answer should include three of these countries: Guatemala, Argentina, Brazil, Chile, and Paraguay. They all had civilian governments by the early 1990s.

On a sheet of paper, write the letter of the answer that correctly completes each sentence.

1. The _____ controlled the Nicaraguan government after the 1979 revolution.

   A military   **B** Sandinistas   **C** Contras   **D** civilians

2. The United States provided _____ military and economic aid because they rebelled against the Sandinistas.

   A Communists   **B** Panamanians   **C** Contras   **D** civilians

3. Nicaragua's civil war ended in _____ when the president signed a treaty with Contra rebels.

   A 1979   **B** 1984   **C** 1989   **D** 1990

4. The U.S. government sent money to support El Salvador's _____ government.

   A military   **B** Communist   **C** rebel   **D** Contra

5. El Salvador's civil war ended after a peace treaty promised _____ and political reform.

   A economic   **B** military   **C** social   **D** Communism

6. _____ was finally sworn in as president after U.S. troops invaded Panama.

   A General Manuel Noriega   **C** George H.W. Bush
   B Eric Arturo Delvalle   **D** Guillermo Endara

On a sheet of paper, write the answer to each question. Use complete sentences.

7. Why did U.S. President Reagan believe it was important to support anti-Communist forces in Latin America?

8. Why were some U.S. citizens upset at the aid sent to El Salvador?

9. Why did U.S. troops invade Panama in 1989?

10. Name three Latin American nations where civilian governments replaced military governments by the early 1990s.

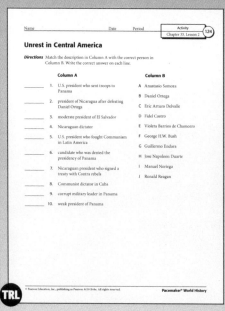

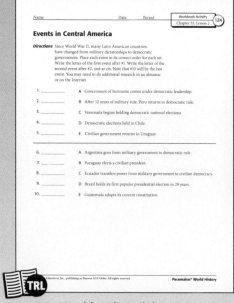

Trouble in Mexico and Haiti

Objectives

■ To explain Mexico's political and economic situation
■ To explain why so many Haitians are fleeing their country

Mexico and Haiti have similar political and economic situations—they are unstable. Both have large gaps between the rich and the poor. Both have people who flee their country to try and make a home in the United States. This has strained the relationships between these two countries and the United States.

What Changes Were Happening in Mexico?

Political corruption and a growing population put Mexico into an economic crisis during the 1980s. During the 1970s, the discovery of vast oil fields in southern Mexico had promised new riches. The government increased spending on public works and on industry. It expected to pay for new development with income from oil. In the early 1980s, however, the price of oil fell, and so did Mexico's hopes for success. The country was left in serious debt.

This cathedral in Mexico City was built on top of the ruins of an Aztec temple.

1945–PRESENT   *Latin America After World War II*   Chapter 33   **715**

Ask:

- How did oil play a part in the Mexican economy? (When it was discovered, the Mexican government increased spending, and went into debt when the oil prices dropped.)
- Which nations are part of the North American Free Trade Agreement? (Canada, Mexico, the United States)
- Name three problems that have encouraged Haitians to emigrate. (poverty, hurricanes, hunger)

ELL/ESL STRATEGY

Language Objective: *To extract causes and effects from a reading and use them to summarize*

Ask students to read "What Changes Were Happening in Mexico?" on pages 715–716. Ask students to list the causes and effects of Mexico's economic problems. Have students use their lists to write a summary.

Reading Strategy:
Visualizing

Discuss the ideas they have. If possible, have students produce addenda to the lesson that they share with classmates.

History Fact

International organizations, such as *Human Rights Watch*, oversee elections to make sure they are fair.

Background Information

Mexico is a developing country, with per capita income of $10,600 (in 2006, estimated). Its population was estimated at 109 million in 2007. Its population doubled between 1970 and 2000, but the rate of increase has slowed. About 4 people per 1000 emigrate each year. Mexico's people can expect to live to 75.5 years, just a few years less than Canadians (80 years) or Americans (78 years). The literacy rate in Mexico is also high, 92% in 2007.

LEARNING STYLES

Logical/Mathematical

Students may be interested in the estimates of damage done by hurricanes in the Caribbean every year. Have them research the data on the Internet, make a table for a few of the islands for each year, and create a bar graph of their data. Students might be interested in comparing their graph to the hurricane-severity graph at NOAA's Web site: www.agsglobepmwh.com/page716

COMMON ERROR

A common misperception about international migration is that migrants come from the poorest countries. More typically, they come from developing and growing nations, such as Mexico. Point out that Mexico's per capita income is nearly as high as Russia's, and that Mexicans have good health care and a high life expectancy.

Tariff

A tax that countries put on goods they import or export

Immigration

The act of coming into a country or region to live there

Reading Strategy:
Visualizing

How could this section on Mexico be written differently to create a stronger picture in your mind?

History Fact

On July 2, 2000, Vincent Fox Quesada became the president of Mexico. The election may have been the fairest in Mexican history.

Mexico's economic crisis caused rising unemployment. The population kept growing rapidly, adding to the number of unemployed. A growing population, high foreign debt, and falling oil income meant economic troubles for Mexico.

Many Mexicans turned their anger and disappointment toward the government. Political unrest increased. During the oil boom, Mexico's peasants and the poor who lived in the city saw hope for their future. Now that hope was gone. They became more aware than ever of the great gap that existed between the few rich people and the many poor ones. As Mexico's economy weakened, the number of Mexicans illegally entering the United States grew. They crossed the border in search of work and a better standard of living.

In 1992, the United States, Canada, and Mexico announced plans for the North American Free Trade Agreement (NAFTA). The agreement offered a chance for economic growth for all three nations. Among the terms of the agreement were proposals to eventually end **tariffs** on all farm products and many other goods. A tariff is a tax that a country puts on goods they import or export. The treaty also aimed to ease **immigration** laws for business executives and professionals (when a person immigrates, he or she comes into a country to live there). Finally, the treaty allowed trucks free access to border routes between the three countries. The agreement was approved by the governments of the three nations. It promised a boost to Mexico's economy. After some difficult years, the Mexican economy grew from 1997 to 2000.

In the mid-1990s, rebels in the state of Chiapas demanded more land for the people. The Mexican government is in control of the state today. However, some fighting between armed civilians over land claims still happens.

Refuge
Shelter or protection from danger

Reading Strategy: Visualizing
Draw a picture to help you visualize what you are reading in this section on Haiti. How does this image help you remember?

Why Was There Unrest in Haiti?

Civil unrest has plagued the Caribbean island nation of Haiti in recent years. Revolutions and government takeovers have been spurred by poverty, drought, hurricanes, and famine. Between early 1986 and mid-1990, Haiti had five different governments. In the 1990s, the United States led a force from many nations to restore Haiti's elected leader to office.

Violence against civilians has led many Haitians to flee their country. In 1991 and 1992, over 65,000 Haitian refugees were stopped by the U.S. Coast Guard. They were trying to enter the United States illegally. Most of them were returned to Haiti, although many in the United States felt they should be allowed to seek **refuge** (shelter) in the United States.

Violence against civilians forced many Haitians to flee their country in 1991 and 1992.

Reading Strategy: Visualizing

Post the drawings so that classmates can use them to form or reinforce their own impressions.

LEARNING STYLES

Visual/Spatial
Huge murals on building walls decorate some neighborhoods where Latin Americans live, in native and adopted countries. Have students visit local examples or discover some on the Internet. Encourage them to create their own murals, too.

3 | Reinforce and Extend

COMMON ERROR

Latin Americans of Spanish descent often have three names: the first name is their given name, the second is their mother's family name, and the third is their father's family name. Their mother's family name functions as the surname. So, Vicente Fox Quesada might be shortened to Vicente Fox or Fox Quesada, but not Vicente Quesada.

Lesson 33–3 Review Answers

1. B **2.** C **3.** A **4.** B **5.** D **6.** A **7.** B
8. Possible answer: A high rate of unemployment, a growing population, and high foreign debt all contributed to Mexico's economic troubles. **9.** The agreement promised to end tariffs on farm products and many other goods. It aimed to ease immigration laws, and to allow trucks free access to border routes between the three countries. **10.** Civilians are fleeing Haiti because there is so much violence.

LESSON 33-3 REVIEW

On a sheet of paper, write the letter of the answer that correctly completes each sentence.

1. _____ was discovered in Mexico during the 1970s, and promised new riches.

   A Gold   **B** Oil   **C** An ancient ruin   **D** NAFTA

2. In the early 1980s, the price of oil fell, leaving Mexico in serious _____.

   A drought   **B** success   **C** debt   **D** riches

3. As Mexico's economy weakened, more Mexicans entered the United States _____.

   A illegally   **B** to avoid work   **C** in search of water   **D** looking for oil

4. Mexicans came to the United States in search of _____ and a better standard of living.

   A oil   **B** work   **C** food   **D** water

5. The North American Free Trade Agreement (NAFTA) offered economic growth for the United States, _____, and Mexico.

   A Cuba   **B** El Salvador   **C** Haiti   **D** Canada

6. Poverty, drought, hurricanes, and _____ have prompted civil unrest in Haiti.

   A famine   **B** the military   **C** unemployment   **D** violence

7. Haiti had _____ different governments between early 1986 and mid-1990.

   A three   **B** five   **C** seven   **D** nine

On a sheet of paper, write the answer to each question. Use complete sentences.

8. What are three factors that have contributed to the economic troubles in Mexico?

9. What were the terms of the North American Free Trade Agreement?

10. Why are so many Haitians fleeing their country?

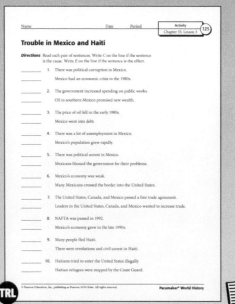

Latin America Today

Objectives

- To explain what happened to the Latin American economy by the late 1970s
- To explain the positive changes that have taken place in Latin America since 2000

Throughout its history, Latin America has faced many problems. However, in recent years the region has become more democratic and financially stable.

What Is Latin America Like Today?

Latin America's economy grew during the 1960s and early 1970s. By the late 1970s, however, economic growth declined. Latin American industry depended upon certain imports. It needed refined goods and machinery. This became a problem when prices on these imports rose sharply. At the same time, the prices on Latin America's raw agricultural and mineral exports dropped.

Latin America Today

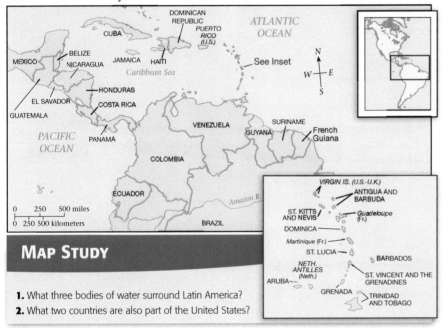

MAP STUDY

1. What three bodies of water surround Latin America?
2. What two countries are also part of the United States?

Point out that these timelines can be useful in reviewing what they have learned.

Answer: 1959

Have students make questions based on the timeline, and write them on a separate piece of paper. They should exchange their questions with another student and answer them.

2 Teaching the Lesson

As students read this lesson, have them focus on the trends that are mentioned. It might be helpful to compare these trends with those in their own country.

Ask:

* What caused the Latin American countries to go into debt? (Prices of imports rose and prices of exports dropped. The imbalance meant borrowing and cash outflow.)

* In 2000, were the economies of most Latin Americans growing or shrinking? (growing)

* If you wanted to visit an American tropical rain forest, where would you go? (Central America, Brazil)

Background Information

Brazil's efforts to preserve its rain forests include setting aside huge tracts as protected reserves. Tumucumaque Mountains National Park, set aside in 2002, is the largest tropical national park in the world. It covers 9.6 million acres of mountains, covered with rain forest. The first people to use the park were scientists, who studied the area to make informed decisions on what degree of tourism is consistent with protecting the habitats.

During this period, the Latin American nations were spending more and making less. Many had to borrow huge sums of money. Some of these nations have had trouble raising the money they need to repay their loans. By 2000, many positive changes had taken place in Latin America. In most countries, the economy had been improving. Democracy was growing. Women were gaining rights. Education had become a priority.

Brazil has the largest economy in South America. In fact, Brazil has the ninth largest economy in the world. Although the Brazilian government had to devalue its money in 1999, the economy still grew.

Reading Strategy:
Visualizing

Study the timeline in this lesson. How does it help you visualize the events in this chapter?

TIMELINE STUDY: LATIN AMERICA: 1945–2010

In what year did Cuba become a Communist country?

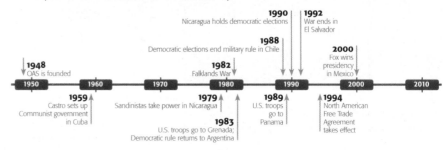

1948 OAS is founded

1959 Castro sets up Communist government in Cuba

1979 Sandinistas take power in Nicaragua

1982 Falklands War

1983 U.S. troops go to Grenada; Democratic rule returns to Argentina

1988 Democratic elections end military rule in Chile

1989 U.S. troops go to Panama

1990 Nicaragua holds democratic elections

1992 War ends in El Salvador

1994 North American Free Trade Agreement takes effect

2000 Fox wins presidency in Mexico

1950 | 1960 | 1970 | 1980 | 1990 | 2000 | 2010

Global warming
The heating up
of Earth from the
burning of wood, coal,
oil, and gasoline

Environment
The land, sea, and air
of our world

*Destruction of the
rain forests not only
threatens the world's
climate. It also threatens
the one-of-a-kind
animals, such as this
Cassowary, that
live there.*

LEARN MORE ABOUT IT

Brazil Pledges to Protect Its Rain Forest

The rain forests of South and Central America are an important resource to the whole world. The forests are not only beautiful. They have a direct effect on the world's climate. Yet in many regions, vast areas of the rain forests have been burned or cut down to make way for cattle ranches and farms. In 1987 and 1988, pictures taken from space showed the huge damage being done to Brazilian forest lands.

The world will pay a price for the destruction, or ruin, of its rain forests. Trees remove carbon dioxide (CO_2) from the air. Many scientists believe that a buildup of CO_2 will result in **global warming.** Global warming is the term used to describe the heating up of Earth from the burning of wood, coal, oil, and gasoline.

Global warming is sometimes called the "greenhouse effect." In addition, Brazilian fires set to burn the rain forests add CO_2 to the atmosphere. This increases the greenhouse effect.

In 1988, Brazil's president promised an end to the mass burning of the Amazon forests. In 1989, Brazil began a program aimed at protecting its rain forests. Brazil demonstrated its concern for the **environment** by hosting representatives from 178 countries at an Earth Day Summit in June 1992. Today, Brazil has adopted an environmental plan. It has also adopted the Environmental Crimes Law with strong penalties.

LEARN MORE ABOUT IT

Have students read "Brazil Pledges to Protect Its Rain Forest."

Ask:

- What can people do to help save the environment? (Possible answers: reduce the kinds of packages manufactures sell things in, plant trees, reuse and recycle)

- What can the government do to help save the environment? (Possible answers: pass laws that preserve places where animals live and protect endangered animals, promote the use of cleaner power and technology)

LEARNING STYLES

Auditory/Verbal

Ask students to research sports that are popular in Latin America today or that have a long history in Latin America. Have students organize their research into a short speech.

ELL/ESL STRATEGY

Language Objective:
To create a chart based on reading the text

Ask students to read "Brazil Pledges to Protect Its Rain Forest." Have them create a *Who, What, Why, Where, When,* and *How* chart. Have students write *Who benefits from rain forests? What is a rain forest? Why are rain forests important? Where are the world's rain forests located? When did Brazil initiate an environmental program to protect the rain forests?* and *How do rain forests affect people's lives?* Have students complete their charts using the information from the text or an additional online source.

LEARNING STYLES

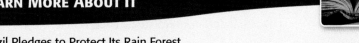

Interpersonal/Group Learning

Ask students why it is important to preserve the world's rain forests. Ask students to review the *Who, What, Why, Where, When,* and *How* chart they created for rain forests and work in groups to list ways they can contribute to the preservation of the world's rain forests. You might want to suggest that students research environmental organizations that work to preserve the rain forests. Ask students to make a wall-sized class poster that explains and illustrates problems and solutions for the world's rain forests.

3 Reinforce and Extend

CAREER CONNECTION

Latin America has tremendously diverse plants, many of which have traditionally been used in healing. These special plants are being sought as potential sources of medically valuable chemicals. Ethnobotanists are the people who explore how plants are used for medicine, as well as for food, shelter, clothing, hunting, and religious ceremonies. Ethnobotanists must understand not only plants, but also how cultures work and how to help preserve tropical forests. They train primarily in botany or biology, and study other subjects, such as archaeology, chemistry, ecology, anthropology, pharmacology, and religion.

Lesson 33–3 Review Answers

1. machinery 2. mineral 3. loans
4. economies 5. democracy 6. Brazil
7. climate 8. carbon dioxide (CO_2)
9. Global warming 10. Amazon

Word Bank

Amazon

Brazil

carbon dioxide (CO_2)

climate

democracy

economies

global warming

loans

machinery

mineral

On a sheet of paper, write the word from the Word Bank to complete each sentence correctly.

1. Latin American industry was dependent on refined goods and _____.

2. The price of Latin America's raw agricultural and _____ exports dropped as the price for imports rose.

3. Some Latin American nations were having trouble repaying their _____.

4. By 2000, many Latin American _____ were improving.

5. Also, _____ was growing, women were gaining rights, and education was becoming a priority.

6. _____ has the ninth largest economy in the world.

7. Rain forests have a direct effect on the world's _____.

8. By cutting down trees in the rain forests, _____ is being removed from the air.

9. _____ is also known as the "greenhouse effect."

10. Since 1988, Brazil has worked to protect the _____ forests.

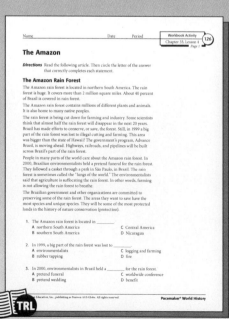

- After World War II, the United States tried to keep Communism out of Latin America.

- In a 1959 revolution, Fidel Castro set up a Communist dictatorship in Cuba.

- A Communist group called the Sandinistas took over the government of Nicaragua in 1979. The United States provided aid to a group called the Contras, a rebel group opposed to the Sandinistas. A civil war went on until 1989.

- A civil war in El Salvador went on for over 12 years. It took the lives of nearly 13,000 people.

- The United States invaded Panama to remove General Manuel Noriega from power.

- Many Latin Americans and U.S. citizens criticized the U.S. government for interfering in the affairs of other nations. They also did not think the United States should aid harsh governments.

- Mexico faced an economic and political crisis in the 1980s and 1990s.

- In 1992, the United States, Canada, and Mexico announced plans for the North American Free Trade Agreement.

- The island nation of Haiti has faced great hardship in recent years. Poverty, drought, hunger, and damage from hurricanes have caused many revolutions.

- The countries of Latin America have struggled with many different problems. However, in recent years some have become more democratic and financially stable.

Chapter 33 Summary

Have students read the Chapter Summary on page 723 to review the main ideas presented in Chapter 33.

Ask:

- Why did the United States intervene in Latin America after World War II? (to keep out the Communists)

- Who became the Communist dictator of Cuba? (Fidel Castro)

- Which two groups were fighting a civil war in Nicaragua in the 1980s? (the Sandinistas and the Contras)

- How long did the civil war in El Salvador last? (12 years)

- Why did the United States invade Panama in 1989? (to arrest General Noriega)

- Why were so many Latin Americans critical of U.S. involvement in their countries? (They did not want other nations interfering in their countries' political affairs.)

- What set off Mexico's economic crisis in the 1980s and 1990s? (reliance on oil income, followed by dropping oil prices)

- What is NAFTA? (a trade agreement among Canada, Mexico, and the United States)

- Which Caribbean island is one of the poorest nations in the world? (Haiti)

- Are Latin American countries generally becoming more democratic or more Communist? (more democratic)

TEACHER'S RESOURCE

The AGS Globe Teaching Strategies in Social Studies Transparencies may be used with this chapter. The transparencies add an interactive dimension to expand and enhance the Pacemaker® *World History* program content.

CHAPTER PROJECT FOLLOW-UP

Have each group display and explain its collage. Ask a student who enjoys creating displays to use the posters to develop a current-events display for the classroom.

Chapter 33 Review

Use the Chapter Review to prepare students for tests and to reteach content from the chapter.

Chapter 33 Mastery Test

The Teacher's Resource Library includes two forms of the Chapter 33 Mastery Test. Each test addresses the chapter Goals for Learning. An optional third page of additional critical-thinking items is included for each test. The difficulty level of the two forms is equivalent.

Chapter 33 Review Answers

Vocabulary Review

1. stronghold
2. humane
3. politics
4. moderate
5. global warming
6. Immigration
7. environment
8. tariff
9. ban
10. refuge

Chapter Review Questions

11. Friendly relations between Cuba and the United States ended.

12. In Nicaragua, the United States was afraid the Sandinista government would become a Communist stronghold in Central America.

Word Bank

ban
environment
global warming
humane
immigration
moderate
politics
refuge
stronghold
tariff

Vocabulary Review

On a sheet of paper, use the words from the Word Bank to complete each sentence correctly.

1. The U.S. feared a Communist _____ in Central America.

2. A(n) _____ government cares about poor people.

3. Some people believe that the United States should not interfere in the _____ of other nations.

4. A(n) _____ government is not extreme in its policies or actions.

5. Burning wood, coal, oil, and gasoline heats up Earth, causing _____.

6. _____ laws are rules about people coming into a country or region to live there.

7. The rain forests are an important part of our _____.

8. A(n) _____ is a tax a country puts on goods they import or export.

9. When you _____ aid to someone or something, you make providing aid illegal.

10. A(n) _____ is a safe place away from danger.

Chapter Review Questions

On a sheet of paper, write the answer to each question. Use complete sentences.

11. What happened to Cuba-U.S. relations after Castro took power in Cuba?

12. Why did the United States fight on the side of the rebels in Nicaragua?

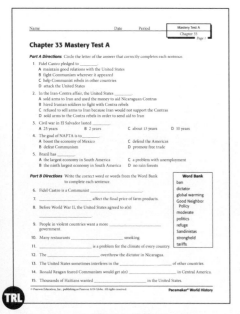

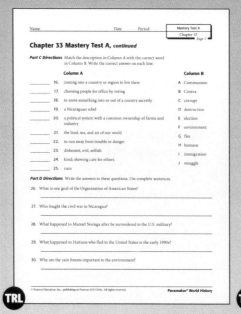

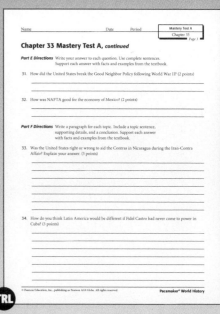

Test Tip

When studying for a test, work with a partner to write your own test questions. Then answer each other's questions. Check your answers.

13. Why did the United States fight on the side of the government in El Salvador?

14. What happened after General Manuel Noriega claimed victory in Panama's 1989 election?

15. What countries does NAFTA include and what does the agreement offer?

16. What four factors have contributed to the unrest (the revolutions and government takeovers) in Haiti?

Critical Thinking

On a sheet of paper, write your response to each question. Use complete sentences.

17. Why do events in Mexico affect the United States?

18. How could the destruction of the rain forests in Brazil affect your life?

Using the Timeline

Use the timeline on page 720 to answer the questions.

19. Which came first, the Falklands War or the U.S. invasion of Panama?

20. When was the Organization of American States founded?

GROUP ACTIVITY

With a group of three or four students, discuss U.S. relations with Cuba. Do you think the United States should have friendly relations with Cuba even if it is a Communist country? List the reasons your group says yes or no.

---

13. In El Salvador, the United States thought the rebels were backed by Communist governments in Cuba and Nicaragua.

14. The United States sent troops to remove General Noriega, an accused drug smuggler, from power. (He had claimed victory in the election even though his opponent, Guillermo Endara, won the most votes.)

15. NAFTA offers economic growth for the U.S., Canada, and Mexico.

16. Haiti has battled poverty, drought, hurricanes, and famine.

Critical Thinking

17. Possible answers: Mexico shares a border with the United States. Many people in the United States have relatives and friends in Mexico. Mexico is a major trading partner of the United States.

18. Possible answers: The rain forests probably affect the climate of the world. Even small climate changes could affect the way we live and grow food.

Using the Timeline

19. Falklands War

20. 1948

GROUP ACTIVITY

Some students may think that the United States can help the Cuban people by normalizing relations. Other students may think Castro must be isolated for holding to Communist ideas.

Chapter 33 Mastery Test B

Name _____ Date _____ Period _____   Mastery Test B / Chapter 33 / Page 1

Part A Directions Circle the letter of the answer that correctly completes each sentence.

1. The goal of the Organization of American States is to _____
   A promote free trade C support the U.S. government
   B settle arguments peacefully D conquer Communist nations
2. The war in Nicaragua was between _____
   A the Sandinistas and the Contras C Nicaragua and El Salvador
   B the United States and the Contras D the Sandinistas and the Communists
3. Manuel Noriega was taken from Panama to _____
   A vacation in Europe C be executed
   B attend peace talks in the Middle East D stand trial in the United States
4. Haitians fleeing to the United States _____
   A have been welcomed C helped build the U.S. economy
   B were stopped by the U.S. Coast Guard D used violence against civilians
5. The rain forests are important to the environment because _____
   A their wood is valuable C the trees remove carbon dioxide from the air
   B they are a source of food for Brazil D coffee beans are grown there

Part B Directions Write the correct word from the Word Bank to complete each sentence.

Word Bank: Communist, Contra, corrupt, destruction, elections, environment, flee, humane, immigration, smuggling

6. Voters in El Salvador wanted a more _____ government.
7. The _____ of the rain forest would be felt by everyone on Earth.
8. Violence caused Haitians to _____ their country.
9. Fidel Castro set up a(n) _____ dictatorship in Cuba.
10. The United States sent aid to the _____ rebels.
11. Economic and political problems in Mexico caused increased _____ to the United States.
12. Pollution is a problem for the _____.
13. Manuel Noriega was a(n) _____ leader.
14. Noriega was accused of _____ drugs.
15. Noriega also interfered with _____.

© Pearson Education, Inc., publishing as Pearson AGS Globe. All rights reserved.   Pacemaker® World History

---

Chapter 33 Mastery Test B, continued

Name _____ Date _____ Period _____   Mastery Test B / Chapter 33 / Page 2

Part C Directions Match the description in Column A with the correct word or words in Column B. Write the correct answer on each line.

Column A
16. shelter or protection from danger
17. to make or become less extreme or violent
18. the heating of Earth from the burning of wood, coal, oil, and gasoline
19. to make something not legal
20. a tax that countries put on goods they import or export
21. a Communist rebel in Nicaragua
22. a government in which one person has complete control
23. the work of government
24. a place dominated by a certain group
25. the policy in which the United States said it would not interfere with Latin American affairs

Column B
A ban
B dictatorship
C global warming
D Good Neighbor Policy
E moderate
F politics
G refuge
H Sandinista
I stronghold
J tariff

Part D Directions Write the answers to these questions. Use complete sentences.

26. What did Fidel Castro pledge to do in Latin America?
27. What happened in the Iran-Contra affair?
28. How long did the civil war in El Salvador last?
29. What is the goal of NAFTA?
30. How does Brazil's economy compare to the rest of South America?

© Pearson Education, Inc., publishing as Pearson AGS Globe. All rights reserved.   Pacemaker® World History

---

Chapter 33 Mastery Test B, continued

Name _____ Date _____ Period _____   Mastery Test B / Chapter 33 / Page 3

Part E Directions Write your answer to each question. Use complete sentences. Support each answer with facts and examples from the textbook.

31. Why has the United States interfered in the affairs of Latin American countries since World War II? Give examples to explain your answer. (2 points)

32. Describe the conflict between the Sandinistas and the Contras in Nicaragua. (2 points)

Part F Directions Write a paragraph for each topic. Include a topic sentence, supporting details, and a conclusion. Support each answer with facts and examples from the textbook.

33. Explain why the politics and economy of Mexico are important to the United States. (3 points)

34. Explain why many people are concerned about the future of the rain forests in Central and South America. (3 points)

© Pearson Education, Inc., publishing as Pearson AGS Globe. All rights reserved.   Pacemaker® World History

Introducing the Chapter

This chapter discusses the advances of modern technology, particularly in energy, space, and communication. It also describes the challenges facing the modern world, such as overpopulation, global terrorism, and environmental degradation.

The World Today

People call the present time the "Nuclear Age," the "Computer Age," or the "Age of Technology." Today's world is full of brand new inventions and discoveries. People today are seeing advances in technology at a faster rate than ever before. At the same time, the world's challenges are rapidly increasing. Overpopulation, food shortages, and disease present important needs for change. Damage to the environment threatens the well-being of generations to come. Preventing ongoing global terrorism is a main concern of many world governments.

GOALS FOR LEARNING

- To describe the uses of nuclear power
- To explain the advances made in space exploration
- To describe the many ways we can get information in today's world
- To explain the global issues we face today
- To describe the current state of our environment and population
- To tell about the threat of global terrorism
- To consider what the future holds

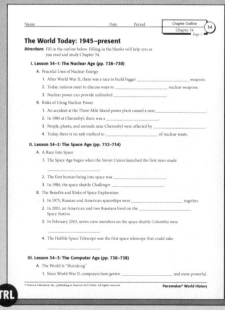

Reading Strategy: Inferencing

You have to infer the meaning of a text when it is not directly stated. When making inferences, start with what you already know. Then try to think "beyond the text" by considering what you have just read.

What You Know + What You Read = Inference

When inferencing, consider what you are reading and then predict what will happen next. Also, explain cause and effect to help you make quality inferences.

Key Vocabulary Words

Lesson 1
Nonrenewable Cannot be replaced once it is used up

Lesson 2
Satellite An object put into orbit around the earth

Astronaut A person trained to make space flights

Cosmonaut Russian word meaning "astronaut"

Lesson 4
Multinational corporation A company that hires people and has business interests around the world

Technology Science put to use in practical work

Lesson 5
Overpopulation The state of having too many people; can ruin the environment or the quality of life

Extinction The act of bringing to an end; dying out

Epidemic The rapid spread of a disease

Lesson 6
Agency A group that provides a service

Humanity The human race

Ask:

- What developments have made the world seem smaller? (developments in transportation and communications)
- Why does it seem as if history has repeated itself throughout the course of time? (Sample answer: Wars still occur for the same reasons. Leaders still rise to power and then fall.)

Reading Strategy:
Inferencing

Remind students that an inference is a conclusion based on prior knowledge and newly acquired information. Suggest that students read the introductory paragraph of each lesson and then make an inference based on what they read. When they have finished reading the lessons, have them check to see if their inferences were correct.

Key Vocabulary Words

Point out that these chapter words are presented in the order they appear in each lesson. They are also found in the glossary.

LIFE SKILLS CONNECTION

Students learn how to create a business plan for their futures. They discuss short- and long-term goals. Let students brainstorm ideas for goals; write them all on the board.

KEY VOCABULARY

Students choose the correct word from the Word Bank to complete each sentence. Have students review each lesson's vocabulary before they begin.

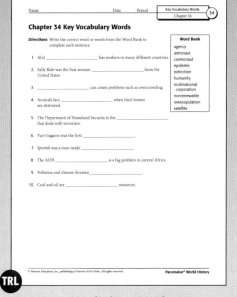

TRL

Life Skills Connection 34

TRL

Key Vocabulary Words 34

Lesson at a Glance

Chapter 34 Lesson 1

Overview This lesson discusses uses of and the advantages and disadvantages of using nuclear power for war and for energy.

Objectives

- To name two uses of nuclear power
- To explain the arguments for and against nuclear power

Student Pages 728–731

Teacher's Resource Library

Workbook Activity 127

Activity 127

Modified Activity 127

Vocabulary

nonrenewable

Before students read this lesson, tell them they can often infer the meanings of words by using prefixes and suffixes. Have them look up the prefix *non-* and the word *renewable* in a dictionary. Based on what they have learned, ask them to infer the meaning of the vocabulary word *nonrenewable*. Tell students to compare their answer to the definition of *nonrenewable* in the text to see if they were correct.

Reading Strategy:
Inferencing

Students may say that nuclear energy is a controversial issue because of the potential for accidents and the need to safely store hazardous waste for thousands of years.

You Decide

Answers will vary. Some students may say that the world is a safer place because relations between countries have improved. Others may say that the world is not safer because the former Soviet states may not be able to handle their nuclear arms responsibly.

The Nuclear Age

Objectives

- To name two uses of nuclear power
- To explain the arguments for and against nuclear power

Reading Strategy:
Inferencing

What do you already know about the use of nuclear energy?

You Decide
Do you think the world is a safer or more dangerous place since the breakup of the Soviet Union? Explain why or why not.

The last half of the 20th century is sometimes called the "Nuclear Age." Actually, the idea of nuclear power began about 1905, with Albert Einstein. Einstein suggested that energy was contained in every atom. The first use of that energy came in 1945 when the United States exploded two atomic bombs over Japan. Those explosions ended World War II and began an age of development for atomic energy.

The explosion of the first atomic bomb started the powerful nations of the world on a race. It was a deadly race to build bigger weapons. Countries tried to outdo each other in the number and size of the bombs they built.

Now many nations have a weapon so destructive that the results of another world war are impossible to imagine. So, nations try to avoid that war. They meet and talk about peace. They discuss ways to limit the buildup of nuclear arms. The United States and the Soviet Union held talks and signed treaties.

In 1991, the Soviet Union broke up. Its separate republics became 15 new nations. The nuclear weapons of the old Soviet Union are no longer under control of a single government. The cold war is over, and old enemies have friendlier relations. However, there is concern whether these new nations will handle their nuclear arms responsibly. Nuclear weapons in the hands of unstable governments or of terrorists threaten the safety of the whole world. It is a reality that today's people must live with.

LEARNING STYLES

Visual/Spatial
Place students in small groups. Have each group create a timeline that illustrates advances in technology during the period from 1990 to the present. Tell students to create a title for their timeline, and to divide it into appropriate time intervals. Suggest that students add information to the timeline as they read this chapter.

CHAPTER PROJECT

Have the class work together to create a classroom museum. Students should create a display that will show future generations what life was like in the early 21st century. Ask each student to bring in an item that he or she thinks is representative of the world today. Discourage students from bringing in expensive or irreplaceable items. Students will write a short description of their item to include in the display.

Nonrenewable
Cannot be replaced once it is used up

What Are Some Peaceful Uses of Nuclear Energy?

Although it was first used in a bomb, nuclear power has peacetime uses, too. The most important use is as a source of energy.

All nations use oil, coal, and natural gas for energy. These are all **nonrenewable** energy sources. Once they are used up, they are gone. As the population grows, the demand for energy also grows. People worry that we will run out of those traditional sources of energy.

The energy created in the nucleus of an atom can be used to run factories, heat homes, and light cities. Today this energy is produced in nuclear power plants around the world. Nuclear power is expensive. However, it can provide unlimited energy for thousands of years. The question is: Is it safe?

What Are the Risks to Using Nuclear Power?

History Fact
In a meltdown, the cooling system fails and the core of the nuclear reactor actually melts.

Nuclear power plants have strict safety regulations, or rules. Accidents, however, can happen. In 1979, there was an accident at the Three-Mile Island nuclear power plant in Pennsylvania. Failing equipment and human mistakes caused a near meltdown. While there were no tragic results, the public was frightened. People became aware that a disaster could happen. Stricter safety rules were set up. Yet, some people still wondered about the future of nuclear power. They worried that the risk was too great.

In 1986, a nuclear disaster occurred in the Soviet Union. There was a meltdown and explosion at the Chernobyl nuclear power plant. Nuclear explosions cause radiation. Radiation is when the rays and tiny pieces from a nuclear explosion are spread out. These rays and tiny pieces are very harmful and dangerous to anything living.

Reading Strategy:
Inferencing

Students may say that nuclear energy will not expand because of the risks associated with its use. Others will argue that use of nuclear power will expand as society depletes nonrenewable resources.

Background Information

The Chernobyl nuclear disaster released a radioactive cloud that killed at least 23 people directly. However, many more people were impacted indirectly. Some 4,000 children alone have developed various cancers. The damaged reactor has been sealed inside a concrete structure. But the structure is crumbling and could release more radioactive material if it collapses. The area surrounding the power plant is still radioactive some 20 years after the accident. People are not allowed near the site, but plants and animals have moved back into the area—partly because it is undisturbed by humans.

Reading Strategy:
Inferencing

After reading this section, what can you infer about the future use of nuclear energy? What words helped you make your inference?

The explosion at the Chernobyl nuclear power plant killed 23 people. It also forced many people to evacuate, or leave, nearby towns. The radiation from the explosion badly polluted the soil for 1,000 square miles. It sent a cloud of radiation across the Ukraine and other parts of the Soviet Union, and across several other European nations. Thousands of Soviet citizens—men, women, and children—were exposed to the radiation. Many of these people may die of cancer or other diseases. Traces of radiation were also found in animals, milk, and plant life far from the site of the accident. No one is sure just what the long-range effects of such radiation might be.

Many people protest the building of nuclear power plants. They say that no amount of energy is worth the risk of nuclear disaster. Others maintain that nuclear power is a safe answer to the world's energy crisis. They point out that many people have died in coal mine accidents over the years. Compared to this, only a few have died in accidents related to nuclear power plants.

Those in favor of nuclear power also point out that it is clean. It causes much less pollution than coal or oil. However, those against nuclear power have one very solid argument for their point of view. No safe method has yet been discovered for disposing of nuclear waste.

3   **Reinforce and Extend**

Word Bank

Einstein

energy

Japan

meltdown

nuclear

nucleus

Soviet Union

On a sheet of paper, write the word from the Word Bank to complete each sentence correctly.

1. The last half of the 20th century is sometimes called the "_____ Age."

2. In 1905, nuclear power began with the idea from _____.

3. In 1945, the United States exploded two atomic bombs over _____.

4. The most important peacetime use of nuclear power is as a renewable source of _____.

5. The _____ of an atom creates enough energy to heat homes and light cities.

6. In 1979, there was almost a(n) _____ at the Three-Mile Island nuclear power plant.

7. In 1986, a nuclear disaster happened in the _____.

On a sheet of paper, write the letter of the answer that correctly completes each sentence.

8. Nuclear explosions cause _____.

   A heat   B radiation   C energy   D light

9. Nuclear power causes much less _____ than coal or oil.

   A pollution   B energy   C heat   D light

10. There is not a safe method yet to dispose of nuclear _____.

   A energy   B power   C weapons   D waste

3   Reinforce and Extend

COMMON ERROR

Given the concerns about nuclear power, students might think that nuclear power provides little to no energy for most countries. Tell them that about 70 percent of the electricity in France comes from nuclear power. Nuclear power provides about 20 percent of the electricity in the United States, Japan, and Great Britain.

STUDY SKILLS

Ask students to rewrite each lesson heading in the chapter in the form of a question. For example, the lesson titled "The Nuclear Age" could be rewritten as "What Is the Nuclear Age?" The lesson titled "The Threat of Global Terrorism" could be rewritten as "How Can Global Terrorism be Stopped?" Once students have written each lesson heading as a question, have them write answers for each question.

Lesson 34–1 Review Answers

1. Nuclear **2.** Einstein **3.** Japan
4. energy **5.** nucleus **6.** meltdown
7. Soviet Union **8.** B **9.** A **10.** D

The Nuclear Age

Directions Read each statement. If it is a fact, write F on the line. If it is an opinion, write O on the line.

_____ 1. The United States dropped two atomic bombs on Japan.

_____ 2. Dropping the atomic bombs saved American lives.

_____ 3. The Soviet Union raced to build an atomic bomb.

_____ 4. The Soviet Union did not trust the United States with the atomic bomb.

_____ 5. The end of the Soviet Union was good for the world.

_____ 6. The Soviet Union broke up in 1991.

_____ 7. Nuclear power is better than coal or oil.

_____ 8. Coal and oil are nonrenewable sources of energy.

_____ 9. Nuclear power is safe.

_____ 10. Nuclear power creates dangerous waste.

_____ 11. There will never be a safe way to dispose of nuclear waste.

_____ 12. There was a meltdown at the Chernobyl nuclear power plant.

_____ 13. The Russians cannot be trusted with nuclear power.

_____ 14. No amount of energy is worth the risk of nuclear disaster.

_____ 15. Thousands of Soviet citizens were exposed to the radiation from Chernobyl.

Activity 127

The Nuclear Age Word Find

Part A Directions Write the correct word from the Word Bank to complete each sentence.

Word Bank
Albert
energy
expensive
meltdown
nonrenewable
Nuclear
oil
Soviet
Three

1. The last half of the 20th century is called the "_____ Age."

2. There was an accident at the _____-Mile Island nuclear power plant.

3. The republics of the _____ Union became 15 new nations.

4. When _____ energy sources are used up, they are gone.

5. Nuclear power can be _____.

6. Coal and _____ are fossil fuels.

7. _____ Einstein came up with the idea of nuclear power.

8. People are afraid that nuclear _____ is not safe.

9. An accident at a nuclear power plant can cause a(n) _____.

Part B Directions Use the words from the sentences above to fill in the words in this puzzle. The letters in the box reading down spell out the location of a nuclear disaster.

1. ___ ___ ___ | ___
2. ___ ___ | ___ ___
3. ___ ___ | ___ ___ ___
4. ___ ___ | ___ ___ ___
5. ___ ___ | ___ ___
6. ___ | ___ ___
7. ___ ___ | ___ ___ ___
8. ___ ___ | ___ ___ ___
9. ___ ___ | ___ ___

Hidden place: _____

Workbook Activity 127

Chapter 34 Lesson 2

Overview This lesson discusses the race for space between the United States and the Soviet Union. It also describes different technology used to explore space.

Objectives

- To explain why the late 20th century is sometimes called the "Space Age"
- To describe the advances in space technology

Student Pages 732–735

Teacher's Resource Library 🅣🅡🅛

Workbook Activity 128

Activity 128

Modified Activity 128

....

Vocabulary

astronaut
cosmonaut
satellite

Have each student make a Venn diagram that compares and contrasts the vocabulary words *astronaut* and *cosmonaut*. Tell students to make two overlapping circles, then label them *astronaut* and *cosmonaut*, respectively. In the parts of the circles that do not overlap, tell them to write unique details about each vocabulary word. In the overlapping part of the circles, have them write details or characteristics that both words share. Students can repeat the activity with the vocabulary word *satellite*, comparing it to a space shuttle or space station.

History Fact

Following the launch of *Sputnik I*, the United States accelerated its efforts to explore space. A big step forward was the creation of the National Aeronautics and Space Administration (NASA) in 1958.

The Space Age

Objectives

- To explain why the late 20th century is sometimes called the "Space Age"
- To describe the advances in space technology

Satellite
An object put into orbit around the earth

Astronaut
A person trained to make space flights

Cosmonaut
Russian word meaning "astronaut"

History Fact
Sputnik I weighed 184 pounds and was only 23 inches wide. It looked like a shooting star as it moved across the sky.

Sometimes the present era is called the "Space Age." The Space Age began in 1957. That is when the Soviet Union launched the first **satellite** made by humans into orbit around the earth. The satellite was called *Sputnik I*. Soon after, the United States launched its first satellite, *Explorer I*. The space race had begun.

Why Was There a Race Into Space?

An **astronaut** is a person who is trained to make space flights. In 1961, the Russians put the first human being into space. He was **cosmonaut** Yuri Gagarin (*cosmonaut* is the Russian word for "astronaut"). Then, in 1969, U.S. astronaut Neil Armstrong became the first person to walk on the moon. This event was watched on TV by 600 million people around the world.

The first woman went into space in 1963. She was the Soviet cosmonaut Valentina V. Tereshkova. In 1983, the United States sent its first woman astronaut, Sally Ride, into space aboard the shuttle *Challenger*.

The exploration of space is exciting. But it is also difficult, expensive, and dangerous. In January 1986, the space shuttle *Challenger* exploded shortly after takeoff. All the people on board were killed. There have been other accidents in which people have died. However, many people feel that the rewards from space exploration are worth the risks.

The space shuttle program provides a way for astronauts to learn more about our universe.

What Are the Benefits and Risks of Space Exploration?

Space has been an area in which the United States and the Soviet Union race to be the best. Space, however, can also be an arena for peace. In July 1975, three American astronauts and two Russian cosmonauts met in space. As planned, their two spaceships hooked up. U.S. space shuttles regularly delivered supplies and people to the Russian space station *Mir*. American and Russian astronauts lived and worked together in space. They conducted scientific experiments together and both nations shared the results.

In early 2001, an American and two Russians were living on the International Space Station (ISS). The ISS is an orbiting science laboratory. It will be completed in space.

By the beginning of the 21st century, 25 percent of American astronauts were women. Perhaps the best-known woman in space, however, was Sharon Christa McAuliffe. She was the New Hampshire teacher who was selected for the NASA Teacher In Space Project. McAuliffe was tragically killed, along with the rest of the crew, when the *Challenger* exploded.

Reading Strategy:
Inferencing

(Sample answer: People will continue to explore space. Perhaps someday, we will send spaceships with astronauts to other planets.)

TECHNOLOGY CONNECTION

Tell students that the Hubble Space Telescope was named after U.S. astronomer Edwin Hubble. In the 1920s, Hubble was instrumental in proving that distant fuzzy patches of light were actually galaxies, located outside of our own galaxy. He also discovered that distant galaxies are moving away from us. This meant that the universe is expanding. This idea led to the big bang theory.

LEARNING STYLES

Interpersonal/Group Learning

Have students create a "talk show" starring Christopher Columbus and his crew and the crew of a space shuttle. Ask for volunteers to act in the skit. One student should play the host of the show. Students who do not participate in the skit can film the show, set up the stage, and play the role of a studio audience. The host and the audience should ask questions of the two crews. Explain that the questions should focus on how exploration has changed over the years. *What was Columbus searching for? What are astronauts searching for? What kind of technology did each crew use?* As they listen, have the audience evaluate the skit by noting any historical discrepancies.

Reading Strategy:
Inferencing

Consider what you just read. What can you infer about the future progress of space exploration?

The *Columbia* was the first space shuttle to be launched into orbit, in April 1981. During the next 22 years it flew a total of 28 missions. It was completely rebuilt three times, most recently in 1999. On February 1, 2003, the *Columbia* was returning from a 16-day scientific mission. It broke apart as it reentered the earth's atmosphere. The *Columbia's* seven crew members were killed. Researchers believe that a piece of insulation broke off the shuttle's outside fuel tank. (Insulation is material used to cover and protect something.) The falling insulation seriously damaged one of the shuttle's wings.

The Space Age has only begun. Many people expect that before too long, we will have colonies on the moon. People from Earth may someday live on Mars and on other planets. Spaceships that do not include humans to operate them have already landed on Mars and Venus and sent back pictures. Other ships have flown close to Jupiter, Saturn, Uranus, and Neptune. Perhaps someday, we may even go to other solar systems!

TECHNOLOGY CONNECTION

The Hubble Space Telescope
In the late 1970s, the National Aeronautics and Space Agency (NASA) teamed up with the European Space Agency. Together they built the Hubble Space Telescope. In 1990, the space shuttle *Discovery* sent the telescope into space, about 350 miles above the earth. This was the first telescope in space that could take photographs. Since that time, the telescope has sent back better photos of the universe than any taken from the ground. Among the many images captured by the Hubble were those of two distant galaxies. A galaxy is a large group of stars and planets. In 1997 these galaxies, named *Antennae*, collided. At first, this crash created blue light from gases and hot star clusters. Scientists counted over 1,000 clusters of new stars. The brightest cluster was believed to have contained a million new stars.

ELL/ESL STRATEGY

Language Objective:
To learn how to take notes and summarize text

Place students in pairs. Ask each pair to find out more about an upcoming space mission. Tell them to focus on main points, such as the goal of the mission, destination, timeframe, type of technology used, cost, and other pertinent points. They should compile their information into a summary to share with the class. Remind students that when taking notes from reference materials, they can summarize important information using outlines or bulleted points. They do not need to copy the reference word for word, nor do they need to write in complete sentences while taking notes. Explain that only the final summary need be in paragraph form.

Word Bank

astronaut

Challenger

Neil Armstrong

Soviet Union

Space Age

Sputnik I

Yuri Gagarin

On a sheet of paper, write the word from the Word Bank to complete each sentence correctly.

1. The _____ began in 1957.

2. The _____ launched the first satellite made by humans into orbit around the earth.

3. The first satellite to orbit around the earth was called _____.

4. A(n) _____ is a person who is trained to make space flights.

5. In 1961, the Russians launched the first human into space. The cosmonaut's name was _____.

6. _____ was the first person to walk on the moon.

7. In 1986, the space shuttle _____ exploded shortly after takeoff.

On a sheet of paper, write the letter of the answer that correctly completes each sentence.

8. In 1975, Americans and Russians started working together in a Russian space station named _____.

    A *Columbia* **B** *Mir* **C** *Challenger* **D** *Explorer*

9. In _____, the *Columbia* was the first space shuttle to be launched into orbit.

    A 1957 **B** 1975 **C** 1981 **D** 2004

10. More than _____ people watched on television as the first man walked on the moon.

    A 12 million **C** 200 million
    B 60 million **D** 600 million

1945–PRESENT *The World Today   Chapter 34* **735**

---

3 Reinforce and Extend

ONLINE CONNECTION

Students can gain additional information by accessing the following Web site: www. agsglobepmwh.com/page735 (This site contains a wealth of information and images about objects in space and space exploration. It discusses past and future space missions. It also has interactive educational pages for students.)

COMMON ERROR

Students may think that the Hubble Space Telescope takes clearer pictures than Earth-based telescopes because it is relatively closer to objects in space. Explain that the earth's atmosphere contains dust and gases that distort images. The Hubble takes clearer images because it orbits above the earth's atmosphere.

Lesson 34–2 Review Answers

1. Space Age **2.** Soviet Union **3.** *Sputnik I* **4.** astronaut **5.** Yuri Gagarin **6.** Neil Armstrong **7.** *Challenger* **8.** B **9.** C **10.** D

The Space Age

Directions Read the following article. Then circle the letter of the answer that correctly completes each statement.

Women in Space

Many women have been part of the U.S. space program. They have been engineers, scientists, mathematicians, technicians, and astronauts. Most of these women have been highly educated. Many have a Ph.D. or a medical degree.

In January 1978, the first women joined the corps of astronauts. They were Anna Fisher, Shannon Lucid, Judith Resnick, Sally Ride, Rhea Seddon, and Kathryn D. Sullivan.

In 1983, Sally Ride became the first American woman in space. She flew two missions. Today, she is a physics professor and writes children's books. In 1984, Kathryn D. Sullivan became the first American woman to walk in space. In 1985, Anna Fisher was sent to bring back a broken satellite. In 1992, Mae Jemison became the first African American woman in space.

Women have been responsible for many other "firsts" in space. For example, Eileen Collins piloted the first space shuttle flight to meet up with the Russian's *Mir* space station. Shannon Lucid stayed in space longer than any other American. In 1999, Air Force Colonel Eileen Collins became the first woman to command a space mission.

By the end of the 20th century, 25 percent of American astronauts were women. Perhaps the best-known woman in space, however, was Christa McAuliffe. She was selected for the NASA Teacher In Space Project. McAuliffe was tragically killed, along with the rest of the crew, when the *Challenger* exploded.

1. The first women astronauts joined the American space program _____
    A when the space program began   C in 1983
    B in 1978   D in 1999

2. The first African American woman in space was _____
    A Mae Jemison   B Christa McAuliffe   C Eileen Collins   D Sally Ride

The Space Age Chart

Directions The words and phrases below refer to the United States, the Soviet Union, or both the United States and the Soviet Union. Write each word or phrase in the correct column on the chart.

first woman in space   flew into space in 1975
first person on the moon   Hubble Space Telescope
people lived in space   *Challenger*
Explorer I   scientists performed experiments in space
Sputnik I   first person into space
the International Space Station   space race
the space shuttle   *Columbia*
Mir

The United States	Both the U.S. and the USSR	The Soviet Union

Activity 128, pages 1–2   Workbook Activity 128   *The World Today Chapter 34*   **735**

Lesson at a Glance

Chapter 34 Lesson 3

Overview This lesson discusses how communication, transportation, and daily life have been changed by computers.

Objectives

- To detail the many uses of computers
- To explain how advances in communication and transportation make the world seem smaller

Student Pages 736–739

Teacher's Resource Library

Workbook Activity 129

Activity 129

Modified Activity 129

Reading Strategy:
Inferencing

Students will likely know that computers can be used to do research, play games, and chat with friends. They might also say that computers are helpful for writing papers and creating graphs and tables.

History Fact
The first person to travel at or beyond the speed of sound was U.S. Major Charles E. Yeager. Yeager accomplished this task in 1947 in an Air Force rocket-plane, which was carried into the sky by a B-29 and then released. Two years later, the first supersonic jet exceeded the speed of sound.

You Decide
Sample answer: Yes, the name fits because we can get information in seconds from the Internet and telephones. We also get information about events around the world from television, radio, and newspapers.

The Computer Age

Objectives

- To detail the many uses of computers
- To explain how advances in communication and transportation make the world seem smaller

Reading Strategy:
Inferencing

What do you already know about computers?

History Fact
Supersonic airplanes fly faster than sound can travel. (At sea level, sound travels 740 miles per hour.)

You Decide
The present era is often called the "Information Age." Do you think the name fits? Why or why not?

Computers are electronic machines. They solve problems, answer questions, and store information. Computers are used around the world to help people do their work, find information, communicate with others, and play games.

Computers have improved steadily since World War II. At first they were very large, very expensive, and difficult to run. Now they are much smaller and are used by millions of people. A computer that once filled an entire room now fits into the palm of a hand!

At first people worried that computers would replace humans in many jobs. In some cases, this has happened. However, computers have created many more new jobs. Computers give people the time and freedom to get more work done. They also provide entertainment for millions of people.

In What Ways Is the World "Shrinking"?

Developments in transportation and communication have made the world seem smaller. People in one part of the world now know what is happening across the ocean. In fact, a trip across an ocean that used to take months, now takes only hours!

Television also has the ability to transport people across the ocean—all while they sit on their couch! Without a doubt, TV has greatly changed 21st-century life. Many Americans protested involvement in the Vietnam War because television cameras brought the action to them. They saw for themselves the suffering of American soldiers and Vietnamese villagers.

Television news brought the Israeli-Arab conflict into millions of homes. People of the world witnessed the injustices of apartheid in South Africa. They also saw hunger in Ethiopia and Somalia with their own eyes.

We also get information from the hundreds of communication satellites that circle the earth. They beam radio, television, telephone, and computer signals around the world. Satellites in space can take weather pictures to make forecasts anywhere in the world.

Reading Strategy:
Inferencing

How does what you already know about computers add to what you have just read?

With computers and the Internet, workers can trade or share information almost instantly.

Although use of the Internet did not explode until the late 20th century, the Internet has been around since the 1960s. The concept of a shared computer network was created by the U.S. Department of Defense Advanced Research Projects Agency as a way to share data among researchers.

ELL/ESL STRATEGY

Language Objective:
To compare and contrast the use of cell phones around the world

Have ELL students research cell phone use in the United States and in their native countries. Tell them to focus on the following points: number of people who use cell phones, different uses of the phones, and average cost of owning a cell phone. Ask students to present their results to the class. Encourage them to use visuals to display their data, such as bar graphs and circle graphs. As a class, discuss any reasons for similarities and differences between cell phone use in the United States and other countries.

3 | Reinforce and Extend

AT HOME

Have students talk with family members about how technology affects their lives. Which type of technology does each family member consider most important, and why? Encourage students to talk to older family members as well. Having seen vast changes in technology during their lifetimes, senior citizens should have interesting views on the matter. Have students compile a list of their family's top 10 technologies. Ask volunteers to share their lists with the class.

Words from the Past

The Internet

Communication around the world is advancing almost daily. Satellites and under-ocean cables provide connections for global telephone and Internet service.

The Internet links people all over the world in a way like never before. We can write to one another, send photos and videos, and even communicate "live" using webcam. Consumers can buy countless products from companies all over the world. We can book a hotel room in Tokyo, arrange car rental in Cairo, or sign up for scuba lessons in New Zealand. The number of people using the Internet has tripled since 1997. More than one billion people worldwide now use the Internet regularly.

Personal computers and cell phones bring people together, even when they are on the move. Using handheld devices, people can type instant messages (IMs), share music, and talk. They can snap and then send photos. They can surf the Internet while riding on a bus, or send e-mails from a coffee shop in a foreign country. They can watch movies or do research while sitting under a tree in a park.

Thousands of people have created their own spaces on the Internet. They can link to friends through these sites, and share ideas instantly with other people all over the world. Workers can trade or share files with one another using other Internet sites.

Word Bank

bigger
billion
cell phones
computers
humans
Internet
satellites
smaller
Vietnam War
World War II

On a sheet of paper, write the word from the Word Bank to complete each sentence correctly.

1. _____ solve problems, answer questions, and store information.

2. Computers have improved steadily since _____.

3. People were afraid computers would replace _____ in many jobs.

4. Development in transportation and communication make the world seem _____.

5. Many Americans did not like the _____ because television cameras showed the action to them.

6. Communication _____ beam radio, television, and computer signals all over the world.

7. The _____ links people all over the world.

8. More than one _____ people worldwide regularly use the Internet.

9. Personal computers and _____ bring people together, even when they are on the move.

10. Computers used to be much _____ than they are today.

WORLD CULTURES

Technology can dominate modern lives. Cell phones keep us in close touch with family and friends. Videos allow us to watch movies in the privacy of our homes. Internet shopping helps us to avoid bustling crowds.

Technology can have a price, though. Cell phones interrupt intimate conversations. Internet shopping is an impersonal transaction. Videos keep us from enjoying a shared experience with others in a theater.

The Amish is one group that will likely never face the problems associated with technology. For more than 300 years, Amish communities have clung to traditional ways. Their religion dictates that they live simply. This belief is reflected in all parts of their lives, from their clothes to their food to their avoidance of television and modern farming equipment. The world may have changed around them, but the Amish have steadfastly remained true to their beliefs.

Lesson 34–3 Review Answers

1. computers **2.** World War II **3.** humans **4.** smaller **5.** Vietnam War **6.** satellites **7.** Internet **8.** billion **9.** cell phones **10.** bigger

---

Activity 129   Workbook Activity 129   *The World Today Chapter 34*   **739**

Lesson at a Glance

Chapter 34 Lesson 4

Overview This lesson explains the advantages and disadvantages of a global economy, and compares and contrasts developed and developing nations.

Objectives

■ To describe a global economy

■ To explain the relationship between developed nations and developing nations

Student Pages 740–744

Teacher's Resource Library **TRL**

Workbook Activity 130

Activity 130

Modified Activity 130

Vocabulary

multinational corporation
technology

Ask students to work in pairs. Have one partner read a definition of a vocabulary word. Have the other partner identify the word that matches the definition, and then write the definition in his or her own words.

1   Warm-Up Activity

Help students understand the relationship between resources and manufactured goods. Ask a volunteer to come to the board and draw a manufactured product, such as a bicycle. Next to the drawing, write the name of a raw material, such as iron ore, that is used to make the product. Ask students how a shortage of the raw material would affect the price of the product.

Global Issues

Objectives

■ To describe a global economy

■ To explain the relationship between developed nations and developing nations

As the world seems to grow smaller, nations have a greater influence on each other. Trade has long affected cultures and civilizations, and ideas have always been shared while trading. Now it is common for nations to trade their goods and ideas worldwide. They depend on each other for an exchange of raw materials and manufactured goods.

What Is a "Global Economy"?

The Pacific Rim is a term used to describe lands bordering the Pacific Ocean. During the 1980s, the Pacific Rim became the world's fastest-growing trading area. Electronic equipment, cars, and other products leave Japan, Taiwan, and Korea for foreign markets.

The popularity of foreign products weakened the economy of the United States. Since the 1970s, the United States has imported more goods from other nations than it has exported. Since that time, hundreds of U.S. factories have closed or laid off workers. This is because these foreign products are being purchased in large quantities by U.S. consumers.

At first the United States tried to solve its economic problems by setting up trade restrictions. Congress set limits on the number of imports that could enter the country. Foreign companies found ways to get around the restrictions. Japanese automakers built factories in the United States. By 1989, many "American-made" cars were manufactured in U.S. plants owned by Japanese companies.

COMMON ERROR

 Students may think that the Pacific Rim only includes Asian nations such as Japan, Taiwan, and Korea. The Pacific Rim actually includes all areas that border the Pacific Ocean. This includes parts of North America, Central America, South America, and Australia. In fact, the Pacific Rim National Park is located in Canada. Show students a globe and have them trace the outline of the Pacific Rim with their fingertips.

This was not a new strategy. The United States had been setting up factories all over the world for years. During the 1980s, many U.S. companies built factories in foreign lands to take advantage of cheap labor. Today many are **multinational corporations**—companies that hire people and have business interests around the world. Japanese companies own some entertainment and food business in the United States. U.S. auto companies have interests in auto companies in other countries.

The health of one nation's economy depends greatly on that of other nations. All countries need places to export the goods they make. All countries need to import some. Countries made trade alliances and free-trade agreements to tear down barriers and encourage fair trade. In 1988, the United States and Canada signed a free-trade pact. It ended restrictions and tariffs on almost all products. In 1994, the United States, Canada, and Mexico began free trade between all three nations.

European nations have joined together in the European Union (EU). The goal of the EU is to ensure completely free trade and free movement of money and people between member nations. The World Trade Organization (WTO) has 150 member nations. In 2000, some people in the United States protested against the WTO. In Seattle, protesters included workers who were afraid their jobs would go to other countries. Environmentalists who wanted stronger protection for the environment were there, too.

What Is the Difference Between a Developed Nation and a Developing Nation?

The Industrial Revolution split the nations of the world into two camps: developed nations and developing nations. Developed nations have many industries. They import and export products. Most people who live in developed nations have a fairly high standard of living.

2 Teaching the Lesson

Have students explain how their actions affect other people. (Answers will vary. Sample answer: If I have soccer practice after school, one of my parents has to rearrange their day to pick me up.) Tell students that countries can also affect one another. In a global economy, the actions of one nation can have a big impact on other nations.

Ask:

- Why are developing nations more dependent on other nations? (The economies of developing nations can be easily upset.)
- How do multinational companies help the world economy? (Sample answer: Because of multinational companies, each nation must depend on the other for financial success.)
- What is the goal of the European Union? (to ensure free trade and free movement between member nations)

Background Information

A global economy can have severe ramifications if one nation's economy collapses. In June 1997, Thailand experienced one such collapse. The impacts were felt in South Korea, Indonesia, Malaysia, and Russia. Many businesses and banks went bankrupt. Such an economic downswing characterized by low consumer spending is called a recession.

Japan also felt the sting of the recession, as did the United States. Consumers in key nations did not have the money to buy U.S. goods. Some workers were laid off. The recession did bring about some relief in the form of oil prices. Because the demand for oil dropped dramatically in Asian nations, the prices of oil fell. U.S. consumers noticed the difference at the gas pumps.

Most people there can read and write. They benefit from the advances of modern science and its practical uses, or **technology.** The United States, Russia, Canada, France, Great Britain, Japan, the Scandinavian countries, and Germany are just some of the developed nations.

Developing nations are the countries that are less developed. Many people in developing nations are poor. Many people farm the land, but their methods of agriculture are often outdated. There are fewer industries in developing nations. Their standard of living is lower, and many people cannot read or write.

In developing countries, many people live in traditional ways. It is important to preserve aspects of traditional life while making economic gains. Haiti, Afghanistan, and Mexico are examples of developing countries. Many South American and African nations are developing countries. Some of these nations, like Nigeria and Venezuela, have rich oil deposits.

Developed nations have many industries and a fairly high standard of living. New York City is an excellent example of a city in a developed nation.

Developing countries are more dependent on other nations. Their economies can be easily upset by weather, a year of bad farm crops, or a war. Sometimes the more developed nations help the developing nations by lending money or sending supplies. The United States has sent thousands of Peace Corps volunteers to developing countries all over the world. There the volunteers teach modern farming methods, health care, and engineering.

Developing nations often use outdated methods of agriculture and live in traditional ways. Afghanistan is an example of a developing country.

Reading Strategy:
Inferencing

After reading this section, what inference can you make about the problems of hunger in developing nations?

GREAT NAMES IN HISTORY

Mother Teresa of Calcutta

Agnes Gonxha Bojaxhiu was born in Macedonia in 1910. At age 18, she joined the Sisters of Loreto, an order of nuns with missions in India. She became Sister Teresa. She started teaching in a convent school in Calcutta, India. Sister Teresa saw great suffering beyond the convent walls. After many years she left the school to work in the poorest neighborhoods of Calcutta. By this time she was known as Mother Teresa.

Mother Teresa started helping people who were sick and had little food. She had no money, yet she founded an open-air school for the children of the poor neighborhoods. She began to attract volunteers to help her. Organizations started giving money for the school. In 1959, she founded the Missionaries of Charity to help needy people in other parts of the world. Mother Teresa won many awards for her kindness, including the Nobel Peace Prize in 1979.

Reading Strategy:
Inferencing

(Sample answer: Hunger is a big problem in developing nations. Volunteers try to help farmers and teach health care. Developed nations lend money or send supplies. However, many people are still hungry.)

GREAT NAMES IN HISTORY

Use the example of Mother Teresa to discuss how one person can make a vast difference in the lives of others. Ask students to describe in their own words how Mother Teresa evolved from a young nun into a Nobel Peace Prize winner. Have them brainstorm a list of historical figures whom they have learned about who have also made a difference.

3 Reinforce and Extend

CAREER CONNECTION

Scientists and engineers constantly work to discover ways to increase crop production and to assess the safety of food. These are especially relevant concerns in developing countries. An agricultural lab technician is a person who works to ensure a safe food supply. He or she might be employed by private or public labs, county extension agencies, and dairy processing plants, to name a few places. An agricultural lab technician must have solid math skills and a solid background in science. Suggest that interested students find out more about this career by talking to their guidance counselor and conducting research on the Internet.

On a sheet of paper, write the letter of the answer that correctly completes
each sentence.

1. It is now common for nations to trade their goods and ideas _____.

   A worldwide   **B** yearly   **C** monthly   **D** by telegraph

2. During the 1980s, the _____ became the world's fastest-growing trading area.

   A United States   **B** Soviet Union   **C** Pacific Rim   **D** Canadian border

3. The popularity of _____ weakened the economy in the United States.

   A farming   **B** the Internet   **C** gold   **D** foreign products

4. The United States set up _____ to try and solve economic problems.

   A allowances   **B** restrictions   **C** agreements   **D** companies

5. In 1988, the United States and Canada signed a _____.

   A peace treaty   **B** free-trade pact **C** trade restriction **D** technology pact

6. There is free trade and movement of resources between nations in the _____.

   A free-trade pact **B** WTO   **C** Peace Corps   **D** European Union

7. The _____ has 150 member nations.

   A World Trade Organization   **C** Pacific Rim
   B European Union   **D** United States

8. The _____ split nations into developed nations and developing nations.

   A Agricultural Revolution   **C** European Union
   B World Trade Organization   **D** Industrial Revolution

9. Many people in developing countries are _____.

   A wealthy   **B** scientists   **C** poor   **D** exporters

10. U.S. _____ volunteers teach modern farming methods in developing countries.

    A Army   **B** Navy   **C** Peace Corps   **D** Air Force

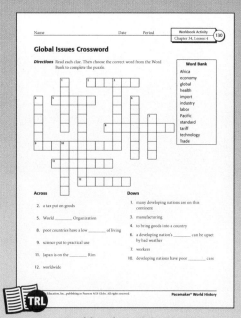

Activity 130   Workbook Activity 130

Environment, Overpopulation, and Disease

Objectives

- To describe the effects of overpopulation
- To explain some alternative sources of energy
- To describe the diseases that threaten our world today

Reading Strategy: Inferencing

What do you already know about concerns regarding the environment, overpopulation, and disease?

Overpopulation
The state of having too many people; can ruin the environment or the quality of life

Humankind has made big progress since the first civilizations in Sumer. However, with progress comes problems. The technological advances we have made, along with our growing population, can negatively affect Earth.

What Is the Growing Population Doing to Our Environment?

As the number of people increases around the world, so does the damage to the environment. More people are driving cars. More factories are using more energy to make products. More space is needed to house and grow food for the population. Indeed, our planet has reached a state of **overpopulation.** Overpopulation, the state of having too many people, can ruin the environment or quality of life.

Vehicles, factories, and some plants produce gases from burning fuels such as oil or coal. These gases pollute the air. They may contribute to breathing illnesses in people. They produce acid rain, which damages plants and harms animals that eat those plants. Dangerous global warming happens when gases surrounding the earth trap the heat from sunlight. Factories, careless farming practices, and misplaced trash is affecting water quality in many countries of the world.

Reading Strategy:
Inferencing

Students will likely know about air and water pollution. They may have heard about acid rain and global warming. Students might also know about diseases such as AIDS.

Lesson at a Glance

Chapter 34 Lesson 5

Overview This lesson discusses global problems, such as overpopulation and pollution, and describes potential remedies for these problems.

Objectives

- To describe the effects of overpopulation
- To explain some alternative sources of energy
- To describe the diseases that threaten our world today

Student Pages 745–749

Teacher's Resource Library

Workbook Activity 131

Activity 131

Modified Activity 131

Vocabulary

epidemic
extinction
overpopulation

Place students in pairs. Have each pair write the name of a vocabulary word on an index card. The definition of the word should be written on the opposite side of the card. Tell students to repeat the activity for each vocabulary term. Then have them quiz one another using the cards.

PRONUNCIATION GUIDE

Use this list to help students pronounce difficult words in this lesson.

tsunami (tsoo nä´ mə)

Sri Lanka (srē läng´ kə)

malaria (mə lâr´ ē ə)

Haiti (hā´ tē)

Warm-Up Activity

Place enough pencils on your desk for each student in the class. Ask students how many pencils each students gets. (1 pencil per student) Take away 10 pencils. Ask students how the supply of pencils has changed. (Students should say that there are not enough pencils to go around.) Tell them that the pencils are like resources. There are only so many resources to go around. Explain that this is a danger of overpopulation—there is not enough space, minerals, fossil fuels, food, and water to meet everyone's needs.

2 Teaching the Lesson

Ask students what they already know about alternative sources of energy such as solar power, hydroelectric power, wind power, and geothermal energy. Discuss which of these sources might be suited to their area. Also discuss which sources, if any, are currently used in their area.

Ask:

- What can overpopulation do? (ruin the environment or people's quality of life)

- How does deforestation affect animals? (Animals lose their homes when forests are destroyed)

- Since the 1980s, what has become the most widespread epidemic in Central Africa? (AIDS)

Extinction
The act of bringing to an end; dying out

Lands that were once wilderness are becoming farms or towns. Deforestation, or the destruction of forests, is taking place all over the globe. Deforestation affects trees and other plants that produce oxygen (which is valuable to the earth's air). It also affects animals—when the forests are destroyed, animals lose their homes. Many of those animals and the plants that once surrounded them are facing **extinction.** When something faces extinction, it is coming to an end—it is dying out. Scientists estimate that up to 100 animal species become extinct every day!

What Are Some Alternative Sources of Energy?

The world's energy needs are increasing. However, the supplies of fossil fuels such as oil, coal, and natural gas are decreasing. Scientists in many countries are working to find ways to use energy from renewable sources. Renewable sources are sources that can be replaced.

Wind, sunlight, water, and heat from the ground are renewable sources, because supplies are endless. Many countries now have wind farms in open areas, often near oceans, which get strong winds. One such collection of windmills near Ireland produces electricity for 16,000 homes. Since the 1980s, many homes and office buildings have used solar panels to collect energy from the sun. New technology is making the use of solar energy better and less expensive. An increasing number of cities are capturing underground heat for use in buildings. Areas near oceans and rivers are exploring new ways of using waves or falling water to produce electricity.

Manufacturers have developed cars that run on electricity or ethanol. Ethanol is a fuel that is made from something that can be grown, such as sugar. People of many nations are working to create laws to improve air and water quality. Laws are being passed to preserve animal homes and to protect animals that are facing extinction.

Governments are working to encourage the use of alternative energy such as wind energy.

ELL/ESL Strategy

Language Objective:
To form a plan of action using a written step-by-step procedure

Show students a photograph of a polluted stream. Be sure litter and discolored water are visible in and around the stream. Have students work in small groups to develop a plan to clean the stream. Tell them to create a step-by-step plan of the actions they would take. Tell them to be sure their steps are in proper order. Ask students to consider the following points before they write their plans: *Who owns the stream? How will they get permission to clean the stream? What materials will they need? How will they get the materials? What safety measures will they take? How will they dispose of the waste?* Have groups exchange plans with one another and critique each other's work.

Deadly Storms

Horrible natural disasters have occurred in recent years on opposite sides of the globe.

A tsunami up to 30 feet high hit the Indian Ocean in late 2004. A tsunami is a giant wall of water usually caused by an earthquake under the sea. It killed nearly 200,000 people, mostly in Indonesia, India, and on the island of Sri Lanka. A second tsunami hit Java, Indonesia's main island, in 2006, killing 530 people. This wave was six feet high, small compared to the one in 2004.

Hurricane Katrina hit the Florida coast on August 25, 2005. Then it moved into the Gulf of Mexico and gained strength. It hit the coast of Louisiana and Mississippi on August 29. The force of the storm broke the levees around New Orleans, Louisiana. The levees were made to hold back water. Almost all of that city became badly flooded. More than 1,800 people were killed and more than a million were left homeless by this storm.

What Diseases Are Threatening Our World?

Millions of poor people die from illnesses related to dirty living conditions. Others simply do not have enough of the right foods to remain healthy. In wealthier countries, many people overeat, use tobacco, and get too little exercise. These habits often lead to heart disease and diabetes, two major causes of early deaths in these countries.

Various new diseases prompted concern in the 1990s and 2000s. Insects and other flying creatures spread many of them. A disease called SARS (Severe Acute Respiratory Syndrome) is spread by close person-to-person contact. More than 8,000 people in 26 countries have become infected with SARS. Lyme disease, spread by deer ticks, infected 25,000 people in the United States alone during 2002. The West Nile virus is most often spread to people and animals through mosquitoes.

1945–PRESENT   *The World Today*   Chapter 34   **747**

LEARNING STYLES

Body/Kinesthetic

Place students in small groups. Have each group research a different alternative energy source such as solar, geothermal, tide, hydroelectric, wind, and biomass. Tell each group to make a model showing how their energy source works. For example, students can build a model of a solar-powered house. They can use a fan to show the power of wind. Encourage students to be creative and to follow proper safety procedures. Have the groups demonstrate their model to the class.

Since 1880, when people first began recording weather conditions, global temperatures have risen 2°F. In comparison, it took 18,000 years for global temperatures to rise by 9°F during the last ice age. Some experts believe that global warming may be causing an increase in the severity of weather events, such as hurricanes, droughts, and floods. Hurricane Katrina is a case in point.

Background Information

Recent scientific studies warn that global temperatures could rise as much as 10.5 degrees during the next 100 years. The reports say that poor countries and island states will be hardest hit by global warming. Coastal areas in the United States, such as Florida, will be at risk from rising sea levels.

Global warming is a rise in Earth's surface temperatures. On Earth, certain gases in the air help trap energy from the sun. This is called the greenhouse effect. It is a natural phenomenon; without the greenhouse effect, life on Earth could not exist. However, the burning of fossil fuels and deforestation has led to an increase of greenhouse gases in the atmosphere, particularly carbon dioxide. Such an increase can lead to global warming.

New scientific studies discuss global warming and its impact on specific areas all over the world. The studies say that in certain parts of the world, there will be fewer crops, more droughts, more floods, and coastal erosion. The ice around polar regions will melt, putting many animals at risk of extinction. Increases in heat-related diseases and deaths are also predicted, as well as the disruption of economies.

Reading Strategy:
Inferencing

Students probably know that AIDS exists, but they might not realize how widely spread it is and the impact it has, particularly in Africa.

TEACHER ALERT

Consider asking the school's health teacher or school nurse to come into the class and discuss disease prevention. Ask him or her to talk about the diseases discussed in this lesson, as well as other common diseases, such as colds. Have students prepare a list of questions to ask the teacher or school nurse beforehand.

Epidemic
The rapid spread of a disease

Reading Strategy:
Inferencing

How does what you already know about these issues add to what you have just read?

The bird flu, spread through infected poultry, has infected about 300 people worldwide. Scientists are working to learn more about how to control all of these diseases.

Malaria is not a new disease, by any means, but it is also transmitted by mosquitoes. About a million people in Africa die each year from malaria. During the 1950s, the disease was eliminated (gone) from the United States. In recent years it has returned, with over 1,000 cases reported in America in 2002.

AIDS (acquired immune deficiency syndrome) continues to infect people all over the world. Doctors discovered that AIDS was caused by a virus—the human immunodeficiency virus (HIV). Since 1981, AIDS has shown up in some 140 countries around the world. It exploded into the most widespread **epidemic**—the rapid spread of a disease—in central Africa. High numbers were also found in the small Caribbean nation of Haiti. By the end of the 1990s, there were very few countries in which this killer disease had not struck. In 2006, nearly 40 million people worldwide were living with HIV. New medications are helping more people with HIV avoid developing AIDS. Despite these new advances, the number of AIDS cases is growing worldwide. Doctors continue to search for ways to stop the AIDS epidemic and to save those who already have the virus.

REVIEW

Word Bank

AIDS
deforestation
fossil fuels
global warming
malaria
overpopulation
renewable

On a sheet of paper, write the word from the Word Bank to complete each sentence correctly.

1. _____ happens when gases surrounding the earth trap heat from the sunlight.

2. _____ can ruin the environment or quality of life for people.

3. _____ affects animals' homes as well as trees and plants that produce oxygen.

4. The supplies of _____, such as oil, coal, and natural gas, are decreasing.

5. _____ sources are energy sources that can be replaced. Wind, sunlight, water, and heat from the ground are examples.

6. About a million people die in Africa each year because of _____.

7. Since 1981, _____ has shown up in 140 countries around the world.

On a sheet of paper, write the answer to each question. Use complete sentences.

8. What are two forms of alternative energy sources?

9. What are governments doing to help the environment?

10. What are two common diseases in wealthier countries that are major causes of death?

Lesson 34–5 Review Answers

1. global warming 2. overpopulation
3. deforestation 4. fossil fuels
5. renewable 6. malaria 7. AIDS
8. Alternative energy sources include wind, sunlight, water, and heat from the ground. 9. Governments are working to create laws to improve air and water quality. Laws are also being passed to preserve animal homes and to protect animals from facing extinction. 10. Heart disease and diabetes are two common diseases in wealthier countries.

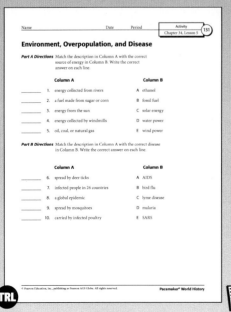

Lesson at a Glance

Chapter 34 Lesson 6

Overview This lesson discusses the effects of global terrorism and efforts to stop future attacks.

Objectives

- To explain how terrorism has affected the entire world
- To describe what can be done to prevent future terrorist attacks

Student Pages 750–753

Teacher's Resource Library

Workbook Activity 132

Activity 132

Modified Activity 132

....

Vocabulary

agency
humanity

Ask a volunteer to write a sentence on the board that uses one of the vocabulary words. Ask a second volunteer to write a related sentence on the board using the other vocabulary word. Sample sentences might include the following: "Nonprofit agencies work in different countries around the world. They teach children, provide medical care, and do other things to help humanity." Encourage other student pairs to come to the board to write two related sentences that incorporate the vocabulary words.

PRONUNCIATION GUIDE

Use this list to help students pronounce difficult words in this lesson.

Afghanistan (af gan´ ə stan´)

al Qaeda (äl kä´ də)

Osama bin Laden
 (ōsä´mə bïn läd´ən)

Saddam Hussein (sädäm´ hōō sān´)

Taliban (täl´ ə bän)

Objectives

- To explain how terrorism has affected the entire world
- To describe what can be done to prevent future terrorist attacks

The Threat of Global Terrorism

As you may remember from Chapter 31, Middle Eastern terrorism has spread to the larger world. With the threat of terrorism so real, nations are coming together to prevent future attacks.

How Has the Threat of Terrorism Changed the World?

Terrorism has existed for many years. It has not been limited to the Middle East. Terrorists throughout the world use violence to frighten people and leaders. They use fear in hope of having their demands met.

After the September 11 terrorist attacks on the United States, all planes were grounded for two days. When they started flying again, airport security screening for all passengers was much stricter. Security was also increased near public places where large groups of people gather, such as sports arenas.

Lawmakers in the United States began developing the new Department of Homeland Security. This department would organize all security and emergency agencies as one branch of government. By doing so, the department wanted to better prepare for and prevent future terrorist attacks.

How Did Wars Start in Iraq and Afghanistan?

The Taliban in Afghanistan was known to allow training camps for al Qaeda members. (The Taliban is the group that controls the government in Afghanistan.) The United States government had asked that the Taliban turn over Osama bin Laden. He had admitted leading the 9/11 terror attacks on America. The Taliban refused to turn bin Laden in.

Agency
A group that provides
a service

Humanity
The human race

So, the United States attacked Taliban sites in Afghanistan in October 2001. They destroyed al Qaeda camps. The Taliban and al Qaeda members fled the country, as did bin Laden. American and NATO troops stayed in Afghanistan to help rebuild the country under a new government.

A report published by the American CIA (Central Intelligence **Agency**) in 2002 warned that Iraq was hiding weapons of mass destruction. Iraq refused to cooperate with United Nations inspectors looking for weapons. President George W. Bush insisted that Saddam Hussein's government was aiding terrorist groups. Hussein had to be removed and the people of Iraq had to be freed of his tyranny. On March 19, 2003, troops from the United States, Britain, and many smaller nations invaded Baghdad, the capital of Iraq. Operation Iraqi Freedom had begun. Saddam Hussein went into hiding. Within 43 days the troops had taken over the country.

Saddam Hussein's sons were killed in a raid in July 2003. Hussein was captured in December of the same year. An Iraqi court found him guilty of crimes against the human race, or **humanity**. He was executed in December 2006. The American and British troops found no weapons of mass destruction.

The Americans wanted to help establish a democratic government in Iraq. Aided by other governments, the Iraqis began forming a representative government. They wrote a constitution and held their first free elections in 2005. Unfortunately, since that time, fighting between groups for control of the country has increased. As of early 2007, more than 10,000 Iraqis had been killed. More than 3,000 American soldiers were killed and about 20,000 had been injured. Many Americans did not support increasing troop activity in the country.

Reading Strategy:
Inferencing

After reading this section, what inference can you make about the best way to control terrorism? What words helped you make your inference?

---

1 **Warm-Up Activity**

As a class, discuss how the events of September 11, 2001, have changed life in America and Canada. Point out that people are more cautious and alert to potential terrorism. It takes longer to get through security checkpoints, including those at airports and large stadiums. Ask students if they think that the new laws and regulations are too strict or not strict enough.

2 **Teaching the Lesson**

Read aloud the lesson title, then have students discuss the meaning of the term *terrorism*. How does it differ from war? What do they think governments can do to stop terrorism? Afterwards, have students read the lesson to see what measures have been taken to prevent future attacks.

Ask:

- What is the function of the Department of Homeland Security? (to organize all security and emergency agencies as one branch of government)

- Why did the United States attack Taliban sites in Afghanistan? (The Taliban would not turn in bin Laden, the man behind the 9/11 attacks on America.)

- Why are liquids banned from air flights? (Terrorists attempted to use liquid bombs that they had in carry-on bags to blow up planes traveling from London to the United States.)

Reading Strategy:
Inferencing

Students might say that increasing awareness of potential dangers is the best way to control terrorism. They may state phrases such as "noticed another passenger acting suspiciously," "discovered a plot," and "monitor the activities of [terrorist] groups."

Reading Strategy:
Inferencing

Students may say that the threat of global terrorism will likely be around for many years and that we may develop new ways of dealing with global terrorism in the future.

Background Information

The U.S. Patriot Act became law soon after the 9/11 attacks on America. This law gave the government broad leeway to fight terrorism. Government and law agencies could more easily access financial and medical records, email, and telephone records of citizens. Immigration authorities could now detain or deport immigrants with suspected ties to terrorism. Did the Patriot Act grant too much power to government agencies at the expense of civil liberties? This issue was hotly debated when the law came up for renewal in 2005. The final bill stayed nearly the same as the original bill and became law in 2006.

Have There Been Other Terrorist Attacks?

According to the U.S. State Department, there were 9,474 terrorist attacks worldwide between 1982 and 2003. In the five-year period between 1998 and 2003, there were 1,865. Regular acts of terror continue in both Iraq and Afghanistan.

In many countries of the world, increased security seems to be reducing the number of terrorist attacks. However, they continue to happen. For instance, bombs planted on a subway and buses in London killed 52 people in 2005.

What Can Be Done to Prevent Further Attacks?

Further attacks can be prevented by increasing our awareness of dangers. This is especially important with travel and in situations involving large groups of people.

Passengers on a flight from Paris to New York in December 2001 noticed another passenger acting suspiciously. They were able to control him before he could light bombs in his shoes.

In August 2006, British officials discovered a plot to blow up nine or ten planes. The planes were traveling from London to the United States. The 24 men arrested planned to blow up the planes mid-air. They would use liquid bombs that they had in their carry-on bags. As a result, all liquids in carry-on bags were banned for future flights.

Reading Strategy:
Inferencing

Based on what you have read, what can you infer about the threat of global terrorism in the years to come?

The U.S. State Department has identified dozens of terrorist groups training members in different countries. One important task for the Department of Homeland Security is to monitor the activities of such groups. Agents and offices in foreign countries help them do this. A law called the Patriot Act helps too. It gives the U.S. government more power to check on backgrounds of people in the country. Firmer rules on entering the United States will also help prevent terrorist acts.

Lesson 34–6 Review Answers
1. D **2.** C **3.** C **4.** D **5.** B **6.** A **7.** B **8.** D
9. A **10.** A

On a sheet of paper, write the letter of the answer that correctly completes each sentence.

1. _____ became much stricter at airports and public places after September 11.

   A Troops   **B** Governments   **C** Lawmakers   **D** Security

2. U.S. lawmakers began developing the Department of _____ after the attacks.

   A Defense   **B** Transportation   **C** Homeland Security **D** Terrorism

3. The _____ in Afghanistan allowed training camps for al Qaeda members.

   A Iraqis   **B** Americans   **C** Taliban   **D** CIA

4. The American CIA warned that Iraq was hiding _____ in 2002.

   A guns   **C** energy sources
   B military troops   **D** weapons of mass destruction

5. In 2003, _____ was found guilty of crimes against the human race.

   A Tony Blair   **B** Saddam Hussein   **C** Osama bin Laden   **D** George W. Bush

6. In 2005, Iraq wrote a _____ and held free elections.

   A constitution   **B** trade-pact   **C** news release   **D** speech

7. According to the U.S. State Department, _____ terrorist attacks were made between 1982 and 2003.

   A 7,000   **B** 9,474   **C** 16,300   **D** 42,714

8. Bombs planted on a subway and in buses in _____ killed 52 people in 2005.

   A Kuwait   **B** New York City   **C** Washington, D.C.   **D** London

9. The _____ gives the U.S. government power to check people's backgrounds.

   A Patriot Act   **B** Terrorism Act   **C** Security Act   **D** Humanity Bill

10. The United States has identified _____ of terrorist groups in different countries.

   A dozens   **B** hundreds   **C** thousands   **D** millions

---

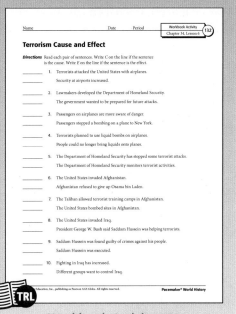

Activity 132   Workbook Activity 132   *The World Today Chapter 34* **753**

Looking to the Future

Lesson at a Glance

Chapter 34 Lesson 7

Overview This lesson describes future challenges that people may face and summarizes how civilization has changed since the early Greeks.

Objective

- To compare ancient times and today

Student Pages 754–756

Teacher's Resource Library

Workbook Activity 133

Activity 133

Modified Activity 133

---

1 Warm-Up Activity

Have students read the title of the lesson. Ask them what they think life will be like 100 years from now. Discuss different aspects of society such as technology, medicine, politics, economics, and the environment. As students read this lesson, have them add to their lists of what the future might hold.

---

2 Teaching the Lesson

Before reading this lesson, have students brainstorm a list of the most pressing problems facing society today. Discuss how this list might change in the future. Which problems might be solved? Which might still present a challenge?

Ask:

- How does the scene surrounding the ancient Greek athlete change? (He races on a dusty road and expects to be crowned with olive leaves. Instead, he finds himself in a crowded, modern stadium and receives a shiny, gold medal.)

Objective

- To compare ancient times and today

Picture the days of ancient Greece and a Greek athlete running an Olympic race. It is 776 B.C. The young man pulls ahead of the other racers on a dusty road. He gasps the warm air. His lungs ache with the effort. As he crosses the finish line, he closes his eyes and raises his arms over his head in victory.

When he opens his eyes again, he expects to find himself surrounded by cheering Greeks. He can almost feel the crown of olive leaves about to be placed on his head.

Instead the racer finds himself in a crowded, modern stadium. It is A.D. 2004, Athens, Greece, the 28th Summer Olympics. People are cheering, but they are not all Greeks. There are people from around the whole world. Furthermore, no olive leaves await the racer. Instead he is awarded a shiny, gold medal. Somehow our racer has been jolted forward in time more than 2,000 years.

What will he find? What undreamed-of wonders will our racer discover?

What Does the Future Hold?

The racer will find a whole new world of medicine. Doctors can actually replace worn-out or diseased body parts. Sometimes those replacements come from people who have died. Other times the parts are manufactured. The young Greek time-traveler can hardly believe it. These modern doctors can even replace a person's heart!

People treat each other in a different way now. The Greek racer is surprised to find women athletes around him. Women, he will discover, have a whole new role in society. In many places they are treated as equals with men.

- What modern wonders might await the ancient athlete? (Sample answer: He might find that spaceships have traveled to the moon and that doctors can replace body parts. Airplanes, telephones, and television would be new to him, as well.)

- Do you believe people will ever live in peace? Explain your answer. (Answers will vary.)

COMMON ERROR

Students may think that body parts are taken from dead people and used to help living people. Explain that body parts are sometimes taken from still-living people who have fatal injuries or diseases. For example, a person in a severe accident may not have his or her brain functioning. However, other body parts may still be functioning. Shortly before this person dies, doctors remove these body parts and transplant them into someone who desperately needs them.

They work side by side with men in all kinds of jobs. Women have become leaders in science, medicine, and business.

Spaceships to the moon, automobiles that speed people to their destinations, airplanes, television, telephones . . . the list of new wonders is endless.

Has anything remained the same? Most people still live in family groups, although many of those groups are smaller. People still have the same basic needs for food and shelter. People still have trouble getting along. There are still those who want to be conquerors and who seek power at all costs. There are still those who must struggle to hold on to their cultures and their homes. People from different backgrounds still do not know and understand each other well enough. People still fear what they do not understand.

Human beings are still curious, too. They still need to learn, explore, and discover. There will always be some questions to answer: What lies beyond the sun? Are there worlds and peoples other than our own? Can the people of this world ever live together completely at peace?

Reading Strategy:
Inferencing

What can you infer about the most important concerns as we look to the future? What details helped you make your inference?

TIMELINE STUDY:

THE WORLD: 1945–2010

Who was the first woman in space? When did she make her flight?

1945 United States drops atomic bombs on Japan

1952 Great Britain tests atomic bomb

1961 Soviet cosmonaut Yuri Gagarin makes first manned space flight

1963 Cosmonaut Valentina V. Tereshkova is first woman in space

1979 Accident at Three-Mile Island nuclear plant

2000 Millennium celebrations take place around the world

2003 Operation Iraqi Freedom begins

2006 Saddam Hussein executed

1949 Soviet Union tests atomic bomb

1957 First satellite to orbit the earth (Sputnik) launched by Soviets

1969 American astronaut Neil Armstrong is first human to walk on moon

1967 First human heart transplant (South Africa)

1986 Accident at Chernobyl nuclear power plant (USSR); U.S. space shuttle Challenger explodes after take-off

1950 | 1960 | 1970 | 1980 | 1990 | 2000 | 2010

Reading Strategy:
Inferencing

Students may infer that the need for food and shelter ranks high as a future concern. They may also mention the need for world peace. These inferences might be based on sentence in the text such as, "People still have trouble getting along."

TIMELINE STUDY

Answer: Cosmonaut Valentina V. Tereshkova; 1963

Background Information

In order to ensure a large food supply, many farmers grow genetically altered plants. These plants are hardier and more resistant to pests. The branch of science that deals with changes in the genetic make-up of living things is called biotechnology. The resulting plants are called genetically modified (GM) or transgenic plants. Although the U.S. Food and Drug Administration has said that GM plants pose no threat to human health, some people question whether the plants are safe. They also have concerns about how the plants will impact pollinating organisms and other parts of ecosystems. Ask students to research and discuss the pros and cons of using genetically altered plants.

ELL/ESL STRATEGY

Language Objective:
To research and write a report

Ask students to write about the changing role of women in the fields of science, space exploration, politics, and the military. Have students research a particular period in history and compare the role of women then and now. Tell students to takes notes from their various sources and then compile the notes into a written report. Students should include a list of references written in alphabetical order. Ask volunteers to share their reports with the class.

Lesson 34–7 Review Answers

1. Greece 2. olive leaves 3. doctors
4. women 5. groups 6. backgrounds
7. fear 8. curious 9. science
10. questions

LESSON 34-7

REVIEW

Word Bank

backgrounds
curious
doctors
fear
Greece
groups
olive leaves
questions
science
women

On a sheet of paper, write the word from the Word Bank to complete each sentence correctly.

1. In 2004, the Summer Olympics were held in _____.

2. At the first Olympics, winners received _____ instead of shiny, gold medals.

3. _____ can now replace worn-out or diseased body parts.

4. In many places in society, _____ are now treated as equals with men.

5. Many people today still live in family _____.

6. People from different _____ still do not know and understand each other well enough.

7. Even today, people _____ what they do not understand.

8. Still today, humans are as _____ as they were before.

9. Women have become leaders in _____, medicine, and business.

10. Throughout time, there will always be _____ to be answered.

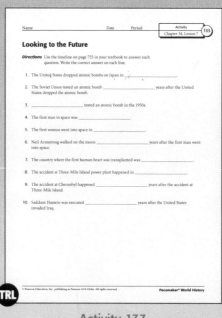

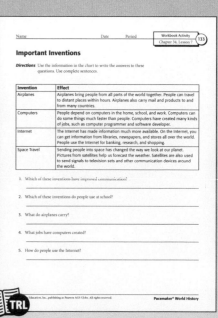

- Nuclear power is used for weapons and as a source of energy in peacetime. People worry about the dangers of an accident in a nuclear power plant. There are also concerns about how to safely get rid of nuclear waste.

- Countries can explore space by working together. Space exploration is both costly and, at times, dangerous. Many people feel that the knowledge gained is well worth the sacrifices.

- Television and other forms of international communication help bring people of the world closer together.

- Computers and the Internet are improving the ways of communication like never before. Handheld devices and the chance to "talk" to people anywhere at any time shrink the distance across the globe.

- Nations have become economically dependent on each other. Many are forming free-trade alliances that remove barriers to international trade.

- Developed nations have advanced technology, a higher standard of living, and strong trade programs. Developing nations are less developed, poorer, and more dependent on other countries.

- It is important to improve living conditions for everyone on Earth.

- The world has much to learn about controlling deadly diseases. Oftentimes, these diseases affect people without doctors or medicines.

- The increase in terrorist attacks in recent years has prompted nations to increase their security.

- Many breakthroughs in energy, space, and communication have taken place in the present age. However, people still have to deal with problems of ignorance, prejudice, persecution, and war.

Chapter 34 Summary

Have students read the Chapter Summary on page 757 to review the main ideas presented in Chapter 34.

Ask:

- What is nuclear power used for? (It is used as a source of energy and as a weapon.)

- What are the advantages and disadvantages of space exploration? (Space exploration helps us gain knowledge about the universe. It is costly and can be dangerous.)

- What technology helps to bring people together? (television and other forms of international communication)

- How do nations remove barriers to trade? (by forming free-trade alliances)

- What are some differences between developed nations and developing nations? (Developed nations have advanced technology, a higher standard of living, and strong trade programs. Developing nations are less developed, poorer, and more dependent on other countries.)

- Whom do deadly diseases often affect? (people without doctors or medicines)

- Why have many nations increased their security? (because of the increase in terrorist attacks)

CHAPTER PROJECT FOLLOW-UP

 Display students' items around the class. Invite other classes to view "the museum." Assess students' work on the written description of their displays and on the originality of their choice of item to display.

TEACHER'S RESOURCE

The AGS Globe Teaching Strategies in Social Studies Transparencies may be used with this chapter. The transparencies add an interactive dimension to expand and enhance the Pacemaker® *World History* program content.

Chapter 34 Review

Use the Chapter Review to prepare students for tests and to reteach content from the chapter.

Chapter 34 Mastery Test 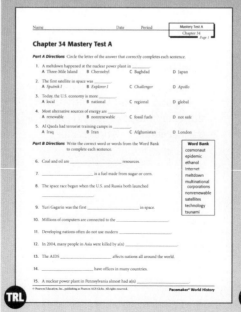TRL

The Teacher's Resource Library includes two forms of the Chapter 34 Mastery Test. Each test addresses the chapter Goals for Learning. An optional third page of additional critical-thinking items is included for each test. The difficulty level of the two forms is equivalent.

Final Mastery Test

The Teacher's Resource Library includes the Final Mastery Test. This test is pictured on page XXX of this Teacher's Edition. The Final Mastery Test assesses the major learning objectives for Chapters 1–34.

Chapter 34 Review Answers

Vocabulary Review

1. astronaut
2. cosmonaut
3. nonrenewable
4. technology
5. satellite
6. agency
7. extinction
8. epidemic
9. humanity
10. overpopulation

CHAPTER 34 REVIEW

Word Bank

agency
astronaut
cosmonaut
epidemic
extinction
humanity
nonrenewable
overpopulation
satellite
technology

Vocabulary Review

On a sheet of paper, use the words from the Word Bank to complete each sentence correctly.

1. A(n) _____ travels into space for the United States.

2. A(n) _____ from the Soviet Union was the first person into space.

3. A(n) _____ resource cannot be replaced once people use it all.

4. Computers, the Internet, and cell phones are examples of _____.

5. The United States has put a(n) _____ into space, which orbits around Earth.

6. A group that provides a service is called a(n) _____.

7. Deforestation is causing the _____ of plants and animals.

8. The rapid spread of AIDS is an example of a(n) _____.

9. _____ means "the human race."

10. The state of having too many people is called _____.

Chapter Review Questions

On a sheet of paper, write the answer to each question. Use complete sentences.

11. What are two uses of nuclear power?

12. When did the Space Age begin?

13. Why does the world seem to be shrinking?

14. Why is the last half of the 20th century sometimes called the "Nuclear Age"?

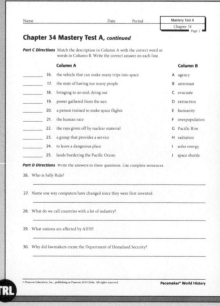

Chapter 34 Mastery Test A, pages 1–3

11. Nuclear power can be used in weapons and as a source of energy.

12. The Space Age began when the Soviets launched *Sputnik I* in 1957.

13. Television and the Internet bring news from around the world each day. Jet planes make it possible to cross oceans within hours.

14. The name "Nuclear Age" is used to describe the time after the first atom bomb was exploded in 1945. This began an age of development for atomic energy.

Critical Thinking

15. Possible answer: The economy of one nation can affect other nations.

16. Possible answer: Developed nations have more technology and a higher standard of living than developing nations.

17. Possible answers: Yes. The energy can be used to run factories, to heat homes, and to light cities. It is renewable. No. Nuclear power is too expensive and too dangerous. There is not a good way yet to dispose of the waste.

Using the Timeline

18. 1967

19. 1969

20. *Sputnik I*

GROUP ACTIVITY

Students' conversations should highlight some important problems and progress in the world since 776 B.C. You might suggest that students review the earlier chapters of the book before they write their dialogue.

Test Tip

When you reread a written answer, imagine that you are someone reading it for the first time. Ask yourself if the ideas and information make sense. Revise your answer to make it clearer and more organized.

Critical Thinking

On a sheet of paper, write your response to each question. Use complete sentences.

15. What are some dangers of a global economy?

16. What is the major difference between a developed nation and a developing nation?

17. Do you think that nuclear energy is worth the possible risks?

Using the Timeline

Use the timeline on page 755 to answer the questions.

18. When was the first human heart transplant?

19. When did Neil Armstrong walk on the moon?

20. What satellite orbited the earth in 1957?

GROUP ACTIVITY

Suppose you are an Olympic racer from 776 B.C. Your partner is an Olympic athlete at the 2008 Olympics. Write a conversation the two of you would have about changes in the world. Practice the conversation and share it with some of your classmates.

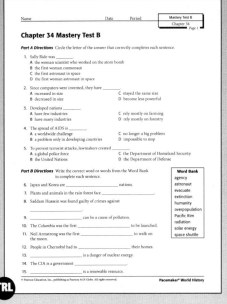

Chapter 34 Mastery Test B, pages 1–3

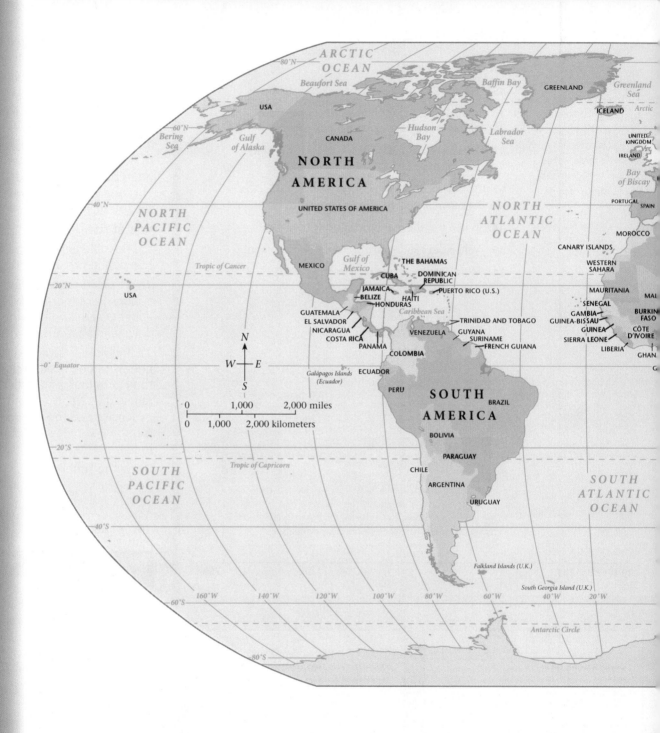

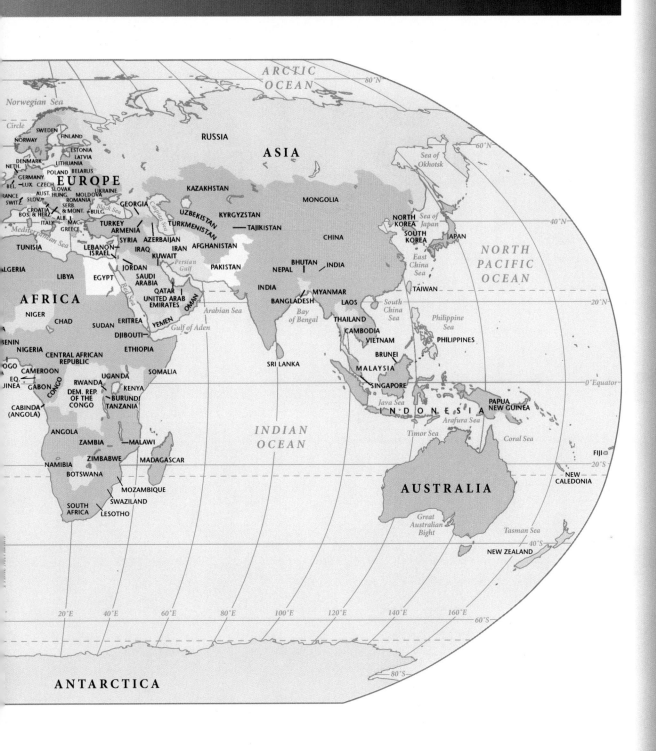

ARCTIC OCEAN
80°N

Norwegian Sea

Circle

SWEDEN
NORWAY
FINLAND
DENMARK
NETH.
ESTONIA
LATVIA
LITHUANIA
POLAND BELARUS
GERMANY
EUROPE
BEL LUX CZECH
FRANCE AUST. SLOVAK.
SWIT. HUNG. MOLDOVA
SLOV. ROMANIA UKRAINE
CROATIA SERB.
BOS & HERZ. & MONT. BULG.
ITALY MAC. GREECE
ALB.
Mediterranean Sea

RUSSIA
ASIA
60°N
Sea of Okhotsk

KAZAKHSTAN

GEORGIA
TURKEY
ARMENIA
SYRIA AZERBAIJAN
LEBANON IRAN
ISRAEL IRAQ
JORDAN KUWAIT
SAUDI
EGYPT ARABIA
QATAR
UNITED ARAB
EMIRATES
YEMEN
Gulf of Aden
DJIBOUTI

Black Sea
Caspian Sea
UZBEKISTAN
TURKMENISTAN
KYRGYZSTAN
TAJIKISTAN
MONGOLIA
CHINA

Persian Gulf
AFGHANISTAN
PAKISTAN
NEPAL
BHUTAN
INDIA
INDIA
BANGLADESH
MYANMAR
LAOS
THAILAND
CAMBODIA
VIETNAM

NORTH KOREA
SOUTH KOREA
Sea of Japan
JAPAN
40°N

East China Sea
TAIWAN
NORTH PACIFIC OCEAN

South China Sea
Philippine Sea
PHILIPPINES
20°N

TUNISIA
ALGERIA
LIBYA

AFRICA
NIGER
CHAD
SUDAN
ERITREA
ETHIOPIA
SOMALIA

Arabian Sea
Bay of Bengal
SRI LANKA

BENIN
NIGERIA
CENTRAL AFRICAN REPUBLIC
TOGO
CAMEROON
EQ. GUINEA GABON
CONGO
DEM. REP. OF THE CONGO
RWANDA
BURUNDI
UGANDA
KENYA
TANZANIA
CABINDA (ANGOLA)

BRUNEI
MALAYSIA
SINGAPORE
INDONESIA
0° Equator

ANGOLA
ZAMBIA MALAWI
ZIMBABWE
NAMIBIA
BOTSWANA
MADAGASCAR

INDIAN OCEAN

Timor Sea
Java Sea
Arafura Sea
PAPUA NEW GUINEA
Coral Sea
FIJI
20°S
NEW CALEDONIA

SOUTH AFRICA
MOZAMBIQUE
SWAZILAND
LESOTHO

AUSTRALIA

Great Australian Bight
40°S
Tasman Sea
NEW ZEALAND

20°E 40°E 60°E 80°E 100°E 120°E 140°E 160°E
60°S
80°S

ANTARCTICA

World Physical

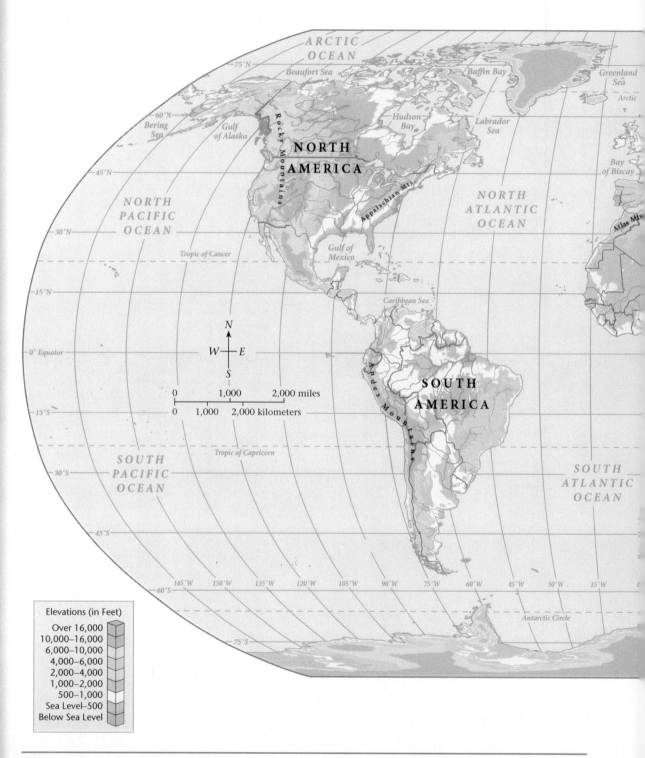

ARCTIC
OCEAN

Beaufort Sea

Baffin Bay

Greenland
Sea

Arctic

75°N

60°N

Bering
Sea

Gulf
of Alaska

Hudson
Bay

Labrador
Sea

Bay
of Biscay

NORTH
AMERICA

45°N

NORTH
PACIFIC
OCEAN

NORTH
ATLANTIC
OCEAN

Atlas Mts

30°N

Tropic of Cancer

Gulf of
Mexico

15°N

Caribbean Sea

N

W   E

S

0   1,000   2,000 miles

0   1,000   2,000 kilometers

0° Equator

SOUTH
AMERICA

15°S

Tropic of Capricorn

SOUTH
PACIFIC
OCEAN

30°S

SOUTH
ATLANTIC
OCEAN

45°S

165°W   150°W   135°W   120°W   105°W   90°W   75°W   60°W   45°W   30°W   15°W

60°S

Antarctic Circle

75°S

Elevations (in Feet)

Over 16,000
10,000–16,000
6,000–10,000
4,000–6,000
2,000–4,000
1,000–2,000
500–1,000
Sea Level–500
Below Sea Level

ARCTIC
OCEAN

Norwegian Sea

Circle

75°N

Siberia

ASIA

EUROPE

60°N

Ural Mts.

Sea of
Okhotsk

45°N

Gobi Desert

Alps

Black Sea

Caucasus

Caspian Sea

Sea of
Japan

Mediterranean Sea

AFRICA

Plateau of Tibet

Himalaya

Persian
Gulf

NORTH
PACIFIC
OCEAN

30°N

East
China
Sea

Sahara
Desert

Red Sea

Arabian Sea

Bay
of Bengal

South
China
Sea

15°N

Gulf of Aden

Philippine
Sea

0° Equator

Java Sea

Arafura Sea

INDIAN
OCEAN

Timor Sea

Coral Sea

15°S

Kalahari
Desert

AUSTRALIA
Victoria Desert

30°S

Great
Australian
Bight

Tasman Sea

45°S

15°E   30°E   45°E   60°E   75°E   90°E   105°E   120°E   135°E   150°E   165°E

60°S

ANTARCTICA

75°S

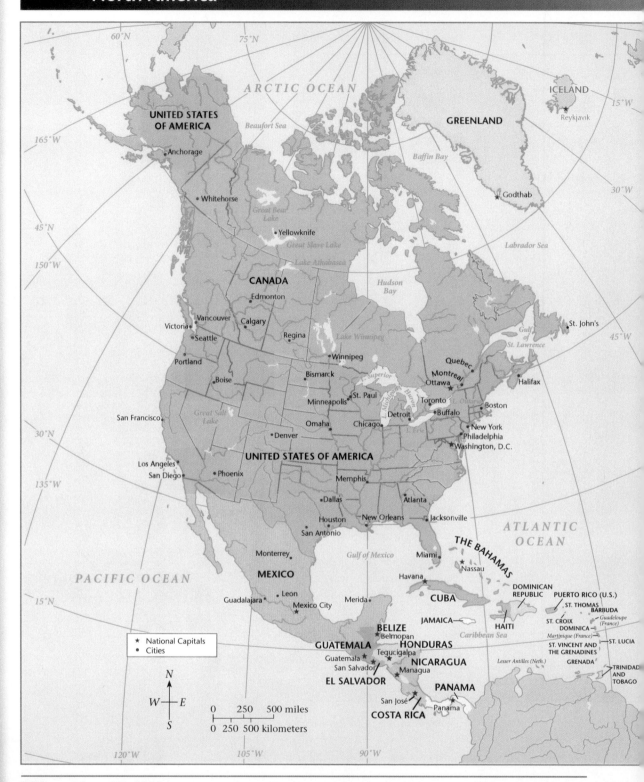

ARCTIC OCEAN

UNITED STATES
OF AMERICA

Beaufort Sea

GREENLAND

ICELAND

Reykjavik

• Anchorage

Baffin Bay

• Whitehorse

• Godthab

Great Bear
Lake

• Yellowknife

Great Slave Lake

Lake Athabasca

Labrador Sea

CANADA

Hudson
Bay

• Edmonton

St. John's

Vancouver
Victoria •
• Seattle

• Calgary

• Regina

Lake Winnipeg

Gulf
of
St. Lawrence

Portland

• Winnipeg

Montreal
Ottawa
★

Quebec

Halifax

Boise •

Bismarck •

Lake Superior

San Francisco •

Minneapolis
•

• St. Paul

Toronto
Detroit

Buffalo

Boston

Omaha •

Chicago •

New York
Philadelphia
Washington, D.C.

• Denver

UNITED STATES OF AMERICA

Los Angeles •
San Diego •

• Phoenix

Memphis •

ATLANTIC
OCEAN

Great Salt
Lake

• Dallas

Atlanta •

Houston •
San Antonio

New Orleans •

Jacksonville •

Monterrey •

Gulf of Mexico

Miami •

THE BAHAMAS

PACIFIC OCEAN

MEXICO

Nassau ★

• Leon

Havana ★

DOMINICAN
REPUBLIC

PUERTO RICO (U.S.)

Guadalajara •

Mexico City
★

Merida •

CUBA

ST. THOMAS
BARBUDA

JAMAICA

St. CROIX

Guadeloupe
(France)

HAITI

DOMINICA

BELIZE

Caribbean Sea

Martinique (France)

★ National Capitals
• Cities

GUATEMALA

Belmopan ★
Tegucigalpa
HONDURAS

St. VINCENT AND
THE GRENADINES

St. LUCIA

Guatemala ★
San Salvador

Managua ★
NICARAGUA

Lesser Antilles (Neth.)

GRENADA

TRINIDAD
AND
TOBAGO

EL SALVADOR

N

W   E

S

PANAMA

San José ★

COSTA RICA

Panama •

0   250   500 miles

0   250 500 kilometers

Caribbean Sea

Managua

Barranquilla

San José

Panamá

Caracas

TRINIDAD AND TOBAGO

Valencia

VENEZUELA

Cúcuta

Georgetown

Medellín

GUYANA

Paramaribo

Bogotá

SURINAME

Cayenne

COLOMBIA

FRENCH GUIANA

Mitú

Quito

Belém

ECUADOR

Guayaquil

Manaus

Fortaleza

Galápagos Islands (Ecuador)

Talara

PERU

Recife

Trujillo

Pôrto Velho

Huánuco

BRAZIL

Lima

Salvador

Ica

Cuzco

BOLIVIA

La Paz

Brásilia

Santa Cruz

Goiânia

Sucre

Iquique

20°S

PACIFIC OCEAN

Antofagasta

PARAGUAY

Rio de Janeiro

São Paulo

CHILE

Asunción

30°S

Córdoba

Rosario

URUGUAY

Santiago

Buenos Aires

Montevideo

Concepción

ARGENTINA

ATLANTIC OCEAN

N

Valdivia

W — E

Puerto Montt

S

Comodoro Rivadavia

★ National Capitals
● Cities

Falkland Islands (U.K.)

0   250   500 miles

South Georgia Island (U.K.)

0   250   500 kilometers

90°W   80°W   70°W   60°W   50°W   40°W

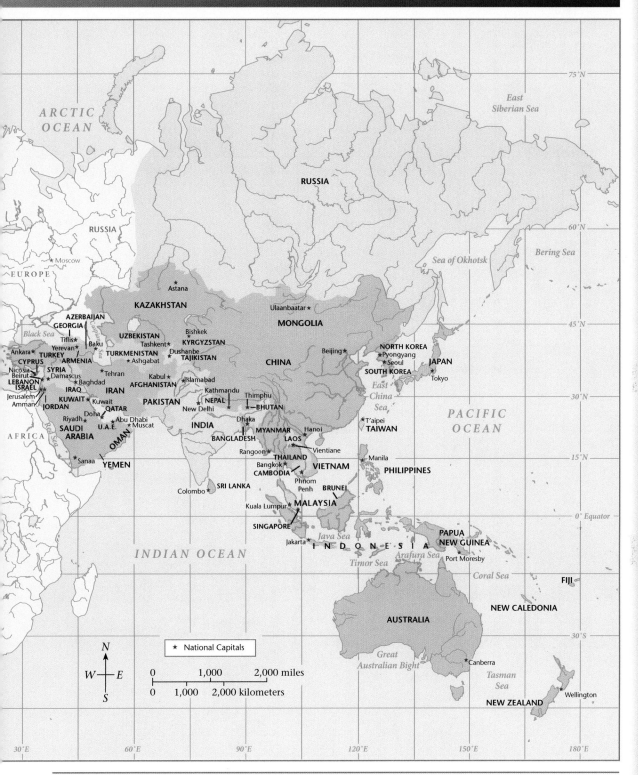

ARCTIC OCEAN

RUSSIA

Moscow ★

EUROPE

Black Sea

Astana ★

KAZAKHSTAN

AZERBAIJAN

GEORGIA

Tiflis ★

Ankara ★ TURKEY   Yerevan ★ Baku ★   Bishkek ★

CYPRUS   ARMENIA   UZBEKISTAN   KYRGYZSTAN

Nicosia ★   Tashkent ★

Beirut ★ SYRIA   TURKMENISTAN   Dushanbe ★

LEBANON ★ Damascus   ★ Ashgabat   TAJIKISTAN

ISRAEL   Tehran ★

Jerusalem ★ IRAQ   IRAN   Kabul ★ Islamabad

Amman ★ JORDAN   Baghdad ★   AFGHANISTAN ★

KUWAIT   Kathmandu ★

Kuwait ★   PAKISTAN   ★ NEPAL   Thimphu ★

Doha ★ QATAR   New Delhi ★   ★ BHUTAN

Riyadh ★   ★ Abu Dhabi   Dhaka ★

SAUDI   U.A.E.   ★ Muscat   INDIA   MYANMAR   Hanoi

ARABIA   OMAN   BANGLADESH   LAOS ★

AFRICA   ★ Sanaa   Rangoon ★   ★ Vientiane

YEMEN   THAILAND   VIETNAM

Red Sea   Bangkok ★ CAMBODIA

Colombo ★ SRI LANKA   Phnom   BRUNEI

Penh

Kuala Lumpur ★ MALAYSIA

SINGAPORE ★

Jakarta ★ INDONESIA

Java Sea

INDIAN OCEAN

RUSSIA

East Siberian Sea

Sea of Okhotsk   Bering Sea

MONGOLIA

Ulaanbaatar ★

Beijing ★   NORTH KOREA

★ Pyongyang   JAPAN

CHINA   ★ Seoul   Tokyo ★

SOUTH KOREA

East

China

Sea

T'aipei ★   PACIFIC

TAIWAN   OCEAN

Manila ★

PHILIPPINES

PAPUA

NEW GUINEA

Port Moresby ★

Arafura Sea

Timor Sea   Coral Sea   FIJI

NEW CALEDONIA

AUSTRALIA

30°S

Great

Australian Bight   ★ Canberra

Tasman

Sea

NEW ZEALAND   Wellington ★

N
W ⊕ E
S

★ National Capitals

0   1,000   2,000 miles
0   1,000   2,000 kilometers

75°N
60°N
45°N
30°N
15°N
0° Equator

30°E   60°E   90°E   120°E   150°E   180°E

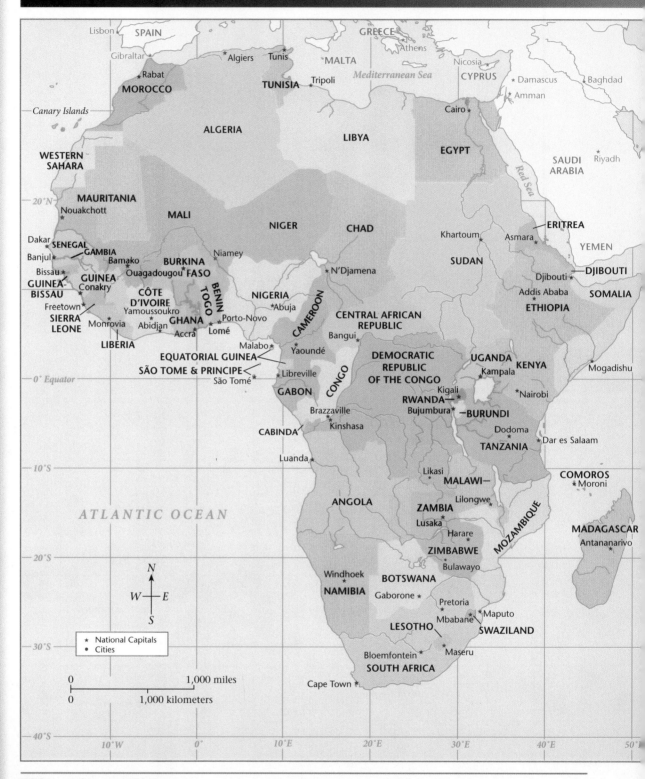

Lisbon SPAIN GREECE Athens
Gibraltar MALTA Nicosia CYPRUS Damascus Baghdad
Algiers Tunis Mediterranean Sea Amman
Rabat Tripoli
MOROCCO TUNISIA Cairo SAUDI Riyadh
ALGERIA LIBYA EGYPT ARABIA
Canary Islands
WESTERN
SAHARA
20°N ERITREA
MAURITANIA Khartoum Asmara YEMEN
Nouakchott MALI NIGER CHAD Djibouti DJIBOUTI
Dakar SENEGAL Niamey SUDAN
Banjul GAMBIA Bamako N'Djamena Addis Ababa SOMALIA
Bissau BURKINA ETHIOPIA
GUINEA- GUINEA Ouagadougou FASO NIGERIA
BISSAU Conakry CÔTE BENIN Abuja CAMEROON CENTRAL AFRICAN
Freetown D'IVOIRE TOGO REPUBLIC
SIERRA Yamoussoukro GHANA Porto-Novo Bangui UGANDA KENYA
LEONE Monrovia Abidjan Lomé Yaoundé DEMOCRATIC Kampala Mogadishu
Accra EQUATORIAL GUINEA REPUBLIC
LIBERIA SÃO TOMÉ & PRINCIPE Libreville CONGO OF THE CONGO Kigali Nairobi
0° Equator São Tomé GABON Malabo RWANDA
Brazzaville Bujumbura BURUNDI
CABINDA Kinshasa Dodoma
TANZANIA Dar es Salaam
Luanda
10°S Likasi COMOROS
MALAWI Moroni
ATLANTIC OCEAN ANGOLA ZAMBIA Lilongwe
Lusaka MOZAMBIQUE MADAGASCAR
Harare Antananarivo
20°S ZIMBABWE
Bulawayo
Windhoek BOTSWANA
NAMIBIA Gaborone
Pretoria
Mbabane Maputo
LESOTHO SWAZILAND
30°S Maseru
Bloemfontein
SOUTH AFRICA
Cape Town
40°S
10°W 0° 10°E 20°E 30°E 40°E 50°E

N
W E
S

★ National Capitals
• Cities

0 — 1,000 miles
0 — 1,000 kilometers

World Climate Zones

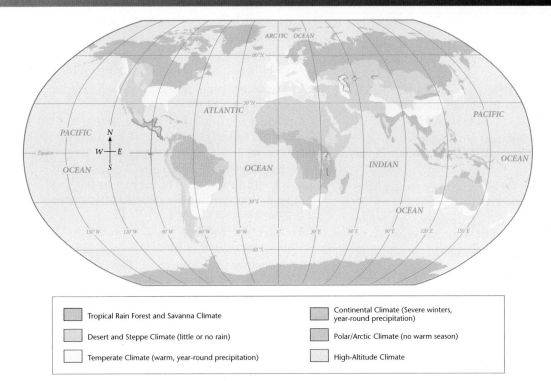

Tropical Rain Forest and Savanna Climate

Desert and Steppe Climate (little or no rain)

Temperate Climate (warm, year-round precipitation)

Continental Climate (Severe winters, year-round precipitation)

Polar/Arctic Climate (no warm season)

High-Altitude Climate

World Time Zones

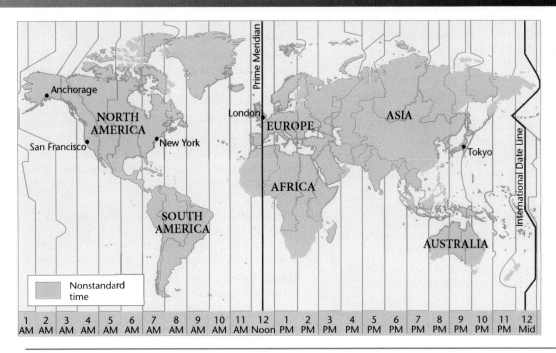

Nonstandard time

Glossary

A

Acropolis (ə krop´ ə lis) The hill on which the people in a Greek city built their main temple (p. 126)

Acupuncture (ak´ yù pungk chər) Treating pain or illness by putting needles into certain parts of the body (p. 308)

A.D. (Anno Domini) (an´ ō dom´ ə nī) Dating from the time Jesus Christ was born (p. 12)

Addicted (ad´ ikt əd) Having a strong habit that is hard to give up (p. 458)

Advanced (ad vanst´) Ahead of most others in knowledge, skill, or progress (p. 324)

Agency (ā´ jən sē) A group that provides a service (p. 751)

Agent (ā´ jənt) A person who has the authority to act for some other person or company (p. 477)

Agriculture (ag´ rə kul chər) The use of land for growing crops and raising animals; farming (p. 5)

Alliance (e lī´ əns) A group of nations joined together for some purpose; an agreement to help one another (p. 534)

Allied Powers (al´ īd pou´ ərs) The nations of Great Britain, France, Russia, Italy, and eventually, the United States and Japan during World War I (p. 534); The nations united against the Axis powers in World War II; includes Britain, France, and later the United States and the Soviet Union (p. 577)

Ambition (am bish´ ən) The drive to become powerful, successful, or famous (p. 145)

American Revolution (ə mar´ ə kən rev ə lü´ shən) The American struggle against Great Britain for independence (p. 365)

Ancestor (an´ ses tər) A person from whom one is descended; for example, your grandfathers, grandmothers, and so on back, are your ancestors (p. 106)

Annul (ə nul´) To cancel; to make something no longer binding under law (p. 296)

Anthem (an´ thəm) The official song of a country (p. 516)

Anti-Semitism (an ti - sem´ ə tiz əm) Prejudice against Jews (p. 576)

Apartheid (ə pärt´ hīt) The separation of races based mainly on skin color (p. 648)

Apprentice (ə pren´ tis) A person who learns a trade under a master (p. 244)

Aqueduct (ak´ wə dukt) A channel that carries flowing water over a long distance (p. 172)

Archaeologist (är kē ol´ ə jist) A scientist who studies cultures of the past by digging up and examining the remains of ancient towns and cities (p. 9)

Architect (är´ kə tekt) A person who draws plans for buildings (p. 262)

Architecture (är´ kə tek chər) The art of building (p. 136)

Armada (är mä´ də) A large fleet of warships (p. 290)

Armistice (är´ mə stis) An agreement to stop fighting; a truce before a formal peace treaty (p. 542)

Arms (ärmz) Weapons used to attack or defend (p. 663)

Arsenal (är´ sə nəl) A place where guns and ammunition are stored (p. 378)

Artifact (är´ tə fakt) A handmade object, such as a tool or weapon (p. 9)

Artisan (är´ tə zən) A person who works with his or her hands to create something (p. 217)

Assassinate (ə sas´ n āt) To kill a leader or other important person (p. 145)

Astronaut (as´ trə nôt) A person trained to make space flights (p. 732)

Astronomer (ə stron´ ə mər) A person who keeps track of the sun, the planets, and the stars (p. 268)

Athlete (ath´ lēt) A person trained to take part in competitive sports; the ancient Greek word *athlete* means "one who tries to win a prize in a contest" (p. 137)

Atomic bomb (ə tom´ ik bom) A bomb that uses nuclear energy and has much destructive power (p. 592)

Authority (ə thôr´ ə tē) Power; the right to tell someone what to do (p. 275)

Axis Powers (ak´ is pou´ ərs) The alliance of Germany, Italy, and Japan during World War II (p. 577)

Ayatollah (ä yä tō´ lə) A Muslim religious leader (p. 669)

B

Balance of power (bal´ əns ov pou´ ər) The condition that exists when all countries or all sections of government have equal strength (p. 534)

Ban (ban) To get rid of; to make something not legal (p. 710)

Barbarians (bär bâr´ ē ənz) Uncivilized, primitive people; people living outside Greece or Rome in the days of the Roman Empire (p. 193)

Barrier (bar´ ē ər) Something that blocks the way; a wall (p. 109)

Barter (bär´ tər) To trade goods or services without using money (p. 325)

Bastille (ba stēl´) A prison in Paris (p. 377)

B.C. (Before Christ) (bi fôr´ krīst) Dating from before the time Jesus Christ was born (p. 12)

Berlin Wall (bər lin´ wȯl) The wall that divided the people of East and West Berlin (p. 607)

Betray (bi trā´) To give help to the enemy; to be unfaithful to (p. 379)

Bible (bī´ bəl) The ancient Israelite and Christian book that is thought to be holy (p. 78)

Bishop (bish´ əp) A high-ranking church official in charge of other priests and a number of churches; from the Latin word that means "overseer" (p. 181)

Bolshevik (bōl´ shə vik) A revolutionary Communist group in Russia; means "member of the majority" (p. 562)

Border (bôr´ dər) The dividing line between two countries (p. 8)

Boundary (boun´ dər ē) The dividing line between one country and another (p. 517)

Buddha (bü´ də) A name meaning the "Enlightened One"; the name given to Siddhartha Gautama, the founder of Buddhism (p. 102)

Buddhism (bü´ də izm) A religion based on the teachings of Buddha (p. 102)

C

Campaign (kam pān´) A series of battles all aimed at one military end (p. 145)

Canal (kə nal´) A man-made waterway (p. 41)

Capital (kap´ ə təl) A city or town where the government of a nation or state is located (p. 80)

Capitalist (kap´ ə təl ist) Having business and industry privately owned and operated for profit (p. 610)

Caravan (kar´ ə van) A group of people traveling together, often through a desert (p. 493)

Cartridge (kär´ trij) A small metal or cardboard tube that holds gunpowder and a bullet (p. 478)

Caste (kast) A social class in India (p. 100)

Casualty (kazh´ ü əl tē) A soldier who has been killed, wounded, captured, or is missing (p. 544)

Cease-fire (sēs´ - fīr) An end in military operations, especially to try and discuss peace (p. 663)

Censor (sen´ sər) To examine communications before they are released and to remove any parts that are objected to (p. 566)

Central Powers (sen´ trəl pou´ ərs) The nations of Germany, Austria-Hungary, Turkey, and later Bulgaria (p. 534)

Chancellor (chan´ sə lər) The head of government, or prime minister, in some European countries (p. 526)

Chariot (char´ ē ət) An open two-wheeled cart, pulled by horses (p. 47)

a	hat	e	let	ī	ice	ȯ	order	ů	put	sh	she		ə	a	in about
ā	age	ē	equal	o	hot	oi	oil	ü	rule	th	thin			e	in taken
ä	far	ėr	term	ō	open	ou	out	ch	child	ᴛʜ	then			i	in pencil
â	care	i	it	ȯ	saw	u	cup	ng	long	zh	measure			o	in lemon
														u	in circus

World History   Glossary   **771**

World History   Glossary   **771**

Charter (chär´ tər) A constitution; a set of statements that explains a group's purpose (p. 248)

Christianity (kris chē an´ ə tē) The religion based on the teachings of Jesus Christ and the Bible (p. 79)

Citizen (sit´ ə zən) A person who has certain rights and duties because he or she lives in a particular city or town (p. 126)

City-state (sit´ ē - stāt) An independent city and the surrounding land it controls (p. 43)

Civil disobedience (siv´ əl dis´ ə bē´ dē əns) The refusal to obey rules, orders, or laws (p. 483)

Civilian (sə vil´ yən) A person who is not in the military (p. 581)

Civilization (siv ə lə zā´ shən) A group of people who have cities and government; a large group of people with a high level of development as a group (p. 9)

Civil war (siv´ əl wôr) Fighting between people who live in the same country (p. 166)

Class (klas) A group of people according to social rank (p. 100)

Clergy (klėr´ jē) The people who lead a religion (p. 213)

Code (kōd) A group of laws (p. 84)

Cold war (kōld wôr) The tension and hostility between the United States and the Soviet Union after World War II; was a war of ideas (p. 610)

Collapse (kə laps´) To fall apart (p. 109)

Collective (kə lek´ tiv) Run by a group; for example, a collective farm (p. 565)

Colonial (kə lō´ nē əl) Having settlements in far-off lands (p. 387)

Colony (kol´ ə nē) A group of people who settle in a far-off land but are still under the rule of the land they came from (p. 74)

Commandment (kə mand´ mənt) A law or order, most often a religious law, as in the Ten Commandments in the Bible (p. 78)

Commonwealth (kom´ ən welth) A nation in which the people hold the ruling power; a republic or democracy (p. 361)

Commune (kə myün´) A group of people working or living closely together, often sharing property and tasks (p. 630)

Communism (kom´ yə niz əm) A political system where there are no social classes and a common ownership of industries and farms, as well as a sharing of work and of goods produced (p. 559)

Compass (kum´ pəs) A tool for finding direction by using a magnet (p. 308)

Concentration camp (kon sən trā´ shən kamp) A prison camp for people thought to be dangerous to a ruling group (p. 576)

Confederation (kən fed ə rā´ shən) A group of independent states joined together for a purpose (p. 523)

Conference (kon´ fər əns) A meeting of people to discuss something (p. 505)

Conflict (kon´ flikt) Fighting; not being able to agree on something (p. 544)

Conquer (kong´ kər) To get control by using force, as in a war (p. 80)

Conqueror (kong´ kər ər) A person who gains control by winning a war (p. 99)

Conquistador (kon kē´ stə dôr) A Spanish conqueror (p. 338)

Consent (kən sent´) To agree to something (p. 360)

Constitution (kon stə tü´ shən) The basic laws and rules of a government (p. 130)

Contract (kon´ trakt) A written agreement between two or more people (p. 47)

Convert (kən vėrt´) Change from one religion to another (p. 180)

Corrupt (kə rupt´) Dishonest, evil, selfish (p. 629)

Cosmonaut (koz´ mə nôt) Russian word meaning "astronaut" (p. 732)

Counter-Reformation (koun´ tər - ref ər mā´ shən) The Catholic Church's reforms that attempted to fight Protestant beliefs; also known as the Catholic Reformation (p. 278)

Coup (kü) A bold, sudden move to bring about change in a government (p. 688)

Craft (kraft) A trade or art that takes special skill with the hands (p. 26)

Create (krē āt´) To make something (p. 48)

Crisis (krī′ sis) A time of danger; a turning point in events (p. 614)

Criticize (krit′ ə sīz) To say that someone has done wrong; to find wrong in something (p. 259)

Crusade (krü sād′) Any of the military journeys taken by Christians to win the Holy Land from the Muslims (p. 232)

Culture (kul′ chər) The way of life—religion, ideas, arts, tools—of a certain people in a certain time (p. 5)

Cuneiform (kyü nē′ ə fôrm) A wedge-shaped form of writing used in ancient Sumer (p. 46)

Curfew (kėr′ fyü) A time after which certain people cannot be on the streets (p. 648)

Currency (kėr′ ən sē) The form of money a country uses (p. 612)

Czar (zär) The ruler of Russia; a Russian title that means "caesar" (p. 553)

D

D-Day (dē′ - dā) The Allied invasion of France in 1944 (p. 589)

Declaration of Independence (dek lə rā′ shən ov in di pen′ dəns) A document the American colonists signed in which they declared their freedom from Great Britain (p. 366)

Decline (di klīn′) A period of increasing weakness (p. 286)

Democracy (di mok′ rə sē) A government that gives the people the ruling power (p. 126)

Democratic (dem ə krat′ ik) Having to do with a government in which all people have equal rights (p. 133)

Depression (di presh′ ən) A period of low business activity and high unemployment (p. 574)

Descendant (di sen′ dənt) A person who comes from a specific group of people; a family member (p. 420)

Desert (dez′ ərt) Dry, sandy land with little or no plant life (p. 58)

Détente (dā tänt′) An easing of tensions between countries (p. 616)

Developed country (di vel′ əpəd kun′ trē) A nation that has many industries and that imports and exports products (p. 410)

Developing country (di vel′ ə ping kun′ trē) A nation that is slowly growing its industry and economy (p. 410)

Development (di vel′ əp mənt) Growth of something (p. 5)

Dialect (dī′ ə lekt) A form of a language used only in a certain place or among a certain group (p. 552)

Dictator (dik′ tā tər) A ruler who has total power (p. 382)

Dike (dīk) A wall built along a river or sea to hold back the water from low land (p. 41)

Diplomat (dip′ lə mat) A person in government whose job is dealing with other countries (p. 520)

Disarm (dis ärm′) To stop having armed forces or to reduce their size (p. 542)

Disaster (də zas′ tər) Something that causes harm or problems (p. 616)

Disband (dis band′) To break up (p. 690)

Discrimination (dis krim ə nā′ shən) Treating a person or people unfairly because of his or her race or religion (p. 420)

Divine right (də vīn′ rīt) The idea that a monarch's right to rule comes directly from God (p. 359)

Document (dôk′ yə mənt) An important paper (p. 248)

Dominance (dom′ ə nəns) The act of ruling, controlling, or being most powerful (p. 505)

Dominate (dom′ ə nāt) To control; to be most important, most powerful, strongest (p. 428)

Domino theory (dom′ ə nō thir′ ē) The belief that if one country became Communist, neighbors would fall to Communism too (p. 641)

a	hat	e	let	ī	ice	ȯ	order	u̇	put	sh	she	ə {	a	in about
ā	age	ē	equal	o	hot	oi	oil	ü	rule	th	thin		e	in taken
ä	far	ėr	term	ō	open	ou	out	ch	child	ᴙн	then		i	in pencil
â	care	i	it	ȯ	saw	u	cup	ng	long	zh	measure		o	in lemon
													u	in circus

World History   Glossary   **773**

Drought (drout) A long period of time without much rain (p. 647)

Dweller (dwel´ ər) A person who lives in a place (p. 321)

Dynasty (dī´ nə stē) A family that rules a country for a long period of time (p. 107)

E

Economic (ek ə nom´ ik) Having to do with money (p. 449)

Economy (i kon´ ə mē) The system of making and trading things (p. 554)

Edict (ē´ dikt) A public order by some authority (p. 292)

Elect (i lekt´) To choose someone for an office by voting (p. 161)

Electronic (i lek tron´ ik) Powered by electricity (p. 638)

Embassy (em´ bə sē) The home and offices of a person sent to represent his or her government in another country (p. 669)

Emperor (em´ pər ər) A person who rules a group of different countries, lands, or peoples (p. 104)

Empire (em´ pīr) A group of lands all ruled by the same government or ruler (p. 84)

Energy (en´ ər jē) Power that comes from wood, coal, electricity, oil, the sun, water, and wind; makes machines work; and produces heat (p. 396)

Enforce (en fôrs´) To make sure that people follow the laws and rules (p. 315)

Enlightened (en līt´ nd) Knowing the truth (p. 102)

Enlightenment (en līt´ n mənt) A time in European history when thinkers and writers tried to solve the problems of society by using reason; also known as the Age of Reason (p. 356)

Enslaved (en slāvd´) When a person is forced to become a slave (p. 177)

Environment (en vī´ rən mənt) The land, sea, and air of our world (p. 721)

Epidemic (ep ə dem´ ik) The rapid spread of a disease (p. 748)

Equality (i kwol´ ə tē) The same rights for everyone (p. 356)

Estate (e stāt´) A large piece of land with a large home on it (pp. 210–211)

Estates-General (e stāts´ - jen´ ər el) The French governmental body made up of representatives from the three estates (p. 376)

Execute (ek´ sə kyüt) To kill someone for a crime (p. 380)

Exiled (eg´ zīld) Forced to live away from home in a foreign land (p. 200)

Expand (ek spand´) To grow; to stretch (p. 126)

Expansion (ek span´ shən) Growth; to increase in size (p. 446)

Exploration (ek splə rā´ shən) The act of looking around some unknown place (p. 238)

Export (ek spôrt´) To send a product out of one country and into another to sell; a product that is sent from one country to another (p. 410)

Extinction (ek stingkt´ shən) The act of bringing to an end; dying out (p. 746)

F

Factory (fak´ tər ē) A building where goods are made by machinery (p. 397)

Faith (fāth) To believe in God; a religion (p. 228)

Famine (fam´ ən) A time when crops do not grow and there is no food (p. 647)

Fascist (fash´ ist) People who follow the political system that honors the state over the individual (p. 574)

Fast (fast) To go without food (p. 485)

Fertile (fėr´ tl) Able to produce large crops, as in rich soil (p. 28)

Fertile Crescent (fėr´ tl kres´ nt) The area of land in the Middle East shaped like a quarter moon (crescent) (p. 28)

Feudalism (fyü´ dl iz əm) A political and military system based on the holding of land (p. 210)

Fleet (flēt) A group of warships under one command (p. 290)

Foreign (fôr´ ən) From another country; having to do with another country (p. 104)

Forge (fôrj) To work into shape by heating and hammering (p. 308)

Fortress (fôr´ tris) A building with strong walls for defense against an enemy (p. 211)

Forum (fôr´ əm) A public square in an ancient Roman city; lawmakers met there (p. 167)

Founded (foun´ ded) To have begun a country or city; to have built a city (p. 148)

Fraternity (frə tėr´ nə tē) Brotherhood (p. 379)

Freemen (frē´ men) People who are free, not slaves, and who have the rights of citizens (pp. 210–211)

French Revolution (french rev ə lü´ shən) The war that the common people of France fought against the king, nobles, and one another to achieve freedom (p. 379)

Front (frunt) A place where the actual fighting is going on during a war (p. 538)

Frontier (frun tir´) Land just beyond the border of a country (p. 192)

G

General (jen´ ər əl) A high-ranking military officer (p. 149)

Genocide (jen´ ə sīd) An attempt to kill all the people of a certain race or religious group (p. 585)

Geography (jē og´ rə fē) The natural surface features of the earth, or any part of it (p. 552)

Glacier (glā´ shər) A large, slow-moving mass of ice and snow (p. 20)

Glasnost (glas´ nost) The Soviet policy of open discussion of political and social issues (p. 687)

Global warming (glō´ bəl wôrm´ ing) The heating up of Earth from the burning of wood, coal, oil, and gasoline (p. 721)

Glorious Revolution (glôr´ ē əs rev ə lü´ shən) The period in England that involved the overthrow of James II and the crowning of William and Mary (p. 363)

Goddess (god´ is) A female god (p. 43)

Good Neighbor Policy (gùd nā´ bər pol´ ə sē) The policy in which the United States said it would not interfere with Latin American affairs (p. 706)

Goods (gùdz) The things for sale or trade (p. 41)

Gospel (gos´ pəl) One of four books of the New Testament part of the Bible; a word that means "good news" (p. 177)

Govern (guv´ ərn) To rule (p. 125)

Governor (guv´ ər nər) A person chosen to run a province or territory (p. 165)

Guerilla (gə ril´ ə) One of a group of fighters who are not part of a regular army, and who usually make surprise raids behind enemy lines (p. 641)

Guild (gild) An organization formed to protect the interests of workers in one craft or trade (p. 244)

Guillotine (gil´ ə tēn) An instrument used for cutting off a person's head; it has two posts crossed by a heavy blade (p. 380)

H

Heretic (her´ ə tik) A person who is against the teachings of a church (p. 276)

Hieroglyphics (hī ər ə glif´ iks) A system of writing using pictures or symbols to represent objects, ideas, or sounds (p. 66)

Hinduism (hin´ dü iz əm) The main religion of India; Hindus worship many gods (p. 99)

Historian (hi stôr´ ē ən) Someone who writes about the past; an expert in history (p. 8)

History (his´ tər ē) The record of past events and the story of what happened to people in the past (p. 4)

Holocaust (hol´ ə kòst) Hitler's killing of many of the Jews in Europe (p. 585)

a	hat	e	let	ī	ice	ȯ	order	ù	put	sh	she		ə	a	in about
ā	age	ē	equal	o	hot	oi	oil	ü	rule	th	thin			e	in taken
ä	far	ėr	term	ō	open	ou	out	ch	child	ᵀH	then			i	in pencil
â	care	i	it	ȯ	saw	u	cup	ng	long	zh	measure			o	in lemon
														u	in circus

Holy Land (hō´ lē land) Palestine; the area where Jesus of Nazareth lived (p. 227)

Homage (hom´ ij) A pledge of loyalty; a promise to serve that was made to kings and lords during the Middle Ages (p. 210)

Homeland (hōm´ land) The land that belongs to people (p. 661)

Hostages (hos´ tij ez) People held prisoner by an enemy until certain demands are met (p. 669)

Hostile (hos´ tl) Unfriendly, showing hate or dislike (p. 663)

Hostility (ho stil´ ə tē) Feelings of hate or acts of war (p. 126)

Humane (hyü mān´) Kind; showing care for others (p. 712)

Humanism (hyü´ mə niz əm) A concern with the needs and interests of human beings rather than religious ideas (p. 258)

Humanity (hyü man´ ə tē) The human race (p. 751)

Human rights (hyü´ mən rīts) The right to life, liberty, and pursuit of (the attempt to get) happiness (p. 248)

I

Ice Age (īs āj) A period of time when much of Earth and Earth's water was frozen (p. 20)

Idol (ī´ dl) An image of a god that is used as an object of worship (p. 224)

Immigration (im ə grā´ shən) The act of coming into a country or region to live there (p. 716)

Imperialism (im pir´ ē ə liz əm) The practice of conquering other lands, forming colonies in other lands, or controlling the government and wealth of weaker lands (p. 5)

Import (im pôrt´) To bring into one country from another (p. 397)

Impose (im pōz´) To force one's ideas or wishes on another (p. 477)

Independence (in di pen´ dəns) Being free; being able to govern one's self (p. 235)

Independent (in di pen´ dənt) Self-governing, separate, free (p. 43)

Indirectly (in də rekt´ lē) In a roundabout way (p. 477)

Industrial Revolution (in dus´ trē əl rev ə lü´ shən) The important changes that took place in the way work was done during the 18th and 19th century (p. 396)

Industry (in´ də strē) Business and manufacturing (p. 5)

Inferior (in fir´ ē ər) Not as good as someone or something else (p. 507)

Influence (in´ flü əns) The power to affect other people or things (p. 428)

Inquisition (in kwə zish´ ən) A special court set up by the Roman Catholic Church to question the beliefs of people to see if they were heretics (p. 276)

Insurance (in shùr´ əns) A guarantee that a person or company will be paid money to cover losses (p. 346)

Interest (in´ tər ist) Money paid for the use of other people's money (p. 346)

Interfere (in tər fir´) To mix in another's affairs without being asked (p. 439)

Interference (in tər fir´ əns) Mixing in another's affairs without being asked (p. 462)

Internal combustion engine (in tėr´ nl kəm bus´ chən en´ jən) An engine that burns gasoline to produce power (p. 403)

International (in tər nash´ ə nəl) Having to do with many nations (p. 449)

Invade (in vād´) To attack or march into another country (p. 575)

Invest (in vest´) To put money into something with the hope of making more money (p. 638)

Investment (in vest´ ment) Money given to businesses in order to get even more money back (p. 346)

Investor (in ves´ tər) A person who expects to make a profit by lending money to a business (p. 397)

Iron Curtain (ī´ərn kėrt´ n) The invisible boundary between Western Europe and Eastern Europe after World War II (p. 566)

Irrigate (ir´ ə gāt) To bring water to dry land by means of canals (p. 41)

Isolate (ī´ sə lāt) To set apart from others; alone (p. 109)

Isolationism (ī sə lā´ shə niz əm) A policy of staying out of the affairs, or business, of other countries (p. 608)

J

Judaism (jü´ dē iz əm) The religion developed by the ancient Israelites that Jews practice today (p. 79)

Jury (jür´ ē) A group of people who listen to the facts and decide if a person on trial is guilty or not guilty (p. 130)

K

Kaiser (kī´ zər) The emperor of Germany (p. 526)

Kamikaze (kä mi kä´ zē) A Japanese pilot who crashed his plane into an enemy ship, destroying it and killing himself (p. 592)

Knight (nīt) A high-ranking soldier of the Middle Ages who received his title from a noble (p. 213)

Koran (kô rän´) The holy book of the Muslims that contains the teachings of Islam; also spelled *Qur'an* (p. 227)

L

Laborer (lā´ bər ər) A person who does hard work with his or her hands (p. 129)

Labor union (lā´ bər yü´ nyən) A group of workers who join together to protect their wages, working conditions, and job benefits (p. 408)

Legal (lē´ gəl) Lawful; based on the law of the government (p. 180)

Legislature (lej´ ə slā chər) A group of people who make the laws of a nation or state (p. 523)

Liberator (lib´ ə rā´ tôr) One who frees a group of people (p. 423)

Liberty (lib´ ər tē) Freedom (p. 365)

Locomotive (lō kə mō´ tiv) A self-propelled vehicle that runs on rails (pp. 396–397)

Lord (lôrd) A king or noble who gave land to someone else (pp. 210–211)

Lutheranism (lü´ thər ə niz əm) The religious movement founded by Martin Luther (p. 275)

M

Majority (mə jôr´ ə tē) A greater number, more than half (p. 648)

Manor (man´ ər) The lands belonging to a medieval lord, including farmland, a village, and the home of the owner (pp. 210–211)

Market (mär´ kit) A place to sell goods (p. 397)

Marshall Plan (mär´ shəl plan) The American plan to rebuild Europe after World War II (p. 606)

Massacre (mas´ ə kər) The act of killing many people who are often defenseless (p. 292)

Masterpiece (mas´ tər pēs) A piece of art that seems almost perfect (p. 262)

Medieval (med ē´ vəl) Belonging to the Middle Ages (p. 211)

Merchant (mėr´ chənt) A person who buys and sells goods for a profit; a trader (p. 41)

Mesoamerica (mes ō ə mer´ ə kə) The area of North America (including Mexico and Central America) where civilizations developed before Europeans entered the continent (p. 321)

Middle Ages (mid´ l āj´ əz) The period of European history extending from the Fall of Rome in A.D. 476 to about A.D. 1450 (p. 192)

Migrate (mī´ grāt) To move away from one country or region to settle in another (p. 243)

Militarism (mil´ ə tə riz əm) A national policy of maintaining a powerful army and constant readiness for war (p. 527)

Military (mil´ ə ter ē) Having to do with soldiers or the armed forces (p. 89)

Minority (mə nôr´ ə tē) A smaller number, less than half (p. 647)

a	hat	e	let	ī	ice	ȯ	order	u̇	put	sh	she	ə	a	in about
ā	age	ē	equal	o	hot	oi	oil	ü	rule	th	thin		e	in taken
ä	far	ėr	term	ō	open	ou	out	ch	child	ᵺ	then		i	in pencil
â	care	i	it	ȯ	saw	u	cup	ng	long	zh	measure		o	in lemon
													u	in circus

Missionary (mish´ ə ner ē) A person sent by a church to other countries to spread a religion (p. 315)

Moderate (mod´ ər it) To make or become less extreme or violent (p. 712)

Monarch (mon´ ərk) A ruler, like a king, queen, or emperor (p. 286)

Monk (mungk) A man who has taken religious vows and usually lives in a monastery (p. 213)

Monroe Doctrine (mən rō´ dok´ trən) The doctrine stating that Europe should not try to get more territory in North or South America; taken from U.S. President James Monroe's speech to Congress (p. 436)

Mosaic (mō zā´ ik) A design made by putting together small pieces of colored stone, glass, or other material (p. 325)

Mother country (muŦH´ ər kun´ trē) A nation that controls a colony (p. 418)

Motto (mot´ ō) A word or phrase that expresses goals, ideas, or ideals (p. 379)

Multinational corporation (mul ti nash´ ə nəl kôr pə rā´ shən) A company that hires people and has business interests around the world (p. 741)

Mummy (mum´ ē) A dead body kept from rotting by being treated with chemicals and wrapped in cloth (p. 63)

Mural (myùr´ əl) A large picture painted on a wall (p. 427)

Muslim (muz´ ləm) A follower of the religion that Muhammad founded in Arabia in the seventh century (p. 225)

Myth (mith) A story, often about gods or goddesses, that is handed down through the years and sometimes used to explain natural events (p. 128)

N

Napoleonic Code (nə pō´ lē ən ik kōd) The constitution Napoleon set up that contained a single set of laws for all of France and its territories; it remains the basis of French law today (p. 382)

Nationalism (nash´ ə nə liz əm) Love of one's nation; patriotism (p. 286)

Natural resource (nach´ ər əl ri sôrs´) Materials that are provided by nature, such as forests, minerals, and water (p. 396)

Navigate (nav´ ə gāt) To plan the course of a ship; to sail or steer (p. 74)

Negotiate (ni gō´ shē āt) To talk together, make bargains, and agree on something (p. 668)

Neutral (nü´ trəl) Joining neither side in a war (p. 538)

Noble (nō´ bəl) A person of high social rank (p. 51)

Nomad (nō´ mad) A person who moves from place to place (p. 78)

Nonrenewable (non ri nü´ ə bl) Cannot be replaced once it is used up (p. 729)

Nonviolent resistance (non vī´ ə lənt ri zis´ təns) The act of opposing or working against without using force or causing injury (p. 483)

Nuclear (nü´ klē ər) Having to do with atoms or energy from atoms (p. 592)

Nuclear weapon (nü´ klē ər wep´ ən) A powerful weapon, such as an atomic bomb or missile (p. 613)

Nun (nun) A woman who has taken religious vows and enters a convent (p. 213)

O

Oath (ōth) A serious promise, often pledged in the name of God (p. 377)

Open-Door Policy (ō´ pən - dôr pol´ ə sē) The American approach to China around 1900 that allowed open trade relations between China and other nations (p. 462)

Oppose (ə pōz´) To be against something (p. 565)

Organization (ôr gə nə zā´ shən) A group of people joined together for a common purpose (p. 596)

Organize (ôr´ gə nīz) To set up (p. 210)

Overpopulation (ō vər pop yə lā´ shən) The state of having too many people; can ruin the environment or the quality of life (p. 745)

P

Pact (pakt) An agreement (p. 587)

Papyrus (pə pī´ rəs) A writing paper the Egyptians made from water plants of the same name (p. 66)

Parliament (pär´ lə mənt) England's body of lawmakers (p. 296)

Patriot (pā´ trē ət) A person who is loyal to his or her own country and shows a great love for that country (p. 365)

Patron (pā´ trən) A wealthy person who supports artists (p. 261)

Pax Romana (paks rō mä´ nə) The Roman peace that began during the reign of Augustus Caesar (p. 169)

Peasant (pez´ nt) A poor farmer or farm worker (p. 217)

Peninsula (pə nin´ sə lə) A long piece of land almost completely surrounded by water; from the Latin word meaning "almost an island" (p. 160)

Perestroika (per ə stoi´ kə) The Soviet policy of economic and government reform (p. 687)

Persecute (pėr´ sə kyüt) To treat in a cruel way; to hurt or injure (p. 178)

Petition (pə tish´ ən) A written request, often with many signatures, to a person or group in authority (p. 360)

Petition of Right (pə tish´ ən ov rīt) An English document that brought about more democracy (p. 360)

Pharaoh (fâr´ ō) A ruler of ancient Egypt (p. 60)

Pictograph (pik´ tə graf) A drawing that represents an actual thing; for example, a picture of an eye represents an eye (p. 48)

Pilgrim (pil´ grəm) A person who came to North America for religious freedom and settled in Plymouth, Massachusetts (p. 342)

Pilgrimage (pil´ grə mij) A visit to a holy place (p. 231)

Piracy (pī´ rə sē) The robbing of ships on the ocean (p. 341)

Plague (plāg) A deadly disease that spreads quickly (p. 134)

Policy (pol´ ə sē) A rule; a method of action or conduct (p. 458)

Political (pə lit´ ə kəl) Having to do with governing (p. 424)

Politics (pol´ ə tiks) The work of government (p. 709)

Pollution (pə lü´ shən) Waste materials in the air or water (p. 638)

Pope (pōp) The head of the Roman Catholic Church (p. 181)

Population (pop yə lā´ shən) People living in a place, or the total number of those people (p. 243)

Prejudice (prej´ ə dis) Dislike of people just because they are of a different race or religion, or are from another country (p. 505)

Priest (prēst) A religious leader (p. 43)

Primary source (prī´ mer ē sôrs) A first-hand account of a historical event (p. 8)

Prime minister (prīm min´ ə stər) The chief official of the government in some countries (p. 520)

Primitive (prim´ ə tiv) Of long ago; very simple (p. 192)

Privilege (priv´ ə lij) A special right given to a person or group (p. 313)

Profit (prof´ it) The amount of money left over after paying for the cost of doing business (p. 396)

Prophet (prof´ it) A religious leader who claims to speak for God; one who tells what will happen in the future (p. 225)

Protestant (prot´ ə stənt) A reformer who protested against the Catholic Church (p. 275)

Province (prov´ əns) A part of a country, with its own local government; much like a state in the United States (p. 165)

a	hat	e	let	ī	ice	ô	order	u̇	put	sh	she	ə	a	in about
ā	age	ē	equal	o	hot	oi	oil	ü	rule	th	thin		e	in taken
ä	far	ėr	term	ō	open	ou	out	ch	child	ᴛʜ	then		i	in pencil
â	care	i	it	ȯ	saw	u	cup	ng	long	zh	measure		o	in lemon
													u	in circus

Puritan (pyür´ ə tən) A member of a 16th- or 17th-century English group of Protestants who wanted to make the Church of England simpler and stricter (p. 342)

Pyramid (pir´ ə mid) A huge stone structure with a square base and four triangular sides that meet in a point at the top; Egyptian rulers were buried in the pyramids (p. 62)

R

Racism (rā´ siz əm) The idea that one race is better than another (p. 505)

Raid (rād) To attack suddenly; a surprise attack (p. 109)

Ratify (rat´ ə fī) To formally approve (p. 617)

Raw material (rȯ mə tir´ ē əl) Matter in its natural condition, not changed by some human process (p. 397)

Rebellion (ri bel´ yən) A fight by people against a government (p. 449)

Reformation (ref ər mā´ shən) A movement that challenged and changed the Catholic religion in Europe (p. 274)

Refuge (ref´ yüj) Shelter or protection from danger (p. 717)

Refugee (ref yə jē´) A person who flees his or her country or home (p. 643)

Reich (rīk) The German word for "empire" (p. 526)

Reign (rān) The rule of a monarch; to rule as a king, queen, or emperor (p. 288)

Reign of Terror (rān ov ter´ ər) The one-year period in French history when radical leaders put many people to death (p. 380)

Reincarnation (rē in kär nā´ shən) A belief that living souls are reborn in a new body (p. 100)

Religious (ri lij´ əs) Having to do with a belief in a higher being (p. 80)

Renaissance (ren´ ə säns) The revival of art, literature, and learning in Europe in the 14th through 16th centuries (p. 258)

Repeal (ri pēl´) To cancel; put an end to (p. 649)

Representation (rep ri zen tā´ shən) Sending one or more people to speak for the rights of others before a body of the government (p. 365)

Representative (rep ri zen´ tə tiv) A person who is chosen to act or speak for others (p. 161)

Republic (ri pub´ lik) A government in which the citizens have the right to elect (or choose) their representatives to make laws (p. 160)

Reunification (rē yü nə fi kā´ shən) The act of joining together again (p. 694)

Revolt (ri vōlt´) To rise up against a government; to refuse to obey the people in charge (p. 130)

Revolution (rev ə lü´ shən) A complete change, especially in a way of life or a government (p. 4)

Riot (rī´ ət) A violent disturbance created by a crowd of people (p. 378)

Roundhead (round´ hed) A Puritan who fought for Parliament in the English Civil War (p. 360)

Royalist (roi´ ə list) A supporter of the king or queen during the English Civil War (p. 360)

S

Saga (sä´ gə) A long story of brave deeds (p. 201)

Samurai (sam´ ů rī) A class of warriors in the Japanese feudal system (p. 313)

Sanction (sangk´ shən) An action taken by one nation against another for breaking international law (p. 647)

Satellite (sat´ l īt) A country that depends on and is controlled by a more powerful country (p. 606); an object put into orbit around the earth (p. 732)

Scapegoat (skāp´ gōt) A person or group blamed for the mistakes and problems of others (p. 576)

Scribe (skrīb) A person whose job it was to write out copies of contracts and other important papers; people worked as scribes before the invention of printing (p. 46)

Sculptor (skulp´ tər) A person who makes statues out of wood, stone, marble, or other material (p. 262)

Sculpture (skulp´ chər) A carving from stone or other hard material (p. 262)

Security (si kyùr´ ə tē) Safety (p. 624)

Senate (sen´ it) A governing or lawmaking body (p. 161)

Senator (sen´ ə tər) A person who is a member of the senate (p. 165)

Serf (sėrf) A poor farm worker who was bound to the land and whose life was controlled by the lord of the manor (pp. 210–211)

Settlement (set´ l mənt) A small group of homes in a newly established place or region (p. 24)

Shah (shä) An Iranian ruler (p. 669)

Shareholder (sher´ hōl dər) A person who owns one or more parts (shares) of a business (p. 346)

Shogun (shō´ gun) A great general governing Japan (p. 315)

Shortage (shôr´ tij) Too small of an amount; not enough (p. 559)

Shrine (shrīn) A place of worship believed to be sacred or holy (p. 114)

Siege (sēj) The surrounding of a city by soldiers who are trying to capture it so that food, water, and other supplies cannot get in or out (p. 89)

Slavery (slā´ vər ē) The owning of human beings with the belief that they are property (p. 4)

Smuggle (smug´ əl) To move something into or out of a country secretly because it is against the law (p. 458)

Sniper (snī´ pər) A person who shoots from a hidden spot (p. 535)

Socialism (sō´ shə liz əm) An economic and political system where the government owns and controls all industry (p. 559)

Society (sə sī´ ə tē) A group of people joined together for a common purpose (p. 517)

Soul (sōl) A person's spirit (p. 100)

Soviet (sō´ vē et) A Russian council (p. 562)

Specialize (spesh´ ə līz) To work in, and know a lot about, one job or field (p. 26)

Stalemate (stāl´ māt) To put in a position in which no action can be taken (p. 668)

Standard of living (stan´ dərd ov liv´ ing) A way to judge how well a person or a family is living (p. 653)

Starvation (stär vā´ shən) The condition of dying from not having enough food to eat (p. 647)

Steppe (step) A wide plain (p. 552)

Stock (stok) Shares in a business or company (p. 346)

Stone Age (stōn āj) The earliest known period of human culture where people used tools and weapons made from stone (p. 21)

Stronghold (strông´ hōld) A place dominated by a certain group which they have made safe and secure (p. 709)

Superiority (sə pir ē ôr´ ə tē) A feeling of being better than others (p. 480)

Superpower (sü´ pər pou ər) A nation that has more power and money than other countries (p. 610)

Surplus (sėr´ pləs) More than what is needed (p. 240)

Swamp (swomp) An area of low, wet land (p. 41)

Symbol (sim´ bəl) An object that stands for an idea; for example, the dove is a symbol of peace (p. 377)

Sympathy (sim´ pə thē) Feeling sorry for another's suffering (p. 448)

T

Tablet (tab´ lit) A small, flat piece of clay used for writing (p. 46)

Tariff (tar´ if) A tax that countries put on goods they import or export (p. 716)

Tax (taks) Money paid to support a government (p. 60)

Technology (tek nol´ ə jē) Science put to use in practical work (p. 742)

Temple (tem´ pəl) A building used to honor and praise a god or gods (p. 43)

a	hat	e	let	ī	ice	ô	order	ù	put	sh	she		a in about
ā	age	ē	equal	o	hot	oi	oil	ü	rule	th	thin	ə	e in taken
ä	far	ėr	term	ō	open	ou	out	ch	child	ᴛʜ	then		i in pencil
â	care	i	it	ò	saw	u	cup	ng	long	zh	measure		o in lemon
													u in circus

Terraced (ter´ ist) Going upward like steps (p. 324)

Territory (ter´ ə tôr ē) The land ruled by a nation or state (p. 436)

Terrorism (ter´ ər ism) The use of force or random violence to frighten people or groups (p. 668)

Terrorist (ter´ ər ist) A fighter who hopes to achieve certain goals by using force or violence (p. 667)

Textile (tek´ stīl) Cloth made by weaving (p. 397)

Theory (thir´ ē) An explanation of how and why something happens, usually based on scientific study (p. 268)

Tomb (tüm) A grave, usually one that is enclosed in stone or cement (p. 62)

Torpedo (tôr pē´ dō) To attack or destroy with a large, exploding, underwater missile (p. 539)

Tradition (trə dish´ ən) A custom, idea, or belief handed down from one person to the next (p. 202)

Traitor (trā´ tər) One who betrays a cause, a friend, or a nation (p. 664)

Translate (tran slāt´) To change the words of one language to another (p. 67)

Transport (tran spôrt´) To move from one place to another (p. 62)

Transportation (tran spər tā´ shən) The act of carrying from one place to another (pp. 396–397)

Trapper (trap´ ər) A person who traps wild animals for their furs (p. 344)

Treaty (trē´ tē) An agreement, usually having to do with peace or trade (p. 87)

Treaty of Versailles (trē´ tē ov ver sī) The treaty that ended World War I (p. 542)

Trench (trench) A long ditch dug in the ground to protect soldiers in battle (p. 538)

Tribute (trib´ yüt) A payment or gift demanded by rulers of ancient kingdoms (p. 90)

Truce (trüs) A time when enemies agree to stop fighting (p. 234)

Truman Doctrine (trü´ mən dok´ trən) U.S. President Truman's plan to stop the spread of Communism (p. 611)

Tyrant (tī´ rənt) A ruler who has complete power (p. 125)

U

U-boat (yü´ - bōt) A German submarine (p. 540)

Uncivilized (un siv´ ə līzd) Without training in arts, science, or government (p. 192)

Unification (yü nə fə kā´ shən) Bringing together into one whole (p. 516)

Unify (yü´ nə fī) To connect; to bring together as one (p. 517)

Unite (yü nīt´) To bring together as one (p. 60)

Upstream (up´ strēm) In the direction against the flow of the river; at the upper part of a river (p. 59)

V

Vassal (vas´ əl) A noble who received land from a king in return for loyalty and service (p. 210)

Viceroy (vīs´ roi) The governor of a country or province who rules as the representative of the king (p. 424)

Victor (vik´ tər) The winner of a battle, war, struggle, or contest (p. 448)

Violence (vī´ ə ləns) Great physical force; actions that hurt others (p. 624)

Vision (vizh´ ən) Something seen in the mind or in a dream (p. 225)

Vote (vōt) To choose leaders and pass laws (p. 126)

W

Weapons of mass destruction (wep´ ənz ov mas di struk´ shən) A means of attack or defense that uses powerful weapons; an atomic bomb is an example (p. 671)

Worship (wėr´ ship) To honor and praise a god (p. 78)

Z

Zionism (zī´ ə niz əm) The movement to set up a Jewish nation in Palestine (p. 661)

Index

Atomic bomb, 592–593, 728
   defined, 592
Attila the Hun, 194
Augustus, 169–170, 185
Aurangzeb, 319, 476
Australia, gold rush, 441
Austria, Germany and, 523
Authority, defined, 275
Avignon, 385
Axis Powers, 577–587, 599
   defined, 577
Ayatollah, defined, 669
Aztecs, 324–326, 329, 338–339

B

Babylonian empire, 51, 53, 81,
   83–84, 93, 152–153
Balance of power, defined, 534
Ban, defined, 710
Bangladesh, 625, 655
Barbarians, 193–195, 205
   defined, 193
Barrier, defined, 109
Barter, defined, 325
Bastille, 377–379, 389
   defined, 377
Batista, Fulgencio, 707
Battle of Tyre, 148, 155
Battle of Waterloo, 385–386
B.C. (Before Christ), defined, 12
Ben-Gurion, David, 662
Berlin Wall, 695, 701
   defined, 607
Betray, defined, 379
Bhopal disaster, 625
Bible, defined, 78
Bill of Rights, English, 363, 369,
   379
Bird flu, 748
Bishop, defined, 181
Bismarck, Otto von, 523–526,
   529, 535
Black Death, 216–217, 219
Blitzkrieg, 579, 581
Bloody Sunday revolt, 558–559,
   569
Bolívar, Simón, 423, 431
Bolshevik, defined, 562
Bolshevik Revolution, 562–564,
   569
Bonaparte, Napoleon, 382–387,
   516–517, 556
Border, defined, 8
Bosnia-Herzegovina, 697

Boundary, defined, 517
Boxer Rebellion, 463, 471
Brazil, 425, 720–721
Britain, Battle of, 581–582
British East India Company, 346,
   476–477, 487
British textile industry, 400–401,
   413
Brutus, 167, 169
Buddha, 102, 117
   defined, 102
Buddhism, 102–104, 117, 318
   defined, 102
Bush, George H. W., 691, 712, 751
Bush, George W., 751
Byzantine Empire, 197–198, 205,
   550

C

Cabot, John, 344
Cabral, Pedro, 336
Calvin, John, 275–276
Campaign, defined, 145
Canaan, 78
Canada, 344, 439
Canal, defined, 41
Capital, defined, 80
Capitalist, defined, 610
Caravan, defined, 493
Carthage, 74, 93, 161–162, 185
Cartridge, defined, 478
Cartwright, Edmund, 401
Cassius, 167, 169
Caste, 100, 104, 626
   defined, 100
Castro, Fidel, 614, 707, 723
Casualty, defined, 544
Catherine II, 556, 569
Cavour, Camillo di, 520–521, 529
Cease-fire, defined, 663
Censor, defined, 566
Central Intelligence Agency
   (CIA), 751
Central Powers, 534, 536, 547
   defined, 534
Chad, 651–652, 675
Chamorro, Violeta Barrios de,
   710
Chancellor, defined, 526
Chariot, defined, 47
Charlemagne, 197–198, 205
Charles I, 359–361
Charles II, 363

Charles the Great. *See*
   Charlemagne
Charter, defined, 248
Chechnya, Russia and, 699, 701
Chernobyl disaster, 729–730
Chiang Kai-shek, 464, 628–629
Chiapas unrest, 716
Child labor, 406
Chile, 424
China, 308, 311, 329, 464. *See also*
   Early China
   Boxer Rebellion, 463
   Chinese-Japanese war,
      462–463, 471
   dynasties, 456, 463, 471
   Great Britain and, 458–459,
      632
   gunpowder, 308, 329
   Hong Kong, 459
   inventions, 308, 329
   isolation, 308, 329, 454, 458
   Japan and, 313, 469
   Korea and, 462, 471
   Macao, 309
   Manchurian rule, 456–459,
      461–463, 480
   Ming dynasty, 456
   Mongols, 309–310, 329
   Nationalist Party, 464, 471
   Open Door Policy, 462, 471
   opium trade, 458
   Qing dynasty, 456–459,
      461–463
   Silk Road, 309
   Taiping Rebellion, 461–462
   trade, 309
   Treaty of Nanjing, 458
   Unequal Treaties, 459
China, Communist, 628–631
   Communists *vs.* Nationalists,
      628–629, 655
   Cultural Revolution, 630
   Great Britain and, 632
   Hong Kong and, 632
   political freedom in, 631,
      655
   private ownership, trade
      631, 655
   U.S. and, 629
   USSR and, 629
China's Sorrow, 106
Chinese-Japanese war, 462–463,
   471

Christianity, 79, 177–181, 185, 493
  defined, 79
Churchill, Winston, 567, 580
Church of England, 295–296, 298, 301
CIA. *See* Central Intelligence Agency
Circus Maximus, 173
CIS. *See* Commonwealth of Independent States
Cities, development of, 26, 33, 43–44
Citizen, defined, 126
City-state, 43–44, 51, 53, 122, 125–126, 128–130, 139
  defined, 43
Civil disobedience, defined, 483
Civilian, defined, 581
Civilization, defined, 9
Civil war, defined, 166
Cixi, 463
Class, defined, 100
Cleopatra, 169, 185
Clergy, 213, 256
  defined, 213
Clinton, Bill, 668
Code, defined, 84
Code of Hammurabi, 84, 93, 152
Cold war, 610–614, 619, 691
  defined, 610
Collapse, defined, 109
Collective, defined, 565
Colonial, defined, 387
Colony, defined, 74
Colonies/Colonization, 397, 413, 418–420, 431, 509
Columbus, Christopher, 334–335, 349
Commandment, defined, 78
Commonwealth, defined, 361
Commonwealth of Independent States (CIS), 690–691, 701
Commune, defined, 630
Communism, 559–561, 567, 569
  after World War II spread of, 606–607, 611, 614, 619
  Cuba and, 707
  defined, 559
  domino theory and, 641, 710
  Latin America and, 704, 706–707, 709, 723
  North Korea and, 634

North Vietnam and, 640–641, 655
  Red Guard, 630
  U.S. and, 704, 706–707, 723
Communist Manifesto, 560
Communist Party, 562–565, 569, 614, 687
Compass, defined, 308
The Computer Age, 736–737, 757
Concentration camp, 576–577
  defined, 576
Confederation, defined, 523
Conference, defined, 505
Conflict, defined, 544
Confucius, 110
Conquer, defined, 80
Conquerors, defined, 99
Conquistador, defined, 338
Consent, defined, 360
Constantine, 179–180, 185
Constitution, defined, 130
Contract, defined, 47
Contras, 709–710, 723
Convert, defined, 180
Copernicus, Nicholas, 268
Corrupt, defined, 629
Cortés, Hernando, 325–326, 339, 349
Cosmonaut, defined, 732
Council of Trent, 278
Counter-Reformation, 278–279, 281
  defined, 278
Coup, defined, 688
Crafts, 26, 33
  defined, 26
Create, defined, 48
Creoles, 419
Crisis, defined, 614
Criticize, defined, 259
Croatia, 697
Cromwell, Oliver, 360–361, 369
Crusades, 231–235, 237–238, 248, 251
  defined, 232
Cuba, 707, 723
Cuban missile crisis, 614
Cultural Revolution, 630
Culture, 5–6, 65–66, 106–107, 152, 155, 306, 427–428, 431
  defined, 5
Cuneiform, 46, 48
  defined, 46
Curfew, defined, 648

Currency, defined, 612
Cyrus the Great, 132
Czar, defined, 553
Czechoslovakia, 579, 693–694, 698

D

Darius III, 147, 149
Das Kapital, 560
David and Goliath, 80
Dayton Accords, 697
D-Day, 589–599
  defined, 589
Declaration by United Nations, 596
Declaration of Independence, 366–367, 369, 379
  defined, 366
Declaration of the Rights of Man, 379
Decline, defined, 286
Democracy, 126, 136, 139, 354, 356–357, 376–380, 624, 720
  defined, 126
Democratic, defined, 133
Department of Homeland Security, 750
Depression, defined, 574
Descendant, defined, 420
Description of the World, 311
Desert, defined, 58
Détente, defined, 616
Developed country, 410, 741, 757
  defined, 410
Developing country, 410, 741, 757
  defined, 410
Development, defined, 5
Dialect, defined, 552
Diaspora, 661
Dictators, 382, 425, 431, 574–577
  defined, 382
Dike, defined, 41
Diocletian, 179
Diplomat, defined, 520
The Directory, France, 382
Disarm, defined, 542
Disaster, defined, 616
Disband, defined, 690
Discrimination, defined, 420
Diseases, 747–748
Divine right, 359, 374
  defined, 359
Document, defined, 248
Dominance, defined, 505

Tennis Court Oath, 377
Third Republic, 387, 389
Vietnam and, 640
Frank, Ann, 587
Franks, 197, 205
Fraternity, defined, 379
Freemen, defined, 210–211
French and Indian War, 344
French East India Company, 346, 477, 487
French monarchs, 198, 292–293, 297, 301, 376–380, 382–387, 389
French Revolution, 378–380, 389
    defined, 379
Front, defined, 538
Frontier, defined, 192
Fulton, Robert, 403

G

Gagarin, Yuri, 732
Galilei, Galileo, 268–269, 281
Da Gama, Vasco, 335, 499
Gandhi, Indira, 624
Gandhi, Mahatma, 483–485, 487
Gandhi, Rajiv, 624
Garibaldi, Giuseppe, 520–521, 529
Gaza, 667
General, defined, 149
Genghis Khan, 309–310, 329, 553, 569
Genocide, defined, 585
Geography, defined, 552
Geography Note, 30, 65, 173, 201, 289, 309, 385, 441, 593, 698
George III, 365–366, 369
Germanic tribes, 192–194, 205
Germany, 524, 527, 535, 542
    after World War II, 606–607, 619
    Austria and, 523
    Bismarck, 523–526, 529
    chancellor, 526, 529
    East and West reunification, 694–695
    government, 526
    Hitler era of, 575–577, 579, 581–583, 591, 599
    militarism, 527, 529
    nationalism in, 523–527, 576, 599
    Nazi party, 576
    Second Reich formation, 526

Soviet Union and, 606–607, 619
    Treaty of Versailles and, 542, 547
    U-boats, 539, 547
    unification, 523–524
Ghana, 495–496, 646
Glacier, defined, 20
Glasnost, defined, 687
Global economy, global issues, 740–741
Global issues, 740–743, 757
Global threat, terrorism, 750, 757
Global warming, defined, 721
Glorious Revolution, 363, 369
    defined, 363
Goddess, defined, 43
Golden Age of Athens, 133
Golden Age of China, 109
Gold rush, 441
Good Neighbor Policy, defined, 706
Goods, defined, 41
Gorbachev, Mikhail, 686–688, 690, 701
Gospel, defined, 177
Goths, 195, 205
Govern, defined, 125
Governor, defined, 165
Grant, Ulysses S., 444
Graphs and charts
    bar graph, xxx
    circle graph (pie graph), xxx
    line graphs, xxxi
    reading, xxx–xxxi
    tables, xxxi, 544
Great Britain, 295–299
    Battle of Britain, 581–582
    China and, 458–459
    colonies, 397, 413
    Communist China and, 632
    Falkland Islands war, 713
    Hong Kong and, 459
    India and, 480–481, 487
    Industrial Revolution, 396–397, 413
    labor unions, 408
    London Blitz, 582
    markets, raw materials, factories, 397
    natural resources, 396, 413
    Scotland, Wales and, 398
    The Sepoy Rebellion, 478

textile industry, 397–398, 400–401, 413
    transportation, 396
    Treaty of Nanjing, 458
    War of 1812, 439, 451
    World War II, 581–583
Great Council, 356–357
Great Depression, 574
Great Names in History, xx
    Anne Frank, 587
    Aung San Suu Kyi, 632
    Confucius, 110
    Golda Meir, 662
    Hammurabi, 84
    Hannibal, 163
    José de San Martín, 424
    Kublai Khan, 310
    Louis and Mary Leakey, 9
    Mother Teresa of Calcutta, 743
    Saladin, 234
    William Shakespeare, 299
Great Pyramid, 62–63, 69
Great Wall of China, 108–109, 117
The Great War. *See* World War I
Greece. *See* Ancient Greece
Greek culture, 152, 155
Guadalupe Hidalgo, treaty of, 441, 451
Guerilla, defined, 641
Guild, defined, 244
Guillotine, defined, 380
Gutenberg Bible, 266
Gutenberg's printing press, 265–266

H

Hadrian, 193, 205
Haiti, 422, 431, 715, 717, 723, 748
Halley, Edmond, 359
Hammurabi, 84, 93, 152
Han dynasty, 109
Hanging Gardens of Babylon, 83
Hannibal, 163
Hastings, Battle of, 203
Henry IV, 292–293, 301
Henry VII, 295
Henry VIII, 295–296, 301
Heretic, defined, 276
Hidalgo, Miguel, 423, 431
Hieroglyphics, 66–67, 69
    defined, 66

INF Treaty. *See* Intermediate Range Nuclear Force Treaty
Inquisition, 275–276
  defined, 276
Insurance, defined, 346
Inter-Allied Declaration, 596
Interest, defined, 346
Interfere, defined, 439
Interference, defined, 462
Intermediate Range Nuclear Force Treaty (INF Treaty), 686
Internal combustion engine, defined, 403
International, defined, 449
International Space Station (ISS), 733
Internet, 738
Intifada, 667
Inuit, 322, 329
Invade, defined, 575
Inventions, 46–47, 53, 66, 75–76, 91, 265–266, 281, 308, 329, 400–403, 406, 413, 540
Invest, defined, 638
Investment, defined, 346
Investor, defined, 397
Iran, 669–670, 676, 681
Iran-Contra Affair, 710
Iran-Iraq war, 669–670, 681
Iraq, 670–671, 751
Iron Curtain, 566–567
  defined, 566
Irrigate, defined, 41
Islam, 224–228, 251, 318–319, 329, 493. *See also* Muslims
Isolate, defined, 109
Isolationism, defined, 608
Israel, 661–662, 667, 678, 681. *See also* Ancient Israelites
Israelites. *See* Ancient Israelites
ISS. *See* International Space Station
Italy, 518, 520–521, 527, 529
  fascism and, 574–575, 591, 599
  nationalism in, 516–521, 529
  Rome, 521, 529
  secret societies, 517
  World War I and, 538, 547
  Young Italy secret society, 517
Ivan the Terrible, 553–554, 567, 569

J

James II, 363
Japan, 466–469
  after World War II, 637
  China and, 313, 469
  Chinese-Japanese war, 462–463, 471
  craftworkers, traders, 314
  economy, 638
  exports, 638
  feudal society, 313–314, 329, 467
  foreign trade, 466
  imperialism, 469, 471
  industry, 638
  investment in, 638
  isolation of, 315–316, 329, 454, 466
  kamikaze, 315
  Korea and, 462, 471
  mikado, 315
  modernization, 467–468
  nation-state formation, 315
  pollution, 638
  raw materials, 469, 471
  Russia and, 469, 471
  Southeast Asia and, 637
  trade, 315–316, 638
  treaties with, 467
  world economy and, 638
  World War II and, 575, 586–587, 592–593, 599, 637
Jefferson, Thomas, 365–366
Jericho, 28–29
Jerusalem, 81, 93, 227, 231–233, 251
Jesuits, 279
Jesus Christ, 177–179, 185
Jews, diaspora, 661
Johnson, Lyndon, 641
Judaism, 79, 81, 93
  defined, 79
Julius Caesar, 165–167, 185
Jury, defined, 130

K

Kaiser, defined, 526
Kamikaze, 315, 592
  defined, 592
Kay, John, 400
Kennedy, John F., 614
Kenya, 646
Kenyatta, Jomo, 646

Khomeini, Ayatollah, 669
Khrushchev, Nikita, 613–614
Kingdoms, development of, 26, 33
Klerk, F. W. de, 648–649
Knights, 213–214
  defined, 213
Kohl, 65
The Koran, 227, 229
  defined, 227
Korea, 655. *See also* North Korea; South Korea
  Chinese-Japanese war, 462–463, 471
Kublai Khan, 310–311, 315, 329
Kush civilization, 492–493, 509
Kuwait, Persian Gulf War, 676, 670–671, 679, 681

L

Laborer, defined, 129
Labor union, defined, 408
Laden, Osama bin, 671, 750
Lafayette, 374
Land bridge, 112, 117
Latin, 174, 197, 265
Latin America, 429, 719. *See also specific countries*
  architecture, 428
  colonies, 422–425
  Communism and, 704, 706–707, 709, 723
  Creoles, 419
  culture, 427–428, 431
  democracy in, 720
  dictators, 425, 431
  discrimination, 420, 431
  independence, 416, 422–425, 428, 429
  Industrial Revolution and, 419
  languages, 428
  mestizos, 420
  native people, 420, 431
  1945–present, 719–720, 723
  protest against military governments, 713
  social structure, 420
  U.S. and, 704, 706–707, 723
Laws, 26, 174, 185, 192, 384
League of Nations, 544–545, 547, 595
Leakey, Louis and Mary, 9

Ratify, defined, 617
Raw materials, defined, 397
Reading Strategy, xx
  Inferencing, xxv, 97, 100, 103,
      104, 106, 109, 114, 257, 259,
      263, 265, 268 272, 275, 279,
      417, 420, 422, 428, 551, 552,
      556, 558, 559, 562, 563, 727,
      728, 730, 734, 736, 743, 745,
      748, 751, 752, 755
  Metacognition, xxv, 123, 125,
      126, 130, 132, 136, 285, 286,
      288, 289, 292, 295, 296, 435,
      436, 439, 443, 444, 446, 447,
      544, 573, 576, 579, 582, 585,
      589, 591, 595, 597, 737
  Predicting, xxv, 39, 41, 44, 46,
      51, 191, 192, 195, 197, 200,
      355, 356, 359, 361, 363, 365,
      491, 492, 496, 498, 499, 501,
      659, 660, 664, 667, 671, 674,
      676, 678
  Questioning, xxv, 19, 20, 26,
      30, 159, 160, 161, 167, 169,
      172, 173, 177, 183, 333, 334,
      335, 339, 341, 343, 347, 475,
      476, 478, 480, 481, 483, 484,
      623, 624, 625, 628, 632, 634,
      637, 640, 643, 646, 651
  Summarizing, xxv, 3, 6, 9, 12,
      13, 143, 144, 145, 148, 153,
      307, 310, 313, 316, 318, 319,
      322, 455, 456, 461, 464, 466,
      469, 605, 606, 608, 611, 616
  Text Structure, xxv, 57, 58, 59,
      63, 66, 209, 210, 214, 373,
      374, 376, 379, 383, 387, 515,
      516, 517, 524, 526, 685, 686,
      688, 690, 693, 696
  Visualizing, xxv, 73, 75, 80, 84,
      86, 90, 91, 223, 224, 225,
      231, 237, 238, 241, 243, 248,
      395, 398, 400, 402, 405, 407,
      411, 533, 535, 538, 539, 705,
      706, 709, 711, 716, 717, 720
Reagan, Ronald, 686, 710, 711
Rebellion, defined, 449
Red Guard, 630
Reformation, 274–276
  defined, 274
Refuge, defined, 717
Refugee, defined, 643
Reich, defined, 526
Reign, defined, 288

Reign of Terror, 380, 389
  defined, 380
Reincarnation, 100, 103, 117
  defined, 100
Religious, defined, 80
The Renaissance, 225–256,
      258–259, 261–263, 265–266,
      268–269, 271–272, 279, 281
  defined, 258
Repeal, defined, 649
Representation, defined, 365
Representative, defined, 161
Republic, defined, 160
Republic of China. *See* Taiwan
Reunification, defined, 694
Revolt, defined, 130
Revolution, 4–5, 15, 394
  defined, 4
Rhodesia, 647–648
Richard the Lionhearted, 234
Ride, Sally, 732
Riot, defined, 378
Robespierre, 380
Roman Catholic Church, 256,
      274–276, 278–279, 281, 295–296
Romance languages, 175
Roman Empire, 12, 158, 162–163,
      167, 169–170, 174, 180, 183,
      185
  Ancient Greece and, 162, 185
  Appian Way, 173
  Appius Claudius Caecus, 173
  art, architecture, 172–173, 185
  Carthage and, 161–162, 185
  Christianity in, 177–181, 185
  Circus Maximus, 173
  Eastern, Western, 179–180,
      197, 205
  end of, 183
  entertainment, holidays, 173
  Etruscans and, 160, 185
  extent, 163
  fall of Western, 192–195, 205
  generals, 165
  Germanic tribes and, 192
  Goths and, 195, 205
  government, 161, 165–166, 185
  Greek influence, 162
  languages, 174–175, 185
  Latin, 174
  laws, 174, 185
  life in, 172–173, 185
  Macedonia and, 162
  Messina, 161

  origins, 160, 185
  Pantheon, 172
  Pax Romana, 169, 183, 185
  persecution in, 178, 185
  political equality, 161, 185
  provinces, 165, 185
  Punic Wars, 161–162, 185
  roads, 173
  Roman calendar, 166
  Roman Forum, 172
  shared rule, 179–180
  slavery, 162
  society, 172–174
  temples in, 172
  Tiber River, 160, 185
  Vandals and, 195, 205
Roosevelt, Eleanor, 596
Roosevelt, Franklin D., 587, 596
Rosetta Stone, 67
Roundhead, defined, 360
Rousseau, Jean Jacques, 356, 374
Royalist, defined, 360
Russia, 310, 552–556, 558–559,
      562–567, 569, 699. *See
      also* Commonwealth of
      Independent States; Russian
      Federation; Union of Soviet
      Socialist Republics
  Bloody Sunday revolt, 558–559,
      569
  Bolshevik Revolution,
      562–564, 569
  Byzantine Empire and, 550
  Chechnya and, 699, 701
  Communist Party, 562–565,
      569
  dialects, languages, 552
  Duma, 559
  early rulers, 553
  Europe and, 554–556, 569
  geography, 552
  industrialization, 558
  Japan and, 469, 471
  lands, size, 552
  Mongol Empire and, 552–553,
      569
  people, 552
  tyrants, 567
  Vikings and, 553, 569
  World War I and, 534, 559, 569
Russian Federation, 691, 701

Acknowledgments

Photo Credits

Cover (Bkgd) (T) © Royalty-Free/Corbis; Cover (Bkgd) (T) © Getty Images; Cover (Bkgd) (B) © Getty Images; Cover (C) © Val Duncan/Kenebec Images/ Alamy; Cover (B) © Royalty-Free/Corbis; Cover (R) © Getty Images; page xviii © Blend Images/ SuperStock; page xxxii © SuperStock, Inc./SuperStock; page 5 © Tamir Niv/Shutterstock; page 6 © Bettman/ CORBIS; page 9 © Nancy Carter/North Wind Picture Archives; page 20 © Charles Knight/National Geographic Image Collection; page 25 © Robert Adrian Hillman/Shutterstock; page 29 The Granger Collection, New York; page 36 © Peter M. Wilson/ CORBIS; page 44 The Granger Collection, New York; page 46 The Art Archive/Musee du Louvre Paris/ Dagli Orti; page 50 © Tom Lovell/National Geographic Image Collection; page 63 The Art Archive/Dagli Orti; page 65 © Vova Pomortzeff/Shutterstock; page 67 © Vladimir Korostyshevskiy/Shutterstock; page 76 © Scala/Art Resource, NY; page 79 © Topham/The Image Works; page 83 © Francoise de Mulder/ CORBIS; page 87 The Art Archive/Museum of Anatolian Civilisations Ankara/Dagli Orti; page 90 The Art Archive/British Museum/Dagli Orti (A); page 103 The Art Archive/Musee Guimet Paris/Dagli Orti (A); page 108 © Thomas Barrat/Shutterstock; page 115 © Ales Liska/Shutterstock; page 120 © Peter M. Wilson/Alamy; page 126 © Palis Michael/ Shutterstock; page 129 © Emily Goodwin/ Shutterstock; page 133 Bust of Pericles (495–429 B.C.) copy of a Greek original, Roman, 2nd century A.D. (marble) (see also 99060)/British Museum, London, UK, Index/The Bridgeman Art Library International; page 145 © Dhoxax/Shutterstock; page 147 © Mimmo Jodice/CORBIS; page 152 © Mansell/Time&Life Pictures/Getty Images; page 163 © Araldo de Luca/ CORBIS; page 166 Bust of Julius Caesar (100–44 B.C.) (marble), Roman, (1st century B.C.)/Galleria degli Uffizi, Florence, Italy, Alinari/The Bridgeman Art Library International; page 174 © Will Iredale/ Shutterstock; page 178 © Erich Lessing/Art Resource, NY; page 179 The Art Archive/Museo Capitolino Rome/Dagli Orti (A); page 188 The Granger Collection, New York; page 194 © Erich Lessing/Art Resource, NY; page 198 © Giraudon/Art Resource, NY; page 201 © Hulton Archive/Getty Images; page 202 © Ted Spiegel/CORBIS; page 214 The Art Archive/Museo di Roma Palazzo Braschi/Dagli Orti (A); page 216 © North Wind/North Wind Picture Archives; page 224 © Keren Su/CORBIS; page 229 © Archivo Iconografico, S.A./CORBIS; page 234 © Ann Ronan Picture Library/HIP/Art Resource, NY; page 238 The Granger Collection, New York; page 241 © Gianni Dagli Orti/CORBIS; page 246 © Snark/Art Resource, NY; page 249 © Bettman/CORBIS; page 254 © Scala/Art Resource, NY; page 263 © Bartlomiej K. Kwieciszewski/Shutterstock; page 269 © Bettman/ CORBIS; page 271 Facsimile of Codex Atlanticus f.386v Water Wheel with Cups (original copy in Biblioteca Ambrosiana, Milan, 1503/4-07), Vinci, Leonardo da (1452–1519)/Private Collection,/The Bridgeman Art Library; page 272 © Scala/Art Resource, NY; page 274 Portrait of Martin Luther (1483–1546) (oil on panel), Cranach, Lucas, the Elder (1472–1553) / Germanisches Nationalmuseum, Nuremberg, Germany/The Bridgeman Art Library; page 278 The Art Archive/Farnese Palace Caprarola/ Dagli Orti (A); page 286 Queen Mary I of England (1516–58) 1550s (oil on panel), Mor, Anthonis (Antonio Moro) (c.1519–1576/77) (studio of)/© Isabella Stewart Gardner Museum, Boston, MA, USA,/The Bridgeman Art Library; page 290 The Art Archive/Eileen Tweedy; page 293 St. Bartholomew's Day Massacre, 24th August 1572 (oil on panel), Dubois, Francois (1529–1584)/Musee Cantonal des Beaux-Arts de Lausanne, Switzerland, Photo © Held Collection/The Bridgeman Art Library; page 298 © Scala/Art Resource, NY; page 304 © Mary Evans Picture Library/The Image Works; page 308 Celebration with Fireworks and Kites (painted textile), Chinese School, (19th century)/Private Collection, Archives Charmet/The Bridgeman Art Library; page 314 © Hulton Archive/Getty Images; page 319 © Taolmor/Shutterstock; page 322 © Nancy Carter/North Wind Picture Archives; page 325 Wikipedia.org; page 336 Ferdinand Magellan (c.1480–1521) from the 'Sala del Mappamondo' (Hall of the World Maps) (fresco), Varese, Antonio Giovanni de (16th century)/Villa Farnese, Caprarola, Lazio, Italy,/The Bridgeman Art Library; page 338 © Michel Zabe/Art Resource, NY; page 342 © Burstein Collection/CORBIS; page 347 Wijdships offshore running in a stiff breeze on a cloudy day (oil on panel), Vlieger, Simon Jacobsz. (c.1600–53)/Private Collection, Johnny Van Haeften Ltd., London/The Bridgeman Art Library; page 352 The Granger Collection, New York; page 357 Edward I (1239–1307) King of England (engraving), English School, (19th century)/Private Collection, Ken Welsh/The Bridgeman Art Library; page 361 © Nancy Carter/North Wind Picture Archives; page 363 Presentation of the Bill of Rights to William III (1650–1702) of Orange and Mary II (1662–94) (engraving) (b/w photo), English School/British Museum, London, UK,/The Bridgeman Art Library; page 366 © Victorian Traditions/Shutterstock; page 378 ullstein bild/The Granger Collection, New York; page 380 The Art Archive/Musee Carnavalet Paris/Dagli Orti (A); page 384 © Reunion des Musees Nationaux/Art Resource, NY; page 386 Battle of Waterloo, 18th June 1815, 1898 (colour litho), Sullivan, William Holmes (fl.1870–d.1908)/Private Collection,/The Bridgeman Art Library; page 392 The Art Archive/Bibliotheque Municipale Dijon/Dagli Orti; page 398 Interior of a Weaver's Cottage with a Mother and Child, 1663 (oil on panel), Decker, Cornelius (d.1678)/Private Collection, Johnny Van Haeften Ltd., London/The Bridgeman Art Library; page 401 The Granger Collection, New York; page 402 The Granger Collection, New York; page 406 © Bettmann/CORBIS; page 408 © John Thomson/Hulton Archive/Getty Images; page 419 © CORBIS; page 422 © British Library/HIP/Art Resource, NY; page 427 © Galen Rowell/CORBIS; page 440 © Brandon Seidel/Shutterstock; page 444 The Granger Collection, New York; page 447 The Granger Collection, New York; page 449 © Kevin Schafer/CORBIS; page 456 © Bettmann/CORBIS; page 459 The Granger Collection, New York; page 461 The Granger Collection, New York; page 467 © Bettmann/CORBIS; page 477 © David Cumming; Eye Ubiquitous/CORBIS; page 478 The Granger Collection, New York; page 481 © Jeremy Horner/CORBIS; page 485 © Hulton-Deutsch Collection/CORBIS; page 493 © Jonathan Blair/CORBIS; page 496 The Granger Collection, New York; page 499 The Granger Collection, New York; page 501 © Kenneth V. Pilon/Shutterstock; page 503 © Henry Guttmann/Hulton Archive/Getty Images; page 512 The Art Archive/National Archives Washington DC; page 520 The Art Archive/Museo Civico Modigliana Italy/Dagli Orti (A); page 525 © Bettmann/CORBIS; page 535 © Bettmann/CORBIS; page 539 © Hulton Archive/Getty Images; page 544 © Hulton-Deutsch Collection/CORBIS; page 553 © Bettmann/CORBIS; page 555 The Granger Collection, New York; page 558 © Archivo Iconografico, S.A./CORBIS; page 560 Library of Congress; page 563 © Erich Lessing/Art Resource, NY; page 566 The Granger Collection, New York; page 574 © Topham/The Image Works; page 575 The Granger Collection, New York; page 576 The Art Archive/Imperial War Museum/Eileen Tweedy; page 577 © A/P Images; page 581 © Hulton Archive/Getty Images; page 586 © Keystone/Hulton Archive/Getty Images; page 589 © Hulton Archive/Getty Images; page 597 © Natalia Bratslavsky/Shutterstock; page 602 © The Image Bank/Getty Images; page 612a © Mario Lopes/Shutterstock; page 612b © CORBIS; page 616 © Wally McNamee/CORBIS; page 626 © Jeremy Horner/CORBIS; page 628 © BoonLeng Woo/Shutterstock; page 631 © Bettmann/CORBIS; page 635 © Jeon Heon-Kyun/epa/Corbis; page 638 © Bettmann/CORBIS; page 643 © Peter Turnley/CORBIS; page 649 © UN Photo/A Tannenbaum; page 651 © David Turnley/CORBIS; page 663 © Peter Turnley/CORBIS; page 668 © Reuters/CORBIS; page 670 © Bob Strong/epa/Corbis; page 672 © Spencer Platt/Getty Images; page 675 © John Moore/The Image Works; page 679 © Hanan Isachar/CORBIS; page 688 © Don Emmert/AFP/Getty Images; page 690 © Peter Turnley/CORBIS; page 694 © Lionel Cironneau/AP Images; page 697 © Danilo Krstanovic/Reuters/Corbis; page 707 © Alejandro Ernesto/epa/Corbis; page 711 © John Hoagland/Getty Images; page 715 © Colman Lerner Gerardo/Shutterstock; page 717 © Jacques Langevin/CORBIS SYGMA; page 721 © Luc Sesselle/Shutterstock; page 733 NASA; page 737 © LWA-Dann Tardif/zefa/Corbis; page 742 © Mityukhin Oleg Petrovich/Shutterstock; page 743 © Kevin Frayer/AP Images; page 746 © ExaMedia Photography/Shutterstock

Staff Credits

Mel Benzinger, Nancy Condon, Barb Drewlo, Marti Erding, Daren Hastings, Brian Holl, Mariann Johanneck, Julie Johnston, Patrick Keithahn, Mary Kaye Kuzma, Marie Mattson, Daniel Milowski, Carol Nelson, Carrie O'Connor, Jeff Sculthorp, Julie Theisen, LeAnn Velde, Mike Vineski, Peggy Vlahos, Amber Wegwerth, Charmaine Whitman, Sue Will

Unit Mastery Test

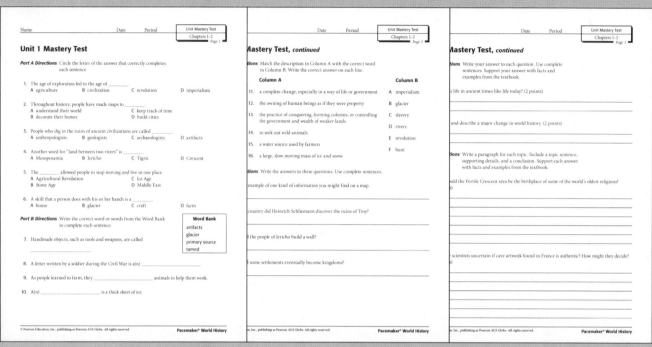

Unit 1 Mastery Test Page 1   Unit 1 Mastery Test Page 2   Unit 1 Mastery Test Page 3

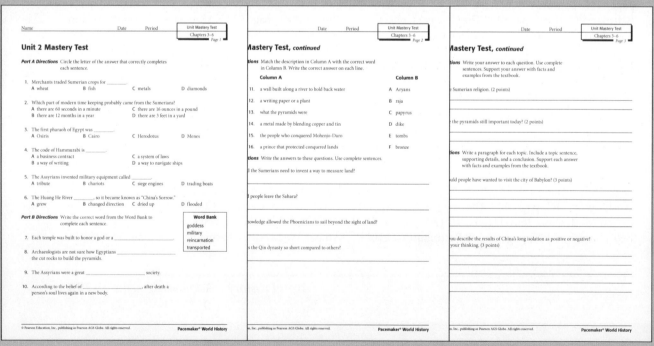

Unit 2 Mastery Test Page 1   Unit 2 Mastery Test Page 2   Unit 2 Mastery Test Page 3

Unit Mastery Test

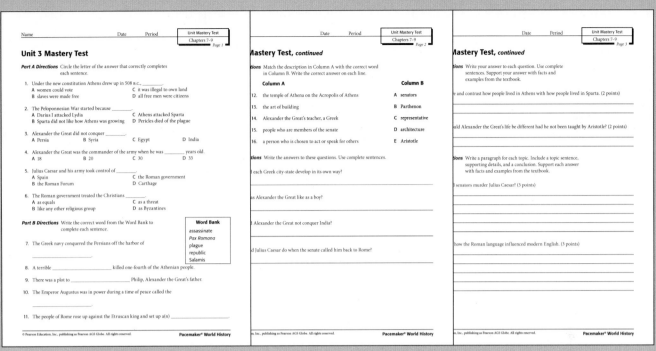

Unit 3 Mastery Test Page 1   Unit 3 Mastery Test Page 2   Unit 3 Mastery Test Page 3

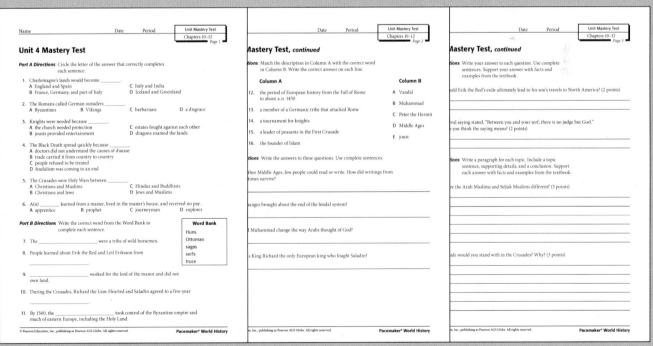

Unit 4 Mastery Test Page 1   Unit 4 Mastery Test Page 2   Unit 4 Mastery Test Page 3

Unit Mastery Test

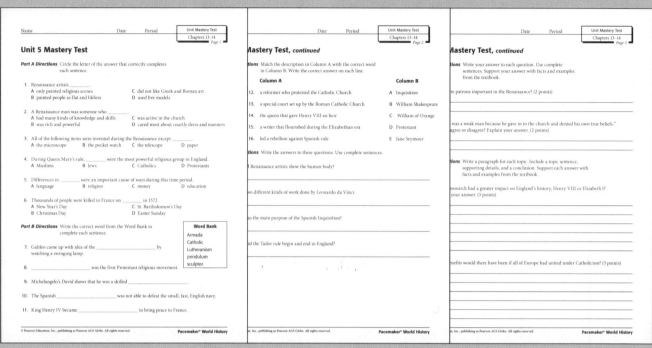

Unit 5 Mastery Test Page 1   Unit 5 Mastery Test Page 2   Unit 5 Mastery Test Page 3

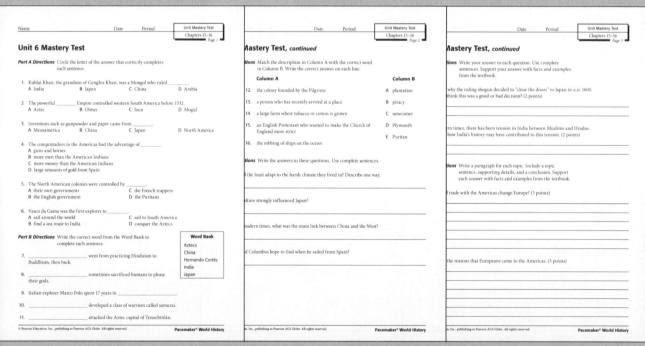

Unit 6 Mastery Test Page 1   Unit 6 Mastery Test Page 2   Unit 6 Mastery Test Page 3

Unit Mastery Test

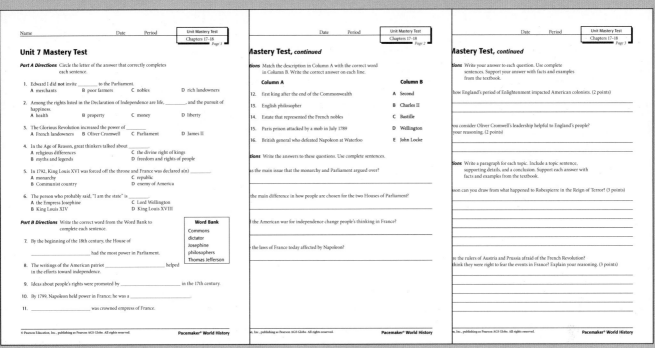

Unit 7 Mastery Test Page 1

Unit 7 Mastery Test

Part A Directions Circle the letter of the answer that correctly completes each sentence.

1. Edward I did **not** invite _____ to the Parliament.
   A merchants   B poor farmers   C nobles   D rich landowners

2. Among the rights listed in the Declaration of Independence are life, _____, and the pursuit of happiness.
   A health   B property   C money   D liberty

3. The Glorious Revolution increased the power of _____.
   A French landowners   B Oliver Cromwell   C Parliament   D James II

4. In the Age of Reason, great thinkers talked about _____.
   A religious differences   C the divine right of kings
   B myths and legends   D freedom and rights of people

5. In 1792, King Louis XVI was forced off the throne and France was declared a(n) _____.
   A monarchy   C republic
   B Communist country   D enemy of America

6. The person who probably said, "I am the state" is _____.
   A the Empress Josephine   C Lord Wellington
   B King Louis XIV   D King Louis XVIII

Part B Directions Write the correct word from the Word Bank to complete each sentence.

Word Bank
Commons
dictator
Josephine
philosophers
Thomas Jefferson

7. By the beginning of the 18th century, the House of _____ had the most power in Parliament.

8. The writings of the American patriot _____ helped in the efforts toward independence.

9. Ideas about people's rights were promoted by _____ in the 17th century.

10. By 1799, Napoleon held power in France; he was a _____.

11. _____ was crowned empress of France.

Pacemaker® World History

Unit 7 Mastery Test Page 2

Mastery Test, continued

Directions Match the description in Column A with the correct word in Column B. Write the correct answer on each line.

Column A

12. first king after the end of the Commonwealth
13. English philosopher
14. Estate that represented the French nobles
15. Paris prison attacked by a mob in July 1789
16. British general who defeated Napoleon at Waterloo

Column B

A Second
B Charles II
C Bastille
D Wellington
E John Locke

Directions Write the answers to these questions. Use complete sentences.

_____ was the main issue that the monarchy and Parliament argued over?

_____ the main difference in how people are chosen for the two Houses of Parliament?

_____ the American war for independence change people's thinking in France?

_____ the laws of France today affected by Napoleon?

Pacemaker® World History

Unit 7 Mastery Test Page 3

Mastery Test, continued

Directions Write your answer to each question. Use complete sentences. Support your answer with facts and examples from the textbook.

_____ how England's period of Enlightenment impacted American colonists. (2 points)

_____ you consider Oliver Cromwell's leadership helpful to England's people? _____ your reasoning. (2 points)

Directions Write a paragraph for each topic. Include a topic sentence, supporting details, and a conclusion. Support each answer with facts and examples from the textbook.

_____ lesson can you draw from what happened to Robespierre in the Reign of Terror? (3 points)

_____ re the rulers of Austria and Prussia afraid of the French Revolution? _____ think they were right to fear the events in France? Explain your reasoning. (3 points)

Pacemaker® World History

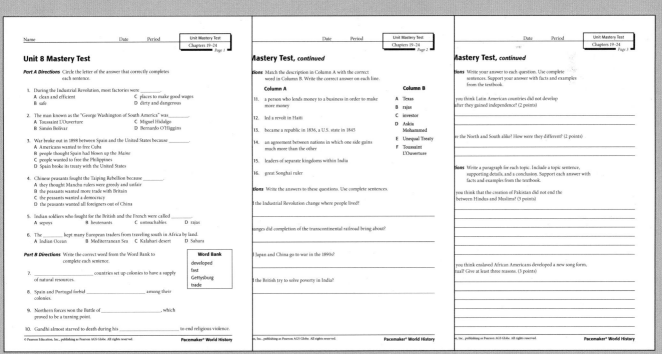

Unit 8 Mastery Test Page 1

Unit 8 Mastery Test

Part A Directions Circle the letter of the answer that correctly completes each sentence.

1. During the Industrial Revolution, most factories were _____.
   A clean and efficient   C places to make good wages
   B safe   D dirty and dangerous

2. The man known as the "George Washington of South America" was _____.
   A Toussaint L'Ouverture   C Miguel Hidalgo
   B Simón Bolívar   D Bernardo O'Higgins

3. War broke out in 1898 between Spain and the United States because _____.
   A Americans wanted to free Cuba
   B people thought Spain had blown up the *Maine*
   C people wanted to free the Philippines
   D Spain broke its treaty with the United States

4. Chinese peasants fought the Taiping Rebellion because _____.
   A they thought Manchu rulers were greedy and unfair
   B the peasants wanted more trade with Britain
   C the peasants wanted a democracy
   D the peasants wanted all foreigners out of China

5. Indian soldiers who fought for the British and the French were called _____.
   A sepoys   B lieutenants   C untouchables   D rajas

6. The _____ kept many European traders from traveling south in Africa by land.
   A Indian Ocean   B Mediterranean Sea   C Kalahari desert   D Sahara

Part B Directions Write the correct word from the Word Bank to complete each sentence.

Word Bank
developed
fast
Gettysburg
trade

7. _____ countries set up colonies to have a supply of natural resources.

8. Spain and Portugal forbid _____ among their colonies.

9. Northern forces won the Battle of _____, which proved to be a turning point.

10. Gandhi almost starved to death during his _____ to end religious violence.

Pacemaker® World History

Unit 8 Mastery Test Page 2

Mastery Test, continued

Directions Match the description in Column A with the correct word in Column B. Write the correct answer on each line.

Column A

11. a person who lends money to a business in order to make more money
12. led a revolt in Haiti
13. became a republic in 1836, a U.S. state in 1845
14. an agreement between nations in which one side gains much more than the other
15. leaders of separate kingdoms within India
16. great Songhai ruler

Column B

A Texas
B rajas
C investor
D Askia Mohammed
E Unequal Treaty
F Toussaint L'Ouverture

Directions Write the answers to these questions. Use complete sentences.

_____ the Industrial Revolution change where people lived?

_____ anges did completion of the transcontinental railroad bring about?

_____ Japan and China go to war in the 1890s?

_____ the British try to solve poverty in India?

Pacemaker® World History

Unit 8 Mastery Test Page 3

Mastery Test, continued

Directions Write your answer to each question. Use complete sentences. Support your answer with facts and examples from the textbook.

_____ you think Latin American countries did not develop _____ after they gained independence? (2 points)

_____ re the North and South alike? How were they different? (2 points)

Directions Write a paragraph for each topic. Include a topic sentence, supporting details, and a conclusion. Support each answer with facts and examples from the textbook.

_____ you think that the creation of Pakistan did not end the _____ between Hindus and Muslims? (3 points)

_____ you think enslaved African Americans developed a new song form, _____ tual? Give at least three reasons. (3 points)

Pacemaker® World History

Unit Mastery Test

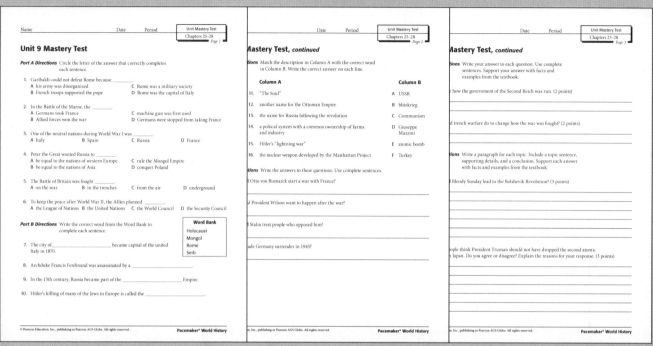

Unit 9 Mastery Test Page 1   Unit 9 Mastery Test Page 2   Unit 9 Mastery Test Page 3

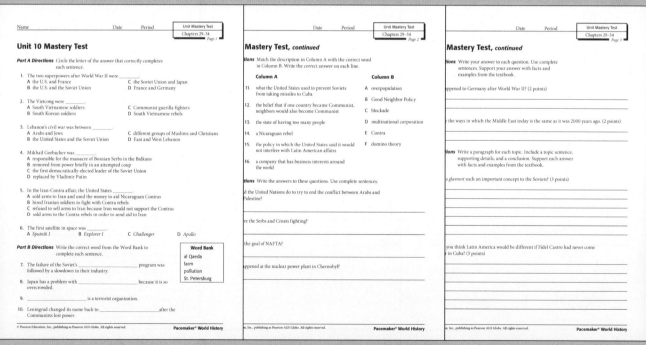

Unit 10 Mastery Test Page 1   Unit 10 Mastery Test Page 2   Unit 10 Mastery Test Page 3

Midterm Mastery Test

Midterm Mastery Test Page 1

Midterm Mastery Test

Part A Directions Circle the letter of the answer that correctly completes each sentence or answers each question.

1. Timelines show _____.
   - A when something took place
   - B where something took place
   - C how something took place
   - D why something took place

2. Which Sumerian invention has helped us learn the most about their civilization?
   - A the chariot
   - B an irrigation system
   - C trading boats
   - D cuneiform writing

3. The Babylonian empire _____.
   - A was built on rocky shores
   - B included the land that had once been Sumer
   - C conquered Egypt
   - D traded with Africa

4. Alexander the Great did **not** conquer _____.
   - A Persia
   - B Syria
   - C Egypt
   - D India

5. During the Middle Ages, _____ became less important.
   - A money
   - B learning
   - C trade
   - D military

6. The Inquisition was set up to _____.
   - A promote Lutheranism
   - B punish heretics
   - C spread Christianity to far-off lands
   - D spell out the beliefs of the church

7. Parliament presented Charles I with the _____.
   - A Petition of Right
   - B Magna Carta
   - C Bill of Rights
   - D Declaration of Independence

8. What brought an end to the Sumerian civilization?
   - A famine
   - B fighting among the city-states
   - C disease
   - D attack from invaders

9. Who was Alexander the Great's teacher? _____
   - A Philip
   - B King Darius
   - C Ptolemy
   - D Aristotle

10. Which one of these cities did **not** flourish during the Middle Ages?
    - A Constantinople
    - B Córdoba
    - C Alexandria
    - D Baghdad

Midterm Mastery Test Page 2

Midterm Mastery Test, *continued*

Part B Directions Write the correct word from the Word Bank to complete each sentence.

Word Bank
- aqueduct
- Carthage
- Christians
- Enlightenment
- gods
- Judaism
- Muslims
- myths
- temple
- Tenochtitlán

11. Sumerians built a(n) _____ at the center of their cities.

12. Sumerians and Egyptians both believed in many _____.

13. We still read about the acts of the Greek gods and goddesses in the _____ that have been written down.

14. A(n) _____ was a man made channel that brought fresh water into Rome.

15. The Crusades were Holy Wars between _____ and Muslims.

16. The city of _____ was built in the Aztec empire.

17. The Ten Commandments are an important part of Christianity and _____.

18. Rome battled _____ during the Punic Wars.

19. In the late 1400s, Spanish _____ were called Moors.

20. The Age of Reason was also called the _____.

Part C Directions Match the description in Column A with the correct word or words in Column B. Write the correct answer on each line.

	Column A	Column B
____ 21.	a thick sheet of ice that moves over land	A theory
____ 22.	a religion that believes greed and selfishness causes all problems	B John Locke
____ 23.	to rise up against a government	C knight
____ 24.	a high-ranking soldier of the Middle Ages	D dynasty
____ 25.	an explanation of how and why something happens	E glacier
____ 26.	an English philosopher	F Michelangelo
____ 27.	a family that rules a country for a long period of time	G conquistadors
____ 28.	the Germanic ruler of the Roman Empire in A.D. 800.	H Buddhism
____ 29.	the artist who painted the Sistine Chapel	I Charlemagne
____ 30.	Spanish explorers who traveled to Mexico and South America	J revolt

Midterm Mastery Test Page 3

Midterm Mastery Test, *continued*

Part D Directions Write the answers to these questions. Use complete sentences.

31. How did the Agricultural Revolution lead to people learning crafts?

32. Why did the pharaohs have people build the pyramids?

33. How were the castes in ancient India structured?

34. What happened to King Darius?

35. Give one reason the Black Death spread across Europe.

36. What was the difference between the Catholic Church and the Church of England?

37. Before modern times, what was the main link between China and the West?

38. Explain the significance of the Acropolis in ancient Greece.

39. Describe the system of feudalism.

40. What were the advantages of being a samurai in Japan?

Midterm Mastery Test Page 4

Midterm Mastery Test, *continued*

Part E Directions Write your answer to each question. Use complete sentences. Support your answer with facts and examples from the textbook.

41. Identify and describe a major change in world history. (2 points)

42. What made the Phoenician civilization different from most other Mediterranean civilizations? (2 points)

Part F Directions Write a paragraph for each topic. Include a topic sentence, supporting details, and a conclusion. Support your answer with facts and examples from the textbook.

43. Why did senators murder Julius Caesar? (3 points)

44. What do you think the world would be like today if the European settlers had never arrived in North America? (3 points)

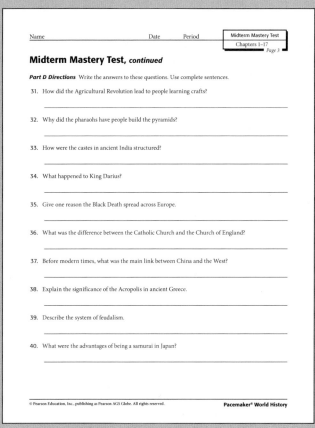

Final Mastery Test

Final Mastery Test

Part A Directions Circle the letter of the answer that correctly completes each sentence.

1. Historians call letters and diaries _____.
   A primary sources
   B secondary sources
   C unreliable sources
   D cultural sources

2. The secret knowledge of the Hittites was _____.
   A how to make iron.
   B how to irrigate fields.
   C how to write using the alphabet.
   D how to sail beyond the sight of land.

3. Roman art and architecture were influenced by the _____.
   A Etruscans   B provinces   C Senate   D Greeks

4. Renaissance artists _____.
   A only painted religious scenes
   B painted people as flat and lifeless
   C did not like Greek and Roman art
   D used live models

5. Parliament persuaded _____ to sign the Bill of Rights.
   A Edward I   B Charles II   C William and Mary   D George III

6. By the late 1700s, the population of China had grown too large for its _____.
   A government   B land area   C food supply   D housing supply

7. Karl Marx thought government _____.
   A should be socialist
   B should be ruled by industry
   C should be soviet
   D should not be necessary

8. Manuel Noriega was taken from Panama to _____.
   A vacation in Europe
   B attend peace talks in the Middle East
   C be executed
   D stand trial in the United States

9. The Enlightenment was also called the Age of _____.
   A Intellect   B Rejoice   C Reason   D Wonder

10. _____ signed the first treaty with Japan.
    A France   B America   C Russia   D Great Britain

Final Mastery Test Page 1

Final Mastery Test, *continued*

11. Peter the Great was given his name because he _____.
    A was a great warrior
    B brought Western ideas to Russia
    C was generous to the common people
    D built a great navy

12. OPEC is powerful because it _____.
    A controls the supply of oil to many other countries
    B controls the supply of fresh water to the Middle East
    C is run by the U.S. and Great Britain
    D produces many different natural resources

13. The term *glasnost* means _____.
    A tension   B freedom   C openness   D conflict

14. A _____ is an unmanned object that orbits around the earth.
    A cosmonaut   B satellite   C *Sputnik*   D shuttle

15. AIDS is most widespread in _____.
    A Africa   B western Europe   C Australia   D South America

Part B Directions Write the correct word from the Word Bank to complete each sentence.

Word Bank
Armada
Communist
Huns
labor unions
locomotives
Mesopotamia
nirvana
nonviolent resistance
nuclear
Zulus

16. Another word for "land between two rivers" is _____.

17. The Buddhists believe that _____ breaks the cycle of death and suffering.

18. The _____ were a tribe of wild horsemen.

19. The Spanish _____ was not able to defeat the small, fast English navy.

20. British _____ protested the working conditions in the factories.

21. Gandhi sought independence through _____, refraining from harming or injuring any British soldiers.

22. The United States used a(n) _____ weapon against Japan.

23. Fidel Castro set up a(n) _____ dictatorship in Cuba.

24. Early steam _____ changed transportation in Europe and the United States.

25. The African kingdom of the _____ fought against European rule.

Final Mastery Test Page 2

Final Mastery Test, *continued*

Part C Directions Match the description in Column A with the correct word in Column B. Write the correct answer on each line.

	Column A		Column B
_____ 26.	a person of high social rank	A	homage
_____ 27.	a deadly disease that spreads quickly	B	Portuguese
_____ 28.	a pledge of loyalty made to kings and lords	C	Haiti
_____ 29.	a large city where many Aztecs lived	D	noble
_____ 30.	the children of native women and Spanish settlers	E	isolationism
_____ 31.	the earliest European slave traders	F	mestizos
_____ 32.	the easing of tensions between countries	G	legislature
_____ 33.	the first Latin American colony to fight for freedom	H	plague
_____ 34.	a group of people who make the laws of a nation	I	détente
_____ 35.	the policy of staying out of the affairs of other nations	J	Tenochtitlán

---

Final Mastery Test Page 3

Final Mastery Test, *continued*

Part D Directions Write the answers to these questions. Use complete sentences.

36. How were Sumer and Egypt's religions alike?
_____

37. How would you describe the city of Alexandria, Egypt?
_____

38. How did Muhammad change the way Arabs thought of God?
_____

39. How did most Africans come to the Americas?
_____

40. Why did U.S. leaders want the Panama Canal?
_____

41. Who ruled most of the Italian kingdoms and states in 1815?
_____

42. What two religious groups fought in Lebanon's civil war?
_____
_____

Final Mastery Test Page 4

Final Mastery Test

Page 5

Name _____ Date _____ Period _____

Final Mastery Test
Chapters 1–34
Page 5

Final Mastery Test, *continued*

43. What was the purpose of the Monroe Doctrine?
_____
_____

44. Why did the United States enter World War I?
_____
_____

45. Why are the United States and other nations concerned about North Korea?
_____
_____

Part E Directions Put the following events in order from earliest to latest.
For instance, if the event happened first, write a 1 next
to the event on the line.

_____ 46. the beginning of World War II

_____ 47. the French Revolution

_____ 48. the terrorist attacks in New York City

_____ 49. the beginning of British rule in India

_____ 50. the end of the cold war

Pacemaker® **World History**

Page 6

Name _____ Date _____ Period _____

Final Mastery Test
Chapters 1–34
Page 6

Final Mastery Test, *continued*

Part F Directions Write your answer to each question. Use complete
sentences. Support your answer with facts and
examples from the textbook.

51. Why did the French Revolution result in widespread war in Europe? (2 points)
_____
_____

52. What did trench warfare do to change how World War I was fought? (2 points)
_____
_____

Part G Directions Write a paragraph for each topic. Include a topic
sentence, supporting details, and a conclusion. Support
your answer with facts and examples from the textbook.

53. How did being defeated in World War II help Japan become more powerful? (3 points)
_____
_____
_____
_____
_____

54. Do you think the United States has a responsibility to help keep peace in Europe?
Why or why not? (3 points)
_____
_____
_____
_____
_____

Pacemaker® **World History**

Midterm and Final Mastery Test

The lists below show how the items from the Midterm and Final Mastery Tests correlate to the chapters in the student edition.

Activities

Activity 1—History Is All About Change
Part A: 1. history **2.** business **3.** slavery **4.** culture **5.** revolution
6. growth **7.** nationalism **8.** imperialism **9.** farming
Part B: Hidden word: historian

Activity 2—Historians and Archaeologists
1. primary **2.** secondary **3.** primary **4.** primary **5.** secondary
6. primary **7.** primary **8.** secondary **9.** primary **10.** primary
11. primary **12.** secondary **13.** primary **14.** secondary **15.** primary

Activity 3—Maps and Timelines
1. 10,000 B.C. **2.** A.D. 2000 **3.** before **4.** Egyptian **5.** Renaissance
6. 4000 B.C. **7.** 1500 B.C. **8.** A.D. 1400 **9.** A.D. **10.** David

Activity 4—The Hunters
1. summer **2.** heavy **3.** Ice Age **4.** successful **5.** south **6.** melt
7. metal **8.** weapons **9.** food **10.** Stone Age

Activity 5—The Agricultural Revolution
1. FS **2.** FS **3.** LC **4.** FS **5.** LC **6.** LC **7.** LC **8.** FS **9.** FS **10.** LC

Activity 6—The Fertile Crescent
1. A **2.** G **3.** D **4.** B **5.** C **6.** F **7.** E **8.** H **9.** J **10.** I

Activity 7—The Sumerian Civilization
Part A: 1. Tigris, Euphrates **2.** Euphrates **3.** Persian Gulf **4.** Caspian Sea **5.** Nile
Part B: 6. A **7.** D **8.** B **9.** C **10.** B

Activity 8—Sumerian City-States
1. reeds **2.** swamp **3.** bricks **4.** cooler **5.** temple **6.** gods **7.** crops
8. wealthy **9.** city-states **10.** government **11.** independent
12. fought **13.** walls **14.** Ur **15.** ziggurat

Activity 9—Sumerian Inventions
Part A: 1. created **2.** tablets **3.** scribes **4.** contract **5.** merchants
6. pictographs **7.** wedge **8.** cuneiform **9.** chariots **10.** writing
Part B: 11. created **12.** tablets **13.** scribes **14.** contract **15.** merchants
16. pictographs **17.** wedge **18.** cuneiform **19.** chariots **20.** writing

Activity 10—Life in Sumer
1. B **2.** A **3.** D **4.** C **5.** B

Activity 11—Egypt and the Nile
1. B **2.** A **3.** B **4.** C **5.** D **6.** D **7.** B **8.** A **9.** C **10.** B

Activity 12—The Pyramids
1. transport **2.** powerful **3.** ramps **4.** mummy **5.** museums
6. pyramids **7.** Herodotus **8.** rich **9.** Cairo **10.** tombs

Activity 13—Egyptian Culture
1. rich **2.** kohl **3.** hair **4.** gods **5.** death **6.** hieroglyphics **7.** paper
8. metal **9.** music **10.** pyramids

Activity 14—The Phoenicians
1. eastern **2.** wood **3.** navigate **4.** colony **5.** Gibraltar **6.** Atlantic
7. Carthage **8.** gold **9.** pottery **10.** taxes **11.** sails **12.** alphabet
13. letters **14.** snails **15.** Tyre

Activity 15—The Israelites
1. D **2.** A **3.** C **4.** B **5.** C **6.** A **7.** C **8.** D **9.** B **10.** A

Activity 16—The Babylonians
1. capital **2.** Euphrates **3.** temples **4.** bricks **5.** bronze **6.** Tower
7. Hanging Gardens **8.** empire **9.** Hammurabi **10.** code

Activity 17—The Hittites
1. D **2.** C **3.** G **4.** A **5.** H **6.** B **7.** E **8.** F **9.** D **10.** F **11.** C **12.** A
13. B **14.** G **15.** E

Activity 18—The Assyrians
Part A: 1. P, I, H **2.** B **3.** P, I, B, H, A **4.** I **5.** I **6.** H, A **7.** H **8.** I
9. P **10.** B
Part B: Students' paragraphs should be supported by facts and examples from the textbook.

Activity 19—Ancient India
1. C **2.** B **3.** A **4.** B **5.** D **6.** B **7.** A **8.** B **9.** A **10.** D

Activity 20—Buddhism
1. nirvana **2.** selfishness **3.** forest **4.** reincarnation **5.** brotherly
6. Maurya **7.** Asoka **8.** caste **9.** empire **10.** pagodas

Activity 21—Early China
1. flood control **2.** north **3.** Chang Jiang **4.** silkworms **5.** mountain
6. isolated **7.** 15 years **8.** mud **9.** 25 feet **10.** Han dynasty

Activity 22—Early America
1. H **2.** A **3.** F **4.** J **5.** D **6.** G **7.** I **8.** B **9.** E **10.** C

Activity 23—The Sea and Ancient Greece
1. grapevines **2.** colonies **3.** papyrus **4.** ebony **5.** Naples
6. mountain **7.** government **8.** tyrant **9.** democracy **10.** citizen
11. fought **12.** Sparta **13.** invaders **14.** Acropolis **15.** Athena

Activity 24—Athens and Sparta
1. S **2.** A **3.** S **4.** A **5.** A **6.** S **7.** A **8.** S **9.** A, S **10.** A **11.** A, S
12. A **13.** S **14.** A, S **15.** A

Activity 25—Fighting in Greece
1. C **2.** A **3.** B **4.** C **5.** D **6.** A **7.** B **8.** A **9.** B **10.** D

Activity 26—Gifts from the Greeks
Part A: 1. athletes **2.** Pericles **3.** architecture **4.** classical **5.** truth
6. columns **7.** wrestling **8.** Olympia **9.** Zeus
Part B: Hidden word: Aristotle

Activity 27—King Philip and Alexander
1. C **2.** A **3.** D **4.** A **5.** B **6.** D **7.** C **8.** A **9.** B **10.** C

Activity 28—Alexander's Conquests
1. Persia 2. escaped 3. Syria 4. bridge 5. Egypt 6. cities 7. Ptolemy
8. Persepolis 9. India 10. Alexander

Activity 29—The End of an Empire
1. thirty 2. unite 3. Babylon 4. plants 5. largest 6. ill 7. medicines
8. Alexandria 9. divided 10. Greek

Activity 30—How Rome Grew Powerful
1. E 2. B 3. D 4. A 5. C 6. D 7. E 8. C 9. A 10. B 11. B 12. A 13. C 14. E
15. D

Activity 31—Julius Caesar
1. A 2. D 3. B 4. D 5. C 6. B 7. D 8. A 9. C 10. B

Activity 32—The Roman Empire
1. A 2. A 3. O 4. O 5. A 6. O 7. A 8. O 9. O 10. A

Activity 33—Roman Society
1. paved 2. fountains 3. temple 4. Forum 5. columns 6. social
7. holidays 8. chariot 9. arches 10. roads 11. sewer 12. Latin
13. dining 14. apartment 15. useful

Activity 34—Christianity in Rome
1. D 2. I 3. A 4. F 5. G 6. H 7. B 8. J 9. E 10. C

Activity 35—The End of the Empire
I. 2, 4, 7, 10, 14 II. 6, 8, 11, 12, 15 III. 1, 3, 5, 9, 13

Activity 36—The Fall of the Western Roman Empire
1. C 2. A 3. A 4. D 5. C 6. A 7. B 8. D 9. D 10. A

Activity 37—The Byzantine Empire
1. Byzantine 2. Charlemagne 3. Franks 4. emperor 5. Christian
6. Greek 7. schools 8. Christmas 9. crumbled 10. divided

Activity 38—The Vikings
Part A: 1. 4 2. 3 3. 2 4. 5 5. 1
Part B: 6. tradition 7. Hastings 8. sailors 9. Normandy 10. exiled

Activity 39—Feudalism
1. N, F 2. N 3. N, F, S 4. N 5. F, S 6. F, S 7. F 8. N 9. S 10. F
11. N 12. S 13. N 14. F, S 15. N, F, S

Activity 40—Religion During the Middle Ages
1. church 2. Christian 3. nobility 4. land 5. clergy 6. powerful
7. warriors 8. monks 9. convents 10. studying

Activity 41—Life in the Middle Ages
1. D 2. C 3. A 4. B 5. C

Activity 42—Muhammad and Islam
1. C 2. B 3. D 4. A 5. B 6. D 7. A 8. C 10. D

Activity 43—The Crusades
1. pilgrimage 2. Crusade 3. peasants 4. Jerusalem 5. Christians
6. Turks 7. Saladin 8. Frederick 9. Richard 10. truce

Activity 44—The Costs of the Crusades
1. give them glory 2. cost much money and many lives 3. Jerusalem
4. none 5. meat and plants that grew in Europe 6. rice, apricots,
lemons, melons, and spices 7. cotton and wool from what they grew
in Europe 8. brightly-colored silks 9. from the European leaders and
feudal lords 10. from ideas shared with other cultures during travel and
trade

Activity 45—Changes in Agriculture
1. C 2. D 3. E 4. G 5. B 6. F 7. I 8. J 9. H 10. A

Activity 46—Changes in City Life
1. fewer 2. city 3. stone 4. disease 5. money 6. free 7. stronger
8. apprentice 9. no pay 10. silver

Activity 47—The Magna Carta
Part A: 1. 3 2. 5 3. 2 4. 1 5. 4
Part B: 6. happiness 7. nobles 8. power 9. army 10. charter

Activity 48—A Time of New Ideas
Part A: 1. M 2. R 3. M 4. R 5. R 6. M 7. M 8. R 9. M 10. R
Part B: 11. M 12. R 13. R 14. M 15. R

Activity 49—Renaissance Art
1. F 2. I 3. I 4. F 5. F 6. F 7. I 8. I 9. F 10. I 11. F 12. F 13. I
14. I 15. I

Activity 50—Advances in Knowledge, Technology, and Science
1. C 2. E 3. A 4. B 5. D 6. G 7. J 8. F 9. H 10. I

Activity 51—The Renaissance Man
Part A: 1. talents 2. poetry 3. sculptor 4. inventor 5. architect
6. sketchbooks 7. machines 8. Duke 9. birds 10. engineer
11. parachute 12. *Mona Lisa*
Part B: Hidden place: Louvre Museum

Activity 52—The Reformation
1. criticize 2. power 3. Reformation 4. monk 5. sermons
6. Wittenberg 7. authority 8. recant 9. outlaw 10. Lutheranism
11. Protestants 12. Switzerland 13. Huguenots 14. Inquisition
15. heretics

Activity 53—The Counter-Reformation
Part A: 1. B 2. C 3. D 4. A 5. E
Part B: 6. Loyola 7. Protestants 8. Paris 9. Society of Jesus
10. Council of Trent

Activity 54—Rule by Monarchs
1. C 2. A 3. D 4. B 5. D 6. A 7. B 8. A 9. B 10. D

Activity 55—Spanish Monarchs
1. Ferdinand 2. Catholic 3. Moors 4. Inquisition 5. Philip
6. Protestantism 7. Netherlands 8. independence 9. Mary
10. Elizabeth

Activity 56—French Monarchs
1. Huguenots 2. civil 3. massacre 4. Navarre 5. Protestant
6. Catholic 7. freedom 8. rich 9. Quebec 10. assassinated

Activity 57—English Monarchs
1. H **2.** M **3.** H **4.** H **5.** M **6.** H **7.** E **8.** M **9.** H **10.** E

Activity 58—China
Part A: Students should enter checkmarks in the following numbered boxes: 4, 7, 8, 14, 16, 18, 19, and 24.
Part B: 25. Accept any well-written answer in which students use complete sentences with proper punctuation.

Activity 59—Japan
Part A: 1. C **2.** D **3.** C **4.** B **5.** A **6.** C **7.** D **8.** D **9.** A **10.** B **11.** D **12.** D
Part B: 13. Answers will vary. Accept any answer based on details from the first paragraph of the student text on page 313. The people of Japan copied writing, arts and crafts, and the calendar system from China. **14.** The nobles and the samurai looked down on people involved in trade. **15.** The shogun closed the doors to Japan because he feared that foreign ideas would upset Japanese culture.

Activity 60—India
Akbar
1. He was Babar's grandson. **2.** He extended Mogul rule to most of India. **3.** He allowed freedom of religion. [Alternatively 1–3: He was a Muslim.]
Asoka
4. He became emperor in 268 B.C. **5.** He converted to Buddhism.
Aurangzeb
6. He was Shah Jahan's son. **7.** He put his father in prison. **8.** He destroyed Hindu temples. [Alternatively 6–8: He made Hindus pay a special tax.]
Babar
9. He was a direct descendant of Genghis Khan. **10.** He conquered northern India. **11.** He established the Mogul Empire and made himself emperor.
Shah Jahan
12. He was the grandson of Akbar. **13.** He had the Taj Mahal built.
Tamerlane
14. He invaded India. **15.** He captured Delhi.

Activity 61—The Americas
Part A: 1. D **2.** A **3.** C **4.** D **5.** B **6.** A **7.** C **8.** A
Part B: 9. The mound builders buried people and built temples on top of giant mounds. **10.** The Pueblo Indians are descendants of the Anasazi. **11.** The Anasazi abandoned their cliff villages around A.D. 1300 and moved on. **12.** The Aztecs favored the pyramid style for building their temples. **13.** The Aztecs did not have money; instead, they bartered for goods they needed. **14.** Tenochtitlán was larger than any Spanish city of the day. It had floating gardens, drawbridges, and markets. **15.** Stories of gold, silver, and jewels drew Pizarro to the Inca Empire.

Activity 62— Exploring New Lands
1. C **2.** B **3.** D **4.** B **5.** A

Activity 63—Conquering South America
1. Vikings **2.** Vasco da Gama **3.** Pedro Cabral **4.** Ferdinand Magellan **5.** Aztecs **6.** Incas **7.** Hernando Cortés **8.** Tenochtitlán **9.** Francisco Pizarro **10.** Sir John Hawkins

Activity 64—Settling in North America
Across: 3. Quebec **4.** nation **5.** east **6.** plantation **10.** Dragon **11.** corn **12.** pirate
Down: 1. Puritan **2.** Hudson **6.** Pilgrim **7.** trappers **8.** tobacco **9.** wary **10.** Drake

Activity 65—Trading with the Colonies
1. 1492 **2.** 1500 **3.** eight **4.** 1519 **5.** three **6.** 1521 **7.** 11 **8.** 1562 **9.** six **10.** 30 **11.** 13 **12.** Quebec **13.** 74 **14.** 1759 **15.** 151

Activity 66—The Beginnings of Democracy
1. C **2.** D **3.** A **4.** A **5.** C **6.** A **7.** B **8.** D **9.** A **10.** A

Activity 67—The Kind Tries to Limit Democracy
1. divine **2.** jail **3.** petition **4.** consent **5.** Scotland **6.** Royalists **7.** Roundheads **8.** Cromwell **9.** Commonwealth **10.** Ireland

Activity 68—The Glorious Revolution
1. C **2.** I **3.** J **4.** F **5.** B **6.** H **7.** A **8.** D **9.** E **10.** G

Activity 69—Revolution in America
1. taxes **2.** revolution **3.** approved **4.** loyalty **5.** leader **6.** representation **7.** colonists **8.** patriot **9.** rights **10.** liberty

Activity 70—The Age of Reason in France
Part A: Answers will vary. **1.** King Louis XIV the King of France in the early 1700s. He believed he ruled by divine right, so no one could challenge him. **2.** Rousseau wrote about freedom and political rights. **3.** Lafayette helped George Washington fight for freedom in America. **4.** Voltaire wrote about freedom and political rights. **5.** George Washington led the American war for independence from British rule.
Part B: Answers will vary. **6.** The nobles lived in luxury under rule by the French kings. **7.** The peasants lived badly under the rule of the French kings. They had hardly anything to eat. **8.** The Age of Reason was a time when people talked about freedom and rights for people. **9.** The French nobles supported the American war for independence because they were happy to see their enemy, Britain, defeated by anyone. **10.** The French peasants supported the American war for independence because they liked the idea of a fight against tyranny.

Activity 71—The King Tries to Limit Democracy
Part A: 1. Estates-General **2.** Second **3.** Third **4.** Bastille **5.** Assembly **6.** Prussia **7.** Convention **8.** republic **9.** Robespierre **10.** guillotine
Part B: 11. The Third Estate asked the king for more voting power because it could be outvoted by the First and Second estates, even though the Third Estate represented about 98 percent of the population. **12.** The French Declaration of the Rights of Man is similar to the American Declaration of Independence. **13.** The nobles lost all of their special privileges during the French Revolution. **14.** It meant freedom, the same rights for everyone, and the brotherhood of all. **15.** The leaders of the revolution forced the king off the throne because they believed he had betrayed France by plotting with enemies such as Austria and Prussia.

Activity 72—Napoleon Bonaparte
Part A: 1. D **2.** E **3.** A **4.** C **5.** B
Part B: 6. B **7.** C **8.** A **9.** E **10.** D

Part C: **11.** The nobles came back because Napoleon said they would be safe if they would be loyal to him. **12.** Napoleon strengthened and reorganized French schools. **13.** Prussia, Sweden, Austria, and Russia joined with Great Britain to defeat Napoleon. **14.** A group of Prussian soldiers arrived during the Battle of Waterloo to help the British and their allies fight against Napoleon. **15.** After Napoleon, France's political life was unstable, with a number of revolutions and changes in government.

Activity 73—Industries Develop
1. B **2.** C **3.** A **4.** C **5.** D **6.** C **7.** B **8.** D **9.** A **10.** C

Activity 74—New Inventions
Part A: 1. steam engine **2.** flying shuttle **3.** spinning jenny **4.** water frame **5.** mule **6.** steam-powered loom **7.** steam locomotive **8.** steamboat **9.** dynamo **10.** telegraph
Part B: 11. Michael Faraday **12.** John Kay **13.** James Watt **14.** Samuel Crompton **15.** James Hargreaves **16.** Robert Fulton **17.** Thomas Savery **18.** Richard Trevithick **19.** Edmund Cartwright **20.** Richard Arkwright

Activity 75—The Industrial Revolution Changes Life
Part A: Checked statements should be 1, 2, 4, 7, 8, and 10.
Part B: 11. NR **12.** NR **13.** FP **14.** NR **15.** FP **16.** NR **17.** NR **18.** FP **19.** NR **20.** FP

Activity 76—The Industrial Revolution Spreads
1. B **2.** C **3.** D **4.** A **5.** D **6.** B **7.** C **8.** C **9.** A **10.** B

Activity 77—Colonization
1. A **2.** B **3.** B **4.** C **5.** D **6.** C **7.** A **8.** C **9.** D **10.** C

Activity 78—Colonies Fight for Independence
1. slave **2.** France **3.** priests **4.** Spain **5.** Colombia **6.** dictator **7.** Argentina **8.** Portugal **9.** Brazil **10.** dictators

Activity 79—Latin American Culture
1. culture **2.** rural **3.** mural **4.** sadness **5.** dominate **6.** Spain **7.** Portugal **8.** African **9.** influence **10.** French

Activity 80—Imperialism and Growth
Part A: 1. LP **2.** MD **3.** LP **4.** LP **5.** LP **6.** LP **7.** MD **8.** MD **9.** LP **10.** MD
Part B: 11. No. The Monroe Doctrine was only concerned with European nations meddling in the Americas. The admission of a new U.S. state concerned only the United States. **12.** Yes. The Monroe Doctrine warns European nations not to start new colonies in the Americas or to expand existing ones. This warning would apply to such action by Britain. **13.** No. The Monroe Doctrine would only apply if Spain were trying to meddle in American affairs. **14.** No. The Monroe Doctrine was only concerned with European nations meddling in the Americas. The admission of a new U.S. state concerned only the United States. **15.** Yes. The situation describes France meddling in the affairs of Mexico and trying to control that Latin American nation. This situation is precisely what the Monroe Doctrine warned European nations against.

Activity 81—Border Problems
Part A: 1. border **2.** Alamo **3.** treaty **4.** Santa Anna **5.** Davy Crockett **6.** California **7.** Rio Grande **8.** Texas
Part B: 9. A **10.** D **11.** C **12.** B **13.** C **14.** C **15.** B

Activity 82—The American Civil War
Part A: 1. A **2.** H **3.** G **4.** E **5.** B **6.** C **7.** F **8.** D
Part B: 9. President Lincoln decided to go to war because he wanted to save the Union. **10.** Northerners expected to win the war quickly because the North had more manufacturing and industry and could produce more guns and cannons. **11.** Southern plantations used enslaved workers. **12.** The South was able to win many battles because its armies were led by brilliant generals. **13.** The turning point in the war was the Battle of Gettysburg, which the North won. **14.** Lincoln's *Emancipation Proclamation* outlawed slavery in areas that were rebelling against the Union. **15.** Lincoln did achieve his goal. He wanted to save the Union, and the North did this (even though the war was long and terrible).

Activity 83—U.S. Expansion
Part A: 1. industrial **2.** pineapple **3.** Harbor **4.** territory **5.** Spain **6.** Cuba **7.** Philippines **8.** Colombia **9.** Zone **10.** Pacific
Part B: 11. Samuel F.B. Morse invented the telegraph, which greatly improved communications. **12.** Cyrus McCormick invented a mechanical reaper, which allowed farmers to harvest grain more quickly. **13.** Queen Liliuokalani ruled Hawaii until she was overthrown in 1893. **14.** Secretary of State William Seward persuaded the U.S. government to buy Alaska from Russia in 1867. **15.** President Theodore Roosevelt wanted the United States to build the Panama Canal.

Activity 84—China Under Manchurian Rule
1. B **2.** A **3.** D **4.** C **5.** C **6.** B **7.** A **8.** C **9.** D **10.** A

Activity 85—Chinese Rebellion
Part A: 1. 5 **2.** 3 **3.** 2 **4.** 1 **5.** 4
Part B: 6. G **7.** E **8.** D **9.** C **10.** I **11.** B **12.** J **13.** H **14.** F **15.** A

Activity 86—Japan Opens Its Doors
Part A: 1. Meiji **2.** shogun **3.** trade **4.** warships **5.** Russia **6.** Harris **7.** advised **8.** industry **9.** Commodore
Part B: Hidden word: Mutsuhito

Activity 87—The British East India Company
1. D **2.** A **3.** B **4.** D **5.** B **6.** D **7.** B **8.** A **9.** D **10.** B

Activity 88—British Rule
1. I **2.** I **3.** B **4.** I **5.** B **6.** I **7.** I **8.** B **9.** B **10.** I

Activity 89—Mahatma Gandhi
1. lawyer **2.** Congress **3.** refuse **4.** bloodshed **5.** Mahatma **6.** stronger **7.** poor **8.** trains **9.** jail **10.** Pakistan

Activity 90—Early Kingdoms in Africa
Part A: 1. D **2.** F **3.** H **4.** E **5.** G **6.** B **7.** C **8.** A
Part B: 9. The Kushites learned how to mine iron ore and make iron weapons. These skills helped the Kushites grow strong enough to conquer Egypt. **10.** Christianity influenced Kush and Aksum around A.D. 350. **11.** The Arab traders and people of Ghana traded salt for gold. **12.** The Arab caravans brought Islam to Ghana, which created tensions between Muslim converts and people who kept the

old religions. **13.** Timbuktu became a center of Muslim learning after Mali's king Mansa Musa invited Arab scholars to come to his kingdom and teach. **14.** Accept any two examples: Mansa Musa took hundreds of enslaved people. Each slave carried a solid gold staff. There were 80 camels, each loaded with a bag of gold dust. Mansa Musa gave out gold and other gifts. **15.** King Mohamed al-Mansur of Morocco was able to defeat Songhai warriors because the Moroccans had guns, but the Songhai warriors had only spears.

Activity 91—Africa After the First Century A.D.
Part A: **1.** C **2.** D **3.** C **4.** B **5.** A **6.** D **7.** D **8.** B
Part B: **9.** Shaka was a fierce ruler of the Zulus. Under Shaka, the Zulus were very strong. **10.** Vasco da Gama was a Portuguese sea captain. He discovered the sea route around Africa while searching for a trade route to India.

Activity 92—The African Slave Trade
1. Portuguese **2.** gold **3.** Spanish **4.** French **5.** Dutch (Answers to 4 and 5 may be transposed.) **6.** Americas **7.** ships **8.** Africans **9.** Britain **10.** slavery

Activity 93—European Imperialism
Part A: **1.** raw **2.** rules **3.** missionaries **4.** Liberia **5.** tribes **6.** inferior **7.** railroads
Part B: **8.** The Europeans wanted raw materials for their industries, and they wanted markets for their finished products. **9.** It took 30 years. The conference was in 1884, and by 1914 Europeans had taken over all of Africa except Liberia and Ethiopia. **10.** The Europeans made agreements with local tribal chiefs, gave them presents, and offered them chances for trade. However, they paid little or no attention to tribal differences. So they ended up putting very different groups of people into artificial "countries" that they created.

Activity 94—Nationalism in Italy
1. D **2.** B **3.** A **4.** C **5.** B **6.** A **7.** C **8.** D **9.** A **10.** B

Activity 95—Nationalism in Germany
Part A: **1.** D **2.** A **3.** B **4.** C **5.** E **6.** B **7.** E **8.** A **9.** C **10.** D
Part B: **11.** C **12.** J **13.** E **14.** A **15.** G **16.** D **17.** F **18.** B **19.** H **20.** I

Activity 96—The War Begins in Europe
1. B **2.** A **3.** D **4.** C **5.** B **6.** C **7.** D **8.** A **9.** B **10.** C

Activity 97—The Fighting
1. C **2.** A **3.** C **4.** A **5.** A **6.** C **7.** A **8.** A **9.** C **10.** A

Activity 98—The End of the War
1. Germany **2.** armistice **3.** France **4.** blame **5.** rebuild **6.** Britain **7.** conflicts **8.** Switzerland **9.** support **10.** Article Ten

Activity 99—The Early History of Russia
Part A: **1.** D **2.** C **3.** F **4.** J **5.** A **6.** G **7.** B **8.** I **9.** E **10.** H
Part B: **11.** B **12.** D **13.** E **14.** A **15.** C

Activity 100—Unrest in the Early 1900s
Part A: **1.** F **2.** I **3.** I **4.** F **5.** I **6.** F **7.** I **8.** F **9.** I **10.** I
Part B: Circled phrases should be B, D, E, H, and J.

Activity 101—Russia Becomes the USSR
1. C **2.** D **3.** A **4.** B **5.** D

Activity 102—The Rise of Dictators
1. C; E **2.** E; C **3.** E; C **4.** C; E **5.** E; C **6.** C; E **7.** E; C **8.** C; E **9.** E; C **10.** E; C

Activity 103—World War II Begins in Europe
1. C **2.** B **3.** E **4.** A **5.** D **6.** B **7.** D **8.** A **9.** E **10.** C

Activity 104—The Holocaust and Allied Victories
1. B **2.** A **3.** D **4.** C **5.** D

Activity 105—The End of the War
1. Bulge **2.** Berlin **3.** executed **4.** kamikaze **5.** Pacific **6.** nuclear **7.** atomic **8.** surrender **9.** Truman **10.** Nagasaki

Activity 106—The Results of the War
Part A: Checked statements should be 1, 2, 4, 6, 9, and 10.
Part B: **11.** after **12.** after **13.** before **14.** after **15.** before

Activity 107—The World After World War II
1. B **2.** D **3.** A **4.** D **5.** C **6.** C **7.** C **8.** D **9.** D **10.** B

Activity 108—The Cold War Begins
1. U **2.** U **3.** S **4.** S **5.** U **6.** S **7.** S **8.** S **9.** U **10.** U

Activity 109—Changing Relations Between the Soviets and Americans
Part A: **1.** Afghanistan **2.** shot down **3.** détente **4.** missiles **5.** Arms
Part B: **6.** The Soviet Union and the United States set up a détente and agreed to cooperate. **7.** The countries held Strategic Arms Limitation Talks. **8.** The Communists took over Afghanistan. **9.** The United States sends more missiles to Europe. **10.** A Korean Air Lines jet was shot down by the Soviets.

Activity 110—India
1. C; E **2.** E; C **3.** E; C **4.** C; E **5.** E; C **6.** E; C **7.** C; E **8.** E; C **9.** C; E **10.** E; C

Activity 111—China
1. Chiang Kai-shek was the leader of the Nationalist Party. **2.** Mao Zedong got his support from the peasants. **3.** Chiang Kai-shek left mainland China to live in Taiwan. **4.** The United States now recognizes the People's Republic of China. **5.** More than one-fifth of the population of the world lives in China. **6.** Farm workers live and work in communes. **7.** China's economy declined during the Cultural Revolution. **8.** Deng Xiaoping gave the Chinese people more economic freedom. **9.** China trades with the West. **10.** Great Britain returned Hong Kong to China in 1997.

Activity 112—Korea
1. C **2.** B **3.** A **4.** C **5.** D **6.** B **7.** D **8.** A **9.** C **10.** B

Activity 113—Japan and Southeast Asia
1. occupied **2.** democratic **3.** military **4.** colonized **5.** independence **6.** civil **7.** manufacturer **8.** electronics **9.** resources **10.** pollution **11.** imports **12.** invested **13.** competition **14.** exports **15.** restrictions

Activity 114—Vietnam
1. B **2.** D **3.** B **4.** C **5.** A

Activity 115—Asia and Africa: 1945–present
1. B **2.** A **3.** D **4.** C **5.** B **6.** D **7.** A **8.** B **9.** C **10.** D

Activity 116—The Fight for Palestine
1. C **2.** A **3.** D **4.** B **5.** C

Activity 117—The Middle East Remains in Conflict
1. D **2.** A **3.** C **4.** E **5.** B **6.** C **7.** E **8.** B **9.** A **10.** D

Activity 118—Oil
1. F **2.** O **3.** O **4.** F **5.** O **6.** F **7.** F **8.** O **9.** F **10.** F **11.** F **12.** O **13.** O **14.** F **15.** O

Activity 119—Life in the Middle East
1. conflict **2.** industrialized **3.** modern **4.** rocky **5.** agricultural **6.** irrigation **7.** saltwater **8.** Red Sea **9.** civilizations **10.** common

Activity 120—Changes in the Soviet Union
1. A **2.** C **3.** D **4.** B **5.** A **6.** D **7.** C **8.** D **9.** A **10.** C

Activity 121— The End of the Soviet Union and Cold War
1. D **2.** E **3.** B **4.** A **5.** F **6.** H **7.** J **8.** G **9.** I **10.** C

Activity 122— Changes in Eastern Europe
1. troops **2.** Solidarity **3.** Lech Walesa **4.** reunification **5.** executed **6.** Yugoslavia **7.** Dayton Accords **8.** Serbia **9.** Slobodan Milosevic **10.** Chechnya

Activity 123—The United States in Latin American Affairs
1. The Pan-American conference took place before World War II. **2.** The Good Neighbor Policy said that the United States would not interfere in Latin America. **3.** The members of OAS include the United States and independent countries of Latin America. **4.** U.S. aid was sometimes unwelcome in Latin America. **5.** Latin America was not stable for the first half of the 20th century. **6.** There was a revolution in Cuba in 1959. **7.** Fidel Castro set up a Communist dictatorship. **8.** Fidel Castro pledged to help Communist rebels in Latin America. **9.** The collapse of the Soviet Union upset Cuba's economy. **10.** Relations between the United States and Cuba have been strained.

Activity 124—Unrest in Central America
1. F **2.** E **3.** H **4.** A **5.** J **6.** G **7.** B **8.** D **9.** I **10.** C

Activity 125—Trouble in Mexico and Haiti
1. C; E **2.** E; C **3.** C; E **4.** E; C **5.** E; C **6.** C; E **7.** E; C **8.** C; E **9.** E; C **10.** C; E

Activity 126—Latin America Today
Part A: 1. D **2.** B **3.** C **4.** A **5.** D
Part B: 6. B **7.** C **8.** D **9.** A **10.** D

Activity 127—The Nuclear Age
1. F **2.** O **3.** F **4.** O **5.** O **6.** F **7.** O **8.** F **9.** O **10.** F **11.** O **12.** F **13.** O **14.** O **15.** F

Activity 128—The Space Age
1. B **2.** A **3.** C **4.** D **5.** B

Activity 129—The Computer Age
1. electronic **2.** information **3.** entertainment **4.** expensive **5.** communication **6.** airplane **7.** television **8.** protesting **9.** satellites **10.** forecast **11.** Internet **12.** billion **13.** webcams **14.** cell phones **15.** files

Activity 130—Global Issues
1. Developed **2.** Developing **3.** Developing **4.** Developing **5.** Developed **6.** Developing **7.** Developed **8.** Developed **9.** Developed **10.** Developing **11.** Developed **12.** Developing **13.** Developing **14.** Developed **15.** Developing

Activity 131—Environment, Overpopulation, and Disease
Part A: 1. D **2.** A **3.** C **4.** E **5.** B
Part B: 6. C **7.** E **8.** A **9.** D **10.** B

Activity 132—The Threat of Global Terrorism
1. A **2.** C **3.** D **4.** C **5.** B **6.** A **7.** C **8.** D **9.** A **10.** B

Activity 133—Looking to the Future
1. 1945 **2.** four **3.** Great Britain **4.** Yuri Gagarin **5.** 1963 **6.** eight **7.** South Africa **8.** 1979 **9.** seven **10.** three

Modified Activities

Modified Activity 1—History Is All About Change
Part A: 1. history 2. business 3. slavery 4. culture 5. revolution
6. growth 7. nationalism 8. imperialism 9. farming
Part B: Hidden word: historian

Modified Activity 2—Historians and Archaeologists
1. primary 2. secondary 3. primary 4. primary 5. secondary
6. primary 7. primary 8. secondary 9. primary 10. primary
11. primary 12. secondary

Modified Activity 3—Maps and Timelines
1. A.D. 2. Medieval Times 3. 10,000 B.C. 4. Egyptian 7. 1500 B.C.
8. A.D. 1400 9. David 10. A.D. 2000

Modified Activity 4—The Hunters
1. summer 2. south 3. heavy 4. Ice Age 5. melt 6. weapons
7. food 8. cave art

Modified Activity 5—The Agricultural Revolution
1. Farming Settlements 2. Farming Settlements 3. Large
Communities 4. Large Communities 5. Large Communities
6. Farming Settlements 7. Farming Settlements 8. Large Communities

Modified Activity 6—The Fertile Crescent
1. F 2. B 3. D 4. E 5. C 6. G 7. I 8. H

Modified Activity 7—The Sumerian Civilization
Part A: 1. Persian Gulf 2. Caspian Sea 3. Tigris, Euphrates
4. Euphrates
Part B: 5. B 6. C 7. D 8. A

Modified Activity 8—Sumerian City-States
1. temple 2. crops 3. wealthy 4. reeds 5. bricks 6. city-states
7. government 8. independent 9. fought 10. walls 11. Ur 12. ziggurat

Modified Activity 9—Sumerian Inventions
Part A: 1. writing 2. tablets 3. scribes 4. contract 5. merchants
6. wedge 7. cuneiform 8. chariots
Part B: 9. writing 10. tablets 11. scribes 12. contract 13. merchants
14. wedge 15. cuneiform 16. chariots

Modified Activity 10—Life in Sumer
1. A 2. D 3. C 4. B

Modified Activity 11—Egypt and the Nile
1. B 2. B 3. C 4. D 5. B 6. A 7. C 8. B

Modified Activity 12—The Pyramids
1. transport 2. powerful 3. ramps 4. mummy 5. museums
6. pyramds 7. rich 8. tombs

Modified Activity 13—Egyptian Culture
1. rich 2. kohl 3. hair 4. gods 5. death 6. hieroglyphics 7. paper
8. metal

Modified Activity 14—The Phoenicians
1. navigate 2. colony 3. Gibraltar 4. Atlantic 5. Carthage 6. gold
7. pottery 8. taxes 9. sails 10. alphabet 11. letters 12. snails

Modified Activity 15—The Israelites
1. B 2. C 3. D 4. A 5. C 6. B 7. A 8. D

Modified Activity 16—The Babylonians
1. temples 2. bricks 3. bronze 4. capital 5. Tower 6. empire
7. Hammurabi 8. code

Modified Activity 17—The Hittites
1. A 2. F 3. B 4. D 5. E 6. C 7. B 8. E 9. D 10. A 11. C 12. F

Modified Activity 18—The Assyrians
Part A: 1. I 2. H, A 3. P, I, H 4. B 5. I 6. I 7. H 8. P
Part B: Students' paragraphs should be supported by facts and
examples from the textbook.

Modified Activity 19—Ancient India
1. C 2. B 3. A 4. B 5. D 6. B 7. B 8. D

Modified Activity 20—Buddhism
1. nirvana 2. selfishness 3. forest 4. reincarnation 5. Maurya
6. Asoka 7. caste 8. pagodas

Modified Activity 21—Early China
1. flood control 2. north 3. Chang Jiang 4. silkworms 5. 15 years
6. mud 7. 25 feet 8. Han dynasty

Modified Activity 22—Early America
1. G 2. A 3. D 4. H 5. C 6. F 7. E 8. B

Modified Activity 23—The Sea and Ancient Greece
1. rocky 2. papyrus 3. colonies 4. Naples 5. mountains 6. tyrant
7. democracy 8. citizen 9. fought 10. Sparta 11. Acropolis 12. Athena

Modified Activity 24—Athens and Sparta
1. S 2. A 3. A 4. S 5. A 6. S 7. A, S 8. A 9. A 10. S 11. A, S 12. A

Modified Activity 25—Fighting in Greece
1. A 2. D 3. C 4. B 5. C 6. D 7. A 8. B

Modified Activity 26—Gifts from the Greeks
Part A: 1. athletes 2. Pericles 3. architecture 4. classical 5. truth
6. columns 7. wrestling 8. Olympia 9. Zeus
Part B: Hidden word: Aristotle

Modified Activity 27—King Philip and Alexander
1. B 2. C 3. D 4. D 5. C 6. A 7. B 8. C

Modified Activity 28—Alexander's Conquests
1. Darius 2. Tyre 3. bridge 4. Egypt 5. cities 6. Ptolemy 7. India
8. Alexander

Modified Activity 29—The End of an Empire
1. twelve 2. unite 3. Babylon 4. largest 5. ill 6. medicines
7. Alexandria 8. divided

Modified Activity 30—How Rome Grew Powerful
1. D 2. B 3. C 4. A 5. C 6. D 7. B 8. A 9. B 10. A 11. D 12. C

Modified Activity 31—Julius Caesar
1. A 2. D 3. C 4. B 5. D 6. A 7. C 8. B

Modified Activity 32—The Roman Empire
1. A 2. A 3. A 4. O 5. A 6. O 7. A 8. O

Modified Activity 33—Roman Society
1. Forum 2. social 3. holidays 4. chariot 5. arches 6. roads
7. sewer 8. Latin 9. dining 10. apartment 11. paved 12. temple

Modified Activity 34—Christianity in Rome
1. C 2. G 3. D 4. B 5. A 6. F 7. H 8. E

Modified Activity 35—The End of the Empire
I. 4, 6, 7, 9, 10 II. 2, 8, 11, 12 III. 1, 3, 5

Modified Activity 36—The Fall of the Western Roman Empire
1. C 2. B 3. A 4. C 5. B 6. D 7. D 8. A

Modified Activity 37—The Byzantine Empire
1. Constantinople 2. Franks 3. Byzantine 4. Charlemagne
5. emperor 6. Greek 7. schools 8. Christmas

Modified Activity 38—The Vikings
Part A: 1. 3 2. 2 3. 4 4. 1
Part B: 5. Hastings 6. sailors 7. Normandy 8. exiled

Modified Activity 39—Feudalism
1. N 2. F, S 3. N 4. N, F 5. N 6. N, F, S 7. S 8. F 9. N 10. S
11. N 12. F, S

Modified Activity 40—Religion During the Middle Ages
1. noble 2. land 3. clergy 4. powerful 5. monks 6. convents
7. studying 8. Christian

Modified Activity 41—Life in the Middle Ages
1. C 2. D 3. A 4. B

Modified Activity 42—Muhammad and Islam
1. C 2. B 3. A 4. D 5. A 6. C 7. D 8. B

Modified Activity 43—The Crusades
1. Crusade 2. peasants 3. Jerusalem 4. Christians 5. pilgrimage
6. Saladin 7. Richard 8. truce

Modified Activity 44—The Costs of the Crusades
1. give them glory 2. cost much money and many lives 3. Jerusalem
4. none 5. meat and plants that grew in Europe 6. rice, apricots,
lemons, melons, and spices 7. cotton and wool from what they grew in
Europe 8. brightly-colored silks

Modified Activity 45—Changes in Agriculture
1. D 2. C 3. E 4. G 5. B 6. F 7. H 8. A

Modified Activity 46— Changes in City Life
1. fewer 2. stone 3. disease 4. money 5. free 6. stronger 7. no pay

Modified Activity 47—The Magna Carta
Part A: 1. 3 2. 2 3. 1 4. 4
Part B: 5. happiness 6. nobles 7. power 8. army

Modified Activity 48—A Time of New Ideas
Part A: 1. R 2. R 3. M 4. M 5. R 6. M 7. R 8. M
Part B: 9. R 10. M 11. M 12. R

Modified Activity 49—Renaissance Art
1. I 2. F 3. F 4. F 5. I 6. I 7. F 8. I 9. F 10. I 11. F 12. I

Modified Activity 50—Advances in Knowledge, Technology, and
Science
1. C 2. E 3. H 4. D 5. F 6. A 7. B 8. G

Modified Activity 51—The Renaissance Man
Part A: 1. talents 2. poetry 3. sculptor 4. inventor 5. architect
6. sketchbooks 7. machines 8. Duke 9. birds 10. engineer
11. parachute 12. *Mona Lisa*
Part B: Hidden place: Louvre Museum

Modified Activity 52—The Reformation
1. Reformation 2. monk 3. sermons 4. Wittenberg 5. authority
6. recant 7. outlaw 8. Lutheranism 9. Protestants 10. Switzerland
11. Inquisition 12. heretics

Modified Activity 53—The Counter-Reformation
Part A: 1. B 2. C 3. A 4. D
Part B: 5. Loyola 6. Protestants 7. Society of Jesus 8. Council of Trent

Modified Activity 54—Rule by Monarchs
1. C 2. A 3. D 4. B 5. D 6. A 7. B 8. D

Modified Activity 55—Spanish Monarchs
1. Catholic 2. Moors 3. Inquisition 4. Philip 5. Netherlands
6. independence 7. Mary 8. Elizabeth

Modified Activity 56—French Monarchs
1. civil 2. massacre 3. Navarre 4. Protestant 5. Catholic
6. freedom 7. Quebec 8. assassinated

Modified Activity 57—English Monarchs
1. M 2. H 3. H 4. M 5. H 6. E 7. H 8. E

Modified Activity 58—China
Students should enter checkmarks in the following numbered boxes:
1, 4, 7, 9, 10, 14, 18, and 19.

Modified Activity 59—Japan
Part A: 1. C 2. D 3. C 4. B 5. A 6. D 7. A 8. B
Part B: 9. Answers will vary. Accept any answer based on details from
the first paragraph of the student text on page 313. The people of Japan
copied writing and the calendar system from China. 10. The shogun
feared that contact with other countries would upset Japanese culture.
He stopped almost all contact with foreigners.

Modified Activity 60—India

Akbar

1. He was Babar's grandson. **2.** He allowed freedom of religion. [Alternatively 1–2: He was a Muslim; He extended Mogul rule to most of India.]

Asoka

3. He became emperor in 268 B.C. **4.** He converted to Buddhism.

Aurangzeb

5. He put his father in prison. **6.** He destroyed Hindu temples. [Alternatively: He made Hindus pay a special tax; He was Shah Jahan's son.]

Babar

7. He conquered northern India. **8.** He established the Mogul Empire and made himself emperor. [Alternatively 7–8: He was a direct descendant of Genghis Khan.]

Shah Jahan

9. He was the grandson of Akbar. **10.** He had the Taj Mahal built.

Modified Activity 61—The Americas

Part A: 1. D **2.** C **3.** D **4.** A **5.** B **6.** A **7.** A **8.** C

Part B: 9. The mound builders built temples on top of their giant mounds. **10.** The Aztecs bartered for their goods, rather than buying and selling with money.

Modified Activity 62— Exploring New Lands

1. B **2.** D **3.** C **4.** A

Modified Activity 63—Conquering South America

1. Pedro Cabral **2.** Ferdinand Magellan **3.** Aztecs **4.** Incas **5.** Hernando Cortés **6.** Tenochtitlán **7.** Francisco Pizarro **8.** Sir John Hawkins

Modified Activity 64—Settling in North America

Across: 3. Quebec **4.** nation **5.** east **6.** plantation **10.** Dragon **11.** corn **12.** pirate

Down: 1. Puritan **2.** Hudson **6.** Pilgrim **7.** trappers **8.** tobacco **9.** wary **10.** Drake

Modified Activity 65—Trading with the Colonies

1. 1519 **2.** 1492 **3.** 1500 **4.** eight **5.** 1521 **6.** 11 **7.** 1562 **8.** six **9.** 13 **10.** one year **11.** 74 **12.** 1759

Modified Activity 66—The Beginnings of Democracy

1. C **2.** D **3.** A **4.** C **5.** A **6.** B **7.** A **8.** A

Modified Activity 67—The King Tries to Limit Democracy

1. Charles **2.** jail **3.** petition **4.** consent **5.** Royalists **6.** Roundheads **7.** Cromwell **8.** Commonwealth

Modified Activity 68—The Glorious Revolution

1. G **2.** H **3.** E **4.** B **5.** A **6.** C **7.** D **8.** F

Modified Activity 69—Revolution in America

1. wars **2.** taxes **3.** revolution **4.** approved **5.** leader **6.** representation **7.** patriot **8.** liberty

Modified Activity 70—The Age of Reason in France

Part A: Answers will vary. Verify that students have used the listed words and have written complete sentences with proper punctuation. **1.** King Louis XIV was the king of France in the early 1700s. His rule was unfair to everyone but the nobles. **2.** Voltaire was an important writer who spoke of freedom and the rights of people. **3.** Lafayette was a French noble who helped George Washington fight against the British in the American war for independence. **4.** George Washington was the leader of the Americans in the war for independence from the British. **Part B: 5.** state **6.** nobles **7.** peasants **8.** Reason **9.** American

Modified Activity 71—The King Tries to Limit Democracy

Part A: 1. Estates-General **2.** Third **3.** Assembly **4.** Bastille **5.** Prussia **6.** republic **7.** Robespierre **8.** guillotine **Part B: 9.** D **10.** C **11.** B **12.** A

Modified Activity 72—Napoleon Bonaparte

Part A: 1. E **2.** D **3.** B **4.** A **5.** C **Part B: 6.** Great Britain **7.** schools **8.** nobles **9.** empress **10.** Russia **11.** Prussian **12.** government

Modified Activity 73—Industries Develop

1. A **2.** C **3.** D **4.** C **5.** B **6.** D **7.** B **8.** A

Modified Activity 74—New Inventions

Part A: 1. steam engine **2.** flying shuttle **3.** spinning jenny **4.** water frame **5.** mule **6.** steam-powered loom **7.** steam locomotive **8.** steamboat

Part B: 9. John Kay **10.** Samuel Crompton **11.** James Hargreaves **12.** Robert Fulton **13.** Thomas Savery **14.** Richard Trevithick **15.** Edmund Cartwright **16.** Richard Arkwright

Modified Activity 75—The Industrial Revolution Changes Life

Part A: Checked statements should be 1, 5, 6, and 7. **Part B: 9.** FP **10.** NR **11.** FP **12.** NR **13.** NR **14.** NR **15.** FP **16.** NR

Modified Activity 76—The Industrial Revolution Spreads

1. A **2.** C **3.** B **4.** C **5.** D **6.** D **7.** B **8.** C

Modified Activity 77—Colonization

1. A **2.** B **3.** B **4.** C **5.** C **6.** A **7.** D **8.** C

Modified Activity 78—Colonies Fight for Independence

1. France **2.** priests **3.** Spain **4.** Colombia **5.** dictator **6.** Argentina **7.** Brazil **8.** Portugal

Modified Activity 79—Latin American Culture

1. cultures **2.** rural **3.** mural **4.** dominate **5.** Spain **6.** Portugal **7.** African **8.** influence

Modified Activity 80—Imperialism and Growth

1. MD **2.** LP **3.** LP **4.** LP **5.** MD **6.** MD **7.** LP **8.** LP **9.** MD **10.** LP **11.** LP **12.** MD

Modified Activity 81—Border Problems

Part A: 1. Alamo **2.** treaty **3.** Santa Anna **4.** Davy Crockett **5.** California **6.** border **7.** Texas **Part B: 8.** A **9.** D **10.** B **11.** C **12.** D

Modified Activity 82—The American Civil War
Part A: 1. C 2. E 3. H 4. A 5. B 6. G 7. F 8. D
Part B: 9. C 10. B 11. D 12. A

Modified Activity 83—U.S. Expansion
Part A: 1. B 2. C 3. D 4. B 5. B 6. C 7. D
Part B: 8. Samuel F.B. Morse 9. William Seward 10. Cyrus McCormick
11. President Theodore Roosevelt 12. Queen Liliuokalani

Modified Activity 84—China Under Manchurian Rule
1. D 2. C 3. C 4. B 5. A 6. C 7. D 8. A

Modified Activity 85—Chinese Rebellion
Part A: 1. 1 2. 3 3. 4 4. 2
Part B: 5. D 6. B 7. H 8. C 9. G 10. A 11. F 12. E

Modified Activity 86—Japan Opens Its Doors
Part A: 1. Meiji 2. shogun 3. trade 4. warships 5. Russia 6. Harris
7. advice 8. industry 9. Commodore
Part B: Hidden word: Mutsuhito

Modified Activity 87—The British East India Company
1. A 2. B 3. D 4. D 5. B 6. A 7. D 8. B

Modified Activity 88—British Rule
1. I 2. B 3. B 4. I 5. I 6. B 7. B 8. I

Modified Activity 89—Mahatma Gandhi
1. lawyer 2. Congress 3. refuse 4. Mahatma 5. poor 6. trains
7. jail 8. Pakistan

Modified Activity 90—Early Kingdoms in Africa
1. iron 2. Arab 3. salt 4. Ghana 5. Christianity 6. Islam
7. Timbuktu 8. Mansa Musa 9. Songhai 10. Morocco

Modified Activity 91—Africa After the First Century A.D.
1. Arab 2. Bantu 3. Shaka 4. Britain 5. Sahara 6. Gold Coast
7. Portugal 8. Angola

Modified Activity 92—The African Slave Trade
1. D 2. C 3. B 4. D 5. D 6. C 7. B 8. A

Modified Activity 93—European Imperialism
1. D 2. C 3. B 4. C 5. D 6. D 7. B 8. C

Modified Activity 94—Nationalism in Italy
1. A 2. B 3. C 4. B 5. A 6. C 7. D 8. A

Modified Activity 95—Nationalism in Germany
Part A: 1. D 2. B 3. A 4. C 5. B 6. A 7. D 8. C
Part B: 9. G 10. A 11. F 12. D 13. E 14. B 15. H 16. C

Modified Activity 96—The War Begins in Europe
1. B 2. A 3. D 4. C 5. B 6. D 7. B 8. C

Modified Activity 97—The Fighting
1. C 2. A 3. C 4. A 5. C 6. A 7. A 8. C

Modified Activity 98—The End of the War
1. Germany 2. armistice 3. France 4. rebuild 5. conflicts
6. Switzerland 7. support 8. Article Ten

Modified Activity 99—The Early History of Russia
Part A: 1. C 2. B 3. E 4. H 5. F 6. A 7. D 8. G
Part B: 9. B 10. D 11. A 12. C

Modified Activity 100—Unrest in the Early 1900s
Part A: 1. F 2. I 3. F 4. I 5. I 6. F 7. F 8. I
Part B: Circled phrases should be B, C, F, and H.

Modified Activity 101—Russia Becomes the USSR
1. B 2. A 3. C 4. D

Modified Activity 102—The Rise of Dictators
1. C; E 2. E; C 3. C; E 4. E; C 5. C; E 6. E; C 7. E; C 8. C; E

Modified Activity 103—World War II Begins in Europe
1. C 2. B 3. A 4. D 5. B 6. A 7. D 8. C

Modified Activity 104—The Holocaust and Allied Victories
1. B 2. D 3. A 4. D

Modified Activity 105—The End of the War
1. shot 2. nuclear 3. Bulge 4. Berlin 5. pilots 6. Pacific 7. atomic
8. Truman

Modified Activity 106—The Results of the War
Part A: Checked statements should be 2, 3, 5, 7, and 8.
Part B: 9. after 10. after 11. before 12. before

Modified Activity 107—The World After World War II
1. B 2. D 3. A 4. D 5. C 6. D 7. D 8. B

Modified Activity 108—The Cold War Begins
1. U 2. U 3. S 4. U 5. S 6. S 7. U 8. U

Modified Activity 109—Changing Relations Between the Soviets and Americans
Part A: 1. Afghanistan 2. shot down 3. détente 4. Arms
Part B: 5. The Soviet Union and the United States set up a détente and agreed to cooperate. 6. The countries held Strategic Arms Limitation Talks. 7. The Communists took over Afghanistan. 8. A Korean Air Lines jet was shot down by the Soviets.

Modified Activity 110—India
1. C; E 2. E; C 3. C; E 4. E; C 5. E; C 6. C; E 7. E; C 8. E; C

Modified Activity 111—China
1. More than one-fifth of the world's people live in China. 2. Great Britain gave Hong Kong to China in 1997. 3. Mao Zedong led the Communist Party. 4. Mao Zedong was supported by the peasants. 5. Farm workers live in communes. 6. China's economy declined during the Cultural Revolution. 7. The Chinese people do not have political freedom. 8. China does trade with the West.

Modified Activity 112—Korea
1. C 2. B 3. A 4. C 5. B 6. D 7. C 8. B

Modified Activity 113—Japan and Southeast Asia
1. independent **2.** military **3.** occupied **4.** democracy **5.** colony
6. civil **7.** manufactures **8.** electronics **9.** resources **10.** pollution
11. imports **12.** exports

Modified Activity 114—Vietnam
1. D **2.** B **3.** C **4.** A

Modified Activity 115—Asia and Africa: 1945–present
1. D **2.** C **3.** B **4.** A **5.** B **6.** A **7.** B **8.** C

Modified Activity 116—The Fight for Palestine
1. C **2.** A **3.** B **4.** C

Modified Activity 117—The Middle East Remains in Conflict
1. B **2.** D **3.** C **4.** A **5.** D **6.** B **7.** A **8.** C

Modified Activity 118—Oil
1. F **2.** F **3.** O **4.** O **5.** F **6.** F **7.** O **8.** F **9.** F **10.** F **11.** O **12.** F

Modified Activity 119—Life in the Middle East
1. modern **2.** rocky **3.** conflicts **4.** industrialized **5.** irrigation
6. saltwater **7.** Mediterranean **8.** civilizations

Modified Activity 120—Changes in the Soviet Union
1. A **2.** C **3.** D **4.** B **5.** A **6.** C **7.** A **8.** C

Modified Activity 121—The End of the Soviet Union
and Cold War
1. B **2.** A **3.** D **4.** F **5.** H **6.** E **7.** G **8.** C

Modified Activity 122—Changes in Eastern Europe
1. Lech Walesa **2.** reunification **3.** executed **4.** Yugoslavia **5.** Dayton
Accords **6.** Serbia **7.** Slobodan Milosevic **8.** Chechnya

Modified Activity 123—The United States in Latin American
Affairs
1. The United States and the independent countries of Latin America
make up the OAS. **2.** The Latin American countries are not all
stable. **3.** Latin American countries are not always happy to have
help from the United States. **4.** The revolution in Cuba happened in
1959. **5.** Fidel Castro set up a Communist dictatorship in Cuba.
6. Fidel Castro was for Communism. **7.** Cuba's economy was upset after
Communism ended. **8.** The United States and Cuba have had strained
relations.

Modified Activity 124—Unrest in Central America
1. F **2.** D **3.** A **4.** E **5.** H **6.** B **7.** G **8.** C

Modified Activity 125—Trouble in Mexico and Haiti
1. C; E **2.** C; E **3.** E; C **4.** C; E **5.** C; E **6.** C; E **7.** E; C **8.** C; E

Modified Activity 126—Latin America Today
Part A: 1. A **2.** D **3.** D **4.** B
Part B: 5. C **6.** B **7.** C **8.** A

Modified Activity 127—The Nuclear Age
1. F **2.** O **3.** F **4.** O **5.** O **6.** F **7.** O **8.** F **9.** O **10.** F **11.** F **12.** O

Modified Activity 128—The Space Age
1. B **2.** A **3.** D **4.** B

Modified Activity 129—The Computer Age
1. communication **2.** airplanes **3.** electronic **4.** entertainment
5. expensive **6.** television **7.** satellites **8.** forecast **9.** Internet
10. billion **11.** cell phones **12.** information

Modified Activity 130—Global Issues
1. Developed **2.** Developing **3.** Developing **4.** Developing
5. Developed **6.** Developing **7.** Developed **8.** Developed
9. Developed **10.** Developing **11.** Developed **12.** Developing

Modified Activity 131—Environment, Overpopulation,
and Disease
Part A: 1. A **2.** C **3.** B **4.** D
Part B: 5. B **6.** C **7.** A **8.** D

Modified Activity 132—The Threat of Global Terrorism
1. D **2.** C **3.** B **4.** A **5.** A **6.** C **7.** D **8.** B

Modified Activity 133—Looking to the Future
1. 1961 **2.** 1963 **3.** eight **4.** 1945 **5.** four **6.** 1979 **7.** seven **8.** three

Workbook Activities

Workbook Activity 1—Historic Events
Answers will vary, but students should include both items from their own history and from their family history.

Workbook Activity 2—Backyard Artifacts
Answers will vary, but students should demonstrate an understanding of how everyday items can communicate information about the modern world. Students should clearly explain the reasons behind their choices of artifacts to include.

Workbook Activity 3—Personal Timeline
Answers will vary, but students should include at least five events. In addition, they should demonstrate an understanding of how to construct a timeline.

Workbook Activity 4—The Hunters Crossword
Across: 4. valleys **6.** herds **8.** lakes **9.** Ice Age
Down: 1. glaciers **2.** caves **3.** million **5.** animals **6.** hunting
7. Stone Age

Workbook Activity 5—The Agricultural Revolution Word Find
1. store **2.** seeds **3.** revolution **4.** tools **5.** rules **6.** specialize
7. tame **8.** trade **9.** farming **10.** crafts
Hidden word: settlement

Workbook Activity 6—The Fertile Crescent Crossword
Across: 4. fertile **7.** Africa **8.** Europe **10.** crescent
Down: 1. Jericho **2.** civilizations **3.** Mesopotamia **5.** Euphrates
6. Tigris **9.** rice

Workbook Activity 7—The Sumerian Civilization Fact Find
1. F **2.** O **3.** F **4.** F **5.** F **6.** O **7.** O **8.** F **9.** F **10.** O **11.** F **12.** O
13. F **14.** F **15.** 0

Workbook Activity 8—Sumerian City-States Crossword
Across: 2. ziggurat **4.** crops **7.** priest **10.** independent
Down: 1. bricks **3.** goddess **5.** city-state **6.** Ur. **8.** temple **9.** reeds

Workbook Activity 9—Cuneiform Symbols
Part A: 1–4. Students' answers should match the symbols on page 48 of the student edition.
Part B: 5–10. Answers will vary. Accept answers with a combination of symbols and words.

Workbook Activity 10—Life in Sumer Compare and Contrast
Part A: 1. They would have worshipped the same gods. **2.** They would have had arranged marriages. **3.** The farm boy would work in the field while the son of a scribe would go to school. **4.** The farm boy would have a hard life while the son of a merchant would have better things. **5.** The farm boy would have to work because his family needed everyone to pitch in.
Part B: 6. we both write in horizontal rows **7.** we both write symbols that stand for words **8.** our symbols are letters, while Sumerian symbols stood for the entire word **9.** we write on paper, while they wrote on clay **10.** every person has the opportunity to learn to write (and attend school), not just the rich

Workbook Activity 11—The Egyptians
Part B: 1. 2 **2.** 4 **3.** 1 **4.** 3 **5.** 5
Part B: 6. Red **7.** 300 **8.** Lower **9.** Sinai **10.** Mediterranean

Workbook Activity 12—The Pyramids Word Find
1. copper **2.** pharaoh **3.** ancient **4.** great **5.** tomb **6.** sled
7. archaeologists **8.** pyramids **9.** picture **10.** statues
Hidden place: Cairo, Egypt

Workbook Activity 13—Egyptian Culture Fact Find
1. The craftworkers had time to become better at their skills. **2.** Osiris is the Egyptian god of death. **3.** Archaeologists have found Egyptian instruments and songs. **4.** The pictures Egyptians used for writing are called *hieroglyphics*. **5.** The Egyptians were able to travel by ship. **6.** Papyrus is the type of plant used to make paper. **7.** Only the pharaohs and nobles were rich. **8.** Egyptian men and women wore makeup. **9.** Men and women drew with kohl around their eyes. **10.** Egyptians thought their dead were carried across a river.

Workbook Activity 14—The Phoenicians Map Study
Part A: 1. Spain **2.** North Africa **3.** Mediterranean Sea **4.** Cyprus
5. Gibraltar
Part B: 6. D **7.** A **8.** B **9.** D **10.** B

Workbook Activity 15—The Israelites Word Find
Part A: 1. Canaan **2.** worship **3.** nomads **4.** Moses **5.** Yahweh
6. Christianity **7.** Judaism **8.** Solomon **9.** slaves **10.** conquered
11. capital
Part B: Hidden word: commandment

Workbook Activity 16—Comparing Civilizations
1. Sumer **2.** both **3.** Babylon **4.** Sumer **5.** both **6.** Babylon
7. Babylon **8.** Sumer **9.** Sumer **10.** both

Workbook Activity 17—Civilization Sequence
1. D **2.** J **3.** E **4.** B **5.** C **6.** F **7.** G **8.** A **9.** I **10.** H

Workbook Activity 18—Matching Mediterranean Civilizations
1. Israelites **2.** Israelites **3.** Hittites **4.** Phoenicians **5.** Assyrians
6. Phoenicians **7.** Babylonians **8.** Phoenicians **9.** Hittites **10.** Assyrians

Workbook Activity 19—Ancient India Crossword
Across: 1. brick **3.** Hinduism **5.** Mohenjo-Daro **10.** nobleman
12. Vishnu **14.** soul **15.** raja
Down: 2. castes **4.** four **6.** outcastes **7.** Aryans **8.** Indus **9.** reincarnation
11. Brahma **13.** Shiva

Workbook Activity 20—Buddhism Word Find
1. six **2.** India **3.** death **4.** Hindu **5.** Enlightened **6.** wealth **7.** greed
8. poverty **9.** northern **10.** nirvana
Hidden word: Siddhartha

Workbook Activity 21—Early China Fact Find

1. The people were separated from the rest of the world. **2.** The people lived in the Huang He Valley. **3.** The Chinese have one of the oldest written languages. **4.** The Huang He River flooded terribly. **5.** Threads from silkworms were used to make fine cloth. **6.** Families in China lived together in large groups. **7.** The Shang kings ruled for about 500 years. **8.** The Zhou dynasty brought many changes to China. **9.** The emperor Shi Huangdi planned the Great Wall. **10.** Most people in China call themselves "People of the Han."

Workbook Activity 22—Early America Crossword

Across: 2. Mexico **3.** Olmec **6.** shrines **8.** number **10.** Asia
Down: 1. Bering Straits **4.** Mayan **5.** cotton **7.** llamas **9.** maize

Workbook Activity 23—The Sea and Ancient Greece Map Study

1. Aegean Sea **2.** Mediterranean Sea **3.** Athens **4.** Macedonia **5.** Crete **6.** northwest **7.** southeast **8.** about 100 km **9.** about 150 km **10.** Sparta is not on the sea coast

Workbook Activity 24—Gods and Goddesses

1. D **2.** B **3.** C **4.** B **5.** A

Workbook Activity 25—Events in Greek Wars

Part A: A. 3 **B.** 4 **C.** 2 **D.** 1 **E.** 5
Part B: A. 3 **B.** 1 **C.** 5 **D.** 4 **E.** 2

Workbook Activity 26—Greek Mathematicians

Philosopher	City/Colony	Field of Study	Major discoveries and achievements
Archimedes	Syracuse	mathematician and engineer	cranes and catapults, principle of the lever, why things float
Eratosthenes	Alexandria	librarian and geographer	figured the circumference of Earth, figured the distance from Earth to the sun, divided Earth using lines going north, south, east, and west
Pythagoras	Samos	philosopher and religious leader	important ideas in mathematics, astronomy, and music; politician; studied triangles; the Pythagorean theorem

Workbook Activity 27—King Philip and Alexander Word Find

1. ambition **2.** conquered **3.** Macedonia **4.** Persia **5.** Philip **6.** Thebes **7.** assassinate **8.** military **9.** adventure **10.** Aristotle
Hidden word: Bucephalus

Workbook Activity 28—Alexander's Empire

Part A: 1. 4 **2.** 3 **3.** 1 **4.** 5 **5.** 2
Part B: 6. Mediterranean Sea **7.** Babylon **8.** 400 miles **9.** Nile River **10.** Caucasus Mountains

Workbook Activity 29—Alexander's Influence

1. Alexander fought for 12 years. **2.** Alexander shared Greek culture with all of the lands he conquered. **3.** Alexander wanted Europe and Asia as one country. **4.** Alexander shared plants from one part of the world with another. **5.** Alexander died from illness. **6.** Alexander was buried in a gold coffin. **7.** The Macedonian empire was split among the generals. **8.** Alexander wanted unity among people. **9.** Alexander married a woman from Asia. **10.** Every conquered country had some Greek style or custom.

Workbook Activity 30—Spartacus

1. C **2.** B **3.** C **4.** A **5.** D

Workbook Activity 31—Julius Caesar Word Find

Part A: 1. coins **2.** calendar **3.** Egypt **4.** governor **5.** popular **6.** Gaul **7.** senators **8.** Brutus **9.** Mark Antony
Part B: Hidden word: Cleopatra

Workbook Activity 32—The Roman Empire Map Study

1. C **2.** A **3.** D **4.** C **5.** B

Workbook Activity 33—Rome and Greece

1. B **2.** R **3.** G **4.** R **5.** B **6.** B **7.** R **8.** G **9.** G **10.** R **11.** G **12.** R **13.** R **14.** G **15.** R

Workbook Activity 34—Constantinople

1. C **2.** A **3.** D **4.** B **5.** C

Workbook Activity 35—Roman Empire Timeline Study

1. 753 B.C. **2.** 509 B.C. **3.** 244 **4.** 264 B.C. **5.** 146 B.C. **6.** 118 **7.** 44 B.C. **8.** 27 B.C. **9.** 17 **10.** 482 **11.** A.D. 180 **12.** A.D. 286 **13.** A.D. 476 **14.** 296 **15.** A.D. 1

Workbook Activity 36—The Fall of the Western Roman Empire Crossword

Across: 2. Hadrian **4.** adventure **6.** Germans **8.** buried **9.** Goths **12.** barbarians **13.** uncivilized **14.** wigs
Down: 1. primitive **3.** test **4.** Attila **5.** Angles **7.** Middle Ages **10.** Odoacer **11.** Vandals

Workbook Activity 37—The Byzantine Empire Word Find

1. Pepin **2.** Byzantine **3.** Charles **4.** Orthodox **5.** Louis **6.** Roman **7.** Latin **8.** Greek **9.** pope **10.** divided
Hidden word: encouraged

Workbook Activity 38—The Vikings Fact Find

1. They came from Norway, Sweden, and Denmark. **2.** They traveled in very fast boats. **3.** They started raiding the cities in England. **4.** The Vikings that settled in France became known as the Normans. **5.** Erik the Red was exiled and settled in Greenland. **6.** Leif Eriksson found an area in North America he called Vinland. **7.** The Vikings sailed to North America for centuries. **8.** King William won the Battle of Hastings. **9.** Sagas tell the stories of Erik the Red and Leif Eriksson. **10.** Valhalla is the Viking hall of the gods.

Workbook Activity 39—Feudalism Crossword

Across: 2. fortress **4.** blacksmith **6.** feudalism **7.** serf **8.** medieval **10.** manor **11.** estate **12.** lord
Down: 1. homage **3.** organize **5.** miller **6.** freemen **9.** vassal

Workbook Activity 40—Knights During the Middle Ages

1. A **2.** D **3.** B **4.** **5.** C **6.** D **7.** B **8.** A **9.** C **10.** B

Workbook Activity 41—Life in the Middle Ages Fact Chart
Answers will vary. Possible responses: **Nobles: 1.** owned land, **2.** fought for the king, **3.** lived in a manor house; **Knights: 1.** members of the nobility; **2.** began training at age 7, **3.** fought each other in jousts; **Clergy: 1.** could own land, **2.** often rich and powerful, **3.** could read and write; **Serfs: 1.** tied to the land, **2.** worked for the lord of the manor, **3.** lived in small huts

Workbook Activity 42—Muhammad and Islam Crossword
Across: 1. idols **3.** Muslim **4.** Mecca **6.** vision **8.** Ramadan **10.** Allah **12.** Koran **13.** verses
Down: 1. Islam **2.** Sunnis **4.** Muhammad **5.** Ali **7.** Palestine **9.** faith **11.** prophet

Workbook Activity 43—The Crusades Word Find
1. Philip **2.** Richard **3.** Saladin **4.** glory **5.** Jerusalem **6.** Hermit **7.** Muslim **8.** Crusade **9.** German **10.** Seljuk
Hidden word: pilgrimage

Workbook Activity 44—The Costs of the Crusades Fact Find
1. The Crusades cost a lot of money. **2.** Muslims, Jews, and Christians died during the Crusades. **3.** The Crusades caused the Christians to suffer a great deal. **4.** None of the Middle East remained in Christian hands. **5.** The Crusades led to Europe making great changes in their culture. **6.** Europeans got new foods from Middle-Eastern traders. **7.** Europe's economy grew strong after the Crusades because trade increased. **8.** Mapmaking improved because of the travels during the Crusades. **9.** The fighting for the Holy Land caused Europeans to improve their weapons. **10.** Children formed their own armies during the Crusades.

Workbook Activity 45—Drawing a Medieval Farm
Drawing should include:
- tools such as plowshares, axes, or hoes
- oxen or horses
- shoulder-yokes or horseshoes
- three fields in different phases of growth
- blacksmiths or traders

Workbook Activity 46—Middle Ages Journal
Part A: 1. a person who learns a trade under a master **2.** an organization formed to protect the interest of workers in one craft or trade **3.** a piece of craftwork that earns an apprentice the status of master **4.** to move away from one country or region to settle in another **5.** people living in a place, or the total number of people
Part B: Journal entries should reflect content of Lesson 12–5.

Workbook Activity 47—The Magna Carta: Fact or Opinion
1. O **2.** F **3.** F **4.** F **5.** O **6.** O **7.** F **8.** F **9.** O **10.** F

Workbook Activity 48—The Birth of the Renaissance
1. A **2.** C **3.** D **4.** C **5.** B

Workbook Activity 49—Michelangelo
1. C **2.** B **3.** D **4.** A **5.** C

Workbook Activity 50—Major Events of the Renaissance
1. D **2.** B **3.** B **4.** A **5.** C

Workbook Activity 51—Renaissance Style
The following items should be circled: pointed-toed shoes, hoop skirts, undergarments showing, starched collars, velvet and silk, tights for men

Workbook Activity 52—The Two Sides of the Reformation
1. C **2.** P **3.** P **4.** C **5.** P **6.** C **7.** P **8.** P **9.** C **10.** P **11.** C **12.** P **13.** P **14.** C **15.** P

Workbook Activity 53—Changes to the Catholic Church
Part A: Reformation: John Calvin, Huguenots, Inquisition, Martin Luther, Protestantism; **Counter-Reformation:** 1545, Council of Trent, Jesuits, Society of Jesus, St. Ignatius Loyola
Part B: Spain, Roman Catholic; Italy, Roman Catholic; Hungary, Roman Catholic; Norway, Lutheran; France, Roman Catholic; Poland, Roman Catholic; Sweden, Lutheran; Denmark, Lutheran; Finland, Lutheran; Portugal, Roman Catholic

Workbook Activity 54—Monarchs and Nationalism Match-Up
1. E **2.** A **3.** H **4.** B **5.** C **6.** F **7.** I **8.** G **9.** J **10.** D

Workbook Activity 55—Interviewing King Philip of Spain
Questions and answers should reflect King Philip II's ardent support of the Catholic Church.

Workbook Activity 56—Unrest in France
1. The Huguenots, or French Protestants, and the Catholics were fighting. **2.** He was not a Catholic, even though the king before him was. **3.** Henry IV declared himself to be Catholic. **4.** He issued the Edict of Nantes giving Protestants religious freedom. **5.** He built new roads, passed laws to help farmers, encouraged trade and manufacturing, and supported French exploration.

Workbook Activity 57—English Monarchs Puzzle
1. Elizabeth **2.** Parliament **3.** Anne **4.** monarch **5.** Seymour **6.** Catherine **7.** annul **8.** England **9.** son **10.** Mary
Hidden words: Henry Tudor

Workbook Activity 58—China Crossword
Across: 2. yurts **3.** gunpowder **6.** Forbidden **7.** Marco **8.** Mongols **10.** Silk **11.** Ming **12.** Kublai Khan **13.** compass
Down: 1. Buddhism **4.** junks **5.** Genghis Khan **6.** forge **9.** Canal

Workbook Activity 59—Japan Riddle
1. Buddhism **2.** mikado **3.** shogun **4.** Cipango **5.** feudalism **6.** nobles **7.** Dutch **8.** Yorimoto **9.** kamikaze **10.** China **11.** samurai **12.** Nagasaki
Riddle solution: hermit nation

Workbook Activity 60—India Under Mogul Rule
1. E **2.** B **3.** C **4.** D **5.** A **6.** D **7.** A **8.** C **9.** E **10.** B

Workbook Activity 61—The Americas Crossword
Across: 5. Mesoamerica **7.** Aztec **8.** dwellers **9.** Montezuma
Down: 1. Cortés **2.** Tenochtitlán **3.** Inuit **4.** Pizarro **5.** mound **6.** Anasazi

Workbook Activity 62—Exploring New Lands Map Study
1. C **2.** D **3.** B **4.** D **5.** C **6.** A **7.** C **8.** B **9.** B **10.** D

Workbook Activity 63—Fighting for South America
1. conquerors **2.** gold **3.** horses **4.** New Spain **5.** convert
6. burned **7.** cruelly **8.** slaves **9.** savages **10.** diseases

Workbook Activity 64—Early Settlements in North America
1. The selection compares the English settlers in Jamestown, Plymouth, and the Massachusetts Bay Colony. **2.** Tobacco was the basis of the economy in Jamestown. **3.** Animal skins were the basis of the economy in Plymouth Colony. **4.** The American Indians taught the Pilgrims to use fish for fertilizer, to grow corn, and to trap beavers. **5.** The Massachusetts Bay Colony had the advantage of visiting the Pilgrims before they set up their colony. Also, the Puritans brought their household goods, farm tools, and livestock with them.

Workbook Activity 65—Goods in Each Colony
1. four **2.** whale products and raw wool **3.** Delaware, Maryland, Virginia, North Carolina, South Carolina, and Georgia **4.** Rhode Island, Massachusetts, and Maryland **5.** furniture

Workbook Activity 66—Understanding the Beginnings of Democracy
Students' paragraphs should discuss the idea of natural rights such freedom to think, decide, and reason. Students should also explain that the ruler should be subject to the approval of the ruled, rather than having the ultimate authority.

Workbook Activity 67—Support for Democracy
1. D **2.** M **3.** D **4.** M **5.** D **6.** D **7.** M **8.** D **9.** D **10.** D

Workbook Activity 68—The Glorious Revolution Timeline
(A) Rights **(B)** Netherlands **(C)** Charles **(D)** James **(E)** democratic
1. C **2.** D **3.** B **4.** A **5.** E

Workbook Activity 69—The Bill of Rights
Part A: Students' lists should include five of the freedoms offered by the Bill of Rights.
Part B: Students' lists should include rights that would be reasonable to want in a school, work, or home setting.

Workbook 70—The Age of Reason in France Quiz
Part A: **1.** E **2.** D **3.** G **4.** F **5.** A **6.** H **7.** C **8.** B
Part B: **9.** B **10.** D **11.** D **12.** C **13.** B **14.** A **15.** D

Workbook Activity 71—The King Tries to Limit Democracy Crossword
Across: **4.** Declaration **6.** fraternity **7.** oath **8.** Bastille
Down: **1.** Revolution **2.** Third Estate **3.** riot **5.** court

Workbook Activity 72—Napoleon Bonaparte Riddle
Part A: **1.** Napoleonic Code **2.** dictator **3.** Saint Helena **4.** Great Britain **5.** directory **6.** Josephine **7.** Waterloo **8.** Wellington **9.** Elba
Part B: Riddle solution: Bonaparte

Workbook Activity 73—Industries Develop Word Find
Part A: **1.** textile **2.** profit **3.** factory **4.** resource **5.** markets
6. transportation **7.** Industrial **8.** material **9.** investor **10.** energy
Part B: Hidden word: locomotive

Workbook Activity 74—Inventions that Changed the World
1. Thomas Savery **2.** flying shuttle **3.** spinning jenny **4.** Richard Arkwright **5.** Scottish **6.** Samuel Crompton **7.** steam-powered loom **8.** Richard Trevithick **9.** American **10.** Michael Faraday

Workbook Activity 75—Labor Unions During the Industrial Revolution
1. C **2.** A **3.** B **4.** D **5.** A

Workbook Activity 76—Agriculture and Industry
Part A: **1.** A **2.** I **3.** I **4.** I **5.** A **6.** A **7.** I **8.** I **9.** A **10.** I
Part B: **11.** B **12.** D **13.** C **14.** B **15.** A

Workbook Activity 77—Colonization Crossword
Across: **4.** Latin America **5.** colonies **9.** discrimination **10.** descendent
Down: **1.** mestizos **2.** Creole **3.** haciendas **6.** Portugal **7.** revolution
8. trade

Workbook Activity 78—Fighting for Independence
1. G **2.** A **3.** J **4.** C **5.** D **6.** H **7.** B **8.** F **9.** E **10.** I

Workbook Activity 79—Latin American Culture Map Study
1. 1816 **2.** 1825 **3.** 1822 **4.** 1810 **5.** 1902 **6.** 1822 **7.** 1804 **8.** 1821
9. 1824 **10.** 1821

Workbook Activity 80—Jefferson and Monroe
Part A: **1.** year **2.** France **3.** Louisiana **4.** west **5.** million **6.** miles
7. doubled **8.** Missouri
Part B: **9.** Congress **10.** imperialism **11.** strong **12.** Latin
13. colonies **14.** enlarge **15.** Doctrine

Workbook Activity 81—Border Problems Crossword
Across: **1.** James Bowie **5.** Santa Anna **6.** Hidalgo **7.** United States
10. Grande **11.** Mexico **12.** million
Down: **2.** mission **3.** San Antonio **4.** borders **8.** Texas **9.** Alamo

Workbook Activity 82—The American Civil War Riddle
1. Union **2.** tobacco **3.** enslaved **4.** Virginia **5.** Robert E. Lee
6. Grant **7.** Pennsylvania **8.** cotton **9.** Bull Run **10.** Confederate
Riddle answer: Gettysburg

Workbook Activity 83—U.S. Expansion Crossword
Across: **1.** Pearl **5.** Cuba **8.** transcontinental **9.** Panama Canal
10. William Seward
Down: **2.** Liliuokalani **3.** *Maine* **4.** Alaska **6.** Guam **7.** Hawaii

Workbook Activity 84—China Under Manchurian Rule Map Study
1. Gobi desert **2.** Beijing (Peking) **3.** Himalayas **4.** Sea of Japan and the Pacific Ocean **5.** Macao and Guangzhou (Canton)

Workbook Activity 85—Foreign Interference
1. C **2.** A **3.** D **4.** B **5.** D

Workbook Activity 86—Japan and China
1. C, J **2.** C **3.** J **4.** C **5.** C, J **6.** C, J **7.** C, J **8.** J **9.** J **10.** J

Workbook Activity 87—The British East India Company Crossword
Across: 1. customs **2.** indirectly **4.** Bombay **5.** trade **6.** agent **7.** sepoys
Down: 1. cartridge **2.** impose **3.** Java **4.** British

Workbook Activity 88—British Rule Matching
1. G **2.** F **3.** B **4.** I **5.** E **6.** D **7.** H **8.** A **9.** J **10.** C

Workbook Activity 89—Mahatma Gandhi Diary Entry
Diary entries should reflect Gandhi's nonviolent protests using civil disobedience.

Workbook Activity 90—Early Kingdoms in Africa Chart Study
Part A: 1. Built pyramids and temples. **2.** Kush **3.** western Africa **4.** Mali **5.** Timbuktu became a center of trade and learning.
Part B: 6. C **7.** D **8.** E **9.** B **10.** A

Workbook Activity 91—Africa After the First Century A.D. Crossword
Across: 3. Zimbabwe **5.** Shaka **6.** Muslim **7.** Henry **8.** Portugal
Down: 1. great migration **2.** Swahili **3.** Zulus **4.** Bantu **9.** Arab

Workbook Activity 92—The Slave Trade Timeline
Part A: 1. 5 **2.** 3 **3.** 4 **4.** 2 **5.** 1
Part B: 6. The Africans treated their slaves like human beings. The Europeans, on the other hand, treated their slaves like goods to be traded. **7.** Slaves were brought to the New World to work in mines and on plantations. **8.** The removal of so many Africans took away some of the strongest, finest people. Those people would be missed greatly when European imperialism threatened Africa. **9.** By 1888, slavery was against the law throughout the Americas. **10.** Enslaved African Americans developed music called spirituals to express their struggles in slavery. Later forms of music that were popular in American culture, such as jazz and blues, came out of the spirituals.

Workbook Activity 93—European Imperialism Riddle
Part A: 1. independence **2.** industrial **3.** Suez **4.** Ethiopia **5.** missionaries **6.** Liberia **7.** schools **8.** Germany **9.** imperialism **10.** Ferdinand de Lesseps
Part B: Riddle answer: colonizing

Workbook Activity 94—Nationalism in Italy Crossword
Across: 3. Sword **4.** shirts **5.** radio **7.** boundary **9.** Italian **13.** nationalism **14.** Young **15.** minister
Down: 1. Marconi **2.** Brain **4.** secret **6.** anthem **8.** diplomat **10.** Austria **11.** Venetia **12.** unify

Workbook Activity 95—Germany and Italy
Italy: Cavour, The Brain; Garibaldi, The Sword; Mazzini, The Soul; once center of the Roman Empire; Red Shirts; Sardinia; Sicily; Victor Emmanuel II
Both Italy and Germany: affected by Napoleon; problems with Austria; rise of nationalism; unification
Germany: Bismarck; Blood and Iron; Confederation of the Rhine; kaiser; Prussia; Second Reich; Wilhelm I; won Alsace and Lorraine

Workbook Activity 96—The War Begins in Europe Map Study
1. N **2.** A **3.** C **4.** C **5.** N **6.** A **7.** C **8.** C **9.** N **10.** A

Workbook Activity 97—Fighting the War
1. C **2.** I **3.** D **4.** F **5.** E **6.** A **7.** H **8.** G **9.** B **10.** J

Workbook Activity 98—Europe After World War I
Part A: 1. Finland **2.** Estonia **3.** Latvia **4.** Lithuania **5.** Poland **6.** Czechoslovakia **7.** Yugoslavia **8.** East Prussia
Part B: 9. Germany and Turkey lost the most in the war. **10.** The war put an end to the Ottoman Empire. Most of the Arab lands that had been ruled by the Turks fell under British control.

Workbook Activity 99—Events in the Early History of Russia
1. E **2.** D **3.** B **4.** A **5.** C **6.** C **7.** E **8.** B **9.** D **10.** A

Workbook Activity 100—Unrest in the Early 1900s Puzzle
Part A: 1. Nicholas **2.** Bloody **3.** Karl Marx **4.** democratic **5.** struggles **6.** Germany **7.** socialist **8.** Prussia **9.** Duma
Part B: Hidden word: Communism

Workbook Activity 101—Lenin and Stalin
Lenin: was exiled, was the "Father of the Revolution," fought in a civil war, led the Bolsheviks, overthrew the government
Both Lenin and Stalin: read Karl Marx, had a strong police force, ruled by fear, ran a strict Communist government, killed his enemies
Stalin: was the "man of steel," built up Russia's economy, censored newspapers, did not allow people to travel, rewrote Soviet history

Workbook Activity 102—Sorting Dictators
Mussolini: absolute rule, Ethiopia, fascist, Italy
Tojo: Asian empire, Japan, Manchuria, military took over government, premier
Hitler: anti-Semitism, concentration camp, Germany, National Socialist, super race, Third Reich

Workbook Activity 103—World War II Begins in Europe Puzzle
Part A: 1. Britain **2.** Royal **3.** civilians **4.** Treaty **5.** Nazi **6.** tanks **7.** Churchill **8.** winter **9.** defeat **10.** Greece
Part B: Hidden word: blitzkrieg

Workbook Activity 104—Poland Fights Back
1. A **2.** D **3.** B **4.** A **5.** C

Workbook Activity 105—The End of the War—Fact or Opinion
1. O **2.** F **3.** F **4.** O **5.** O **6.** F **7.** O **8.** F **9.** O **10.** O **11.** F **12.** O
13. O **14.** F **15.** O

Workbook Activity 106—Soldiers Killed in the War
1. Italy **2.** USSR, 7.5 million **3.** Japan, Germany, USSR **4.** Italy,
France, Britain **5.** Germany

Workbook Activity 107—The World After World War II Map Study
1. France, Soviet Union, Britain, and America **2.** France, Britain, and
America **3.** Students should correctly show the Berlin Wall between
East and West Berlin.

Workbook Activity 108—Alliances During the Cold War
Part A: Students should place asterisks by Belgium, Canada, Denmark,
France, Iceland, Italy, Luxembourg, the Netherlands, Norway, Portugal,
the United Kingdom, and the United States.
Part B: NATO was formed to create an allied defense against
Communism. If one of the countries was attacked, the others would
support them in battle. It was also a way to show strength to the Soviet
Union in the face of the growth of Communism.
The Warsaw Pact was formed in response to NATO, so the Communist
countries could have an alliance should the other countries attack. It
also showed the non-Communist countries that there was strength in
the Communist alliance.

Workbook Activity 109—Cold War Matching
1. G **2.** H **3.** I **4.** D **5.** J **6.** F **7.** B **8.** A **9.** C **10.** E

Workbook Activity 110—India and Pakistan
1. I **2.** I **3.** P **4.** I **5.** P **6.** I **7.** P **8.** I **9.** I **10.** B **11.** P **12.** I **13.** B
14. I **15.** B

Workbook Activity 111—China Word Find
Part A: **1.** Cultural **2.** Xiaoping **3.** Mao **4.** communes **5.** Republic
6. Chiang **7.** Taiwan **8.** students **9.** Tiananmen
Part B: Hidden word: Communism

Workbook Activity 112—Korea's Important Dates
1. 2007 **2.** 2002 **3.** 1953 **4.** 1950 **5.** 1945

Workbook Activity 113—Japan and Southeast Asia Fact Find
1. O **2.** F **3.** O **4.** O **5.** F **6.** F **7.** O **8.** F **9.** O **10.** O **11.** F **12.** O
13. O **14.** F **15.** O

Workbook Activity 114—Vietnam's Important Dates
1. 1957 **2.** 1954 **3.** 1965 **4.** 1969 **5.** 1973

Workbook Activity 115—African Nations
Part A: **1.** South Africa **2.** Sudan **3.** Ghana **4.** Kenya **5.** Zimbabwe
Part B: **6.** D **7.** E **8.** A **9.** I **10.** C **11.** J **12.** G **13.** H **14.** B **15.** F

Workbook Activity 116—Middle East Map Review
1. Cairo **2.** Beirut **3.** Suez Canal **4.** Students should name two: Eliat,
Gaza, Jerusalem, Tel Aviv-Yafo **5.** Dead Sea

Workbook Activity 117—Middle East Conflict Articles
1. A **2.** B **3.** D **4.** C **5.** B

Workbook Activity 118—Oil Production
1. less **2.** less **3.** more **4.** 10 million **5.** five times as many

Workbook Activity 119—Middle East Timeline Study
1. D **2.** B **3.** C **4.** B **5.** A **6.** B **7.** D **8.** A **9.** C **10.** D

Workbook Activity 120—Soviet Union News Report
Articles should contain pertinent facts regarding the event that students
chose to write about.

Workbook Activity 121—Soviet Union and Cold War Crossword
Across: **4.** Russia **6.** fifteen **8.** independent **9.** Gorbachev **10.** hostility
Down: **1.** terrorism **2.** disband **3.** president **5.** Putin **7.** Yeltsin

Workbook Activity 122—Eastern Europe Map Study
1. August 1991 **2.** Turkmenistan **3.** Baltic Sea **4.** Tajikistan **5.** Arctic
Ocean

Workbook Activity 123—The United States in Latin American
Affairs Word Find
Part A: **1.** Policy **2.** States **3.** Castro **4.** Latin **5.** Batista **6.** rebels
7. guerrilla **8.** dictator **9.** economy
Part B: Hidden word: Caribbean

Workbook Activity 124—Events in Central America
1. C (1959) **2.** B (1980) **3.** E (1985) **4.** A (1988) **5.** D (1989)
6. C (1979) **7.** A (1983) **8.** E (1985) **9.** D (1989) **10.** B (1993)

Workbook Activity 125—Facts About Mexico
1. A **2.** C **3.** D **4.** B **5.** D

Workbook Activity 126—The Amazon
1. A **2.** C **3.** A **4.** B **5.** D

Workbook Activity 127—The Nuclear Age Word Find
Part A: **1.** Nuclear **2.** Three **3.** Soviet **4.** nonrenewable
5. expensive **6.** oil **7.** Albert **8.** energy **9.** meltdown
Part B: Hidden place: Chernobyl

Workbook Activity 128—The Space Age Chart
The United States: first person on the moon, *Explorer I,* the space
shuttle, Hubble Space Telescope, *Challenger, Columbia*
Both the U.S. and the USSR: people lived in space, the International
Space Station, flew into space in 1975, scientists performed experiments
in space, space race
The Soviet Union: first woman in space, *Sputnik I, Mir,* first person
into space

Workbook Activity 129—Communication in the Computer Age
Answers will vary. Possible answers include: **1.** personal, handwritten,
can take time to think out what you want to say **2.** slow, delayed
response **3.** can hear other person's voice, immediate response
4. both people have to be at the phone at the same time, expensive
5. easy, can send messages any time, can take time to be clear about
your message **6.** hard to communicate emotion, cannot always get
an immediate response **7.** immediate, quick, easy **8.** limited space
for message, easy to be misunderstood **9.** can communicate to a lot
of people at one time, can include more information, can include
images **10.** public, not good for immediate communication

Workbook Activity 130—Global Issues Crossword

Across: **2.** tariff **5.** Trade **8.** standard **9.** technology **11.** Pacific
12. global
Down: **1.** Africa **3.** industry **4.** import **6.** economy **7.** labor
10. health

Workbook Activity 131—Global Warming

Part A: **1.** D **2.** A **3.** C **4.** E **5.** B
Part B: **6.** C **7.** E **8.** A **9.** D **10.** B

Workbook Activity 132—Terrorism Cause and Effect

Part A: **1.** C; E **2.** E; C **3.** C; E **4.** C; E **5.** E; C
Part B: **6.** E; C **7.** C; E **8.** E; C **9.** C; E **10.** E; C

Workbook Activity 133—Important Inventions

1. All of these inventions have improved communication. **2.** People use computers and the Internet at school. **3.** Airplanes carry people, mail, and products. **4.** Computers have created the jobs of computer programmer and software developer. **5.** People use the Internet for banking, research, and shopping.

Chapter Outlines

Chapter 1 Outline

I. A. 1. Slavery
        2. industry, agriculture
        3. imperialism
II. A. 1. primary
        2. artifacts
III. A. 1. world
     B. 1. B.C., A.D.
        2. left

Chapter 2 Outline

I.   A. 1. glaciers
         2. south
     B. 1. stone, stick, bone
         2. Stone Age
     C. 1. herds
         2. food
         3. struggle
II. A. 1. seeds
         2. sickles, plows
     B. 1. store
         2. settlements
         3. tame
     C. 1. Agricultural Revolution
         2. control
         3. specialize
     D. 1. baskets, pottery, cloth
         2. laws
         3. armies
         4. kingdoms
III. A. 1. Jordan, Syria, Iraq, Iran, Kuwait,
            Lebanon, Israel, Turkey
         2. quarter moon
         3. Tigris, Euphrates
         4. Mesopotamia
     B. 1. 8000
         2. rounded
         3. rich
         4. wall
     C. 1. 7000
         2. square corners
     D. 1. Europe, China, Africa
         2. soil
         3. civilizations

Chapter 3 Outline

I.   A. 1. irrigate
         2. dikes
         3. oxen
     B. 1. metal, stone, timber
         2. river
         3. sails
II. A. 1. temple
         2. independent
         3. ziggurat
III. A. 1. writing
         2. scribes
         3. cuneiform
     B. 1. land
         2. time
         3. wheel
IV. A. 1. wealthy
         2. jewelry
     B. 1. Babylonians

Chapter 4 Outline
I. A. 1. Nile
    2. jungle
    3. cleared
  B. 1. farm, tame animals, make pottery, and weave
    2. metal
    3. canal
    4. fertile
  C. 1. 3200 B.C.
    2. Lower
    3. Upper
    4. south, north
    5. conquered
  D. 1. double
    2. pharaoh
    3. taxes
II. A. 1. rich, powerful
    2. tombs
    3. Wonders
  B. 1. Great
    2. 10
    3. 2
    4. tons
    5. machinery, tools
    6. ramps, planks
  C. 1. artifacts
    2. picture
  D. 1. bowls, pictures, jewelry, pottery
    2. pharaohs
  E. 1. chemicals
    2. brains, organs
    3. bandages
    4. museums
III. A. 1. craftworkers
    2. ringlets, braids
    3. makeup
    4. kohl
    5. perfume
  B. 1. many
    2. city
    3. Osiris
    4. river
  C. 1. hieroglyphics
    2. papyrus
    3. stars
    4. 365
    5. jewelry, tools, weapons
    6. instruments
    7. trade

Chapter 5 Outline
I. A. 1. navigate
    2. colonies
    3. soldiers
  B. 1. oars, sails
    2. alphabet
    3. dye
II. A. 1. god
    2. Abraham
    3. slaves
    4. Moses
  B. 1. Canaan
    2. Philistines
    3. Jerusalem
    4. temple
  C. 1. Israel, Judah
    2. Assyrians
    3. Chaldeans
III. A. 1. Euphrates
    2. Sumerians
    3. Code
IV. A. 1. warriors
    2. iron
    3. peace treaty
V. A. 1. army
    2. siege engines
    3. tribute
  B. 1. library
    2. Chaldeans

Chapter 6 Outline
I. A. 1. India, Pakistan
    2. Fertile Crescent
  B. 1. 1,000
    2. 1500
  C. 1. north
    2. conquer, control
  D. 1. Hindu
    2. god
  E. 1. castes
    2. outcastes
  F. 1. life
    2. soul
    3. reincarnated
  G. 1. east, south
    2. rajas
II. A. 1. 563
    2. Hindu, raja
    3. wealth
  B. 1. greed
    2. nirvana
    3. suffering
  C. 1. 321
    2. caste
  D. 1. 185
    2. foreign
III. A. 1. Yellow
    2. cut
  B. 1. farmers
    2. Sorrow
    3. pits
  C. 1. write
    2. histories
    3. cloth, silkworms
  D. 1. ancestors
    2. homes, families, land
    3. courtesy
  E. 1. dynasty
    2. Shang, 500
    3. 1028, 750
IV. A. 1. Asia, Alaska
    2. North, Central, South
  B. 1. 5,000
    2. maize, squash, tomatoes, beans
    3. cotton, llamas
  C. 1. Mexico
    2. heads, shrines
  D. 1. Mexico, Central
    2. rain, towns

Chapter 7 Outline

I. **A.** **1.** rocky
    2. Aegean, Mediterranean
    3. olive oil
 B. **1.** colonies
    2. mountains
    3. tyrant
    4. democracy
 C. **1.** hill
    2. theaters
    3. Parthenon

II. **A.** **1.** military
    2. the state
    3. slaves
 B. **1.** statues
    2. Socrates
    3. landowners
    4. constitution

III. **A.** **1.** colonies
    2. Marathon
    3. Athens
    4. Salamis
 B. **1.** 50
    2. Pericles
    3. money
 C. **1.** 27
    2. plague

IV. **A.** **1.** architecture
    2. thinkers
    3. Olympic

Chapter 8 Outline

I. **A.** **1.** north
    2. poor
    3. farm, roads
 B. **1.** army
    2. foot, horseback
    3. Persian
    4. strength
 C. **1.** Sparta
    2. Persia
    3. enemies
    4. assassinated
 D. **1.** ambitious, angered
    2. horse
    3. Aristotle
    4. 18
    5. 20

II. **A.** **1.** Persia
    2. Middle East
    3. 333
    4. Alexander, Darius
    5. Tyre, bridge
 B. **1.** Egypt
    2. happy
    3. Alexandria
    4. Ptolemy
 C. **1.** rulers
    2. Darius
    3. Persepolis
 D. **1.** elephants
    2. horses
    3. deeper, India
    4. tired

III. **A.** **1.** 30
    2. 12
    3. Greek
    4. Europe, Asia
    5. Babylon
 B. **1.** ill, 33
    2. gold, Alexandria
    3. divided, generals
    4. style, customs

Chapter 9 Outline

I. **A.** **1.** north
    2. 100
    3. republic
 B. **1.** elected
    2. representatives, senate
 C. **1.** Carthage
    2. Messina
    3. Macedonia
    4. Africa
    5. Greek

II. **A.** **1.** province
    2. general
    3. army
    4. civil
    5. Cleopatra
    6. 45 B.C.
 B. **1.** king
    2. Brutus, Cassius
    3. Senate

III. **A.** **1.** Octavian
    2. Cleopatra
    3. emperor
    4. Augustus
    5. *Pax Romana*

IV. **A.** **1.** aqueducts
    2. Forum
    3. baths
    4. Circus Maximus
 B. **1.** arches
    2. useful
    3. highways
 C. **1.** romance
    2. courts

V. **A.** **1.** the Bible
    2. messiah
    3. Paul
 B. **1.** persecuted
    2. catacombs
 C. **1.** cross
    2. Constantinople
    3. converted
    4. bishops

VI. **A.** **1.** invaders
    2. taxes

Chapter 10 Outline

I.   **A.**   **1.** north
             2. Middle Ages
    B.   **1.** Germans
             2. uncivilized, primitive
    C.   **1.** clothing
             2. laws
    D.   **1.** barbarians
             2. protected
             3. mixed
    E.   **1.** power, riches
             2. Huns
             3. Goths
             4. Vandals
    F.   **1.** Goths
             2. Angles, Saxons, Jutes
             3. Franks
             4. buried
             5. emperor

II.   **A.**   **1.** Constantinople
             2. Byzantine
             3. 1,000
             4. Greek
             5. Roman Catholic, Eastern Orthodox
    B.   **1.** Great
             2. Franks
             3. France
             4. Germany, Italy
    C.   **1.** Holy Roman Empire
             2. schools, artists
             3. died
             4. France, Germany, Italy

III.   **A.**   **1.** Norway, Sweden, Denmark
             2. sailing, fighting
             3. Vikings
             4. 793
             5. France, Spain, Italy
             6. plundered, home
             7. ships
    B.   **1.** Russia, England, France
             2. Normandy
             3. exiled, Iceland, Greenland
             4. North America, Vinland
             5. centuries
             6. sagas
    C.   **1.** Vikings
             2. England
             3. Hastings
             4. Conqueror
    D.   **1.** trade
             2. buildings, ships

Chapter 11 Outline

I.   **A.**   **1.** land
             2. estate
             3. freemen, serfs
    B.   **1.** trade
             2. cold
             3. fairs

II.   **A.**   **1.** nobles
             2. monks, nuns
    B.   **1.** warriors
             2. king
             3. squire

III.   **A.**   **1.** Italy
             2. blood
             3. fleas
             4. labor
    B.   **1.** 700
             2. trade
             3. knights

Chapter 12 Outline

I.   **A.**   **1.** idols
             2. poorer
    B.   **1.** vision
             2. prophet
             3. slaves
             4. rebellion *or* revolution
             5. Medina
    C.   **1.** hundreds
             2. Jews, Christians
    D.   **1.** two
             2. vote
             3. relative

II.   **A.**   **1.** pilgrimage
             2. Jerusalem
             3. Turks
             4. Urban II
             5. 200
             6. 1099
    B.   **1.** 1187
             2. rulers
             3. fighting
             4. Byzantine

III.   **A.**   **1.** money
             2. misery
    B.   **1.** foods
             2. exploration
             3. maps

IV.   **A.**   **1.** Mediterranean
             2. iron
             3. plowshare
             4. surplus
             5. harness
             6. crop rotation

V.   **A.**   **1.** towns
             2. fire, disease
             3. money
    B.   **1.** trade *or* business
             2. deeds
    C.   **1.** guild
             2. apprentice
    D.   **1.** thousand
             2. Venice
             3. art, science, education

VI.   **A.**   **1.** human rights
             2. power
    B.   **1.** King John
             2. 1215
             3. Magna Carta

Chapter 13 Outline

I. A. 1. Christianity
2. universities, cathedrals
3. renaissance
B. 1. life
2. humanism
C. 1. simple
2. criticize
II. A. 1. Italy
2. Greece, Rome
3. real
4. patrons
B. 1. architect
2. bones, muscles
3. *Pietà*
4. ceiling
III. A. 1. China
2. moveable
3. quickly
4. translated
B. 1. springs
2. cast iron
3. microscope
C. 1. earth
2. Copernicus
D. 1. the same
2. telescope
3. moons
4. Copernicus
5. church
IV. A. 1. scientist
2. sketchbooks
3. flying
4. *Mona Lisa*
5. talent
V. A. 1. monk
2. complaints
3. pope
4. Protestants
B. 1. Calvin
2. Huguenots
3. heretics
VI. A. 1. clergy
2. faith
B. 1. army
2. far-off

Chapter 14 Outline

I. A. 1. monarch
2. France
B. 1. nationalism
2. religion
3. personality
II. A. 1. Americas
2. Catholic
B. 1. taxes *or* money
2. independence
C. 1. Mary I
2. Netherlands
III. A. 1. Huguenots
2. assassinated
B. 1. Catholic
2. Edict
3. Quebec
IV. A. 1. Anne Boleyn
2. annul
3. Parliament
4. six
B. 1. Protestantism
2. six
C. 1. Protestants
2. Philip
D. 1. 45
2. Tudor
E. 1. writers
2. Armada
3. Raleigh, Drake

Chapter 15 Outline

I. A. 1. paper
B. 1. Buddhism
C. 1. Mongols
D. 1. Italy
2. coal
E. 1. Forbidden
II. A. 1. samurai
2. emperor
3. shogun
B. 1. Cipango
2. Missionaries
3. Dutch
III. A. 1. eigth
2. Babar
3. Akbar
4. Taj Mahal
IV. A. 1. Ohio
2. Anasazi
B. 1. America
2. vitamins
C. 1. Tenochtitlán
2. Montezuma II
3. Cortés
D. 1. Inca
2. Cuzco
3. Pizarro

Chapter 16 Outline

I.   A. 1. Asia
         2. San Salvador
         3. India
         4. Amerigo Vespucci
     B. 1. 1497
         2. South America
         3. the world
II. A. 1. Mexico
         2. guns, horses
         3. Aztec
         4. Inca
         5. diseases
III. A. 1. pirates
         2. Dutch
         3. culture
         4. wary
         5. Jamestown
         6. Hudson
         7. tobacco
     B. 1. furs
         2. French
     C. 1. John Cabot
         2. Quebec
IV. A. 1. shareholders
         2. Amsterdam
         3. England, France, the Netherlands
         4. losses
     B. 1. middle
         2. nobility

Chapter 17 Outline

I.   A. 1. reason
         2. revolution
     B. 1. nobles
         2. King Edward I
     C. 1. speak
         2. Commons
II. A. 1. jury
         2. arrested
     B. 1. Parliament
         2. Oliver Cromwell
     C. 1. Commonwealth
         2. Lord Protector
III. A. 1. power
         2. William, Mary
     B. 1. consult
         2. Lords
IV. A. 1. taxes
         2. representation
     B. 1. freedom
         2. George Washington

Chapter 18 Chapter Outline

I.   A. 1. Reason
         2. Lafayette
II. A. 1. three
         2. Third
     B. 1. Assembly
         2. oath
     C. 1. symbol
         2. July
     D. 1. nobles
         2. Declaration
     E. 1. republic
     F. 1. executed
         2. Robespierre
III. A. 1. emperor
         2. schools
     B. 1. Russia
         2. Louis XVIII
         3. Elba
     C. 1. Belgium
         2. Wellington
         3. Saint Helena
     D. 1. revolutions
         2. Third

Chapter 19 Outline

I. A. 1. natural resources
2. transportation
3. investors
4. colonies
5. government
B. 1. cloth
2. Cottage weavers
II. A. 1. flying shuttle
2. spinning jenny
3. water power
4. mule
5. steam
B. 1. 1698
2. improved
3. transportation
4. locomotives, ships
C. 1. electricity
2. Petroleum
3. internal combustion engine
III. A. 1. 30 times
2. middle class
3. telegraph
4. women, children
B. 1. population
2. Slum
3. disease
4. labor unions
IV. A. 1. industrialized
2. export
3. cheap

Chapter 20 Outline

I. A. 1. Latin
2. haciendas
B. 1. trade
2. revolution
C. 1. Creoles
2. mestizos
3. discrimination
II. A. 1. revolt
2. French
B. 1. priests
2. September 16
C. 1. wealthy
2. liberated
D. 1. Chile
2. dictator
E. 1. kingdom
2. independent
F. 1. dictators
2. mestizos
III. A. 1. influenced
2. mural
B. 1. Spanish
2. dominate

Chapter 21 Outline

I. A. 1. Monroe
B. 1. France
II. A. 1. Alamo
2. Anna
B. 1. Mexico
2. Treaty
3. 15
III. A. 1. South
2. Lincoln
3. Run
4. Lee
B. 1. Gettysburg
2. Emancipation
3. Grant
4. Appomattox
IV. A. 1. McCormick
2. telegraph
3. transcontinental
4. industrial
B. 1. Seward
2. Pearl
3. territory
C. 1. *Maine*
2. Cuba
3. Guam
D. 1. Roosevelt
2. Colombia
3. South

Chapter 22 Outline

I. **A.** **1.** northeastern
   2. foreign
   3. population
   4. isolationist
   B. **1.** opium
   2. trading
   3. Unequal
II. **A.** **1.** peasants
   2. interference
   B. **1.** Korea
   2. weak
   3. Open Door
   C. **1.** overthrow
   2. president
   3. Nationalist
III. **A.** **1.** warships
   2. president
   3. shogun
   B. **1.** treaties
   2. enlightened rule
   3. constitution
   4. industrial
   C. **1.** Taiwan
   2. Russia
   3. Korea

Chapter 23 Outline

I. **A.** **1.** Hindu
   2. kingdoms
   B. **1.** Portugal
   2. Madras
   3. sepoys
   C. **1.** agents
   2. colony
II. **A.** **1.** viceroy
   2. Jewel
   B. **1.** manufactured
   2. superiority
   C. **1.** 1885
   2. government
   3. Amritsar
III. **A.** **1.** nonviolent
   2. untouchables
   3. arrested
   B. **1.** Pakistan
   2. fast

Chapter 24 Outline

I. **A.** **1.** Egypt
   2. iron
   3. 350
   B. **1.** Arab
   2. salt
   C. **1.** gold
   2. Muslim
   D. **1.** Mansa Musa
   2. Timbuktu
   E. **1.** Mali
   2. Mohammed
   3. Moroccans
II. **A.** **1.** migration
   2. Bantu
   3. Zimbabwe
   4. Shaka
   B. **1.** Navigator
   2. Gama
   3. Angola
III. **A.** **1.** Portuguese
   2. Dutch
   3. 10
   4. 1834
   B. **1.** spirituals
   2. jazz
IV. **A.** **1.** raw
   2. Berlin, Germany
   3. Liberia
   B. **1.** French
   2. Britain
   C. **1.** tribes
   2. inferior
   3. schools

Chapter 25 Outline

I. A. 1. divided
       2. invaded
       3. joined
    B. 1. Austria, the pope
       2. unify
    C. 1. "Young Italy"
       2. revolutionaries
       3. Victor Emmanuel II
    D. 1. prime minister
       2. France
       3. Austria
    E. 1. soldier
       2. "Red Shirts"
       3. Sicily
       4. north, south
    F. 1. The pope, Austria
       2. The Italians
       3. France, the Prussians
II. A. 1. landowner, soldier
       2. prime minister
    B. 1. North German Confederation
       2. France
       3. kaiser
    C. 1. democracy
       2. military
       3. privilege

Chapter 26 Outline

I. A. 1. Central
       2. Allied
    B. 1. Alsace, Lorraine
       2. Austria-Hungary
       3. military
    C. 1. Bosnia
       2. assassinated *or* killed
       3. July 28, 1914
II. A. 1. 30
       2. Italy
    B. 1. the Marne
       2. fronts
    C. 1. submarines
       2. power
III. A. 1. colonies
       2 costs
       3. Britain
    B. 1. conflicts
       2. Article Ten
       3. against

Chapter 27 Outline

I. A. 1. Rus
       2. Prince Oleg
       3. Church
       4. warriors
    B. 1. czar
       2. terror
       3. upper classes, peasants
       4. engineers, doctors
    C. 1. westernize
       2. port
       3. St. Petersburg
    D. 1. peasant revolt
       2. Poland
       3. Napoleon Bonaparte
II. A. 1. factories
       2. protesting
       3. parliament
    B. 1. socialism
       2. Communism
    C. 1. shortages
       2. overthrew
       3. against
III. A. 1. Communist
       2. soviets
    B. 1. civil war
       2. police force
       3. enemies
    C. 1. steel
       2. factories, machinery
       3. collectives
       4. Siberia
       5. censored
       6. Curtain

Chapter 28 Outline

I.   **A.**   **1.** "Great Depression"
                2. fascists
                3. Ethiopia
       B.   **1.** Manchuria
                2. China
       C.   **1.** military
                2. Nazi
                3. Reich
       D.   **1.** hatred, fear
                2. Jewish
                3. concentration
       E.   **1.** Axis
                2. Allied

II.   **A.**   **1.** Austria
                2. Great Britain, France
                3. "lightning war"
                4. Italy
       B.   **1.** air
                2. civilians
                3. defeat
       C.   **1.** Romania, Greece, Yugoslavia
       D.   **1.** million
                2. supplies, machinery, factories
                3. weather

III.   **A.**   **1.** secret, undercover
                2. solution
                3. executed
       B.   **1.** neutral
                2. Pearl Harbor
                3. war
       C.   **1.** surrendered
                2. offensive
                3. North Africa
                4. Italy
       D.   **1.** Normandy
                2. Eisenhower
                3. France, Belgium, Luxembourg

IV.   **A.**   **1.** Bulge
                2. executed
                3. killed
       B.   **1.** MacArthur
                2. duty and honor
                3. bombs
       C.   **1.** Manhattan
                2. Hiroshima, Nagasaki
                3. hanged

V.   **A.**   **1.** expensive
                2. 55 million
       B.   **1.** Declaration
                2. Charter
                3. Security Council
                4. world peace, human rights

Chapter 29 Outline

I.   **A.**   **1.** 13 billion
                2. satellites
       B.   **1.** West Germany *or* Federal Republic of Germany
                2. East Germany *or* German Democratic Republic
                3. Berlin Wall
       C.   **1.** isolationism
                2. United Nations

II.   **A.**   **1.** allies
                2. capitalist
                3. Truman
       B.   **1.** Atlantic
                2. Warsaw
       C.   **1.** materials
                2. Union
       D.   **1.** 1945
                2. hydrogen
       E.   **1.** food, clothing
                2. Khrushchev
       F.   **1.** Cuba
                2. blockade
                3. retire

III.   **A.**   **1.** hot line
                2. space exploration
       B.   **1.** Muslim
                2. missiles

Chapter 30 Outline

I.   **A.**   **1.** Punjab
                2. assassinated
       B.   **1.** Kashmir
                2. East Pakistan
       C.   **1.** population
                2. production
                3. economic
                4. untouchable

II.   **A.**   **1.** landowners, businesspeople
                2. peasants
                3. Taiwan
       B.   **1.** communes
                2. industry
       C.   **1.** brainwashed
                2. Red Guard
                3. modern
                4. Tiananmen
       D.   **1.** manufacturing, business
                2. port

III.   **A.**   **1.** South Korea
                2. the United Nations
       B.   **1.** nuclear
                2. nuclear

IV.   **A.**   **1.** World War II
                2. civil
       B.   **1.** defense budget
                2. automobiles, electronics equipment
                3. restrictions

V.   **A.**   **1.** France
                2. Geneva, Switzerland
                3. Vietcong
       B.   **1.** domino
                2. Communist
       C.   **1.** assassinations
                2. rioted
       D.   **1.** Saigon
                2. Khmer Rouge
       E.   **1.** Soviet Union

VI.   **A.**   **1.** Algeria
                2. Kenya
       B.   **1.** starvation
                2. Uganda
                3. Ethiopia
       C.   **1.** minority
                2. majority
                3. Zimbabwe
       D.   **1.** Dutch colonists
                2. separated
                3. Nelson Mandela
       E.   **1.** Islamic
                2. military
                3. Chad
       F.   **1.** Somalia
                2. African

Chapter 31 Outline

I. **A.** **1.** nation
           2. Britain
    B. **1.** divided
           2. independence
           3. Syria, Egypt, Lebanon, Iraq, Jordan
    C. **1.** refugees
           2. Palestine
    D. **1.** Suez Canal
           2. Egypt, Jordan, Syria
           3. the Sinai Peninsula, the Gaza Strip, the West Bank
           4. Yom Kippur
II. **A.** **1.** Gaza
           2. Christians, Muslims
           3. terrorism
           4. Bill Clinton
    B. **1.** the Ayatollah Khomeini
           2. 1979, Tehran
           3. Iraq
           4. oil
    C. **1.** Kuwait's
           2. United Nations
           3. Kuwait
           4. mass destruction
    D. **1.** Russia
           2. Golan Heights
    E. **1.** al Qaeda
           2. World Trade Center
           3. Madrid, Spain
III. **A.** **1.** oil fields
           2. shortage
    B. **1.** Muammar al-Qaddafi
           2. West Berlin
           3. nuclear
    C. **1.** fields
           2. North Korea, Iran
IV. **A.** **1.** industrialized
           2. irrigation

Chapter 32 Outline

I. **A.** **1.** nuclear
           2. Afghanistan
    B. **1.** speech
           2. violence *or* hostilities
           3. businesses
    C. **1.** coup
           2. death *or* fall
II. **A.** **1.** 15
           2. Boris Yeltsin
    B. **1.** food, medicine
           2. Russia
    C. **1.** president
           2. terrorism
III. **A.** **1.** Czechoslovakia
           2. Solidarity
           3. West Germany
    B. **1.** six
           2. Serbs
           3. Dayton
           4. Serbia
    C. **1.** Russia
           2. suicide

Chapter 33 Outline

I. **A.** **1.** Good Neighbor
           2. American States
           3. rebels
           4. Communist
           5. economy
II. **A.** **1.** Front
           2. Contras
           3. economic
           4. elections
    B. **1.** military
           2. president
           3. peace
    C. **1.** defense
           2. elections
           3. drug
III. **A.** **1.** economic
           2. Free Trade
           3. land
    B. **1.** revolutions, government takeovers
           2. violence
IV. **A.** **1.** imports
           2. exports
           3. grow
           4. rain forests

Chapter 34 Outline

I. A. 1. nuclear
        2. limit
        3. energy
    B. 1. meltdown
        2. meltdown and explosion
        3. radiation
        4. dispose
II. A. 1. satellite
        2. Yuri Gagarin
        3. exploded
    B. 1. hooked
        2. International
        3. killed
        4. pictures
III. A. 1. smaller
        2. transportation, communication
        3. Television
        4. Communication
        5. Internet
IV. A. 1. Pacific
        2. trade
        3. Multinational
        4. tariffs, restrictions
        5. European Union
    B. 1. industries
        2. living
        3. life, economic
        4. lending, aid
V. A. 1. environment, quality
        2. pollute
        3. oxygen
    B. 1. wind, sunlight, water, heat from
           the ground
        2. electricity, ethanol
        3. tsunami
    C. 1. Severe Acute Respiratory
           Syndrome
        2. Malaria
        3. AIDS
VI. A. 1. grounded
        2. Homeland Security
    B. 1. Taliban
        2. Osama bin Laden
        3. mass destruction
        4. executed
        5. increased
    C. 1. subway, buses
    D. 1. awareness
        2. airplanes
        3. terrorist
VII. A. 1. body
        2. equals
        3. smaller

Key Vocabulary Words

Chapter 1 Key Vocabulary Words
Part A: 1. historian **2.** archaeologist **3.** A.D. **4.** artifact **5.** B.C.
6. revolution **7.** agriculture **8.** border **9.** slavery **10.** civilization
Part B: 11. C 12. E **13.** D **14.** A **15.** B

Chapter 2 Key Vocabulary Words
Part A: 1. B **2.** F **3.** C **4.** E **5.** D **6.** A
Part B: 7. B **8.** A **9.** B **10.** D

Chapter 3 Key Vocabulary Words
1. B **2.** A **3.** B **4.** D **5.** C **6.** A **7.** D **8.** B **9.** C **10.** A **11.** D **12.** A
13. D **14.** C **15.** B

Chapter 4 Key Vocabulary Words
Part A: 1. dry and sandy **2.** brought together **3.** money paid to
support the government **4.** graves enclosed in stone or cement
5. direction opposite of the flow of a river
Part B: The following should be circled: hieroglyphics, mummy,
papyrus, pharaoh, pyramids

Chapter 5 Key Vocabulary Words
Part A: 1. conquer **2.** iron **3.** nomad **4.** alphabet **5.** navigate **6.** treaty
7. commandment **8.** siege **9.** tribute **10.** colony
Part B: 11. J **12.** G **13.** I **14.** C **15.** A **16.** E **17.** B **18.** F **19.** H **20.** D

Chapter 6 Key Vocabulary Words
Part A: 1. E **2.** C **3.** D **4.** A **5.** G **6.** F **7.** H **8.** B
Part B: 9. Hinduism **10.** "Enlightened One" **11.** barrier **12.** raid
13. from another country **14.** emperor **15.** collapse

Chapter 7 Key Vocabulary Words
1. citizen **2.** revolt **3.** tyrant **4.** constitution **5.** democracy
6. vote **7.** jury **8.** democratic **9.** govern **10.** expand **11.** hostility
12. Acropolis **13.** myths **14.** architecture **15.** laborers

Chapter 8 Key Vocabulary Words
1. E **2.** D **3.** C **4.** A **5.** B

Chapter 9 Key Vocabulary Words
1. peninsula **2.** elected **3.** representative **4.** republic **5.** aqueducts
6. governors **7.** civil war **8.** senators **9.** emperor **10.** provinces
11. Gospels **12.** pope **13.** bishop **14.** persecute **15.** convert
16. enslaved **17.** senate **18.** legal **19.** *Pax Romana* **20.** Forum

Chapter 10 Key Vocabulary Words
Part A: 1. have no manners **2.** forced to live away from home **3.** just
beyond a country's border **4.** long story **5.** primitive **6.** idea handed
down from one person to the next **7.** about 1,000 years
Part B: 8. B **9.** A **10.** C

Chapter 11 Key Vocabulary Words
Part A: 1. manor **2.** fortress **3.** estate **4.** knight **5.** lord **6.** serf
7. feudalism **8.** medieval **9.** homage **10.** vassal
Part B: 11. clergy **12.** knight **13.** artisan **14.** monks **15.** nun
16. organized **17.** freemen **18.** lord **19.** peasants **20.** fortress

Chapter 12 Key Vocabulary Words
Part A: 1. population **2.** migrate **3.** pilgrimage **4.** Muslim
5. prophet **6.** vision **7.** truce **8.** exploration **9.** apprentice **10.** guild
Part B: 11. D **12.** E **13.** F **14.** J **15.** G **16.** A **17.** B **18.** C **19.** I **20.** H

Chapter 13 Key Vocabulary Words
Part A: 1. A **2.** C **3.** D **4.** B **5.** A **6.** B **7.** C **8.** A **9.** D **10.** C
Part B: 11. D **12.** A **13.** F **14.** B **15.** E **16.** G **17.** J **18.** H **19.** I **20.** C

Chapter 14 Key Vocabulary Words
1. reign **2.** nationalism **3.** Armada **4.** fleet **5.** monarch
6. decline **7.** annul **8.** Parliament **9.** massacre **10.** edict

Chapter 15 Key Vocabulary Words
Part A: 1. B **2.** H **3.** C **4.** E **5.** G **6.** D **7.** A **8.** F
Part B: 9. terraced **10.** samurai **11.** acupuncture **12.** mosaic
13. compass **14.** barter **15.** shogun

Chapter 16 Key Vocabulary Words
1. Pilgrims **2.** conquistadors **3.** piracy **4.** Puritans **5.** trappers
6. insurance **7.** stock **8.** investments **9.** shareholders **10.** interest

Chapter 17 Key Vocabulary Words
1. liberty **2.** commonwealth **3.** representation **4.** patriot
5. petition **6.** divine right **7.** Declaration of Independence **8.** Royalists
9. Enlightenment **10.** consent **11.** Glorious Revolution **12.** equality
13. Roundheads **14.** Petition of Right **15.** American Revolution

Chapter 18 Key Vocabulary Words
Part A: 1. H **2.** A **3.** E **4.** D **5.** F **6.** G **7.** B **8.** C
Part B: 9. Estates-General **10.** Bastille **11.** execute **12.** betray
13. symbol **14.** Reign of Terror **15.** Napoleonic Code

Chapter 19 Key Vocabulary Words
1. Industrial Revolution **2.** profits **3.** raw materials **4.** natural
resources **5.** energy **6.** developing countries **7.** textile **8.** cottage
weavers **9.** developed countries **10.** investors **11.** locomotives
12. export **13.** labor unions **14.** internal combustion engine **15.** import

Chapter 20 Key Vocabulary Words
1. mural **2.** hacienda **3.** political **4.** liberator **5.** viceroy
6. descendant **7.** dominate **8.** influence **9.** discrimination **10.** mother
country

Chapter 21 Key Vocabulary Words
1. expansion **2.** dominate **3.** Monroe Doctrine **4.** interfere
5. rebellion **6.** victor **7.** sympathy **8.** territory **9.** economic
10. international

Chapter 22 Key Vocabulary Words
1. policies **2.** smuggled **3.** addicted **4.** interference **5.** Open-Door
Policy

Chapter 23 Key Vocabulary Words
1. fast 2. nonviolent resistance 3. civil disobedience 4. agents
5. impose 6. loincloth 7. superiority 8. indirectly 9. Muslims
10. cartridge

Chapter 24 Key Vocabulary Words
1. conference 2. dominance 3. prejudice 4. sympathy 5. impose
6. caravan 7. inferior 8. interfere 9. racism 10. expansion

Chapter 25 Key Vocabulary Words
1. unification 2. nationalism 3. boundary 4. society 5. prime
minister 6. diplomat 7. unify 8. transmit 9. anthem
10. confederation 11. kaiser 12. legislature 13. Reich
14. chancellor 15. militarism

Chapter 26 Key Vocabulary Words
Part A: 1. C 2. H 3. F 4. I 5. B 6. J 7. A 8. G 9. E 10. D
Part B: 11. conflict 12. Central Powers 13. Treaty of Versailles
14. balance of power 15. Allied Powers

Chapter 27 Key Vocabulary Words
1. geography 2. steppes 3. dialects 4. terror 5. economy
6. shortages 7. Bolshevik 8. czar 9. soviets 10. socialism
11. Communism 12. opposed 13. collective 14. censor 15. Iron
Curtain

Chapter 28 Key Vocabulary Words
1. depression 2. Axis Powers 3. scapegoat 4. concentration camp
5. Nazi 6. anti-Semitism 7. Holocaust 8. fascist 9. pact
10. invaded 11. *blitzkrieg* 12. genocide 13. D-Day 14. surrender
15. kamikaze 16. atomic bomb 17. nuclear 18. Allied Powers
19. organization 20. civilian

Chapter 29 Key Vocabulary Words
Part A: 1. Truman Doctrine 2. Berlin Wall 3. cold war
4. satellite 5. ratify 6. détente 7. capitalist 8. nuclear weapons
9. Marshall Plan 10. crisis
Part B: 11. D 12. A 13. E 14. B 15. C

Chapter 30 Key Vocabulary Words
1. electronics 2. domino theory 3. sanctions 4. pollution 5. invest
6. curfew 7. refugees 8. standard of living 9. majority 10. guerilla
11. drought 12. starvation 13. minority 14. apartheid 15. repeal
16. security 17. corrupt 18. violence 19. famine 20. communes

Chapter 31 Key Vocabulary Words
1. homeland 2. Zionism 3. embassy 4. weapons of mass
destruction 5. traitor 6. shah 7. terrorist 8. arms 9. stalemate
10. cease-fire 11. terrorism 12. Ayatollah 13. negotiate 14. hostages
15. hostile

Chapter 32 Key Vocabulary Words
1. *glasnost* 2. coup 3. *perestroika* 4. reunification 5. disbanded

Chapter 33 Key Vocabulary Words
1. Good Neighbor Policy 2. ban 3. stronghold 4. environment
5. corrupt 6. politics 7. immigration 8. destruction 9. humane
10. smuggled 11. moderate 12. tariffs 13. dictatorship 14. refuge
15. global warming

Chapter 34 Key Vocabulary Words
1. multinational corporation 2. astronaut 3. overpopulation
4. extinction 5. agency 6. cosmonaut 7. satellite 8. epidemic
9. humanity 10. nonrenewable

Life Skills Connections

Chapter 1 Life Skills Connection
1. secondary 2. primary 3. primary 4. secondary 5. primary
6. primary 7. secondary 8. primary 9. primary 10. primary

Chapter 2 Life Skills Connection
Answers will vary. Students should have detailed answers for each question as well as a final statement about whether they are still satisfied with the city they chose.

Chapter 3 Life Skills Connection
Answers will vary. Students' résumés should include the items listed in the checklist: name, address, phone number, email address; work experience; and educational background. Also check to make sure the student used formal, professional language.

Chapter 4 Life Skills Connection
Answers will vary. Students' reports should include the pertinent details related to their chosen career. Students should list the job responsibilities and education requirements.

Chapter 5 Life Skills Connection
Part A: Answers will vary. Students should list known driving laws, laws they do not agree with, and laws that they feel should exist.
Part B: Answers will vary. Students should be creative and create their own set of laws.

Chapter 6 Life Skills Connection
Students should find the compass rose, distance scale, and key on the maps they chose.

Chapter 7 Life Skills Connection
Answers will vary according to location. Students should provide accurate information based on research of local voting regulations.

Chapter 8 Life Skills Connection
Answers will vary. Students should add reasonable items to both lists. Students should note that both lists would be dependent on the destination.

Chapter 9 Life Skills Connection
Answers will vary. Students should find a real estate ad with a listing price and calculate the total monthly cost using an Internet mortgage calculator. Students should see that the monthly cost of a home includes the payment, taxes, and insurance.

Chapter 10 Life Skills Connection
Answers will vary. Students should list reasonable ideas for preventing identity theft. Students should attempt to contact a local bank for more information.

Chapter 11 Life Skills Connection
Answers will vary. Students should find at least 10 sources of locally produced foods in or near their community. These may include independent farmers, grocery stores, farmers' markets, and restaurants.

Chapter 12 Life Skills Connection
Answers will vary. Students should provide the key words that resulted from their initial search, the results of searching with key words, and the results of searching with quote marks.

Chapter 13 Life Skills Connection
Answers will vary. Students should be able to list at least one venue for each of the cultural topics listed. Students essays should include a detailed description of the event they attended along with a statement about what they learned there.

Chapter 14 Life Skills Connection
Answers will vary. Students should list at least five benefits for Public Transportation and five benefits for a Personal Car. Students should also explain which type of transportation they would choose.

Chapter 15 Life Skills Connection
1. Should not be trusted because the web address ends with .com and typically a reputable organization does not put fliers on cars. 2. Should be trusted because the web address ends with .org and it is reasonable to assume that a minister can be trusted. 3. Should be trusted because the web address ends with .org and it is reasonable to assume that a daily newspaper can be trusted. 4. Should not be trusted because the web address ends with .com and browser pop-ups should be considered advertisements. 5. Should be trusted because the web address ends .org and it is reasonable to assume that a news network can be trusted.

Chapter 16 Life Skills Connection
Answers will vary. Students should find ample information about tourism in their state, whether online or at a tourism office. If students are able to visit a tourist attraction, they should provide a report detailing what they saw and how it is important to the state.

Chapter 17 Life Skills Connection
Answers will vary depending on location. Students should find accurate information for each of the services listed.

Chapter 18 Life Skills Connection
Answers will vary depending on the local sales tax. Check students' calculations for each item.

Chapter 19 Life Skills Connection
Part A: Answers will vary. Students should list five different kinds of workers protected by unions.
Part B: Answers will vary. Students should find accurate answers to questions about a local union.

Chapter 20 Life Skills Connection
Maps will vary. Make sure that each map includes a compass rose, distance scale, color-coding, labels, and a key. Students should test their maps by trading with another group and following it through the school.

Chapter 21 Life Skills Connection
(These answers assume students are in the United States.) 1. Yes 2. No 3. No 4. Yes 5. Yes

Chapter 22 Life Skills Connection

Part A: Answers will vary. Students should list jobs that involve trading.
Part B: Answers will vary. Students should report on the job they research. Reports should include the required background and any special training. Students should report on their informational interviews if possible.

Chapter 23 Life Skills Connection

Answers will vary. Students should find accurate information about income tax in their state or country. Students should find data that shows where their income tax is being spent. Students should report on their interview with an accountant if possible.

Chapter 24 Life Skills Connection

Answers will vary. Students should provide research about the labor laws in their own country as well as another. Students should provide a comparison of the labor laws in each country and offer an analysis.

Chapter 25 Life Skills Connection

Part A: Students' debates should be well supported.
Part B: Answers will vary. Students should explain their preference for one of the branches of the military. Students should report on their visit to a recruiting center if possible.

Chapter 26 Life Skills Connection

Answers will vary. Students should find detailed, accurate information to answer each of the four questions about a lawyer or law firm.

Chapter 27 Life Skills Connection

Answers will vary. Students should find a news story, an editorial, a letter to the editor, a help wanted ad, and a feature story in their local newspaper. Students should compare their local newspaper to a national newspaper.

Chapter 28 Life Skills Connection

Answers will vary. Students should create a budget that realistically shows income, expenses, and savings. Students should be able to evaluate their budgets and make changes to balance it.

Chapter 29 Life Skills Connection

Answers will vary. Students should choose a foreign country and learn what the country's currency is called. Students should find the exchange rate and make the correct calculations.

Chapter 30 Life Skills Connection

Answers will vary. Students' research should include the requirements to join AmeriCorps. Groups should create a list of local volunteer opportunities. Students should provide further information on at least one of the organizations.

Chapter 31 Life Skills Connection

Answers will vary. Students should list possible emergencies, list and organize ideas for an emergency kit, make an evacuation plan, and outline the differences between a home emergency kit and a car emergency kit.

Chapter 32 Life Skills Connection

Answers will vary depending on location. Students should list differences between a current local map and an older local map. Differences might include new roads or new neighborhoods.

Chapter 33 Life Skills Connection

Answers will vary. Students should provide research on preparing products for recycling, local recycling centers, and careers in waste management.

Chapter 34 Life Skills Connection

Answers will vary. Students should write a "business plan" for life that includes short-term goals, long-term goals, and a to-do list.

Self-Study Guides

Self-Study Guides outline suggested sections from the text and workbook. These assignments provide flexibility for individualized instruction or independent study.

Mastery Tests

See page 876 for the Scoring Rubric for the Short-Response Items and Essay Items on page three of the Mastery Tests. The rubric can be used for page three of the Chapter Mastery Tests, Unit Mastery Tests, Midterm Mastery Test, and Final Mastery Test.

Chapter Mastery Tests
Chapter 1 Mastery Test A
Part A: **1.** B **2.** D **3.** A **4.** C **5.** A

Part B: **6.** change **7.** business **8.** archaeologists **9.** nationalism **10.** Troy **11.** primary source **12.** A.D. **13.** understand **14.** timeline **15.** right

Part C: **16.** F **17.** J **18.** A **19.** D **20.** I **21.** B **22.** C **23.** G **24.** H **25.** E

Part D: **26.** Accept any two of the following: Culture is made up of religion, ideas, art, and tools. **27.** Imperialism is the practice of conquering, forming colonies, or controlling the government and wealth of weaker lands. **28.** Accept any of the following: Letters, diaries, speeches, and news articles are all examples of primary sources. **29.** The Sumerian civilization is older. **30.** You can find borders, oceans, waterways, and cities on a map.

Part E: **31.** Answers will vary. Students should support their answers with at least some of these facts: primary sources are documents created at the time of the event; primary sources provide information about events in the actual words of people who were there; they show how people thought and felt about events at the time they happened; they show how people understood current events. **32.** Answers will vary. Students should support their answers with at least some of these facts: timelines put events in order; timelines show the length of time various civilizations existed; they show which civilizations were active at the same time; they help historians compare civilizations that were active during the same period.

Part F: **33.** Answers will vary. Students' paragraphs should include at least some of these ideas: people in ancient times had many of the same worries as people of today; they worried about having enough food, about defending themselves, and about the dangers of nature; they set up governments and made laws; they tried to explain their existence through religion; they educated their children; they celebrated life through art and writing. Throughout history, people have found discovery and change exciting. **34.** Answers will vary. Students' paragraphs should include at least some of these ideas: artifacts are man-made objects that are used in everyday life. Cars, bicycles, and airplanes demonstrate that we were a mobile society, and that getting from place to place was important to us. Computers, iPods, and cell phones show the importance of communication. Traditional artifacts, such as cookware, are light, flexible, and durable. Students should demonstrate an understanding of what artifacts are, and the important role they play in daily life.

Chapter 1 Mastery Test B
Part A: **1.** B **2.** C **3.** D **4.** C **5.** A

Part B: **6.** imperialism **7.** agriculture **8.** development **9.** primary **10.** artifacts **11.** maps **12.** Borders **13.** B.C. **14.** left **15.** waterways

Part C: **16.** E **17.** G **18.** C **19.** F **20.** I **21.** B **22.** H **23.** J **24.** A **25.** D

Part D: **26.** Revolution is the term used to describe a complete change in a way of life or government. **27.** Nationalism is the spirit that leads people to unite under their own flag. **28.** The ruins of Troy were discovered in Turkey. **29.** Historians use primary sources and artifacts

to learn about the past. **30.** An interval on a timeline is an equal unit of time.

Part E: **31.** Answers will vary. Students should support their answers with at least some of these facts: historians study primary sources created at the time of the event; archaeologists study artifacts; artifacts are handmade objects; artifacts include such items as tools and weapons. **32.** Answers will vary. Students should support their answers with at least some of these facts: maps show how countries' borders have changed over time; they show places where cities developed; they show routes traveled by various civilizations; they indicate how various civilizations may have interacted.

Part F: **33.** Answers will vary. Students' paragraphs should include at least some of these ideas: history is all about change. In the past, slavery was an accepted part of life, but today most people think slavery is wrong. The discovery that the world is round led to explorers setting out from Europe on voyages of discovery; the age of discovery led to an age of imperialism. Ideas of freedom, democracy, and independence later swept across the world, resulting in growing nationalism, during which people united under common flags. **34.** Answers will vary. Students' paragraphs should include at least some of these ideas: a primary source is a first-hand account of a historical event. Television programs show how people looked and dressed; TV shows also show people's behavior, and what their interests were. Movies are another source for judging how people lived. Students may point out that TV and movies often show fantasy worlds, and that characters' behavior is not always realistic. Newspapers and magazines contain stories and photographs about important people. Video records of many important events are available.

Chapter 2 Mastery Test A
Part A: **1.** D **2.** B **3.** A **4.** C **5.** A

Part B: **6.** settlement **7.** craft **8.** Stone Age **9.** Ice Age **10.** Fertile Crescent **11.** tamed **12.** glacier **13.** trade

Part C: **14.** E **15.** D **16.** B **17.** C **18.** F **19.** E **20.** I **21.** G **22.** A

Part D: **23.** Valleys and lakes were formed by glaciers slowly moving and pushing the land as it traveled. **24.** People could only live in settlements when they did not have to follow herds to feed themselves. **25.** Tamed animals could carry loads, help break up soil, and provide food and wool. **26.** Since farming allowed people to grow and store food, people had more time to learn one skill instead of spend time finding food. **27.** The Agricultural Revolution gave people wealth. People were afraid that people would take their things away, so they needed laws for protection. **28.** The houses in Jericho changed from rounded mud homes to homes built with square corners. **29.** People started planning how much food to plant to be sure they had enough for winter and for trade. **30.** Farming was done near rivers because the soil was good for growing and water was easy to get.

Part E: **31.** Answers will vary. Students should support their answers with at least some of these facts: People in the Agricultural Revolution built cities near water to have fertile soil and ready water. Today, farming is not done in the cities, but water is used to transport goods for trade. **32.** Answers will vary. Students should support their answers with at least some of these facts: People learned crafts during the Agricultural Revolution. They also learned to trade. Making better cloth or more beautiful pots would increase the likelihood of people wanting the items.

Part F: 33. Answers will vary. Students' paragraphs should include at least some of these ideas: Because people lived in caves, they would look for art on cave walls. They might also find simple tools made of stone and bone. Because people depended very strongly on hunting, the tools might look like spears or clubs. There may also be evidence of animal hide or bones. **34.** Answers will vary. Students' paragraphs should include at least some of these ideas: This part of the world was home to some of the first great civilizations because the Agricultural Revolution started there. This would mean that the population in the Fertile Crescent was probably larger than in other parts of the world. Large groups of people would develop religions to help them understand the earth and give them a sense of control over their lives. These religions developed into the religions many people practice today.

Chapter 2 Mastery Test B
Part A: 1. A **2.** C **3.** D **4.** A **5.** B
Part B: 6. hunt **7.** rules **8.** Mesopotamia **9.** trade **10.** Agricultural Revolution **11.** wall **12.** houses **13.** settlements
Part C: 14. D **15.** E **16.** F **17.** D **18.** I **19.** A **20.** C **21.** G **22.** H
Part D: 23. People had more time to learn new trades such as pottery, weaving, and basket-making. **24.** They had plenty of fertile soil and water. **25.** They would eat berries, nuts, and fruit. **26.** The wall would protect the houses, herds, and belongings of people in the city from thieves. **27.** The Ice Age was over one million years ago. **28.** The area called Mesopotamia is between the Tigris and Euphrates rivers. **29.** The homes had rounded walls, usually made of mud. **30.** Settlements grew in size, leaders developed, and they conquered other cities to rule over.
Part E: 31. Answers will vary. Students should support their answers with at least some of these facts: Using primitive tools and supplies such as mud and branches, rounded corners would be more likely. Not until people could cut timber with tools could they build square corners. **32.** Answers will vary. Students should support their answers with at least some of these facts: Both of these arts would have started from more essential household tools. As they made the tools more easily, they could give attention to making the items artistic, too.
Part F: 33. Answers will vary. Students' paragraphs should include at least some of these ideas: There is no way to be sure that the cave paintings are thousands of years old. Someone may have entered the cave to paint the pictures at a later date. Scientists may possibly be able to compare styles or test the materials used to paint to determine the age of the art. **34.** Answers will vary. Students' paragraphs should include at least some of these ideas: Taming animals made farmers' lives easier. Animals could help cultivate soil and carry grain. The animals could also serve as a source of meat and fur.

Chapter 3 Mastery Test A
Part A: 1. B **2.** C **3.** A **4.** A **5.** D
Part B: 6. swamp **7.** floods **8.** canals **9.** goods **10.** independent **11.** temple **12.** pictographs **13.** contracts **14.** created **15.** nobles
Part C: 16. C **17.** E **18.** B **19.** J **20.** H **21.** I **22.** F **23.** A **24.** D **25.** G
Part D: 26. They dug waterways called canals. **27.** Sumerians built temples to honor their gods in the center of their cities. **28.** They found a way to measure land in order to figure taxes. **29.** Boys from wealthy families were allowed to go to school. **30.** The Babylonians attacked the Sumerians.
Part E: 31. Answers will vary. Students should support their answers with at least some of these facts: Sumer had little stone, metal, or timber; Sumerians depended on trade to get these things; Sumer had

rich farm land, so Sumerians traded their crops for the things they needed; trade was responsible for Sumerians developing sailing ships; Sumerians worked the gold, silver, and copper they received in trade into fine jewelry. **32.** Answers will vary. Students should support their answers with at least some of these facts: writing allowed Sumerians to keep track of what they owned; writing was used in creating contacts for business agreements; writing led to the invention of a way to measure land; scribes became rich and powerful.
Part F: 33. Answers will vary. Students' paragraphs should include at least some of these ideas: priests, scribes, and nobles were the highest classes in Sumerian society; priests were rich and powerful; sons of wealthy families were educated; scribes knew how to read and write and were paid well for it; scribes wrote contracts for merchants, and worked in temples and the palace. **34.** Answers will vary. Students' paragraphs should include at least some of these ideas: Sumerians invented new things; Sumerians invented writing; Sumerian writing spread to other cultures as the Sumerians traded with their neighbors; Sumerians invented sailing ships, which increased the number of cultures they could reach; Sumerians were probably the first people to use the wheel; Sumerians also developed ways to measure land and keep time.

Chapter 3 Mastery Test B
Part A: 1. A **2.** B **3.** D **4.** C **5.** A
Part B: 6. irrigate **7.** scribes **8.** tablets **9.** city-state **10.** cuneiform **11.** ziggurat **12.** merchants **13.** chariots **14.** goddess **15.** priests
Part C: 16. C **17.** J **18.** B **19.** F **20.** D **21.** I **22.** E **23.** A **24.** G **25.** H
Part D: 26. They protected their land by building dikes. **27.** The merchants brought metal, stone, timber, gold, silver, pearls, and copper into Sumer. **28.** The scribes wrote contracts and other documents. **29.** The Sumerians invented a way to measure land so they could find a way to tax it. **30.** We still use the 60-second minute and the 60-minute hour.
Part E: 31. Answers will vary. Students should support their answers with at least some of these facts: early Sumerian writing used pictographs; pictographs looked like the things they represented; pictographs were written in horizontal columns; pictographs developed into symbols which were easier to draw; later Sumerian writing, called *cuneiform,* consisted of wedge-shaped strokes. **32.** Answers will vary. Students should support their answers with at least some of these facts: Sumerians worshipped many gods; each city-state honored a god, who the people hoped would protect them; villages and city-states were built around the god's temple; people brought offerings to the temple to keep the gods happy; Sumerian priests grew rich and powerful.
Part F: 33. Answers will vary. Students' paragraphs should include at least some of these ideas: life was hard for the ordinary Sumerian; many Sumerians worked all day long; Sumerian farmers had to dig canals to irrigate their fields; Sumerians made their own bricks for building by drying mud in the sun; building and maintaining dikes and city walls were some of the work they had to do; Sumerians were religious, with temples at the center of every village; Sumerians worshipped many gods. **34.** Answers will vary. Students' paragraphs should include at least some of these ideas: Sumerians invented many things that we still use today; Sumerians created the first writing; Sumerian writing gives us a first-hand look into their lives; Sumerians were probably the first people to use the wheel; Sumerians also developed ways to measure land and keep time; some elements of Sumerian time-keeping, such as the 60-second minute and the 60-minute hour, are still with

us; Sumerians invented the first sailing ships; trade spread Sumerian culture to other lands.

Chapter 4 Mastery Test A
Part A: 1. A **2.** D **3.** B **4.** B **5.** D
Part B: 6. desert **7.** floods **8.** kohl **9.** Osiris **10.** museums **11.** double **12.** machinery **13.** transported
Part C: 14. B **15.** D **16.** C **17.** A **18.** E **19.** C **20.** B **21.** A
Part D: 22. The Nile River flowed from south to north, thus downstream, or Lower Egypt, is to the north. **23.** Flooding made the soil very fertile. **24.** Archaeologists found statues that showed men and women with makeup. **25.** Both countries had many gods, and each city had a special god. **26.** The pharaohs believed they would need their favorite things in the next world. **27.** Ships could take people and goods to other lands. **28.** Archaeologists found musical instruments and words to songs. **29.** Farmers built canals to take water to the fields. **30.** The Rosetta Stone was a stone that has writing in different languages that taught archaeologists how to read hieroglyphics.
Part E: 31. Answers will vary. Students should support their answers with at least some of these facts: Most people in Egypt lived simple lives. The pharaohs and nobles used taxes to pay for extravagant lives. All people cared about appearance, and because the farms were successful, they were able to develop art and other crafts. **32.** Answers will vary. Students should support their answers with at least some of these facts: Archaeologists are not able to determine how the pyramids were built. The pyramids were huge, and the rocks used to build them were so large and heavy, that nobody knows how they were carved or moved into place.
Part F: 33. Answers will vary. Students' paragraphs should include at least some of these ideas: A Wonder should be something unique and historically important. The pyramids are both. There are no buildings that old that took so much ingenuity and strength. They were also filled with important historical artifacts that provided information about the ancient Egyptian culture. **34.** Answers will vary. Students' paragraphs should include at least some of these ideas: Archaeologists have to look for patterns in writing and use the patterns to decide what the writing means. The patterns are much like a code. Once part of the code is broken, they can use the pieces of information to determine the meanings of more of the writing.

Chapter 4 Mastery Test B
Part A: 1. A **2.** D **3.** B **4.** B **5.** D
Part B: 6. makeup **7.** gods **8.** ships **9.** music **10.** canals **11.** Rosetta Stone **12.** tools **13.** rocks
Part C: 14. A **15.** C **16.** E **17.** B **18.** D **19.** C **20.** B **21.** A
Part D: 22. People went looking for a place that had water. **23.** The ancient Egyptians wanted to look attractive. **24.** The Sahara had become a desert and they could not farm. **25.** The Nile would flood the farmland and fields. **26.** The Egyptian pharaohs wanted people to remember how rich and powerful they were. **27.** Kohl was used to line their eyes. **28.** They believed that they would meet the god Osiris. **29.** You can see Egyptian artifacts in museums. **30.** He wore a double crown because he unified the two parts of Egypt.
Part E: 31. Answers will vary. Students should support their answers with at least some of these facts: Most Egyptians believed in many gods. Each of the gods had a special power. Death was an important part of religion. Osiris was the god of death. **32.** Answers will vary. Students should support their answers with at least some of these facts: Archaeologists are not able to determine how the pyramids were built.

The stones were cut, transported, and raised into place. They may have used a system of ramps and planks to place the stones.
Part F: 33. Answers will vary. Students' paragraphs should include at least some of these ideas: They are unique and historically important. There are no other structures of that age with such complexity in design. They are also filled with important historical artifacts that provide information about the ancient Egyptian culture. **34.** Answers will vary. Students' paragraphs should include at least some of these ideas: Archaeologists have learned to read hieroglyphics. They have also found many different artifacts in the pyramids, everything from extravagant jewelry to common household items.

Chapter 5 Mastery Test A
Part A: 1. B **2.** D **3.** C **4.** A **5.** C
Part B: 6. colony **7.** nomad **8.** worship **9.** Judaism **10.** capital **11.** Bible **12.** iron **13.** conquer **14.** military **15.** tribute
Part C: 16. G **17.** D **18.** H **19.** B **20.** E **21.** C **22.** J **23.** I **24.** A **25.** F
Part D: 26. The Phoenicians learned to use the stars to navigate. **27.** King Solomon's kingdom split into two parts, with the tribes in the north becoming Israel and the tribes in the south becoming Judah. **28.** The Sumerian civilization lived in Mesopotamia. **29.** The Hittites signed a peace treaty and a Hittite princess married an Egyptian pharaoh. **30.** All Assyrian men had to go into the well-trained army. Assyrians built military equipment such as siege engines to use against their enemies.
Part E: 31. Answers will vary. Students should support their answers with at least some of these facts: the Phoenicians were traders instead of farmers; they knew how to navigate by the stars, so they could sail beyond the sight of land; they set up colonies, rather than conquering other civilizations; they did not have an army, but hired soldiers from other lands. **32.** Answers will vary. Students should support their answers with at least some of these facts: the ancient Israelites believed God promised them their own land, called the "Promised Land;" they wanted to be free to worship one God; they had been slaves in Egypt, so a land of their own was important to them; they were nomads for many years, and wanted a place to settle.
Part F: 33. Answers will vary. Students' paragraphs should include at least some of these ideas: Phoenicians could navigate by the stars, so they had a wider influence than most cultures; they were active traders, bringing both goods and ideas from one culture to another; they set up colonies throughout the Mediterranean, helping to spread their culture; by traveling so far, they developed a better idea of the size and shape of the world than other civilizations had; one of the ideas they spread was using the alphabet to write. **34.** Answers will vary. Students' paragraphs should include at least some of these ideas: the ancient Israelites gave us the Ten Commandments, which was a written code of behavior; the commandments became the basis of Jewish law; Jewish law was the base of Christian law which followed it; the Babylonians gave us the Code of Hammurabi, which was a system of nearly 300 laws; the Code listed both laws and punishments for breaking the law; the Hittites and Egyptians signed the first treaty, which is the basis of international law; Assyrian culture had strict laws and stiff penalties.

Chapter 5 Mastery Test B
Part A: 1. C **2.** A **3.** B **4.** A **5.** D
Part B: 6. navigate **7.** commandment **8.** Christianity **9.** religious **10.** empire **11.** Code **12.** bronze **13.** treaty **14.** siege **15.** library
Part C: 16. J **17.** F **18.** C **1 9.** D **20.** A **21.** H **22.** G **23.** I **24.** E **25.** B

Part D: 26. Trade brought gold, ivory, and ebony. 27. The ancient Israelites believed the land of Canaan has been promised to them by God. 28. The Code was a system of laws written by Hammurabi, a king of the Babylonians. 29. The Hittites knew how to make weapons out of iron. 30. Siege engines were huge machines used by the Assyrians to knock down city gates and walls.

Part E: 31. Answers will vary. Students should support their answers with at least some of these facts: Babylon was one of the greatest cities of the ancient world; it had beautiful temples and palaces; the buildings were decorated with glazed blue bricks and pictures of mythical beasts; the city contained many wonders, such as the Tower of Babel and the Hanging Gardens of Babylon. 32. Answers will vary. Students should support their answers with at least some of these facts: both the Hittites and the Assyrians were military cultures; they both developed military advances; the Hittites had iron spears and the Assyrians had siege engines; they both conquered neighboring kingdoms.

Part F: 33. Answers will vary. Students' paragraphs should include at least some of these ideas: neither the Phoenicians nor the Assyrians were farming cultures; the Phoenicians were traders and the Assyrians were warriors; both cultures developed advances in building; the Phoenicians built better ships, the Assyrians built war machinery; both cultures spread their influence, but in different ways; Phoenicians set up colonies for trading, while the Assyrians conquered cities and made them pay tribute; the Phoenicians had no military, but hired soldiers from other lands; the Phoenicians explored the sea, while the Assyrians lived in interior lands. 34. Answers will vary. Students' paragraphs should include at least some of these ideas: the ancient Israelite culture was one of the first to believe in one God; the Ten Commandments were the basis of Jewish law, and later Christian law; the Jewish religion is still practiced today; the Bible of the ancient Israelites became the basis of the Bible of the Christians; King David established Jerusalem as his capital and a religious center; Jerusalem is still an important religious center for Jewish people, Christians, and Muslims.

Chapter 6 Mastery Test A
Part A: 1. C 2. B 3. A 4. D 5. D
Part B: 6. caste 7. reincarnation 8. shrine 9. dynasty 10. ancestors 11. isolate 12. bridge 13. wool 14. foreign 15. maize
Part C: 16. E 17. F 18. G 19. H 20. A 21. D 22. B 23. C
Part D: 24. It was clean and well-planned, with homes, apartments buildings, drainage, and pools. 25. Brahma is the creator of life, Vishnu preserves life, and Shiva destroys life. 26. Buddhists believe that greed and selfishness cause all problems, and that being unselfish and following Buddhist law will lead to nirvana. Nirvana breaks the cycle of suffering and death. They also believe in reincarnation. 27. Asoka made Buddhism the official state religion. The caste system was weakened. 28. The early Chinese of the Huang He Valley are remembered for being farmers and fighting floods, learning to write and leaving one of the world's earliest written histories, making fine cloth from silk, and respecting their ancestors. 29. The Chinese were angry with the Qin dynasty because the Great Wall required them to pay such high taxes. 30. It probably took people a very long time to move from Asia to the Americas and settle in communities. They also would have to learn about the plants that would grow well in this new area.

Part E: 31. Answers will vary. Students should support their answers with at least some of these facts: The Zhou dynasty was made up of warlike people who extended their rule southward in China. They were a powerful dynasty that lasted more than 750 years. They helped

China by developing systems of irrigation and flood control. The Qin dynasty had a much shorter rule, from 221 B.C. to 206 B.C. The first Qin emperor, Shi Huangdi, had the first empire with a strong central government. However, as Shi Huangdi taxed people to pay for building the Great Wall of China, he caused a civil war to break out, which led to the collapse of the Qin dynasty. 32. Answers will vary. Students should support their answers with at least some of these facts: The Olmecs settled in Mexico, and built statues and mound shrines. They created a counting system and a calendar, and lasted for more than 1,000 years. The Maya settled farther south in Mexico and Central America. They also had a calendar, and learned about astronomy. They lasted only about 550 years.

Part F: 33. Answers will vary. Students' paragraphs should include at least some of these ideas: The main beliefs of Hinduism were based on the idea that some people were better than others. The impact this had on civilizations where it was practiced was that people were divided into groups based on their social rank, or classes. These classes were called *castes*. The Hindu belief was that the only way out of a caste was through reincarnation. 34. Answers will vary. Students' paragraphs should include at least some of these ideas: Farming is critical because the food it provides allows people to spend time developing other skills instead of hunting and gathering. It also provides income. Religion gives a culture structure and moral rules to live by, and gives people meaning in their lives aside from the day-to-day tasks they must participate in.

Chapter 6 Mastery Test B
Part A: 1. C 2. B 3. A 4. D 5. D
Part B: 6. Aryans 7. raja 8. barrier 9. Hinduism 10. nirvana 11. untouchable 12. Buddhist 13. emperor 14. Qin 15. history
Part C: 16. D 17. A 18. G 19. F 20. C 21. E 22. H 23. B
Part D: 24. The highest level were priests and scholars. The second level were rulers and warriors. The third level were craftworkers, merchants, and farmers, The lowest level was unskilled workers. 25. Scientists think that the American Indians first came to America from Asia over a bridge of land and ice at the Bering Strait that led them to Alaska. 26. The Han dynasty built up the military and expanded China into a larger empire. 27. The Huang He River flooded often and very badly. 28. The Olmecs built huge statues, great shrines without using wheels or metal tools, created a counting system, and made a simple calendar. 29. India was invaded by many foreign lands, and most people reverted to Hinduism. 30. People in America grew maize, squash, beans, tomatoes, and cotton.

Part E: 31. Answers will vary. Students should support their answers with at least some of these facts: Hinduism and Buddhism developed in ancient India. They both believe in reincarnation. However Hinduism believes in three specific gods; Brahma, Vishnu, and Shiva. It also teaches the caste system, where people can only change their place in life through reincarnation. Buddhism does not use a caste system, and teaches unselfishness. Its goal is to reach nirvana to break the cycle of suffering and death. 32. Answers will vary. Students should support their answers with at least some of these facts: Siddhartha Gautama was the son of a wealthy Hindu raja. He saw many of his people living in poverty and sorrow and felt sorry for them. He could have become a rich prince, but instead he gave up his wealth and lived in the forest for six years, wandering about India. He came upon the "truth" when he decided that the sorrows of the world are caused by selfishness. He developed Buddhism based on this idea of brotherly love.

Part F: 33. Answers will vary. Students' paragraphs should include at least some of these ideas: Since the Zhou dynasty was made of warlike people, it is possible that the common farmers were exposed to war and fighting as the dynasty extended their rule to the south. The Zhou also developed new systems for irrigation and flood control, so these could have made a positive difference in the farmer's life as floods became less of a problem and watering crops became more possible. In the Qin dynasty, a farmer may have liked the idea of building up the Great Wall, as Emperor Shi Huangdi planned, because this would stop invaders from attacking their farms. However, as they were forced to pay high taxes for the building of the wall, this would have caused great difficulty, leading to hatred of the dynasty and a civil war. **34.** Answers will vary. Students' paragraphs should include at least some of these ideas: China's isolation allowed them to develop a very rich culture and a people who respect its ancestors and traditions. Families are very close. However, they may have been slow to develop more modern skills and had limited access to new ideas because they were not in contact with people from other cultures.

Chapter 7 Mastery Test A
Part A: **1.** A **2.** D **3.** C **4.** B **5.** D
Part B: **6.** expand **7.** govern **8.** democracy **9.** architecture **10.** laborers **11.** Salamis **12.** citizens **13.** Acropolis **14.** revolt **15.** plague
Part C: **16.** D **17.** G **18.** B **19.** A **20.** I **21.** E **22.** J **23.** H **24.** F **25.** C
Part D: **26.** The Acropolis was a hill near a city where the Greeks built their main temple. **27.** Spartan boys were raised by the government to be soldiers. **28.** Athens had slaves, but some people thought slavery was wrong. **29.** Pericles was the leader of Athens during the Golden Age. **30.** Some ideas the Greeks gave us are democracy, architecture, and geometry. They also gave us ideas about the sun, the earth, and the stars.
Part E: 31. Answers will vary. Students should support their answers with at least some of these facts: Greece had rocky soil that was not good for farming; the Greeks depended on trade for their wheat and other grains; trade helped spread Greek culture; the Greeks set up colonies in the lands they visited; trade made city-states such as Athens wealthy. **32.** Answers will vary. Students should support their answers with at least some of these facts: the Golden Age of Athens was the period of peace following the Persian Wars; during this time Athens grew in power and wealth; the Greeks wrote their finest plays and created their best art and architecture; Greek thinkers studied science and geography; Pericles rebuilt the Parthenon, which was destroyed during the war; most of our gifts from Greece come from the Golden Age.
Part F: 33. Answers will vary. Students' paragraphs should include at least some of these ideas: Athens and Sparta had a lot in common; they were both powerful city-states; their people spoke the same language; they believed in the same gods and told the same myths; the two city-states joined together to fight the Persians. In other ways, they were different. Sparta was a military society; children belonged to the state; women were not important; the government was ruled by a small group of people. Athens was a democracy; all free men could vote; the leaders were elected by the people; the people of Athens were interested in art and architecture; Athens had many great thinkers and teachers; they left many written records. **34.** Answers will vary. Students' paragraphs should include at least some of these ideas: many things in modern culture can be traced back to the Greeks; Greece developed democracy, which we still practice today; Greek law included trial by jury; Greek

plays are still produced and Greek statues are still enjoyed; Greek architecture still influences modern building; Greece was one of the first cultures to question slavery; we still read and study the works of Greek philosophers; some Greek ideas in science and mathematics are still in use today.

Chapter 7 Mastery Test B
Part A: **1.** B **2.** A **3.** C **4.** D **5.** B
Part B: **6.** hostility **7.** democratic **8.** Parthenon **9.** jury **10.** constitution **11.** vote **12.** tyrant **13.** athlete **14.** Marathon **15.** myths
Part C: **16.** C **17.** F **18.** J **19.** H **20.** D **21.** B **22.** I **23.** A **24.** E **25.** G
Part D: **26.** Greek city-states were separated from each other by mountain ranges, so they had limited contact. **27.** The new constitution made all free men citizens. **28.** The final battle of the Persian Wars was the Greek defeat of the Persians at Salamis. **29.** The Peloponnesian War started because the Spartans did not like the way Athens was building and growing, and the Spartans were angry that Athens had been collecting money from the rest of Greece. **30.** Athletes from all the Greek city-states competed in the Olympic games.
Part E: 31. Answers will vary. Students should support their answers with at least some of these facts: Greek gods looked and acted like humans; they had a human form and personality; they were married and had families; they laughed and argued and played tricks on each other; they felt love and jealousy; this shows us that the Greeks believed in the importance of human beings and human lives. **32.** Answers will vary. Students should support their answers with at least some of these facts: democracy is the most important gift the Greeks gave to the world; democracy is a government that gives the people the ruling power; at first, only landowners could vote, but later all free men could vote too; Greek democracy was not perfect, because women still could not vote.
Part F: 33. Answers will vary. Students' paragraphs should include at least some of these ideas: the Spartan culture was a military one; the Spartan army was well trained and disciplined; Spartan boys were raised to be soldiers; during the Golden Age, when the Athenians devoted their time to science and the arts, Sparta maintained its military; Sparta was a land power, while Athens was mostly a sea power; Spartan soldiers knew how to surround a city and cut off supplies; Sparta joined with other city-states in its war against Athens. **34.** Answers will vary. Students' paragraphs should include at least some of these ideas: if Persia had conquered Greece, we would not have many of the gifts we received from the Greeks; the Greeks wrote their most important plays and created their best art and architecture during the period of peace following the Persian Wars; we would not have the advances in science and math that developed during this period; our language might be different, since we have so many Greek words in English; we might have a different system of government, since the Greeks developed democracy; the Peloponnesian War would never have happened.

Chapter 8 Mastery Test A
Part A: **1.** C **2.** A **3.** D **4.** B **5.** B
Part B: **6.** ambition **7.** conqueror **8.** assassinate **9.** campaign **10.** general **11.** founded
Part C: **12.** D **13.** E **14.** A **15.** B **16.** C
Part D: **17.** D **18.** E **19.** F **20.** A **21.** C **22.** B
Part E: **23.** B **24.** C **25.** A **26.** D

Part F: 27. Alexander was easily angered, very ambitious, and fearless. **28.** Alexandria was very large and wealthy. It had a lot of Greek architecture, libraries, schools, and a lighthouse that was one of the Wonders of the Ancient World. **29.** Alexander conquered Egypt, Persia, Syria, Phoenicia, and the Indus River Valley. **30.** His military conquests were greater than any leader before him, and his empire was the largest of its time.

Part G: 31. Answers will vary. Students should support their answers with at least some of these facts: Aristotle was a great thinker, so he probably taught Alexander how to reason and think out problems. He also was Greek, so he would have taught Alexander Greek customs and history. **32.** Answers will vary. Students should support their answers with at least some of these facts: Alexander fulfilled his father's wishes by defeating the Persian Empire and taking King Darius from power. He further fulfilled Philip's wishes by destroying Persepolis as revenge.

Part H: 33. Answers will vary. Students' paragraphs should include at least some of these ideas: Asia would not have been as isolated, and they would have developed trade relationships with other cultures much sooner. There would be evidence of Greek style in their culture as well. **34.** Answers will vary. Students' paragraphs should include at least some of these ideas: Alexander was a masterful leader, as he was able to conquer so many powerful nations. He could also be considered ruthless, as he destroyed Perepolis and defeated the Persian Empire out of ambition and a wish to please his father. He was not satisfied when he reached that goal, and intended to enlarge his empire.

Chapter 8 Mastery Test B
Part A: 1. C **2.** A **3.** D **4.** B **5.** B
Part B: 6. teach **7.** conquer **8.** Egypt **9.** India **10.** Sparta **11.** Macedonia
Part C: 12. D **13.** E **14.** A **15.** B **16.** C
Part D: 17. E **18.** A **19.** F **20.** B **21.** C **22.** D
Part E: 23. B **24.** C **25.** A **26.** D
Part F: 27. They both dreamed of getting revenge on the Persian Empire by conquering it. **28.** Alexander had his army build a bridge to the city. **29.** King Darius was able to escape Alexander twice, but was killed by his own men. **30.** Alexander's troops were too tired to take on another battle and wanted to return home.

Part G: 31. Answers will vary. Students should support their answers with at least some of these facts: Alexander shared Greek customs and styles with the places he conquered. He also made plans for Alexandria to create a Greek-style city with Greek architecture, schools, and libraries. **32.** Answers will vary. Students should support their answers with at least some of these facts: Alexander had the ambition that his father had, and was trained by Aristotle. He was very well educated and likely was groomed for the job.

Part H: 33. Answers will vary. Students' paragraphs should include at least some of these ideas: Alexander would not have had as strong an understanding of Greek culture since he was not Greek himself. He also may not have valued education and reading as strongly without the scholar's influence. **34.** Answers will vary. Students' paragraphs should include at least some of these ideas: Alexander shared the style of architecture and stressed the importance of education. Cities under his reign would encourage education and learning.

Chapter 9 Mastery Test A
Part A: 1. A **2.** C **3.** B **4.** D **5.** C

Part B: 6. peninsula **7.** republic **8.** representatives **9.** provinces **10.** senator **11.** Forum **12.** *Pax Romana* **13.** Gospels **14.** persecuted **15.** bishop
Part C: 16. G **17.** D **18.** A **19.** F **20.** E **21.** I **22.** C **23.** J **24.** H **25.** B
Part D: 26. Rome fought Carthage in the Punic Wars. **27.** Julius Caesar was asked to return to Rome from Gaul, but he brought his army with him and they took control of the Roman government. **28.** Constantine stopped the persecution of Christians, made Christianity legal, and helped it become established as a religion. **29.** Constantinople was the city Constantine made his capital. It was previously called Byzantium. **30.** Roman emperors brought about the end of the empire because some were greedy, some wanted more power, and they fought among themselves.

Part E: 31. Answers will vary. Students should support their answers with at least some of these facts: before Octavian, Rome was a republic; Octavian became the first emperor of Rome; Octavian was called Augustus, which put him above all others; he had complete power; he chose new senators, rather than having elections. **32.** Answers will vary. Students should support their answers with at least some of these facts: the teachings of Jesus appealed most to the poor and enslaved people; his teaching offered hope for a better life in the next world; other religions said that wealthy people and nobility would have a high rank in the afterlife; Jesus taught that all good people would be treated equally well.

Part F: 33. Answers will vary. Students' paragraphs should include at least some of these ideas: the Romans conquered the Greek city-states during the Punic Wars; they brought Greek art and style back to Rome; some of the Greeks who were slaves became teachers in Rome; many of the Roman gods and goddesses were based on the Greek gods; Greek ideas of architecture were used in Rome; Greek statues were taken back to Rome; Romans copied the style of Greek art; Roman government is similar to Greek government; as Roman civilization spread, the things they took from the Greeks spread throughout the world; Rome preserved many of the things about Greek culture that other civilizations might have destroyed. **34.** Answers will vary. Students' paragraphs should include at least some of these ideas: Latin is the language of ancient Rome; as Roman civilization spread, its language spread with it; Roman soldiers and settlers brought the common Roman language, or Vulgar Latin, with them; countries such as France and Spain speak languages called *Romance languages* (they are called this because they are based on the Roman language). English is not a Romance language, but it contains words from a number of other languages; English has words that come from French, Italian, and Spanish, which are Romance languages; many of our words are based on Latin words.

Chapter 9 Mastery Test B
Part A: 1. A **2.** D **3.** D **4.** C **5.** B
Part B: 6. elected **7.** governor **8.** legal **9.** aqueduct **10.** enslaved **11.** convert **12.** civil war **13.** pope **14.** senate **15.** emperor
Part C: 16. D **17.** G **18.** C **19.** I **20.** F **21.** J **22.** H **23.** A **24.** B **25.** E
Part D: 26. Julius Caesar brought his army to Rome and took control of the government. **27.** The title "Augustus" meant Octavian was above all others and was to be worshipped. **28.** The Romans copied styles of art and architecture from the Greeks. **29.** The Roman government decided the Christians were a threat because they would not bow down to the Roman emperor or call him a god. **30.** Invaders from northern and eastern Europe attacked Rome.

Part E: 31. Answers will vary. Students should support their answers with at least some of these facts: In a republic, the government is a democracy that is controlled by the people. The citizens of Rome elected representatives to make laws and run their government. The members of the Roman Senate were usually wealthy landowners who held office for life. **32.** Answers will vary. Students should support their answers with at least some of these facts: the senators worried about how popular Caesar was with the Roman people; they thought he was too powerful; they were afraid that he wanted to be king; they thought he wanted to end the Republic; the senators thought they were doing the right thing by killing Caesar.

Part F: 33. Answers will vary. Students' paragraphs should include at least some of these ideas: if Constantine had not converted, Christianity would have had a harder time becoming established; the emperors before Constantine persecuted the Christians; Christians were killed and had to meet in secret; Constantine made Christianity legal; after he converted, more and more Romans became Christian; Constantine built the first Christian cathedral in Rome; the Roman government and the Christian church became linked; the bishop of Rome became the leader of the Roman Catholic Church. **34.** Answers will vary. Students' paragraphs should include at least some of these ideas: in Caesar's time, Rome was a republic; citizens elected people to represent them in the government; Augustus had complete power, and appointed senators who would carry out his laws; Caesar fought civil wars against other Roman armies; civil wars came to an end under Augustus; life was better for many people under Augustus; he built roads and improved the harbors; trade became easier; Augustus ruled a much longer time than Caesar.

Chapter 10 Mastery Test A

Part A: 1. B **2.** B **3.** A **4.** D **5.** C
Part B: 6. learning **7.** barbarians **8.** laws **9.** Huns **10.** Byzantine
11. Charlemagne **12.** Hastings **13.** sagas **14.** Vikings **15.** Goths
Part C: 16. F **17.** H **18.** A **19.** E **20.** G **21.** C **22.** D **23.** B
Part D: 24. They wanted the Roman riches and power. They were also being forced out of their lands by the Huns. **25.** The Romans used a system of justice that had courts and people to determine if laws were broken or not. The German system allowed for a group of leaders that would test how the gods treated accused people to see if they are innocent or guilty. **26.** Charlemagne died, and his son was not able to keep the empire together. The land was divided among Charlemagne's three grandsons. **27.** Erik the Red was exiled from Iceland where other Vikings had settled. He traveled to Greenland and settled there.
28. The Romans had natural barriers such as mountains and seas, and built a wall in England where there were not natural barriers.
29. Charlemagne had a good relationship with the pope, and shared similar values. The pope named him Emperor of the Holy Roman Empire. **30.** Because the Vikings sailed and traded to so many parts of the world, they spread their influence.
Part E: 31. Answers will vary. Students should support their answers with at least some of these facts: After A.D. 476, the Western Roman Empire was gone. The Germans had taken control of the area, and tribes such as the Vandals, Goths, Angles, Saxons, and Jutes took control of different areas. Eventually the Vikings took control of some of this land as well. Learning and the arts suffered. During the same period, the Eastern Roman Empire thrived, particularly under the reign of Charlemagne. Only after both he and his son was the empire split up, and throughout that time, the culture, learning, and the arts thrived. **32.** Answers will vary. Students should support their answers

with at least some of these facts: Charlemagne was a German, but he spoke Greek. In addition, he read a great deal and learned Latin. He also developed a strong relationship with the pope. He was eventually made ruler of the Holy Roman Empire.

Part F: 33. Answers will vary. Students' paragraphs should include at least some of these ideas: The barbarians were very fierce fighters, and they were motivated by both greed and the need for new lands to settle. The Romans had the advantage of their natural barriers, and enough infrastructure to be able to build walls. **34.** Answers will vary. Students' paragraphs should include at least some of these ideas: Historians might review more than one saga to compare details. They would also look for evidence of Viking settlements in places such as Iceland, Greenland, and North America. They would look for information about Viking history in their artwork. Finally, the Vikings would interact with other people, so the history of those peoples should also mention the Vikings.

Chapter 10 Mastery Test B

Part A: 1. C **2.** B **3.** A **4.** C **5.** D
Part B: 6. Constantinople **7.** France **8.** sailors **9.** Great
10. barbarian **11.** saga **12.** Vandals **13.** Germans **14.** Middle Ages
15. uncivilized
Part C: 16. C **17.** E **18.** F **19.** H **20.** D **21.** G **22.** A **23.** B
Part D: 24. The Huns were invading their land from Asia. **25.** A frontier is land on or just beyond the border of a country. **26.** The final Roman emperor of the Western Roman Empire was defeated by the Germans. **27.** After Charlemagne died, his empire went to his son, Louis I, and began to crumble. It was divided among Charlemagne's three grandsons, and would become France, Germany, and part of Italy. **28.** The Romans had riches and power. **29.** The Goths were a barbarian tribe who captured Rome and destroyed much of the city and later settled in Italy and Spain.
Part E: 31. Answers will vary. Students should support their answers with at least some of these facts: Charlemagne spoke Greek, which was the language of the pope. He read and learned Latin, which would show that he was more civilized than the typical Germans. He also showed an interest in Christianity. **32.** Answers will vary. Students should support their answers with at least some of these facts: Erik the Red traveled further east from Iceland to settle in Greenland. This put Erik and Leif closer to North American territories. It would take Leif Eriksson less distance to travel to North America than it would have from Iceland.
Part F: 33. Answers will vary. Students' paragraphs should include at least some of these ideas: The Norse were known for plundering towns and sailing, both of these would require a great deal of strength. Also, Norse gods were known for their great strength. Exercise manufacturers would use the image of strength to promote their equipment.
34. Answers will vary. Students' paragraphs should include at least some of these ideas: Barbarians are uncivilized and primitive. In today's terms, someone uncivilized may not use proper etiquette, not make use of modern technologies, or depend on physical intimidation instead of common modern negotiation and communication.

Chapter 11 Mastery Test A

Part A: 1. A **2.** D **3.** C **4.** B **5.** A
Part B: 6. organized **7.** vassals **8.** homage **9.** estate **10.** freemen
11. serfs **12.** clergy **13.** knights **14.** artisans **15.** medieval
Part C: 16. G **17.** J **18.** C **19.** H **20.** F **21.** A **22.** I **23.** B **24.** E **25.** D
Part D: 26. The church saved writings from ancient times. **27.** In the feudal system, the each class owed their loyalty to the class above it.

28. In monasteries, monks and nuns prayed, studied, worked, and took part in religious services. **29.** Changes in society, trade, warfare, and weapons brought about the end of the feudal system. **30.** The feudal system lasted almost 700 years.

Part E: 31. Answers will vary. Students should support their answers with at least some of these facts: the bishop was describing the class system of the feudal world; serfs worked for the lord of the manor; they were tied to the land and had no rights; knights were the warriors of the feudal world; they were nobles, and fought for the king; freemen also fought for the nobles; the clergy prayed; they were the only important people who did not fight. **32.** Answers will vary. Students should support their answers with at least some of these facts: except for the clergy, every important person in the Middle Ages was a fighter; nobles swore to protect their kings, and knights were needed to fight; knights fought to protect their own estates from other estates and outsiders; knights also fought to protect Christianity; being a knight was an honor; young men in noble families were expected to become knights; being a knight was exciting; knights were respected.

Part F: 33. Answers will vary. Students' paragraphs should include at least some of these ideas: in the feudal system, everything was organized by classes, so people knew where they belonged; they knew what was expected from them; serfs had hard lives, but they also had the protection of the lord and his knights; every class owed loyalty to the class above it, which made life more predictable; kings and lords knew they had knights and other soldiers, such as freemen, who would fight for them; the nobles lived well, and had their needs taken care of by the serfs; clergy were often wealthy and powerful. **34.** Answers will vary. Students' paragraphs should include at least some of these ideas: the Black Death probably would not happen today because doctors know more about disease; doctors understand what causes disease and how disease spreads; we understand how germs work, and how to fight them; our cities and towns are much cleaner, so there is less chance of disease; doctors use sterilization and other advanced medical techniques. Something like the Black Death could happen today because many parts of the world are still poor; many countries do not have clean drinking water; some countries do not have enough doctors; some people are not educated enough to know how to protect themselves from disease; some diseases are still hard to control; we have diseases like AIDS that still kill many people.

Chapter 11 Mastery Test B

Part A: 1. B **2.** A **3.** D **4.** C **5.** B

Part B: 6. lord **7.** manor **8.** feudalism **9.** fortress **10.** peasants **11.** monks **12.** nuns **13.** jousts **14.** squire **15.** plague

Part C: 16. D **17.** F **18.** G **19.** A **20.** J **21.** E **22.** B **23.** I **24.** H **25.** C

Part D: 26. In return for land, the nobles paid homage, or pledged their loyalty, to the king. **27.** Nobles built fortresses as protection against enemies. **28.** Warriors were important during the Middle Ages because estates fought against each other, robbers had to be controlled, and tribes of people came looking for new lands. **29.** High officials of the church belonged to the nobility. **30.** The Black Death spread across Europe because the villages were not clean, there were large populations of rats, and there was not much medical knowledge.

Part E: 31. Answers will vary. Students should support their answers with at least some of these facts: serfs worked for the lord of the manor; they were bound to the land and had no rights; serfs had to do everything for the lord; they worked the land and took care of the manor house; the lord could treat the serfs as he wanted; there was no legal system to protect the serfs; the medieval world was a Christian

society, so if a lord treated his serfs poorly, he would pay for it in the next world. **32.** Answers will vary. Students should support their answers with at least some of these facts: changes in society, trade, and warfare brought about the end of the feudal system; trade picked up and money came back into use; the Black Death resulted in a shortage of labor, so artisans and peasants could demand higher wages; since people could buy and sell goods, estates no longer had to meet all their own needs; people began moving back into towns, rather than living in feudal villages; gunpowder and new weapons, such as cannons, started being used; these new weapons made knights on horseback less important; nobles no longer received land from the king, so they no longer owed their loyalty.

Part F: 33. Answers will vary. Students' paragraphs should include at least some of these ideas: some people joined the clergy to devote their lives to God; men became monks and lived in monasteries; women became nuns and lived in convents; life was hard in the Middle Ages, members of the clergy knew they would be taken care of; the clergy could read and write, unlike most of the other classes, so people might join the clergy to learn; the church kept the writings from earlier times, so the clergy was able to study those writings; the clergy owned land and many were rich and powerful; the clergy did not have to fight in battles. **34.** Answers will vary. Students' paragraphs should include at least some of these ideas: life today is easier than it was in feudal times; more people are educated; homes are more comfortable; we have glass in our windows and better heat; we have indoor plumbing; we live much cleaner lives, so there is less chance of disease; in the United States, all people are free and can come and go as they wish; people are not tied to the class they were born into. Life is still very difficult today; it is hard for poor people to advance; though people can better their lives, for poor people it is still hard to get a good education; people are not tied to the land, but they are often tied to their jobs; it is not always easy to get a better job, or any job at all; today, nobody owes loyalty to anyone, so life is less predictable; there is still a big difference between rich people and poor people and how they are treated.

Chapter 12 Mastery Test A

Part A: 1. A **2.** D **3.** B **4.** B **5.** C

Part B: 6. pilgrimage **7.** apprentice **8.** guild **9.** fallow **10.** prophet **11.** truce **12.** idols **13.** Jews **14.** Ottoman **15.** drowned

Part C: 16. F **17.** C **18.** A **19.** D **20.** E **21.** B

Part D: 22. With more food, people were healthier and would live longer. **23.** Having a surplus of food created more opportunities for trade. This benefited people living in cities as much as it did the farmers. **24.** If a serf was able to hide from their lord for one day more than a year, then they were free. **25.** The Magna Carta made King John follow the laws like other nobles and freemen. **26.** The Magna Carta assured basic human rights for people who were free. It also guaranteed that they would be allowed a trial by jury. **27.** Muslims would be eager to die in a war that was fought for Allah. It would ensure that they would reach paradise. **28.** They disagreed on who would succeed Muhammad. The Sunnis believed that the next leader did not have to be appointed by Muhammad or be a relative of him. The Shi'ites felt that Muhammad appointed a relative to follow him. **29.** The Turks took over control of Jerusalem and no longer allowed Christians to make pilgrimages. **30.** The availability of iron led farmers to make stronger tools such as plowshares and axes. These tools made farming easier, and farmers were able to grow more crops.

Part E: 31. Answers will vary. Students should support their answers with at least some of these facts: Islam spread throughout Arabia and into the Middle East and Asia. The Muslims eventually took control of Jerusalem. As the less tolerant Turkish Islamic took over control of Jerusalem, they refused to let Christians make pilgrimages to the holy city. The pope rallied Christians to declare a Holy War. **32.** Answers will vary. Students should support their answers with at least some of these facts: As long as young people were not serfs under the control of a lord, they could learn a trade as an apprentice. They could learn a specific craft, such as leatherwork or blacksmithing. The master would train them for seven years before having to pay a wage as a journeyman. Once the journeyman completed a masterpiece to the master's liking, the journeyman could set out to work independently.

Part F: 33. Answers will vary. Students' paragraphs should include at least some of these ideas: There were many lives lost and the cost of the wars brought great debt to the Europeans. However, the Europeans also benefited by improved skills in warfare, increased trade, and a better ability to explore the world. The economy in Europe actually improved because of the Crusades. **34.** Answers will vary. Students' paragraphs should include at least some of these ideas: A guild helped set working conditions, wages, prices, working hours, etc. This is similar to the role of the government in some ways, in that minimum wage is set by the government, and minimum standards for workers and their working conditions are as well. In addition, some groups have labor unions that operate much like guilds did in the Middle Ages.

Chapter 12 Mastery Test B
Part A: 1. D **2.** A **3.** C **4.** B **5.** B
Part B: 6. Christians **7.** conquered **8.** Turks **9.** Muslims **10.** trade **11.** iron **12.** disease **13.** serfs **14.** army **15.** rights
Part C: 16. C **17.** F **18.** E **19.** A **20.** B **21.** D
Part D: 22. King Richard and Saladin agreed on a truce so that Christians could resume their pilgrimages. **23.** Muhammad changed the Arabs from believing in many gods and idols to believing in one God, Allah. **24.** Jerusalem was the holy land for Muslims, Christians, and Jews. **25.** Muhammad taught the poor people that there was paradise for them if they fought and died for Allah. They had nothing to count on until they were taught this. **26.** The French king drowned and the German king returned to Europe before reaching Jerusalem. **27.** He conquered areas such as Egypt, and built many mosques. **28.** The Ottoman Turks took control of the Byzantine Empire, the Middle East, northern Africa, and much of eastern Europe, including the Holy Land. **29.** They wanted to make basic rules that all free men, including the king, would have to follow. **30.** Pope Urban II talked to people from all over Europe and made them want to take Jerusalem back from the Turks. He told people that the Christians were in danger.
Part E: 31. Answers will vary. Students should support their answers with at least some of these facts: Arab Muslims were tolerant of Jews and Christians because they also believed in one God. The Seljuk Turks did not tolerate people who were not Muslim worshipping in their holy land. **32.** Answers will vary. Students should support their answers with at least some of these facts: The three religions share many common holy sites. They are also three major religions of the world. All three religions believe in only one God, and they all agree on some prophets, such as Moses and Abraham.
Part F: 33. Answers will vary. Students' paragraphs should include at least some of these ideas: The Crusades were a violent attack on another religion, the Muslims, who were doing the same thing that every other nation was—expanding their territory. The Muslims were not attacking Christians, they had simply gained control of a Christian holy city.

The Christians forced children into war that resulted in their deaths and enslavement. **34.** Answers will vary. Students' paragraphs should include at least some of these ideas: The pope acted as both a political and religious leader in the Middle Ages. He gave Charlemagne the role of Emperor of the Holy Roman Empire, which is a political statement. He also called for Christians to attack the Muslims in order to take Jerusalem back from them. This is also a political move. The pope called for the Crusades for what could be called a religious reason.

Chapter 13 Mastery Test A
Part A: 1. B **2.** D **3.** C **4.** A **5.** C
Part B: 6. humanism **7.** sculptor **8.** Lutheranism **9.** heretics **10.** translated **11.** masterpiece **12.** pendulum **13.** theory **14.** astronomers **15.** microscope
Part C: 16. G **17.** I **18.** H **19.** J **20.** A **21.** F **22.** D **23.** E **24.** B **25.** C
Part D: 26. Michelangelo painted scenes from the Bible on the ceiling of the Sistine Chapel. **27.** The microscope, the spring, the pocket watch, cast iron, and the telescope are inventions other than the printing press that were developed during the Renaissance. **28.** Leonardo da Vinci worked as an artist, a scientist, an architect, a musician, an inventor, a geologist, and an engineer. **29.** The Catholic Church created the Inquisition to punish people who spoke out against the teachings of the church, or heretics. **30.** The Council of Trent clearly spelled out the beliefs of the church and approved new religious orders.
Part E: 31. Answers will vary. Students should support their answers with at least some of these facts: during the Renaissance, people were interested in human life and activity; newspapers told about what was going on in this life, rather than the next one; they told about what was going on in other countries; newspapers helped spread new ideas; newspapers encouraged more people to learn to read and write; newspapers helped people feel more connected. **32.** Answers will vary. Students should support their answers with at least some of these facts: patrons were wealthy people who provided food, housing, and money for young artists; because of patrons, artists were able to study and work on their art; artists with patrons did not have to find other work; most of the important artists in the Renaissance had patrons; Michelangelo and Leonardo da Vinci both had patrons.
Part F: 33. Answers will vary. Students' paragraphs should include at least some of these ideas: humanism was a belief in the importance of human beings; humanists were interested in people rather than religion; humanists were concerned with this life rather than the life after death; Renaissance art reflected this interest in human beings; although subject matter was still religious, the people in the paintings were more real and lifelike; Renaissance artists used live models; painters such as Michelangelo studied the human body at work and at rest; Michelangelo even studied dead bodies to understand how the bones and muscles work; Leonardo da Vinci filled his sketchbooks with drawings of human beings; the goal was to make the paintings and sculptures seem alive and real. **34.** Answers will vary. Students' paragraphs should include at least some of these ideas: Galileo was weak for giving into the church; Galileo was a scientist, and the truth should have been the most important thing to him; he made observations with his telescope, so he knew what he said was right; other people depended on Galileo to speak the truth; since Galileo had some power and influence, he could afford to go against the church. (1) Galileo was not weak for giving into the church; in Galileo's time, the church was very powerful; the Inquisition punished people who went against the church; people who were thought to be heretics were tortured and put to death; Galileo's ideas were already in print, so

people could still read them; Galileo was an old man (68) at the time of his trial, so punishment would have been hard for him; even after taking back his ideas, he was still confined to his home; who knows what worse punishment he would have received if he did not take back his ideas.

Chapter 13 Mastery Test B
Part A: 1. C **2.** D **3.** A **4.** B **5.** D
Part B: 6. Renaissance **7.** patrons **8.** architect **9.** criticize **10.** telescope **11.** Inquisition **12.** Reformation **13.** authority **14.** Protestants **15.** Counter-Reformation
Part C: 16. D **17.** F **18.** I **19.** J **20.** A **21.** C **22.** E **23.** G **24.** B **25.** H
Part D: 26. Erasmus criticized the church for being concerned with wealth and power. **27.** Renaissance artists painted the human body as lifelike. **28.** Johannes Gutenberg invented moveable type. **29.** A Renaissance man is someone who has many different talents or skills. **30.** Followers of Martin Luther were called Protestants because they spoke out, or protested, against the Catholic Church.
Part E: 31. Answers will vary. Students should support their answers with at least some of these facts: the Inquisition was a special court set up to punish people who spoke out against the church; during the Renaissance, many people were questioning the church; Martin Luther challenged the power of the church, and many people followed him; scientists such as Copernicus and Galileo had theories that went against the church; the church was afraid it was losing power; the spread of Protestantism was a serious challenge to the control the church had over Europe. **32.** Answers will vary. Students should support their answers with at least some of these facts: a Renaissance man had many different talents and skills; he was active in different fields, such as art and science; this is true of Leonardo; he was an artist, a scientist, an architect, a musician, an inventor, and an engineer; he is known today both for his art, such as *Mona Lisa,* and his inventions, such as the flying machine and the parachute; he used one talent to benefit another; he was always interested in new ideas and new inventions, which is what the Renaissance was all about.
Part F: 33. Answers will vary. Students' paragraphs should include at least some of these ideas: Erasmus was one of the first scholars to question the church and its leaders; Erasmus said the church was too concerned with wealth and power; he thought there was too much ritual and ceremony in the church; he believed simple ways were best; Martin Luther also questioned the church; his complaints were similar to Erasmus; he thought there was too much ritual in the church; he thought the pope had too much power and authority; the church that Luther set up simplified religion; other people who agreed with Luther also protested against the Catholic Church, and set up other Protestant churches. **34.** Answers will vary. Students' paragraphs should include at least some of these ideas: before the invention of moveable type, books had to be copied by hand; it took a long time to make a book, and books were expensive; the invention of moveable type meant that books could be made quickly and for less money. During the Renaissance, people were interested in the writings of the ancient Greeks and Romans; printing gave more people an opportunity to read those writings; because books were easier to produce, new ideas, such as those in the books of Copernicus and Galileo, spread faster; the Bible was translated into the language of the common people; now people did not have to depend on the church for their information about the Bible, but could get it firsthand.

Chapter 14 Mastery Test A
Part A: 1. A **2.** C **3.** C **4.** B **5.** B
Part B: 6. Elizabeth I **7.** freedom **8.** the Netherlands **9.** pope **10.** money **11.** Spain **12.** Moors **13.** Mary I **14.** nationalism **15.** Huguenots
Part C: 16. C **17.** D **18** F **19.** E **20.** B **21.** A
Part D: 22. Henry VIII wanted to annul his marriage to Catherine. The pope refused to grant his request. **23.** The main purpose of the Inquisition was to hunt down Spanish citizens who were not Catholic, and try to convert them to Catholicism. Many of those who refused were killed. **24.** The Church of England practiced religion much like the Catholic Church, but they were not under the control of Rome and the pope. **25.** Queen Mary's death ended Catholic control in England. Also, the Spanish Armada was defeated by the English navy. **26.** Elizabeth chose to make the Church of England a Protestant church, and the country became united. **27.** The Dutch wanted the freedom to choose their religion. They also felt they were paying too many taxes to the Spanish. **28.** Queen Mary made new laws to enforce Catholicism. She also married Philip II of Spain, a Catholic. **29.** Henry IV encouraged farming, trade, and manufacturing. He also sent out explorers to found the colony of Quebec. **30.** Henry VII kept England out of wars, and improved the country's economy.
Part E: 31. Answers will vary. Students should support their answers with at least some of these facts: The Armada was the largest fleet of ships, and represented the most powerful country in Europe. Losing so many ships was both a military and economic defeat to Spain. It also was the end of King Philip's dream of an entirely Catholic Europe. **32.** Answers will vary. Students should support their answers with at least some of these facts: England flourished in many areas. The arts increased with famous writers and the construction of the Globe Theater. The country became richer, and Elizabeth helped the poor. Trade increased, as did exploration.
Part F: 33. Answers will vary. Students' paragraphs should include at least some of these ideas: Having all of Europe share the same religion would have spared many lives lost during religious wars. The countries would have also shared common values. It would also have allowed the pope to work with all of the leaders, as they all would have looked to Rome for religious leadership. **34.** Answers will vary. Students' paragraphs should include at least some of these ideas: The Inquisition involved killing and torturing people who did not follow the Catholic faith. In areas such as Iraq and parts of Africa, people of one faith are persecuting followers of other faiths.

Chapter 14 Mastery Test B
Part A: 1. C **2.** B **3.** D **4.** C **5.** A
Part B: 6. Armada **7.** Catholic **8.** Mary **9.** Dutch **10.** religion **11.** Huguenot **12.** England **13.** Orange **14.** Spanish **15.** Inquisition
Part C: 16. C **17.** D **18.** F **19.** E **20.** B **21.** A
Part D: 22. He changed religions from Protestant to Catholic, and then granted religious freedom to the Protestants. **23.** Elizabeth sent money to the Netherlands and had her navy attack Spanish ships. **24.** Henry VIII wanted his marriage to Catherine annulled, but the pope refused to do so. **25.** The Dutch wanted religious freedom and did not want to pay taxes to Spain. **26.** Spain held many lands and controlled rich colonies overseas. **27.** The Moors were the Muslims that lived in Spain. **28.** Henry VII's Catholic daughter was Queen Mary I. **29.** Edward became king at age nine, and died before he reached adulthood. **30.** The Church of England practiced religion much like the Catholic Church, but they were not under the control of Rome and the pope.

Part E: **31.** Answers will vary. Students should support their answers with at least some of these facts: Mary was Catholic and wanted all English to be Catholic. She was also very unpopular with the Parliament. She reigned for a short period of time. Elizabeth was Protestant, and brought peace to England. She was able to work with Parliament to pass laws helping the poor, and she was also popular with the people. She reigned for decades. **32.** Answers will vary. Students should support their answers with at least some of these facts: The Tudor reign started with Henry VII. His son, Henry VIII, was his successor. Henry VIII was followed by Edward VI, then Henry's daughters Mary I and Elizabeth I.

Part F **33.** Answers will vary. Students' paragraphs should include at least some of these ideas: Henry VIII changed the course of the country by breaking with the Catholic Church. Had he not, the Church of England would never have existed, and he would not have been able to marry after Catherine. Elizabeth brought a cultural and financial boom to England during her reign. She also brought peace to the country. **34.** Answers will vary. Students' paragraphs should include at least some of these ideas: The pope would use religious reasons to convince Henry to remain Catholic, such as the sanctity of marriage and the sin of wanting to be with another woman. The pope would also use political reasons, such as the alliance England would have with other Catholic leaders, such as Philip in Spain.

Chapter 15 Mastery Test A
Part A: **1.** B **2.** C **3.** D **4.** A **5.** C
Part B: **6.** Inuit **7.** India **8.** Anasazi **9.** Aztecs **10.** Japan **11.** China **12.** China
Part C: **13.** B **14.** A **15.** D **16.** C
Part D: **17.** The Vikings were the first Europeans to meet the Inuit (they did so in Greenland). **18.** Cortés came to Tenochtitlán in 1519. **19.** Kublai Khan developed a postal service in China. **20.** Spanish explorers, like Francisco Pizzaro, brought about the end to the Inca civilization.
Part E: **21.** Answers will vary. Students should support their answers with at least some of these facts: Both Japanese society and Western European society during the Middle Ages were feudal societies. In feudal societies, the people were divided into a system of classes from top to bottom. **22.** Answers will vary. Students should support their answers with at least some of these facts: To the European explorers, the Americas were previously unknown, so the region was "new" to them. It also seemed vast, like a whole world in itself. The American Indians had long lived in the Americas, however. The region was not "new" to them.
Part F: **23.** Answers will vary. Students' paragraphs should include at least some of these ideas: The shogun closed the doors to Japan because he thought that Christianity and European ways might upset the Japanese culture. While this did preserve the unique culture in Japan, it restricted the freedom of people to enter and leave the country. Students will have different opinions about whether the benefits outweighed the harm done. **24.** Answers will vary. Students' paragraphs should include at least some of these ideas: Genghis Khan and Kublai Khan probably had very different points of view about China. Genghis would have seen it as an enemy to conquer. We know that Genghis was brutal, so he probably would have told his warriors to kill as many Chinese as it took to get control of the country. Kublai, on the other hand, lived in China and probably appreciated its many wonders. We know that he improved things and built things, such as the Grand Canal. He wanted to make China an even better place, and he probably considered that his great achievement.

Chapter 15 Mastery Test B
Part A: **1.** D **2.** B **3.** A **4.** D **5.** C
Part B: **6.** The Inca Empire was in western South America. **7.** The Inuit built houses of blocks of snow. [Alternatively: The Inuit hunted caribou, whales, and seals for meat.] **8.** Babar and Akbar ruled the Mogul Empire in India. **9.** The main link between China and the West was the Silk Road. **10.** The culture of China strongly influenced Japan. **11.** The Mongols, led by their ruler Genghis Khan, invaded China. **12.** The Italian explorer Marco Polo visited China for 17 years.
Part C: 13. D **14.** C **15.** B **16.** A
Part D: 17. the Vikings **18.** Cortés **19.** Kublai Khan **20.** Spanish explorers
Part E: **21.** Answers will vary. Students should support their answers with at least some of these facts: Kublai Khan allowed religious freedom. He maintained good roads, developed a postal service, and promoted the building of the Grand Canal. **22.** Answers will vary. Students should support their answers with at least some of these facts: Students should conclude that the shoguns were indeed very powerful. A weak ruler would not be able to stop people from traveling and trading. The Japanese people must have been afraid to break the shoguns' rules precisely because these leaders were so powerful.
Part F: **23.** Answers will vary. Students' paragraphs should include at least some of these ideas: I'd probably want to understand that for these people, the "new" planet is their home and therefore not "new." I would realize that we team of explorers were the guests of the planet people. I could draw on the experience of the Spanish in the Americas. They destroyed empires and killed many people, sometimes by tricking the leaders. Our team would want to come in peace, to make friends with the local people. Then we could trade with them and have them as allies instead of enemies. **24.** Answers will vary. Students' paragraphs should include at least some of these ideas: The Mogul ruler Aurangzeb made Hindus pay a special tax. He destroyed Hindu temples. He tried to force conversion to Islam. For these reasons, Hindus revolted against Mogul rule.

Chapter 16 Mastery Test A
Part A: **1.** D **2.** A **3.** C **4.** B **5.** C
Part B: **6.** Vasco da Gama **7.** insurance **8.** newcomers **9.** Plymouth **10.** Ferdinand Magellan **11.** Sir Francis Drake **12.** stock **13.** conquistadors **14.** interest **15.** plantations
Part C: 16. G **17.** E **18.** C **19.** B **20.** H **21.** I **22.** D **23.** J **24.** A **25.** F
Part D: 26. The English, French, and Dutch explored and settled in North America. **27.** Most Africans came to the Americas on ships as slaves. **28.** The Pilgrims were seeking religious freedom in North America. **29.** Most colonists were farmers. **30.** Trade created a new middle class in Europe.
Part E: **31.** Answers will vary. Students should support their answers with at least some of these facts: the Spaniards treated the people of South America cruelly; they did not accept that the people who lived there had civilizations and cultures of their own; the Spaniards thought of the native people as savages; Pizarro attacked and conquered the Inca Empire in order to take their gold; the Spaniards tried to make the Indians accept Christianity; many Indians who refused were burned; other Indians were used as slaves; thousands of Indians died from the diseases the Spaniards brought with them. **32.** Answers will vary. Students should support their answers with at least some of these facts: trade brought about new businesses in banking and investing; the Amsterdam Stock Exchange was built for the buying and selling of stocks; new banks were set up to help pay for trading trips; insurance

companies were founded to cover merchants' losses; the English East India Company, the Dutch East India Company, and the French East India Company were powerful trading companies.

Part F: 33. Answers will vary. Students' paragraphs should include at least some of these ideas: the Europeans came to the Americas for many reasons; some came for adventure; some of the early explorers, such as Columbus and Cabral, came accidentally; some came to make money; the conquistadors came for the gold of Mexico and South America; the French trappers came to make money selling animal furs; the traders came to establish new markets; some, such as the Pilgrims and Puritans, came for religious freedom; other colonists came to make a better life for themselves in the new world. **34.** Answers will vary. Students' paragraphs should include at least some of these ideas: North America would be very different today if the European settlers had never arrived; there were many American Indian nations, each with its own culture; these would have grown in ways we cannot predict; the American Indian people of the east would not have been driven from their lands; other people in the world would not have some of the crops that came from North America, such as corn and tobacco; the slave trade, which brought African slaves to the Americas, would not have existed; the English language would not have the words that came from the culture of the Americas; English might not be spoken in as many places as it now is; the United States would never have been born.

Chapter 16 Mastery Test B

Part A: 1. B **2.** C **3.** A **4.** B **5.** D

Part B: 6. Pilgrims **7.** Puritans **8.** trappers **9.** Quebec
10. Hernando Cortés **11.** Francisco Pizarro **12.** Amerigo Vespucci
13. shareholders **14.** investment **15.** piracy

Part C: 16. J **17.** H **18.** G **19.** A **20.** E **21.** B **22.** F **23.** D **24.** I **25.** C

Part D: 26. Columbus hoped to find a water route to Asia. **27.** Guns and horses helped the conquistadors conquer the American Indians. **28.** The American Indians in North America were driven westward. **29.** The English government controlled the colonies on the east coast of North America. **30.** The Netherlands, England, and France were the three European trading powers of the 1600s.

Part E: 31. Answers will vary. Students should support their answers with at least some of these facts: at first, the European settlers and the native people lived together in peace; the Europeans did not understand the American Indians; some of the Europeans thought the Indians were savages; the diseases the Europeans brought with them killed many of the native people; as more Europeans came, they drove the Indians westward; over time, the American Indians lost their lands to the settlers. **32.** Answers will vary. Students should support their answers with at least some of these facts: there was slavery in both North and South America; the native people of South America were used as slaves by the conquistadors; the native people of North America did not become slaves; African people were sold into slavery in the Americas; the first African slaves were brought to South America by Spanish and Portuguese traders; later, English traders started bringing slaves to North America; African slaves worked on the plantations of the southern colonies of North America.

Part F: 33. Answers will vary. Students' paragraphs should include at least some of these ideas: Mexico would be very different today if the conquistadors had never arrived; the Aztec people had a powerful civilization in Mexico; if they had not been conquered, their civilization may have grown larger; many people would not have died from the diseases the conquistadors brought with them; Mexico would not be a Spanish-speaking country today; Mexico might not be a Christian

country without the influence of the Spaniards; Mexico might be a much richer country today; since the Aztecs had a strong class system, there might still be a great division between rich and poor in Mexico even if the Spaniards had never arrived. **34.** Answers will vary. Students' paragraphs should include at least some of these ideas: trade with the Americas brought many changes to Europe; banks were set up to help pay for trading voyages; buying and selling stock in trading companies became a big business; the Amsterdam Stock Exchange was built just for the buying and selling of stocks; insurance companies were set up to cover merchants' losses; merchants grew wealthy; trade created a new middle class in Europe; slave trading started between Africa and the Americas; the Spanish, Portuguese, and English worked as slave traders; trade brought many new products, such as corn, tobacco, and animal skins, to European markets.

Chapter 17 Mastery Test A

Part A: 1. B **2.** B **3.** D **4.** C **5.** C

Part B: 6. Commons **7.** taxes **8.** democracy **9.** Thomas Jefferson
10. consent **11.** Charles I **12.** representation **13.** philosophers
14. Oliver Cromwell **15.** Lords

Part C: 16. A **17.** E **18.** B **19.** C **20.** D **21.** F

Part D: 22. Edward expanded the Parliament to include merchants, knights and others who were not nobles. This gave more people a voice in his government. **23.** Answers may vary. People had natural rights to speak freely and live the way they wanted to live. Also, they said a monarch could be overthrown for not following the will of the people. **24.** Charles I arrested five members of Parliament. **25.** The king and the nobles who supported him were called Royalists. Oliver Cromwell was supported by Parliament, as well as Puritans who were called Roundheads. **26.** Answers may vary. Cromwell brought Scotland and Ireland under English rule. But he also fought with Parliament and ruled by himself. **27.** James II became a Catholic and he tried to get too much power. Parliament asked William and Mary to come over from the Netherlands to become monarchs. **28.** Parliament grew more powerful because monarchs had to consult them before acting. Also, Parliament became more democratic. **29.** Many American colonists wanted a voice in English government on issues that affected them—like taxes. **30.** Jefferson stressed ideals like freedom from control by Parliament, and unfair acts by the king.

Part E: 31. Answers will vary. Students should support their answers with at least some of these facts: The English civil war involved Oliver Cromwell leading a group who wanted to overthrow the king and restore the rights of Parliament and the people of England. The American Revolution also sought to get out from under control of the king, but they were intent on becoming their own country and breaking from England. **32.** Answers will vary. Students should support their answers with at least some of these facts: Both leaders disbanded Parliament in order to make decisions without having to get permission from Parliament. Charles did not want his powers limited, as he believed his authority was given to him by God. Cromwell wanted to bring Scotland and Ireland under England's control without worrying about approval of others.

Part F: 33. Answers will vary. Students' paragraphs should include at least some of these ideas: The Seven Years' War was fought in America. Defeating France and the Indian tribes allowed the colonists to expand their holdings and not worry about attack from the French. Americans should help pay for these benefits. **34.** Answers will vary. Students' paragraphs should include at least some of these ideas: Oliver Cromwell was able to remove the king from leadership and give rights back to the people of England. However, Cromwell disbanded Parliament and was especially violent to the Irish.

Chapter 17 Mastery Test B
Part A: 1. B **2.** A **3.** B **4.** D **5.** A
Part B: 6. Declaration of Independence **7.** Parliament **8.** Bill of Rights **9.** participation **10.** philosophers **11.** arrested **12.** Roundheads **13.** Commonwealth **14.** representation **15.** independence
Part C: 16. E **17.** B **18.** A **19.** D **20.** C **21.** F
Part D: 22. Through the Petition of Right, the Glorious Revolution and the Bill of Rights, Parliament was able to gain power over the government that had been reserved for the monarch. **23.** The main issue they argued over was taxes. The monarch wanted to raise taxes, and Parliament resisted. **24.** Answers may vary. Rights that are critical to a democracy are free speech, a trial by jury, and the ability to choose your representatives. **25.** Locke's writings stressed the value of freedom of speech and thought. These ideas were realized in documents like the Bill of Rights and the Declaration of Independence. **26.** For a few years, Cromwell worked with Parliament to run the country. But after many arguments, he dismissed them and ran the country himself. **27.** Members of the House of Lords must be part of the nobility, and can inherit their position. Members of the House of Commons are elected. **28.** George III tried to force the colonists to pay higher taxes in order to pay for the war. **29.** James I was the first monarch in the Stuart line. **30.** Charles I was considered a public enemy of the nation.
Part E: 31. Answers will vary. Students should support their answers with at least some of these facts: The writings of philosophers would have come to America. In addition, American colonists knew the rights given to the English in their Bill of Rights. They wanted rights similar to those that were discussed by philosophers. This is evident by the wording of the Declaration of Independence. **32.** Answers will vary. Students should support their answers with at least some of these facts: Both revolutions gave power back to citizens of the areas impacted. The Glorious Revolution allowed English citizens to go back to a Parliamentary government, although still under the rule of the monarchy. The American Revolution allowed the American colonies to gain self-government.
Part F: 33. Answers will vary. Students' paragraphs should include at least some of these ideas: The quotations of the Enlightenment philosophers are still significant today. There are countries where all people do not have rights as we do in a democracy, In addition, when our government makes a mistake or a leader tries to take too much power, the people have the ability to act to limit the actions.
34. Answers will vary. Students' paragraphs should include at least some of these ideas: Americans can vote leaders in and out of office. They can also work with government leaders to change laws and ways that the government handles problems.

Chapter 18 Mastery Test A
Part A: 1. C **2.** D **3.** C **4.** A **5.** C
Part B: 6. Voltaire **7.** Estates-General **8.** Second **9.** Third **10.** Bastille **11.** Austria **12.** Convention **13.** Liberty **14.** guillotine **15.** Napoleon
Part C: 16. E **17.** H **18.** D **19.** G **20.** B **21.** F **22.** A **23.** C
Part D: 24. The American war of independence made many French people think about freedom from tyranny and the rights of people. Before then, most people had accepted the king's right to rule. **25.** The Third Estate represented 98 percent of French people. Members of the

Third Estate realized it was unfair to be outvoted by the combination of the First and Second estates. **26.** The storming of the Bastille was an important event because the Bastille was a symbol of the king's tyranny and also because it allowed the common people to show their support for revolution. **27.** King Louis XVI and Queen Marie Antoinette were both beheaded by the guillotine in 1793, on the orders of the revolutionary leaders. **28.** In 1795, Napoleon Bonaparte successfully defended the National Convention, France's lawful government, from a group of armed rebels. **29.** The laws of France today are based on the Napoleonic Code, which Napoleon sponsored soon after he came to power. **30.** The French government after Napoleon was unstable, and there were many changes for half a century.
Part E: 31. Answers will vary. Students should support their answers with at least some of these facts: Apparently, King Louis XVI did not understand the feelings of the French people in 1789. If he had understood how angry they were he either would not have called the Estates-General or he would have tried harder to work with the Third Estate. **32.** Answers will vary. Students should support their answers with at least some of these facts: The rulers of Austria and Prussia were afraid that the ideas of the French Revolution would spread to their countries and create opposition to their rule. They were probably right to be fearful, because all the monarchies in Europe probably had enemies who would have been glad to listen to revolutionary ideas.
Part F: 33. Answers will vary. Students' paragraphs should include at least some of these ideas: Robespierre turned violence on his enemies during the Reign of Terror. Before long, however, Robespierre himself fell to the violence. The lesson could be that when powerful people use violence against others, that violence comes back on them in the end. **34.** Answers will vary. Students' paragraphs should include at least some of these ideas: The French Revolution shows that ideas are more powerful than brute force. The kings and nobles had used force to keep the peasants and other members of the Third Estate in "their place." New ideas about freedom and rights flowed back into France from the American war for independence. These ideas inspired the members of the Third Estate and the common people to fight for freedom and rights in the revolution. Eventually, they won freedom and those rights.

Chapter 18 Mastery Test B
Part A: 1. B **2.** A **3.** C **4.** D **5.** A
Part B: 6. H **7.** D **8.** A **9.** G **10.** F **11.** E **12.** C **13.** B
Part C: 14. guillotine **15.** Directory **16.** dictator **17.** fraternity **18.** Elba **19.** colonies **20.** Josephine **21.** Louis XVIII **22.** Wellington **23.** Saint Helena
Part D: 24. The American War for Independence gave the French people ideas about freedom from tyranny and the rights of people. **25.** Members of the Third Estate felt they had the right to represent the French people because 98 percent of the French people belonged to the Third Estate. Although the First and Second estates represented a tiny minority of French people, they could outvote the Third Estate under the old royal system. **26.** The angry mob expected to find lots of people who had been locked away in the Bastille for falling behind in their taxes or for disagreeing with the king. **27.** The revolutionary leaders executed the king and queen, by the guillotine, in 1793. **28.** Napoleon Bonaparte first became powerful in 1795 by successfully defending the National Convention, France's lawful government, against a group of armed rebels. **29.** Napoleon's system of laws, the Napoleonic Code, still affects French laws today. **30.** In the 50 years after Napoleon, France's government was unstable with many frequent changes.

Part E: 31. Answers will vary. Students should support their answers with at least some of these facts: Merchants, workers, and peasants were very angry with King Louis XVI in 1789 because they had long been underrepresented in government, yet they had paid most of the taxes. They saw how much wealth the king and nobles displayed and wondered why all of the wealth had to be used to support the royals and the nobles. **32.** Answers will vary. Students should support their answers with at least some of these facts. The Reign of Terror lasted through 1793 and 1794 (about two years). (Reasons for the end of the Reign of Terror will vary.) The common people got sick and tired of so many bloody executions. Many of the leaders who supported the Reign of Terror were eventually executed, such as Robespierre. Napoleon Bonaparte brought order and stability when he gained power.

Part F: 33. Answers will vary. Students' paragraphs should include at least some of these ideas: The French Revolution resulted in widespread warfare for several reasons. Most countries in Europe were ruled by monarchs—that is, kings and queens. In those countries, the monarchs were afraid of talk of freedom and rights for people. They believed that such ideas, if they spread, would harm their own positions in their own countries. Also, after French troops began to fight countries such as Austria and Prussia, other neighboring countries may have become alarmed about France. The chaos of the revolution allowed Napoleon to take power. His plans of conquest and glory drew more enemy countries into war. The French Revolution showed how a revolution can lead to widespread war. **34.** Answers will vary. Students' paragraphs should include at least some of these ideas: (1) I think Napoleon is a hero of history. He brought ideas of the French Revolution, including freedom and equality, to all parts of Europe. He outlawed special tax privileges for the wealthy and powerful, improved education, and drew up a system of laws. It is true that his rule caused war in Europe, but on the balance, Napoleon was a force for good. (2) I think Napoleon is a villain of history. He unleashed decades of war in Europe. This was because he could not be satisfied with ruling France only. Instead he had to conquer and rule many other nations. Many people must have died in Napoleon's battles. Many others must have been forced away from their homes. It is true that Napoleon achieved some reforms inside France, but these count for little against his crimes of war.

Chapter 19 Mastery Test A
Part A: 1. A **2.** C **3.** B **4.** D **5.** B
Part B: 6. Industrial Revolution **7.** cottage weavers **8.** factories **9.** raw material **10.** textile **11.** developed countries **12.** developing countries **13.** petroleum **14.** internal combustion engine **15.** energy
Part C: 16. H **17.** E **18.** C **19.** I **20.** D **21.** B **22.** J **23.** G **24.** A **25.** F
Part D: 26. The Industrial Revolution helped people make a profit by increasing the production of goods. **27.** People feared the new machines because they thought they would lose their jobs. **28.** Locomotives, ships, and steamboats were powered by the steam engine. **29.** Factory owners lowered wages by hiring women and children. **30.** During the Industrial Revolution, people moved from the country to the cities.
Part E: 31. Answers will vary. Students should support their answers with at least some of these facts: the steam engine powered many of the machines that made the Industrial Revolution possible; heavy machines needed more power than water power could provide; the steam engine ran machines such as the power loom; the steam engine changed transportation; the steam locomotive crossed Great Britain, France, Germany, and the United States; steamships carried raw material and finished goods across the ocean. **32.** Answers will vary. Students should support their answers with at least some of these facts: factories were dirty and dangerous places; factory owners cared more about making money than how they treated their workers; factory owners hired women and children to do the work; they paid terrible wages; workers protested against the conditions; they wanted higher wages and safer working conditions; workers found they had to band together to have their demands met.

Part F: 33. Answers will vary. Students' paragraphs should include at least some of these ideas: the Industrial Revolution made life better in many ways; incomes increase 30 times over between 1815 and 1836; people had better food to eat; better transportation meant that food was fresher; increased trade meant that people had more access to things like sugar, tea, and coffee; more efficient transportation meant that food was less expensive; coal provided people with better ways to heat their homes and cook their food; since textiles could be made quickly in factories, cloth was not as expensive; the middle class benefited the most; merchants, bankers, and factory owners grew wealthy; the middle class had a greater voice in government; improvements in communication made it easier for people to stay in contact; people knew more about what was going on in the rest of the world. **34.** Answers will vary. Students' paragraphs should include at least some of these ideas: trade was important in spreading the Industrial Revolution; developed countries needed raw material to make into finished products; they also needed markets for their goods; developed nations formed colonies in places such as Africa and Asia; they imported raw materials from their colonies and sold finished products there; in time, developed nations set up factories in undeveloped nations; developed nations also traded with each other; as they traded goods, they also traded ideas; improvements in transportation also helped the ideas of the Industrial Revolution to spread; steam-powered locomotives and ships meant that goods could travel more quickly.

Chapter 19 Mastery Test B
Part A: 1. C **2.** B **3.** A **4.** D **5.** B
Part B: 6. practical **7.** profit **8.** Transportation **9.** Locomotives **10.** natural resources **11.** imported **12.** markets **13.** investors **14.** labor unions **15.** exported
Part C: 16. H **17.** D **18.** G **19.** E **20.** C **21.** A **22.** I **23.** B **24.** J **25.** F
Part D: 26. Cottage weavers were farm families who produced cloth at home. **27.** The mule spun finer threads very rapidly. **28.** The dynamo led to the widespread use of electricity as a source of power. **29.** During the Industrial Revolution, factories were dirty and dangerous, and workers were paid poorly. **30.** In the 1800s, the Industrial Revolution spread to France, Germany, the United States, Russia, and Japan.
Part E: 31. Answers will vary. Students should support their answers with at least some of these facts: industrialized countries needed raw materials to make their goods; they set up colonies to provide them with these raw materials; Great Britain took over lands in Africa and Asia in order to have access to their natural resources; colonies also needed the finished goods that the factories produced; developed nations imported raw materials from their colonies, and exported their finished goods to markets there. **32.** Answers will vary. Students should support their answers with at least some of these facts: the Industrial Revolution made life harder in many ways; factory work was often dangerous; factories employed women and children, and paid them less than men; cities grew overcrowded; workers lived in poorly built slum buildings; sometimes whole families had to share one room; cities were often dirty; overcrowding led to the spread of disease.

Part F: 33. Answers will vary. Students' paragraphs should include at least some of these ideas: Great Britain had the natural resources needed for industry; Britain had a good supply of coal and iron; coal was an important source of fuel to power the steam engine; Britain had colonies that could provide it with raw materials, and where it could sell its goods; Britain had the transportation necessary to support industry; Britain had been engaged in shipping and trade for many years; the steam-powered locomotive and steam-powered ships made transportation more efficient; Britain had a large supply of workers; farmers operated spinning wheels and looms in their homes, so when that work moved to the cities, many of them followed; British investors had been investing in trade for years, so they were ready to back new businesses; the British government supported growing industry in the country. 34. Answers will vary. Students' paragraphs should include at least some of these ideas: the internal combustion engine was the most important invention to come out of the Industrial Revolution; it improved transportation; it led to the development of the automobile; trucks now carry many goods that were once carried by trains; it made petroleum an important natural resource; it allowed people to move out of the cities. Other inventions of the Industrial Revolution were as important as the internal combustion engine; the telegraph improved communication; it led to other inventions, such as the telephone, which made improved communication even more; today, much of our economy is based on communication; the dynamo generated electric power; it led to more powerful electric generators and motors; the use of electricity became widespread; today, electricity is our most important source of power.

Chapter 20 Mastery Test A

Part A: 1. C 2. B 3. D 4. B 5. A
Part B: 6. mestizos 7. Mexico 8. descendants 9. haciendas
10. murals 11. discrimination 12. landowners 13. viceroy
14. natives 15. liberators
Part C: 16. F 17. D 18. C 19. A 20. E 21. B
Part D: 22. Spain and Portugal forbid their colonies from trading between themselves or other countries. Also, the colonies could not make any finished goods, and had to buy their products from the mother country. 23. The Europeans used natives or enslaved Africans as field hands on their haciendas. 24. The Haitians were excited to learn about events of the French Revolution, and started thinking about freedom for themselves. 25. Bolívar used his own money to back revolutions. He also organized his own army to fight the Spanish soldiers. 26. O'Higgins became the dictator of Chile, and tried to break up the estates of the large landowners. 27. Most of the new nations were ruled by dictators or kings, with the power of the military behind them. 28. Many Latin Americans of today still produce the same type of music, clothing, and art that their ancestors did. 29. The languages of the colonizing nations—Spain, Portugal and France—were based in Latin. 30. Even though they were the children of Spaniards, the mestizos were often treated poorly and discriminated against.
Part E: 31. Answers will vary. Students should support their answers with at least some of these facts: People in Haiti heard about the revolution in France. Because Haiti was under French rule, they wanted freedom as well. Toussaint L'Ouverture led a slave revolt, then became governor of Haiti. Napoleon sent an army to Haiti and war broke out. L'Ouverture was imprisoned, but the people overthrew the French. 32. Answers will vary. Students should support their answers with at least some of these facts: Latin America is a blend of the cultures that ruled and were used for labor. Architecture is mainly Spanish, and

music is influenced by Africa. People in rural areas still live much as their ancestors did.
Part F: 33. Answers will vary. Students' paragraphs should include at least some of these ideas: The Latin American countries led revolutions with slaves and the poorer people. They did not have money or education after their freedom was earned to start building businesses and industry. The governments they lived under after overthrowing Europeans were often not democracies, so people did not have rights as more developed countries did. 34. Answers will vary. Students' paragraphs should include at least some of these ideas: Bolívar was the most well-known, and he liberated many countries, including Colombia, Venezuela, Ecuador, and Peru. He also became an important political leader. Dom Pedro led Brazil to independence without any bloodshed. Toussaint L'Ouverture led the first Latin American fight for freedom, and was a former slave himself. He went on to become the governor of Haiti.

Chapter 20 Mastery Test B

Part A: 1. B 2. B 3. C 4. D 5. A
Part B: 6. trade 7. mestizo 8. freedom 9. Gran Colombia
10. Chile 11. dictators 12. music 13. Creole 14. discrimination
15. mural
Part C: 16. C 17. E 18. F 19. B 20. A 21. D
Part D: 22. He became governor of Haiti. However, he died in prison after being captured by the French. 23. The raw materials were sent back to the mother country. Once there, it was made into finished products and sold back to the colonists. 24. The revolutions in the British colonies and France inspired the colonists to think about freedom. 25. Bolívar earned that name because he led so many countries to independence. 26. Hidalgo rang the church bells in Dolores. He also shouted "the cry of Dolores." 27. They marched their army through the Andes Mountains, and attacked the Spanish by surprise. 28. The European powers forced the natives to work on their own land. They also imported slaves from Africa. 29. The revolutionaries were mostly from the poor. Many of these were natives, slaves and mestizos. 30. Many of the settlers were only interested in getting rich, and then returning to the mother country.
Part E: 31. Answers will vary. Students should support their answers with at least some of these facts: Two Catholic priests, Hidalgo and Morelos, rallied people starting in the city of Dolores. They were killed, but the Mexican people were able to defeat the Spanish. 32. Answers will vary. Students should support their answers with at least some of these facts: Both leaders helped their countries gain freedom by leading revolts. Both men were leaders that the people became unhappy with, as Bolívar had to resign and O'Higgins was exiled.
Part F: 33. Answers will vary. Students' paragraphs should include at least some of these ideas: European rule allowed only Europeans to get rich and live well in Latin America. People had no say over taxation, laws, etc. Dictatorship was bad because there was no democracy, but the leadership was closer, so coups and takeovers might be easier to accomplish. 34. Answers will vary. Students' paragraphs should include at least some of these ideas: Latin American architecture is used in some communities. Latin American music has become mainstream. There are Latin American characters on television shows. In addition, Latin American art and food is also very prominent.

Chapter 21 Mastery Test A

Part A: 1. B 2. D 3. A 4. B 5. C
Part B: 6. D 7. F 8. A 9. E 10. H 11. G 12. B 13. C

Part C: **14.** imperialism **15.** Thomas Jefferson **16.** Britain
17. independence **18.** Mexico **19.** Treaty **20.** Confederate
21. enslaved **22.** Bull **23.** Gettysburg
Part D: **24.** The completion of the transcontinental railroad tied the East and West together and opened up the West for settlement. **25.** They thought that Alaska was a frozen wasteland without any useful resources. **26.** Americans who were farming or running businesses in Hawaii pushed Queen Liliuokalani off the throne. **27.** Samuel Morse invented the telegraph to improve communication and Cyrus McCormick invented the mechanical reaper to improve farming. **28.** By winning the Spanish-American War, the United States gained Puerto Rico, Guam, and the Philippines. **29.** U.S. battleships that went from the Atlantic to the Pacific oceans had to travel all around the southern tip of South America, an enormous distance. With a canal across Central America, they could cut the distance to a fraction. **30.** Panama rebelled against rule by Colombia because Colombia would not grant land to the United States to build a canal. The United States encouraged Panama in its rebellion.
Part E: **31.** Answers will vary. Students should support their answers with at least some of these facts: Not everyone in Mexico had accepted the treaty which gave Texas independence from Mexico. As long as Texas remained by itself, this was not a big problem. However, when Texas decided to join the United States, Mexicans opposed to the treaty realized that they would lose Texas forever. These Mexicans then wanted to fight over Texas. **32.** Answers will vary. Students should support their answers with at least some of these facts: The North was stronger because it had more people and more industry. More people meant that the North could keep more troops in the field. More industry meant that the North could make more guns and bullets.
Part F: **33.** Answers will vary. Students' paragraphs should include at least some of these ideas: (1) The Louisiana Purchase was more important than the Monroe Doctrine. The Louisiana Purchase was such a huge chunk of North America that it made the United States a major power. It put the United States in a good position to gain more land, including the Pacific coast, later on. Also, the purchase gave the United States complete control over the Mississippi River, the most important waterway on the continent. (2) The Monroe Doctrine was more important than the Louisiana Purchase. The Louisiana Purchase merely added land to the United States. The Monroe Doctrine, however, made the United States an important international power. It showed European powers that the U.S. would use military force to stop European meddling in the Americas. **34.** Answers will vary. Students' paragraphs should include at least some of these ideas: Colombia probably strongly disliked U.S. President Theodore Roosevelt. The land that became the nation of Panama had originally been part of Colombia. U.S. representatives encouraged Panama to rebel against its Colombian rulers so that the U.S. could buy a strip of land on which to build a canal. Colombian rulers would probably have seen this involvement as meddling in Colombia's affairs. They might have thought that Roosevelt and the Americans were dishonest, because with their Monroe Doctrine, they warned others not to meddle in the Americas, but they themselves meddled in their American neighbors' affairs.

Chapter 21 Mastery Test B
Part A: **1.** B **2.** D **3.** D **4.** B **5.** A
Part B: **6.** Atlantic **7.** France **8.** Britain **9.** Monroe Doctrine
10. Mexico **11.** Alamo **12.** Guadalupe **13.** Union **14.** Confederate
15. Spain
Part C: **16.** E **17.** C **18.** B **19.** D **20.** A **21.** H **22.** G **23.** F
Part D: **24.** The Transcontinental Railroad linked the eastern United States with the western United States and provided an easy way for settlers to go to the West. **25.** The Alaska purchase proved to be a good decision when gold was discovered in Alaska in 1897. Later, oil was found there. **26.** The reign of Queen Liliuokalani was cut short when American settlers led a revolt to remove her from the throne and set up a republic that would be friendly to the United States. **27.** The telegraph, invented by Samuel Morse, improved communication and the mechanical reaper, invented by Cyrus McCormick, improved farming. **28.** Spain lost the Philippines, Puerto Rico, and Guam to the United States. It also had to grant independence to Cuba. **29.** U.S. leaders wanted the Panama Canal because the Spanish-American War proved how difficult it would be to move battleships between the Atlantic and the Pacific oceans without a canal. **30.** Agents of the U.S. government persuaded Panama to rebel against Colombia. They knew that if Panama became independent, it would sell land to the United States. That is exactly what happened.
Part E: **31.** Answers will vary. Students should support their answers with at least some of these facts: The Louisiana Purchase was an important development in U.S. history because it almost doubled the size of the United States and it also gave the U.S. complete control of the Mississippi River. Additionally, possession of the Louisiana Territory put the U.S. in position to reach, in time, all the way to the Pacific Ocean. **32.** Answers will vary. Students should support their answers with at least some of these facts: The North and South both had traditions based on fighting the war for American independence against Britain and the founding of the United States. They also mostly spoke the same language, English. The North and South were different in many ways, however. The North had many more factories and much more industry. It also had more people. The South had fewer factories, so it was not able to produce as many guns and cannons. Also, southerners used enslaved labor on many of their larger farms, or plantations. By 1861, on the other hand, there were no enslaved people in the North.
Part F: **33.** Answers will vary. Students' paragraphs should include at least some of these ideas: Sample answer: I think the Mexican officials were right to stop the immigration of Americans into Texas. The Mexicans would have wanted to hold on to their lands, including Texas. They probably realized that if a large population of English-speaking Americans settled in Texas, those people might, after a while, want to join the United States instead of being part of Mexico. The Mexican officials were simply trying to protect their own country when they outlawed immigration. **34.** Answers will vary. Students' paragraphs should include at least some of these ideas: Sample answer: If a European country had gotten land from Panama to build a canal, the United States would probably have protested. The U.S. may even have gone to war over such an action. Ever since President Monroe stated his Monroe Doctrine in 1823, the U.S. had enforced a policy of no European expansion in the Americas. The U.S. would have been justified in enforcing this long-established policy. On the other hand, the governments of other countries would probably have thought that the U.S. was being dishonest—since it wanted land itself in Panama to build a canal.

Chapter 22 Mastery Test A

Part A: 1. B **2.** A **3.** C **4.** B **5.** D

Part B: 6. Manchus **7.** Qing dynasty **8.** smuggled **9.** Taiping Rebellion **10.** Boxer Rebellion **11.** Open-Door Policy **12.** Sun Yatsen **13.** policy **14.** industrialized **15.** constitution

Part C: 16. E **17.** H **18.** J **19.** F **20.** A **21.** B **22.** D **23.** C **24.** I **25.** G

Part D: 26. After the Opium War, China opened five ports to British trade. **27.** The United States suggested the Open-Door Policy to China. **28.** The population of China increased rapidly and became too big for its food supply. **29.** Emperor Mutsuhito welcomed foreigners, and invited them to teach in Japan. **30.** Because of industrialization, Japan set up overseas colonies and waged war with its neighbors.

Part E: 31. Answers will vary. Students should support their answers with at least some of these facts: the Manchus looked down on the rest of the world; they refused trade with Europe and the United States; China had been a leader in science and medicine; because of its policies, China fell behind the Europeans; as the population increased more than the food supply, the people suffered; in order to make money, Europeans began smuggling opium into China; many Chinese people became addicted to opium; when China seized opium from a British trader, it led to war; China lost the war, and was forced to accept Unequal Treaties with the British; the Chinese felt helpless to stop the British. **32.** Answers will vary. Students should support their answers with at least some of these facts: Sun Yatsen led a revolution in China; he overthrew the Manchu empire; he became the first president of China; after Yatsen was removed from power, he and his followers formed the Nationalist Party; he trained an army with help from the Soviet Union and Chinese Communists; his followers set up a Nationalist government in China in 1928.

Part F: 33. Answers will vary. Students' paragraphs should include at least some of these ideas: foreigners interfered in China in many ways; British smugglers brought opium into China; Great Britain forced China to open its ports to foreign trade; Western nations helped the Manchu government put down the Taiping Rebellion; Japan fought China for control of Korea; Japan took control of the Chinese island of Taiwan; the United States forced China to accept an Open-Door Policy following the Chinese-Japanese war; Americans gave Sun Yatsen money to help overthrow the Manchu government; the Soviet Union supported the Nationalist Party in their efforts to control China. **34.** Answers will vary. Students' paragraphs should include at least some of these ideas: Matthew C. Perry helped make Japan into a modern nation; before Perry came, Japan was an isolated nation; Japan did not trade with other countries; Perry brought a letter from the U.S. president, asking the Japanese to change their policies; Perry brought warships to back up his efforts; as a result, Japan opened its ports to U.S. ships; Japan then signed trade agreements with other European nations; foreign trade brought in new ideas along with new goods; open trade led Emperor Mutsuhito to want to modernize Japan; he brought in foreign teachers; Japan wanted to learn all it could about industry, transportation, and banking; within 40 years of Perry's visit, Japan was an industrialized nation.

Chapter 22 Mastery Test B

Part A: 1. B **2.** D **3.** C **4.** B **5.** D

Part B: 6. isolationist **7.** opium **8.** addicted **9.** queue **10.** Unequal Treaties **11.** interference **12.** Nationalist Party **13.** Commodore Perry **14.** Emperor Mutsuhito **15.** imperialism

Part C: 16. C **17.** E **18.** H **19.** A **20.** G **21.** F **22.** I **23.** J **24.** B **25.** D

Part D: 26. The Manchu rulers restricted foreign trade. **27.** Chinese peasants rebelled because they thought Manchu rulers were greedy and unfair. **28.** Manchu rule of China ended when Chinese Nationalists overthrew the government. **29.** Japan and China went to war in the 1890s because they both had claims on Korea. **30.** In 1910, Japan took complete control of Korea.

Part E: 31. Answers will vary. Students should support their answers with at least some of these facts: the Manchus looked down at the Chinese people; they made it illegal for a Manchu to marry a Chinese; they made Chinese men wear the Manchu hairstyle; the Manchus set up isolationist policies which hurt the Chinese people; the Manchu leaders were greedy and unfair; when the Chinese peasants rebelled against Manchu rule, the Manchus put down the rebellion with the help of Western governments. **32.** Answers will vary. Students should support their answers with at least some of these facts: as Japan became more industrialized, it needed more raw materials; Japan decided to set up colonies in order to supply their industries with raw materials; in order to set up colonies, Japan went to war; it fought China for control of Korea; after it won the war, Japan took the Chinese island of Taiwan; Japan also fought Russia for control of Korea; by 1910, Japan had complete control of Korea.

Part F: 33. Answers will vary. Students' paragraphs should include at least some of these ideas: many Chinese people became addicted to the opium that the British brought into China; China outlawed the opium trade; the British and other Europeans continued to smuggle the drug into China; after a Manchu official seized opium from British traders, Great Britain went to war with China; the British won the war with China; Great Britain forced China to accept Unequal Treaties, which gave Britain power over China; Britain forced China to open five ports to British trade; after this, Great Britain, the United States, and other powers interfered with Chinese affairs; China grew weaker and more open to foreign influence. **34.** Answers will vary. Students' paragraphs should include at least some of these ideas: before Emperor Mutsuhito came to power, Japan was torn between its old ways and the new ways; Mutsuhito decided to modernize Japan; during his rule, Japanese people traveled to other nations to learn about industry, banking, education, and transportation; the Japanese built thousands of schools in Japan and brought foreigners into Japan to teach; within 25 years, Japan was an industrial nation. Along with new factories and industries, Japan built up its army and navy; Japan used its military to conquer other lands; Japan took the island of Taiwan from China; it fought both China and Russia in Korea; by 1910, it controlled all of Korea; Japan established colonies and brought more raw materials home to feed its industries. Japan modernized its government as well; it wrote a new constitution, giving some power to the people; the emperor still ruled, but with advice from elected officials. All of these changes gave Japan new power in the world; it now had the industry and military might to be a world power.

Chapter 23 Mastery Test A

Part A: 1. C **2.** A **3.** D **4.** B **5.** C

Part B: 6. Hindu **7.** Muslim **8.** civil disobedience **9.** fast **10.** impose **11.** wealthy **12.** educate **13.** massacre **14.** Parliament **15.** independent

Part C: 16. F **17.** E **18.** B **19.** G **20.** H **21.** D **22.** A **23.** C

Part D: 24. India split up into several kingdoms, each ruled by its own raja. They constantly fought with each other. **25.** The British tried to impose Christianity, and criticized the Hindu caste system. **26.** The East India Company caused a rebellion in the sepoy army when they to ordered the Indians to bite a cartridge covered with animal fat. **27.** The British helped the Indians build railroads, hospitals, schools, and other things to improve the country. **28.** The Indians claimed the Congress was to improve relations with Britain. Secretly, the Congress was planning revolution. **29.** Gandhi worked as a lawyer in South Africa for many years. **30.** After the Amritsar massacre, the Indians learned that the British would try to keep their colony by force.

Part E: 31. Answers will vary. Students should support their answers with at least some of these facts: The British were concerned about the quality of living in terms of the caste systems and the number of poor. They made improvements to society with schools, hospitals, etc. However, they also looked upon the Indian people and land as British assets, used for the benefit of the British. This caused a loss of skills and culture in India. **32.** Answers will vary. Students should support their answers with at least some of these facts: Indian people were beginning to rebel against British rule in instances such as the Sepoy Rebellion. Mahatma Gandhi came to India after working in South Africa. He used the legal system to fight for Indian's rights. In addition, he taught Indians how to use nonviolent forms of protest to damage the British in India.

Part F: 33. Answers will vary. Students' paragraphs should include at least some of these ideas: Students' opinions may vary, but students should mention the oppression that Indians were subject to, including the disregard of their religious beliefs and the destruction of the Indian culture and traditions. **34.** Answers will vary. Students' paragraphs should include at least some of these ideas: Gandhi taught people to make changes in government and society by using civil disobedience. People were not hurt in the protests, but the government and British companies would be hurt economically by the actions of the Indians.

Chapter 23 Mastery Test B

Part A: 1. D **2.** A **3.** C **4.** C **5.** B
Part B: 6. Mogul **7.** British **8.** civil disobedience **9.** Java
10. massacre **11.** revolution **12.** nonviolent resistance
13. superiority **14.** Madras **15.** lawyer
Part C: 16. A **17.** E **18.** D **19.** F **20.** C **21.** B **22.** G
Part D: 23. France tried to establish trade in India with the French East India Company. England successfully drove them out of India.
24. The British East India Company was formed to establish trade with India. **25.** The Muslim population demanded their own country. This led to bloody fighting between Muslims and Hindus. **26.** Gandhi was killed by a Hindu gunman shortly after independence. **27.** The British started including Indians in important positions in their government. **28.** Indian soldiers were ordered to bite cartridges that were greased with animal fat. This was not permitted in their religion. **29.** Gandhi taught the Indians that they can achieve independence through civil disobedience and nonviolent resistance. **30.** The British started building roads, hospitals, schools, and railroads. They also tried to get rid of the caste system.

Part E: 31. Answers will vary. Students should support their answers with at least some of these facts: The British wanted to control all of the trade in and out of India. The French were powerful, and Britain did not want to give up any monies to them in lost trade. **32.** Answers will vary. Students should support their answers with at least some of these facts: The raw materials that were generated in India were sent to Britain, so Indians could not make their products anymore. Factories shut down. Manufactured goods were imported from Britain, so people in India lost the skills needed to manufacture.

Part F: 33. Answers will vary. Students' paragraphs should include at least some of these ideas: The poor had no means of gaining weapons, so they would be motivated to find another way to resist the British. The wealthy could afford weapons, and were probably benefiting from British trade, so they would not be as willing to do things differently. **34.** Answers will vary. Students' paragraphs should include at least some of these ideas: Pakistan is a smaller country than India, and there is not nearly as much coastland. This would limit the amount of ports that Pakistan could have. Muslims might feel that they did not get equal treatment. In addition, Hindus may have been unhappy to lose a significant portion of land to the Muslims, especially if that land was their home before Pakistan was created.

Chapter 24 Mastery Test A

Part A: 1. B **2.** D **3.** B **4.** B **5.** D **6.** D **7.** C
Part B: 8. D **9.** G **10.** F **11.** E **12.** A **13.** B **14.** C
Part C: 15. B **16.** B **17.** A **18.** D **19.** B **20.** C
Part D: 21. C **22.** D **23.** E **24.** A **25.** B

Part E: 26. Answers will vary. Students should support their answers with at least some of these facts: Enslaved African Americans created their own song form—spirituals. Out of the rhythms and the harmony of the spirituals developed jazz, gospel music, and blues. These are all highly popular musical styles in modern America. **27.** Answers will vary. Students should support their answers with at least some of these facts: The Suez Canal illustrates a good part of imperialism. It shows how Europeans brought knowledge and technology to Africa to modernize it. However, the Canal illustrates bad parts of imperialism, too. It is an example of Europeans holding on to an important African resource for a long time for their own benefit.

Part F: 28. Answers will vary. Students' paragraphs should include at least some of these ideas: The 19th century was indeed a time of great change in attitudes toward human rights and freedom. The fact that most countries, including Britain and the United States, abolished slavery in the 1800s shows that the people of these countries came to realize that slavery was wrong. Attitudes about slavery did change, but unfortunately, attitudes about imperialism did not change until much later. Still, the 19th century was an important watershed in the development of human rights and freedom. **29.** Answers will vary. Students' paragraphs should include at least some of these ideas: Invaders try to convert others to their religion for a number of reasons. One important reason is that many of the invaders are sincere in their beliefs and want to share them with others. Some of the invaders, however, realize that by converting foreigners, they can make them more like themselves and therefore easier to rule. Converting others to a religion is important because religion is a very basic part of a culture. If invaders want to export (carry) their culture to other places, they need to spread their religion.

Chapter 24 Mastery Test B

Part A: 1. B **2.** D **3.** C **4.** A **5.** B
Part B: 6. A **7.** C **8.** D **9.** F **10.** G **11.** B **12.** E
Part C: 13. C **14.** G **15.** E **16.** F **17.** D **18.** A **19.** B
Part D: 20. The kingdom of Ghana was rich in gold. **21.** Ghana lasted the longest (it lasted about 775 years). **22.** The Songhai kingdom ended in a battle with the Moroccans (in 1591). **23.** Timbuktu was the center of Muslim learning in ancient Mali. **24.** The United States outlawed slavery about 20 years after Britain outlawed it. **25.** A conference of European nations in Berlin in 1884 led to the rapid colonization of Africa.

Part E: 26. Answers will vary. Students should support their answers with at least some of these facts: Slavery changed the most during the 19th century (1800s). That is the century during which Britain, the United States, and other countries in the Americas outlawed slavery. **27.** Answers will vary. Students should support their answers with at least some of these facts: The Muslim religion arrived with Arab caravan traders in western and central Africa. It also came to the eastern coast of Africa by traders who stopped at ports there. Christianity, on the other hand, came to many parts of Africa by means of missionaries who spent time in Africa spreading their faith.

Part F: 28. Answers will vary. Students' paragraphs should include at least some of these ideas: The Europeans could have managed the canal in such a way as to give Africans a bigger stake. It was important for Europeans to build the canal in the first place, because they had the money and the know-how to do so. However, they could have set up schools to train engineers and encouraged the new engineers to manage the canal. Then, after just a few years of training, they could have turned the canal over to Africans, rather than waiting almost 100 years to do so. **29.** Answers will vary. Students' paragraphs should include at least some of these ideas: Enslaved African Americans probably wanted to remember traditions they had enjoyed in Africa, so they put them in their music. The music also probably helped them to keep hope of freedom alive. Singing the songs helped them keep their minds free while they worked on the masters' plantations.

Chapter 25 Mastery Test A

Part A: 1. C **2.** D **3.** B **4.** A **5.** D

Part B: 6. nationalism **7.** Rome **8.** boundary **9.** diplomat **10.** prime minister **11.** Giuseppe Garibaldi **12.** confederation **13.** Otto von Bismarck **14.** kaiser **15.** Victor Emmanuel II

Part C: 16. E **17.** D **18.** I **19.** J **20.** G **21.** H **22.** B **23.** A **24.** C **25.** F

Part D: 26. Napoleon created a spirit of nationalism in Italy by joining the kingdoms together. **27.** Giuseppe Mazzini founded "Young Italy" and its goal was to free Italy from Austrian rule and join the country together. **28.** Otto von Bismarck came to power when Wilhelm I made him prime minister of Prussia. **29.** Bismarck started a war with France to bring the German states together against a common enemy. **30.** The Second Reich was an empire ruled by one person.

Part E: 31. Answers will vary. Students should support their answers with at least some of these facts: Cavour was a diplomat and a master of foreign affairs; he was the prime minister of King Victor Emmanuel II of Sardinia, who wanted to unify Italy; Austria controlled Venetia and other Italian lands; Cavour arranged a defense agreement with France; when Austria declared war on Sardinia, France helped Sardinia beat the Austrians; their success made other Italian lands unite with Sardinia against Austria; in 1860, Cavour sent an army south to meet up with Garibaldi's army, which was marching north; the two armies freed most of Italy. **32.** Answers will vary. Students should support their answers with at least some of these facts: militarism is a policy in which a country maintains a strong army; Bismarck believed the strength of a country was measured by the number of soldiers it had; Germany was always ready for war; German nationalism meant pride in their strong army; soldiers got great respect and honor from the people; it was considered a privilege to belong to the army; it was an honor to fight for the empire; large businesses supported the military; factories were devoted to making war machines; everyone stood behind the war effort.

Part F: 33. Answers will vary. Students' paragraphs should include at least some of these ideas: before Napoleon, both Italy and Germany

were divided countries; after the fall of Rome, Italy was divided into many small kingdoms; for many years, different nations fought over the Italian lands; when Napoleon invaded Italy, he did away with the boundaries that divided the countries; he joined the kingdoms together to make them easier to control; for the first time since the Roman Empire, Italians saw themselves as one people; they started to feel the spirit of nationalism. Germany was also divided into many small kingdoms; Napoleon joined them together into the Confederation of the Rhine; people living in the Confederation became loyal to each other; they started to feel like members of a German nation; after Napoleon was defeated, the German states formed a new Confederation of 39 states. **34.** Answers will vary. Students' paragraphs should include at least some of these ideas: several different foreign powers influenced Italy's unification; Napoleon gave control of Venetia to Austria; after Napoleon was defeated, Austria took over other Italian lands; Mazzini wanted to join the country together; French and Austrian armies put down the Italian revolt of 1848; after the war, the Austrians forced the king of Sardinia from his throne; the new king, Victor Emmanuel II, was important in bringing about unification; his prime minister, Camillo do Cavour arranged a defense agreement between Sardinia and France; France helped Sardinia defeat Austria the next year; then other Italian lands joined with Sardinia against Austria; in 1866, Italy joined with Prussia in a war against Austria; after the war, Prussia gave Venetia to Italy; France helped Rome fight against Garibaldi; when France had to take its troops out of Rome to fight against Prussia, Rome became part of Italy.

Chapter 25 Mastery Test B

Part A: 1. A **2.** C **3.** D **4.** B **5.** C

Part B: 6. Giuseppe Mazzini **7.** society **8.** transmitted **9.** unify **10.** anthem **11.** Camillo di Cavour **12.** Wilhelm I **13.** legislature **14.** Otto von Bismarck **15.** militarism

Part C: 16. B **17.** H **18.** D **19.** G **20.** E **21.** I **22.** J **23.** F **24.** A **25.** C

Part D: 26. Austria and the pope ruled most of the Italian kingdoms and states in 1815. **27.** Victor Emmanuel II wanted to unify Italy. **28.** Garibaldi failed to take Rome because he was defeated by French troops. **29.** Otto von Bismarck's military policy was called "blood and iron." **30.** The Second Reich was the name for the united German empire.

Part E: 31. Answers will vary. Students should support their answers with at least some of these facts: Garibaldi was a revolutionary and a soldier; he joined the fight for freedom led by King Victor Emmanuel; he led an army that freed Sicily; after freeing Sicily, he led his army north on the Italian mainland; his army met up with the army of Cavour and freed most of Italy; Garibaldi then tried to take Rome; he was defeated by the French troops who came to help the pope defend Rome; finally, when France was at war with Prussia, Garibaldi was able to conquer Rome. **32.** Answers will vary. Students should support their answers with at least some of these facts: the Second Reich was an empire; Wilhelm I was the kaiser, or emperor; he had complete power; Otto von Bismarck was chancellor; he ran to government; he was responsible only to Kaiser Wilhelm; there was no legislature or any elected representatives.

Part F: 33. Answers will vary. Students' paragraphs should include at least some of these ideas: nationalism is a strong feeling of loyalty to one's country and culture; nationalism develops among people who speak the same language and follow similar customs; for many years, people living in Italy and Germany did not feel nationalism; the countries were divided into many small kingdoms, and people felt loyal to their own kingdom; for example, people living in Venice thought of themselves as Venetians, not as Italians; Napoleon joined kingdoms together in Italy and Germany to make them easier to rule; when he did this, people started looking at themselves as members of one group; after Napoleon left Italy, many of the Italian lands were ruled by Austria or the pope; many Italians wanted a free and united Italy; they formed secret societies and fought other countries in order to be united; in Germany, Napoleon formed the German states into a Confederation; after he was defeated, the spirit of nationalism caused the German people to form a new Confederation on their own. **34.** Answers will vary. Students' paragraphs should include at least some of these ideas: Bismarck followed a policy of "blood and iron;" this was a policy of war; Bismarck thought the goals of the people and the goals of the state were the same; he encouraged King Wilhelm to unite the German states under Prussian rule; Prussia went to war with Denmark to gain land; Prussia defeated Austria to get the lands Austria controlled; Bismarck started a war with France to rally the German states together; his idea worked, and the other German states joined with Prussia to form the united German empire; Prussia also won lands from France in the war; after Germany was unified, its military continued to hold its people together; the whole nation stood behind the military.

Chapter 26 Mastery Test A
Part A: 1. B **2.** D **3.** D **4.** B **5.** C
Part B: 6. alliances **7.** Switzerland **8.** Allied **9.** Germany **10.** Poland **11.** Turkey **12.** Central **13.** fronts **14.** treaty **15.** neutral
Part C: 16. D **17.** H **18.** E **19.** B **20.** A **21.** G **22.** C **23.** F
Part D: 24. Many European nations built up their military might to keep up with other countries. **25.** After the Russian Revolution, Russia signed a peace treaty with Germany **26.** The Germans used submarines to attack ships under the water. **27.** Germany had to disarm, and could only keep a small army. **28.** It was called the Great War because over 30 nations were involved. **29.** Russia and Austria-Hungary argued over the ownership of different territories, including Bosnia. **30.** Airplanes were used for scouting the enemy and taking pictures. Later, they had machine guns and bombs for attacking.
Part E: 31. Answers will vary. Students should support their answers with at least some of these facts: Archduke Ferdinand was heir to the Austria-Hungary throne. When he was killed, his country blamed the Serbs. Since Russia backed the Serbian government, they went to the defense of Serbia. Then each country's allies became involved and much of Europe was then involved in the war. **32.** Answers will vary. Students should support their answers with at least some of these facts: Americans felt like they were dragged into a war that did not need to involve them. The battles were related to disputes between countries in Europe. Since fighting the war came at a personal and financial cost to Americans, they did not want to make a commitment to help European nations keep the peace.
Part F: 33. Answers will vary. Students' paragraphs should include at least some of these ideas: Students' opinions may vary, but students should mention that Article Ten of the pact would have tied Americans to Europe to continue to keep the peace. The article made the League of Nations responsible for settling disputes, which could potentially cost American money and lives. There was no clear direction of how this was to be done. American involvement may have prevented further disputes. **34.** Answers will vary. Students' paragraphs should include at least some of these ideas: The world powers recognized the need for a forum to handle disputes among nations. There was also a great increase in inventions that would benefit people after the war, such as

improvement in the speed of airplanes. People would be able to travel more quickly.

Chapter 26 Mastery Test B
Part A: 1. B **2.** D **3.** A **4.** C **5.** B
Part B: 6. torpedoed **7.** conflicts **8.** revolution **9.** Serb **10.** Germany **11.** Versailles **12.** Allied **13.** armistice **14.** Marne **15.** Geneva
Part C: 16. A **17.** B **18.** F **19.** G **20.** C **21.** E **22.** D
Part D: 23. Austria-Hungary's Archduke Francis Ferdinand was assassinated while visiting Serbia. War was declared on Serbia, Germany took Serbia's side, and other countries defended the countries they were allied with. **24.** Wilson wanted the United States to become a part of the League of Nations. **25.** Russia had the most casualties in the war. **26.** A neutral party is one that does not take sides. **27.** Germans used submarines, or U-boats, to attack ships. They could not be seen. **28.** Russia had a revolution and needed to pull out of the war to take care of issues at home. **29.** The allies used depth chargers and fast boats that could zig-zag and avoid attack. **30.** The Treaty of Versailles restricted Germany's military, telling the country not to rebuild its navy or air force.
Part E: 31. Answers will vary. Students should support their answers with at least some of these facts: Trade would have been impacted in a number of ways. Countries would not be able to trade with countries involved in war as much as before, as fighting countries would not have time or money to devote to trade. It also became dangerous to send ships to Europe because German submarines were attacking ships from countries that had no part in the war. **32.** Answers will vary. Students should support their answers with at least some of these facts: Trenches kept troops from moving around, as it would take a great deal of time to dig trenches every time the troops needed to move.
Part F: 33. Answers will vary. Students' paragraphs should include at least some of these ideas: The Central Powers would have divided the Allies' territory. This would have made it difficult to have Allied troops move from Italy to France and into Britain. They would be forced to the seas or to travel in Central territory over land. **34.** Answers will vary. Students' paragraphs should include at least some of these ideas: Democracy means that people have freedom to make choices about their rule. If the Allied countries were taken over by Central Powers, they would not live under the rule of their choice.

Chapter 27 Mastery Test A
Part A: 1. C **2.** B **3.** D **4.** C **5.** A
Part B: 6. geography **7.** dialects **8.** Mongol **9.** czar **10.** territory **11.** industry **12.** shortages **13.** socialism **14.** Bolshevik **15.** Iron Curtain
Part C: 16. H **17.** F **18.** D **19.** G **20.** B **21.** E **22.** A **23.** J **24.** I **25.** C
Part D: 26. Ivan IV controlled the Russian people by threatening them with cruel punishment and murder. **27.** St. Petersburg was the "Window to the West," and Empress Catherine II kept it open after it was established by Peter the Great. (Peter the Great's port on the Baltic Sea is also an acceptable description for "Window of the West.") **28.** Karl Marx felt government should be unnecessary. **29.** The Reds were the Communists and the Whites were the anti-Communists in Russia's civil war. **30.** Stalin killed or exiled people who opposed him.
Part E: 31. Answers will vary. Students should support their answers with at least some of these facts: Russian socialists wanted changes in their society; they wanted better treatment for workers; workers wanted higher wages and better working conditions; after soldiers

killed workers on Bloody Sunday, the people did not trust the government; the people wanted a voice in government; the people did not want Russia to be involved in World War I; the war created food shortages, and the people blamed the government; the people wanted a democratic government. **32.** Answers will vary. Students should support their answers with at least some of these facts: many Soviet people led difficult lives under Joseph Stalin; Stalin set up collective farms, which the people did not like; he forced them to use government machines, but did not show them how to run them; this made farming more difficult, rather than easier; farm production went down, so there were food shortages; good clothing was hard to come by; people could not travel outside Russia; Stalin controlled newspapers and radios, so the people had a limited view of what was happening outside Russia; people who opposed Stalin were exiled or killed.

Part F: 33. Answers will vary. Students' paragraphs should include at least some of these ideas: Peter the Great wanted to westernize Russia; he brought industrialization into Russia; he brought in engineers to build new factories; new industry brought people from the farms into the cities; the working conditions in the factories led to the people protesting against factory owners and the government; Peter the Great made life better for the upper classes, but the peasants were still poor; peasant revolts started during the rule of Catherine the Great; these revolts were the beginning of the unrest that led to the Bolshevik Revolution; Peter the Great opened Russia to new ideas; Karl Marx was born in Prussia and later lived in England; Marx's ideas were some of the new ideas that came into Russia; opening Russia to western Europe led to Russia being involved in World War I; the problems caused by World War I led to the Revolution. **34.** Answers will vary. Students' paragraphs should include at least some of these ideas: in some ways, people were better off after the Revolution; they had more say in government; government was run by soviet councils instead of by a czar; people were given more control of factories and farms. In many ways, people's lives were more difficult; both Lenin and Stalin used fear to control the people; there was a strong police force which arrested and killed people who opposed the government; religion was outlawed and many members of the clergy were arrested; members of the middle class were arrested and the government took their businesses; Jewish people were treated badly; there were shortages of food and clothing; the government had total control over people's lives.

Chapter 27 Mastery Test B
Part A: 1. A **2.** C **3.** D **4.** A **5.** D
Part B: 6. steppes **7.** peasants **8.** USSR **9.** Communism **10.** soviets **11.** collective **12.** economy **13.** terror **14.** opposed **15.** censored
Part C: 16. D **17.** C **18.** H **19.** A **20.** E **21.** J **22.** B **23.** G **24.** I **25.** F
Part D: 26. The early inhabitants of Russia were Slavs and Vikings (or Rus). **27.** Peter the Great wanted to westernize Russia because he wanted Russia to be equal to the nations of western Europe. **28.** January 22, 1905, was called "Bloody Sunday" because soldiers killed hundreds of men, women, and children on that day. **29.** USSR stands for the Union of Soviet Socialist Republics. **30.** Czar Nicholas II was overthrown because he led Russia into World War I, and the resulting food shortages led to revolt by starving workers and peasants.
Part E: 31. Answers will vary. Students should support their answers with at least some of these facts: Peter the Great wanted to westernize Russia; he brought western Europeans into Russia to teach Russians the ways of western Europe; he brought industry into Russia; he ordered the people to wear European style clothing and cut their beards; he changed the calendar to match the European calendar; he

put the Russian orthodox church under government control; he built St. Petersburg as a "Window to the West" and moved the government there; he fought a war with Sweden to gain a port on the Baltic Sea; he brought new ideas into Russia. **32.** Answers will vary. Students should support their answers with at least some of these facts: Ivan the Terrible and Joseph Stalin both ruled by terror; Ivan frightened people into doing what he wanted by threatening them with cruel punishment; he had a strong police force which murdered hundreds of people; Stalin also had a strong police force; he exiled and executed his enemies; he kept the Russian people separated from the rest of Europe; both Ivan and Stalin set up new kinds of governments; both had total control of the government.

Part F: 33. Answers will vary. Students' paragraphs should include at least some of these ideas: Bloody Sunday started as a worker protest; workers and their families wanted better working conditions and a voice in government; the czar's soldiers killed hundreds of men, women, and children; this made the protests even more violent; riots broke out; people started talking about revolution; people did not trust the government; Nicholas II set up a parliament to give the people a voice, but many people felt it was not enough; Russia continued to have problems; when Russia entered World War I, there were food shortages; people wanted change; some people had read the works of Karl Marx; Marx said government was not necessary; Marx called for the workers of the world to unite; many of the workers became Bolsheviks; in 1917, the starving workers and peasants revolted. **34.** Answers will vary. Students' paragraphs should include at least some of these ideas: Karl Marx and Joseph Stalin were both Communists; they both believed that workers should control the farms and factories; they were both against religion; Marx's ideas were important in developing Communist Russia; they were different because Marx said government was not necessary, but Stalin believed in a strong government; Marx believed in a classless society, but under Stalin, the Soviet government had all the power; Stalin controlled the factories and the farms, so the people did not have much more power than they did under the czar; Marx wanted the workers of the world to come together, but Stalin kept the Russian people separate, behind the Iron Curtain.

Chapter 28 Mastery Test A
Part A: 1. D **2.** C **3.** B **4.** A **5.** B
Part B: 6. Axis Powers **7.** fascist **8.** Nazi **9.** anti-Semitism **10.** genocide **11.** *blitzkrieg* **12.** invaded **13.** surrender **14.** kamikaze **15.** atomic bomb
Part C: 16. D **17.** H **18.** B **19.** E **20.** J **21.** A **22.** F **23.** C **24.** G **25.** I
Part D: 26. Benito Mussolini, Hideko Tojo, and Adolf Hitler were dictators of Axis Powers. **27.** Germany invaded Poland in 1939 and Great Britain and France declared war on Germany, starting World War II. **28.** The Allied forces invaded France (or Normandy) on D-Day. **29.** The United States ended the war with Japan by dropping atomic bombs on Hiroshima and Nagasaki. **30.** The goal of the United Nations was to end war and protect human rights.
Part E: 31. Answers will vary. Students should support their answers with at least some of these facts: life was hard during the depressions; millions of people were out of work; businesses went broke and banks closed; many people were poor and hungry; people did not have any hope; they could not see things getting better; people wanted big changes; leaders such as Hitler and Mussolini offered hope; Mussolini built roads and factories; Hitler supported German nationalism; people saw these dictators as strong men who could make the changes they wanted; by attacking other countries the dictators made the people

feel better about their own countries. **32.** Answers will vary. Students should support their answers with at least some of these facts: after World War II, people wondered how such terrible things had happened; millions of people died in the war and it made people afraid of war; leaders wanted to prevent further wars; leaders wanted a way to control dictators such as Hitler and Mussolini; the League of Nations had not been able to prevent World War II; since so many countries had fought in World War II, there were a lot of nations that supported an organization to keep the peace; men such as Roosevelt and Churchill were strong leaders who could get other nations to follow them.
Part F: 33. Answers will vary. Students' paragraphs should include at least some of these ideas: nations such as the United States may have had more hope than the nations that turned to dictators; leaders such as Franklin Roosevelt and Winston Churchill gave their people hope; the United States and Great Britain had won World War I, so their people were not as angry; people in the United States felt they had a voice in their government, so they may have had more hope; the United States was more isolated, unlike Germany, which was "next door" to the countries that had defeated it; Germany and Japan had traditions of militarism, so they turned to military leaders; since people in the U.S. believed that people were equal, they were not as quick to make scapegoats of people as the Germans were. **34.** Answers will vary. Students' paragraphs should include at least some of these ideas: If Hitler had not come to power, Germany might not have been involved in World War II; Hitler was a strong leader, who got the people to follow him; Hitler hated the Jews, so he started to kill them all, Germany had signed the Treaty of Versailles, and another leader might have followed it; a different leader might have been able to rebuild Germany without using hate and terror. If Hitler had not come to power, Germany would still have been involved in World War II; the German people were angry, and wanted to get even; even without Hitler, there was anti-Semitism in Germany; the people wanted a leader like Hitler, so someone else might have taken his place; Germany was proud of being a military nation, and would have wanted to rebuild its military no matter what; the success of Mussolini in Italy might have made the German people interested in rebuilding their empire.

Chapter 28 Mastery Test B
Part A: 1. C **2.** D **3.** A **4.** C **5.** B
Part B: 6. depression **7.** Allied Powers **8.** concentration camps **9.** scapegoat **10.** civilians **11.** pact **12.** D-Day **13.** Holocaust **14.** nuclear **15.** organization
Part C: 16. D **17.** H **18.** F **19.** A **20.** E **21.** J **22.** B **23.** G **24.** I **25.** C
Part D: 26. The Great Depression was a period of hard times during the 1930s. **27.** The Battle of Britain was the first major air war in history. **28.** The United States declared war because Japan attacked its naval base at Pearl Harbor. **29.** Germany surrendered after the Allies captured Berlin. **30.** The Allies created the United Nations to keep the peace after World War II.
Part E: 31. Answers will vary. Students should support their answers with at least some of these facts: Hitler's soldiers marched into Russia in June 1941; Hitler expected to conquer the country quickly; he expected the war with Russia to be over before the weather got cold; Hitler had defeated other nations, so he had reason to be confident; by the time he attacked Russia, Hitler controlled most of Europe; since he had lost the Battle of Britain, he needed a quick victory; Hitler did not expect the Russian people to fight as hard as they did; Hitler did not expect the winter to be as bad as it was. **32.** Answers will vary. Students should support their answers with at least some of these facts:

Japan kept fighting even after Germany and Italy had surrendered; even though General MacArthur had beaten them in the Pacific, Japan would not surrender; the Japanese felt it was their duty to fight to the end; President Truman felt the atomic bomb would be the quickest way to end the war; on August 6, 1945, an American plane dropped an atomic bomb on Hiroshima; three days later, the U.S. dropped a bomb on Nagasaki; in September, Japan finally surrendered; General Tojo was arrested and hanged.
Part F: 33. Answers will vary. Students' paragraphs should include at least some of these ideas: Germany was defeated in World War I; the nation signed the Treaty of Versailles, which did not allow them to rebuild their military; German pride was crushed; Germany was a very nationalistic country, and its people were angry; Germany had a tradition of militarism, so its military was important to it; Germany had been hit by depression, so the people were poor and starving; Germany wanted change; Germans wanted someone they could blame for their problems; the German people wanted a strong leader who would make them feel better about themselves; Hitler was a strong leader; Hitler blamed the Jews for Germany's problems; the people liked having a scapegoat; Hitler ignored the Treaty of Versailles and rebuilt the military; this made the people feel stronger and more confident; Hitler ignored the League of Nations, which made the people feel powerful; when the League did not do anything, the people felt they were right to support Hitler. **34.** Answers will vary. Students' paragraphs should include at least some of these ideas: Truman should have dropped the second atomic bomb on Japan; Japan refused to surrender; kamikaze pilots were flying their planes into ships, killing American soldiers; every day that the U.S. fought Japan, more people died; Japan was warned about the atomic bomb, but still did not surrender; Japan had three days to respond after the U.S. dropped the first atomic bomb; dropping the bomb was the quickest way to end the war. Truman should not have dropped the second bomb; the war was almost over; Japan's navy and air force had been destroyed; Japan would have had to surrender soon, whether or not Truman dropped the second bomb; dropping the first atomic bomb should have been enough to let Japan now they could not win; Truman could have given Japan more time to respond after he dropped the first bomb; Japan still did not surrender for almost a month, so the U.S. could have given them more time after the first bomb.

Chapter 29 Mastery Test A
Part A: 1. B **2.** B **3.** D **4.** C **5.** D
Part B: 6. farm program **7.** Truman Doctrine **8.** satellite **9.** crisis **10.** currency **11.** ratified **12.** détente **13.** cold war **14.** nuclear weapons **15.** isolationism
Part C: 16. D **17.** E **18.** F **19.** H **20.** C **21.** G **22.** B **23.** A **24.** I
Part D: 25. The Berlin Wall was built to keep East and West Berlin separate. Also, the wall prevented East Berliners from escaping to the West. **26.** Most of the countries that refused Marshall Plan funds were in Eastern Europe, under Soviet control. **27.** Under capitalism, businesses are privately owned and operated for a profit. **28.** Khrushchev stopped some of the activities of the secret police. He also allowed more freedom of speech. **29.** The United States boycotted the 1980 Summer Olympics in Moscow. **30.** The U.S., Britain, France, and the Soviet Union took over parts of Germany. They sent soldiers in to restore order. After a few years, East and West Germany were formed.
Part E: 31. Answers will vary. Students should support their answers with at least some of these facts: NATO is the North Atlantic Treaty

Organization, and it was formed by the United States and other non-Communist nations from Europe. This was a military alliance so that if one country was threatened, the others would support them. The Warsaw Pact was a Communist military alliance that was formed in response to NATO. The Warsaw Pact would provide the same support for a nation under attack. **32.** Answers will vary. Students should support their answers with at least some of these facts: Events may include: The Cuban missile crisis, where the Soviet Union tried to build missile bases in Cuba, placing them very near the United States. President Kennedy responded by placing a blockade around Cuba, and the standoff nearly became a war. In the 1970s, the countries started negotiating arms reductions at SALT I and SALT II. In the 1980s, the Soviets shot down a Korean Air Lines jet, killing many people, including Americans.

Part F: 33. Answers will vary. Students' paragraphs should include at least some of these ideas: Students' opinions may vary, but students should mention that the relationship between the Soviet Union and the United States may not have been as strained. However, without the United States as part of NATO, Communism may have spread and war broken out among European countries. **34.** Answers will vary. Students' paragraphs should include at least some of these ideas: Nuclear weapons can ensure that countries consider other options before attacking a nuclear armed country. However, a country that tries to assert their position and gain strength might use a nuclear weapon hastily and kill many innocent people. In addition, one nuclear attack is likely to cause many others.

Chapter 29 Mastery Test B

Part A: 1. D **2.** A **3.** C **4.** C **5.** B

Part B: 6. profit **7.** atomic **8.** hydrogen **9.** isolationism
10. Muslim **11.** Cuban **12.** United States **13.** Communist
14. superpowers **15.** euro

Part C: 16. B **17.** H **18.** C **19.** D **20.** G **21.** E **22.** I **23.** A **24.** F

Part D: 25. Marshall was the United States Secretary of State during Harry Truman's administration. **26.** The Warsaw Pact was a military alliance between Communist countries in answer to NATO.
27. Stalin set up labor camps to force people to work. **28.** Khrushchev said that Stalin was responsible for many arrests and deaths of Soviet citizens. **29.** The "hot line" was a phone line between the United States and Soviet Union so that the leaders could talk in an emergency to prevent war. **30.** The Marshall Plan was used to help countries in Europe that were hurt by the war rebuild.

Part E: 31. Answers will vary. Students should support their answers with at least some of these facts: Germany was divided up into four sectors, controlled by the United States, Britain, France, and the Soviet Union. The first three countries joined together to form West Germany, and the Soviet Union refused to join them. The Soviet-controlled section became East Germany. Berlin was divided in a similar way. West Berlin was separated from East Berlin by a wall used to keep people from escaping to the West. **32.** Answers will vary. Students should support their answers with at least some of these facts: The cold war developed as the United States formed strong alliances with the countries in NATO, and the Soviet Union created allies with the Warsaw Pact. The two factions developed arms to use against the other side should a war erupt. The two sides refused to cooperate, and each thought the other's system of government was wrong.

Part F: 33. Answers will vary. Students' paragraphs should include at least some of these ideas: The United States would have stronger allies in Europe if these countries recovered from the war. These European

countries would be more democratic and eager to work with the United States. They would also be stronger militarily if the Soviets or their satellites would attack. **34.** Answers will vary. Students' paragraphs should include at least some of these ideas: Khrushchev helped the Soviet Union by decreasing the activities of the Secret Police and the attacks on the Soviet citizens. He made working conditions better for citizens. He made life more comfortable for people, and planned on more manufacturing. He also had a plan to help farmers.

Chapter 30 Mastery Test A

Part A: 1. B **2.** C **3.** D **4.** C **5.** A

Part B: 6. electronics **7.** communes **8.** pollution **9.** guerillas
10. secure **11.** sanctions **12.** drought **13.** starvation **14.** apartheid
15. standard of living

Part C: 16. C **17.** H **18.** D **19.** F **20.** A **21.** I **22.** E **23.** G **24.** B **25.** J

Part D: 26. The Nationalists left to live in Taiwan after the Communists gained power in China. **27.** The goal of China's Cultural Revolution was to build loyalty for the Communists. **28.** The new constitution said Japan would not maintain a strong military, so Japan invested in industry. **29.** The "boat people" were refugees from Southeast Asia who did not want to live under Communist rule.
30. Nelson Mandela was the jailed leader of the African National Congress who eventually became president of South Africa.

Part E: 31. Answers will vary. Students should support their answers with at least some of these facts: poverty and food shortages are problems in India; the government is teaching farmers better ways to grow more food; India has allowed Western businesses to build chemical factories, in order to grow more crops; the government has started programs for economic growth; the government is finding ways to make better use of India's natural resources; India has built dams to provide electricity; India has reformed its caste system, to make life better for those in the lower classes. **32.** Answers will vary. Students should support their answers with at least some of these facts: the United States got involved in Korea as part of the United Nations; the UN troops were able to push the North Koreans out of South Korea; the Korean War lasted for only three years; the war ended with a truce between North and South Korea; the United States got involved in Vietnam on its own; the U.S. first sent money and supplies, but later sent troops; U.S. troops fought in Vietnam for eight years; the U.S. was not able to force the Vietcong out of South Vietnam; when U.S. troops left Vietnam, the war was not over; the Communists eventually took over South Vietnam.

Part F: 33. Answers will vary. Students' paragraphs should include at least some of these ideas: (1) The United States was right to give China permanent normal trade relations; China is a large nation with a growing economy, so it makes sense to trade with China; trade is a good way to bring Western ideas into China; the U.S. should encourage China to become more modern; Chinese leaders should be encouraged to give their people more economic freedom; trade will give people a chance to own their own businesses in China; the United States learned from the cold war with the Soviet Union that there is value in exchanging goods and ideas with Communist nations. (2) The United States should not have given China permanent normal trade relations; as a Communist country, China is our enemy; China helped North Korea in the Korean War and North Vietnam in the Vietnam War; China helped spread Communism to the rest of Southeast Asia; China does not give its people equal rights; the Chinese need political freedom; when students protested against the government in Tiananmen Square, the government used tanks to put down the

demonstration; trade sanctions are a way to get the Chinese government to give their people more freedom and human rights.
34. Answers will vary. Students' paragraphs should include at least some of these ideas: there are many problems in Africa today; hunger is a major problem; droughts have caused starvation in several countries; Ethiopia suffered through famine in the 1980s and in 2000; many people died in Somalia in the 1990s because of drought; civil wars make life hard for people; armies in Somalia kept food from people who needed it; the United Nations tried to help the people of Somalia, but had to leave because of the fighting; fighting in Sudan has led to violence against innocent people; Janjaweed soldiers have killed people in Sudan and the neighboring country of Chad; many African nations are underdeveloped; they do not have enough hospitals or schools; many people suffer from poverty and disease.

Chapter 30 Mastery Test B

Part A: 1. B **2.** A **3.** C **4.** D **5.** C
Part B: 6. violence **7.** corrupt **8.** invested **9.** domino theory
10. refugees **11.** famine **12.** minority **13.** curfew **14.** repealed
15. majority
Part C: 16. G **17.** E **18.** C **19.** B **20.** D **21.** J **22.** H **23.** A **24.** I **25.** F
Part D: 26. Bangladesh was formed because of the 1971 civil war in Pakistan. **27.** The Communists and the Nationalists struggled for control of China. **28.** In February 2007, North Korea agreed to shut down its main nuclear facility. **29.** The Vietcong were North Vietnamese Communist guerilla fighters. **30.** Civil war and drought are two causes of starvation in Africa.
Part E: 31. Answers will vary. Students should support their answers with at least some of these facts: the United States got involved in Vietnam because it believed in the domino theory; the domino theory said that if Vietnam became Communist, other countries in Southeast Asia would also become Communist; after World War II, the Soviet Union took control of many countries in Eastern Europe; the United States was involved in the cold war with the Soviet Union; the U.S. did not want to see Communist China have control in Southeast Asia; the U.S. had allies in Asia, such as Thailand and Korea, that it wanted to protect. **32.** Answers will vary. Students should support their answers with at least some of these facts: since the death of Mao Zedong, China has become more modern; leaders such as Deng Xiaoping have given Chinese people more economic freedom; China has a growing economy; Chinese people can now own businesses and trade with the West; the United States has given China normal trade relations; there is still not much political freedom in China; Chinese students have protested against the government, but their demonstration was crushed; Western nations are trying to get China to improve attitudes toward their human rights.
Part F: 33. Answers will vary. Students' paragraphs should include at least some of these ideas: after World War II, Japan was occupied by Allied forces; they worked to make Japan stronger; Japan wrote a new constitution, which made Japan a democracy; this gave more people a voice in the future of Japan; women were given the right to vote; politically, Japan became similar to powerful Western nations such as the United States and Britain; Japan was not allowed to rebuild its military; that meant that money and supplies that would have gone into the military in the past now went into private industry; Japan became an industrial leader; it now makes cars instead of war machines; it makes electronics for people instead of for the military; because of their low defense budget, the Japanese can invest more money in industry; this has made Japan economically powerful. **34.** Answers will vary.

Students' paragraphs should include at least some of these ideas: young people were unhappy for many reasons during the 1960s; they did not like the war in Vietnam; many young people did not understand why we were fighting in Vietnam; many of them did not believe in the reasons the United States was in the war; the more soldiers who died, the more they protested against the war; young people were being sent to fight in Vietnam, so the ones still at home had friends fighting in the war; they may have been afraid of going to Vietnam to fight; some of the young people in the 1960s had parents who fought in World War II; this led to conflicts between the young people and their parents; this conflict made them see more things they did not like about their parents' values. A series of political assassinations also affected people during the 1960s; the victims were people like President Kennedy and Martin Luther King, Jr., who were fighting to make things better; their deaths made people even more angry.

Chapter 31 Mastery Test A

Part A: 1. B **2.** C **3.** B **4.** A **5.** D
Part B: 6. hostages **7.** Shah **8.** arms **9.** terrorist **10.** intifada **11.** al Qaeda **12.** stalemate **13.** weapons of mass destruction **14.** hostile
15. traitor
Part C: 16. D **17.** B **18.** J **19.** G **20.** E **21.** H **22.** A **23.** I **24.** F **25.** C
Part D: 26. Israel expanded its borders as a result of its war with the Arab nations in 1967. **27.** The Camp David Accords were peace agreements between Egypt and Israel. **28.** The Iranians who took hostages at the American embassy demanded that the Shah return to Iran to stand trial. **29.** Iraq attacked Iran in 1980 in a fight over territory. **30.** Scientists in Israel are trying to turn saltwater into fresh water to use in farming.
Part E: 31. Answers will vary. Students should support their answers with at least some of these facts: Zionism was the movement to set up a Jewish nation in Palestine; this movement grew out of the persecution of Jews across Europe; by the late 1800s, Jews started settling in Palestine; following World War I, Britain controlled most of the Middle East; Britain promised to create a Jewish homeland in Palestine; Hitler's persecution of the Jews in World War II made Zionism even more popular; there was conflict between the Arabs who had been living in Palestine and the Jews who were immigrating there; to resolve the conflict, the United Nations divided Palestine in 1947. **32.** Answers will vary. Students should support their answers with at least some of these facts: oil is an important resource for all nations; oil is refined into fuels that run our cars, trucks, and airplanes; oil is used to heat homes and run industry; the world's supply of oil is limited; there are large oil fields throughout the Middle East; the United States and other countries depend on oil from the Middle East; in the 1970s, when the Arabs cut off oil to the West, there was a severe oil shortage in the United States; drivers had to wait in long lines for gasoline and had to pay high prices; as long as the Western nations depend on oil, the nations of the Middle East will have control.
Part F: 33. Answers will vary. Students' paragraphs should include at least some of these ideas: (1) The Jews have claims on Palestine that go back to the times of the Bible; Israel is the land that they believe was promised to them by God; the Jewish king Solomon founded Jerusalem as his capital; Jerusalem is a holy city to the Jews; the Jews were driven out of Palestine by the Romans and other conquering civilizations; for thousands of years, the Jews have not had a homeland; it is right that every people should have a land they can call their own; after hundreds of years of persecution, the Jews deserve a Jewish state. (2) The Arabs have been living in Palestine for thousands of years; the lands

surrounding Palestine are all Arab nations; Palestine had been the homeland for many people for thousands of years; the United Nations forced these people to leave their homes; Arabs living in Palestine became refugees; forcing the Arabs out of Palestine is the same as the persecution of the Jews; two wrongs do not make a right. **34.** Answers will vary. Students' paragraphs should include at least some of these ideas: Israel is an important ally of the United States; Israel is a strong democracy in the Middle East; the spread of democracy is important to the United States; a strong state of Israel can be a stabilizing force in the Middle East; there are many Jewish people living in the United States; so it is important to the United States that Israel stay strong. The United States depends on the OPEC nations for oil; conflict causes the price of oil to rise; OPEC has used oil as a weapon in the past, thus the United States wants the Arab nations to be stable. Conflict in the Middle East leads to terrorism; terrorist attacks have spread beyond the Middle East to the rest of the world; the United States and its allies have been victims of terrorist attacks; many U.S. companies do business in the Middle East; peace in the Middle East means that Americans are safer.

Chapter 31 Mastery Test B
Part A: 1. D **2.** B **3.** C **4.** A **5.** B
Part B: 6. OPEC **7.** homeland **8.** refugees **9.** Zionism **10.** negotiated **11.** irrigation **12.** cease-fire **13.** ayatollah **14.** embassy **15.** terrorism
Part C: 16. G **17.** D **18.** J **19.** E **20.** B **21.** H **22.** C **23.** A **24.** I **25.** F
Part D: 26. The United Nations tried to end the conflict between Arabs and Jews by dividing Palestine. **27.** Christians and Muslims fought in Lebanon's civil war. **28.** The United States attacked Iraq in 1991 because Iraq invaded Kuwait. **29.** Many Arab nations took control of their oil fields after World War II. **30.** Many people in Israel (85 percent) live and work in modern cities.
Part E: 31. Answers will vary. Students should support their answers with at least some of these facts: Saddam Hussein was a dangerous leader; he attacked other nations in the Middle East; in 1980, Hussein attacked Iran; during that war, both Iran and Iraq attacked oil tankers in the Persian Gulf; the United States was forced to protect the flow of oil; in 1990, Hussein invaded Kuwait; he kept his armies in Kuwait despite warnings from the United Nations; in 1991, the United States went to war in the Persian Gulf to drive Hussein's armies out of Kuwait; even after the Gulf War, Hussein was suspected of having weapons of mass destruction; he refused to cooperate with weapons inspectors from the United Nations; Saddam Hussein was a destabilizing force in the Middle East. **32.** Answers will vary. Students should support their answers with at least some of these facts: many of the problems the Middle East faces today are the same as problems it faced thousands of years ago; much of the land of the Middle East is dry and difficult to farm; people have been using irrigation in the Middle East back to the time of the Sumerians; in ancient times, there were conflicts between the civilizations living in the Middle East; the Assyrians, Hittites, and Babylonians all fought over land in the Middle East; nations still fight over the same land; different people in the Middle East worshiped different gods; those conflicts still exist between Christians, Jews, and Muslims; the conflict between the Jews and the Egyptians goes back to Biblical times; many of the conflicts in the Middle East go back for thousands of years.
Part F: 33. Answers will vary. Students' paragraphs should include at least some of these ideas: OPEC is the organization of oil-producing nations in the Middle East; OPEC controls the price of oil; oil is important to the rest of the world; oil is refined into fuel that runs our cars, trucks, and airplanes; oil heats our homes and runs industry; there are large oil fields in the Middle East; control over these oil fields has made the nations which control them rich and powerful; OPEC manages this power; OPEC not only controls the oil that comes out of the Middle East, but also oil from fields in Asia, Africa, and South America; OPEC sets the price of oil; in this way, the OPEC nations work together, rather than competing with each other; competition can drive prices down, but by cooperating, OPEC gets to set the price; they can also use oil as a weapon; in 1973, OPEC cut off the flow of oil to the West because of conflict with Israel; this caused oil prices in the United States to rise dramatically; drivers in the United States had to wait in long lines for gasoline; after the Persian Gulf War, oil prices rose because Saddam Hussein set fire to the oil fields of Kuwait; OPEC helped bring prices down by increasing the supply of oil from other nations; in this way, OPEC can drive prices up or down. **34.** Answers will vary. Students' paragraphs should include at least some of these ideas: terrorism is a new kind of warfare; terrorists are fighters who use violence to get what they want; like other soldiers, terrorists work together to plan and carry out their attacks; they use weapons of war, such as bombs; terrorist demands are sometimes the same sort of conflicts that countries fight wars over; terrorists often fight over politics or religion; they may not like the presence of a foreign government in their country. Terrorists are guerilla fighters; they are not members of a regular army; they do not wear uniforms or fight like a regular army; sometimes terrorist attacks are against government buildings, such as the attack on the U.S. embassy in Nairobi; sometimes they are against ships or other military targets; unlike regular armies, terrorists also target civilians; the attacks on the United States in 2001 and Spain in 2004 were against civilians; anyone can be a victim of a terrorist attack.

Chapter 32 Mastery Test A
Part A: 1. C **2.** B **3.** D **4.** B **5.** A
Part B: 6. coup **7.** *perestroika* **8.** disband **9.** reunify **10.** *glasnost* **11.** St. Petersburg **12.** reforms **13.** Muslims **14.** rebels **15.** Sarajevo
Part C: 16. D **17.** I **18.** H **19.** F **20.** E **21.** C **22.** G **23.** A **24.** B
Part D: 25. An unfortunate consequence of *glasnost* was an increase in violence among different ethic groups within the Soviet Union. **26.** Putin got two weapons reduction agreements passed by the Russian legislature. **27.** Hungary tried to break away from Soviet control in 1956. **28.** The United States convinced the Bosnians and Serbs to sign the Dayton Accords, ending the fighting. **29.** He forced ethnic Albanians out of Serbia. **30.** East Germans started to tear down the wall when East Germany agreed to open the gates and allow people to travel through freely.
Part E: 31. Answers will vary. Students should support their answers with at least some of these facts: The CIS allowed countries freedom they were not allowed in the Soviet Union. Before, the country was Communist, with no private companies and little trade with Western countries. In the CIS, the Communist Party was not in charge, and people were able to work for themselves, work with non-Communist countries, and speak and live more freely. **32.** Answers will vary. Students should support their answers with at least some of these facts: Yugoslavia had people of 30 different nationalities, many of whom did not get along. It broke up into different countries, but there was still violence. There was civil war among Croats and Serbs, and Serbs and Bosnians. There was also violence between Serbs and Albanians, and war crimes committed against Albanians. Troops from other nations had to come to many of the locations to keep the peace.

Part F: 33. Answers will vary. Students' paragraphs should include at least some of these ideas: The Berlin wall separated Communist Germany from democratic Germany. The wall symbolized how Communism kept people from freedom, and how the politics kept people from seeing what the rest of the world was like. When Communism fell, people rebelled and insisted on independence. When the wall fell, it was torn down by people who were also demanding their freedom. **34.** Answers will vary. Students' paragraphs should include at least some of these ideas: With United States aid, Soviet businesses have Western goods to trade for, and money to start new businesses. U.S. aid also provided people with food when it was short. A stronger Russian economy can mean a better opportunity for U.S. businesses to make money for themselves in Russia as well. This will benefit Americans.

Chapter 32 Mastery Test B

Part A: 1. C **2.** B **3.** D **4.** B **5.** A

Part B: 6. Berlin Wall **7.** George H.W. Bush **8.** prime minister **9.** United Nations **10.** elect **11.** union **12.** chancellor **13.** assassinating **14.** Russian Federation **15.** Fidel Castro

Part C: 16. F **17.** C **18.** G **19.** D **20.** I **21.** B **22.** E **23.** A **24.** H

Part D: 25. Solidarity was a labor union in Poland. It was outlawed by the Communists, then made legal again. As Poland gained more freedom, the union became a political party that elected Lech Walesa. **26.** Gorbachev and Reagan signed the INF treaty which reduced nuclear weapons and eliminated an entire class of weapons. **27.** They split into 15 separate nations and most joined the Commonwealth of Independent States. **28.** The Croats and ethnic Serbs were fighting for control over Croatia. **29.** They declared the end of cold war hostilities. **30.** The Communists did not agree with Gorbachev's policies, and the country was in an economic crisis.

Part E: 31. Answers will vary. Students should support their answers with at least some of these facts: *Glasnost* was a policy of open discussion of political and social issues. Soviets were not free to speak and discuss policies of the Communist government before *glasnost*. It created a desire for independence among many of the republics.

32. Answers will vary. Students should support their answers with at least some of these facts: People in the Soviet Union had a taste of freedom, and were not willing to return to the Communist rule before Gorbachev. Citizens revolted against more Communist symbols and ideas after the coup than they did before the coup.

Part F: 33. Answers will vary. Students' paragraphs should include at least some of these ideas: Keeping the peace in Europe may prevent wars from reaching the United States. It also keeps people safe, which would be considered morally correct. On the other hand, providing security forces in countries outside the United States can create political enemies and make the United States vulnerable without a full legion of troops at home. **34.** Answers will vary. Students' paragraphs should include at least some of these ideas: Bosnians and Chechens have freedoms that they did not have under Communism. They have control over earning money for themselves, and speak freely about the government. However, without the strict control of a Communist government, the people were not safe. Groups that disagree with each other's cultures attacked each other. This prompted attacks on the countries, which also caused people harm.

Chapter 33 Mastery Test A

Part A: 1. C **2.** A **3.** C **4.** D **5.** A

Part B: 6. dictator **7.** tariffs **8.** Good Neighbor Policy **9.** moderate **10.** ban **11.** global warming **12.** Sandinistas **13.** politics **14.** stronghold **15.** refuge

Part C: 16. I **17.** E **18.** J **19.** B **20.** A **21.** F **22.** G **23.** C **24.** H **25.** D

Part D: 26. The goals of the Organization of American States are to defend the Americas and to settle any quarrels peacefully. **27.** The civil war in Nicaragua was between the Sandinistas and the Contras. **28.** Manuel Noriega was brought back to the United States, where he was convicted of drug trafficking. **29.** Haitians who fled to the United States were stopped by the U.S. Coast Guard. **30.** The rain forests are important to the environment because they remove carbon dioxide from the air.

Part E: 31. Answers will vary. Students should support their answers with at least some of these facts: the Good Neighbor Policy promised that the United States would not interfere with the affairs of other nations; since the 1950s, the U.S. has interfered in Latin American affairs on many occasions; some Latin Americans say the U.S. sends aid to protect its own interests in Central and South America; the United States supported the Contra rebels against the Sandinistas in Nicaragua; the U.S. continued to send aid to the Contras, even after though it was against the law; the U.S. sent aid to the military government in El Salvador; the U.S. sent troops to Panama to remove Manuel Noriega from power. **32.** Answers will vary. Students should support their answers with at least some of these facts: NAFTA was the North American Free Trade Agreement; NAFTA ended tariffs on farm products and other goods; a tariff is a tax placed on exports and imports; NAFTA made it easier for Mexico to sell its goods in the United States; NAFTA made it easier for U.S. companies to do business in Mexico; NAFTA eased immigration laws for professionals and business executives; this helped Mexican companies do more business in the U.S., which brought more money into Mexico; NAFTA also helped the U.S. and Mexico do more business by making it easier for trucks to cross the border; easing these restrictions boosted Mexico's economy in the late 1990s.

Part F: 33. Answers will vary. Students' paragraphs should include at least some of these ideas: The United States was right to aid the Contras; the Contras were fighting against the Communist government; it is in the interests of the United States to fight Communism in Central America; the U.S. learned from its involvement in Vietnam that it is important to keep Communism from getting a stronghold in developing nations; helping the Contras forced Nicaragua to hold democratic elections. The United States was wrong to help the Contras; the U.S. had agreed not to interfere in other nations' affairs; the Sandinistas overthrew Anastasio Somoza, who was a military dictator; the Sandinistas were fighting for freedom; Somoza was a bad leader, even though he supported the United States; the Sandinistas were better leaders than Somoza, even though they were Communists; the aid that the United States sent to the Contras was against the law; the U.S. government got money to send to the Contras by selling arms to Iran; Iran was an enemy of the United States, and had taken hostages in 1979. **34.** Answers will vary. Students' paragraphs should include at least some of these ideas: Castro gave the Soviet Union a stronghold in the Western hemisphere; Castro was a Communist and received aid from the Soviet Union; Castro promised to help Communist rebels in Latin America; the Sandinistas who overthrew the military government in Nicaragua were Communists; the Sandinistas were accused of relying on the Soviet Union for aid and support; if Castro was not in power in Cuba, the Soviet Union might not have been able to help the Sandinistas; if the Soviets did not aid the Sandinistas, there might not have been a civil war in Nicaragua; Nicaragua might have developed a democratic government sooner than it did; the Sandinistas were suspected of helping the Communists in El Salvador; Cuba helped back the rebels in El Salvador; if Cuba was not Communist, the rebels might not have relied on Communist aid; the rebels in El Salvador were fighting against a military government; the United States backed the military government, which promoted violence and had killed thousands of Salvadoran civilians; if Cuba did not back the Communists and the United States did not back the military government, the civil war in El Salvador might not have lasted as long as it did.

Chapter 33 Mastery Test B

Part A: **1.** B **2.** A **3.** D **4.** B **5.** C

Part B: **6.** humane **7.** destruction **8.** flee **9.** Communist **10.** Contra **11.** immigration **12.** environment **13.** corrupt **14.** smuggling **15.** elections

Part C: **16.** G **17.** E **18.** C **19.** A **20.** J **21.** H **22.** B **23.** F **24.** I **25.** D

Part D: **26.** Fidel Castro pledged to help Communist rebels in other Latin American countries. **27.** In the Iran-Contra affair, the United States sold arms to Iran and used the money to aid Nicaraguan Contras. **28.** Civil war in El Salvador lasted about 13 years. **29.** The goal of NAFTA is to promote free trade between the United States, Mexico, and Canada. **30.** Brazil has the largest economy in South America.

Part E: **31.** Answers will vary. Students should support their answers with at least some of these facts: the United States has interfered in the affairs of Latin American countries since World War II to stop the spread of Communism; the United States refused to recognize the Castro government in Cuba; the United States supported the Contra rebels against the Sandinistas; the Sandinistas received aid from the Communists, so the United States supported the Contras; the United States supported the military government in El Salvador; the military took control of the government; the military promoted violence against the people of El Salvador; the rebels who were against the military were supported by Cuba and the Communists, so the United States supported the military. **32.** Answers will vary. Students should support their answers with at least some of these facts: the Contras and Sandinistas fought against each other in a civil war in Nicaragua; Nicaragua was ruled by a dictator named Anastasio Somoza; the Sandinista National Liberation Front overthrew the dictator; the Sandinistas were Communists; the Contras were a group of rebels who were against the Sandinista government; the Contras were anti-Communists; the United States supported the Contras against the Sandinistas; the Soviet Union supported the Sandinistas; the civil war ended with a peace treaty signed by Nicaraguan President Daniel Ortega; the treaty promised democratic elections in 1990.

Part F: **33.** Answers will vary. Students' paragraphs should include at least some of these ideas: the politics and economy of Mexico are important to the United States because Mexico and Canada are the United States' nearest neighbors; actions in Mexico directly affect the United States; the United States wants to have friendly relations with Mexico; Mexico is an important market for American businesses; the United States signed NAFTA to help ease trade between Mexico and the United States; the United States depends on food and other products coming out of Mexico; problems in Mexico causes Mexican people to immigrate to the United States; many of the immigrants

come to the United States illegally; immigration from Mexico affects the economy of the United States; many Mexican immigrants send money home, rather than buying goods and services in the United States; a stronger economy in Mexico means a stronger economy in the United States. **34.** Answers will vary. Students' paragraphs should include at least some of these ideas: people are concerned about the future of the rain forests in Central and South America because the rain forests affect the climate of the rest of the world; trees in the rain forest take in carbon dioxide and give off oxygen; carbon dioxide is called a greenhouse gas; scientists believe that the buildup of greenhouse gases leads to global warming; global warming is the heating up of the temperature of Earth; global warming is a problem for the entire world; higher temperatures mean more droughts and famines; it could also lead to higher sea levels; cutting the rain forests means fewer trees to take the carbon dioxide out of the air; much of the land covered by rain forests is cleared by burning; burning the trees puts even more carbon dioxide into the air, which makes the problem even worse.

Chapter 34 Mastery Test A

Part A: **1.** B **2.** A **3.** D **4.** A **5.** C

Part B: **6.** nonrenewable **7.** ethanol **8.** satellites **9.** cosmonaut **10.** Internet **11.** technology **12.** tsunami **13.** epidemic **14.** multinational corporations **15.** meltdown

Part C: **16.** J **17.** F **18.** D **19.** I **20.** B **21.** E **22.** H **23.** A **24.** C **25.** G

Part D: **26.** Sally Ride was the first American woman astronaut in space. **27.** Since they were first invented, computers have gotten smaller, more powerful, and less expensive. **28.** Countries with a lot of industry are called developed nations. **29.** Every country in the world is affected by AIDS. **30.** Lawmakers created the Department of Homeland Security to prepare for and prevent terrorist attacks.

Part E: **31.** Answers will vary. Students should support their answers with at least some of these facts: the United States believed Saddam Hussein had weapons of mass destruction; a CIA report warned that Saddam had weapons; Saddam refused to cooperate with United Nations weapons inspectors; President George W. Bush believed that Saddam Hussein was aiding terrorist groups; Saddam Hussein was a dictator who had used terror against his own people; the United States wanted to set up a democratic government in Iraq. **32.** Answers will vary. Students should support their answers with at least some of these facts: the economy of the United States has become more global for the past 30 years; U.S. companies have been setting up factories all over the world for years; factories in other nations take advantage of cheap labor; since the 1970s, the U.S. has imported more than goods than it exported; at first it tried to fight competition with trade restrictions and tariffs; foreign companies found ways to get around the restrictions; the U.S. now pursues a strategy of free trade; NAFTA is a free trade agreement between the U.S., Canada, and Mexico; today many U.S. companies are multinational; they hire people and have business interests around the world.

Part F: **33.** Answers will vary. Students' paragraphs should include at least some of these ideas: Nuclear energy is a good alternative source of power; nuclear energy is renewable; it does not depend on fossil fuels (which are running out); nuclear power plants are already in operation around the world; nuclear power can provide unlimited energy for thousands of years; nuclear power is clean; it causes much less pollution that burning fossil fuels; nuclear power can be safe if safety regulations are followed; stricter safety regulations were set up after the accident at Three-Mile Island; there has not been an accident at a nuclear power plant in 20 years. Nuclear energy is not a good alternative source of power; nuclear energy is dangerous; the accident at Chernobyl killed 23 people; it also forced people to leave their homes for miles around; the explosion at Chernobyl sent radiation across parts of the Soviet Union and Europe; people, plants, and animals were exposed to radiation; many of these people may die of cancer or other diseases; we do not know what the long-range effects of this exposure to radiation will be; nuclear waste is hazardous; there is no safe way to dispose of nuclear waste; other forms of alternative energy, such as solar power; are much safer. **34.** Answers will vary. Students' paragraphs should include at least some of these ideas: television has changed daily life; many people get most of their news and entertainment from television; without television, we would not be as connected as we are; television shows us life in other places; television makes news from other countries seem more immediate and important; television was an important influence on the Internet; television made people want to be able to access video over the Internet; without television, other forms of entertainment would be more popular; if there was no television, people might get out of their homes more; people might be in better shape; people might read more.

Chapter 34 Mastery Test B
Part A: 1. D **2.** B **3.** B **4.** A **5.** C
Part B: 6. Pacific Rim **7.** extinction **8.** humanity **9.** overpopulation **10.** space shuttle **11.** astronaut **12.** evacuate **13.** radiation **14.** agency **15.** solar energy
Part C: 16. F **17.** B **18.** D **19.** I **20.** A **21.** E **22.** H **23.** C **24.** J **25.** G
Part D: 26. There was a meltdown and an explosion at the nuclear power plant in Chernobyl. **27.** The first satellite in space was *Sputnik I.* **28.** The United States has a global economy because companies in the United States hire people and have business interests around the world. **29.** Scientists are looking for alternative sources of energy because fossil fuels are decreasing. **30.** Al Qaeda was the terrorist organization in Afghanistan.
Part E: 31. Answers will vary. Students should support their answers with at least some of these facts: the United States invaded Afghanistan because of the terrorist attacks on America on September 11; Osama bin Laden admitted to leading the attacks; Osama bin Laden was in Afghanistan; the United States asked the Taliban to turn over Osama bin Laden; the Taliban refused, so the U.S. invaded Afghanistan; al Qaeda had terrorist training camps in Afghanistan; the United States wanted to destroy those training camps; the people of Afghanistan suffered under the Taliban; the United States wanted to set up a democratic government in Afghanistan. **32.** Answers will vary. Students should support their answers with at least some of these facts: developed nations have many industries; they import and export products; people who live in developed nations have a high standard of living; most people can read and write; people in developed countries benefit from science and technology. Developing nations do not have many industries; many people farm the land; their farming methods are often outdated; many people are poor; their standard of living is lower; many people cannot read or write; they do not have access to services such as health care; their living conditions are often poor; their economies are easily upset by bad weather, drought, or war.
Part F: 33. Answers will vary. Students' paragraphs should include at least some of these ideas: in a global economy, the health of one nation's economy depends on the health of other nations; countries import and export goods from each other; companies hire people and have business interests around the world; terrorism makes a global economy difficult because what affects one nation affects all nations;

a terrorist attack in one nation is felt by other nations; since U.S. citizens work in countries around the world, they are always open to threats of terror; even if terrorists do not attack the United States, they may kill U.S. citizens in other countries; a terrorist attack in the Middle East affects every county that does business in the Middle East; the global economy depends on travel, and terrorism makes travel dangerous; terrorists often target airplanes; people working in a global economy may be afraid to travel; a global economy depends on communication; if terrorists blow up communication stations or cables, it can affect countries around the world. **34.** Answers will vary. Students' paragraphs should include at least some of these ideas: Despite the space shuttle accidents, the United States should continue to explore space; there have only been two accidents in 20 years; most space travel is safe; the United States has learned from the space shuttle accidents how to make space travel safer; the *Columbia* flew more than 20 missions safely; there is much we can learn from space exploration; we can perform experiments in space that we cannot perform on Earth; what we learn about the universe, we can use on Earth; the future of mankind is in outer space; people from Earth may some day live on the moon or Mars; people have always wanted to explore; exploration has always been dangerous; we should not stop exploring just because it is dangerous. The United States should not continue to explore space; space travel is dangerous; people have died in other accidents beside the two shuttle disasters; we can learn just as much from sending up spaceships that do not have people in them; most of the universe is too far away to explore with manned flights; we have learned more from machines such as the Hubble Space Telescope than from manned missions; we have a lot of problems here on Earth; the money we spend on space exploration could be better spent solving the problems in our country; we should put our energy into things like safe and clean sources of energy instead of space exploration.

Unit Mastery Tests

Unit 1 Mastery Test Answers
Part A: 1. D **2.** A **3.** C **4.** A **5.** A **6.** C
Part B: 7. artifacts **8.** primary source **9.** tamed **10.** glacier
Part C: 11. E **12.** C **13.** A **14.** F **15.** D **16.** B
Part D: 17. Sample answers: Examples of information you might find on a map are borders, oceans, waterways, and cities. **18.** Heinrich Schliemann discovered the ruins of Troy in Turkey. **19.** The wall would protect the houses, herds, and belongings of people in the city from thieves. **20.** Settlements grew in size, leaders developed, and they conquered other cities to rule over.
Part E: 21. Answers will vary. Students should support their answers with at least some of these facts: people in ancient times had many of the same worries as people of today; they worried about having enough food, about defending themselves, and about the dangers of nature; they set up governments and made laws; they tried to explain their existence through religion; they educated their children; they celebrated life through art and writing. Throughout history, people have found discovery and change exciting. **22.** Answers will vary. Students should support their answers with at least some of these facts: history is all about change. In the past, slavery was an accepted part of life, but today most people think slavery is wrong. The discovery that the world is round led to explorers setting out from Europe on voyages of discovery; the age of discovery led to an age of imperialism. Ideas of freedom, democracy, and independence later swept across the world, resulting in growing nationalism, during which people united under common flags.
Part F: 23. Answers will vary. Students' paragraphs should include at least some of these ideas: This part of the world was home to some of the first great civilizations because the Agricultural Revolution started there. This would mean that the population in the Fertile Crescent was probably larger than in other parts of the world. Large groups of people would develop religions to help them understand the earth and give them a sense of control over their lives. These religions developed into the religions many people practice today. **24.** Answers will vary. Students' paragraphs should include at least some of these ideas: There is no way to be sure that the cave paintings are thousands of years old. Someone may have entered the cave to paint the pictures at a later date. Scientists may possibly be able to compare styles or test the materials used to paint to determine the age of the art.

Unit 2 Mastery Test Answers
Part A: 1. C **2.** A **3.** D **4.** C **5.** C **6.** D
Part B: 7. goddess **8.** transported **9.** military **10.** reincarnation
Part C: 11. D **12.** C **13.** E **14.** F **15.** A **16.** B
Part D: 17. The Sumerians needed to invent a way to measure land in order to figure the taxes a farmer owed. **18.** The Sahara had become a desert and they could not farm. **19.** The Phoenicians learned to use the stars to navigate. **20.** The Chinese were angry with the Qin dynasty because the Great Wall required them to pay such high taxes.
Part E: 21. Answers will vary. Students should support their answers with at least some of these facts: Sumerians worshipped many gods; each city-state honored a god, who the people hoped would protect them; villages and city-states were built around the god's temple; people brought offerings to the temple to keep the gods happy; Sumerian priests grew rich and powerful. **22.** Answers will vary. Students should support their answers with at least some of these facts: They are unique and historically important. There are no other structures of that age with such complexity in design. They are also filled with important

historical artifacts that provided information about the ancient Egyptian culture.
Part F: 23. Answers will vary. Students' paragraphs should include at least some of these ideas: Babylon was one of the greatest cities of the ancient world; it had beautiful temples and palaces; the buildings were decorated with glazed blue bricks and pictures of mythical beasts; the city contained many wonders, such as the Tower of Babel and the Hanging Gardens of Babylon. **24.** Answers will vary. Students' paragraphs should include at least some of these ideas: China's isolation allowed them to develop a very rich culture and a people who respect its ancestors and traditions. Families are very close. However, they may have been slow to develop more modern skills and had limited access to new ideas because they were not in contact with people from other cultures.

Unit 3 Mastery Test Answers
Part A: 1. D **2.** B **3.** D **4.** B **5.** C **6.** C
Part B: 7. Salamis **8.** plague **9.** assassinate **10.** *Pax Romana* **11.** republic
Part C: 12. B **13.** D **14.** E **15.** A **16.** C
Part D: 17. Greek city-states were separated from each other by mountain ranges, so they had limited contact. **18.** Alexander was easily angered, very ambitious, and fearless. **19.** Alexander's troops were too tired to take on another battle and wanted to return home. **20.** Julius Caesar brought his army to Rome and took control of the government.
Part E: 21. Answers will vary. Students should support their answers with at least some of these facts: Athens and Sparta had a lot in common; they were both powerful city-states; their people spoke the same language; they believed in the same gods and told the same myths; the two city-states joined together to fight the Persians. In some ways they were different. Sparta was a military society; children belonged to the state; women were not important; the government was ruled by a small group of people. Athens was a democracy; all free men could vote; the leaders were elected by the people; the people of Athens were interested in art and architecture; Athens had many great thinkers and teachers; they left many written records. **22.** Answers will vary. Students should support their answers with at least some of these facts: Alexander would not have had as strong an understanding of Greek culture since he was not Greek himself. He also may not have valued education and reading as strongly without the scholar's influence.
Part F: 23. Answers will vary. Students' paragraphs should include at least some of these ideas: the senators worried about how popular Caesar was with the Roman people; they thought he was too powerful; they were afraid that he wanted to be king; they thought he wanted to end the Republic; the senators thought they were doing the right thing by killing Caesar. **24.** Answers will vary. Students' paragraphs should include at least some of these ideas: Latin is the language of ancient Rome; as Roman civilization spread, its language spread with it; Roman soldiers and settlers brought the common Roman language, or Vulgar Latin, with them; countries such as France and Spain speak languages called *Romance languages* (because they are based on the Roman language). English is not a Romance language, but it contains words from a number of other languages; English has words that come from French, Italian, and Spanish, which are Romance languages; many of our words are based on Latin words.

Unit 4 Mastery Test Answers

Part A: **1.** B **2.** C **3.** C **4.** A **5.** A **6.** A

Part B: **7.** Huns **8.** sagas **9.** serfs **10.** truce **11.** Ottoman

Part C: **12.** D **13.** A **14.** E **15.** C **16.** B

Part D: **17.** The church saved writings from ancient times. **18.** Changes in society, trade, warfare, and weapons brought about the end of the feudal system. **19.** Muhammad changed the Arabs from believing in many gods and idols to believing in one God, Allah. **20.** The French king drowned and the German king returned to Europe before reaching Jerusalem.

Part E: **21.** Answers will vary. Students should support their answers with at least some of these facts: Erik the Red traveled further east from Iceland to settle in Greenland. This put Erik and Leif closer to North American territories. It would take Leif Eriksson less distance to travel to North America than it would have from Iceland. **22.** Answers will vary. Students should support their answers with at least some of these facts: serfs worked for the lord of the manor; they were bound to the land and had no rights; serfs had to do everything for the lord; they worked the land and took care of the manor house; the lord could treat the serfs as he wanted; there was no legal system to protect the serfs; the medieval world was a Christian society, so if a lord treated his serfs poorly, he would pay for it in the next world.

Part F: **23.** Answers will vary. Students' paragraphs should include at least some of these ideas: Arab Muslims were tolerant of Jews and Christians because they also believed in one God. The Seljuk Turks did not tolerate people who were not Muslim worshipping in their Holy Land. **24.** Answers will vary. Students' paragraphs should include at least some of these ideas: The Crusades were a violent attack on another religion, the Muslims, who were doing the same thing that every other nation was—expanding their territory. The Muslims were not attacking Christians; they had simply gained control of a Christian Holy City. The Christians forced children into war that resulted in their deaths and enslavement.

Unit 5 Mastery Test Answers

Part A: **1.** D **2.** A **3.** D **4.** C **5.** B **6.** C

Part B: **7.** pendulum **8.** Lutheranism **9.** sculptor **10.** Armada **11.** Catholic

Part C: **12.** D **13.** A **14.** E **15.** B **16.** C

Part D: **17.** Renaissance artists painted the human body as lifelike. **18.** Leonardo da Vinci worked as an artist, a scientist, an architect, a musician, an inventor, a geologist, and an engineer. **19.** The main purpose of the Inquisition was to hunt down Spanish citizens who were not Catholic, and try to convert them to Catholicism. Many of those who refused were killed. **20.** Tudor rule began with King Henry VII in 1485 and ended when Queen Elizabeth died in 1603.

Part E: **21.** Answers will vary. Students should support their answers with at least some of these facts: patrons were wealthy people who provided food, housing, and money for young artists; because of patrons, artists were able to study and work on their art; artists with patrons did not have to find other work; most of the important artists in the Renaissance had patrons; Michelangelo and Leonardo da Vinci both had patrons. **22.** Answers will vary. Students should support their answers with at least some of these facts: (1) Galileo was weak for giving into the church; Galileo was a scientist, and the truth should have been the most important thing to him; he made observations with his telescope, so he knew what he said was right; other people depended on Galileo to speak the truth; since Galileo had some power and influence, he could afford to go against the church. (2) Galileo

was not weak for giving into the church; in Galileo's time, the church was very powerful; the Inquisition punished people who went against the church; people who were thought to be heretics were tortured and put to death; Galileo's ideas were already in print, so people could still read them; Galileo was an old man (68) at the time of his trial, so punishment would have been hard for him; even after taking back his ideas, he was still confined to his home; who knows what worse punishment he would have received if he did not take back his ideas.

Part F: **23.** Answers will vary. Students' paragraphs should include at least some of these ideas: Henry VIII changed the course of the country by breaking with the Catholic Church. Had he not, the Church of England would have never existed, and he would not have been able to marry after Catherine. Elizabeth brought a cultural and financial boom to England during her reign. She also brought peace to the country. **24.** Answers will vary. Students' paragraphs should include at least some of these ideas: Having all of Europe share the same religion would have spared many lives lost during religious wars. The countries would have also shared common values. It would also have allowed the pope to work with all of the leaders, as they all would have looked to Rome for religious leadership.

Unit 6 Mastery Test Answers

Part A: **1.** C **2.** C **3.** B **4.** A **5.** B **6.** B

Part B: **7.** India **8.** Aztecs **9.** China **10.** Japan **11.** Hernando Cortés

Part C: **12.** D **13.** C **14.** A **15.** E **16.** B

Part D: **17.** The Inuit built houses of blocks of snow. [Alternatively: The Inuit hunted caribou, whales, and seals for meat.] **18.** The culture of China strongly influenced Japan. **19.** The main link between China and the West was the Silk Road. **20.** Columbus hoped to find a water route to Asia.

Part E: **21.** Answers will vary. Students should support their answers with at least some of these facts: The shogun closed the doors to Japan because he thought that Christianity and European ways might upset the Japanese culture. While this did preserve the unique culture in Japan, it restricted the freedom of people to enter and leave the country. Students will have different opinions about whether the benefits outweighed the harm done. **22.** Answers will vary. Students should support their answers with at least some of these facts: The Mogul ruler Aurangzeb made Hindus pay a special tax. He destroyed Hindu temples. He tried to force conversion to Islam. For these reasons, Hindus revolted against Mogul rule.

Part F: **23.** Answers will vary. Students' paragraphs should include at least some of these ideas: trade with the Americas brought many changes to Europe; banks were set up to help pay for trading voyages; buying and selling stock in trading companies became a big business; the Amsterdam Stock Exchange was built just for the buying and selling of stocks; insurance companies were set up to cover merchants' losses; merchants grew wealthy; trade created a new middle class in Europe; slave trading started between Africa and the Americas; the Spanish, Portuguese, and English worked as slave traders; trade brought many new products, such as corn, tobacco, and animal skins, to European markets. **24.** Answers will vary. Students' paragraphs should include at least some of these ideas: the Europeans came to the Americas for many reasons; some came for adventure; some of the early explorers, such as Columbus and Cabral, came accidentally; some came to make money; the conquistadors came for the gold of Mexico and South America; the French trappers came to make money selling animal furs; the traders came to establish new markets; some, such as the Pilgrims, and Puritans, came for religious freedom; other colonists came to make a better life for themselves in the new world.

Unit 7 Mastery Test Answers

Part A: 1. B 2. D 3. C 4. D 5. C 6. B

Part B: 7. Commons 8. Thomas Jefferson 9. philosophers 10. dictator 11. Josephine

Part C: 12. B 13. E 14. A 15. C 16. D

Part D: 17. The main issue they argued over was taxes. The monarch wanted to raise taxes, and Parliament resisted. 18. Members of the House of Lords must be part of the nobility, and can inherit their position. Members of the House of Commons are elected. 19. The American war of independence made many French people think about freedom from tyranny and the rights of people. Before then, most people had accepted the king's right to rule. 20. The laws of France today are based on the Napoleonic Code, which Napoleon sponsored soon after he came to power.

Part E: 21. Answers will vary. Students should support their answers with at least some of these facts: The writings of philosophers would have come to America. In addition, American colonists knew the rights given to the English in their Bill of Rights. They wanted rights similar to those that were discussed by philosophers. This is evident by the wording of the Declaration of Independence. 22. Answers will vary. Students should support their answers with at least some of these facts: Oliver Cromwell was able to remove the king from leadership and give rights back to the people of England. However, Cromwell disbanded Parliament and was especially violent to the Irish.

Part F: 23. Answers will vary. Students' paragraphs should include at least some of these ideas: Robespierre turned violence on his enemies during the Reign of Terror. Before long, however, Robespierre himself fell to the violence. The lesson could be that when powerful people use violence against others, that violence comes back on them in the end. 24. Answers will vary. Students' paragraphs should include at least some of these ideas: The rulers of Austria and Prussia were afraid that the ideas of the French Revolution would spread to their countries and create opposition to their rule. They were probably right to be fearful, because all the monarchies in Europe probably had enemies who would have been glad to listen to revolutionary ideas.

Unit 8 Mastery Test

Part A: 1. D 2. B 3. B 4. A 5. A 6. D

Part B: 7. developed 8. trade 9. Gettysburg 10. fast

Part C: 11. C 12. F 13. A 14. E 15. B 16. D

Part D: 17. During the Industrial Revolution, people moved from the country to the cities. 18. The completion of the transcontinental railroad tied the East and West together and opened up the West for settlement. 19. Japan and China went to war in the 1890s because they both had claims on Korea. 20. The British helped the Indians build railroads, hospitals, schools and other things to improve the country.

Part E: 21. Answers will vary. Students should support their answers with at least some of these facts: The Latin American countries led revolutions with slaves and the poorer people. They did not have money or education after their freedom was earned to start building businesses and industry. The governments they lived under after overthrowing Europeans were often not democracies, so people did not have rights as more developed countries did. 22. Answers will vary. Students should support their answers with at least some of these facts: The North and South both had traditions based on fighting the war for American independence against Britain and the founding of the United States. They also mostly spoke the same language, English. The North and South were different in many ways, however. The North had many more factories and much more industry. It also had more people. The South had fewer factories, so it was not able to produce as many guns and cannons. Also, southerners used enslaved labor on many of their larger farms, or plantations. By 1861, on the other hand, there were no enslaved people in the North.

Part F: 23. Answers will vary. Students' paragraphs should include at least some of these ideas: Pakistan is a smaller country than India, and there is not nearly as much coastland. This would limit the amount of ports that Pakistan could have. Muslims might feel that they did not get equal treatment. In addition, Hindus may have been unhappy to lose a significant portion of land to the Muslims, especially if that land was their home before Pakistan was created. 24. Answers will vary. Students' paragraphs should include at least some of these ideas: Enslaved African Americans probably wanted to remember traditions they had enjoyed in Africa, so they put them in their music. The music also probably helped them to keep the hope of freedom alive. Singing the songs helped them keep their minds free while they worked on the masters' plantations.

Unit 9 Mastery Test

Part A: 1. B 2. D 3. B 4. A 5. C 6. B

Part B: 7. Rome 8. Serb 9. Mongol 10. Holocaust

Part C: 11. D 12. F 13. A 14. C 15. B 16. E

Part D: 17. Bismarck started a war with France to bring the German states together against a common enemy. 18. Wilson wanted the United States to become a part of the League of Nations. 19. Stalin killed or exiled people who opposed him. 20. Germany surrendered after the Allies captured Berlin.

Part E: 21. Answers will vary. Students should support their answers with at least some of these facts: the Second Reich was an empire; Wilhelm I was the kaiser, or emperor; he had complete power; Otto von Bismarck was chancellor; he ran the legislature; he was responsible only to Kaiser Wilhelm; there was no legislature or any elected representatives. 22. Answers will vary. Students should support their answers with at least some of these facts: Trenches kept troops from moving around, as it would take a great deal of time to dig trenches every time the troops needed to move.

Part F: 23. Answers will vary. Students' paragraphs should include at least some of these ideas: Bloody Sunday started as a worker protest; workers and their families wanted better working conditions and a voice in government; the czar's soldiers killed hundreds of men, women, and children; this made the protests even more violent; riots broke out; people started talking about revolution; people did not trust the government; Nicholas II set up a parliament to give the people a voice, but many people felt it was not enough; Russia continued to have problems; when Russia entered World War I, there were food shortages; people wanted change; some people had read the works of Karl Marx; Marx said government was not necessary; Marx called for the workers of the world to unite; many of the workers became Bolsheviks; in 1917, the starving workers and peasants revolted. 24. Answers will vary. Students' paragraphs should include at least some of these ideas: (1) Truman should have dropped the second atomic bomb on Japan; Japan refused to surrender; kamikaze pilots were flying their planes into ships, killing American soldiers; every day that the U.S. fought Japan, more people died; Japan was warned about the atomic bomb, but still did not surrender; Japan had three days to respond after the U.S. dropped the first atomic bomb; dropping the bomb was the quickest way to end the war. (2) Truman should not have dropped the second bomb; the war was almost over; Japan's navy and air force had been destroyed; Japan would have had to surrender soon, whether or not Truman dropped the second bomb; dropping the first atomic bomb should have been enough to let Japan know they could not win; Truman could have given Japan more time to respond after he dropped the first bomb; Japan still did not surrender for almost a month, so the U.S. could have given them more time after the first bomb.

Unit 10 Mastery Test Answers

Part A: 1. B **2.** C **3.** C **4.** B **5.** A **6.** A

Part B: 7. farm **8.** pollution **9.** al Qaeda **10.** St. Petersburg

Part C: 11. C **12.** F **13.** A **14.** E **15.** B **16.** D

Part D: 17. The United Nations tried to end the conflict between Arabs and Jews by dividing Palestine. **18.** The Croats and ethnic Serbs were fighting for control over Croatia. **19.** The goal of NAFTA is to promote free trade between the United States, Mexico, and Canada. **20.** There was a meltdown and an explosion at the nuclear power plant in Chernobyl.

Part E: 21. Answers will vary. Students should support their answers with at least some of these facts: Germany was divided up into four sectors, controlled by the United States, Britain, France, and the Soviet Union. The first three countries joined together to form West Germany, and the Soviet Union refused to join them. The Soviet-controlled section became East Germany. Berlin was divided in a similar way. West Berlin was separated from East Berlin by a wall used to keep people from escaping to the West. **22.** Answers will vary. Students should support their answers with at least some of these facts: many of the problems the Middle East faces today are the same as problems it faced thousands of years ago; much of the land of the Middle East is dry and difficult to farm; people have been using irrigation in the Middle East back to the time of the Sumerians; in ancient times, there were conflicts between the civilizations living in the Middle East; the Assyrians, Hittites, and Babylonians all fought over land in the Middle East; nations still fight over the same land; different people in the Middle East worshipped different gods; those conflicts still exist between Christians, Jews, and Muslims; the conflict between the Jews and the Egyptians goes back to Biblical times; many of the conflicts in the Middle East go back thousands of years.

Part F: 23. Answers will vary. Students' paragraphs should include at least some of these ideas: *Glasnost* was a policy of open discussion of political and social issues. Soviets were not free to speak and discuss policies of the Communist government before *glasnost*. It created a desire for independence among many of the republics. **24.** Answers will vary. Students' paragraphs should include at least some of these ideas: Castro gave the Soviet Union a stronghold in the Western hemisphere; Castro was a Communist and received aid from the Soviet Union; Castro promised to help Communist rebels in Latin America; the Sandinistas who overthrew the military government in Nicaragua were Communists; the Sandinistas were accused of relying on the Soviet Union for aid and support; if Castro was not in power in Cuba, the Soviet Union might not have been able to help the Sandinistas; if the Soviets did not aid the Sandinistas, there might not have been a civil war in Nicaragua; Nicaragua might have developed a democratic government sooner than it did; the Sandinistas were suspected of helping the Communists in El Salvador; Cuba helped back the rebels in El Salvador; if Cuba was not Communist, the rebels might not have relied on Communist aid; the rebels in El Salvador were fighting against a military government; the United States backed the military government, which promoted violence and had killed thousands of Salvadoran civilians; if Cuba did not back the Communists and the United States did not back the military government, the civil war in El Salvador might not have lasted as long as it did.

Midterm Mastery Test

Part A: **1.** A **2.** D **3.** B **4.** D **5.** B **6.** B **7.** A **8.** B **9.** D **10.** C

Part B: **11.** temple **12.** gods **13.** myths **14.** aqueduct **15.** Christians
16. Tenochtitlán **17.** Judaism **18.** Carthage **19.** Muslims
20. Enlightenment

Part C: **21.** E **22.** H **23.** J **24.** C **25.** A **26.** B **27.** D **28.** I **29.** F **30.** G

Part D: **31.** People had more time to learn new trades such as pottery, weaving, and basket making. **32.** The Egyptian pharaohs wanted people to remember how rich and powerful they were. **33.** The highest level were priests and scholars. The second level were rulers and warriors. The third level were craftworkers, merchants, and farmers. The lowest level consisted of unskilled workers. **34.** King Darius was able to escape Alexander the Great twice, but was killed by his own men. **35.** The Black Death spread across Europe because the villages were not clean, there were large populations of rats, and there was not much medical knowledge. **36.** The Church of England practiced religion much like the Catholic Church, but they were not under the control of Rome and the pope. **37.** The main link between China and the West was the Silk Road. **38.** The Acropolis was the hill upon which Greeks built special buildings. They placed temples and theaters there to honor their gods and goddesses. **39.** Feudalism was a political and military system based on the holding of land. The king gave land to nobles in exchange for loyalty; the nobles allowed serfs to live and work on the land for a tax. **40.** Samurais fought for the nobles, who provided them with special privileges, wealth, and land.

Part E: **41.** Answers will vary. Students should support their answers with at least some of these facts: history is all about change. In the past, slavery was an accepted part of life, but today most people think slavery is wrong. The discovery that the world is round led to explorers setting out from Europe on voyages of discovery; the age of discovery led to an age of imperialism. Ideas of freedom, democracy, and independence later swept across the world, resulting in growing nationalism, during which people united under common flags. **42.** Answers will vary. Students should support their answers with at least some of these facts: the Phoenicians were traders instead of farmers; they knew how to navigate by the stars, so they could sail beyond the sight of land; they set up colonies, rather than conquering other civilizations; they did not have an army, but hired soldiers from other lands.

Part F: **43.** Answers will vary. Students' paragraphs should include at least some of these ideas: the senators worried about how popular Caesar was with the Roman people; they thought he was too powerful; they were afraid that he wanted to be king; they thought he wanted to end the republic; the senators thought they were doing the right thing by killing Caesar. **44.** Answers will vary. Students' paragraphs should include at least some of these ideas: North America would be very different today if the European settlers had never arrived; there were many American Indian nations, each with its own culture; these would have grown in ways we cannot predict; the American Indian people of the east would not have been driven from their lands; other people in the world would not have some of the crops that came from North America, such as corn and tobacco; the slave trade, which brought African slaves to the Americas, would not have existed; the English language would not have the words that came from the culture of the Americas; English might not be spoken in as many places as it now is; the United States would never have been born.

Final Mastery Test

Part A: 1. A **2.** A **3.** D **4.** D **5.** C **6.** C **7.** D **8.** D **9.** C **10.** B **11.** B **12.** A **13.** C **14.** B **15.** A

Part B: 16. Mesopotamia **17.** nirvana **18.** Huns **19.** Armada **20.** labor unions **21.** nonviolent resistance **22.** nuclear **23.** Communist **24.** locomotives **25.** Zulus

Part C: 26. D **27.** H **28.** A **29.** J **30.** F **31.** B **32.** I **33.** C **34.** G **35.** E

Part D: 36. Both countries had many gods, and each city had a special god. **37.** Alexandria was very large and wealthy. It had a lot of Greek architecture, libraries, schools, and a lighthouse that was one of the Wonders of the Ancient World. **38.** Muhammad changed the Arabs from believing in many gods and idols to believing in one God, Allah. **39.** Most Africans came to the Americas on ships as slaves. **40.** U.S. leaders wanted the Panama Canal because the Spanish-American War proved how difficult it would be to move battleships between the Atlantic and the Pacific oceans without a canal. **41.** Austria and the pope ruled most of the Italian kingdoms and states in 1815. **42.** Christians and Muslims fought in Lebanon's civil war. **43.** The Monroe Doctrine was intended to stop Europe from gaining any more colonies in North or South America. It also prevented existing colonies from expanding. **44.** German submarines were attacking the ships of neutral nations along with several American merchant ships. **45.** North Korea has built up a supply of nuclear weapons over many years. After agreeing in 2007 to stop production on nuclear weapons, they reversed their decision and said production was only stopped temporarily.

Part E: 46. 3 **47.** 1 **48.** 5 **49.** 2 **50.** 4

Part F: 51. Students should support their answers with at least some of these facts: The French Revolution resulted in widespread warfare for several reasons. Most countries in Europe were ruled by monarchs—that is, kings and queens. In those countries, the monarchs were afraid of talk of freedom and rights for people. They believed that such ideas, if they spread, would harm their own positions in their own countries. Also, after French troops began to fight countries such as Austria and Prussia, other neighboring countries may have become alarmed about France. The chaos of the revolution allowed Napoleon to take power. His plans of conquest and glory drew more enemy countries into war. The French Revolution showed how a revolution can lead to widespread war. **52.** Answers will vary. Students should support their answers with at least some of these facts: Trenches kept troops from moving around, as it would take a great deal of time to dig trenches every time the troops needed to move.

Part G: 53. Answers will vary. Students' paragraphs should include at least some of these ideas: after World War II, Japan was occupied by Allied forces; they worked to make Japan stronger; Japan wrote a new constitution, which made Japan a democracy; this gave more people a voice in the future of Japan; women were given the right to vote; politically, Japan became similar to powerful Western nations such as the United States and Britain; Japan was not allowed to rebuild its military; that meant that money and supplies that would have gone into the military in the past now went into private industry; Japan became an industrial leader; it now makes cars instead of war machines; it makes electronics for people instead of for the military; because of their low defense budget, the Japanese can invest more money in industry; this has made Japan economically powerful. **54.** Answers will vary. Students' paragraphs should include at least some of these ideas: Keeping the peace in Europe may prevent wars from reaching the United States. It also keeps people safe, which would be considered morally correct. On the other hand, providing security forces in countries outside the United States can create political enemies and make the United States vulnerable without a full legion of troops at home.

Scoring Rubric for Short-Response Items on the last page of the Mastery Tests

2 points— The student demonstrates a solid understanding of the content by providing:
- a complete set of accurate facts that support the answer
- a clearly stated answer to the question

1 point— The student demonstrates a partial understanding of the content by providing *one* of the following:
- a complete set of accurate facts that support the answer
- a clearly stated answer to the question

0 points— The student fails to demonstrate understanding of the content by doing *one* of the following:
- includes no facts or incorrect facts, and fails to provide a clearly stated answer
- provides no answer at all

Scoring Rubric for Essay Items on the last page of the Mastery Tests

3 points— The student demonstrates a solid understanding of the content by providing:
- a complete set of accurate facts that support the answer
- a clearly stated answer to the essay's primary question
- a standard essay response (topic sentence, body, conclusion)

2 points— The student demonstrates a good understanding of the content by providing *two* of the following:
- a complete set of accurate facts that support the answer
- a clearly stated answer to the essay's primary question
- a standard essay response (topic sentence, body, conclusion)

1 point— The student demonstrates a partial understanding of the content by providing *one* of the following:
- a complete set of accurate facts that support the answer
- a clearly stated answer to the essay's primary question
- a standard essay response (topic sentence, body, conclusion)

0 points— The student fails to demonstrate understanding of the content by doing *one* of the following:
- includes no facts or incorrect facts, fails to answer the essay's primary question, and fails to include a standard essay response (topic sentence, body, conclusion)
- provides no answer at all

Teacher Questionnaire

Attention Teachers! As publishers of Pacemaker® *World History,* we would like your help in making this textbook more valuable to you. Please take a few minutes to fill out this survey. Your feedback will help us to better serve you and your students.

1. What is your position and major area of responsibility? _____
    _____
    _____

2. Briefly describe your setting:

    _____ regular education _____ special education _____ adult basic education

    _____ community college _____ university _____ other _____

3. The enrollment in your classroom includes students with the following (check all that apply):

    _____ at risk for failure _____ low reading ability _____ behavior problems

    _____ learning disabilities _____ ESL _____ other _____

4. Grade level of your students: _____

5. Racial/ethnic groups represented in your classes (check all that apply):

    _____ African-American _____ Asian _____ Caucasian _____ Hispanic

    _____ American Indian _____ other

6. School location:

    _____ urban _____ suburban _____ rural _____ other_____

7. What reaction did your students have to the materials? Include comments about the cover design, lesson format, illustrations, etc.
    _____
    _____
    _____

8. What features in the student text helped your students the most?
    _____
    _____
    _____

9. What features in the student text helped your students the least? Please include suggestions for changing these to make the text more relevant.

_____

_____

10. How did you use the Teacher's Edition and support materials, and what features did you find to be the most helpful?

_____

_____

11. What activity from the program did your students benefit from the most? Please briefly explain.

_____

_____

_____

12. Optional: Share an activity that you used to teach the materials in your classroom that enhanced the learning and motivation of your students.

_____

_____

_____

Several activities will be selected to be included in future editions. Please include your name, address, and phone number so we may contact you for permission and possible payment.

Thank you!

▼ fold in thirds and tape shut at the top ▼

Name: _____
School: _____
Address: _____
City/State/ZIP: _____
Phone: _____